[redacted]

[redacted]

BRITISH HERBAL COMPENDIUM

BRITISH HERBAL COMPENDIUM

Volume 2

A handbook of scientific information on widely used plant drugs

Companion to the
British Herbal Pharmacopoeia

Peter Bradley

BRITISH HERBAL MEDICINE ASSOCIATION, BOURNEMOUTH

ISBN 0 903032 12 0

First published 2006 by the
British Herbal Medicine Association,
1 Wickham Road, Bournemouth BH7 6JX

British Library Cataloguing-in-Publication Data
A catalogue record for this book is available from the British Library

Design and phytochemical structure diagrams by
Martin J. Willoughby BSc PhD CSci CChem FRSC

Typeset by Roberta Hutchins BSc MNIMH MCPP

Printed and bound in Great Britain by
Biddles Limited, King's Lynn

CONTENTS

MONOGRAPHS

FOREWORD

After a long and arduous struggle lasting forty years the British Herbal Medicine Association can now say that Herbal Medicine has been recognised in this country by those in authority.

The wording of the Medicines Bill in the early 1960s posed such a threat to the herbal practitioners of those days that the BHMA, realising that there must be standards whereby the quality of the medicinal herbs they used could be controlled, set up a Scientific Committee in 1965 under Frederick Fletcher-Hyde. This led to the progressive publication, in parts, of the British Herbal Pharmacopoeia, with a consolidated edition in 1983. In these publications identification of the herbal material was almost entirely botanical and clinical therapeutics were based on the reports of herbal practitioners, whereas in a completely revised edition in 1990 identification was confirmed by a chromatographic method but no therapeutics were included. Yet it was necessary for modern herbal practitioners to understand the scientific reasons for the therapeutic activities of the herbs they were using.

For more than fifty years modern medicine has been depending, in the main, on the prescribing of organic chemicals, made synthetically and foreign to the human body, to correct the irregularities of biochemical reactions in the body which lead to diseases. But organic molecules foreign to the human body have been produced by plants from time immemorial and it is these chemical substances, unknown until recent times (and many still unknown), that account for the pharmacological actions of herbs, often as a result of their combined activity.

It is the British Herbal Compendium Volumes 1 and 2, so diligently prepared and with such great skill by Peter Bradley, which now provide the modern herbal practitioners with all this information. It is fitting, therefore, that the British Herbal Medicine Association can celebrate its long sought recognition of Herbal Medicine by the publication of Volume 2.

E. J. Shellard
Emeritus Professor of Pharmacognosy
University of London

ACKNOWLEDGEMENTS

When the BHMA launched Volume 1 of the British Herbal Compendium in 1992, as a "Companion to the British Herbal Pharmacopoeia", no-one was more keenly aware than its Editor of two imperatives. Firstly, sooner or later and however it might be achieved, there would have to be a Volume 2. Secondly, which monographs would feature in Volume 2 was not a matter of choice; it was preordained by the content of the BHP 1996, then in preparation. In accepting the task of writing Volume 2, on top of a demanding job at that time and a longstanding commitment to ESCOP work on monographs, it was clear that it was going to be a long haul but I had little appreciation of just how long or what a challenge it would prove to be.

That it has been completed at all depended on help and encouragement from many colleagues. Foremost among them is Martin Willoughby, to whom I am particularly indebted not only for his preparation of the elegant phytochemical structure diagrams which appear in every monograph, but for magnificent support in other ways, from book design to the supply of scientific information and computer assistance. The other member of our production team, Roberta Hutchins, has played an invaluable role in typesetting the text with care and patience over a long period, and I am most grateful for all her splendid work.

My thanks also to the other members of the BHMA Scientific Committee for encouragement and guidance and, when called upon, technical advice and items of scientific literature; their names are listed on a separate page and all contributed in some way. Continental delegates in ESCOP Scientific Committee provided stimulating discussion and considerably improved my familiarity with certain plant drugs while working with them on numerous herbal projects. Having spent a great deal of time in scientific libraries, the helpful assistance on many occasions of library staff at the Royal Society of Chemistry, the Royal Pharmaceutical Society of Great Britain and the University of Surrey is gratefully acknowledged.

Particular thanks are expressed to Hugh Mitchell, the BHMA President Emeritus, for wise counsel on many occasions, to both Hugh and the BHMA Secretary, Diana Foreman, for general support and patience in awaiting this book as the years slipped by, and to Victor Perfitt of Bio-Health for the provision of a new computer, which certainly enhanced my word processing. Finally, I am delighted that Professor Joe Shellard, a major contributor to the BHP 1990 and now a sprightly nonagenarian, kindly agreed to write a Foreword to this book.

Peter R. Bradley

PREFACE

The BHMA set itself on a path in the late 1980s to revise the 232 monographs of the British Herbal Pharmacopoeia (BHP) 1983. For each plant drug, two monographs would henceforth be produced; one defining quality standards for inclusion in a redesigned BHP and one containing summaries of phytochemical, pharmacological, toxicological and clinical data to be published in what would become the British Herbal Compendium.

Because of the enormity of the task herbal drugs were prioritized for revision, partly on the basis of the level of interest expressed by BHMA company members in a survey. The 86 plant drugs selected were scheduled for inclusion in an abridged BHP published in 1990 and a first volume of the Compendium.

A review of that original priority list 18 years on serves to illustrate just how far the science, commerce and practice of herbal medicine has evolved. Notably absent from the Compendium Volume 1 were Ginkgo Leaf, St. Johns Wort and Saw Palmetto - some of today's most prominent herbal medicines. During the original planning phase, these and others were considered "second tier" and scheduled for coverage in the BHP 1996 and Volume 2 of the Compendium.

It is interesting to note a comment in the preface to the Compendium Volume 1 (1992) that scientific information was *"being published worldwide at an unprecedented rate"*. Contributors to that volume would undoubtedly agree that the extent, depth and quality of scientific literature now available was unimaginable at that time.

All this led to monumental challenges for Volume 2. Firstly, a diverse selection of herbal medicines to cover, including many of the major plant drugs. Secondly, an enormously expanded literature base, much of it good, some poor, but all needing review in order to produce concise yet comprehensive summaries of the most relevant data.

Unlike Volume 1, which was a collaborative work with contributions from various members of the Scientific Committee, the texts in this volume are entirely the work of Peter Bradley, who has devoted his available time over the past 14 years to completion of the manuscript. To some observers this may have seemed an eternity, but the finished publication should give some indication of the countless hours that went into its preparation.

Although the format of Volume 2 broadly follows that of Volume 1, the level of coverage and detail represents a quantum leap forward. In particular, in-depth pharmacological summaries are now included and comprehensive tabulations of clinical data are provided for some important plant drugs. The text cites over 3000 scientific references but I know that many more have been reviewed in the preparation of this book.

On behalf of the Scientific Committee and Board of the BHMA, I would like to extend our gratitude for Peter's dedicated work over past years. His endeavour has produced a unique and invaluable book, in my view unequalled by any other single publication in the field.

Martin J. Willoughby
Chairman, BHMA Scientific Committee

THE BRITISH HERBAL MEDICINE ASSOCIATION

Founded in 1964, the BHMA represents the interests of herbal medicine in the United Kingdom. Its members include companies involved in the supply of herbal raw materials and extracts, manufacturers of herbal medicines, herbal practitioners, pharmacists, retailers, academics and students of phytotherapy, with a number of individual overseas members. The BHMA Board endeavours to support the members through a wide spectrum of activities and keeps a close watch on legislative developments affecting herbal medicine, liaising with regulatory authorities, industry forums and the media, providing advice and comment on new EU or UK legislation and guidelines, and commenting on specific issues of quality, safety or efficacy. Encouraging wider knowledge and recognition of the value of herbal medicine, and promoting high standards of quality and safety, are also key objectives of the Association.

The BHMA Scientific Committee, formed in 1965, has played an important role in the Association's activities and has a long record of achievement in developing monographs on plant drugs as well as in providing technical information to BHMA members and public bodies. With many distinguished contributors, the Committee prepared the original 232 monographs of the British Herbal Pharmacopoeia (BHP), the culmination of 16 years of dedicated study and practical work, which formed the basis of the unified BHP 1983 - a classic still in print and valued for its therapeutic information. The current edition, the British Herbal Pharmacopoeia 1996, with 169 monographs, provides updated specifications for herbal drugs, particularly those not listed in official pharmacopoeias. Its companion, the British Herbal Compendium, now in two volumes, Volume 1 (1992) and this new Volume 2, provides a wealth of scientific and regulatory information on the same range of plant drugs. A Guide to Traditional Herbal Medicines (2003), providing information on traditional uses of medicinal plants within Europe, completes the range of BHMA books.

ESCOP

The BHMA is a leading member of the European Scientific Cooperative on Phytotherapy (ESCOP), founded in 1989 as an umbrella organization to bring together phytotherapy associations from individual European countries and to represent their interests at the European level. Some 15 national societies, which in earlier days had little contact with each other, now participate in ESCOP. The organization has flourished and achieved wide recognition. One of its major activities is the preparation by ESCOP Scientific Committee of monographs on the medicinal uses of plant drugs, primarily to support the work of the Committee on Herbal Medicinal Products at the European Medicines Agency in establishing Community herbal monographs for use throughout the European Union. A book of 80 monographs prepared by ESCOP was published in 2003 as *ESCOP Monographs - The Scientific Foundation for Herbal Medicinal Products.*

MEMBERS OF THE BHMA SCIENTIFIC COMMITTEE

Peter R. Bradley MSc CChem FRSC
Former Chairman, ESCOP Scientific Committee

Paul Henly CChem MRSC
Technical Manager, G.R. Lane Health Products Limited

Roberta Hutchins BSc (Phytotherapy) MNIMH MCPP
Secretary, BHMA Scientific Committee
Herbal Practitioner, Argyle House, Exeter

Richard Middleton BSc PhD MRPharmS
Chairman, BHMA
Technical Director, Medic Herb UK Limited

Simon Y. Mills MA FNIMH MCPP
Teaching Fellow, Peninsula Medical School
Honorary Secretary, ESCOP

Hugh W. Mitchell HonMNIMH
President Emeritus, BHMA
Chairman, Mitchfield Botanics Limited

Victor Perfitt MBE HonMNIMH
President, BHMA
Managing Director, Bio-Health Limited

Ann F. Walker PhD MIBiol RNutr MNIMH MCPP
Senior Lecturer in Human Nutrition
The Hugh Sinclair Unit of Human Nutrition, University of Reading

Martin J. Willoughby BSc PhD CSci CChem FRSC
Chairman, BHMA Scientific Committee
Associate Director - Technology, Wyeth Consumer Healthcare

INTRODUCTION

In historical context this second volume of the British Herbal Compendium is the result of an evolution going back to the earliest days of the BHMA and the inspiration of its founders to commence work on the British Herbal Pharmacopoeia (BHP). The original BHP monographs were prepared over the years 1965-1981, published in stages and then combined into the BHP 1983, which is still in print. As well as a specification for the quality of the herbal material each of those relatively brief monographs included a Therapeutics section, unique in that it was based on a survey of British herbal practitioners and thus reflected indications and dosages prevalent in the UK at that time. A different approach was adopted in subsequent editions. In line with official pharmacopoeias, the BHP 1990 and the current edition, the BHP 1996 with 169 monographs, focussed almost entirely on quality requirements for herbal materials. At the same time the concept of a companion book to the BHP, to provide revised Therapeutics sections together with scientific data supporting medicinal use of the herbal drugs in question, led to preparation of the British Herbal Compendium. Taken together, Volume 1 (1992) and this second volume of the Compendium cover almost all the plant drugs for which specifications appear in the BHP 1996; the only ones omitted for various reasons are Ispaghula Seed, Linseed, Lucerne, Mistletoe Herb, Psyllium Seed and Wild Cherry Bark, while a revised monograph on Echinacea covering three species has been included in this book.

Each Compendium monograph summarizes in a concise form the most useful scientific research and review information on a plant drug, together with brief information on its regulatory status as a medicine in the UK, France and Germany and, where applicable, the degree of acceptance in foods under USA and Council of Europe requirements. The format of Volume 1 has been largely maintained except that much greater emphasis has been given to Pharmacology and Clinical Studies in separate and in some cases quite lengthy sections, and a Safety section has been introduced.

The Compendium is based primarily on data from published research, hence the monographs are extensively referenced to scientific journals and other publications. As a reflection of the volume of scientific literature available, in most of the monographs the proportion of reference papers published since 1990 (when Volume 1 was in preparation) is remarkably high. Internet access to free databases and abstracts of new papers, especially from major journals published in English, has greatly enhanced awareness of the available literature. On the other hand, the acquisition of large numbers of full papers and their efficient organization into a convenient retrieval system will always be a time-consuming and costly, but essential, exercise for documentary research of this kind.

Over 3000 references are included in the text and it has been considered important to give the citations in full since they add a certain perspective to the monographs. In contrast to Volume 1, no "standard texts" (with abbreviated citations in monographs and a list of standard texts at the front of the book) have been used in Volume 2 on the basis that full citations for all the references in a monograph are more convenient to the reader. A considerable number of references relate to scientific papers published in languages other than English. In these cases the original language has been indicated in brackets at the end of the citation, together with mention of an English summary if one is included in the paper. With regard to titles of such papers the policy adopted has been to give, in those cases where the journal included an English translation of the title, only the title in English; otherwise to give the title in the original language, followed by an English translation in brackets.

The author of this volume is closely involved in the work of the Scientific Committee of the European Scientific Cooperative on Phytotherapy which also produces monographs on plant drugs, published in book form in 2003 as *ESCOP Monographs*. No less than 33 herbal drugs feature in both the Compendium Volume 2 and the ESCOP book, but the format and content of the monographs are markedly different and in some ways complement each other. The Compendium offers more comprehensive phytochemical data on plant constituents, for example, and in summaries of clinical data in major monographs tends to concentrate on systematic reviews and meta-analyses, with tabulations of clinical studies where appropriate, while the longer ESCOP monographs usually include a detailed summary of every controlled study and in some cases much more comprehensive coverage of *in vitro* and *in vivo* pharmacological studies.

The question of whether particular herbal drugs are safe for use during pregnancy and lactation is frequently difficult to answer satisfactorily in the absence of human data on such use, or even teratogenicity and other toxicological data from animals. Contraindications against the use of certain plant drugs during pregnancy and lactation are stated in the respective monographs where there appears to be a compelling reason to do so. Going beyond that, common sense and caution are also essential and it is obviously prudent to seek professional advice before taking any medicines during pregnancy. On this subject, the monograph on Raspberry Leaf may be of particular interest since some clinical data is now available on the safe use and possible benefit of this traditional remedy, which has been taken for generations during the latter stages of pregnancy.

As one measure of the recognition and importance of herbal medicinal products, it is encouraging to note the very substantial increase in the number of monographs on herbal materials which have been introduced into the European Pharmacopoeia (Ph. Eur.) in recent years. Of the 80 plant drugs featured in this volume, 46 are now covered by a Ph. Eur. monograph and a further 20 appear in national pharmacopoeias, leaving 14 to be found only in unofficial pharmacopoeias (of which 11 only in the BHP). This trend makes a further edition of the BHP unlikely, since it was never intended to compete with official pharmacopoeias and the number of unofficial plant drugs suitable for inclusion is now too small to be viable in a separate publication. The world has moved on, but the original purpose of the BHP and the efforts of its creators have been well served. It would be premature to speculate on further BHMA publications but, just as the Compendium has evolved to replace the Therapeutics of the original BHP, perhaps some way will ultimately be found to maintain its other great strength, quality standards for unofficial plant drugs.

ABBREVIATIONS

ADP	Adenosine diphosphate
ALT	Alanine aminotransferase (= GPT)
AST	Aspartate aminotransferase (= GOT)
ATP	Adenosine triphosphate
AUASI	American Urological Association Symptom Index (for BPH)
AUC	Area under the curve
BPH	Benign prostatic hyperplasia
cAMP	Cyclic adenosine monophosphate
CGI	Clinical Global Impressions scale
CNS	Central nervous system
DSM-III-R	Diagnostic and Statistical Manual of Mental Disorders, 3rd ed., revised (American Psychiatric Association)
DSM-IV	Diagnostic and Statistical Manual of Mental Disorders, 4th ed. (American Psychiatric Association)
ED_{50}	Median effective dose; the amount estimated to be effective in 50% of the organisms tested
FDA	Food and Drug Administration (USA)
FSH	Follicle-stimulating hormone
GOT	Glutamic-oxaloacetic transaminase (= AST)
GPT	Glutamic-pyruvic transaminase (= ALT)
GRAS	Generally recognized as safe (for intended use)
HAMA	Hamilton Anxiety Scale
HAMD	Hamilton depression scale
HDL	High density lipoprotein
IC_{50}	Median inhibitory concentration; the concentration estimated to produce 50% inhibition
ICD-10	International Statistical Classification of Diseases and Related Health Problems, Tenth Revision. Geneva: World Health Organization, 1992.
kDa	kiloDaltons
LC_{50}	Median lethal concentration; the concentration estimated to be fatal to 50% of the organisms tested
LD_{50}	Median lethal dose; the amount estimated to be fatal to 50% of the organisms tested
LDL	Low density lipoprotein
LH	Luteinizing hormone
LUTS	Lower urinary tract symptoms
MIC	Minimum inhibitory concentration
MW	Molecular weight
Na^+,K^+-ATPase	Sodium-potassium-activated adenosine triphosphatase
NYHA	New York Heart Association
IPSS	International Prostate Symptom Score
PSA	Prostate-specific antigen
ROS	Reactive oxygen species
SSRI	Selective serotonin reuptake inhibitor
TNF	Tumour necrosis factor
TRH	Thyrotrophin-releasing hormone
URT	Upper respiratory tract
VLDL	Very low density lipoprotein

GENERAL REFERENCES

REGULATORY PUBLICATIONS

In Regulatory Status sections of the monographs, brief information is given on legislation or guidelines relating to the acceptability of specific herbal substances in medicines (in the UK, France and Germany) and, where relevant, in foods (Council of Europe and USA publications). Although the sources of information are referenced to brief citations in each text, the following additional details may be helpful.

UNITED KINGDOM

Under UK legislation, medicinal products for which marketing authorizations have been granted are classified as 'Pharmacy Only' unless, by their active ingredient(s) being listed in a specific Order, their status is amended (i.e. further restricted or relaxed). The website of the Medicines and Healthcare Products Regulatory Agency (www.mhra.gov.uk), under Licensing of medicines - legal status, offers guidance on which substances fall into particular categories, which include:

- General Sale List (GSL)
  The majority of herbal drugs described in this volume fall into this category and medicinal products containing them may be sold in any retail outlet. The Order governing the sale of such products is Statutory Instrument (S.I.) 1984/769: *The Medicines (Products other than Veterinary Drugs) (General Sale List) Order 1984*, as amended. Numerous Amendment Orders over more than 20 years make it rather tedious to refer to the original series of SIs but further details may be obtained from the MHRA website, including a full list of GSL substances as *List B: Consolidated list of substances in authorised medicines for general sale.*
  The General Sale List is not intended as a 'positive list', implying unacceptability of other substances. It merely lists those active substances in GSL medicines for which a marketing authorization has been granted and imposes certain limitations, for example maximum dose or maximum daily dose, for specific substances. The list is divided into two tables: Table A lists substances accepted for internal or external use, while Table B lists substances accepted for external use only.
- Prescription Only
  None of the herbal drugs described in this volume are in this category.

A few Orders relate specifically to herbal drugs and impose restrictions, in some cases prohibition, on certain substances. Guidance is available on the MHRA website including a *List of herbal substances which are prohibited or restricted in medicines.* The only such Order relevant to a monograph in this volume is:

- Statutory Instrument 1977 No. 2130. *The Medicines (Retail Sale or Supply of Herbal Remedies) Order 1977.*
  This includes a Part I list of plant substances which are Pharmacy Only and may not be sold or supplied by a herbal practitioner, and a Part II list of plant substances which are Pharmacy Only except when sold or supplied by a herbal practitioner to a patient under specified conditions.
  Lily of the Valley appears in the Part II list.

FRANCE

The document to which the monographs refer is: *Médicaments à base de plantes.* ISBN 2-911473-02-7. Saint-Denis Cedex, France: Agence du Médicament, 1998.

As well as guidance on the preparation of dossiers for marketing authorizations, this helpful booklet includes a list of herbal drugs and a linked list of therapeutic indications (with standard wording; all commencing with "Traditionally used") which may be applied to them.

GERMANY

Hundreds of monographs prepared by Commission E (phytotherapeutic methods and substances group) of the German health authority, now the Bundesinstitut für Azneimittel und Medizinprodukte (BfArM), were issued during the years 1983-1994 and originally published in the *Bundesanzeiger* (official gazette). Each monograph presents an officially accepted summary of therapeutic information for a plant drug or a fixed combination of plant drugs, which at that time could be used in Germany in relation to marketing authorizations for phytomedicines. Although lacking references to scientific literature, and now somewhat dated, they offer a great deal of information on indications, dosages and other criteria.

The accessibility of these monographs was much improved by publication of English translations in: Blumenthal M, senior editor. *The Complete German Commission E Monographs - Therapeutic Guide to Herbal Medicines.* ISBN 0-9655555-0-X. Austin, Texas: American Botanical Council, 1998.

USA

Information on the acceptability of herbal substances in foods in the United States is given in a 600-page paperback publication, revised annually: *Code of Federal Regulations, Title 21 (Food and Drugs), Parts 170 to 199.* Washington DC: U.S. Government Printing Office.

As an example of abbreviated notation used in the monographs, "21 CFR 182.10" refers to Title 21, Part 182, Section 182.10: Spices and other natural seasonings and flavourings that are generally recognized as safe for their intended use.

COUNCIL OF EUROPE

Almost 500 plant substances used as flavourings are defined and, based primarily on toxicological assessment, classified into four categories in: *Flavouring Substances and Natural Sources of Flavourings,* 3rd ed. ISBN 2-7160-0081-6. Strasbourg: Council of Europe, 1981 (known colloquially as the "Blue Book"). Categories N1, N2 and N3 denote acceptable natural sources of flavourings; category N4 denotes flavourings used at present but with insufficient information to be classed as N1, N2 or N3. An Appendix lists examples of flavourings considered toxicologically unacceptable.

To replace this ageing publication, the Committee of Experts on Flavouring Substances is gradually reviewing the safety-in-use of over 600 natural flavouring source materials. Its first interim report, with evaluations of 101 herbal materials, was published as: *Natural Sources of Flavourings. Report No. 1.* ISBN 92-871-4324-2. Strasbourg: Council of Europe Publishing, 2000.

PHARMACOPOEIAS

The following pharmacopoeias are mentioned in the monographs.

Official Pharmacopoeias

BP	British Pharmacopoeia	*United Kingdom*
DAB	Deutsches Arzneibuch	*Germany*
JP	Japanese Pharmacopoeia, English version	*Japan*
Ph. Eur.	European Pharmacopoeia	*Council of Europe*
Ph. Fr.	Pharmacopée Française	*France*
Ph. Helv.	Pharmacopoea Helvetica	*Switzerland*
ÖAB	Österreichisches Arzneibuch	*Austria*
PPRC	Pharmacopoeia of the People's Republic of China, English edition	*China*
USP	United States Pharmacopeia and National Formulary	*USA*

Unofficial Pharmacopoeias

BHP	British Herbal Pharmacopoeia	*United Kingdom*
DAC	Deutscher Arzneimittel-Codex	*Germany*

MONOGRAPHS

AGNUS CASTUS

Verbenaceae

Agni casti fructus

Synonym: Chaste Tree Fruit.

Definition

Agnus Castus consists of the dried, ripe fruits of *Vitex agnus-castus* L.

Native to the eastern Mediterranean and western Asia, *Vitex agnus-castus* is a shrub that grows to a height of 5-6 metres.

CONSTITUENTS

□ ***Diterpenes*** Labdane-type diterpenes, 0.08-0.4%, principally rotundifuran (0.04-0.3%), vitexilactone (0.016-0.17%) and 6β,7β-diacetoxy-13-hydroxy-labda-8,14-diene (0.02-0.10%) [1-3], with smaller amounts of three other labdane compounds [4,5]. Six clerodane-type diterpenes have also been identified in the non-polar fraction, five clerodadien-13-ols and one clerodatrien-13-ol [4].

□ ***Iridoid glycosides*** Agnuside (0.02-0.4%) [6-10] and aucubin [9,10], the former being the *p*-hydroxybenzoyl ester of the latter.

□ ***Flavonoids***, 0.4-1% [11], principally the lipophilic, highly methylated 6-hydroxyflavonols casticin (quercetagetin 3,6,7,4′-tetramethyl ether, 0.1-0.2%) [7,8,12,13] (Ph. Eur. min. 0.08%) and 6-hydroxykaempferol 3,6,7,4′-tetramethyl ether, with minor amounts of chrysosplenol-D and penduletin (the 3,6,7-trimethyl ethers of quercetagetin and 6-hydroxykaempferol respectively) [12]. Hydrophilic flavone *C*-glycosides including isoorientin [6,7,14], orientin and isovitexin [14], and the flavone apigenin [15], are also present.

□ ***Essential oil***, 0.5-1.6%, of variable composition according to source but composed largely of monoterpenes and sesquiterpenes; at least 85 components have been identified [16]. The main components usually include 1,8-cineole and sabinene [16-19], sometimes with substantial amounts of α-pinene [18-20], γ-elemene [18], α-terpinyl acetate [21], β-caryophyllene [16,20,21] and/or germacrene B [20,21].

□ ***Other constituents*** include *p*-hydroxybenzoic acid (0.006-0.06%) [6,7]; tannins (up to 1.6%) [22]; triglycerides in which the fatty acids include capric, myristic, palmitic, palmitoleic and stearic acids [23], and a small amount of free linoleic acid [24,25].

Contrary to a brief report claiming the isolation of ketosteroids from *Vitex agnus-castus* fruits [26], none were detected in a more recent investigation [25].

Published Assay Methods

Diterpenoids [1], agnuside [6] and casticin [Ph. Eur.] by HPLC.

PHARMACOLOGY

Agnus castus has a long history of use in female complaints related to the menstrual cycle and extracts from agnus castus are widely used in the treatment of premenstrual symptoms. An elevated level of serum prolactin, a hormone secreted by lactotroph cells in the pituitary gland, is one of the most frequent causes of cycle disorders. Manifest hyperprolactinaemia is a common cause of infertility and even minor changes in prolactin secretion can cause pathophysiological changes in the women concerned. "Latent" hyperprolactinaemia, in which prolactin levels are only slightly above the norm (often with normal basal values during the day and peak values during sleep or in stress situations), can cause disturbances of the menstrual cycle, mastodynia and even sterility. One of the factors regulating prolactin secretion

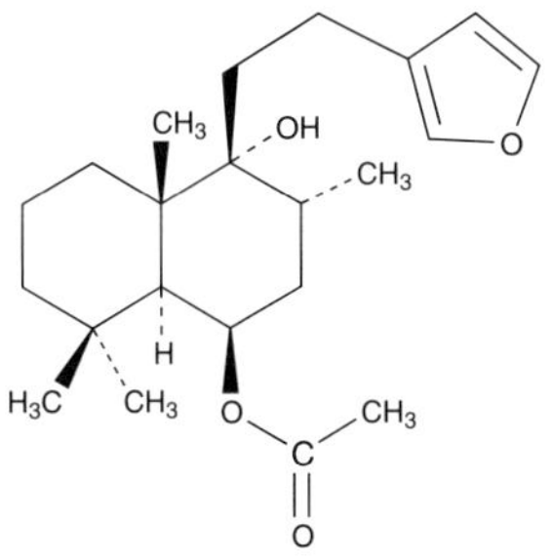

Rotundifuran

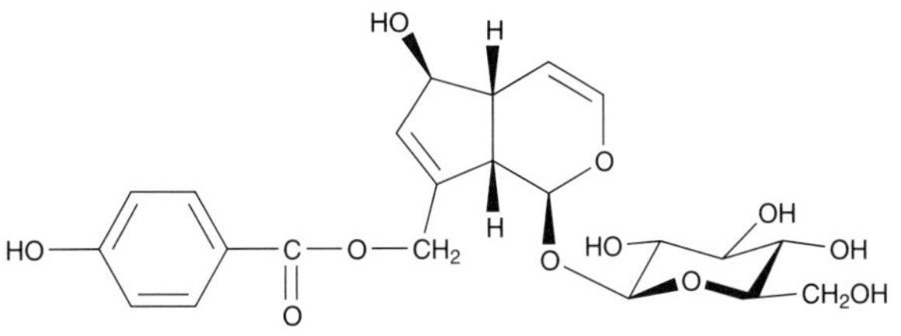

Agnuside

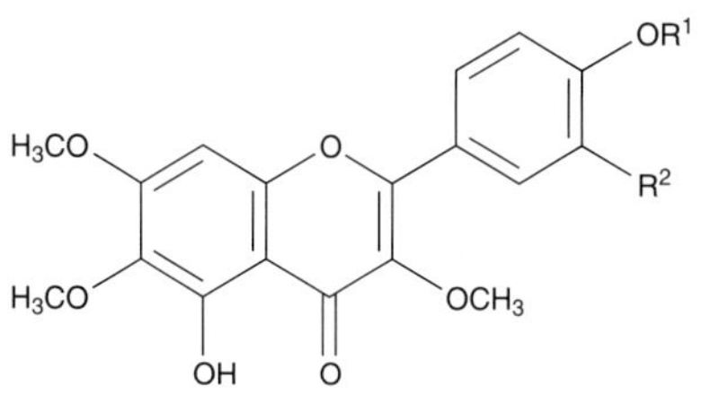

	R^1	R^2
Casticin	CH_3	OH
6-Hydroxykaempferol-3,6,7,4′-tetramethyl ether	CH_3	H
Chrysosplenol-D	H	OH
Penduletin	H	H

by pituitary cells is dopamine, which is inhibitory to prolactin release, and this effect is mediated via dopamine D_2 receptors. Dopamine-agonists (dopaminergic drugs which act as stimulants of dopamine receptors) have a prolactin-lowering effect. Although the aetiopathogenesis for the varied symptoms of premenstrual syndrome is not entirely clear, treatment with dopaminergics can be effective. A number of experimental and clinical studies support the assumption that agnus castus can reduce circulating prolactin levels by a dopaminergic mode of action [27-29].

In vitro

Dopaminergic activity and inhibition of prolactin release

Ethanolic agnus castus extracts significantly inhibited prolactin secretion from cultured rat pituitary cells [30,31], but had no effect on the release of luteinizing hormone (LH) or follicle-stimulating hormone (FSH) [31]. The inhibition of prolactin secretion could be blocked by adding a dopamine receptor antagonist such as haloperidol [30]. It was subsequently demonstrated that agnus castus contains a dopaminergic active principle that binds to the dopamine D_2 receptor, and the researchers postulated that this active principle may inhibit prolactin release [31].

Ethanolic agnus castus native extracts inhibited the binding of a radioligand (^{3}H-spiperone) to the dopamine D_2 receptor with IC_{50} values of 40-70 µg/ml. Bioguided fractionation of a methanolic extract revealed that only a hexane fraction containing diterpenes and fatty acids inhibited D_2 binding. Rotundifuran, 6β,7β-diacetoxy-13-hydroxy-labda-8,14-diene and linoleic acid were identified as active compounds with IC_{50} values of 40, 79 and 45 µg/ml respectively. Inhibition of the binding of radioligands to opioid (µ and κ subtype) receptors was also observed, but no significant inhibition was evident with respect to histamine H_1, benzodiazepine or serotonin receptors [32].

In subsequent dopamine D_2 receptor assays, all the diterpenes identified in agnus castus showed dopaminergic activity to varying degrees, the most potent being a labdadiene (designated as B-115) with about one fifth of the activity of dopamine. On a molar basis the clerodadienols had slightly less activity (about one eighth of that of dopamine), but due to their quantitative predominance they represented the major dopaminergic compounds in an agnus castus extract. At concentrations about 50-fold higher than that of dopamine the clerodadienols proved to be potent inhibitors of prolactin release and cAMP release from rat pituitary cells (lactotrophs), while rotundifuran did not inhibit prolactin release at this concentration [4].

Oestrogen receptor binding

At concentrations of 0.1-1.0% V/V a 50%-ethanolic extract from agnus castus significantly inhibited serum-stimulated growth of oestrogen-receptive T47D breast cancer cells ($p<0.001$), indicating that the extract may contain phyto-oestrogens [33].

A methanolic agnus castus extract was shown to contain compounds that competitively bind to recombinant human oestrogen receptors alpha (ERα) and beta (ERβ), with IC_{50} values for the extract of 46 µg/ml and 64 µg/ml respectively [34]. From bioguided fractionation of the extract using ER binding assays linoleic acid (a fatty acid ubiquitous in nature) was identified as a corresponding receptor ligand, with IC_{50} values of 27 µg/ml and 30 µg/ml for ERα and ERβ respectively. Both the agnus castus extract and linoleic acid stimulated mRNA expression of ERβ in T47D:A18 breast cancer cells and mRNA expression of progesterone in ER-positive Ishikawa endometrial cancer cells but, unlike other oestrogenic plant extracts such as red clover and hops, not alkaline phosphatase activity in Ishikawa cells [24]. The physiological significance of this data is not yet clear.

Other workers have found only ERβ-selective phyto-oestrogens in agnus castus extract, namely the flavone apigenin (the strongest ERβ-binding constituent) and the flavonoid glycosides vitexin and penduletin [15]. Compounds with selectivity for the oestrogen receptor β-subtype appear to be involved in the regulation of fat tissue but exert no oestrogenic effects in the uterus and have little effect on bone [4].

In vivo

Stressful situations can lead to an increase in

blood prolactin levels. Brief exposure of rats to an ether-saturated atmosphere dramatically increased prolactin in the blood within 2 minutes, reaching a maximum after 10 minutes. However, intravenous pre-treatment of the rats with an agnus castus extract (in saline) at 60 mg/animal markedly reduced the ether stress-induced prolactin release in comparison with animals receiving saline only [29].

Subcutaneous administration of a dilute agnus castus tincture to lactating rats led to decreased milk production, which was interpreted as indirect evidence of lowering of the prolactin level [35].

Pharmacological studies in humans
In an open, intra-individual comparison study, 20 healthy males (aged 18-40 years) with basal prolactin levels of ≥ 80 µIU/ml were treated consecutively for 14-day periods (separated by wash-out phases of at least one week) with placebo and then with increasing daily dose levels of an agnus castus extract, equivalent to 120 mg (dose A), 240 mg (dose B) and 480 mg (dose C) of crude drug respectively. During each phase the 24-hour prolactin secretion profile of each participant was measured from the penultimate to the final day, and the amount of prolactin release was monitored one hour after stimulation with thyrotrophin-releasing hormone (TRH) on the last day (performing the study in males avoided the problem in females of menstrual cycle-associated and oestradiol-dependent variations in prolactin levels). Compared to placebo, a significant 11% increase in 24-hour serum prolactin AUC was registered with dose A (p = 0.033), while doses B and C caused decreases of 3-10%. The $AUC_{0\text{-}1\,h}$ after TRH was about 16% higher with dose A, around the initial level with dose B and about 10% lower after dose C. The results suggested effects of agnus castus which are dependent on the dose administered and the initial prolactin concentration but tended towards "smoothing out" of variations in the prolactin daily profile. No changes were observed in blood pressure, heart rate, serum levels of FSH, LH and testosterone, or in a wide range of clinical biochemistry parameters [36,37].

CLINICAL STUDIES

Premenstrual syndrome (PMS) and premenstrual dysphoric disorder (PMDD)
The term premenstrual dysphoric disorder (or late luteal phase dysphoric disorder) is a recently described variant of PMS that covers the more severe psychological symptoms. In some recent clinical studies a diagnosis of PMDD has been used as the basis for patient inclusion [38,39]. Whereas 20-30% of women have complaints that that may be classified as PMS, only 3-5% meet criteria for PMDD [40].

Controlled studies
In a randomized, double-blind, placebo-controlled, multicentre study (in general medicine community clinics), 170 women with PMS diagnosed in accordance with DSM-III-R were treated daily with 20 mg of an agnus castus dry extract (6-12:1, 60% ethanol; n = 86) or placebo (n = 84) during three consecutive menstrual cycles. Improvement in the main efficacy variable (combined patients' self assessment scores for irritability, mood alteration, anger, headache, breast fullness and other menstrual symptoms including bloating) was significantly greater in the agnus castus group than in the placebo group (p<0.001). Responder rates (a responder defined as a patient showing a reduction of ≥ 50% in self-assessed symptoms) were 52% in the agnus castus group and 24% in the placebo group. Using the CGI scale (three items) to evaluate efficacy, the physicians found significant superiority of verum treatment (p<0.001) [41].

An earlier randomized, double-blind, placebo-controlled study over a period of 3 months found no statistical difference between a high daily dosage of 1800 mg of agnus castus (tablets containing crude drug, 3 × 600 mg/day) and placebo in the treatment of self-diagnosed sufferers from PMS, recruited by mail as volunteers following advertisements in the popular press. Out of 1300 volunteers, 600 women were selected, of whom only 217 completed the full 3 months of treatment: 105 on agnus castus and 112 on placebo. Self-assessment of 50 symptoms by the volunteers using the Moos Menstrual Distress Questionnaire indicated a dramatic improvement in both groups by the end of the first menstrual cycle with relative stability over the next two cycles. Although some trends in favour of agnus castus were evident, statistical significance was found with respect to only one symptom, restlessness [42].

In a randomized, double-blind, comparative study over a treatment period of three menstrual cycles, women with PMS were assigned to treatment with an agnus castus dry extract (9.6-11.5:1, 60% ethanol; corresponding to 40 mg of crude drug daily) or pyridoxine hydrochloride (2 × 100 mg daily on days 16-35 of the cycle; placebo only on days 1-15). The intention-to-treat analysis included 127 patients, 61 in the agnus castus group and 66 in the pyridoxine group. Using the main efficacy parameter, a self-assessment premenstrual tension scale, scores decreased from 15.2 to 5.1 in the agnus castus group and from 11.9 to 5.1 in the pyridoxine group. In comparison with pyridoxine, agnus castus treatment led to more marked alleviation of typical PMS symptoms such as breast tenderness, oedema, inner tension, headache, constipation and depression. Results on the Clinical Global Impressions scale indicated a marked or very marked improvement in 77.1% and 60.6%

of patients in the agnus castus and pyridoxine groups respectively. Other study parameters also showed favourable results for agnus castus. It was concluded that the agnus castus treatment was as effective as, and to some extent superior to, pyridoxine treatment [43].

In a randomized, single-blind (i.e. drug assignments known by the prescribing physician, but not the patient or assessor) comparative study, patients with premenstrual dysphoric disorder diagnosed in accordance with DSM IV were randomly assigned to treatment with either 20-40 mg of an agnus castus dry extract (not further defined; n = 20) or 20-40 mg of fluoxetine (a selective serotonin reuptake inhibitor, n = 21) daily for 8 weeks. Evaluation using daily symptom reports, the Hamilton depression rating scale (HAMD) and the Clinical Global Impressions scale showed that after 8 weeks the patients had responded well to both treatments, with significant improvements from baseline ($p<0.01$) for all three outcome measures in both groups and no significant difference with respect to rates of responders to treatment (58% in the agnus castus group; 68% in the fluoxetine group). From the daily symptom reports fluoxetine seemed to some extent to be more effective for psychological symptoms, while agnus castus extract appeared more effective for physical symptoms [39].

Open studies

In a prospective, open, multicentre study, 43 patients (out of 50 originally enrolled) with premenstrual syndrome diagnosed in accordance with DSM-III (late luteal phase dysphoric disorder) were evaluated over 8 menstrual cycles: 2 cycles to establish the baseline, 3 cycles in which they received daily treatment with 20 mg of an agnus castus native dry extract (6-12:1, 60% ethanol; corresponding to 120-240 mg of crude drug) and 2 cycles of post-treatment observation. At the end of treatment, compared to baseline, a significant reduction of 45% in scores from the Moos menstrual distress questionnaire (MMDQ; patients' self-assessment of 47 symptoms) was achieved ($p<0.001$). The symptoms gradually reverted towards baseline values after cessation of treatment, but even 3 cycles after treatment the average MMDQ score remained 20% below baseline ($p<0.001$). The number of patients classified as "responders", with a reduction in MMDQ score of at least 50% from baseline, was 20 out of 43. Further self-assessments using a visual analogue scale and a global impressions scale corroborated the improvement in symptoms [38].

In an open study gynaecologists completed questionnaires based on interviews with 1634 patients suffering from PMS, before and after treatment for a period of three menstrual cycles with an agnus castus extract (6.7-12.5:1) corresponding to 2 × 20 mg of crude drug daily. At the end of treatment, 42% of patients reported that they were no longer suffering from PMS; a further 51% reported a decrease in symptoms such as depression, anxiety, craving and hyperhydration. The most frequently reported symptom, mastodynia, decreased substantially in frequency and severity. In global assessments, 85% of the physicians rated the clinical efficacy as good or very good and 81% of the patients assessed their status after treatment as very much or much better [44].

Numerous other open studies with agnus castus preparations have been published over the past 50 years, ranging from large, multicentric observational studies on patients with PMS or other complaints [45-47] to case reports on patients with amenorrhoea [48]. By today's standards, many of the studies had shortcomings in design or procedure. Furthermore, the value of uncontrolled studies in PMS is limited by the high "placebo effect".

Menstrual cycle irregularities

In a randomized, double-blind, placebo-controlled study, 52 women with menstrual cycle abnormalities (luteal phase defects) due to latent hyperprolactinaemia were assigned to daily treatment with 20 mg of an agnus castus dry extract (50-70% ethanol) or placebo for 3 months. Data from 17 verum and 20 placebo patients were available for evaluation. Luteal phases before treatment were too short in both groups (mean: 5.5 and 3.4 days in the verum and placebo groups respectively). In the agnus castus group the luteal phase lengthened significantly to 10.5 days ($p<0.005$) with no effect on overall cycle duration since initially prolonged follicular phases were correspondingly shortened; no change was observed in the placebo group. Significant increases in mid-luteal progesterone and oestradiol levels were observed during treatment with agnus castus ($p<0.001$ and $p<0.05$ respectively in comparison with placebo). A significant reduction in releasable pituitary prolactin reserve during the mid-follicular phase in the agnus castus group ($p<0.001$) was considered sufficient to improve or normalize the disturbed ovarian function, while no change was observed in the placebo group. From those patients initially suffering from PMS, only 2 out of 9 in the verum group reported the complaint after 3 months of treatment compared to 11 out of 13 in the placebo group ($p<0.05$). In the verum group 2 women became pregnant [49].

Female infertility

Observations in a number of clinical studies have suggested that agnus castus may be helpful in restoring fertility to women with cycle disorders, particularly corpus luteum insufficiency, and hence in facilitating the induction of pregnancy.

In a double-blind, placebo-controlled study, 66 women with fertility disorders (28 with secondary amenorrhoea, 21 with luteal insufficiency and 17 with idiopathic infertility) were evaluated after taking 2 × 30 drops of a combination preparation containing agnus castus daily for 3 months; in women with secondary amenorrhoea or luteal insufficiency, pregnancy occurred more than twice as often in the verum groups (5/15 and 3/11 respectively) than in the placebo groups (2/13 and 1/10 respectively). While these numbers are too small for statistical significance, the results are encouraging [50].

Several open studies also suggest a restoration of fertility in some women after treatment with agnus castus:

- 7 out of 45 women (15.5%) with infertility problems due to corpus luteum insufficiency achieved pregnancy during treatment for three menstrual cycles with 40 drops daily of an agnus castus extract solution (corresponding to 30 mg of crude drug) [51].

- 33 patients undergoing therapy for corpus luteum insufficiency were given 30 drops of an agnus castus liquid preparation daily for 5 months. Six of the patients (18%) became pregnant, roughly corresponding to the pregnancy rate in spontaneous cycles [52].

- In the open study summarized above in which 1634 patients were treated for PMS with an agnus castus extract, 19 of the 23 women who conceived during treatment were among the 126 women in the study who had hitherto been unsuccessful in achieving pregnancy [44].

Other studies

Only a few placebo-controlled studies (as summarized above) have been published on agnus castus mono-preparations. In this situation, the following placebo-controlled studies on a long-established combination product offer useful data, since the preparation is a 55%-ethanolic solution containing only agnus-castus extract at a phytotherapeutic level together with low (homoeopathic) levels of five other herbal extracts.

Premenstrual mastalgia

In three randomized, double-blind, placebo-controlled studies positive results were achieved with this combination product in women patients with cyclical premenstrual mastalgia (breast pain). The dosage of 2 × 30 drops (1.8 ml) daily, equivalent to 32.4 mg of agnus castus, was given for the duration of 3-4 menstrual cycles and the intensity of breast pain was assessed by the patients on a visual analogue scale:

- In the first study, at the end of four menstrual cycles the rate of success (i.e. symptoms of premenstrual breast pain and tension no longer present or so reduced that no further treatment required) was significantly greater ($p<0.01$) in the verum group (n = 55) at 75% than in the placebo group (n = 38) at 37%. The success rate in a third group (n = 28) taking the progestogen lynestrenol (2 × 5 mg daily) was even higher at 82% [53].

- In the second study, in comparison with the placebo group (n = 38) at the end of three menstrual cycles, the intensity of breast pain had diminished significantly more in the verum group (n = 34; p = 0.00067) and basal prolactin levels had fallen significantly more in the verum group (p = 0.039) [54].

- In the third study, in comparison with the placebo group (n = 49), the mean decrease in breast pain intensity was significant in the verum group (n = 48) after the first and second treatment cycles (p = 0.018 and p = 0.006 respectively), while the result after three treatment cycles was not quite significant (p = 0.064) [55].

THERAPEUTICS

Actions

Dopaminergic [31,32], inhibits the release of prolactin from the pituitary gland [29-31,35].

Indications

Premenstrual syndrome [39-41] including premenstrual mastalgia [53-56]; menstrual cycle irregularities [49,56].

Contraindications

Should be avoided by women taking oral contraceptives [40], during pregnancy [56] and, in view of the inhibitory effect of agnus castus on prolactin secretion, during lactation.

Side effects

Occasional gastrointestinal disturbances or skin reactions.

Interactions with other drugs

None known. Interaction with dopamine receptor antagonists appears possible [56].

Dosage

Daily dose: dried fruits, 40-240 mg, usually in the form of a dry extract (50-70% ethanol) or tincture [39,41,43,49].

SAFETY

Agnus castus is usually well tolerated at the recommended dosage. In some 40 clinical studies during the past 50 years about 8000 women have taken agnus castus preparations in daily doses corresponding to 40-240 mg (in one study 1800 mg) of crude drug for periods of 3 months or more. The reported adverse effects have been generally mild, predominantly nausea and gastrointestinal complaints, skin reactions and headaches. In three large open studies involving a total of over 4800 women the overall incidence of reported adverse events was about 2.1% (not all of which would be attributable to the drug) [44,46,47].

In the most recent placebo-controlled study, out of 86 women taking a daily dose of 20 mg of an agnus castus dry extract (6-12:1, 60% ethanol) for three consecutive menstrual cycles only 4 adverse events were reported (once each: acne, multiple abscesses, intermenstrual bleeding and urticaria); all were mild and none led to discontinuation of treatment. In the placebo group of 84 women, 3 adverse events were reported (one each: acne, early menstrual period, gastric upset) [41].

No systematic toxicological data on agnus castus appear to have been published.

REGULATORY STATUS

Medicines

UK	Accepted for general sale, internal or external use [57].
France	Accepted for specified indications [58].
Germany	Commission E monograph published, with approved uses [56].

Food

Not used in foods.

REFERENCES

Current Pharmacopoeial Monographs

Ph. Eur.	Agnus Castus Fruit
USP	Chaste Tree

Literature References

1. Hoberg E, Meier B and Sticher O. Quantitative High Performance Liquid Chromatographic Analysis of Diterpenoids in Agni-Casti Fructus. *Planta Medica* 2000, **66**, 352-355.
2. Hoberg E, Orjala J, Meier B and Sticher O. Diterpenoids from the fruits of *Vitex agnus-castus*. *Phytochemistry* 1999, **52**, 1555-1558.
3. Hoberg E, Sticher O, Orjala JE and Meier B. Diterpene aus Agni-casti fructus [Diterpenes from Agni-casti fructus]. Pages 149-150 in: Meier B and Hoberg E. Agni-casti fructus. Neue Erkenntnisse zur Qualität und Wirksamkeit [Agni-casti fructus. New information on quality and efficacy]. *Z. Phytotherapie* 1999, **20**, 140-158 [GERMAN/English summary].
4. Wuttke W, Jarry H, Christoffel V, Spengler B, Seidlová-Wuttke D. Chaste tree (*Vitex agnus-castus*) - Pharmacology and clinical indications. *Phytomedicine* 2003, **10**, 348-357.
5. Christoffel V, Spengler B, Jarry H and Wuttke W. Prolactin inhibiting dopaminergic activity of diterpenes from Vitex agnus castus. In: Loew D, Blume H and Dingermann T, editors. *Phytopharmaka V*. Darmstadt: Steinkopff, 1999: 209-214.
6. Hoberg E, Meier B and Sticher O. An Analytical High Performance Liquid Chromatographic Method for the Determination of Agnuside and *p*-Hydroxybenzoic Acid Contents in Agni-casti Fructus. *Phytochem. Analysis* 2000, **11**, 327-329.
7. Meier B. Probleme der Standardisierung pharmazeutischer Zubereitungen [Problems in the standardization of pharmaceutical preparations]. Pages 145-147 in: Meier B and Hoberg E. Agni-casti fructus. Neue Erkenntnisse zur Qualität und Wirksamkeit [Agni-casti fructus. New information on quality and efficacy]. *Z. Phytotherapie* 1999, **20**, 140-158 [GERMAN/English summary].
8. Abel G. Erfahrungen mit der Analytik von der Droge bis zum Fertigarzneimittel [Experience with analysis from the crude drug to the finished product]. Pages 147-148 in: Meier B and Hoberg E. Agni-casti fructus. Neue Erkenntnisse zur Qualität und Wirksamkeit [Agni-casti fructus. New information on quality and efficacy]. *Z. Phytotherapie* 1999, **20**, 140-158 [GERMAN/English summary].
9. Castagnou MR, Larcebau S and Nicou O. Contribution à l'étude des graines de *Vitex agnus castus*. Deuxième partie [Contribution to the study of the fruits of *Vitex agnus castus*. Part 2]. *Bull. Soc. Pharm. Bordeaux* 1964, **103**, 189-192 [FRENCH].
10. Hänsel R and Winde E. Agnoside, a new Glycoside obtained from *Vitex agnus castus* L. *Arzneim.-Forsch./Drug Res.* 1959, **9**, 189-190 [GERMAN/English summary].
11. Kustrak D, Antolic A and Males Z. Determination of the flavonoid content of Chaste Tree (*Vitex agnus castus* L.). *Farm. Glas.* 1993, **49**, 299-303 [SERBO-CROAT/English summary].
12. Wollenweber E and Mann K. Flavonols from Fruits of Vitex agnus castus. *Planta Medica* 1983, **48**, 126-127 [GERMAN/English summary].
13. Belic I, Bergant-Dolar J and Morton RA. Constituents of *Vitex agnus castus Seeds*. Part I. Casticin. *J. Chem. Soc.* 1961, 2523-2525.
14. Gomaa CS, El-Moghazy MA, Halim FA and El-Sayyad AE. Flavonoids and Iridoids from Vitex agnus castus. *Planta Medica* 1978, **33**, 277.
15. Jarry H, Spengler B, Porzel A, Schmidt J, Wuttke W and Christoffel V. Evidence for Estrogen Receptor β-Selective Activity of *Vitex agnus-castus* and Isolated Flavones. *Planta Medica* 2003, **69**, 945-947.
16. Senatore F, Porta GD and Reverchon E. Constituents of *Vitex agnus-castus* L. Essential Oil. *Flavour Fragr. J.* 1996, **11**, 179-182.
17. Sørensen JM and Katsiotis ST. Parameters Influencing the Yield and Composition of the Essential Oil from Cretan *Vitex agnus-castus* Fruits. *Planta Medica* 2000, **66**, 245-250.
18. Valentini G, Bellomaria B and Arnold N. L'olio essenziale di *Vitex agnus-castus* [The essential oil of *Vitex agnus-castus*]. *Riv. Ital. EPPOS* 1998, 24 (April), 13-18 [ITALIAN/English summary].
19. Kustrak D, Kuftinec J and Blazevic N. Composition of the Essential Oil of *Vitex agnus castus* L. *J. Essent. Oil Res.* 1994, **6**, 341-344.
20. Zwaving JH and Bos R. Composition of the Essential Fruit Oil of *Vitex agnus-castus*. *Planta Medica* 1996, **62**, 83-84.
21. Galletti GC, Russo MT and Bocchini P. Essential Oil Composition of Leaves and Berries of *Vitex agnus-castus* L. from Calabria, Southern Italy. *Rapid Commun. Mass Spect.* 1996, **10**, 1345-1350.

22. Antolic A and Males Z. Quantitative analysis of the polyphenols and tannins of *Vitex agnus-castus* L. *Acta Pharm. (Zagreb)* 1997, **47**, 207-211.
23. Katyuzhanskaya AN. The composition of the organic acids of carbon dioxide extracts of some spice-aromatic plants. *Khim. Prir. Soedin.* 1977, (6), 763-767 [RUSSIAN], translated into English as: *Chem. Nat. Compd.* 1977, **13**, 643-646.
24. Liu J, Burdette JE, Sun Y, Deng S, Schlecht SM, Zheng W et al. Isolation of linoleic acid as an estrogenic compound from the fruits of *Vitex agnus-castus* L. (chaste-berry). *Phytomedicine* 2004, **11**, 18-23.
25. Hoberg E. Phytochemical and analytical investigations of *Vitex agnus-castus* L. [Dissertation]. Swiss Federal Institute of Technology (ETH) Zürich, 1999.
26. Saden-Krehula M and Kustrak D. Δ^4-3-Ketosteroide in *Vitex agnus castus* Früchten. In: Abstracts of 3rd Phytotherapie-Kongreß (Gesellschaft für Phytotherapie), Lübeck-Travemünde, Germany. 3-6 October 1991:34 (Abstract P16) [GERMAN].
27. Winterhoff H. *Vitex agnus-castus* (Chaste Tree): Pharmacological and Clinical Data. In: Lawson LD and Bauer R, editors. *Phytomedicines of Europe - Chemistry and Biological Activity. ACS Symposium Series 691.* ISBN 0-8412-3559-7. Washington DC: American Chemical Society, 1998:299-308.
28. Gorkow C. Klinischer Kenntnisstand von Agni-casti fructus. Klinisch-pharmakologische Untersuchungen und Wirksamkeitsbelege. [The current state of clinical knowledge on Agni casti fructus. Clinical-pharmacological studies and evidence of efficacy]. *Z. Phytotherapie* 1999, **20**, 159-168 [GERMAN/English summary].
29. Wuttke W, Gorkow C and Jarry H. Dopaminergic Compounds in *Vitex agnus-castus.* In: Loew D and Rietbrock N, editors. Phytopharmaka in Forschung und klinischer Anwendung. Darmstadt: Steinkopff, 1995:81-91.
30. Sliutz G, Speiser P, Schulz AM, Spona J and Zeillinger R. Agnus Castus Extracts Inhibit Prolactin Secretion of Rat Pituitary Cells. *Horm. metab. Res.* 1993, **25**, 253-255.
31. Jarry H, Leonhardt S, Gorkow C, Wuttke W. In vitro prolactin but not LH and FSH release is inhibited by compounds in extracts of Agnus castus: direct evidence for a dopaminergic principle by the dopamine receptor assay. *Exp. Clin. Endocrinol.* 1994, **102**, 448-454.
32. Meier B, Berger D, Hoberg E, Sticher O and Schaffner W. Pharmacological activities of *Vitex agnus-castus* extracts in vitro. *Phytomedicine* 2000, **7**, 373-381.
33. Dixon-Shanies D and Shaikh N. Growth inhibition of human breast cancer cells by herbs and phytoestrogens. *Oncol. Rep.* 1999, **6**, 1383-1387.
34. Liu J, Burdette JE, Xu H, Gu C, van Breemen RB, Bhat KPL et al. Evaluation of Estrogenic Activity of Plant Extracts for the Potential Treatment of Menopausal Symptoms. *J. Agric. Food Chem.* 2001, **49**, 2472-2479.
35. Winterhoff H, Gorkow C and Behr B. Die Hemmung der Laktation bei Ratten als indirekter Beweis für die Senkung von Prolaktin durch *Agnus castus* [Inhibition of lactation in rats as indirect evidence for the prolactin-lowering activity of agnus castus]. *Z. Phytotherapie* 1991, **12**, 175-179 [GERMAN].
36. Merz P-G, Gorkow C, Schrödter A, Rietbrock S, Sieder C, Loew D et al. The effects of a special Agnus castus extract (BP1095E1) on prolactin secretion in healthy male subjects. *Exp. Clin. Endocrinol. Diabetes* 1996, **104**, 447-453.
37. Loew D, Gorkow C, Schrödter A, Rietbrock S, Merz P-G, Schnieders M and Sieder C. Zur dosisabhängigen Verträglichkeit eines Agnus-castus-Spezialextraktes [Dose-dependent tolerability of an agnus castus special extract]. *Z. Phytotherapie* 1996, **17**, 237-243 [GERMAN/English summary].
38. Berger D, Schaffner W, Schrader E, Meier B and Brattström A. Efficacy of *Vitex agnus-castus* L. extract Ze 440 in patients with pre-menstrual syndrome (PMS). *Arch. Gynecol. Obstet.* 2000, **264**, 150-153.
39. Atmaca M, Kumru S and Tezcan E. Fluoxetine versus *Vitex agnus castus* extract in the treatment of premenstrual dysphoric disorder. *Hum. Psychopharmacol. Clin. Exp.* 2003, **18**, 191-195.
40. Parfitt K, editor. Premenstrual syndrome. In: *Martindale - The complete drug reference, 32nd edition.* ISBN 0-85369-429-X. London: Pharmaceutical Press, 1999:1456-1457.
41. Schellenberg R. Treatment for the premenstrual syndrome with agnus castus fruit extract: prospective randomised, placebo controlled study. *BMJ* 2001, **322**, 134-137.
42. Turner S and Mills S. A double-blind clinical trial on a herbal remedy for premenstrual syndrome: a case study. *Complementary Therap. Med.* 1993, **1**, 73-77.
43. Lauritzen C, Reuter HD, Repges R, Böhnert K-J and Schmidt U. Treatment of premenstrual tension syndrome with *Vitex agnus castus.* Controlled, double-blind study versus pyridoxine. *Phytomedicine* 1997, **4**, 183-189.
44. Loch E-G, Selle H and Boblitz N. Treatment of Premenstrual Syndrome with a Phytopharmaceutical Formulation Containing *Vitex agnus-castus. J. Women's Health Gender-Based Med.* 2000, **9**, 315-320.
45. Peters-Welte C and Albrecht M. Regeltempostörungen und PMS. Vitex agnus-castus in einer Anwendungsbeobachtung. [Menstrual cycle disturbances and PMS. Vitex agnus-castus in an observational study]. *TW Gynäkologie* 1994, **7**, 49-52 [GERMAN/English summary].
46. Dittmar FW, Böhnert K-J, Peeters M, Albrecht M, Lamertz M and Schmidt U. Prämenstruelles Syndrom. Behandlung mit einem Phytopharmakon. [Premenstrual syndrome. Treatment with a phytomedicine]. *TW Gynäkologie* 1992, **5**, 60-68 [GERMAN/English summary].
47. Feldmann HU, Albrecht M, Lamertz M and Böhnert K-J. Therapie bei Gelbkörperschwäche bzw. prämenstruellem Syndrom mit Vitex-agnus-castus-Tinktur. [Therapy for corpus luteum insufficiency or premenstrual syndrome with Vitex agnus-castus tincture]. *Gyne* 1990, (12), 421-425 [GERMAN/English summary].
48. Amann W. Amenorrhoe. Günstige Wirkung von Agnus castus (Agnolyt®) auf Amenorrhoe. [Favourable effect of Agnus castus (Agnolyt®) on amenorrhoea]. *Z. Allg. Med.* 1982, **58**, 228-231 [GERMAN].
49. Milewicz A, Gejdel E, Sworen H, Sienkiewicz K, Jedrzejak J, Teucher T and Schmitz H. *Vitex agnus castus* Extract in the Treatment of Luteal Phase Defects due to Latent Hyperprolactinaemia. Results of a randomized placebo-controlled double blind trial. *Arzneim.-Forsch./Drug Res.* 1993, **43**, 752-756 [GERMAN/English summary].
Also published as:
Teucher T. Der gestörte Menstruationszyklus. Indikation für *Vitex agnus castus* [The distorted menstrual cycle. Indication für *Vitex agnus castus*]. Therapeutikon 1993, **7**, 375-382 [GERMAN/English summary].
50. Gerhard I, Patek A, Monga B, Blank A and Gorkow C. Mastodynon® for Female Infertility. Randomized, Placebo-Controlled, Clinical Double-Blind Study. *Forsch. Komplementärmed.* 1998, **5**, 272-278 [GERMAN/English summary].
51. Propping D, Katzorke T and Belkien L. Diagnostik und Therapie der Gelbkörperschwäche in der Praxis [Diagnosis and therapy for corpus luteum insufficiency in practice]. *Therapiewoche* 1988, **38**, 2992-3001 [GERMAN/English summary].
52. Neumann-Kühnelt B, Stief G, Schmiady H and Kentenich H. Investigations of possible effects of the phytotherapeutic agent Agnus Castus on the follicular and corpus luteum phases. In: Abstracts of 9th Annual Meeting of the ESHRE, Thessaloniki, 1993 (Abstract 323). Published as: *Human Reproduction* 1993, **8** (Suppl. 1), 110.
53. Kubista E, Müller G and Spona J. Treatment of Mastopathy Associated with Cyclic Mastodynia: Clinical Results and Hormonal Profiles. *Gynäk. Rdsch.* 1986, **26**, 65-79 [GERMAN/English summary].
54. Wuttke W, Splitt G, Gorkow C and Sieder C. Behandlung zyklusabhängiger Brustschmerzen mit einem Agnus castus-haltigen Arzneimittel. Ergebnisse einer randomisierten, plazebo-kontrollierten Doppelblindstudie [Treatment of cyclical mastalgia with an agnus castus-containing preparation. Results of a randomized, placebo-controlled,

double-blind study]. *Geburtshilfe Frauenheilkunde* 1997, **57**, 569-574 [GERMAN/English summary].

55. Halaska M, Beles P, Gorkow C and Sieder C. Treatment of cyclical mastalgia with a solution containing a *Vitex agnus castus* extract: results of a placebo-controlled double-blind study. *The Breast* 1999, **8**, 175-181.
Also published as:
Halaska M, Raus K, Beles P, Martan A and Paithner KG. Treatment of the Cyclical Mastalgia with *Vitex agnus castus* Extract: Results of the Double Blind Placebo Controlled Study. *Ces. Gynek.* 1998, **63**, 388-392 [CZECH/English summary].
56. Agni casti fructus. German Commission E Monograph published in: Bundesanzeiger No. 226 of 2 December 1992.
57. Agnus castus (Chaste Tree). In: UK Statutory Instrument 1994 No. 2410. The Medicines (Products Other Than Veterinary Drugs) (General Sale List) Amendment Order 1994. Schedule 1, Table A.
58. Gattillier, fruit, sommité fleurie. In: *Médicaments à base de plantes*. ISBN 2-911473-02-7. Saint-Denis Cedex, France: Agence du Médicament, 1998.

REGULATORY GUIDELINES FROM OTHER EU COUNTRIES

FRANCE

Médicaments à base de plantes [58]: Gattillier, fruit.

Therapeutic indications accepted

Oral use
Traditionally used: for painful periods; in the symptomatic treatment of neurotonic states in adults and children, particularly in cases of minor sleep disorders.

GERMANY

Commission E monograph [56]: Agni casti fructus (Keuschlammfrüchte).

Uses
Menstrual cycle irregularities; premenstrual complaints, mastodynia.

Note: In cases of a feeling of tension and swelling in the breasts or menstrual bleeding disorders, a physician should first be consulted for diagnostic clarification.

Contraindications
None known.

Side effects
Occasional occurrence of an itching, urticarial rash.

Special precautions for use
None known.

Use during pregnancy and lactation
Not used during pregnancy.
A diminution of lactation output has been observed in animal studies.

Interactions with other drugs and other forms of interaction
No interactions are known.
Animal studies have pointed to a dopaminergic effect; therefore a reciprocal reduction in activity could occur if taking dopamine receptor antagonists.

Dosage
Unless otherwise prescribed, daily dose: hydroalcoholic extracts equivalent to 30-40 mg of crude drug.

Mode of administration
Liquid or dry hydroalcoholic extracts (50-70% V/V) from the comminuted fruits, taken orally.

Overdosage
None known.

Special warnings
None known.

Effects of ability to drive and operate machines
None known.

AGRIMONY **Rosaceae**

Agrimoniae herba

Synonyms: Common Agrimony (*A. eupatoria*); Fragrant Agrimony (*A. procera*) [1].

Definition
Agrimony consists of the dried flowering tops of *Agrimonia eupatoria* L. or *Agrimonia procera* Wallr.

CONSTITUENTS

☐ ***Tannins,*** 3-11% in *Agrimonia eupatoria*, 7-13% in *A. procera* [2-6], consisting mainly of proanthocyanidins (condensed tannins) [4,7] with a small proportion of ellagitannins [7]. Reported amounts are highly dependent on the method of determination [6].

The proanthocyanidins are present mainly in the form of leucoanthocyanins which yield cyanidin on acid hydrolysis [8,9].

☐ ***Flavonoids***, ca. 1.9% [10], principally hyperoside (0.37% in *A. eupatoria* and 0.18% in *A. procera* on average) [2], together with rutin, isoquercitrin, quercitrin, luteolin and apigenin [2,4,8,11,12]; also kaempferol, its 3-glucoside, 3-rhamnoside, 3-rutinoside and 4′-methyl ether (kaempferide) [13,14], and kaempferide 3-rhamnoside [13].

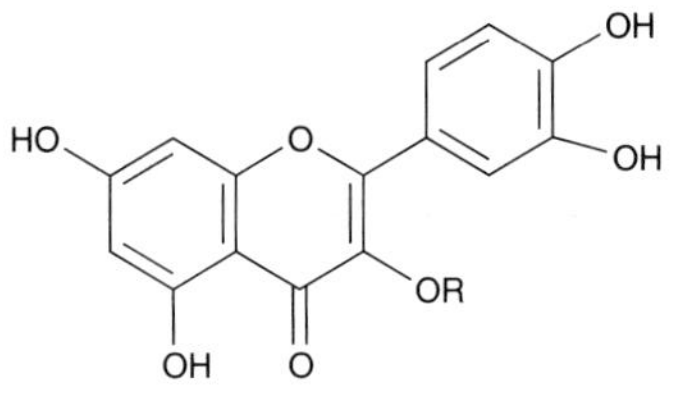

	R
Hyperoside	galactosyl
Rutin	rutinosyl
Quercitrin	rhamnosyl
Isoquercitrin	glucosyl

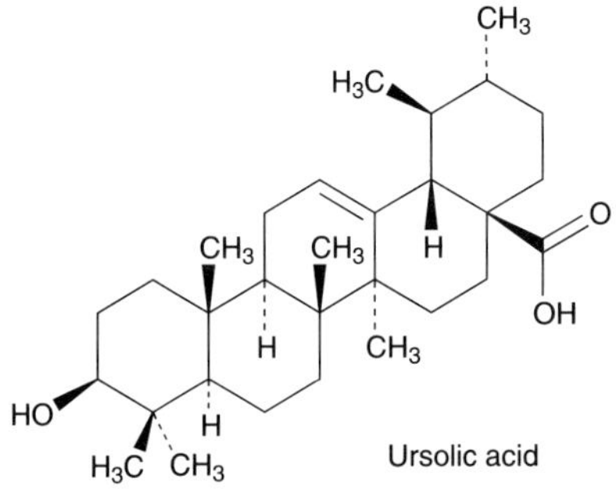

Ursolic acid

☐ ***Triterpenoids*** Ursolic acid (0.6%) [15]; also euscapic acid and the 28-glucosyl esters of euscapic acid and tormentic acid [14].

☐ ***Phenolic acids*** Chlorogenic, caffeic and ellagic acids in both species [16,17]; also *p*-hydroxybenzoic, protocatechuic, homoprotocatechuic, gentisic, vanillic, salicylic, *p*-coumaric and ferulic acids in *A. eupatoria* [17].

☐ ***Minerals*** 7.3-7.9% in *A. eupatoria*, 6.5-7.6% in *A. procera* [2], with a relatively high silica content [7]. Potassium and sodium concentrations in the dried herb were determined as 12,882 μg/g and 37.2 μg/g respectively, a ratio of 346:1 [18].

☐ ***Other constituents*** include β-sitosterol [14], polysaccharides (19.5%) and unidentified coumarins [4].

Published Assay Methods
Determination of tannins in herbal drugs [Ph. Eur. method 2.8.14]. Hyperoside, quercitrin, isoquercitrin, rutin, luteolin 7-glucoside and apigenin 7-glucoside by HPLC [2].

PHARMACOLOGY

In vitro
An aqueous extract of agrimony (1 mg of dried extract per ml) stimulated 2-deoxyglucose transport (1.4-fold), glucose oxidation (1.4-fold) and incorporation of glucose into glycogen (2.0-fold) in mouse abdominal muscle, comparable to 0.1 μM insulin. In acute 20-minute tests, 0.25-1 mg/ml of aqueous extract of agrimony evoked a stepwise 1.9- to 3.8-fold stimulation of insulin secretion from the BRIN-BD11 rat pancreatic B-cell line with no detrimental effect on cell viability. These experiments demonstrated the presence of insulin-like, insulin-releasing activity in agrimony [19].

A hydromethanolic extract (*Agrimonia eupatoria*; 50% V/V) showed no spasmolytic activity on spontaneous or induced contractions of isolated guinea-pig ileum at concentrations up to 800 μg/ml [20].

In vivo
After oral administration to rats of an infusion or decoction of agrimony at a dose equivalent to 3 g of dried herb per kg body weight, the volume of urine excreted over the following 6 hours was significantly less ($p<0.01$) than that from rats treated with distilled water. The amount of uric acid in the urine was significantly greater ($p<0.01$), over

twice the amount in 4 hours compared to rats treated with distilled water, suggesting a uricosuric effect, while the amount of urea remained largely unchanged [21]. Further experiments with rats showed that, while diuresis resulting from distilled water provoked loss of electrolytes, agrimony compensated for electrolyte loss, particularly that of potassium [22].

Agrimony incorporated into the diet, 62.5 g/kg in food and 2.5 g/litre (a diluted decoction) in drinking water for 20 days, countered the weight loss, polydipsia, hyperphagia and hyperglycaemia of streptozotocin (STZ)-induced diabetic mice. Which constituent of agrimony has anti-hyperglycaemic activity is not clear but, from in vitro experiments (above), it appears to be water-soluble and heat stable [19].

According to Drozd et al. [4], luteolin 7-glucoside is known to have a cholagogic action, which "explains and justifies the wide use of the herb agrimony in folk medicine for the treatment of diseases of the liver".

CLINICAL STUDIES

In an open study, 20 patients with cutaneous porphyria were treated orally with infusions of *Agrimonia eupatoria* 3-4 times daily (and no other treatment). Substantial improvements in skin eruptions were observed after 15 days together with decreases in serum iron levels and urinary porphyrins (intensely hyperchromic urine after initial doses, decolorizing to normal over the following days). All the patients showed improvements in general health (appetite, lack of dyspepsia, regularity) [23].

THERAPEUTICS

Actions
Mildly astringent [24-26], uricosuric [21], anti-hyperglycaemic [19], anti-inflammatory [26], probably cholagogic [4].

Indications
None adequately substantiated by pharmacological or clinical studies.

Uses based on experience or tradition
Internal use: Mild diarrhoea [27,28], especially in children [24]. Cutaneous porphyria [23].

As a gargle for inflammation of the oral and pharyngeal mucosa [28], including acute sore throat [24,26] and chronic pharyngeal catarrh [24].
External use: Skin disorders including inflammation [28], rashes [26], sores, eruptions and ulcers [25,26], and in wound healing [8].

Agrimony has also been used internally for liver and gall bladder disorders [4,8,25,26,29]; kidney disorders, especially kidney stones [26]; gastritis and enteritis [26], urinary incontinence, cystitis [24]; venous insufficiency, such as 'heavy legs' and haemorrhoids [27], and diabetes mellitus [19,30].

Contraindications
None known.

Side effects
None known.

Interactions with other drugs
None known.

Dosage
Internal use: Three times daily, 1-3 g of dried herb or as an infusion or equivalent preparation [24,28]; liquid extract (1:1) in 25% ethanol, 1-3 ml [24]; tincture (1:5 in 45% ethanol), 5-10 ml.
External use: 10% decoction, in compresses several times daily [28].

SAFETY

Few specific safety data are available on agrimony but extensive traditional use and wide regulatory acceptance are reassuring with regard to its use at therapeutic dosage levels. *Agrimonia eupatoria* has been assessed as a herb that can be safely consumed when used appropriately [31].

No adverse effects were observed when an infusion of *Agrimonia eupatoria* herb was administered orally 3-4 times daily for 15 days to 20 patients with cutaneous porphyria [23].

No mutagenic potential was shown in the *Salmonella* microsome reversion assay (Ames test) by a methanolic extract [14] or a tincture (1:5, ethanol 70%) of agrimony [32].

REGULATORY STATUS

Medicines

UK	Accepted for general sale, internal or external use [33].
France	Accepted for specified indications [27].
Germany	Commission E monograph published, with approved uses [28].

Foods

Council of Europe	Permitted as flavouring, category N2 [34].

REFERENCES

Current Pharmacopoeial Monographs

Ph. Eur. Agrimony

Literature References

1. Blamey M and Grey-Wilson C. *The Illustrated Flora of Britain and Northern Europe.* ISBN 0-340-40170-2. London: Hodder & Stoughton, 1989.
2. Carnat A, Lamaison JL and Petitjean-Freytet C. L'Aigremoine: Étude comparée d'*Agrimonia eupatoria* L. et *Agrimonia procera* Wallr. [Agrimony: Comparative study of *Agrimonia eupatoria* L. and *Agrimonia procera* Wallr.]. *Plantes Méd. Phytothér.* 1991, **25**, 202-211 [FRENCH/English summary].
3. Lamaison JL, Carnat A and Petitjean-Freytet C. Tannin content and elastase inhibiting activity in the Rosaceae family. *Ann. Pharm. Fr.* 1990, **48**, 335-340 [FRENCH/English summary].
4. Drozd GA, Yavlyanskaya SF and Inozemtseva TM. Phytochemical investigation of *Agrimonia eupatoria. Khim. Prir. Soedin.* 1983, (1), 106 [RUSSIAN]; translated into English as *Chem. Nat. Compd.* 1983, **19**, 104.
5. Bucková A, Leifertová I, Nátherová L and Skalický V. Pharmacobotanical Study of the Genus *Agrimonia*. II. Evaluation of Tannins in European Agrimony. *Ceskoslov. Farm.* 1971, **20**, 136-140 [CZECH/English summary].
6. Péter MH and Rácz G. Der Gerbstoffgehalt verschiedener Agrimoniaarten [The tannin content of various Agrimonia species]. *Pharmazie* 1973, **28**, 539-541 [GERMAN].
7. Gyzicki F. *Agrimonia eupatoria* L. - Der Odermennig. 2. Mitteilung. [*Agrimonia eupatoria* L. - Agrimony. Part 2]. *Pharmazie* 1949, **4**, 463-471.
8. Gorunovic M, Stosic D and Lukic P. La valeur de l'Aigremoine (*Agrimonia eupatoria* L.) comme plante médicinale. [The value of Agrimony (*Agrimonia eupatoria* L.) as a medicinal plant]. *Herba Hungarica* 1989, **28**, 45-49 [FRENCH].
9. Bate-Smith EC. Tannins of herbaceous Leguminosae. *Phytochemistry* 1973, **12**, 1809-1812.
10. Karatodorov K and Kolarova R. Study of the flavonoid composition of some Bulgarian medicinal plants. *Durzh. Inst. Kontrol Lek. Sredstva* 1977, **10**, 103-109 [BULGARIAN]; through *Chem. Abstr.* 1978, **89**, 72948.
11. Sendra J and Zieba J. Isolation and identification of flavonoid compounds from herb of agrimony (*Agrimonia eupatoria* L.). *Diss. Pharm. Pharmacol.* 1972, **24**, 79-83.
12. Ivanov V and Nikolov N. Flavonoids from the Rosaceae family. I. Isolation of flavonoid mixtures from the aerial part of *Agrimonia eupatoria* and from flowers of *Prunus spinosa. Farmatsiya (Sofia)* 1969, **19** (4), 36-41 [BULGARIAN] through *Chem. Abstr.* 1970, **72**, 51781.
13. Bilia AR, Palme E, Marsili A, Pistelli L and Morelli I. A flavonol glycoside from *Agrimonia eupatoria. Phytochemistry* 1993, **32**, 1078-1079.
14. Bilia AR, Palme E, Catalano S, Pistelli L and Morelli I. Constituents and biological assay of *Agrimonia eupatoria. Fitoterapia* 1993, **64**, 549-550.
15. Le Men J and Pourrat H. Répartition de l'acide ursolique dans les feuilles de diverses Rosacées – Acide ursolique (Cinquième mémoire). [Distribution of ursolic acid in the leaves of various Rosaceae - Ursolic acid (Fifth report)]. *Ann. Pharm. Fr.* 1955, **13**, 169-170 [FRENCH].
16. Bucková A, Eisenreichová E, Leifertová I and Lichá K. Pharmacobotanical Study of the Genus *Agrimonia*. III. Phenolic Substances and Saccharides in *Agrimonia eupatoria* L. ssp. *eupatoria* and *Agrimonia procera* Wallr. *Ceskoslov. Farm.* 1972, **21**, 244-248 [SLOVAK/English summary].
17. Krzaczek T. Phenolic acids in some tannin drugs from the Rosaceae family. *Farm. Pol.* 1984, **40**, 475-477 [POLISH]; through *Chem. Abstr.* 1985, **102**, 146198.
18. Szentmihályi K, Kéry Á, Then M, Lakatos B, Sándor Z and Vinkler P. Potassium-Sodium Ratio for the Characterization of Medicinal Plant Extracts with Diuretic Activity. *Phytotherapy Res.* 1998, **12**, 163-166.
19. Gray AM and Flatt PR. Actions of the traditional anti-diabetic plant, *Agrimonia eupatoria* (agrimony): effects on hyperglycaemia, cellular glucose metabolism and insulin secretion. *Brit. J. Nutr.* 1998, **80**, 109-114.
20. Izzo AA, Capasso R, Senatore F, Seccia S and Morrica P. Spasmolytic Activity of Medicinal Plants Used for the Treatment of Disorders Involving Smooth Muscles. *Phytotherapy Res.* 1996, **10** (Suppl.), S107-S108.
21. Giachetti D, Taddei E and Taddei I. Ricerche sull'attività diuretica ed uricosurica di *Agrimonia eupatoria* L. [Investigation on the diuretic and uricosuric activity of *Agrimonia eupatoria* L.]. *Boll. Soc. Ital. Biol. Sper.* 1986, **62**, 705-711 [ITALIAN/English summary].
22. Giachetti D, Taddei I, Cenni A and Taddei E. Diuresis from Distilled Water Compared with that from Vegetable Drugs. *Planta Medica* 1989, **55**, 97.
23. Patrascu V, Chebac-Patrascu I and Gheorghiu G. Favourable therapeutic results in cutaneous porphyria obtained with *Agrimonia eupatoria. Dermato-Venerologia* 1984, **29**, 153-157 [ROMANIAN/English summary].
24. Agrimonia. In: *British Herbal Pharmacopoeia 1983.* ISBN 0-903032-07-4. Bournemouth: British Herbal Medicine Association, 1983.
25. Grieve M, edited by Leyel CF. Agrimony. In: *A Modern Herbal* (first published in 1931). ISBN 1-85501-249-9. London: Tiger Books International, 1994:12-14.
26. Stodola J and Volák J. Agrimony. Translated into English in: Bunney S, editor. *The Illustrated Book of Herbs.* ISBN 0-7064-1489-6. London: Octopus Books, 1984:55.
27. Aigremoine. In: *Médicaments à base de plantes.* ISBN 2-911473-02-7. Saint-Denis Cedex, France: Agence du Médicament, 1998.
28. Agrimoniae herba (Odermennigkraut). German Commission E Monograph published in: Bundesanzeiger No. 50 of 13.03.86; amended in Bundesanzeiger No. 50 of 13.03.90.
29. Weiss RF. *Agrimonia eupatoria* (Agrimony). In: *Herbal Medicine* (translated from the 6th German edition of *Lehrbuch der Phytotherapie*). ISBN 0-906584-19-1. Beaconsfield, UK: Beaconsfield Publishers, 1988:92-93.
30. Gray AM and Flatt PR. Nature's own pharmacy: the diabetes perspective. *Proc. Nutr. Soc.* 1997, **56**, 507-517.
31. McGuffin M, Hobbs C, Upton R and Goldberg A, editors. *Agrimonia eupatoria* L. In: American Herbal Products Association's *Botanical Safety Handbook.* Boca Raton-Boston-London: CRC Press, 1997:5.
32. Schimmer O, Krüger A, Paulini H and Haefele F. An evaluation of 55 commercial plant extracts in the Ames mutagenicity test. *Pharmazie* 1994, **49**, 448-452.
33. Agrimony. In: UK Statutory Instrument 1984 No. 769. The Medicines (Products other than Veterinary Drugs) (General Sale List) Order 1984. Schedule 1, Table A.
34. *Agrimonia eupatoria* L., herb. In: *Flavouring Substances and Natural Sources of Flavourings,* 3rd ed. ISBN 2-7160-0081-6. Strasbourg: Council of Europe, 1981.

REGULATORY GUIDELINES FROM OTHER EU COUNTRIES

FRANCE

Médicaments à base de plantes [27]: Aigremoine, sommité fleurie.

Therapeutic indications accepted

Oral use

Traditionally used in subjective manifestations of venous insufficiency, such as heavy legs, and for haemorrhoidal symptoms.

Traditionally used in the symptomatic treatment of mild diarrhoea.

Topical use
Traditionally used in subjective manifestations of venous insufficiency, such as heavy legs.
Traditionally used for haemorrhoidal symptoms.
Traditionally used topically in mouthwashes, for buccal hygiene.

GERMANY

Commission E monograph [28]: Agrimoniae herba (Odermennigkraut).

Uses
Internal use: Mild, non-specific acute diarrhoea. Inflammation of the oral and pharyngeal mucosa.
External use: Mild, superficial inflammation of the skin.

Contraindications
None known.

Side effects
None known.

Interactions with other drugs
None known.

Dosage
Unless otherwise prescribed, oral daily dose: 3-6 g of the drug or equivalent preparations. For external use, compresses with a 10% decoction several times daily.

Mode of administration
Finely cut or powdered drug for infusions; other galenic preparations for internal or external use.

Action
Astringent.

AMMONIACUM

Umbelliferae

Gummi-resina Ammoniacum

Synonyms: Ammoniac, gum ammoniac; known in India and Pakistan as Ushaq or Ushak.

Definition

Ammoniacum consists of the gum-resin exuded from flowering and fruiting stems of *Dorema ammoniacum* D. Don [*D. aitchisonii* Korovin, *D. aucheri* Boisson, *Diserneston gummiferum* Jaub. et Spach].

Dorema ammoniacum grows in Iran (the principal source of ammoniacum) and other central Asian countries such as Afghanistan, Pakistan and Uzbekhistan. The plant stems are punctured by beetles, causing the secretion of an exudate from the cortex. The exudate dries on the stem in the form of tears, which are collected [1].

Only ammoniacum in the form of tears (5-25 cm in diameter) or nodular masses of tears is of pharmacopoeial quality. Material in large lumps (up to 600 g), consisting of exudate which fell to the ground and agglutinated, is usually inferior and often contaminated with plant parts, stones and other debris [1-3].

The name of the drug is said to originate from the Temple of Jupiter Ammon in the Libyan Desert, an area from where it was collected in ancient times [4]. However, Cyrenaican 'ammoniacum' and other types from north Africa are derived from *Ferula* species [1,5] and no longer used medicinally.

CONSTITUENTS

Ammoniacum is composed of 50-70% resin, 18-26% gum and up to 0.5% essential oil.

□ ***Coumarins*** Ammoresinol (a major component of the resin) [6-8], the pyranocoumarin 7-hydroxyferprenin (ca. 1.2%) [9] and the furanocoumarins bergapten and imperatorin [10].

A phenolic compound, 2′,4′-dihydroxyphenyl-4,8,12-trimethyl-3,7,11-tridecatrienylketone, which is related to (and can readily be converted to, or derived from) ammoresinol, has also been isolated [11].

□ ***Chromandiones*** A spirosesquiterpenoid chroman-2,4-dione was identified simultaneously in 1991 by two Italian research groups. Arnone et al. named it doremone A [12], while Appendino et al. isolated the same compound as a mixture of C-3′ epimers and named it ammodoremin [9]. Its structure is related to coumarins and it is probably formed biogenetically from a dioxygenated coumarin and a farnesyl unit [9,12].

□ ***Polysaccharides*** The gum fraction of ammoniacum contains a branched galactan (MW ca. 21,600) with 57% of D-galactose and attached residues of L-arabinose (19%), D-glucuronic acid and 4-

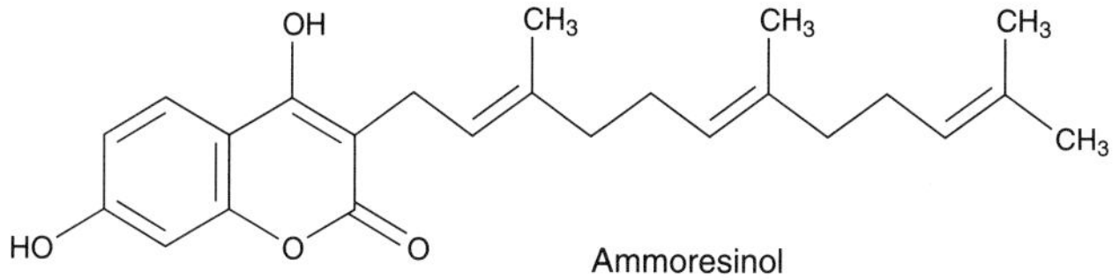

Ammoresinol

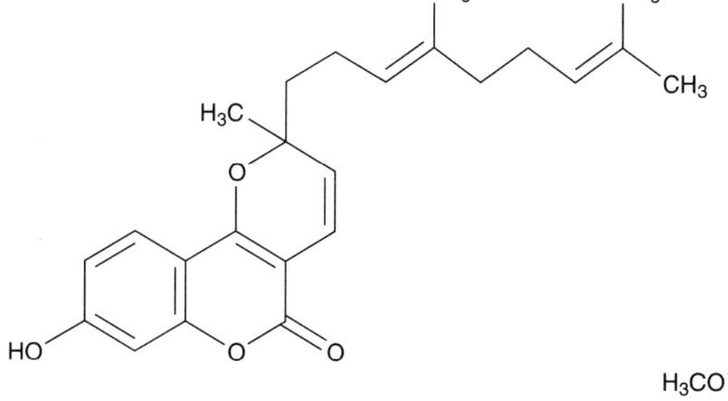

7-Hydroxyferprenin

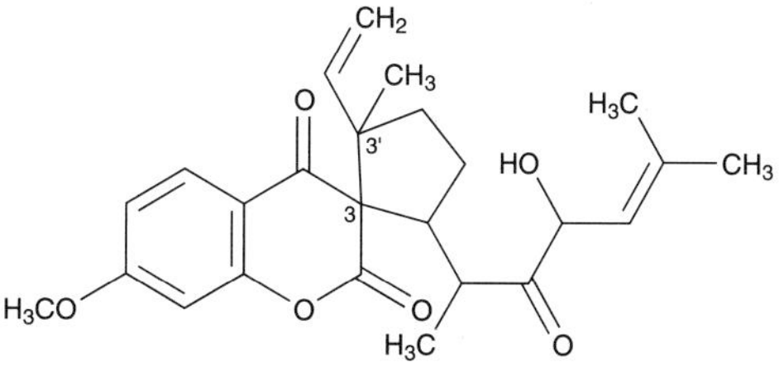

Doremone A

methyl-D-glucuronic acid (16%), and L-rhamnose (8%) [13,14].
□ ***Essential oil***, 0.3-0.5%, containing citronellyl acetate (39%), ferulene (20%), doremyl alcohol (ca. 13%), doremone (3%), α-pinene (4%) and other terpenes [10,15]. The higher boiling fraction contains cetyl alcohol [15].
□ ***Other constituents*** include salicylic acid [1,16] and methyl salicylate [3].

Published Assay Methods
No quantitative methods published. Qualitative and semi-quantitative phytochemical fingerprinting of ammoniacum by HPTLC and densitometric scanning has been described [17].

PHARMACOLOGY

No relevant *in vitro* or *in vivo* data have been traced in the literature.

Pharmacological studies in humans
According to a patent application, preparations containing ammoniacum and vitamin K3 have been used in the treatment of malignant tumours [18].

CLINICAL STUDIES

None published on mono-preparations of ammoniacum.

THERAPEUTICS

Actions
Expectorant [1-4,19,20], spasmolytic [3,4,19], stimulant [2,4,5], mildly diaphoretic [3,4,19,20], mildly diuretic [1,3,4,6], emmenagogic [3,4,20].

Indications
None adequately substantiated by pharmacological or clinical studies.

Uses based on experience or tradition
Internal: Chronic bronchitis [1-4,19,20], particularly when the secretion is viscid [4]; asthma [2,3,19] and persistent coughs [20].
Joint pains and sciatica; liver and spleen complaints [3].
External: Treatment of wounds and sciatica [3,5]; as a plaster for white swellings of the joints [3-5] and benign tumours [4].

Contraindications
Should not be used internally during pregnancy.

Side effects
None known.

Interactions with other drugs
None known.

Dosage
Three times daily: powdered gum-resin, 0.3-1 g [1,19].

Has also been used in liquid preparations, usually in combination, e.g. Ammoniacum Mixture BPC 1934: powdered ammoniacum, syrup of tolu and water (3:6:100); single dose, 15-30 ml.

SAFETY

Preparations containing ammoniacum have been used internally in humans without causing side effects [18]. The essential oil from ammoniacum is considered unlikely to present any hazard in aromatherapy [21].

Blood from groups of rats which received ammodoremin intragastrically at 2, 107, 214 or 1068 mmol/kg for 2 days had a significantly increased prothrombin time (>100 seconds, compared to 12 seconds for controls) only at the highest dose, which was 80 times the warfarin dose required to obtain a similar response. Liver damage was also observed only at the highest dose [9]. These results are reassuring with respect to ammoniacum at therapeutic dose levels.

Very old reports that ammoniacum taken internally can cause sight disorders (from a 1928 book) [3] and has an abortifacient action (apparently dating back to the writings of Dioscorides) [5] have not been substantiated but add a note of caution.

REGULATORY STATUS

Medicines

UK	Accepted for general sale, internal or external use [22].
France	Not listed in *Médicaments à base de plantes* [23].
Germany	No Commission E monograph published.

Food
Not used in foods.

REFERENCES

Current Pharmacopoeial Monographs
BHP Ammoniacum

Literature References

1. Pharmaceutical Society of Great Britain. Ammoniacum. In: *British Pharmaceutical Codex (BPC) 1949*. London:

Pharmaceutical Press, 1949:81.
2. Wood HC and LaWall CH, editors. Ammoniacum. In: *United States Dispensatory*, Centennial (22nd) Edition. Philadelphia-London: JB Lippincott Company, 1937:1232-1233.
3. Martinetz D. Dorema. In: Blaschek W, Hänsel R, Keller K, Reichling J, Rimpler H and Schneider G, editors. *Hagers Handbuch der Pharmazeutischen Praxis, 5th ed. Supplement Volume 2: Drogen A-K.* ISBN 3-540-61618-7. Berlin-Heidelberg-New York-London: Springer, 1998:530-534 [GERMAN].
4. Grieve M (edited by Leyel CF). Ammoniacum. In: *A Modern Herbal* (First published 1931; revised 1973). ISBN 1-85501-249-9. London: Tiger Books International, 1994:31.
5. Breckle S-W and Unger W. Afghanische Drogen und ihre Stammpflanzen (I). Gummiharze von Umbelliferen [Afghan drugs and their botanical sources (I). Gum-resins from Umbelliferae]. *Afghanistan J.* (Graz, Austria; ISSN 03046125) 1977, **4**, 86-95 [GERMAN/English summary].
6. Späth E, Simon AFJ and Lintner J. Die Konstitution des Ammoresinols (XIX. Mitteil. über natürliche Cumarine) [The constitution of ammoresinol (Natural coumarins, Part XIX)]. *Ber.* 1936, **69**, 1656-1664 [GERMAN].
7. Kunz K and Hoops L. Über die Harzbestandteile des Ammoniacums, II. Mitteil.: Die Konstitution des Ammoresinols [The resin component of ammoniacum. Part II. The constitution of ammoresinol]. *Ber.* 1936, **69**, 2174-2182 [GERMAN].
8. Späth E and Kesztler F. Zur Konstitution des Ammoresinols (XXXI. Mitteil. über natürliche Cumarine) [The constitution of ammoresinol (Natural coumarins, Part XXXI)]. *Ber.* 1937, **70**, 1255-1258 [GERMAN].
9. Appendino G, Nano GM, Viterbo D, De Munno G, Cisero M, Palmisano G and Aragno M. Ammodoremin, an Epimeric Mixture of Prenylated Chromandiones from Ammoniacum. *Helv. Chim. Acta* 1991, **74**, 495-500.
10. Ashraf M, Munir A, Karim A and Batty MK. Studies on the essential oils of the Pakistani species of the family Umbelliferae. Part XIV. *Dorema ammoniacum* ("Ushak") gum. *Pakistan J. Sci. Ind. Res.* 1977, **20**, 298-299.
11. Cardillo G, Cricchio R and Merlini L. Un nuovo costituente fenolico della gomma ammoniaco [A new phenolic constituent of ammoniacum gum]. *Ricerca Scientifica* 1968, **38**, 804-805 [ITALIAN].
12. Arnone A, Nasini G, Vajna de Parva O and Camarda L. Isolation and structure elucidation of doremone A, a new spiro-sesquiterpenoidic chroman-2,4-dione from ammoniac gum resin. *Gazz. Chim. Ital.* 1991, **121**, 383-386.
13. Guarnieri A and Amorosa M. Sulla struttura della gomma contenuta nella gommo-resina "ammoniaco". Nota I. Caratteri generali, idrolisi acida, metilazione e metanolisi [Structure of the gum in gum-resin "ammoniacum". Part 1. General characteristics, acid hydrolysis, methylation and methanolysis]. *Ann. Chim. (Rome)* 1970, **60**, 3-16 [ITALIAN/English summary].
14. Guarnieri A and Amorosa M. Sulla struttura della gomma contenuta nella gommo-resina "ammoniaco". Part II. Idrolisi parziale e gomma degradata [Structure of the gum in gum-resin "ammoniacum". Part 2. Partial hydrolysis and degraded gum]. *Ann. Chim. (Rome)* 1970, **60**, 17-28 [ITALIAN/English summary].
15. Semmler FW, Jonas KG and Roenisch P. Gum ammoniac oil, and synthetic experiments on the nature of its constituents. Ber. 1917, **50**, 1823-1837 [GERMAN]; through *Chem. Abstr.* 1918, **12**, 1461-1462.
16. Leclerc H. The pharmacology of gum ammoniac. *Bull. Sci. Pharmacol.* 1941, **48**, 81-87 [FRENCH]; through *Chem. Abstr.* 1942, **36**, 1140.
17. Rajani M, Ravishankara MN, Shrivastava N and Padh H. HPTLC-Aided Phytochemical Fingerprinting Analysis as a Tool for Evaluation of Herbal Drugs. A Case Study of Ushaq (Ammoniacum Gum). *J. Planar Chromatogr.* 2001, **14**, 34-41.
18. Chekroun M. Pharmaceuticals containing ammoniac gum for use in treating malignant tumors. Fr. Demande FR 2,502,008 (Cl. A61K35/78), 24 September 1982; through *Chem. Abstr.* 1983, **98**, 40602.
19. Ammoniacum. In: *British Herbal Pharmacopoeia 1983.* ISBN 0-903032-07-4. Bournemouth: British Herbal Medicine Association, 1983.
20. Chevallier A. In: *The Encyclopedia of Medicinal Plants.* ISBN 0-7513-0314-3. London-New York-Stuttgart: Dorling Kindersley, 1996:200.
21. Tisserand R and Balacs T. Safety Index, Part 2: Ammoniac (gum). In: *Essential Oil Safety - A Guide for Health Care Professionals.* ISBN 0-443-05260-3. Edinburgh: Churchill-Livingstone, 1995:212.
22. Gum Ammoniacum. In: UK Statutory Instrument 2001 No. 2068. The Medicines (Products Other Than Veterinary Drugs) (General Sale List) Amendment Order 2001. Schedule 1, Table A.
23. *Médicaments à base de plantes.* ISBN 2-911473-02-7. Saint-Denis Cedex, France: Agence du Médicament, 1998.

ANGELICA ROOT

Umbelliferae

Angelicae radix

Definition

Angelica Root consists of the dried rhizome and roots of *Angelica archangelica* L. [*Archangelica officinalis* Hoffm.].

There are several subspecies of *Angelica archangelica* L. The angelica cultivated in Europe for flavouring, perfumery and medicinal use is mainly ssp. *archangelica* var. *sativa*, the garden angelica. Another variety of ssp. *archangelica*, found particularly in Scandinavia, is var. *archangelica* (mountain angelica, also called var. *norvegica* or simply *Angelica norvegica*). A further European subspecies is ssp. *litoralis*. In the Indian subcontinent ssp. *himalaica* is used medicinally [1,2].

CONSTITUENTS

□ ***Coumarins*** Osthenol (0.04%) and osthol [3-5].

□ ***Furanocoumarins*** Over 20 furanocoumarin compounds have been reported [3] including bergapten, angelicin, imperatorin, isoimperatorin, oxypeucedanin, oxypeucedanin hydrate, phellopterin, ostruthol, byakangelicin angelate, xanthotoxin, psoralen and isopimpinellin, and the dihydrofuranocoumarins archangelicin and 2′-angeloyl-3′-isovaleryl vaginate [3,4].

Quantitative data on the total and individual amounts of coumarins and furanocoumarins are scarce in the literature.

□ ***Essential oil***, 0.2-2% [6,7] (Ph. Eur. min. 0.2% V/m), of varied composition depending on the source, the plant variety and whether the oil is steam-distilled or extracted, but consisting predominantly of monoterpenes: α-pinene (19-32%), δ-3-carene (10-25%), limonene (7-10%), *p*-cymene (3-9%), myrcene (2-6%) and many others among over 80 components of the oil [6,8,9]. β-Phellandrene is sometimes the predominant monoterpene, especially in root oil from ssp. *archangelica* var. *archangelica* [8-10]; in one investigation β-pinene was found to be predominant [11].

Small amounts of sesquiterpenes, such as α-copaene, germacrene D, β-bisabolene and caryophyllenes [6-10], and macrocyclic lactones [12] are also present.

□ ***Phenolic acids*** Chlorogenic and caffeic acids [13].

□ ***Other constituents*** include sitosteryl esters, angelic acid and various fatty acids [14], tannins [1] and starch.

Further compounds identified in (what was stated to be, or probably was) ssp. *himalaica* include two prenylated flavanones, archangelenone (= 4′-*O*-prenyl naringenin) and a diprenyl naringenin [15], pregnenolone, peucenin 7-ethyl ether (a chromone) [16] and angelicain (a furanochromone) [17].

Published Assay Methods

Essential oil composition by GC and GC-MS [6]. HPLC of furanocoumarins [18]. Osthenol by TLC densitometry [5].

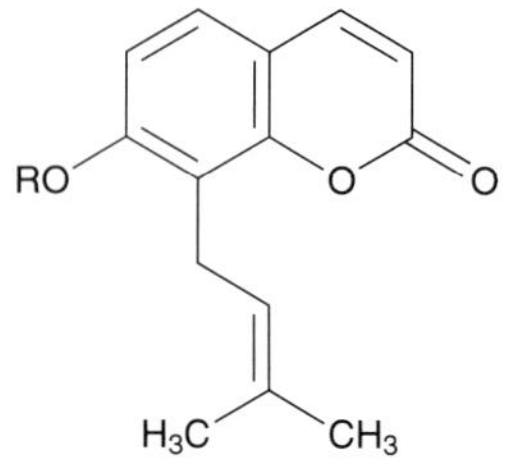

Osthenol R = H
Osthol R = CH_3

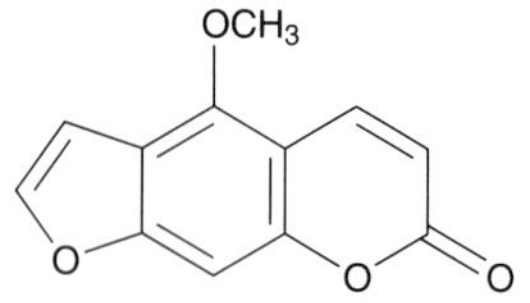

Bergapten

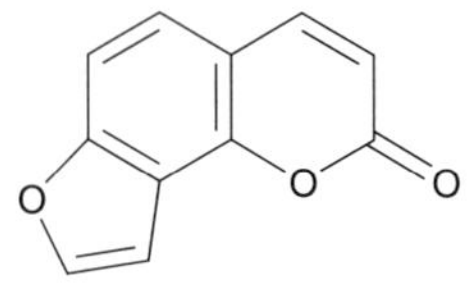

Angelicin

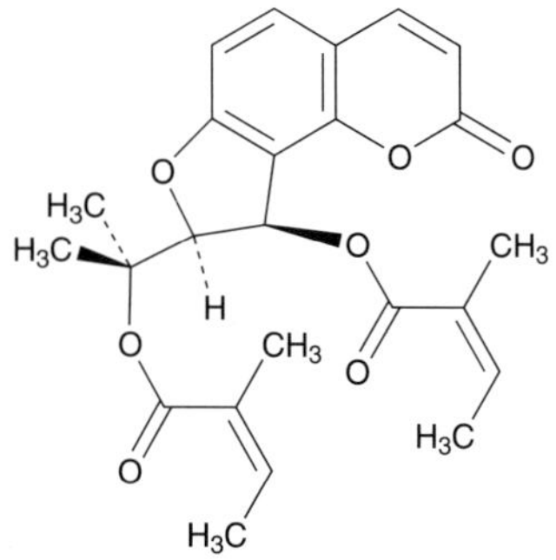

Archangelicin

PHARMACOLOGY

In vitro

Calcium-blocking activity
Extracts of angelica root exerted significant calcium blocking activity, inhibiting depolarization-induced uptake of calcium ions ($^{45}Ca^{2+}$) into rat pituitary cells, an effect attributed to coumarins and furanocoumarins in the extract. When isolated compounds were tested in the same system, osthol, imperatorin, isoimperatorin and phellopterin had IC_{50} values in the range 4-12 µg/ml, and others caused significant, if lesser, inhibition of 39-46% at 20 µg/ml. A methanolic extract of angelica root and the most potent furanocoumarin extracted from it, archangelicin, had IC_{50} values of 3.9 µg/ml [19,20] and 1.2 µg/ml (2.8 µM) [3,21] respectively, compared to 2.0 µg/ml for verapamil, a commonly used calcium-channel blocker. The main therapeutic influence of calcium-channel blockers is on cardiac function and blood circulation; they are coronary vasodilators and reduce peripheral vascular resistance [20].

Spasmolytic and relaxant activity
A 50%-methanolic extract of angelica root exhibited significant spasmolytic activity in isolated guinea pig ileum ($p<0.05$), inhibiting spontaneous contractions of the circular smooth muscle (IC_{50} 265 µg/ml) and acetylcholine- and barium chloride-induced contractions of the longitudinal smooth muscle (IC_{50} values of 242 and 146 µg/ml respectively) [22].

Angelica root oil had a potent relaxant effect on isolated guinea pig tracheal and ileal smooth muscle, inhibiting contractions with IC_{50} values of 2.5 mg/litre and 10 mg/litre respectively [23].

Angelicin at 20 µg/ml produced marked relaxation of isolated rabbit duodenum and inhibited acetylcholine-, histamine- and barium chloride-induced contractions in guinea pig ileum by 50% [24].

Anti-inflammatory activity
A dichloromethane/petroleum ether extract of angelica root inhibited the enzymes cycloxygenase-1 (COX-1) by 55% and 5-lipoxygenase (5-LO) by 85% at a concentration of 50 µg/ml. In similar assays, coumarins isolated from angelica root showed no remarkable inhibitory activity on COX-1, but concentration-dependent inhibition of 5-LO was observed with osthol (IC_{50} 36.2 µM) [4].

Other activities of furanocoumarins
Phellopterin strongly inhibited the binding of [^{3}H]diazepam to CNS benzodiazepine receptors in isolated rat cortical membrane with an IC_{50} of 0.36 µM. Although less potent than diazepam itself (IC_{50} 0.018 µM), the selectivity of the benzodiazepine receptor for phellopterin was considered remarkable [25].

Various furanocoumarins present in angelica root inhibited cell proliferation when incubated at 25 µg/ml for 48 hours with HeLa cancer cell cultures. Xanthotoxin and imperatorin have also been shown to inhibit the proliferation of lymphocytes *in vitro*, and xanthotoxin to inhibit the growth of induced tumours in mice [26].

In vivo

Activities of furanocoumarins
Angelicin has potent sedative, anticonvulsant and central muscle relaxant effects in mice, rats and rabbits. When administered intraperitoneally at 20-80 mg/kg or orally at 40-300 mg/kg it caused marked sedation, flaccidity, inhibition of spontaneous motor activity (77% at 80 mg/kg i.p.) and hypothermia [24].

Anti-inflammatory and analgesic activity of osthol
Osthol inhibited carrageenan-induced rat paw oedema, by 65% when administered intraperitoneally at 50 mg/kg body weight ($p<0.01$) compared to 47% for indometacin at 10 mg/kg, and by 62% when administered orally at 500 mg/kg. It also inhibited acetic acid-induced writhing in mice, by 61% at 50 mg/kg ($p<0.01$) compared to 70% for aspirin at 100 mg/kg, and by 54% when administered orally at 250 mg/kg [27].

CLINICAL STUDIES

None published on mono-preparations of angelica root.

THERAPEUTICS

Actions
Aromatic bitter [1,28,29], warming tonic and stomachic [30,31], spasmolytic [22-24,29], carminative [1,28-31], diaphoretic and expectorant [29,30,33].

Indications
None adequately substantiated by pharmacological or clinical studies.

Uses based on experience or tradition
Main uses Dyspeptic complaints such as mild gastrointestinal spasms, flatulence, eructation, bloating or sluggish digestion [29-31,34,35]; loss of appetite [34], anorexia nervosa [29].
Other uses Bronchitis [29-31] and pleurisy [30], respiratory catarrh [29,32]; rheumatic and arthritic

conditions [21,28,29,32], internally, or externally as a compress of tincture or decoction [32] or as diluted essential oil [28]; peripheral vascular disease [29] - considered a specific treatment for Buerger's disease (a condition that narrows the arteries of the hands and feet) [31]; as a diaphoretic in feverish conditions [30].

Contraindications
Pregnancy [31]; gastric and duodenal ulcers.

Side effects
Photosensitization of skin is possible due to furanocoumarins, hence prolonged exposure to sunlight should be avoided while taking angelica root.

Interactions with other drugs
None known.

Dosage
Three times daily: dried root and rhizome, 0.6-2 g or as an infusion (1 in 20) [29,33,34]; liquid extract 1:1 in 25% alcohol, 0.5-2 ml; tincture 1:5 in 50% alcohol, 0.5-2 ml [29,34].

SAFETY

As a food flavouring, angelica root is accepted by the Council of Europe and is generally recognized as safe by the United States FDA; it is used as a flavouring in liqueurs such as Chartreuse and Benedictine.

Angelica root oil is considered to be safe for oral use at therapeutic dose levels [34,36]. The acute oral LD50 was determined as 2.2 g/kg body weight in mice and 11.2 g/kg in rats. When the oil was administered to rats for 8 weeks in daily doses of 0.5-3.0 g/kg, the tolerated dose was 1.5 g/kg; however, the rats receiving 0.5 or 1.0 g/kg daily weighed less than control animals [37].

The oral LD_{50} of angelicin was determined as 322 mg/kg in rats [24].

In the Ames mutagenicity test a tincture and a fluid extract showed weak mutagenic potential in *S. typhimurium* strains TA 98 and TA 100 [38].

REGULATORY STATUS

Medicines

UK	Accepted for general sale, internal or external use [39].
France	Accepted for specified indications [35].
Germany	Commission E monograph published, with approved uses [34].

Food

USA	Generally recognized as safe (21 CFR 182.10 and 182.20) [40].
Council of Europe	Permitted as flavouring, category N2 [41].

REFERENCES

Current Pharmacopoeial Monographs
Ph. Eur. Angelica Root

Literature References

1. Czygan F-C. Engelwurz oder Angelikawurzel - *Angelica archangelica* L. *Z. Phytotherapie* 1998, **19**, 342-348 [GERMAN/English summary].
2. Vieweger U. Angelica. In: Blaschek W, Hänsel R, Keller K, Reichling J, Rimpler H and Schneider G, editors. *Hagers Handbuch der Pharmazeutischen Praxis, 5th ed. Supplement Volume 2: Drogen A-K.* ISBN 3-540-61618-7. Berlin-Heidelberg-New York-London: Springer, 1998:91-125 [GERMAN].
3. Härmälä P, Vuorela H, Hiltunen R, Nyiredy S, Sticher O, Törnquist K and Kaltia S. Strategy for the Isolation and Identification of Coumarins with Calcium Antagonistic Properties from the Roots of *Angelica archangelica. Phytochem. Analysis* 1992, **3**, 42-48.
4. Roos G, Waiblinger J, Zschocke S, Liu JH, Klaiber I, Kraus W and Bauer R. Isolation, Identification and Screening for COX-1- and 5-LO-Inhibition of Coumarins from *Angelica archangelica. Pharm. Pharmacol. Lett.* 1997, **4**, 157-160.
5. Genius OB. Radix Angelicae archangelicae. Identitätsnachweis und Gehaltsbestimmung auf der Basis von Osthenol [Radix Angelicae archangelicae. Identification and content determination on the basis of osthenol]. *Dtsch. Apoth. Ztg.* 1981, **121**, 386-387 [GERMAN/English summary].
6. Chalchat J-C and Garry R-P. Essential Oil of Angelica Roots (*Angelica archangelica* L.): Optimization of Distillation, Location in Plant and Chemical Composition. *J. Essent. Oil. Res.* 1997, **9**, 311-319.
7. Lawrence BM. Progress in Essential Oils. *Perfumer & Flavorist* 1989, **14** (Jul/Aug), 41-56.
8. Lawrence BM. Progress in Essential Oils. *Perfumer & Flavorist* 1996, **21** (Sept-Oct), 57-68.
9. Kerrola K, Galambosi B and Kallio H. Characterization of Volatile Composition and Odor of Angelica (*Angelica archangelica* subsp. *archangelica* L.) Root Extracts. *J. Agric. Food Chem.* 1994, **42**, 1979-1988.
10. Kerrola KM and Kallio HP. Extraction of Volatile Compounds of Angelica (*Angelica archangelica* L.) Root by Liquid Carbon Dioxide. *J. Agric. Food Chem.* 1994, **42**, 2235-2245.
11. Héthelyi I, Tétényi P, Kálmán-Pál Á, Turiák G and Grezál G. Mass-spectrometric examination of the oil components of *Angelica archangelica. Herba Hung.* 1985, **24**, 148-163 [HUNGARIAN/English summary].
12. Taskinen J. 12-Methyl-ω-tridecanolide, a New Macrocyclic Lactone from Angelica Root Oil. *Acta Chem. Scand. B* 1975, **29**, 637-638.
13. Baerheim Svendsen A. Über das Vorkommen der Chlorogen- und Kaffesäure in der Pflanzenfamilie der Umbelliferen. 2. Mitteilung über Papierchromatographie in der phytochemischen Analyse [The occurrence of chlorogenic and caffeic acids in the Umbelliferae family. Part 2. Paper chromatography in the phytochemical analysis]. *Pharm. Acta Helv.* 1951, **26**, 253-258 [GERMAN].
14. Eichstedt Nielsen B and Kofod H. Constituents of Umbelliferous Plants. I. Constituents of the Root of *Angelica archangelica* L. *Acta Chem. Scand.* 1963, **17**, 1161-1163.
15. Basa SC, Basu D and Chatterjee A. Occurrence of flavonoid

in *Angelica*: archangelenone, a new flavanone from the root of *Angelica archangelica* Linn. *Chem. Ind. (London)* 1971, 355.
16. Harkar S, Razdan TK and Waight ES. Steroids, chromone and coumarins from *Angelica officinalis. Phytochemistry* 1984, **23**, 419-426.
17. Kaul VK and Weyerstahl P. Further evidence for the revised structure of angelicain. *Fitoterapia* 1987, **58**, 129-132.
18. Zogg GC, Nyiredy S and Sticher O. Qualitative und quantitative Furanocumarinbestimmung in Apiaceen-wurzeln [Qualitative and quantitative determination of furanocoumarins in roots of Apiaceae]. *Dtsch. Apoth. Ztg.* 1989, **129**, 717-722 [GERMAN].
19. Härmälä P, Vuorela H, Törnquist K and Hiltunen R. Choice of Solvent in the Extraction of *Angelica archangelica* Roots with Reference to Calcium Blocking Activity. *Planta Medica* 1992, **58**, 176-183.
20. Vuorela H, Vuorela P, Törnquist K and Alaranta S. Calcium channel blocking activity: Screening methods for plant derived compounds. *Phytomedicine* 1997, **4**, 167-181.
21. Härmälä P, Vuorela H, Törnquist K, Kaltia S, Galambosi B and Hiltunen R. Isolation and Testing of the Calcium Blocking Activity of Furanocoumarins from *Angelica archangelica. Planta Medica* 1991, **57**, A58-A59.
22. Izzo AA, Capasso R, Senatore F, Seccia S and Morrica P. Spasmolytic Activity of Medicinal Plants Used for the Treatment of Disorders Involving Smooth Muscles. *Phytotherapy Res.* 1996, **10**, S107-S108.
23. Reiter M and Brandt W. Relaxant Effects on Tracheal and Ileal Smooth Muscles of the Guinea Pig. *Arzneim.-Forsch./Drug Res.* 1985, **35**, 408-414.
24. Chandhoke N and Ghatak BJR. Pharmacological Investigations of Angelicin - A Tranquillosedative and Anticonvulsant Agent. *Indian J. Med. Res.* 1975, **63**, 833-841.
25. Bergendorff O, Dekermendjian K, Nielsen M, Shan R, Witt R, Ai J and Sterner O. Furanocoumarins with affinity to brain benzodiazepine receptors *in vitro. Phytochemistry* 1997, **44**, 1121-1124.
26. Gawron A and Glowniak K. Cytostatic Activity of Coumarins *in vitro. Planta Medica* 1987, **52**, 526-529.
27. Kosuge T, Yokota M, Sugiyama K, Yamamoto T, Mure T and Yamazawa H. Studies on Bioactive Substances in Crude Drugs Used for Arthritic Diseases in Traditional Chinese Medicine. II. Isolation and Identification of an Anti-inflammatory and Analgesic Principle from the Root of *Angelica pubescens* Maxim. *Chem. Pharm. Bull.* 1985, **33**, 5351-5354.
28. Weiss RF and Fintelmann V. Aromatic Bitters: Angelica archangelica. In: *Herbal Medicine, 2nd ed.* (translated from the 9th German edition of *Lehrbuch der Phytotherapie*). ISBN 3-13-126332-6. Stuttgart-New York: Thieme, 2000:56-57.
29. Angelica Root. In: *British Herbal Pharmacopoeia 1983*. ISBN 0-903032-07-4. Bournemouth: British Herbal Medicine Association, 1983.
30. Grieve M (edited by Leyel CF). Angelica. In: *A Modern Herbal* (first published 1931; revised 1973). ISBN 1-85501-249-9. London: Tiger Books International, 1994:35-40.
31. Chevallier A. Angelica. In: *The Encyclopedia of Medicinal Plants*. ISBN 0-7513-0314-3. London-New York-Stuttgart: Dorling Kindersley, 1996:166.
32. Ody P. Angelica. In: *The Complete Guide Medicinal Herbal*. ISBN 0-7513-3005-1. London-New York: Dorling Kindersley, 2000:38.
33. Todd RG, editor. Angelica. In: Extra Pharmacopoeia: Martindale, 25th edition. London: Pharmaceutical Press, 1967:223.
34. Angelicae radix. German Commission E Monograph published in: Bundesanzeiger No. 101 of 1 June 1990.
35. Angélique. In: *Médicaments à base de plantes*. ISBN 2-911473-02-7. Saint-Denis Cedex, France: Agence du Médicament, 1998.
36. Tisserand R and Balacs T. Angelica Root. In: *Essential Oil Safety - A Guide for Health Care Professionals*. Edinburgh: Churchill-Livingstone, 1995:116 and 201-203.
37. Opdyke DLJ. Monographs on fragrance raw materials: Angelica root oil. *Food Cosmet. Toxicol.* 1975, **13**, 713-714.
38. Göggelmann W and Schimmer O. Mutagenic activity of phytotherapeutical drugs. In: *Genetic Toxicology of the Diet*. New York: Alan R Liss, 1986:63-72.
39. Angelica. In: UK Statutory Instrument 1984 No. 769. The Medicines (Products Other Than Veterinary Drugs) (General Sale List) Order 1984. Schedule 1, Table A.
40. Angelica root. In: Sections 182.10 and 182.20 of USA Code of Federal Regulations, Title 21, Food and Drugs, Parts 170 to 199. Revised as of April 1, 2000.
41. Archangelica officinalis Hoff. (Angelica archangelica L.), roots. In: *Flavouring Substances and Natural Sources of Flavourings, 3rd ed.* ISBN 2-7160-0081-6. Strasbourg: Council of Europe, 1981.

REGULATORY GUIDELINES FROM OTHER EU COUNTRIES

FRANCE

Médicaments à base de plantes [35]: Angélique, souche radicante.

Therapeutic indications accepted

Oral use
Traditionally used: in the symptomatic treatment of digestive disorders such as epigastric distension, sluggish digestion, eructation, flatulence; as adjuvant treatment of the painful component of functional digestive disorders.

GERMANY

Commission E monograph [34]: Angelicae radix (Angelikawurzel).

Uses
Loss of appetite; dyspeptic complaints such as mild gastrointestinal spasms, bloating, flatulence.

Contraindications
None known.

Side effects
The furocoumarins in angelica root make the skin sensitive to light and can lead to skin inflammation on exposure to UV rays. When using angelica root or preparations from it, prolonged sunbathing and intensive UV rays should therefore be avoided.

Interactions with other drugs
None known.

Dosage
Unless otherwise prescribed, daily dose: 4.5 g of the drug, 1.5-3 g of fluid extract, 1.5 g of tincture (1:5) or equivalent preparations. 10-20 drops of essential oil.

Mode of administration
Comminuted drug and other galenic preparations for internal use.

Actions
Spasmolytic, cholagogic, promotes secretion of gastric juice.

ANISEED

Umbelliferae

Anisi fructus

Synonym: Anise.

Definition

Aniseed consists of the whole dry cremocarps of *Pimpinella anisum* L.

Native to the eastern Mediteranean region, *Pimpinella anisum* is an umbelliferous annual, about 50 cm high. Botanically, aniseed is a fruit, not a seed.

CONSTITUENTS

□ ***Essential oil***, 1.5-5% [1] (Ph. Eur. min. 2.0% V/m) consisting mainly of *trans*-anethole (85-96%) with small amounts of *cis*-anethole (0.3-2.3%), estragole (methylchavicol; up to 5%, but usually below 2.5%), *p*-anisaldehyde (0.5-2.5%), γ-himachalene (0.7-2.0%), linalool (0.2-0.3%) and other mono- and sesquiterpenes [2-5].

It should be noted that steam-distilled essential oil from either aniseed or star anise (the dry ripe fruits of *Illicium verum* Hook. f.) are accepted as Anise Oil Ph. Eur.

□ ***Fixed oil***, about 15% [5], in which the predominant fatty acid is petroselinic acid (*cis*-6-octadecenoic acid, about 60%) together with oleic acid (*cis*-9-octadecenoic acid, 15%) and various dienoic acids (19%) [6].

Stigmasterol and its palmitate and stearate have also been isolated from the lipid fraction [7].

□ ***Phenylpropenyl esters***, of which eight have been identified [8]. The principal compound, the 2-methylbutyrate of 2-hydroxy-5-methoxy-propenylbenzene (also called pseudoisoeugenyl 2-methylbutyrate) represented over 5% of a supercritical carbon dioxide extract from aniseed [9]; it can be detected in aniseed essential oil, a useful means of distinction from star anise oil [3,10].

□ ***Flavonoids***, about 0.5%: the flavone luteolin [11] together with flavone *O*-glycosides (luteolin 7-*O*-xyloside, luteolin 7-*O*-glucoside and apigenin 7-*O*-glucoside), flavone *C*-glycosides (luteolin 6-*C*-glucoside = isoorientin, apigenin 6-*C*-glucoside = isovitexin) and flavonol *O*-glycosides (quercetin 3-*O*-glucuronide and quercetin 3-*O*-rutinoside = rutin) [11,12].

□ ***Coumarins*** Umbelliferone, scopoletin, umbelliprenin and the furanocoumarin bergapten [7].

□ ***Hydroxycinnamic acid derivatives*** Chlorogenic acid (3-caffeoylquinic acid, 0.1-0.2%) with smaller amounts of 4- and 5-caffeoylquinic acids [13]. Also caffeic acid (0.2%) and small amounts of *p*-coumaric and ferulic acids [14,15].

□ ***Benzoic acid derivatives*** *p*-Hydroxybenzoic acid (0.1%) and small amounts of gentisic, vanillic, salicylic and related acids [14,15]; also *p*-hydroxybenzoic acid glucoside [13,16].

□ ***Other constituents*** include, on the dry weight basis, starch (29%), protein (28%), fibre (11%), sugars (3%) and minerals (8%) [5].

Published Assay Methods

Anise oil components by GC [Ph. Eur.] and GC-MS [9]. Direct mass spectrometric analysis of the fruits [2].

PHARMACOLOGY

In vitro

Expectorant activity

Application of 200 μl of an infusion from aniseed to isolated epithelium from the frog oesophagus stimulated the cilia, resulting in a modest increase in mucociliary transport velocity after 90 seconds [17].

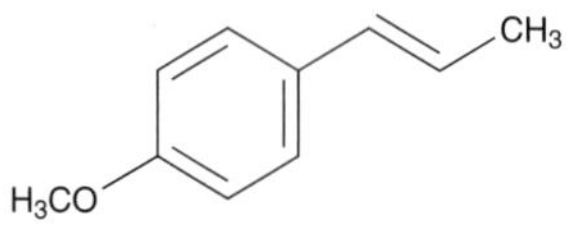

trans-Anethole

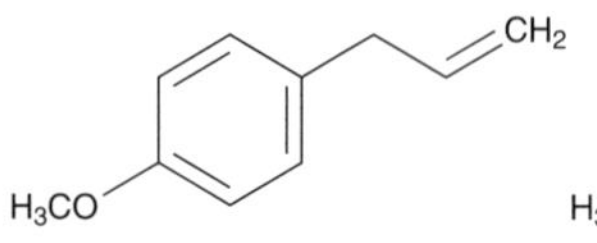

Estragole
(Methylchavicol)

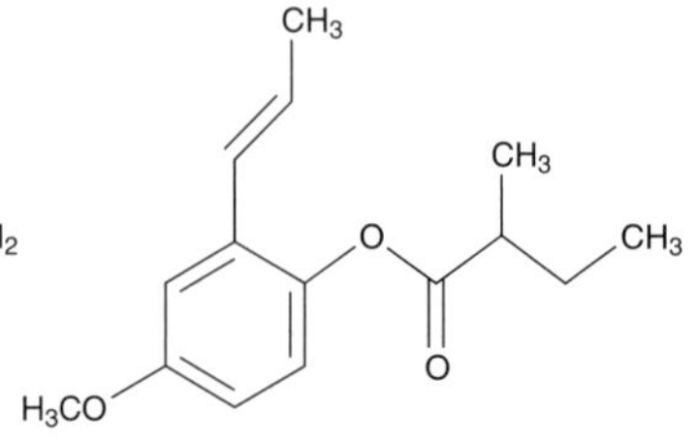

2-Methylbutyrate of
2-hydroxy-5-methoxy-propenylbenzene

Spasmolytic activity
Significant relaxant effects on methacholine-induced contractions of guinea pig tracheal chains (prepared from rings of isolated tracheal smooth muscle) were produced by an aqueous extract ($p<0.005$), an ethanolic extract ($p<0.001$) and the essential oil ($p<0.05$) from aniseed. The results indicated bronchodilatory activity of the extracts and essential oil, attributed to inhibitory effects on muscarinic receptors [18].

In an earlier study, the essential oil at 200 mg/litre produced complete relaxation of carbachol-induced contractions of isolated guinea pig tracheal muscle. In contrast, the contraction force in electrically-stimulated guinea pig ileal smooth muscle was increased by anise oil with an EC_{50} of 6-7 mg/litre (a positive inotropic effect) [19].

Oestrogenic activity
Aniseed has a long tradition of use as a galactagogue [20] and is reputed to be mildly oestrogenic [21], although the mechanism of such activity is unclear. A recent experiment demonstrated that anise oil at 10-100 µg/ml did not stimulate the secretion of prolactin in pituitary cells *in vitro*. However, anise oil at concentrations of 0.01-10 µg/ml stimulated the proliferation of oestrogen-dependent human MCF-7 breast cancer cells ($p<0.05$ compared to the control), confirming oestrogenic activity comparable to that of 1 nM oestradiol. In one sense, this oestrogenic activity does not appear to fit well with the traditional use of aniseed as a galactagogue during the lactation period, since oestrogens themselves inhibit lactation. On the other hand, *trans*-anethole, the main component of anise oil, has been reported to be a dopamine antagonist, a property which should favour galactagogic activity (dopamine inhibits prolactin secretion) [22].

Antimicrobial activity
Anise oil at 0.25-2.0% V/V exhibited moderate inhibitory activity against a range of Gram-positive (e.g. *Staphylococcus aureus*) and Gram-negative (e.g. *Escherichia coli, Salmonella typhimurium*) bacteria, but not against Gram-negative *Pseudomonas aeruginosa* or *Klebsiella pneumoniae*; at 0.25 V/V it also inhibited the yeast *Candida albicans* [23]. An acetone extract from aniseed had comparable effects [24]. In another study, the oil at 0.1% and anethole at 0.06% totally inhibited the growth of a wide range of fungi [25].

Inhibition of TNF
Trans-anethole has been shown to be a potent inhibitor of tumour necrosis factor (TNF), a cytokine known to mediate inflammation and carcinogenesis, even at concentrations lower than 1 mM. Various inhibitory actions on TNF signalling are thought to be a possible explanation for the anti-inflammatory and anticarcinogenic effects of anethole [26].

In vivo

Expectorant effects
Oral administration (by gastric tube) to cats of 2 drops of anise oil in an emulsion produced hypersecretion of mucus in the air passages and stimulated upward ciliary movement of mucus (previously inhibited by opium alkaloids) [27].

In a series of studies between 1946 and 1968, the effect of orally administered anise oil on the output of respiratory tract fluid (RTF) was examined in anaesthetized animals. A 3- to 6-fold increase in RTF was induced in guinea pigs [28], a 28% increase in RTF in rats [29] and, from inhalation of the oil vapour (in steam) at rather toxic dose levels, a 19-82% increase in RTF in rabbits [30]. Anise oil is not a "reflex expectorant"; the expectorant action appears to result from direct stimulation of the secretory cells of the respiratory tract [28].

Oestrogenic activity of anethole
Oral administration of *trans*-anethole to immature female rats at 80 mg/kg for 3 days increased their uterine weight to 2 g/kg compared to 3 g/kg in animals given oestradiol valerate subcutaneously at 0.1 µg/rat/day and 0.5 g/kg in controls. The results confirmed that *trans*-anethole has oestrogenic activity [31].

Other effects
Trans-anethole had an antigenotoxic effect in the mouse bone marrow micronucleus test. Significant protective effects ($p<0.05$ to $p<0.01$) against known genotoxins such as cyclophosphamide, procarbazine, N-methyl-N′-nitrosoguanidine and urethane were observed after oral pre-treatment of mice with *trans*-anethole at 40-400 mg/kg by gavage 2 and 20 hours before intraperitoneal injection of the genotoxins [32]. Furthermore, anethole administered orally at 500 or 1000 mg/kg on alternate days for 60 days to mice bearing Ehrlich ascites tumour (EAT) reduced tumour weight and volume compared to EAT-bearing controls [33].

Intraperitoneal administration of anise oil to mice at 50 mg/kg at the same time as pentobarbital prolonged (almost doubled) the pentobarbital-induced sleeping time ($p<0.01$); *trans*-anethole gave similar results [34].

Pharmacokinetics
The metabolic fate of *trans*-anethole in humans was studied after oral administration of the radioactively-labelled *methoxy*-^{14}C compound to 5 healthy volunteers at three dose levels on separate occasions: 1, 50 and 250 mg. Following rapid absorption, 54-69% of the ^{14}C dose was eliminated in the urine, mainly as 4-methoxyhippuric acid,

and 13-17% was exhaled as carbon dioxide, while none was detected in the faeces. Dose size had no major effect on the rate or route of excretion and most of the elimination occurred within 8 hours [35].

CLINICAL STUDIES

None published on mono-preparations of aniseed.

THERAPEUTICS

Actions

Mildly expectorant [17,36-38], spasmolytic [1,18, 36,37], carminative [25,36,38], antibacterial [37] and parasiticidal [36]. Also stated to be diuretic [25,39] and galactagogic [20,39]

Few pharmacological studies have been performed with the fruits or aqueous/ethanolic extracts; most have been carried out on the essential oil and/or anethole, which have been shown to have expectorant [27-29], spasmolytic [18], antimicrobial [23-25], anti-tumour [33] and mildly oestrogenic [22,31] activity.

Umbelliferous fruits have been ranked as follows, in order of decreasing carminative effect and increasing expectorant effect: caraway, fennel, anise [40].

Indications

None adequately substantiated by pharmacological or clinical studies.

Uses based on experience or tradition

Internal: Catarrhs of the respiratory tract [36,37], bronchitis, whooping cough [36,41], spasmodic cough [36]. Dyspeptic complaints such as flatulence and colic [25,36,37,41,42], especially in children [1,41].

Has also been used to stimulate lactation [20, 41].

External: As diluted anise oil, to treat lice and scabies [36,41].

Contraindications

None known.
In view of the reported oestrogenic and antifertility effects of *trans*-anethole [31], it may be prudent to avoid anise oil during pregnancy and take only aqueous infusions.

Side effects

Occasional allergic reactions [37] or dermatitis [38].

Interactions with other drugs

None known.

Dosage

Average daily dose: dried, crushed fruits, 3 g as an infusion or equivalent preparation; anise oil, 0.3 g in suitable preparations [36,37].
External use: Preparations containing 5-10% of anise oil [37].

SAFETY

Most of the available toxicity data relate to anise oil or its main component *trans*-anisole. Toxicological data on *trans*-anethole was comprehensively reviewed in 1991 by the FAO/WHO [43].

The oral LD_{50} of anise oil has been determined as 2.7 g/kg body weight in rats [44]; for *trans*-anethole the values are 2.1-3.2 g/kg in rats, 1.8-5.0 g/kg in mice and 2.2 g/kg in guinea pigs [43]. Rats receiving 0.25% of anethole in their diet for 1 year showed no adverse effects, while others receiving 1.0% for 15 weeks showed slight oedematous alterations in liver cells [43,45]. In a similar study in rats over 90 days, 0.1% of *trans*-anethole in the diet caused no toxic effects, but dose-related hepatic cell oedema was evident at 0.3% and higher [43].

Allergic reactions to aniseed occasionally occur and these may involve a wider sensitivity to other umbelliferous plants [46].

Trans-anethole has been reported to have a dose-dependent antifertility effect in adult female rats after oral administration at 50-80 mg/kg body weight on days 1-10 of pregnancy; implantation was completely inhibited by 80 mg/kg. No gross malformations were observed in any of the offspring [31].

An ethanolic aniseed extract [47], anise oil and *trans*-anethole [43,48] proved weakly mutagenic in tests using various strains of *Salmonella typhimurium*. However, an ethanolic aniseed extract gave negative results in chromosomal aberration tests [49] and *trans*-anethole gave negative results in a *Bacillus subtilis* rec assay [43,48]. Estragole was found to be non-mutagenic or very weakly mutagenic in *S. typhimurium* [50]. No evidence of carcinogenic potential of *trans*-anethole has been revealed from long-term studies in rats and mice [43].

In 1999 *trans*-anethole was reaffirmed as GRAS by the Flavour and Extract Manufacturers' Association (USA) after a safety evaluation in which it was concluded that "*trans*-anethole undergoes efficient metabolic detoxication in humans at low levels of exposure" [51].

REGULATORY STATUS

Medicines

UK	Accepted for general sale, internal or external use [52].
France	Accepted for specified indications [42].
Germany	Commission E monograph published, with approved uses [37].

Food

USA	Generally recognized as safe (21 CFR 182.10 and 182.20) [53].
Council of Europe	Permitted as flavouring, category N2 [54].

REFERENCES

Current Pharmacopoeial Monographs

Ph. Eur. Aniseed

Literature References

1. Wichtl M and Schäfer-Korting M. Anis - Anisi fructus. In: Hartke K, Hartke H, Mutschler E, Rücker G and Wichtl M, editors. *Kommentar zum Europäischen Arzneibuch.* Stuttgart: Wissenschaftliche Verlagsgesellschaft, 1999 (11 Lfg.):A 47 [GERMAN].
2. Schultze W, Lange G and Heinrich G. Massenspektrometrische Untersuchungen an Arzneipflanzen. II. Direkte massenspektrometrische Analyse von Anisi fructus [Mass spectrometric studies on medicinal plants. II. Direct mass-spectrometric analysis of Anisi fructus]. *Dtsch. Apoth. Ztg.* 1986, **126**, 2787-2793 [GERMAN].
3. FormácekV and Kubeczka K-H. Anise seed oil. In: *Essential oils analysis by capillary gas chromatography and carbon-13 NMR spectroscopy.* ISBN 0-471-26218-8. Chichester: John Wiley, 1982:7-11.
4. Lawrence BM. New Trends in Essential Oils. *Perfumer & Flavorist* 1980, (Aug/Sept), 6-16.
5. El-Wakeil F, Khairy M, Morsi S, Farag RS, Shihata AA and Badel AZMA. Biochemical Studies on the Essential Oils of some Fruits of Umbelliferae Family. *Seifen-Öle-Fette-Wachse* 1986, **112**, 77-80.
6. Nikolova-Damyanova B, Momchilova S and Christie WW. Determination of Petroselinic, *cis*-Vaccenic and Oleic Acids in Some Seed Oils of the Umbelliferae by Silver Ion Thin Layer Chromatography of their Phenacyl Esters. *Phytochem. Analysis* 1996, **7**, 136-139.
7. Kartnig T and Scholz G. Component Lipids of the Fruits of *Pimpinella anisum* (L.) und *Carum carvi* (L.). *Fette Seifen Anstrichmittel* 1969, **71**, 276-280 [GERMAN/English summary].
8. Kleiman R, Plattner RD and Weisleder D. Antigermination activity of phenylpropenoids from the genus *Pimpinella. J. Nat. Prod.* 1988, **51**, 249-256.
9. Rodrigues VM, Rosa PTV, Marques MOM, Petenate AJ and Meireles MAA. Supercritical Extraction of Essential Oil from Aniseed (*Pimpinella anisum* L.) Using CO_2: Solubility, Kinetics and Composition Data. *J. Agric. Food Chem.* 2003, **51**, 1518-1523.
10. Kubeczka KH. Grundlagen der Qualitätsbeurteilung arzneilich verwendeter ätherischer Öle [Fundamentals of quality assessment of medicinally used essential oils]. *Acta Horticulturae* 1978, **73**, 85-93.
11. El-Moghazi AM, Ali AA, Ross SA and Mottaleb MA. Flavonoids of *Pimpinella anisum* L. Growing in Egypt. *Fitoterapia* 1979, **50**, 267-268.
12. Kunzemann J and Herrmann K. Isolation and Identification of Flavon(ol)-O-glycosides in Caraway (*Carum carvi* L.), Fennel (*Foeniculum vulgare* Mill.), Anise (*Pimpinella anisum* L.) and Coriander (*Coriandrum sativum* L.) and of Flavone-C-glycosides in Anise. I. Phenolics of Spices. *Z. Lebensm. Unters.-Forsch.* 1977, **164**, 194-200 [GERMAN/English summary].
13. Dirks U and Herrmann K. High Performance Liquid Chromatography of Hydroxycinnamoylquinic Acids and 4-(β-D-Glucopyranosyloxy)-benzoic Acid in Spices. 10. Phenolics of Spices. *Z. Lebensm. Unters. Forsch.* 1984, **179**, 12-16 [GERMAN/English summary].
14. Schulz JM and Herrmann K. Analysis of hydroxybenzoic and hydroxycinnamic acids in plant material. II. Determination by gas-liquid chromatography. *J. Chromatogr.* 1980, **195**, 95-104.
15. Schulz JM and Herrmann K. Occurrence of Hydroxybenzoic Acids and Hydroxycinnamic Acids in Spices. IV. Phenolics of Spices. *Z. Lebensm. Unters. Forsch.* 1980, **171**, 193-199 [GERMAN/English summary].
16. Dirks U and Herrmann K. 4-(β-D-glucopyranosyloxy) benzoic acid, a characteristic phenolic constituent of the Apiaceae. *Phytochemistry* 1984, **23**, 1811-1812.
17. Müller-Limmroth W and Fröhlich H-H. Wirkungsnachweis einiger phytotherapeutischer Expektorantien auf den mukoziliaren Transport [Evidence of the effects of some phytotherapeutic expectorants on mucociliary transport]. *Fortschr. Med.* 1980, **98**, 95-101 [GERMAN].
18. Boskabady MH and Ramazani-Assari M. Relaxant effect of *Pimpinella anisum* on isolated guinea pig tracheal chains and its possible mechanism(s). *J. Ethnopharmacol.* 2001, **74**, 83-88.
19. Reiter M and Brandt W. Relaxant Effects on Tracheal and Ileal Smooth Muscles of the Guinea Pig. *Arzneim.-Forsch./Drug Res.* 1985, **35**, 408-414.
20. Brückner C. Anwendung und Wert in Europa gebräuchlicher lactationsfördernder Heilpflanzen (Galactagoga) [The use and merit of the more common lactation-promoting medicinal plants (galactagogues) in Europe]. *Pädiatr. Grenzgeb.* 1989, **28**, 403-410 [GERMAN/English summary].
21. Albert-Puleo M. Fennel and anise as estrogenic agents. *J. Ethnopharmacol.* 1980, **2**, 337-344.
22. Melzig MF, Möller I and Jarry H. New investigations of the *in vitro* pharmacological activity of essential oils from Apiaceae. *Z. Phytotherapie* 2003, **24**, 112-116 [GERMAN/English summary].
23. Hammer KA, Carson CF and Riley TV. Antimicrobial activity of essential oils and other plant extracts. *J. Applied Microbiol.* 1999, **86**, 985-990.
24. Maruzzella JC and Freundlich M. Antimicrobial Substances from Seeds. *J. Am. Pharm. Assoc.* 1959, **48**, 356-358.
25. Shukla HS and Tripathi SC. Antifungal Substance in the Essential Oil of Anise (*Pimpinella anisum* L.). *Agric. Biol. Chem.* 1987, **51**, 1991-1993.
26. Chainy GBN, Manna SK, Chaturvedi MM and Aggarwal BB. Anethole blocks both early and late cellular responses transduced by tumor necrosis factor: effect on NF-κB, AP-1, JNK, MAPKK and apoptosis. *Oncogene* 2000, **19**, 2943-2950.
27. van Dongen K and Leusink H. The action of opium-alkaloids and expectorants on the ciliary movements in the air passages. *Arch. Int. Pharmacodyn.* 1953, **93**, 261-276.
28. Boyd EM and Pearson GL. On the expectorant action of volatile oils. *Am. J. Med. Sci.* 1946, **211**, 602-610.
29. Boyd EM. Expectorants and respiratory tract fluid. *Pharmacol. Rev.* 1954, **6**, 521-542.
30. Boyd EM and Sheppard EP. The effect of steam inhalation of volatile oils on the output and composition of respiratory tract fluid. *J. Pharmacol. Exp. Therap.* 1968, **163**, 250-256.
31. Dhar SK. Anti-fertility activity and hormonal profile of *trans*-anethole in rats. *Indian J. Physiol. Pharmacol.* 1995, **39**, 63-67.
32. Abraham SK. Anti-genotoxicity of *trans*-anethole and eugenol in mice. *Food Chem. Toxicol.* 2001, **39**, 493-498.
33. Al-Harbi MM, Qureshi S, Raza M, Ahmed MM, Giangreco AB and Shah AH. Influence of anethole treatment on the tumour induced by Ehrlich ascites carcinoma cells in paw of

Swiss albino mice. *Eur. J. Cancer Prev.* 1995, **4**, 307-318.
34. Marcus C and Lichtenstein EP. Interactions of Naturally Occurring Food Plant Components with Insecticides and Pentobarbital in Rats and Mice. *J. Agric. Food Chem.* 1982, **30**, 563-568.
35. Caldwell J and Sutton JD. Influence of dose size on the disposition of *trans*-[*methoxy*-^{14}C]anethole in human volunteers. *Food Chem. Toxicol.* 1988, **26**, 87-91.
36. Pimpinella. In: *British Herbal Pharmacopoeia 1983.* ISBN 0-903032-07-4. Bournemouth: British Herbal Medicine Association, 1983.
37. Anisi fructus. German Commission E Monograph published in: Bundesanzeiger No. 122 of 6 July 1988.
38. Parfitt K, editor. Aniseed and Anise Oil. In: *Martindale - The complete drug reference, 32nd ed.* ISBN 0-85369-429-X. London: Pharmaceutical Press, 1999:1549-1550.
39. Stodola J and Volák J. Anise - *Pimpinella anisum.* Translated into English in: Bunney S, editor. *The Illustrated Book of Herbs.* ISBN 0-7064-1489-6. London: Octopus Books, 1984:215.
40. Schulz V, Hänsel R and Tyler VE. Typical Carminative Herbs. In: *Rational Phytotherapy - A Physicians' Guide to Herbal Medicine, 4th ed.* ISBN 3-540-67096-3. Berlin-Heidelberg-New York-London: Springer-Verlag, 2001:219-220.
41. Chevallier A. Anise - *Pimpinella anisum.* In: *Encyclopedia of Medicinal Plants, 2nd ed.* ISBN 0-7513-1209-6. London-New York: Dorling Kindersley, 2001:248.
42. Anis. In: *Médicaments à base de plantes.* ISBN 2-911473-02-7. Saint-Denis Cedex, France: Agence du Médicament, 1998.
43. Lin FSD. *Trans*-anethole. In: Joint FAO/WHO Expert Committee on Food Additives. *Toxicological evaluation of certain food additives and contaminants. WHO Food Additives Series 28.* Geneva: World Health Organization, 1991:135-152. www.inchem.org/documents/jecfa/jecmono/v28je10.htm
44. von Skramlik E. Über die Giftigkeit und Verträglichkeit von ätherischen Ölen. *Pharmazie* 1959, **14**, 435-445 [GERMAN].
45. Hagan EC, Hansen WH, Fitzhugh OG, Jenner PM, Jones WI, Taylor JM et al. Food Flavourings and Compounds of Related Structure. II. Subacute and Chronic Toxicity. *Food Cosmet. Toxicol.* 1967, **5**, 141-157.
46. Stäger J, Wüthrich B and Johansson SGO. Spice allergy in celery-sensitive patients. *Allergy* 1991, **46**, 475-478.
47. Shashikanth KN and Hosono A. *In vitro* Mutagenicity of Tropical Spices to Streptomycin-dependent Strains of *Salmonella typhimurium* TA 98. *Agric. Biol. Chem.* 1986, **50**, 2947-2948.
48. Sekizawa J and Shibamoto T. Genotoxicity of safrole-related chemicals in microbial test systems. *Mutat. Res.* 1982, **101**, 127-140.
49. Ishidate M, Sofuni T, Yoshikawa K, Hayashi M, Nohmi T, Sawada M and Matsuoka A. Primary mutagenicity screening of food additives currently used in Japan. *Food Chem. Toxicol.* 1984, **22**, 623-636.
50. European Commission: Scientific Committee on Food. Opinion of the Scientific Committee on Food on Estragole (1-Allyl-4-methoxybenzene). Ref. No. SCF/CS/FLAV/FLAVOUR/6 ADD2 FINAL, adopted on 26 September 2001. http://europa.eu.int (under Food Safety).
51. Newberne P, Smith RL, Doull J, Goodman JI, Munro IC, Portoghese PS et al. The FEMA GRAS assessment of *trans*-anethole used as a flavouring substance. Flavour and Extract Manufacturers' Association. *Food Chem. Toxicol.* 1999, **37**, 789-811.
52. Aniseed (Anise). In: UK Statutory Instrument 1994 No. 2410. The Medicines (Products Other Than Veterinary Drugs) (General Sale List) Amendment Order 1994. Schedule 1, Table A.
53. Anise. In: Sections 182.10 and 182.20 of USA Code of Federal Regulations, Title 21, Food and Drugs, Parts 170 to 199. Revised as of April 1, 2000.
54. Pimpinella anisum L., fruits. In: *Flavouring Substances and Natural Sources of Flavourings, 3rd ed.* ISBN 2-7160-0081-6. Strasbourg: Council of Europe, 1981.

REGULATORY GUIDELINES FROM OTHER EU COUNTRIES

FRANCE

Médicaments à base de plantes [42]: Anis, fruit.

Therapeutic indications accepted

Oral use
Traditionally used: in the symptomatic treatment of digestive disorders such as epigastric distension, sluggish digestion, eructation, flatulence; as adjuvant treatment of the painful component of functional digestive disorders.

GERMANY

Commission E monograph [37]: Anisi fructus (Anis).

Uses
Internal use Dyspeptic complaints.
Internal and external use Catarrhs of the upper respiratory tract.

Contraindications
Allergy to aniseed or anethole.

Side effects
Occasional allergic reactions of the skin, respiratory tract and gastrointestinal tract.

Interactions with other drugs
None known.

Dosage
Unless otherwise prescribed:
Internal use Average daily dose: 3 g of the drug, 0.3 g of essential oil or equivalent preparations.

External use Preparations containing 5-10% of essential oil.

Mode of administration
Crushed or milled drug for infusions and other galenic preparations for oral use or for inhalation.
Note: The objective of external use of aniseed preparations is inhalation of the essential oil.

Actions
Expectorant, weakly spasmolytic, antibacterial.

ARNICA FLOWER

Compositae

Arnicae flos

Definition
Arnica Flower consists of the dried flower-heads of *Arnica montana* L.

Since *Arnica montana* is a protected species in the wild [1] and initially proved difficult to cultivate, material obtained from *Arnica chamissonis* Less. ssp. *foliosa* (Nutt.) Maguire was also accepted for some years in the definition of Arnica flower (Arnikablüten) in the Deutsches Arzneibuch. However, success has now been achieved in the field cultivation of *Arnica montana,* notably with the variety "Arbo" in Bavaria [2,3]. Since the flowers of *A. chamissonis* ssp. *foliosa* show greater qualitative and quantitative variability in constituents [2,4] the European Pharmacopoeia monograph specifies only *Arnica montana* L.

CONSTITUENTS

☐ ***Sesquiterpene lactones*** of the pseudoguaianolide type, 0.3-0.9% [5] (Ph. Eur. min. 0.4% m/m, expressed as helenalin tiglate), mainly esters of helenalin and 11α,13-dihydrohelenalin with short-chain fatty acids such as acetic, isobutyric, isovaleric, methacrylic and tiglic acids [6]. These compounds are known as helenanolides, i.e. pseudoguaian-7β,8β-olides with an α-methyl group at C-10.

Two geographically separated chemotypes exist: central European *Arnica montana* flowers with a consistent qualitative sesquiterpene lactone profile in which helenalin esters are dominant (principally the tiglate, isobutyrate, methacrylate and 2-methylbutyrate), and flowers from Spain in which 11α,13-dihydrohelenalin esters are highly predominant (principally the methacrylate and tiglate) [3,7,8].

☐ ***Flavonoids***, 0.4-0.6% [9], comprising a mixture of flavonols and flavones (most of which have one or two methoxy groups) and their glycosides.

The flavonols include patuletin, isorhamnetin, 6-methoxykaempferol, spinacetin [10] and betuletol [11] and their 3-glucosides, as well as the 3-glucosides of quercetin (i.e. isoquercitrin), kaempferol (i.e. astragalin) and quercetagetin 6,3′,4′-trimethyl ether [12,13]. Also the 3,7-diglucosides of patuletin and quercetin [13], and the 3-glucuronides of patuletin, isorhamnetin, 6-methoxykaempferol, kaempferol and quercetin [14]. Patuletin 3-glucoside and isoquercitrin are among the principal flavonoid glycosides present [15].

The flavones include pectolinarigenin, hispidulin, jaceosidin [11], eupafolin and traces of chrysoeriol and apigenin [19], together with the 7-glucosides of pectolinarigenin [13] and hispidulin [12].

Flowers of *A. montana* can be distinguished from those of *A. chamossonis* ssp. *foliosa* (using TLC or HPLC) by the absence of kaempferol 3-(6″-acetyl)-glucoside [15].

☐ ***Caffeoylquinic acids*** Chlorogenic acid (5-caffeoylquinic acid), cynarin (1,3-dicaffeoylquinic acid), 1,5-dicaffeoylquinic acid and 1,4,5-tricaffeoylquinic acid [16].

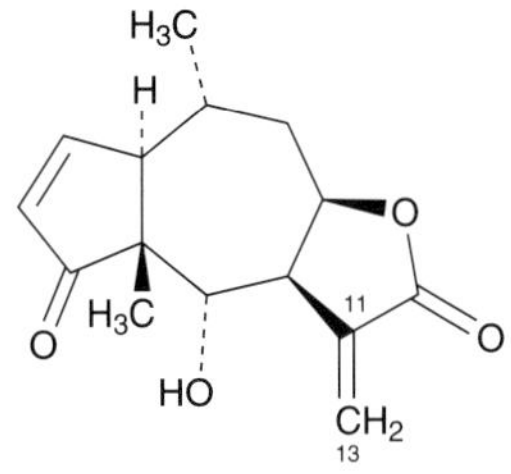

Helenalin

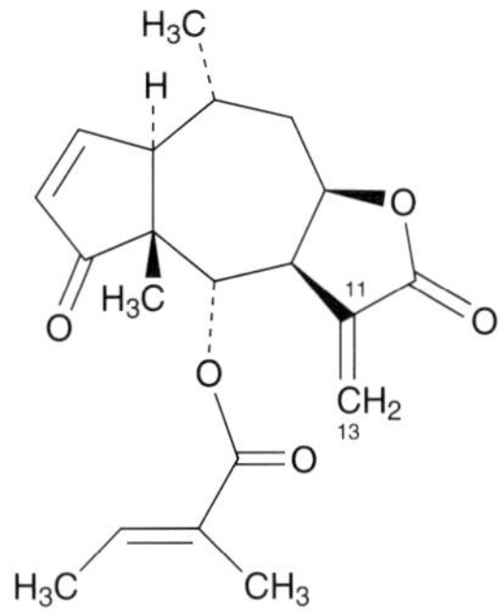

Helenalin tiglate

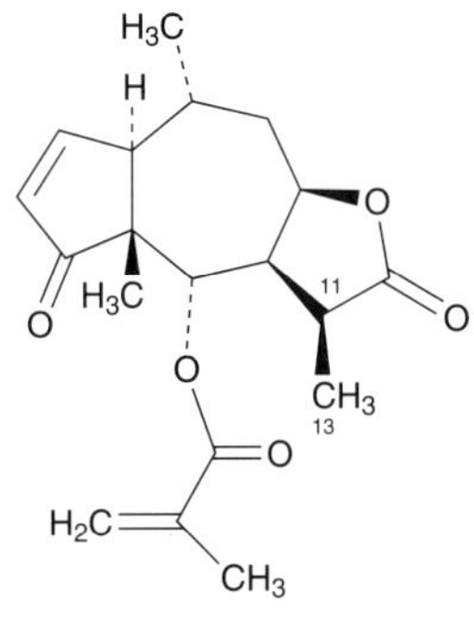

11α,13-Dihydrohelenalin methacrylate

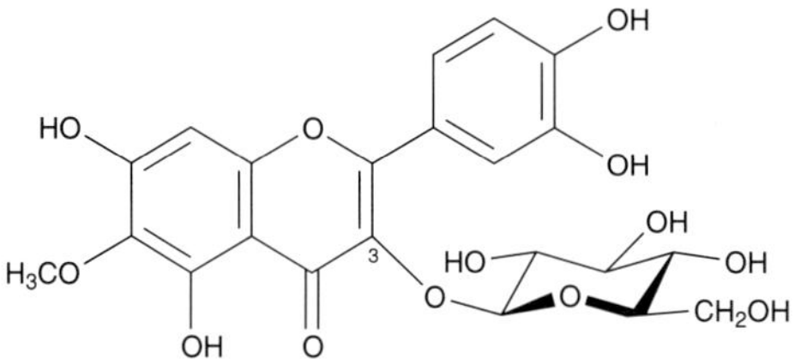

Patuletin 3-glucoside

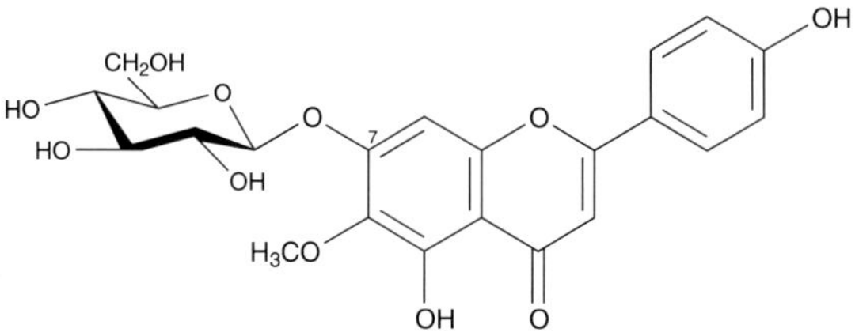

Hispidulin 7-glucoside

☐ ***Polysaccharides*** of undetermined structure. A crude fraction was found to contain mainly galactose and glucose with smaller amounts of rhamnose, xylose and mannose [17].
☐ ***Essential oil***, 0.23-0.35% [5], of a buttery consistency and containing 40-60% of fatty acids (mainly palmitic) [18] as well as sesquiterpenes, thymol derivatives and other monoterpenes [5].
☐ ***Diterpenes*** A diterpene of the labdane type, *Z*-labd-13-ene-8α,15-diol [19].
☐ ***Pyrrolizidine alkaloids*** Trace amounts (about 0.01%) of tussilaginic acid and its C-2 epimer isotussilaginic acid, and the C-1 epimers of both compounds. 2-Pyrrolidineacetic acid, a possible precursor of these pyrrolizidine alkaloids, was also isolated [20].

Tussilagine and isotussilagine (the methyl esters of tussilaginic acid and isotussilaginic acid respectively), previously reported as present in arnica flower [21], were subsequently shown to be artefacts arising from extraction of the flowers with methanol [20].
☐ ***Other constituents*** Polyacetylenes [22], the coumarins scopoletin and umbelliferone [23], carotenoids [5] and alkane-6,8-diols [24].

Published Assay Methods
Total sesquiterpene lactones by HPLC [Ph. Eur.]. Sesquiterpene lactones by GC and GC-MS [25].

PHARMACOLOGY

Sesquiterpene lactones are major contributors to the pharmacological activity of arnica flower, not least to its anti-inflammatory properties. Their mechanism of action at the molecular level, established by numerous *in vitro* and *in vivo* studies, involves α,β-unsaturated carbonyl structures, of which helenalin has two: the α-methylene-γ-lactone ring and also an α,β-unsaturated cyclopentenone moeity. These structural elements can bind to thiol (sulfhydryl) groups in proteins by what is known as "Michael-type" addition, a type of alkylation. Thus exposed thiol groups, such as those on the amino acid cysteine in certain proteins (including enzymes and transcription factors), appear to be primary targets of sequiterpene lactones [5,26].

In vitro

Anti-inflammatory activity
Helenalin proved to be the most potent of twenty sesquiterpene lactones in a range of *in vitro* tests for anti-inflammatory activity. It inhibited the migration (chemotaxis) of human polymorphonuclear neutrophils by 54% at 10^{-6} M and 100% at 5×10^{-5} M, and suppressed prostaglandin synthetase activity by 29% at 10^{-3} M [27].

Studies to investigate how sesquiterpene lactones exert their anti-inflammatory activity demonstrated that helenalin is a potent inhibitor of the transcription factor NF-κB (nuclear factor-kappa B), a central mediator of the human immune response which regulates the transcription of inflammatory cytokines such as the interleukins IL-1, IL-2, IL-6 and IL-8 and tumour necrosis factor-α (TNF-α). By inhibiting NF-κB activation, helenalin simultaneously decreases the production of many inflammatory cytokines. In turn this prevents the recruitment of immune cells, T- and B-cells, as well as macrophages and neutrophils, to the afflicted site, thereby reducing inflammation. It has been shown that helenalin can inactivate previously activated NF-κB, a property crucial to the treatment of inflammation, where active NF-κB is sustaining inflammatory processes [28]. The concentration of arnica tincture (DAB) required to completely inhibit activation of NF-κB in a cell culture was found to be 100 µl in 5 ml of medium [29].

Helenalin binds directly to thiol (sulfhydryl) groups on the amino acid cysteine in NF-κB (a protein), thus blocking its transcription activities [26]. Both the α-methylene-γ-lactone and α,β-unsaturated cyclopentenone structures in helenalin are involved in this mechanism, which explains why 11α,13-dihydrohelenalin, lacking the α-methylene-γ-lactone group, is less active and inhibits NF-κB only at about 20-fold higher concentrations than helenalin [26,30].

Cytotoxic activity
Helenalin exhibited potent cytotoxicity (greater than that of cisplatin, as a reference compound) against human small cell lung carcinoma and colorectal cancer cells, while 11,13-dihydrohelenalin was about 100 times less cytotoxic [31]. The acetate and isobutyrate of helenalin were more cytotoxic than helenalin itself, whereas larger acyl groups such as tiglate had lower toxicity due to steric hindrance [32].

Antimicrobial actvity
Helenalin and 11,13-dihydrohelenalin acetates and other esters exhibited moderate antibacterial activity against Gram-positive organisms such as *Bacillus subtilis* and *Staphylococcus aureus* [33,34] but not generally against Gram-negative organisms such as *Escherichia coli* [34].

Other effects
Helenalin and 11,13-dihydrohelenalin at 3-300 μM dose-dependently inhibited collagen-induced aggregation of human platelets and thromboxane B_2 formation. This effect was shown to be due to interaction of the sesquiterpene lactones with cellular sulfhydryl groups [35].

A crude polysaccharide fraction from arnica flower at 0.001 mg/ml stimulated phagocytosis in human granulocytes by 44%, indicating immunostimulant activity [17].

In vivo

Anti-inflammatory effects
A dry 80%-ethanolic extract from arnica significantly inhibited carrageenan-induced paw oedema in rats by 29% ($p<0.05$) after oral administration at 100 mg/kg body weight, while indometacin at 5 mg/kg produced 45% inhibition ($p<0.01$) [36].

Helenalin showed very potent anti-inflammatory activity when pre-administered intraperitoneally to rodents. It inhibited carrageenan-induced paw oedema in rats by 72% ($p<0.001$) at 2 × 2.5 mg/kg body weight, an effect comparable to the 78% inhibition produced by indometacin at 2 × 10 mg/kg, and at 20 mg/kg it inhibited the acetic acid-induced writhing reflex (an indicator of inflammation pain) in mice by 93% ($p<0.001$) compared to 57% inhibition by indometacin at 2 × 10 mg/kg ($p<0.001$) [37].

The α-methylene-γ-lactone ring of helenalin proved particularly important to the anti-inflammatory activity, which decreased when the 11,13-double bond was saturated [5,27]. This was also confirmed by a chronic adjuvant arthritis test in rats, in which intraperitoneal treatment with helenalin at 2.5 mg/kg/day on days 3-20 inhibited swelling by 77% ($p<0.001$) compared to 45% inhibition by indometacin at 10 mg/kg/day [37].

Although 11α,13-dihydrohelenalin (lacking an α-methylene-γ-lactone ring) has less anti-inflammatory activity than helenalin, esters of 11α,13-dihydrohelenalin (which are the main sesquiterpene lactones in the Spanish chemotype of arnica flower) and particularly those bearing unsaturated acyl groups have been shown to have significant anti-inflammatory properties. The methacrylate and acetate esters of 11α,13-dihydrohelenalin inhibited croton oil-induced mouse ear oedema by 77% and 54% respectively ($p<0.001$) when applied topically at 1.0 μmol/cm^2, compared to 44% inhibition by indometacin at 0.2 μmol/cm^2 [3].

Tumour-inhibiting effects
Helenalin inhibited Ehrlich ascites tumour growth in mice and Walker 256 carcinosarcoma in rats [38].

Immunostimulant effect
In the carbon clearance test in mice, a crude polysaccharide fraction from arnica flower showed considerable immunostimulating activity [17].

CLINICAL STUDIES

In a randomized, double-blind, placebo-controlled study to evaluate the efficacy of an arnica gel in the treatment of bruises, 19 patients scheduled for laser treatment of facial telangiectases (a procedure which causes bruising) were divided into pretreatment (n = 9) and post-treatment (n = 10) groups. Each patient received two gels, labelled A and B, one containing an arnica tincture (1×) in an aqueous vehicle (which also contained hamamelis water + excipients) and the other the vehicle alone. In accordance with random assignments, patients in the pre-treatment group applied gel A to one side and gel B to the other side of the face twice a day for 2 weeks prior to laser treatment. The post-treatment group patients similarly applied the gels for 2 weeks following laser treatment. All patients were given laser treatment on day 0, as far as possible standardizing the laser treatment on each side of the face, and bruising was assessed on a visual analogue scale (VAS; 0 = no bruising, 10 = worst bruising) on days 0, 3, 7, 10, 14 and 17 by both patient and physician. Additionally, photographs taken at each follow-up visit were assessed by a second physician using the VAS. Although mean scores were very slightly in favour of arnica (pretreatment: 4.335 vs 4.572, $p = 0.496$; post-treatment 3.901 vs 4.128, $p = 0.359$), no statistically significant differences between scores for arnica gel and vehicle treatment were evident in either the pre- or post-treatment groups [39].

In a randomized, double-blind, placebo-controlled study, patients with chronic venous insufficiency (primary varicosis of the legs) undergoing basic hydrotherapy treatment were also treated, by topical application to the lower legs and feet for 3 weeks, with either an arnica flower extract ointment ($n = 39$) or a placebo ointment ($n = 39$). From objective plethysmographic measurements and subjective assessment of pain, tension and swelling in the legs, improvements were observed in both groups. The plethysmography results showed a "significantly better effect from verum therapy" (no quantitave data reported) but no difference between groups was evident from the subjective assessments. In a subsequent study under identical conditions except using an arnica flower extract *gel* ($n = 50$) and a placebo *gel* ($n = 50$) comparable improvements were observed, but neither objective measurements nor subjective assessments showed a significant difference between the verum and placebo groups. Overall, these results are not convincing in favour of arnica extract treatment [40].

In an open multicentre study, 26 men and 53 women with mild to moderate osteoarthritis of the knee received an arnica gel, of which 50% by weight was a tincture from fresh arnica flower (1:20, 50% ethanol), to be applied as a thin layer to the affected knee morning and evening for 6 weeks. Compared to initial scores, substantial decreases were evident in median total scores on the Western Ontario and McMaster Universities (WOMAC) Osteoarthritis Index (a 24-item questionnaire concerning pain, joint stiffness and restriction of everday activities) after 3 and 6 weeks in both the intention-to-treat (ITT; $n = 79$) and per-protocol (PP; $n = 54$) populations. The physicians rated the efficacy of treatment as good or very good in 63% of PP patients. In a subgroup of patients who took concomitant analgesics, the decrease in WOMAC scores was not statistically significant [41].

THERAPEUTICS

Actions

Anti-inflammatory [3,36] and immunostimulant [17].

To varying degrees helenalin, 11α,13-dihydrohelenalin and their esters are anti-inflammatory [3, 37], cytotoxic [32,38] and moderately antibacterial against Gram-positive organisms [33,34].

Arnica flower is also stated to be topically counter irritant [42], to promote resorption of haemorrhages and to accelerate wound healing [4,43].

After topical application, arnica preparations have anti-inflammatory and then analgesic effects on inflammation [44].

Indications

None adequately substantiated by pharmacological or clinical studies.

Uses based on experience or tradition

External use on unbroken skin: Haematoma, contusions [4,44,45], bruises, sprains, dislocations and associated swellings resulting from blunt injuries or accidents [4,42-44,46]; chilblains [42], pains and/or inflammation in muscles and joints [4,43,44], particularly in acute stages of chronic arthritic conditions [4]; furunculosis, inflammation due to insect bites, and superficial phlebitis [44].
As a mouthwash or gargle: Inflammation of the mouth and throat mucosa [4,44].

According to Weiss, "the great benefit to be derived from external applications of arnica [to treat acute inflammation of the joints] is repeatedly confirmed in practice" [47].

Contraindications

Known hypersensitivity to arnica or other Compositae [44]. For use only on unbroken skin. Discontinue treatment on first sign of dermatitis [42,48].

Side effects

Skin irritation and inflammation are fairly common when arnica flower preparations are applied to the skin of sensitive persons [4,46]. Prolonged use may lead to more severe skin reactions with blistering [44].

Interactions with other drugs

None known.

Dosage

Using a tincture 1:10 in 70% ethanol: for compresses, tincture diluted 3- to 10-fold with water; for mouthwashes, tincture diluted 10-fold with water; in ointments or gels, 10-25% of tincture [44,48].

Alternatively in ointments or gels, up to 15% of "arnica oil" (an infusion of 1 part of arnica flower to 5 parts of fatty vegetable oil) [44,48].

An infusion from 2.0 g of arnica flower to 100 ml of water is also suitable for compresses [44,48].

SAFETY

Arnica flower is not used internally (except in dilute

homoeopathic preparations) since oral ingestion has been known to produce severe gastrointestinal and nervous system disturbances, irregularities of heart rate and collapse [Martindale 1999]. Data relating to oral or intraperitoneal toxicity and mutagenicity are not therefore summarized here, but may be found elsewhere [5,49,50].

When used as recommended, no restriction appears necessary on external use of arnica preparations during pregnancy and lactation [48].

No adverse effects were noted or reported from topical application of an arnica gel twice daily for 2 weeks by 19 patients [39]. In another study, minor skin reactions were reported by 6 out of 79 patients (7.6%), including one allergic reaction which persisted beyond the end of treatment, after topical application of an arnica gel twice daily for 6 weeks [41].

In view of the paucity of evidence of efficacy and the possibility of undesirable skin reactions [51], even the external use of arnica preparations is today regarded somewhat critically in terms of the benefit-to-risk ratio [52,53].

REGULATORY STATUS

Medicines

UK	Accepted for general sale, external use only [54].
France	Accepted for specified indications [45].
Germany	Commission E monograph published, with approved uses [44].

Food

USA	Permitted as flavouring in alcoholic beverages only (21 CFR 172.510) [55].
Council of Europe	Permitted as flavouring, category N2 [56].

REFERENCES

Current Pharmacopoeial Monographs

Ph. Eur. Arnica Flower

Literature References

1. Lange D and Schippmann U. *Checklist of medicinal and aromatic plants and their trade names covered by CITES and EU Regulation 2307/97, Version 3.0.* Bonn: German Federal Agency for Nature Conservation (Bundesamt für Naturschutz), 1999.
2. Meyer-Chlond G. Arnika - Arzneipflanze mit Tradition und Zukunft [Arnica - Medicinal plant with tradition and a future]. *Dtsch. Apoth. Ztg.* 1999, **139**, 3229-3232.
3. Klaas CA, Wagner G, Laufer S, Sosa S, Della Loggia R, Bomme U et al. Studies on the Anti-Inflammatory Activity of Phytopharmaceuticals Prepared from *Arnica* Flowers. *Planta Medica* 2002, **68**, 385-391.
4. Stahl-Biskup E, Wichtl M and Neubeck M. Arnikablüten - Arnicae flos. In: Hartke K, Hartke H, Mutschler E, Rücker G and Wichtl M, editors. *Kommentar zum Europäischen Arzneibuch.* Stuttgart: Wissenschaftliche Verlagsgesellschaft, 2001 (14 Lfg.):A 54 [GERMAN].
5. Willuhn G. *Arnica* Flowers: Pharmacology, Toxicology and Analysis of the Sesquiterpene Lactones - Their Main Active Substances. In: Lawson LD and Bauer R, editors. *Phytomedicines of Europe - Chemistry and Biological Activity.* ACS Symposium Series 691. ISBN 0-8412-3559-7. Washington DC: American Chemical Society, 1998:118-132.
6. Willuhn G, Röttger P-M and Matthiesen U. Helenalin and 11,13-Dihydrohelenalin esters from Flowers of *Arnica montana. Planta Medica* 1983, **49**, 226-231 [GERMAN/English summary].
7. Merfort I, Pietta PG, Mauri PL, Zini L, Catalano G and Willuhn G. Separation of Sesquiterpene Lactones from Arnicae Flos DAB 10 by Micellar Electrokinetic Chromatography. *Phytochem. Analysis* 1997, **8**, 5-8.
8. Willuhn G, Leven W and Luley C. Arnikablüten DAB 10. Untersuchungen zur qualitativen und quantitativen Variabilität des Sesquiterpenlactongehaltes der offizinellen Arnikadrogen [Arnica flower DAB 10. Investigations on the qualitative and quantitative variability in sesquiterpene lactone content of the official Arnica drug]. *Dtsch. Apoth. Ztg.* l994, **134**, 4077-4085.
9. Wijnsma R, Woerdenbag HJ and Busse W. Die Bedeutung von Arnika-Arten in der Phytotherapie. Portrait einer Arzneipflanze [The importance of *Arnica* species in phytomedicine. Portrait of a medicinal plant]. *Z. Phytotherapie* 1995, **16**, 48-62 [GERMAN/English summary].
10. Merfort I. Flavonoids from *Arnica montana* and *Arnica chamissonis. Planta Medica* 1985, **51**, 136-138 [GERMAN/English summary].
11. Merfort I. Methylated Flavonoids from *Arnica montana* and *Arnica chamissonis. Planta Medica* 1984, **50**, 107-108 [GERMAN/English summary].
12. Merfort I and Wendisch D. Flavonoid Glycosides from *Arnica montana* and *Arnica chamissonis. Planta Medica* 1987, **53**, 434-437 [GERMAN/English summary].
13. Merfort I and Wendisch D. New flavonoid glycosides from Arnicae flos DAB 9. *Planta Medica* 1992, **58**, 355-357.
14. Merfort I and Wendisch D. Flavonol Glucuronides from the Flowers of *Arnica montana. Planta Medica* 1988, **54**, 247-250 [GERMAN/English summary].
15. Merfort I, Willuhn G and Jerga C. Arnikablüten DAB 9 - Reinheitsprüfung. Zuordnung und Zusammensetzung der Flavonoidglykosid-Banden im DC und HPLC sowie Vergleich mit den "Mexikanischen Arnikablüten" [Arnica Flower DAB 9 - Purity testing. Assignment and composition of the flavonoid glycoside bands in TLC and HPLC, and comparison with "Mexican arnica flower"]. *Dtsch. Apoth. Ztg.* 1990, **130**, 980-984 [GERMAN].
16. Merfort I. Caffeoylquinic acids from flowers of *Arnica montana* and *Arnica chamissonis. Phytochemistry* 1992, **31**, 2111-2113.
17. Wagner H, Proksch A, Riess-Maurer I, Vollmar A, Odenthal S, Stuppner H et al. Immunstimulierend wirkende Polysaccharide (Heteroglykane) aus höheren Pflanzen [Immunostimulant polysaccharides (heteroglycans) from higher plants]. *Arzneim.-Forsch./Drug Res.* 1985, **35**, 1069-1075 [GERMAN/English summary].
18. Kating H, Rinn W and Willuhn G. Untersuchungen über die Inhaltsstoffe von *Arnica*-Arten. III. Die Fettsäuren in den ätherischen Ölen der Blüten verschiedener *Arnica*-Arten [Investigations into the constituents of *Arnica* species. III. Fatty acids in volatile oils from the flowers of various *Arnica* species]. *Planta Medica* 1970, **18**, 130-146 [GERMAN/English summary].
19. Schmidt T, Paßreiter CM, Wendisch D and Willuhn G. First diterpenes from *Arnica. Planta Medica* 1992, **58** (Suppl. 1), A713.
20. Paßreiter CM. Co-occurrence of 2-pyrrolidineacetic acid with the pyrrolizidines tussilaginic acid and isotussilaginic

acid and their 1-epimers in *Arnica* species and *Tussilago farfara*. *Phytochemistry* 1992, **31**, 4135-4137.
21. Paßreiter CM, Willuhn G and Röder E. Tussilagine and Isotussilagine: Two Pyrrolizidine Alkaloids in the Genus *Arnica*. *Planta Medica* 1992, **58**, 556-557.
22. Schulte KE, Rücker G and Reithmayr K. Einige Inhaltsstoffe von *Arnica chamissonis* und anderer *Arnica*-Arten [Some constituents of *Arnica chamissonis* and other *Arnica* species]. *Lloydia* 1969, **32**, 360-368 [GERMAN/English summary].
23. Marchishin SM and Komissarenko NF. Components of *Arnica montana* and *Arnica foliosa*. *Khim. Prir. Soedin.* 1981 (5), 662 [RUSSIAN], through *Chem. Abstr.* 1982, **96**, 31675.
24. Akihisa T, Inoue Y, Yasukawa K, Kasahara Y, Yamanouchi S, Kumaki K and Tamura T. Widespread occurrence of *syn*-alkane-6,8-diols in the flowers of the Compositae. *Phytochemistry* 1998, **49**, 1637-1640.
25. Schmidt TJ, Matthiesen U and Willuhn G. On the Stability of Sesquiterpene Lactones in the Official Arnica Tincture of the German Pharmacopoeia. *Planta Medica* 2000, **66**, 678-681.
26. Rüngeler P, Castro V, Mora G, Gören N, Vichnewski W, Pahl HL et al. Inhibition of Transcription Factor NF-κB by Sesquiterpene Lactones: a Proposed Molecular Mechanism of Action. *Bioorg. Med. Chem.* 1999, **7**, 2343-2352.
27. Hall IH, Lee KH, Starnes CO, Sumida Y, Wu RY, Waddell TG et al. Anti-inflammatory activity of sesquiterpene lactones and related compounds. *J. Pharm. Sci.* 1979, **68**, 537-542.
28. Lyß G, Knorre A, Schmidt TJ, Pahl HL and Merfort I. The Anti-inflammatory Sesquiterpene Lactone Helenalin Inhibits the Transcription Factor NF-κB by Directly Targeting p65. *J. Biol. Chem.* 1998, **273**, 33508-33516.
29. Lyß G, Schmidt TJ, Pahl HL and Merfort I. Anti-inflammatory activity of Arnica tincture (DAB 1998) using the transcription factor NF-κB as molecular target. *Pharm. Pharmacol. Lett.* 1999, **9**, 5-8.
30. Lyss G, Schmidt TJ, Merfort I and Pahl HL. Helenalin, an anti-inflammatory sesquiterpene lactone from *Arnica*, selectively inhibits transcription factor NF-κB. *Biol. Chem.* 1997, **378**, 951-961.
31. Woerdenbag HJ, Merfort I, Paßreiter CM, Schmidt TJ, Willuhn G, van Uden W et al. Cytotoxicity of Flavonoids and Sesquiterpene Lactones from *Arnica* Species Against the GLC_4 and the COLO 320 Cell Lines. *Planta Medica* 1994, **60**, 434-437.
32. Beekman AC, Woerdenbag HJ, van Uden W, Pras N, Konings AWT, Wikström HV and Schmidt TJ. Structure-Cytotoxicity Relationships of Some Helenanolide-Type Sesquiterpene Lactones. *J. Nat. Prod.* 1997, **60**, 252-257.
33. Lee KH, Ibuka T, Wu RY and Geissman TA. Structural-antimicrobial activity relationships among the sesquiterpene lactones and related compounds. *Phytochemistry* 1977, **16**, 1177-1181.
34. Willuhn G, Röttger P-M and Quack W. Untersuchungen zur antimikrobiellen Aktivität der Sesquiterpenlactone der Arnikablüten [Investigation of the antimicrobial activity of sesquiterpene lactones in arnica flowers]. *Pharm. Ztg.* 1982, **127**, 2183-2185 [GERMAN].
35. Schröder H, Lösche W, Strobach H, Leven W, Willuhn G, Till U and Schrör K. Helenalin and 11α,13-dihydrohelenalin, two constituents from *Arnica montana* L., inhibit human platelet function via thiol-dependent pathways. *Thrombosis Res.* 1990, **57**, 839-845.
36. Mascolo N, Autore G, Capasso F, Menghini A and Fasulo MP. Biological Screening of Italian Medicinal Plants for Anti-inflammatory Activity. *Phytotherapy Res.* 1987, **1**, 28-31.
37. Hall IH, Starnes CO, Lee KH and Waddell TG. Mode of action of sesquiterpene lactones as anti-inflammatory agents. *J. Pharm. Sci.* 1980, **69**, 537-543.
38. Hall IH, Lee K-H, Starnes CO, Eigebaly SA, Ibuka T, Wu Y-S et al. Antitumor agents XXX: Evaluation of α-methylene-γ-lactone-containing agents for inhibition of tumor growth, respiration and nucleic acid synthesis. *J. Pharm. Sci.* 1978, **67**, 1235-1239.
39. Alonso D, Lazarus MC and Baumann L. Effects of Topical Arnica Gel on Post-Laser Treatment Bruises. *Dermatol. Surg.* 2002, **28**, 686-688.
40. Brock FE. Ergebnisse klinischer Studien bei Patienten mit chronisch venöser Insuffizienz [Results of a clinical study in patients with chronic venous insufficiency]. Pages 49-50 in: von Raison J, Heilmann J, Merfort I, Schmidt TJ, Brock FE, Leven W et al. Arnika - Arzneipflanze mit Tradition und Zukunft [Arnica - Medicinal plant with tradition and a future]. *Z. Phytotherapie* 2000, **21**, 39-54 [GERMAN/English summary].
41. Knuesel O, Weber M and Suter A. *Arnica montana* Gel in Osteoarthritis of the Knee: An Open, Multicenter Clinical Trial. *Adv. Ther.* 2002, **19**, 209-217.
42. Arnica. In: *British Herbal Pharmacopoeia 1983.* ISBN 0-903032-07-4. Bournemouth: British Herbal Medicine Association, 1983.
43. Chevallier A. Arnica - *Arnica montana*. In: *Encyclopedia of Medicinal Plants, 2nd ed.* ISBN 0-7513-1209-6. London-New York: Dorling Kindersley, 2001:172.
44. Arnicae flos. German Commission E Monograph published in: Bundesanzeiger No. 228 of 5 December 1984.
45. Arnica. In: *Médicaments à base de plantes.* ISBN 2-911473-02-7. Saint-Denis Cedex, France: Agence du Médicament, 1998.
46. Parfitt K. editor. Arnica. In: *Martindale - The complete drug reference, 32nd edition.* ISBN 0-85369-429-X. London: Pharmaceutical Press, 1999:1550.
47. Weiss RF. External Use of Herbal Medicines for Rheumatic Conditions. In: *Herbal Medicine* (translated from the 6th German edition of *Lehrbuch der Phytotherapie*). ISBN 0-906584-19-1. Gothenburg: AB Arcanum, Beaconsfield, UK: Beaconsfield Publishers, 1988:267-270.
48. Mills S and Bone K. Arnica flowers (*Arnica montana* L.). In: *Principles and Practice of Phytotherapy. Modern Herbal Medicine.* ISBN 0-443-06016-9. Edinburgh-London-New York: Churchill Livingstone, 2000:269-272.
49. European Scientific Cooperative on Phytotherapy. Arnicae flos - Arnica Flower. In: *ESCOP Monographs - The Scientific Foundation for Herbal Medicinal Products*, 2nd ed. ISBN 3-13-129421-3. Stuttgart: Georg Thieme Verlag, 2003:43-47.
50. Cosmetic Ingredient Review Expert Panel. Final Report on the Safety Assessment of *Arnica montana* Extract and *Arnica montana*. *Int. J. Toxicol.* 2001, **20** (Suppl. 2), 1-11.
51. Hörmann HP and Korting HC. Allergic acute contact dermatitis due to *Arnica* tincture self-medication. *Phytomedicine* 1995, **2**, 315-317.
52. Hörmann HP and Korting HC. Evidence for the Efficacy and Safety of Topical Herbal Drugs in Dermatology. Part 1: Anti-inflammatory agents. *Phytomedicine* 1994, **1**, 161-171.
53. Schulz V, Hänsel R and Tyler VE. Arnica. In: *Rational Phytotherapy - A Physicians' Guide to Herbal Medicine, 4th ed.* ISBN 3-540-67096-3. Berlin-Heidelberg-New York-London: Springer-Verlag, 2001:314-315.
54. Arnica. In: UK Statutory Instrument 1994 No. 2410. The Medicines (Products Other Than Veterinary Drugs) (General Sale List) Amendment Order 1994. Schedule 1, Table B (External use only).
55. Arnica flowers. In: Section 172.510 of USA Code of Federal Regulations, Title 21, Food and Drugs, Parts 170 to 199. Revised as of April 1, 2000.
56. Arnica montana L., flowers. In: *Flavouring Substances and Natural Sources of Flavourings, 3rd ed.* ISBN 2-7160-0081-6. Strasbourg: Council of Europe, 1981.

REGULATORY GUIDELINES FROM OTHER EU COUNTRIES

FRANCE

Médicaments à base de plantes [45]: Arnica, capitule.

Therapeutic indications accepted

Topical use
Traditionally used in the symptomatic treatment of ecchymoses.

GERMANY

Commission E monograph [44]: Arnicae flos (Arnikablüten).

Uses
For external use on the outcomes of injuries or accidents, such as haematoma, dislocations, bruises, contusions and oedema associated with fractures; rheumatic complaints in muscles and joints; inflammation of the mouth and throat mucosa; furunculosis, inflammation due to insect bites, superficial phlebitis.

Contraindications
Allergy to arnica.

Side effects
Prolonged use on damaged skin, e.g. on injuries or crural ulcer, relatively frequently causes oedematous dermatitis with blistering. Eczema may also arise with prolonged use. With dosage forms of higher concentration, primary toxic skin reactions with blistering or even necrosis are also possible.

Interactions with other drugs
None known.

Dosage
Unless otherwise prescribed,
Infusion: 2.0 g of the drug to 100 ml of water.
Tincture: for compresses, tincture diluted 3- to 10-fold with water; for mouthwashes, tincture diluted 10-fold; in ointments, not more than 20-25% of tincture.
"Arnica oil": an infusion of 1 part of drug to 5 parts of fatty vegetable oil; in ointments, not more than 15% of "arnica oil".

Mode of administration
Whole, cut or powdered drug for infusions, liquid and semi-solid dosage forms for external use.

Actions
Particularly after topical application, arnica preparations have anti-inflammatory and then analgesic effects on inflammation, and are antiseptic.

ARTICHOKE LEAF

Compositae

Cynarae folium

Synonym: Globe artichoke leaf.

Definition

Artichoke Leaf consists of the dried leaves of *Cynara scolymus* L.

The globe artichoke head, of which tender parts are eaten as an hors d'oeuvre, is the immature flower of *Cynara scolymus*, a plant related to thistles. In the cultivation of artichoke leaf for pharmaceutical purposes, the basal leaves, which form a large rosette close to the ground, offer the optimal material when harvested before the flower stalk develops, since the content of caffeoylquinic acids declines thereafter [1]. However, some of the commercial material used in making extracts is leaf or aerial parts available as a by-product of cultivation for flower heads [2,3]. This is more variable in quality than leaf cultivated specifically for pharmaceutical use [2], but not necessarily lower in constituent levels [3]. What appears to be most important for good quality in terms of efficacy-determing constituents is gentle drying (at no higher than 40°C) to minimise loss of caffeoylquinic acids in the dried material [1,3]. Both dried and fresh leaf are used in medicinal preparations, which include pressed juice from fresh leaf [1].

The Jerusalem artichoke, cultivated for its edible tuber, is a quite different species, *Helianthus tuberosus* L., a member of the sunflower family. Its common name is a corruption of *girasole*, the Italian word for sunflower.

In a taxonomic revision of the genus *Cynara*, published in 1992, the cultivated globe artichoke (*Cynara scolymus*) and the cardoon (formerly *Cynara cardunculus*) were united as a new subspecies, *Cynara cardunculus* L. subsp. *flavescens* Wikl. [4]. Although no doubt sound from a botanical perspective, the change does not help to distinguish the morphological type of plant cultivated as a source of pharmaceutical grade artichoke leaf [5,6] and the new name has not yet caught on. The name *Cynara scolymus* continues to be used very widely and is retained in this text in order to relate to published literature.

CONSTITUENTS

☐ ***Caffeoylquinic acids***, principally 1,5-dicaffeoylquinic acid* and chlorogenic acid (5-caffeoylquinic acid; Ph. Eur. min. 0.8%) with small amounts of neo- and cryptochlorogenic acids [3,8,9], and 3,4-, 3,5- and 4,5-dicaffeoylquinic acids [8]. The minimum content of total caffeoylquinic acids, calculated as chlorogenic acid, should be 1.0% in good dried material [1] while up to 6% is attained in selected dried leaf [2]. Samples containing 4.1-4.7% of chlorogenic acid and 5.9-6.4% of total caffeoylquinic acids have been reported [10].

Cynarin (1,3-dicaffeoylquinic acid), a key constituent of the aqueous dry extracts used in many

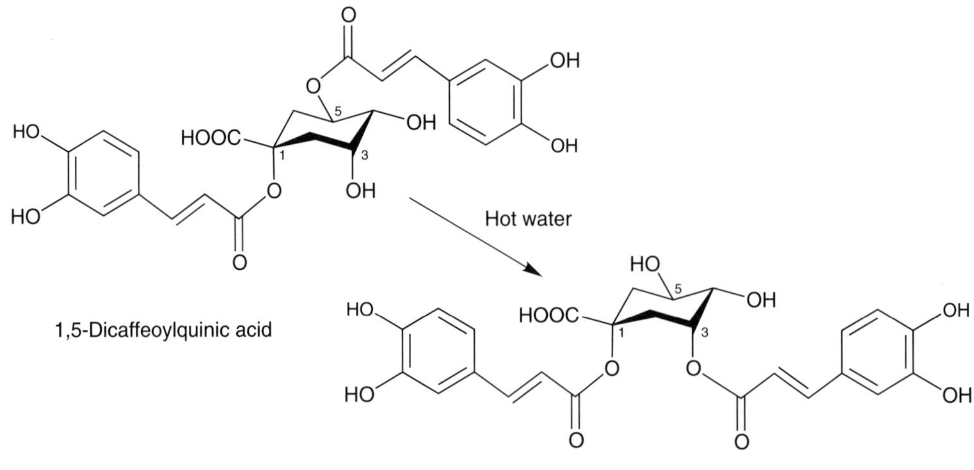

1,5-Dicaffeoylquinic acid

Cynarin (1,3-Dicaffeoylquinic acid)

* Numbered in accordance with IUPAC recommendations for cyclitols [7]. Some texts on artichoke describe 1,5-dicaffeoylquinic acid as 1,3-dicaffeoylquinic acid and cynarin as 1,5-dicaffeoylquinic acid.

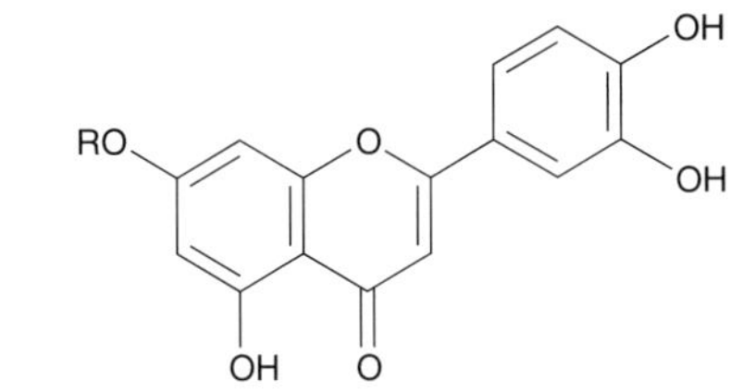

Luteolin 7-glucoside (cynaroside) R = glucosyl
Luteolin 7-rutinoside (scolymoside) R = rutinosyl

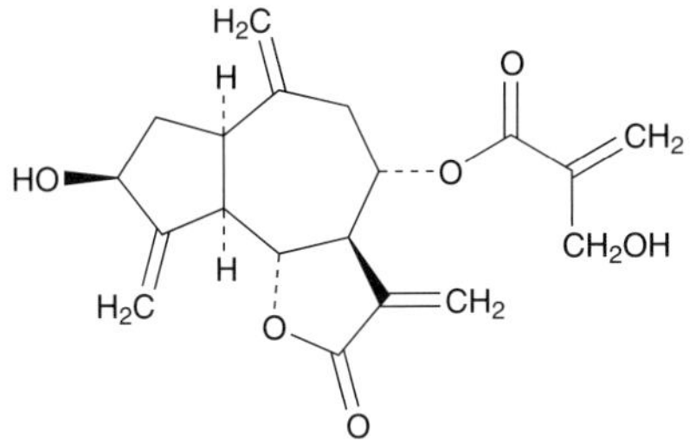

Cynaropicrin

artichoke preparations, is present only in traces in fresh or carefully dried leaf; it is formed as an artefact by rearrangement (transesterification) from 1,5-dicaffeoylquinic acid in hot water during the extraction process [1].

Caffeoylquinic acids are not very stable to drying processes. Under laboratory conditions, drying of fresh leaf at room temperature led to a loss of 20-40% of caffeoylquinic acids, while drying at 60°C caused 80-85% loss [11].

☐ ***Flavonoids***, 0.3-0.75% [1,2,12], mainly luteolin 7-rutinoside (scolymoside) and 7-glucoside (cynaroside) with a smaller amount of free luteolin [3,8,12-14].

Other flavonoids reported include luteolin 7-glucuronide [15], 7-gentiobioside, 4′-glucoside [9,16] and 7-rutinosyl-4′-glucoside (cynarotrioside) [11]; free apigenin, apigenin 7-glucoside (cosmosiin) and 7-rutinoside [14,16]; quercetin, rutin, hesperetin and hesperidin [16].

☐ ***Sesquiterpene lactones*** of the guaianolide type, up to 4%, principally cynaropicrin (47-83% of total sesquiterpene lactones; bitterness value 400,000), grosheimin and cynaratriol [11,17]. At least 7 other sesquiterpene lactones, including grosulfeimin, have also been isolated [18,19] as well as 4 sequiterpene glucosides [19].

Due to their low solubility in water, sesquiterpene lactones are scarcely present in aqueous extracts of artichoke [20].

☐ ***Coumarins*** Scopoletin and esculin [16].

☐ ***Aliphatic acids***, particularly hydroxy acids such as lactic, glycolic, malic and citric acids [21]; also hydroxymethylacrylic acid [22].

☐ ***Other constituents*** include caffeic acid [8,16] and the aurone maritimein [16].

For a review of the constituents of artichoke leaf see Brand [11].

Published Assay Methods

Chlorogenic acid [Ph. Eur.], caffeoylquinic acids and flavonoids [1,3,10,20] by HPLC. Sesquiterpene lactones by GC [17] and HPLC [19]. Hydroxycinnamic metabolites in human plasma [23].

PHARMACOLOGY

Antioxidative, hepatoprotective and choleretic effects of artichoke leaf extracts as well as lipid-lowering and anti-atherogenic activity, with increased elimination of cholesterol and inhibition of hepatocellular *de novo* cholesterol biosynthesis, have been demonstrated in various *in vitro* and *in vivo* test systems. Active constituents mainly responsible for the effects have been identified and include caffeoylquinic acids, luteolin and luteolin 7-glucoside (cynaroside). Antidyspeptic effects are mainly attributed to increased choleresis. For summaries of *in vitro* and animal studies with artichoke leaf extracts see Kraft [24] and the ESCOP monograph [25].

Pharmacological studies in humans

Choleretic effects

A single dose of 1.92 g of a dry aqueous extract (4.5-5:1) of artichoke leaf, or placebo, was administered intraduodenally to one of two randomized groups of 10 male volunteers with acute or chronic metabolic disorders in a double-blind study. Cross-over to the alternative medication followed after an 8-day washout phase. Compared to initial values, intraduodenal bile secretion (monitored with duodenal probes) increased in the artichoke group by 127% after 30 minutes, 151% after 60 minutes (the maximum effect) and 94% after 90 minutes. Bile secretion in the placebo group also increased, but to a much lesser extent, by a maximum of 39% after 30 minutes. The difference between verum and placebo groups was significant ($p<0.01$ after 30, 60 and 90 minutes, $p<0.05$ after 120 and 150 minutes). No adverse effects were observed [26].

Lipid lowering effects

In a randomized double-blind study, healthy volunteers received either 3 × 640 mg of artichoke leaf aqueous dry extract or placebo daily for 12 weeks. Mean initial total cholesterol (ITC) levels were relatively low in both the verum (204.2 mg/dl,

n_v = 22) and placebo (203.0 mg/dl, n_p = 22) groups. In subgroups with ITC of over 210 mg/dl (n_v = 10, n_p = 7) and over 220 mg/dl (n_v = n_p = 5), differences (p = 0.022 and p = 0.012 respectively) in favour of the extract could be detected for triglycerides but not for cholesterol. In volunteers with ITC higher than 230 mg/dl (n_v = n_p = 3), the artichoke extract significantly decreased concentrations of both triglycerides (p = 0.01) and total cholesterol (p = 0.015) compared to placebo [27].

Daily administration of 0.9 g of an artichoke extract to 30 healthy elderly subjects for 6 weeks significantly reduced serum levels of total lipids ($p<0.01$), triglycerides ($p<0.01$) and free fatty acids ($p<0.05$) [28].

Administration of a single large dose (1.92 g) of dry aqueous extract of artichoke to 4 healthy young volunteers did not produce any increases in thermometric (energy expenditure, respiratory quotient) or cardiovascular (heart rate, systolic and diastolic blood pressure) parameters which might have indicated a potential for artichoke leaf as a thermogenic agent in the treatment of human obesity [29].

Pharmacokinetics in humans
In a crossover study involving 14 healthy volunteers, who received an otherwise plant material-free diet for 2 days before, and during, the 24-hour test periods, no mono- or dicaffeoylquinic acids or luteolin glycosides were detected in blood plasma or urine after administration of single oral doses of two different artichoke extracts. The metabolites of caffeoylquinic acids detected, mainly as sulphate or glucuronide conjugates, were caffeic acid, its methylated derivatives ferulic and isoferulic acids, and the hydrogenated derivatives dihydrocaffeic acid and dihydroferulic acid. Luteolin was recovered only as sulphate or glucuronide. The amounts recovered in urine within 24 hours represented only 4-5% of the caffeoylquinic acids and about 2% of the luteolin intake [6,30].

CLINICAL STUDIES

Controlled studies
The four controlled clinical studies published to date present a rather mixed bag, investigating the effects of artichoke leaf extracts in very different indications: functional dyspepsia [31], alcohol-induced hangovers [32], hyperlipoproteinaemia [33] and adjuvant treatment of malaria [34].

In a double-blind, randomized, placebo-controlled study, 244 patients with functional dyspepsia were treated daily for 6 weeks with 1.92 g (3 × 640 mg) of a dry aqueous artichoke leaf extract (3.8-5.5:1, n = 129) or placebo (n = 115). Based on patient self-rating, the overall improvement of symptoms during the 6-week period was significantly greater in the artichoke group (score reduction of 8.3 points; $p<0.01$) than in the placebo group (score reduction of 6.7 points). Global quality of life scores also reflected greater improvement in the artichoke group ($p<0.01$). All patients reported improvement in six individual symptoms over the 6-week period; compared to the placebo group, significantly better responses were shown by the artichoke group for fullness, early satiety and flatulence (each $p<0.05$), but differences were not significant for nausea, vomiting or epigastric pain [31].

Although artichoke leaf preparations have been promoted as having beneficial effects on the symptoms of alcohol-induced hangover, the results (hangover severity scores, mood questionnaires and cognitive performance tests) of a randomized, double-blind, placebo-controlled crossover study involving 15 healthy adult volunteers offered no evidence in support of this theory [32].

Patients with hyperlipoproteinaemia (cholesterol > 280 mg/dl) received daily for 6 weeks either 1800 mg of an artichoke leaf dry aqueous extract (25-35:1, derived from fresh leaf and presented in coated tablets) (n = 71) or placebo (n = 72) in a randomized, double-blind study. From baseline to end of treatment the reductions in blood levels of total cholesterol and LDL-cholesterol were 18.5% and 22.9% respectively in the verum group compared to 8.6% and 6.3% in the placebo group, demonstrating significant superiority of the artichoke leaf extract (p = 0.0001). The LDL/HDL ratio decreased by 20.2% in the artichoke group and 7.2% in the placebo group [33].

In addition to conventional quinine therapy, malaria patients participating in a placebo-controlled study were treated with either a purified aqueous dry extract from fresh artichoke leaf juice, administered orally at 1600 mg/day and intramuscularly at 100 mg/day for 3 days then continuing the oral treatment on days 4-7 (n = 46), or placebo (n = 46). In patients treated with artichoke extract, more rapid improvements in clinical symptoms of malaria were observed and attributed to hepatoprotective effects of the extract [34].

Open studies
In a surveillance study involving 553 patients, non-specific digestive disorders (dyspeptic symptom complex) such as vomiting, stomach pains, loss of appetite, constipation, flatulence or fat intolerance were treated on average for 6 weeks with capsules providing 960-1920 mg (average 1520 mg) per day of an artichoke leaf aqueous dry extract (3.8-5.5:1, equivalent to about 4.7-8.9 g of dried artichoke leaf per day). During the treatment period, patients' subjective symptom scores declined significantly,

by 46-88% compared to initial values, with reductions of 88% for vomiting, 76% for stomach pains, 72% for loss of appetite and 59% for fat intolerance. Within a sample of 302 patients, serum cholesterol levels decreased by 11.5% and triglycerides by 12.5%, while HDL-cholesterol showed a small increase of 2.3%. The physicians' global assessment of efficacy was excellent or good in 87% of cases [35]. Comparable results were obtained in a similar but longer-term study involving the treatment of 203 patients with dyspeptic symptoms for 21 weeks with the same extract and dosage range [36].

As there is a symptom overlap between dyspeptic symptom complex (dyspeptic syndrome) and irritable bowel syndrome (IBS), data arising from one of the above studies [35] was further analysed with respect to a subgroup of 279 dyspeptic patients who had reported at least 3 out of 5 defined symptoms of IBS: abdominal pain, right-sided abdominal cramps, bloating, flatulence or constipation. Within the IBS subgroup, scores for all five of these symptoms dropped substantially over the 6-week period ($p<0.05$ compared to baseline values), with an overall reduction of 71%, and this was taken as encouragement for further work [37].

Patients with self-reported dyspepsia (but otherwise healthy), recruited through the media, were randomly allocated to daily treatment for 2 months with either 320 mg or 640 mg of a dry aqueous artichoke leaf extract (4-6:1, minimum 0.3% of flavonoids and 2.4% of caffeoylquinic acids). From an initial 516 participants, 454 completed the open study. Using the Nepean Dyspepsia Index, completed at baseline and end of treatment, substantial reductions in dyspeptic symptoms were evident in both dosage groups, with an average reduction of 40% in global dyspepsia score, but no significant difference between groups [38]. In a subgroup of 208 patients identified as suffering from irritable bowel syndrome, the incidence of IBS had declined by 26.4% after 2 months, with no significant difference between dosage groups, and 55 subjects no longer fell within the criteria for IBS [39].

In a comparative study, patients with primary hypertriglyceridaemia resistant to treatment with clofibrate were treated daily for 1 month with an artichoke extract providing 45 mg of polyphenolic acids (n = 25) or with 0.75 g of cynarin (n = 28) or 1.5 g of cynarin (n = 20). The artichoke extract significantly reduced total serum lipids, triglycerides and phospholipids in 56% of patients, while 0.75 g or 1.5 g of cynarin improved these parameters in 61% or 40% of patients respectively [40].

THERAPEUTICS

Actions

Choleretic, lipid-lowering, hepatoprotective, anti-atherogenic and antioxidative [24,25,41].

Also stated to be diuretic and hepatostimulant [41,42].

Indications

Dyspeptic complaints [31,35,36,43] including flatulence, early satiety, feeling of fullness [31], vomiting, nausea, stomach pains, loss of appetite, constipation, fat intolerance [35,36,38] and irritable bowel syndrome [37,39].

Adjuvant to a low fat diet in the treatment of mild to moderate hyperlipidaemia [25,27,28,33,40].

Contraindications

Known allergy to artichoke and other Compositae; obstruction of the bile duct [43].

Side effects

None known.

Interactions with other drugs

None known.

Dosage

Daily dose (usually as three divided doses): dried leaf, 6 g on average [43]; dry aqueous extracts corresponding to 4.5-9 g of dried leaf [31,35,36] or 27-54 g of *fresh* leaf [33].

SAFETY

The comparative safety of artichoke leaf extracts is to some extent implied by the popularity of artichoke heads (immature flowers) as an hors d'oeuvre and no major adverse events have been reported by patients during clinical studies. From 1471 patients treated with artichoke leaf extracts in six clinical studies [32-36,38] only 7 adverse events were reported, none at all in three of these studies [33,34,36]. Unusually, therefore, in a recent controlled study in which 129 patients with functional dyspepsia received 1.92 g of artichoke leaf extract daily for 6 weeks, 29 patients reported 45 adverse events, predominantly mild to moderate and relating to the gastrointestinal tract or "the body as a whole"; the majority of adverse events resolved themselves by the end of the study and, in any case, the incidence should be seen in the context of patients already suffering from gastrointestinal ailments [31].

Preclinical (*in vitro* and *in vivo*) safety data on artichoke leaf extracts and cynarin can be found in the ESCOP monograph [25].

REGULATORY STATUS

Medicines

UK	Accepted for general sale, internal or external use [44].
France	Accepted for specified indications [42].
Germany	Commission E monograph published, with approved uses [43].

Food

USA	Permitted as flavouring in alcoholic beverages only (21 CFR 172.510) [45].
Council of Europe	Permitted as flavouring, category N2 [46].

REFERENCES

Current Pharmacopoeial Monographs

Ph. Eur. Artichoke Leaf

Literature References

1. Brand N. Der Extrakt in Artischockenpräparaten [The extract in artichoke preparations]. *Dtsch. Apoth. Ztg.* 1997, **137**, 3564-3578 [GERMAN].
2. Wagenbreth D, Grün M, Wagenbreth A-N and Wegener T. Artischocke - Qualitätsdroge aus Arzneipflanzenanbau [Artichoke - Crude drug of quality from medicinal plant cultivation]. *Dtsch. Apoth. Ztg.* 1996, **136**, 3818-3826 [GERMAN].
3. Brand N and Weschta H. Die analytische Bewertung der Artischocke und ihrer Präparate [The analytical evaluation of artichoke and its preparations]. *Z. Phytotherapie* 1991, **12**, 15-21 [GERMAN/English summary].
4. Wiklund A. The genus *Cynara* L. (Asteraceae-Cardueae). *Bot. J. Linn. Soc.* 1992, **109**, 75-123.
5. Brand N. Die Artischocke - eine Dekade interdisziplinärer Forschung [The Artichoke - A Decade of Interdisciplinary Research]. *Z. Phytotherapie* 1999, **20**, 292-302 [GERMAN/English summary].
6. van Rensen I and Wittemer SM. *Cynara cardunculus* subsp. *flavescens* (bisher *Cynara scolymus*) - die Artischocke. Bioverfügbarkeit und Pharmakokinetik der Inhaltstoffe [*Cynara cardunculus* subsp. *flavescens* (formerly *Cynara scolymus*) – the Artichoke. Bioavailability and pharmacokinetics of the constituents]. *Z. Phytotherapie* 2003, **24**, 267-276 [GERMAN/English summary].
7. IUPAC Commission on the Nomenclature of Organic Chemistry (CNOC) and IUPAC-IUB Commission on Bio-chemical Nomenclature (CBN). Nomenclature of Cyclitols: Recommendations, 1973. *Biochem. J.* 1976, **153**, 23-31.
8. Adzet T and Puigmacia M. High-performance liquid chromatography of caffeoylquinic acid derivatives of *Cynara scolymus* L. leaves. *J. Chromatogr.* 1985, **348**, 447-453.
9. Bombardelli E, Gabetta B and Martinelli EM. Gas-Liquid Chromatographic and Mass Spectrometric Investigation on *Cynara scolymus* Extracts. *Fitoterapia* 1977, **48**,143-152.
10. Wang M, Simon JE, Aviles IF, He K, Zheng Q-Y and Tadmor Y. Analysis of Antioxidative Phenolic Compounds in Artichoke (*Cynara scolymus* L.). *J. Agric. Food. Chem.* 2003, **51**, 601-608.
11. Brand N. *Cynara scolymus* L. - Die Artischocke [The artichoke]. *Z. Phytotherapie* 1990, **11**, 169-175 [GERMAN].
12. Hammouda FM, Seif El-Nasr MM, Ismail SI and Shahat AA. Quantitative Determination of the Active Constituents in Egyptian Cultivated *Cynara scolymus*. *Int. J. Pharmacognosy* 1993, **31**, 299-304.
13. Hammouda FM, Seif El-Nesr MM, Ismail SI and Shahat AA. HPLC Evaluation of the Active Constituents in the Newly Introduced Romanian Strain of *Cynara scolymus* cultivated in Egypt. *Planta Medica* 1991, **57** (Suppl. 2), A119-A120.
14. El-Negoumy SI, El-Sayed NH and Saleh NAM. Flavonoid glycosides of *Cynara scolymus*. *Fitoterapia* 1987, **58**, 178-180.
15. Eich J, Paper DH and Grün M. Luteolin-7-*O*-β-glucuronide from artichoke leaves. *Pharm. Pharmacol. Lett.* 2001, (1), 9-10.
16. Hinou J, Harvala C and Philianos S. Polyphenolic substances of *Cynara scolymus* L. leaves. *Ann. Pharm. Fr.* 1989, **47**, 95-98 [FRENCH/English summary].
17. Bernhard H. Quantitative Bestimmung der Bitter-Sesquiterpene von *Cynara scolymus* L. (Artischocke) und *Cynara cardunculus* L. (Kardone) (Compositae) [Quantitative determination of bitter sesquiterpenes of *Cynara scolymus* L. (artichoke) and *Cynara cardunculus* L. (cardoon) (Compositae)]. *Pharm. Acta Helv.* 1982, **57**, 179-180 [GERMAN/English summary].
18. Barbetti P, Chiappini I, Fardella G and Grandolini G. Grosulfeimin and new related guaianolides from *Cynara scolymus* L. *Nat. Prod. Lett.* 1993, **3**, 21-30.
19. Shimoda H, Ninomiya K, Nishida N, Yoshino T, Morikawa T, Matsuda H and Yoshikawa M. Anti-Hyperlipidemic Sesquiterpenes and New Sesquiterpene Glycosides from the Leaves of Artichoke (*Cynara scolymus* L.): Structure Requirement and Mode of Action. *Bioorg. Med. Chem. Lett.* 2003, **13**, 223-228.
20. Wiedenfeld H. Artischockenpräparate. Getrocknet und extrahiert oder lieber frisch gepreßt [Artichoke preparations. Dried and extracted or better freshly pressed]. *Pharm. Ztg.* 1999, **144**, 118-124 [GERMAN].
21. Bogaert JP, Mortier F, Jouany JM, Pelt JM and Delaveau P. Organic acids, particularly acids-alcohols, in *Cynara scolymus* L. *Ann. Pharm. Fr.* 1972, **30**, 401-408 [FRENCH/English summary].
22. Bogaert JP, Mortier F, Jouany JM, Delaveau P and Pelt JM. Caractérisation et dosage de l'acide hydroxyméthyl-acrylique dans les feuilles de *Cynara scolymus* L. (Compositae) [Characterization and assay of hydroxymethylacrylic acid in the leaves of *Cynara scolymus* L. (Compositae)]. *Plantes Méd. Phytothér.* 1974, **8**, 199-203 [FRENCH/English summary].
23. Wittemer SM and Veit M. Validated method for the determination of six metabolites derived from artichoke leaf extract in human plasma by high-performance liquid chromatography-coulometric array detection. *J. Chromatogr. B* 2003, **793**, 367-375.
24. Kraft K. Artichoke leaf extract - Recent findings reflecting effects on lipid metabolism, liver and gastrointestinal effects. *Phytomedicine* 1997, **4**, 369-378.
25. European Scientific Cooperative on Phytotherapy. Cynarae folium - Artichoke Leaf. In: *ESCOP Monographs - The Scientific Foundation for Herbal Medicinal Products, 2nd ed.* Stuttgart-New York: Thieme; Exeter, UK: ESCOP, 2003:118-125.
26. Kirchhoff R, Beckers C, Kirchhoff GM, Trinczek-Gärtner H, Petrowicz O and Reimann HJ. Increase in choleresis by means of artichoke extract. *Phytomedicine* 1994, **1**, 107-115.
Also published as:
Kirchhoff R, Beckers C, Kirchhoff G, Trinczek-Gärtner H, Petrowicz O and Reimann H-J. Steigerung der Cholerese durch Artischockenextrakt. Ergebnisse einer plazebok**on**trollierten Doppelblindstudie. *Ärztl. Forsch.* **1993,** 40 (6), 1-12 [GERMAN].
27. Petrowicz O, Gebhardt R, Donner M, Schwandt P and Kraft K. Effects of artichoke leaf extract (ALE) on lipoprotein metabolism in vitro and in vivo [Abstract]. *Atherosclerosis* 1997, **129**, 147 (Abstract 41).
28. Wójcicki J, Samochowiec L and Kosmider K. Influence of an extract from artichoke (*Cynara scolymus* L.) on the level

of lipids in serum of aged men. *Herba Polonica* 1981, **27**, 265-268 [POLISH/English summary].
29. Martinet A, Hostettmann K and Schutz Y. Thermogenic effects of commercially available plant preparations aimed at treating human obesity. *Phytomedicine* 1999, **6**, 231-238.
30. Wittemer SM, Ploch M, Windeck T, Muller SC, Drewelow B, Derendorf H and Veit M. Bioavailability and pharmacokinetics of caffeoylquinic acids and flavonoids after oral administration of Artichoke leaf extracts in humans. *Phytomedicine* 2005, **12**, 28-38.
31. Holtmann G, Adam B, Haag S, Collet W, Grünewald E and Windeck T. Efficacy of artichoke leaf extract in the treatment of patients with functional dyspepsia: a six-week placebo-controlled, double-blind, multicentre trial. *Aliment. Pharmacol. Ther.* 2003, **18**, 1099-1105.
32. Pittler MH, White AR, Stevinson C and Ernst E. Effectiveness of artichoke extract in preventing alcohol-induced hangovers: a randomized controlled trial. *CMAJ (Can. Med. Assoc. J.)* 2003, **169**, 1269-1273.
33. Englisch W, Beckers C, Unkauf M, Ruepp M and Zinserling V. Efficacy of Artichoke Dry Extract in Patients with Hyperlipoproteinemia. *Arzneim.-Forsch./Drug Res.* 2000, **50**, 260-265.
34. Wone E, Barondra-Haaby E, de Lauture H. Intérêt de l'intégration systématique du Chophytol dans le traitement ambulatoire du paludisme [Interest in the systematic integration of Chophytol into the ambulant treatment of malaria]. *Afrique Médicale* 1986, **25**, 233-240 [FRENCH].
35. Fintelmann V and Menßen HG. Artischockenblätterextrakt. Aktuelle Erkentnisse zur Wirkung als Lipidsenker und Antidyspeptikum [Artichoke leaf extract. Current knowledge concerning its efficacy as a lipid-lowering and antidyspeptic agent]. *Dtsch. Apoth. Ztg.* 1996, **136**, 1405-1414 [GERMAN].
Also published as:
Fintelmann V. Antidyspeptische und lipidsenkende Wirkungen von Artischockenblätterextrakt. Ergebnisse klinischer Untersuchungen zur Wirksamkeit und Verträglichkeit von Hepar-SL® forte an 553 Patienten [Antidyspeptic and lipid-lowering effects of Artichoke leaf extract. Results of clinical investigations into the efficacy and tolerability of Hepar-SL® forte in 553 patients]. *Z. Allg. Med.* 1996, **72** (Suppl. 2), 3-19 [GERMAN].
36. Fintelmann V and Petrowicz O. Langzeitanwendung eines Artischocken-Extraktes bei dyspeptischem Symptomkomplex. Ergebnisse einer Beobachtungsstudie [Long-term use of an artichoke extract in dyspeptic symptom complex. Results of a surveillance study]. *Naturamed* 1998, **13**, 17-26 [GERMAN].
37. Walker AF, Middleton RW and Petrowicz O. Artichoke Leaf Extract Reduces Symptoms of Irritable Bowel Syndrome in a Post-marketing Surveillance Study. *Phytotherapy Res.* 2001, **15**, 58-61.
38. Marakis G, Walker AF, Middleton RW, Booth JCL, Wright J and Pike DJ. Artichoke leaf extract reduces mild dyspepsia in an open study. *Phytomedicine* 2002, **9**, 694-699.
39. Bundy R, Walker AF, Middleton RW, Marakis G and Booth JCL. Artichoke Leaf Extract Reduces Symptoms of Irritable Bowel Syndrome and Improves Quality of Life in Otherwise Healthy Volunteers Suffering from Concomitant Dyspepsia: A Subset Analysis. *J. Altern. Complement. Med.* 2004, **10**, 667-669.
40. Wójcicki J, Olejak B, Pieczul-Mróz J, Torbus-Lisiecka B, Bukowska H, Gregorczyk J. The use of 1,5-dicaffeoylquinic acid in the treatment of hypertriglyceridemia. *Przeglad Lekarski* 1982, **39**, 601-606 [POLISH/English summary].
41. Barnes J, Anderson LA and Phillipson JD. Artichoke. In: *Herbal Medicines - A guide for healthcare professionals, 2nd ed.* ISBN 0-85369-474-5. London-Chicago: Pharmaceutical Press, 2002:61-66.
42. Artichaut, feuille. In: *Médicaments à base de plantes.* ISBN 2-911473-02-7. Saint-Denis Cedex, France: Agence du Médicament, 1998.
43. Cynarae folium. German Commission E Monograph published in: Bundesanzeiger No. 122 of 6 July 1988; amended in Bundesanzeiger No. 164 of 1 September 1990.
44. Artichoke. In: UK Statutory Instrument 1984 No. 769. The Medicines (Products Other Than Veterinary Drugs) (General Sale List) Order 1984. Schedule 1, Table A.
45. Artichoke leaves. In: Section 172.510 of USA Code of Federal Regulations, Title 21, Food and Drugs, Parts 170 to 199. Revised as of April 1, 2000.
46. Cynara scolymus L.,leaves. In: *Flavouring Substances and Natural Sources of Flavourings, 3rd ed.* ISBN 2-7160-0081-6. Strasbourg: Council of Europe, 1981.

REGULATORY GUIDELINES FROM OTHER EU COUNTRIES

FRANCE

Médicaments à base de plantes [42]: Artichaut, feuille.

Therapeutic indications accepted

Oral use
Traditionally used: to facilitate urinary and digestive elimination functions; to promote the renal elimination of water; as a choleretic or cholagogue.

GERMANY

Commission E monograph [43]: Cynarae folium (Artischockenblätter).

Uses
Dyspeptic complaints.

Contraindications
Known allergy to artichoke and other Compositae. Bile duct obstruction. In cases of gall stones to be used only after consultation with a doctor.

Side effects
None known.

Interactions with other drugs
None known.

Dosage
Unless otherwise prescribed, average daily dose: 6 g of the drug; equivalent preparations.

Mode of administration
Dried, comminuted drug, pressed juice from fresh plant and other galenic preparations for internal use.

Action
Choleretic.

ASCOPHYLLUM **Fucaceae**

Ascophylli thallus

Synonyms: Knotted wrack. Kelp, in the sense of 'dried brown seaweed'.

Definition
Ascophyllum consists of the dried thallus of *Ascophyllum nodosum* Le Jolis.

This brown seaweed, found in the intertidal zone on rocky shores, generally grows at a level somewhat lower than, but often adjacent to or overlapping, that of bladderwrack (*Fucus vesiculosus* L.). Commercial ascophyllum may therefore contain up to about 10% of bladderwrack. The best material is harvested mechanically (at high tide) and dried within hours of collection.

CONSTITUENTS

☐ ***Polysaccharides*** A complex array of the following types:
Alginic acid, 23-30% [1,2], a linear polysaccharide (MW ca. 200,000) composed of β-(1→4)-linked D-mannuronic acid (M) and α-(1→4)-linked L-guluronic acid (G) residues, occurring in blocks of $(\text{-M-})_n$, $(\text{-G-})_n$ and $(\text{-MG-})_n$ as calcium and magnesium salts [3].
Laminaran (laminarin), 3-7% [2], a polysaccharide composed mainly of β-(1→3)-linked D-glucose with some branching [4].
Fucans The collective term 'fucans' refers to a family of sulphated polysaccharides found in the cell walls of brown algae. Two types, fucoidans and ascophyllans, occur in *Ascophyllum nodosum* [3].

Fucoidans have a sulphated fucose backbone and xylose, galactose and glucuronic acid as minor components [3]. Their structure is poorly understood, largely because no commercial endofucosidase is available and chemical cleavage of glycosidic linkages causes structural alterations [5]. Although long considered to consist mainly of α-(1→2)-linked fucose units [3], an α-(1→3)-linked structure was proposed in 1993 [6]. However, recent work suggested that the fucoidan in *Ascophyllum nodosum* has a high proportion of α-(1→4)-linked L-fucose units, sulphated mainly at O-2 and to a lesser extent at O-3, with some 2,3-di-O-sulphate residues [5].

Ascophyllans have a backbone composed mainly of β-(1→4)-D-glucuronic acid units, with short branches of sulphated or neutral residues of xylose and fucose [7,8].

☐ ***Mannitol***, a monosaccharide, 7-12% [1,2].
☐ ***Minerals*** Iodine, usually 0.07-0.1% [1,2,9,10] but seasonally variable and may occasionally reach 0.2% [2] (Ph. Eur. limits: 0.03-0.2% of total iodine). Commercial ascophyllum harvested from two areas on the Norwegian coast and analysed monthly for 12 months gave iodine levels of 0.067-0.110% (average 0.088%) [10].

The iodine content is somewhat higher than that of bladderwrack (usually 0.03-0.07%) [1,9] and other *Fucus* species [1]. Over 60% of the iodine is organically bound, mainly to protein [9].

Potassium (ca. 2%) [1], calcium, magnesium, zinc, iron and various trace elements are present, including arsenic (22-44 ppm) [11]. The total ash content is 17-24% [2,11].
☐ ***Lipids*** Three glycolipids represent over 50% of the total lipids: monogalactosyldiacyl-glycerol (MGDG), sulphoquinovosyldiacyl-glycerol (SQDG), and digalactosyldiacyl-glycerol (DGDG)

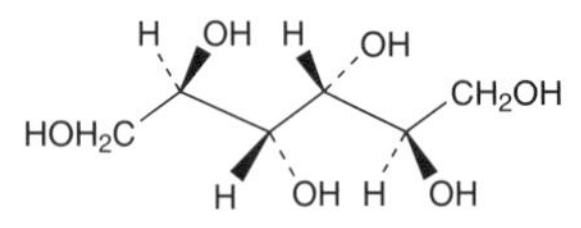

Mannitol

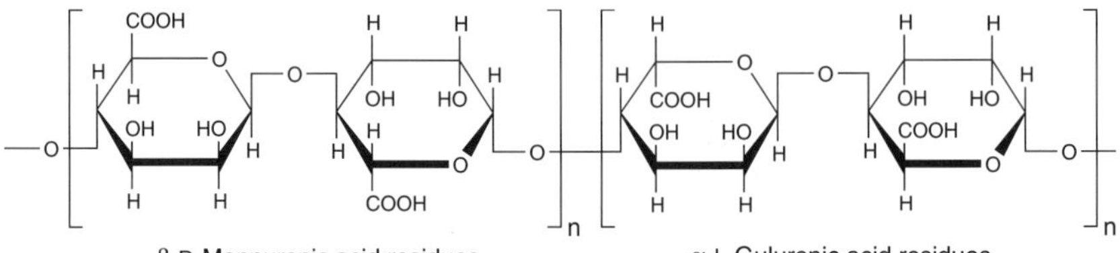

Alginic acid

[12]. MGDG is the most unsaturated, with high proportions of eicosapentaenoic (20:5) and octadecatetraenoic (18:4) acids in the acyl chains [12,13].

Phospholipids are also present, the most abundant being phosphatidylethanolamine [12].

□ ***Other constituents*** Sterols, ca. 0.04%, mainly as free fucosterol [14]; abscisic acid (0.03-0.15 µg/g) [15]; crude protein 3-10% [2].

Polyphenols consisting of polymers (phlorotannins) and oligomers (fucols and fucophlorethols) of phloroglucinol are probably present, as they are in *Fucus vesiculosus* and other brown algae [16].

Published Assay Methods

Total iodine by titrimetry [Ph. Eur].

PHARMACOLOGY

Considerable research has been published on anticoagulant, anti-inflammatory, antiviral, antitumoral and other activities of purified fucan fractions of various molecular weights; see reviews by Boisson-Vidal et al. [3,17]. The anticoagulant and antithrombotic characteristics of fucoidan fractions are probably the most investigated to date, particularly in comparison with the anticoagulant heparin (a sulphated polysaccharide present in mammalian tissues), which has structural resemblances to fucoidan. Heparin from animals is used as anticoagulant therapy in thrombosis and other conditions. The anticoagulant activity of both heparin and fucoidan is related to the presence of sulphate groups [5].

As an example, the antithrombotic activity of a homogeneous, highly purified fucoidan fraction (MW ca. 20,000) extracted from ascophyllum was demonstrated after intravenous administration to rabbits. Bovine factor Xa-induced thrombus formation was inhibited with an ED_{80} of 1.8 mg/kg, comparable to the activity of 0.1 mg/kg of heparin but with a more persistent effect (30 minutes vs. 15) than heparin and a significantly prolonged thrombin clotting time (73 seconds vs. 29 for the control and 53 for heparin) [18]. A fucoidan fraction of MW 600,000 also showed anticoagulant activity *in vitro* by increasing activated partial thromboplastin time [8].

Antitumour effects of a heterogeneous fucoidan fraction (MW 40,000-500,000) from ascophyllum have been demonstrated *in vitro* and *in vivo* against human bronchopulmonary carcinoma cells (NSCLC-N6) [19]. A low MW fucan fraction (MW ca. 20,000) from ascophylllum showed in vitro antiproliferative activity against fibroblasts CCL39 and sigmoid colon adenocarcinoma cells COLO 320 DM (but not lymphocytic leukaemia P388 or human breast carcinoma MCF7 cells [20]. A fucan fraction of MW 19 kDa from ascophyllum inhibited proliferation of rat aortic smooth muscle cells in vitro [21]. Fucan fractions of MW 4,100-214,000 from ascophyllum inhibited human complement activation *in vitro*, suggesting anti-inflammatory activity [22].

However, while such studies demonstrate that certain fucoidan fractions may have therapeutic potential, this research may be of little relevance to the oral use of ascophyllum, since high MW fucoidan is unlikely to be absorbed or hydrolysed after ingestion.

CLINICAL STUDIES

None published on mono-preparations of ascophyllum.

Since bladderwrack (*Fucus vesiculosus* L.) is regarded as similar in composition and action to ascophyllum, it is worth mentioning a randomized, double-blind, placebo-controlled clinical study reported in 1976 using a bladderwrack extract in the treatment of obesity. Groups of obese patients on the same controlled diet (1200 calories/day) received daily for 60 days either 3 tablets each containing 126 mg of the bladderwrack extract plus anthranoid laxatives (n = 25) or 3 tablets containing the anthranoid laxatives only (n = 25). Those taking the preparation containing *Fucus vesiculosus* extract achieved a significantly greater ($p<0.01$) average reduction in excess weight (in relation to 'ideal' weight for the patients height and build) of 31% and an average weight loss of ca. 1 kg per week, compared to 14% and ca. 0.5 kg per week achieved by those taking laxatives only. Unfortunately, the type of extract and its iodine content were not stated, nor was the thyroid status of the patients reported [23].

On the other hand, administration of a single large dose of a tincture of *Fucus vesiculosus* (3 ml; iodine content not determined) to 4 healthy, non-obese, young volunteers did not produce any changes in thermometric (energy expenditure, respiratory quotient) or cardiovascular (heart rate, systolic and diastolic blood pressure) parameters which would indicate a potential for bladderwrack as a thermogenic agent in the treatment of human obesity [24]. It may be that, in the treatment of obesity, kelp supplements are effective only in persons with poor thyroid function, by increasing the metabolic rate.

THERAPEUTICS

Actions

Supplementation of dietary iodine.

Normal thyroid function requires an adequate intake of iodine. Iodine forms part of the thyroid hormones thyroxine and triiodothyronine, which play an important role in energy metabolism. The only rich natural sources of iodine commonly eaten are those derived from marine life; sea fish contain 200-1000 μg/kg and shellfish a slightly larger amount, but for those who do not eat fish the element can be scarce in the diet [25].

Indications
None adequately substantiated by pharmacological or clinical studies.

The iodine content of ascophyllum can obviously help to prevent iodine deficiency and conditions arising from it.

Uses (including those of bladderwrack) based on experience or tradition
Prevention or treatment of iodine deficiency goitre, lymphadenoid goitre [26] or hypothyroidism. Obesity associated with hypothyroidism [26]; as an adjuvant in slimming regimes [1,27]. Rheumatism and rheumatoid arthritis [26].

Contraindications
Pregnancy and breast feeding.
In cases of thyroid illness, should only be taken under professional advice.

Side effects
None in normal individuals at therapeutic dosage levels.
Excessive use may induce or aggravate hyperthyroidism [28].

Interactions with other drugs
None reported, but should not be taken in conjunction with any treatment for abnormal thyroid function (unless on medical advice).

Dosage
Daily dose: dried thallus, 150-500 mg.

SAFETY

Safety in the use of ascophyllum is primarily related to its iodine content. From analysis of seaweed-based food supplements in the UK in 1987, the levels of both total and inorganic arsenic were found to be generally low and within acceptable limits, while iodine levels varied widely; in a few cases the potential iodine intake from the maximum recommended dosage was very high (up to 5000 μg per day) [29].

An intake of 1000 μg of iodine per day is considered to be safe [29]. At its maximum content of 0.2% iodine (which is rarely attained) this equates to 500 mg of ascophyllum per day.

Excessive intake of iodine can lead to hyperthyroidism, but susceptibility varies from person to person and may depend on hereditary factors or physiology [29]. Case reports have revealed symptoms of hyperthyroidism in patients, with and without family histories of thyroid problems, after taking kelp products for periods of several months or years at daily dosages equivalent to 1,000-10,000 μg of iodine. Since the symptoms included weight loss, interpreted as a sign of thyrotoxicosis, it has been argued that the use of kelp products as anti-obesity agents, in the belief that the iodine content stimulates production of thyroid hormones known to affect metabolic processes, is inadvisable [30].

As a drastic precautionary measure for use in radiation emergencies such as accidents involving nuclear reactors, a one-off dose of 100-200 mg of iodine in the form of potassium iodate or iodide tablets has been proposed as a thyroid blocking agent to reduce absorption of radioactive iodine. Stocks of tablets are maintained in some areas near to nuclear reactors for distribution to populations at risk in the event of an emergency [31]. Although the Chernobyl disaster in 1986 had only a limited impact on the UK, stocks of 'kelp' supplements, many of which contained ascophyllum, rapidly sold out in shops as customers apparently took their own precautions.

REGULATORY STATUS

Medicines

UK	Accepted for general sale, internal or external use [32].
France	Accepted for specified indications [27].
Germany	Commission E monograph published; not approved for any indications [28].

Food

Council of Europe	Ascophyllum not listed. However, *Fucus vesiculosus* (thallus) is permitted as flavouring, category N2 [33].

REFERENCES

Current Pharmacopoeial Monographs

Ph. Eur.	Kelp (defined as the 'dried thallus of *Fucus vesiculosus* L. or *F. serratus* L. or *Ascophyllum nodosum* Le Jolis').
BHP	Ascophyllum

Literature References

1. Muller D, Carnat A and Lamaison JL. Le "Fucus": Étude

comparée de *Fucus vesiculosus* L., *Fucus serratus* L. et *Ascophyllum nodosum* Le Jolis. *Plantes Méd. Phytothér.* 1991, **25**, 194-201 {FRENCH/English summary].
2. Black WAP. The seasonal variation in chemical composition of some of the littoral seaweeds common to Scotland. Part I. *Ascophyllum nodosum. J. Soc. Chem. Ind. (London)* 1948, **67**, 355-357.
3. Boisson-Vidal C, Haroun F, Ellouali M, Blondin C, Fischer AM, de Agostini A and Jozefonvicz J. Biological activities of polysaccharides from marine algae. *Drugs of the Future* 1995, **20**, 1237-1249.
4. Harborne JB and Baxter H. Laminaran. In: *Phytochemical Dictionary - A Handbook of Bioactive Compounds from Plants.* ISBN 0-85066-736-4. London: Taylor & Francis, 1995:18.
5. Chevolot L, Foucault A, Chaubet F, Kervarec N, Sinquin C, Fisher A-M and Boisson-Vidal C. Further data on the structure of brown seaweed fucans: relationships with anticoagulant activity. *Carbohydr. Res.* 1999, **319**, 154-165.
6. Patankar MS, Oehninger S, Barnett T, Williams RL and Clark GF. A Revised Structure for Fucoidan May Explain Some of Its Biological Activities. *J. Biol. Chem.* 1993, **268**, 21770-21776.
7. Larsen B, Haug A and Painter T. Sulphated Polysaccharides in Brown Algae. III. The Native State of Fucoidan in *Ascophyllum nodosum* and *Fucus vesiculosus. Acta Chem. Scand.* 1970, **24**, 3339-3352.
8. Nardella A, Chaubet F, Boisson-Vidal C, Blondin C, Durand P and Jozefonvicz J. Anticoagulant low molecular weight fucans produced by radical process and ion exchange chromatography of high molecular weight fucans extracted from the brown seaweed *Ascophyllum nodosum. Carbohydr. Res.* 1996, **289**, 201-208.
9. Stahl E, Menßen HG, Staesche K and Bachmann H. Knoten- und Blasentang als Arzneibuchdroge. Jodbestimmung, Morphologie und Anatomie von *Ascophyllum nodosum* und *Fucus vesiculosus* [Knotted wrack and bladderwrack as pharmacopoeial drugs. Iodine determination, morphology and anatomy of *Ascophyllum nodosum* and *Fucus vesiculosus*]. *Dtsch. Apoth. Ztg.* 1975, **115**, 1893-1896 [GERMAN].
10. Norwegian Institute of Seaweed Research, Trondheim; unpublished data, 1965.
11. Lunde G. Analysis of trace elements in seaweed. *J. Sci. Food. Agric.* 1970, **21**, 416-418.
12. Jones AL and Harwood JL. Lipid composition of the brown algae *Fucus vesiculosus* and *Ascophyllum nodosum. Phytochemistry* 1992, **31**, 3397-3403.
13. Jamieson GR and Reid EH. The component fatty acids of some marine algal lipids. *Phytochemistry* 1972, **11**, 1423-1432.
14. Duperon R, Thiersault M and Duperon P. Occurrence of steryl glycosides and acylated steryl glycosides in some marine algae. *Phytochemistry* 1983, **22**, 535-538.
15. Boyer GL and Dougherty SS. Identification of abscisic acid in the seaweed *Ascophyllum nodosum. Phytochemistry* 1988, **27**, 1521-1522.
16. Ragan MA and Jamieson WD. Oligomeric polyphloroglucinols from *Fucus vesiculosus*: photoplate mass spectrometric investigation. *Phytochemistry* 1982, **21**, 2709-2711.
17. Boisson-Vidal C, Colliec-Jouault S, Fischer AM, Tapon-Bretaudiere J, Sternberg C, Durand P and Jozefonvicz J. Biological activities of fucans extracted from brown seaweeds. *Drugs of the Future* 1991, **16**, 539-545.
18. Mauray S, Sternberg C, Theveniaux J, Millet J, Sinquin C, Tapon-Bretaudière J and Fischer A-M. Venous Antithrombotic and Anticoagulant Activities of a Fucoïdan Fraction. *Thrombosis and Haemostasis* 1995, **74**, 1280-1285.
19. Riou D, Colliec-Jouault S, Pinczon du Sel D, Bôsch S, Siavoshian S, Le Bert V et al. Antitumor and Antiproliferative Effects of a Fucan Extracted from *Ascophyllum nodosum* against a Non-Small-Cell Bronchopulmonary Carcinoma Line. *Anticancer Res.* 1996, **16**, 1213-1218.
20. Ellouali M, Boisson-Vidal C, Durand P and Jozefonvicz J. Antitumor Activity of Low Molecular Weight Fucans Extracted from Brown Seaweed *Ascophyllum nodosum. Anticancer Res.* 1993, **13**, 2011-2020.
21. Logeart D, Prigent-Richard S, Jozefonvicz J and Letourneur D. Fucans, sulfated polysaccharides extracted from brown seaweeds, inhibit vascular smooth muscle cell proliferation. I. Comparison with heparin for antiproliferative activity, binding and internalization. *Eur. J. Cell Biol.* 1997, **74**, 376-384.
22. Blondin C, Chaubet F, Nardella A, Sinquin C and Jozefonvicz J. Relationships between chemical characteristics and anticomplementary activity of fucans. *Biomaterials* 1996, **17**, 597-603.
23. Curro F and Amadeo A. L'Estratto di Fucus vesiculosus L. nel Trattamento Medico dell'Obesità e delle Alterazioni Metaboliche Connesse [Extract of *Fucus vesiculosus* L. in the medical treatment of obesity and related metabolic disorders]. *Arch. Med. Interna* 1976, **28**, 19-32 [ITALIAN].
24. Martinet A, Hostettmann K and Schutz Y. Thermogenic effects of commercially available plant preparations aimed at treating human obesity. *Phytomedicine* 1999, **6**, 231-238.
25. Haynes RC. Thyroid and antithyroid drugs. In: Goodman Gilman A, Rall TW, Nies AS and Taylor P, editors. *Goodman and Gilman's The Pharmacological Basis of Therapeutics, 8th ed.* ISBN 0-08-040296-8. New York-Oxford: Pergamon, 1990:1361-1383.
26. Fucus. In: *British Herbal Pharmacopoeia 1983.* ISBN 0-903032-07-4. Bournemouth: British Herbal Medicine Association, 1983.
27. Ascophyllum. In: *Médicaments à base de plantes.* ISBN 2-911473-02-7. Saint-Denis Cedex, France: Agence du Médicament, 1998.
28. Fucus (Tang). German Commission E Monograph published in: Bundesanzeiger No. 101 of 1 June 1990.
29. Norman JA, Pickford CJ, Sanders TW and Waller M. Human intake of arsenic and iodine from seaweed-based food supplements and health foods available in the UK. *Food Additives Contam.* 1987, **5**, 103-109.
30. De Smet PAGM. Toxicological Outlook on the Quality Assurance of Herbal Remedies: Special Considerations, including case reports of hyperthyroidism in users of kelp products. In: De Smet PAGM, Keller K, Hänsel R and Chandler RF, editors. *Adverse Effects of Herbal Drugs, Volume 1.* ISBN 3-540-53100-9. Berlin-Heidelberg-New York: Springer-Verlag, 1992:51-53.
31. Reynolds JEF, editor. Potassium iodate. In: *Martindale - The Extra Pharmacopoeia, 29th edition.* ISBN 0-85369-210-6. London: Pharmaceutical Press, 1989:1186.
32. Kelp. In: UK Statutory Instrument 1994 No. 2410. The Medicines (Products Other Than Veterinary Drugs) (General Sale List) Amendment Order 1994. Schedule 1, Table A.
33. *Flavouring Substances and Natural Sources of Flavourings, 3rd ed.* ISBN 2-7160-0081-6. Strasbourg: Council of Europe, 1981.

REGULATORY GUIDELINES FROM OTHER EU COUNTRIES

FRANCE

Médicaments à base de plantes [27]: Ascophyllum, thalle.

Therapeutic indications accepted

Oral use
Traditionally used as an adjuvant in slimming regimes.
As a bulk-forming laxative, for the symptomatic treatment of constipation.

Ascophyllum

GERMANY

Commission E monograph [28]: Fucus (Tang) [Fucus (seaweed/kelp)].

Composition of the drug
Kelp consists of the dried thallus of *Fucus vesiculosus* Linné, of *Ascophyllum nodosum* Le Jolis, or of both species, as well as preparations thereof.

Uses
Preparations from kelp are used in thyroid gland illnesses, obesity, excessive weight, arteriosclerosis and digestive disorders, as well as for 'blood purifying'.

Efficacy in the claimed areas of use is not substantiated.

Risks
Preparations with a daily dose up to 150 µg of iodine; none known.

Above a daily dose of 150 µg of iodine there is a risk of induction or aggravation of hyperthyroidism. In rare cases hypersensitivity reactions can occur in the form of a severe general reaction.

Assessment
Since the efficacy of a daily dose of less than 150 µg of iodine is not substantiated in the claimed areas of use, therapeutic use cannot be recommended.

Therapeutic use of a daily dose above 150 µg of iodine cannot be justified due to lack of efficacy and in view of the risks.

BARBERRY BARK

Berberidaceae

Berberidis cortex

Definition
Barberry Bark consists of the dried stem-bark or root-bark of *Berberis vulgaris* L.

Berberis vulgaris L. is a shrub indigenous to Great Britain and distributed over the greater part of Europe and western Asia. Only the stem-bark was included in the BPC 1934 [1], but root-bark has been more commonly used in continental Europe [2].

CONSTITUENTS

☐ ***Isoquinoline alkaloids*** The alkaloids in stem-bark and root-bark are qualitatively similar and of three structural types [2]:

- ***Protoberberine alkaloids***, including berberine (the major alkaloid), jatrorrhizine, palmatine, columbamine and others.
- ***Bisbenzylisoquinoline alkaloids***, including berbamine and oxyacanthine.
- ***Aporphine alkaloids***, principally magnoflorine.

Samples collected in the Czech Republic at the beginning of the vegetation period gave exceptionally high total yields of alkaloids (stem-bark 6.0%, root-bark 16.2%, calculated as bases) and the main alkaloids were isolated in the following amounts, calculated as bases [3]:

	Stem-bark	Root-bark
Berberine	1.8%	6.8%
Jatrorrhizine	0.5%	3.1%
Berbamine	1.4%	1.9%
Oxyacanthine	0.4%	2.3%
Magnoflorine	1.5%	1.3%

Lower total yields (stem-bark 5.5%, root-bark 12.8%) but fairly similar ratios of alkaloids were found in material from Romania in an earlier study [4], while stem-bark from the Caucasus yielded only 1.5% of total alkaloids [5]. Berberine assays on five samples of root-bark gave results in the range 1.9-6.1% (average 3.9%), expressed as base [6].

☐ ***Other constituents*** Very little information is available; in older literature tannins, resin, polysaccharides and chelidonic acid were reported in the root-bark [7].

Published Analytical Methods
Berberine and other protoberberine alkaloids by selective extraction and HPLC [8]. Isoquinoline alkaloids by capillary electrophoresis-mass spectrometry [Sturm 1998/3026]. Berberine by TLC and spectrophotometry [6].

PHARMACOLOGY

The available pharmacological data on barberry bark itself are very limited, but considerable research (including clinical studies) has been, and is being, carried out on berberine as a pure alkaloid. Overviews of berberine studies have been published [10,11].

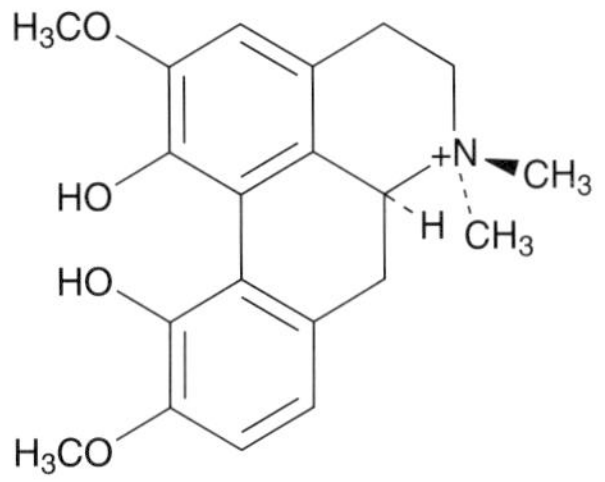

Berberine

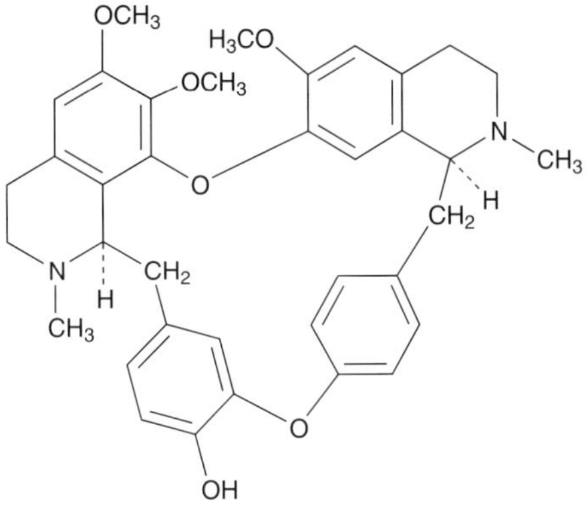

Berbamine

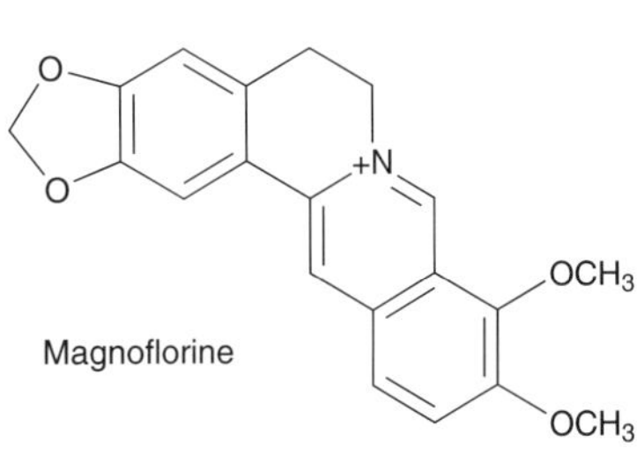

Magnoflorine

In vitro

Antibacterial activity
An extract from barberry bark, an alkaloid fraction [12] and individual alkaloid salts [12,13] exhibited moderate bactericidal activity. Although the published data vary, perhaps depending on methodology, berberine is only weakly antibacterial, as demonstrated against a range of pathogens [14,15]; for example, it was ineffective against Gram-positive *Bacillus subtilis* (MIC 1000 µg/ml) and Gram-negative *Salmonella enteridis* (MIC 500 µg/ml) [15] and *E. coli* (MIC > 1000 µg/ml) [14]. However, aside from direct antibacterial activity, berberine is reported to inhibit bacterial adherence, which might explain its anti-infectious activity in *E. coli* infections of the urinary tract [10].

Cardiovascular actions of berberine
Berberine is positively inotropic, negatively chronotropic, antiarrhythmic and vasodilatory. These effects have been extensively studied and the research has been summarized by Lau et al. The inotropic effect was found to improve the haemodynamics in patients with heart failure [16].

Anti-inflammatory activity of berbamine
In a range of tests to evaluate the anti-inflammatory properties of bisbenzylisoquinoline alkaloids, berbamine at 10 µg/ml exerted significant suppressive effects ($p<0.05$) on the adherence, locomotion (random movement and chemotaxis) and ^{3}H-deoxyglucose uptake of neutrophils [17]. Another study showed that berbamine inhibited production of the inflammatory cytokines interleukin-1 (ED_{50}: 28.5 µg/ml) and tumour necrosis factor-α (ED_{50}: 10.3-20.2 µg/ml) by human monocytes and macrophages, and tumour necrosis factor-β by human lymphocytes (ED_{50}: 28.3 µg/ml) [18].

In vivo

Anti-inflammatory effects
A 95% ethanolic extract from powdered barberry root, injected intraperitoneally, had a moderate inhibitory effect on carrageenan-induced inflammation (24% reduction at a dose of 200 mg/kg; $p<0.001$) and a pronounced, dose-dependent inhibitory effect on zymosan-induced inflammation (68% reduction at a dose of 200 mg/kg; $p<0.001$) in mouse paw oedema tests, compared to reductions of 40% and 9.4% respectively for aspirin at 100 mg/kg ($p<0.001$) [19].

Berberine administered intraperitoneally at 2 mg/kg daily on days 0-14 significantly inhibited adjuvant-induced arthritis (degree of paw swelling) in mice ($p<0.001$ on both day 14 and day 28). When the mice were treated with indometacin only, at 10 mg/kg on days −3 to + 10, paw swelling was reduced by 26.1% ($p<0.05$). A stronger inhibitory effect (44.6%, $p<0.01$) was obtained after a single dose of indometacin (10 mg/kg on day −1) combined with 10 days on berberine (2 mg/kg on days 0 to + 10). Even stronger inhibition (56.9%; $p<0.001$) was achieved with the combination of indometacin (5 mg/kg on days −3 to + 3) and berberine (2 mg/kg on days + 4 to + 10). Thus berberine augmented the suppressive effect of indometacin when administered after it (but not before it) [20].

Cholagogic effect
Intraduodenal administration of 1 ml of a barberry bark tincture (freed from ethanol and made up to half the original volume with water) increased bile flow in guinea pigs by 20%, but did not have a similar effect in rats. Since the tincture increased the tone and amplitude of contractions in guinea pig isolated ileal smooth muscle *in vitro*, the cholagogic effect was interpreted as cholekinetic (influencing the gall bladder) rather than choleretic (true increase in bile secretion) and attributed to berberine [21].

In a later study, an alkaloid fraction from barberry root containing 80% of berbamine, administered intraperitoneally at 5 mg/kg, stimulated bile secretion in rats by 72% [22].

Uterine effect
An acetone-alcohol extract from barberry stem-bark enhanced the contractility of the uterus of guinea pigs, cats and rabbits *in vivo* [23].

Other effects of berberine
In models of osteoporosis, berberine prevented ovariectomy-related bone loss (decrease in bone density) in rats after oral administration for 4 weeks at 30 and 50 mg/kg/day [24], and increased bone density in senescence-accelerated mice after oral administration for 22 weeks at 10 mg/kg/day [25].

Pretreatment of rats with berberine at 2 × 4 mg/kg daily for 2 days gave significant protection against acetaminophen (paracetamol)- or carbon tetrachloride-induced hepatotoxicity ($p<0.05$ to $p<0.001$ for serum levels of alkaline phosphatase and serum transaminases) [26].

Pretreatment of mice with a single oral dose (4 mg/kg) of berberine significantly prolonged pentobarbital-induced sleeping time ($p<0.05$). The same treatment increased strychnine-induced toxicity in mice, leading to 100% mortality from what was otherwise a sublethal dose of strychnine. Both these effects were attributed to the inhibition of cytochrome P450 enzymes in the animal liver, resulting in slower metabolization of pentobarbital and strychnine [26].

CLINICAL STUDIES

None published on mono-preparations of barberry bark.

THERAPEUTICS

Actions

Cholagogic [10,21,22,27,28], anti-inflammatory [19,28], moderately antimicrobial [10,12], a bitter tonic [1,28,29] and digestive stimulant [10].

Also stated to be antiemetic [10,27], mildly laxative [10,29,30] and antidiarrhoeal [11,31].

Indications

None adequately substantiated by pharmacological or clinical studies.

Uses based on experience or tradition

Internal: Hepatic and biliary disorders including gall-stones, cholecystitis, jaundice (when there is no obstruction of the bile ducts) and biliousness [2,10,27,29,31]; as a bitter stomachic tonic for dyspepsia [2,29,30].

Barberry bark has also been used for leishmaniasis, malaria and other protozoal infections [2,10,27].

External: Cutaneous eruptions [29] and chronic skin conditions such as eczema and psoriasis [31]; in eyewashes as an eye tonic [31].

Contraindications

Avoid during pregnancy [10,27,31].

Side effects

None at normal dosage levels.

Interactions with other drugs

None known with barberry bark. However, an influence on the metabolization of certain drugs due to inhibition of hepatic enzymes appears possible [26].

Dosage

Daily dose: dried stem- or root-bark, 1.5-3 g or as a decoction; liquid extract (1:2 in 60% alcohol), 3-6 ml; tincture 1:5 in 60% alcohol, 7-14 ml [10].

SAFETY

No adverse effects are expected from barberry bark when used at the recommended dosage [10].

Safety data on barberry bark itself are very limited. The available safety information on berberine has been summarized by Lampe [11].

The oral LD_{50} of berberine in mice was reported as 329 mg/kg [10]. Oral doses of 100 mg/kg of berberine sulphate were well tolerated by rats, but caused persistent emesis in cats and death within 8-10 days [11]. Therapeutic doses of 0.5 g of berberine have been well tolerated in man [11]; in terms of total alkaloids, 0.5 g equates to about 4 g of barberry bark. Large doses may lead to stupor, nosebleed, vomiting, diarrhoea and kidney irritation [2].

REGULATORY STATUS

Medicines

UK	Accepted for general sale, internal or external use [32].
France	Not listed in *Médicaments à base de plantes* [33].
Germany	Commission E monograph published; not approved for any indications [34].

Food

Council of Europe	Root bark permitted as flavouring, category N3 [35].

REFERENCES

Current Pharmacopoeial Monographs

BHP	Barberry Bark

Literature References

1. Pharmaceutical Society of Great Britain. Berberidis cortex. In: *The British Pharmaceutical Codex 1934*. London: Pharmaceutical Press, 1934:201-202.
2. Hänsel R, Keller K, Rimpler H and Schneider G, editors. Berberis. In: *Hagers Handbuch der Pharmazeutischen Praxis, 5th ed. Volume 4: Drogen A-D*. ISBN 3-540-52631-5. Berlin-Heidelberg-New York-London: Springer-Verlag, 1992:480-497 [GERMAN].
3. Slavík J and Slavíková L. Quaternary isoquinoline alkaloids and some diterpenoid alkaloids in plants of the Czech Republic. *Collect. Czech. Chem. Commun.* 1995, **60**, 1034-1041.
4. Petcu P and Goina T. Neue Methoden zur Extrahierung der Alkaloide aus *Berberis vulgaris* [New methods for extraction of alkaloids from *Berberis vulgaris*]. *Planta Medica* 1970, **18**, 372-375 [GERMAN/English summary].
5. Yusupov MM, Karimov A and Lutfullin KL. Alkaloids of *Berberis vulgaris*. XII. *Khim. Prir. Soedin* 1990, (1), 128-129 [RUSSIAN], translated into English as: *Chem. Nat. Compds.* 1990, **26**, 105-106.
6. Csupor L. Berberinbestimmung in Radix Berberidis [Determination of berberine in Berberidis radix]. *Dtsch. Apoth. Ztg.* 1971, **111**, 481-482 [GERMAN].
7. List PH and Hörhammer L, editors. Berberis. In: *Hagers Handbuch der Pharmazeutischen Praxis, 4th ed. Band 3*. Berlin-Heidelberg-New York: Springer-Verlag, 1972:415-424 [GERMAN].
8. Lee HS, Eom YE and Eom DO. Narrowbore high performance liquid chromatography of berberine and palmatine in crude drugs and pharmaceuticals with ion-pair extraction using cobalt thiocyanate reagent. *J. Pharmaceut. Biomed. Analysis* 1999, **21**, 59-63.
9. Sturm S and Stuppner H. Analysis of isoquinoline alkaloids in medicinal plants by capillary electrophoresis-mass spectrometry. *Electrophoresis* 1998, **19**, 3026-3032.

10. Mills S and Bone K. Berberis bark and Hydrastis root (*Berberis vulgaris* L., *Hydrastis canadensis* L.). In: *Principles and Practice of Phytotherapy. Modern Herbal Medicine.* ISBN 0-443-06016-9. Edinburgh-London-New York: Churchill Livingstone, 2000:286-296.
11. Lampe KF. Berberine. In: De Smet PAGM, Keller K, Hänsel R and Chandler RF. *Adverse Effects of Herbal Drugs, Volume 1.* ISBN 3-540-53100-9. Berlin-Heidelberg-New York: Springer-Verlag, 1992:97-104.
12. Andronescu E, Petcu P, Goina T and Radu A. Antibiotic activity of the extract and the alkaloid isolate from Berberis vulgaris. *Clujul Med.* 1973, **46**, 627-631 [ROMANIAN]; through *Chem. Abstr.* 1974, **81**, 100062.
13. Kowalewski Z, Kedzia W and Mirska I. Effect of berberine sulfate on Staphylococci. *Arch. Immunol. Ther. Exp.* 1972, **20**, 353-360; through *Chem. Abstr.* 1972, **77**, 135606.
14. Tegos G, Stermitz FR, Lomovskaya O and Lewis K. Multidrug Pump Inhibitors Uncover Remarkable Activity of Plant Antimicrobials. *Antimicrob. Agents Chemother.* 2002, **46**, 3133-3141.
15. Iwasa K, Nanba H, Lee D-U and Kang S-I. Structure-Activity Relationships of Protoberberines Having Antimicrobial Activity. *Planta Medica* 1998, **64**, 748-751.
16. Lau C-W, Yao X-Q, Chen Z-Y, Ko W-H and Huang Y. Cardiovascular Actions of Berberine. *Cardiovasc. Drug Rev.* 2001, **19**, 234-244.
17. Li S-Y, Ling L-H, Teh BS, Seow WK and Thong YH. Anti-inflammatory and immunosuppressive properties of the bisbenzylisoquinolines: *in vitro* comparisons of tetrandrine and berbamine. *Int. J. Immunopharmacol.* 1989, **11**, 395-401.
18. Seow WK, Ferrante A, Summors A and Thong YH. Comparative effects of tetrandrine and berbamine on production of the inflammatory cytokines interleukin-1 and tumor necrosis factor. *Life Sciences* 1992, **50**, PL53-PL58.
19. Ivanovska N and Philipov S. Study on the anti-inflammatory action of Berberis vulgaris root extract, alkaloid fractions and pure alkaloids. *Int. J. Immunopharmacol.* 1996, **18**, 553-561.
20. Ivanovska N, Philipov S and Nikolova P. Effect of berberine and its combination with immunosuppressive drugs in adjuvant arthritis and DTH reaction in mice. *Pharm. Pharmacol. Lett.* 1997, **7**, 55-58.
21. Rentz E. Zum Wirkungsmechanismus einiger bei Leber- und Gallenleiden angewandter pflanzlicher Mittel (Berberis, Chelidonium, Chelone) [The mechanism of action of some medicinal plants used to treat liver- and gall-stones (Berberis, Chelidonium, Chelone)]. *Arch. Exp. Pathol. Pharmakol.* 1948, **205**, 332-339 [GERMAN].
22. Manolov P, Nikolov N, Markov M and Toneva M. Experimental studies on *Berberis vulgaris. Eksp. Med. Morfol.* 1985, **24** (2), 41-45 [BULGARIAN]; through *Chem. Abstr.* 1985, **103**, 189503.
23. Aliev RK and Yuzbashinskaya PA. Nature of chemical composition of barberry leaves and the effect of a preparation made from them on the contractility of smooth muscles of the uterus. *Doklady Akad. Nauk Azerbaidzhan. S.S.R.* 1953, **9**, 306-307 [RUSSIAN]; through *Chem. Abstr.* 1955, **49**, 1961.
24. Li H, Miyahara T, Tezuka Y, Namba T, Suzuki T, Dowaki R et al. The Effect of Kampo Formulae on Bone Resorption *in Vitro* and *in Vivo*. II. Detailed Study of Berberine. *Biol. Pharm. Bull.* 1999, **22**, 391-396.
25. Li H, Miyahara T, Tezuka Y, Tran QL, Seto H and Kadota S. Effect of Berberine on Bone Mineral Density in SAMP6 as a Senile Osteoporosis Model. *Biol. Pharm. Bull.* 2003, **26**, 110-111.
26. Janbaz KH and Gilani AH. Studies on preventive and curative effects of berberine on chemical-induced hepatotoxicity in rodents. *Fitoterapia* 2000, **71**, 25-33.
27. Berberis. In: *British Herbal Pharmacopoeia* 1983. ISBN 0-903032-07-4. Bournemouth: British Herbal Medicine Association, 1983.
28. Ody P. In: *The Complete Guide - Medicinal Herbal.* ISBN 0-7513-3005-1. London-New York: Dorling Kindersley, 2000.
29. Grieve M (edited by Leyel CF). Common Barberry - *Berberis vulgaris.* In: *A Modern Herbal* (first published 1931; revised 1973). ISBN 1-85501-249-9. London: Tiger Books International, 1994:82-84.
30. Stodola J and Volák J. Barberry. Translated into English in: Bunney S, editor. *The Illustrated Book of Herbs.* ISBN 0-7064-1489-6. London: Octopus Books, 1984:85.
31. Chevallier A. Barberry - *Berberis vulgaris.* In: *Encyclopedia of Medicinal Plants, 2nd ed.* ISBN 0-7513-1209-6. London-New York: Dorling Kindersley, 2001:177.
32. Barberry Bark. In: UK Statutory Instrument 1984 No. 769. The Medicines (Products Other Than Veterinary Drugs) (General Sale List) Order 1984. Schedule 1, Table A.
33. *Médicaments à base de plantes.* ISBN 2-911473-02-7. Saint-Denis Cedex, France: Agence du Médicament, 1998.
34. Berberis vulgaris (Berberitze). German Commission E Monograph published in: Bundesanzeiger No. 43 of 2 March 1989.
35. Berberis vulgaris L., root bark. In: *Flavouring Substances and Natural Sources of Flavourings, 3rd ed.* ISBN 2-7160-0081-6. Strasbourg: Council of Europe, 1981.

REGULATORY GUIDELINES FROM OTHER EU COUNTRIES

GERMANY

Commission E monograph [34]: *Berberis vulgaris* (Berberitze), fructus, cortex, radicis cortex, radix.

Uses

Barberry root, bark and/or root bark are used for ailments and complaints of the gastrointestinal tract, the liver and biliary system, the kidney and lower urinary tract, the respiratory tract and the heart and circulatory system as well as in febrifuges and "blood purifiers". Efficacy in the claimed areas is not proven.

Risks

For barberry fruits: none known.
The other parts of *Berberis vulgaris* contain alkaloids, the main one being berberine.
Berberine is well tolerated in doses of up to 0.5 g. Inadvertent ingestion of more than 0.5 g causes stupor, nosebleed, dyspnoea, and skin and eye irritation. Kidney irritation and nephritis, gastrointestinal disorders with nausea, vomiting and diarrhoea, and even cases of death through poisoning, have been reported.
The intraperitoneal LD_{50} of berberine sulphate in mice is 24.3 mg/kg. Small doses of berberine stimulate the respiratory system; higher doses lead to more severe dyspnoea and convulsions ending in lethal primary respiratory paralysis. Lethal doses also cause haemorrhagic nephritis. In anaesthetized cats and dogs death occurs through respiratory failure at 25 mg/kg; marked inhibition of cardiac activity was also observed.
There are no reports of poisoning with *Berberis vulgaris.*

Assessment

Since efficacy in the claimed areas of use is not substantiated, therapeutic use cannot be recommended.

BAYBERRY BARK

Myricaceae

Myricae radicis cortex

Synonyms: Southern bayberry bark, wax myrtle bark, candleberry bark, Myrica.

Definition
Bayberry Bark consists of the dried root bark of *Myrica cerifera* L.

CONSTITUENTS

□ ***Triterpenes*** The pentacyclic triterpenes myricadiol, taraxerol and taraxerone [1].
□ ***Flavonoids*** Myricitrin (= myricetin 3-rhamnoside) [1].
□ ***Other constituents*** include starch, tannins [2], a little volatile oil and an acrid, astringent resin [3].

No other phytochemical studies specifically on the root bark appear to have been reported. However, the following constituents have been isolated from aerial bark or twigs of *Myrica cerifera* and might be present in the root bark, especially since known constituents of the root bark have also been found in aerial bark or twigs:
□ ***Cyclophanes from aerial bark*** Two [7.0]metacyclophanes, (±)-myricanol and myricanone, have been isolated from unspecified (assumed to be aerial) bark; myricadiol and taraxerol (previously found in the root bark) were isolated from the same material [4].
□ ***Triterpenoids from twigs*** Myrica acid (an oleanane triterpenic acid) and myricalactone (a diketonic lactone of an oleanane triterpene) have been isolated from dried twigs. Myricadiol and taraxerol, and also (±)-myricanol, myricanone, myriceric acid C, oleanolic acid and β-sitosterol, were identified in the same material [5].

Myriceric acids A, B, C and D have been isolated from fresh twigs; all are 27-caffeoyl esters of oleanane acids, myriceric acid A being myricerone 27-caffeoyl ester [6].

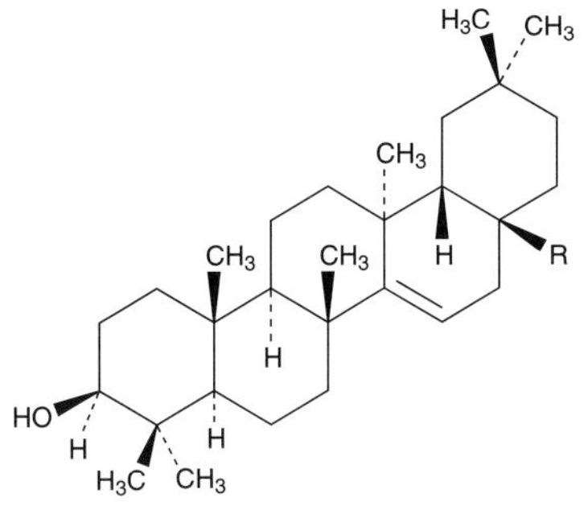

Myricadiol R = CH_2OH
Taraxerol R = CH_3

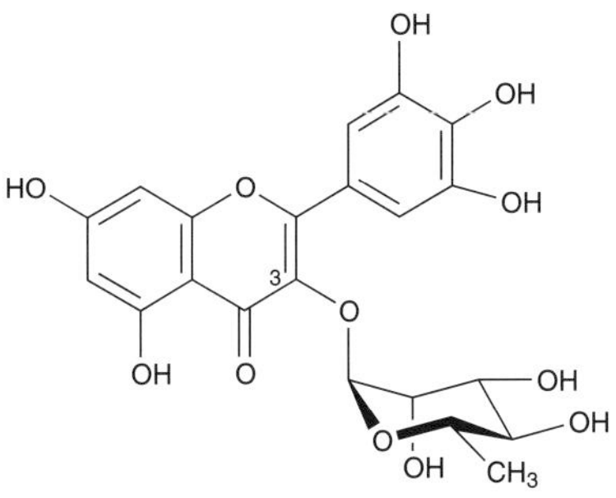

Myricitrin

PHARMACOLOGY

In vitro
Myriceric acid A (= myricerone 27-caffeoyl ester, designated as compound 50-235), has been a subject of research interest in recent times, since it is a potent non-peptide endothelin receptor antagonist, specific to the endothelin ET_A receptor and the first such compound to be isolated from a higher plant [6-9]. Endothelin, a potent vasoconstrictor consisting of three isopeptides produced by vascular endothelial cells, is involved in many regulatory functions in the body; its physiological and pathological roles are not entirely clear, but it may be involved in cardiovascular diseases [7,8].

In vivo
A tincture of bayberry bark significantly increased choleresis in rats by a maximum of 20% [10].

Myricetin (the aglycone of myricitrin) had strong anti-inflammatory effects in rats after intraperitoneal administration, simultaneously inhibiting carrageenan-induced paw oedema and croton oil-induced ear oedema (both $p<0.001$ at 25-50 mg/kg) [11].

CLINICAL STUDIES

None published on mono-preparations of bayberry bark.

THERAPEUTICS

Actions
Astringent [1-3,12,13], circulatory stimulant, mildly diaphoretic [12,14], mildly choleretic [10]. Emetic in large doses [1-3,13]. Also stated to be antipyretic [1].

Myricadiol has mineralocorticoid activity [1]. Myricitrin has anti-inflammatory [11], choleretic, bactericidal, paramecicidal and spermatocidal [1] activities.

Indications
None adequately substantiated by pharmacological or clinical studies.

Uses based on experience or tradition
Diarrhoea [12,13]; colds [12,14], at one time in combination with ginger, capsicum and clove as a domestic remedy for colds and chills [3]; mucous colitis [12,14]; gall bladder dysfunction [4].

Infusions have been used for sore throat (as a gargle), leucorrhoea (as a douche) [2,12,13], or as a mouthwash to strengthen the gums [13,14].
External use: Ulcers and sores [1,2,14].

Contraindications
Pregnancy [14].

Side effects
None known at therapeutic dose levels.

Interactions with other drugs
None known.

Dosage
Three times daily: Powdered bark, 0.6-2 g, usually as an infusion or decoction [2,12]. Liquid extract (1:1 in 45% alcohol), 0.6-2 ml [12].

SAFETY

Bayberry bark has been assessed as safe for internal use when used appropriately [15].

REGULATORY STATUS

Medicines

UK	Accepted for general sale, internal or external use [16].
France	Not listed in *Médicaments à base de plantes* [17].
Germany	No Commission E monograph published.

Food
Not used in foods.

REFERENCES

Current Pharmacopoeial Monographs
BHP Bayberry Bark

Literature References

1. Paul BD, Rao GS and Kapadia GJ. Isolation of Myricadiol, Myricitrin, Taraxerol and Taraxerone from *Myrica cerifera* L. Root Bark. *J. Pharm. Sci.* 1974, **63**, 958-959.
2. Wood HC and LaWall CH, editors. Myrica. In: *United States Dispensatory, Centennial (22nd) Edition.* Philadelphia-London: JB Lippincott Company, 1937:1483-1484.
3. Pharmaceutical Society of Great Britain. Myrica. In: *British Pharmaceutical Codex 1949.* London: Pharmaceutical Press, 1949:542-543.
4. Joshi BS, Pelletier SW, Newton MG, Lee D, McGaughey GB and Puar MS. Extensive 1D,2D NMR Spectra of Some [7.0]Metacyclophanes and X-ray Analysis of (±)-Myricanol. *J. Nat. Prod.* 1996, **59**, 759-764.
5. Nagai M, Sakurai N, Yumoto N, Nagumo S and Seo S. Oleanane Acid from *Myrica cerifera. Chem. Pharm. Bull.* 2000, **48**, 1427-1428.
6. Sakurawi K, Yasuda F, Tozyo T, Nakamura M, Sato T, Kikuchi J et al. Endothelin Receptor Antagonist Triterpenoid, Myriceric Acid A, Isolated from *Myrica cerifera*, and Structure Activity Relationships of Its Derivatives. *Chem. Pharm. Bull.* 1996, **44**, 343-351.
7. Fujimoto M, Mihara S, Nakajima S, Ueda M, Nakamura M and Sakurai K. A novel non-peptide endothelin antagonist isolated from bayberry, *Myrica cerifera. FEBS Lett.* 1992, **305**, 41-44.
8. Mihara S and Fujimoto M. The endothelin ET_A receptor-specific effect of 50-235, a non-peptide endothelin antagonist. *Eur. J. Pharmacol.* 1993, **246**, 33-38.
9. Mihara S, Sakurai K, Nakamura M, Konoike T and Fujimoto M. Structure-activity relationships of an endothelin ET_A receptor antagonist, 50-235, and its derivatives. *Eur. J. Pharmacol.* 1993, **247**, 219-221.
10. Pirtkien R, Surke E and Seybold G. Vergleichende Untersuchungen über die choleretische Wirkung verschiedener Arzneimittel bei der Ratte [Comparative studies on the choleretic effect of various drugs in the rat]. *Med. Welt* 1960, **33**, 1417-1422.
11. Gábor M and Rázga Z. Effect of benzopyrone derivatives on simultaneously induced croton oil ear oedema and carrageenin paw oedema in rats. *Acta Physiol. Hung.* 1991, **77**, 197-207.
12. Myrica. In: *British Herbal Pharmacopoeia 1983.* ISBN 0-903032-07-4. Bournemouth: British Herbal Medicine Association, 1983.
13. Grieve M (edited by Leyel CF). Bayberry. In: *A Modern Herbal* (first published 1931; revised 1973). ISBN 1-85501-249-9. London: Tiger Books International, 1994:87-88.
14. Chevallier A. Bayberry - *Myrica cerifera.* In: *Encyclopedia of Medicinal Plants, 2nd ed.* ISBN 0-7513-1209-6. London-New York: Dorling Kindersley, 2001:237.
15. McGuffin M, Hobbs C, Upton R and Goldberg A, editors. *Myrica cerifera* L. In: American Herbal Products Association's *Botanical Safety Handbook.* Boca Raton-Boston-London: CRC Press, 1997:77.
16. Bayberry. In: UK Statutory Instrument 1994 No. 2410. The Medicines (Products Other Than Veterinary Drugs) (General Sale List) Amendment Order 1994. Schedule 1, Table A.
17. *Médicaments à base de plantes.* ISBN 2-911473-02-7. Saint-Denis Cedex, France: Agence du Médicament, 1998.

BIRCH LEAF

Betulaceae

Betulae folium

Synonyms: Silver Birch Leaf (*Betula pendula*); Downy Birch Leaf (*Betula pubescens*).

The names *Betula alba* and White Birch have been used for both species in older literature and are not definitive. In recent times the name White Birch has been applied specifically to *Betula pubescens* [1,2].

Definition

Birch Leaf consists of the dried leaves of *Betula pendula* Roth [*Betula verrucosa* Ehrh.] or *Betula pubescens* Ehrh. and hybrids of the two species.

The leaves are usually harvested in the Spring.

CONSTITUENTS

☐ ***Flavonoids*** Flavonol glycosides (1-2%), principally hyperoside (= hyperin, quercetin 3-galactoside, 0.6-0.8%) [3,4] together with myricetin 3-galactoside (ca. 0.55% in *B. pendula*) [3], and quercetin 3-glucuronide (0.2-0.4%), 3-(4″-acetyl)-rhamnoside, 3-rhamnoside (quercitrin), 3-glucoside (isoquercitrin), 3-arabinoside and 3-rutinoside (rutin) [1-7].

Other glycosides of myricetin are present [1,2, 7,8], as well as glycosides of kaempferol [2,7], isorhamnetin, luteolin, acacetin and scutellarein [9], methyl ethers of kaempferol, apigenin and naringenin [10], and (+)-catechin [1,3].

The content of flavonoids increases steadily during the period of growth [11].

☐ ***Non-flavonoid phenolics of low MW*** 3,4′-Dihydroxypropiophenone 3-glucoside [3,12], also called 1-(4″-hydroxyphenyl)-3′-oxopropyl-glucose [1], predominates in *B. pendula* (ca. 0.8%, compared to ca. 0.08% in *B. pubescens*) [1,3] while chlorogenic acid predominates in *B. pubescens* (ca. 2.0% [1] compared to 0.1% or less [1,3] in *B. pendula*). Small amounts of neochlorogenic acid, 3- and 5-*p*-coumaroyl-quinic acids and other phenolics occur in both species [1].

The total content of low-MW phenolics including flavonoids is higher in *B. pubescens* (ca. 4.5%) than in *B. pendula* (ca. 2.7%) [1].

☐ ***Tannins*** *B. pubescens* leaves contain a complex mixture of hydrolysable tannins comprising 14 gallotannins and 20 ellagitannins; all are galloyl and/or hexahydroxydiphenoyl (HHDP) esters of glucose, for example, trigalloyl-HHDP-glucose [13]. Hydrolysable tannins are the predominant phenolics in young leaves but condensed tannins (proanthocyanidins), mainly delphinidin-type oligomers and polymers, become predominant in mature leaves, reaching over 10% of dry weight [14].

☐ ***Terpenes*** Eight dammarane triterpenes with a malonate group at C-3 and acetate at C-12 have been isolated from leaves of *B. pendula* [15,16]. Various other dammarane compounds are present [10,17-20], including the alcohols betulafolientriol and betulafolientetraol [17-19].

The sesquiterpene 14-hydroxycaryophyllene 4,5-oxide [21] and stereoisomeric glucosides (betulalbusides A and B) of the monoterpene hydroxylinalool [22] have also been isolated.

☐ ***Other constituents*** include the cyclohexenone derivative roseoside [23], β-sitosterol and citrostadienol [20]. Potassium and sodium contents of dried leaf have been determined as ca. 8000 and 40 μg/g respectively, a ratio of 200:1 [24].

Haemolytic compounds originally thought to be saponins, reported in 1924 by Kroeber [25] and later by others [11,26] but never elucidated, are now known to be dammarane triterpenes [16].

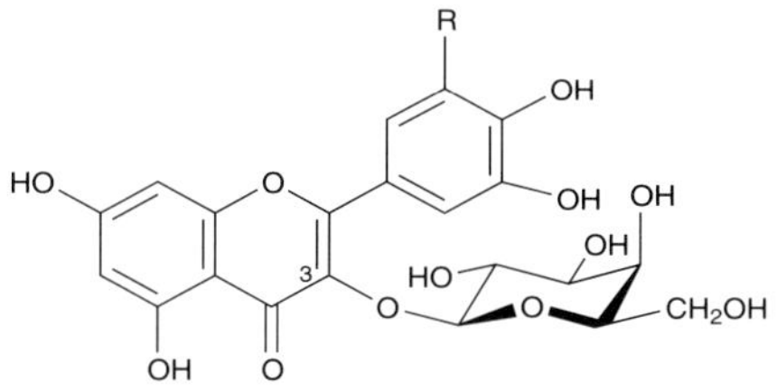

Hyperoside (hyperin) R = H
Myricetin 3-galactoside R = OH

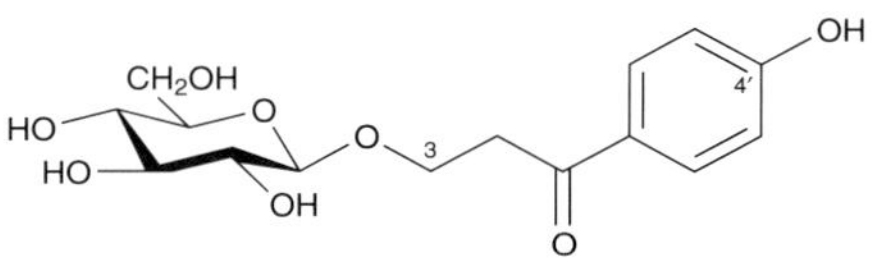

3,4′–Dihydroxypropiophenone 3-glucoside

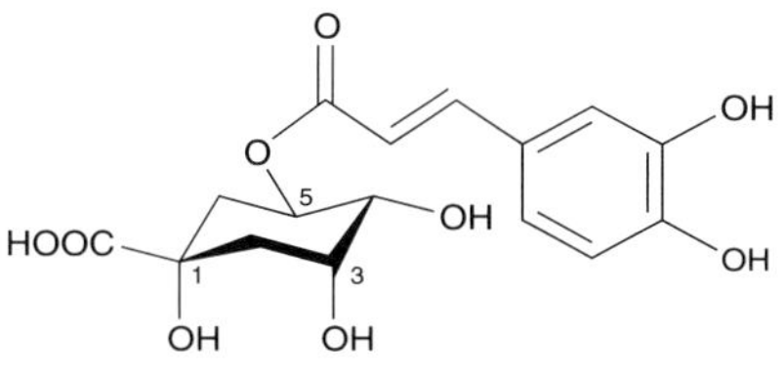

Chlorogenic acid

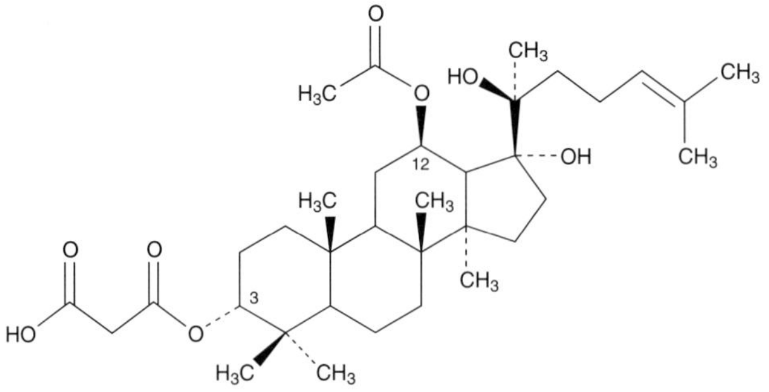

A dammarane triterpene

Published Assay Methods
Flavonoids [1-3,27] and other low MW phenolics [1,3] by HPLC.

PHARMACOLOGY

In vitro

From an investigation of enzyme systems (neutral endopeptidase and angiotensin-converting enzyme) which regulate the formation of urine in the body via excretion of sodium ions, it was concluded that certain flavonoids present in birch leaf, particularly quercetin and its metabolites, may contribute to the accelerated formation of urine [28].

So far as a high potassium content may contribute to a diuretic effect, the potassium content of birch leaf has been determined as ca. 8 mg/g, with potassium-sodium ratios of 200:1 in the leaf and 170:1 in a decoction [24].

An aqueous extract of birch leaf exhibited no antimicrobial activity [29].

Haemolytic activity of birch leaf [11] and isolated dammarane triterpenes [16] has been demonstrated.

In vivo

Diuretic effects
Oral administration of a birch leaf infusion to rabbits increased urine volume by 17-30% and chloride excretion by 35-48% compared to animals given water only; in mice, urine volume increased by 42% and chloride excretion by 128% [30]. In other experiments, birch leaf infusion produced no increase in urine volume in rats but increased urea excretion by 30% and chloride excretion by 45% [31]. Young (just spread) birch leaves produced no diuretic effect in rats or mice [11].

Birch leaf administered orally to dogs at 240 mg/kg body weight increased urine volume by 13.8% after 2 hours; a flavonoid fraction at 14 mg/kg increased urine volume by only 2.8% [32].

Oral administration of an aqueous extract of birch leaf (total flavonoids: 148 mg/100 ml) to male rats in single doses of 1.33-10.64 ml/kg body weight dose-dependently increased excretion of urine, by 91% at 10.64 ml/kg compared to control animals; a 50%-hydroethanolic extract produced somewhat smaller increases. Excretion of sodium, potassium or chloride was unaffected. The authors concluded that the diuretic effect of birch leaf was partly, but not entirely, due to flavonoids and estimated that in humans at least 50 mg of flavonoids per day would be necessary to produce a diuretic effect [33].

Neither a total extract of birch leaf nor various fractions (chloroform fraction; butanol fraction; flavonoid-deficient butanol fraction; aqueous fraction; dammarane ester-containing fraction) produced any significant increase in diuretic or saluretic effects after oral administration to rats [34].

Thus in vivo studies on the diuretic effect of birch leaf have shown variable results, weakly positive in rabbits and dogs but contradictory in rodents. The rat, particularly the female rat, is not considered a very suitable model for diuresis experiments [33].

Other effects
An aqueous extract of birch leaf exhibited no anti-inflammatory activity; it showed weak antipyretic activity against yeast-induced fever in rats [29].

Pharmacological studies in humans
In a 1937 study, no increases in urine volume

were observed after oral administration of birch leaf tea, in comparison with water, in short term (4 hours) and long term (10-14 days) experiments on 5 healthy volunteers and 12 patients with chronic nephritis and other ailments [35]. Similarly, in a 1941 study, oral administration of an infusion of birch leaf produced no diuretic effect in healthy volunteers and only a very weak effect in patients with cardiac oedema [36].

CLINICAL STUDIES

Only one clinical study has been reported, a post-marketing study involving 258 urological practices in Germany. A birch leaf dry extract preparation was administered daily for around 2-4 weeks to 1066 patients, mainly with infections or inflammatory complaints of the urinary tract, to promote irrigation of the urinary tract. Over half of the patients also received antibiotics and some took other medications. At the end of treatment 80% of patients who received antibiotics, and 75% who did not, were symptom-free. Over 90% of physicians and patients assessed the efficacy of the birch leaf preparation as good or very good [37]. However, it is difficult to draw any conclusion regarding beneficial effects of birch leaf from this study.

THERAPEUTICS

Actions
Weak diuretic [30,32,33].

Indications
None adequately substantiated by pharmacological or clinical studies.

Uses based on experience or tradition
To promote diuresis in the treatment of ailments which require it [38,39], including irrigation in bacterial and inflammatory disorders of the urinary tract [39,40]; prevention of renal gravel [39-41]; rheumatic complaints [40-42].

Has also been used in gout [41,42].

Contraindications
Oedema in cardiac or renal insufficiency [39, 40].

Side effects
None known.

Interactions with other drugs
None known.

Dosage
2-3 g of dried leaf several times daily [39,40], in infusion or as an equivalent aqueous or hydroethanolic extract.

SAFETY

An extract of birch leaf showed weak mutagenicity in the Ames test, a common response from plant drugs containing flavonols [43].

No significant adverse effects have been reported from human studies with birch leaf; in the clinical study involving 1066 urological patients, only 8 reported mild adverse effects [37].

REGULATORY STATUS

Medicines

UK	Accepted for general sale, external use only [44].
France	Accepted for specified indications [38].
Germany	Commission E monograph published, with approved uses [40].

REFERENCES

Current Pharmacopoeial Monographs
Ph. Eur. Birch Leaf

Literature References

1. Ossipov V, Nurmi K, Loponen J, Haukioja E and Pihlaja K. High-performance liquid chromatographic separation and identification of phenolic compounds from leaves of *Betula pubescens* and *Betula pendula*. *J. Chromatogr. A* 1996, **721**, 59-68.
2. Ossipov V, Nurmi K, Loponen J, Prokopiev N, Haukioja E and Pihlaja K. HPLC Isolation and Identification of Flavonoids from White Birch *Betula pubescens* Leaves. *Biochem. Syst. Ecol.* 1995, **23**, 213-222.
3. Keinänen M and Julkunen-Tiitto R. Effect of Sample Preparation Method on Birch (*Betula pendula* Roth) Leaf Phenolics. *J. Agric. Food Chem.* 1996, **44**, 2724-2727.
4. Dallenbach-Tölke, Nyiredy S and Sticher O. Birkenblätter-Qualität. Vergleich der Einzel- und Gesamtbestimmungsmethoden der Flavonoid-glykoside von Betulae folium [Birch leaf quality. Comparison of methods for the determination of individual and total flavonoid glycosides of Betulae folium]. *Dtsch. Apoth. Ztg.* 1987, **127**, 1167-1171 [GERMAN].
5. Dallenbach-Tölke K, Nyiredy S, Meier B and Sticher O. HPLC Analysis of the Flavonoid Glycosides from Betulae folium. *Planta Medica* 1987, **53**, 189-192 [GERMAN/English summary].
6. Dallenbach-Tölke K, Nyiredy S, Gross GA and Sticher O. Flavonoid glycosides from *Betula pubescens* and *Betula pendula*. *J. Nat. Prod.* 1986, **49**, 1155-1156.
7. Tissut M and Egger K. Les glycosides flavoniques foliares de quelques arbres, au cours du cycle vegetatif [Flavone glycosides of the leaves of certain trees in the course of the vegetative cycle]. *Phytochemistry* 1972, **11**, 631-634 [FRENCH/English summary].
8. Hörhammer L, Wagner H and Luck R. Isolierung eines Myricetin-3-digalaktosides aus *Betula verrucosa* und *Betula pubescens* [Isolation of myricetin 3-digalactoside from *Betula verrucosa* und *Betula pubescens*]. *Arch. Pharm. (Weinheim)* 1957, **290**, 338-341 [GERMAN].
9. Pawlowska L. Flavonoids in the leaves of Polish species of the genus Betula L. IV. Flavonoids of *Betula pubescens*

Ehrh., *B. carpatica* Waldst., *B. tortuosa* Ledeb. and *B. nana* L. leaves. *Acta Soc. Bot. Pol.* 1982, **51**, 403-411 through *Chem. Abstr.* 1983, **99**, 155204.
10. Pokhilo ND, Denisenko VA, Makhan'kov VV and Uvarova NI. Terpenoids and flavonoids from the leaves of Siberian species of the genus Betula. *Khim. Prir. Soedin.* 1983, 392-393 [RUSSIAN] as English translation in: *Chem. Nat. Compd.* 1983, **19**, 374-375.
11. Elbanowska A and Kaczmarek F. Investigations on the flavonoid compounds content and the diuretic activity of *Betula verrucosa* Ehrh. leaves at different phases of growth. *Herba Polonica* 1966, **11**, 47-56 [POLISH/English summary].
12. Tschesche R, Harz A and Wulff G. 3,4 -Dihydroxypropiophenon-3-β-D-glucopyranosid aus *Betula alba*. *Phytochemistry* 1974, **13**, 518-519 [GERMAN].
13. Salminen J-P, Ossipov V, Loponen J, Haukioja E and Pihlaja K. Characterization of hydrolysable tannins from leaves of *Betula pubescens* by high-performance liquid chromatography-mass spectrometry. *J. Chromatogr. A* 1999, **864**, 283-291.
14. Ossipova S, Ossipov V, Haukioja E, Loponen J and Pihlaja K. Proanthocyanidins of Mountain Birch Leaves: Quantification and Properties. *Phytochem. Analysis* 2001, **12**, 128-133.
15. Hilpisch U, Hartmann R and Glombitza K-W. New Dammaranes, Esterified with Malonic Acid, from Leaves of *Betula pendula*. *Planta Medica* 1997, **63**, 347-351.
16. Rickling B and Glombitza K-W. Saponins in the Leaves of Birch? Hemolytic Dammarane Triterpenoid Esters of *Betula pendula*. *Planta Medica* 1993, **59**, 76-79.
17. Fischer FG and Seiler N. Die Triterpenalkohole der Birkenblätter, II [The triterpene alcohols of birch leaf, II]. *Liebigs Ann. Chem.* 1961, **644**, 146-162 [GERMAN].
18. Fischer FG and Seiler N. Die Triterpenalkohole der Birkenblätter [The triterpene alcohols of birch leaf]. *Liebigs Ann. Chem.* 1959, **626**, 185-205 [GERMAN].
19. Pokhilo ND, Makhnev AK and Uvarova NI. Triterpenoids of leaves of *Betula pendula* growing in high mountain regions of the Altai. Khim. Prir. Soedin. 1988, (3), 460-461 [RUSSIAN], translated into English as: *Chem. Nat. Compd.* 1988, **24**, 396-397.
20. Pokhilo ND, Denisenko VA, Makhan'kov VV and Uvarova NI. Triterpenoids of the leaves of *Betula pendula* from different growth sites. *Khim. Prir. Soedin* 1986, (2), 179-185 [RUSSIAN], translated into English as: *Chem. Nat. Compd.* 1986, **22**, 166-171.
21. Pokhilo ND, Denisenko VA, Novikov VL and Uvarova NI. 14-Hydroxycaryophyllene 4,5-oxide - a new sesquiterpene from *Betula pubescens*. *Khim. Prir. Soedin.* 1984, (5), 598-603 [RUSSIAN], translated into English as: *Chem. Nat. Compd.* 1984, **20**, 563-567.
22. Tschesche R, Ciper F and Breitmaier E. Monoterpen-Glucoside aus den Blättern von *Betula alba* und den Früchten von *Chaenomeles japonica* [Monoterpene glucosides from the leaves of *Betula alba* and the fruits of *Chaenomeles japonica*]. Chem. Ber. 1977, **110**, 3111-3117 [GERMAN/English summary].
23. Tschesche R, Ciper F and Harz A. Roseosid aus *Betula alba* und *Cydonia oblonga*. *Phytochemistry* 1976, **15**, 1990-1991 [GERMAN].
24. Szentmihályi K, Kéry A, Then M, Lakatos B, Sándor Z and Vinkler P. Potassium-Sodium Ratio for the Characterization of Medicinal Plant Extracts with Diuretic Activity. *Phytotherapy Res.* 1998, **12**, 163-166.
25. Kroeber L. Studienergebnisse einer Reihe von Fluidextrakten aus heimischen Arzneipflanzen [Results of a study on a series of fluid extracts from native medicinal plants]. *Pharm. Zentralhalle* 1924, 400-404 [GERMAN].
26. Tamas M, Hodisan V, Grecu L, Fagarasan E, Baciu M and Muica I. Investigations on triterpenoid saponins in medicinal indigenous plants. *Studii Cerc. Biochim.* 1978, **21**, 89-94. ROMANIAN/English summary].
27. Wagner H, Tittel G and Bladt S. Analyse und Standardisierung von Arzneidrogen und Phytopräparaten durch Hochleistungsflüssigchromatographie (HPLC) und andere chromatographische Verfahren [Analysis and standardization of medicinal plant drugs and phytopreparations by high performance liquid chromatography (HPLC) and other chromatographic methods]. *Dtsch. Apoth. Ztg.* 1983, **123**, 515-521 [GERMAN].
28. Melzig MF and Major H. New aspects for understanding the aquaretic mechanism of Betulae folium and Solidaginis virgaureae herba. *Z. Phytotherapie* 2000, **21**, 193-196 [GERMAN/English summary].
29. Klinger W, Hirschelmann R and Süss J. Birch sap and birch leaves extract: screening for antimicrobial, phagocytosis-inducing, antiphlogistic and antipyretic activity. *Pharmazie* 1989, **44**, 558-560.
30. Vollmer H. Untersuchungen über die diuretische Wirkung der Folia betulae an Kaninchen und Mäusen. Vergleich mit anderen Drogen [Investigations on the diuretic effect of birch leaf in rabbits and mice. Comparison with other plant drugs]. *Naunyn-Schmiederbergs Arch. exp. Path. Pharmakol.* 1937, **186**, 584-591 [GERMAN].
31. Vollmer H and Hübner K. Untersuchungen über die diuretische Wirkung der Fructus juniperi, Radix levistici, Radix ononidis, Folia betulae, Radix liquiritiae und Herba equiseti an Ratten [Investigations on the diuretic effect of Fructus juniperi, Radix levistici, Radix ononidis, Folia betulae, Radix liquiritiae and Herba equiseti in rats]. *Naunyn-Schmiederbergs Arch. exp. Path. Pharmakol.* 1937, **186**, 592-605 [GERMAN].
32. Borkowski B. Diuretische Wirkung einiger Flavondrogen [Diuretic effect of some flavone drugs]. *Planta Medica* 1960, **8**, 95-104 [GERMAN].
33. Schilcher H and Rau H. Nachweis der aquaretischen Wirkung von Birkenblätter- und Goldrutenkrautauszügen im Tierversuch [Evidence of the aquaretic effect of birch leaf and golden rod infusions in animal experiments]. *Urologe [B]* 1988, **28**, 274-280 [GERMAN].
34. Rickling B. Identifizierung hämolytisch aktiver Triterpenester aus *Betula pendula* [Identification of haemolytically active triterpene esters from *Betula pendula*]. Dissertation: Rheinischen Friedrich-Wilhelms-Universität, Bonn, 1992.
35. Marx H and Büchmann R. Über harntreibende Heilpflanzen [Urine-promoting medicinal plants]. *Dtsch. Med. Wochenschr.* 1937, **63**, 384-386 [GERMAN].
36. Braun H. Die therapeutische Verwendung wichtiger Drogen der Volksmedizin in der täglichen Praxis. IV. *Betula alba* (Birke) [Therapeutic use of the more important plant drugs of folk medicine in daily practice. IV. *Betula alba* (Birch)]. *Fortschr. Med.* 1941, **59**, 114-116 [GERMAN].
37. Müller B, Schneider B. Anwendungsbereiche eines Trockenextrakts aus Birkenblättern bei Harnwegserkrankungen: Ergebnisse einer Anwendungsbeobachtung [Use of a dry extract from birch leaf in urinary tract complaints: results of a post-marketing surveillance study]. In: Abstracts of Phytotherapie an der Schwelle zum neuen Jahrtausend - 10. Jahrestagung der Gesellschaft für Phytotherapie. Münster, 11-13 November 1999:106-8 (Abstract P16).
38. Bouleau. In: *Médicaments à base de plantes.* ISBN 2-911473-02-7. Saint-Denis Cedex, France: Agence du Médicament, 1998.
39. Wichtl M and Neubeck M. Birkenblätter. In: Hartke K, Hartke H, Mutschler E, Rücker G and Wichtl M, editors. *Arzneibuch-Kommentar. Wissenschaftliche Erläuterungen zum Europäischen Arzneibuch und zum Deutschen Arzneibuch.* ISBN 3-8047-1738-1. Stuttgart: Wissenschaftliche Verlagsgesellschaft, 1999 (Suppl. 11): B39 [GERMAN].
40. Betulae folium: German Commission E Monograph published in: Bundesanzeiger No. 50 of 13 March 1986.
41. Grieve M (edited by Leyel CF). Common Birch. In: *A Modern Herbal* (First published 1931; revised 1973). ISBN 1-85501-249-9. London: Tiger Books International, 1994:103-104.
42. Bartram T. Birch, European. In: *Encyclopaedia of Herbal Medicine.* ISBN 0-9515984-1-4. Christchurch, UK: Grace Publishers, 1995:57.
43. Göggelmann W, Schimmer O. Mutagenic activity of phytotherapeutical drugs. In: Knudsen I, editor. *Genetic Toxicology of the Diet.* New York: Alan R. Liss, 1986:63-72.

44. European Birch. In: UK Statutory Instrument 1994 No. 2410. The Medicines (Products Other Than Veterinary Drugs) (General Sale List) Amendment Order 1994. Schedule 1, Table B (External use only).

REGULATORY GUIDELINES FROM OTHER EU COUNTRIES

FRANCE

Médicaments à base de plantes [38]: Bouleau, feuille.

Therapeutic indications accepted

Oral use

Traditionally used to facilitate urinary and digestive elimination functions.

Traditionally used to promote renal elimination of water.

GERMANY

Commission E monograph [40]: Betulae folium (Birkenblätter).

Uses

For irrigation in bacterial and inflammatory ailments of the lower urinary tract and for renal gravel; supportive treatment of rheumatic complaints.

Contraindications

None known.

Note: Irrigation therapy not to be used in oedema due to impaired cardiac or renal function.

Side effects

None known.

Interactions with other drugs

None known.

Dosage

Unless otherwise prescribed, average dose: 2-3 g of dried leaf several times daily; equivalent preparations.

Mode of administration

Internal use as comminuted dried leaf or dry extract for infusions, other galenic preparations or pressed juice from fresh leaf.

Note: In irrigation therapy ensure copious intake of fluid.

Action

Diuretic.

BLACK HAW BARK

Caprifoliaceae

Viburni prunifolii cortex

Definition
Black Haw Bark consists of the dried stem bark of *Viburnum prunifolium* L.

Although earlier monographs of the U.S. National Formulary and BPC specified root bark, from 1942 the N.F. permitted 'dried bark of the root or stem' [1]. Stem bark is now more commonly used and is official in the Pharmacopée Française. The more recent phytochemical and pharmacological research has been carried out on stem bark.

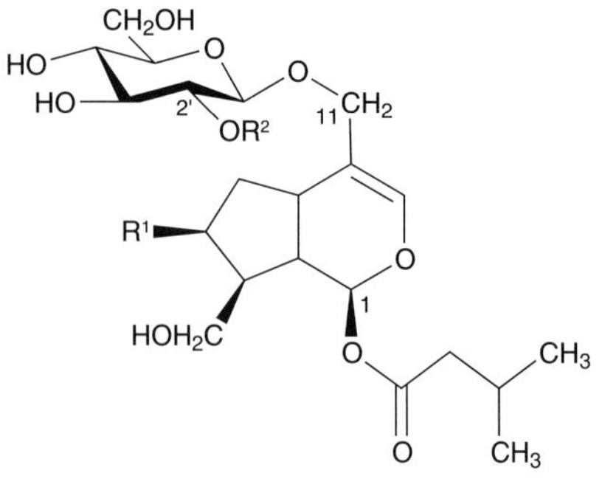

	R¹	R²
Patrinoside	OH	H
2′-Acetylpatrinoside	OH	acetyl
2′-Acetyl-dihydropenstemide	H	acetyl
2′-*p*-Coumaroyl-dihydropenstemide	H	*p*-coumaroyl

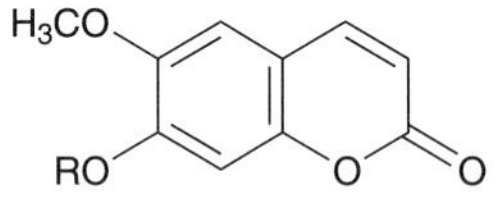

Scopoletin R = H
Scopolin R = glucosyl

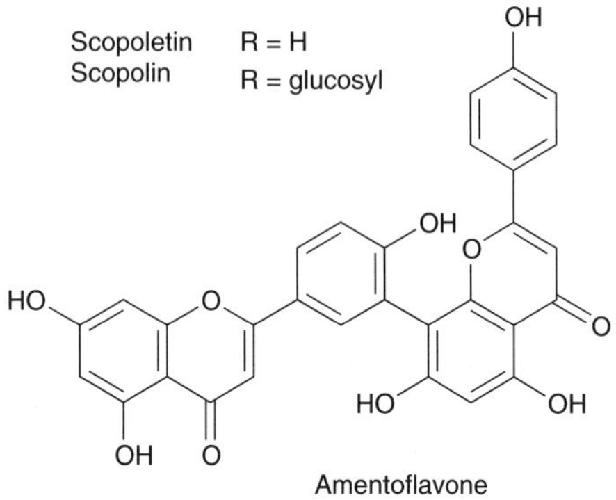

Amentoflavone

CONSTITUENTS

☐ ***Iridoid glucosides***, 0.4-0.5%, with an isovaleryl group at C-1 and glucosyl group at C-11: patrinoside, 2′-acetylpatrinoside, 2′-acetyldihydropenstemide and 2′-trans-*p*-coumaroyldihydropenstemide [2].
☐ ***Coumarins*** Scopoletin [3,4], its glucoside scopolin [4,5], and esculetin [3,5].
☐ ***Amentoflavone*** (= 3′,8″-biapigenin or I3′,II8-biapigenin) [3-6]. Since amentoflavone does not occur in *Viburnum opulus* or other *Viburnum* barks it can be used for TLC differentiation [4,5].
☐ ***Phenylpropanoids*** Chlorogenic and isochlorogenic acids [4].
☐ ***Triterpenes***: α- and β-amyrin, and ursolic and oleanolic acids [3,5] and their acetates [5].
☐ ***Other constituents*** include condensed tannins (proanthocyanidins) [7], 1-methyl 2,3-dibutyl hemimellitate [8], arbutin (hydroquinone glucoside) and β-sitosterol [3,5].

The reported presence of salicin [9] was subsequently disputed [5].

PHARMACOLOGY

In 1951 Woodbury reviewed the pharmacological studies on black haw bark, in vitro, in vivo and in humans, reported up to that time (carried out between 1913 and 1945); while the studies generally demonstrated a significant effect on the uterus, he concluded that most results were of rather limited value due to inadequate methodology [10]. No subsequent studies on uterine activity in vivo or in humans appear to have been published.

In vitro
Early studies to identify the uterine relaxant substances in black haw bark led to disputed findings. A 'glycosidal principle', isolated from authenticated (root) bark [11] and subsequently identified as salicin [9], had a marked relaxant effect, antagonised by cocaine or atropine, on rat uterine horn and on human uterine strips [11,12]. Later researchers could not detect salicin in the (stem) bark, but found that esculetin had one-eighth, scopoletin and an ethyl actetate extract of black haw bark one-twentieth, and amentoflavone one-fiftieth, of the spasmolytic activity of papaverine on isolated guinea pig ileum [5]. The recently isolated iridoid glucoside constituents [2] may be of pharmacological interest but have not yet been investigated.

A methanolic extract of black haw bark exhibited

spasmolytic activity, producing complete relaxation of regular contractions in isolated rat uterine horns. The effect appeared to be due to selective uterine relaxant activity by certain constituents directly on the muscle [13] and scopoletin was subsequently shown to be active in this respect, producing concentration-dependent decreases in contraction amplitude of single uterine horns, with a 50% decrease at 0.09 mg/ml [14].

In tests on isolated uterus from rats in oestrus, the spasmolytic activity of a lyophilised black haw bark extract prepared with 30° (ca. 17% V/V) ethanol (ED_{50}: 2,450 µg/ml) was about 5 times greater than that of an extract prepared with 60° (ca. 34% V/V) ethanol (ED_{50}: 13,300 µg/ml), both having considerably less activity than papaverine (ED_{50}: 4.8 µg/ml) [7].

Amentoflavone has high affinity for benzodiazepine receptors in rat brain in vitro, but showed only a small inhibition of ^{3}H-flunitrazepam in mousebrain in vivo, indicating that it is either rapidly metabolized or does not penetrate the blood-brain barrier [15].

In vivo
Lyophilised black haw bark extracts at a concentration of 300 mg/litre exhibited a venotonic action on the perfused hind quarters of the rabbit, a 30° alcoholic extract having a greater effect than a 60° alcoholic extract [7].

CLINICAL STUDIES

None published on mono-preparations of black haw bark.

A number of case studies published between 1866 and 1939, reporting relief from dysmenorrhoea or amenorrhoea, have been criticised as largely superficial, with inadequate data and, in some cases, involving concurrent use of other medicines [10].

THERAPEUTICS

Actions
Spasmolytic, uterine relaxant [7,16-18], venotonic [7].
Also reported to be hypotensive and astringent [16].

Indications
None adequately substantiated by pharmacological or clinical studies.

Uses based on experience or tradition
Dysmenorrhoea [10,16,19].
False labour pains; threatened miscarriage [16,18], especially with rise in arterial tension [16]; pain after childbirth [17,18]; capillary fragility; venous insufficiency [20]; asthma [16].

Contraindications
None known.

Side effects
None known.

Interactions with other drugs
None known.

Dosage
Three times daily: powdered bark, 2.5-5 g by infusion or decoction [16]; liquid extract 1:1 in 70% ethanol, 4-8 ml [16,19]; tincture 1:5 in 70% ethanol, 5-10 ml [16].

Note: Extracts prepared with a lower percentage of ethanol may be appropriate. Extracts prepared with ethanol 17% V/V had 5 times the spasmolytic activity in vitro and higher venotonic activity in vivo than extracts prepared with ethanol 34% V/V [7].

SAFETY

In the Ames mutagenicity test, a fluid extract of black haw bark at 200 µl/plate showed no mutagenic potential in *Salmonella typhimurium* strains TA98 or TA100, with or without activation [21].

REGULATORY STATUS

Medicines

UK	Accepted for general sale, internal or external use [22].
France	Accepted for specified indications [20].
Germany	No Commission E monograph issued.

Foods

USA	Permitted as flavouring (21 CFR 172.510) [23].
Council of Europe	Permitted as flavouring, category N3 [24].

REFERENCES

Current Pharmacopoeial Monographs

Ph. Fr.	Viburnum
BHP	Black Haw Bark

Literature References

1. Viburnum prunifolium. In: The National Formulary, 7th edition. Washington DC: American Pharmaceutical Association, 1942:482.
2. Tomassini L, Cometa MF, Foddai S and Nicoletti M. Iridoid

Glucosides from *Viburnum prunifolium*. *Planta Medica* 1999, **65**, 195.
3. Hörhammer L, Wagner H and Reinhardt H. Chemistry, pharmacology and pharmaceutics of the components from Viburnum prunifolium and V. opulus L. *Botan. Mag. (Tokyo)* 1966, **79**, 510-525 [GERMAN]; through *Chem. Abstr.* 1967, **67**, 14807.
4. Hörhammer L, Wagner H and Reinhardt H. Neue Methoden im pharmakognostischen Unterricht. 11. Mitteilung. Chromatographische Unterscheidung handelsüblicher Viburnum-Drogen [New methods in pharmacognostic teaching. Part 11. Chromatographic differentiation of commercial Viburnum drugs]. *Dtsch. Apoth. Ztg.* 1965, **105**, 1371-1373 [GERMAN].
5. Hörhammer L, Wagner H and Reinhardt H. Über neue Inhaltsstoffe aus den Rinden von *Viburnum prunifolium* L. (Amerikanischer Schneeball) und *Viburnum opulus* L. (Gemeiner Schneeball) [New constituents from the bark of *Viburnum prunifolium* L. (American Snowball) and *Viburnum opulus* L. (Common Snowball)]. *Z. Naturforsch.* 1967, **22b**, 768-776 [GERMAN].
6. Hörhammer L, Wagner H and Reinhardt H. Isolierung des Bis-(5,7,4'-Trihydroxy)-flavons "Amentoflavon" aus der Rinde von *Viburnum prunifolium* L. (Amerikan. Schneeball) [Isolation of the bis-(5,7,4'-trihydroxy)-flavone "amentoflavone" from the bark of *Viburnum prunifolium* L. (American Snowball)]. Naturwiss. 1965, **52**, 161 [GERMAN].
7. Balansard G, Chausse D, Boukef K, Toumi A, Jadot G and Boudon G. Critères de choix d'un extrait de *Viburnum, Viburnum prunifolium* L., en fonction de ses actions toniveineuse et spasmolytique [Criteria in the choice of an extract of *Viburnum, Viburnum prunifolium* L., with respect to its venotonic and spasmolytic activity]. *Plantes Méd. Phytothér.* 1983, **17**, 123-132 [FRENCH/English summary].
8. Jarboe CH, Zirvi KA, Schmidt CM, McLafferty FW and Haddon WF. 1-Methyl-2,3-Dibutyl Hemimellitate. A Novel Component of *Viburnum prunifolium*. *J. Org. Chem.* 1969, **34**, 4202-4203.
9. Iwamoto HK, Evans WE and Krantz JC. Characterization of the Glycosidal Principle of *Viburnum prunifolium*. *J. Am. Pharm. Assoc.* 1945, **34**, 205-207.
10. Woodbury RA. The Viburnums. *Drug Standards* (formerly *Bulletin of the National Formulary Committee*) 1951, **19**, 143-152.
11. Evans WE, Harne WG and Krantz JC. A uterine principle from Viburnum prunifolium. *J. Pharmacol. Exp. Therap.* 1942, **75**, 174-177.
12. Evans WE, Iwamoto HK and Krantz JC. A Note on the Pharmacology of *Viburnum prunifolium* and its Glycoside. *J. Am. Pharm. Assoc.* 1945, **34**, 207-208.
13. Jarboe CH, Schmidt CM, Nicholson JA and Zirvi KA. Uterine Relaxant Properties of *Viburnum*. *Nature* 1966, **212**, 837.
14. Jarboe CH, Zirvi KA, Nicholson JA and Schmidt CM. Scopoletin, an Antispasmodic Component of *Viburnum opulus* and *prunifolium*. *J. Med. Chem.* 1967, **10**, 488-489.
15. Nielsen M, Froekjaer S and Braestrup C. High affinity of the naturally-occurring biflavonoid, amentoflavone, to brain benzodiazepine receptors in vitro. *Biochem. Pharmacol.* 1988, **37**, 3285-3287.
16. Viburnum prunifolium. In: *British Herbal Pharmacopoeia 1983*. ISBN 0-903032-07-9. Bournemouth: British Herbal Medicine Association, 1983.
17. Ody P. *Viburnum* spp. - Black Haw. In: *Medicinal Herbal, 2nd ed.* ISBN 0-7513-3005-1. London-New York: Dorling Kindersley, 2000:136.
18. McIntyre A. Black Haw. In: *The Complete Woman's Herbal*. ISBN 1-85675-135-X. London: Gaia Books, 1994:33.
19. Viburnum: Black Haw. In: *The British Pharmaceutical Codex 1934*. London: Pharmaceutical Society of Great Britain, 1934:1108-1109.
20. Viburnum. In: *Médicaments à base de plantes*. ISBN 2-911473-02-7. Saint-Denis Cedex, France: Agence du Médicament, 1998.
21. Schimmer O, Krüger A, Paulini H and Haefele F. An evaluation of 55 commercial plant extracts in the Ames mutagenicity test. *Pharmazie* 1994, **49**, 448-451.
22. Black Haw. In: UK Statutory Instrument 1994 No. 2410. The Medicines (Products Other Than Veterinary Drugs) (General Sale List) Amendment Order 1994. Schedule 1, Table A.
23. Haw, black, bark (Section 172.510). In: USA Code of Federal Regulations, Title 21, Food and Drugs, Parts 170 to 199. Revised as of April 1, 2000.
24. Viburnum prunifolium L., bark of branches. In: *Flavouring Substances and Natural Sources of Flavourings, 3rd ed.* ISBN 2-7160-0081-6. Strasbourg: Council of Europe, 1981.

REGULATORY GUIDELINES FROM OTHER EU COUNTRIES

FRANCE

Médicaments à base de plantes [20]: Viburnum, écorce de tige.

Therapeutic indications accepted

Oral and/or topical use
Traditionally used in the symptomatic treatment of functional disorders of cutaneous capillary fragility, such as ecchymoses or petechiae.
Traditionally used in subjective manifestations of venous insufficiency, such as 'heavy legs'.
Traditionally used in haemorrhoidal symptomatology.

BLACK HOREHOUND **Labiatae**

Ballotae nigrae herba

Definition

Black Horehound consists of the dried flowering tops of *Ballota nigra* L.

A strongly aromatic perennial herb, 30-80 cm in height, with dense whorls of lilac flowers along the upright leafy stems, *Ballota nigra* is widespread from Europe to central Asia and naturalized or casual in Britain. It is polymorphic; at least six European subspecies can be distinguished, the two most common in western Europe being *B. nigra* L. ssp. *nigra* and *B. nigra* L. ssp. *foetida* Hayek [1].

CONSTITUENTS

□ ***Phenylpropanoids***, up to 5.5%, principally *ortho*-dihydroxycinnamic acid derivatives (Ph. Eur. min. 1.5%, calculated as acteoside) including the glycosides verbascoside (= acteoside), forsythoside B, arenarioside and ballotetroside [1-4], estimated at ca. 1% each [2], very small amounts of three other glycosides, alyssonoside, lavandulifolioside and angoroside, and ca. 1% of non-glycosidic (+)-*E*-caffeoyl-L-malic acid [2].

From a Ukrainian research group, and perhaps from a different subspecies of *Ballota nigra*, chlorogenic (ca. 3.8%), caffeic (ca. 0.15%) and ferulic (ca. 0.15%) acids have been reported in the flowering aerial parts [5].

□ ***Diterpenoids*** The labdane diterpene lactones ballotinone (= 7-oxomarrubiin) [6], ballonigrine [7], 7α-acetoxymarrubiin [8], ballotenol [9], 13-hydroxyballonigrinolide [10] and traces of marrubiin [6]; all these compounds have a furan ring on the C-9 side chain. Preleosibirin (a prefuranic diterpenoid) has also been isolated [11].

□ ***Flavonoids*** Luteolin 7-lactate and 7-glucosyl-lactate are the major flavonoids [12]. Apigenin 7-*O*-glucoside and vicenin-2 (apigenin 6,8-*C*-diglucoside) also occur in the leaves [13].

Acacetin, apigenin, chrysoeriol and luteolin monosides, apigenin and acacetin biosides and scutellarein have been identified in the flowers [5].

A highly methoxylated flavone, tangeretin (5,6,7,8,4′-pentamethoxyflavone), has also been isolated, but from a sample of *Ballota nigra* aerial parts containing no labdane diterpenoids [14].

□ ***Other constituents*** include β-sitosterol, phytol [15], stachydrine, choline [16] and essential oil (0.01%) [17].

Published Assay Methods

Total *ortho*-dihydroxycinnamic acid derivatives by spectrophotometry [2, Ph. Eur.]. 13-Hydroxyballonigrinolide by TLC densitometry [10].

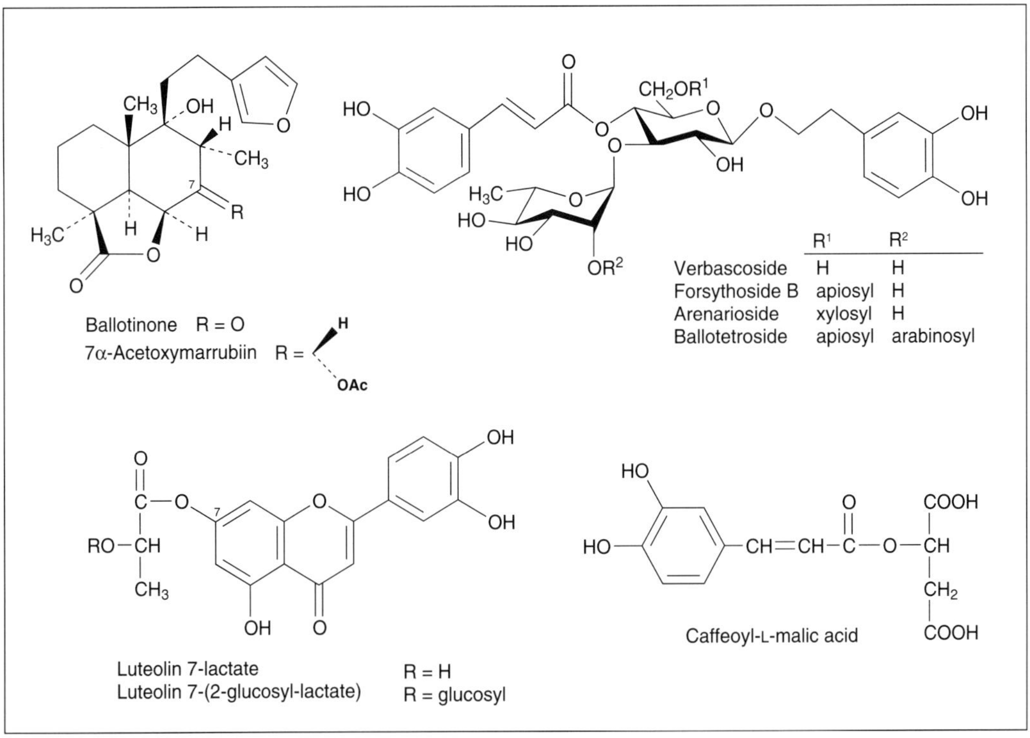

PHARMACOLOGY

In vitro

Four phenylpropanoid glycosides present in black horehound, verbascoside, forsythoside B, arenarioside and ballotetroside, and the non-glycosidic phenylpropanoid caffeoyl-L-malic acid, have been subjected to a range of *in vitro* tests [2,18,19]:

In competitive receptor affinity studies verbascoside, forsythoside B, arenarioside and caffeoyl-L-malic acid, but not ballotetroside, showed affinity for benzodiazepine, dopaminergic and morphinic receptors from rat brain with 50% inhibitory concentrations (IC_{50}) of between 0.4 mg/ml and 4.8 mg/ml. Verbascoside, for example, gave IC_{50} values of 1.2 mg/ml, 4.8 mg/ml, and 0.5 mg/ml for benzodiazepine, dopaminergic and morphinic receptors respectively. The neurosedative properties of black horehound may therefore be due, in part, to the major phenylpropanoid esters present [18].

The phenylpropanoids exhibited antioxidant activity, scavenging the reactive oxygen species (ROS) superoxide anion, peroxide hydrogen, hypochlorous acid and hydroxyl radical, all of which can be produced by polymorphonuclear neutrophils (PMNs) in response to infectious agents, with IC_{50} values comparable to that of N-acetylcysteine. In subsequent tests with stimulated PMNs from human blood the phenylpropanoids significantly ($p<0.05$) and dose-dependently reduced the release of ROS from PMNs, with activity in the order verbascoside > forsythoside B > caffeoyl-L-malic acid > arenarioside > ballotetroside. This effect on PMN oxidative metabolism suggests therapeutic potential in inflammatory conditions [18].

Oxidized low-density lipoprotein (LDL) is thought to play an important role in the pathogenesis of atherosclerosis. The phenylpropanoids strongly inhibited Cu^{2+}-induced peroxidation of LDL in a dose-dependent manner with ED_{50} values of 1 mM for verbascoside and forsythoside B, 1.8 mM for arenarioside, 7.5 mM for ballotetroside and 9.5 mM for caffeoyl-L-malic acid, compared to 2.3 mM for quercetin (a well-known inhibitor of Cu^{2+}-induced LDL oxidation). In contrast to quercetin, the phenylpropanoids were shown not to be Cu^{2+} chelators; their inhibitory activity is linked to scavenging of free radicals [19].

Verbascoside, forsythoside B and arenarioside, but not ballotetroside or caffeoyl-L-malic acid, exhibited moderate antibacterial activity against *Staphylococcus aureus* (Gram-positive) and *Proteus mirabilis* (Gram-negative) at a concentration of 128 mg/ml [2].

In vivo

From a range of tests to investigate the psychotropic effects of a black horehound extract intraperitoneally administered to rodents, 200 mg/kg significantly reduced mobility and, to a lesser extent, curiosity in mice; produced a significant tranquillizing effect in mice; significantly reduced anxiety but not locomotor activity in rats; and significantly prolonged barbiturate-induced sleeping time in rats. No muscle relaxant effect was evident in mice from doses of 200 or 400 mg/kg. It was concluded that black horehound extract is suitable for the symptomatic treatment of stress, anxiety and sleep disturbances [20].

Black horehound extract administered intraperitoneally to mice produced a marked sedative effect on the central nervous system, reducing spontaneous motor activity by 60% after 1 hour and 65% after 3 hours [21].

In the forced swimming test an aqueous extract from aerial parts of *Ballota nigra* subsp. *anatolica*, administered intraperitoneally to rats as a single dose at 240 mg/kg, had a significant antidepressant effect. The mean duration of immobility was 496 seconds ($p<0.001$) compared to 570 seconds for untreated controls, 379 seconds after amitriptyline at 5 mg/kg ($p<0.001$) and 389 seconds after *Passiflora* extract at 60 mg/kg ($p<0.001$). No significant anxiolytic activity of the black horehound extract was observed in the elevated plus-maze test [22].

A 55:45 mixture of two phenylpropanoid glycosides, verbascoside and orobanchoside (of which only verbascoside is present in black horehound) significantly reduced locomotor activity ($p<0.05$) and prolonged pentobarbital-induced sleep ($p<0.05$) in mice after intraperitoneal injection at 100 mg/kg; produced a slowing of the electroencephalographic trace in rabbits after intravenous injection of 50-500 mg/kg in rabbits; and produced epileptiform effects in rabbits when injected into the lateral cerebral ventricle. No significant change was observed on the nociceptive threshold in mice (hot plate test) nor any effect on isolated guinea-pig ileum. From these results it was suggested that the phenylpropanoid glycosides may act as a neuroleptic drug [23].

CLINICAL STUDIES

In an open study, 28 patients with general anxiety (at least 6 of the 18 criteria comprising the DSM III R classification of general anxiety) involving depression and sleep disorders were treated orally for 90 days with the equivalent of 1.5 g of black horehound per day, taken in three part doses as a hydroethanolic liquid preparation. Based on clinical examination and interrogation based on DSM III R at days 0, 15, 30, 60 and 90, 65% of patients showed a distinct improvement in their condition by day 60 and 73% by day 90. Patients with sleep disorders showed particularly marked improvement. Out of 10 patients taking benzodiazepines prior to the study, 3 discontinued and 4 reduced their dose by half [24].

THERAPEUTICS

Actions
Anxiolytic [20,24], sedative [20,21], antidepressant [22], spasmolytic [13,25].

Indications
None adequately substantiated by clinical studies.

Uses based on experience or tradition
Sleep disorders, anxiety, stress [20,24,26]. Nausea, nervous dyspepsia [24,27]; coughs [2,13], whooping cough, digestive spasms [13,24,25], nervous complaints of the menopause [24].

Contraindications
None known.

Side effects
In some cases, feelings of fatigue or nausea in early stages of treatment [24].

Dosage
Up to three times daily, taken after meals: dried herb, 0.5-4 g [24,27], usually as a hydroethanolic extract [24], e.g. liquid extract 1:1 in 25% alcohol, 1-3 ml [27].

SAFETY

Black horehound has been classified as a herb that can be safely consumed when used appropriately [28].

No major adverse effects were reported in an open clinical study on 28 patients, summarized above. During early stages of treatment 14 patients reported feelings of fatigue, which later diminished. 9 patients reported nausea, which was alleviated by taking the black horehound preparation after meals [24].

In an acute oral toxicity test, after administration to mice of a single large dose of black horehound extract at 2 g/kg body weight, no mortality occurred and no signs of toxicity were evident from 15-day observation or post-mortem examination [20].

REGULATORY STATUS

Medicines

UK	No licences issued for products containing black horehound.
France	Accepted for specified indications [26].
Germany	No Commission E monograph issued.

Foods

Council of Europe	Permitted as flavouring, category N3 [29].

REFERENCES

Current Pharmacopoeial Monographs
Ph. Eur. Black Horehound

Literature References

1. Seidel V, Bailleul F and Tillequin F. Diterpene and phenylpropanoid glycosides from *Ballota nigra* L. *Ann. Pharm. Franç.* 1998, **56**, 31-35 [FRENCH/English summary].
2. Didry N, Seidel V, Dubreuil L, Tillequin F and Bailleul F. Isolation and antibacterial activity of phenylpropanoid derivatives from *Ballota nigra. J. Ethnopharmacol.* 1999, **67**, 197-202.
3. Seidel V, Bailleul F and Tillequin F. Phenylpropanoid Glycosides from *Ballota nigra. Planta Medica* 1996, **62**, 186-187.
4. Seidel V, Bailleul F, Libot F and Tillequin F. A phenylpropanoid glycoside from *Ballota nigra. Phytochemistry* 1997, **44**, 691-693.
5. Zhukov IM and Belikov VV. Chromatospectrophotometric determination of flavonoids and dioxycinnamic acids in the above-ground parts of *Ballota nigra* L. *Farm. Zh. (Kiev)* 1989, (5), 55-58 [UKRAINIAN]; through *Chem. Abstr.* 1990, **112**, 18874.
6. Savona G, Piozzi F, Hanson JR and Siverns M. Structure of Ballotinone, a Diterpenoid from *Ballota nigra. J. Chem. Soc. Perkin I* 1976, 1607-1609.
7. Savona G, Piozzi F, Hanson JR and Siverns M. Nuovi diterpenoidi provenienti da specie del genere Ballota. [New diterpenoids from species of the genus Ballota]. *Chim. Ind.* (Milan) 1976, **58**, 378 [ITALIAN].
8. Savona G, Piozzi F, Hanson JR and Siverns M. Structures of Three New Diterpenoids from *Ballota* Species. *J. Chem. Soc. Perkin I* 1977, 322-324.
9. Savona G, Piozzi F, Hanson JR and Siverns M. The Structure of Ballotenol, a New Diterpenoid from *Ballota nigra. J. Chem. Soc. Perkin I* 1977, 497-499.
10. Seidel V, Bailleul F and Tillequin F. Isolation from *Ballota nigra* L. of 13-hydroxyballonigrinolide, a diterpene useful for the standardization of the drug. *J. Pharm. Belg.* 1996, **51**, 72-73.
11. Bruno M, Savona G, Pascual C and Rodriguez B. Preleosibirin, a prefuranic labdane diterpene from *Ballota nigra* subsp. *foetida. Phytochemistry* 1986, **25**, 538-539.
12. Bertrand M-C, Tillequin F and Bailleul F. Two major flavonoids from *Ballota nigra. Biochem. Syst. Ecol.* 2000, **28**, 1031-1033.
13. Darbour N, Baltassat F and Raynaud J. Sur la présence d'un O-hétéroside et d'un C-hétéroside d'apigénine dans les feuilles de Ballota foetida Lamk. (Labiées). [On the presence of an O-glycoside and a C-glycoside of apigenin in leaves of Ballota foetida Lamk. (Labiatae)]. *Pharmazie* 1986, **41**, 605-606 [FRENCH].
14. Kisiel W and Piozzi F. Tangeretin from *Ballota nigra. Polish. J. Chem.* 1995, **69**, 476-477.
15. Popa DP and Pasechnik GS. Higher terpenoids in some species of Labiatae. *Khim. Prir. Soedin.* 1974, (4), 529-530 [RUSSIAN]; through *Chem. Abstr.* 1975, **82**, 54181.
16. Balansard J. Essais pharmacologiques sur la Ballote fétide. [Pharmacological tests on Ballota foetida]. *Comptes Rend. Soc. Biol. (Paris)* 1934, **115**, 1295-1297 [FRENCH].

17. Strzelecka H, Dobrowolska B and Twardowska K. Anatomical investigation and preliminary phytochemical examinations of Herba Galeopsidis and Herba Ballotae nigrae. *Herba Polonica* 1975, **21**, 3-16 [POLISH/English summary].
18. Daels-Rakotoarison DA, Seidel V, Gressier B, Brunet C, Tillequin F, Bailleul F et al. Neurosedative and Antioxidant Activities of Phenylpropanoids from *Ballota nigra. Arzneim.-Forsch./Drug Res.* 2000, **50**, 16-23.
19. Seidel V, Verholle M, Malard Y, Tillequin F, Fruchart J-C, Duriez P et al. Phenylpropanoids from *Ballota nigra* L. Inhibit in vitro LDL Peroxidation. *Phytotherapy Res.* 2000, **14**, 93-98.
20. Mongold JJ, Camilleri S, Serrano JJ, Taillade C, Masse JP and Susplugas P. Étude experimentale de l'activité psychotrope de *Ballota nigra* [Experimental study of the psychotropic activity of *Ballota nigra*]. *Phytotherapy (Paris)* 1991, **36/37**, 5-11 [FRENCH].
21. Rácz-Kotilla E, Rácz G and Józsa J. Activity of some species belonging to Labiatae on the central nervous system in mice. *Herba Hungarica* 1980, **19**, 49-53.
22. Vural K, Ezer N, Erol K and Sahin FP. Anxiolytic and antidepressant activities of some *Ballota* species. *J. Fac. Pharm. Gazi* 1996, **13**, 29-32.
23. Pieretti S, Di Giannuario A, Capasso A and Nicoletti M. Pharmacological Effects of Phenylpropanoid Glycosides from *Orobanche hederae. Phytother. Res.* 1992, **6**, 89-93.
24. Huriez A. L'utilisation du M.D.E. de Ballota chez des patients anxieux (A propos de 28 cas). [The use of M.D.E. (Medicinal Drug Extract) of Ballota in anxious patients (with reference to 28 cases)]. *Phytotherapy (Paris)* 1991, **36/37**, 12-19 [FRENCH].
25. Ballota. In: Hänsel R, Keller K, Rimpler H and Schneider G, editors. *Hagers Handbuch der Pharmazeutischen Praxis. 5th ed, Volume 4: Drogen A-D.* ISBN 3-540-52631-5. Berlin-Heidelberg-New York-London: Springer-Verlag, 1992:453-457 [GERMAN].
26. Ballote noire ou Marroube noir. In: *Médicaments à base de plantes.* ISBN 2-911473-02-7. Saint-Denis Cedex, France: Agence du Médicament, 1998.
27. Ballota. In: *British Herbal Pharmacopoeia 1983.* [ISBN 0-903032-07-9. Bournemouth: British Herbal Medicine Association, 1983.
28. McGuffin M, Hobbs C, Upton R and Goldberg A, editors. *Ballota nigra* L. In: American Herbal Products Association's *Botanical Safety Handbook.* Boca Raton-Boston-London: CRC Press, 1997:18.
29. Ballota nigra L. (Ballota foetida Lam.), herb. In: *Flavouring Substances and Natural Sources of Flavourings, 3rd ed.* ISBN 2-7160-0081-6. Strasbourg: Council of Europe, 1981.

REGULATORY GUIDELINES FROM OTHER EU COUNTRIES

FRANCE

Médicaments à base de plantes [27]: Ballote noire ou Marroube noir, sommité fleurie.

Therapeutic indications accepted

Oral use
Traditionally used in the symptomatic treatment of neurotonic states in adults and children, particularly in cases of minor sleep disorders.
Traditionally used in the symptomatic treatment of coughs.

BOLDO LEAF

Monimiaceae

Boldi folium

Definition
Boldo Leaf consists of the dried leaves of *Peumus boldus* Molina.

Boldo is an evergreen tree native to central regions of Chile between latitudes 33° and 39°S.

CONSTITUENTS

□ ***Isoquinoline alkaloids***, 0.2-0.5% [1] (Ph. Eur. min. 0.1% of total alkaloids expressed as boldine), mainly of the aporphine type; at least 17 alkaloids have been identified [2].

Boldine is usually the major alkaloid, reported as 14-36% of the total alkaloids [3-5], together with isoboldine, isocorydine, norisocorydine, laurotetanine, N-methyllaurotetanine and others [2,3,6]. Perplexingly, in recent determinations on leaf from northern, central and southern parts of the natural geographic range of boldo in Chile, boldine (0.007-0.009% in dried leaf) was found not to be a major alkaloid, representing only 2.6% of the total alkaloid content of the leaf (0.28-0.32%); unfortunately the proportions of other specific alkaloids were not reported [1].

□ ***Essential oil***, 1.6-2.6% [1,7] (Ph. Eur. 2.0-4.0% V/m in whole leaf; not less than 1.5% V/m in fragmented leaf), of very variable composition.

The major components usually include ascaridole (16-38%) [7-9], 1,8-cineole (11-39%) and *p*-cymene (9-29%) together with smaller amounts of other monoterpenes [7-10].

Data from three recent investigations illustrate the high variability of the oil. Hexane-extracted oil from leaves of three different *Peumus boldus* populations, taken from northern, central and southern parts of the natural geographic range in Chile, contained ascaridole (26-35%), but only small amounts of cineole (0.1-0.5%) and *p*-cymene (1.8-3.9%) [1]. In steam-distilled oil, Miraldi et al. reported ascaridole (21.2%), 1,8-cineole (21.1%), and *p*-cymene (8.6%) but also substantial amounts of four compounds not previously found in boldo leaf oil: α-thujone (14.3%), β-thujone (7.1%), *cis*-verbenol (9.9%) and guaiazulene (8.8%) [7]. Vila et al. reported major components to be limonene (17.0%), 1,8-cineole (11.8%) and *p*-cymene (13.6%), with only 1% of ascaridole (no thujones) [10].

Steam-distilled oil from boldo leaf grown in Italy (Tuscany) contained equal amounts of ascaridole (38.6%) and 1,8-cineole (38.6%) together with *p*-cymene (9.5%) and only traces of thujones [7].

□ ***Flavonoids*** Isorhamnetin 3-glucoside-7-rhamnoside (boldoside), rhamnetin 3-arabinoside-3′-rhamnoside (peumoside), kaempferol 3-glucoside-7-rhamnoside, an isorhamnetin dirhamnoside [11, 12] and isorhamnetin 3-arabinoside-7-rhamnoside [13] have been identified. Other flavonol glycosides appear to be present in small amounts [11].

Published Assay Methods
Total of six alkaloids (boldine, isoboldine, isocorydine, isocorydine N-oxide, laurotetanine and N-methyllaurotetanine) by HPLC with spectrophotometric detection) [Ph. Eur.]. Total alkaloids by spectrophotometry; boldine by HPLC [1]. Boldine in pharmaceutical preparations by HPLC [14]. Boldine, isocorydine and N-methyllaurotetanine by HPLC [15]. Total alkaloids by acidimetric titration [16]. Essential oil by GC [1,10] and GC-MS [7,10].

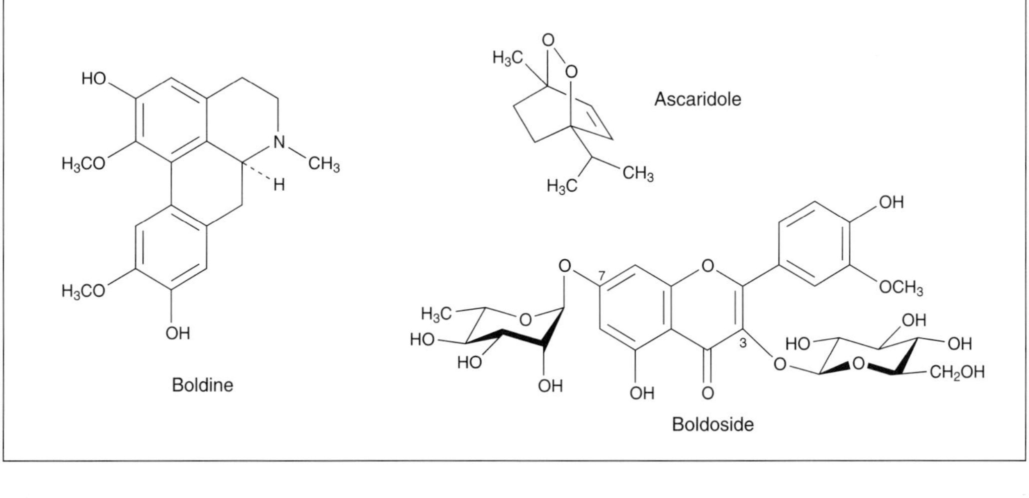

PHARMACOLOGY

In vitro

Antimicrobial activity
The essential oil from boldo leaf showed activity against both Gram-positive and Gram-negative bacteria as well as strong activity against *Candida* species [10].

Spasmolytic effect of boldine
Boldine concentration-dependently relaxed acetylcholine-induced contractions of smooth muscle from isolated rat ileum with an EC_{50} of 1.7×10^{-4}M [17].

Cytoprotective effects of boldine
Strong free radical scavenging and antioxidant properties of boldine have been demonstrated [18]. Free radicals are implicated as major initiators and/or mediators of biochemical events leading to hepatocellular injury induced by oxidative stress [19]. Boldine afforded significant protection against *tert*-butyl hydroperoxide-induced damage to isolated rat hepatocytes [19,20], and inhibited rat [21] and human [22] liver microsomal lipid peroxidation.

In other studies, boldine protected rat erythrocytes against haemolytic damage induced by free radicals [18], prevented auto-oxidation of rat brain homogenate [23] and reduced the lethal effect induced by stannous chloride on the survival of *Escherichia coli* [24].

Other effects of boldine
Boldine strongly inhibited arachidonic acid- and collagen-induced platelet aggregation ($p<0.001$), and inhibited high K^+- and norepinephrine-induced aortic contractions ($p<0.01$) [25].

In vivo

Choleretic effects
Choleretic effects have been reported after oral or intraduodenal administration of aqueous [26,27] or ethanolic [4,28] boldo extracts or pure boldine [26,29,30] to rats or dogs. However, more recent studies found no significant increase in bile secretion after oral [31] or intravenous [20] administration of hydroethanolic boldo extracts to rats or guinea pigs. The choleretic activity therefore remains controversial and appears, at best, to require high doses [20].

Hepatoprotective effects
A dry hydroethanolic extract containing 0.2-0.4% of alkaloids, administered intraperitoneally to mice, exerted 70% protection ($p<0.001$) against carbon tetrachloride-induced hepatotoxicity at a dose equivalent to 500 mg/kg of boldo leaf; boldine at 10 mg/kg provided 49% protection [20].

Anti-inflammatory effects
The same extract, administered intraperitoneally at doses equivalent to 100-400 mg/kg of boldo leaf, dose-dependently inhibited carrageenan-induced rat paw oedema by 55-89%, whereas boldine at 10-20 mg/kg produced no significant anti-inflammatory effect [20,32]. On the other hand, boldine administered orally to guinea pigs dose-dependently inhibited carrageenan-induced paw oedema with an ED_{50} of 34 mg/kg [33]. When administered intrarectally to rats at 100 mg/kg in an experimental model of acute colitis, boldine afforded significant protection against acid-induced oedema ($p<0.01$) and also against macroscopic ($p<0.00002$) and histologic ($p<0.001$) injuries caused by acetic acid [34].

Laxative effect
Oral administration of 400 or 800 mg/kg of a soft hydroethanolic extract from boldo leaf daily for 8 weeks had a mild laxative effect (from the third day) in rats [31].

Antipyretic effect of boldine
Boldine at an oral dose of 60 mg/kg reduced *E. coli* endotoxin-induced pyrexia in rabbits by 84% (AUC) during the first 90 minutes after pyrogen administration, but had no effect in the 90-180 minute period [33].

Pharmacological studies in humans

Daily administration of 2.5 g of a dry 75%-ethanolic extract of boldo leaf (4:1, 0.4% of alkaloids) to healthy volunteers for periods of 4 days significantly increased orocaecal transit time, to 112.5 minutes compared to 87 minutes with placebo ($p<0.05$), as measured by collection of breath hydrogen after the ingestion of 20 g of lactulose on day 4 [35].

Pharmacokinetics

When boldine was added to a suspension of rat hepatocytes at 200 μM, the extracellular concentration steadily declined. Meanwhile, the concentration of boldine within the hepatic cells swiftly accumulated to 1600 μM within 2 minutes and then gradually declined, but remained substantially greater than that in the extracellular medium, being 17-fold higher at the end of a 60-minute incubation. Isolated rat livers portally perfused with boldine concentration-dependently removed it from the extracellular medium [36].

In vivo studies in rats revealed that after oral administration of boldine at 50-75 mg/kg it was absorbed within 30 minutes and preferentially concentrated in the liver, with substantially lower concentrations in the brain and heart [36].

CLINICAL STUDIES

None published on mono-preparations of boldo leaf.

THERAPEUTICS

Actions

Choleretic [4,26-28,37-44], liver stimulant [38-40], hepatoprotective [20]; anti-inflammatory [20,32], mildly laxative [31,41], antimicrobial [10].

Also stated to increase secretion of gastric juice [42-44] and to be diuretic [20,38,41,44], urinary tract antiseptic [20] and sedative [20,44]

Boldine is spasmolytic [17], hepatoprotective [19-22] and antipyretic [33].

Indications

None adequately substantiated by pharmacological or clinical studies.

Uses based on experience or tradition

Mild spasmodic disorders of the gastrointestinal tract [42,44], especially functional disorders of the bile duct [44], gall-stones, liver or gall-bladder pains [37-40]; dyspeptic complaints [42-44]; urinary tract inflammation [20] including cystitis [38-40]; rheumatism [20,38].

Contraindications

Pregnancy [39,45].
Obstruction of the bile duct, severe liver disorders [42]. Use of boldo leaf in cases of gallstones should be based on professional diagnosis and advice.

Side effects

None known.

Interactions with other drugs

None known.

Dosage

Three times daily: dried leaf, 60-200 mg, or as an infusion; liquid extract 1:1 in 45% alcohol, 0.1-0.3 ml; tincture 1:10 in 60% alcohol, 0.5-2 ml [38].

German recommended dosages are generally higher: dried leaf, average *daily* dose: 3.0 g [42]; dried leaf, 1-2 g as an infusion in 150 ml of water, 2-3 times daily [44]. The UK General Sale List maximum *single* dose is 1.5 g [46].

In view of its high content of ascaridole the essential oil should never be used, internally or externally [42,47].

SAFETY

Boldo leaf [37] and boldine [21,22] are considered to have relatively low toxicity. The essential oil is, however, very toxic due to the ascaridole content; the oral LD_{50} in rats is 0.13 g/kg and it produces convulsions in rats at 0.07 g/kg [47]. Intraperitoneal LD_{50} values for total boldo leaf alkaloids and pure boldine were determined as 420 mg/kg and 250 mg/kg (equivalent to 125 g and 75 g of boldo leaf) respectively; the LD_{50} of a hydroethanolic fluid extract (1:1) was 6 g/kg [4].

Boldine showed no genotoxic potential in the SOS chromotest or the Ames mutagenicity test and did not induce mutations in haploid *Saccharomyces cerevisiae* cells [48]. When tested *in vitro* on human peripheral blood lymphocytes or *in vivo* in mice (analysis of bone marrow cells), boldine did not induce a statistically significant increase in the frequency of chromosomal aberrations or sister-chromatid exchanges [49].

Groups of pregnant rats treated orally with 500 mg or 800 mg of a hydroethanolic dry extract of boldo leaf daily, or 500 mg or 800 mg of boldine daily, on either days 1-5 or days 7-12 of pregnancy, were compared with control groups on day 19 of gestation. Doses of 500 mg produced no fetal toxicity but the extract and boldine at 800 mg/kg, in both the days 1-5 and 7-12 groups, led to a low level of fetal toxicity and malformations of the implant and viable fetus [45].

REGULATORY STATUS

Medicines

UK	Accepted for general sale, internal or external use. Maximum dose: 1.5 g [46].
France	Accepted for specified indications [41].
Germany	Commission E monograph published, with approved uses [42].

Food

USA	Permitted as flavouring in alcoholic beverages only (21 CFR 172.510) [50].
Council of Europe	Permitted as flavouring, category N3 [51].

REFERENCES

Current Pharmacopoeial Monographs

Ph. Eur. Boldo Leaf

Literature References

1. Vogel H, Razmilic I, Muñoz M, Doll U and San Martin J. Studies of Genetic Variation of Essential Oil and Alkaloid Content in Boldo (*Peumus boldus*). *Planta Medica* 1999, **65**, 90-91.
2. Hughes DW, Genest K and Skakum W. Alkaloids of *Peumus boldus*. Isolation of (+)-Reticuline and Isoboldine. *J. Pharm. Sci.* 1968, **57**, 1023-1025.
3. Rüegger A. Neue Alkaloide aus *Peumus boldus* Molina [New alkaloids from *Peumus boldus* Molina]. *Helv. Chim. Acta.* 1959, **42**, 754-762 [GERMAN].
4. Lévy-Appert-Collin M-C and Lévy J. Sur quelques préparations galéniques de feuilles de boldo (*Peumus boldus* Monimiacées) [Several galenic preparations from leaves

of boldo (*Peumus boldus*, Monimiaceae)]. *J. Pharm. Belg.* 1977, **32**, 13-22 [FRENCH/English summary].
5. Van Hulle C, Braeckman P and Van Severen R. Influence of the preparation technique on the boldine content of boldo dry extract. *J. Pharm. Belg.* 1983, **38**, 97-100.
6. Hughes DW, Genest K and Skakum W. Alkaloids of *Peumus boldus*. Isolation of Laurotetanine and Laurolitsine. *J. Pharm. Sci.* 1968, **57**, 1619-1620.
7. Miraldi E, Ferri S, Franchi GG and Giorgi G. *Peumus boldus* essential oil: new constituents and comparison of oils from leaves of different origin. *Fitoterapia* 1996, **67**, 227-230.
8. Montes Guyot MA, Wilkomirsky T and Valenzuela L. Aceite esencial de hojas de boldo (*Peumus boldus* Mol.). Rendimiento y variación estacional [Essential oil of boldo leaf (*Peumus boldus* Mol.). Yield and seasonal variation]. *An. Real Acad. Farm.* 1980, **46**, 325-334 [SPANISH/English summary].
9. Bruns K and Köhler M. Über die Zusammensetzung des Boldoblätteröls [The composition of boldo leaf oil]. *Parfüm. Kosmet.* 1974, **55**, 225-227 [GERMAN/English summary].
10. Vila R, Valenzuela L, Bello H, Cañigueral S, Montes M and Adzet T. Composition and Antimicrobial Activity of the Essential Oil of *Peumus boldus* leaves. *Planta Medica* 1999, **65**, 178-179.
11. Krug H and Borkowski B. Neue Flavonol-Glykoside aus den Blättern von *Peumus boldus* Molina [New flavonol glycosides from the leaves of *Peumus boldus* Molina]. *Pharmazie* 1965, **20**, 692-698 [GERMAN].
12. Krug H and Borkowski B. Flavonoidverbindungen in den Blättern von *Peumus boldus* Molina [Flavonoid compounds in the leaves of *Peumus boldus* Molina]. *Naturwissenschaften* 1965, **52**, 161 [GERMAN].
13. Bombardelli E, Martinelli EM and Mustich G. A new flavonol glycoside from *Peumus boldus*. *Fitoterapia* 1976, **47**, 3-5.
14. De Orsi D, Gagliardi L, Manna F and Tonelli D. HPLC Analysis of Boldine in Pharmaceuticals. *Chromatographia* 1997, **44**, 619-622.
15. Pietta P, Mauri P, Manera E and Ceva P. Determination of isoquinoline alkaloids from *Peumus boldus* by high-performance liquid chromatography. *J. Chromatogr.* 1988, **457**, 442-445.
16. Boldo folium. In: Pharmacopoea Helvetica VII (1991). This monograph was superseded by the current European Pharmacopoeia monograph on Boldo leaf.
17. Speisky H, Squella JA and Núnez-Vergara LJ. Activity of Boldine on Rat Ileum. *Planta Medica* 1991, **57**, 519-522.
18. Jiménez I, Garrido A, Bannach R, Gotteland M and Speisky H. Protective Effects of Boldine against Free Radical-induced Erythrocyte Lysis. *Phytotherapy Res.* 2000, **14**, 339-343.
19. Bannach R, Valenzuela A, Cassels BK, Núnez-Vergara LJ and Speisky H. Cytoprotective and antioxidant effects of boldine on *tert*-butyl hydroperoxide-induced damage to isolated hepatocytes. *Cell. Biol. Toxicol.* 1996, **12**, 89-100.
20. Lanhers MC, Joyeux M, Soulimani R, Fleurentin J, Sayag M, Mortier F et al. Hepatoprotective and Anti-Inflammatory Effects of a Traditional Medicinal Plant of Chile, *Peumus boldus*. *Planta Medica* 1991, **57**, 110-115.
21. Cederbaum AI, Kukielka E and Speisky H. Inhibition of rat liver microsomal lipid peroxidation by boldine. *Biochem. Pharmacol.* 1992, **44**, 1765-1772.
22. Kringstein P and Cederbaum AI. Boldine prevents human liver microsomal lipid peroxidation and inactivation of cytochrome P4502E1. *Free Rad. Biol. Med.* 1995, **18**, 559-563.
23. Speisky H, Cassels BK, Lissi EA and Videla LA. Antioxidant properties of the alkaloid boldine in systems undergoing lipid peroxidation and enzyme inactivation. *Biochem. Pharmacol.* 1991, **41**, 1575-1581.
24. Reiniger IW, da Silva CR, Felzenszwalb I, de Mattos JCP, de Oliveira JF, da Silva Dantas FJ *et al.* Boldine action against the stannous chloride effect. *J. Ethnopharmacol.* 1999, **68**, 345-348.
25. Chen K-S, Ko F-N, Teng C-M ands Wu Y-C. Antiplatelet and Vasorelaxing Actions of Some Aporphinoids. *Planta Medica* 1996, **62**, 133-136.
26. Delso Jimeno JL. Coleréticos y colagogos: estudio farmacologico de la hoja del boldo [Choleretics and cholagogues: pharmacological study of boldo leaf]. *Anales. Inst. Farmacol. Española.* 1956, **5**, 395-441 [SPANISH].
27. Pirtkien R, Surke E and Seybold G. Vergleichende Untersuchungen über die choleretische Wirkung verschiedener Arzneimittel bei der Ratte [Comparative studies on the choleretic effect of various drugs in the rat]. *Med. Welt* 1960, **33**, 1417-1422 [GERMAN].
28. Böhm K. Untersuchungen über choleretische Wirkungen einiger Arzneipflanzen [Investigations on choleretic effects of some medicinal plants]. *Arzneim.-Forsch./Drug Res.* 1959, **9**, 376-378 [GERMAN/English summary].
29. Kreitmair H. Pharmakologische Wirkung des Alkaloids aus *Peumus boldus* Molina [Pharmacological effect of the alkaloids from *Peumus boldus* Molina]. *Pharmazie* 1952, **7**, 507-511 [GERMAN].
30. Borkowski B, Desperak-Naciazek A, Obojska K and Szmal Z. The effect of some aporphine alkaloids on bile secretion in rats. *Diss. Pharm. Pharmacol.* 1966, **18**, 455-465 [POLISH/English summary].
31. Magistretti MJ. Remarks on the Pharmacological Examination of Plant Extracts. *Fitoterapia* 1980, **51**, 67-79.
32. Lanhers MC, Fleurentin J, Rolland A and Vinche A. Activité anti-inflammatoire d'un extrait de *Peumus boldus* Molina (Monimiaceae) [Anti-inflammatory activity of an extract from *Peumus boldus* Molina (Monimiaceae)]. *Phytotherapy (Paris)* 1992, **38/39**, 12-13 [FRENCH].
33. Backhouse N, Delporte C, Givernau M, Cassels BK, Valenzuela A and Speisky H. Anti-inflammatory and antipyretic effects of boldine. *Agents Actions* 1994, **42**, 114-117.
34. Gotteland M, Jimenez I, Brunser O, Guzman L, Romero S, Cassels BK and Speisky H. Protective Effect of Boldine in Experimental Colitis. *Planta Medica* 1997, **63**, 311-315.
35. Gotteland M, Espinoza JM, Cassels BK and Speisky HC. Effect of a dry boldo extract on oro-cecal intestinal transit time in healthy volunteers. *Rev. Méd. Chile* 1995, **123**, 955-960 [SPANISH/English summary].
36. Jiménez I and Speisky H. Biological Disposition of Boldine: *in vitro* and *in vivo* studies. *Phytotherapy Res.* 2000, **14**, 254-260.
37. Genest K and Hughes DW. Natural products in Canadian pharmaceuticals. II. *Peumus boldus. Can. J. Pharm. Sci.* 1968, **3**, 84-90.
38. Peumus. In: *British Herbal Pharmacopoeia 1983.* ISBN 0-903032-07-4. Bournemouth: British Herbal Medicine Association, 1983.
39. Chevallier A. Boldo. In: *The Encyclopedia of Medicinal Plants.* ISBN 0-7513-0314-3. London-New York-Stuttgart: Dorling Kindersley, 1996:244.
40. Bartram T. Boldo. In: *Encyclopaedia of Herbal Medicine.* ISBN 0-9515984-1-4. Christchurch, UK: Grace Publishers, 1995:64.
41. Boldo. In: *Médicaments à base de plantes.* ISBN 2-911473-02-7. Saint-Denis Cedex, France: Agence du Médicament, 1998.
42. Boldo folium. German Commission E Monograph published in: Bundesanzeiger No. 76 of 23 April 1987; amended in Bundesanzeiger No. 164 of 1 September 1990.
43. Weiss RF and Fintelmann V. *Peumus boldus*, Boldo. In: *Herbal Medicine, 2nd ed.* (translated from the 9th German edition of *Lehrbuch der Phytotherapie*). ISBN 3-13-126332-6. Stuttgart-New York: Thieme, 2000: 122.
44. Stahl-Biskup E and Henke D. Boldoblätter. In: Hartke K, Hartke H, Mutschler E, Rücker G and Wichtl M, editors. *Kommentar zum Europäischen Arzneibuch [Commentary on the European Pharmacopoeia]*. Stuttgart: Wissenschaftliche Verlagsgesellschaft, 2001 (14. Lfg.):B 47/5 [GERMAN].
45. de Almeida ER, Melo AM and Xavier H. Toxicological Evaluation of the Hydro-alcohol Extract of the Dry Leaves of *Peumus boldus* and Boldine in Rats. *Phytotherapy Res.*

2000, **14**, 99-102.
46. Boldo. In: UK Statutory Instrument 1990 No. 1129. The Medicines (Products Other Than Veterinary Drugs) (General Sale List) Amendment Order 1990. Schedule 1, Table A.
47. Tisserand R and Balacs T. Boldo. In: *Essential Oil Safety - A Guide for Health Care Professionals.* ISBN 0-443-05260-3. Edinburgh: Churchill-Livingstone, 1995:123.
48. Moreno PRH, Vargas VMF, Andrade HHR, Henriques AT and Henriques JAP. Genotoxicity of the boldine aporphine alkaloid in prokaryotic and eukaryotic organisms. *Mutation Res.* 1991, **260**, 145-152.
49. Tavares DC and Takahashi CS. Evaluation of the genotoxic potential of the alkaloid boldine in mammalian cell systems in vitro and in vivo. *Mutation Res.* 1994, **321**, 139-145.
50. Boldus (boldo) leaves. In: Section 172.510 of USA Code of Federal Regulations, Title 21, Food and Drugs, Parts 170 to 199. Revised as of April 1, 2000.
51. Peumus boldus Molina, leaves. In: *Flavouring Substances and Natural Sources of Flavourings, 3rd ed.* ISBN 2-7160-0081-6. Strasbourg: Council of Europe, 1981.

REGULATORY GUIDELINES FROM OTHER EU COUNTRIES

FRANCE

Médicaments à base de plantes [41]: Boldo, feuille.

Therapeutic indications accepted

Oral use
Traditionally used to facilitate urinary and digestive elimination functions.
Traditionally used as a choleretic or cholagogue.

GERMANY

Commission E monograph [42]: Boldo folium (Boldoblätter).

Uses
Mild spasmodic disorders of the gastrointestinal tract; dyspeptic complaints.

Contraindications
Obstruction of the bile duct, severe liver illnesses. In cases of gallstones, to be used only after consultation with a doctor.

Side effects
None known.

Interactions with other drugs
None known.

Dosage
Unless otherwise prescribed, average daily dose: 3.0 g of the drug; equivalent preparations.

Note: On account of the ascaridole content, neither the essential oil nor distillates must be used.

Mode of administration
Comminuted drug for infusions and other practically ascaridole-free preparations for internal use.

Actions
Spasmolytic, choleretic, increases secretion of gastric juice.

BROOM TOP

Leguminosae-Papilionoideae

Cytisi scoparii herba

Synonyms: Scoparium, Scotch broom top, common broom top.

Definition

Broom Top consists of the dried flowering tops of *Cytisus scoparius* (L.) Link [*Sarothamnus scoparius* (L.) Wimm. ex W.D.J. Koch].

The part of the plant defined in pharmacopoeias varies from one country to another: in the BHP, dried flowering tops (as above); in the DAC, aerial parts collected in spring or late autumn; the Pharmacopée Française includes only dried flowers.

The name of the Plantagenet dynasty of kings, who ruled England for three centuries commencing with the reign of Henry II in 1154, is derived from broom (medieval name: *planta genista*, French: *genêt à balai*), which had been used as a heraldic device in the badge of Brittany from an earlier period. Geoffrey of Anjou, Henry's father, wore a sprig of broom on his helmet when going into battle and broom is depicted on the Great Seal of Richard I [1,2].

CONSTITUENTS

☐ ***Quinolizidine alkaloids***, 0.18-0.55% of the dry weight of tops during the flowering period, but only 0.04-0.06% in dried flowers [3]; for dried aerial parts (not limited to the flowering period) the DAC minimum is 0.7% total alkaloids. Sparteine is the main alkaloid, usually 76-98% of the total, together with 11,12-dehydrosparteine, 17-oxosparteine and others [3,4].

Earlier investigations reported varying amounts of total and individual alkaloids [5-7], and indeed the total alkaloid content of young shoots fluctuates considerably during the vegetation period; it can be 4- to 10-fold higher at the end (July onwards) than at the beginning (April-May) [3].

☐ ***Aromatic amines*** Tyramine, 0.005-0.04% of the dry weight of tops during the flowering period (but up to 0.28% in dried flowers) [3], and also 3-hydroxytyramine (oxytyramine) [4,5,8].

☐ ***Flavonoids***, 0.2-0.6%, of several types: the flavone C-glycosides scoparin [9-11], 6″-O-acetylscoparin [12] and vitexin [9]; the flavonol O-glycosides isoquercitrin, astragalin, spiraeoside, and other quercetin and kaempferol derivatives [9,10]; the isoflavones genistein [13-15] and, in the flowers, orobol 3′-methyl ether and its 7-glucoside [15].

☐ ***Essential oil*** from fresh flowers contained *cis*-3-hexen-1-ol, 1-octen-3-ol, benzyl and phenylethyl alcohols, phenol, cresols, guaiacol, eugenol, isovaleric acid, benzoic acid and *n*-paraffins [16].

☐ ***Other constituents*** Tannins [4] and, in the flowers, terephthalic acid dimethyl ester [17], caffeic and *p*-coumaric acids, and the coumarin esculetin [16].

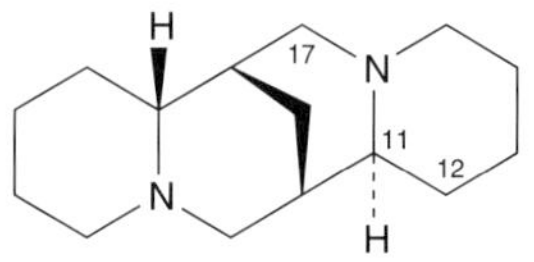

Sparteine

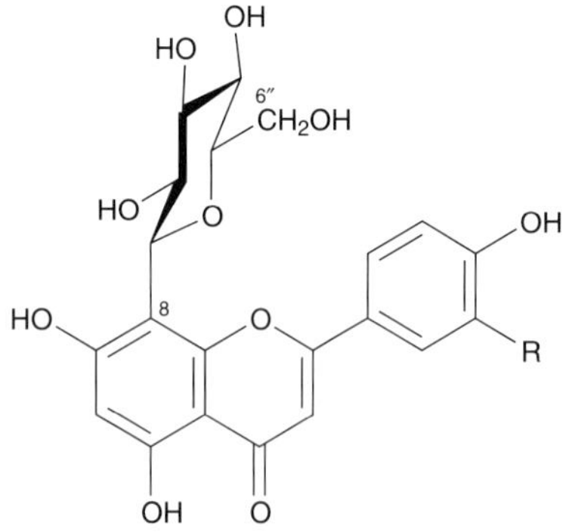

Scoparin R = OCH_3
Vitexin R = H

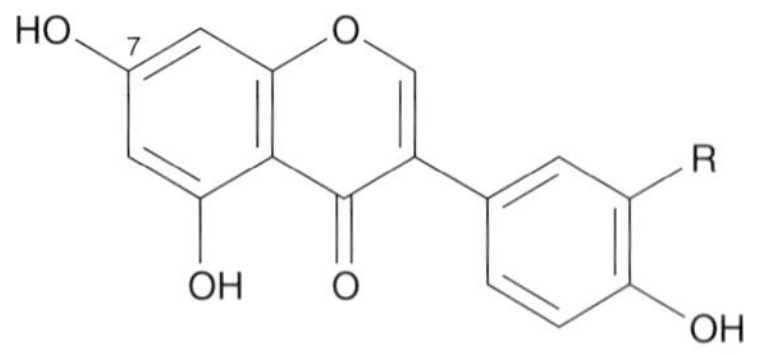

Genistein R = H
Orobol 3-methyl ether R = OCH_3

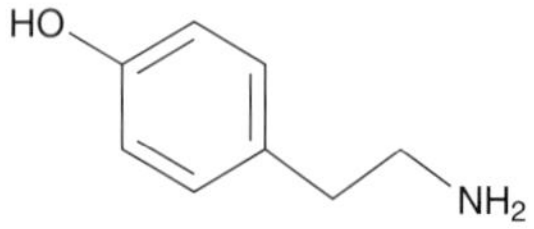

Tyramine

Published Assay Methods

Quinolizidine alkaloids and tyramine by GC and GC-MS [3]. Total alkaloids by spectrophotometry [DAC]. Simultaneous determination of sparteine and its 2-dehydro and 5-dehydro metabolites in urine by HPLC [18].

PHARMACOLOGY

Not many pharmacological studies have been published specifically on broom top preparations. However, much of the activity of broom top is related to its alkaloid content and considerable research has been carried out on sparteine; for a review see Seeger and Neumann [19].

Sparteine has an antiarrhythmic effect on the heart and an oxytocic effect on the uterus; in higher doses it has a nicotine-like action on ganglions, which it blocks after previous excitation, and a curare-like action on skeletal muscle. Its activity spectrum resembles that of quinidine, from which it is, however, differentiated in particular components of the antiarrhythmic effect. Sparteine is a class I antiarrthymic [19]; in general terms it acts on electrical conductance of the heart, slowing the transmission of impulses.

Tyramine and 3-hydroxytyramine have hypertensive and peripheral vasoconstrictive effects, but only after parenteral administration. Whether these compounds contribute to the efficacy of broom after oral intake is not clear [9].

In vitro

Sparteine stimulated the amplitude, rate and/or tone of contractions in isolated rabbit uterus with a minimal concentration of 1:100,000; the magnitude of response was greatest in uteri from pregnant rabbits [20].

In vivo

Sparteine showed antiarrhythmic activity in experimental cardiac arrhythmias of various origins and localisations: sinus arrhythmia in unanaesthetized dogs, ventricular tachycardia and ventricular flutter provoked in rats by intravenous infusion of aconitine, and ischaemic ventricular arrhythmias in conscious dogs following partial coronary artery occlusion. In the conscious normotensive dog with normal heart rate, sparteine had a positive chronotropic action without decreasing blood pressure [21].

Pharmacological studies in humans

At one time sparteine was used in maternity hospitals as an oxytocic and a number of studies were carried out during the early 1960s to evaluate its effectiveness in inducing labour. In one study sparteine sulphate was given to 640 patients for comparison with a control group of 200. The usual dose was 150 mg intramuscularly every hour, but occasionally it was given every 20 minutes. The number of doses given ranged from 1 to 11 (sic) with an average of 1.9. If sparteine was given during the first stage of labour, the length of nulliparous labours was reduced by 2.7 hours and multiparous by 0.4 hours. When given before labour, labour was shortened in nulliparas by 5.6 hours and multiparas by 2.7 hours. No deleterious effects on the babies were observed in that study [22]. However, severe complications and in some cases fatalities of mother or baby associated with administration of sparteine in childbirth led to abandonment of this use by the mid-1960s [19].

Pharmacokinetics

After oral administration, sparteine is almost completely absorbed. In 'good metabolizers' it is metabolized in the liver and eliminated in the urine as 2-dehydrosparteine (mainly), 5-dehydrosparteine and unchanged sparteine (15-20%); in 'poor metabolizers' most of the sparteine is eliminated unchanged in the urine. The rate and type of elimination varies widely according to the individual and sparteine is used in human diagnostic tests of liver function with respect to the activity of the cytochrome P450 isoenzyme [19]. The incidence of 'poor metabolizers' has been found to be 5-8% in Caucasians, 2-4% in Japanese, 4.1% in South African Barakwena subjects and none in Ghanaians. Genetic deficiencies in the oxidation of sparteine appear to be the reason for the severe effects multiple dosage generates in some individuals [18].

CLINICAL STUDIES

None published on mono-preparations of broom top.

THERAPEUTICS

Broom top is unsuitable for self-medication; it should be used only under professional advice [23,24].

Actions

Antiarrhythmic [9,19], mild diuretic [23-28] and oxytocic [20,28].

Also stated to be a peripheral vasoconstrictor [23,25] and antihaemorrhagic [23-25].

Indications

None adequately substantiated by pharmacological or clinical studies.

Uses based on experience or tradition

Functional cardiac and circulatory disorders [23-

25,29,30]; as a mild diuretic [26,28] in cardiac oedema [23,25]; to inhibit blood loss during menstruation [23,25] or after childbirth [24].

Contraindications
Pregnancy [23-25,28] and lactation; high blood pressure [23-25].

Side effects
None known.

Interactions with other drugs
Concomitant use of monoamine oxidase (MAO)-inhibitors should be avoided [29,31], since tyramine is hypertensive. However, the tyramine content is very low in dried top (less than 0.05%); even in dried flower it was found to be less than 0.3% [3], compared to 'over 2%' suggested in the Commission E monograph [31].

Dosage
Three times daily: 300-500 mg of dried top or equivalent hydroethanolic extracts; preparations equivalent to 2-4 mg of sparteine [29,32].

Higher doses of dried top or herb, or equivalent aqueous or hydroethanolic preparations, are also recommended in the literature: single dose, 1-2 g [25]; daily dose, 3-8 g [30] or 6-12 g [23]. Single doses recommended in BPC 1949 for Concentrated Decoction of Scoparium or Concentrated Infusion of Broom were equivalent to 3-6 g of dried top [26].

SAFETY

The oral LD_{50} of sparteine has been determined as 350 mg/kg in male (510 mg/kg in female) mice, with death after 1-5 hours [19]. Sparteine sulphate administered intraperitoneally to guinea pigs was toxic at 27-55 mg/kg, the minimum lethal dose being 42-55 mg/kg [20].

As the main active constituent of broom top, sparteine also presents the greatest risk since sparteine levels in the crude drug are quite variable, the rate of elimination varies widely according to the individual and a proportion of 'poor metabolisers' (unidentifiable without diagnostic testing) exist in the population. The use of preparations with known sparteine content, and only under professional advice, is therefore prudent.

To put dosage into perspective, a single dose of 150 mg of sparteine sulphate pentahydrate, in earlier days administered intramuscularly to induce labour, was equivalent to 83 mg of sparteine - and additional doses at 2-hour intervals up to a total of 332 mg of sparteine were considered safe up to the 1960s [22]. In contrast, the BPC 1949 maximum single dose (equivalent to 6 g of dried top) [26] contained no more than 33 mg of sparteine. Daily dose levels recommended for currently marketed German products [32] provide up to about 11 mg of sparteine.

REGULATORY STATUS

Medicines

UK	No licences issued for products containing broom top.
France	Accepted for specified indications [27].
Germany	Two Commission E monographs published: approved uses for broom herb [29]; therapeutic use of broom flower not justifiable [31].

Food

USA	Designated by the FDA as an unsafe herb, which should not be used in foods, beverages or drugs [33].
Council of Europe	Permitted as flavouring, category N3 [34].

REFERENCES

Current Pharmacopoeial Monographs

Ph. Fr.	Genêt à balai (flowers only)
DAC	Besenginsterkraut (aerial parts)
BHP	Broom Top

Literature References

1. Strong R. The First Plantagenet. In: The Story of Britain. ISBN 1-85681-099-2. London: Hutchinson, 1996:63-69.
2. Grieve M (edited by Leyel CF). Broom. In: *A Modern Herbal* (first published 1931; revised 1973). ISBN 1-85501-249-9. London: Tiger Books International, 1994:124-127.
3. Gresser G, Witte L, Dedkov VP and Czygan F-C. A Survey of Quinolizidine Alkaloids and Phenylethylamine Tyramine in *Cytisus scoparius* (Leguminosae) from Different Origins. *Z. Naturforsch.* 1996, **51c**, 791-801.
4. Gresser G. Der Besenginster - *Cytisus scoparius* (L.) Link. Portrait einer Arzneipflanze [Broom - *Cytisus scoparius* (L.) Link. Portrait of a medicinal plant]. *Z. Phytotherapie* 1996, **17**, 320-330 [GERMAN/English summary].
5. Murakoshi I, Yamashita Y, Ohmiya S and Otomasu H. (–)-3β,13α-Dihydroxylupanine from *Cytisus scoparius*. *Phytochemistry* 1986, **25**, 521-524.
6. Wink M, Witte L and Hartmann T. Quinolizidine Alkaloid Composition of Plants and of Photomixotrophic Cell Suspension Cultures of Sarothamnus scoparius and Orobanche rapum-genistae. *Planta Medica* 1981, **43**, 342-352.
7. Wink M, Hartmann T, Witte L and Rheinheimer J. Interrelationship between Quinolizidine Alkaloid Producing Legumes and Infesting Insects: Exploitation of the Alkaloid-Containing Phloem Sap of *Cytisus scoparius* by the Broom Aphid *Aphis cytisorum*. *Z. Naturforsch.* 1982, **37c**, 1081-1086.
8. Jaminet F. Contribution à l'étude biochimique du genêt à balais (*Sarothamnus scoparius* L.). I. Les amines vasoconstrictives [Contribution to the biochemical study of broom (*Sarothamnus scoparius* L.). I. The vasoconstrictive amines]. *J. Pharm. Belg.* 1953, **8**, 23-35 [FRENCH].

9. Gresser G. Der Besenginster. Arznei- und Giftpflanze, Plantagenet und Teufelsbesen [Broom. Medicinal and poisonous plant, Plantagenet and devil's broom]. *Dtsch. Apoth. Ztg.* 1998, **138**, 807-813 [GERMAN].
10. Brum-Bousquet M and Delaveau P. Sur les flavonoïdes de *Sarothamnus scoparius* et de *S. patiens.* Étude particulière des fleurs [The flavonoids of *Sarothamnus scoparius* and *S. patiens.* A study particularly of the flowers]. *Plantes Méd. Phytothér.* 1981, **15**, 201-209 [FRENCH/English summary].
11. Hörhammer L, Wagner H and Beyersdorff P. Über die Struktur des Scoparins und weitere Vorkommen von C-Glykosiden der Flavon-Reihe [The structure of scoparin and further occurrence of C-glycosides in the flavone series]. *Naturwissenschaften* 1962, **49**, 392-393 [GERMAN].
12. Brum-Bousquet M, Tillequin F and Paris R-R. Sur les C-Flavonosides de Sarothamnus scoparius. Isolement d'un nouveau composé, le 6''-O-acétylscoparoside [Flavone C-glycosides of *Sarothamnus scoparius.* Isolation of a new compound, 6''-O-acetylscoparin]. *Lloydia* 1977, **40**, 591-592 [FRENCH/English summary].
13. Harborne JB. Chemosystematics of the Leguminosae. Flavonoid and isoflavonoid patterns in the tribe Genisteae. *Phytochemistry* 1969, **8**, 1449-1456.
14. Harborne JB. Distribution of Flavonoids in the Leguminosae. In: Harborne JB, Boulter D and Turner BL. *Chemotaxonomy of the Leguminosae.* ISBN 0-12-324652-0. London-New York: Academic Press, 1971:31-71.
15. Viscardi P, Reynaud J and Raynaud J. A New Isoflavone Glucoside from the Flowers of *Cytisus scoparius* Link. (Leguminosae). *Pharmazie* 1984, **39**, 781.
16. Kurihara T and Kikuchi M. Studies on the constituents of flowers. XIII. On the components of the flower of *Cytisus scoparius* Link. *Yakugaku Zasshi* 1980, **100**, 1054-1057 [JAPANESE]; through *Chem. Abstr.* 1980, **93**, 235183.
17. Hörhammer L, Wagner H and Krämer-Heydweiler D. Terephthalsäuredimethylester in den Blüten von Sarothamnus scoparius L. [Terephthalic acid dimethyl ester in the flowers of Sarothamnus scoparius L.]. *Naturwissenschaften* 1966, **53**, 584 [GERMAN].
18. Moncrieff J. Simultaneous determination of sparteine and its 2-dehydro and 5-dehydro metabolites in urine by high-performance liquid chromatography with electrochemical detection. *J. Chromatogr.* 1990, **529**, 194-200.
19. Seeger R and Neumann H-G. DAZ-Giftlexikon: Spartein [Deutsche Apotheker Zeitung (German Pharmacists' Journal) - Poison Lexicon: Sparteine]. *Dtsch. Apoth. Ztg.* 1992, **132**, 1577-1581 [GERMAN].
20. Ligon EW. The action of lupine alkaloids on the motility of the isolated rabbit uterus. *J. Pharmacol. Exptl. Therap.* 1941, **73**, 151-158.
21. Raschack M. Cardiovascular Effects of Sparteine and Sparteine Derivatives. *Arzneim.-Forsch./Drug Res.* 1974, **24**, 753-759 [GERMAN/English summary].
22. Todd RG, editor. Sparteine Sulphate. Extra Pharmacopoeia: Martindale, 25th edition. London: Pharmaceutical Press, 1967:592-593.
23. Mills S. Broom. In: *The A-Z of Modern Herbalism.* ISBN 0-7225-1882-X. Wellingborough, UK: Thorsons, 1989:44-45.
24. Chevallier A. Broom. In: *The Encyclopedia of Medicinal Plants.* ISBN 0-7513-0314-3. London-New York-Stuttgart: Dorling Kindersley, 1996:265.
25. Scoparium. In: *British Herbal Pharmacopoeia 1983.* ISBN 0-903032-07-4. Bournemouth: British Herbal Medicine Association, 1983.
26. Pharmaceutical Society of Great Britain. Scoparium (and preparations from it). In: British Pharmaceutical Codex 1949. London: Pharmaceutical Press, 1949: 792, 1093-1094 and 1156-1157.
27. Genêt à balai, fleur [Broom, flower]. In: *Médicaments à base de plantes.* ISBN 2-911473-02-7. Saint-Denis Cedex, France: Agence du Médicament, 1998.
28. Reynolds JEF, editor. Scoparium. In: Martindale - The Extra Pharmacopoeia, 31st edition. London: Royal Pharmaceutical Society, 1996.
29. Cytisi scoparii herba. German Commission E Monograph published in: Bundesanzeiger No. 11 of 17 January 1991.
30. Braun R, editor. Besenginsterkraut [Broom herb]. In: Standardzulassungen für Fertigarzneimittel - Text und Kommentar. Stuttgart: Deutscher Apotheker Verlag, Frankfurt: Govi-Verlag, 1988.
31. Cytisi scoparii flos. German Commission E Monograph published in: Bundesanzeiger No. 11 of 17 January 1991.
32. Rote Liste Service GmbH, editor. Cefacor and Spartiol®. In: Rote Liste 2001. Arzneimittelverzeichnis für Deutschland (einschließlich EU-Zulassungen und bestimmter Medizinprodukte [Red List. Index of medicines for Germany (including EU-authorizations and clearly medicinal products]. Aulendorf: Editio Cantor Verlag, 2001: Section 09 A.1. [GERMAN]
33. Anon. Unsafe Herbs. *FDA Consumer* 1983, (October), 8-10.
34. Cytisus scoparius Link (Sarothamnus scoparius Koch), whole plant. In: *Flavouring Substances and Natural Sources of Flavourings, 3rd ed.* ISBN 2-7160-0081-6. Strasbourg: Council of Europe, 1981.

REGULATORY GUIDELINES FROM OTHER EU COUNTRIES

FRANCE

Médicaments à base de plantes [27]: Genêt à balai, fleur [Broom, flower].

Therapeutic indications accepted

Oral use
Traditionally used to facilitate urinary and digestive elimination functions.
Traditionally used to promote the renal elimination of water.

GERMANY

Commission E monograph [29]: Cytisi scoparii herba (Besenginsterkraut = broom herb).

Components of the drug

Broom herb consists of the aerial parts of *Cytisus scoparius* (L.) Link and its preparations in effective dosage. The drug contains alkaloids, principally sparteine. Preparations contain not more than 1 mg of sparteine per ml.

Uses

Functional cardiac and circulatory disorders.

Contraindications

None known.

Side effects

None known.

Interactions with other drugs

Due to its tyramine content, taking the drug at the same time as treatment with MAO-inhibitors can lead to a blood pressure crisis.

Dosage

Unless otherwise prescribed, daily dose: hydroethanolic extracts equivalent to 1-1.5 g of the drug.

Mode of administration

Hydroethanolic extracts for internal use.

Broom Top

Commission E monograph [31]: Cytisi scoparii flos (Besenginsterblüten = broom flower).

Components of the drug
Broom flower consists of the flowers of *Cytisus scoparius* (Linné) Link [syn. *Sarothamnus scoparius* (Linné) Wimm. ex W.D.J Koch] and its preparations.

Pharmacological Properties, Pharmacokinetics, Toxicology
The drug can contain over 2% of tyramine. It contains small amounts of alkaloids, principally sparteine.

Tyramine acts indirectly as a sympathomimetic, vasoconstrictive and hypertensive.

Sparteine has a negative inotropic and negative chronotropic effect. Due to the very low amount of sparteine, corresponding effects would not be expected from use of the (crude) drug.

Clinical Data
Medical-clinical reports and other literature on medicinal experience in the use of broom flower are not available.

This is followed by a list of combination products (none with less than 5 components) in which broom flower is, or was, used in Germany and a list of claimed uses of the combination products.

Risks
Contraindications: treatment with MAO-inhibitors; high blood pressure.

Side effects
None known.

Precautions for use
None known.

Medicinal and other interactions
Due to its tyramine content, taking the drug at the same time as treatment with MAO-inhibitors can lead to a blood pressure crisis.

Dosage and mode of administration
The drug is used in tea mixtures and extract preparations.

Overdosage
Nothing known.

Special warnings
None known.

Effects on driving and operation of machines
None known.

Assessment
Due to inadequately substantiated efficacy and in view of possible interactions, therapeutic use is not justifiable.

There are no objections to use in tea mixtures as an embellishment in amounts up to 1%.

CALAMUS

Acoraceae

Calami rhizoma

Synonym: Sweet Flag Root.

Definition

Calamus consists of the dried rhizomes of *Acorus calamus* L. var. *americanus* (Raf.) Wulff or *A. calamus* L. var. *calamus* (= var. *vulgaris*), free from roots and leaf bases, peeled or unpeeled.

Acorus calamus is a reed-like, semi-aquatic, perennial herb, 0.5-2 metres in height, widely distributed in Europe, Asia and North America. Three varieties can be distinguished taxonomically since the species exhibits polyploidy (differing numbers of chromosomes) [1]:

- *Acorus calamus* L. var. *americanus* (Raf.) Wulff, a diploid variety (2n = 24) occurring mainly in North America and to some extent in Siberia.
- *Acorus calamus* L. var. *calamus*, a triploid variety (2n = 36) occurring mainly in Europe but to some extent in the Himalayan region of India and, introduced by European settlers, in North America. It is cultivated in Eastern European countries and the Netherlands [2].
- *Acorus calamus* L. var. *angustatus* Bess., a tetraploid variety (2n = 48) found in subtropical/tropical South and South-East Asia, and in temperate Far East Asia.

The presence or absence of the phenylpropanoid β-asarone (= *cis*-isoasarone), a known carcinogen, is therapeutically and toxicologically important. Stahl and Keller [3-5] classified four types of calamus on the basis of the β-asarone content of the rhizomes, which increases with ploidy.

Type I: Diploid, β-asarone-free.
Type II: Triploid, β-asarone content of about 0.3% on average.
Type III: Tetraploid, β-asarone content 2-3% (from the former USSR and Korea).
Type IV: Tetraploid, β-asarone content 4-8% (from India, Pakistan and the Philippines).

In view of the carcinogenicity of β-asarone, monographs on calamus in official pharmacopoeias limit the β-asarone content of the dried rhizome to 0.5%, which can be met only by rhizome from diploid and some triploid plants. With its lack of β-asarone and higher spasmolytic activity, rhizome from diploid *Acorus calamus* L. var. *americanus* (Raf.) Wulff is preferable for use in phytomedicines [6]. In practice, however, eastern European countries continue to be the major source of calamus for the European market.

CONSTITUENTS

☐ ***Essential oil***, 4.7-6.0% in rhizomes of North American diploid plants, 1.7-4.9% in European triploid plants and 2.8-9.3% in Asian tetraploid plants [4,7] (Ph. Helv. and ÖAB min. 2.0% V/m).

The main constituents reported in steam distilled oils are:
North American diploid Shyobunones (13-45%), principally 2,6-diepi-shyobunone [8,9], hydrocarbon (mainly sesqui-) terpenes (15%), acorenone (13%), acorones (10%), pre-isocalamenediol (7%) and other mono- and sesquiterpenes [9].
European triploid Shyobunone and derivatives (3.6-32%), β-asarone (= *cis*-isoasarone, 3.6-19%) [2,8,10], acorenone (8.1-8.4%) [2,10], acorone and derivatives (6.9%), calamendiol (2.0%) [10], pre-isocalamendiol (1-7%) [2,10], β-gurjunene (6.7%), α-selinene (3.8%), calamusenone (3.7%) and camphor (3.1%) [2].
Indian tetraploid β-Asarone (48-84%), shyobunone and derivatives (1.4-6.2%) [2,10], α-asarone (2.7-3.7%), γ-asarone (1.0-1.4%), calamenene (0.5-1%) [10] and pre-isocalamendiol (0.9%) [2].
Japanese tetraploid β-Asarone (20-76%), *cis*-methylisoeugenol (2-49%) [11], shyobunone, epishyobunone, isoshyobunone, calamendiol, isocalamendiol [12] and other phenylpropanoids and terpenes [11].

The composition of steam-distilled calamus oils is variable, not only due to ploidy and geographic or seasonal factors, but also due to structural rearrangement of thermolabile sesquiterpenes (particularly ketones such as acoragermacrone) [12-14], which gives rise to artefacts. Gentler methods of extraction yield rather different results:
North American diploid Essential oil extracted with supercritical carbon dioxide contained acorone and isoacorone (37%), acoragermacrone (12%), acorenone (6%) and shyobunone isomers (2%) [14].
European triploid An oleoresin extracted with diethyl ether contained acorenone (18.1%), isocalamendiol (11.3%), shyobunone and derivatives

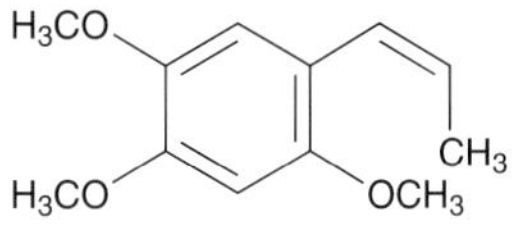

β-Asarone
(*cis*-Isoasarone)

(9.0%), β-asarone (8.2%), acorone (6.1%), isoacorone (3.3%), calamendiol (2.0%), pre-isocalamendiol (2%) and α-asarone (0.4%) [10]. Among 243 compounds detected in an ethanolic extract the main ones were acorone (5245 ppm), β-asarone (1723 ppm), calamendiol (1709 ppm), pre-isocalamendiol (1557 ppm), acorenone (1431 ppm), shyobunones (689 ppm) and camphor (619 ppm) [15].
Japanese tetraploid From oil extracted with hexane, acoragermacrone and pre-isocalamendiol were isolated by TLC. Acoragermacrone could be completely converted to shyobunone and epishyobunone by heating at 110°C [13].
☐ ***Other constituents*** include tannins (0.6-1%) [7] and starch [16]. Fatty acids (mainly oleic and linoleic acids) and sugars (fructose and glucose) have been identified in Indian rhizomes [17].

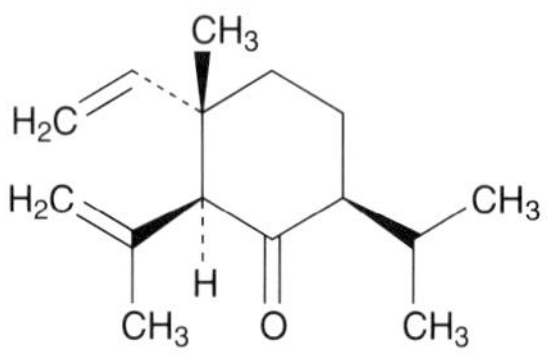

Shyobunone

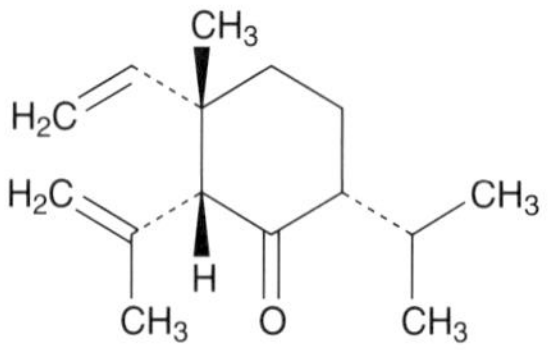

2,6-Diepi-shyobunone

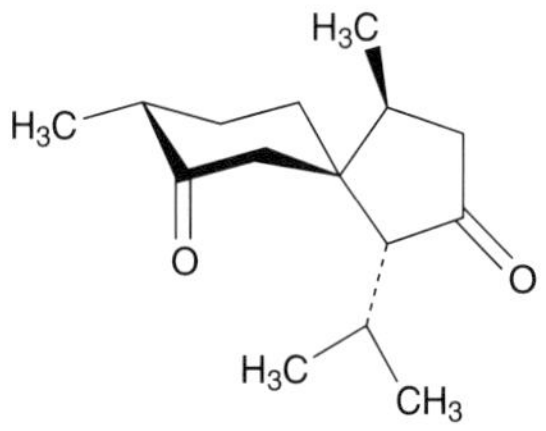

Acorone

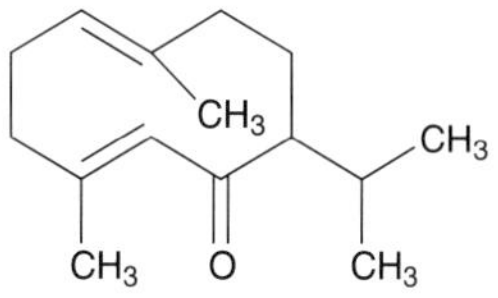

Acoragermacrone

Published Assay Methods
β-Asarone content by TLC [Ph. Helv.], spectrophotometry [ÖAB] or HPLC with fluorimetric detection [18]. Components of essential oil or extracts by GC and GC-MS [2,10,15,19].

PHARMACOLOGY

In vitro
Essential oils from calamus with various β-asarone contents were tested for their spasmolytic activity on histamine-induced contractions of isolated guinea pig ileum. The results broadly showed that the lower the β-asarone content the stronger the spasmolytic activity. Type I oil (β-asarone-free, from *Acorus calamus* L. var. *americanus*) at 10 µg/ml exhibited strong spasmolytic activity ($p<0.001$ with histamine dihydrochloride at 58 µg/ml), comparable to that of mepyramine maleate at 4 µg/ml as a standard antagonist. Type II oil (less than 10% of β-asarone, from triploid calamus) had a marked but inferior spasmolytic effect to that of β-asarone-free oil, while Type IV oil (high β-asarone content) showed no spasmolytic activity. Thus the spasmolytic activity is high in the absence of β-asarone, although it is not clear which components of the oil cause the spasmolytic effect [6].

An earlier Polish study (using native calamus) also demonstrated the spasmolytic activity of calamus oil against contractions induced by acetylcholine and other agents in isolated smooth muscle (rat intestine and uterus, rabbit intestine and aorta, cat trachea) with a potency of about one tenth of that of papaverine [20].

In vivo
Alcoholic and aqueous extracts from European calamus, administered intraperitoneally, exhibited hypothermic activity in rats and had a hypotensive effect in rabbits and cats, but showed neither anticonvulsant nor analgesic activity in rodents. The aqueous extract at doses up to 4 g/kg had a sedative effect in mice, while the alcoholic (but not the aqueous) extract potentiated the effect of narcotics and diminished the toxicity of amphetamine in mice [21,22].

Essential oil from European calamus exerted a significant depressant effect on the central nervous system. In mice it reduced spontaneous motility by 76% at 200 mg/kg ($p<0.001$), caused ptosis, had an analgesic effect, increasing response time to thermal stimuli by 166% after 2 hours at 200 mg/kg and 266% after 30 minutes at 400 mg/kg, enhanced the effect of barbiturates and potentiated the effects of morphine. The oil also had a hypothermic effect in rats and a hypotensive effect in rabbits [23].

Calamus oils of types I (no β-asarone) and II (β-asarone10%) had no effect on stress-, ethanol- or phenylbutazone-induced ulcers in rats. Type III oil (β-asarone 95%) administered orally at 50-200 mg/kg dose-dependently reduced phenylbutazone-induced ulcers by 50-60% but did not influence stress- or ethanol-induced ulcers [24].

Numerous pharmacological studies have demonstrated central depressant, sedative, anticonvulsive, hypothermic and other effects in animals of extracts from Indian calamus [25,26] and of β-asarone [27]. However, since only calamus low in, or free from, β-asarone is now acceptable, these studies are less relevant to European herbal medicine. The pharmacological effects of calamus have been summarized by Motley [28].

CLINICAL STUDIES

None published on mono-preparations of calamus.

THERAPEUTICS

Calamus should be used only under professional supervision [29].

Actions
Spasmolytic [6,20,30], carminative [6,16,29-31], aromatic bitter [16,32], digestive stimulant [29,31,32], appetite stimulant [29,32].

Indications
None adequately substantiated by pharmacological or clinical studies.

Uses based on experience or tradition
Acute and chronic dyspepsia [3,29,30], flatulence, intestinal colic [29,30], gastritis [30]; lack of appetite [29,32] and anorexia [30,32]. As a tonic for the nervous system [29].

Contraindications
Pregnancy.

Side effects
None known.

Interactions with other drugs
None known.

Dosage
Three times daily: dried rhizome, 1-3 g or as an infusion; liquid extract 1:1 in 60% alcohol, 1-3 ml; tincture 1:5 in 60% alcohol, 2-4 ml [16,30].

Excessive doses and prolonged use of calamus should be avoided.

SAFETY

In a 2-year study carried out by the United States FDA, calamus oil of the Jammu (India) variety containing 76% of β-asarone was mixed into the diet of rats at levels of 500, 1000, 2500 and 5000 ppm. Dose-related growth inhibition and degenerative changes in the liver and heart were observed at all dose levels. Malignant tumours became evident after 59 weeks at all dose levels, whereas tumours of the same type were not found in control animals [33]. A further FDA report in 1971 confirmed the carcinogenicity of β-asarone [3,34]. In other studies β-asarone has been shown to be mutagenic in the Ames test and to induce chromosome aberrations in human lymphocyte cultures after metabolic activation with rat liver microsomes [34].

To give perspective to the question of whether calamus with a relatively low β-asarone content is safe for human use it has been pointed out that β-asarone is only a weak carcinogen [3,7] and no carcinogenic effects in humans have been reported, even from use of Indian calamus with a high β-asarone content. Data on the metabolic pathway of β-asarone in humans appears to be unavailable. In a benefit-risk assessment of calamus, it was concluded that, while only β-asarone-free diploid calamus completely excludes any conceivable risk, taking a pragmatic view the use of triploid, low-asarone European calamus is justifiable on the basis of restriction of β-asarone content (as exemplified by pharmacopoeial limits) and avoidance of excessive or prolonged use [7].

The acute oral LD_{50} of calamus oil in rats has been determined as 777 mg/kg and also as 888 mg/100 g rat [22], the wide variation probably reflecting differences in β-asarone content.

REGULATORY STATUS

Medicines

UK	Accepted for general sale, internal or external use [35].
France	Not listed in *Médicaments à base de plantes* [36].
Germany	No Commission E monograph published.

Food

USA	Prohibited from use in human food (21 CFR 189.110) [37].
Council of Europe	Permitted as flavouring, category N3 [38] with β-asarone content of food and beverages limited to 0.05 mg/kg, except 0.5 mg/kg in alcoholic beverages traditionally flavoured with calamus [39].

REFERENCES

Current Pharmacopoeial Monographs

Ph. Helv. Acore vrai
ÖAB Radix Calami
BHP Calamus

Literature References

1. Röst LCM. Biosystematic Investigations with Acorus L. 4. A Synthetic Approach to the Classification of the Genus. *Planta Medica* 1979, **37**, 289-307.
2. Mazza G. Gas chromatographic and mass spectrometric studies of the constituents of the rhizome of calamus. I. The volatile constituents of the essential oil. *J. Chromatogr.* 1985, **328**, 179-194.
3. Stahl E and Keller K. Zur Klassifizierung handelsüblicher Kalmusdrogen [The classification of commercial calamus crude drugs]. *Planta Medica* 1981, **43**, 128-140 [GERMAN/English summary].
4. Stahl E and Keller K. Über den unterschiedlichen β-Asarongehalt handelsüblicher Kalmusdrogen [The variable β-asarone content of commercial calamus crude drugs]. *Pharmazie* 1981, **36**, 53-57 [GERMAN].
5. Keller K and Stahl E. Kalmus: Inhaltsstoffe und β-Asarongehalt bei verschiedenen Herkünften [Calamus: constituents and β-asarone content of material from various sources]. *Dtsch. Apoth. Ztg.* 1982, **122**, 2463-2466 [GERMAN].
6. Keller K, Odenthal KP and Leng-Peschlow E. Spasmolytische Wirkung des Isoasaronfreien Kalmus [Spasmolytic effect of isoasarone-free calamus]. *Planta Medica* 1985, **51**, 6-9 [GERMAN/English summary].
7. Schneider K and Jurenitsch J. Kalmus als Arzneidroge: Nutzen oder Risiko? [Calamus as a medicinal drug: Benefit or risk?]. *Pharmazie* 1992, **47**, 79-85 [GERMAN].
8. Röst LCM and Bos R. Biosystematic Investigations with *Acorus* L. 3. Constituents of Essential Oils. *Planta Medica* 1979, **36**, 350-361.
9. Keller K and Stahl E. Composition of the Essential Oil from β-Asarone Free Calamus. *Planta Medica* 1983, **47**, 71-74 [GERMAN/English summary].
10. Lander V and Schreier P. Acorenone and γ-Asarone: Indicators of the Origin of Calamus Oils (*Acorus calamus* L.). *Flavour Fragrance J.* 1990, **5**, 75-79.
11. Fujita S, Enomoto Y, Suemitsu R and Fujita Y. Essential oils of the plants from various territories. XXVIII. Components of the essential oils of *Acorus calamus* var. *angustatus*. *Yakugaku Zasshi* 1971, **91**, 571-574 [JAPANESE]; through *Chem. Abstr.* 1971, **75**, 59759.
12. Yamamura S, Iguchi M, Nishiyama A, Niwa M, Koyama H and Hirata Y. Sesquiterpenes from *Acorus calamus* L. *Tetrahedron* 1971, **27**, 5419-5431.
13. Iguchi M, Niwa M, Nishiyama A and Yamamura S. Isolation and structure of acoragermacrone. *Tetrahedron Lett.* 1973, (29), 2759-2762.
14. Gorecki P and Keller K. Acorus. In: Blaschek W, Hänsel R, Keller K, Reichling J, Rimpler H and Schneider G, editors. *Hagers Handbuch der Pharmazeutischen Praxis, 5th ed. Supplement Volume 2: Drogen A-K.* ISBN 3-540-61618-7. Berlin-Heidelberg-New York-London: Springer, 1998:18-35 [GERMAN].
15. Mazza G. Gas chromatographic and mass spectrometric studies of the constituents of the rhizome of calamus. II. The volatile constituents of alcoholic extracts. *J. Chromatogr.* 1985, **328**, 195-206.
16. Pharmaceutical Society of Great Britain. Calamus. In: *British Pharmaceutical Codex 1934*. London: Pharmaceutical Press, 1934:241.
17. Asif M, Siddiqi MTA and Ahmad MU. Fatty Acid and Sugar Composition of Acorus calamus Linn. *Fette-Seifen-Anstrichmittel* 1984, **86**, 24-25.
18. Micali G, Curro P and Calabro G. Reversed-phase high-performance liquid chromatography for the determination of β-asarone. *J. Chromatogr.* 1980, **194**, 245-250.
19. Oprean R, Tamas M and Roman L. Comparison of GC-MS and TLC techniques for asarone isomers determination. *J. Pharmaceut. Biomed. Analysis* 1998, **18**, 227-234.
20. Maj J, Malec D and Lastowski Z. Pharmacological Properties of the Native Calamus (*Acorus calamus* L.). III. Spasmolytic Action of the Volatile Oil. *Acta Polon. Pharm.* 1966, **23**, 477-482 [POLISH/English summary].
21. Maj J, Lastowski Z and Lukowski K. Pharmacological properties of the native calamus (*Acorus calamus* L.). Part II. Central action of extracts. *Dissertationes Pharmaceuticae* 1965, **17**, 157-161 [POLISH/English summary].
22. Opdyke DLJ. Monographs on fragrance raw materials: Calamus oil. *Food Cosmet. Toxicol.* 1977, **15**, 623-626.
23. Maj J, Malec D and Lastowski Z. Pharmacological properties of the native calamus (*Acorus calamus* L.). Part I. Effect of the essential oil on the central nervous system. *Dissertationes Pharmaceuticae* 1964, **16**, 447-456 [POLISH/English summary].
24. Keller K, Leng-Peschlow E and Odenthal KP. Pharmacological activity of calamus oils with different amounts of cis-asarone. *Naunyn-Schmiedeberg's Arch. Pharmacol.* 1983, **324** (Suppl.), R55 (Abstract 220).
25. Vohora SB, Shah SA and Dandiya PC. Central nervous system studies on an ethanol extract of *Acorus calamus* rhizomes. *J. Ethnopharmacol.* 1990, **28**, 53-62.
26. Martis G, Rao A and Karanth KS. Neuropharmacological activity of *Acorus calamus*. *Fitoterapia* 1991, **62**, 331-337.
27. Zanoli P, Avallone R and Baraldi M. Sedative and Hypothermic Effects Induced by β-Asarone, a Main Component of *Acorus calamus*. *Phytotherapy Res.* 1998, **12**, S114-S116.
28. Motley TJ. The Ethnobotany of Sweet Flag, *Acorus calamus* (Araceae). *Econ. Bot.* 1994, **48**, 397-412.
29. Chevallier A. Sweet Flag. In: *The Encyclopedia of Medicinal Plants*. ISBN 0-7513-0314-3. London-New York-Stuttgart: Dorling Kindersley, 1996:55.
30. Acorus. In: *British Herbal Pharmacopoeia 1983*. ISBN 0-903032-07-4. Bournemouth: British Herbal Medicine Association, 1983.
31. Stodola J and Volák J. Sweet Flag. Translated into English in: Bunney S, editor. *The Illustrated Book of Herbs*. ISBN 0-7064-1489-6. London: Octopus Books, 1984:52.
32. Weiss RF. *Acorus calamus* (Calamus, Sweet Flag Root). In: *Herbal Medicine* (translated from the 6th German edition of *Lehrbuch der Phytotherapie*). ISBN 0-906584-19-1. Gothenburg: AB Arcanum, Beaconsfield, UK: Beaconsfield Publishers, 1988:44-46.
33. Taylor JM, Jones WI, Hagan EC, Gross MA, Davis DA and Cook EL. Toxicity of Oil of Calamus (Jammu variety). *Toxicol. Applied Pharmacol.* 1967, **10**, 405 (Abstract 72).
34. Abel G. Chromosome Damaging Effect on Human Lymphocytes by β-Asarone. *Planta Medica* 1987, **53**, 251-253 [GERMAN/English summary].
35. Calamus (Sweet Flag). In: UK Statutory Instrument 1994 No. 2410. The Medicines (Products Other Than Veterinary Drugs) (General Sale List) Amendment Order 1994. Schedule 1, Table A.
36. *Médicaments à base de plantes*. ISBN 2-911473-02-7. Saint-Denis Cedex, France: Agence du Médicament, 1998.
37. Calamus and its derivatives. In: Section 189.110 of USA Code of Federal Regulations, Title 21, Food and Drugs, Parts 170 to 199. Revised as of April 1, 2000.
38. Acorus calamus L., rhizome. In: *Flavouring Substances and Natural Sources of Flavourings, 3rd ed.* ISBN 2-7160-0081-6. Strasbourg: Council of Europe, 1981.
39. β-Asarone. In: Appendix 2 of *Natural Sources of Flavourings. Report No. 1*. ISBN 92-871-4324-2. Strasbourg: Council of Europe Publishing, 2000:19-20.

CALENDULA FLOWER

Compositae

Calendulae flos

Synonyms: Pot, common, Scotch or European marigold flower.

Definition
Calendula Flower consists of the dried, fully opened flowers, detached from the receptacle, of cultivated, double-flowered varieties of *Calendula officinalis* L.

The 'flower' is a compound inflorescence with two types of florets (small flowers): ligulate or ray florets (sometimes wrongly referred to as 'petals') in several series around the periphery, and tubular or disc florets in the centre. In 'filled' flowers, practically all the florets are ligulate. As well as being a common garden plant, the flowers are cultivated in eastern Europe and in Mediterranean countries, particularly Egypt.

The common name 'marigold' is also used for certain unrelated species, particularly of *Tagetes*, which are mainly indigenous to Central and South America. *Tagetes erecta* (African marigold) is grown commercially in Mexico, Peru and Ecuador for extraction of carotenoids [1].

CONSTITUENTS

□ ***Triterpene saponins***, 2-10% [2,3]. Six saponins based on oleanolic acid 3-glucuronide (which is glycoside F) have been isolated: glycosides A, B, C, D, D_2 and F. Glycosides A-D have a galactosyl (1→3) residue, and glycosides A and B also a glucosyl (1→2) residue, attached to the 3-glucuronyl group; furthermore, saponins A, C and D_2 are 28-glucosyl esters [4].

In smaller amounts, other saponins with slightly different pentacyclic sapogenins or glycosyl groups have been identified: calenduloside D, calendasaponins A-D and arvensoside [5].

□ ***Triterpene alcohols*** A complex mixture of pentacyclic triterpene mono-, di- and triols, derived from ψ-taraxene, taraxene, lupene, oleanene and ursene. 10% of the monools and 98% of the diols are esterified, mainly as 3-palmitates, myristates or laurates [3,6]. The mixture includes:

Triterpene diol 3-monoesters, ca. 4% in dried flowers, of which 75% or more are faradiol (3β,16β-dihydroxy-ψ-taraxene) and arnidiol (3β,16β-dihydroxytaraxene) monoesters [6-8]: in ligulate florets, faradiol 3-palmitate (1.4%), faradiol 3-myristate (1.3%) and faradiol 3-laurate (0.2%); in tubular florets about one tenth of these amounts [9].

The others include 3-monoesters of calendula-diol, brein and ursadiol [6-8].

Free triterpene monools, ca. 0.8% in dried flowers [2], including ψ-taraxasterol, β-amyrin, lupeol, α-amyrin and taraxasterol [6,7,10]. A high proportion of helianol has been reported in tubular florets, but virtually none in ligulate florets [10].

Triterpene triols including heliantriols A_1, B_0, B_1, B_2, C and F, longispinogenine, lupentriol and ursatriol [2,11].

□ ***Flavonoids*** (Ph. Eur. min. 0.4%, calculated as hyperoside), consisting of flavonol 3-glycosides based on isorhamnetin and quercetin, including their 3-*O*-glucosides, 3-*O*-rutinosides, 3-*O*-2^G-rhamnosylrutinosides, and 3-*O*-neohesperidosides [5,12,13]; the isorhamnetin glycosides

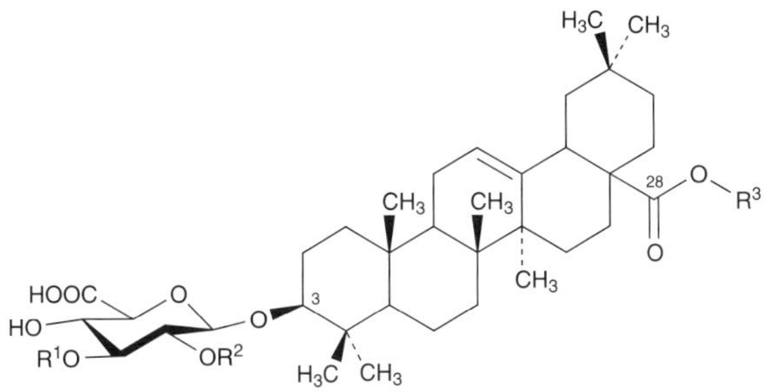

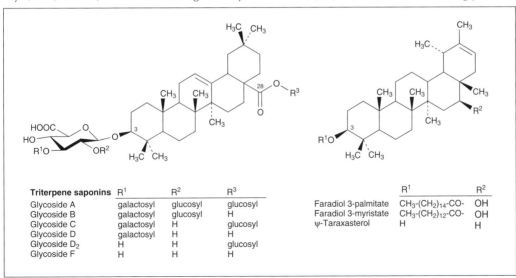

Triterpene saponins	R^1	R^2	R^3
Glycoside A	galactosyl	glucosyl	glucosyl
Glycoside B	galactosyl	glucosyl	H
Glycoside C	galactosyl	H	glucosyl
Glycoside D	galactosyl	H	H
Glycoside D_2	H	H	glucosyl
Glycoside F	H	H	H

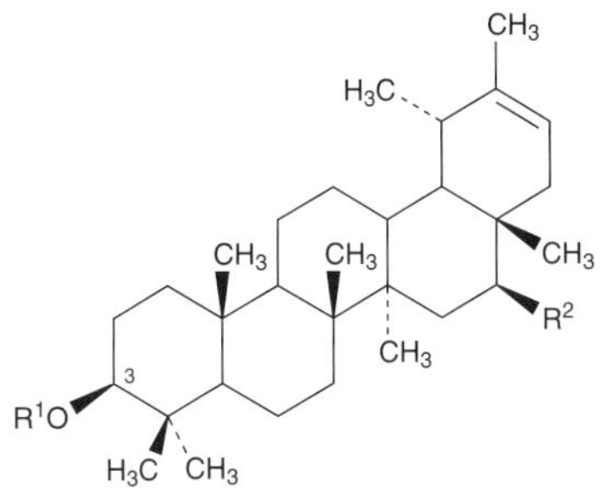

	R^1	R^2
Faradiol 3-palmitate	CH_3-$(CH_2)_{14}$-CO-	OH
Faradiol 3-myristate	CH_3-$(CH_2)_{12}$-CO-	OH
ψ-Taraxasterol	H	H

are quantitatively predominant [5,14,15]. Small amounts of free quercetin and isorhamnetin are also present [12,13].

☐ ***Carotenoids***, which give the colour to the flowers; the content can reach 1.5% or more. Lutein is predominant, and lutein and zeaxanthin account for 88-92% of total carotenoids. However, the colour intensity of orange-flowered varieties is primarily due to lycopene, which is absent from yellow-flowered varieties [2].

☐ ***Polysaccharides*** Three homogeneous polysaccharides with (1→3)-linked β-D-galactan backbones and branching at C-6 have been isolated: rhamnoarabinogalactan PS-I (galactose 41.0%, arabinose 34.2%, rhamnose 24.8%; MW 15,000) and two arabinogalactans, PS-II (galactose 72.4%, arabinose 27.6%; MW 25,000) and PS-III (galactose 51.4%, arabinose 48.7%; MW 35,000) [16].

☐ ***Phenolic acids***, ca. 0.1%, principally salicylic, vanillic and gentisic acids in the free form, and vanillic, syringic and ferulic acids in bound form [17].

☐ ***Coumarins*** Scopoletin and small amounts of umbelliferone and esculetin [18].

☐ ***Essential oil***, ca. 0.3%, containing mainly sesquiterpene alcohols, principally cadinol (20-25%) together with eudesmol, nerolidol, epicubenol, α-muurolol and others, and smaller amounts of sesquiterpene hydrocarbons [19].

☐ ***Other constituents*** Sterols, ca. 0.06% of dry weight, mainly as free stigmasterol and sitosterol [6]; two ionone glucosides (officinosides A and B), two sesquiterpene oligosides (officinosides C and D) [20] and a sesquiterpene glucoside (icariside C3) [5]; loliolide, a bitter substance arising from oxidation of certain carotenoids [21]; and tannins (11.2% in ligulate flowers) [22].

Published Assay Methods

Total flavonoids by spectrophotometry [Ph. Eur.]. Flavonol glycosides by HPLC [14] and thermospray LC-MS [23]. Faradiol monoesters by HPLC [9]. Essential oil components by GC and GC-MS [19].

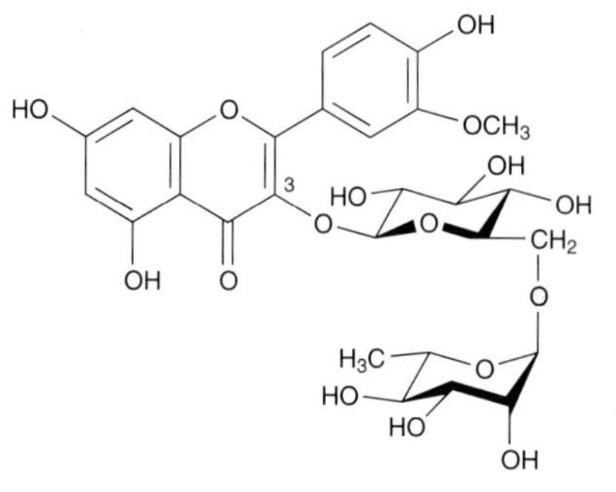

Isorhamnetin 3-rutinoside

PHARMACOLOGY

In vitro

Wound healing

The wound healing process involves several distinct phases in which the formation of new blood vessels (angiogenesis) plays an important role. In the chick chorioallantoic membrane (CAM) test using incubated hen eggs, a freeze-dried, cold aqueous infusion of calendula flower proved highly angiogenic, the number of microvessels counted in treated tissue sections being significantly higher than in control CAMs ($p<0.0001$). Hyaluronan, which is known to be involved in the formation, alignment and migration of newly formed capillaries, was detected in all calendula flower-treated CAMs, while none was found in untreated CAMs. The high level of neovascularization observed in treated CAMs was attributed to effects of the calendula flower extract, in which the predominant constituents were flavonoids [24].

Anti-inflammatory activity

Isorhamnetin 3-glycosides isolated from calendula flower inhibited lipoxygenase (a key enzyme in the synthesis of leukotrienes) from rat lung cytosol at a concentration of 1.5×10^{-5} M [15].

Immunomodulatory activity

At a concentration of 10^{-5} to 10^{-6} mg/ml, polysaccharides isolated from marigold exhibited immunostimulating activity by enhancing the phagocytosis of human granulocytes: the rhamnoarabinogalactan PS-I by 40-57%, arabinogalactan PS-II by 20-30% and, with very high activity, arabinogalactan PS-III by 54-100% [16].

A dry 70%-ethanolic extract of calendula flower had no direct mitogenic effect on human lymphocytes but inhibited mitogen-induced proliferation of lymphocytes. Treatment of mixed lymphocytes with calendula flower extract at 0.1-10 μg/ml stimulated cell proliferation but higher concentrations of the extract caused inhibition [25].

Adhesion to mucous membranes

A raw polysaccharide fraction (>95% carbohydrates) from calendula flower exhibited strong adhesion to isolated porcine buccal membranes; the bioadhesive effect was greater than that observed with a comparable extract from marshmallow root [26].

Antimicrobial effects

Moderate antibacterial activity was exhibited by a dry hydroethanolic extract from calendula flower at 50 mg/ml against *Escherichia coli* and *Pseudomonas aeruginosa*, and particularly against *Staphylococcus aureus* and *Streptococcus faecalis*, although an aqueous extract appeared to be devoid of activity [27].

A 10%-methanolic extract showed fungistatic activity [28]. A tincture had high virucidal activity against influenza viruses and marked virustatic activity against herpes simplex virus in vitro, but was not effective against flu virus in chick embryos or flu-induced pneumonia in mice [29]. Potent anti-HIV properties were exhibited by a dichloromethane-methanol (1:1) extract [30].

A 10% infusion of calendula flower exhibited high *in vitro* activity against *Trichomonas vaginalis* protozoa, being effective within 15 minutes of contact [31]; a 50% alcoholic extract and a tincture also showed trichomonacidal activity against this organism [32].

Other effects
An aqueous infusion diluted to the equivalent of 1-2 mg of crude drug per ml enhanced the tonus of isolated rabbit and guinea pig uterine horn [33].

In vivo

Wound healing
Accelerated healing of wounds after treatment with calendula flower preparations has been demonstrated in several animal species.

Complete cicatrization of experimental wounds in rabbits was achieved in 14 days with a dry alcoholic extract of calendula flower, applied topically as a 10% hydrogel or 10% powder (in lactose), compared to 18-19 days with vehicle-only controls [34].

Healing of experimental wounds in buffalo calves was accelerated by topical treatment on alternate days with 5% of a dry extract of calendula flower in petroleum jelly compared to wounds treated with normal saline [35].

Dry 70%-ethanolic (E) and aqueous (A) extracts of calendula flower, applied topically as 5% ointments, accelerated the healing of surgically inflicted skin wounds in rats; the degree of epithelization was 73% (E) and 65% (A) by the 5th day, and 90% (E) and 88% (A) by the 10th day compared to 60% and 79% in control animals treated with vehicle only [36]. In similar experiments, addition of allantoin to the ointment enhanced the effect of the extracts; by the 14th day, compared to 70% in controls and 79% with allantoin alone, the degree of healing was 80% with A + E, and 90% with A + E + allantoin in a 2:2:1 ratio ($p<0.01$) [37].

Topical treatment of *Staphylococcus epidermides*-infected skin wounds in rats with a calendula flower cream accelerated cicatrization compared to control animals [38].

Anti-inflammatory activity
Calendula flower extracts have exhibited anti-inflammatory activity in several tests. After oral administration at 100 mg/kg body weight, a dry 80%-ethanolic extract inhibited carrageenan-induced rat paw oedema by 11%, compared to 45% inhibition by oral indometacin at 5 mg/kg [39]. A freeze-dried extract of calendula flower suppressed inflammatory effects and leukocyte infiltration induced in rats by simultaneous injection of carrageenan and prostaglandin E1 [40].

When applied topically in the croton oil ear oedema test in mice, a 70%-alcoholic extract had a dose-dependent anti-inflammatory effect with 20% inhibition of oedema at 1200 µg/ear (equivalent to 4.2 mg of dried flower). A supercritical carbon dioxide extract, which contained only lipophilic constituents, was more effective, producing 31% inhibition at 150 µg/ear (equivalent to 3.6 mg of dried flower) and 71% inhibition at 1200 µg/ear (equivalent to 28.6 mg of dried flower); the latter effect was similar to that of indometacin at 120 µg/ear (73.3% inhibition) [41].

Subsequently, using the same test, it was shown that triterpenoids are the most important anti-inflammatory principles in calendula flower and that the anti-inflammatory activity of various carbon dioxide extracts was proportional to their content of faradiol 3-monoesters (the quantitatively predominant triterpenoids) [7]. In fact, on a molar basis, unesterified faradiol (not present in the extracts) has anti-inflammatory activity equal to that of indometacin, but as 3-monesters the activity is reduced by more than 50%. Free monools, especially ψ-taraxasterol, also showed substantial and apparently synergistic anti-inflammatory activity, but their contribution to the effect of an extract appeared to be of lesser importance due to their low concentration [7,42]. Inhibitions of oedema produced by topical application of faradiol 3-myristate, faradiol 3-palmitate and ψ-taraxasterol were 46%, 45% and 49% respectively at 240 $\mu g/cm^2$, and 65%, 66% and 86% at 480 $\mu g/cm^2$ (on a molar basis the 3-monesters are more potent than ψ-taraxasterol); in comparison, faradiol produced 73% inhibition at 120 $\mu g/cm^2$ and indometacin 75% at 100 $\mu g/cm^2$ [42].

In another study, using 12-*O*-tetradecanoylphorbol-13-acetate to induce ear inflammation in mice, topically applied helianol, taraxasterol and ψ-taraxasterol dose-dependently inhibited inflammation with ID_{50} values of 0.1, 0.3 and 0.4 mg/ear respectively, compared to 0.3 mg/ear for indometacin and 0.03 mg/ear for hydrocortisone [10].

Anti-inflammatory activity has been reported for the saponin calenduloside B [43], but no data appear to be available with respect to other calendula flower saponins.

Gastroprotective effects
A methanolic extract from calendula flower, orally administered to rats at 100-200 mg/kg body weight, had a strong dose-dependent inhibitory effect ($p<0.01$) on gastric lesions induced in rats by ethanol or indometacin. The effect was shown to be due to saponins in the extract; glycosides A, B, C and D at 20 mg/kg, and F at 10 mg/kg, produced significant inhibition ($p<0.01$), and glycosides B, D and F reduced the length of ethanol-induced gastric lesions more effectively than the anti-ulcer drug omeprazole at 20 mg/kg [5].

Hypoglycaemic effect
Orally-administered methanolic extract from calendula flower at 1000 mg/kg had a mild, and certain isolated saponins a potent, hypoglycaemic effect, reducing serum glucose levels in glucose-loaded rodents. The effect of glycosides D and F at 50 mg/kg in rats was comparable to that of the hypoglycaemic drug tolbutamide at 25 mg/kg ($p<0.01$). These two saponins also inhibited gastric emptying in rats ($p<0.01$ at 25-50 mg/kg), apparently the mode of action for hypoglycaemic activity [5].

Immunomodulatory effects
In the carbon clearance test in mice, a polysaccharide fraction from calendula flower showed moderate immunostimulating activity [44,45].

The unsaponifiable fraction from a hydroalcoholic extract, administered intraperitoneally to mice, stimulated phagocytic activity of the reticulo-endothelial system and protected 3 out of 5 mice from lethal septicaemia after injection of *Escherichia coli* [46].

CLINICAL STUDIES

Patients with second or third degree burns were treated topically for 17 days in an open, controlled, randomized study with one of three preparations: a calendula flower ointment (prepared by digestion in vaseline) (n = 53) or vaseline (n = 50) or a proteolytic ointment (to promote elimination of devitalized tissue) (n = 53). The success rates were considered to be 37/53 for calendula flower ointment, 27/50 for vaseline and 35/53 for the proteolytic ointment. Calendula flower ointment was marginally superior ($p = 0.05$) to its base, vaseline, and better tolerated than the proteolytic ointment [47].

In an open study, 30 patients with first (reddening and soft swellings) or second degree (2a superficial; stronger reddening and blisters) burns or scalds were treated at least 3 times daily for up to 14 days, depending on the severity of symptoms, with a hydrogel containing 10% of a calendula flower tincture. Scores for reddening, swelling, blistering, pain, soreness and sensitivity to heat steadily improved; by the end of the study only a few patients had slight but perceptible symptoms [48].

In an open study, calendula flower preparations consisting of diluted tincture (6.6:1, 70% ethanol; diluted 10:1 with water) or a hydrogel (containing 2% of soft ethanolic extract) were used for topical treatment of patients with burns (n = 8; 3-6 days of treatment), cuts or dermatitic lesions (n = 5; 5-10 days of treatment) and varicose ulcer (n = 6, mainly chronic cases; 10-30 days of treatment). By the end of treatment all patients with burns were cured; 3/5 patients with cuts were cured, the other 2 improved; 3/6 patients with varicose ulcer were cured, the other 3 improved [49].

Positive results from open studies and case reports on the topical use of calendula flower ointment in venous circulatory disorders such as varicosis, thrombophlebitis and crural ulcer, and the resulting inflammation and skin ailments, and also in the prophylaxis and treatment of bedsores (decubitus ulcer), have been summarized by Isaac [3].

THERAPEUTICS

Actions
Vulnerary [34-38,50-52], promoting granulation [3,50] and cicatrization [4,34] of wounds when applied topically; anti-inflammatory [7,39-41,50-52], gastroprotective [5], immunomodulatory [44-46] and moderately antimicrobial [27-30].

Also stated to be antihaemorrhagic [24,51,52] and styptic [3,51]; mildly oestrogenic [52,53], emmenagogic [3,4,51], diaphoretic [3,51,54] and spasmolytic [51-53].

Indications
External use: Minor wounds [2,3,24,50,55], particularly those with a tendency to poor healing [3,50]; minor burns and scalds (up to second degree) [3,47-49,55] including sunburn [52,55]; inflammatory skin lesions [24,51] and a wide range of skin problems including abrasions, sores and rashes [3,52,55]; varicose veins, haemorrhoids [3,51], crural ulcer [3,50,51]. Regarded as outstanding for the treatment of insect stings, and long used for the prophylaxis and treatment of bedsores [3].

Other uses, based on experience or tradition
External use: Conjunctivitis [51] and other ocular irritations [55], as an eye lotion; sebaceous cysts, enlarged or inflamed lymphatic nodes [51]; sprains and bruises [54]; proctitis [51], frostbite [3].
Local internal use: Inflammation of the mouth and throat mucosa [3,50,55] including stomatitis, apthous ulcer, gingivitis and periodontitis [3].

Internal use: Inflammatory complaints of the digestive system such as gastric and duodenal ulcer, gastritis and colitis [3,24,51-53]; amenorrhoea and dysmenorrhoea [51-54].

Contraindications
Internal use in pregnancy [53].

Side effects
None known.

Interactions with other drugs
None known.

Dosage
External use Ointment containing the equivalent to 2-5 g [50] or, in more concentrated form, 10-12 g [3,52] of dried flower per 100 g. Infused oil, and ointments, creams or gels containing about 10% of tincture or fluid extract, are also used. Semi-solid preparations or liquids (infusion or diluted tincture) are often applied to wounds and skin disorders with a compress, changed several times daily [3].
Local internal use As a gargle or mouthrinse, a warm infusion or a 2% solution of tincture every 2 hours [3].
Internal use Three times daily: dried flower, 2-3 g as an infusion in 150 ml of water [50-52]; liquid extract 1:1 in 40% alcohol, 0.5-1 ml; tincture 1:5 in 90% alcohol, 0.3-1.2 ml [51]. Up to 10 g of tincture daily (divided into 3 doses) has also been recommended [3].

SAFETY

Calendula flower is considered to be largely non-toxic at therapeutic dose levels and, since it lacks sequiterpene lactones, the risk of allergic reactions is low [3]. No adverse effects were observed in 30 patients with burns or scalds treated with a hydrogel containing calendula flower hydroethanolic extract for up to 14 days [48]. In a 17-day study, 53 patients with 2nd to 3rd degree burns tolerated a calendula flower ointment better, with less pain, than a parallel group treated with a proteolytic ointment [47].

The intravenous LD_{50} was 526 mg/100 g in rats for a 30%-hydroethanolic extract of calendula flower [56] and 375 mg/kg in mice for an aqueous extract [57]. Rats tolerated daily oral doses of calenduloside B at 200 mg/kg for 2 months with no adverse response [43].

No carcinogenic effects were observed in rats or hamsters after daily oral administration of a calendula flower extract at 0.15 g/kg daily for 18-22 months [58]. A 60%-ethanolic fluid extract at concentrations of 50-5000 µg/plate gave negative results in the Ames mutagenicity test using *Salmonella typhimurium* strains TA153S, TA1537, TA98 and TA100 with or without activation. Genotoxicity to *Aspergillus nidulans* was detected, but was not confirmed in the mouse bone marrow micronucleus test after oral doses of up to 1 g/kg for 2 days [59].

REGULATORY STATUS

Medicines

UK	Accepted for general sale, *external use only* [60].
France	Accepted for specified indications [55].
Germany	Commission E monograph published, with approved uses [50].

Food

USA	Generally recognized as safe (21 CFR 182.10) [61].
Council of Europe	Permitted as flavouring, category N2 [62].

REFERENCES

Current Pharmacopoeial Monographs
Ph. Eur. Calendula Flower

Literature References

1. Evans WC. Marigold flowers. In: *Trease and Evans' Pharmacognosy, 14th ed.* ISBN 0-7020-1899-6. London-Philadelphia: WB Saunders, 1996:459.
2. Isaac O. Calendula. In: Hänsel R, Keller K, Rimpler H and Schneider G, editors. *Hagers Handbuch der Pharmazeutischen Praxis, 5th ed. Volume 4: Drogen A-D.* ISBN 3-540-52631-5. Berlin-Heidelberg-New York-London: Springer-Verlag, 1992:597-615 [GERMAN].
3. Isaac O. *Calendula officinalis* L. - Die Ringelblume. Portrait einer Arzneipflanze [*Calendula officinalis* L. - Marigold flower. Portrait of a medicinal plant]. *Z. Phytotherapie* 1994, **15**, 356-370 [GERMAN/English summary].
4. Vidal-Ollivier E, Balansard G, Faure R and Babadjamian A. Revised structures of triterpenoid saponins from the flowers of *Calendula officinalis. J. Nat. Prod.* 1989, **52**, 1156-1159.
5. Yoshikawa M, Murakami T, Kishi A, Kageura T and Matsuda H. Medicinal Flowers. III. Marigold. (1): Hypoglycemic, Gastric Emptying Inhibitory and Gastroprotective Principles and New Oleanane-Type Triterpene Oligoglycosides, Calendasaponins A, B, C and D, from Egyptian *Calendula officinalis. Chem. Pharm. Bull.* 2001, **49**, 863-870.
6. Wilkomirski B and Kasprzyk Z. Free and ester-bound triterpene alcohols and sterols in cellular subfractions of *Calendula officinalis* flowers. *Phytochemistry* 1979, **18**, 253-255.
7. Della Loggia R, Tubaro A, Sosa S, Becker H, Saar S and Isaac O. The Role of Triterpenoids in the Topical Anti-Inflammatory Activity of *Calendula officinalis* Flowers. *Planta Medica* 1994, **60**, 516-520.
8. Wojciechowski Z, Bochenska-Hryniewicz M, Kucharczak B and Kasprzyk Z. Sterol and triterpene alcohol esters from *Calendula officinalis. Phytochemistry* 1972, **11**, 1165-1168.
9. Zitterl-Eglseer K, Reznicek G, Jurenitsch J, Novak J,

Zitterl W and Franz C. Morphogenetic Variability of Faradiol Monoesters in Marigold, *Calendula officinalis* L. *Phytochem. Analysis* 2001, **12**, 199-201.
10. Akihisa T, Yasukawa K, Oinuma H, Kasahara Y, Yamanouchi S, Takido M et al. Triterpene alcohols from the flowers of Compositae and their anti-inflammatory effects. *Phytochemistry* 1996, **43**, 1255-1260.
11. Wilkomirski B. Pentacyclic triterpene triols from *Calendula officinalis* flowers. *Phytochemistry* 1985, **24**, 3066-3067.
12. Komissarenko NF, Chernobai VT and Derkach AI. Flavonoids of inflorescences of *Calendula officinalis*. *Khim. Prir. Soedin.* 1988, (6), 795-801 [RUSSIAN]; translated into English as *Chem. Nat. Compd.* 1988, **24**, 675-680.
13. Vidal-Ollivier E, Elias R, Faure F, Babadjamian A, Crespin F, Balansard G and Boudon G. Flavonol Glycosides from *Calendula officinalis* Flowers. *Planta Medica* 1989, **55**, 73-74.
14. Pietta P, Bruno A, Mauri P and Rava A. Separation of flavonol-3-O-glycosides from *Calendula officinalis* and *Sambucus nigra* by high-performance liquid and micellar electrokinetic capillary chromatography. *J. Chromatogr.* 1992, **593**, 165-170.
15. Bezákova L, Masterová I, Paulíková I and Psenák M. Inhibitory activity of isorhamnetin glycosides from *Calendula officinalis* L. on the activity of lipoxygenase. *Pharmazie* 1996, **51**, 126-127.
16. Varljen J, Lipták A and Wagner H. Structural analysis of a rhamnoarabinogalactan and arabinogalactans with immuno-stimulating activity from *Calendula officinalis*. *Phytochemistry* 1989, **28**, 2379-2383.
17. Kurowska A, Kalemba D, Góra J and Zadernowski R. Quantitative and qualitative analysis of phenolic acids from the inflorescences of marigold (*Calendula officinalis* L.). *Acta Polon. Pharm.* 1985, **42**, 473-477 [POLISH/English summary].
18. Derkach AI, Komissarenko NF and Chernobai VT. Coumarins of the inflorescences of *Calendula officinalis* and *Helichrysum arenarium*. *Khim. Prir. Soedin.* 1986, (6), 777 [RUSSIAN], translated into English as: *Chem. Nat. Compd.* 1986, **22**, 722-723.
19. Chalchat JC, Garry RP and Michet A. Chemical Composition of Essential Oil of *Calendula officinalis* L. (Pot Marigold). *Flavour Fragrance J.* 1991, **6**, 189-192.
20. Murakami T, Kishi A and Yoshikawa M. Medicinal Flowers. IV. Marigold. (2): Structures of New Ionone and Sesquiterpene Glycosides from *Calendula officinalis*. *Chem. Pharm. Bull.* 2001, **49**, 974-978.
21. Willuhn G and Westhaus R-G. Loliolide (Calendin) from *Calendula officinalis*. *Planta Medica* 1987, **53**, 304.
22. Ocioszynska I, Nartowska J and Strzelecka H. Study of the chemistry of marigold (*Calendula officinalis* L.) inflorescence. *Herba Pol.* 1977, **23**, 191-199 [POLISH]; through *Chem. Abstr.* 1978, **88**, 148980.
23. Pietta P, Maffei Facino R, Carini M and Mauri P. Thermospray liquid chromatography-mass spectrometry of flavonol glycosides from medicinal plants. *J. Chromatogr. A* 1994, **661**, 121-126.
24. Patrick KFM, Kumar S, Edwardson PAD, Hutchinson JJ. Induction of vascularisation by an aqueous extract of the flowers of *Calendula officinalis* L. the European marigold. *Phytomedicine* 1996, **3**, 11-18.
25. Amirghofran Z, Azadbakht M and Karimi MH. Evaluation of the immunomodulatory effects of five herbal plants. *J. Ethnopharmacol.* 2000, **72**, 167-172.
26. Schmidgall J, Schnetz E and Hensel A. Evidence for Bioadhesive Effects of Polysaccharides and Polysaccharide-Containing Herbs in an ex vivo Bioadhesion Assay on Buccal Membranes. *Planta Medica* 2000, **66**, 48-53.
27. Dumenil G, Chemli R, Balansard G, Guiraud H and Lallemand M. Evaluation of antibacterial properties of marigold flowers (*Calendula officinalis* L.) and mother homeopathic tinctures of *C. officinalis* L. and *C. arvensis* L. *Ann. Pharm. Fr.* 1980, **38**, 493-499 [FRENCH/English summary].
28. Wolters B. Die Verbreitung antibiotischer Eigenschaften bei Saponindrogen [The range of antibiotic properties of saponin drugs]. *Dtsch. Apoth. Ztg.* 1966, **106**, 1729-1733 [GERMAN].
29. Bogdanova NS, Nikolaeva IS, Scherbakova LI, Tolstova TI, Moskalenko NY and Pershin GN. A study into antiviral properties of *Calendula officinalis*. *Farmakol. Toksikol.* 1970, **33**, 349-355 [RUSSIAN/English summary].
30. Kalvatchev Z, Walder R and Garzaro D. Anti-HIV activity of extracts from *Calendula officinalis* flowers. *Biomed. & Pharmacother.* 1997, **51**, 176-180.
31. Fazakas B and Rácz G. Actiunea unor produse vegetale asupra protozoarului *Trichomonas vaginalis* [Activity of some plant products on *Trichomonas vaginalis* protozoa]. *Farmacia (Bucharest)* 1965, **13**, 91-93 [RUMANIAN].
32. Samochowiec E, Urbanska L, Manka W and Stolarska E. Assessment of the action of *Calendula officinalis* and *Echinacea angustifolia* extracts on *Trichomonas vaginalis* in vitro. *Wiad. Parazytol.* 1979, **25**, 77-81 [POLISH/English summary].
33. Shipochliev T. Extracts from a group of plant extracts enhancing the uterine tonus. *Veterinarno-Meditsinski Nauki* 1981, **18** (4), 94-98 [RUSSIAN/English summary].
34. Oana L, Mates N, Ognean L, Muste A, Aldea M, Neculoiu D and Banciu C. Studies concerning the wound healing action of some medicinal herb extracts. *Buletinul Universitatii de Stiinte Agricole - Seria Zootehnie Medicina si Veterinara* 1995, **49**, 461-465 [RUMANIAN/English summary].
35. Ansari MA, Jadon NS, Singh SP, Kumar A and Singh H. Effect of *Calendula officinalis* ointment, charmil and gelatin granules on wound healing in buffaloes - a histological study. *Indian Vet. J.* 1997, **74**, 594-597.
36. Klouchek-Popova E, Popov A, Pavlova N and Krusteva K. Experimental phytochemical, pharmacological and cytomorphological studies of the regenerative action of fractions C1 and C5 isolated from *Calendula officinalis*. *Savremenna Med* 1981, **32**, 395-399 [RUSSIAN/English summary].
37. Klouchek-Popova E, Popov A, Pavlova N and Krusteva S. Influence on Physiological Regeneration and Epithelization Using Fractions Isolated from *Calendula Officinalis*. *Acta Physiol. Pharmacol. Bulg.* 1982, **8**, 63-67.
38. Perri de Carvalho PS, Tagliavini DG and Tagliavini RL. Cutaneous cicatrization after topical application of calendula cream or comfrey, propolis and honey combination in infected wounds of skin. Clinical and histological study in rats. *Rev. Ciênc. Bioméd.* (São Paulo) 1991, **12**, 39-50 [PORTUGUESE/English summary].
39. Mascolo N, Autore G, Capasso F, Menghini A and Fasulo MP. Biological Screening of Italian Medicinal Plants for Anti-inflammatory Activity. *Phytotherapy Res.* 1987, **1**, 28-31.
40. Shipochliev T, Dimitrov A and Aleksandrova E. Study on the anti-inflammatory effect of a group of plant extracts. *Veterinarno-Meditsinski Nauki* 1981, **18** (6), 87-94 [RUSSIAN/English summary].
41. Della Loggia R, Becker H, Isaac O and Tubaro A. Topical Anti-Inflammatory Activity of *Calendula officinalis* Extracts. *Planta Medica* 1990, **56**, 658.
42. Zitterl-Eglseer K, Sosa S, Jurenitsch J, Schubert-Zsilavecz M, Della Loggia R, Tubaro A et al. Anti-oedematous activities of the main triterpendiol esters of marigold (*Calendula officinalis* L.). *J. Ethnopharmacol.* 1997, **57**, 139-144.
43. Yatsyno AI, Belova LF, Lipkina GS, Sokolov SY and Trutneva EA. Pharmacology of calenduloside B - a new triterpene glycoside from rhizomes of *Calendula officinalis*. *Farmakol. Toksikol. (Moscow)* 1978, **41**, 556-560 [RUSSIAN]; through *Chem. Abstr.* 1978, **89**, 209164.
44. Wagner H, Proksch A, Riess-Maurer I, Vollmar A, Odenthal S, Stuppner H et al. Immunstimulierend wirkende Polysaccharide (Heteroglykane) aus höheren Pflanzen. Vorläufige Mitteilung. *Arzneim.-Forsch./Drug Res.* 1984, **34**, 659-661 [GERMAN/English summary].
45. Wagner H, Proksch A, Riess-Maurer I, Vollmar A, Odenthal S, Stuppner H et al. Immunstimulierend wirkende Polysaccharide (Heteroglykane) aus höheren Pflanzen. *Arzneim.-Forsch./Drug Res.* 1985, **35**, 1069-1075 [GERMAN/English summary].

46. Delaveau P, Lallouette P and Tessier AM. Stimulation of the Phagocytic Activity of the Reticulo-Endothelial System by Plant Extracts. *Planta Medica* 1980, **40**, 49-54 [FRENCH/English summary].
47. Lievre M, Marichy J, Baux S, Foyatier JL, Perrot J and Boissel JP. Controlled study of three ointments for the local management of 2nd and 3rd degree burns. *Clinical Trials and Meta-Analysis* 1992, **28**, 9-12.
48. Baranov AP. Calendula. Wie ist die Wirksamkeit bei Verbrennungen und Verbrühungen? [Calendula. How effective is it for burns and scalds?]. *Dtsch. Apoth. Ztg.* 1999, **139**, 2135-2138 [GERMAN].
49. Neto JJ, Fracasso JF, Camargo Neves MCL, dos Santos LE and Banuth VL. Treatment of varicose ulcer and skin lesions with *Calendula officinalis* L. or *Stryphnodendron barbadetiman* (Velloso) Martius. *Rev. Ciênc. Farm. São Paulo* 1996, **17**, 181-186 [PORTUGUESE/English summary].
50. Calendulae flos. German Commission E Monograph published in: Bundesanzeiger No. 50 of 13 March 1986.
51. Calendula. In: *British Herbal Pharmacopoeia 1983*. ISBN 0-903032-07-4. Bournemouth: British Herbal Medicine Association, 1983.
52. Chevallier A. Marigold. In: *Encyclopedia of Medicinal Plants, 2nd ed.* ISBN 0-7513-1209-6. London-New York: Dorling Kindersley, 2001:73.
53. McIntyre A. Calendula. In: *The Complete Woman's Herbal*. ISBN 1-85675-135-X. London: Gaia Books, 1994:62.
54. Pharmaceutical Society of Great Britain. Calendula; Tincture of Calendula. In: *British Pharmaceutical Codex 1934*. London: Pharmaceutical Press, 1934:257-258 and 1471.
55. Souci. In: *Médicaments à base de plantes*. ISBN 2-911473-02-7. Saint-Denis Cedex, France: Agence du Médicament, 1998.
56. Boyadzhiev T. Sedative and hypotensive effect of preparations from the plant *Calendula officinalis*. *Nauchni Tr. Vissh. Med. Inst. Sofia* 1964, **43**, 15-20; through *Chem. Abstr.* 1965, **63**, 1114.
57. Manolov P, Boyadzhiev T and Nikolov P. Antitumorigenic effect of preparations of *Calendula officinalis* on Crocker sarcoma 180. *Eksperim. Med. Morfol.* 1964, **3**, 41-5 [BULGARIAN]; through *Chem Abstr* 1965, **62**, 9652.
58. Avramova S, Portarska F, Apostolova B, Petkova S, Konteva M, Tsekova M et al. Marigold (*Calendula officinalis* L.). - Source of new products for the cosmetic industry. *MBI (Med. Biol. Inf.)* 1988, (4), 28-32.
59. Ramos A, Edreira A, Vizoso A, Betancourt J, López M and Décalo M. Genotoxicity of an extract of *Calendula officinalis* L. *J. Ethnopharmacol.* 1998, **61**, 49-55.
60. Calendula (Marigold). In: UK Statutory Instrument 1994 No. 2410. The Medicines (Products Other Than Veterinary Drugs) (General Sale List) Amendment Order 1994. Schedule 1, Table B (External use only).
61. Calendula. In: Section 182.10 of USA Code of Federal Regulations, Title 21, Food and Drugs, Parts 170 to 199. Revised as of April 1, 2000.
62. Calendula officinalis L., flowers. In: *Flavouring Substances and Natural Sources of Flavourings, 3rd ed.* ISBN 2-7160-0081-6. Strasbourg: Council of Europe, 1981.

REGULATORY GUIDELINES FROM OTHER EU COUNTRIES

FRANCE

Médicaments à base de plantes [55]: Souci, capitule.

Therapeutic indications accepted

Local use
Traditionally used: for the treatment of small wounds and sores after copious washing (with soap and water) and for the elimination of spots; as a soothing and antipruriginous local treatment of dermatological ailments, as a trophic protector in the treatment of chaps, abrasions or fissures and against insect stings; in cases of sunburn, superficial and limited burns, and erythema of the buttocks; in cases of ocular irritation or discomfort due to various causes (smoky atmosphere, sustained visual effort, bathing in the sea or swimming pool); locally (mouthwash/gargle, pastille) to alleviate pain in ailments of the buccal cavity and/or the pharynx.

GERMANY

Commission E monograph [50]: Calendulae flos (Ringelblumenblüten).

Uses
Local internal use: inflammation of the mouth and throat mucosa.
External use: wounds, including those with a tendency to poor healing. Ulcus cruris.

Contraindications
None known.

Side effects
None known.

Interactions with other drugs
None known.

Dosage
Unless otherwise prescribed, 1-2 g of dried flower to a cup of water (150 ml), or 1-2 teaspoonsful (2-4 ml) of tincture to 250-500 ml of water, or as ointments corresponding to 2-5 g of dried flower in 100 g of ointment.

Mode of administration
Comminuted drug for preparation of infusions and other galenic preparations for local use.

Action
Promotes wound healing; anti-inflammatory and granulation-promoting effects in local use have been described.

CAPSICUM

Solanaceae

Capsici fructus

Synonyms: Chillies, Cayenne pepper (ground, dried fruits).

Definition

Capsicum consists of the dried ripe fruits of *Capsicum annuum* L. var. *minimum* (Miller) Heiser and small-fruited varieties of *Capsicum frutescens* L.

Originating from Central and South America, *Capsicum* plants have been cultivated around the world for centuries, especially in tropical and subtropical regions, to provide staple foods and spices. Consequently, numerous cultivated forms have arisen, differentiated in various ways but particularly by the shape, colour, size and degree of pungency or "hotness" of their fruits. The pungency depends on the concentration of capsaicinoids, 90% or more of the spiciness usually coming from two major compounds, capsaicin and dihydrocapsaicin.

The European Pharmacopoeia definition (as above) specifies the same botanical sources of capsicum as did the BPC 1973 [1] and also defines a minimum content of total capsaicinoids (0.4% of dry weight) - a more important criterion from the medicinal viewpoint than the particular species or variety of *Capsicum* used.

Botanical classification of members of the *Capsicum* genus is rather confused and unreliable [2]. It should also be said that trivial names used for some of the more popular varieties and cultivars are far from consistent in scientific texts or from one country to another. Furthermore, generalizations as to which species or variety produces the hottest peppers tend to prove misleading; it seems to depend on the specific cultivar.

There may be exceptions, but in most cases larger and less pungent peppers tend to be varieties of *C. annuum*, while smaller, hotter peppers (such as hot chillies, jalapeños and tabasco peppers) tend to be varieties of *C. frutescens* [2]. Large, fleshy, non-pungent bell peppers enjoyed as a fresh vegetable and valued for their aroma, taste, colour and texture, are types of *Capsicum annuum* var *annuum* [3]. Paprika, grown in temperate regions and valued particularly for its brilliant red colour, is also derived from mild races of *C. annuum* [1].

CONSTITUENTS

□ *Capsaicinoids*, 0.3-1.2% in *C. frutescens* [4] (Ph. Eur. min. 0.4%, as the total of the three major capsaicinoids), principally capsaicin (61-77%), dihydrocapsaicin (17-29%) and nordihydrocapsaicin (0.5-6%) together with small amounts of at least 7 other capsaicinoids (i.e. *N*-vanillyl amides of saturated or mono-unsaturated C_8-C_{11} fatty acids) [5-8].

Nonivamide (nonanoic acid vanillylamide), a compound with a straight C_9 chain, is naturally present to the extent of 0.35-2.2% of total capsaicinoids in *C. frutescens* [5-7,9]; the Ph. Eur. limit is 5.0%. This compound can be readily synthesized and is often used as an adulterant - so much so that, of 20 topical non-prescription products available in the USA in 1993 and reported to contain capsaicin or capsicum oleoresin, analysis revealed that 5 contained only nonivamide, with no detectable capsaicin present [8].

Capsicum oleoresin (also known as "capsicin"), a dark red oily liquid and a powerful irritant, is a capsaicinoid-rich extract obtained from capsicum by solvent extraction with yields of 8.0-16.5% [4].

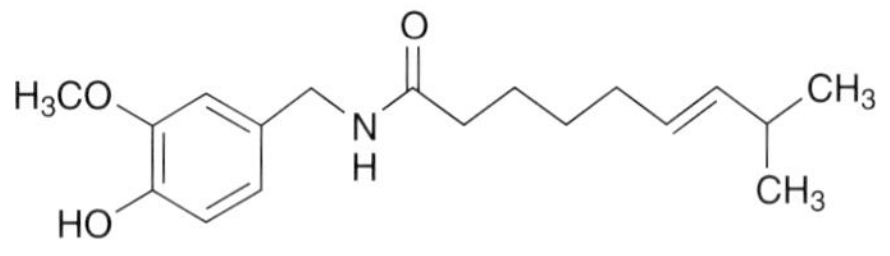

Capsaicin

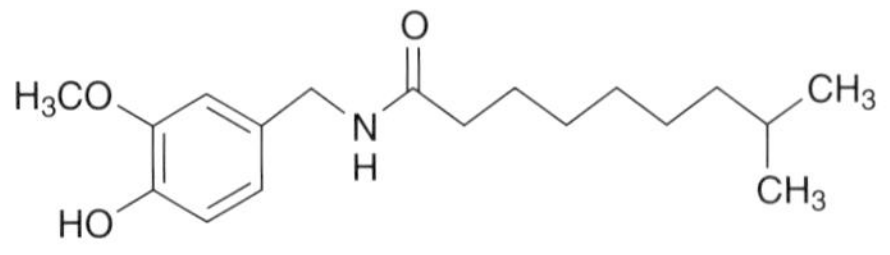

Dihydrocapsaicin

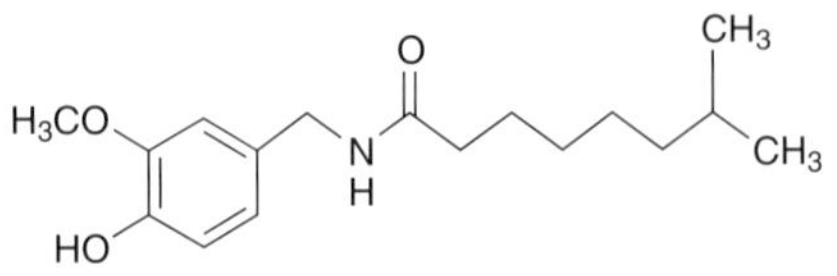

Nordihydrocapsaicin

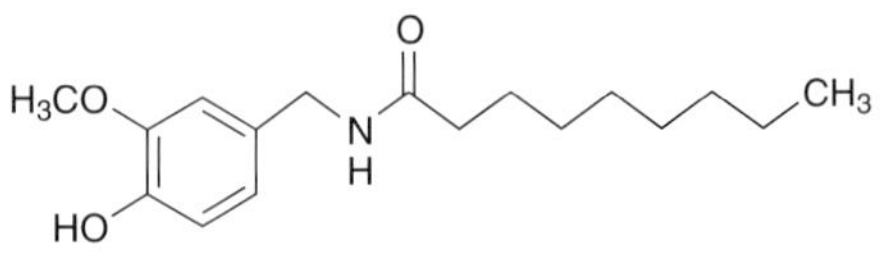

Nonivamide

The USP monograph defines it as an ethanolic extract containing not less than 8.0% of total capsaicins (defined as capsaicin, dihydrocapsaicin and nordihydrocapsaicin) by HPLC, whereas the earlier monograph of the BPC 1973 [1] allowed extraction with acetone or ethanol 90% and required not less than 8.0% of capsaicinoids by spectrophotometry.

Capsaicin USP, an even more potent mixture of capsaicinoids is also used in pharmaceutical preparations; it is a solid mixture of isolated capsaicinoids containing not less than 55% of capsaicin, not less than 75% of capsaicin + dihydrocapsaicin, and not more than 15% of other capsaicinoids.

□ ***Carotenoids***, about 0.2% in mature red fruits of *Capsicum annum* comprising capsanthin (0.06%), β-carotene (0.03%), β-cryptoxanthin (0.02%), capsorubin (0.02%) and lesser amounts of other carotenoids [10]. Ketocarotenoids such as capsanthin and capsorubin are unique to red pepper fruits and the main contributors to the red colour [11]; they are present mainly as diesters [10].

□ ***Flavonoids*** Quercetin 3-*O*-rhamnoside and 3-*O*-rhamnoside-7-glucoside; luteolin 6-*C*-glucoside-8-*C*-arabinoside, 7-*O*-(2-apiosyl)-glucoside and 7-*O*-(2-apiosyl-4-glucosyl-6-malonyl)-glucoside; and apigenin 6-*C*-glucoside-8-*C*-arabinoside (schaftoside) [12].

□ ***Phenolic acids***: Small amounts of hydroxycinnamic (e.g. sinapic, *p*-coumaric, ferulic) and hydroxybenzoic (e.g. vanillic) acids [13], and the glycosides *trans-p*-feruloyl-glucoside and *trans-p*-sinapoyl-glucoside [12].

□ ***Other constituents*** include *trans-p*-ferulyl alcohol 4-*O*-6-(2-methyl-3-hydroxypropionyl)-glucoside [12], ascorbic acid (4-6 mg/100 g in dried chillies) [14] and a complex volatile fraction containing over 100 compounds, particularly fatty acid esters [2,15].

Published Assay Methods

Total capsaicins (defined as capsaicin, dihydrocapsaicin and nordihydrocapsaicin) in capsicum oleoresin by HPLC [USP,16]. Total capsaicinoids by spectrophotometry [1,17]. Individual capsaicinoids by HPLC [4], complexation HPLC [18] or capillary GC [19].

PHARMACOLOGY

It should be noted that many of the published pharmacological and clinical studies relating to capsicum have been carried out with preparations containing Capsaicin USP. While some would regard such preparations as falling outside the realm of herbal medicine, they are included here on the basis that capsicum oleoresin preparations or capsicum tinctures of similar capsaicinoid potency would produce broadly similar effects.

Substance P (SP), a neuropeptide known to influence inflammatory processes and pain transmission, is present in sensory neurons that innervate the dermis and epidermis, and is released in the skin in response to endogenous (stress) and exogenous (injury) factors. Release of SP in the dermis causes vasodilatation and plasma extravasation in rats and humans. SP release has been associated with activation of cytokines, mast cell degranulation resulting in release of histamine, and macrophage chemotaxis. It has also been implicated in the pathogenesis of psoriasis and pruritus. Topically-applied capsaicin first stimulates the release of SP and subsequently depletes cutaneous sensory neurons of SP [20,21]. The treated area of skin then becomes less sensitive to painful stimuli and itching sensations.

Capsaicin is highly specific in its effect and is thought to exert its pharmacological action at the "vanilloid" receptor. The release of substance P is believed to stimulate secretions (gastrointestinal, salivary), to contract smooth muscles, to dilate microvessels and to increase vascular permeability, thereby allowing the leakage of plasma proteins. Repeated administration of capsaicin desensitizes and inactivates sensory neurons through receptor-dependent block of calcium channels [22].

Pharmacological studies in humans

Topical effects

To evaluate the storage of neuropeptides (substance P and others, identified by incubation with rabbit monoclonal antibodies) in cutaneous nerve fibres of patients with aquagenic pruritus, previously untreated with capsaicin, direct immunofluorescence was performed on skin biopsy samples obtained before and after topical application of capsaicin cream (0.025%, 0.5% or 1.0%; three times daily for 4 weeks). The neuropeptidergic fibres appeared to be filled with neuropeptides before, and depleted of them after, capsaicin treatment, to a degree unaffected by the concentration of the capsaicin cream. No change in neuropeptide content was observed in patients treated with cream base only [23].

After repeated application of 1% capsaicin (in ethanol) to human forearm skin for 10 minutes, seven times on average, the skin would no longer develop flare (vasodilatation) around a small injury. Heat pain thresholds were initially reduced, on average by 3.5°C (from 46.3°C to 42.9°C, for up to 10 hours after the last application of capsaicin), but were subsequently higher than normal by 1.9°C in the period 2-10 days after last application. Sensitivity reverted to normal within a few weeks [24].

In 13 healthy volunteers the effects were compared

of repeated topical application of capsaicin (1% in 50% ethanol), 3 times daily for 7 days, to the volar skin (i.e. same side as the palm of the hand) of one forearm and the application of vehicle only to the other forearm. The first application of capsaicin solution caused marked erythema and burning sensation, but these effects became less evident on subsequent applications. By the last day of treatment capsaicin did not cause pain or erythema in any of the subjects. On the capsaicin-pretreated side, pain sensation and increase in blood flow induced by intradermal injection of acidic media (pH 4 and pH 2.5) were markedly reduced, thus both sensory (pain) and 'efferent' (vasodilatation) responses to low pH media had been inhibited [25].

Oral effects
Animal studies with orally administered capsaicin have indicated gastroprotective effects on the stomach. Stimulation of capsaicin-sensitive sensory nerves with low intragastric concentrations of capsaicin protected the rat gastric mucosa against injury produced by various ulcerogenic agents, while high local desensitizing concentrations of capsaicin markedly enhanced the susceptibility of the rat gastric mucosa to later noxious challenge. In most studies, capsaicin given into the stomach of rats or cats inhibited gastric acid secretion [26].

Human studies also provide evidence in favour of a beneficial effect of capsaicin on the gastric mucosa [26]. A significant protective effect ($p<0.05$) of capsicum, taken orally as 20 g of powder with 200 ml of water, against aspirin-induced gastric mucosal injury was demonstrated in a crossover study involving 18 healthy volunteers [27]. Capsaicin also influences gastrointestinal motility; the gastric emptying rates of 10 healthy human subjects were significantly enhanced ($p<0.05$) after intragastric administration of 400 µg of capsaicin [28].

Pharmacokinetics
In a study of the uptake and elimination kinetics of capsaicinoids in stratum corneum (outer layer of the epidermis) of the forearms of 12 healthy volunteers after single topical application of solutions of 30 mg/ml of capsaicinoids, capsaicinoids were detected in the stratum corneum within 1 minute and reached a pseudo-steady state shortly thereafter. The estimated half-lives of capsaicin and dihydrocapsaicin were about 24 hours [29].

CLINICAL STUDIES

A considerable number of clinical studies have been carried out with topical preparations containing capsaicinoid-rich capsicum extracts, i.e. capsicum oleoresin or capsaicin USP, in the treatment of pain arising from various causes. Although many were placebo-controlled, there is an obvious problem with double-blinding due to the stinging and burning sensation from capsaicin.

Chronic pain
In a systematic review [30] of 16 controlled studies (14 placebo-controlled) in the topical application of capsaicinoid preparations for the relief of chronic pain, the studies were separated into two basic categories, in both of which treatment with capsaicin was significantly more effective than placebo: neuropathic conditions, mainly using capsaicin 0.075% cream, and musculoskeletal conditions, mainly using capsaicin 0.025% cream. Some of the studies permitted concomitant oral drugs for pain relief.
Neuropathic pain: 10 studies involved a total of 1035 patients suffering from pain due to neuropathic conditions, classified as post-herpetic neuralgia [31, 32], diabetic neuropathy [33-35], neuropathic pain [36,37], polyneuropathy [38], post-mastectomy pain [39] and HIV-associated neuropathy [40]. The mean response rate (percentage of patients with at least 50% pain relief) at 8 weeks was 60% after capsaicin 0.075% treatment compared to 42% after placebo. Meta-analysis from pooling the 8-week data from six studies (a total of 656 patients) [31-33,36,38,39] indicated a relative benefit of 1.4 from capsaicin 0.075% cream compared to placebo, and the number needed to treat was 5.7, i.e. for every six patients, one would achieve at least 50% reduction in pain who would not have done so if given placebo.
Musculoskeletal pain: 6 studies involved 521 patients suffering from pain due to musculoskeletal conditions, classified as osteoarthritis [41-43], osteoarthritis and rheumatoid arthritis [44], back pain [45] and jaw pain [46]. The mean response rate at 4 weeks was 38% after capsaicin 0.025% treatment compared to 25% after placebo. Meta-analysis from pooling the 4-week data from three studies (a total of 368 patients) [41,44,45] indicated a relative benefit of 1.5 from capsaicin 0.025% cream compared to placebo and the number needed to treat was 8.1.
While these meta-analyses indicated only moderate to poor efficacy, the authors pointed out that most of the patients had chronic moderate to severe pain and some had proved unresponsive to other treatments; in such conditions even a small reduction in pain can be beneficial [30].

An earlier review in 1994 [47] identified sufficient double-blind, placebo-controlled studies to enable pooling of data for meta-analysis in two categories of chronic pain.
Diabetic neuropathy: Capsaicin 0.075% cream produced significantly higher response rates in pain relief than placebo cream in two studies [33,48] but not in two others [34,49]. Nevertheless, in all four studies the trends were in favour of capsaicin

cream, as confirmed by an odds ratio of 2.74 from meta-analysis.
Osteoarthritis: Results were in favour of capsaicin cream in all three available studies, one using 0.075% cream [50] and two using 0.025% cream [43,44]; the pooled results gave an odds ratio of 4.36.

Low back pain
Two randomized, double-blind, placebo-controlled studies by the same clinical research unit in patients suffering from non-specific chronic low back pain involved the application of plasters impregnated with an ethanolic soft extract from capsicum (providing 37.4 µg of capsaicinoids per sq. cm. and complying with a German Commission E monograph [51]), or placebo plasters, to the site of maximum pain for 4-12 hours per day for 3 weeks. Significantly higher responder rates, defined as the proportion of patients with a reduction of at least 30% from baseline in total pain score using the Arhus Index, were reported after verum treatment in both studies:

- In the first study, 61% of responders in the capsicum group (n = 77) compared to 42% in the placebo group (n = 77) (p = 0.022) [45].
- In the second study, 67% of responders in the verum group (n = 160) compared to 49% in the placebo group (n = 160) (p = 0.002) [52].

Pruritus
Significant benefit from the daily application of capsaicin 0.025% cream has been demonstrated in a number of double-blind, placebo-controlled studies in complaints involving pruritus:

- Patients with pruritic psoriasis applied the cream (n = 98) or vehicle only (n = 99) four times daily for 6 weeks. After 4 weeks and 6 weeks respectively in comparison with vehicle-treated patients, capsaicin-treated patients experienced significantly greater relief from pruritus (p = 0.002 and p = 0.060) and had significantly greater reduction in psoriasis severity scores (p = 0.030 and p = 0.036), while the physician's global evaluations indicated significantly greater improvement (p = 0.024 and p = 0.030) [21].
- In a crossover study, 14 out of 17 patients gained marked relief from moderate to severe idiopathic haemodialysis-related pruritus by application of the cream to localised areas four times daily and 5 had complete remission from pruritus during capsaicin treatment (p<0.001 compared to cream base as placebo). Further evaluation 8 weeks after the end of treatment revealed that 5 patients relapsed but 9 maintained the original states (4 complete resolution, 5 improvements) [53].
- A small study demonstrated that aquagenic pruritus (itching provoked by contact with water) can be effectively relieved by application of the cream 3 times daily for 4 weeks [23].

Patients with chronic idiopathic and intractable pruritus ani were treated three times daily for four weeks with a thin perianal layer of either capsaicin 0.006% cream or menthol 1% cream, and vice versa after a washout period, in a crossover study. Out of 44 patients, 31 experienced significant relief during capsaicin treatment (p<0.0001) but did not respond to menthol treatment. Thereafter, 29 of the responders needed a single application of capsaicin daily to remain free or nearly free from anal itching [54].

THERAPEUTICS

Actions
External use: Hyperaemic, rubefacient, counter-irritant [24,25,51,55,56].
Internal use: Carminative [1,55,56], analgesic [22, 55], warming stimulant, spasmolytic, diaphoretic [55,56].

Indications
External use: Relief of pain arising from osteoarthritis and rheumatoid arthritis [41-44,50, 56,57] and other musculoskeletal conditions such as backache, lumbago, sciatica and fibrositis [45, 51,52,56,57]; relief of neuropathic pain, such as postherpetic neuralgia (shingles) and diabetic neuropathy [31-33,35-38,56], and pruritus arising from various causes [21,23,53,54].

Other uses, based on experience or tradition
Internal use: Flatulent dyspepsia and colic [55, 56]; insufficiency of peripheral circulation; atony of the digestive organs, especially in debility of senescence [56].
Topical use: Unbroken chilblains [55,56]; as a gargle for chronic laryngitis [56] and sore throat [55].

Contraindications
Internal use during pregnancy and lactation, except in amounts normally ingested in foods [55,58]. Topical use on damaged skin or open lesions [51].

Side effects
After topical application, a transient stinging or burning sensation at treatment sites that usually diminishes after repeated application; this is part of the normal and expected action.

Interactions with other drugs
None known.

Dosage
External use Several times daily, cream or lotion containing 0.025-0.075% of capsaicinoids [30,47];

impregnated plasters (10-40 µg of capsaicinoids per cm²) [45,51,52]; infused oil from dried fruits [55,58].

Internal use Three times daily: dried fruits, 30-120 mg; Capsicum Tincture BPC 1968 (1:20 in 60% alcohol; not less than 0.025% w/v of capsaicin), 0.3-1 ml [56]. As a gargle, 5-10 drops of tincture in half a glass of water [58].

Caution: Even in small amounts capsicum preparations irritate the mucosa very strongly and cause a painful burning sensation. Contact of capsicum preparations with mucous membranes, especially the eyes, should be carefully avoided.

SAFETY

Capsicum and capsicum oleoresin preparations in oral or topical use, and capsaicin preparations in topical use, are usually well tolerated.

Due to the mechanism of action of capsaicinoids, localised skin reactions and an initial burning sensation are to be expected from topical treatments and are acceptable to most patients, but may lead to discontinuation of use by some individuals.

The oral LD_{50} of capsaicin was determined as 97-118 mg/kg body weight in mice and 148-161 mg/kg in rats [59], while the LD_{50} of capsaicin after dermal application to mice was greater than 512 mg/kg [3]. The acute oral toxicity of capsaicinoids as a food additive in man is considered to be negligible [3,60].

From a standard battery of genotoxicity assays, capsaicin was found to have no genotoxic activity in bacterial mutation, chromosome aberration or rat bone marrow micronucleus tests [61].

REGULATORY STATUS

Medicines

UK	Accepted for general sale, internal or external use: capsicum (dried fruits) [62]; capsicum oleoresin (min. 8% of capsaicin) with limits on dosage* [63].
France	Accepted for specified indications [57].
Germany	Commission E monograph published, with approved uses [51].

* Internal use: 1.2 mg maximum single dose, 1.8 mg maximum daily dose. External use: 2.5% maximum strength.

Food

USA	Generally recognized as safe (21 CFR 182.10 and 182.20) [64].
Council of Europe	Permitted as flavouring, category N2 [65].

REFERENCES

Current Pharmacopoeial Monographs

Ph. Eur.	Capsicum
USP	Capsicum
USP	Capsicum Oleoresin

Literature References

1. Pharmaceutical Society of Great Britain. Capsicum; Capsicum Oleoresin. In: British Pharmaceutical Codex 1973. London: Pharmaceutical Press, 1973:72-73 and 764.
2. Keller U, Flath RA, Mon TR and Teranishi R. Volatiles from Red Pepper (*Capsicum* spp.). In: Teranishi R and Barrera-Benitez H, editors. *Quality of Selected Fruits and Vegetables of North America*. ACS Symposium Series 170. ISBN 0-8412-0662-7. Washington DC: American Chemical Society, 1981:137-146.
3. Govindarajan VS and Sathyanarayana MN. Capsicum - Production, Technology, Chemistry and Quality. Part V. Impact on Physiology, Pharmacology, Nutrition and Metabolism; Structure, Pungency, Pain and Desensitisation Sequences. *Crit. Rev. Food Sci. Nutr.* 1991, **29**, 435-474.
4. Maillard M-N, Giampaoli P and Richard HMJ. Analysis of Eleven Capsaicinoids by Reversed-phase High Performance Liquid Chromatography. *Flavour Fragrance J.* 1997, **12**, 409-413.
5. Jurenitsch J and Leinmüller R. Quantification of nonylic acid vanillylamide and other capsaicinoids in the pungent principles of Capsicum fruits and preparations by gas-liquid chromatography on glass capillary columns. *J. Chromatogr.* 1980, **189**, 389-397 [GERMAN/English summary].
6. Jurenitsch J. Scharfstoffzusammensetzung in Früchten definierter Capsicum-Sippen - Konsequenzen für Qualitätsforderungen und taxonomische Aspekte [Composition of pungent substances in fruits of defined *Capsicum* species - Inferences for quality requirements and taxonomical aspects]. *Sci. Pharm.* 1981, **49**, 321-328 [GERMAN].
7. Jurenitsch J and Kastner U. Klassische Pharmakognosie - eine Wissenschaft mit Zukunft? [Classical pharmacognosy - a science with a future?]. *Pharm. unserer Zeit* 1994, **23**, 93-99 [GERMAN].
8. Cordell GA and Araujo OE. Capsaicin: Identification, nomenclature and pharmacotherapy. *Ann. Pharmacother.* 1993, **27**, 330-336.
9. Constant HL, Cordell GA and West DP. Nonivamide, a Constituent of *Capsicum* oleoresin. *J. Nat. Prod.* 1996, **59**, 425-426.
10. Camara B and Monéger R. Free and esterified carotenoids in green and red fruits of *Capsicum annuum*. *Phytochemistry* 1978, **17**, 91-93.
11. Ittah Y, Kanner J and Granit R. Hydrolysis Study of Carotenoid Pigments of Paprika (*Capsicum annuum* L. variety Lehava) by HPLC/Photodiode Array Detection. *J. Agric. Food Chem.* 1993, **41**, 899-901.
12. Materska M, Piacente S, Stochmal A, Pizza C, Oleszek W and Perucka I. Isolation and structure elucidation of flavonoid and phenolic acid glycosides from pericarp of hot pepper fruit (*Capsicum annuum* L.). *Phytochemistry* 2003, **63**, 893-898.
13. Schulz JM and Herrmann K. Occurrence of Hydroxybenzoic Acids and Hydroxycinnamic Acids in Spices. IV. Phenolics of Spices. *Z. Lebensm. Unters. Forsch.* 1980, **171**, 193-199 [GERMAN/English summary].
14. Keshinro OO and Ketiku OA. The Contribution of Tropical Chillies to Ascorbic Acid Consumption. *Food Chem.* 1983, **11**, 43-49.
15. Haymon LW and Aurand LW. Volatile Constituents of

Tabasco Peppers. *J. Agric. Food Chem.* 1971, **19**, 1131-1134.
16. International Organization for Standardization (ISO). ISO 7543-2:1993 (E). Chillies and chilli oleoresins - Determination of total capsaicinoid content. Part 2: Method using high-performance liquid chromatography. Geneva: ISO, 1993:1-5.
17. International Organization for Standardization (ISO). ISO 7543-1:1994 (E). Chillies and chilli oleoresins - Determination of total capsaicinoid content. Part 1: Spectrometric method. Geneva: ISO, 1994:1-4.
18. Constant HL, Cordell GA, West DP and Johnson JH. Separation and quantification of capsaicinoids using complexation chromatography. *J. Nat. Prod.* 1995, **58**, 1925-1928.
19. Thomas BV, Schreiber AA and Weisskopf CP. Simple Method for Quantitation of Capsaicinoids in Peppers Using Capillary Gas Chromatography. *J. Agric. Food Chem.* 1998, **46**, 2655-2663.
20. Buck SH and Burks TF. The Neuropharmacology of Capsaicin: Review of Some Recent Observations. *Pharmacol. Rev.* 1986, **38**, 179-226.
21. Ellis CN, Berberian B, Sulica VI, Dodd WA, Jarratt MT, Katz HI et al. A double-blind evaluation of topical capsaicin in pruritic psoriasis. *J. Am. Acad. Dermatol.* 1993, **29**, 438-442.
22. Hautkappe M, Roizen MF, Toledano A, Roth S, Jeffries JA and Ostermeier AM. Review of the Effectiveness of Capsaicin for Painful Cutaneous Disorders and Neural Dysfunction. *Clin. J. Pain* 1998, **14**, 97-106.
23. Lotti T, Teofoli P and Tsampau D. Treatment of aquagenic pruritus with topical capsaicin cream. *J. Am. Acad. Dermatol.* 1994, **30**, 232-235.
24. Carpenter SE and Lynn B. Vascular and sensory responses of human skin to mild injury after topical treatment with capsaicin. *Br. J. Pharmacol.* 1981, **73**, 755-758.
25. Del Bianco E, Geppetti P, Zippi P, Isolani D, Magini B and Cappugi P. The effects of repeated dermal application of capsaicin to the human skin on pain and vasodilatation induced by intradermal injection of acid and hypertonic solutions. *Br. J. Clin. Pharmacol.* 1996, **41**, 1-6.
26. Abdel-Salam OM, Szolcsányi J, Mózsik G. Capsaicin and the stomach. A review of experimental and clinical data. *J. Physiol. (Paris)* 1997, **91**, 151-171.
27. Yeoh KG, Kang JY, Yap I, Guan R, Tan CC, Wee A and Teng CH. Chili protects against aspirin-induced gastroduodenal mucosal injury in humans. *Dig. Dis. Sci.* 1995, **40**, 580-583.
28. Debreceni A, Abdel-Salam OM, Figler M, Juricskay I, Szolcsanyi J and Mozsik G. Capsaicin increases gastric emptying rate in healthy human subjects measured by 13C-labeled octanoic acid breath test. *J. Physiol. (Paris)* 1999, **93**, 455-460.
29. Pershing LK, Reilly CA, Corlett JL and Crouch DJ. Effects of vehicle on the uptake and elimination kinetics of capsaicinoids in human skin in vivo. *Toxicol. Appl. Pharmacol.* 2004, **200**, 73-81.
30. Mason L, Moore RA, Derry S, Edwards JE and McQuay HJ. Systematic review of topical capsaicin for the treatment of chronic pain. *BMJ* 2004, **328**, 991-995.
31. Bernstein JE, Korman NJ, Bickers DR, Dahl MV and Millikan LE. Topical capsaicin treatment of chronic postherpetic neuralgia. *J. Am. Acad. Dermatol.* 1989, **21**, 265-270.
32. Watson CP and Evans RJ. The postmastectomy pain syndrome and topical capsaicin: a randomized trial. *Pain* 1992, **51**, 375-379.
33. The Capsaicin Study Group. Treatment of Painful Diabetic Neuropathy with Topical Capsaicin. A Multicenter, Double-Blind, Vehicle-Controlled Study. *Arch. Intern. Med.* 1991, **151**, 2225-2229.
34. Chad DA, Aronin N, Lundstrom R, McKeon P, Ross D, Molitch M et al. Does capsaicin relieve the pain of diabetic neuropathy? *Pain* 1990, **42**, 387-388.
35. Biesbroeck R, Bril V, Hollander P, Kabadi U, Schwartz S, Singh SP et al. A Double-Blind Comparison of Topical Capsaicin and Oral Amitriptyline in Painful Diabetic Neuropathy. *Advances Ther.* 1995, **12**, 111-120.
36. Ellison N, Loprinzi CL, Kugler J, Hatfield AK, Miser A, Sloan JA et al. Phase III Placebo-Controlled Trial of Capsaicin Cream in the Management of Surgical Neuropathic Pain in Cancer Patients. *J. Clin. Oncol.* 1997, **15**, 2974-2980.
37. McCleane G. The analgesic efficacy of topical capsaicin is enhanced by glyceryl trinitrate in painful osteoarthritis: a randomized, double blind, placebo controlled study. *Eur. J. Pain* 2000, **4**, 355-360.
38. Low PA, Opfer-Gehrking TL, Dyck PJ, Litchy WJ and O'Brien PC. Double-blind, placebo-controlled study of the application of capsaicin cream in chronic distal painful polyneuropathy. *Pain* 1995, **62**, 163-168.
39. Watson CPN, Tyler KL, Bickers DR, Millikan LE, Smith S and Coleman E. A Randomised Vehicle-Controlled Trial of Topical Capsaicin in the Treatment of Postherpetic Neuralgia. *Clin. Ther.* 1993, **15**, 510-526.
40. Paice JA, Ferrans CE, Lashley FR, Shott S, Vizgirda V and Pitrak D. Topical capsaicin in the management of HIV-associated peripheral neuropathy. *J. Pain Symptom Manage.* 2000, **19**, 45-52.
41. Altman RD, Aven A, Holmburg CE, Pfeifer LM, Sack M and Young GT. Capsaicin Cream 0.025% as Monotherapy for Osteoarthritis: A Double-Blind Study. *Semin. Arthritis Rheum.* 1994, **23** (Suppl. 3), 25-33.
42. Schnitzer TJ, Posner M and Lawrence ID. High strength capsaicin cream for osteoarthritis pain: rapid onset of action and improved efficacy with twice daily dosing. *J. Clin. Rheumatol.* 1995, **1**, 268-273.
43. Schnitzer T, Morton C and Coker S. Topical Capsaicin Therapy for Osteoarthritis Pain: Achieving a Maintenance Regimen. *Semin. Arthritis Rheum.* 1994, **23** (Suppl. 3), 34-40.
44. Deal CL, Schnitzer TJ, Lipstein E, Seibold JR, Stevens RM, Levy MD et al. Treatment of Arthritis with Topical Capsaicin: A Double-Blind Trial. *Clin. Ther.* 1991, **13**, 383-395.
45. Keitel W, Frerick H, Kuhn U, Schmidt U, Kuhlmann M and Bredehorst A. Capsicum Pain Plaster in Chronic Non-specific Low Back Pain. *Arzneim.-Forsch./Drug Res.* 2001, **51**, 896-903.
46. Winocur E, Gavish A, Halachmi M, Eli I and Gazit E. Topical application of capsaicin for the treatment of localized pain in the temporomandibular joint area. *J. Orofac. Pain* 2000, **14**, 31-36.
47. Zhang WY and Li Wan Po A. The effectiveness of topically applied capsaicin. A meta-analysis. *Eur. J. Clin. Pharmacol.* 1994, **46**, 517-522.
48. Scheffler NM, Sheitel PL and Lipton MN. Treatment of Painful Diabetic Neuropathy with Capsaicin 0.075%. *J. Am. Podiatric Med. Assoc.* 1991, **81**, 288-293.
49. Tandan R, Lewis GA, Krusinski PB, Badger GB and Fries TJ. Topical Capsaicin in Painful Diabetic Neuropathy. Controlled Study with Long-Term Follow-Up. *Diabetes Care* 1992, **15**, 8-14.
50. McCarthy GM and McCarty DJ. Effect of Topical Capsaicin in the Therapy of Painful Osteoarthritis of the Hands. *J. Rheumatol.* 1992, **19**, 604-607.
51. Capsicum (Paprika): Capsici fructus (Paprika), Capsici fructus acer (Cayennepfeffer). German Commission E Monograph published in: Bundesanzeiger No. 22 of 1 February 1990.
52. Frerick H, Keitel W, Kuhn U, Schmidt S, Bredehorst A and Kuhlmann M. Topical treatment of chronic low back pain with a capsicum plaster. *Pain* 2003, **106**, 59-64.
53. Tarng D-C, Cho Y-L, Liu H-N and Huang T-P. Hemodialysis-Related Pruritus: A Double-Blind, Placebo-Controlled, Crossover Study of Capsaicin 0.025% Cream. *Nephron* 1996, **72**, 617-622.
54. Lysy J, Sistiery-Ittah M, Israelit Y, Shmueli A, Strauss-Liviatan N, Mindrul V et al. Topical capsaicin - a novel and effective treatment for idiopathic intractable pruritus ani: a randomised, placebo controlled, crossover study. *Gut* 2003, **52**, 1323-1326.
55. Chevallier A. Cayenne, Chilli - *Capsicum frutescens.* In: *Encyclopedia of Medicinal Plants, 2nd ed.* ISBN 0-7513-1209-6. London-New York: Dorling Kindersley, 2001:74.

56. Capsicum. In: *British Herbal Pharmacopoeia 1983*. ISBN 0-903032-07-4. Bournemouth: British Herbal Medicine Association, 1983.
57. Piment, fruit. In: *Médicaments à base de plantes*. ISBN 2-911473-02-7. Saint-Denis Cedex, France: Agence du Médicament, 1998.
58. Ody P. *Capsicum frutescens* - Cayenne. In: *The Complete Guide - Medicinal Herbal*. ISBN 0-7513-3005-1. London-New York: Dorling Kindersley, 2000:50.
59. Saito A and Yamamoto M. Acute oral toxicity of capsaicin in mice and rats. *J. Toxicol. Sci.* 1996, **21**, 195-200.
60. Glinsukon T, Stitmunnaithum V, Toskulkao C, Buranawuti T and Tangkrisanavinont V. Acute toxicity of capsaicin in several animal species. *Toxikon* 1980, **18**, 215-220.
61. Proudlock R, Thompson C and Longstaff E. Examination of the Potential Genotoxicity of Pure Capsaicin in Bacterial Mutation, Chromosome Aberration and Rodent Micronucleus Tests. *Environ. Mol. Mutagen.* 2004, **44**, 441-447.
62. Capsicum. In: UK Statutory Instrument 1984 No. 769. The Medicines (Products Other Than Veterinary Drugs) (General Sale List) Order 1984. Schedule 1, Table A.
63. Capsicum Oleoresin BPC 1973. In: UK Statutory Instrument 1994 No. 2410. The Medicines (Products Other Than Veterinary Drugs) (General Sale List) Amendment Order 1994. Schedule 1, Table A.
64. Capsicum (Capsicum frutescens L. and Capsicum annuum L.). In: Sections 182.10 and 182.20 of USA Code of Federal Regulations, Title 21, Food and Drugs, Parts 170 to 199. Revised as of April 1, 2000.
65. Capsicum annuum L. and Capsicum frutescens L., fruits. In: *Flavouring Substances and Natural Sources of Flavourings, 3rd ed.* ISBN 2-7160-0081-6. Strasbourg: Council of Europe, 1981.

REGULATORY GUIDELINES FROM OTHER EU COUNTRIES

FRANCE

Médicaments à base de plantes [57]: Piment, fruit.

Therapeutic indications accepted

Topical use
Traditionally used in the symptomatic treatment of minor painful articular complaints.

GERMANY

Commission E monograph [51]: Capsici fructus (Paprika) and Capsici fructus acer (Cayennepfeffer) under the general heading Capsicum (Paprika).

Uses
Painful muscle tension in the region of the shoulder-arm and spinal column in adults and schoolchildren.

Contraindications
Use on damaged skin; hypersensitivity to capsicum preparations.

Side effects
In rare cases, hypersensitivity reactions (urticaria) may occur.

Interactions with other drugs
None known.
Note: No additional application of warmth.

Dosage
Unless otherwise prescribed, semi-solid preparations containing 0.02-0.05% of capsaicinoids; liquid preparations containing 0.005-0.01% of capsaicinoids; plasters containing 10-40 µg of capsaicinoids per sq. cm.

Mode of administration
Capsicum preparations exclusively for external use.

Duration of administration
No longer than 2 days. Then 14 days must elapse before repeated application to the same area. Longer use on the same area could damage sensory nerves.

Caution: Even in small amounts capsicum preparations irritate the mucosa very strongly and cause a painful burning sensation. Contact of capsicum preparations with mucous membranes, especially the eyes, should be avoided.

Actions
Locally hyperaemic and nerve-damaging.

CARAWAY FRUIT

Carvi fructus

Synonym: Caraway seed.

Definition
Caraway Fruit consists of the whole dried mericarps of *Carum carvi* L.

Caraway is a biennial herb, 30-100 cm high. It is cultivated in northern and central European countries and in other parts of the world such as Morocco, Egypt, China and Australia.

CONSTITUENTS

□ ***Essential oil,*** 3-6% [1] (Ph. Eur. min. 3% V/m). (+)-Carvone (49-70%) and (+)-limonene (30-47%) are the main components, often accounting for over 95% of the oil; none of the other components (about 30, mainly monoterpenes) are present in amounts greater than 1% [1-6].

In green fruits limonene is predominant, but the proportion of carvone in the oil increases sharply as the fruits ripen and turn brown [6].

□ ***Fixed oil,*** 9-14%, containing fatty acids (as glycerides), principally petroselinic acid (= *cis*-6-octadecenoic acid; 33-43%) and linoleic acid (35-37%) together with oleic (15-24%), palmitic (4-5%), stearic (1-2%) and *cis*-vaccenic (= *cis*-11-octadecenoic; 0.6-0.7%) acids, as percentages of the total fruit oil [7].

□ ***Flavonoids***, ca. 0.1% [8], including isoquercitrin, hyperin, and the 3-glucosides and 3-galactosides of kaempferol and isorhamnetin [9]; also quercetin 3-glucuronide [8].

□ ***Phenylpropanoids*** Caffeic acid (0.3%) [10,11], chlorogenic acid (5-caffeoylquinic acid, 0.1%) [11,12] and small amounts of other hydroxycinnamic [10] and caffeoylquinic [12] acids; also traces of hydroxybenzoic acids [10] including 4-glucosyloxy-benzoic acid [13].

□ ***Coumarins*** Small amounts of umbelliferone and scopoletin [14], and traces (less than 0.005 µg/g) of the furanocoumarins 5-methoxypsoralen and 8-methoxypsoralen [15].

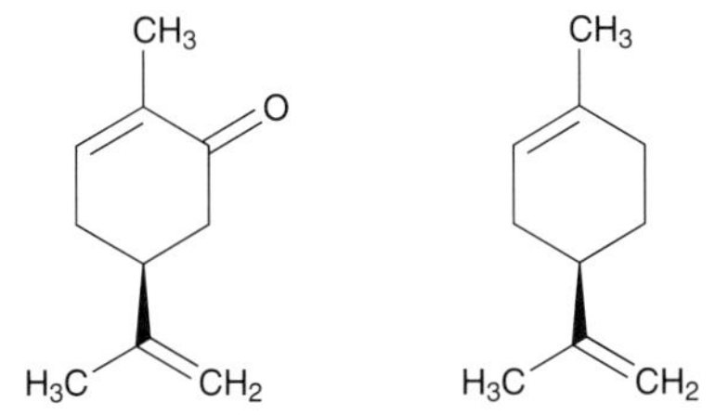

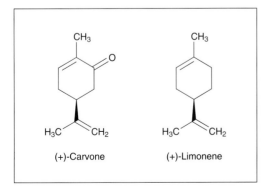

(+)-Carvone (+)-Limonene

□ ***Polysaccharides*** The reserve polysaccharide in the endosperm of caraway fruits (about 14% of the weight of dry fruits) consists largely of a β-(1-4)-mannan [16].

□ ***Other constituents*** include protein (27%), sugars (3%) and minerals [17]. From a water-soluble fraction, ten *p*-menthanetriols (eight of which are stereoisomers of *p*-menthane-2,8,9-triol) and five *p*-menthanetriol glucosides have been isolated [18].

Published Assay Methods
Essential oil components by GC [1]. Fatty acids as butyl esters by GC [7].

PHARMACOLOGY

In vitro

Spasmolytic activity
An ethanolic extract of caraway fruit at 2.5 and 10.0 ml/litre significantly and dose-dependently decreased acetylcholine- and histamine-induced contractions in isolated guinea pig ileum ($p<0.05$ and $p<0.01$ respectively at 10.0 ml/litre); the maximum contractility also decreased [19]. Similar effects were observed with carbachol-induced contractions [20].

Caraway oil had a relaxant effect on guinea pig tracheal smooth muscle, decreasing the force of phasic contractions by 50% at 27 mg/litre, but no antispasmodic effect was observed on electrically-stimulated guinea pig ileum [21].

Antimicrobial activity
The antimicrobial activity of caraway fruit is fairly strong, although somewhat weaker than that of clove or thyme, and is due largely to its essential oil.

Extracts of caraway fruit prepared with organic solvents exhibited moderate antimicrobial activity against *Escherichia coli, Staphylococcus aureus, Candida albicans* and *Streptomyces venezuelae* [22] and strong activity against two *Shigella* species [23]. A methanolic extract inhibited *Helicobacter pylori* with an MIC of 100 µg/ml [24]. Powdered caraway fruit inhibited growth and toxin production of two toxigenic *Aspergillus* fungal strains [25] and an aqueous extract inhibited the growth of a range of fungi [26].

Caraway fruit essential oil showed antimicrobial activity against *S. aureus* (MIC 700 ppm), *E. coli, Salmonella typhi, Shigella dysentery* and *Vibrio cholera* [27]. It also showed good inhibitory activity against dermatophytic fungi which cause infections such as athlete's foot [28] and completely inhibited mould growth and aflatoxin production by *Aspergillus parasiticus* at 0.8 mg/ml [29]. (+)-Carvone showed moderate inhibitory activity against bacteria and fungi, and good activity against vermiforms [30].

Other effects
A dry 80%-methanolic extract of caraway fruit at 20 mg/ml significantly increased Ca^{2+} fluxes into clonal rat pituitary cells by 27% [31].

On the assumption that a carminative effect is probably due to several responses, one of which is antifoaming and another antispasmodic, it has been demonstrated that the foam height of simulated gastric juice was reduced by caraway oil at concentrations of 0.025-0.1% [32].

In vivo

Effects on respiratory tract fluid
Carvone inhaled by urethanized rabbits as vapour (2 mg/kg body weight) in steam increased the volume output of respiratory tract fluid by 89.6% during autumn months ($p<0.01$) but by only 17.5% during the rest of the year; the reason for the greater effect in autumn is not clear. At 1-9 mg/kg body weight it produced a dose-dependent 4-9% decrease in the specific gravity of respiratory tract fluid in non-autumn months. Limonene has also been shown to increase output of respiratory tract fluid [33].

Antiulcerogenic effects
An alcoholic extract of caraway fruit, administered orally to rats at 2.5-10 ml/kg, had a dose-dependent protective effect against indometacin-induced ulcers; 80% protection at 10 ml/kg was similar to the effect of oral cimetidine at 50 mg/kg. Oral pre-treatment of rats with the same extract (but lyophilized and reconstituted with water only) at 2.5 ml/kg significantly reduced gastric juice acidity and increased mucin concentration compared to indometacin-treated animals [34].

Antidiabetic effects
Oral administration of caraway oil to alloxan-induced diabetic rats at 10 mg/kg body weight daily for 6 weeks significantly reduced ($p<0.001$) blood glucose by 55% and serum cholesterol by 74% compared to an untreated diabetic control group [35].

Anticarcinogenic activity
Carvone (and separately limonene) isolated from caraway oil was orally administered to mice at 20 mg per animal three times over 6 days. Subsequent assays of cytosolic fractions from various organs and tissues of the mice showed that, compared to control animals, carvone had significantly in-creased ($p<0.05$ to $p<0.005$) the activity of the detoxifying enzyme glutathione S-transferase in the liver, forestomach, small intestinal mucosa and colon; limonene was also effective, but less so. Carvone significantly increased glutathione levels in the lung, small intestinal mucosa and colon. The results suggested that carvone and limonene may have potential as inhibitors of carcinogenesis [36].

When fed to rats as 20% of their diet for 25 weeks, powdered caraway fruit significantly decreased ($p<0.05$) the incidence of 7,12-dimethylbenz(*a*)anthracene-induced tumours (42.8% protection) and the mean number of tumours per rat (50.6% protection) compared to control animals. The latency period of tumour appearance significantly increased (17.6 weeks compared to 14.4 weeks; $p<0.05$) [37].

Pharmacological studies in humans

Antispasmodic effect
'Real time' sonographic measurements on volunteers who took a capsule containing 50 mg of caraway oil on an empty stomach, followed 15 minutes later by a test drink (400 ml apple juice + 10 ml lactulose), showed that the gall bladder emptied (volume decrease of 20%) in response to the drink. When the gall bladder subsequently filled up again, a volume increase of 90% (from initial), compared to about 40% in those who had taken only the test drink, confirmed that caraway oil inhibited contraction of the gall bladder [38].

CLINICAL STUDIES

None published on mono-preparations of caraway fruit or caraway oil.

In a double-blind clinical study using a combination preparation, patients with painful but non-ulcer dyspepsia (plus other digestive disorders) who took daily for four weeks 3 enteric-coated capsules, each containing 90 mg of peppermint oil and 50 mg of caraway oil ($n = 19$), showed significant improvements in pain intensity ($p = 0.015$) and Clinical Global Impressions ($p = 0.008$) compared to those who received placebo ($n = 20$) [39].

THERAPEUTICS

Actions
Carminative [32,40-43], spasmolytic [19-21,38,42-45] and antimicrobial [22-30].

Also stated to be expectorant [42,44], galactagogic [41,44] and emmenagogic [42].

Caraway fruit has been described as the strongest and most reliable of the herbal carminatives, and it is well tolerated [46]. Small doses of caraway fruit liquid preparations may be used in infant feeding bottles [41], although no medicines should be given to babies under 6 months without professional advice [44]. Caraway water has been used as a vehicle for children's medicines [43].

Indications
None adequately substantiated by pharmacological or clinical studies.

Uses based on experience or tradition
Main use Dyspeptic complaints such as flatulence, eructation, bloating and mild spasmodic pains in the gastrointestinal tract [42,44,45,47], including flatulent colic of infants [40-42].
Other uses Loss of appetite; dysmenorrhoea [42, 44]; to stimulate the flow of milk in breast-feeding mothers [41,44]; bronchitis and (as a gargle) laryngitis [42].

Contraindications
None known.

Side effects
None known.

Interactions with other drugs
None known.

Dosage

Adults Three times daily: powdered fruits (crushed immediately before use), 0.5-2 g, usually as an infusion [42,45]; tincture (1:5 in 45% alcohol), 0.5-4 ml [42]; caraway oil, 0.05-0.2 ml [43]; Concentrated Caraway Water BPC 1973, 0.3-1 ml (contains 0.006-0.02 ml of caraway oil in 50% ethanol) [43].
One teaspoonful of dried caraway fruit weighs about 3.6 g [41].

Infants over 6 months A suitable dose for use in feeding bottles (equivalent to about 60 mg of caraway fruit) is 2-3 drops of Concentrated Caraway Water BPC 1973. Alternatively, one teaspoonful of fresh infusion, prepared from half a teaspoonful (ca. 1.8 g) of caraway fruit in 150 ml of boiling water [41].

SAFETY

Caraway fruit is widely used as a flavouring in food, accepted as category 1 (no restriction) by the Council of Europe and accorded GRAS status by the FDA for the amounts normally used. Although a few persons hypersensitive to plants of the Umbelliferae (especially celery) show allergic responses [48], caraway fruit is considered to have low sensitizing potential [49].

Caraway oil has been assessed as non-toxic (at therapeutic dose levels), very mildly irritant but non-sensitizing to skin, and moderately irritant to mucous membranes [50]. The acute oral LD_{50} of caraway oil in rats was determined as 3.5 ml/kg. Caraway oil was non-irritating when applied to the backs of hairless mice but irritant to intact or abraded skin of rabbits. When tested on the skin of 25 volunteers at a concentration of 4% in petrolatum, it produced neither irritation nor sensitization reactions [51].

No adverse effects were observed from addition of 0.25% of carvone to the diet of rats for one year [52]. Based on short- and long-term toxicity studies in rodents the World Health Organization established an acceptable daily intake (ADI) for (+)-carvone of 0-1 mg/kg body weight per day [53].

In the *Salmonella typhimurium* assay (Ames test), an ethanolic extract of caraway fruit showed no mutagenic potential using strain TA 98 but was moderately mutagenic in strain TA 102, although the activity was less than that observed with clove or ginger [54]. In another evaluation, aqueous, methanolic and hexanic extracts equivalent to 75 mg of caraway fruit showed no mutagenic potential in *Salmonella typhimurium* strains TA 98 and TA 100 [55]. A hot water extract inhibited methylation and mutation induced by alkylating agents in the Ames test using *Salmonella typhimurium* TA 100 and other strains, and inhibited tumour formation in the colon of rats [56]. Other studies, summarized in the Pharmacology *in vivo* section above, have demonstrated the anticarcinogenic potential of caraway fruit, carvone and limonene [36,37].

REGULATORY STATUS

Medicines

UK	Accepted for general sale, internal or external use [57].
France	Accepted for specified indications [47].
Germany	Commission E monograph published, with approved uses [45].

Food

USA	Generally recognized as safe (21 CFR 182.10 and 182.20) [58].
Council of Europe	Permitted as flavouring, category 1 [59].

REFERENCES

Current Pharmacopoeial Monographs

Ph. Eur. Caraway Fruit

Literature References

1. Analytical Methods Committee, Royal Society of Chemistry. Application of Gas-Liquid Chromatography to the Analysis of Essential Oils. Part XIV. Monographs for Five Essential Oils. *Analyst* 1988, **113**, 1125-1136.
2. Lawrence BM. Progress in Essential Oils. *Perfumer & Flavorist* 1996, **21** (May-Jun), 55-68.
3. Lawrence BM. Progress in Essential Oils. *Perfumer & Flavorist* 1992, **17** (Jan-Feb), 45-56.
4. Kallio H, Kerrola K and Alhonmäki P. Carvone and Limonene in Caraway Fruits (*Carum carvi* L.) Analyzed by Supercritical Carbon Dioxide Extraction-Gas Chromatography. *J. Agric. Food Chem.* 1994, **42**, 2478-2485.
5. Gorunovic M, Panov I, Chalchat JC, Garry R-P and Michet A. The quality of wild-growing caraway, *Carum carvi* L., from Montenegro. *Acta Pharm. Jugosl.* 1991, **41**, 267-271.
6. von Schantz M and Ek BS. Über die Bildung von ätherischem Öl in Kümmel, *Carum carvi* L. [The formation of essential oil in caraway, *Carum carvi* L.]. *Sci. Pharm.* 1971, **39**, 82-101 [GERMAN].
7. Reiter B, Lechner M and Lorbeer E. The fatty acid profiles - including petroselinic and cis-vaccenic acid - of different Umbelliferae seed oils. *Fett/Lipid* 1998, **100**, 498-502.
8. Kunzemann J and Herrmann K. Isolation and Identification of Flavon(ol)-O-glycosides in Caraway (*Carum carvi* L.), Fennel (*Foeniculum vulgare* Mill.), Anise (*Pimpinella anisum* L.) and Coriander (*Coriandrum sativum* L.) and of Flavone-C-glycosides in Anise. I. Phenolics of Spices. *Z. Lebensm. Unters. Forsch.* 1977, **164**, 194-200 [GERMAN/English summary].
9. Harborne JB and Williams CA. Flavonoid patterns in the fruits of the Umbelliferae. *Phytochemistry* 1972, **11**, 1741-1750.
10. Schulz JM and Herrmann K. Occurrence of Hydroxybenzoic Acids and Hydroxycinnamic Acids in Spices. IV. Phenolics of Spices. *Z. Lebensm. Unters. Forsch.* 1980, **171**, 193-199 [GERMAN/English summary].
11. Baerheim Svendsen A. Über das Vorkommen der Chlorogen- und Kaffeesäure in der Pflanzenfamilie der Umbelliferen. 2. Mitteilung über Papierchromatographie in der phytochemischen Analyse [The occurrence of chlorogenic and caffeic acids in the Umbelliferae family. 2. Paper chromatography in phytochemical analysis]. *Pharm. Acta Helv.* 1951, **26**, 253-258 [GERMAN].
12. Dirks U and Herrmann K. High Performance Liquid Chromatography of Hydroxycinnamoyl-quinic Acids and 4-(β-D-Glucopyranosyloxy)-benzoic Acid in Spices. 10. Phenolics of Spices. *Z. Lebensm. Unters. Forsch.* 1984, **179**, 12-16 [GERMAN/English summary].
13. Dirks U and Herrmann K. 4-(β-D-Glucopyranosyloxy)-benzoic acid, a characteristic phenolic constituent of the Apiaceae. *Phytochemistry* 1984, **23**, 1811-1812.
14. Kartnig T, Scholz G. Component Lipids of the Fruits of *Pimpinella anisum* L. und *Carum carvi* L. *Fette Seifen Anstrichmittel* 1969, **71**, 276-280 [GERMAN/English summary].
15. Ceska O, Chaudhary SK, Warrington PJ and Ashwood-Smith MJ. Photoactive furocoumarins in fruits of some Umbellifers. *Phytochemistry* 1987, **26**, 165-169.
16. Hopf H and Kandler O. Characterization of the 'reserve cellulose' of the endosperm of *Carum carvi* as a β-(1-4)-mannan. *Phytochemistry* 1977, **16**, 1715-1717.
17. El-Wakeil F, Khairy M, Morsi S, Farag RS, Shihata AA and Badel AZMA. Biochemical Studies on the Essential Oils of some Fruits of Umbelliferae Family. *Seifen Öle Fette Wachse* 1986, **112**, 77-80.
18. Matsumura T, Ishikawa T and Kitajima J. New *p*-menthanetriols and their glucosides from the fruit of caraway. *Tetrahedron* 2001, **57**, 8067-8074.
19. Forster HB, Niklas H and Lutz S. Antispasmodic Effects of Some Medicinal Plants. *Planta Medica* 1980, **40**, 309-319.
20. Forster H. Spasmolytische Wirkung pflanzlicher Carminativa. Tierexperimentelle Untersuchungen [Spasmolytic effect of herbal carminatives. Studies in animals]. *Z. Allg. Med.* 1983, **59**, 1327-1333 [GERMAN].
21. Reiter M and Brandt W. Relaxant Effects on Tracheal and Ileal Smooth Muscles of the Guinea Pig. *Arzneim.-Forsch./Drug Res.* 1985, **35**, 408-414.
22. Maruzzella JC and Freundlich M. Antimicrobial Substances from Seeds. *J. Am. Pharm. Assoc.* 1959, **48**, 356-358.
23. Ali MA, Kabir MH, Quaiyyum MA, Rahman MM and Uddin A. Antibacterial activity of caraway against *Shigella* spp. *Bangladesh J. Microbiol.* 1995, **12**, 81-85.
24. Mahady GB, Pendland SL, Stoia A and Hamill FA. *In vitro* susceptibility of *Helicobacter pylori* to botanicals used traditionally for the treatment of gastrointestinal disorders [Poster]. In: Abstracts of 3rd International Congress on Phytomedicine. Munich, 11-13 October 2000. Published as: *Phytomedicine* 2000, **7** (Suppl. 2), 95 (Poster P-79).
25. Hitokoto H, Morozumi S, Wauke T, Sakai S and Kurata H. Inhibitory Effects of Spices on Growth and Toxin Production of Toxigenic Fungi. *Applied Environ. Microbiol.* 1980, **39**, 818-822.
26. Guérin J-C and Réveillère H-P. Antifungal activity of plant extracts used in therapy. II. Study of 49 plant extracts against 9 fungi species. *Ann. Pharm. Fr.* 1985, **43**, 77-81 [FRENCH/English summary].
27. Syed M, Khalid MR, Chaudhary FM and Bhatty MK. Antimicrobial activity of the essential oils of the Umbelliferae family. Part V. *Carum carvi, Petroselinum crispum* and *Dorema ammoniacum* oils. *Pakistan J. Sci. Ind. Res.* 1987, **30**, 106-110.
28. Janssen AM, Scheffer JJC, Parhan-Van Atten AW and Baerheim Svendsen A. Screening of some essential oils for their activities on dermatophytes. *Pharm. Weekblad Sci. Ed.* 1988, **10**, 277-280.
29. Farag RS, Daw ZY and Abo-Raya SH. Influence of Some Spice Essential Oils on *Aspergillus parasiticus* Growth and Production of Aflatoxins in a Synthetic Medium. *J. Food. Sci.* 1989, **54**, 74-76.
30. Göckeritz D, Weuffen W and Höppe H. Terpene und Terpenderivate vom Carvon- und Camphertyp - ihre antimikrobiellen und verminoxen Eigenschaften [Terpenes and terpene derivatives of the carvone and camphor types - their antimicrobial and anthelmintic properties]. *Pharmazie* 1974, **29**, 339-344 [GERMAN].
31. Rauha J-P, Tammela P, Summanen J, Vuorela P, Kähkönen M, Heinonen M et al. Actions of some plant extracts containing flavonoids and other phenolic compounds on calcium fluxes in clonal rat pituitary GH_4C_1 cells. *Pharm. Pharmacol. Lett.* 1999, **9**, 66-69.
32. Harries N, James KC and Pugh WK. Antifoaming and carminative actions of volatile oils. *J. Clin. Pharmacy* 1978, **2**, 171-177.
33. Boyd EM and Sheppard EP. An Autumn-Enhanced Mucotropic Action of Inhaled Terpenes and Related Volatile Agents. *Pharmacology* 1971, **6**, 65-80.
34. Khayyal MT, El-Ghazaly MA, Kenawy SA, Seif-El-Nasr M, Mahran LG, Kafafi YAH and Okpanyi SN. Antiulcerogenic Effect of Some Gastrointestinally Acting Plant Extracts and their Combination. *Arzneim.-Forsch./Drug Res.* 2001, **51**, 545-553.
35. Modu S, Gohla K and Umar IA. The hypoglycaemic and hypocholesterolaemic properties of black caraway (*Carum carvi* L.) oil in alloxan diabetic rats. *Biokemistri (Nigeria)* 1997, **7**, 91-97.
36. Zheng G-Q, Kenney PM and Lam LKT. Anethofuran, Carvone and Limonene: Potential Cancer Chemopreventive Agents from Dill Weed Oil and Caraway Oil. *Planta Medica* 1992, **58**, 338-341.
37. Shwaireb MH, El-Mofty MM, Rizk AM, Abdel-Galil A-MM and Harasani HA. Inhibition of mammary gland tumorigenesis in the rat by caraway seeds and dried leaves

of watercress. *Oncology Reports* 1995, **2**, 689-692.

38. Goerg KJ and Spilker T. Simultane sonographische Messung der Magen- und Gallenblasenentleerung mit gleichzeitiger Bestimmung der orozökalen Transitzeit mittels H_2-Atemtest [Real-time sonographic measurement of gastric and gallbladder emptying with simultaneous determination of orocaecal transit time by means of respiratory hydrogen test]. In: Loew D and Rietbrock N, editors. *Phytopharmaka II: Forschung und klinische Anwendung*. ISBN 3-7895-1066-0. Darmstadt: Steinkopff, 1996:63-72 [GERMAN].
39. May B, Kuntz H-D, Kieser M and Köhler S. Efficacy of a Fixed Peppermint Oil/Caraway Oil Combination in Non-ulcer Dyspepsia. *Arzneim.-Forsch./Drug Res.* 1996, **46**, 1149-1153.
40. Parfitt K, editor. Caraway; Caraway Oil. In: *Martindale - The complete drug reference, 32nd edition*. ISBN 0-85369-429-X. London: Pharmaceutical Press, 1999:1559-1560.
41. Wichtl M and Henke D. Kümmel - Carvi fructus. In: Hartke K, Hartke H, Mutschler E, Rücker G and Wichtl M, editors. *Kommentar zum Europäischen Arzneibuch* [Commentary on the European Pharmacopoeia]. Stuttgart: Wissenschaftliche Verlagsgesellschaft, 1998 (9. Lfg.):K 32 [GERMAN].
42. Carum. In: *British Herbal Pharmacopoeia 1983*. ISBN 0-903032-07-4. Bournemouth: British Herbal Medicine Association, 1983.
43. Pharmaceutical Society of Great Britain. Caraway; Caraway Oil; Caraway Water, Concentrated. In: British Pharmaceutical Codex 1973. London: Pharmaceutical Press, 1973:74-75 and 825.
44. Chevallier A. Caraway. In: *The Encyclopedia of Medicinal Plants*. ISBN 0-7513-0314-3. London-New York-Stuttgart: Dorling Kindersley, 1996:182.
45. Carvi fructus. German Commission E Monograph published in: Bundesanzeiger No. 22 of 1 February 1990.
46. Weiss RF and Fintelmann V. Carum carvi, Caraway. In: *Herbal Medicine, 2nd ed.* (translated from the 9th German edition of *Lehrbuch der Phytotherapie*). ISBN 3-13-126332-6. Stuttgart-New York: Thieme, 2000:74-75.
47. Carvi, fruit. In: *Médicaments à base de plantes*. ISBN 2-911473-02-7. Saint-Denis Cedex, France: Agence du Médicament, 1998.
48. Wüthrich B and Dietschi R. Das "Sellerie-Karotten-Beifuss-Gewürz-Syndrom": Hauttest- und RAST-Ergebnisse [The 'celery-carrot-mugwort-spice syndrome'. Skin test and RAST data]. *Schweiz. Med. Wschr.* 1985, **115**, 358-364 [GERMAN/English summary].
49. Hausen BM and Vieluf IK. In: *Allergiepflanzen - Pflanzenallergene. Handbuch und Atlas der allergie-induzierenden Wild- und Kulturpflanzen [Allergy plants - Plant allergies. Handbook and atlas of allergy-inducing wild and cultivated plants], 2nd ed.* ISBN 3-609-64080-4. Landsberg/München: Ecomed, 1997:304 [GERMAN].
50. Tisserand R and Balacs T. Safety Index: Part 1: Caraway. In: *Essential Oil Safety - A Guide for Health Care Professionals*. Edinburgh: Churchill-Livingstone, 1995:201-211.
51. Opdyke DLJ. Fragrance raw materials monographs: Caraway oil. *Food Cosmet. Toxicol.* 1973, **11**, 1051.
52. Hagan EC, Hansen WH, Fitzhugh OG, Jenner PM, Jones WI, Taylor JM et al. Food Flavourings and Compounds of Related Structure. II. Subacute and Chronic Toxicity. *Food Cosmet. Toxicol.* 1967, **5**, 141-157.
53. World Health Organization. Toxicological evaluation of certain food additives and contaminants: (+)- and (–)-carvone. WHO Food Additives Series: 28. Geneva: World Health Organization,1991:155-167.
54. Mahmoud I, Alkofahi A and Abdelaziz A. Mutagenic and Toxic Activities of Several Spices and Some Jordanian Medicinal Plants. *Int. J. Pharmacognosy* 1992, **30**, 81-85.
55. Higashimoto M, Purintrapiban J, Kataoka K, Kinouchi T, Vinitketkumnuen U, Akimoto S et al. Mutagenicity and antimutagenicity of extracts of three spices and a medicinal plant in Thailand. *Mutation Res.* 1993, **303**, 135-142.
56. Purintrapiban J, Shaheduzzaman SM, Vinitketkumnuen U, Kinouchi T, Kataoka K, Higashimoto M et al. Inhibitory effect of caraway seeds on mutation by alkylating agents. *Environ. Mut. Res. Commun.* 1995, **17**, 99-105 [JAPANESE/English summary].
57. Caraway. In: UK Statutory Instrument 1984 No. 769. The Medicines (Products Other Than Veterinary Drugs) (General Sale List) Order 1984. Schedule 1, Table A.
58. Caraway. In: Sections 182.10 and 182.20 of USA Code of Federal Regulations, Title 21, Food and Drugs, Parts 170 to 199. Revised as of April 1, 2000.
59. Carum carvi L. In: *Natural Sources of Flavourings. Report No. 1*. ISBN 92-871-4324-2. Strasbourg: Council of Europe Publishing, 2000;105-106.

REGULATORY GUIDELINES FROM OTHER EU COUNTRIES

FRANCE

Médicaments à base de plantes [47]: Carvi, fruit.

Therapeutic indications accepted

Oral use
Traditionally used: in the symptomatic treatment of digestive disorders such as epigastric distension, sluggish digestion, eructation, flatulence; as adjuvant treatment of the painful component of functional digestive disorders.

GERMANY

Commission E monograph [45]: Carvi fructus (Kümmel).

Uses
Dyspeptic complaints such as mild spasmodic pains in the gastrointestinal tract, flatulence and feeling of fullness.

Contraindications
None known.

Side effects
None known.

Interactions with other drugs
None known.

Dosage
Unless otherwise prescribed, daily dose: 1.5-6 g of dried fruits or equivalent preparations.

Mode of administration
Freshly powdered drug for infusions and other galenic preparations for internal use.

Actions
Spasmolytic, antimicrobial.

CARDAMOM FRUIT

Zingiberaceae

Cardamomi fructus

Definition

Cardamom Fruit consists of the dried, nearly ripe fruits of *Elettaria cardamomum* Maton var. *minuscula* Burkill.

The true or small cardamom, *Elettaria cardamomum* Maton var. *minuscula* Burkill, is grown principally in southern India but also in Sri Lanka, Tanzania, Guatemala and Costa Rica. There are two distinct cultivars, cv. Mysore (eg. the Alleppey Green variety) and cv. Malabar (eg. the Coorg Green variety), and one natural hybrid called 'Vazzukka'. Paradoxically, cv. Mysore is grown in the Kerala and Tamil Nadu regions of India, and cv. Malabar in the Mysore (now Karnataka) region, which has led to some confusion in the literature [1].

The fruits, harvested before full ripeness to avoid splitting, are dried to yield, at least in the higher and unbleached grades, green three-celled capsules tightly packed with dark brown seeds. International trade is mainly in the form of dried capsules, but to a lesser extent as seeds sealed in tins to prevent loss of volatiles [1]. Only the seeds are used medicinally.

For a comprehensive review of the cultivation and technical aspects of cardamom fruits see Govindarajan [1].

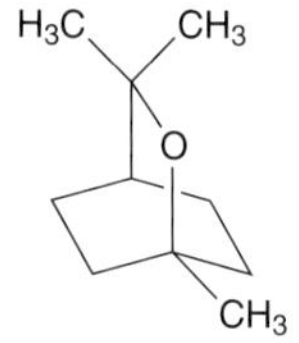

1,8-Cineole

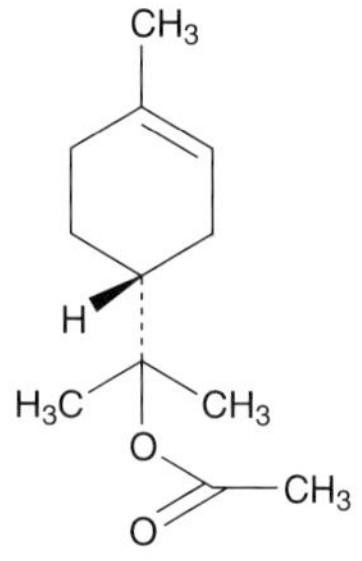

α-Terpinyl acetate

CONSTITUENTS

☐ ***Essential oil***, 6-10% in the seeds, only 0.2% in the husk [1,2], of which the principal constituents are 1,8-cineole and α-terpinyl acetate.

In cold-pressed cardamom essential oil of the 'Malabar type' (= cv. Mysore), α-terpinyl acetate (50-52%) predominated over 1,8-cineole (23-31%), whereas in the 'Mysore type' (= cv. Malabar) 1,8-cineole (44%) predominated over α-terpinyl acetate (37%) [1,3].

In distilled oil, either 1,8-cineole (24-45%) or α-terpinyl acetate (24-49%) may be predominant [1,2,4-7] depending on the cultivar and, to some extent, duration of storage of the oil (details often not stated). In an ambient storage trial on freshly-distilled commercial oil, the α-terpinyl acetate content increased from 25% to 43% while 1,8-cineole decreased from 39% to 28% over a period of 90 days [4].

Minor components of the distilled oil, mainly monoterpenes, include limonene (0.2-12%), linalyl acetate (1-8%), linalool (0.4-6%), β-pinene (0.15-6%), α-terpineol (1-6%), sabinene (1-5%), terpinen-4-ol (2-3%) and various others [1-7]. Cold-pressed oil contains low amounts of β-pinene and limonene (< 0.5%) and terpinen-4-ol (< 1%) [1,3].

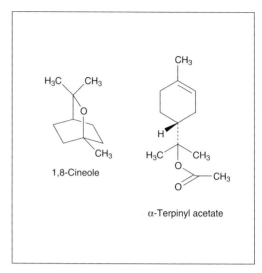

A trace amount, less than 10 ppm, of Z-3-(but-1-enyl) pyridine has been identified in the oil [8].

☐ ***Fatty oil***, 2-4%, containing oleic (42-44%), palmitic (28-38%), linoleic, linolenic and other fatty acids [1,9]; also α-tocopherol, phytosterols and C_{22}-C_{33} hydrocarbons [9].

☐ ***Other constituents*** of the seeds include crude fibre (6-13%), starch (38-46%) and protein (7-14%) [1].

Published Assay Methods

Essential oil by GC [2,4,6] and GC-MS [6,7]. Fatty acids and other lipids by GC [9].

PHARMACOLOGY

In vitro

An aqueous extract of cardamom moderately increased trypsin activity in buffer solution [10]. Ether and acetone extracts of cardamom exhibited a wide spectrum of antibacterial and antifungal activity [11].

Cardamom essential oil had concentration-dependent relaxant effects on isolated guinea pig tracheal (EC_{50} 27 mg/litre) and ileal (EC_{50} 15 mg/litre) muscles [12], and showed antispasmodic activity on isolated mouse intestine [13].

In vivo

Aqueous (127 mg/kg body weight) or methanolic (109 mg/kg) extracts of cardamom caused significant decreases ($p<0.05$) in the secretion of gastric juice, acid and pepsin in the period 3-5 hours after oral administration to rabbits. The aqueous extract produced a greater decrease in acid output, and the methanolic extract a greater decrease in pepsin output, than in gastric juice volume [14].

An acetone extract of cardamon seed produced cholagogic effects after intraduodenal administration to rats, significantly increasing bile secretion ($p<0.01$ at 100 mg/kg body weight). Pure terpineol and terpinyl acetate also significantly increased bile secretion after oral or duodenal administration [15].

CLINICAL STUDIES

None published on mono-preparations of cardamom fruit.

THERAPEUTICS

Actions
Carminative [16-18], antispasmodic [13,17], smooth muscle relaxant [12], cholagogic [15, 18], appetite and digestive stimulant [16,17], antimicrobial [11].

Also reputed to be aphrodisiac [1,17].

Indications
None adequately substantiated by pharmacological or clinical studies.

Other traditional uses
Flatulent dyspepsia [16] and dyspeptic complaints generally [17,19].

Has also been used as a mouth freshener [1].

Contraindications
Not advisable in cases of gallstones (due to cholagogic action) [19].

Side effects
None known.

Interactions with other drugs
None known.

Dosage
Up to three times daily: powdered seeds, 0.5-2 g or by infusion [16,19]; liquid extract 0.3-2 ml. Cardamom oil, 0.03-0.2 ml; Aromatic Cardamom Tincture BP, 0.12-0.6 ml; Compound Cardamom Tincture BP, 2-5 ml [18].

SAFETY

Cardamom fruit showed no mutagenic potential in the Ames test using *Salmonella typhimurium* strains TA98 and TA102, nor any significant toxicity (LC_{50} > 1000 ppm) in the brine shrimp bioassay [20].

Cardamom essential oil has been categorised as non-irritant, non-sensitising, non-phototoxic and non-toxic in normal use, with an oral LD_{50} > 5 g/kg in rodents and dermal LD_{50} > 5 g/kg in rabbits [21,22].

REGULATORY STATUS

Medicines

UK	Accepted for general sale, internal or external use [23].
France	Not listed in *Médicaments à base de plantes* [24].
Germany	Commission E monograph published, with approved uses [19].

Food

USA	Generally recognized as safe (21 CFR 182.10 and 182.20) [25]
Council of Europe	Permitted as flavouring, category N2 [26].

REFERENCES

Current Pharmacopoeial Monographs
BP Cardamom Fruit

Literature References

1. Govindarajan VS, Narasimhan S, Raghuveer KG and Lewis YS. Cardamom - Production, Technology, Chemistry and Quality. *CRC Crit. Rev. Food Sci. Nutr.* 1982, March, 229-326.
2. Variyar PS and Bandyopadhyay C. On the volatiles of clove, cardamom, nutmeg and mace. *Pafai J.* 1995, Jan-Mar, 19-25.
3. Bernhard RA, Wijesekera ROB and Chichester CO. Terpenoids of cardamom oil and their comparative distribution among varieties. *Phytochemistry* 1971, **10**, 177-184.
4. Gopalakrishnan N. Studies on the Storage Quality of CO_2-Extracted Cardamom and Clove Bud Oils. *J. Agric. Food Chem.* 1994, **42**, 796-798.
5. Lawrence BM. Progress in Essential Oils. *Perfumer & Flavorist* 1998, **23**, 47-57.
6. Pieribattesti JC, Smadja J and Mondon JM. Composition of the essential oil of cardamom (*Elettaria cardamomum* Maton) from Reunion. In: Lawrence BM, Mookherjee BD and Willis BJ, editors. *Flavors and Fragrances: A World Perspective.* Amsterdam: Elsevier, 1988:697-706.
7. Noleau I, Toulemonde B and Richard H. Volatile Constituents of Cardamom (*Elettaria cardamomum* Maton) Cultivated in Costa Rica. *Flavour Fragrance J.* 1987, **2**, 123-127.
8. Maurer B and Hauser A. New Pyridine Derivatives from Essential Oils. *Chimia* 1992, **46**, 93-95.
9. Shaban MAE, Kandeel KM, Yacout GA and Mehaseb S. Gas-liquid-chromatographic analysis of the lipid composition of *Elettaria cardamomum Seeds. Acta Alimentaria* 1988, **17**, 95-101.
10. Kato Y. Effects of spice extracts on hydrolases. No. 1. On trypsin. *Koryo* 1975, **113**, 17-23 [JAPANESE]; through

Chem. Abstr. 1976, **84**, 149393.
11. Maruzzella JC and Freundlich M. Antimicrobial Substances from Seeds. *J. Am. Pharm. Assoc.* 1959, **48**, 356-358.
12. Reiter M and Brandt W. Relaxant Effects on Tracheal and Ileal Smooth Muscles of the Guinea Pig. *Arzneim.-Forsch./Drug Res.* 1985, **35**, 408-414.
13. Haginiwa J, Harada M and Morishita I. Pharmacological studies on crude drugs. VII. Properties of essential oil components of aromatics and their pharmacological effect on mouse intestine. *Yakugaku Zasshi* 1963, **83**, 624-628; through *Chem. Abstr.* 1964, **60**, 999.
14. Sakai K, Miyazaki Y, Yamane T, Saitoh Y, Ikawa C and Nishihata T. Effect of Extracts of Zingiberaceae Herbs on Gastric Secretion in Rabbits. *Chem. Pharm. Bull.* 1989, **37**, 215-217.
15. Yamahara J, Kimura H, Kobayashi M, Sawada T, Fujimura H and Chisaka T. Biologically Active Principles of Crude Drugs. Cholagogic Substances in Cardamom Seed and Its Properties. *Yakugaku Zasshi* 1983, **103**, 979-985 [JAPANESE/English summary].
16. Elettaria. In: *British Herbal Pharmacopoeia 1983.* ISBN 0-903032-07-4. Bournemouth: British Herbal Medicine Association, 1983.
17. Chevallier A. Cardamom. In: *The Encyclopedia of Medicinal Plants.* ISBN 0-7513-0314-3. London-New York-Stuttgart: Dorling Kindersley, 1996:91.
18. Cardamom Fruit and Cardamom Oil. In: Pharmaceutical Society of Great Britain. *British Pharmaceutical Codex 1973.* London: Pharmaceutical Press, 1973.
19. Cardamomi fructus (Kardamomen). German Commission E Monograph published in: Bundesanzeiger No. 223 of 30 November 1985, with amendments in Bundesanzeiger No. 50 of 13 March 1990 and No. 164 of 1 September 1990.
20. Mahmoud I, Alkofahi A and Abdelaziz A. Mutagenic and Toxic Activities of Several Spices and Some Jordanian Medicinal Plants. *Int. J. Pharmacognosy* 1992, **30**, 81-85.
21. Opdyke DLJ. Fragrance raw materials monographs: Cardamom oil. *Food Cosmet. Toxicol.* 1974, **12** (Suppl.), 837-838.
22. Tisserand R and Balacs T. Safety Index: Part 1. In: *Essential Oil Safety - A Guide for Health Care Professionals.* Edinburgh: Churchill-Livingstone, 1995:201-211.
23. Cardamom. In: UK Statutory Instrument 1990 No. 1129. The Medicines (Products Other Than Veterinary Drugs) (General Sale List) Amendment Order 1990. Schedule 1, Table A.
24. *Médicaments à base de plantes.* ISBN 2-911473-02-7. Saint-Denis Cedex, France: Agence du Médicament, 1998.
25. Cardamom. In: Sections 182.10 and 182.20 of USA Code of Federal Regulations, Title 21, Food and Drugs, Parts 170 to 199. Revised as of April 1, 2000.
26. Elettaria cardamomum L. Maton, fruit. In: *Flavouring Substances and Natural Sources of Flavourings, 3rd ed.* ISBN 2-7160-0081-6. Strasbourg: Council of Europe, 1981.

REGULATORY GUIDELINES FROM OTHER EU COUNTRIES

GERMANY

Commission E monograph [19]: Cardamomi fructus (Kardamomen).

Uses
Dyspeptic complaints.

Contraindications
In cases of gallstones, to be used only after consulting a doctor.

Side effects
None known.

Interactions with other drugs
None known.

Dosage
Unless otherwise prescribed, average daily dose: 1.5 g of the drug or equivalent preparations; tincture (in accordance with DAB Ergänzung B6), 1-2 g.

Mode of administration
Ground seeds or other galenic preparations for internal use.

Actions
Cholagogic, virustatic.

CASSIA BARK

Lauraceae

Cinnamomi cassiae cortex

Synonyms: Chinese cinnamon, Chinese cassia lignea.

Definition

Cassia Bark consists of the dried bark of the trunk or older branches of *Cinnamomum cassia* Blume [*Cinnamomum aromaticum* Nees] from which the outer tissues have been wholly or partly removed.

Cinnamomum cassia is cultivated mainly in the south-eastern provinces of China (Guangxi and Guangdong). When the trees are about 6 years old, the bark is harvested and the cork and cortex are partly removed by planing. The bark has many of the same uses as that of Ceylon cinnamon (from *Cinnamomum zeylanicum*), but the outer surface is darker, the odour is coarser and the taste more astringent [1].

In publications originating from China and Japan (e.g. the Pharmacopoeia of Japan), the terms 'Cinnamomi cortex', 'cinnamon bark' or 'cinnamon' usually refer to the bark of *Cinnamomum cassia*.

CONSTITUENTS

□ ***Essential oil***, 1-3%. Few modern analyses have been published of oil distilled solely from the bark. From one determination, cinnamaldehyde (97.1%) and small amounts (< 1%) of α-copaene, δ-cadinene, cinnamyl acetate, cinnamic acid and benzaldehyde were reported [2]; this may or may not be typical.

Average cinnamaldehyde contents of dried bark from HPLC assays were 2.6% (range 0.8-3.4%) [3] and 2.9% (range 2.0-4.5%) [4]; much higher results of 7.9% (HPLC), 8.9% (GC) and 9.1% (fluorimetry) have also been reported [5].

Cassia oil of commerce, a pharmacopoeial oil [Ph. Eur.] and an ingredient of cola-type beverages [6], is distilled not from the bark but from leaves and twigs of *C. cassia* [7]. It contains cinnamaldehyde (55-90%), cinnamyl acetate (1-9%), 2-methoxycinnamaldehyde (0.4-12%), benzaldehyde (0.7-6%), coumarin (up to 8.7%) and benzyl benzoate (up to 3%) among nearly 100 components [2,7].

□ ***Other aromatic compounds*** include 2′-hydroxy-

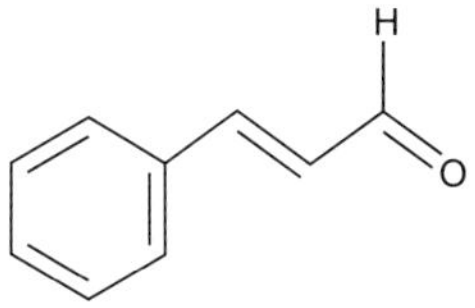

Cinnamaldehyde

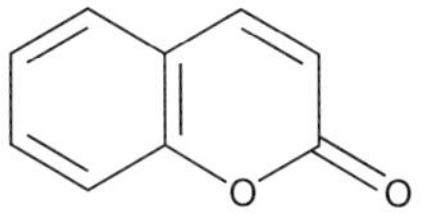

Coumarin

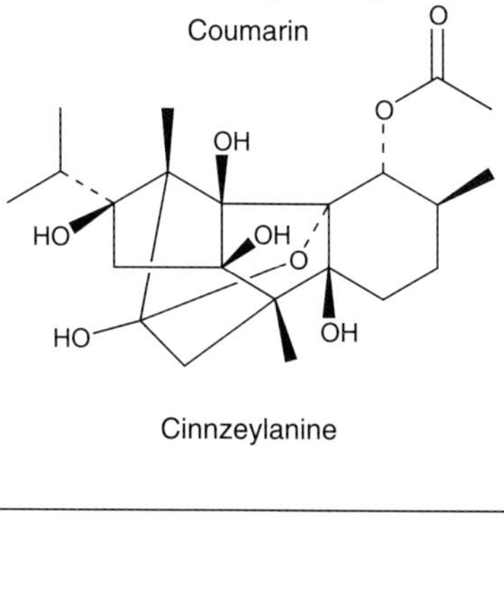

Cinnzeylanine

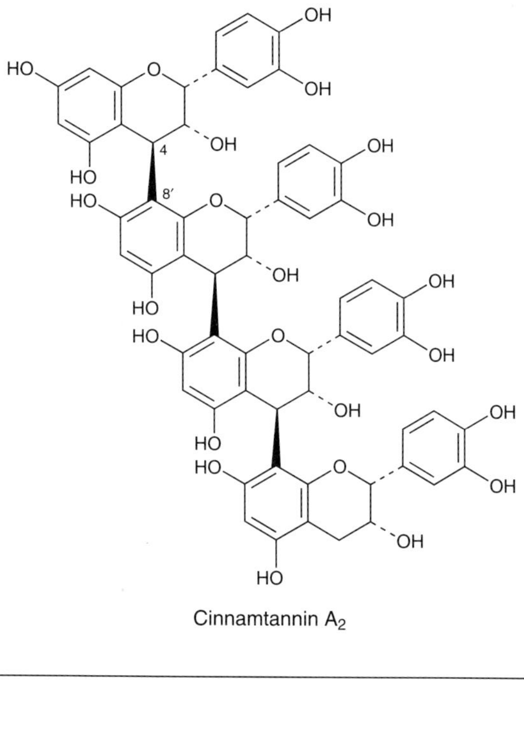

Cinnamtannin A_2

cinnamaldehyde [8], two cinnamaldehyde cyclic glycerol 1,3-acetals [9] and small amounts of cinnamic [4], 3-(2-hydroxyphenyl)-propanoic [10], protocatechuic, *p*-coumaric, ferulic and other phenolic acids [11,12].

Lyoniresinol 3-glucoside (a lignan), 3,4,5-trimethoxyphenol apiosyl-(1→6)-glucoside and (±)-syringaresinol have also been isolated [9].

☐ ***Coumarin***, 0.14-1.1% [3,4,12]. The presence of coumarin is a distinguishing feature from cinnamon bark (*Cinnamomum zeylanicum*) [3].

☐ ***Diterpenes*** A series of highly oxygenated diterpenes with related tetra-, penta- or hexacyclic structures, including cinnzeylanine, cinnzeylanol and cinncassiols A [13], B [14], C_1 [15], C_2, C_3 [16], D_1 [17,18], D_2, D_3 [18], D_4 [19] and E [20].

The 19-glucosides of cinncassiols A [13], B [14], C_1 [16], D_1 [17,18] and D_2 [18], and the 2-glucoside of cinncassiol D_4 [19], are also present.

☐ ***Polysaccharides*** An arabinoxylan has been isolated, composed of L-arabinose and D-xylose residues in a ratio of 4:3 and with a MW of ca. 1,000,000 [21]. The bark is reported to contain about 10% of mucilage and starch is present [1].

☐ ***Condensed tannins (proanthocyanidins)*** Three oligomeric procyanidins have been isolated, cinnamtannins A_2 (tetrameric), A_3 (pentameric) and A_4 (hexameric), each consisting of linearly-(4β→8)-linked (−)-epicatechin units [22], together with procyanidin dimers B-2, B-5 [22,23], B-1, B-7 [23] and C-1 [22], the trimer A-2 [22,23] and the 6-C- and 8-C-glucosides of procyanidin B-2 [23].

Related monomeric compounds present include (−)-epicatechin [22], methylated derivatives of (−)-epicatechin [9,24] and (+)-catechin [24], and the 3-O-, 6-C- and 8-C-glucosides of (−)-epicatechin [22].

Published Assay Methods

Cinnamaldehyde, cinnamic acid, coumarin and other compounds by HPLC [3,4]. Cinnamaldehyde content by fluorimetry [5]. Cassia oil components by GC [Ph. Eur.].

PHARMACOLOGY

In vitro

An ethanolic extract from cassia bark exhibited broad antimicrobial activity against a range of bacteria (except *Staphylococcus aureus*), yeasts and moulds [25]. A methanolic extract exhibited strong inhibitory activity against two intestinal bacteria, *Clostridium perfringens* and *Bacteroides fragilis*, the activity being attributed to the cinnamaldehyde content [26].

An aqueous extract from cassia bark at 10^{-5} g/ml had a significant ($p<0.01$) and dose-dependent protective effect against glutamate-induced neuronal death in cultured cerebellar granule cells, suggesting that cassia bark could potentially have a protective effect against ischaemic brain injury [27].

Aqueous extracts of cassia bark exhibited potent anti-complement activity; cinncassiols were assumed to be the active constituents [13,17].

A neutral arabinoxylan, isolated from an aqueous extract of cassia bark and administered intraperitoneally to mice at 5-50 µg/g body weight for 5 days, significantly and dose-dependently increased the phagocytic index in a carbon clearance test ($p<0.05$), suggesting powerful activation of the reticulo-endothelial system [21].

Cinnamaldehyde inhibited acetylcholine- and histamine-induced contractions of isolated mouse and guinea pig ileum with 7-10% of the potency of papaverine, and increased cardiac contractile force and beating rate of isolated guinea pig atria and perfusing heart [28].

In vivo

Formation of stress-induced gastric ulcer in mice was significantly inhibited ($p<0.05$) by oral administration of a decoction of cassia bark [29].

A dry aqueous extract of cassia bark, administered intraperitoneally to rats at 25, 50 and 100 mg/kg, prevented the occurrence of cold stress-induced gastric ulcers in rats as effectively as cimetidine, with 100% inhibition at 100 mg/kg ($p<0.05$). It was less effective than cimetidine on water immersion stress-induced ulcers, but again significantly inhibited ulcerogenesis at 100 mg/kg ($p<0.05$). Against serotonin-induced gastric ulcer the extract at 100 mg/kg was effective after both intraperitoneal ($p<0.01$) and oral ($p<0.001$) administration, while cimetidine failed to prevent ulcerogenesis. The extract (100 mg/kg i.p.) significantly reduced the output of gastric juice ($p<0.001$) and pepsin ($p<0.01$) in rats, showed a tendency to reduce gastric acidity, and increased gastric mucus output and gastric mucosal blood flow ($p<0.05$ after 60 minutes) [30].

Subsequent testing of aqueous extract fractions led to the isolation of two compounds which inhibited serotonin-induced ulcerogenesis in rats: 3-(2-hydroxyphenyl)-propanoic acid (HPPA) and its O-glucoside. When administered intravenously to rats at a very low dose of 40 µg/kg body weight, HPPA inhibited gastric ulcers induced by phenylbutazone (46% inhibition, $p<0.001$) and water immersion stress (42%, $p<0.05$); oral administration at 40 µg/kg inhibited ethanol-induced gastric ulcers by 53% ($p<0.05$). The antiulcerogenic effect was attributed to potentiation of defensive factors, such as stimulation of gastric blood flow, since HPPA did not significantly inhibit gastric secretions (in contrast to the aqueous extract) [10].

An aqueous solution of cassia bark equivalent to 150 mg/kg body weight/day had a uraemic toxin-decreasing effect when administered to rats with adenine-induced renal failure, reducing serum levels of urea nitrogen, creatinine and guanidinosuccinic acid, and especially methylguanidine ($p<0.001$ compared to the control) [31].

A dry methanolic extract of cassia bark had an anti-inflammatory effect when applied topically to the ears of mice at 2 mg/ear, markedly inhibiting 12-O-tetradecanoyl-13-acetate-induced ear oedema by 75% ($p<0.01$) compared to the control vehicle [32].

The traditional Japanese herbal medicine Kakkon-to, used in the treatment of influenza and common cold infections (more than 20 million doses prescribed annually in Japan), has seven components. Of these, cassia bark showed the strongest antipyretic activity ($p<0.001$) after oral administration of 3 × 5 mg of an aqueous extract daily for 4 days to mice infected with a mouse-adapted influenza virus. It was shown that the anti-inflammatory activity of the extract was due to suppression of interleukin-1α production ($p<0.001$) subsequent to interferon production caused by the influenza infection [33].

Central effects of orally-administered cinnamaldehyde have been demonstrated in mice: sedative activity (decrease of spontaneous motor activity, antagonistic effect to methamphetamine-induced hyperactivity, motor incoordination in a rotor-rod test), and also hypothermic and antipyretic activities. An aqueous extract from cassia bark produced no significant response in these tests, but both the extract and cinnamaldehyde showed analgesic activity in the writhing test in mice [34].

Cinnamaldehyde administered intravenously produced a hypotensive effect in anaesthetised dogs and guinea pigs, and moderately inhibited rat stomach movement and mouse intestinal propulsion; when administered orally it protected stress-induced gastric erosions in mice and increased biliary secretions in rats [28].

2′-hydroxycinnamaldehyde isolated from cassia bark [8] strongly inhibited the *in vitro* growth of 29 kinds of human cancer cells with an average ID_{50} of 2.64 µg/ml and, when administered intraperitoneally at 30-100 mg/kg, the *in vivo* growth of SW-620 human colon tumour xenograft in nude mice without loss of body weight [35].

CLINICAL STUDIES

None published on mono-preparations of cassia bark.

THERAPEUTICS

Actions
Carminative [36-38] and stomachic [38], mildly astringent [36], spasmolytic [28,37], antipyretic [33], anti-ulcerogenic [10,29,30], moderately antimicrobial [25,26], topical anti-inflammatory [32].

Cinnamaldehyde is sedative, analgesic [34] and hypotensive [28].

Indications
None adequately substantiated by pharmacological or clinical studies.

Uses based on experience or tradition
Dyspeptic complaints such as flatulence, eructation, colic and nausea [37-40].

Common cold [37]; loss of appetite [39,40]; functional asthenia [40]; diarrhoea [37,38].

Cassia bark is used in Chinese medicine [13] for indigestion, hypertension [8], headache, fevers [21] and conditions caused by poor circulation [27].

Contraindications
Avoid in pregnancy (except in amounts normally used in foods).

Side effects
Allergic or sensitization reactions are possible from cassia oil [41], but unlikely from oral use of cassia bark preparations.

Interactions with other drugs
None known.

Dosage
Three times daily: dried bark, 0.5-1 g or by infusion [37,39]; tincture (BPC 1949), 2-4 ml [36]. Cassia oil, 0.05-0.2 ml [37,39].

SAFETY

The intraperitoneal LD_{50} of an aqueous extract of cassia bark was determined as 4.98 g/kg body weight, thus it is essentially non-toxic [34].

Aqueous and methanolic extracts from cassia bark showed no mutagenic potential in the rec-assay with Bacillus subtilis or in the Ames test with *Salmonella typhimurium* strains TA98 and TA100 [42].

Cassia oil is considered to be non-toxic at appropriate oral dose levels, but is moderately irritating and may cause sensitization if applied to the skin [41]. The acute oral LD_{50} of cassia oil (from leaves and twigs) in rats was reported as 2.8 ml/kg [43] and in a different study as 5.2 g/kg [44]; the dermal LD_{50} in rabbits was 0.32 ml/kg [43]. The oral LD_{50} of cinnamaldehyde in mice was found to be 2.225 g/kg [34].

REGULATORY STATUS

Medicines

UK	No licences issued for products containing cassia bark, but cassia oil is accepted for general sale, internal or external use [45].
France	Accepted for specified indications [40].
Germany	Commission E monograph published, with approved uses [39].

Food

USA	Generally recognized as safe (21 CFR 182.10 and 182.20) [46].
Council of Europe	Permitted as flavouring, category N2 [47].

REFERENCES

Current Pharmacopoeial Monographs

JP	Cinnamon Bark
BHP	Cassia Bark

Literature References

1. Evans WC. Cassia, Chinese cinnamon or cassia lignea. In: *Trease and Evans' Pharmacognosy, 13th ed.* ISBN 0-7020-1357-9. London-Philadelphia: Baillière Tindall, 1989:457-458.
2. Lawrence BM. Progress in Essential Oils. *Perfumer and Flavorist* 1994, **19**, 33-40.
3. Archer AW. Determination of cinnamaldehyde, coumarin and cinnamyl alcohol in cinnamon and cassia by high-performance liquid chromatography. *J. Chromatogr.* 1988, **447**, 272-276.
4. Sagara K, Oshima T, Yoshida T, Tong Y-Y, Zhang G and Chen Y-H. Determination of Cinnamomi Cortex by high-performance liquid chromatography. *J. Chromatogr.* 1987, **409**, 365-370.
5. Tsai S-Y and Chen S-C. A fluorimetric assay of transcinnamaldehyde in cinnamon. *J. Nat. Prod.* 1984, **47**, 536-538.
6. Zhu L, Ding D and Lawrence BM. The Cinnamomum Species in China: Resources for the Present and Future. *Perfumer and Flavorist* 1994, **19**, 17-22.
7. ter Heide R. Qualitative Analysis of the Essential Oil of Cassia (*Cinnamomum cassia* Blume). *J. Agric. Food Chem.* 1972, **20**, 747-751.
8. Kwon B-M, Cho Y-K, Lee S-H, Nam J-H, Bok S-H, Chun S-K et al. 2'-Hydroxycinnamaldehyde from Stem bark of *Cinnamomum cassia*. *Planta Medica* 1996, **62**, 183-184.
9. Miyamura M, Nohara T, Tomimatsu T and Nishioka I. Seven aromatic compounds from bark of *Cinnamomum cassia*. *Phytochemistry* 1983, **22**, 215-218.
10. Tanaka S, Yoon Y, Fukui H, Tabata M, Akira T, Okana K et al. Antiulcerogenic Compounds Isolated from Chinese Cinnamon. *Planta Medica* 1989, **55**, 245-248.
11. Schulz JM and Herrmann K. Occurrence of Hydroxybenzoic Acids and Hydroxycinnamic Acids in Spices. IV. Phenolics of Spices. *Z. Lebensm. Unters. Forsch.* 1980, **171**, 193-199 [GERMAN/English summary].
12. Yuan A, Tan L and Jiang D. Studies on chemical constituents of Rou Gui (*Cinnamomum cassia* Presl.). *Zhongyao Tongbao* 1982, **7** (2), 26-28 [CHINESE]; through *Chem. Abstr.* 1982, **97**, 141659.
13. Yagi A, Tokubuchi N, Nohara T, Nonaka G, Nishioka I and Koda A. The Constituents of Cinnamomi Cortex. I. Structures of Cinncassiol A and its Glucoside. *Chem. Pharm. Bull.* 1980, **28**, 1432-1436.
14. Nohara T, Tokubuchi N, Kuroiwa M and Nishioka I. The Constituents of Cinnamomi Cortex. III. Structures of Cinncassiol B and its Glucoside. *Chem. Pharm. Bull.* 1980, **28**, 2682-2686.
15. Nohara T, Nishioka I, Tokubuchi N, Miyahara K and Kawasaki T. Cinncassiol C_1, a Novel Type of Diterpene from Cinnamomi Cortex. (The Constituents of Cinnamomi Cortex, Part II.). *Chem. Pharm. Bull.* 1980, **28**, 1969-1970.
16. Kashiwada Y, Nohara T, Tomimatsu T and Nishioka I. Constituents of Cinnamomi Cortex. IV. Structures of Cinncassiols C_1 Glucoside, C_2 and C_3. *Chem. Pharm. Bull.* 1981, **29**, 2686-2688.
17. Nohara T, Kashiwada Y, Tomimatsu T, Kido M, Tokubuchi N and Nishioka I. Cinncassiol D_1 and its Glucoside, Novel Pentacyclic Diterpenes from Cinnamomi Cortex. *Tetrahedron Lett.* 1980, **21**, 2647-2648.
18. Nohara T, Kashiwada Y, Murakami K, Tomimatsu T, Kido M, Yagi A and Nishioka I. Constituents of Cinnamomi Cortex. V. Structures of Five Novel Diterpenes, Cinncassiols D_1, D_1 Glucoside, D_2, D_2 Glucoside and D_3. *Chem. Pharm. Bull.* 1981, **29**, 2451-2459.
19. Nohara T, Kashiwada Y, Tomimatsu T and Nishioka I. Two Novel Diterpenes from Bark of *Cinnamomum cassia*. *Phytochemistry* 1982, **21**, 2130-2132.
20. Nohara T, Kashiwada Y and Nishioka I. Cinncassiol E, a Diterpene from the Bark of *Cinnamomum cassia*. *Phytochemistry* 1985, **24**, 1849-1850.
21. Kanari M, Tomoda M, Gonda R, Shimizu N, Kimura M, Kawaguchi M and Kawabe C. A Reticuloendothelial System-Activating Arabinoxylan fron the Bark of *Cinnamomum cassia*. *Chem. Pharm. Bull.* 1989, **37**, 3191-3194.
22. Morimoto S, Nonaka G and Nishioka I. Tannins and Related Compounds. XXXVIII. Isolation and Characterization of Flavan-3-ol Glucosides and Procyanidin Oligomers from Cassia Bark (*Cinnamomum cassia* Blume). *Chem. Pharm. Bull.* 1986, **34**, 633-642.
23. Morimoto S, Nonaka G and Nishioka I. Tannins and Related Compounds. XXXIX. Procyanidin C-Glucosides and an Acylated Flavan-3-ol Glucoside from the Barks of *Cinnamomum cassia* Blume and *C. obtusifolium* Nees. *Chem. Pharm. Bull.* 1986, **34**, 643-649.
24. Morimoto S, Nonaka G, Nishioka I, Ezaki N and Takizawa N. Tannins and Related Compounds. XXIX. Seven New Methyl Derivatives of Flavan-3-ols and a 1,3-Diarylpropan-2-ol from *Cinnamomum cassia, C. obtusifolium* and *Lindera umbellata* var. *membranacea*. *Chem. Pharm. Bull.* 1985, **33**, 2281-2286.
25. Mau J-L, Chen C-P and Hsieh P-C. Antimicrobial Effect of Extracts from Chinese Chive, Cinnamon and Corni Fructus. *J. Agric. Food Chem.* 2001, **49**, 183-188.
26. Lee H-S and Ahn Y-J. Growth-Inhibiting Effects of *Cinnamomum cassia* Bark-Derived Materials on Human Intestinal Bacteria. *J. Agric. Food. Chem.* 1998, **46**, 8-12.
27. Shimada Y, Goto H, Kogure T, Kohta K, Shintani T, Itoh T and Terasawa K. Extract Prepared from the Bark of *Cinnamomum cassia* Blume Prevents Glutamate-induced Neuronal Death in Cultured Cerebellar Granule Cells. *Phytotherapy Res.* 2000, **14**, 466-468.
28. Harada M and Yano S. Pharmacological Studies on Chinese Cinnamon. II. Effects of Cinnamaldehyde on the Cardiovascular and Digestive Systems. *Chem. Pharm. Bull.* 1975, **23**, 941-947.
29. Tanaka S, Akira T and Tabata M. Pharmacological Analysis of the Traditional Chinese Prescription "Goreisan-ryo". *Yakugaku Zasshi* 1984, **104**, 601-606 [JAPANESE/English summary].
30. Akira T, Tanaka S and Tabata M. Pharmacological Studies on the Antiulcerogenic activity of Chinese Cinnamon. *Planta Medica* 1986, **52**, 440-443.
31. Yokozawa T, Fujioka K, Oura H, Tanaka T, Nonaka G

and Nishioka I. Confirmation that Tannin-containing Crude Drugs have a Uraemic Toxin-decreasing Action. *Phytotherapy Res.* 1995, **9**, 1-5.
32. Yasukawa K, Yamaguchi A, Arita J, Sakurai S, Ikeda A and Takido M. Inhibitory Effect of Edible Plant Extracts on 12-O-Tetradecanoylphorbol-13-acetate-induced Ear Oedema in Mice. *Phytotherapy Res.* 1993, **7**, 185-189.
33. Kurokawa M, Kumeda CA, Yamamura J, Kamiyama T and Shiraki K. Antipyretic activity of cinnamyl derivatives and related compounds in influenza virus-infected mice. *Eur. J. Pharmacol.* 1998, **348**, 45-51.
34. Harada M and Ozaki Y. Pharmacological Studies on Chinese Cinnamon. I. Central Effects of Cinnamaldehyde. *Yakugaku Zasshi* 1972, **92**, 135-140 [JAPANESE/English summary].
35. Lee CW, Hong DH, Han SB, Park SH, Kim HK, Kwon B-M and Kim HM. Inhibition of Human Tumor Growth by 2'-Hydroxy- and 2'-Benzoyloxycinnamaldehydes. *Planta Medica* 1999, **65**, 263-266.
36. Pharmaceutical Society of Great Britain. Cassia Bark. In: *British Pharmaceutical Codex (BPC) 1949*. London: Pharmaceutical Press, 1949.
37. Cinnamomum cassia. In: *British Herbal Pharmacopoeia 1983*. ISBN 0-903032-07-4. Bournemouth: British Herbal Medicine Association, 1983.
38. Grieve M (edited by Leyel CF). Cassia (Cinnamon). In: *A Modern Herbal* (first published 1931; revised 1973). ISBN 1-85501-249-9. London: Tiger Books International, 1994:168-169.
39. Cinnamomi cassiae cortex. German Commission E Monograph published in: Bundesanzeiger No. 22 of 1 February 1990.
40. Canneliers de Ceylan et de Chine. In: *Médicaments à base de plantes*. ISBN 2-911473-02-7. Saint-Denis Cedex, France: Agence du Médicament, 1998.
41. Tisserand R and Balacs T. Safety Index, Part 1: Cassia. In: *Essential Oil Safety - A Guide for Health Care Professionals*. Edinburgh: Churchill-Livingstone, 1995:201-211.
42. Morimoto I, Watanabe F, Osawa T, Okitsu T and Kada T. Mutagenicity screening of crude drugs with *Bacillus subtilis* rec-assay and Salmonella/microsome reversion assay. *Mutation Res.* 1982, **97**, 81-102.
43. Opdyke DLJ. Monographs on fragrance raw materials: Cassia oil. *Food Cosmet Toxicol.* 1975, **13**, 109-110.
44. von Skramlik E. Über die Giftigkeit und Verträglichkeit von ätherischen Ölen [The toxicity and tolerability of essential oils]. *Pharmazie* 1959, **14**, 435-445 [GERMAN].
45. Cassia Oil. In: UK Statutory Instrument 1984 No. 769. The Medicines (Products Other Than Veterinary Drugs) (General Sale List) Order 1984. Schedule 1, Table A.
46. Cinnamon bark, Chinese. In: Sections 182.10 and 182.20 of USA Code of Federal Regulations, Title 21, Food and Drugs, Parts 170 to 199. Revised as of April 1, 2000.
47. Cinnamomum aromaticum Nees, bark. In: *Flavouring Substances and Natural Sources of Flavourings, 3rd ed.* ISBN 2-7160-0081-6. Strasbourg: Council of Europe, 1981.

REGULATORY GUIDELINES FROM OTHER EU COUNTRIES

FRANCE

Médicaments à base de plantes [40]: Canneliers de Ceylan et de Chine, écorce de tige = cannelle.

Therapeutic indications accepted

Oral use
Traditionally used in the symptomatic treatment of digestive disorders such as epigastric distension, sluggish digestion, eructation or flatulence; in functional asthenia; to facilitate weight gain.

GERMANY

Commission E monograph [39]: Cinnamomi cassiae cortex (Chinesischer Zimt).

Uses
Loss of appetite; dyspeptic complaints such as mild, spasmodic disorders of the gastrointestinal tract, bloatedness, flatulence.

Contraindications
Hypersensitivity to cinnamon or Peru balsam.
Pregnancy.

Side effects
Frequently allergic skin and mucosal reactions.

Interactions with other drugs
None known.

Dosage
Unless otherwise prescribed, daily dose: 2-4 g of dried bark, 0.05-0.2 g of essential oil; equivalent preparations.

Mode of administration
Comminuted drug for tea infusions; essential oil and other galenic preparations for internal use.

Actions
Antibacterial, fungistatic, motility-promoting.

CENTAURY

Gentianaceae

Centaurii herba

Synonym: Common Centaury.

Definition

Centaury consists of the dried flowering aerial parts of *Centaurium erythraea* Rafn [*C. minus* Moench, *C. umbellatum* Gilib., *Erythraea centaurium* (L.) Pers.].

CONSTITUENTS

☐ ***Secoiridoid glucosides***, principally swertiamarin (4-9%) together with gentiopicrin (=gentiopicroside, 0.3-0.9%) [1-3] and sweroside [3,4]; these compounds have a bitterness value of ca. 12,000 [5]. Some samples give lower results, e.g. 0.5% of swertiamarin, only traces of gentiopicrin and/or absence of sweroside [2].

Two intensely bitter esters of sweroside, centapicrin (= 2′-*m*-hydroxybenzoyl-3′-acetylsweroside) [3,4] and deacetylcentapicrin [3], occurring in small amounts in the flower ovaries, provide most of the bitterness of the drug. Centapicrin has a bitterness value of ca. 4,000,000 [6]; that of deacetylcentapicrin is lower, but over 1,000,000 [7].

The secoiridoid gentioflavoside and the iridoid dihydrocornin have also been isolated from centaury [8].

☐ ***Xanthones*** Eustomin (1-hydroxy-3,5,6,7,8-pentamethoxyxanthone, 0.04-0.06%) [9,10], demethyleustomin (0.03-0.04%) [9-11] and various other highly oxygenated xanthones [12-15].

☐ ***Phenolic acids*** in free and bound forms, principally *p*-coumaric acid (227 μmol/100 g = ca. 0.04%) [16] together with other cinnamic acid derivatives (caffeic, ferulic and sinapic acids) and derivatives of benzoic acid (*m*- and *p*-hydroxybenzoic, protocatechuic, vanillic and syringic acids) [16-19]. Hydroxyterephthalic acid and 2,5-dihydroxyterephthalic acid have also been isolated [20].

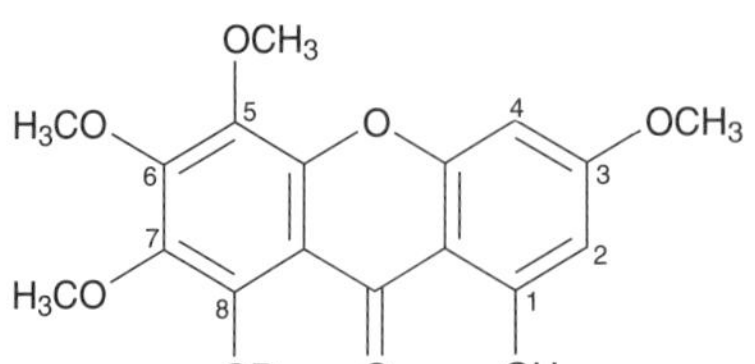

Eustomin R = CH_3
Demethyleustomin R = H

☐ ***Triterpenes*** including β-amyrin, oleanolic acid, oleanolic acid lactone and maslinic acid [21].

☐ ***Alkaloids***, especially gentianine (0.3%) [22].

☐ ***Flavonols*** Kaempferol and quercetin glycosides [18,23].

☐ ***Phytosterols*** β-Sitosterol, stigmasterol, campesterol and others [24].

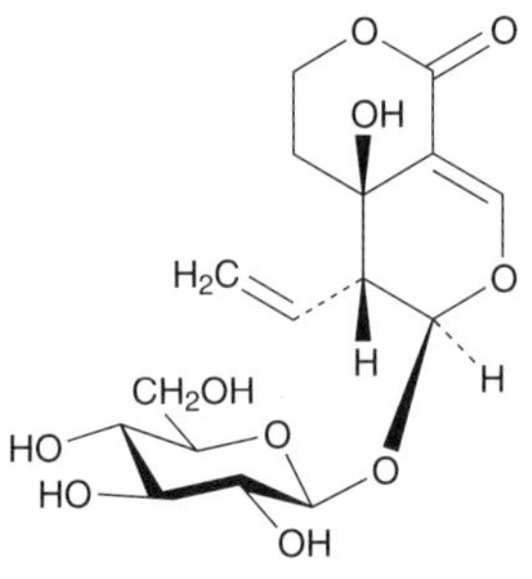

Swertiamarin

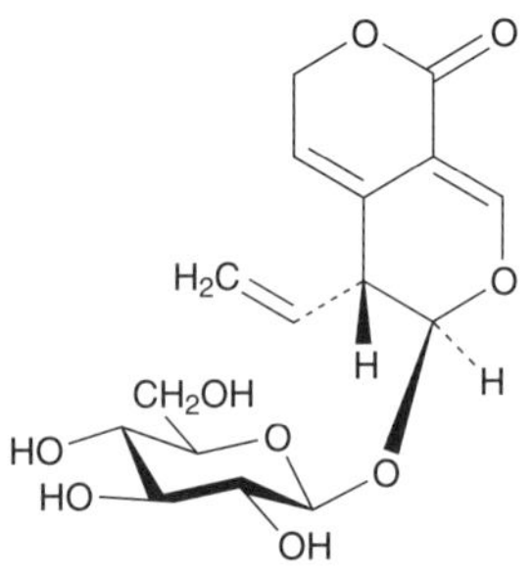

Gentiopicrin

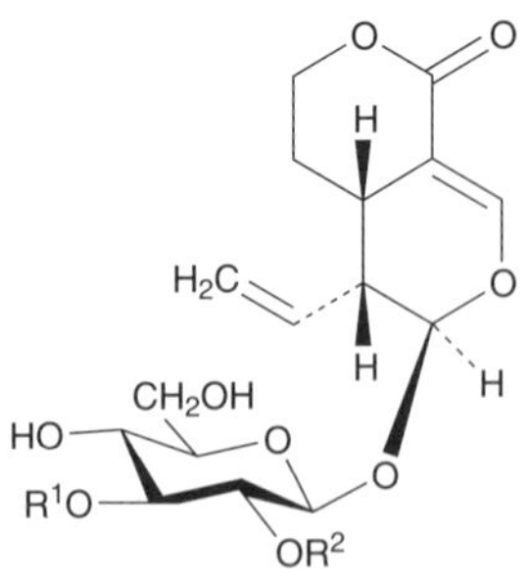

	R^1	R^2
Sweroside	H	H
Centapicrin	acetyl	*m*-hydroxybenzoyl
Deacetylcentapicrin	H	*m*-hydroxybenzoyl

Published Assay Methods
Swertiamarin [1] and gentiopicroside [1,25] by HPLC; by TLC densitometry [2]. Eustomin and demethyleustomin by HPLC [9]. Phenolic acids by GC [16]. Flavonoids and phenolic acids simultaneously by HPLC [18].

PHARMACOLOGY

In vitro
A lyophilised infusion of centaury exhibited antioxidant activity, scavenging the superoxide radical and inhibiting xanthine oxidase; the activity was attributed mainly to phenolic acids and kaempferol [19].

In vivo

Anti-inflammatory activity
Centaury extracts have exhibited mild anti-inflammatory activity in several tests. After oral administration at 100 mg/kg body weight, a dry 80%-ethanolic extract inhibited carrageenan-induced rat paw oedema by 19-22%, compared to 45-55% inhibition by indometacin at 5 mg/kg [26,27].

In the Freund's adjuvant-induced polyarthritis test a dry aqueous extract, orally-administered to rats at 10-500 mg per animal on days 12 and 16 following adjuvant injection, significantly and dose-dependently reduced oedema ($p<0.01$; 20.6% inhibition at 100 mg/day), although with less effect than indometacin at 1 mg/kg/day (70% inhibition) [28].

In the air pouch granuloma test in rats, topically administered creams containing 2.5-10% of a dry aqueous extract of centaury inhibited exudate formation by 19-47% ($p<0.01$) [28].

Antipyretic activity
A dry aqueous extract of centaury administered by gavage to rats at 50-100 mg per animal reduced yeast-induced hyperthermia ($p<0.05$), with somewhat less effect than indometacin at 5 mg/kg [28].

Activities of constituents
Orally administered swertiamarin exhibited anticholinergic (antispasmodic) activity, inhibiting carbachol-induced contractions of the proximal colon in rats in a dose-dependent manner at 150-300 mg/kg body weight ($p<0.05$) [29].

Gentiopicrin administered intraperitoneally to mice at 30-60 mg/kg/day for 5 days inhibited hepatic injury in two model systems, in part by suppressing the increase in tumour necrosis factor (a major mediator of inflammation) [30].

Orally administered gentianine had a CNS depressant effect in mice, significantly inhibiting spontaneous movement ($p<0.001$ after 50 minutes) and increasing hexobarbital-induced sleeping time ($p<0.05$) at 30 mg/kg. In rats it exhibited anti-ulcerogenic activity in the water immersion stress test ($p<0.01$) at a high dose of 100 mg/kg [31].

Pharmacological studies in humans
Tonic bitters such as centaury reflexively stimulate digestive secretions (saliva, gastric juice, bile and pancreatic juice) and increase gastric motility and the acidity of gastric juice by primary stimulation of bitter receptors in the taste buds and secondary stimulation when the bitter principles reach the stomach. Although not easy to demonstrate, a number of human pharmacological studies (not specifically with centaury) have confirmed these effects. However, bitters do not appear to increase digestive secretions in healthy subjects with a normal appetite, in whom normal reflex secretion is already functioning at an optimum level [32,33].

Pharmacokinetics
It has been demonstrated in vitro that numerous species of intestinal bacteria have the ability to tranform swertiamarin into the seco-iridoid metabolites erythrocentaurin and its reduced product, 5-hydroxymethyl-isochroman-1-one. Some species also have the ability to transform it into nitrogen-containing gentianine [34].

CLINICAL STUDIES

None published on mono-preparations of centaury.

THERAPEUTICS

Actions
Tonic bitter, digestive stimulant [32,33,35,36]; mildly anti-inflammatory [26-28] and antipyretic [28].

The relative bitterness of centaury is 2,000-10,000 compared to 10,000-20,000 for gentian and 10,000-30,000 for wormwood [32].

Indications
None adequately substantiated by pharmacological or clinical studies.

Uses based on experience or tradition
Loss of appetite [37,38], anorexia, especially in children [33,35]; dyspeptic complaints [35,37] including those due to inadequate gastric juice formation or achylia gastrica (lack of acid and pepsin in gastric juice) [33].

Contraindications
None known.

Side effects
None known.

Interactions with other drugs
None known.

Dosage
3-4 times daily: dried herb, 1-3 g, usually as an infusion [35,37]; liquid extract 1:1 in 25% alcohol, 1-3 ml [35].

Centaury should be taken 20-30 minutes before meals [32,33] and sipped slowly so that the bitter principles reflexively stimulate digestive secretory activity [36]. The tonic effects take time to fully develop and several weeks of treatment may be advisable [33,36].

SAFETY

Conflicting results have been obtained with centaury extracts in the Ames mutagenicity test. A tincture and a fluid extract revealed no mutagenic potential in *Salmonella typhimurium* strains TA 98 or TA 100, whereas a soft (inspissated) extract showed weak mutagenicity in strain TA 98 [39]. In a different study, a tincture and a fluid extract appeared to be weakly mutagenic in *S. typhimurium* strain TA 100, but not in TA 98 [40]. On the other hand, the methoxylated xanthones eustomin and demethyleustomin isolated from centaury showed strongly antimutagenic properties in *S. typhimurium* strains TA 98 and TA 100 [41].

REGULATORY STATUS

Medicines

UK	Accepted for general sale, internal or external use [42].
France	Accepted for specified indications [38].
Germany	Commission E monograph published, with approved uses [37].

Food

USA	Permitted as flavouring in alcoholic beverages only (21 CFR 172.510) [43].
Council of Europe	Permitted as flavouring, category 4 (with limits on xanthones under evaluation) [44].

REFERENCES

Current Pharmacopoeial Monographs

Ph. Eur. Centaury

Literature References

1. Jankovic T, Krstic D, Savikin-Fodulivic K, Menkovic N and Grubisic D. Comparative investigation of secoiridoid compounds of *Centaurium erythraea* grown in nature and cultured *in vitro*. *Pharm. Pharmacol. Lett.* 1998, **8**, 30-32.
2. Nikolova-Damyanova B and Handjieva N. Quantitative Determination of Swertiamarin and Gentiopicroside in *Centaurium erythrea* and *C. turcicum* by Densitometry. *Phytochem. Analysis* 1996, **7**, 140-142.
3. van der Sluis WG. Chemotaxonomical Investigations of the Genera *Blackstonia* and *Centaurium* (Gentianaceae). *Plant Syst. Evol.* 1985, **149**, 253-286.
4. Sakina K and Aota K. Studies on the Constituents of *Erythraea centaurium* (Linné) Persoon. I. The Structure of Centapicrin, a New Bitter Secoiridoid Glucoside. *Yakugaku Zasshi* 1976, **96**, 683-688 [JAPANESE/English summary].
5. Wagner H and Vasirian K. Zur Chromatographie der Enzianbitterstoffe [Chromatography of the bitter substances of gentian]. *Dtsch. Apoth. Ztg.* 1974, **114**, 1245-1248 [GERMAN].
6. van der Sluis WG and Labadie RP. Secoiridoid glucosides occurring in Gentianaceae. *Pharm. Weekblad* 1978, **113**, 21-32 [DUTCH/English summary].
7. van der Sluis WG and Labadie RP. Secoiridoids and Xanthones in the Genus Centaurium. Part III. Decentapicrins A, B and C, new *m*-hydroxybenzoyl esters of sweroside from Centaurium littorale. *Planta Medica* 1981, **41**, 150-160.
8. Do T, Marekov N and Trifonov A. Iridoids from Gentianaceae Plants growing in Bulgaria. *Planta Medica* 1987, **53**, 580.
9. Jankovic T, Krstic D, Savikin-Fodulivic K, Menkovic N and Grubisic D. Xanthone compounds of *Centaurium erythraea* grown in nature and cultured *in vitro*. *Pharm. Pharmacol. Lett.* 2000, **8**, 23-25.
10. Schimmer O and Mauthner H. Polymethoxylated xanthones from the herb of *Centaurium erythraea* with strong antimutagenic properties in *Salmonella typhimurium*. *Planta Medica* 1996, **62**, 561-564.
11. Neshta NM, Glyzin VI, Nikolaeva GG and Sheichenko VI. A new xanthone compound from *Centaurium erythraea*. *Khim. Prir. Soedin.* 1983, 106-107 [RUSSIAN], translated into English as *Chem. Nat. Compd.* 1983, **19**, 105.
12. Neshta NM, Nikolaeva GG, Sheichenko VI and Patudin AV. A new xanthone compound from *Centaurium erythraea*. *Khim. Prir. Soedin.* 1982, 258 [RUSSIAN], translated into English as *Chem. Nat. Compd.* 1982, **18**, 240-241.
13. Neshta NM, Glyzin VI, Savina AA and Patudin AV. A new xanthone compound from *Centaurium erythraea*. III. *Khim. Prir. Soedin.* 1983, 787 [RUSSIAN], translated into English as *Chem. Nat. Compd.* 1983, **19**, 750-751.
14. Neshta NM, Glyzin VI and Patudin AV. A new xanthone compound from *Centaurium erythraea*. IV. *Khim. Prir. Soedin.* 1984, 110 [RUSSIAN], translated into English as Chem. Nat. Compd. 1984, **20**, 108.
15. Valentão P, Areias F, Amaral J, Andrade P and Seabra R. Tetraoxygenated xanthones from *Centaurium erythraea*. *Nat. Prod. Lett.* 2000, **14**, 319-323.
16. Dombrówicz E, Swiatek L and Zadernowski R. Phenolic acids in bitter drugs. Part III. Examination of Herba Centaurii. *Farm. Pol.* 1988, **44**, 657-660 [POLISH/English summary].
17. Hatjimanoli M and Debelmas A-M. Phenolic acids from *Centaurium umbellatum* Gil. *Ann. Pharm. Fr.* 1977, **35**, 107-111 [FRENCH/English summary].
18. Andrade PB, Seabra RM, Valentão P and Areias F. Simultaneous determination of flavonoids, phenolic acids and coumarins in seven medicinal species by HPLC/diode-array detector. *J. Liq. Chrom. Rel. Technol.* 1998, **21**, 2813-2820.
19. Valentão P, Fernandes E, Carvalho F, Andrade PB, Seabra RM and Bastos ML. Antioxidant Activity of *Centaurium erythraea* Infusion Evidenced by Its Superoxide Radical Scavenging and Xanthine Oxidase Inhibitory Activity. *J. Agric. Food. Chem.* 2001, **49**, 3476-3479.

20. Hatjimanoli M, Favre-Bonvin J, Kaouadji M and Mariotte A-M. Monohydroxy- and 2,5- dihydroxy terephthalic acids, two unusual phenolics isolated from *Centaurium erythraea* and identified in other Gentianaceae members. *J. Nat. Prod.* 1988, **51**, 977-980.
21. Bellavita V, Schiaffella F and Mezzetti T. Triterpenoids of *Centaurium erythraea*. *Phytochemistry* 1974, **13**, 289-290.
22. Bishay DW, Shelver WH and Wahba Khalil SK. Alkaloids of *Erythraea centaurium* Pers. growing in Egypt. I. Isolation of Gentianine. *Planta Medica* 1978, **33**, 422-423.
23. Lebreton P and Dangy-Caye MP. Contribution biochimique à l'étude taxonomique des Gentianacées [Biochemical contribution to the taxonomical study of Gentianaceae]. *Plantes Méd. Phytothér.* 1973, **7**, 87-94 [FRENCH/English summary].
24. Aquino R, Behar I, Garzarella P, Dini A and Pizza C. Composizione chimica e proprietà biologiche della *Erythraea centaurium* Rafn [Chemical composition and biological properties of *Erythraea centaurium* Rafn]. *Boll. Soc. Ital. Biol. Sper* 1985, **61**, 165-169 [ITALIAN/English summary].
25. Kaluzová L, Glatz Z, Pospísilová J, Musil P and Unar J. Determination of Gentiopicroside in *Centaurium erythraea* by Means of High-Performance Liquid Chromatography [CZECH/English summary]. *Cesk. Slov. Farm.* 1995, **44**, 203-205.
26. Mascolo N, Autore G, Capasso F, Menghini A and Fasulo MP. Biological Screening of Italian Medicinal Plants for Anti-inflammatory Activity. *Phytotherapy Res.* 1987, **1**, 28-31.
27. Capasso F, Mascolo N, Morrica P and Ramundo E. Phytotherapeutic profile of some plants used in folk medicine. *Boll. Soc. Ital. Biol. Sper.* 1983, **59**, 1398-1404.
28. Berkan T, Üstünes L, Lermioglu F and Özer A. Antiinflammatory, Analgesic and Antipyretic Effects of an Aqueous Extract of *Erythraea centaurium*. *Planta Medica* 1991, **57**, 34-37.
29. Yamahara J, Kobayashi M, Matsuda H and Aoki S. Anticholinergic action of *Swertia japonica* and an active constituent. *J. Ethnopharmacol.* 1991, **33**, 31-35.
30. Kondo Y, Takano F and Hojo H. Suppression of Chemically and Immunologically Induced Hepatic Injuries by Gentiopicroside in Mice. *Planta Medica* 1994, **60**, 414-416.
31. Yamahara J, Konoshima T, Sawada T and Fujimura H. Biologically Active Principles of Crude Drugs: Pharmacological Actions of Swertia japonica Extracts, Swertiamarin and Gentianine. *Yakugaku Zasshi (J. Pharm. Soc. Japan)* 1978, **98**, 1446-1451 [JAPANESE/English summary].
32. Schulz V, Hänsel R and Tyler VE. Bitter Herbs (Bitters). In: *Rational Phytotherapy - A Physicians' Guide to Herbal Medicine, 4th ed.* ISBN 3-540-67096-3. Berlin-Heidelberg-New York-London: Springer-Verlag, 2001:204-209.
33. Weiss RF and Fintelmann V. Amara, Bitters; Centaurium minus (C. erythraea), Lesser Centaury. In: *Herbal Medicine, 2nd ed.* (translated from the 9th German edition of *Lehrbuch der Phytotherapie*). ISBN 3-13-126332-6 and 0-86577-970-8. Stuttgart-New York: Thieme, 2000:51-54.
34. El-Sedawy AI, Shu Y-Z, Hattori M, Kobashi K and Namba T. Metabolism of Swertiamarin from *Swertia japonica* by Human Intestinal Bacteria. *Planta Medica* 1989, **55**, 147-150.
35. Centaurium. In: *British Herbal Pharmacopoeia 1983.* ISBN 0-903032-07-4. Bournemouth: British Herbal Medicine Association, 1983.
36. Chevallier A. Centaury. In: *The Encyclopedia of Medicinal Plants.* ISBN 0-7513-0314-3. London-New York-Stuttgart: Dorling Kindersley, 1996:204.
37. Centaurii herba. German Commission E Monograph published in: Bundesanzeiger No. 122 of 6 July 1988; amended in Bundesanzeiger No. 50 of 13 March 1990.
38. Centaurée (Petite). In: *Médicaments à base de plantes.* ISBN 2-911473-02-7. Saint-Denis Cedex, France: Agence du Médicament, 1998.
39. Schimmer O, Krüger A, Paulini H and Haefele F. An evaluation of 55 commercial plant extracts in the Ames mutagenicity test. *Pharmazie* 1994, **49**, 448-451.
40. Göggelmann W and Schimmer O. Mutagenic activity of phytotherapeutical drugs. In: *Genetic Toxicology of the Diet.* New York: Alan R Liss, 1986:63-72.
41. Schimmer O and Mauthner H. Polymethoxylated Xanthones from the Herb of Centaurium erythraea with Strong Antimutagenic Properties in Salmonella typhimurium. *Planta Medica* 1996, 62, 561-564.
42. Centaury. In: UK Statutory Instrument 1994 No. 2410. The Medicines (Products Other Than Veterinary Drugs) (General Sale List) Amendment Order 1994. Schedule 1, Table A.
43. Centaury. In: Section 172.510 of USA Code of Federal Regulations, Title 21, Food and Drugs, Parts 170 to 199. Revised as of April 1, 2000.
44. Centaurium erythraea Rafn. In: *Natural Sources of Flavourings. Report No. 1.* ISBN 92-871-4324-2. Strasbourg: Council of Europe Publishing, 2000:109-111.

REGULATORY GUIDELINES FROM OTHER EU COUNTRIES

FRANCE

Médicaments à base de plantes [38]: Centaurée (Petite), sommité fleurie.

Therapeutic indications accepted

Oral use
Traditionally used to stimulate the appetite.
Traditionally used to facilitate weight gain.

GERMANY

Commission E monograph [37]: Centaurii herba (Tausendgüldenkraut).

Uses
Loss of appetite; dyspeptic complaints.

Contraindications
None known.

Side effects
None known.

Interactions with other drugs
None known.

Dosage
Unless otherwise prescribed, average daily dose: 6 g of herb; 1-2 g of extract (in accordance with DAB Ergänzung B6); equivalent preparations.

Mode of administration
Comminuted herb for tea infusions and other bitter-tasting preparations for internal use.

Action
Increases the secretion of gastric juice.

CINNAMON

Lauraceae

Cinnamomi cortex

Synonym: Ceylon cinnamon.

Definition

Cinnamon consists of the dried bark, freed from the outer cork and underlying parenchyma, of shoots grown on cut stock of *Cinnamomum zeylanicum* Nees [*C. verum* J. Presl].

Cinnamomum zeylanicum is indigenous to Sri Lanka and southern India and for the most part is now grown commercially in Sri Lanka, the Seychelles and Madagascar.

In the United Kingdom, much of the British Commonwealth and most of Europe the term 'cinnamon' is reserved almost exclusively for the dried bark of *Cinnamomum zeylanicum*. However, in the USA the term cinnamon embraces material from a wider range of botanical sources including *Cinnamomum cassia* Blume (see the monograph on Cassia Bark), *C. loureirii* Nees and *C. burmanii* Blume, as well as *C. zeylanicum* Nees [1]. In publications originating from China and Japan (e.g. the Pharmacopoeia of Japan), the terms 'Cinnamomi cortex','cinnamon bark' and 'cinnamon' usually refer to the bark of *Cinnamomum cassia*.

CONSTITUENTS

☐ ***Essential oil***, 0.5-2.5% [2] (Ph. Eur. min. 1.2% V/m). The European Pharmacopoeia monograph for Ceylon cinnamon bark oil specifies the following profile of components: *trans*-cinnamaldehyde (55-75%), linalool (1.0-6.0%), β-caryophyllene (1.0-4.0%), eugenol (<7.5%), 1,8-cineole (<3.0%), *trans*-2-methoxycinnamaldehyde (0.1-1.0%), benzyl benzoate (< 1.0%), coumarin (< 0.5%) and safrole (< 0.5%). Even though this does not form part of the Ph. Eur. specification for the bark itself, a comparable profile is obviously desirable for essential oil distilled from a bark sample.

GC analysis of essential oil distilled from 16 cinnamon samples from varied sources gave the following results: *trans*-cinnamaldehyde (85-93%), *cis*-cinnamaldehyde (0.8-3.5%), linalool (0.3-2.5%), β-caryophyllene (0.4-4.5%), eugenol (0.8-4.0%), 2-methoxycinnamaldehyde (0.08-1.3%) and benzyl benzoate (0.05-1.2%) [1]. Disconcertingly, the Ph. Eur. upper limit for *trans*-cinnamaldehyde is well below the minimum found here.

While other fairly similar data can be found in the literature [3-5], essential oils from some cinnamon (bark) samples may contain more than 10% of safrole and/or eugenol [6] or, in more unusual cases, 65-74% of eugenol (material from Madagascar) [7] or 84.7% of benzyl benzoate (material from Assam) [8]. Careful selection and monitoring of raw material is therefore necessary.

☐ ***Polysaccharides*** A water-insoluble glucan (as crude material, about 10% of the dry bark) and a water-soluble arabinoxylan (about 6%) [9]. The glucan has a (1→4)-linked α-D-glucan backbone in which some of the glucose units carry oligoglucosyl units as substituents at O-6 [10]. The arabinoxylan has a linear (1→4)-linked β-D-xylan backbone in which each xylose unit is substituted both at O-2 and O-3 with arabinosyl, 3-xylosyl-arabinosyl or 3-arabinosyl-arabinosyl groups [9].

☐ ***Condensed tannins (proanthocyanidins)*** (–)-Epicatechin and four dimers, two trimers, two tetramers and one pentamer of epicatechin have been isolated. Amounts were very small, the highest being that of the trimer epicatechin (4β→8, 2β→7)-epicatechin-(4α→8)-epicatechin (ca. 0.1%) [11].

☐ ***Phenolic acids*** Cinnamic acid (0.05%), protocatechuic acid (0.02%) and smaller amounts of gentisic, vanillic and various other phenolic acids [12].

☐ ***Diterpenes*** Small amounts of two highly-oxygenated pentacyclic diterpenes, cinnzeylanine (structure illustrated in the Cassia Bark monograph) and cinnzeylanol [13,14].

☐ ***Other constituents*** An absence of coumarin distinguishes cinnamon from cassia bark (*Cinnamomum cassia*) [15].

Published Assay Methods

Essential oil components by GC and GC-MS [16]. Cinnamaldehyde, cinnamyl alcohol, coumarin and other compounds by HPLC [15]. Cinnamaldehyde by fluorimetry [17].

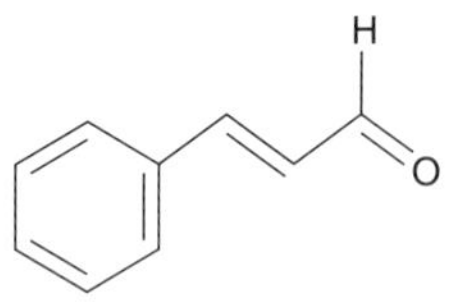

Cinnamaldehyde

Linalool

PHARMACOLOGY

In vitro

Antimicrobial activity
Cinnamon (bark) oil exhibited strong antibacterial activity over a wide spectrum of both Gram-negative (e.g. *Escherichia coli, Pseudomonas aeruginosa*) and Gram-positive (e.g. *Staphylococcus aureus, Bacillus subtilis*) organisms [18-20]. A supercritical carbon dioxide extract from cinnamon showed comparable activity [21].

Strong antifungal activity of cinnamon oil against *Aspergillus niger* [18], *Candida albicans* [18,19] and three common dermatophytic fungi [22] has been demonstrated. The essential oil and a dry chloroform extract from cinnamon also strongly inhibited aflatoxin production by *Aspergillus parasiticus* [23].

Spasmolytic activity
Cinnamon bark oil and cinnamaldehyde exerted spasmolytic effects on guinea pig tracheal and ileal smooth muscle, the EC_{50} values for the oil being 41 and 12 mg/litre respectively [24]. In another study, cinnamaldehyde inhibited acetylcholine- and histamine-induced contractions of isolated mouse and guinea pig ileum with 7-10% of the potency of papaverine [25].

Carminative action of cinnamon oil
On the basis that the carminative effect of cinnamon oil is due to an antifoaming action, as well as spasmolytic activity, a foam generator was used to demonstrate that the oil reduced foam volume in artificial gastric and intestinal fluids [26].

Anti-inflammatory activity
Cinnamon bark oil at a concentration of about 37 μM (based on the average MW of components) inhibited cyclooxygenase activity and hence the biosynthesis of prostaglandins (mediators of inflammation) by 51.9% in sheep seminal vesicles; this activity was attributed mainly to the presence of about 5% of eugenol [27].

In vivo

Anti-inflammatory and antinociceptive effects
A dry 80%-ethanolic extract from cinnamon showed significant anti-inflammatory activity in the cotton pellet granuloma test in rats ($p<0.05$) after oral administration at 400 mg/kg, but had no effect on xylene-induced ear oedema in mice. The same extract produced significant and dose-dependent antinociceptive effects in the hot-plate test ($p<0.001$ at 400 mg/kg) and acetic acid-induced writhing test ($p<0.001$ at 200 mg/kg) in mice [28].

Wound-healing effects
A dry 90%-ethanolic extract from cinnamon (6.5:1) produced dose-dependent wound-healing effects, promoting all the crucial phases of healing (collagenation, wound contraction and epithelization), when administered orally at 250 or 500 mg/kg daily to rats bearing different types of wounds. The breaking strength increased in an incision wound model ($p<0.01$), while the number of days to achieve epithelization and wound contraction decreased in an excision wound model ($p<0.01$). In a dead space wound model, the weight of granulation tissue and the breaking strength increased ($p<0.01$) [29].

Effects of cinnamaldehyde
Cinnamaldehyde administered intravenously produced a hypotensive effect in anaesthetized dogs and guinea pigs, and moderately inhibited rat stomach movement (contraction and tone) and mouse intestinal propulsion; when administered orally it protected stress-induced gastric erosions in mice and increased biliary secretions in rats [25].

Central effects of orally-administered cinnamaldehyde have been demonstrated in mice: sedative activity (decrease of spontaneous motor activity, antagonistic effect to methamphetamine-induced hyperactivity, motor incoordination in a rotor-rod test), and also hypothermic and antipyretic activities [30].

CLINICAL STUDIES

Negative results were obtained in a randomized, placebo-controlled pilot study in which patients aged 16-79 years testing positive for *Helicobacter pylori* (a common human pathogen associated with gastritis and duodenal and gastric ulcers) were treated daily for 4 weeks with either 2 × 40 mg of an ethanolic extract of cinnamon (n = 15) or plac-ebo (n = 8). Mean counts in the ^{13}C-urea breath test (taken as a measurement of the degree of *H. pylori* colonization) before and after therapy were 22.1 and 23.9 in the cinnamon group compared to 24.4 and 25.9 in the control group [31].

THERAPEUTICS

Actions
Carminative [32,33], spasmolytic [24,25,33], appetite stimulant [33], antibacterial [18-21] and antifungal [18,19,22], anti-inflammatory [28], vulnerary [29], anthelmintic [33], circulatory stimulant [34,35].

Indications
None adequately substantiated by pharmacological or clinical studies.

Uses based on experience or tradition
Internal: Digestive complaints such as nausea,

flatulence, dyspepsia and gastrointestinal colic; to stimulate the appetite [2,33,36,37]; as a digestive stimulant in debility or convalescence [34]; common cold, influenza and winter chills [33,35,38]; diarrhoea in children [33,38]; worm infestations [38].
External: Wound-healing [38].

Contraindications
Avoid in pregnancy [2,36], except in amounts normally used in foods.

Side effects
Allergic skin and mucosal reactions may occur in sensitive individuals [36,39], arising mainly from cinnamaldehyde (the major component of the essential oil) [40].

Interactions with other drugs
None known.

Dosage
Three times daily: dried bark, 0.5-1 g as an infusion [2,33]; liquid extract 1:1 in 70% alcohol, 0.5-1 ml; tincture BPC 1949 (1:5 in 70% ethanol), 2-4 ml [33].

SAFETY

Cinnamon is usually well tolerated at recommended dosage levels. During 4 weeks of treatment with a daily oral dose of 2 × 40 mg of an ethanolic extract of cinnamon, 23 patients with *Helicobacter pylori* infections reported 5 minor adverse gastrointestinal effects [31].

Allergic reactions to contact with cinnamon, or more often the essential oil, are not uncommon and arise mainly from cinnamaldehyde, a skin irritant. Cinnamaldehyde tops the list of substances causing allergic reactions to perfumes and cosmetics [39,41].

Ames mutagenicity tests on cinnamon extracts and cinnamaldehyde have given conflicting results, mostly negative but some positive; this may be due to botanical and chemical variability as well as antimicrobial and cytotoxic activities [39]. Cinnamon extracts exhibited mutagenic activity in the *Bacillus subtilis* rec assay [42-44]. Cinnamaldehyde induced chromosomal aberrations in Chinese hamster cells [45,46] and mutations in *Drosophila* [47]. Overall, the mutagenicity data relating to cinnamon are considered inadequate for full evaluation of carcinogenic risk [39].

Cinnamon is not considered to present any special risk in pregnancy, despite old and rather vague reports to the contrary. However, since the data on mutagenicity remain insufficient, use of the oil should be restricted during pregnancy [39].

The acute oral LD_{50} of cinnamon bark oil in rats was determined as 3.4 ml/kg body weight [48]. Cinnamaldehyde given orally to rats for 16 weeks as 0.25% of their diet had no apparent adverse effect and 1% caused only slight abnormalities in the liver and stomach [49].

REGULATORY STATUS

Medicines

UK	Accepted for general sale, internal or external use [50].
France	Accepted for specified indications [37].
Germany	Commission E monograph published, with approved uses [36].

Foods

USA	Generally recognized as safe (21 CFR 182.10 and 182.20) [51].
Council of Europe	Permitted as flavouring, category N2 [52].

REFERENCES

Current Pharmacopoeial Monographs
Ph. Eur. Cinnamon

Literature References

1. Jayatilaka A, Poole SK, Poole CF and Chichila TMP. Simultaneous micro steam distillation/solvent extraction for the isolation of semivolatile flavor compounds from cinnamon and their separation by series coupled-column gas chromatography. *Analytica Chim. Acta* 1995, **302**, 147-162.
2. Wichtl M and Schäfer-Korting M. Zimtrinde - Cinnamomi cortex. In: Hartke K, Hartke H, Mutschler E, Rücker G and Wichtl M, editors. *Kommentar zum Europäischen Arzneibuch.* Stuttgart: Wissenschaftliche Verlagsgesellschaft, 1999 (11 Lfg.):Z 1 [GERMAN].
3. Lawrence BM. Progress in Essential Oils. *Perfumer & Flavorist* 1998, **23** (Jan/Feb), 39-50.
4. Senanayake UM, Lee TH and Wills RBH. Volatile Constituents of Cinnamon (*Cinnamomum zeylanicum*) Oils. *J. Agric. Food Chem.* 1978, **26**, 822-824.
5. Wijesekera ROB, Jayewardene AL and Rajapakse LS. Volatile Constituents of Leaf, Stem and Root Oils of Cinnamon (*Cinnamomum zeylanicum*). *J. Sci. Food. Agric.* 1974, **25**, 1211-1220.
6. Wijesekera ROB. The chemistry and technology of cinnamon. *Crit. Rev. Food. Sci. Nutr.* 1978, **10**, 1-30.
7. De Medici D, Pieretti S, Salvatore G, Nicoletti M and Rasoanaivo P. Chemical Analysis of Essential Oils of Malagasy Medicinal Plants by Gas Chromatography and NMR Spectroscopy. *Flavour Fragrance J.* 1992, **7**, 275-281.
8. Nath SC, Pathak MG and Baruah A. Benzyl Benzoate, the Major Component of the Leaf and Stem Bark Oil of *Cinnamomum zeylanicum* Blume. *J. Essent. Oil Res.* 1996, **8**, 327-328.
9. Gowda DC and Sarathy C. Structure of an L-arabino-D-xylan from the bark of *Cinnamomum zeylanicum*. *Carbohydrate*

Res. 1987, **166**, 263-269.
10. Sarathy C and Gowda DC. Structural Features of a D-Glucan from the Stem bark of *Cinnamomum zeylanicum*. *Indian J. Chem.* 1988, **27B**, 694-695.
11. Nonaka G-I, Morimoto S and Nishioka I. Tannins and Related Compounds. Part 13. Isolation and Structures of Trimeric, Tetrameric and Pentameric Proanthocyanidins from Cinnamon. *J. Chem. Soc. Perkin Trans. I* 1983, 2139-2145.
12. Schulz JM and Herrmann K. Occurrence of Hydroxybenzoic Acids and Hydroxycinnamic Acids in Spices. IV. Phenolics of Spices. *Z. Lebensm. Unters. Forsch.* 1980, **171**, 193-199 [GERMAN/English summary].
13. Isogai A, Suzuki A, Tamura S, Murakoshi S, Ohashi Y and Sasada Y. Structures of Cinnzeylanine and Cinnzeylanol, Polyhydroxylated Pentacyclic Diterpenes from *Cinnamomum zeylanicum* Nees. *Agric. Biol. Chem.* 1976, **40**, 2305-2306.
14. Isogai A, Suzuki A, Tamura S, Ohashi Y and Sasada Y. Cinnzeylanine, a New Pentacyclic Diterpene Acetate from *Cinnamomum zeylanicum*. *Acta Cryst.* 1977, **B33**, 623-626.
15. Archer AW. Determination of cinnamaldehyde, coumarin and cinnamyl alcohol in cinnamon and cassia by high-performance liquid chromatography. *J. Chromatogr.* 1988, **447**, 272-276.
16. Jirovetz L, Buchbauer G, Ngassoum MB, Essia-Ngang JJ, Tatsadjieu LN and Adjoudji O. Chemical composition and antibacterial activities of the essential oils of *Plectranthus glandulosus* and *Cinnamomum zeylanicum* from Cameroon. *Sci. Pharm.* 2002, **70**, 93-99.
17. Tsai S-Y and Chen S-C. A fluorimetric assay of trans-cinnamaldehyde in cinnamon. *J. Nat. Prod.* 1984, **47**, 536-538.
18. Raharivelomanna PJ, Terrom GP, Bianchini JP and Coulanges P. Contribution a l'étude de l'action antimicrobienne de quelques huiles essentielles extraites de plantes Malgaches. II: Les Lauracées [Contribution to the study of antimicrobial activity of some essential oils from Madagascan plants. II: the Lauraceae]. *Arch. Inst. Pasteur Madagascar.* 1989, **56**, 261-271 [FRENCH/English summary].
19. Janssen AM, Chin NLJ, Scheffer JJC and Baerheim Svendsen A. Screening for antimicrobial activity of some essential oils by the agar overlay technique. *Pharm. Weekblad. Sci. Ed.* 1986, **8**, 289-292.
20. Inouye S, Takizawa T and Yamaguchi H. Antibacterial activity of essential oils and their major constituents against respiratory tract pathogens by gaseous contact. *J. Antimicrob. Chemother.* 2001, **47**, 565-573.
21. Ehrich J, Bauermann U and Thomann R. Antimikrobielle Wirkung von CO_2-Gewürzextrakten von Bohnenkraut bis Ceylon-Zimt [Antimicrobial activity of CO_2 extracts of seasonings from summer savory to Ceylon cinnamon]. *Lebensmitteltechnik* 1995, (11), 51-53 [GERMAN].
22. Janssen AM, Scheffer JJC, Parhan-Van Atten AW and Baerheim Svendsen A. Screening of some essential oils for their activities on dermatophytes. *Pharm. Weekblad Sci. Ed.* 1988, **10**, 277-280.
23. Sharma A, Ghanekar AS, Padwal-Desai SR and Nadkarni GB. Microbiological Status and Antifungal Properties of Irradiated Spices. *J. Agric. Food Chem.* 1984, **32**, 1061-1063.
24. Reiter M and Brandt W. Relaxant Effects on Tracheal and Ileal Smooth Muscles of the Guinea Pig. *Arzneim.-Forsch./Drug Res.* 1985, **35**, 408-414.
25. Harada M and Yano S. Pharmacological Studies on Chinese Cinnamon. II. Effects of Cinnamaldehyde on the Cardiovascular and Digestive Systems. *Chem. Pharm. Bull.* 1975, **23**, 941-947.
26. Harries N, James KC and Pugh WK. Antifoaming and carminative actions of volatile oils. *J. Clin. Pharmacy* 1978, **2**, 171-177.
27. Wagner H, Wierer M and Bauer R. *In vitro* Inhibition of Prostaglandin Biosynthesis by Essential Oils and Phenolic Compounds. *Planta Medica* 1986, **52**, 184-187 [GERMAN/English summary].
28. Atta AH and Alkofahi A. Anti-nociceptive and anti-inflammatory effects of some Jordanian medicinal plant extracts. *J. Ethnopharmacol.* 1998, **60**, 117-124.
29. Kamath JV, Rana AC and Chowdhury AR. Pro-healing Effect of *Cinnamomum zeylanicum* Bark. *Phytotherapy Res.* 2003, **17**, 970-972.
30. Harada M and Ozaki Y. Pharmacological Studies on Chinese Cinnamon. I. Central Effects of Cinnamaldehyde. *Yakugaku Zasshi* 1972, **92**, 135-140 [JAPANESE/English summary].
31. Nir Y, Potasman I, Stermer E, Tabak M and Neeman I. Controlled Trial of the Effect of Cinnamon Extract on *Helicobacter pylori*. *Helicobacter* 2000, **5**, 94-97.
32. Pharmaceutical Society of Great Britain. Cinnamon. In: *British Pharmaceutical Codex 1973*. London: Pharmaceutical Press, 1973.
33. Cinnamomum. In: *British Herbal Pharmacopoeia 1983*. ISBN 0-903032-07-4. Bournemouth: British Herbal Medicine Association, 1983.
34. Chevallier A. Cinnamon. In: *Encyclopedia of Medicinal Plants, 2nd ed.* ISBN 0-7513-1209-6. London-New York: Dorling Kindersley, 2001:84.
35. McIntyre A. Cinnamon - *Cinnamomum zeylanicum*. In: *The Complete Woman's Herbal*. ISBN 1-85675-135-X. London: Gaia Books, 1999:155.
36. Cinnamomi ceylanici cortex (Zimtrinde). German Commission E Monograph published in: Bundesanzeiger No. 22 of 1 February 1990.
37. Canneliers de Ceylan et de Chine. In: *Médicaments à base de plantes*. ISBN 2-911473-02-7. Saint-Denis Cedex, France: Agence du Médicament, 1998.
38. Hänsel R, Keller K, Rimpler H and Schneider G, editors. Cinnamomum. In: *Hagers Handbuch der Pharmazeutischen Praxis, 5th ed. Volume 4: Drogen A-D.* ISBN 3-540-52631-5. Berlin-Heidelberg-New York-London: Springer-Verlag, 1992:884-911 [GERMAN].
39. Keller K. *Cinnamomum Species*. In: De Smet PAGM, Keller K, Hänsel R, Chandler RF, editors. *Adverse Effects of Herbal Drugs, Volume 1*. ISBN 3-540-53100-9. Berlin-Heidelberg-New York: Springer-Verlag, 1992:105-114.
40. Mathias CGT, Chappler RR and Maibach HI. Contact Urticaria from Cinnamic Aldehyde. *Arch. Dermatol.* 1980, **116**, 74-76.
41. Hausen BM. *Cinnamomum zeylanicum* Blume. In: *Allergiepflanzen - Pflanzenallergene. Handbuch und Atlas der allergie-induzierenden Wild- und Kulturpflanzen. Teil 1. Kontaktallergene.* ISBN 3-609-64080-4. Landsberg/Munich: ecomed, 1988:95-97 [GERMAN].
42. Ungsurungsie M, Paovalo C and Noonai A. Mutagenicity of extracts from Ceylon cinnamon in the *rec* assay. *Food Chem. Toxic.* 1984, **22**, 109-112.
43. Ungsurungsie M, Suthienkul O and Paovalo C. Mutagenicity screening of popular Thai spices. *Food Chem. Toxicol.* 1982, **20**, 527-530.
44. Paovalo C and Chulasiri MU. Bacterial Mutagenicity of Fractions from Chloroform Extracts of Ceylon Cinnamon. *J. Food Protection* 1986, **49**, 12-13.
45. Kamasaki A, Takahashi H, Tsumura N, Niwa J, Fujita T and Urasawa S. Genotoxicity of flavouring agents. *Mutation Res.* 1982, **105**, 387-392.
46. Ishidate M, Sofuni T, Yoshikawa K, Hayashi M, Nohmi T, Sawada M and Matsuoka A. Primary mutagenicity screening of food additives currently used in Japan. *Food Chem. Toxicol.* 1984, **22**, 623-636.
47. Woodruff RC, Mason JM, Valencia R and Zimmering S. Chemical Mutagenesis Testing in *Drosophila*. V. Results of 53 Coded Compounds Tested for the National Toxicology Program. *Environmental Mutagenesis* 1985, **7**, 677-702.
48. Opdyke DLJ. Fragrance raw materials monographs: Cinnamon bark oil, Ceylon. *Food Cosmet. Toxicol.* 1975, **13** (Suppl.), 111-112.
49. Hagan EC, Hansen WH, Fitzhugh OG, Jenner PM, Jones WI, Taylor JM et al. Food Flavourings and Compounds of Related Structure. II. Subacute and Chronic Toxicity. *Food Cosmet. Toxicol.* 1967, **5**, 141-157.
50. Cinnamon. In: UK Statutory Instrument 1990 No. 1129. The Medicines (Products Other Than Veterinary Drugs) (General Sale List) Amendment Order 1990. Schedule 1, Table A.

51. Cinnamon bark, Ceylon. In: Sections 182.10 and 182.20 of USA Code of Federal Regulations, Title 21, Food and Drugs, Parts 170 to 199. Revised as of April 1, 2000.
52. Cinnamomum zeylanicum Blume, bark. In: *Flavouring Substances and Natural Sources of Flavourings, 3rd ed.* ISBN 2-7160-0081-6. Strasbourg: Council of Europe, 1981.

REGULATORY GUIDELINES FROM OTHER EU COUNTRIES

FRANCE

Médicaments à base de plantes [37]: Canneliers de Ceylan et de Chine, écorce de tige = cannelle.

Therapeutic indications accepted

Oral use
Traditionally used in the symptomatic treatment of digestive disorders such as epigastric distension, sluggish digestion, eructation and flatulence; in functional asthenia; to facilitate weight gain.

GERMANY

Commission E monograph [36]: Cinnamomi ceylanici cortex (Zimtrinde).

Uses
Loss of appetite; dyspeptic complaints such as mild, spasmodic disorders of the gastrointestinal tract, bloatedness, flatulence.

Contraindications
Hypersensitivity to cinnamon or Peru balsam.
Pregnancy.

Side effects
Frequently allergic skin and mucosal reactions.

Interactions with other drugs
None known.

Dosage
Unless otherwise prescribed, daily dose: 2-4 g of dried bark, 0.05-0.2 g of essential oil; equivalent preparations.

Mode of administration
Comminuted drug for tea infusions; essential oil and other galenic preparations for internal use.

Actions
Antibacterial, fungistatic, motility-promoting.

CLOVE

Myrtaceae

Caryophylli flos

Definition

Clove consists of the whole flower buds of *Syzygium aromaticum* (L.) Merr. et L.M. Perry [*Eugenia caryophyllus* (Spreng.) Bull. et Harr.], dried until they become reddish-brown.

The clove tree, some 10-20 metres high, originated in the Molucca Islands in Indonesia, where the Dutch maintained a monopoly on cloves until 1770. The French then succeeded in introducing cloves to Mauritius and cultivation spread to other countries. For about 150 years Zanzibar produced most of the world supply but the industry there has declined somewhat and from the 1970s Madagascar, Indonesia and Brazil have emerged as major producers of cloves [1,2].

CONSTITUENTS

☐ ***Essential oil***, 14-21% [2] (Ph. Eur. min. 15% V/m). Three components usually comprise over 95% of the oil: eugenol (64-89%), acetyleugenol (4-20%) and β-caryophyllene (4-12%); minor components include α-humulene (0.5-1.9%), caryophyllene oxide (0.2-0.4%) and other sesquiterpenes [3-6].

For medicinal clove oil the European Pharmacopoeia specifies steam-distilled oil from dried flower buds containing eugenol (75-88%), acetyleugenol (4-15%) and β-caryophyllene (5-14%).

Clove oils for other commercial uses are also distilled from leaves of the clove tree and from stems separated from the flower buds, and often rectified, yielding oils of fairly similar composition but usually with a lower content of acetyleugenol and an aroma inferior to that of the flower bud oil [7].

☐ ***Flavonoids***, ca 0.2%, including (as aglycones) kaempferol, rhamnetin [8,9], quercetin, kaempferide [8] and myricetin [9], together with small amounts of quercetin 3-glucoside (isoquercitrin), 3-galactoside (hyperin) and 3,4′-diglucoside, and kaempferol 3-glucoside [8].

☐ ***Chromones*** 5,7-Dihydroxy-2-methylchromone 8-*C*-glucoside and 5,7-dihydroxy-2-methylchromone 6-*C*-glucoside (biflorin) [9].

☐ ***Phenolic acids*** Gallic acid (1.3%), p-coumaric acid (0.03%), protocatechuic acid (0.02%), ferulic, gentisic and vanillic acids (ca. 0.01% each) and traces of other hydroxycinnamic and hydroxybenzoic acids [10]; ellagic acid [9]; chlorogenic acid (0.1%) and small amounts of other caffeoylquinic acids [11].

☐ ***Tannins***, 10-13% [2], notably eugeniin (an ellagitannin) [12,13].

☐ ***Triterpenes*** Oleanolic acid (1%) [9,14] and crataegolic acid (= 2α-hydroxyoleanolic acid) methyl ester [15].

☐ ***Polysaccharides*** Two rhamnogalacturonans, both with arabinan side-chains and 10-15% of sulphate groups, have been partially characterized; one has a low MW of ca. 36,000, the other a MW of ca. 103,000 [16].

☐ ***Sterol glucosides***, of sitosterol, stigmasterol and campesterol [15].

Published Assay Methods

Eugenol, acetyleugenol and β-caryophyllene in clove oil by GC [Ph. Eur.]. Essential oil components by GC [5] and GC-MS [3]. Eugenol by spectrophotometry [17].

PHARMACOLOGY

Most of the pharmacological activity of clove relates to the essential oil and particularly to its phenolic component, eugenol.

In vitro

Antimicrobial activity

Powdered clove completely inhibited the growth of two toxigenic *Aspergillus* fungal strains [18] and

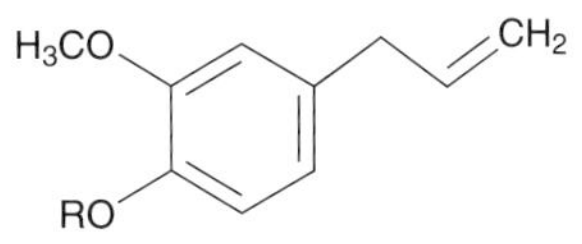

Eugenol R = H
Acetyleugenol R = $COCH_3$

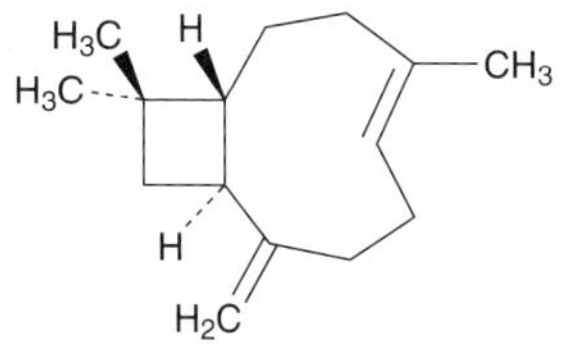

β-Caryophyllene

a hydroalcoholic extract of clove strongly inhibited the growth of a range of nine fungi [19].

A methanolic extract from clove inhibited growth of the Gram-negative anaerobic periodontal oral pathogens *Prevotella intermedia* and *Porphyromonas gingivalis* with minimum inhibitory concentrations (MICs) of 156 and 625 µg/ml respectively. Among eight active compounds identified by bioassay-guided fractionation, the flavones kaempferol and myricetin had the most potent inhibitory activity with MICs of 20 µg/ml compared to 2 µg/ml for sanguinarine [9].

Clove bud oil exhibited moderate to strong antimicrobial activity against a wide range of bacteria [20,21] and the yeast *Candida albicans* [21], and strongly inhibited dermatophytic fungi which cause infections such as athlete's foot [22]. Eugenol at 1 mg/ml inhibited the growth of 6 out of 10 Gram-positive and Gram-negative bacteria with activity comparable to neomycin at 500 µg/ml, and of *Candida* species more strongly than nystatin at 5000 U/ml [23].

Spasmolytic activity
Clove oil had a potent relaxant effect on isolated guinea pig tracheal and ileal smooth muscle, inhibiting contractions with EC_{50} values of 3.8 and 6.8 mg/litre respectively [24].

Eugenol at 300 ng/ml reduced spontaneous contractions, and at 0.2-100 µg/ml the tone, in isolated human longitudinal muscle strips from stomach and colon; at 22 µg/ml it reduced acetylcholine-induced contractions and the tone in human uterine strips. Prostaglandin E_2-, 5-hydroxytrytamine- and acetylcholine-induced contractions in rat stomach muscle strips, bradykinin-induced contractions in rat uterine strips and spontaneous contractions in rabbit jejunum were concentration-dependently reduced by eugenol [25].

The force of rested state contractions in guinea pig papillary muscle under the influence of catecholamine, which are determined by calcium influx through calcium channels, was diminished by eugenol, acetyleugenol, β-caryophyllene and caryophyllene oxide with EC_{50} values of 183, 300, 270 and 29 µmol/litre respectively. Eugenol and β-caryophyllene oxide were shown to concentration-dependently and reversibly reduce the calcium-inward current in isolated cardiac ventricular cells with EC_{50} values of 32 and 200 µmol/litre respectively. The results indicated that constituents of clove oil have a blocking effect on calcium channels and thereby diminish the intracellular calcium concentration [26].

Anti-inflammatory activity
In evaluation of herbal drugs used in the treatment of inflammatory diseases in traditional Korean medicine, an 80%-methanolic extract from clove inhibited induction of a cytokine of the interleukin-8 (IL-8) type in lipopolysaccharide-activated peritoneal macrophages from rats by more than 50% at 0.1 mg/ml. Sequential dichloromethane, ethyl acetate and butanolic fractions from the extract produced 59%, 51% and 62% inhibition respectively at 0.05 mg/ml. Induction of the IL-8 was also significantly inhibited by steroidal anti-inflammatory drugs such as dexamethasone at 1 µM, but not by non-steroidal drugs such as aspirin and ibuprofen. In pathophysiology, IL-8 is known to be involved in several inflammatory diseases such as rheumatoid arthritis, psoriasis and pulmonary fibrosis [27].

In a cyclooxygenase test system using sheep seminal vesicles, clove oil and isolated eugenol inhibited the biosynthesis of prostaglandins by 84% and 69.5% respectively at 37 µM (calculating the clove oil concentration from the average MW of principal constituents). Acetyleugenol (IC_{50} 3.0) had a stronger inhibitory effect than eugenol (IC_{50} 11.0) [28].

Inhibition of platelet aggregation
Clove oil and two of its constituents, eugenol and acetyleugenol, have been shown to be inhibitors of platelet aggregation. Eugenol and acetyleugenol inhibited arachidonic acid-induced platelet aggregation in platelet-rich human plasma (IC_{50} values of 0.8 and 2 µM respectively) more potently than aspirin (IC_{50} 28 µM); this was also the case with adrenaline- and collagen-induced aggegation. A combination of eugenol and acetyleugenol produced an additive effect ($p<0.01$) [29].

Eugenol strongly inhibited platelet aggregation in human plasma induced by platelet-activating factor (PAF), with lesser effects on arachidonic acid- or collagen-induced platelet aggregation, the respective IC_{50} values being 0.2, 0.5 and 0.7 µM [30]. In rabbit plasma eugenol inhibited arachidonic acid-induced platelet aggregation with an IC_{50} of 0.3 µM [23].

Antioxidant activity
In tests on methanolic extracts from twelve herbal drugs reported to exhibit strong antioxidative activity, a clove extract showed by far the strongest activity by an electrochemical method and had the strongest radical scavenging effect against the 1,1-diphenyl-2-picrylhydrazyl (DPPH) radical [31].

Copper-catalyzed oxidation of low-density lipoprotein in human plasma was strongly inhibited by clove oil and other essential oils with a high eugenol content [32]. Clove oil and eugenol showed exceptionally potent activity in trapping free radicals in an antioxidant assay; their activities at 1000 ppm in terms of 'Trolox equivalents' were

69 and 68 mmol/litre, similar to that of butylated hydroxyanisole (BHA) at 2.5 mmol/litre [3].

Antithrombotic activity
Two sulphated rhamnogalacturonans isolated from clove exhibited significant antithrombotic activity. In human plasma clotting assays, the activated partial thromboplastin times of the higher and lower MW rhamnogalacturonans were 145 and 90 seconds respectively at 25 μg/ml ($p<0.01$), compared to 29 seconds for the control and 177 for heparin at 4 μg/ml [16].

In vivo

Cholagogic effect
A dry acetone extract of clove, administered intraduodenally to rats at 500 mg/kg, exerted a potent and lasting cholagogic effect, significantly increasing bile flow ($p<0.01$). At 100 mg/kg, isolated eugenol and to a lesser extent acetyleugenol (but not β-caryophyllene) produced similar effects, and a significant increase in solids content of the bile was confirmed ($p<0.01$) [33].

Local anaesthetic activity
Eugenol failed to show positive results in tests to evaluate local anaesthetic activity. At 10-1000 μg/ml it did not induce an increase in the number of stimuli required to evoke the conjunctival reflex in rabbits; nor, in an *in vitro* test, did it cause a significant reduction in electrically-evoked contractions of rat phrenic nerve-hemidiaphragm. In contrast, anethole and terpineol (not present in clove oil) produced highly positive results in these tests, comparable to those of procaine [34].

Anti-inflammatory effect
Eugenol inhibited carrageenan-induced rat paw oedema by 28% at 25 mg/kg body weight ($p<0.005$) and 78% at 100 mg/kg ($p<0.001$); in this respect it was about five times more potent than aspirin, which produced 25% inhibition at 150 mg/kg and 71% at 300 mg/kg [30]. In a similar experiment, eugenol at 100 mg/kg inhibited rat paw oedema by 30% after 4 hours ($p<0.05$), comparable to the effect of phenylbutazone at 100 mg/kg [25].

Effect of eugenol on platelet aggregation
Arachidonic acid (AA; 2 mg/kg) or platelet activating factor (PAF; 11 μg/kg) injected into the ear vein of rabbits caused fatal pulmonary thrombosis associated with occlusive platelet aggregates in the vasculature of the lung in all control animals. However, if the animals had been pretreated intraperitoneally with eugenol at 100 mg/kg, 4/7 of AA animals and 7/7 of PAF animals survived, compared to 7/7 of AA animals and 5/7 PAF animals after pretreatment with aspirin (a known inhibitor of platelet aggregation) at 50 mg/kg. The results were taken as evidence that eugenol acts as a dual antagonist of arachidonic acid and platelet activating factor [30].

Prophylactic effect against herpes simplex
In mice intradermally infected with herpes simplex virus type 1 (HSV-1) in the pinna (external part of the ear), a lyophilized hot aqueous extract of clove showed significant prophylactic efficacy against recurrent outbreaks of the disease from latently infected ganglia. When administered orally at 3 × 250 mg/kg/day for 10 days, the extract arrested the progression of HSV-1 reactivated (4 months after primary infection) by UV irradiation, reducing the incidence and shortening the period of severe erythema and/or vesicles in the pinna ($p<0.01$ to 0.05). Recurrent disease induced by stripping the infected pinna with cellophane tape was similarly alleviated ($p<0.01$) [35].

From *in vitro* testing, eugeniin (an ellagitannin) was identified as a clove constituent with potent anti-herpes simplex virus activity [12,13].

Antioxidant effects
Daily administration of 3.9 mg of clove oil in the diet of rats over a period of 17 months (from rat age 11 to 28 months) resulted in much higher levels of polysunsaturated fatty acids, particularly docosahexaenoic acid (DHA, $p<0.001$ compared to control animals), within the retinal phospholipids of the aged rats, mainly at the expense of a reduction in oleic acid. This antioxidant effect was thought to have possible application in the prevention of age-related macular degeneration (a reduction in tissue retina levels of DHA is a feature of ageing) [36].

Pharmacokinetics
The mean biological half-life of eugenol after oral administration to rabbits was 95 minutes [23].

CLINICAL STUDIES

None published on mono-preparations of clove.

THERAPEUTICS

Actions
Stimulant aromatic [2,37,38], spasmolytic [24-26], carminative [37-40], cholagogic [33] and antimicrobial [9,18-23] including inhibition of herpes simplex [35]. Also said to be antiemetic [37,38].

Clove oil and eugenol are locally irritant, mildly anaesthetic [39,41], anti-inflammatory [25,30] and antioxidant [36], and have been shown to inhibit platelet aggregation [23,29,30].

Indications
None adequately substantiated by pharmacological or clinical studies.

Uses based on experience or tradition

Main uses
Internal: Digestive complaints such as flatulence, colic, abdominal bloating, languid digestion [37,38,40,42], nausea or emesis [37].
Local: As undiluted clove oil for the relief of toothache [38,41,42]; as a mouthwash or gargle to alleviate pain and inflammation of the mouth or throat mucosa [41,42], or for buccal hygiene [42].

Other uses
Internal: Coughs [38] and bronchial complaints [37].
Local: Treatment of small wounds, sores or acne [38,42]; muscle spasms [38]; as a liniment for rheumatic and other inflammatory conditions [27,28], neuralgia, bronchitis or whooping cough [40].

Contraindications
Avoid clove oil if liver function is impaired, or if taking paracetamol (acetaminophen) or anticoagulants [43].

Side effects
Clove oil in concentrated form is irritant to tissues [41].

Interactions with other drugs
None known.

Dosage
Internal Three times daily: dried buds, 120-300 mg [40] or an infusion of 2 cloves to a cupful of hot water [38]; tincture (1:5, about 40% ethanol), 20 drops [38]; Concentrated Infusion of Clove BPC 1954 (about 1 in 5, ethanol 25%), 2-3 ml [44]; clove oil, 0.05-0.1 ml (2-4 drops) [39,40].
Local For toothache, undiluted oil [38,41] - dab 1-2 drops of clove oil on to cotton wool and rub over affected tooth [38]. In mouthwashes, the equivalent of 1-5% of essential oil [41]. As a liniment for pain relief, 1 part of clove oil to 2 parts of a suitable diluent oil [40].

Caution should be exercised in the use of undiluted oil for toothache; repeated use may damage gingival tissue [39].

SAFETY

The acute oral LD_{50} of clove bud oil in rats was determined as 2.65 g/kg and previously as 3.72 g/kg. Oral doses of 35-70 mg/day of clove bud oil were well tolerated by rats for 8 weeks; 105 mg/day was fatal after 2-3 weeks and 140 mg rapidly after one dose, accompanied by severe liver and kidney damage [45].

Clove bud oil has been assessed as non-toxic (i.e. safe for use at therapeutic dose levels), unlikely to cause skin sensitization (in diluted form) and non-phototoxic, but irritant to mucous membranes [43]. The Joint FAO/WHO Expert Committee on Food Additives estimated the acceptable daily intake of eugenol to be 2.5 mg/kg body weight and did not consider it to have carcinogenic potential [46].

In the Ames mutagenicity test, an ethanolic extract of clove exhibited weak mutagenic potential in *Salmonella typhimurium* strain TA 98 and strong mutagenic potential in strain TA 100; it showed significant toxicity in the brine shrimp lethality bioassay [47]. In another investigation, aqueous and methanolic extracts of clove showed no mutagenic potential in the Ames test but gave strongly positive results in the *Bacillus subtilis* spore rec-assay [48].

REGULATORY STATUS

Medicines

UK	Accepted for general sale, internal or external use [49].
France	Accepted for specified indications [42].
Germany	Commission E monograph published, with approved uses [41].

Food

USA	Generally recognized as safe (21 CFR 184.1257) [50].
Council of Europe	Permitted as flavouring, category N2 [51].

REFERENCES

Current Pharmacopoeial Monographs
Ph. Eur. Clove

Literature References

1. Martin PJ. The Zanzibar clove industry. *Econ. Bot.* 1991, **45**, 450-459.
2. Evans WC. Clove and Clove Oil. In: *Trease and Evans' Pharmacognosy, 14th ed.* ISBN 0-7020-1899-6. London-Philadelphia: WB Saunders, 1996:279-281.
3. Dorman HJD, Surai P and Deans SG. *In Vitro* Antioxidant Activity of a Number of Plant Essential Oils and Phytoconstituents. *J. Essent. Oil. Res.* 2000, **12**, 241-248.
4. Lawrence BM. Progress in Essential Oils. *Perfumer Flavorist* 1988, **13** (Dec), 57-63.
5. Gopalakrishnan N. Studies on the Storage Quality of CO_2-Extracted Cardamom and Clove Bud Oils. *J. Agric. Food Chem.* 1994, **42**, 796-798.
6. Variyar PS and Bandyopadhyay C. On the volatiles of clove, cardamom, nutmeg and mace. *Pafai J.* 1995, (Jan-Mar), 19-25.
7. Steinegger E and Hänsel R. Nelkenöl und Eugenol in der konservierenden Zahnheilkunde [Clove oil and eugenol in dental preventive medicine]. In: *Pharmakognosie, 5th ed.* ISBN 3-540-55649-4. Berlin-Heidelberg-New York: Springer-Verlag, 1992:360-361 [GERMAN].
8. Vösgen B and Herrmann K. Flavonol Glycosides of Pepper

[Piper nigrum L.], Clove [Syzygium aromaticum (L.) Merr. et Perry] and Allspice [Pimenta dioica (L.) Merr.]. 3. Phenolics of Spices. *Z. Lebensm. Unters. Forsch.* 1980, **170**, 204-207 [GERMAN/English summary].

9. Cai L and Wu CD. Compounds from *Syzygium aromaticum* Possessing Growth Inhibitory Activity Against Oral Pathogens. *J. Nat. Prod.* 1996, **59**, 987-990.
10. Schulz JM and Herrmann K. Occurrence of Hydroxybenzoic Acids and Hydroxycinnamic Acids in Spices. IV. Phenolics of Spices. *Z. Lebensm. Unters. Forsch.* 1980, **171**, 193-199 [GERMAN/English summary].
11. Dirks U and Herrmann K. High Performance Liquid Chromatography of Hydroxycinnamoyl-quinic Acids and 4-(β-D-Glucopyranosyloxy)-benzoic Acid in Spices. 10. Phenolics of Spices. *Z. Lebensm. Unters. Forsch.* 1984, **179**, 12-16 [GERMAN/English summary].
12. Kurokawa M, Hozumi T, Basnet P, Nakano M, Kadota S, Namba T et al. Purification and Characterization of Eugeniin as an Anti-herpesvirus Compound from *Geum japonicum* and *Syzygium aromaticum*. *J. Pharmacol. Exptl. Ther.* 1998, **284**, 728-735.
13. Takechi M and Tanaka Y. Purification and Characterization of Antiviral Substance from the Bud of Syzygium aromatica. *Planta Medica* 1981, **42**, 69-74.
14. Narayanan CR and Natu AA. Triterpene acids of Indian clove buds. *Phytochemistry* 1974, **13**, 1999-2000.
15. Brieskorn CH, Münzhuber K and Unger G. Crataegolsäure und Steroidglukoside aus dem Blütenknospen von *Syzygium aromaticum* [Crataegolic acid and steroid glucosides from the flower buds of *Syzygium aromaticum*]. *Phytochemistry* 1975, **14**, 2308-2309 [GERMAN].
16. Lee JI, Lee HS, Jun WJ, Yu KW, Shin DH, Hong BS et al. Purification and Characterization of Antithrombotics from *Syzygium aromaticum* (L.) Merr. & Perry. *Biol. Pharm. Bull.* 2001, **24**, 181-187.
17. Backheet EY. Micro Determination of Eugenol, Thymol and Vanillin in Volatile Oils and Plants. *Phytochem. Analysis* 1998, **9**, 134-140.
18. Hitokoto H, Morozumi S, Wauke T, Sakai S and Kurata H. Inhibitory Effects of Spices on Growth and Toxin Production of Toxigenic Fungi. *Appl. Environ. Microbiol.* 1980, **39**, 818-822.
19. Guérin J-C and Réveillère H-P. Antifungal activity of plant extracts used in therapy. II. Study of 49 plant extracts against 9 fungi species. *Ann. Pharm. Fr.* 1985, **43**, 77-81 [FRENCH/English summary].
20. Dorman HJD and Deans SG. Antimicrobial agents from plants: antibacterial activity of plant volatile oils. *J. Applied Microbiol.* 2000, **88**, 308-316.
21. Hammer KA, Carson CF and Riley TV. Antimicrobial activity of essential oils and other plant extracts. *J. Applied Microbiol.* 1999, **86**, 985-990.
22. Janssen AM, Scheffer JJC, Parhan-Van Atten AW and Baerheim Svendsen A. Screening of some essential oils for their activities on dermatophytes. *Pharm. Weekblad Sci. Ed.* 1988, **10**, 277-280.
23. Laekeman GM, Van Hoof L, Haemers A, Vanden Berghe DA, Herman AG and Vlietinck AJ. Eugenol a Valuable Compound for *In Vitro* Experimental Research and Worthwhile for Further *In Vivo* Investigation. *Phytotherapy Res.* 1990, **4**, 90-96.
24. Reiter M and Brandt W. Relaxant Effects on Tracheal and Ileal Smooth Muscles of the Guinea Pig. *Arzneim.-Forsch./Drug Res.* 1985, **35**, 408-414.
25. Bennett A, Stamford IF, Tavares IA, Jacobs S, Capasso F, Mascolo N et al. The Biological Activity of Eugenol, a Major Constituent of Nutmeg (*Myristica fragrans*): Studies on Prostaglandins, the Intestine and other Tissues. *Phytotherapy Res.* 1988, **2**, 124-130.
26. Sensch O, Vierling W, Brandt W and Reiter M. Calcium-Channel Blocking Effect of Constituents of Clove Oil. *Planta Medica* 1993, **59** (Suppl.), A687.
27. Lee G-I, Ha JY, Min KR, Nakagawa H, Tsurufuji S, Chang I-M and Kim Y. Inhibitory Effects of Oriental Herbal Medicines on IL-8 Induction in Lipopolysaccharide-Activated Rat Macrophages. *Planta Medica* 1995, **61**, 26-30.
28. Wagner H, Wierer M and Bauer R. *In vitro*-Hemmung der Prostaglandin-Biosynthese durch etherische Öle und phenolische Verbindungen [*In vitro* inhibition of prostaglandin biosynthesis by volatile oils and phenolic compounds]. *Planta Medica* 1986, **52**, 184-187 [GERMAN/English summary].
29. Srivastava KC. Antiplatelet Principles from a Food Spice, Clove (*Syzygium aromaticum* L.). *Prostagland. Leukotr. Essent. Fatty Acids* 1993, **48**, 363-372.
30. Saeed SA, Simjee RU, Shamim G and Gilani AH. Eugenol: a dual inhibitor of platelet-activating factor and arachidonic acid metabolism. *Phytomedicine* 1995, **2**, 23-28.
31. Yamasaki K, Hashimoto A, Kokusenya Y, Miyamoto T and Sato T. Electrochemical Method for Estimating the Antioxidative Effects of Methanol Extracts of Crude Drugs. *Chem. Pharm. Bull.* 1994, **42**, 1663-1665.
32. Teissedre PL and Waterhouse AL. Inhibition of Oxidation of Human Low-Density Lipoproteins by Phenolic Substances in Different Essential Oils Varieties. *J. Agric. Food Chem.* 2000, **48**, 3801-3805.
33. Yamahara J, Kobayashi M, Saiki Y, Sawada T and Fujimura H. Biologically active principles of crude drugs. Pharmacological evaluation of cholagogue substances in clove and its properties. *J. Pharmacobiodyn.* 1983, **6**, 281-286.
34. Ghelardini C, Galeotti N and Mazzanti G. Local Anaesthetic Activity of Monoterpenes and Phenylpropanes of Essential Oils. *Planta Medica* 2001, **67**, 564-566.
35. Kurokawa M, Nakano M, Ohyama H, Hozumi T, Kageyama S, Namba T and Shiraki K. Prophylactic efficacy of traditional herbal medicines against recurrent herpes simplex virus type 1 infection from latently infected ganglia in mice. *J. Dermatol. Sci.* 1997, **14**, 76-84.
36. Recsan Z, Pagliuca G, Piretti MV, Penzes LG, Youdim KA, Noble RC and Deans SG. Effect of Essential Oils on the Lipids of the Retina in the Aging Rat: A Possible Therapeutic Use. *J. Essent. Oil. Res.* 1997, **9**, 53-56.
37. Grieve M (edited by Leyel CF). Cloves. In: *A Modern Herbal* (first published 1931; revised 1973). ISBN 1-85501-249-9. London: Tiger Books International, 1994:208.
38. Chevallier A. Clove. In: *The Encyclopedia of Medicinal Plants.* ISBN 0-7513-0314-3. London-New York-Stuttgart: Dorling Kindersley, 1996:95.
39. Pharmaceutical Society of Great Britain. Cloves; Clove oil. In: *British Pharmaceutical Codex 1973.* London: Pharmaceutical Press, 1973:118-119.
40. Todd RG, editor. Clove; Clove oil. In: *Extra Pharmacopoeia: Martindale*, 25th edition. London: Pharmaceutical Press, 1967:853.
41. Caryophylli flos. German Commission E Monograph published in: Bundesanzeiger No. 223 of 30 November 1985.
42. Giroflier. In: *Médicaments à base de plantes.* ISBN 2-911473-02-7. Saint-Denis Cedex, France: Agence du Médicament, 1998.
43. Tisserand R and Balacs T. Clove; clove bud (oil). In: *Essential Oil Safety - A Guide for Health Care Professionals.* ISBN 0-443-05260-3. Edinburgh: Churchill-Livingstone, 1995:131-132 and 201-205.
44. Pharmaceutical Society of Great Britain. Infusion of Clove, Concentrated. In: *British Pharmaceutical Codex 1954.* London: Pharmaceutical Press, 1954:1008.
45. Opdyke DLJ. Monographs on fragrance raw materials: clove bud oil. *Food Cosmet. Toxicol.* 1975, **13**, 761-762.
46. Reynolds JEF, editor. Eugenol. In: *Martindale - The Extra Pharmacopoeia*, 29th edition. ISBN 0-85369-210-6. London: Pharmaceutical Press, 1989:1063.
47. Mahmoud I, Alkofahi A and Abdelaziz A. Mutagenic and Toxic Activities of Several Spices and Some Jordanian Medicinal Plants. *Int. J. Pharmacognosy* 1992, **30**, 81-85.
48. Morimoto I, Watanabe F, Osawa T, Okitsu T and Kada T. Mutagenicity screening of crude drugs with *Bacillus subtilis* rec-assay and *Salmonella*/microsome reversion assay. *Mutation Res.* 1982, **97**, 81-102.
49. Clove. In: UK Statutory Instrument 1994 No. 2410. The Medicines (Products Other Than Veterinary Drugs) (General Sale List) Amendment Order 1994. Schedule 1, Table A.

50. Clove and its derivatives. In: Section 184.1257 of USA Code of Federal Regulations, Title 21, Food and Drugs, Parts 170 to 199. Revised as of April 1, 2000.
51. Eugenia caryophyllus (C. Spreng.) Bull. et Harr., flowers. In: *Flavouring Substances and Natural Sources of Flavourings, 3rd ed.* ISBN 2-7160-0081-6. Strasbourg: Council of Europe, 1981.

REGULATORY GUIDELINES FROM OTHER EU COUNTRIES

FRANCE

Médicaments à base de plantes [42]: Giroflier, bouton floral = clou de girofle.

Therapeutic indications accepted

Oral use
Traditionally used in the symptomatic treatment of digestive disorders, such as epigastric distension, sluggish digestion, eructation, flatulence.

Topical use
Traditionally used: for the treatment of small wounds and sores after copious washing (with soap and water) and for the elimination of spots; to alleviate pain (headaches, toothache); locally (mouthwash/gargle, pastille) to alleviate pain in ailments of the buccal cavity and/or the pharynx; locally in mouthwashes, for buccal hygiene.

GERMANY

Commission E monograph [41]: Caryophylli flos (Gewürznelken).

Uses
Inflammatory changes in mouth and throat mucosa. In dental therapy for local relief from pain.

Contraindications
None known.

Side effects
Clove oil in concentrated form is irritant to tissues.

Interactions with other drugs
None known.

Dosage
Unless otherwise prescribed: in mouthwashes, the equivalent of 1-5% of essential oil; in dental therapy, undiluted essential oil.

Mode of administration
Powdered, whole or cut drug to obtain the essential oil and other galenic preparations for local use.

Action
Antiseptic, antibacterial, antifungal, antiviral, local anaesthetic, spasmolytic.

CORIANDER

Umbelliferae

Coriandri fructus

Definition
Coriander consists of the dried cremocarps of *Coriandrum sativum* L.

CONSTITUENTS

□ ***Essential oil***, 0.5-2% (Ph. Eur. min 0.3% V/m with reference to the dried drug), consisting predominantly of linalool (65-87%) together with γ-terpinene (3-10%), α-pinene (0.5-7%), camphor (4-8%, sometimes absent), limonene (1-6%), geranyl acetate (1-4%), and other terpenes [1-5].
□ ***Fatty acids***, principally petroselinic acid [*cis*-6-octadecenoic acid; 67-73%] together with linoleic (14-18%), oleic (8-9%), palmitic (3-4%), stearic (0.6-1%) and *cis*-vaccenic [= *cis*-11-octadecenoic; 0.7-0.8%] acids, as percentages of the total seed oil [6,7].

The total oil content of coriander seeds is 9-16% on the dry basis [6].
□ ***Flavonoids*** Isoquercitrin, quercetin 3-glucuronide and rutin [8].
□ ***Phenolic acids*** Caffeic acid (ca. 0.08%), ferulic acid (ca. 0.02%) and small amounts of various other hydroxycinnamic and hydroxybenzoic acids [9]; also a trace of *p*-hydroxybenzoic acid glucoside [10,11].

Chlorogenic acid (= 3-caffeoylquinic acid, ca. 0.02%) [11,12] and traces of other hydroxycinnamoylquinic acids [11] are also present.
□ ***Coumarins*** Small amounts of umbelliferone and scopoletin [13] and traces (less than 0.005 µg/g) of the furanocoumarins bergapten (= 5-methoxypsoralen), xanthotoxin (= 8-methoxypsoralen) and probably imperatorin [14].
□ ***Other constituents*** include the triterpene alcohol coriandrinonediol [15], γ-sitosterol [13], the phthalide neocnidilide (ca. 0.03%) [16] and probably polyacetylenic compounds [17].

Published Assay Methods
Essential oil by GC and GC-MS [1,3]. Fatty acids profile as butyl esters by GC [6].

PHARMACOLOGY

In vitro

Extracts of coriander showed insulin-releasing and insulin-like activity in a series of experiments. An aqueous extract at 1 mg/ml increased 2-deoxyglucose transport 1.6-fold, glucose oxidation 1.4-fold and incorporation of glucose into glycogen 1.7-fold in abdominal muscle isolated from mice, comparable to the activity of human insulin at 10^{-8} M. In acute 20-minute tests, 0.25-10 mg/ml of aqueous extract evoked a concentration-dependent 1.3-1.7-fold stimulation of insulin secretion from a clonal B-cell line; a hexane extract of coriander produced a similar effect [18].

A methanolic extract of coriander showed antiproliferative activity against tumour cells, with ED_{50} values of 40 and 50 µg/ml against human gastric adenocarcinoma (MK-1) and murine malignant melanoma (B16F10) cells respectively. The activity was attributed to unidentified polyacetylene compounds [17].

Ether and acetone extracts of coriander exhibited moderate antibacterial and weak antifungal activity against certain microorganisms [19]. In another study, coriander essential oil showed moderate antibacterial activity, but no antifungal activity [20].

In vivo

Anti-inflammatory activity
An orally administered 80%-ethanolic extract of coriander inhibited carrageenan-induced rat paw oedema by 31% (p<0.01) at 100 mg/kg body weight [21].

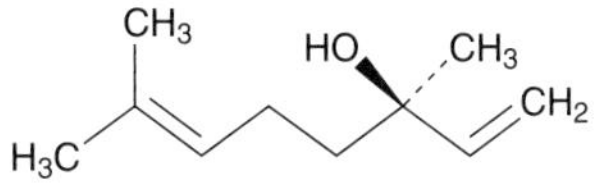

Linalool

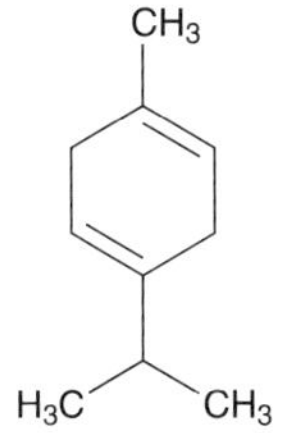

γ-Terpinene

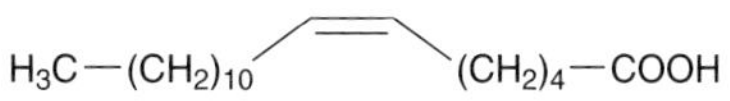

Petroselinic acid $C_{18}H_{34}O_2$

Coriander essential oil orally administered at 37.5 mg/kg inhibited formalin-induced rat paw oedema by 25% after 3 hours ($p<0.005$), comparable to the effect of phenylbutazone at 15 mg/kg [20].

Hypolipidaemic effect
Addition of 10% of powdered coriander to the diet of rats fed on a high fat diet with added cholesterol produced a significant decrease ($p<0.01$) in cholesterol and triglyceride levels (serum, liver and heart). From changes in various metabolic parameters, the lowering of cholesterol levels in serum and tissues seemed to be mediated through its increased rate of degradation to bile acids and neutral sterols [22].

Similarly, 10% of powdered coriander added to the diet of rats with 1,2-dimethylhydrazine (DMH)-induced colon cancer reduced the concentrations of choleresterol and phospholipids in the gut while faecal bile acids and neutral sterols showed a sharp increase compared with a DMH control group ($p<0.01$). The number of colon/intestinal tumours was significantly lower in the coriander group, demonstrating a protective effect of coriander against deleterious metabolic effects of lipids in experimental colon cancer [23].

Antidiabetic effect
Coriander has been documented as a traditional remedy for diabetes [24]. When incorporated into the diet (62.5 g/kg) and drinking water (2.5 g/litre as a decoction) of streptozotocin (STZ)-induced diabetic mice, coriander seed significantly ($p<0.05$) decreased hyperglycaemia by day 20 compared to STZ-treated mice on a normal diet. At the same time, polydipsia increased ($p<0.01$) in the coriander-treated mice [18].

Post-coital antifertility activity
An aqueous dry extract (about 6:1) of coriander, orally administered at 250 or 500 mg/kg body weight per day for 5 days to female rats following coitus, produced a significant and dose-dependent anti-implantation effect ($p<0.01$), which appeared to be due to lowering of the serum progesterone level; complete infertility was not attained. In pregnant rats which received similar doses of extract during days 8-12 and 12-20 of their pregnancy no significant abortifacient effects and no teratogenic effects were observed [25].

Analgesic effect of essential oil
Coriander essential oil orally administered at 37.5 mg/kg body weight markedly decreased *p*-benzoquinone-induced writhing in mice, comparable to the effect of aspirin at 50 mg/kg [20].

Sedative effects of linalool
(±)-Linalool administered intraperitoneally to mice significantly increased sodium pentobarbital-induced sleeping time ($p<0.05$) at 200 mg/kg; dose-dependently protected against tonic convulsions induced by pentylenetetrazole (ED_{50} 64 mg/kg) or transcorneal electroshock (ED_{50} 112 mg/kg; 100% protection at 400-500 mg/kg); significantly decreased body temperature at 200 mg/kg ($p<0.05$) and caused marked loss of righting reflex at 500 mg/kg ($p<0.05$) [26].

CLINICAL STUDIES

None published on mono-preparations of coriander.

THERAPEUTICS

Coriander is well known as a flavouring, particularly in curries. Its use in medicines is often more for aromatic qualities than for therapeutic activity [27]. In dyspeptic complaints its efficacy is attributed to the essential oil content [28].

Actions
Carminative [27-30], weakly spasmolytic [16,28] and stimulant to the digestion [28,30].

Anti-inflammatory [21], hypolipidaemic [22] and antidiabetic [18] effects have been demonstrated *in vivo*.

Also said to be diuretic [16], sedative [20,30] and aphrodisiac [20].

Indications
None adequately substantiated by pharmacological or clinical studies.

Uses based on experience or tradition
Internal: Dyspeptic complaints including flatulence, windy colic, stomach ache and sluggish digestion [28,30-32]; loss of appetite [28,31]. Also as an aromatic to flavour medicines [27].
External: In preparations for painful rheumatic joints and muscles [30].

Contraindications
None known.

Side effects
None known.

Interactions with other drugs
None known.

Dosage
Average daily dose: 3 g of crushed fruits or equivalent preparations [31].
As a tea, 1-2 g of crushed fruits in 150 ml of boiling water, several times daily [28].

SAFETY

In the *Salmonella typhimurium* assay (Ames test), coriander proved mildly mutagenic using strain TA98 and strongly mutagenic using strain TA102. In the brine shrimp bioassay, coriander showed significant toxicity (LC_{50}: 173 µg/ml). Several other spices (clove, ginger, nutmeg) gave comparable results [33].

In scratch tests on 70 patients with known allergy to celery or to birch and/or mugwort pollens, 26 patients gave positive results with powdered coriander; a manifestation of the "celery-carrot-mugwort-spice" allergy syndrome. Fennel and aniseed gave comparable results [34].

An aqueous extract of coriander produced anti-implantation effects on the fertility of rats, but no teratogenic effects and only very slight abortifacient activity at the high dosage used [25].

Coriander essential oil has been assessed as non-irritant, non-sensitising and non-toxic at therapeutic dose levels [20,35]. The oral LD_{50} of the oil in mice was determined as 750 mg/kg body weight [20], while the intraperitoneal LD_{50} of linalool was found to be 459 mg/kg [26].

REGULATORY STATUS

Medicines

UK	Accepted for general sale, internal or external use [36].
France	Accepted for specified indications [32].
Germany	Commission E monograph published, with approved uses [31].

Food

USA	Generally recognized as safe (21 CFR 182.10 and 182.20) [37]
Council of Europe	Permitted as flavouring, category N2 [38].

REFERENCES

Current Pharmacopoeial Monographs

Ph. Eur. Coriander

Literature References

1. Smallfield BM, van Klink JW, Perry NB and Dodds KG. Coriander Spice Oil: Effects of Fruit Crushing and Distillation Time on Yield and Composition. *J. Agric. Food Chem.* 2001, **49**, 118-123.
2. Frank C, Dietrich A, Kremer U and Mosandl A. GC-IRMS in the Authenticity Control of the Essential Oil of *Coriandrum sativum* L. *J. Agric. Food Chem.* 1995, **43**, 1634-1637.
3. Kerrola K and Kallio H. Volatile Compounds and Odor Characteristics of Carbon Dioxide Extracts of Coriander (*Coriandrum sativum* L.) Fruits. *J. Agric. Food Chem.* 1993, **41**, 785-790.
4. FormácekV and Kubeczka K-H. Coriander Oil. In: *Essential Oils Analysis by Capillary Gas Chromatography and Carbon-13 NMR Spectroscopy.* ISBN 0-471-26218-8. Chichester-New York: John Wiley, 1982: 67-71.
5. Lawrence BM. New Trends in Essential Oils. *Perfumer & Flavorist* 1980, **5**, 6-16.
6. Reiter B, Lechner M and Lorbeer E. The fatty acid profiles - including petroselinic and cis-vaccenic acid - of different Umbelliferae seed oils. *Fett/Lipid* 1998, **100**, 498-502.
7. Thies W. Determination of the Petroselinic Acid in Seeds of *Coriandrum sativum* by Gas Liquid Chromatography as n-Butyl Esters. *Fat. Sci. Technol.* 1995, **97**, 411-413.
8. Kunzemann J and Herrmann K. Isolation and Identification of Flavon(ol)-O-glycosides in Caraway (*Carum carvi* L.), Fennel (*Foeniculum vulgare* Mill.), Anise (*Pimpinella anisum* L.) and Coriander (*Coriandrum sativum* L.) and of Flavone-C-glycosides in Anise. I. Phenolics of Spices. *Z. Lebensm. Unters.-Forsch.* 1977, **164**, 194-200 [GERMAN/English summary].
9. Schulz JM and Herrmann K. Occurrence of Hydroxybenzoic Acids and Hydroxycinnamic Acids in Spices. IV. Phenolics of Spices. *Z. Lebensm. Unters.-Forsch.* 1980, **171**, 193-199 [GERMAN/English summary].
10. Dirks U and Herrmann K. 4-(β-D-Glucopyranosyloxy)-benzoic acid, a characteristic phenolic constituent of the Apiaceae. *Phytochemistry* 1984, **23**, 1811-1812.
11. Dirks U and Herrmann K. High Performance Liquid Chromatography of Hydroxycinnamoylquinic Acids and 4-(β-D-Glucopyranosyloxy)-benzoic Acid in Spices. 10. Phenolics of Spices. *Z. Lebensm. Unters.-Forsch.* 1984, **179**, 12-16 [GERMAN/English summary].
12. Baerheim Svendsen A. Über das Vorkommen der Chlorogen- und Kaffeesäure in der Pflanzenfamilie der Umbelliferen. 2. Mitteilung über Papierchromatographie in der phytochemischen Analyse [The occurrence of chlorogenic and caffeic acids in the Umbelliferae family. 2. Paper chromatography in the phytochemical analysis]. *Pharm. Acta Helv.* 1951, **26**, 253-258 [GERMAN].
13. Kartnig T. Über einige Lipoid-Inhaltsstoffe aus den Früchten von Anethum graveolens L. und Coriandrum sativum L. [Some lipoid constituents from fruits of Anethum graveolens L. and Coriandrum sativum L.]. *Fette Seifen Anstrichmittel* 1966, **68**, 131-134 [GERMAN/English summary].
14. Ceska O, Chaudhary SK, Warrington PJ and Ashwood-Smith MJ. Photoactive furocoumarins in fruits of some Umbellifers. *Phytochemistry* 1987, **26**, 165-169.
15. Naik CG, Namboori K and Merchant JR. Triterpenoids of *Coriandrum sativum* seeds. *Current Science (Bangalore)* 1983, **52**, 598-599; also through *Chem. Abstr.* 1983, **99**, 119311.
16. Gijbels MJM, Scheffer JJC and Baerheim Svensen A. Phthalides in Roots of *Cenolophium denudatum* and in Roots, Herb and Fruits of *Coriandrum sativum. Fitoterapia* 1982, **53**, 17-20.
17. Nakano Y, Matsunaga H, Saita T, Mori M, Katano M and Okabe H. Antiproliferative Constituents in Umbelliferae Plants II. Screening for Polyacetylenes in Some Umbelliferae Plants and Isolation of Panaxynol and Falcarindiol from the Root of *Heracleum moellendorffii. Biol. Pharm. Bull.* 1998, **21**, 257-261.
18. Gray AM and Flatt PR. Insulin-releasing and insulin-like activity of the traditional anti-diabetic plant *Coriandrum sativum* (coriander). *Brit. J. Nutr.* 1999, **81**, 203-209.
19. Maruzzella JC and Freundlich M. Antimicrobial Substances from Seeds. *J. Am. Pharm. Assoc.* 1959, **48**, 356-358.
20. Afifi NA, Ramadan A, El-Kashoury EA and El-Banna HA. Some pharmacological activities of essential oils of certain Umbelliferous fruits. *Vet. Med. J. Giza* 1994, **42** (3), 85-92.
21. Mascolo N, Autore G, Capasso F, Menghini A and Fasulo MP. Biological Screening of Italian Medicinal Plants for Anti-inflammatory Activity. *Phytotherapy Res.* 1987, **1**, 28-31.

22. Chithra V and Leelamma S. Hypolipidemic effect of coriander seeds (*Coriandrum sativum*): mechanism of action. *Plant Foods for Human Nutrition* 1997, **51**, 167-172.
23. Chithra V and Leelamma S. Coriandrum sativum - effect on lipid metabolism in 1,2-dimethyl hydrazine induced colon cancer. *J. Ethnopharmacol.* 2000, **71**, 457-463.
24. Gray AM and Flatt PR. Nature's own pharmacy: the diabetes perspective. *Proc. Nutr. Soc.* 1997, **56**, 507-517.
25. Al-Said MS, Al-Khamis KI, Islam MW, Parmar NS, Tariq M and Ageel AM. Post-coital antifertility activity of the seeds of *Coriandrum sativum* in rats. *J. Ethnopharmacol.* 1987, **21**, 165-173.
26. Elisabetsky E, Coelho de Souza GP, Dos Santos MAC, Siquieira IR and Amador TA. Sedative properties of linalool. *Fitoterapia* 1995, **66**, 407-414.
27. Weiss RF. *Coriandrum sativum* (Coriander). In: *Herbal Medicine* (translated from the 6th German edition of *Lehrbuch der Phytotherapie*). ISBN 0-906584-19-1. Gothenburg: AB Arcanum, Beaconsfield, UK: Beaconsfield Publishers, 1988: 69-70.
28. Stahl-Biskup E and Neubeck M. Koriander. In: Hartke K, Hartke H, Mutschler E, Rücker G and Wichtl M, editors. *Arzneibuch-Kommentar. Wissenschaftliche Erläuterungen zum Europäischen Arzneibuch und zum Deutschen Arzneibuch* [*Pharmacopoeial Commentary. Scientific Explanations on the European and German Pharmacopoeias*]. Stuttgart: Wissenschaftliche Verlagsgesellschaft, 1999 (Suppl. 12):K28 [GERMAN].
29. Coriandrum. In: *British Pharmaceutical Codex 1973*, London: Pharmaceutical Press, 1973:129.
30. Stodola J and Volák J. Coriander. Translated into English in: Bunney S, editor. *The Illustrated Book of Herbs*. ISBN 0-7064-1489-6. London: Octopus Books, 1984:119.
31. Coriandri fructus. German Commission E Monograph published in: Bundesanzeiger No. 173 of 18 September 1986.
32. Coriandre. In: *Médicaments à base de plantes*. ISBN 2-911473-02-7. Saint-Denis Cedex, France: Agence du Médicament, 1998.
33. Mahmoud I, Alkofahi A and Abdelaziz A. Mutagenic and Toxic Activities of Several Spices and Some Jordanian Medicinal Plants. *Int. J. Pharmacognosy* 1992, **30**, 81-85.
34. Stäger J, Wüthrich B and Johansson SGO. Spice allergy in celery-sensitive patients. *Allergy* 1991, **46**, 475-478.
35. Tisserand R and Balacs T. Safety Index: Part 1. In: *Essential Oil Safety - A Guide for Health Care Professionals*. Edinburgh: Churchill-Livingstone, 1995:201-211.
36. Coriander. In: UK Statutory Instrument 1994 No. 2410. The Medicines (Products Other Than Veterinary Drugs) (General Sale List) Amendment Order 1994. Schedule 1, Table A.
37. Coriander. In: Sections 182.10 and 182.20 of USA Code of Federal Regulations, Title 21, Food and Drugs, Parts 170 to 199. Revised as of April 1, 2000.
38. Coriandrum sativum L., fruits. In: *Flavouring Substances and Natural Sources of Flavourings, 3rd ed.* ISBN 2-7160-0081-6. Strasbourg: Council of Europe, 1981.

REGULATORY GUIDELINES FROM OTHER EU COUNTRIES

FRANCE

Médicaments à base de plantes [32]: Coriandre, fruit.

Therapeutic indications accepted

Oral use
Traditionally used in the symptomatic treatment of digestive disorders such as: epigastric distension, sluggish digestion, eructation, flatulence.
Traditionally used as adjuvant treatment of the painful component of functional digestive disorders.

GERMANY

Commission E monograph [31]: Coriandri fructus (Koriander).

Uses
Dyspeptic complaints. Loss of appetite.

Contraindications
None known.

Side effects
None known.

Interactions with other drugs
None known.

Dosage
Unless otherwise prescribed, average daily dose: 3 g of the drug; equivalent preparations.

Mode of administration
Crushed and powdered drug or other galenic preparations for internal use.

COUCH GRASS RHIZOME — Gramineae

Agropyri repentis rhizoma

Synonyms: Quackgrass, dog grass or twitchgrass rhizome, Graminis rhizoma, Triticum (*Triticum repens* L. is an older botanical name for couch grass).

Definition

Couch Grass Rhizome consists of the washed and dried rhizomes of *Agropyron repens* (L.) Beauv. [*Elymus repens* (L.) Gould]; the adventitious roots are removed.

The rhizomes are usually collected in early spring.

Couch grass is a competitive and persistent perennial weed which propagates vegetatively by its underground rhizomes. It is allelopathic (interacts biochemically with other plants), containing compounds which are released into the soil and inhibit the germination or growth of other plants. Some of the more recent phytochemical studies [1,2] have been directed towards identification of such compounds.

CONSTITUENTS

□ ***Polysaccharides*** Triticin (ca. 12%) [3], a highly branched, short-chain fructan with about 30 fructofuranose units joined through 1→2 and 2→6 linkages, and probably with end units of glucose [3-5].

About 10% of unidentified mucilaginous polysaccharide is also present [5,6].

□ ***Flavonoids*** Quercetin and luteolin glycosides [7]; also small amounts (ca. 0.01%) of tricin (5,7,4′-trihydroxy-3′,5′-dimethoxyflavone) and a related flavone [1], probably present as glycosides [2].

□ ***Phenolic glucosides***, ca. 1.7%, mainly 5-glucosides of 5-hydroxyindole-3-acetic acid and 5-hydroxytryptophan [2]. 6-Hydroxy-1,2,3,4-tetrahydro-β-carboline-3-carboxylic acid is also present as a glucoside [8].

□ ***Essential oil***, ca. 0.02%, containing carvacrol (10.8%), *trans*-anethole (6.8%), carvone (5.5%), thymol (4.3%), menthol (3.5%), various other monoterpenes and small amounts of three sesquiterpenes among a total of 49 components [9].

An acetylenic and aromatic hydrocarbon, agropyren (1-phenylhexa-2,4-diyne) [10], once reported as 95% of the essential oil [11], was not detected in more recent GC-MS analysis [9].

□ ***Phenylpropanoid esters*** Small amounts of (*E*)- and (*Z*)-*p*-coumaric acid hexadecyl ester and (*E*)- and (*Z*)-*p*-coumaric acid-16-hydroxyhexadecyl ester [12]; also bis-(*E*)- and bis-(*Z*)-diesters of similar nature [13].

□ ***Other constituents*** Sugar alcohols (2-3%) including mannitol and inositol [5,6]; free fructose [7];

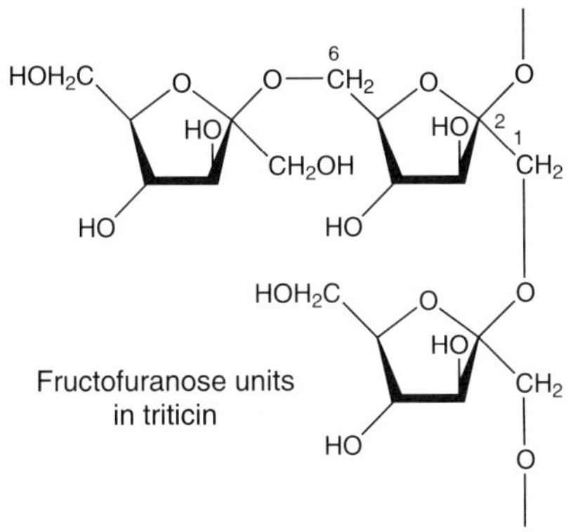

Fructofuranose units in triticin

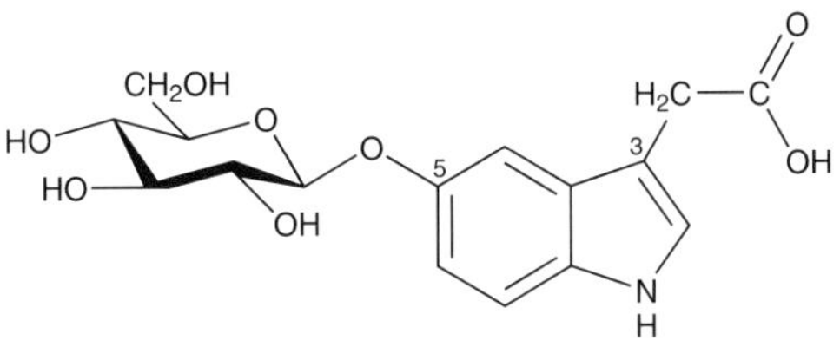

5-Hydroxyindole-3-acetic acid 5-glucoside

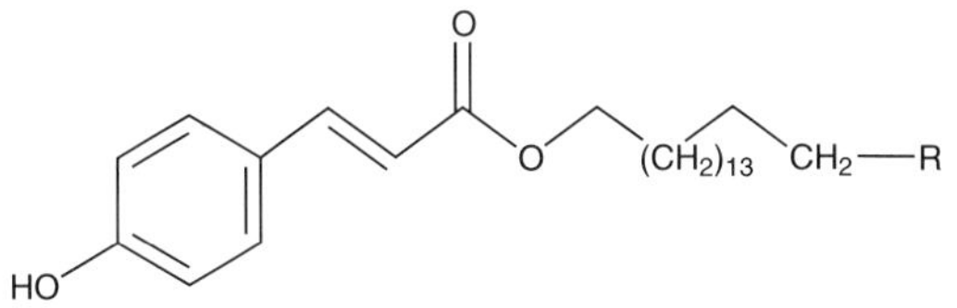

p-Coumaric acid hexadecyl ester R = H
p-Coumaric acid 16-hydroxyhexadecyl ester R = OH

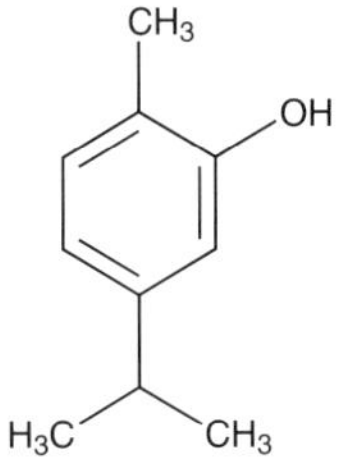

Carvacrol

fatty acids (mainly palmitic) [9]; phytosterols including β-sitosterol [7]; minerals including silicon (0.4%), potassium and iron [14]; and very low levels (5 ppm) of organic acids such as ferulic, *p*-hydroxybenzoic and vanillic acids [2]. Trace amounts of mammalian steroids have also been detected: oestrogen (120 ng/g), androstenone (120 ng/g), progesterone (250 ng/g) and androgens (3 ng/g) [15].

Although saponins are mentioned in some texts [16], their presence has not been confirmed.

Published Assay Methods

Essential oil by GC-MS [9].

PHARMACOLOGY

In vivo

Diuretic effects

An aqueous infusion of couch grass rhizome (3 g/litre), given to rats on a standard diet for 7 days as their water supply, significantly increased urine volume ($p<0.005$) and increased calcium excretion while reducing magnesium excretion ($p<0.005$). No positive effects pertinent to calcium oxalate urolithiasis risk factors were observed [17].

An orally administered aqueous extract (prepared by maceration) from couch grass rhizome increased urine volume in rats; the diuretic index was 1.42 [18].

Other effects

An orally administered 80%-ethanolic extract of couch grass rhizome exhibited only weak anti-inflammatory activity in the carrageenan-induced rat paw oedema test, producing 14% inhibition at 100 mg/kg body weight [19].

CLINICAL STUDIES

In an open post-marketing study, the results of daily treatment with a fluid extract (1:1, 20% ethanol) of couch grass rhizome, on average 50-60 drops three times daily for 12 days, were assessed in 313 patients suffering from urinary tract infections (cystitis, prostatitis and/or urethritis) or irritable bladder; two-thirds of the patients were female and about one-third of patients were taking other drugs concomitantly (23% on antibiotics). Urological symptoms (such as pollakiuria, nycturia, urge to urinate or burning sensation during micturition) declined by 69-91% during the course of therapy and, depending on the underlying diagnosis, between 32% and 53% of patients were symptom-free after the treatment. The physicians' global assessment of efficacy was good to very good in 84% of cases [20].

THERAPEUTICS

Actions

Diuretic [17,18,21-24] and demulcent [22-24].

Indications

None adequately substantiated by pharmacological or clinical studies.

Uses based on experience or tradition

Inflammatory ailments and infections of the urinary tract, particularly cystitis but also including urethritis, prostatitis [16,20-24] and irritable bladder [20].

Has also been used in the treatment of renal calculi [21,24] and lithuria [21], gout and rheumatic disorders [6,23], and chronic skin complaints [5,6].

Contraindications

None known.

Side effects

None known.

Interactions with other drugs

None known.

Dosage

Three times daily: dried rhizome, 4-8 g, usually in decoction or infusion [21,23]; liquid extract 1:1 in 25% alcohol, 4-8 ml [21,22], tincture 1:5 in 40% alcohol, 5-15 ml [21].

SAFETY

No adverse reactions were reported from treatment of 313 patients with a fluid extract of couch grass rhizome (50-60 drops twice daily) for 12 days; the preparation was well tolerated [20].

A fluid extract of couch grass rhizome (1:1, 20% ethanol) showed no mutagenic potential in the Ames test using *Salmonella typhimurium* strains TA98 and TA100 [25].

REGULATORY STATUS

Medicines

UK	Accepted for general sale, internal or external use [26].
France	Accepted for specified indications [27].
Germany	Commission E monograph published, with approved uses [16].

Food

USA	Generally recognized as safe (21 CFR 182.20) [28].

Council of Europe	Permitted as flavouring, category 5 [29].

REFERENCES

Current Pharmacopoeial Monographs

Ph. Eur. Couch Grass Rhizome

Literature References

1. Weston LA, Burke BA and Putnam AR. Isolation, characterization and activity of phytotoxic compounds from quackgrass [*Agropyron repens* (L.) Beauv.]. *J. Chem. Ecol.* 1987, **13**, 403-421.
2. Hagin RD. Isolation and Identification of 5-Hydroxyindole-3-acetic Acid and 5-Hydroxytryptophan, Major Allelopathic Aglycons in Quackgrass (*Agropyron repens* L. Beauv.). *J. Agric. Food Chem.* 1989, **37**, 1143-1149.
3. Arni PC and Percival EGV. Studies on Fructosans. Part II. Triticin from the Rhizomes of Couch Grass (*Triticum repens* L.). *J. Chem. Soc.* 1951, 1822-1830.
4. Percival EGV (revised by Percival E). Triticin. In: *Structural Carbohydrate Chemistry, 2nd ed.* London: J. Garnet Miller, 1962:278.
5. Steinegger E and Hänsel R. Queckenwurzelstock [Couch grass rhizome]. In: *Pharmakognosie*, 5th ed. ISBN 3-540-55649-4. Berlin-Heidelberg-New York: Springer-Verlag, 1992:111 [GERMAN].
6. Hänsel R, Keller K, Rimpler H and Schneider G, editors. Agropyron. In: *Hagers Handbuch der Pharmazeutischen Praxis*, 5th ed. Volume 4: Drogen A-D. ISBN 3-540-52631-5. Berlin-Heidelberg-New York-London: Springer-Verlag, 1992 [GERMAN].
7. Stanic G, Gavric D and Simic I. Phytochemical study of *Elymus repens* Gould and *Cynodon dactylon* (L.) Pers. *Farm. Glas.* 2000, **56**, 1-9 [SERBO-CROAT/English summary].
8. Hagin RD and Bobnick SJ. Isolation and Identification of a Slug-Specific Molluscicide from Quackgrass (*Agropyron repens* L. Beauv.). *J. Agric. Food Chem.* 1991, **39**, 192-196.
9. Boesel R and Schilcher H. Composition of the Essential Oil of *Agropyrum repens* Rhizome. *Planta Medica* 1989, **55**, 399-400.
10. Craig JC and Lack RE. Structure of agropyren. *Chem. Ind. (London)* 1959, 952.
11. Treibs W. Über das Agropyren, einen natürlichen aromatischen *En-in*-Kohlenwasserstoff der Queckenwurzel [Agropyren, a natural aromatic ene-yne hydrocarbon from couch grass root]. *Chem. Ber.* 1947, **80**, 97-100 [GERMAN].
12. Koetter U, Kaloga M and Schilcher H. Isolation and Structure Elucidation of *p*-Hydroxycinnamic Acid Esters from the Rhizome of *Agropyron repens*: Part 1. *Planta Medica* 1993, **59**, 279-280 [GERMAN].
13. Koetter U, Kaloga M and Schilcher H. Isolation and Structure Elucidation of *p*-Hydroxycinnamic Acid Esters from the Rhizome of *Agropyron repens*, Part 2. *Planta Medica* 1994, **60**, 488-489 [GERMAN].
14. Paslawska S and Piekos R. Studies on the optimum conditions of extraction of silicon species from plants with water. IV. Agropyron repens. *Planta Medica* 1976, **30**, 216-220.
15. Simons RG and Grinwich DL. Immunoreactive detection of four mammalian steroids in plants. *Can. J. Bot.* 1989, **67**, 288-296.
16. Graminis rhizoma. German Commission E Monograph published in: Bundesanzeiger No. 22 of 1 February 1990.
17. Grases F, Ramis M, Costa-Bauzá A and March JG. Effect of *Herniaria hirsuta* and *Agropyron repens* on calcium urolithiasis risk in rats. *J. Ethnopharmacol.* 1995, **45**, 211-214.
18. Racz-Kotilla E and Mozes E. Diuretic action of rhizoma graminis. *Rev. Med. (Tirgu-Mures)* 1971, **17**, 82-84 [ROMANIAN]; through *Chem. Abstr.* 1971, **75**, 128341.
19. Mascolo N, Autore G, Capasso F, Menghini A and Fasulo MP. Biological Screening of Italian Medicinal Plants for Anti-inflammatory Activity. *Phytotherapy Res.* 1987, **1**, 28-31.
20. Hautmann C and Scheithe K. Fluid extract of *Agropyron repens* for the treatment of urinary tract infections or irritable bladder. Results of a multicentric post-marketing surveillance. *Z. Phytotherapie* 2000, **21**, 252-255 [GERMAN/English summary].
21. Agropyron. In: *British Herbal Pharmacopoeia 1983*. ISBN 0-903032-07-4. Bournemouth: British Herbal Medicine Association, 1983.
22. Pharmaceutical Society of Great Britain. Agropyrum. In: *British Pharmaceutical Codex 1934*. London: Pharmaceutical Press, 1934:77-78.
23. Grieve M (edited by Leyel CF). Couch-Grass. In: *A Modern Herbal* (First published 1931; revised 1973). ISBN 1-85501-249-9. London: Tiger Books International, 1994:370-371.
24. Chevallier A. Couch Grass. In: *The Encyclopedia of Medicinal Plants*. ISBN 0-7513-0314-3. London-New York-Stuttgart: Dorling Kindersley, 1996:160.
25. Schimmer O, Krüger A, Paulini H and Haefele F. An evaluation of 55 commercial plant extracts in the Ames mutagenicity test. *Pharmazie* 1994, **49**, 448-451.
26. Agropyron (Triticum). In: UK Statutory Instrument 1989 No. 969. The Medicines (Products Other Than Veterinary Drugs) (General Sale List) Amendment Order 1989. Schedule 1, Table A.
27. Chiendent. In: *Médicaments à base de plantes*. ISBN 2-911473-02-7. Saint-Denis Cedex, France: Agence du Médicament, 1998.
28. Dog grass (quackgrass, triticum). In: Section 182.20 of USA Code of Federal Regulations, Title 21, Food and Drugs, Parts 170 to 199. Revised as of April 1, 2000.
29. Agropyron repens (L.) Beauv. In: *Natural Sources of Flavourings. Report No. 1*. ISBN 92-871-4324-2. Strasbourg: Council of Europe Publishing, 2000.

REGULATORY GUIDELINES FROM OTHER EU COUNTRIES

FRANCE

Médicaments à base de plantes [27]: Chiendent, rhizome.

Therapeutic indications accepted

Oral use

Traditionally used: to facilitate urinary and digestive elimination functions; to promote the renal elimination of water; as an adjuvant in slimming regimes.

GERMANY

Commission E monograph [16]: Graminis rhizoma (Queckenwurzelstock).

Uses

For irrigation in inflammatory ailments of the lower urinary tract and for the prevention of renal gravel.

Contraindications

None known.

Note: Irrigation therapy should not be used in oedema due to impaired cardiac or renal function.

Couch Grass Rhizome

Side effects
None known.

Interactions with other drugs
None known.

Dosage
Unless otherwise prescribed, daily dose: dried rhizome, 6-9 g; equivalent preparations.

Mode of administration
Comminuted drug for decoctions and other galenic preparations for internal use.
Note: During irrigation therapy ensure copious intake of fluid.

Action
The essential oil is antimicrobial.

CRANESBILL HERB/ROOT — Geraniaceae

Geranii maculati herba/rhizoma

Synonyms: American Cranesbill, Wild Geranium.

Definition

Cranesbill Herb consists of the dried, flowering aerial parts, and Cranesbill Root of the dried rhizomes, of *Geranium maculatum* L.

The BHP 1996 included only Cranesbill Root, but separate monographs on Geranium Herb and Geranium Root appeared in the BHP 1983. Dried rhizome of *G. maculatum* was at one time official in the U.S. National Formulary as Cranesbill N.F. V [1].

Geranium maculatum is a perennial herb bearing rose-purplish flowers from May to July. It is found in Canada and the eastern USA south to Georgia [2]. The rhizome is collected in autumn [1].

CONSTITUENTS

HERB

□ ***Tannins*** of the hydrolysable type. In a survey of tannins in the leaves of *Geranium* species, *G. maculatum* leaf was found to contain 27.5% of galloyl esters, of which roughly 10.5% were esters of hexahydroxydiphenic acid (i.e. ellagitannins) and the remainder presumably gallotannins (i.e. a glucose core surrounded by 5 or more galloyl ester groups). Only trace amounts of proanthocyanidins were evident [3].

The predominant hydrolysable tannin in the *Geranium* genus is geraniin (an ellagitannin) [3]. Although not confirmed in the herb or the rhizome of *G. maculatum*, it seems likely that geraniin is present in both.

□ ***Flavonoids*** After hydrolysis of leaf material, two flavonol aglycones were identified: quercetin and a lesser amount of kaempferol [4].

□ ***Other constituents*** include gallic, caffeic and *p*-coumaric acids [4].

ROOT

□ ***Tannins***, 10-28%, of the hydrolysable type [1], probably including geraniin as mentioned under Leaf.

Some texts suggest that, in *Geranium* species as a rule, condensed tannins (proanthocyanidins) predominate in the underground organs [5]. However, this is not borne out by the high amounts (21-32%) of hydrolysable tannins reported in the roots of several *Geranium* species [6].

□ ***Other constituents*** include starch and calcium oxalate [1].

PHARMACOLOGY

No pharmacological data are available on cranesbill herb or root.

CLINICAL STUDIES

None published on mono-preparations of cranesbill.

THERAPEUTICS

Actions

Astringent [1,7-11], anti-haemorrhagic, vulnerary [7] and styptic [8,10].

Cranesbill has been described as a particularly palatable herbal astringent, reliable in its action, devoid of unpleasant effects [1,11] and gentle enough for children, the elderly and the debilitated [7,10].

In a review of tannins by Japanese authors, geraniin and an infusion of geraniin-rich *Geranium thunbergii* herb (the Japanese equivalent of cranesbill) were stated to have almost no astringent taste [12].

Indications

None substantiated by pharmacological or clinical studies.

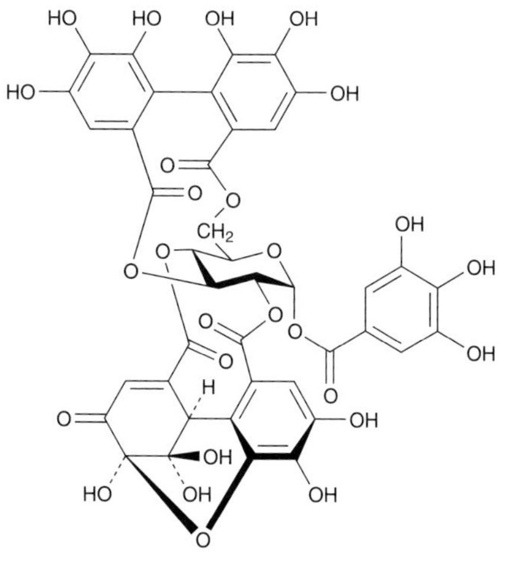

Geraniin

Uses based on experience or tradition

Internal: Diarrhoea [1,7-11], peptic and duodenal ulcers [7], melaena, haemorrhoids [7-9], menorrhagia and metrorrhagia [7-9].

Topical: As a local astringent [1] for external bleeding [9] and indolent ulcers [1,7]; as a gargle or mouthwash for sore throat [1,8,9], mouth ulcers and infected gums [9]; as a douche for leucorrhoea [7,8].

Contraindications
None known.

Side effects
None known.

Interactions with other drugs
None known.

Dosage
Three times daily: dried rhizome, 1-2 g as an infusion (herb) or decoction (root); liquid extract 1:1 in 45% alcohol, 1-2 ml [7].

SAFETY

Cranesbill is considered to be safe for internal consumption when used appropriately [13].

A similar astringent, *Geranium thunbergii* herb, is described as "one of the most popular herb medicines in Japan, taken by enormous numbers of people for hundreds of years...without encountering any notable toxicity" [12].

REGULATORY STATUS

Medicines

UK	All parts of the plant accepted for general sale, internal or external use [14].
France	Not listed in *Médicaments à base de plantes* [15].
Germany	No Commission E monograph issued.

Food
Not used in foods.

REFERENCES

Current Pharmacopoeial Monographs

BHP	Cranesbill Root

Literature References

1. Wood HC and LaWall CH, editors. Geranium. In: *United States Dispensatory, Centennial (22nd) Edition.* Philadelphia-London: JB Lippincott Company, 1937:1390-1391.
2. Budavari S, editor. Geranium - Cranesbill. In: *The Merck Index: An encyclopedia of chemicals, drugs and biologicals, 12th edition.* ISBN 0-911910-12-3. Whitehouse Station, NJ: Merck & Co., 1996:748 (monograph 4412).
3. Bate-Smith EC. Astringent tannins of the leaves of Geranium species. *Phytochemistry* 1981, **20**, 211-216.
4. Bate-Smith EC. Chemotaxonomy of Geranium. *Bot. J. Linn. Soc.* (London) 1973, **67**, 347-359.
5. Hänsel R, Keller K, Rimpler H and Schneider G, editors. Geranium. In: *Hagers Handbuch der Pharmazeutischen Praxis, 5th ed. Volume 5: Drogen E-O.* ISBN 3-540-52638-2. Berlin-Heidelberg-New York-London: Springer-Verlag, 1993:250-260 [GERMAN].
6. Hájková I, Bucková H, Gesková E and Nátherová L. The Study of Tannins in Some Species of the Genus *Geranium. Ceskoslov. Farm.* 1964, **13**, 183-185 [SLOVAK/English summary].
7. Geranium Herb, Geranium Root. In: *British Herbal Pharmacopoeia 1983.* ISBN 0-903032-07-4. Bournemouth: British Herbal Medicine Association, 1983.
8. Grieve M (edited by Leyel CF). Cranesbill Root, American - *Geranium maculatum.* In: *A Modern Herbal* (first published 1931; revised 1973). ISBN 1-85501-249-9. London: Tiger Books International, 1994:233.
9. Chevallier A. American Cranesbill - *Geranium maculatum.* In: *Encyclopedia of Medicinal Plants, 2nd ed.* ISBN 0-7513-1209-6. London-New York: Dorling Kindersley, 2001:215.
10. Ody P. American Cranesbill. In: *The Complete Guide - Medicinal Herbal.* ISBN 0-7513-3005-1. London-New York: Dorling Kindersley, 2000:186, 218 and 228.
11. Ellingwood F. Geranium - *Geranium maculatum.* In: *A Systematic Treatise on Materia Medica and Therapeutics.* Chicago: Chicago Medical Press, 1900:437-438.
12. Okuda T, Yoshida T and Hatano T. Pharmacologically active tannins isolated from medicinal plants. *Basic Life Sciences* 1992, **59**, 539-569.
13. McGuffin M, Hobbs C, Upton R and Goldberg A, editors. *Geranium maculatum* L. In: American Herbal Products Association's *Botanical Safety Handbook.* Boca Raton-Boston-London: CRC Press, 1997:57.
14. Cranesbill Root. In: UK Statutory Instrument 1984 No. 769. The Medicines (Products Other Than Veterinary Drugs) (General Sale List) Order 1984. Schedule 1, Table A. The entry "Cranesbill Root" was amended to "Cranesbill (Geranium)" by Articles 3(1) and 3(2)(e) of S.I. 1994 No. 2410. The Medicines (Products Other Than Veterinary Drugs) (General Sale List) Amendment Order 1994.
15. *Médicaments à base de plantes.* ISBN 2-911473-02-7. Saint-Denis Cedex, France: Agence du Médicament, 1998.

ECHINACEA

Compositae

Echinaceae angustifoliae radix
Echinaceae pallidae radix
Echinaceae purpureae radix
Echinaceae purpureae herba

Synonyms: Narrow-Leaved Coneflower (*Echinacea angustifolia*), Pale Coneflower (*E. pallida*), Purple Coneflower (*E. purpurea*).

Introduction
Three species of *Echinacea* are used medicinally to varying extents: *Echinacea angustifolia* DC, *E. pallida* (Nutt.) Nutt. and *E. purpurea* (L.) Moench.

Usage of *E. angustifolia* and *E. pallida* is generally limited to root material. However, three materials derived from *E. purpurea* are used in phytomedicine: the root, the herb and pressed juice from the fresh herb, the last-mentioned being the most clinically tested type of echinacea preparation. Each of these materials is covered in the following text, with differentiation between them particularly in the sections on Constituents and Clinical Studies.

In 1987 it became apparent that much of the "*Echinacea angustifolia*" cultivated in Europe was, in fact, *E. pallida* [1]. Hence earlier data on *E. angustifolia* from European sources may not be reliable with regard to species.

Definitions
Echinacea angustifolia root consists of the dried rhizome and roots of *Echinacea angustifolia* DC.

Echinacea pallida root consists of the dried rhizome and roots of *Echinacea pallida* (Nutt.) Nutt.

Echinacea purpurea root consists of the dried rhizome and roots of *Echinacea purpurea* (L.) Moench.

Echinacea purpurea herb consists of the dried flowering aerial parts of *Echinacea purpurea* (L.) Moench.

CONSTITUENTS

For an excellent review of the constituents of *Echinacea* species, see Bauer and Wagner [2].

ECHINACEA ANGUSTIFOLIA ROOT

☐ ***Caffeic acid derivatives***, 1.0-1.4%, principally echinacoside (0.5-1.3%) with modest amounts of cynarin (0.12-0.14%), chlorogenic acid and cichoric acid [1,3-5].
☐ ***Alkamides*** At least 15 alkamides (alkylamides; long-chain polyunsaturated fatty acid amides) have been isolated and identified. All of them are isobutylamides or 2-methylbutylamides, most have a 2-monoene moiety and 10 are di-acetylenic compounds [6,7]. The dominant compounds appear to be isomeric dodeca-2*E*,4*E*,8*Z*,10*E*/*Z*-tetraenoic acid isobutylamides [6], up to 0.5% (average 0.22% in 23 batches of dried root) [8], and also isomeric undeca-2*E*/*Z*-ene-8,10-diynoic acid isobutylamides and dodeca-2*E*-ene-8,10-diynoic acid isobutylamide [9].
☐ ***Polysaccharides*** Three glycoproteins of MW 17, 21 and 30 kDa, containing about 3% of protein; the dominant sugars were found to be arabinose (64-84%), galactose (2-5%) and glucosamine (6%) [10]. Fructans are also present [2].
☐ ***Other constituents*** include a trace of essential oil (< 0.1%) in which a principal component is

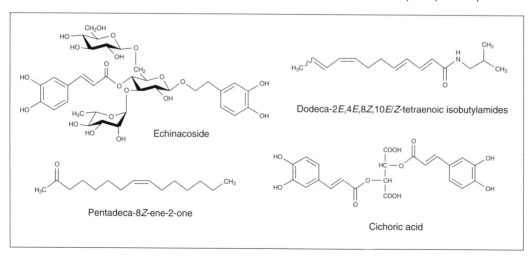

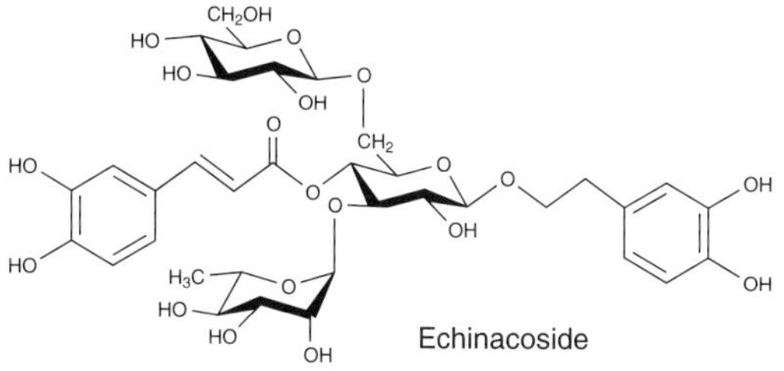

Echinacoside

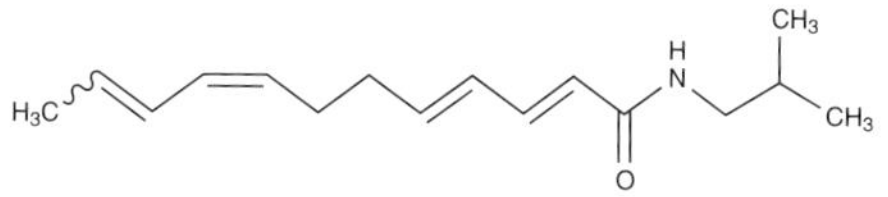

Dodeca-2*E*,4*E*,8*Z*,10*E*/*Z*-tetraenoic isobutylamides

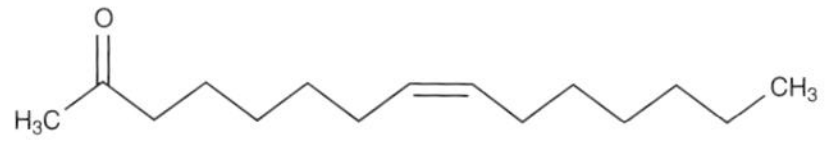

Pentadeca-8*Z*-ene-2-one

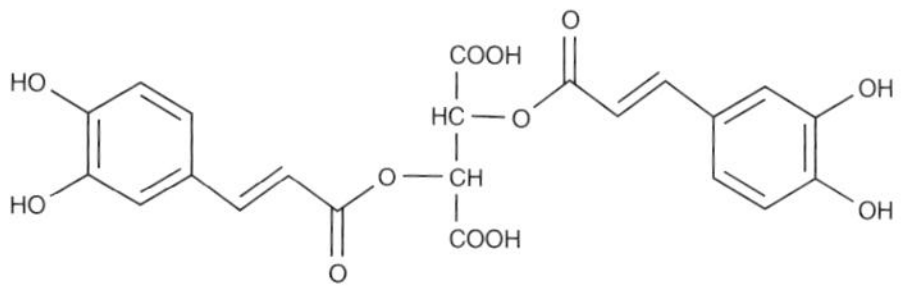

Cichoric acid

8*Z*-pentadecene-2-one [11] and, as 44% of a pentane extract from dried root, pentadeca-1,8*Z*-diene [12].

ECHINACEA PALLIDA ROOT

☐ ***Caffeic acid derivatives***, 0.5-1.8%, principally echinacoside with small amounts of cichoric (0.08%), caftaric (0.04-0.08%) and chlorogenic acids [3,4,8].
☐ ***Alkamides*** Practically free from alkamides [9], although a very small amount (average 0.001%) of isomeric dodeca-2*E*,4*E*,8*Z*,10*E*/*Z*-tetraenoic acid isobutylamides can be detected [8].
☐ ***Essential oil***, 0.2-1.0%, consisting mainly of unsaturated alkyl ketones (ketoalkenes and keto-alkenynes), principally 8*Z*-pentadecene-2-one (about 65% of the oil) together with pentadeca-8*Z*,11*Z*-diene-2-one, pentadeca-8*Z*,13*Z*-diene-11-yne-2-one, tetradeca-8*Z*-ene-11,13-diyne-2-one and others [1,11]. The hydrocarbon pentadeca-1,8*Z*-diene is also a substantial component [11, 12].

Unsaturated alkyl ketones are susceptible to oxidation in the 8-position and are fairly rapidly converted through autoxidation on storage to their 8-hydroxy derivatives, which usually predominate in the dried root. They include 8-hydroxytetradeca-9*E*-ene-11,13-diyne-2-one, 8-hydroxypentadeca-9*E*-ene-11,13-diyne-2-one and 8-hydroxypentadeca-9*E*,13*Z*-diene-11-yne-2-one [1,9].
☐ ***Other constituents*** include glycoproteins and polysaccharides [10,13].

ECHINACEA PURPUREA ROOT

☐ ***Caffeic acid derivatives***, 2.0-2.7%, principally cichoric acid (2,3-*O*-dicaffeoyl-tartaric acid, 1.7-2.4%) and caftaric acid (2-*O*-caffeoyl-tartaric acid, ca. 0.4%) [3,4,14]. Chlorogenic acid is also present [8].

In 18 batches of *Echinacea purpurea* root from various commercial sources, the cichoric acid content ranged from 0.33 to 2.4%, with an average of only 0.94% [8]. On the other hand, using an ultrasound extraction technique, over 4% of cichoric acid was reported in one study [5].
☐ ***Alkamides***, 0.5-0.7% [14,15], principally the isomeric dodeca-2*E*,4*E*,8*Z*,10*E*/*Z*-tetraenoic acid isobutylamides (ca. 0.18%) [15,16]. Undeca-2*Z*,4*E*-diene-8,10-diynoic acid isobutylamide is also prominent [17] among at least 11 alkamides present, most of which have a 2,4-diene structure [2].
☐ ***Polysaccharides*** Arabinogalactans, and an arabinogalactan-containing glycoprotein with a sugar component consisting of arabinose (64-84%), galactose (2-5%) and galactosamine (6%) [18,19].
☐ ***Other constituents*** Small amounts of poly-acetylenic compounds (other than alkamides mentioned above) [20] and a trace of essential oil (less than 0.1%) [11] containing caryophyllene, caryophyllene oxide and humulene [2].

ECHINACEA PURPUREA HERB

☐ ***Caffeic acid derivatives***, 0.7-2.8%, principally cichoric acid (0.5-2.0%) and caftaric acid (0.2-0.8%) [4]. Other compounds, such as 2-*O*-caffeoyl-3-*O*-coumaroyl-tartaric acid, have been isolated [10,21].

A cichoric acid level of 3.0% was found in one study using an ultrasound extraction technique [5]. The distribution of cichoric acid in the plant parts has been found to be 0.4-0.9% in stems, 3.2-4.3% in leaves and 2.2-2.7% in flowerheads [14,17].
☐ ***Alkamides***, about 0.03%, principally isomeric dodeca-2*E*,4*E*,8*Z*,10*E*/*Z*-tetraenoic acid isobutylamides [17,22] together with various other isobutylamides, for example undeca-2*E*,4*Z*-diene-8,10-diynoic acid isobutylamide [22].
☐ ***Polysaccharides*** including a 4-*O*-methyl-glucuronoarabinoxylan of average MW 35 kDa with a (1→4)-linked xylan backbone [10,23,24], an acidic arabinorhamnogalactan of MW 450 kDa [10,24] and a xyloglucan of MW 79.5 kDa [10].
☐ ***Flavonoids***, ca. 0.5% in the leaves, consisting of flavonols such as quercetin, kaempferol, iso-rhamnetin and their glycosides [2], rutin being the major compound [22].
☐ ***Essential oil***, a small amount (about 0.07% in leaves, 0.17% in flowers) [25] containing mono-terpenes such as borneol and bornyl acetate, and sesquiterpenes such as germacrene D, caryophyllene and caryophyllene epoxide [2].

PRESSED JUICE FROM *ECHINACEA PURPUREA* FRESH HERB

The pressed juice contains 12-13% of solids [26].

☐ ***Caffeic acid derivatives***, principally cichoric acid. In samples of commercial pressed juice preparations the content of cichoric acid ranged from nil to 0.4 g/100 ml due to inconsistent inhibition of enzymatic degradation of this constituent. All the nil results related to products stabilised with 20% ethanol, while four samples of a thermally stabilized product contained cichoric acid in the range 0.25-0.4 g/100 ml [27].

Subsequent work has shown that cichoric acid can be stabilized in aqueous preparations by the addition of 40% ethanol and 50 mM ascorbic acid [28].
☐ ***Alkamides*** Isomeric dodeca-2*E*,4*E*,8*Z*,10*E*/*Z*-tetraenoic acid isobutylamides, 0.1-1.8 mg/100 ml [27].
☐ ***Polysaccharides*** An acidic, highly-branched arabinogalactan (MW ca. 70 kDa) [26] and an arabinogalactan-protein (MW 1.2 × 10^3 kDa; 83% polysaccharide) [29] have been partially characterized. Inulin-type fructans [26], which are characteristic for plants of the Compositae

[24], and a pectin-like polysaccharide [10] are also present.

Published Assay Methods
Alkamides and cichoric acid simultaneously by HPLC [17]. Isomeric dodeca-2*E*,4*E*,8*Z*,10*E*/*Z*-tetraenoic acid isobutylamides and cichoric acid by HPLC [27]. Alkamides and caffeic acid derivatives by HPLC [5] or simultaneously by HPLC-MS [30].

PHARMACOLOGY

Summaries of the extensive pharmacological studies carried out on various extracts, fractions and constituents of echinacea can be found in a number of publications [2,10,31-34], among which the 1991 review (in English) [2] and 1990 book (in German) [32] by Bauer and Wagner are outstanding, if now somewhat dated. The following is only a small selection from the published research.

Immunomodulatory activity
Echinacea has been described as a non-specific immunostimulant, implying that it has no antigenic relationship to specific pathogens; its action results from the stimulation of cell-mediated immune responses such as phagocytosis and the release of cytokines and other serum factors. Phagocytosis, the process of ingestion or clearance of microorganisms, cells and particles by cells of the reticulo-endothelial system, has been used as an indicator of the immunostimulant activity of echinacea.

Ethanolic extracts from the roots and aerial parts of *E. angustifolia*, *E. pallida* and *E. purpurea* were tested, both *in vitro* and *in vivo*, to find out whether, irrespective of species or part of plant, they stimulated phagocytosis [2,35,36]:

- In the *in vitro* granulocyte smear test all the root extracts at concentrations of 10^{-2} to 10^{-4} mg/ml caused a 20-30% increase in phagocytosis, the extract from *E. purpurea* being the most active.
- In the *in vivo* carbon clearance test, after oral administration to mice of 3 ×10 ml/kg daily for 2 days, the elimination rate was increased about 3-fold by *E. purpurea* root extract and 2-fold by root extracts from *E. angustifolia* and *E. pallida*. Extracts from aerial parts were also active in this test, stimulating the rate of clearance by 1.5 to 1.7-fold compared to controls.
- Further work indicated that alkamides and cichoric acid possess phagocytosis-stimulating activity, while echinacoside appeared to be inactive.

Thus lipophilic alkamides as well as the more polar caffeic acid derivative cichoric acid (but not echinacoside) probably make a considerable contribution to the immunostimulatory action of alcoholic echinacea extracts [2].

Polysaccharide fractions from both aerial parts and roots of *E. purpurea* have also shown phagocytic activity, in the human granulocyte smear test at concentrations of 10^{-2} to 10^{-3} mg/ml and, after intraperitoneal administration to mice at 10 mg/kg, in the carbon clearance test. Similar fractions from *E. angustifolia* were active in the granulocyte test at 10^{-2} mg/ml [2,24]. However, due to factors such as gastrointestinal breakdown and poor absorption of polysaccharides, these results are unlikely to be relevant to oral preparations of echinacea [33].

Elevation of an immune parameter after oral administration of an echinacea extract has been demonstrated in humans. Healthy male volunteers were treated orally for 5 days with 3 × 30 drops per day of an ethanolic extract from *E. purpurea* root (n = 12) or placebo (n = 12) in a double-blind study. The daily dose of extract contained about 1 mg of cichoric acid and 1 mg of mixed alkamides. Stimulation of granulocyte phagocytosis (measured by a microscopic smear test) reached a peak on day 5 at 120% of the initial value, then phagocytosis activity slowly returned to the normal range over 3 days [37].

Topical anti-inflammatory and wound-healing activity
An aqueous extract from *E. angustifolia* root dose-dependently inhibited oedema in the croton oil ear test in mice, both at the maximum (6 hours) and in the decreasing phase (18 hours), with a potency greater than that of benzydamine [38]; the topical anti-inflammatory activity was attributed to high MW polysaccharides [39].

Twice-daily application of 0.15 ml of an ointment containing pressed juice from *E. purpurea* herb to incision wounds in the flanks of anaesthetized guinea pigs increased the rate of healing in comparison with untreated controls. On the 6th and 9th days after incision, wound areas treated with the echinacea ointment were significantly smaller ($p<0.05$) [40].

In another wound-healing study, gels containing ethanolic dry extract from *E. pallida* root (100 mg/ml; 2% of echinacoside in the extract) or *E. purpurea* root (100 mg/ml; devoid of echinacoside), or pure echinacoside (0.4 mg/ml), were applied once only to abrasion wounds (anti-inflammatory test), and in separate experiments to incision wounds (cicatrizing test), on the backs of rats, while control groups were treated with the vehicle only. The

E. pallida root extract and its constituent echinacoside showed good anti-inflammatory and wound-healing (cicatrizing) properties after 72 hours. The *E. purpurea* root extract was more effective over the first 24 hours but inferior at 48-72 hours. All three treatments increased the collagen content in incision wounds by significantly more than controls after 72 hours ($p<0.05$) [41].

CLINICAL STUDIES

Upper respiratory tract infections

Most of the controlled clinical studies of echinacea have been directed towards the prophylaxis or treatment of upper respiratory tract (URT) infections such as common cold. Tables 1-3 list the randomized, double-blind, placebo-controlled studies [42-55] carried out in this area with oral echinacea *mono*-preparations, separated according to species and plant part used. Studies involving echinacea-containing combination products, which are included in some clinical reviews [34, 56], have been excluded here.

Considering that echinacea preparations constitute one of the top-selling herbal medicines in Europe and North America for the treatment of URT infections, mankind's most common and repetitive minor illnesses, the clinical evidence in support of their popularity is remarkably weak. Overall, the available studies must be considered rather inconclusive with regard to efficacy. As can be seen from Tables 1-3:

- No studies in the prophylaxis of URT infections have produced significant evidence of efficacy [42,43,49,55]. The study by Berg et al. [51] is too small for the numbers to be meaningful.
- In the treatment of URT infections/common cold with root preparations
  - a study with *E. angustifolia* root extracts gave negative results [43].
  - a study with an *E. pallida* root extract showed significant efficacy [44].
  - extracts from *E. purpurea* root gave significantly positive results in one study [45], offset by negative results in another [46].
- A standardized extract from various fresh plant parts of *E. purpurea*, developed to contain specific amounts of key constituents, gave significantly positive results in the treatment of common cold [48].
- In the treatment of URT infections/common cold with preparations from *E. purpurea* fresh herb:
  - one study with a dry extract gave significantly positive results [46].
  - two studies with pressed juice gave significantly positive results [50,52], but are counterbalanced by negative results in two later studies [53,54].

On the basis of published clinical data of statistical significance, therefore, echinacea has been found ineffective in the *prophylaxis* of URT infections. With respect to the *treatment* of URT infections, echinacea preparations were ineffective in 4 studies [43,47,53,54] out of 6 published since 2000 [43,47,48,52-54].

On the other hand, over the past 15 years, with one echinacea preparation or another, significant efficacy has been shown in 6 placebo-controlled studies [44-46,48,50,52]. The therapeutic potential of some echinacea preparations in the treatment of URT infections has therefore been demonstrated, but the exact criteria - species, plant parts, content of key constituents, dosage or whatever - to ensure consistent and reproducible efficacy remains to be clarified. With the complication of three *Echinacea* species and the therapeutic use of different plant parts and preparations, this is a considerable challenge for future studies.

Although the necessity for standardization of extracts (and the avoidance of enzymic degradation of constituents) in order to enable reproducible activity, has been stressed by Bauer on a number of occasions [9,10], quantification of key constituents has been lacking in the majority of echinacea clinical studies. A recent and notable exception is the study (summarized below and in Table 2) in which the preparation used was specifically formulated and standardized to contain known amounts of alkamides, cichoric acid and polysaccharides [48]. Perhaps the fact that this preparation produced a significant result in the treatment of common cold will focus more attention on the question of standardization.

Cichoric acid has been shown to possess phagocytosis-stimulating activity *in vivo*, while echinacoside appeared inactive in that respect [2,35,36] but showed good anti-inflammatory and wound-healing properties in rats [41]. On this basis it could be theorized that *Echinacea purpurea* root and herb (usually high in cichoric acid, devoid of echinacoside) should be the more favourable choice for URT infections (immunostimulant effects), while *E. angustifolia* root and *pallida* root (low in cichoric acid, high in echinacoside) should be the more favourable choice for topical applications in skin disorders. However, the clinical results are too mixed to provide confirmation.

Summaries of clinical studies published before 2003 (and included in Tables 1 and 3) can be found in ESCOP monographs [31]. Only the more recent studies are summarized below.

***Echinacea angustifolia* root**

Using 60% ethanol, 20% ethanol and supercritical carbon dioxide (CO_2) as extraction solvents, three different extracts were prepared from the same batch of *Echinacea angustifolia* root for use in a double-blind, placebo-controlled study involving 427 healthy young adult volunteers, who were randomly assigned to one of seven groups in accordance with the scheme outlined below. After a prophylaxis phase (day -7 to day 0) all the volunteers were inoculated with rhinovirus type 39, a virus which causes common cold, and then isolated in individual hotel rooms while under observation during a treatment phase (day 0 to day 5). Study medications were taken in the form of 3 × 1.5 ml/day of a tincture prepared from the relevant extract, in each case corresponding to 3 × 300 mg/day of dried *E. angustifolia* root, or a placebo tincture:

Prophylaxis phase	Treatment phase	Randomized patients
60% ethanol extract	60% ethanol extract	55
20% ethanol extract	20% ethanol extract	54
CO2 extract	CO2 extract	54
Placebo	60% ethanol extract	55
Placebo	20% ethanol extract	55
Placebo	CO2 extract	55
Placebo	Placebo	109

No statistically significant effects of the three extracts were evident in the prophylaxis or treatment of rhinovirus infections, i.e. from rates of infection or severity of symptoms. Similarly, there were no significant effects of treatment in terms of the volume of nasal secretions, concentrations of polymorphonuclear leucocytes or interleukin-8 (markers of response to inflammation) in nasal lavage specimens, or quantitative virus titre. The authors concluded that extracts of *E. angustifolia* root have no significant effects on infection with a rhinovirus or on the clinical illness resulting from it.

Analytical results reported for the three extracts make rather surprising reading. None contained detectable amounts of echinacoside and only the 60% ethanol extract contained a small amount of cynarin. The CO_2 extract contained no polysaccharides but 73.8% of alkamides; the 60% ethanol extract, 48.9% of polysaccharides and 2.3% of alkamides; and the 20% ethanol extract, 42.1% of polysaccharides and only 0.1% of alkamides [43].

***E. angustifolia* root + *E. purpurea* herb/root**

In another double-blind, placebo-controlled study, the preparation used was an encapsulated mixture of *Echinacea angustifolia* root (50%) + *E. purpurea* dried herb (25%) + root (25%). University students were randomly assigned to treatment with the echinacea preparation (n = 73) or matching placebos (n = 75), at a dosage of 6 × 1 g on the first day of illness with common cold and 3 × 1 g on subsequent days for a maximum of 10 days. Based on self-reported symptoms, no significant differences were detected between the echinacea and placebo groups. Trajectories of the severity of cold symptoms over time were nearly identical in the two groups, while the mean duration of colds was 6.27 days in the echinacea group compared to 5.75 days in the placebo group. The authors concluded that this particular form of echinacea provided no benefit to common cold symptoms in young healthy adults [47].

***Echinacea purpurea* fresh herb/root**

A highly standardized liquid formulation, prepared from water-ethanol extracts of various parts of fresh *Echinacea purpurea* plants and containing alkamides, cichoric acid and polysaccharides at concentrations of 0.25, 2.5 and 25 mg/ml respectively, was used in a double-blind, placebo-controlled study involving adults aged 18-65 years with a history of two or more colds in the previous year, but otherwise in good health. The subjects were randomized and instructed to take either echinacea (4 ml per dose, to be diluted with water) or placebo from onset of the first symptom of a common cold, consuming 10 doses the first day and 4 doses per day thereafter for 7 days. Out of 282 persons initially randomized, 154 remained asymptomatic over the 6-month study period while 128 contracted a cold, 59 taking echinacea and 69 placebo. In those who fully observed the study protocol, 54 taking echinacea and 57 placebo, the total daily symptom score was 23.1% lower in the echinacea group than in the placebo group ($p<0.01$). The response to treatment rate was greater in the echinacea group throughout the treatment period. The authors concluded that early intervention with a standardized echinacea formulation reduced the symptom severity of naturally acquired upper respiratory tract infection [48].

Pressed juice from *Echinacea purpurea* fresh herb

Prior to 2003, two published studies using pressed juice gave positive results in the treatment of URT infections or common cold [50,52]. In contrast, no statistically significant evidence of efficacy was obtained from two more recent studies [53,54], as follows.

The duration and severity of symptoms of upper respiratory tract (URT) infections when they occurred in otherwise healthy children, 2-11 years of age, over a period of 4 months were assessed in a randomized, double-blind, placebo-controlled study. Of 524 children randomized, 263 were assigned to treatment with dried pressed juice from fresh *Echinacea purpurea* aerial parts (in a syrup formulation) and 261 to placebo. Study medications were administered from the onset of

TABLE 1 ECHINACEA ROOT PREPARATIONS: Randomized, double-blind, placebo-controlled clinical studies

First author Year Reference number	Type of study	Duration of treatment	Number of patients Verum/Placebo	Preparation	Daily dosage	Outcome for echinacea group (in comparison with placebo group)
***Echinacea angustifolia* root**						
Melchart 1998 [42]	**Prophylaxis** of URT infections	12 weeks	Adults 100/90	Liquid extract (1:11, ethanol 30%)	2 × 50 drops	No prophylactic effect apparent.
Turner 2005 [43]	**Prophylaxis** of, and **treatment** after, infection with a nasally inoculated rhinovirus	7 days of prophylaxis 5 days of treatment	Young adults 296/103 evaluated	60%-ethanolic, 20%-ethanolic and supercritical CO_2 extracts, as tinctures	3 × 1.5 ml of tincture, corresponding to 3 × 300 mg of root	Neither prophylaxis nor treatment effects apparent.
***Echinacea pallida* root**						
Bräunig 1993 [44] (= Dorn 1997)	**Treatment** of influenza-like URT infections	8-10 days	Adults 80/80	Hydroethanolic liquid extract	90 drops, corresp-onding to 900 mg of root	Significant improvements in duration of illness (p<0.0001), symptom scores (p<0.0004) and clinical scores (p<0.001).
***Echinacea purpurea* root**						
Bräunig 1992 [45]	**Treatment** of influenza	8-10 days	Adults 60/60/60	Tincture (1:5, ethanol 55%)	Corresp. to 450 mg of root or 900 mg of root	450 mg: No significant difference from placebo in symptom score. 900 mg: Significant reduction in symptom score (p<0.0001).
Melchart 1998 [42]	**Prophylaxis** of URT infections	12 weeks (Monday-Friday)	Adults 99/90	Liquid extract (1:11, ethanol 30%)	2 × 50 drops	No prophylactic effect apparent.
Brinkeborn 1999 [46]	**Treatment** of common cold	Up to 7 days from onset of symptoms	Adults 44/46	Dry extract from root, 29.6 mg per tablet.	3 × 2 tablets	No significant difference from placebo in severity of symptoms.

TABLE 2 ECHINACEA ROOT + HERB PREPARATIONS: Randomized, double-blind, placebo-controlled clinical studies

***Echinacea angustifolia* root + *E. purpurea* herb/root**						
Barrett 2002 [47]	**Treatment** of common cold	Up to 10 days from onset of symptoms	Young adults 73/75	*E. angustifolia* dried root (50%) + *E. purpurea* dried herb (25%) and root (25%).	6 × 1 g on day 1. 3 × 1 g thereafter	No significant difference from placebo in duration or severity of symptoms.
***Echinacea purpurea* fresh herb/root**						
Goel 2004 [48]	**Treatment** of common cold	7 days from onset of symptoms	Adults 59/69	Water-ethanol extracts from fresh *E. purpurea* plant parts, combined to provide: Alkamides, 0.25 mg/ml Cichoric acid, 2.5 mg/ml Polysaccharides, 25 mg/ml	10 × 4 ml on day 1. 4 × 4 ml on days 2-7.	Significant reduction in symptom score (p<0.01).

TABLE 3 ECHINACEA HERB PREPARATIONS: Randomized, double-blind, placebo-controlled clinical studies

First author Year Reference number	Type of study	Duration of treatment	Number of patients Verum/Placebo	Preparation	Daily dosage	Outcome for echinacea group (in comparison with placebo group)
***Echinacea purpurea* fresh herb**						
Brinkeborn 1999 [46]	**Treatment** of common cold	Up to 7 days from onset of symptoms	Adults 41 + 49/46	Dry extract from fresh herb (95%) and root (5%): A) 6.78 mg/tablet, or B) 48.27 mg/tablet	 3 × 2 tablets 3 × 2 tablets	Severity of symptoms significantly lower in both verum groups. $p<0.02$ $p<0.003$
Pressed juice from *Echinacea purpurea* fresh herb						
Schöneberger 1992 [49] (= Grimm 1999)	**Prophylaxis** (and **treatment** when necessary) of common cold	8 weeks	Adults 54/54	Pressed juice (80% m/m) in 22% ethanol	2 × 4 ml	No significant reduction in the incidence, duration or severity of colds and respiratory infections.
Hoheisel 1997 [50]	**Treatment** of acute URT infections, in some cases developing to common cold	Up to 10 days from onset of symptoms	Adults 60/60	Pressed juice (80% m/m) in 22% ethanol	20 drops every 2 hours on day 1. 3 × 20 drops daily thereafter.	Significantly fewer 'real' colds developed ($p<0.044$). Shorter duration of URT infections and 'real' colds.
Berg 1998 [51]	**Prophylaxis** of URT infections	28 days preceding a triathlon	Male athletes 14/13	Pressed juice (80% m/m) in 22% ethanol	3 × 40 drops	No URT infections in verum group; 3 in placebo group.
Schulten 2001 [52]	**Treatment** of common cold	10 days from onset of symptoms	Adults 41/39	Pressed juice (80% m/m) in 22% ethanol	2 × 5 ml	Significantly shorter duration of illness ($p = 0.018$).
Taylor 2003 [53]	**Treatment** of URT infections	Up to 10 days from onset of symptoms	Children (2-11 years) 263/261	Dried pressed juice in syrup	2 × 3.75 ml (2-5 years) 2 × 5 ml (6-11 years)	No significant differences from placebo in duration or severity of symptoms.
Yale 2004 [54]	**Treatment** of common cold	Up to 14 days from onset of symptoms	Adults 63/63	Freeze-dried pressed juice	3 × 100 mg	No significant differences in duration or severity of symptoms.
Sperber 2004 [55]	**Prophylaxis** of infection with nasally inoculated rhinovirus	7 days before and 7 days after intranasal inoculation	Adults 24/24	Pressed juice (80% m/m) in 22% ethanol	3 × 2.5 ml	No significant difference in rate of infection.

symptoms of URT infection and continued until all symptoms had resolved, up to a maximum of 10 days. Data were analyzed on 707 URT infections, 337 treated with echinacea and 370 with placebo, that occurred in 407 children, while 79 children completed their 4-month study periods without having an infection. No statistically significant differences between echinacea and placebo groups were observed with respect to duration (median: 9 days) or severity of symptoms, nor with respect to peak severity of symptoms, number of days of peak symptoms, number of days of fever or parental global assessment of severity. Thus pressed juice was ineffective in this study [53].

Patients recruited through advertisements and attending a clinic within 24 hours of the onset of symptoms of common cold were medically examined, and those satisfying the inclusion criteria were admitted to a placebo-controlled study. They were given capsules containing 100 mg of freeze-dried pressed juice from *Echinacea purpurea* aerial parts or lactose placebos, to be taken three times daily until cold symptoms were relieved (up to a maximum of 14 days), and were required to maintain a daily self-assessment record of the severity of a defined range of symptoms (sneezing, nasal discharge, nasal congestion, headache, sore throat, cough etc.). Statistical analysis revealed no significant difference between the echinacea (n = 63) and placebo (n = 63) groups with respect to total symptom scores, mean individual symptom scores or time to resolution of symptoms [54].

To allow better assessment of the effect of echinacea on infection rates, 48 volunteers were intranasally inoculated with a specific rhinovirus, RV-39, in a randomized double-blind, placebo-controlled study. For 7 days before and 7 days after inoculation the subjects received 3 × 2.5 ml daily of either an *Echinacea purpurea* preparation (pressed juice from aerial parts in a 22% alcohol base; n = 24) or placebo (n = 24). Laboratory evidence from virological and serological tests revealed that 92% of echinacea recipients and 95% of placebo recipients became infected with the rhinovirus. Thus echinacea did not decrease the rate of infection. From the frequency and severity of symptoms recorded in participants' diaries, clinical illness, i.e, the presence of a cold, developed in 58% of echinacea recipients and 82% of placebo recipients ($p = 0.114$), a promising trend in favour of echinacea but, unfortunately, not statistically significant with the small sample size [55]. In an earlier and fairly comparable study, 92 volunteers received an undefined echinacea preparation or placebo and were challenged with rhinovirus type 23. Infection occurred in 44 and 57%, and illness in 36 and 43%, of the echinacea- and placebo-treated subjects respectively. It was concluded that this echinacea preparation had no significant effect on either occurrence of infection or severity of illness [57].

Other complaints

In an open study, a control group of patients (n = 43) suffering from recurrent vaginal candidiasis and treated only with locally-applied antifungal cream containing econazole nitrate for 6 days had a very high relapse rate within 6 months of 60.5%. In contrast, a group of patients who (in addition to the econazole cream) were also treated orally with 3 × 30 drops of pressed juice from *E. purpurea* herb daily for 10 weeks (n = 60) had a relapse rate within 6 months of only 17% [58].

Based on the clinical evaluation of 4598 patients, topical application of an ointment containing 16% w/w of pressed juice from *E. purpurea* herb several times daily gave favourable results in the treatment of skin disorders. Healing of wounds, burns and herpes simplex was achieved in over 90% of cases, within 1 week on average. Success rates for inflamed skin ailments, eczema and leg ulcers were 85, 83 and 71% respectively after treatment for 8-15 days [59].

THERAPEUTICS

Actions

Immunomodulatory [2,32,35-37], topical anti-inflammatory [2,10,32,38,39,41] and wound-healing [2,32,33,40,41,60,61].

Any significant clinical antibacterial and antiviral activity probably follows indirectly from immune enhancement [33].

Indications

Internal: Treatment of upper respiratory tract infections including common cold [46,48,50,52] and influenza [44,45].
External: Poorly healing superficial wounds [33, 59,60,62].

Other uses, based on experience or tradition

Internal: Infections in general, including infections of the digestive, respiratory and urinary tracts [33]; inflammatory and purulent conditions including furunculosis, carbuncles, abscesses and acne; mild septicaemia [33,63].
External: Skin complaints [33] including burns, inflamed skin ailments, eczema and leg ulcers [59]; as a gargle for throat infections and tonsillitis [61,63].

Contraindications

None known, other than hypersensitivity to plants of the Compositae [33].

Side effects

Usually none. Increased incidence of skin rash

has been reported in one clinical study in children [53].

Interactions with other drugs
None known.

Dosage

Treatment of upper respiratory tract infections

Adult internal daily dose (as 2-4 divided doses)
Hydroethanolic extracts corresponding to 900 mg of dried root from *E. pallida* [44,64] or *E. purpurea* [45].
Hydroethanolic liquid extract from *Echinacea purpurea* herb and root, standardized to alkamides (0.25 mg/ml) and cichoric acid (2.5 mg/ml), 16 ml [48].
Pressed juice from *Echinacea purpurea* herb, stabilized in 22% ethanol, 8-10 ml [52,62].

During the first 24-48 hours from the onset of acute symptoms it may be beneficial to substantially increase the above daily doses, by a factor of 2 or 3, preferably by increasing the frequency (rather than amount) of unit doses [33,48,50].

For a more comprehensive scheme of dosages (mainly higher than those given above, which reflect only those used in positive clinical studies) see Mills and Bone [33].

External uses
As a gargle for throat infections, 50 ml of a decoction from root, three times daily [61].
For application to skin in wound healing and skin disorders, semi-solid preparations containing not less than 15% of pressed juice from *E. purpurea* herb [62].

SAFETY

A recent systematic review, based on clinical studies, case reports and surveillance programmes of national medicines regulatory authorities and the World Health Organization, concluded that echinacea products have a good safety profile when taken in the short term, while data on long term use is not available. If adverse events occur they tend to be transient and reversible, the most common being gastrointestinal or skin-related. However, atopic patients (i.e. those with a tendency to hypersensitivity states) and those with asthma should be cautious since rare allergic reactions have been reported [65].

Echinacea was generally well tolerated in the clinical studies listed in Tables 1-3, verum groups usually, but not always, reporting slightly more adverse events than placebo groups, but without statistically significant difference. Mild gastrointestinal complaints, headache or dizziness were the main adverse events. The only significantly higher incidence of an adverse event related to skin rash during a large study in children, 7.1% in the echinacea group compared to 2.7% in the placebo group ($p = 0.008$) [53].

An extensive toxicity study on pressed juice from *Echinacea purpurea* fresh herb showed that it is virtually non-toxic to rats and mice. The oral LD_{50} was over 15 g/kg in rats and 30 g/kg in mice, and after oral administration of pressed juice to male and female rats at up to 8 g/kg/day for 4 weeks no evidence of toxicity was revealed by laboratory tests or post-mortem examination. Tests for mutagenicity and carcinogenicity also gave negative results [66]. No embryotoxic effects were evident in rats or rabbits after oral administration of the pressed juice (80% in 22% ethanol) at dose levels up to 2.7 g/kg/day, and post-natal development was not affected when followed up in rats [67].

Pregnancy outcomes were compared between 206 women who took oral echinacea products during pregnancy (112 in the first trimester, 17 in all three trimesters) and a matched control group of 206 women who had not taken echinacea. The products included tablet, capsule and tincture preparations of *Echinacea* (*angustifolia, purpurea* and in one case *pallida*) at various dose levels, usually taken for 5-7 days. No statistical differences between groups were found in pregnancy outcome, delivery method, maternal weight gain, gestational age, birth weight, fetal distress or major malformations [68].

Although the pyrrolizidine alkaloids tussilagine and isotussilagine have been detected in dried whole plants of *Echinacea angustifolia* and *E. purpurea* in trace amounts (0.006%), they lack the 1,2-unsaturated necine ring structure necessary for hepatotoxicity and are considered harmless [2].

REGULATORY STATUS

Medicines

UK	Accepted for general sale, internal or external use [69].
France	Not listed in *Médicaments à base de plantes* [70].
Germany	Four Commission E monographs published [62,64,71,72], but with uses approved only for *Echinacea pallida* root and *E. purpurea* herb.

Food
Not used in foods.

REFERENCES

Current Pharmacopoeial Monographs

Ph. Eur.	Narrow-leaved Coneflower Root
USP	*Echinacea angustifolia* (dried rhizome and roots)
Ph. Eur.	Pale Coneflower Root
USP	*Echinacea pallida* (dried rhizome and roots)
Ph. Eur.	Purple Coneflower Herb†
USP	*Echinacea purpurea* Aerial Parts
Ph. Eur.	Purple Coneflower Root†
USP	*Echinacea purpurea* Root

† In draft form only [*Pharmeuropa* 2004] at time of going to press.

Literature References

1. Bauer R, Khan IA and Wagner H. TLC and HPLC Analysis of *Echinacea pallida* and *E. angustifolia* Roots. *Planta Medica* 1988, **54**, 426-430.
2. Bauer R and Wagner H. *Echinacea* Species as Potential Immunostimulatory Drugs. In: Wagner H and Farnsworth NR, editors. *Economic and Medicinal Plant Research, Volume 5*. ISBN 0-12-730066-X. London-San Diego-New York: Academic Press, 1991:253-321.
3. Pellati F, Benvenuti S, Magro L, Melegari M and Soragni F. Analysis of phenolic compounds and radical scavenging activity of *Echinacea spp. J. Pharmaceut. Biomed. Analysis* 2004, **35**, 289-301.
4. Perry NB, Burgess EJ and Glennie VL. *Echinacea* Standardization: Analytical Methods for Phenolic Compounds and Typical Levels in Medicinal Species. *J. Agric. Food. Chem.* 2001, **49**, 1702-1706.
5. Bergeron C, Livesey JF, Awang DVC, Arnason JT, Rana J, Baum BR and Letchamo W. A Quantitative HPLC Method for the Quality Assurance of *Echinacea* Products on the North American Market. *Phytochem. Analysis* 2000, **11**, 207-215.
6. Bauer R, Remiger P and Wagner H. Alkamides from the roots of *Echinacea angustifolia. Phytochemistry* 1989, **28**, 505-508.
7. Bauer R and Remiger P. TLC and HPLC Analysis of Alkamides in *Echinacea* Drugs. *Planta Medica* 1989, **55**, 367-371.
8. Laasonen M, Wennberg T, Harmia-Pulkkinen T and Vuorela H. Simultaneous Analysis of Alkamides and Caffeic Acid Derivatives for the Identification of *Echinacea purpurea, Echinacea angustifolia, Echinacea pallida* and *Parthenium integrifolium* Roots. *Planta Medica* 2002, **68**, 570-572.
9. Bauer R. Echinacea - Eine Arzneidroge auf dem Weg zum rationalen Phytotherapeutikum [Echinacea - A plant drug on the way to a rational phytomedicine]. *Dtsch. Apoth. Ztg.* 1994, **134**, 94-103 [GERMAN].
10. Bauer R. *Echinacea*: Biological Effects and Active Principles. Chapter 12 in: Lawson LD and Bauer R, editors. *Phytomedicines of Europe. Chemistry and Biological Activity.* ACS Symposium Series 691. Washington DC: American Chemical Society, 1998:140-157.
11. Heinzer F, Chavanne M, Meusy J-P, Maltre H-P, Giger E and Baumann TW. Ein Beitrag zur Klassifizierung der therapeutisch verwendeten Arten der Gattung Echinacea [A contribution to the classification of therapeutically used species of the genus Echinacea]. *Pharm. Acta Helv.* 1988, **63**, 132-136 [GERMAN].
12. Voaden DJ, Jacobson M. Tumor Inhibitors. 3. Identification and Synthesis of an Oncolytic Hydrocarbon from American Coneflower Roots. *J. Med. Chem.* 1972, **15**, 619-623.
13. European Scientific Cooperative on Phytotherapy. Echinaceae pallidae radix - Pale Coneflower Root. In: *ESCOP Monographs - The Scientific Foundation for Herbal Medicinal Products, 2nd ed.* Stuttgart-New York: Thieme; Exeter, UK: ESCOP, 2003:126-128.
14. Stuart DL and Wills RBH. Effect of Drying Temperature on Alkylamide and Cichoric Acid Concentrations of *Echinacea purpurea. J. Agric. Food Chem.* 2003, **51**, 1608-1610.
15. Perry NB, van Klink JW, Burgess EJ and Parmenter GA. Alkamide Levels in *Echinacea purpurea*: Effects of Processing, Drying and Storage. *Planta Medica* 2000, **66**, 54-56.
16. Gray DE, Pallardy SG, Garrett HE and Rottinghaus GE. Acute Drought Stress and Plant Age Effects on Alkamide and Phenolic Acid Content in Purple Coneflower Roots. *Planta Medica* 2003, **69**, 50-55.
17. Mølgaard P, Johnsen S, Christensen P and Cornett C. HPLC Method Validated for the Simultaneous Analysis of Cichoric Acid and Alkamides in *Echinacea purpurea* Plants and Products. *J. Agric. Food Chem.* 2003, **51**, 6922-6933.
18. Bodinet C and Beuscher N. Antiviral and Immunological Activity of Glycoproteins from *Echinacea purpurea* Radix. *Planta Medica* 1991, **57** (Suppl. 2), A33-A34.
19. Beuscher N, Scheit K-H, Bodinet C and Egert D. Modulation of Host Resistance by Polymeric Substances from *Baptisia tinctoria* and *Echinacea purpurea*. In: Masihi KN and Lange W, editors, *Immunotherapeutic Prospects of Infectious Diseases.* Berlin-Heidelberg: Springer-Verlag, 1990:59-63.
20. Schulte KE, Rücker G and Perlick J. Das Vorkommen von Polyacetylen-Verbindungen in *Echinacea purpurea* Mnch. und *Echinacea angustifolia* DC [The occurrence of polyacetylene compounds in *Echinacea purpurea* Mnch. and *Echinacea angustifolia* DC]. *Arzneim.-Forsch./Drug Res.* 1967, **17**, 825-829 [GERMAN/English summary].
21. Soicke H, Al-Hassan G and Görler K. Further Derivatives of Caffeic Acid from *Echinacea purpurea. Planta Medica* 1988, **54**, 175-176 [GERMAN/English summary].
22. Bauer R, Remiger P and Wagner H. Vergleichende DC- und HPLC-Analyse der Herba-Drogen von Echinacea purpurea, E. pallida und E. angustifolia (3. Mitt.) [Comparative TLC and HPLC analysis of the herb drugs of Echinacea purpurea, E. pallida und E. angustifolia (Part 3)]. *Dtsch. Apoth. Ztg.* 1988, **128**, 174-180 [GERMAN/English summary].
23. Proksch A and Wagner H. Structural analysis of a 4-O-methyl-glucuronoarabinoxylan with immunostimulating activity from *Echinacea purpurea. Phytochemistry* 1987, **26**, 1989-1993.
24. Wagner H, Proksch A, Riess-Maurer I, Vollmar A, Odenthal S, Stuppner H et al. Immunostimulierend wirkende Polysaccharide (Heteroglykane) aus höheren Pflanzen [Immunostimulating polysaccharides (heteroglykanes) from higher plants]. *Arzneim.-Forsch./Drug Res.* 1985, **35**, 1069-1075 [GERMAN/English summary].
25. Bomme U, Hölzl J, Heßler C and Stahn T. Wie beeinflußt die Sorte Wirkstoffgehalt und Ertrag von Echinacea purpurea (L.) Moench im Hinblick auf die pharmazeutische Nutzung? 1. Mitt. Ergebnisse des einjährigen Anbaues [How does the variety influence the active constituent content and yield of Echinacea purpurea (L.) Moench in relation to its pharmaceutical use? Part 1. Results of one-year cultivation]. *Landwirtschaftliches Jahrbuch* 1992, **69**, 149-164 [GERMAN/English summary].
26. Blaschek W, Döll M and Franz G. Echinacea polysaccharides: Analytical investigations on pressed juice and the preparation Echinacin®. *Z. Phytotherapie* 1998, **19**, 255-262 [GERMAN/English summary].
27. Bauer R. Standardisierung von *Echinacea-purpurea*-Preßsaft auf Cichoriensäure und Alkamide [Standardization of *Echinace purpurea* pressed juice on cichoric acid and alkamides]. *Z. Phytotherapie* 1997, **18**, 270-276 [GERMAN/English summary].
28. Nüsslein B, Kurzmann M, Bauer R and Kreis W. Enzymatic Degradation of Cichoric Acid in *Echinacea purpurea* Preparations. *J. Nat. Prod.* 2000, **63**, 1615-1618.
29. Classen B, Witthohn K and Blaschek W. Characterization of an arabinogalactan-protein isolated from pressed juice of *Echinacea purpurea* by precipitation with the β-glucosyl Yariv reagent. *Carbohydrate Res.* 2000, **327**, 497-504.

30. Luo X-B, Chen B, Yao S-Z and Zeng J-G. Simultaneous analysis of caffeic acid derivatives and alkamides in roots and extracts of *Echinacea purpurea* by high-performance liquid chromatography-photodiode array detection-electrospray mass spectrometry. *J. Chromatogr. A* 2003, **986**, 73-81.
31. European Scientific Cooperative on Phytotherapy. Echinaceae pallidae radix, Echinaceae purpureae herba, Echinaceae purpureae radix. In: *ESCOP Monographs - The Scientific Foundation for Herbal Medicinal Products, 2nd ed.* Stuttgart-New York: Thieme; Exeter, UK: ESCOP, 2003:126-141.
32. Bauer R and Wagner H. *Echinacea - Handbuch für Ärzte, Apotheker und andere Naturwissenschaftler [Echinacea - Handbook for Physicians, Pharmacists and other Scientists]*. ISBN 3-8047-0999-0. Stuttgart: Wissenschaftliche Verlagsgesellschaft, 1990 (182 pp.) [GERMAN].
33. Mills S and Bone K. Echinacea (*Echinacea* spp.) In: *Principles and Practice of Phytotherapy. Modern Herbal Medicine.* ISBN 0-443-06016-9. Edinburgh-London-New York: Churchill Livingstone, 2000:354-362.
34. Barrett B. Medicinal properties of *Echinacea*: A critical review. *Phytomedicine* 2003, **10**, 66-86.
35. Bauer R, Jurcic K, Puhlmann J and Wagner H. Immunologische In-vivo- und In-vitro-Untersuchungen mit Echinacea-Extrakten [*In vivo* and *in vitro* investigations with *Echinacea* extracts]. *Arzneim.-Forsch./Drug Res.* 1988, **38**, 276-281 [GERMAN/English summary].
36. Bauer R, Remiger P, Jurcic K and Wagner H. Beeinflussung der Phagozytose-Aktivität durch *Echinacea*-Extrakte [The influence of *Echinacea* extracts on phagocytic activity]. *Z. Phytotherapie* 1989, **10**, 43-48 [GERMAN/English summary].
37. Jurcic K, Melchart D, Holzmann M, Martin P, Bauer R, Doenecke A et al. Zwei Probandenstudien zur Stimulierung der Granulozytenphagozytose durch *Echinacea*-Extrakt-haltige Präparate [Two volunteer studies of the stimulation of granulocyte phagocytosis by *Echinacea* extract-containing preparations]. *Z. Phytotherapie* 1989, **10**, 67-70 [GERMAN/English summary].
38. Tragni E, Tubaro A, Melis S and Galli CL. Evidence from two classic irritation tests for an anti-inflammatory action of a natural extract, Echinacina B. *Food Chem. Toxicol.* 1985, **23**, 317-319.
39. Tragni E, Galli CL Tubaro A, Del Negro P and Della Loggia R. Anti-inflammatory activity of *Echinacea angustifolia* fractions separated on the basis of molecular weight. *Pharmacol. Res. Commun.* 1988, **20**, 87-90.
40. Kinkel H-J, Plate M and Tüllner H-U. Effect of Echinacin® ointment in healing of skin lesions. *Med. Klin.* 1984, **79**, 580-583 [GERMAN/English summary].
41. Speroni E, Govoni P, Guizzardi S, Renzulli C and Guerra MC. Anti-inflammatory and cicatrizing activity of *Echinacea pallida* Nutt. root extract. *J. Ethnopharmacol.* 2002, **79**, 265-272.
42. Melchart D, Walther E, Linde K, Brandmaier R and Lersch C. Echinacea Root Extracts for the Prevention of Upper Respiratory Tract Infections. A Double-blind, Placebo-controlled Randomized Trial. *Arch. Fam. Med.* 1998, **7**, 541-545.
43. Turner RB, Bauer R, Woelkart K, Hulsey TC and Gangemi JD. An Evaluation of *Echinacea angustifolia* in Experimental Rhinovirus Infections. *N. Engl. J. Med.* 2005, **353**, 341-348.
44. Bräunig B and Knick E. Therapeutische Erfahrungen mit Echinaceae pallidae radix bei grippalen Infekten. Ergebnisse einer plazebokontrollierten Doppelblindstudie [Therapeutic experiences with Echinaceae pallidae radix in influenzal infections. Results of a placebo-controlled, double-blind study]. *Naturheilpraxis* 1993, **46**, 72-75 [GERMAN].
Also published in English as:
Dorn M, Knick E and Lewith G. Placebo-controlled, double-blind study of Echinaceae pallidae radix in upper respiratory tract infections. *Complementary Therap. Med.* 1997, **5**, 40-42.
45. Bräunig B, Dorn M and Knick E. Echinaceae purpureae radix: zur Stärkung der körpereigenen Abwehr bei grippalen Infekten [Echinaceae purpureae radix: for strengthening the body's resistance in influenzal infections]. *Z. Phytotherapie* 1992, **13**, 7-13 [GERMAN].
46. Brinkeborn RM, Shah DV and Degenring FH. Echinaforce® and other fresh plant preparations in the treatment of common cold. A randomized, placebo-controlled, double-blind clinical trial. *Phytomedicine* 1999, **6**, 1-6.
47. Barrett BP, Brown RL, Locken K, Maberry R, Bobula JA and D'Alessio D. Treatment of the Common Cold with Unrefined Echinacea. A Randomized, Double-Blind, Placebo-Controlled Trial. *Ann. Intern. Med.* 2002, **137**, 939-946.
48. Goel V, Lovlin R, Barton R, Lyon MR, Bauer R, Lee TDG and Basu TK. Efficacy of a standardized echinacea preparation (Echinilin™) for the treatment of the common cold: a randomized, double-blind, placebo-controlled trial. *J. Clin Pharm. Ther.* 2004, **29**, 75-83.
49. Schöneberger D. Einfluss der immunstimulierenden Wirkung von Preßsaft aus Herba Echinaceae purpureae auf Verlauf und Schweregrad von Erkältungskrankheiten [Influence of the immunostimulating effect of pressed juice from Herba Echinaceae purpureae on the course and severity of common colds]. *Forum Immunologie* 1992, **2**, 18-22 [GERMAN].
Also published in English as:
Grimm W, Müller H-H. A Randomized Controlled Trial of the Effect of Fluid Extract of Echinacea purpurea on the Incidence and Severity of Colds and Respiratory Infections. *American J. Med.* 1999, **106**, 138-143.
50. Hoheisel O, Sandberg M, Bertram S, Bulitta M and Schäfer M. Echinagard treatment shortens the course of the common cold: a double-blind, placebo-controlled clinical trial. *Eur. J. Clin. Res.* 1997, **9**, 261-268.
51. Berg A, Northoff H, König D, Weinstock C, Grathwohl D, Parnham MJ et al. Influence of Echinacin (EC31) treatment on the exercise-induced immune response in athletes. *J. Clin. Res.* 1998, **1**, 367-380.
52. Schulten B, Bulitta M, Ballering-Brühl B, Köster U and Schäfer M. Efficacy of *Echinacea purpurea* in patients with a common cold. A placebo-controlled, randomised, double-blind clinical trial. *Arzneim.-Forsch./Drug Res.* 2001, **51**, 563-568.
53. Taylor JA, Weber W, Standish L, Quinn H, Goesling J, McGann M and Calabrese C. Efficacy and Safety of Echinacea in Treating Upper Respiratory Tract Infections in Children. A Randomized Controlled Trial. *JAMA* 2003, **290**, 2824-2830.
54. Yale SH and Liu K. *Echinacea purpurea* Therapy for the Treatment of the Common Cold. A Randomized, Double-blind, Placebo-controlled Clinical Trial. *Arch. Intern. Med.* 2004, **164**, 1237-1241.
55. Sperber SJ, Shah LP, Gilbert RD, Ritchey TW and Monto AS. *Echinacea purpurea* for Prevention of Experimental Rhinovirus Colds. *Clin. Infect. Dis.* 2004, **38**, 1367-1371.
56. Melchart D, Linde K, Worku F, Bauer R and Wagner H. Immunomodulation with Echinacea - a systematic review of controlled clinical trials. *Phytomedicine* 1994, **1**, 245-254.
57. Turner RB, Riker DK and Gangemi JD. Ineffectiveness of Echinacea for Prevention of Experimental Rhinovirus Colds. *Antimicrob. Agents Chemother.* 2000, **44**, 1708-1709.
58. Coeugniet E and Kühnast R. Rezidivierende Candidiasis. Adjuvante Immuntherapie mit verschiedenen Echinacin®-Darreichungsformen [Recurrent candidiasis. Adjuvant immunotherapy with various Echinacin®-dosage forms]. *Therapiewoche* 1986, **36**, 3352-3358 [GERMAN/English summary].
59. Viehmann P. Erfahrungen mit einer Echinacea-haltigen Hautsalbe [Experiences with an echinacea-containing ointment]. *Erfahrungsheilkunde* 1978, **27**, 353-358 [GERMAN].
60. Weiss RF. Wounds and Other Injuries: *Echinacea purpurea*. In: *Herbal Medicine* (translated from the 6th German edition of *Lehrbuch der Phytotherapie*). ISBN 0-906584-19-1. Gothenburg: AB Arcanum, Beaconsfield, UK: Beaconsfield Publishers, 1988: 342-344.

61. Chevallier A. Echinacea - Purple Coneflower. In: *Encyclopedia of Medicinal Plants, 2nd ed.* ISBN 0-7513-1209-6. London-New York: Dorling Kindersley, 2001:94.
62. Echinaceae purpureae herba. German Commission E Monograph published in: Bundesanzeiger No. 43 of 2 March 1989.
63. Echinacea. In: *British Herbal Pharmacopoeia* 1983. ISBN 0-903032-07-4. Bournemouth: British Herbal Medicine Association, 1983.
64. Echinaceae pallidae radix. German Commission E Monograph published in: Bundesanzeiger No. 162 of 29 August 1992.
65. Huntley AL, Thompson Coon J and Ernst E. The Safety of Herbal Medicinal Products Derived from *Echinacea* Species - A Systematic Review. *Drug Safety* 2005, **28**, 387-400.
66. Mengs U, Clare CB and Poiley JA. Toxicity of *Echinacea purpurea*: Acute, subacute and genotoxicity studies. *Arzneim.-Forsch./Drug Res.* 1991, **41**, 1076-1081.
67. Mengs U, Leuschner J and Marshall RR. Toxicity studies with Echinacin. In: Abstracts of 3rd International Congress on Phytomedicine. Munich, 11-13 October 2000. Published as: *Phytomedicine* 2000, **7** (Suppl. 2), 32 (Abstract SL-63).
68. Gallo M, Sarkar M, Au W, Pietrzak K, Comas B, Smith M et al. Pregnancy Outcome Following Gestational Exposure to Echinacea. A Prospective Controlled Study. *Arch. Intern. Med.* 2000, **160**, 3141-3143.
69. Echinacea. In: UK Statutory Instrument 1984 No. 769. The Medicines (Products other than Veterinary Drugs) (General Sale List) Order 1984. Schedule 1, Table A.
70. *Médicaments à base de plantes.* ISBN 2-911473-02-7. Saint-Denis Cedex, France: Agence du Médicament, 1998.
71. Echinaceae angustifoliae herba; Echinaceae angustifoliae radix; Echinaceae pallidae herba. German Commission E Monograph published in: Bundesanzeiger No. 162 of 29 August 1992.
72. Echinaceae purpureae radix. German Commission E "Stoffcharacteristik" (monograph for an unapproved component of herbal combinations) published in: Bundesanzeiger No. 162 of 29 August 1992.
73. Blumenthal M, senior editor. Echinacea Angustifolia herb and root/Pallida herb; Echinacea Purpurea root. In: *The Complete German Commission E Monographs - Therapeutic Guide to Herbal Medicines.* ISBN 0-9655555-0-X. Austin, Texas: American Botanical Council, 1998:327-328 and 391-393.

REGULATORY GUIDELINES FROM OTHER EU COUNTRIES

GERMANY

Commission E monographs:

Echinaceae angustifoliae herba (Schmalblättriges Sonnenhutkraut); Echinaceae angustifoliae radix (Schmalblättrige Sonnenhutwurzel); Echinaceae pallidae herba (Blaßfarbenes Kegelblumenkraut) [71].

Echinaceae purpureae radix (Purpursonnenhutwurzel) [72].

As the above two monographs are negative, i.e. no uses approved for *Echinacea angustifolia* herb or root, *E. pallida* herb or *E. purpurea* root, the texts are not included here, but English translations are available elsewhere [73].

Commission E monograph: Echinaceae pallidae radix (Echinacea-pallida-Wurzel) [64].

Pharmacological properties, pharmacokinetics, toxicology
Experiments in animals: In the carbon clearance test, alcoholic extracts from the root increased the rate of elimination of carbon particles by a factor of 2.2.
In vitro: In granulocyte smears, alcoholic extracts from the root at initial concentrations of 10^{-2} to 10^{-4} mg/ml increased the rate of phagocytosis by 23%.

Uses
As supportive therapy for influenza-like infections.

Contraindications
From fundamental considerations, not to be used in cases of progressive systemic illness such as tuberculosis, leucosis, collagenosis, multiple sclerosis, AIDS, HIV infection and other auto-immune diseases.

Side effects
None known.

Special precautions for use
None known.

Use in pregnancy and lactation
Nothing known.

Interactions with other drugs
None known.

Dosage
Unless otherwise prescribed, daily dose: tincture (1:5, ethanol 50%V/V) from native dry extract (7-11:1, ethanol 50%), corresponding to 900 mg of crude drug.

No information is available on the dosage for children.

Mode of administration
Liquid dosage forms for oral use.

Duration of administration
Not more than 8 weeks.

Overdosage
Nothing known.

Special warnings
None known.

Effects on driving or operating machinery
None known.

Commission E monograph: Echinaceae purpureae herba (Purpursonnenhutkraut) [62].

Uses
Internal: As supportive treatment for recurrent infections of the respiratory tract and the lower urinary tract.
External: Poorly healing superficial wounds.

Contraindications
Internal: Progressive systemic illnesses such as tuberculosis, leucosis, collagenosis and multiple sclerosis.
Not to be administered parenterally to persons prone to allergies, especially to plants of the Compositae, nor during pregnancy.
Note: Parenteral administration of the drug can adversely affect the metabolic status of diabetics.
External: None known.

Side effects
Oral and external use: None known.
Parenteral use: Depending on the dose, shivers, short-lived feverish reactions, nausea and vomiting may occur. In individual cases, allergic reactions of the instant type are possible.

Interactions with other drugs
None known.

Dosage
Unless otherwise prescribed:
Internal daily dose: 6-9 ml of pressed juice or equivalent preparations.
Parenteral use: Individually adjusted to the type and severity of illness and the specific properties of the preparation used. Parenteral use requires, especially for children, a graduated dosage scheme, which must be substantiated by the manufacturer of the particular preparation.
External: Semi-solid preparations containing at least 15% of pressed juice.

Mode of administration
Fresh plant juice and galenic preparations from it, for internal and external use.

Duration of administration
Preparations for parenteral use: Not more than 3 weeks.
Preparations for oral and external use: Not more than 8 weeks.

Actions
In human and/or animal studies echinacea preparations administered parenterally and/or orally have an immunobiological effect. For example, they increase the number of white blood cells and spleen cells, activate the phagocytic activity of human granulocytes and cause fevers.

EUCALYPTUS LEAF **Myrtaceae**

Eucalypti folium

Definition
Eucalyptus Leaf consists of the dried leaves from older branches of *Eucalyptus globulus* Labill.

CONSTITUENTS

☐ ***Essential oil***, 0.7-3.5% V/m (Ph. Eur. min. 2.0% V/m in whole leaf, 1.5% in cut leaf), containing principally 1,8-cineole (= eucalyptol, 36-82%) together with α-pinene (3-33%), *p*-cymene (0.4-8%), limonene (0-9%), α-terpenyl acetate and other monoterpenes. Small amounts of sesquiterpenes such as globulol and aromadendrene are also present [1-5].

Average results from steam distillation of 25 leaf samples from Spain included: 1,8-cineole (69.1%), α-pinene (12.3%), limonene (3.1%), α-terpenyl acetate (2.1%) and globulol (3.4%) [3]. Moroccan oil showed a seasonal variation in 1,8-cineole content of 62-82% (m/m on dry basis) [1].

Steam-distilled oil from *Eucalyptus globulus* leaf does not generally meet the compositional requirements for Eucalyptus Oil Ph. Eur. (not less than 70% of 1,8-cineole, 2-8% of α-pinene, 4-12% of limonene etc.), which may be obtained from certain other *Eucalyptus* species besides *E. globulus* and undergoes a rectification process after distillation.

☐ ***Phloroglucinol-terpene compounds*** Macrocarpals A-E [6] and H-J [7,8], in which isopentyl phloroglucinol dialdehyde is coupled to a sesquiterpene structure. Eucalyptone, with a similar structure, is also present [8,9].

12 compounds with related phloroglucinol-terpene structures (some monoterpenic, others sesquiterpenic), called euglobals, have been isolated from the flower buds of *E. globulus* [10-13]. At least the major compound, euglobal-III (sesquiterpenic), has also been isolated from eucalyptus leaf with a 0.001% yield [10].

☐ ***Leaf wax***, 0.15-0.3% from fresh leaves [14,15], containing a complex mixture of long-chain aliphatic compounds, principally the C_{33} β-diketone *n*-tritriacontane-16,18-dione (ca. 56%) [14] with a smaller amount of its 4-hydroxy derivative [15] and various esters, alcohols, acids and hydrocarbons [14]. 5-Hydroxy-7,4′-dimethoxy-6,8-dimethylflavone (eucalyptin, 2.8%) [14], other flavones [16] and the triterpenoid 11,12-dehydro-ursolic lactone acetate [14] are also present.

☐ ***Tannins*** Proanthocyanidins (2.1-3.5 mg/g) and ellagitannins (ca. 3.7 mg/g) [17] have been identified together with small amount of ellagic and gallic acids [17,18].

The total phenols content of *E. globulus* leaf was determined as 51-59 mg/g by a colorimetric method [17].

☐ ***Flavonoids*** Quercetin and its glycosides rutin [19] and quercitrin [18,19]. Luteolin (32-51 ppm) and apigenin (22-44 ppm) have also been identified in some samples [18].

Published Assay Methods
Flavonoids, phenolic acids and aldehydes by HPLC [20]. Low MW polyphenols by HPLC [18]. Eucalyptus oil components by GC-MS [21]. Cineole in eucalyptus oil by near-infrared spectroscopy [22].

PHARMACOLOGY

In vitro

Eucalyptus leaf extracts
A 50%-methanolic extract from eucalyptus leaf exhibited significant spasmolytic activity in isolated

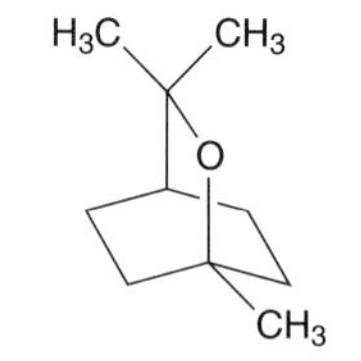

1,8-Cineole (eucalyptol)

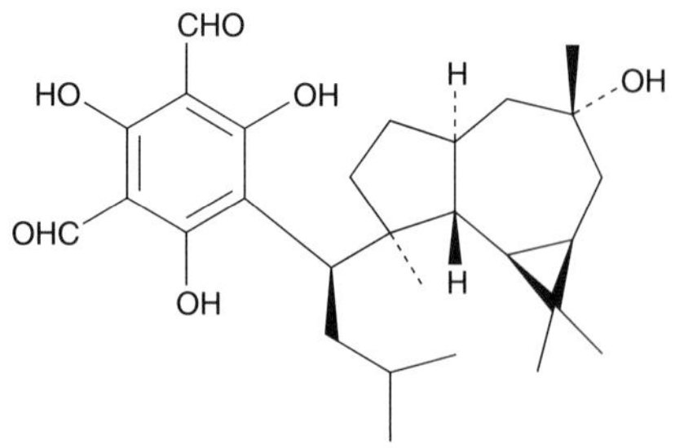

Macrocarpal A

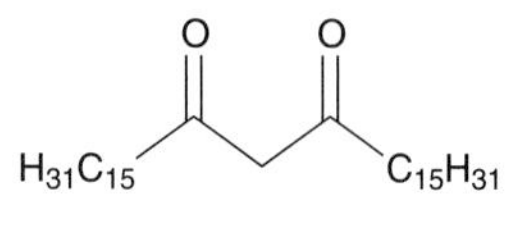

n-Tritriacontane-16,18-dione

guinea pig ileum ($p<0.05$), inhibiting spontaneous contractions of the circular smooth muscle (IC_{50} 753 µg/ml) and acetylcholine- and barium chloride-induced contractions of the longitudinal smooth muscle (IC_{50} values of 227 and 137 µg/ml respectively) [23].

An aqueous extract of *Eucalyptus globulus* leaf exhibited antihyperglycaemic activity in a series of experiments. In mouse abdominal muscle, extract equivalent to 0.5 g leaf/litre enhanced 2-deoxy-glucose transport by 50%, glucose oxidation by 60% and incorporation of glucose into glycogen by 90%. In clonal rat pancreatic cells, acute 20-minute incubations with extract equivalent to 0.25-0.5 g leaf/litre evoked a stepwise 70-160% enhancement of insulin secretion [24].

In antibacterial screening of plants traditionally used in the treatment of infected skin lesions, an aqueous extract from eucalyptus leaf showed outstanding antibacterial activity against *Staphylococcus aureus* (Gram positive) and *Escherichia coli* (Gram negative) with minimum inhibitory concentrations of 0.07-0.09 mg dry extract per ml [25].

Eucalyptus oil
The ciliary beat frequency of human nasal respiratory cells (not protected by a mucus layer), harvested from healthy volunteers and observed *in vitro* by video-interference-contrast microscopy, dose-dependently decreased on exposure for 30 minutes to high concentrations of eucalyptus oil vapour. At a vapour concentration of 7.5 g/m^3, which is higher than would normally be achieved by steam inhalation of essential oils as cold remedies, the decrease was –32.5% ($p<0.01$) compared to ambient air as control [26].

Eucalyptus oil (*E. globulus*) was found to have moderate antibacterial activity against resistant pathogenic bacterial strains found in hospital environments, including *E. coli*, *Staphylococcus aureus*, *Salmonella typhi*, *Pseudomonas aeruginosa* and others, and was particularly effective against a *Streptococcus* strain from bronchial aspirate [27].

Macrocarpals
Macrocarpals A-D and H (and the related compound eucalyptone) inhibited oral Gram-positive cariogenic and Gram-negative periodontopathic bacteria with MICs of 0.20-3.13 and 0.20-6.25 µg/ml respectively, revealing antibacterial properties greater than those of thymol (MIC 200-400 and 50-200 µg/ml respectively), which is used as a wide-spectrum oral antibacterial agent. Macrocarpals A-D and H-J (and eucalyptone) at 100 µg/ml strongly inhibited adherent, water-insoluble glucan synthesis by glucosyltransferase with greater effect than (–)-epigallocatechin, a known glucosyltransferase inhibitor. These substances may therefore be useful for the maintenance of oral health [7].

Macrocarpals A-E are reported to significantly inhibit HIV reverse transcriptase [6]. Euglobal-III had a strong inhibitory effect on Epstein-Barr virus activation (an indication of inhibition of skin tumours) [28].

In vivo

Eucalyptus leaf
Incorporation of eucalyptus leaf into the diet (62.5 g/kg body weight) and drinking water (2.5 g/litre) of streptozotocin (STZ)-treated diabetic mice for 20 days significantly reduced plasma glucose levels ($p<0.05$) and associated weight loss ($p<0.05$), as well as polydipsia ($p<0.001$), compared to STZ mice given a normal diet [24]; this confirmed earlier experiments [29]. It was concluded that *Eucalyptus globulus* leaf represents an effective antihyperglycaemic dietary adjunct for the treament of diabetes [24].

Eucalyptus oil
Eucalyptus oil administered intragastrically to guinea pigs in doses of 10 or 50 mg/kg body weight was effective in increasing the output of respiratory tract fluid (RTF), by 58% and 172% respectively in the second hour, compared to control animals treated with 12% ethanol at 5 ml/kg. Smaller increases in RTF output were also observed in other animals: in the second hour after eucalyptus oil at 50 mg/kg, 71% in rabbits, 76% in cats and 59% in dogs. From other tests it was concluded that eucalyptus oil is not a 'reflex expectorant'; probably it directly stimulates secretory cells of the respiratory tract [30].

Administration of eucalyptus oil to rabbits by steam inhalation had no effect on RTF output at dose levels relevant to therapeutic use in humans [31].

Eucalyptus oil had a repellent effect against mosquitoes (*Aedes* species) of 79% in laboratory trials and 93% in field trials, compared to 95% and 100% respectively for the widely used repellent diethyl toluamide (DEET) [21].

1,8-cineole
Moderate anti-inflammatory activity was exhibited by 1,8-cineole after oral administration to rats. In the rat paw oedema test it produced 26% inhibition at 100 mg/kg ($p<0.01$) and 46% at 400 mg/kg compared to 62% inhibition by indometacin at 5 mg/kg, and in the cotton pellet granuloma test 37-40% inhibition at 400 mg/kg ($p<0.001$) compared to 25-55% by indometacin at 5 mg/kg [32].

Pentobarbital-induced sleeping time was significantly increased and locomotor activity inhibited in mice by 1,8-cineole at 200-400 mg/kg, indicating a central nervous system depressant effect; in other tests cineole exhibited analgesic activity in mice [32].

Pharmacological studies in humans

Air passed through a flask containing eucalyptus oil at 80°C was administered for 5 minutes through a face mask to 31 volunteers, including 8 with nasal catarrh. No effect was observed on nasal resistance to airflow (measured by a nasal resistance meter), but the majority of subjects reported a cold sensation in the nose with a sensation of improved airflow; similar results were obtained with camphor and menthol vapours. Although the experiments provided no objective evidence (and none appears to exist) to support the long usage of these substances as 'decongestants', the authors concluded that stimulation of nasal cold receptors and sensation of improved airflow may be important for patient comfort, and more beneficial than an objective change, in the treatment of nasal congestion [33].

Pharmacokinetics

It has been demonstrated *in vitro* that 1,8-cineole is transformed by human liver microsomes into a single oxidised metabolite, 2-*exo*-hydroxy-1,8-cineole [34].

CLINICAL STUDIES

No modern clinical studies have been published on mono-preparations of eucalyptus leaf.

With regard to the antihyperglycaemic effects summarized above [24], it is interesting to note that in 1902 a Scottish doctor found an infusion of eucalyptus leaf to be very effective in some patients with diabetes, particularly in the early stages. Symptoms were rapidly eliminated in 15 patients, while the treatment was unsuccessful in 26 [35].

THERAPEUTICS

Medicinal use of dried eucalyptus leaf is mainly limited to teas and extemporaneous inhalations. Eucalyptus oil is much more widely employed and is a component of many proprietary inhalations, rubs and pastilles. However, the oil can be regarded as a separate subject, not covered here but summarized in an ESCOP monograph [36].

Actions

Expectorant [37,38], weakly spasmolytic [23,37], antihyperglycaemic [24], antibacterial [25,27,38]. Also stated to be a stimulant and febrifuge [38].

Indications

None adequately substantiated by pharmacological or clinical studies.

Uses based on experience or tradition

Infections of the upper respiratory tract, including common cold [37,38]; catarrh; acute bronchial infections [39]; sore throat; sinusitis [38].

Contraindications

Inflammatory disorders of the gastrointestinal tract; liver complaints [37,40].

Side effects

In rare cases, gastrointestinal upset [40].

Interactions with other drugs

None known.

Dosage

Internal: Dried leaf in infusion, 4-6 g daily [37], average single dose 2 g; the hot infusion may be used as an inhalation [40]. Tincture (1:5 in 45% ethanol), 5-20 ml daily.

SAFETY

A tincture of eucalyptus leaf showed no mutagenic potential in the Ames test using *Salmonella typhimurium* strains TA98 and TA100 [41].

Eucalyptus oil has low toxicity [42,43]; the oral LD_{50} was determined as 3.32 g/kg in mice [44] and 4.44 g/kg in rats [45].

REGULATORY STATUS

Medicines

UK	No licences issued for products containing eucalyptus leaf. However, eucalyptus oil is accepted for general sale, internal or external use [46].
France	Accepted for specified indications [39].
Germany	Commission E monograph published, with approved uses [37].

Food

USA	Permitted as flavouring (21 CFR 172.510) [47].
Council of Europe	Permitted as flavouring, category 4 (with limit on eucalyptol under evaluation) [48].

REFERENCES

Current Pharmacopoeial Monographs

Ph. Eur. Eucalyptus Leaf

Literature References

1. Zrira SS and Benjilali BB. Seasonal Changes in the Volatile Oil and Cineole Contents of Five *Eucalyptus* Species Growing in Morocco. *J. Essent. Oil. Res.* 1996, **8**, 19-24.
2. Chalchat J-C, Muhayimana A, Habimana JB and Chabard JL. Aromatic Plants of Rwanda. II. Chemical Composition of Essential Oils of Ten *Eucalyptus* Species Growing in Ruhande Arboretum, Butare, Rwanda. *J. Essent. Oil Res.* 1997, **9**, 159-165.
3. Renedo J, Otero JA and Mira JR. Huile essentielle d'*Eucalyptus globulus* L. de Cantabrie (Espagne). Variation au cours de la distillation [Essential oil of *Eucalyptus globulus* L. from Cantabria (Spain). Variation in the course of distillation]. *Plantes Méd. Phytothér.* 1990, **24**, 31-35 [FRENCH/English summary].
4. Betts TJ. Solid Phase Microextraction of Volatile Constituents from Individual Fresh *Eucalyptus* Leaves of Three Species. *Planta Medica* 2000, **66**, 193-195.
5. De Medici D, Pieretti S, Salvatore G, Nicoletti M and Rasoanaivo P. Chemical Analysis of Essential Oils of Malagasy Medicinal Plants by Gas Chromatography and NMR Spectroscopy. *Flavour Fragrance J.* 1992, **7**, 275-281.
6. Nishizawa M, Emura M, Kan Y, Yamada H, Ogawa K and Hamanaka N. Macrocarpals: HIV-RTase inhibitors of *Eucalyptus globulus*. *Tetrahedron Letters* 1992, **33**, 2983-2986.
7. Osawa K, Yasuda H, Morita H, Takeya K and Itokawa H. Macrocarpals H, I and J from the Leaves of *Eucalyptus globulus*. *J. Nat. Prod.* 1996, **59**, 823-827.
8. Osawa K, Yasuda H, Morita H, Takeya K and Itokawa H. Configurational and Conformational Analysis of Macrocarpals H, I and J from *Eucalyptus globulus*. *Chem. Pharm. Bull.* 1997, **45**, 1216-1217.
9. Osawa K, Yasuda H, Morita H, Takeya K and Itokawa H. Eucalyptone from *Eucalyptus globulus*. *Phytochemistry* 1995, **40**, 183-184.
10. Sawada T, Kozuka M, Komiya T, Amano T and Goto M. Euglobal-III, a Novel Granulation Inhibiting Agent from *Eucalyptus globulus* Labill. *Chem. Pharm. Bull.* 1980, **28**, 2546-2548.
11. Amano T, Komiya T, Hori M, Goto M, Kozuka M and Sawada T. Isolation and characterization of euglobals from *Eucalyptus globulus* Labill. by preparative reversed-phase liquid chromatography. *J. Chromatogr.* 1981, **208**, 347-355.
12. Kozuka M, Sawada T, Kasahara F, Mizuta E, Amano T, Komiya T and Goto M. The Granulation-Inhibiting Principles from *Eucalyptus globulus* Labill. II. The Structures of Euglobal-Ia_1, -Ia_2, -Ib, -Ic, -IIa, -IIb and –IIc. *Chem. Pharm. Bull.* 1982, **30**, 1952-1963.
13. Kozuka M, Sawada T, Mizuta E, Kasahara F, Amano T, Komiya T and Goto M. The Granulation-Inhibiting Principles from *Eucalyptus globulus* Labill. II. The Structures of Euglobal-III, -IVb and –VII. *Chem. Pharm. Bull.* 1982, **30**, 1964-1973.
14. Horn DHS, Kranz ZH and Lamberton JA. The composition of *Eucalyptus* and some other leaf waxes. *Aust. J. Chem.* 1964, **17**, 464-476.
15. Osawa T and Namiki M. Natural Antioxidants Isolated from *Eucalyptus* Leaf Waxes. *J. Agric. Food. Chem.* 1985, **33**, 777-780.
16. Wollenweber E and Kohorst G. Epicuticular Leaf Flavonoids from *Eucalyptus* Species and from *Kalmia latifolia*. *Z. Naturforsch.* 1981, **36c**, 913-915.
17. Cadahía E, Conde E, García-Vallejo MC and Fernández de Simón B. High Pressure Liquid Chromatographic Analysis of Polyphenols in Leaves of *Eucalyptus camaldulensis, E. globulus* and *E. rudis*: Proanthocyanidins, Ellagitannins and Flavonol Glycosides. *Phytochem. Analysis* 1997, **8**, 78-83.
18. Conde E, Cadahía E and García-Vallejo MC. Low Molecular Weight Polyphenols in Leaves of *Eucalyptus camaldulensis, E. globulus* and *E. rudis. Phytochem. Analysis* 1997, **8** 186-193.
19. Boukef K, Balansard G, Lallemand M and Bernard P. Étude des hétérosides et aglycones flavoniques isolés des feuilles d'*Eucalyptus globulus* Labill. [Study of glycosides and aglycones isolated from leaves of *Eucalyptus globulus* Labill.]. *Plantes Méd. Phytothér.* 1976, **10**, 30-35 [FRENCH/English summary].
20. Conde E, Cadahía E and García-Vallejo MC. HPLC Analysis of Flavonoids and Phenolic Acids and Aldehydes in *Eucalyptus* spp. *Chromatographia* 1995, **41**, 657-659.
21. Thorsell W, Mikiver A, Malander I and Tunón H. Efficacy of plant extracts and oils as mosquito repellents. *Phytomedicine* 1998, **5**, 311-323.
22. Wilson ND, Watt RA and Moffat AC. A near-infrared method for the assay of cineole in eucalyptus oil as an alternative to the official BP method. *J. Pharm. Pharmacol.* 2001, **53**, 95-102.
23. Izzo AA, Capasso R, Senatore F, Seccia S and Morrica P. Spasmolytic Activity of Medicinal Plants Used for the Treatment of Disorders Involving Smooth Muscles. *Phytotherapy Res.* 1996, **10**, S107-S108.
24. Gray AM and Flatt PR. Antihyperglycemic Actions of *Eucalyptus globulus* (Eucalyptus) are Associated with Pancreatic and Extra-Pancreatic Effects in Mice. *J. Nutr.* 1998, **128**, 2319-2323.
25. Brantner A and Grein E. Antibacterial activity of plant extracts used externally in traditional medicine. *J. Ethnopharmacol.* 1994, **44**, 35-40.
26. Riechelmann H, Brommer C, Hinni M and Martin C. Response of Human Ciliated Respiratory Cells to a Mixture of Menthol, Eucalyptus Oil and Pine Needle Oil. *Arzneim.-Forsch./Drug Res.* 1997, **47**, 1035-1039.
27. Benouda A, Hassar M and Benjilali B. Les propriétés antiséptiques des huiles essentielles *in vitro*, testées contre des germes pathogènes hospitaliers [The antiseptic properties of essential oils *in vitro*, tested against pathogenic hospital germs]. *Fitoterapia* 1988, **59**, 115-119 [FRENCH/English summary].
28. Takasaki M, Konoshima T, Fujitani K, Yoshida S, Nishimura H, Tokuda H et al. Inhibitors of Skin-Tumor Promotion. VIII. Inhibitory Effects of Euglobals and Their Related Compounds on Epstein-Barr Virus Activation. *Chem. Pharm. Bull.* 1990, **38**, 2737-2739.
29. Swanston-Flatt SK, Day C, Bailey CJ and Flatt PR. Traditional plant treatments for diabetes. Studies in normal and streptozotocin diabetic mice. *Diabetologia* 1990, **33**, 462-464.
30. Boyd EM and Pearson GL. On the expectorant action of volatile oils. *Am. J. Med. Sci.* 1946, **211**, 602-610.
31. Boyd EM and Sheppard EP. The effect of steam inhalation of volatile oils on the output and composition of respiratory tract fluid. *J. Pharmacol. Exp. Ther.* 1968, **163**, 250-256.
32. Santos FA and Rao VSN. Anti-inflammatory and Antinociceptive Effects of 1,8-Cineole, a Terpene Oxide Present in many Plant Essential Oils. *Phytotherapy Res.* 2000, **14**, 240-244.
33. Burrow A, Eccles R and Jones AS. The effects of camphor, eucalyptus and menthol vapour on nasal resistance to airflow and nasal sensation. *Acta Otolaryngol.* 1983, **96**, 157-161.
34. Miyazawa M and Shindo M. Biotransformation of 1,8-cineole by human liver microsomes. *Nat. Prod. Lett.* 2001, **15**, 49-53.
35. Faulds AG. Eucalyptus in the treatment of diabetes. *Glasgow Med. J.* 1902, **57**, 342-348.
36. European Scientific Cooperative on Phytotherapy. Eucalypti aetheroleum - Eucalyptus Oil. In: *ESCOP Monographs - The Scientific Foundation for Herbal Medicinal Products, 2nd ed.* Stuttgart-New York: Thieme; Exeter, UK: ESCOP, 2003:150-6.
37. Eucalypti folium: German Commission E monograph published in: Bundesanzeiger No. 177a of 24 September 1986, amended in Bundesanzeiger No. 50 of 13 March 1990.
38. Chevallier A. Eucalyptus. In: *The Encyclopedia of Medicinal Plants*. ISBN 0-7513-0314-3. London-New York-Stuttgart: Dorling Kindersley, 1996:94.
39. Eucalyptus. In: *Médicaments à base de plantes*. ISBN 2-911473-02-7. Saint-Denis Cedex, France: Agence du Médicament, 1998.

40. Stahl-Biskup E, Wichtl M and Henke D. Eucalyptusblätter - Eucalypti folium. In: Hartke K, Hartke H, Mutschler E, Rücker G and Wichtl M, editors. *Kommentar zum Europäischen Arzneibuch [Commentary on the European Pharmacopoeia]*. Stuttgart: Wissenschaftliche Verlagsgesellschaft, 1999 (12. Lfg.):E 44 [GERMAN].
41. Schimmer O, Krüger A, Paulini H and Haefele F. An evaluation of 55 commercial plant extracts in the Ames mutagenicity test. *Pharmazie* 1994, **49**, 448-451.
42. Tisserand R and Balacs T. Safety Index: Part 1. In: *Essential Oil Safety - A Guide for Health Care Professionals.* Edinburgh: Churchill-Livingstone, 1995:201-211.
43. Opdyke DLJ. Monographs on fragrance raw materials: Eucalyptus oil. *Food Cosmet. Toxicol.* 1975, **13**, 107-108.
44. Ohsumi T, Kuroki K, Kimura T and Murakami Y. Study on acute toxicities of essential oils used in endodontic treatment. *Kyushu Shika Gakkai Zasshi* 1984, **38**, 1064-1071 [JAPANESE]; through *Chem. Abstr.* 1985, **102**, 179007.
45. von Skramlik E. Über die Giftigkeit und Verträglichkeit von ätherischen Ölen [The toxicity and tolerability of essential oils]. *Pharmazie* 1959, **14**, 435-445 [GERMAN].
46. Eucalyptus Oil. In: UK Statutory Instrument 1984 No. 769. The Medicines (Products other than Veterinary Drugs) (General Sale List) Order 1984. Schedule 1, Table A.
47. Eucalyptus globulus leaves. In: Section 172.510 of USA Code of Federal Regulations, Title 21, Food and Drugs, Parts 170 to 199. Revised as of April 1, 2000.
48. Eucalyptus globulus Labill. In: *Natural Sources of Flavourings. Report No. 1.* ISBN 92-871-4324-2. Strasbourg: Council of Europe Publishing, 2000.

REGULATORY GUIDELINES FROM OTHER EU COUNTRIES

FRANCE

Médicaments à base de plantes [39]: Eucalyptus, feuille.

Therapeutic indications accepted

Oral and topical use
Traditionally used in the course of acute benign bronchial infections.

Topical use
Traditionally used in the event of blocked nose in colds.

GERMANY

Commission E monograph [37]: Eucalypti folium (Eucalyptusblätter).

Uses
Common cold ailments of the respiratory tract.

Contraindications
Inflammatory disorders of the gastrointestinal tract and the bile ducts; serious liver complaints. Eucalyptus preparations should not be applied to the face, especially the nose, of babies and young children.

Side effects
In rare cases nausea, vomiting and diarrhoea may occur after taking eucalyptus preparations.

Interactions with other drugs
None known.
Note: Eucalyptus oil causes induction of the detoxifying enzyme system in the liver. The effect of other medicines can therefore be weakened and/or shortened.

Dosage
Unless otherwise prescribed, average daily internal dose: 4-6 g of leaf; equivalent preparations. Tincture (in accordance with Erg. B6): daily dose 3-9 g.

Mode of administration
Comminuted drug for infusions and other galenic preparations for internal or external use.

Actions
Secretomotoric, expectorant, weakly spasmolytic.

FENNEL

Umbelliferae

Foeniculi fructus

Definitions

The European Pharmacopoeia includes monographs for two varieties of fennel:

Bitter Fennel consists of the dry cremocarps and mericarps of *Foeniculum vulgare* Miller subsp. *vulgare* var. *vulgare* (Miller) Thellung.

Sweet Fennel consists of the dry cremocarps and mericarps of *Foeniculum vulgare* Miller subsp. *vulgare* var. *dulce* (Miller) Thellung.

The literature can be vague or confusing at times with regard to subspecies and varieties of fennel, but the following botanical classification is accepted [1-5].

There are two subspecies of *Foeniculum vulgare* Miller:

- subsp. *piperitum* (Ucria) Coutinho, which is only found in the wild.

- subsp. *capillaceum* (Gilibert) Holmboe [synonym: subsp. *vulgare*], which is often cultivated and has three main varieties,
  - var. *vulgare* (Miller) Thellung, **bitter fennel**
  - var. *dulce* (Miller) Thellung, **sweet fennel**
  - var. *azoricum* (Miller) Thellung, **Florence fennel** - not of pharmaceutical interest but used in cooking and salads.

With experience, organoleptic differentiation between bitter and sweet fennel fruits is often possible, especially when samples of both are available to contrast. However, it is not always easy, and the descriptions and identification tests in the European Pharmacopoeia offer no clear distinction. As a rule, sweet fennel fruits have a lighter colour, and a taste and odour reminiscent of aniseed. Differentiation by TLC may be possible, based on the prominence (bitter fennel) or weakness (sweet fennel) of the fenchone band. However, quantitative determination by GC of anethole, fenchone and estragole levels in the essential oil offers the most reliable means of differentiation and is essential to ensure compliance with the requirements of the European Pharmacopoeia.

Bitter fennel is the more frequently used for medicinal purposes and the only type specified in the BPC 1973 [6] and the German Commission E monograph [7]. On the other hand, only sweet fennel is listed in guidance issued by the French authorities [8].

CONSTITUENTS

☐ ***Essential oil*** The European Pharmacopoeia monographs for bitter and sweet fennel stipulate rather demanding criteria for the essential oils obtained by distillation:

Bitter fennel

Yield:	Not less than 40 ml/kg (4.0% V/m, on dry basis).
Composition:	Not less than 60.0% of anethole and 15.0% of fenchone. Not more than 5.0% of estragole (= methyl chavicol).

Sweet fennel

Yield:	Not less than 20 ml/kg (2.0% V/m, on dry basis).
Composition:	Not less than 80.0% of anethole. Not more than 7.5% of fenchone and 10.0% of estragole.

Besides anethole, fenchone and estragole the oils contain smaller amounts of other monoterpenes such as limonene, α- and β-pinene, myrcene and γ-terpinene [2,9-11]. Data on fennel oils are abundant in the literature, but very varied and it is surprisingly

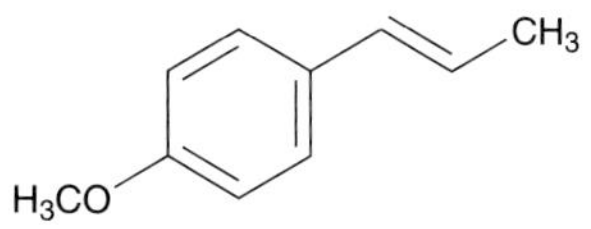

trans-Anethole

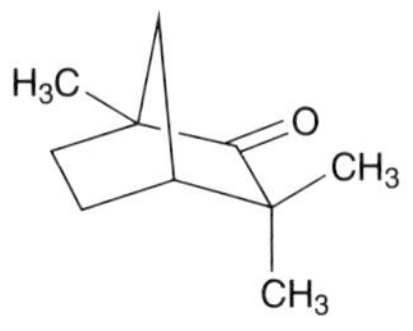

Fenchone

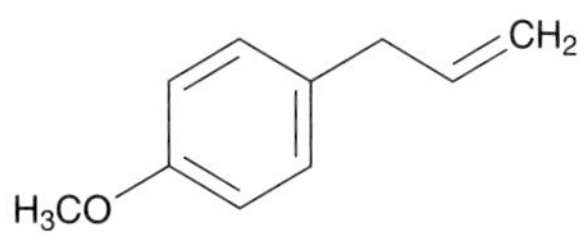

Estragole
(Methyl chavicol)

difficult to find reports describing hydrodistilled oils which satisfy the Ph. Eur. requirements with respect to both yield and composition. For example:

- Bitter fennel oils from fruits grown in Germany (yield 5.4%; *trans*-anethole 61.1%, fenchone 28.2%, estragole 2.1%) and USA (yield 6.1%; *trans*-anethole 75.8%, fenchone 15.1%, estragole 2.7%) [9] met all the Ph. Eur. criteria, whereas some other samples failed due to low content of *trans*-anethole (72.3%) [10] or fenchone (5.5-10.2%) [2] and/or low yields of 2.7-2.8% [2,10]. In a 2-year experiment in Hungary, with 13 different bitter fennel cultivars from Hungary, Italy, Korea, France, Belgium and other sources, the Ph. Eur. criteria were satisfied by essential oil from only 7 out of the 26 crops and only 2 cultivars satisfied the criteria in both years [4].

- Sweet fennel oil from fruits grown in Italy met all the Ph. Eur. criteria when distilled from powdered fruits (yield 2.2%; *trans*-anethole 86.1%, fenchone 1.5%, estragole 3.4%), but the yields were too low (1.6-1.8%) when distilled from crushed fruits [2].

Aspects of the hydrodistillation technique, such as the size of fennel fruit particles [2], the ratio of fruit to water in the distillation vessel and the duration of the distillation process [10], can influence the yield or composition of the oil sufficiently in some cases to make the difference between meeting or failing Ph. Eur. requirements.
□ ***Fixed oil***, 10-15%, containing (as glycerides) principally petroselinic acid (= *cis*-6-octadecenoic acid, C18:1 ω6; 72-74%) and linoleic acid (15-17%) together with oleic (5%), palmitic (4%), stearic (1%) and *cis*-vaccenic (0.4%) acids, as percentages of the total fruit oil [12].
□ ***Phenylpropanoids*** Chlorogenic acid, caffeic acid (0.02%) and small amounts of other caffeoylquinic and hydroxycinnamic acids [13,14].
□ ***Flavonoids*** Small amounts of flavonol glycosides (ca. 0.03% in total) including the 3-glucuronides and 3-arabinosides of quercetin and kaempferol, and also isoquercitrin and rutin [15,16].
□ ***Coumarins*** Very small amounts of several types: the simple hydroxycoumarins scopoletin, umbelliferone, osthenol and scoparone; the furanocoumarins bergapten, columbianetin, marmesin and xanthotoxin; and the pyranocoumarin seselin [17,18]. Sensitive assays revealed traces of photoactive furanocoumarins: ca. 0.5 ppm each of psoralen, 5-methoxypsoralen, isopimpinellin and imperatorin, and ca. 0.005 ppm of 8-methoxypsoralen [19].
□ ***Miscellaneous glycosides*** In a series of papers published from 1995 to 1998, a Japanese group reported isolation for the first time from fennel (in many cases for the first time from any source) of over 80 compounds, predominantly water-soluble glycosides, from methanolic extracts of the fruits [20-28]. The compounds are too numerous and varied to summarize here, and the majority will be present only in small amounts in the fruits. They range from simple alkyl glycosides (e.g. ethyl glucoside) [22] to di- and tri-glucosides of stilbene trimers [20]. The type of fennel investigated was described only as Foeniculi fructus, the fruit of *Foeniculum vulgare* Miller; this corresponds to the monograph of the JP [29].
□ ***Other constituents*** include phytosterols (β-sitosterol and stigmasterol) [17,18], α-amyrin [18] and vanillin [17].

Published Assay Methods

Essential oil components by GC [2,4] and GC-MS [2,30].

PHARMACOLOGY

In vitro

Fennel has a long tradition of use as a galactagogue [31] and is reputed to be mildly oestrogenic [32], although the mechanism of such activities remains unclear. A recent experiment demonstrated that fennel oil at 10-100 µg/ml did not stimulate the secretion of prolactin in pituitary cells *in vitro*. However, fennel oil at concentrations of 0.01-0.1 µg/ml stimulated the proliferation of oestrogen-dependent human MCF-7 breast cancer cells ($p<0.05$ compared to the control), confirming oestrogenic activity comparable to that of 1 nM of oestradiol. In one sense, this oestrogenic activity does not appear to fit well with the traditional use of fennel as a galactagogue during the lactation period, since oestrogens themselves inhibit lactation. On the other hand, *trans*-anethole, the main component of fennel oil, has been reported to be a dopamine antagonist, a property which should favour galactagogic activity (dopamine inhibits prolactin secretion) [33].

The spasmolytic activity of a 30%-ethanolic extract from bitter fennel has been demonstrated against acetylcholine- and carbachol-induced contractions [34], and also against histamine-induced contractions [35], in isolated guinea pig ileum (smooth muscle). On the other hand, fennel oil was shown to have a spasmogenic effect on isolated guinea-pig ileum [36,37], while the oil caused contracture and inhibition of the twitch response to nerve stimulation in a preparation of isolated rat phrenic nerve diaphragm (skeletal muscle) [37]. Fennel oil dose-dependently reduced the intensity of oxytocin-induced contractions ($p<0.01$ at 50 µg/ml) and PGE_2-induced contractions ($p<0.01$ at 10 and 20 µg/ml) in isolated rat uterus. The oil also reduced the frequency of contractions induced by PGE_2 (but not by oxytocin) [38].

Fennel extracts (extracted with ethanol, acetone or ether) [39] and fennel oil [40] exhibited moderate antimicrobial activity against *Escherichia coli*, *Staphylococcus aureus* (but not *Pseudomonas aeruginosa*) and the yeast *Candida albicans*.

An infusion from bitter fennel stimulated mucociliary transport in isolated ciliated epithelium from the frog oesophagus. This was regarded as an indication of expectorant activity [41].

In vivo

Oestrogenic effects
An acetone extract from fennel produced dose-dependent oestrogenic effects when orally administered to adult female ovariectomized rats at 0.5-2.5 mg/kg. It induced oestrus (by the 9th day in 20% of rats at 0.5 mg/kg, in all rats at 2.5 mg/kg) and led to increases in weight of the mammary glands, oviduct, endometrium, myometrium, cervix and vagina ($p<0.01$ to $p<0.001$ at 2.5 mg/kg). Treatment of mature male rats with the extract at 2.5 mg/kg/day for 15 days caused no appreciable changes in body or organ weights, but significant changes were observed in biochemical parameters of genital tissue [42]. Subsequent work by the same group demonstrated that administration of the acetone extract to ovariectomized rats at 1.5-2.5 mg/kg/day for 10 days significantly increased the weights of the cervix and vagina ($p<0.01$) [43].

Oestrogenic activity of *trans*-anethole was demonstrated by administering it orally to immature female rats at 80 mg/kg for 3 days. Uterine weights increased significantly, from 0.5 g/kg in control rats to 2 g/kg in treated animals, compared to 3 g/kg in animals given subcutaneous oestradiol valerate at 0.1 µg/rat/day ($p<0.001$) [44].

Anti-inflammatory effects
An orally administered dry 80%-ethanolic extract from sweet fennel inhibited carrageenan-induced rat paw oedema by 36% at 100 mg/kg ($p<0.01$), compared to 45% inhibition by indometacin at 5 mg/kg [45]. Similarly, a dry 80%-methanolic extract from fennel (type not stated), orally administered at 200 mg/kg, inhibited carrageenan-induced rat paw oedema by 69% after 3 hours ($p<0.05$); this dosage also inhibited arachidonic acid-induced ear oedema in mice by 70% after 3 hours ($p<0.05$). Central analgesic, antioxidant and type IV anti-allergic activities of the methanolic extract were also demonstrated at the same oral dosage [46].

Other effects
A dry ethanolic extract from fennel administered orally at 500 mg/kg showed strong diuretic and choleretic activity in rats, moderate analgesic activity in mice and moderate antipyretic activity in yeast-fevered mice [47].

Aqueous extracts from fennel produced hypotensive and diuretic effects in spontaneously hypertensive rats [48] and increased gastric acid secretion in anaesthetized rats ($p<0.02$) [49]. Addition of 0.5% of fennel to the diet of rats for 6 weeks shortened food transit time by 12% ($p<0.05$) [50] and a single dose of fennel given orally to rabbits stimulated stomach movement [51].

Inhalation of anethole or fenchone vapour (from 3 mg/kg added to a vaporizer) by urethanized rabbits increased the volume output and reduced the specific gravity of respiratory tract fluid [52].

Pharmacokinetics
Radioactively-labelled *trans*-anethole was rapidly absorbed after oral administration in doses of 1-250 mg to human volunteers; 54-69% of the dose was eliminated in the urine (where the principal metabolite was 4-methoxyhippuric acid) and 13-17% in exhaled carbon dioxide, while none was detected in the faeces [53].

CLINICAL STUDIES

Infantile colic
The long-established use of fennel in infantile colic was evaluated in a randomized, double-blind, placebo-controlled study conducted by paediatricians at two large clinics in St. Petersburg, Russia. Babies from 2 to 12 weeks of age with colic, diagnosed in accordance with the Wessel criteria (crying for 3 hours or more per day on at least 3 days per week) after exclusion of other conditions, were treated orally for 7 days, up to 4 times a day before feeding and at the onset of colic episodes, with 5-20 ml of either an emulsion of 0.1% fennel oil in water + 0.4% polysorbate-80 as emulsifier ($n = 65$) or placebo (0.4% polysorbate-80 in water; $n = 60$), with a dosage limit of 12 ml/kg body weight/day (providing 12 mg/kg/day of fennel oil in the verum group - a rather high dosage level). All episodes of infant crying lasting longer than 15 minutes were recorded by the family and cumulative totals calculated for the 7 days prior to, 7 days during and 7 days after the test period. Cumulative crying decreased significantly more ($p<0.01$) in the fennel oil group (from 13.5 to 8.8 hours) than in the placebo group (from 12.9 to 12.3 hours). Colic was eliminated (i.e. crying decreased to less than 9 hours per week) in 65% of infants in the fennel oil group compared to 24% in the placebo group ($p<0.01$). The investigators concluded that fennel oil emulsion is superior to placebo in reducing the intensity of infantile colic [54].

An earlier randomized, double-blind, placebo-controlled study of infantile colic, organized on similar lines by paediatricians at clinics in Beer-Sheva, Israel, gave results significantly in favour of a combination herbal tea (fennel, matricaria flower, vervain, liquorice and melissa leaf). Use of the tea eliminated colic in 19 (57%) out of 33 infants aged 2-8 weeks, whereas placebo was helpful in only 9 (26%) out of 35 ($p<0.01$) [55].

Dysmenorrhoea
Sweet fennel oil was compared with mefenamic acid as an oral treatment for moderate to severe primary dysmenorrhoea in a 3-cycle open study involving 30 women aged 15-24 years (all nulliparous and not using any form of hormonal contraception). During menstrual days, the patients received no medication in the first (control) cycle, 250 mg of mefenamic acid every 6 hours in the second cycle and 25 drops of a 2% sweet fennel oil preparation every 4 hours in the third cycle. Based on patients' daily records using a self-scoring system, the mean duration of menstruation was 6.6 days with a mean cycle of 27 days. Both mefenamic acid and fennel oil effectively relieved menstrual pain ($p<0.001$) compared to control cycles. Mefenamic acid had a more potent pain-relieving effect on days 2 and 3 of menstruation ($p<0.05$) but the difference on other days was not significant. Elapsed times before onset of action were similar: 67.5 minutes for mefenamic acid compared to 75 minutes for sweet fennel oil. The investigators concluded that the sweet fennel oil preparation was a safe and effective treatment for primary dysmenorrhoea, if somewhat less potent than mefenamic acid at the dosage used [56].

Idiopathic hirsutism
Based on the reputation of fennel as an oestrogenic agent, a randomized, double-blind, placebo-controlled study was carried out to evaluate the effects of a topically applied fennel extract in idiopathic hirsutism, the occurrence of excessive male pattern hair growth in women with normal ovulatory menstrual cycles and normal levels of serum androgens. Patients applied creams containing 2% ($n = 15$) or 1% ($n = 11$) of a dry ethanolic fennel extract, or a placebo cream ($n = 12$), to the face twice daily for 12 weeks. Facial hair density and growth were noted clinically, and hair diameter (in µm) on chin, cheek and upper lip was measured every 4 weeks. As the patients were allowed to epilate, decreasing frequency of epilation gave the first indirect sign of efficacy (i.e. reduced hair growth rate) in the 2% and 1% cream groups. Mean values for reduction in hair diameter after 12 weeks were 18.3%, 7.8% and –0.5% in the groups receiving 2%, 1% and placebo creams respectively, both active creams performing significantly better than placebo ($p<0.0001$) and the 2% cream performing significantly better than the 1% ($p<0.001$). The degree of improvement was also apparent from visual tests and patient satisfaction [57].

THERAPEUTICS

Actions
Carminative [3,58-60], spasmolytic [7,34,35,59], mildly expectorant [41,52,59-61], anti-inflammatory [45,46,58], oestrogenic [42,43,59], digestive stimulant [7,49-51], diuretic [47,48,58], choleretic, moderately analgesic and antipyretic [47], and moderately antimicrobial [39].

Fennel is also stated to be orexigenic [58,61] and galactagogic [31,59,61]. Its carminative action is not as powerful as that of caraway, but the flavour of fennel offers advantages [60].

Fennel oil [33] and *trans*-anethole [44] show oestrogenic activity.

Indications
Infantile colic [54,58-61]; dyspeptic complaints [7,8,58-61] including flatulence [7,58], eructation, sluggish digestion [8] and feeling of fullness [7,61]; dysmenorrhoea [56].

External use: Idiopathic hirsutism (a tentative new indication based on one controlled study with a cream containing 2% of a dry ethanolic fennel extract) [57].

Other uses, based on experience or tradition
Catarrh of the upper respiratory tract [7], coughs and bronchitis [3,5]; anorexia [58]; amenorrhoea [3]. As a galactagogue to stimulate milk flow in nursing mothers when necessary [3,31,59].

External use: Conjunctivitis and blepharitis (as an eye wash); sore throat and pharyngitis (as a gargle) [58,59].

Contraindications
Preparations other than aqueous infusions should be avoided during pregnancy [7].

Side effects
In rare cases, allergic reactions of the skin or respiratory tract.

Interactions with other drugs
None known.

Dosage
Adult daily dose: Dried fruits, 0.9-1.8 g or as an infusion [58,59]; liquid extract (1:2), 3-6 ml; tincture (1:5), 7-14 ml [59]. A much higher daily dose of 5-7 g of dried fruits (bitter fennel) was recommended by the German Commission E [7].

Dose for children and babies
Based on the Commission E adult daily dose, average daily doses for children (as crushed fruits in aqueous infusion) have been proposed as: *0-1 year of age*, 1-2 g; *1-4 years*, 1.5-3 g; *4-10 years*,

3-5 g; *10-16 years*, 5-7 g [62]. If the fruits contain 4% of essential oil, a daily dose of 1-2 g of dried fruits for infants 0-1 year of age would potentially contain 40-80 mg of fennel oil; however, it has been shown that only about 10% of the essential oil passes into a fennel tea infusion [63], hence 4-8 mg of fennel oil in the infusion is more realistic.

In a positive clinical study summarized above [54], an emulsion of 0.1% of fennel oil in water (i.e. 1 mg of fennel oil per ml), was given orally to babies aged 2-12 weeks as a treatment for colic. The maximum daily dosage of fennel oil was set at 12 mg/kg/day. For a 5 kg baby, this equated to a maximum daily dosage (divided into small doses) of 60 mg of fennel oil.

SAFETY

No adverse effects were observed when 65 babies (2-12 weeks of age) with colic were treated orally for 7 days with an aqueous emulsion containing fennel oil at up to 12 mg/kg body weight/day [54], or when 26 adults applied creams containing 1-2% of a dry ethanolic fennel extract to the face twice daily for 12 weeks [57]. From 25 patients taking the equivalent of about 0.02 ml of fennel oil every 4 hours during menstruation (as treatment for dysmenorrhoea), no side effects were reported other than one case of slightly increased menstrual flow; 5 patients refused the fennel oil preparation due to its odour [56].

An ethanolic fennel extract administered orally to mice caused no toxic effects after single doses of up to 3 g/kg body weight [47,64]. The oral LD_{50} of bitter fennel oil in rats was found to be 4.52 ml/kg [65].

Antifertility activity of *trans*-anethole was revealed when it was orally administered to adult female rats at 50, 70 or 80 mg/kg on days 1-10 of pregnancy. Compared to control animals (which delivered normal offspring on completion of term), implantation in treated animals was inhibited by 33%, 66% and 100% respectively. Further work showed that normal implantation and delivery occurred in rats given *trans*-anethole at 80 mg/kg only on days 1-2 of pregnancy, while implantation was completely inhibited in those given 80 mg/kg only on days 3-5. In rats given 80 mg/kg of *trans*-anethole only on days 6-10, three out of five rats failed to deliver at term and this was interpreted as a sign of early abortifacient activity. No gross malformations of offspring were observed in any of the groups [44].

Further toxicological data on fennel and its constituents have been summarized in the ESCOP monograph [66] and earlier by Keller [67].

REGULATORY STATUS

Medicines

UK	Accepted for general sale, internal or external use [68].
France	Sweet fennel accepted for specified indications [8].
Germany	Commission E monograph published for bitter fennel, with approved uses [7].

Food

USA	Generally recognized as safe (21 CFR 182.10 and 182.20) [69].
Council of Europe	Permitted as flavouring, category N2 [70].

REFERENCES

Current Pharmacopoeial Monographs

Ph. Eur.	Fennel, Bitter
Ph. Eur.	Fennel, Sweet

Literature References

1. Duquénois P, Anton R and Dupin M. Normalisation des drogues végétales. V. Problèmes posés par les fruits de Fenouils [Standardization of vegetable drugs. V. Problems posed by fennel fruits]. *Ann. Pharm. Fr.* 1977, **35**, 497-502 [FRENCH/English summary].
2. Marotti M and Piccaglia R. The Influence of Distillation Conditions on the Essential Oil Composition of Three Varieties of *Foeniculum vulgare* Mill. *J. Essent. Oil. Res.* 1992, **4**, 569-576.
3. Hänsel R, Keller K, Rimpler H and Schneider G, editors. Foeniculum. In: *Hagers Handbuch der Pharmazeutischen Praxis, 5th ed. Volume 5: Drogen E-O.* ISBN 3-540-52638-2. Berlin-Heidelberg-New York-London: Springer-Verlag, 1993:156-181 [GERMAN].
4. Bernáth J, Németh E, Kattaa A and Héthelyi E. Morphological and Chemical Evaluation of Fennel (*Foeniculum vulgare* Mill.) Populations of Different Origin. *J. Essent. Oil. Res.* 1996, **8**, 247-253.
5. Stahl-Biskup E, Wichtl M and Neubeck M. Bitterer Fenchel - Foeniculi amari fructus; Süßer Fenchel - Foeniculi dulcis fructus. In: Hartke K, Hartke H, Mutschler E, Rücker G and Wichtl M, editors. *Kommentar zum Europäischen Arzneibuch.* Stuttgart: Wissenschaftliche Verlagsgesellschaft, 1999 (12 Lfg.):F6 and F7 [GERMAN].
6. Pharmaceutical Society of Great Britain. Fennel. In: *British Pharmaceutical Codex 1973.* London: Pharmaceutical Press, 1973:194.
7. Foeniculi fructus. German Commission E Monograph published in: Bundesanzeiger No. 74 of 19 April 1991.
8. Fenouil doux, fruit. In: *Médicaments à base de plantes.* ISBN 2-911473-02-7. Saint-Denis Cedex, France: Agence du Médicament, 1998.
9. Ehlers D, Färber J, Martin A, Quirin K-W and Gerard D. Untersuchung von Fenchelölen - Vergleich von CO_2-Extrakten und Wasserdampfdestillaten [Investigation of fennel oils - Comparison of CO_2 extracts and steam distillates]. *Dtsch. Lebensm.-Rundschau* 2000, **96**, 330-335 [GERMAN/English summary].
10. Mimica-Dukic N, Kujundzic S, Sokovic M and Couladis M. Essential Oil Composition and Antifungal Activity of *Foeniculum vulgare* Mill. Obtained by Different Distillation Conditions. *Phytotherapy Res.* 2003, **17**, 368-371.
11. Lawrence BM. Progress in Essential Oils. *Perfumer Flavorist* 1998, **23** (March/April) 47-57.

12. Reiter B, Lechner M and Lorbeer E. The fatty acid profiles - including petroselinic and *cis*-vaccenic acid - of different Umbelliferae seed oils. *Fett/Lipid* 1998, **100**, 498-502.
13. Dirks U and Herrmann K. High Performance Liquid Chromatography of Hydroxycinnamoyl-quinic Acids and 4-(β-D-Glucopyranosyloxy)-benzoic Acid in Spices. 10. Phenolics of Spices. *Z. Lebensm. Unters. Forsch.* 1984, **179**, 12-16 [GERMAN/English summary].
14. Schulz JM and Herrmann K. Occurrence of Hydroxybenzoic Acids and Hydroxycinnamic Acids in Spices. IV. Phenolics of Spices. *Z. Lebensm. Unters. Forsch.* 1980, **171**, 193-199 [GERMAN/English summary].
15. Kunzemann J and Herrmann K. Isolation and Identification of Flavon(ol)-O-glycosides in Caraway (*Carum carvi* L.), Fennel (*Foeniculum vulgare* Mill.), Anise (*Pimpinella anisum* L.) and Coriander (*Coriandrum sativum* L.) and of Flavone-C-glycosides in Anise. I. Phenolics of Spices. *Z. Lebensm. Unters. Forsch.* 1977, **164**, 194-200 [GERMAN/English summary].
16. Harborne JB and Williams CA. Flavonoid patterns in the fruits of the Umbelliferae. *Phytochemistry* 1972, **11**, 1741-1750.
17. Méndez J and Castro-Poceiro J. Coumarins in *Foeniculum vulgare* fruits. *Rev. Latinoam. Quim.* 1981, **12**, 91-92.
18. El-Khrisy EAM, Mahmoud AM and Abu-Mustafa EA. Chemical Constituents of *Foeniculum vulgare* Fruits. *Fitoterapia* 1980, **51**, 273-275.
19. Ceska O, Chaudhary SK, Warrington PJ and Ashwood-Smith MJ. Photoactive furocoumarins in fruits of some Umbellifers. *Phytochemistry* 1987, **26**, 165-169.
20. Ono M, Ito Y, Kinjo J, Yahara S, Nohara T and Niiho Y. Four New Glycosides of Stilbene Trimer from Foeniculi Fructus (Fruit of *Foeniculum vulgare* Miller). *Chem. Pharm. Bull.* 1995, **43**, 868-871.
21. Ono M, Ito Y, Ishikawa T, Kitajima J, Tanaka Y, Niiho Y and Nohara T. Five New Monoterpene Glycosides and Other Compounds from Foeniculi Fructus (Fruit of *Foeniculum vulgare* Miller). *Chem. Pharm. Bull.* 1996, **44**, 337-342.
22. Kitajima J, Ishikawa T and Tanaka Y. Water-Soluble Constituents of Fennel. I. Alkyl Glycosides. *Chem. Pharm. Bull.* 1998, **46**, 1643-1646.
23. Kitajima J, Ishikawa T and Tanaka Y. Water-Soluble Constituents of Fennel. II. Four *erythro*-Anethole Glycol Glycosides and Two *p*-Hydroxyphenylpropylene Glycol Glycosides. *Chem. Pharm. Bull.* 1998, **46**, 1591-1594.
24. Ishikawa T, Kitajima J and Tanaka Y. Water-Soluble Constituents of Fennel. III. Fenchane-Type Monoterpenoid Glycosides. *Chem. Pharm. Bull.* 1998, **46**, 1599-1602.
25. Ishikawa T, Kitajima J and Tanaka Y. Water-Soluble Constituents of Fennel. IV. Menthane-Type Monoterpenoids and Their Glycosides. *Chem. Pharm. Bull.* 1998, **46**, 1603-1606.
26. Kitajima J, Ishikawa T, Tanaka Y, Ono M, Ito Y and Nohara T. Water-Soluble Constituents of Fennel. V. Glycosides of Aromatic Compounds. *Chem. Pharm. Bull.* 1998, **46**, 1587-1590.
27. Ishikawa T, Kitajima J, Tanaka Y, Ono M, Ito Y and Nohara T. Water-Soluble Constituents of Fennel. VI. 1,8-Cineole Type Glycosides. *Chem. Pharm. Bull.* 1998, **46**, 1738-1742.
28. Ishikawa T, Tanaka Y and Kitajima J. Water-Soluble Constituents of Fennel. VII. Acyclic Monoterpenoid Glycosides. *Chem. Pharm. Bull.* 1998, **46**, 1748-1751.
29. Fennel - Foeniculi Fructus. In: The Japanese Pharmacopoeia, 14th ed. (JP XIV). English edition. Tokyo: Society of Japanese Pharmacopoeia, 2001.
30. Barazani O, Fait A, Cohen Y, Diminshtein S, Ravid U, Putievsky E et al. Chemical Variation Among Indigenous Populations of *Foeniculum vulgare* var. *vulgare* in Israel. *Planta Medica* 1999, **65**, 486-489.
31. Brückner C. Anwendung und Wert in Europa gebräuchlicher lactationsfördernder Heilpflanzen (Galactagoga) [The use and merit of the more common lactation-promoting medicinal plants (galactagogues) in Europe]. *Pädiatr. Grenzgeb.* 1989, **28**, 403-410 [GERMAN/English summary].
32. Albert-Puleo M. Fennel and anise as estrogenic agents. *J. Ethnopharmacol.* 1980, **2**, 337-344.
33. Melzig MF, Möller I and Jarry H. Neue Untersuchungen zur in-vitro-pharmakologischen Wirkung ätherischer Öle aus Apiaceenfrüchten [New investigations of the *in vitro* pharmacological activity of essential oils from Apiaceae fruits]. *Z. Phytotherapie* 2003, **24**, 112-116 [GERMAN/English summary].
34. Forster H. Spasmolytische Wirkung pflanzlicher Carminativa. Tierexperimentelle Untersuchungen [Spasmolytic effects of herbal carminatives. Animal studies]. *Z. Allg. Med.* 1983, **59**, 1327-1333 [GERMAN].
35. Forster HB, Niklas H and Lutz S. Antispasmodic Effects of Some Medicinal Plants. *Planta Medica* 1980, **40**, 309-319.
36. Reiter M and Brandt W. Relaxant Effects on Tracheal and Ileal Smooth Muscles of the Guinea Pig. *Arzneim.-Forsch./Drug Res.* 1985, **35**, 408-414.
37. Lis-Balchin M and Hart S. A preliminary study of the effect of essential oils on skeletal and smooth muscle in vitro. *J. Ethnopharmacol.* 1997, **58**, 183-187.
38. Ostad SN, Soodi M, Shariffzadeh M, Khorshidi N and Marzban H. The effect of fennel essential oil on uterine contraction as a model for dysmenorrhea: pharmacology and toxicology study. *J. Ethnopharmacol.* 2001, **76**, 299-304.
39. Maruzzella JC and Freundlich M. Antimicrobial Substances from Seeds. *J. Am. Pharm. Assoc.* 1959, **48**, 356-358.
40. Hammer KA, Carson CF and Riley TV. Antimicrobial activity of essential oils and other plant extracts. *J. Applied Microbiol.* 1999, **86**, 985-990.
41. Müller-Limmroth W and Fröhlich H-H. Wirkungsnachweis einiger phytotherapeutischer Expektorantien auf den mukoziliaren Transport [Evidence of the effects of some phytotherapeutic expectorants on mucociliary transport]. *Fortschr. Med.* 1980, **98**, 95-101 [GERMAN/English summary].
42. Malini T, Vanithakumari G, Megala N, Anusya S, Devi K and Elango V. Effect of *Foeniculum vulgare* Mill. seed extract on the genital organs of male and female rats. *Indian J. Physiol. Pharmacol.* 1985, **29**, 21-26.
43. Annusuya S, Vanithakumari G, Megala N, Devi K, Malini T and Elango V. Effect of *Foeniculum vulgare* seed extracts on cervix and vagina of ovariectomised rats. *Indian J. Med. Res.* 1988, **87**, 364-367.
44. Dhar SK. Anti-fertility activity and hormonal profile of trans-anethole in rats. *Indian J. Physiol. Pharmacol.* 1995, **39**, 63-67.
45. Mascolo N, Autore G, Capasso F, Menghini A and Fasulo MP. Biological Screening of Italian Medicinal Plants for Anti-inflammatory Activity. *Phytotherapy Res.* 1987, **1**, 28-31.
46. Choi E-M and Hwang J-K. Antiinflammatory, analgesic and antioxidant activities of the fruit of *Foeniculum vulgare*. *Fitoterapia* 2004, **75**, 557-565.
47. Tanira MOM, Shah AH, Mohsin A, Ageel AM and Qureshi S. Pharmacological and Toxicological Investigations on *Foeniculum vulgare* Dried Fruit Extract in Experimental Animals. *Phytotherapy Res.* 1996, **10**, 33-36.
48. El Bardai S, Lyoussi B, Wibo M and Morel N. Pharmacological evidence of hypotensive activity of *Marrubium vulgare* and *Foeniculum vulgare* in spontaneously hypertensive rat. *Clin. Exper. Hypertension* 2001, **23**, 329-343.
49. Vasudevan K, Vembar S, Veeraraghavan K and Haranath PSRK. Influence of intragastric perfusion of aqueous spice extracts on acid secretion in anesthetized albino rats. *Indian J. Gastroenterol.* 2000, **19**, 53-56.
50. Platel K and Srinivasan K. Studies on the influence of dietary spices on food transit time in experimental rats. *Nutrition Res.* 2001, **21**, 1309-1314.
51. Niiho Y, Takayanagi I and Takagi K. Effects of a combined stomachic and its ingredients on rabbit stomach motility in situ. *Japan. J. Pharmacol.* 1977, **27**, 177-179.
52. Boyd EM and Sheppard EP. An Autumn-Enhanced Mucotropic Action of Inhaled Terpenes and Related Volatile Agents. *Pharmacology* 1971, **6**, 65-80.
53. Caldwell J and Sutton JD. Influence of dose size on the disposition of *trans*-[*methoxy*-^{14}C]anethole in human volunteers. *Food. Chem. Toxicol.* 1988, **26**, 87-91.

54. Alexandrovich I, Rakovitskaya O, Kolmo E, Sidorova T and Shushunov S. The effect of fennel (*Foeniculum vulgare*) seed oil emulsion in infantile colic: a randomized, placebo-controlled study. *Altern. Ther. Health Med.* 2003, **9**, 58-61.
55. Weizman Z, Alkrinawi S, Goldfarb D and Bitran C. Efficacy of herbal tea preparation in infantile colic. *J. Pediatr.* 1993, **122**, 650-652.
56. Namavar Jahromi B, Tartifizadeh A and Khabnadideh S. Comparison of fennel and mefenamic acid for the treatment of primary dysmenorrhea. *Int. J. Gynecol. Obstet.* 2003, **80**, 153-157.
57. Javidnia K, Dastgheib L, Mohammadi Samani S and Nasiri A. Antihirsutism activity of Fennel (fruits of *Foeniculum vulgare*) extract. A double-blind placebo controlled study. *Phytomedicine* 2003, **10**, 455-458.
58. Foeniculum. In: *British Herbal Pharmacopoeia 1983*. ISBN 0-903032-07-4. Bournemouth: British Herbal Medicine Association, 1983.
59. Mills S and Bone K. Fennel fruit (*Foeniculum vulgare* Mill.). In: *Principles and Practice of Phytotherapy. Modern Herbal Medicine*. ISBN 0-443-06016-9. Edinburgh-London-New York: Churchill Livingstone, 2000:378-384.
60. Weiss RF. *Foeniculum vulgare* (Fennel). In: *Herbal Medicine* (translated from the 6th German edition of *Lehrbuch der Phytotherapie*). ISBN 0-906584-19-1. Gothenburg: AB Arcanum, Beaconsfield, UK: Beaconsfield Publishers, 1988:68-69.
61. Chevallier A. Fennel - *Foeniculum vulgare*. In: *Encyclopedia of Medicinal Plants, 2nd ed.* ISBN 0-7513-1209-6. London-New York: Dorling Kindersley, 2001:211-212.
62. Dorsch W, Loew D, Meyer-Buchtela E and Schilcher H. Foeniculi fructus (Fenchelfrüchte). In: Kooperation Phytopharmaka, editor. *Kinderdosierung von Phytopharmaka, 3. Aufl. Teil I - Empfehlungen zur Anwendung und Dosierung von Phytopharmaka, monographierten Arzneidrogen und ihren Zubereitungen in der Pädiatrie [Children's dosages of phytomedicines. 3rd ed. Part I. Usage and dosage recommendations for phytomedicines, monographed herbal drugs and their preparations in paediatrics]*. Bonn: Kooperation Phytopharmaka, 2002:70-71 [GERMAN].
63. Fehr D. Bestimmung flüchtiger Inhaltsstoffe in Teezubereitungen. 1. Mitteilung: Freisetzung des ätherischen Öls aus Fenchelfrüchten [Determination of volatile constituents in tea preparations. Part 1: Release of essential oil from fennel fruits]. *Pharm. Ztg.* 1982, **127**, 2520-2522 [GERMAN/English summary].
64. Shah AH, Qureshi S and Ageel AM. Toxicity studies in mice of ethanol extracts of *Foeniculum vulgare* fruit and *Ruta chalepensis* aerial parts. *J. Ethnopharmacol.* 1991, **34**, 167-172.
65. Opdyke DLJ. Monographs on fragrance raw materials: fennel oil, bitter. *Food Cosmet. Toxicol.* 1976, **14**, 309.
66. European Scientific Cooperative on Phytotherapy. Foeniculi fructus - Fennel. In: *ESCOP Monographs - The Scientific Foundation for Herbal Medicinal Products, 2nd ed.* Stuttgart-New York: Thieme; Exeter, UK: ESCOP, 2003:162-168.
67. Keller K. *Foeniculum vulgare*. In: De Smet PAGM, Keller K, Hänsel R, Chandler RF, editors. *Adverse Effects of Herbal Drugs, Volume 1*. Berlin-Heidelberg-New York-London: Springer-Verlag, 1992:135-142.
68. Fennel. In: UK Statutory Instrument 1984 No. 769. The Medicines (Products Other Than Veterinary Drugs) (General Sale List) Order 1984. Schedule 1, Table A.
69. Fennel, common; fennel, sweet. In: Sections 182.10 and 182.20 of USA Code of Federal Regulations, Title 21, Food and Drugs, Parts 170 to 199. Revised as of April 1, 2000.
70. Bitter fennel, sweet fennel; fruits. In: *Flavouring Substances and Natural Sources of Flavourings, 3rd ed.* ISBN 2-7160-0081-6. Strasbourg: Council of Europe, 1981.

REGULATORY GUIDELINES FROM OTHER EU COUNTRIES

FRANCE

Médicaments à base de plantes [8]: Fenouil doux, fruit.

Therapeutic indications accepted

Oral use

Traditionally used: in the symptomatic treatment of digestive disorders such as epigastric distension, sluggish digestion, eructation, flatulence; as adjuvant treatment of the painful component of functional digestive disorders.

GERMANY

Commission E monograph [7]: Foeniculi fructus (Fenchel).

The monograph relates to bitter fennel.

Uses

Dyspeptic complaints such as mild spasmodic gastrointestinal ailments, feeling of fullness and flatulence.
Catarrh of the upper respiratory tract.
Fennel syrup and fennel honey: catarrh of the upper respiratory tract in children.

Contraindications

None known for tea infusions from the crude drug or preparations with a comparable content of the essential oil.
Other preparations: pregnancy.

Side effects

In single cases, allergic reactions of the skin and respiratory tract.

Interactions with other drugs

None known.

Dosage

Unless otherwise prescribed, daily dose: 5-7 g of the drug; 10-20 g of fennel syrup or fennel honey, or 5-7.5 g of compound fennel tincture (all three preparations as defined in Erg. DAB 6); equivalent preparations.

Mode of administration

Crushed or milled drug for tea infusions, tea-like products and other galenic preparations for oral use.

Duration of administration

Fennel preparations should not be taken over prolonged periods (several weeks) without consulting a doctor or pharmacist.

Note: Fennel syrup and fennel honey: diabetics must take account of the sugar content (as given in the manufacturers' information).

Actions

Promotes gastrointestinal motility, spasmolytic in higher concentrations. Anethole and fenchone have been found experimentally to have a secretolytic effect in the respiratory tract; aqueous fennel infusions increased mucociliary activity of the ciliary epithelium of frogs.

FENUGREEK

Leguminosae-Papilionoideae

Foenugraeci semen

Synonym: Trigonellae foenugraeci semen.

Definition

Fenugreek consists of the dried, ripe seeds of *Trigonella foenum-graecum* L.

CONSTITUENTS

□ ***Steroidal saponins***, occurring as furostanol 3,26-diglycosides with a chain of 2-6 sugar residues (glucose, rhamnose and/or xylose) at C-3 and a glucosyl group at C-26. At least 30 saponins are present, most of which have been isolated and structurally elucidated, including trigofoenosides A-G, trigonelloside B [1] and a range of 18 trigoneosides [2-4]. On hydrolysis the furostanol saponins yield spirostanol sapogenins, principally diosgenin and its 25β-epimer yamogenin [5,6], but including tigogenin, gitogenin and others [2-5].

GC analysis of mature seeds from 10 accessions of fenugreek gave mean levels of diosgenin + yamogenin in the range 0.7-1.0% for the four best samples [7]. Earlier assays using an IR method indicated 1.27-1.5% of total sapogenins [8].

Fenugreekine, a steroidal sapogenin with a peptide ester group at C-3, is also present [9].

□ ***Mucilage polysaccharide***, 18-45% [10,11], consisting mainly of galactomannan with a backbone of β-(1→4)-linked mannose residues to which α-galactosyl groups are attached at O-6 [12,13].

□ ***Flavonoids*** Flavone *C*-glycosides including vicenin-1 (=apigenin 6-*C*-xyloside-8-*C*-glucoside), vicenin-2 (= apigenin 6,8-di-*C*-glucoside) [14], vitexin (= apigenin 8-*C*-glucoside) [14-16], vitexin 7-glucoside [15], vitexin 2''-*p*-coumarate [17], saponaretin (= apigenin 6-*C*-glucoside) and isoorientin (= luteolin 6-*C*-glucoside) [14].

The flavone tricin and its 7-glucoside, the flavonol quercetin and the flavanone naringenin are also present [16].

□ ***Lipids***, 7-9%, in which over 90% of the fatty acids are unsaturated, principally oleic (18:1), linoleic (18:2) and linolenic (18:3) acids [18,19].

□ ***Sterols*** Over 20 sterols have been detected (12 identified), 42% in the free state, 47% esterified and 7% glycosidically bound. The main sterol (ca. 65%) is 24ξ-ethyl-cholest-5-en-3β-ol [20].

□ ***Volatile compounds***, less than 0.01% from steam distillation, including alkanes, sequiterpenes, oxygenated and aromatic compounds, none comprising more than 10% of the oil [21].

In a fraction obtained by solvent extraction from seed the dominant compound, with a characteristic and persistent odour of fenugreek, was found to be 3-hydroxy-4,5-dimethyl-2(*5H*)-furanone [22]. This powerful flavour compound, known as sotolone, is present at 2-25 ppm in fenugreek; it also contributes to the flavour of certain other seasonings (e.g. lovage) and the burnt/sweet note of coffee [23].

□ ***Other constituents*** include free amino acids, of which 4-hydroxyisoleucine represents 30-50% [20], and the alkaloid trigonelline [20,24].

The composition of a sample of dry fenugreek seeds was determined as: moisture 9%, ash 3%,

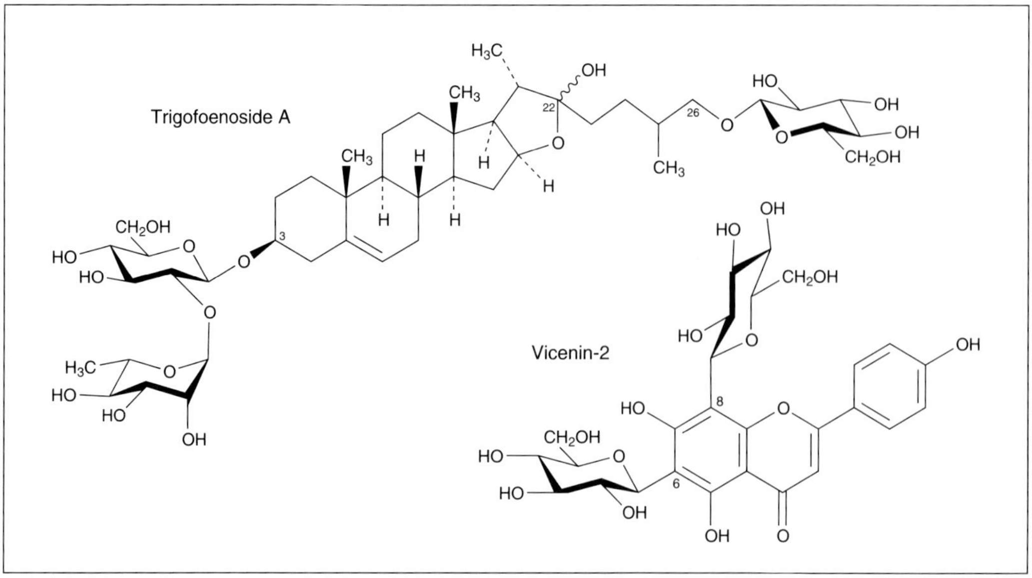

lipids 8%, protein 26%, starch 6% and total fibre 48% (of which gum 20%) [25].

Published Assay Methods
Sapogenins by GC [7,26].

PHARMACOLOGY

Recent research on fenugreek has been mainly related to its hypoglycaemic and hypolipidaemic effects and to its potential use in the treatment of diabetes (carbohydrate intolerance).

Most diabetic patients can be classified as having insulin-dependent diabetes mellitus (IDDM, Type I diabetes) or non-insulin-dependent diabetes mellitus (NIDDM, Type II diabetes), the latter type being more common. Insulin, a hormone secreted by B-cells in the islets of Langerhans in the pancreas, regulates glucose, fat and amino acid metabolism; it lowers the concentration of glucose in blood by inhibiting hepatic glucose production and by stimulating the uptake and metabolism of glucose by muscle and adipose tissue [27].

In vitro

Antidiabetic activity
At concentrations of 100 µM to 1 mM, 4-hydroxyisoleucine (an amino acid extracted from fenugreek and not found in mammalian tissues) stimulated glucose-induced insulin release through a direct effect on both rat and human pancreatic islets. The effect was strictly glucose-dependent [28]. It was subsequently demonstrated that 4-hydroxyisoleucine at 200 µM stimulated glucose (8-16 mM)-induced insulin release from pancreatic islets isolated from NIDDM rats ($p<0.01$) [29].

Other effects
Aqueous and alcoholic extracts from fenugreek had a stimulating effect on isolated, non-pregnant guinea pig uterus. The effect was markedly greater on isolated, pregnant guinea pig uterus, particularly during the last stages of pregnancy, and the extracts were considered to be oxytocic [30].

An aqueous fluid extract of fenugreek had a mild relaxant effect on smooth muscle of isolated rabbit duodenum [31].

An aqueous extract from fenugreek exhibited antioxidant activity, scavenging peroxyl (but not superoxide) radicals and reducing the release of reactive oxygen metabolites from inflamed mucosa (biopsy material from patients with active ulcerative colitis) [32].

In vivo
Numerous studies demonstrating hypoglycaemic and/or hypocholesterolaemic effects of fenugreek in rodents, rabbits and dogs have been summarized in a recent ESCOP monograph [33]. The soluble fibre (galactomannan) in fenugreek, as well as 4-hydroxyisoleucine [29], appear to be the main contributors to the hypoglycaemic effects, while saponins and galactomannan have been shown to contribute to the hypocholesterolaemic effects.

Fenugreek extracts have been shown to have appetite-stimulating effects in rats, increasing food intake and the motivation to eat [33,34], and to promote the healing of experimentally-induced gastric ulcers [31,33].

Pharmacological studies in humans
In a randomized crossover study, glucose tolerance tests were carried out on 8 healthy volunteers after they had consumed 100 g of glucose in 250 ml of water with or, after a 7-day interval, without the addition of 25 g of powdered fenugreek. The addition of fenugreek significantly reduced the rise in blood glucose after 30 and 60 minutes ($p<0.05$) and the glucose AUC by 42% ($p<0.001$), and also reduced serum insulin levels after 30 and 60 minutes ($p<0.05$) and the insulin AUC [35].

To evaluate the hypolipidaemic effect of fenugreek 10 apparently healthy, non-obese subjects with asymptomatic hyperlipidaemia (serum cholesterol > 240 mg/dl) received isocaloric diets for two successive periods of 20 days, the first without and the second with 2 × 50 g daily of debitterized fenugreek powder (free from lipids and saponins). Incorporation of fenugreek into the diet reduced serum total cholesterol by 24.4%, LDL- and VLDL-cholesterol by 31.7% and triglyceride levels by 37.7% (all $p<0.001$) [36].

In contrast to the above results, it was found in a subsequent study that fenugreek given to 30 healthy individuals at 2 × 2.5 g daily for 3 months had no significant effects on blood glucose (fasting or postprandial) or blood lipids [37].

CLINICAL STUDIES

Hypoglycaemic effects in non-insulin-dependent diabetes
As listed in Table 1, three small controlled studies have been carried out on Type II (non-insulin-dependent) diabetes mellitus (NIDDM) patients. It should be pointed out that in each study all or most of the patients were also receiving an oral hypoglycaemic drug (such as glibenclamide).

In the Sharma 1990 crossover study, patients were given standard diets, each for a period of 10 days in a randomized design, balanced with respect to carbohydrate, protein and fat content

TABLE 1 Controlled clinical studies with fenugreek in Type II (non-insulin-dependent) diabetes

First author Year Reference number	Duration of treatment	Number of patients	Type of preparation	Daily dosage	Comparison treatment
Sharma 1990 [38]	2 × 10-day periods (crossover)	15	Debitterized fenugreek powder (free from lipids and saponins)	2 × 50 g	Isocaloric diet without fenugreek
Raghuram 1994 [39]	2 × 15-day periods (crossover)	10	Powdered fenugreek	2 × 12.5 g	Isocaloric diet without fenugreek
Gupta 2001 [40]	2 months	25	Hydroalcoholic extract (n = 12)	2 × 500 mg	Placebo (n = 13)

but with or without the inclusion of 2 × 50 g/day of debitterized fenugreek powder. Incorporation of fenugreek into the diet significantly reduced the mean fasting blood glucose level ($p<0.05$), improved performance in the glucose tolerance test ($p<0.01$ at 30-120 minutes and for the area under the plasma glucose curve, AUC), and reduced 24-hour urinary glucose excretion ($p<0.05$) and serum insulin levels ($p<0.05$). The same protocol followed for 20 days in 5 other patients produced similar changes, but of higher magnitude, in all parameters [38].

The Raghuram 1994 crossover study had a similar design but with the 10 patients receiving for periods of 15 days isocaloric diets with or without the inclusion of 2 × 12.5 g/day of powdered fenugreek (which provided more dietary fibre, $p<0.001$). Intravenous glucose tolerance tests (GTT) showed that fenugreek significantly reduced mean plasma glucose levels after glucose loading ($p<0.05$ after 40 minutes; $p<0.02$ after 60 minutes) and hence the area under the plasma glucose curve (AUC, $p<0.05$) as well as the plasma glucose half-life ($p<0.02$), due to an increase in its metabolic clearance rate. An increase in erythrocyte insulin receptors ($p<0.02$) was also observed. The results suggested that fenugreek can improve peripheral glucose utilization and may exert its hypoglycaemic effect by acting at insulin receptors as well as at the gastrointestinal level [39].

In the placebo-controlled Gupta 2001 study, results from the glucose tolerance test showed that blood glucose levels after glucose loading were lower in the fenugreek group than in the placebo group ($p<0.01$ for the AUC). Glycosylated haemoglobin levels also declined ($p<0.05$) and insulin sensitivity increased ($p<0.05$) in the fenugreek group [40].

In an open study, groups of patients with mild (n = 20) or severe (n = 20) non-insulin-dependent diabetes were given 2 × 2.5 g of fenugreek powder daily for 1 month. In the mild NIDDM group fasting and postprandial blood sugar levels decreased significantly (both $p<0.01$ compared to initial values) but results in the severe NIDDM group were not significant [37].

Consumption by 21 NIDDM patients of a prescribed meal, then 4-7 days later the same meal to which 15 g of powdered fenugreek had been added, demonstrated that fenugreek significantly reduced postprandial glucose levels for 2 hours following the meal ($p<0.05$) [41].

In a larger open study involving 60 patients with NIDDM (40 of whom were taking oral hypoglycaemic drugs), incorporation of 2 × 12.5 g of powdered fenugreek into the diet daily for 24 weeks lowered fasting blood glucose levels, improved performance in the glucose tolerance test ($p<0.001$ for AUC at 8, 12 and 24 weeks compared to baseline values) and reduced serum insulin levels ($p<0.01$). Reductions were also evident after 8 weeks in 24-hour urinary sugars ($p<0.001$) and glycosylated haemoglobin ($p<0.001$) [25].

Hypoglycaemic effects in insulin-dependent diabetes

In a randomized, crossover study, 10 Type I (insulin-dependent) diabetic patients consumed isocaloric diets with or without the addition of 2 × 50 g daily of debitterized fenugreek powder (free from lipids and saponins) for periods of 10 days. Fenugreek significantly reduced mean fasting blood glucose levels ($p<0.01$) and, in the glucose tolerance test, reduced the rise in blood glucose levels at 30, 60 and 90 minutes, and hence significantly reduced the blood glucose AUC ($p<0.05$) [42].

Hypolipidaemic effects

In a study described above [25], progressive lipid-lowering effects of fenugreek in the diabetic patients over the period of 24 weeks were reported in a separate paper [43]. Significant reductions were observed in serum total cholesterol, LDL + VLDL-cholesterol and triglyceride levels (all $p<0.001$ after 24 months).

In the Sharma 1990 crossover study in 15 NIDDM patients (see Table 1), significant changes were observed in serum lipids. Serum total cholesterol, LDL + VLDL-cholesterol and triglyceride levels decreased (all $p<0.001$) during the fenugreek treatment phase without significant change in HDL-cholesterol [38].

Similar findings were reported from a randomized crossover study involving 10 insulin-dependent diabetic patients. Debitterized fenugreek powder (2 × 50 g, free from lipids and saponins) taken daily for 10 days significantly reduced serum total cholesterol ($p<0.001$), LDL + VLDL-cholesterol ($p<0.01$) and triglyceride ($p<0.01$) levels, but not HDL-cholesterol [42].

In conclusion, although most of the published clinical studies on fenugreek are of rather poor quality and involve small numbers of patients (and in some cases high dosage levels, up to 2 × 50 g daily), they offer promising evidence of antidiabetic and hypolipidaemic effects. Two relevant reviews are available [44,45].

THERAPEUTICS

Actions

Hypoglycaemic [38-40], hypolipidaemic and hypocholesterolaemic [38,42,43]; appetite stimulant [34,46,47], nutritive [46,48], demulcent and topically emollient; mildly laxative [46]; uterine stimulant and probably oxytocic [30].

Reputed to promote milk flow in nursing mothers [49-51].

Indications

As an adjuvant in the treatment of non-insulin-dependent diabetes mellitus [33,38-40].

The daily dose necessary for this purpose is, however, comparatively high (see below).

Other uses, based on experience or tradition

Internal: General debility [46] and loss of appetite [46,47], especially in convalescence [46,49,50]; dyspepsia and gastritis [46,49].
External: As a poultice for local inflammations [47], abscesses, swellings, boils, ulcers and burns [46,49,50].

Contraindications

Avoid during pregnancy [49,51], except in small amounts as food flavouring.

Side effects

Skin reactions may arise from repeated external application [47].

Interactions with other drugs

None known.

Dosage

Adjuvant treatment of diabetes mellitus

Adult daily dose: 25 g of powdered seeds [39] or equivalent preparations.

Other uses

Internal: Up to three times daily, about 2 g of crushed seed taken with adequate fluid before a meal [52].
External: 50 g of powdered seed boiled with 250 ml of water for 5 minutes before application as a poultice or compress [52].

SAFETY

As might be expected for seeds which are widely used (albeit in small quantities) as a food flavouring, no serious adverse effects have been reported from clinical studies with fenugreek at dosages from 5 g to 100 g per day. Gastrointestinal complaints such as diarrhoea and excessive flatulence, which subsided within a few days, were initially experienced by some patients [25], as many as 4 out of 10 in a small study involving consumption of 100 g of debitterized fenugreek powder per day for 10 days [42]. Toxicological evaluation of 60 NIDDM patients before and after administration of fenugreek at 25 g/day for 24 weeks revealed no renal or hepatic toxicity and no haematological abnormalities [53]. Comparable results were obtained after incorporation of fenugreek into the diet of rats at levels of up to 20% for 90 days, from which it was concluded that fenugreek appeared to be "essentially non-toxic" [54].

In the Ames mutagenicity test, fenugreek exhibited weak mutagenicity in *Salmonella typhimurium* strain TA102, but none in strain TA98 [55].

Two teratogenicity studies in rats gave highly conflicting results. No teratogenic effects were reported from a 1986 study in which pregnant rats were given fenugreek as 5-20% of their diet for 21 days (corresponding to 890 and 2930 mg/rat/day) [56]. On the other hand, a 1990 study in rats found that a much lower dosage of fenugreek, 175 mg/kg body weight (corresponding to about 31.5 mg/rat/day), caused high antifertility rates and substantial fetal abnormalities [57]. Further studies are needed to clarify the position. In the meantime fenugreek should clearly be avoided during pregnancy, except in the small amounts which may be present in certain foods.

REGULATORY STATUS

Medicines

UK	Accepted for general sale, internal or external use [58].

France	Accepted for specified indications [48].
Germany	Commission E monograph published, with approved uses [47].

Food

USA	Generally recognized as safe (21 CFR 182.10 and 182.20) [59].
Council of Europe	Permitted as flavouring, category N2 [60].

REFERENCES

Current Pharmacopoeial Monographs

Ph. Eur. Fenugreek

Literature References

1. Sauvaire Y, Baissac Y, Leconte O, Petit P and Ribes G. Steroid saponins from fenugreek and some of their biological properties. *Adv. Exp. Med. Biol.* 1996, **405**, 37-46.
2. Yoshikawa M, Murakami T, Komatsu H, Murakami N, Yamahara J and Matsuda H. Medicinal Foodstuffs. IV. Fenugreek Seed. (1): Structures of Trigoneosides Ia, Ib, IIa, IIb, IIIa and IIIb, New Furostanol Saponins from the Seeds of Indian *Trigonella foenum-graecum* L. *Chem. Pharm. Bull.* 1997, **45**, 81-87.
3. Yoshikawa M, Murakami T, Komatsu H, Yamahara J and Matsuda H. Medicinal Foodstuffs. VIII. Fenugreek Seed. (2): Structures of six new furostanol saponins, trigoneosides IVa, Va, Vb, VI, VIIb and VIIIb, from the seeds of Indian *Trigonella foenum-graecum* L. *Heterocycles* 1998, **47**, 397-405.
4. Murakami T, Kishi A, Matsuda H and Yoshikawa M. Medicinal Foodstuffs. XVII. Fenugreek Seed. (3): Structures of New Furostanol-Type Steroid Saponins. Trigoneosides Xa, Xb, XIb, XIIa, XIIb and XIIIa from the Seeds of Egyptian *Trigonella foenum-graecum* L. *Chem. Pharm. Bull.* 2000, **48**, 994-1000.
5. Knight JC. Analysis of Fenugreek sapogenins by gas-liquid chromatography. *J. Chromatogr.* 1977, **133**, 222-225.
6. Hardman R and Brain KR. Variations in the yield of total and individual 25α- and 25β-sapogenins on storage of whole seed of *Trigonella foenum-graecum* L. *Planta Medica* 1972, **21**, 426-430.
7. Taylor WG, Zulyniak HJ, Richards KW, Acharya SN, Bittman S and Elder JL. Variation in Diosgenin Levels among 10 Accessions of Fenugreek Seeds Produced in Western Canada. *J. Agric. Food Chem.* 2002, **50**, 5994-5997.
8. Fazli FRY and Hardman R. Isolation and characterisation of steroids and other constituents from *Trigonella foenum-graecum*. *Phytochemistry* 1971, **10**, 2497-2503.
9. Ghosal S, Srivastava RS, Chatterjee DC and Dutta SK. Fenugreekine, a new steroidal sapogenin-peptide ester of *Trigonella foenum-graecum*. *Phytochemistry* 1974, **13**, 2247-2251.
10. Karawya MS, Wassel GM, Baghdadi HH and Ammar NM. Mucilaginous Contents of Certain Egyptian Plants. *Planta Medica* 1980, **38**, 73-78.
11. Ribes G, Sauvaire Y, Baccou J-C, Valette G, Chenon D, Trimble ER et al. Effects of Fenugreek Seeds on Endocrine Pancreatic Secretions in Dogs. *Ann. Nutr. Metab.* 1984, **28**, 37-43.
12. Chatterjee BP, Sarkar N and Rao AS. Serological and chemical investigations of the anomeric configuration of the sugar units in the D-galacto-D-mannan of fenugreek (*Trigonella foenum-graecum*) seed. *Carbohydr. Res.* 1982, **104**, 348-353.
13. Madar Z and Shomer I. Polysaccharide Composition of a Gel Fraction Derived from Fenugreek and Its Effect on Starch Digestion and Bile Acid Absorption in Rats. *J. Agric. Food Chem.* 1990, **38**, 1535-1539.
14. Wagner H, Iyengar MA and Hörhammer L. Vicenin-1 and -2 in the seeds of *Trigonella foenum-graecum*. *Phytochemistry* 1973, **12**, 2548.
15. Adamska M and Lutomski J. C-Flavonylglycosides in seeds of *Trigonella foenum-graecum* (fenugreek). *Planta Medica* 1971, **20**, 224-229 [GERMAN]; through *Chem. Abstr.* 1972, **76**, 23054.
16. Shang M, Cai S, Han J, Li J, Zhao Y, Zheng J et al. Studies on flavonoids from fenugreek (*Trigonella foenum graecum* L.). *Zhongguo Zhongyao Zha Zhi* 1998, **23**, 614-616, 639 [CHINESE]; through *Chem. Abstr.* **130**:220364.
17. Sood AR, Boutard B, Chadenson M, Chopin J and Lebreton P. A new flavone C-glycoside from *Trigonella foenum graecum*. *Phytochemistry* 1976, **15**, 351-352.
18. Hemavathy J and Prabhakar JV. Lipid Composition of Fenugreek (*Trigonella foenum-graecum* L.) Seeds. *Food Chem.* 1989, **31**, 1-7.
19. Sidhu GS and Oakenfull DG. Lipid Composition of Fenugreek (*Trigonella foenum-graecum* L.) Seeds (Hemavathy & Prabhakar, 1989) [Letter]. *Food Chem.* 1990, **35**, 159-160.
20. Hänsel R, Keller K, Rimpler H and Schneider G, editors. Trigonella. In: *Hagers Handbuch der Pharmazeutischen Praxis, 5th ed. Volume 6: Drogen P-Z.* ISBN 3-540-52639-0. Berlin-Heidelberg-New York-London: Springer-Verlag, 1994:994-1004.
21. Girardon P, Bessiere JM, Baccou JC and Sauvaire Y. Volatile Constituents of Fenugreek Seeds. *Planta Medica* 1985, **51**, 533-534.
22. Girardon P, Sauvaire Y, Baccou J-C and Bessiere J-M. Identification of 3-Hydroxy-4,5-Dimethyl-2(5H)-Furanone in Aroma of Fenugreek Seeds (*Trigonella foenum-graecum* L.). *Lebensm. Wiss. Technol.* 1986, **19**, 44-46 [FRENCH/English summary].
23. Blank I, Lin J, Devaud S, Fumeaux R and Fay LB. Chapter 3: The Principal Flavor Components of Fenugreek (*Trigonella foenum-graecum* L.). In: Risch SJ, Ho C-T, editors. Spices - Flavor Chemistry and Antioxidant Properties. ACS Symposium Series 660. Washington DC: American Chemical Society, 1997:12-28.
24. Mishkinsky J, Joseph B, Sulman FG and Goldschmied AL. Hypoglycaemic Effect Of Trigonelline. *Lancet* 1967, **2**, 1311-1312.
25. Sharma RD, Sarkar A, Hazra DK, Mishra B, Singh JB, Sharma SK et al. Use of fenugreek seed powder in the management of non-insulin dependent diabetes mellitus. *Nutr. Res.* 1996, **16**, 1331-1339.
26. Taylor WG, Elder JL, Chang PR and Richards KW. Microdetermination of Diosgenin from Fenugreek (*Trigonella foenum-graecum*) Seeds. *J. Agric. Food Chem.* 2000, **48**, 5206-5210.
27. Kahn CR and Shechter Y. Chapter 61: Insulin, oral hypoglycemic agents and the pharmacology of the endocrine pancreas. In: Goodman Gilman A, Rall TW, Nies AS and Taylor P, editors. *Goodman and Gilman's The Pharmacological Basis of Therapeutics, 8th ed.* ISBN 0-08-040296-8. New York-Oxford: Pergamon, 1990:1463-1495.
28. Sauvaire Y, Petit P, Broca C, Manteghetti M, Baissac Y, Fernandez-Alvarez J et al. 4-Hydroxyisoleucine: a novel amino acid potentiator of insulin secretion. *Diabetes* 1998, **47**, 206-210.
29. Broca C, Gross R, Petit P, Sauvaire Y, Manteghetti M, Tournier M et al. 4-Hydroxyisoleucine: experimental evidence of its insulinotropic and antidiabetic properties. *Am. J. Physiol.* 1999, **277**, E617-E623.
30. Abdo MS and Al-Kafawi AA. Experimental studies on the effect of *Trigonella foenum-graecum*. *Planta Medica* 1969, **17**, 14-18.
31. Al-Meshal IA, Parmar NS, Tariq M and Ageel AM. Gastric anti-ulcer activity in rats of *Trigonella foenum-graecum* (Hu-Lu-Pa). *Fitoterapia* 1985, **56**, 232-235.
32. Langmead L, Dawson C, Hawkins C, Banna N, Loo S and Rampton DS. Antioxidant effects of herbal therapies used by patients with inflammatory bowel disease: an *in vitro*

study. *Aliment. Pharmacol. Ther.* 2002, **16**, 197-205.
33. European Scientific Cooperative on Phytotherapy. Trigonellae foenugraeci semen - Fenugreek. In: *ESCOP Monographs - The Scientific Foundation for Herbal Medicinal Products, 2nd ed.* Stuttgart-New York: Thieme; Exeter, UK: ESCOP, 2003:511-520.
34. Petit P, Sauvaire Y, Ponsin G, Manteghetti M, Fave A and Ribes G. Effects of a Fenugreek Seed Extract on Feeding Behaviour in the Rat: Metabolic-Endocrine Correlates. *Pharmacol. Biochem. Behav.* 1993, **45**, 369-374.
35. Sharma RD. Effect of fenugreek seeds and leaves on blood glucose and serum insulin responses in human subjects. *Nutr. Res.* 1986, **6**, 1353-1364.
36. Sharma RD, Raghuram TC and Rao VD. Hypolipidaemic Effect of Fenugreek Seeds. A Clinical Study. *Phytotherapy Res.* 1991, **5**, 145-147.
37. Bordia A, Verma SK and Srivastava KC. Effect of ginger (*Zingiber officinale* Rosc.) and fenugreek (*Trigonella foenum graecum* L.) on blood lipids, blood sugar and platelet aggregation in patients with coronary artery disease. *Prostagland. Leukotr. Essent. Fatty Acids* 1997, **56**, 379-384.
38. Sharma RD and Raghuram TC. Hypoglycaemic effect of fenugreek seeds in non-insulin dependent diabetic subjects. *Nutr. Res.* 1990, **10**, 731-739.
39. Raghuram TC, Sharma RD, Sivakumar B and Sahay BK. Effect of Fenugreek Seeds on Intravenous Glucose Disposition in Non-insulin Dependent Diabetic Patients. *Phytotherapy Res.* 1994, **8**, 83-86.
40. Gupta A, Gupta R and Lal B. Effect of *Trigonella foenum graecum* (Fenugreek) Seeds on Glycaemic Control and Insulin Resistance in Type 2 Diabetes Mellitus: A Double Blind Placebo Controlled Study. *J. Assoc. Physicians India* 2001, **49**, 1057-1061.
41. Madar Z, Abel R, Samish S and Arad J. Glucose-lowering effect of fenugreek in non-insulin dependent diabetics. *Eur. J. Clin. Nutr.* 1988, **42**, 51-54.
42. Sharma RD, Raghuram TC and Rao NS. Effect of fenugreek seeds on blood glucose and serum lipids in Type I diabetes. *Eur. J. Clin. Nutr.* 1990, **44**, 301-306.
43. Sharma RD, Sarkar A, Hazra DK, Misra B, Singh JB, Maheshwari BB et al. Hypolipidaemic Effect of Fenugreek Seeds: a Chronic Study in Non-insulin Dependent Diabetic Patients. *Phytotherapy Res.* 1996, **10**, 332-334.
44. Basch E, Ulbricht C, Kuo G, Szapary P and Smith M. Therapeutic Applications of Fenugreek. *Altern. Med. Rev.* 2003, **8**, 20-27.
45. Al-Habori M and Raman A. Review: Antidiabetic and Hypocholesterolaemic Effects of Fenugreek. *Phytotherapy Res.* 1998, **12**, 233-242.
46. Trigonella. In: *British Herbal Pharmacopoeia 1983*. ISBN 0-903032-07-4. Bournemouth: British Herbal Medicine Association, 1983.
47. Foenugraeci semen. German Commission E Monograph published in: Bundesanzeiger No. 22 of 1 February 1990.
48. Fenugrec. In: *Médicaments à base de plantes*. ISBN 2-911473-02-7. Saint-Denis Cedex, France: Agence du Médicament, 1998.
49. Chevallier A. Fenugreek - *Trigonella foenum-graecum*. In: *Encyclopedia of Medicinal Plants, 2nd ed.* ISBN 0-7513-1209-6. London-New York: Dorling Kindersley, 2001:277.
50. Stodola J and Volák J. Fenugreek. Translated into English in: Bunney S, editor. *The Illustrated Book of Herbs*. ISBN 0-7064-1489-6. London: Octopus Books, 1984:286.
51. Ody P. Fenugreek - *Trigonella foenum-graecum*. In: *The Complete Guide - Medicinal Herbal*. ISBN 0-7513-3005-1. London-New York: Dorling Kindersley, 2000:129.
52. Wichtl M and Henke D. Bockshornsamen - Trigonellae foenugraeci semen. In: Hartke K, Hartke H, Mutschler E, Rücker G and Wichtl M, editors. *Kommentar zum Europäischen Arzneibuch*. Stuttgart: Wissenschaftliche Verlagsgesellschaft, 1999 (12 Lfg.):B 47 [GERMAN].
53. Sharma RD, Sarkar A, Hazra DK, Misra B, Singh JB and Maheshwari BB. Toxicological Evaluation of Fenugreek Seeds: a Long Term Feeding Experiment in Diabetic Patients. *Phytotherapy Res.* 1996, **10**, 519-520.
54. Rao PU, Sesikeran B, Rao PS, Naidu AN, Rao VV and Ramachandran EP. Short term nutritional and safety evaluation of fenugreek. *Nutr. Res.* 1996, **16**, 1495-1505.
55. Mahmoud I, Alkofahi A and Abdelaziz A. Mutagenic and Toxic Activities of Several Spices and Some Jordanian Medicinal Plants. *Int. J. Pharmacognosy* 1992, **30**, 81-85.
56. Mital N and Gopaldas T. Effects of fenugreek (*Trigonella foenum graecum*) seed based diets on the birth outcome in albino rats. *Nutr. Rep. Int.* 1986, **33**, 363-369.
57. Sethi N, Nath D, Singh RK and Srivastava RK. Antifertility and teratogenic activity of some indigenous medicinal plants in rats. *Fitoterapia* 1990, **61**, 64-67.
58. Fenugreek. In: UK Statutory Instrument 1994 No. 2410. The Medicines (Products Other Than Veterinary Drugs) (General Sale List) Amendment Order 1994. Schedule 1, Table A.
59. Fenugreek. In: Sections 182.10 and 182.20 of USA Code of Federal Regulations, Title 21, Food and Drugs, Parts 170 to 199. Revised as of April 1, 2000.
60. Trigonella foenum-graecum L., seeds. In: *Flavouring Substances and Natural Sources of Flavourings, 3rd ed.* ISBN 2-7160-0081-6. Strasbourg: Council of Europe, 1981.

REGULATORY GUIDELINES FROM OTHER EU COUNTRIES

FRANCE

Médicaments à base de plantes [48]: Fenugrec, graine.

Therapeutic indications accepted

Oral use
Traditionally used to facilitate weight gain.

GERMANY

Commission E monograph [47]: Foenugraeci semen (Bockshornsamen).

Uses
Internal: Loss of appetite.
External: As a poultice for local inflammation.

Contraindications
None known.

Side effects
Undesirable skin reactions may arise from repeated external application.

Interactions with other drugs
None known.

Dosage
Daily dose unless otherwise prescribed:
Internal: 6 g of the drug or equivalent preparations.
External: 50 g of powdered drug to 250 ml of water.

Mode of administration
Internal: Comminuted drug and other galenic preparations.
External: Boil 50 g of powdered drug with 250 ml of water and use as a moist and warm poultice.

GALANGAL — Zingiberaceae

Galangae rhizoma

Synonyms: Lesser Galangal, Galanga.

Definition

Galangal consists of the dried rhizome of *Alpinia officinarum* Hance.

There are two species of galangal: lesser galangal, *Alpinia officinarum* Hance (the subject of this monograph), which is native to, and mainly grown in, southern China, especially on the island of Hainan; and greater galangal, *Alpinia galanga* Willdenow, which is grown in tropical south-east Asian countries such as Indonesia, Malaysia and the Philippines. Both are members of the Zingiberaceae or ginger family.

CONSTITUENTS

□ ***Diarylheptanoids*** At least 12 closely-related diarylheptanoid compounds have been identified, all with a 3-keto group and a 5-hydroxy, 5-methoxy or 5-keto group [1-6]. The majority have one phenyl ring substituted, the most abundant compound of this type being 5-hydroxy-7-(4′-hydroxy-3′-methoxyphenyl)-1-phenyl-3-heptanone (structure illustrated in the diagram) [2]. However, compounds with neither (i.e. 5-hydroxy-1,7-diphenyl-3-heptanone) or both of the phenyl rings substituted are also present.
□ ***Flavonoids***, occurring as aglycones rather than glycosides: the flavonols galangin (= 3,5,7-trihydroxyflavone) and kaempferide, with smaller amounts of kaempferol, quercetin, rhamnetin, isorhamnetin and izalpin, and the 3-methyl ethers of galangin and quercetin [1,6-10]; also the flavanone pinocembrin [7].

No data appear to be published on flavonoid levels in the crude drug, but an ethanolic extract was reported to contain ca. 10% of galangin [11].

□ ***Essential oil***, ca. 1% (Ph. Helv. min. 0.5% V/m), in which 1,8-cineole (49.6%) was found to be the principal component, together with β-pinene (6.6%), α-pinene (ca. 5%), camphene (4.6%), cadinene (4.6%), limonene (4.0%) and small amounts of other monoterpenes, sequiterpenes and aromatic esters [12].
□ ***Other constituents*** include the glucosides of β-sitosterol, stigmasterol and campesterol [8], starch (20-25%), sugars, lipids and phlobaphenes (red, insoluble, high MW tannins) [13].

Published Assay Methods

Essential oil by GC [12].

PHARMACOLOGY

In vitro

Spasmolytic activity
Hexane and chloroform soluble fractions from galangal inhibited histamine- and barium chloride-induced contractions of isolated guinea pig ileum by 95-100% at 1×10^{-4} g/ml [4]. Essential oil from galangal produced relaxant effects on isolated guinea pig ileal (EC_{50} 27 mg/litre) and tracheal (EC_{50} 122 mg/litre) smooth muscle, more effectively than ginger oil but less effectively than oils from angelica root, cardamom and clove [14].

Inhibition of prostaglandin biosynthesis
A hot aqueous extract of galangal was found to inhibit the prostaglandin (PG) biosynthesizing enzyme PG synthetase; a chloroform fraction produced 99% inhibition at 150 µg/ml [1]. It was subsequently demonstrated that the diarylheptanoids in galangal inhibit PG synthetase and hence prostaglandin biosynthesis, an effect associated with anti-inflammatory and anti-platelet

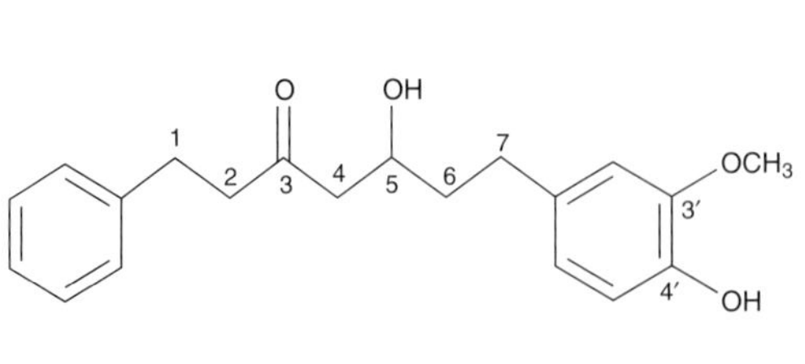

A diarylheptanoid

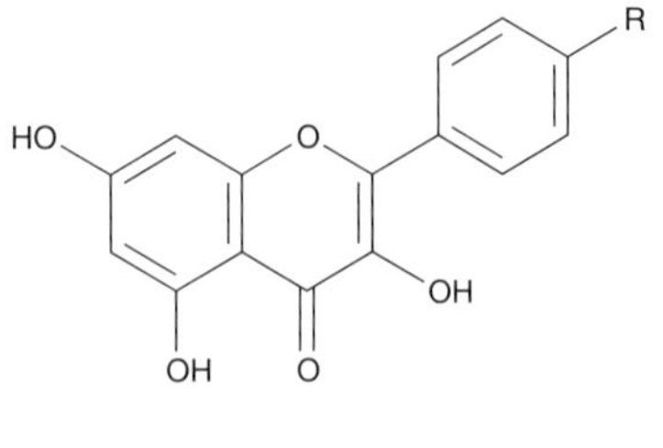

Galangin	R = H
Kaempferol	R = OH
Kaempferide	R = OCH_3

aggregation activities. IC_{50} values were mainly in the range 2.0-19 μM, compared to 4.9 μM for indomethacin [1,3]. Gingerols from ginger, which have structural similarities to diarylheptanoids in galangal, also inhibit prostaglandin biosynthesis [1].

In more recent work, bioassay-guided fractionation of a methanolic extract led to the isolation and identification of five cyclooxygenase-2 (COX-2) inhibitors in galangal, four being flavonoids and one a diarylheptanoid. At a concentration of 2.5 μg/ml galangin and kaempferide inhibited the formation of prostaglandin D_2 by 100%, while galangin 3-methyl ether, pinocembrin and 5-hydroxy-7-(4′-hydroxy-3′-methoxyphenyl)-1-phenyl-3-heptanone inhibited its formation by 89%, 52% and 72% respectively [7].

Antiviral activity
Serum obtained from guinea pigs 2 hours after gastrointestinal administration of 600 mg of a dry aqueous extract of galangal inhibited the growth of herpes simplex virus type 1 by 93% compared to serum from animals which received water only; galangal gave the most favourable result out of 32 herbal extracts tested [15]. An aqueous extract from galangal also showed significant inhibitory activity against hepatitis B virus [16].

The flavonol galangin exhibited significant inhibitory activity against herpes simplex virus type 1 and coxsackie B virus type 1 at concentrations of 12-47 μg/ml [17].

Antigenotoxicity of galangin
Galangin at 600 μg/plate inhibited the mutagenic action of 2-aminoanthracene on *Salmonella typhimurium* strain TA98 by 97% [18] and has shown antigenotoxic activity in various other studies, both *in vitro* and *in vivo* [11].

Other activities
Diarylheptanoids isolated from galangal showed significant antihepatotoxic effects, inhibiting carbon tetrachloride-induced cytotoxicity in primary cultured rat hepatocytes ($p<0.001$ at 1 mg/ml) [19].

Three diarylheptanoids from galangal, and the flavonols galangin, rhamnetin and kaempferide, exhibited antioxidative activity in a microsomal lipid peroxidation assay [6].

In vivo
Gastric secretions were measured and analyzed 3-5 hours after oral administration of aqueous or methanolic dry extracts of galangal to intact, unanaesthetized rabbits at 70-75 mg/kg body weight. The volume of gastric juice decreased to 60-68%, acid output to 44-59% and pepsin output to 34-67% of basal values ($p<0.05$), compared to 60%, 34% and 55% respectively for cimetidine at 50 mg/kg. Fairly similar results were obtained with extracts of other Zingiberaceae, including ginger [20].

Anti-inflammatory effect of galangin
Galangin administered intraperitoneally to rats at 100 mg/kg significantly inhibited simultaneously induced carrageenan paw oedema by 28% ($p<0.01$) and croton oil ear oedema by 55% ($p<0.001$) [21].

Based on its potent enzyme modulating, antimutagenic, antioxidative and free radical scavenging activities, galangin may be a promising candidate as a cancer chemopreventive agent; for a review see Heo et al. [11].

CLINICAL STUDIES

None published on mono-preparations of galangal.

THERAPEUTICS

Actions
Warming digestive tonic [22], carminative [22-24], spasmolytic [4,25], reduces gastric secretions [20], anti-emetic [22,26], anti-inflammatory (inhibits prostaglandin biosynthesis) [1,3,7], antiviral [15, 16].
Diarylheptanoids are antihepatotoxic [19] and antioxidative [6]; galangin is anti-inflammatory [21] and antigenotoxic [11,18].

Indications
None adequately substantiated by pharmacological or clinical studies.

Uses based on experience or tradition
Dyspeptic complaints [1,22-26], flatulence [22-24], nausea and vomiting (including seasickness) [22,23,26] and loss of appetite [25].

Contraindications
None known.

Side effects
None known.

Interactions with other drugs
None known.

Dosage
Three times daily, half an hour before meals: dried rhizome, 1-2 g or by infusion or decoction [23,24]; liquid extract 1:1 in 25% alcohol, 1-2 ml; tincture 1:5 in 45% alcohol, 2-4 ml [23].

SAFETY

Galangal is widely used as a spice and condiment in Asian countries and is considered safe at therapeutic dose levels; excessive doses may be irritant to the digestive system. A tincture of galangal showed no mutagenic potential in the Ames test using *Salmonella typhimurium* strains TA98 and TA100 [27].

Essential oil of galangal is considered unlikely to present any hazard from topical use in aromatherapy [28].

REGULATORY STATUS

Medicines

UK	No licences issued for products containing galangal.
France	Not listed in *Médicaments à base de plantes* [29].
Germany	Commission E monograph published, with approved uses [25].

Food

USA	Generally recognized as safe (21 CFR 182.10 and 182.20) [30].
Council of Europe	Permitted as flavouring, category N2 [31].

REFERENCES

Current Pharmacopoeial Monographs

Ph. Helv.	Galanga
DAC	Galgant
BHP	Galangal

Literature References

1. Kiuchi F, Iwakami S, Shibuya M, Hanaoka F and Sankawa U. Inhibition of Prostaglandin and Leukotriene Biosynthesis by Gingerols and Diarylheptanoids. *Chem. Pharm. Bull.* 1992, **40**, 387-391.
2. Itokawa H, Morita H, Midorikawa I, Aiyama R amd Morita M. Diarylheptanoids from the Rhizome of *Alpinia officinarum* Hance. *Chem. Pharm. Bull.* 1985, **33**, 4889-4893.
3. Kiuchi F, Shibuya M and Sankawa U. Inhibitors of prostaglandin biosynthesis from *Alpinia officinarum. Chem. Pharm. Bull.* 1982, **30**, 2279-2282.
4. Itokawa H, Morita M and Mihashi S. Two New Diarylheptanoids from *Alpinia officinarum* Hance. *Chem. Pharm. Bull.* 1981, **29**, 2383-2385.
5. Inoue T, Shinbori T, Fujioka M, Hashimoto K and Masada Y. Studies on the Pungent Principle of *Alpinia officinarum* Hance. *Yakugaku Zasshi* 1978, **98**, 1255-1257 [JAPANESE/English summary].
6. Shen J, Zhang H, Xu B and Pan J. The antioxidative constituents of rhizomes of *Alpinia officinarum. Nat. Prod. Res. Dev.* 1998, **10** (2), 33-36 [CHINESE/English summary].
7. Kang SS, Kim JS, Son KH, Kim HP and Chang HW. Isolation of COX-2 Inhibitors from *Alpinia officinarum. Korean J. Pharmacogn.* 2000, **31**, 57-62 [KOREAN/English summary].
8. Tunmann P and Tkotz H. Flavonols and Sterol Glycosides in the Root of *Alpinia officinarum* Hance. *Z. Naturforsch.* 1972, **27 b**, 323-324 [GERMAN].
9. Bleier W and Chirikdjian JJ. Über die Flavonoide von Rhizoma Galangae (*Alpinia officinarum* Hance). *Planta Medica* 1972, **22**, 145-151 [GERMAN/English summary].
10. Karlsen J and Beker F. Flavonoids of rhizoma galangae (*Alpinia officinarum*). *Farm. Aikak.* 1971, **80**, 95-97; through *Chem. Abstr.* 1971, **75**, 59751.
11. Heo MY, Sohn SJ and Au WW. Anti-genotoxicity of galangin as a cancer chemopreventive agent candidate. *Mutation Res.* 2001, **488**, 135-150.
12. Lawrence BM, Hogg JW and Terhune SJ. Essential Oils and their Constituents. Part II. The Oil of *Alpinia officinarum* Hance. *Perfumery Ess. Oil. Record* 1969, **60**, 88-96.
13. Steinegger E and Hänsel R. Galgant [Galangal]. In: *Pharmakognosie, 5th ed.* ISBN 3-540-55649-4. Berlin-Heidelberg-New York: Springer-Verlag, 1992:276 [GERMAN].
14. Reiter M and Brandt W. Relaxant Effects on Tracheal and Ileal Smooth Muscles of the Guinea Pig. *Arzneim.-Forsch./Drug Res.* 1985, **35**, 408-414.
15. Kurokawa M, Ohyama H, Hozumi T, Namba T, Nakano M and Shiraki K. Assay for Antiviral Activity of Herbal Extracts Using Their Absorbed Sera. *Chem. Pharm. Bull.* 1996, **44**, 1270-1272.
16. Chung TH, Kim JC, Kim MK, Choi SC, Kim SL, Chung JM et al. Investigation of Korean Plant Extracts for Potential Phytotherapeutic Agents Against B-Virus Hepatitis. *Phytotherapy Res.* 1995, **9**, 429-434.
17. Meyer JJM, Afolayan AJ, Taylor MB and Erasmus D. Antiviral activity of galangin isolated from the aerial parts of *Helichrysum aureonitens. J. Ethnopharmacol.* 1997, **56**, 165-169.
18. Wall ME, Wani MC, Manikumar G, Abraham P, Taylor H, Hughes TJ et al. Plant antimutagenic agents, 2. Flavonoids. *J. Nat. Prod.* 1988, **51**, 1084-1091.
19. Hikino H, Kiso Y, Kato N, Hamada Y, Shioiri T, Aiyama R et al. Antihepatotoxic actions of gingerols and diarylheptanoids. *J. Ethnopharmacol.* 1985, **14**, 31-39.
20. Sakai K, Miyazaki Y, Yamane T, Saitoh Y, Ikawa C and Nishihata T. Effect of Extracts of Zingiberaceae Herbs on Gastric Secretion in Rabbits. *Chem. Pharm. Bull.* 1989, **37**, 215-217.
21. Gábor M and Rázga Z. Effect of benzopyrone derivatives on simultaneously induced croton oil ear oedema and carrageenin paw oedema in rats. *Acta Physiol. Hung.* 1991, **77**, 197-207.
22. Chevallier A. Galangal. In: *The Encyclopedia of Medicinal Plants.* ISBN 0-7513-0314-3. London-New York-Stuttgart: Dorling Kindersley, 1996:58.
23. Alpinia. In: *British Herbal Pharmacopoeia 1983.* ISBN 0-903032-07-4. Bournemouth: British Herbal Medicine Association, 1983.
24. Pharmaceutical Society of Great Britain. *British Pharmaceutical Codex 1934.* London: Pharmaceutical Press, 1934.
25. Galangae rhizoma. German Commission E Monograph published in: Bundesanzeiger No. 173 of 18 September 1986; amended in Bundesanzeiger No. 50 of 13 March 1990.
26. Tang W and Eisenbrand G. Alpinia spp. In: *Chinese Drugs of Plant Origin. Chemistry, Pharmacology and Use in Traditional and Modern Medicine.* ISBN 0-387-19309-X. New York-Berlin-Heidelberg: Springer-Verlag, 1992:87-93.
27. Schimmer O, Krüger A, Paulini H and Haefele F. An evaluation of 55 commercial plant extracts in the Ames mutagenicity test. *Pharmazie* 1994, **49**, 448-51.
28. Tisserand R and Balacs T. Safety Index, Part 2: Galangal (roots). In: *Essential Oil Safety - A Guide for Health Care Professionals.* Edinburgh: Churchill-Livingstone, 1995:212-225.
29. *Médicaments à base de plantes.* ISBN 2-911473-02-7. Saint-Denis Cedex, France: Agence du Médicament, 1998.
30. Galanga (galangal). In: Sections 182.10 and 182.20 of USA Code of Federal Regulations, Title 21, Food and Drugs, Parts 170 to 199. Revised as of April 1, 2000.

31. Alpinia officinarum Hance. In: *Flavouring Substances and Natural Sources of Flavourings, 3rd ed.* ISBN 2-7160-0081-6. Strasbourg: Council of Europe, 1981.

REGULATORY GUIDELINES FROM OTHER EU COUNTRIES

GERMANY

Commission E monograph [25]: Galangae rhizoma (Galgantwurzelstock).

Uses
Dyspeptic complaints. Loss of appetite.

Contraindications
None known.

Side effects
None known.

Interactions with other drugs
None known.

Dosage
Unless otherwise prescribed, daily dose: dried rhizome, 2-4 g; tincture (in accordance with DAB Ergänzung B6), 2-4 g.

Mode of administration
Comminuted or powdered drug and other galenic preparations for internal use.

Actions
Spasmolytic, anti-inflammatory (inhibition of prostaglandin biosynthesis), antibacterial.

GINKGO LEAF

Ginkgoaceae

Ginkgo folium

Definition
Ginkgo Leaf consists of the dried leaves of *Ginkgo biloba* L.

CONSTITUENTS

GINKGO LEAF

☐ ***Flavonoids***, 0.5-3.5% (Ph. Eur. min. 0.5%), of various types [1-3].

Flavonols (as aglycones): kaempferol, quercetin, isorhamnetin and myricetin.

Mono-, di- and triglycosides of the above flavonols.

p-Coumaroyl esters of kaempferol and quercetin di- and triglycosides, some of which are found only in *Ginkgo biloba*.

Flavones: apigenin and luteolin, as aglycones and mono-glucosides.

Dimeric flavones (biflavones): amentoflavone and its methylated derivatives.

Flavan-3-ols: (+)-catechin, (–)-epicatechin, (+)-gallocatechin and (–)-epigallocatechin.

At least 33 flavonoids (22 glycosides, 6 flavonol aglycones and 5 biflavones) can be identified by fingerprint HPLC [3].

☐ ***Terpene trilactones*** Four diterpene trilactones, ginkgolides A, B, C and J (which differ only in the number and positions of hydroxyl groups) and the sesquiterpene trilactone bilobalide [1,2,4]. These compounds are unique to the ginkgo tree and all have a characteristic tertiary butyl group. Ginkgolides are remarkably stable compounds, but bilobalide is unstable in solutions of pH > 7 [4]. Total concentrations of terpene trilactones in leaf samples vary widely depending on the source and season, from less than 0.1% [5] to about 0.4% [6,7], reaching a maximum in late summer or early autumn [8]. Bilobalide is usually the most abundant terpene trilactone. For example, in one recent study the amounts of individual compounds determined by HPLC were: ginkgolide A, 0.032%; B, 0.024%; C, 0.029%; J, 0.015%; bilobalide, 0.15%; total 0.25% [9].

Pharmaceutical dried leaf should contain not less than 0.1% of terpene lactones, calculated as the sum of bilobalide and ginkgolides A, B and C [10].

☐ ***Long-chain alkyl phenols*** of several types, with alkyl chain lengths of C_{13}, C_{15} or C_{17}:

Ginkgolic acids (anarcardic acids, 2-hydroxy-6-alkyl benzoic acids). In one determination the total content of ginkgolic acids in dried leaf was found to be 1.73%, the principal compound (1.20%) having a C_{15} alkyl chain with one double bond at position 8 [11].

Cardanols (ginkgols, 3-alkylphenols), approx. 0.1% [12].

Urushiols (3-alkylcatechols), 7-25 ppm (i.e. up to 0.0025%) [12,13].

☐ ***Condensed tannins*** (proanthocyanidins), 4-12% when determined by acid hydrolysis, predominantly in the form of prodelphinidins [14] but including procyanidin dimers such as catechin-catechin and epicatechin-catechin [1].

☐ ***Other constituents*** include polysaccharides [15], organic acids, phytosterols (ca. 0.2%; mainly β-sitosterol) and a small amount of essential oil with diverse components [1].

STANDARDIZED GINKGO LEAF DRY EXTRACT

In most of the pharmacological and clinical studies relating to ginkgo leaf a standardized dry extract has been used. No extract of this nature is yet official in the European Pharmacopoeia. However, the major extracts manufactured in Europe conform to very specific requirements of a monograph in

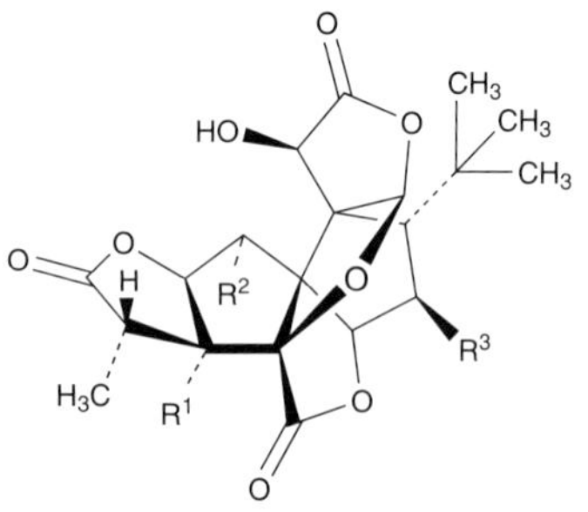

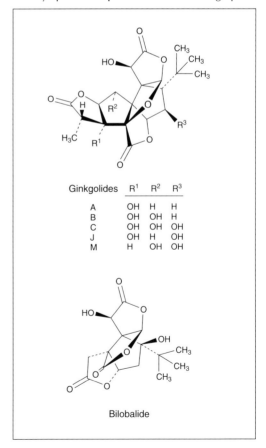

Ginkgolides	R^1	R^2	R^3
A	OH	H	H
B	OH	OH	H
C	OH	OH	OH
J	OH	H	OH
M	H	OH	OH

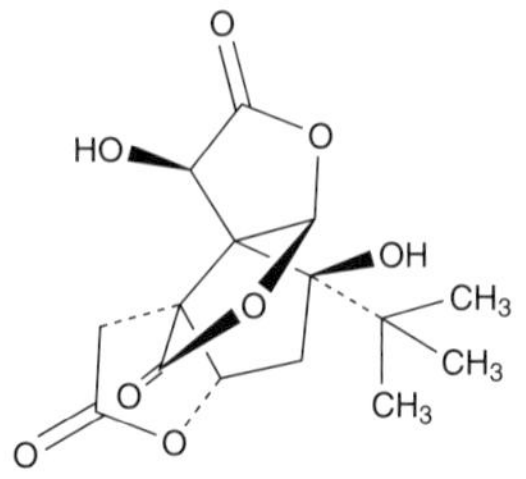

Bilobalide

the *Deutsches Arzneibuch* (DAB) [16]:
Extracted with acetone 60% m/m by a multistage process.
Drug to extract ratio of 35-67:1
22.0-27.0% of flavonoids, expressed as flavone glycosides (MW 756.7).
5.0-7.0% of terpene lactones including 2.8-3.4% of ginkgolides A, B and C, and 2.6-3.2% of bilobalide.
Effectively, the DAB monograph specifies a highly refined 50:1 extract containing about 24% of flavonoids and 6% of terpene lactones. Many other constituents of ginkgo leaf are present only in negligible amounts or are not detectable in the extract, including flavonol and flavone aglycones and monoglycosides, biflavones, flavan-3-ols, long-chain alkyl phenols and steroids [2,17].

Published Assay Methods
Flavonoids by HPLC [Ph. Eur.]. Terpene trilactones by HPLC [5,6,9,18] or capillary GC [7]. Ginkgolic acids by HPLC [19] or HPLC-MS [20].

PHARMACOLOGY

The majority of pharmacological and clinical studies relating to ginkgo leaf have been carried out using standardized ginkgo leaf dry extracts conforming with the requirements described in the Constituents section. Except where stated otherwise, the term "extract" in the following text relates to an extract of this nature.

A large number of human studies have been carried out with ginkgo leaf extracts, ranging from clinical studies since the 1980s in dementia and intermittent claudication to relatively recent studies of cognitive effects in healthy individuals. They reflect not only the importance of ginkgo leaf as a prescription drug but also popular interest in its potential for cognition-enhancing effects. Its broad spectrum of pharmacological activities have been investigated in considerable depth. The numerous *in vitro* and *in vivo* studies are not covered here, but have been summarized by De Feudis [21] and in the ESCOP monograph [10].

Pharmacological studies in humans

Cognition-enhancing effects in healthy individuals
Up to the turn of the millenium only a few studies had investigated the effect of ginkgo leaf extracts on cognitive function in healthy individuals. One of the earliest (1984), a randomized, double-blind, crossover study involving 8 healthy female volunteers aged 25-40 years, demonstrated that a single 600 mg dose of a ginkgo leaf extract significantly improved short-term working memory ($p<0.0001$ for overall reaction time) [22].

In a subsequent study (1999) with a randomized, double-blind, placebo-controlled, 5-way crossover design, 31 healthy volunteers aged 30-59 years were given, on different occasions separated by 5-day wash-out periods, 3 × 50 mg, 3 × 100 mg, 1 × 120 mg or 1 × 240 mg of a ginkgo leaf extract, or placebo, daily for 2 days. Psychometric tests conducted pre-dose and at intervals until 11 hours post-dose confirmed that cognition-enhancing effects of the extract were more pronounced for memory, particularly working memory, than for other aspects of cognitive and psychomotor functioning. The effects were more likely to be apparent in individuals aged 50-59 years and were most evident after 120 mg of extract [23].

More recent randomized, double-blind, placebo-controlled studies have also demonstrated positive effects of ginkgo leaf extracts in healthy participants, usually concentrating on one or the other of two distinct age groups: relatively young participants (18-40 years) or those of more advanced years (over 50) with no cognitive impairment:

Healthy individuals aged 18-40 years
Dose-dependent cognitive effects were assessed after acute administration (on different days at weekly intervals) of 120 mg, 240 mg or 360 mg of a ginkgo leaf extract or placebo to 20 healthy undergraduates (aged 19-24 years) in a crossover design. The most striking effects of the extract were significant and dose-dependent improvements in the 'speed of attention' factor following a 240 mg dose ($p = 0.036$ at 2.5 hours, $p = 0.026$ at 6 hours) or a 360 mg dose ($p = 0.0001$ at 2.5 hours, $p = 0.0004$ at 6 hours), while no significant improvements (but a positive trend) were evident after 120 mg [24].

Cognitive tests and mood assessment carried out at baseline and 1, 2.5, 4 and 6 hours after administration of 360 mg of a ginkgo leaf extract or placebo to 20 healthy young adults in a crossover study demonstrated that the extract improved secondary memory performance, mental arithmetic results and self-rated mood [25].

Neuropsychological tests conducted before and after treatment of 61 healthy participants aged 18-40 years with either 120 mg of a ginkgo leaf extract or placebo daily for 30 days indicated that the extract improved memory processes, particularly with respect to working memory ($p<0.05$) and memory consolidation ($p<0.01$) [26].

Healthy individuals aged 50 years or over
In a study involving 40 adults aged 55-86 years with no history of cognitive dysfunction, the effects of a ginkgo leaf extract (180 mg/day for 6 weeks) on neurocognitive processes were evaluated using a diverse battery of neuropsychological tests and measures. Compared to the placebo group, partici-

pants receiving the extract exhibited significantly greater improvement in a mental task (a colour and word test) assessing speed of processing ability, and more participants in the ginkgo extract group rated their overall ability to remember as "improved" by the end of treatment [27].

The same authors subsequently carried out a larger scale study, using the same extract and dosage regimen but with a wider range of tests to evaluate neuropsychological functioning, involving 262 community-dwelling, cognitively intact volunteers aged 60 years or older (mean 67.8 years) with unremarkable medical histories (no dementia or significant neurocognitive impairment). Compared to the placebo group, participants in the ginkgo group achieved significantly greater improvement in memory tasks involving 30-minute-delayed free recall ($p<0.04$) and recognition ($p<0.01$) of verbal material, and in 30-minute-delayed recognition of visual material (human faces; $p<0.025$). More participants in the ginkgo group rated their overall ability to remember as improved ($p<0.05$) [28].

On the other hand, a study of similar scale involving 219 healthy, community-dwelling volunteers over 60 years of age (average 69) failed to show significant differences in results between those taking a ginkgo leaf extract (3 × 40 mg/day for 6 weeks) and those taking placebos in any of a range of standard neuropsychological tests of learning, memory, attention and concentration [29].

A randomized study in which golf players aged 50-70 years received either 240 mg of a ginkgo leaf extract (n = 35) or placebo (n = 35) daily for 6 weeks suggested that ginkgo leaf can even help to improve golf performance ($p<0.05$), particularly of players benefiting from stabilization of mood and improvement of coordination [30].

Other cognitive function studies

A very large study of randomized older volunteers, in the form of a postal survey using questionnaires on activities of daily living (ADL) and various aspects of mood and sleep, involved 5028 free-living participants, recruited through a magazine, resident in the British Isles and of average age 68.9 years (range 32-97 years). Ginkgo leaf extract (GLE) 120 mg tablets were supplied to 1000 participants with instructions to take one tablet each day for 4 months; the remainder formed the control group and received no tablets (NT). One type of ADL scale was completed by an observer (spouse, caregiver or other informant sufficiently familiar with the individual) at baseline and at the end of month 4, while each participant completed a self-rating ADL scale and also rating scales for mood and sleep on a monthly basis. Significant differences (mainly $p<0.001$) between the ginkgo and control groups were evident on all scales at each time point. The ginkgo group felt better able to cope with their daily activities and showed positive changes in mood and sleep compared to the control group [31]. As a follow-up survey, 1570 of the volunteers continued participation for a further 6 months, selecting their own treatment option and thus creating four groups according to initial and follow-up treatments (GLE + GLE, GLE + NT, NT + GLE and NT + NT). Participants' self-ratings at the end of the 6-month period indicated that overall competence, "mood" and "alertness" deteriorated on cessation of ginkgo leaf extract treatment and improved when treatment was initiated [32].

Haemorheological effects

A randomized, placebo-controlled, cross-over study involving 10 healthy subjects demonstrated that after oral administration of a solution containing 112.5 mg of a ginkgo leaf extract blood flow in nail fold capillaries significantly increased by about 57% within 1 hour ($p<0.004$) and erythrocyte aggregation decreased by 15.6% within 2 hours ($p<0.001$) [33].

Another randomized, placebo-controlled study, involving 48 patients with vascular dementia, demonstrated that intravenously administered doses of 100 or 200 mg of a ginkgo leaf extract significantly increased microperfusion of the skin ($p<0.05$) and 200 mg decreased whole blood viscosity after 60 minutes ($p<0.05$) [34].

Pharmacokinetics

After oral administration of 50-300 mg of a ginkgo leaf extract to 2 healthy volunteers flavonol glycosides reached peak plasma levels within 2-3 hours, had half-lives of 2-4 hours and declined to baseline levels within 24 hours [35].

Following ingestion of 120 mg of a ginkgo leaf extract (in solution) by 12 healthy young volunteers ginkgolides A and B and bilobalide had high bioavailabilities of 80, 88 and 79% respectively. Peak concentrations in blood were 16-33 ng/ml in fasting conditions and 11-21 ng/ml after a meal. Plasma half-lives were 9.5-10.6 hours for ginkgolide B and 3.2-4.5 hours for ginkgolide A and bilobalide [36].

CLINICAL STUDIES

The efficacy of ginkgo leaf extracts has been assessed in a large number of controlled studies, probably more than carried out on any other plant drug and far too numerous to describe here. Indications for which they have been prescribed can be usefully grouped under four main headings: dementia, cerebral insufficiency, neurosensory disturbances and intermittent claudication. This section concentrates primarily on meta-analyses and systematic reviews of clinical studies in these areas, while summaries of the more important individual studies may be found in an ESCOP monograph [10].

Several studies in a field of recent interest, the prophylaxis of acute mountain sickness among climbers, are summarized at the end of this section.

Dementia

Dementia is a form of mental disorder in which cognitive and intellectual functions of the mind are affected, impairment of memory being one of the earliest signs. It is invariably a symptom of organic cerebral disease and implies some degree of permanent change. Totally recoverable confusional states, in which cognitive changes are also prominent, are thus excluded (but may be classified as "cerebral insufficiency" - see below). Controlled clinical studies have assessed the efficacy of ginkgo leaf extracts in mild to moderate dementia of the Alzheimer type, multi-infarct type or mixed types, diagnosed in accordance with DSM-III-R and/or ICD-10 in the more recent studies. Many of the older studies are now considered inadequate, primarily because of lack of clear diagnoses.

In a 1998 meta-analysis [37] focussing specifically on the effects of ginkgo leaf extracts on cognitive function in Alzheimer's disease, only 4 placebo-controlled studies [38-41] met all the inclusion criteria. Overall, from pooled data on a total of 424 patients (212 in verum, 212 in placebo groups), a modest but significant positive effect on objective measures of cognitive function ($p<0.001$) was evident after 3-6 months of daily oral treatment with 120-240 mg of a ginkgo leaf extract. The most prominent studies in terms of size and duration combined with methodological quality were those of Kanowski et al. (data on 156 patients evaluated after 24 weeks) [38] and Le Bars et al. (data on 244 patients evaluated after 26 weeks; 137 after 52 weeks) [39].

The conclusion from a wider systematic review of 9 randomized, double-blind, placebo-controlled studies was that collectively they suggested ginkgo leaf extracts are more effective than placebo in the symptomatic treatment of dementia (Alzheimer, multi-infarct and mixed types) [42].

A review of clinical studies of at least 6 months' duration in the treatment of mild to moderate Alzheimer's dementia [43] found the efficacy of a ginkgo leaf extract, based on two studies [38,39], to be comparable to that of second-generation cholinesterase inhibitors (tacrine, donepezil, rivastigmine and metrifonate), while the drop-out rate in ginkgo groups was much lower than for tacrine.

In sharp contrast with the above meta-analyses and clinical reviews the conclusions from a subsequent double-blind study (2000) were negative. The participants, 214 elderly patients of average age 83 years, all in residential care homes and suffering from mild to moderate dementia of the Alzheimer or vascular type ($n = 63$) or age-associated memory impairment ($n = 151$), were randomly treated with 160-240 mg of a ginkgo leaf extract or placebo daily for 24 weeks in accordance with a rather complex design. In comparison with placebo, no beneficial effects were evident in those participants assigned to ginkgo leaf extract for the entire 24-week period [44]. This study has been criticized for a number of reasons including the composite patient population with a broad and heterogeneous spectrum of cognitive decline, of high average age and high comorbidity, and living in the non-challenging environment of care-assisted homes; the adequacy of procedures has also been questioned [45]. The results cannot be generalized, therefore, and direct comparison with the effects of ginkgo leaf extracts in well-defined outpatient populations, as studied by Kanowski et al. [38] and Le Bars et al. [39], is difficult.

Cerebral Insufficiency

The term *cerebral insufficiency* has rather gone out of favour because of its vagueness. It can be described as a clinical symptom complex embracing a range of cerebral disturbances which fall short of a diagnosis of (but are sometimes considered to be early signs of) dementia. Symptoms described as typical of cerebral insufficiency include difficulties of concentration and memory, absent-mindedness, confusion, lack of energy, tiredness, decrease in physical performance, depressive mood and anxiety. These symptoms have been associated with decreased cerebral circulation [46].

From a complicated meta-analysis of 11 randomized, double-blind, placebo-controlled studies in the treatment of elderly patients suffering from various symptoms of cerebral insufficiency (and other symptoms better described as neurosensory disturbances - see below), it was concluded that ginkgo leaf extracts, in most cases at 150 mg/day, were significantly more effective than placebo [47]. In an earlier critical review of 40 controlled studies of ginkgo leaf extract preparations in the treatment of cerebral insufficiency, the authors found only 8 well-performed studies; all reported positive results but were considered too heterogeneous for meta-analysis [46].

Neurosensory Disturbances

Ginkgo leaf extracts have been used in the treatment of certain types of neurosensory disturbance, particularly complaints associated with the ear (vestibular and auditory systems) and/or eye. Those such as vertigo and dizziness, tinnitus, idiopathic hearing loss and nystagmus, may be regarded as symptoms associated with disturbances of CNS function. Others such as retinal ischaemia and degeneration are related more specifically to dysfunctions of the visual system and its associated neural pathways. Beneficial effects which ginkgo leaf extracts may have on these conditions are considered to be due to a vasoregulatory action [48].

Tinnitus

Although the notion that ginkgo leaf extracts could be helpful in the treatment of tinnitus has created considerable interest, any positive effects appear to be small and statistically insignificant, and reports are contradictory. Various "cerebral insufficiency" studies, in which tinnitus was but one symptom grouped with others such as memory loss and poor concentration, have been dismissed as of inadequate methodological quality. It has also been pointed out that tinnitus in cognitive insufficiency may be caused by central vascular insufficiency or neural metabolic disorder, whereas in primary tinnitus the initiating pathology is a cochlear disorder [49].

Ginkgo leaf extracts have been used in several randomized, double-blind, placebo-controlled studies in primary tinnitus. In a 12-week study involving 99 patients with chronic tinnitus, a modest but significant improvement in tinnitus loudness was claimed (no p-value stated) [50]. However, no significant differences between ginkgo and placebo groups were evident in a 12-week study based on mailed questionnaires and telephone interviews, involving 1121 participants aged 18-70 years and analysis of data from 360 matched pairs [51], nor in another study involving 66 patients [52]. A 1999 systematic review suggested that the results available up to that time were favourable to ginkgo leaf extracts as a treatment for tinnitus [53]. In contrast, a recent meta-analysis of 6 placebo-controlled studies revealed that only 21.6% of ginkgo-treated patients (n = 107/552) gained benefit compared to 18.4% of placebo-treated patients (n = 87/554) and concluded that ginkgo leaf extracts did not significantly benefit patients with tinnitus [52].

Other conditions

Limited evidence, mainly from relatively small controlled studies, that ginkgo leaf extracts may be beneficial to sufferers from vertigo and certain types of visual dysfunction associated with the retina has been summarized in an ESCOP monograph [10].

Intermittent claudication

In the development of peripheral arterial occlusive disease, a manifestation of arteriosclerosis, the most frequent initial symptomatology occurs at stage II (as defined by Fontaine) in the form of intermittent claudication, which can be described as convulsive pain in the calf or thigh after walking for a certain distance. From Fontaine stage III on, pain occurs at rest [54]. Numerous clinical studies have been carried out on patients with intermittent claudication, partly because this condition enables evaluation of objective parameters (pain-free and/or maximum walking distance, often on a treadmill), and two meta-analyses have been published, based on pooled data from randomized, double-blind, placebo-controlled studies.

Data from 9 studies involving a total of 619 patients with intermittent claudication (Fontaine stage II) were found to be suitable for pooling. The patients had been treated daily with 120-160 mg of the same ginkgo leaf acetone-water extract, or placebo, for periods of 6-24 weeks (24 weeks in 7 out of the 9 studies). The meta-analysis indicated a significant effect in favour of the ginkgo leaf extract, the overall pain-free walking distance being 23% greater than in patients taking placebo. Since the studies were to some extent heterogeneous (e.g. in duration of treatment and inclusion or lack of a placebo run-in period), a second stage was limited to data from the four most homogeneous studies (all with 24 weeks of treatment after a 2-week placebo run-in). In the latter case the overall pain-free walking distance was 18% greater in patients taking the extract than in those taking placebo. It was concluded that the ginkgo leaf extract was more effective than placebo for patients with intermittent claudication [54].

This conclusion corroborated an earlier meta-analysis in which data were pooled from 8 studies (6 of which were common to both meta-analyses) involving 415 patients with intermittent claudication (Fontaine stage II). A significant difference was found in favour of ginkgo leaf extract, the overall increase in pain-free walking distance being 34 metres greater in verum patients than in those taking placebo. In the three most homogeneous studies this difference was 33 metres [55].

However, the size of the overall treatment effect from ginkgo leaf extracts was considered modest and of uncertain clinical relevance taking into account that regular physical exercise can lead to increases from baseline in pain-free walking distance ranging from 88% to 190%. In one meta-analysis, exercise training was found to produce an average increase of 139 metres in pain-free walking distance compared to placebo tablets or no intervention. Of course, a disadvantage of exercise therapy is the notoriously poor compliance with such regimes [55,56].

Acute mountain sickness (AMS)

Most persons acutely exposed to altitudes above 3000 m experience varying degrees of mountain sickness, reflected by non-specific symptoms such as headache, lightheadedness, fatigue, nausea, insomnia etc., which can be further classified as cerebral and respiratory symptoms. Inspired by favourable reports from two ginkgo studies in the 1980s, one in the prevention of mountain sickness and the other concerning improvements in microcirculation of the extremities during exposure to cold, 44 healthy male mountaineers, all of whom had experienced acute mountain sickness on previous climbs, were randomly given 160 mg of a ginkgo leaf extract (n = 22) or placebo (n = 22) daily for 8 days during their ascent from below 2000 m to a Himalayan base camp at an altitude of 4900 m. None of the climbers in the ginkgo group experienced cerebral symptoms of AMS compared to 41% of the placebo group ($p = 1.4 \times 10^{-3}$) and only 14% experienced respiratory symptoms compared to 82% in the placebo group ($p = 1.2 \times 10^{-5}$). The ginkgo group also had significantly less vasomotor disorders of the extremities, as demonstrated using plethysmography and a specific questionnaire [57].

Whether ginkgo leaf extract is an effective prophylactic against AMS if begun 1 day prior to a rapid ascent was investigated in a randomized, double-blind, placebo-controlled study. The 26 participants received either the extract (3 × 60 mg daily; n = 12) or placebo (n = 14) starting 24 hours before being transported from sea level to the summit (4205 m) of Mauna Kea, Hawaii, over a period of 3 hours including a stop of 1 hour at 2835 m. Two subjects (17%) on ginkgo leaf extract and nine (64%) on placebo developed severe AMS and required prompt descent for their safety (p = 0.021). Although the median self-report symptom score (from the Lake Louise AMS questionnaire) at 4205 m was significantly lower in the ginkgo group than in the placebo group (p = 0.03), the ginkgo group results did not quite reach statistical significance in lowering the incidence of AMS (ginkgo group 7/12, placebo group 13/14; p = 0.07) [58].

Despite these promising results a more recent study found ginkgo leaf extract ineffective for AMS. On the approach to Mount Everest, at the baseline villages of Pheriche (4280 m) or Dingboche (4358 m), 614 trekkers completed a Lake Louise AMS questionnaire, had pulse oximetry readings taken, provided further data and were then enrolled in the study and randomized to take one of four daily treatments in a double-blind fashion: 2 × 120 mg of a ginkgo leaf extract, 2 × 250 mg of acetazolamide, combined ginkgo leaf extract + acetazolamide at these dosage levels, or placebo. On arrival at the study end point in Lobuje (4928 m), the 487 trekkers who completed the study provided repeat data. The incidence of AMS was 35% for ginkgo, 12% for acetazolamide, 14% for combined ginkgo + acetazolamide and 34% for placebo. The proportion of patients with severe AMS was 18% for ginkgo, 3% for acetazolamide, 7% for combined ginkgo + acetazolamide and 18% for placebo. While acetazolamide (a standard drug for prevention of AMS, but with common side effects) afforded robust protection against AMS symptoms, ginkgo leaf extract was no better than placebo in this study. Since the baseline was at high altitude and many participants would have experienced AMS below this altitude, direct comparison with earlier studies that had a low baseline altitude is difficult, but the authors considered the testing conditions to be adequate for the conclusions drawn [59].

THERAPEUTICS

Actions
Enhances cognitive function [22-28,31,32], increases blood flow [21,33,34], platelet activating factor (PAF) antagonist, antioxidant and free-radical scavenger [10,21,60].

Indications
Symptomatic treatment of mild to moderate dementia including primary degenerative dementia of the Alzheimer type, multi-infarct dementia and mixed forms [37-43].

Treatment of symptoms, attributed to impaired cerebral blood flow and loosely described as cerebral insufficiency, such as difficulties of concentration and memory, confusion, lack of energy and initiative, depressive mood and anxiety [46,47].

Enhancement of cognitive performance in healthy individuals [22-28,31,32].

Neurosensory disturbances such as vertigo and certain types of visual dysfunction [10,60]. Conclusions regarding the efficacy of ginkgo in tinnitus are conflicting [52,53]; a recent meta-analysis of controlled studies revealed no significant benefit [52].

Symptomatic treatment of peripheral arterial occlusive disease (intermittent claudication) [54, 55].

Contraindications
None.

Side effects
Occasional mild gastrointestinal upsets.

Interactions with other drugs
Caution is advisable in concomitant use of ginkgo and anticoagulants such as warfarin and aspirin [60]. However, no interaction with warfarin was

observed in a controlled study [61].

Dosage

Adult daily dose: 120-240 mg of a standardized ginkgo dry extract (as described under Constituents) or equivalent preparation, divided into 2-3 doses [10,38,39,42,55].

Treatment for at least 6 weeks is recommended before clinical benefit is assessed [60,62].

SAFETY

Ginkgo leaf extracts are usually well tolerated with a low frequency of adverse events, the most common being gastrointestinal complaints such as nausea and dyspepsia. The reported incidence of adverse events in clinical studies has often been no greater in ginkgo groups than in corresponding placebo groups [51,54,55]. In a 52-week controlled study in dementia involving 327 patients of mean age 69 years, 16% of patients in the ginkgo group (27/166) attributed at least one adverse event to the study drug compared to 12% in the placebo group (19/161) [39].

Allergic skin reactions in humans after contact with *Ginkgo biloba* fruits (but not ginkgo leaf) have been attributed to the presence of alkyl phenols [11,63] and allergic contact dermatitis can be produced in guinea pigs with ginkgolic acids [64]. However, based on sensitization tests performed in guinea pigs, it was concluded that ginkgo leaf extracts taken orally containing up to 1000 ppm (0.1%) of ginkgolic acids can be considered safe, while no firm advice could be given regarding the oral dose of ginkgolic acids that represents a real hazard [63]. In this perspective, the DAB limit of 5 ppm of ginkgolic acids in standardized ginkgo leaf dry extracts [16], which applied to extracts used in the majority of clinical studies, appears unduly stringent. Nevertheless, it seems desirable and prudent to control ginkgolic acids in extracts to a reasonably low level and this is not always the case with marketed products. Analysis of 27 ginkgo leaf extract preparations on the USA market revealed ginkgolic acid levels of over 1500 ppm (0.15%) in 20 preparations and over 25000 ppm (2.5%) in 4 preparations [65].

A few cases of spontaneous bleeding or haemorrhage, at least one under co-medication with warfarin and one with aspirin, have been reported in patients taking ginkgo leaf extracts [10,66], but no causal link with the extracts has been established. Subsequent controlled studies to investigate the potential for haemorrhagic complications found a lack of interaction between ginkgo leaf extracts and warfarin in long-term warfarin-treated patients [61] and a lack of influence of ginkgo leaf extracts (120-480 mg/day for 14 days) on haemostasiological parameters such as bleeding time, platelet function and coagulation in healthy volunteers [66,67].

A cross-over study in 8 healthy volunteers showed that simultaneous oral administration of 240 mg of a ginkgo leaf extract and 10 mg of nifedipine (a calcium channel blocker) did not significantly affect the *mean* pharmacokinetic parameters of nifedipine. However, the mean C_{max} for nifedipine in the ginkgo group was about 1.3-fold that of the control group and C_{max} values for two of the volunteers were almost doubled [68].

REGULATORY STATUS

Medicines

UK	No licences issued for products containing ginkgo leaf or extracts.
France	Not listed in *Médicaments à base de plantes* [69]; approved as a prescription only medicine [70].
Germany	Two Commission E monographs published: ginkgo leaf and various extracts (including hydroalcoholic extracts) not approved [71], but uses of a closely-defined acetone-water extract approved [62].

Food

Not used in foods.

REFERENCES

Current Pharmacopoeial Monographs

Ph. Eur.	Ginkgo Leaf
USP	Ginkgo

Literature References

1. Hasler A. Chemical constituents of *Ginkgo biloba*. In: van Beek TA, editor. *Ginkgo biloba*. (Medicinal and Aromatic Plants - Industrial Profiles series). Amsterdam: Harwood Academic, 2000:109-142.
2. van Beek TA, Bombardelli E, Morazzoni P and Peterlongo F. *Ginkgo biloba* L. *Fitoterapia* 1998, **69**, 195-244.
3. Hasler A, Sticher O and Meier B. Identification and determination of the flavonoids from *Ginkgo biloba* by high-performance liquid chromatography. *J. Chromatogr.* 1992, **605**, 41-48.
4. Strømgaard K and Nakanishi K. Chemistry and Biology of Terpene Trilactones from *Ginkgo biloba*. *Angew. Chem. Int. Ed.* 2004, **43**, 1640-1658.
5. van Beek TA, Scheeren HA, Rantio T, Melger WC and Lelyveld GP. Determination of ginkgolides and bilobalide in *Ginkgo biloba* leaves and phytopharmaceuticals. *J. Chromatogr.* 1991, **543**, 375-387.
6. Lang Q and Wai CM. An Extraction Method for Determination of Ginkgolides and Bilobalide in Ginkgo Leaf Extracts. *Analyt. Chem.* 1999, **71**, 2929-2933.
7. Hasler A and Meier B. Determination of terpenes from *Ginkgo biloba* L. by capillary gas chromatography. *Pharm. Pharmacol. Lett.* 1992, **2**, 187-190.

8. van Beek TA and Lelyveld GP. Concentration of Ginkgolides and Bilobalide in *Ginkgo biloba* Leaves in Relation to the Time of Year. *Planta Medica* 1992, **58**, 413-416.
9. Ding C, Chen E, Zhou W and Lindsay RC. A Method for Extraction and Quantification of Ginkgo Terpene Trilactones. *Analyt. Chem.* 2004, **76**, 4332-4336.
10. European Scientific Cooperative on Phytotherapy. Ginkgo folium - Ginkgo Leaf. In: *ESCOP Monographs - The Scientific Foundation for Herbal Medicinal Products, 2nd ed.* Stuttgart-New York: Thieme; Exeter, UK: ESCOP, 2003:179-210.
11. Jaggy H and Koch E. Chemistry and biology of alkylphenols from *Ginkgo biloba* L. *Pharmazie* 1997, **52**, 735-738.
12. Schötz K. Detection of allergenic urushiols in *Ginkgo biloba* leaves. *Pharmazie* 2002, **57**, 508-510.
13. Schötz K. Quantification of Allergenic Urushiols in Extracts of *Ginkgo biloba* Leaves, in Simple One-step Extracts and Refined Manufactured Material. *Phytochem. Analysis* 2004, **15**, 1-8.
14. Lang F and Wilhelm E. Quantitative determination of proanthocyanidins in *Ginkgo biloba* special extracts. *Pharmazie* 1996, **51**, 734-737.
15. Kraus J. Water-soluble polysaccharides from *Ginkgo biloba* leaves. *Phytochemistry* 1991, **30**, 3017-3020.
16. Eingestellter Ginkgotrockenextrakt - Ginkgo extractum siccum normatum [Standardized Ginkgo Dry Extract]. In: *Deutsches Arzneibuch.*
17. DeFeudis FV. Substances that are present in Ginkgo biloba leaves but absent or present in negligible amounts in EGb 761 (Table 2.2). In: *Ginkgo biloba extract (EGb 761): from chemistry to the clinic.* ISBN 3-86126-173-1. Wiesbaden: Ullstein Medical, 1998:363.
18. Ganzera M, Zhao J and Khan IA. Analysis of Terpenelactones in *Ginkgo biloba* by High Performance Liquid Chromatography and Evaporative Light Scattering Detection. *Chem. Pharm. Bull.* 2001, **49**, 1170-1173.
19. Fuzzati N, Pace R and Villa F. A simple HPLC-UV method for the assay of ginkgolic acids in *Ginkgo biloba* extracts. *Fitoterapia* 2003, **74**, 247-256.
20. Ndjoko K, Wolfender J-L and Hostettmann K. Determination of trace amounts of ginkgolic acids in *Ginkgo biloba* L. leaf extracts and phytopharmaceuticals by liquid chromatography-electrospray mass spectrometry. *J. Chromatogr. B* 2000, **744**, 249-255.
21. DeFeudis FV. *Ginkgo biloba extract (EGb 761): from chemistry to the clinic.* ISBN 3-86126-173-1. Wiesbaden: Ullstein Medical, 1998.
22. Subhan Z and Hindmarch I. The Psychopharmacological Effects of *Ginkgo biloba* Extract in Normal Healthy Volunteers. *Int. J. Clin. Pharm. Res.* 1984, **4**, 89-93.
23. Rigney U, Kimber S and Hindmarch I. The Effects of Acute Doses of Standardized *Ginkgo biloba* Extract on Memory and Psychomotor Performance in Volunteers. *Phytother. Res.* 1999, **13**, 408-415.
24. Kennedy DO, Scholey AB and Wesnes KA. The dose-dependent cognitive effects of acute administration of *Ginkgo biloba* to healthy young volunteers. *Psychopharmacology* 2000, **151**, 416-423.
25. Kennedy DO, Scholey AB and Wesnes KA. Modulation of cognition and mood following administration of single doses of Ginkgo biloba, ginseng and a ginkgo/ginseng combination to healthy young adults. *Physiol. Behav.* 2002, **75**, 739-751.
26. Stough C, Clarke J, Lloyd J and Nathan PJ. Neuropsychological changes after 30-day *Ginkgo biloba* administration in healthy participants. *Internat. J. Neuropsychopharmacol.* 2001, **4**, 131-134.
27. Mix JA and Crews WD. An examination of the efficacy of *Ginkgo biloba* extract EGb761 on the neuropsychologic functioning of cognitively intact older adults. *J. Altern. Complement. Med.* 2000, **6**, 219-229.
28. Mix JA and Crews WD. A double-blind, placebo-controlled, randomized trial of *Ginkgo biloba* extract EGb 761® in a sample of cognitively intact older adults: neuropsychological findings. *Human Psychopharmacol.* 2002, **17**, 267-277.
29. Solomon PR, Adams F, Silver A, Zimmer J and DeVeaux R. Ginkgo for Memory Enhancement. A Randomized Controlled Trial. *JAMA* 2002, **288**, 835-840.
30. Maier P, Pösl M and Pöppel E. Ginkgo - Wundermittel für ältere Golfspieler? Auswirkung von Ginkgo-biloba-Extrakt auf Stimmung, Konzentration und Feinmotorik am Beispiel von Golfspielern [Ginkgo - Wonder supplement for the older golf player? Effects of *Ginkgo biloba* extract on morale, concentration and coordination, taking the example of golf players]. *Leistungssport* 2003, **33** (4), 57-62 [GERMAN].
31. Cockle SM, Kimber S and Hindmarch I. The Effects of *Ginkgo biloba* Extract (LI 1370) Supplementation on Activities of Daily Living in Free Living Older Volunteers: A Questionnaire Survey. *Human Psychopharmacol. Clin. Exp.* 2000, **15**, 227-235.
32. Trick L, Boyle J and Hindmarch I. The effects of *Ginkgo biloba* extract (LI 1370) supplementation and discontinuation on activities of daily living and mood in free living older volunteers. *Phytotherapy Res.* 2004, **18**, 531-537.
33. Jung F, Mrowietz C, Kiesewetter H and Wenzel E. Effect of *Ginkgo biloba* on Fluidity of Blood and Peripheral Microcirculation in Volunteers. *Arzneim.-Forsch./Drug Res.* 1990, **40**, 589-593.
34. Költringer P, Langsteger W and Eber O. Dose-dependent hemorheological effects and microcirculatory modifications following intravenous administration of *Ginkgo biloba* special extract EGb 761. *Clin. Hemorheol.* 1995, **15**, 649-656.
35. Nieder M. Pharmacokinetics of Ginkgo Flavonols in Plasma. *Münch. med. Wschr.* 1991, **133** (Suppl. 1), S61-S62 [GERMAN/English summary].
36. Fourtillan JB, Brisson AM, Girault J, Ingrand I, Decourt JP, Drieu K et al. Pharmacokinetics of Bilobalide, Ginkgolide A and Ginkgolide B in healthy volunteers following oral and intravenous administrations of *Ginkgo biloba* extract (EGb 761). *Thérapie (Paris)* 1995, **50**, 137-144 [FRENCH/English summary].
37. Oken BS, Storzbach DM and Kaye JA. The Efficacy of *Ginkgo biloba* on Cognitive Function in Alzheimer Disease. *Arch. Neurol.* 1998, **55**, 1409-1415.
38. Kanowski S, Hermann WM, Stephan K, Wierich W and Hörr R. Proof of Efficacy of the Ginkgo biloba Special Extract EGb 761 in Outpatients Suffering from Mild to Moderate Primary Degenerative Dementia of the Alzheimer Type or Multi-Infarct Dementia. *Pharmacopsychiatry* 1996, **29**, 47-56. Republished in: *Phytomedicine* 1997, **4**, 3-13.
Further analysis of the data published as:
Kanowski S and Hoerr R. Ginkgo biloba Extract EGb 761® in Dementia: Intent-to-treat Analyses of a 24-week, Multicenter, Double-blind, Placebo-controlled, Randomized Trial. *Pharmacopsychiatry* 2003, **36**, 297-303.
39. Le Bars PL, Katz MM, Berman N, Itil TM, Freedman AM and Schatzberg AF. A Placebo-controlled, Double-blind, Randomized Trial of an Extract of Ginkgo biloba for Dementia. *JAMA* 1997, **278**, 1327-1332.
Further analysis of the data published as:
Le Bars PL, Kieser M and Itil KZ. A 26-Week Analysis of a Double-Blind, Placebo-Controlled Trial of the *Ginkgo biloba* Extract EGb 761® in Dementia. *Dement. Geriatr. Cogn. Disord.* 2000, **11**, 230-237.
40. Hofferberth B. The Efficacy of EGb 761 in Patients with Senile Dementia of the Alzheimer Type: A Double-Blind, Placebo-Controlled Study on Different Levels of Investigation. *Human Psychopharmacol.* 1994, **9**, 215-222.
41. Wesnes K, Simmons D, Rook M and Simpson P. A Double-blind Placebo-controlled Trial of Tanakan in the Treatment of Idiopathic Cognitive Impairment in the Elderly. *Human Psychopharmacol.* 1987, **2**, 159-169.
42. Ernst E and Pittler MH. Ginkgo biloba for Dementia. A Systematic Review of Double-Blind, Placebo-Controlled Trials. *Clin. Drug Invest.* 1999, **17**, 301-308.
43. Wettstein A. Cholinesterase inhibitors and Ginkgo extracts - are they comparable in the treatment of dementia? Comparison of published placebo-controlled efficacy studies of at least six months' duration. *Phytomedicine* 1999, **6**, 393-401.
44. van Dongen MCJM, van Rossum E, Kessels AGH, Sielhorst

HJG and Knipschild PG. The Efficacy of Ginkgo for Elderly People with Dementia and Age-Associated Memory Impairment: New Results of a Randomized Clinical Trial. *J. Am. Geriatr. Soc.* 2000, **48**, 1183-1194.
45. Le Bars P. Conflicting results on ginkgo research. *Forsch. Komplementärmed. Klass. Naturheilkd.* 2002, **9**, 19-20.
46. Kleijnen J and Knipschild P. *Ginkgo biloba* for cerebral insufficiency. *Br. J. Clin. Pharmacol.* 1992, **34**, 352-358.
47. Hopfenmüller W. Proof of the therapeutic effectiveness of a *Ginkgo biloba* special extract. Meta-analysis of 11 clinical trials in aged patients with cerebral insufficiency. *Arzneim.-Forsch./Drug Res.* 1994, **44**, 1005-1013 [GERMAN/English summary].
48. DeFeudis FV. Clinical Studies on EGb 761 and Neurosensory Disturbances. In: *Ginkgo biloba extract (EGb 761): from chemistry to the clinic.* ISBN 3-86126-173-1. Wiesbaden: Ullstein Medical, 1998:175-183.
49. Hilton M and Stuart E. Ginkgo biloba for tinnitus. *Cochrane Database Syst. Rev.* 2004, (2), CD003852.
50. Morgenstern C and Biermann E. Tinnitus-Langzeittherapie mit Ginkgo-Spezialextrakt EGb 761 [Long term therapy of tinnitus with Ginkgo special extract EGb 761]. *Fortschr. Med.* 1997, **115** (29), 57-58 [GERMAN].
51. Drew S and Davies E. Effectiveness of *Ginkgo biloba* in treating tinnitus: double blind, placebo controlled trial. *BMJ* 2001, **322**, 73-78.
52. Rejali D, Sivakumar A and Balaji N. *Ginkgo biloba* does not benefit patients with tinnitus: a randomized placebo-controlled double-blind trial and meta-analysis of randomized trials. *Clin. Otolaryngol.* 2004, **29**, 226-231.
53. Ernst E and Stevinson C. Ginkgo biloba for tinnitus. A review. *Clin. Otolaryngol.* 1999, **24**, 164-167.
54. Horsch S and Walther C. Ginkgo biloba special extract EGb 761 in the treatment of peripheral arterial occlusive disease (PAOD) - a review based on randomized, controlled studies. *Int. J. Clin. Pharmacol. Ther.* 2004, **42**, 63-72.
55. Pittler MH and Ernst E. Ginkgo biloba Extract for the Treatment of Intermittent Claudication: A Meta-Analysis of Randomized Trials. *Am. J. Med.* 2000, **108**, 276-281.
56. Pittler MH and Ernst E. Complementary therapies for peripheral arterial disease: Systematic review. *Atherosclerosis* 2005, **181**, 1-7.
57. Roncin JP, Schwartz F and d'Arbigny P. EGb 761 in Control of Acute Mountain Sickness and Vascular Reactivity to Cold Exposure. *Aviat. Space Environ. Med.* 1996, **67**, 445-452.
58. Gertsch JH, Seto TB, Mor J and Onopa J. Ginkgo biloba for the prevention of severe acute mountain sickness (AMS) starting one day before rapid ascent. *High Alt. Med. Biol.* 2002, **3**, 29-37.
59. Gertsch JH, Basnyat B, Johnson EW, Onopa J and Holck PS. Randomised, double blind, placebo controlled comparison of ginkgo biloba and acetazolamide for prevention of acute mountain sickness among Himalayan trekkers: the prevention of high altitude illness trial (PHAIT). *BMJ* 2004, **328** (7443), 797-801.
60. Mills S and Bone K. Ginkgo (*Ginkgo biloba* L). In: *Principles and Practice of Phytotherapy. Modern Herbal Medicine.* ISBN 0-443-06016-9. Edinburgh-London-New York: Churchill Livingstone, 2000:404-417.
61. Engelsen J, Nielsen JD and Winther K. Effect of Coenzyme Q_{10} and Ginkgo biloba on Warfarin Dosage in Stable, Long-Term Warfarin Treated Outpatients. A Randomised, Double Blind, Placebo-crossover Trial [Letter]. *Thromb. Haemost.* 2002, **87**, 1075-1076.
62. Trockenextrakt (35-67:1) aus Ginkgo-biloba-Blättern, extrahiert mit Aceton-Wasser [Dry extract (35-67:1) from Ginkgo biloba leaf, extracted with acetone-water]. German Commission E Monograph published in: Bundesanzeiger No. 133 of 19 July 1994.
63. Hausen BM. The Sensitizing Capacity of Ginkgolic Acids in Guinea Pigs. *Am. J. Contact Derm.* 1998, **9**, 146-148.
64. Lepoittevin J-P, Benezra C and Asakawa Y. Allergic contact dermatitis to *Ginkgo biloba* L.: relationship with urushiol. *Arch. Dermatol. Res.* 1989, **281**, 227-230.
65. Kressmann S, Müller WE and Blume HH. Pharmaceutical quality of different *Ginkgo biloba* brands. *J. Pharm. Pharmacol.* 2002, **54**, 661-669.
66. Bal dit Sollier C, Caplain H and Drouet L. No alteration in platelet function or coagulation induced by EGb 761 in a controlled study. *Clin. Lab. Haem.* 2003, **25**, 251-253.
67. Köhler S, Funk P and Kieser M. Influence of a 7-day treatment with *Ginkgo biloba* special extract EGb 761 on bleeding time and coagulation: a randomized, placebo-controlled, double-blind study in healthy volunteers. *Blood Coagul. Fibrinolysis* 2004, **15**, 303-309.
68. Yoshioka M, Ohnishi N, Koishi T, Obata Y, Nakagawa M, Matsumoto T et al. Studies on Interactions between Functional Foods or Dietary Supplements and Medicines. IV. Effects of *Ginkgo biloba* Leaf Extract on the Pharmacokinetics and Pharmacodynamics of Nifedipine in Healthy Volunteers. *Biol. Pharm. Bull.* 2004, **27**, 2006-2009.
69. *Médicaments à base de plantes.* ISBN 2-911473-02-7. Saint-Denis Cedex, France: Agence du Médicament, 1998.
70. Ginkgo biloba. In: *Vidal® 2000. Le Dictionnaire, 76th ed.* Paris: Editions du Vidal, 2000.
71. Ginkgo folium. German Commission E Monograph published in: Bundesanzeiger No. 133 of 19 July 1994.

REGULATORY GUIDELINES FROM OTHER EU COUNTRIES

GERMANY

Two Commission E monographs have been published in relation to ginkgo leaf. The first, on ginkgo leaf and certain types of extracts from it, is negative [71]. The second, on a well-defined acetone-water extract, is positive [62].

Commission E monograph [71]: Ginkgo folium (Ginkgo-biloba-Blätter).

Composition of the drug
Ginkgo leaf and preparations from it: various listed extracts including dry or liquid (hydro)ethanolic, dry (hydro)methanolic and liquid ethanol-wine extracts.

Pharmacological properties, pharmacokinetics and toxicology
Available scientific knowledge on the pharmacology and toxicology of the above preparations is inadequate.

Uses
Ginkgo leaf and the above mono-preparations from it are used: in arterial and cerebral circulatory disorders; in cerebral circulatory insufficiency; in vertigo; to improve circulation in, and to strengthen, the circulatory system, especially the veins; to relieve strain on the circulation; as a "psychotropic" and "neurotropic".

A wide range of indications claimed for combination preparations is also described.

The efficacy of the stated preparations for the indications claimed has not been substantiated.

Risks
Due to the content of ginkgolic acids, which can be potent contact allergens, a risk of allergies cannot be ruled out.

Evaluation
Since efficacy in the claimed indications has not been substantiated, therapeutic use cannot be supported.

Commission E monograph [62]: Trockenextrakt (35-67:1) aus Ginkgo-biloba-Blättern, extrahiert mit Aceton-Wasser [Dry extract from *Ginkgo biloba* leaf extracted with acetone-water].

Composition of the drug
A dry extract manufactured from the dried leaves of *Ginkgo biloba* L. with acetone-water and subsequent purification steps, without admixture of concentrates or isolated constituents. The drug to extract ratio is 35-67:1, on average 50:1. The extract is characterized by:
- 22-27% of flavonol glycosides, determined by HPLC as quercetin and kaempferol including isorhamnetin, and calculated as acylflavonols with molecular weights of 756.7 (quercetin glycosides) and 740.7 (kaempferol glycosides);
- 5-7% of terpene lactones, of which ca. 2.8-3.4% of ginkgolides A, B and C, and ca. 2.6-3.2% of bilobalide;
- Less than 5 ppm of ginkgolic acids.

The stated ranges include production and analytical variances.

The monograph includes a summary of Pharmacological Properties, Pharmacokinetics and Toxicology.

Uses
(a) Symptomatic treatment of performance disorders associated with the organic brain within the framework of an overall therapeutic concept for dementia syndromes with the following primary symptoms:
Memory disorders, concentration disorders, depressive mood, dizziness, tinnitus, headaches.
The primary target groups are dementia syndromes in primary degenerative dementia, vascular dementia and mixed forms of both.
Note: Before commencing treatment with ginkgo extract, it should be clarified that the symptoms of illness are not due to a specific underlying illness requiring treatment.
(b) Improvement in pain-free walking distance in peripheral arterial occlusive disease at Fontaine's Stage II (intermittent claudication) within a regimen of physical-therapeutic measures, especially walking exercise.
(c) Vertigo/dizziness, tinnitus of vascular and involutional origin.

Contraindications
Hypersensitivity to *Ginkgo biloba* preparations.

Side effects
Very rarely, mild gastrointestinal upsets, headaches or allergic skin reactions.

Special precautions for use
None known.

Use during pregnancy and lactation
No restrictions known.

Interaction with other medicaments and other forms of interaction
None known.

Dosage
Unless otherwise prescribed, daily dose:
Indication (a): 120-240 mg of native dry extract, divided into 2 or 3 single doses.
Indications (b) and (c): 120-160 mg of native dry extract, divided into 2 or 3 single doses.

Mode of administration
In liquid or solid oral dosage forms.

Duration of administration
Indication (a): The duration of treatment should be guided by the severity of symptoms and in chronic illnesses should last for at least 8 weeks. After treatment for 3 months, whether continuation of treatment is still justified should be reviewed.
Indication (b): Improved performance in walking distance requires a treatment period of at least 6 weeks.
Indication (c): There is no therapeutic advantage in continuing treatment for longer than 6-8 weeks.

Overdosage
Nothing known.

Special warnings
None.

Effects on driving or operating machinery
None known.

GOLDENROD, EUROPEAN Compositae

Solidaginis virgaureae herba

Definition
European Goldenrod consists of the dried flowering aerial parts of *Solidago virgaurea* L.

The term "European goldenrod" serves to distinguish *Solidago virgaurea* (the only native European species of *Solidago*) from two North American species, *S. canadensis* L. (Canadian goldenrod) and *S. gigantea* Aiton (early goldenrod), which are naturalized in Europe and also used medicinally; some commercial goldenrod may consist of the latter species [1]. The term also distinguishes European *Solidago virgaurea* from the Asian form (e.g. from India or Japan), which appears to have minor differences in constituents.

CONSTITUENTS

□ ***Triterpene glycosides (saponins)*** of the oleanane type (0.2-0.3%, calculated as polygalacic acid 3-glucoside) [2,3]. The four major saponins were isolated and identified as 3,28-bisdesmosidic glycosides of polygalacic acid (2β,3β,16α,23-tetrahydroxyolean-12-en-28-oic acid) with a glucosyl or glucosyl-(1→3)-glucosyl group at the 3-position and a rhamnosyl-(1→3)-xylosyl-(1→4)-rhamnosyl-(1→2)-fucosyl ester group at the 28-position, the fucosyl residue being 4-acylated with a chain of 2 or 3 units of β-hydroxybutyric acid [4]. These four compounds have been designated as virgaureasaponins B, C, D and E [5], virgaureasaponins B and C being identical respectively to solidagosaponins XIV and XVIII.

From fresh whole plants of the Asian form of *Solidago virgaurea* 30 saponins of polygalacic acid (solidagosaponins I-XX) have been isolated. They include 3-mono-, 16-mono-, 3,28-bi, 16,28-bi- and 3,16,28-tridesmosides of polygalacic acid with varying glycosyl and acyl groups [6-8].

□ ***Phenolic diglucosides*** Leiocarposide (0.4-0.8% in aerial parts) [9-11], predominantly in the leaves and flowers [9], and virgaureoside A (0.01-0.14%) [10,12].

Leiocarposide serves as a useful marker substance for European goldenrod since it is not found in *S. canadensis* or *S. gigantea* [9,13].

□ ***Caffeic acid derivatives***, predominantly 3,5-di-*O*-caffeoylquinic acid (2.8%) and chlorogenic acid (5-*O*-caffeoylquinic acid, 1.1%) together with small amounts (less than 0.1% each) of other caffeoylquinic acids [14].

□ ***Flavonoids***, 1.5% expressed as quercetin [2] (Ph. Eur. min. 1.0%, expressed as hyperoside),

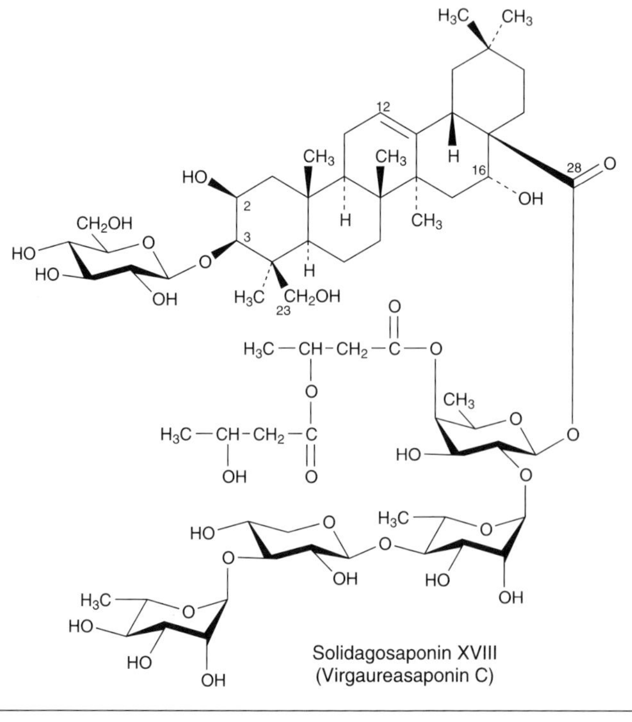

Solidagosaponin XVIII
(Virgaureasaponin C)

comprising the flavonols quercetin, kaempferol and isorhamnetin and their 3-*O*-glycosides such as isoquercitrin, hyperoside, rutin (glycosides of quercetin), nicotiflorin, astragalin, afzelin (glycosides of kaempferol) and isorhamnetin 3-rutinoside [13,15-19]. Rutin (quercetin 3-rutinoside, 0.8%) [2], kaempferol 3-robinobioside, nicotiflorin (kaempferol 3-rutinoside) and isorhamnetin 3-rutinoside are predominant [16].

☐ ***Diterpene lactones*** of the *cis*-clerodane type; 12 such compounds have been isolated from *Solidago virgaurea* plants collected in northeast India [20], although these lactones do not appear to be present in European material [2].

☐ ***Phenolic acids*** Small amounts of free acids have been detected: salicylic (9.9 mg/100g), ferulic (7.7 mg/100g), sinapic (5.1 mg/100g), protocatechuic (4.8 mg/100g), caffeic (1.7 mg/100g) and other acids [21].

☐ ***Polysaccharides***, 5-8%, not yet fully characterized but composed of galacturonic acid (44%) and neutral monosaccharides [22,23]. A β-1,2-fructosan has also been reported [24].

☐ ***Other constituents*** include essential oil (0.4-0.55%) containing mono- and sesquiterpenes [25], and alkane diols (especially C_{29} and C_{31} diols) in the flower-heads [26]. Tannins of the catechin type (10-15%) are reported to be present [27,28], but no modern data is available.

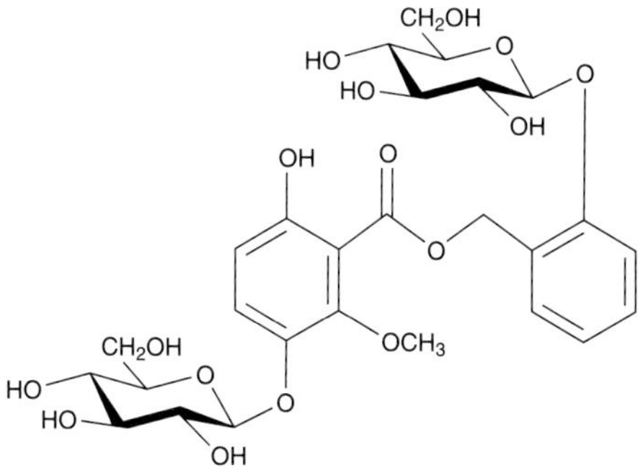

Leiocarposide

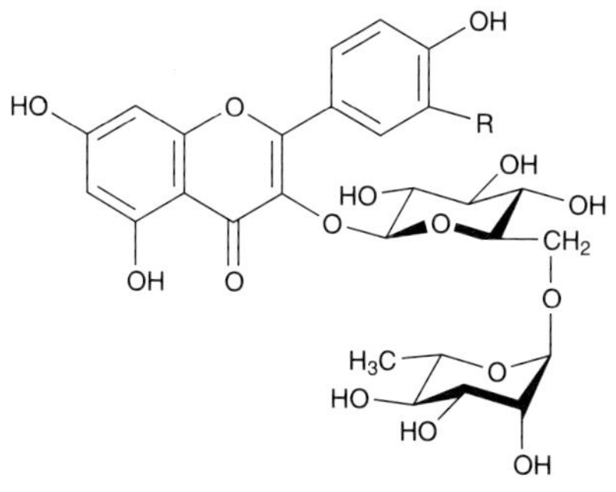

Rutin R = OH
Nicotiflorin R = H

Published Assay Methods

Total flavonoids by spectrophotometry [Ph. Eur.]. Flavonol glycosides by HPLC [16]. Leiocarposide by HPLC [9]; phenolic glucosides by spectrophotometry [10,11]. Caffeic acid derivatives by HPLC [14]. Phenolic acids by GC [21].

PHARMACOLOGY

In vitro

A 60%-ethanolic dry extract from European goldenrod showed spasmolytic activity, strongly inhibiting acetylcholine-induced contractions in isolated guinea pig ileum (ED_{50}: 19.4 mg/litre; 14.7% of the activity of papaverine) [29] and in isolated rat bladder (ED_{50}: 35.7 mg/litre) [30].

An aqueous extract (1:1) from European goldenrod exhibited antioxidant activity in several test systems; it inhibited the peroxidation of phosphatidylcholine liposomes, scavenged hydroxyl radicals and reduced the 1,1′-diphenyl-2-picrylhydrazyl (DPPH) radical [31].

Inhibition of elastase (an enzyme involved in inflammatory processes) in an enzyme preparation from human neutrophils by 3,5-dicaffeoylquinic acid and the flavonoids rutin and quercetin, all of which are present in European goldenrod, was interpreted as supportive evidence for anti-inflammatory activity of the drug [32].

In vivo

Diuretic effects

In a 1960 study, negative diuretic effects (i.e. inhibition of diuresis) were observed in dogs after oral administration of extracts or a flavonoid fraction from European goldenrod [33].

In contrast, oral administration of an aqueous infusion of European goldenrod (total flavonoids: 285 mg/100 ml) to male rats in single doses of 4.64 or 10.0 ml/kg body weight significantly increased the volume of urine excreted over a 4-hour period compared to that of control animals, by 52% at 4.64 ml/kg ($p<0.01$) and, surprisingly, to a lesser extent (40%) at 10.0 ml/kg. Excretion of sodium, potassium and chloride also increased significantly ($p<0.01$), but was considered mainly due to the increased intake of these ions in the infusion. The authors concluded that the diuretic effect was partly due to flavonoids and estimated that in humans at least

50 mg of flavonoids per day would be necessary to produce a diuretic effect [34].

In a later study, oral administration to rats of the flavonoid fraction from European goldenrod at 25 mg/kg significantly increased diuresis (urine volume) by 88% over a 24-hour period ($p<0.05$) compared to control animals [35,36].

Leiocarposide administered orally to rats at 25 mg/kg body weight increased urine volume by 80% in relation to control values ($p<0.05$), compared to 100% after furosemide at 6 mg/kg; stronger effects were observed after intraperitoneal administration, 110% for leiocarposide and 125% for furosemide. The diuretic effect of leiocarposide was evident 5 hours after administration and lasted for up to 24 hours. When administered simultaneously with leiocarposide (25 mg/kg), the flavonoid fraction (25 mg/kg) or the saponin fraction (20 mg/kg orally or 1 mg/kg intraperitoneally) from European goldenrod reduced the diuretic effect of leiocarposide by about 30% and 10% respectively [36-38].

Leiocarposide (25 mg/kg daily) also showed anti-urolithic activity, inhibiting the growth of human urinary calculi implanted in the rat bladder by about 40% after 6 weeks ($p<0.05$), normalizing urinary phosphate and potassium levels and reducing urinary magnesium by more than 3-fold ($p<0.05$) [36,39].

Anti-inflammatory effects
In the Freund's adjuvant-induced arthritis test, oral administration of a 46%-ethanolic extract from European goldenrod (total flavonoids: 0.0715 mg/ml) to rats at 5 ml/kg on days 15-21 after inoculation of adjuvant into the hind paw significantly inhibited paw inflammation; nearly 40% inhibition of the control value was achieved by day 21 ($p<0.05$) [40].

A 45%-ethanolic infusion of European goldenrod, orally administered to rats, showed anti-inflammatory activity in the carrageenan- and dextran-induced rat paw oedema tests at 2 ml/kg and in the cotton pellet granuloma test at 1 ml/kg [41].

Leiocarposide administered subcutaneously inhibited carrageenan-induced rat paw oedema by 20% at 100 mg/kg and 27% at 200 mg/kg ($p<0.05$) after 5 hours, compared to 54% by phenylbutazone at 50 mg/kg. It also had a weak analgesic effect in the hot plate test in mice [42]. However, since less than 10% of leiocarposide is absorbed in rats after oral administration [43] the relevance of these results to humans is questionable.

When applied topically at 10^{-7} mol/ear, leiocarposide inhibited arachidonic acid-induced mouse ear oedema by 41% after 10 minutes ($p<0.01$), compared to 61% by indometacin at 1.3×10^{-7} mol/ear ($p<0.001$) [9].

Intravenous administration of a mixture of saponins isolated from European goldenrod inhibited sodium nucleinate-induced rat paw oedema at 1.25-2.5 mg/kg body weight [44].

Antitumour activity
An active fraction (corresponding to a molecular weight of about 40,000 and probably protein in nature) isolated from an aqueous extract of European goldenrod by bioguided assay exhibited strong cytotoxic activity *in vitro* against various human tumour cell lines including prostate, breast, melanoma and small cell lung cancer. In a subsequent *in vivo* experiment, mice were injected in the flank with rat prostatic tumour cells and then treated, both intraperitoneally and subcutaneously, with the active fraction (5 mg/kg) every 3 days for 25 days; compared to controls, tumour growth was suppressed by 75-80% in mice receiving the active fraction [45].

In an earlier study, polysaccharides isolated from aerial parts of a related goldenrod species, *Solidago canadensis*, also showed activity against tumours implanted in mice; this suggested immunomodulating activity to the authors [46].

Virgaureasaponin E administered intraperitoneally to mice at 1 mg/kg/day for 10 days dose-dependently inhibited sarcoma 180 tumour growth in mice (a model sensitive to immunomodulatory compounds); the inhibition rate was 75% and 6 out of 15 mice had total regression of the tumour. This saponin was able to significantly enhance the release of tumour necrosis factor alpha (TNF-α) in the blood of mice after being triggered by lipopolysaccharide ($p<0.05$) [47].

Pharmacological studies in humans
The diuretic effect of a tincture prepared from fresh European goldenrod was evaluated in 22 healthy volunteers in a double-blind, intraindividual cross-over study. Compared to placebo treatment, urine volume increased by 30% after a single oral dose of 100 drops of the tincture [48].

Pharmacokinetics
Leiocarposide was poorly absorbed after oral administration to rats, most of it being excreted unchanged in the faeces. Less than 10% was detected in the urine as metabolites, mainly leiocarpic acid (3,6-dihydroxy-2-methoxybenzoic acid, 2% of the dose) and its 3-conjugates (2%), and salicylic acid and salicyluric acid (0.5% each). The low absorption is considered due to the high stability and hence very slow hydrolysis of the ester bond [43].

CLINICAL STUDIES

No controlled clinical studies of European goldenrod have been published.

In an open post-marketing study, 1487 patients suffering from urological complaints were treated daily for 3-8 weeks with 3 × 424.8 mg of a European goldenrod dry extract (5.0-7.1:1, ethanol 30% m/m; corresponding to 7.7 g of crude drug per day). The results of treatment were evaluated for three subgroups of patients:

- 555 patients suffering from chronic or recurrent urinary tract infections were treated with the extract for 33 days on average and 45% of the patients took no other medication. Using the Clinical Global Impressions (CGI) Scale, the physicians rated the condition of 78% of the patients as "very much or much better". Treatment with the extract alone was claimed to be just as effective as when combined with an initial 5-day course of an antibiotic [49].
- 427 patients had urinary calculi and/or renal gravel (of whom 32% also had urinary tract infections and 11% also had symptoms of irritable bladder); 25% of the patients were chronic or recurrent cases. After treatment for 4 weeks on average, responder rates ranged from 98% for colics to 84% for pollakisuria and 81% for feeling of pressure in the bladder. Using the CGI scale, the physicians rated the condition of patients to be "very much or much better" in 79% of cases [50]
- 512 patients (average age 56 years; 90% women) suffered from chronic or recurrent irritable bladder (as the sole indication in 53% of patients; accompanied by a urinary infection in 34% and urinary stones or renal gravel in 7%). Patients in this subgroup were treated for 35 days on average, 70% of the patients receiving no other treatment. At the end of the study period, a high response rate (i.e. symptom eliminated or improved) was reported for most symptoms, ranging from 90% for pain/burning during micturition to 86% for pollakisuria, 86% for urge to urinate and 65% for incontinence. Using the CGI scale, the physicians rated the condition of 69% of the patients as "very much or much better" [51].

From case reports, the same extract was found to have a beneficial spasmolytic effect in 10 patients undergoing hospital treatment for calculi by extracorporeal shock wave lithotripsy (ESWL) and during 4-week after-care; no colics occurred and no other spasmolytic drugs were necessary [50].

In another post-marketing study (total number of patients 3927), a subgroup of 745 patients with irritable bladder were treated daily with 3 × 342 mg of a European goldenrod dry extract (5-7:1). After 2 weeks of treatment, micturition frequency had considerably decreased and responder rates for individual symptoms ranged from 69% (pollakisuria) to 87% (pain and burning when passing water) [52].

After daily treatment of 53 patients suffering from urinary tract inflammation with 5 × 20 drops of a tincture from fresh plants of European goldenrod the symptoms (dysuria, frequency of micturition, tenesmus etc.) disappeared in 70-73% of cases [48].

THERAPEUTICS

Actions
Diuretic [34,48,53-56], spasmolytic [29,30,54], anti-inflammatory [40,41,54] and antioxidant [31,56].

Also stated to be diaphoretic [55,57], carminative [55,57,58], astringent [56-59] and vulnerary [58].

Indications
None adequately substantiated by controlled clinical studies.

Uses based on experience or tradition
Inflammatory disorders of the lower urinary tract [54] including infections [49,60], cystitis [55,56], nephritis and urethritis [56]; urinary calculi and renal gravel [50,54,57]; irritable bladder [51,52,60]. Also the prophylaxis of urinary calculi and kidney gravel [54,60], and facilitation of the expulsion of calculi [50,56,60].

Has also been used in the treatment of chronic nasopharyngeal catarrh [55,56] and flatulent dyspepsia [55,58].

Contraindications
Should not be taken by persons with oedema due to impaired cardiac or renal function [54].

Side effects
None known.

Interactions with other drugs
None known.

Dosage
Adult daily dose: 6-8 g of the herb or equivalent preparations [51,52,54,55].

SAFETY

European goldenrod preparations are generally well tolerated. In two large drug monitoring studies [51,52] a total of over 5000 patients were treated with extracts corresponding to 6-8 g of the crude drug for periods of 2-5 weeks; the overall rate of adverse events, principally gastrointestinal disturbances or allergic reactions, was reported to be less than 1%.

REGULATORY STATUS

Medicines

UK	No licences issued for products containing European goldenrod.
France	Accepted for specified indications [53].
Germany	Commission E monograph published, with approved uses [54].

Food

Not used in foods.

REFERENCES

Current Pharmacopoeial Monographs

Ph. Eur. Goldenrod, European

Literature References

1. Bader G. Die Goldrute - Inhaltsstoffe, Pharmakologie, Klinik und Anbau [Goldenrod - Constituents, pharmacology, clinical studies and cultivation]. *Z. Phytotherapie* 1999, **20**, 196-200 [GERMAN]
2. Hiller K and Bader G. Goldruten-Kraut. Die Gattung *Solidago* - eine pharmazeutische Bewertung [Goldenrod herb. The genus *Solidago* - a pharmaceutical evaluation]. *Z. Phytotherapie* 1996, **17**, 123-130 [GERMAN/English summary].
3. Bader G, Grimm A and Hiller K. Quantitative Determination of Triterpenoid Saponins in *Solidago virgaurea. Planta Medica* 1991, **57** (Suppl. 2), A67-A68.
4. Bader G, Wray V and Hiller K. The Main Saponins from the Aerial Parts and the Roots of *Solidago virgaurea* subsp. *virgaurea. Planta Medica* 1995, **61**, 158-161.
5. Bader G, Plohmann B, Hiller K and Franz G. Cytotoxicity of triterpenoid saponins. Part 1: Activities against tumor cells *in vitro* and hemolytical index. *Pharmazie* 1996, **51**, 414-417.
6. Inose Y, Miyase T and Ueno A. Studies on the Constituents of *Solidago virga-aurea* L. I. Structural Elucidation of Saponins in the Herb. *Chem. Pharm. Bull.* 1991, **39**, 2037-2042.
7. Inose Y, Miyase T and Ueno A. Studies on the Constituents of *Solidago virga-aurea* L. II. Structures of Solidagosaponins X-XX. *Chem. Pharm. Bull.* 1992, **40**, 946-953.
8. Miyase T, Inose Y and Ueno A. Studies on the Constituents of *Solidago virga-aurea* L. III. Structures of Solidagosaponins XXI-XXIX. *Chem. Pharm. Bull.* 1994, **42**, 617-624.
9. Bader G, Lück L, Schenk R, Hirschelmann R and Hiller K. Leiocarposid - Leitsubstanz zur Qualitätssicherung von Solidaginis virgaureae herba [Leiocarposide - marker substance for quality assurance of Solidaginis virgaureae herba]. *Pharmazie* 1998, **53**, 805-806 [GERMAN].
10. Hiller K and Fötsch G. Zur quantitativen Verteilung der Phenolglykoside Virgaureosid A und Leiocarposid in *Solidago virgaurea* L. [Quantitative distribution of the phenolic glycosides virgaureoside A and leiocarposide in *Solidago virgaurea* L.]. *Pharmazie* 1986, **41**, 415-416 [GERMAN/English summary].
11. Bader G, Janka M, Hannig H-J and Hiller K. Zur quantitativen Bestimmung von Leiocarposid in *Solidago virgaurea* L. [Quantitative determination of leiocarposide in Solidago virgaurea L.]. *Pharmazie* 1990, **45**, 380-381 [GERMAN].
12. Hiller K, Dube G and Zeigan D. Virgaureoside A - a New Bisdesmosidic Phenol Glycoside from *Solidago virgaurea* L. *Pharmazie* 1985, **40**, 795-796 [GERMAN/English summary].
13. Budzianowski J, Skrzypczak L and Wesolowska M. Flavonoids and Leiocarposide in Four *Solidago* Taxa. *Sci. Pharm.* 1990, **58**, 15-23.
14. Poetsch F. Caffeic Acid Derivatives from *Solidago* Species. *Drogenreport* 1999, **12**, 15-18 [GERMAN/English summary].
15. Wittig J and Veit M. Analysis of Flavonol Glycosides from *Solidago* Species in a Complex Plant Extract. *Drogenreport* 1999, **12**, 18-20 [GERMAN/English summary].
16. Pietta P, Gardana C, Mauri P and Zecca L. High-performance liquid chromatographic analysis of flavonol glycosides of *Solidago virgaurea. J. Chromatogr.* 1991, **558**, 296-301.
17. Schilcher H. Über das Vorkommen von Flavonoiden und Hydroxyzimtsäuren in *Solidago virgaurea* L. und *Solidago serotina* Ait. [The occurrence of flavonoids and hydroxycinnamic acids in *Solidago virgaurea* L. and *Solidago serotina* Ait.]. *Naturwissenschaften* 1964, **51**, 636 [GERMAN].
18. Batyuk VS and Kovaleva SN. Flavonoids of *Solidago canadensis* and *S. virgaurea. Khim. Prir. Soedin.* 1985, (4), 566-567 [RUSSIAN], translated into English as: *Chem. Nat. Compd.* 1985, **21**, 533-534.
19. Skrzypczakowa L. Flavonoids in herb of *Solidago virgaurea* L. II. Separation and identification of further flavonol derivatives. *Acta Pol. Pharm.* 1962, **19**, 481-490 [POLISH/English summary].
20. Goswami A, Barua RN, Sharma RP, Baruah JN, Kulanthaivel P and Herz W. Clerodanes from *Solidago virgaurea. Phytochemistry* 1984, **23**, 837-841.
21. Kalemba D. Phenolic acids in four *Solidago* species. *Pharmazie* 1992, **47**, 471-472.
22. Pychenkova PA. Dynamics of the amount and characteristics of the polysaccharides of *Solidago virgaurea. Khim. Prir. Soedin.* 1987, (2), 291-292 [RUSSIAN], translated into English as: *Chem. Nat. Compd.* 1987, **23**, 246-7.
23. Yakovlev AI and Pychenkova PA. Polysaccharides of *Solidago virgaurea. Khim. Prir. Soedin.* 1981, (6), 790-791 [RUSSIAN], translated into English as: *Chem. Nat. Compd.* 1981, **17**, 580-581.
24. Franz G. Polysaccharides in Pharmacy: Current Applications and Future Concepts. *Planta Medica* 1989, **55**, 493-497.
25. Fujita S. Miscellaneous contributions to the essential oils of plants from various territories. LII. Components of the essential oils of *Solidago virgaurea* Linn. ssp. *Nippon Nogei Kagaku Kaishi* 1990, **64**, 1729-1732 [JAPANESE]; through *Chem. Abstr.* 1991, **114**, 98252.
26. Akihisa T, Inoue Y, Yasukawa K, Kasahara Y, Yamanouchi S, Kumaki K and Tamura T. Widespread occurrence of *syn*-alkane-6,8-diols in the flowers of the Compositae. *Phytochemistry* 1998, **49**, 1637-1640.
27. Mayer RA and Mayer M. *Solidago virga aurea* L., Goldrute. *Pharmazie* 1950, **5**, 82-85 [GERMAN].
28. Hoppe HA. Solidago. In: *Drogenkunde*, 8th ed. Berlin-NewYork: Walter de Gruyter, 1975:110-14-16 [GERMAN].
29. Westendorf J and Vahlensieck W. Spasmolytische und kontraktile Einflüsse eines pflanzlichen Kombinationspräparates auf die glatte Muskulatur des isolierten Meerschweinchendarms [Spasmolytic and contractile influence of a herbal combination preparation on the smooth muscle of isolated guinea pig ileum]. *Arzneim.-Forsch./Drug Res.* 1981, **31**, 40-43 [GERMAN].
30. Westendorf J, Vahlensieck W. Spasmolytische Einflüsse des pflanzlichen Kombinationspräparates Urol® auf die isolierte Rattenharnblase [Spasmolytic influence of the herbal combination preparation Urol® on isolated rat bladder]. *Therapiewoche* 1983, **33**, 936-944 [GERMAN/English summary].
31. Filípek J. Antioxidative properties of *Alchemilla xantho-*

chlora, Salvia officinalis and Solidago virgaurea water extracts. *Biologia (Bratislava)* 1994, **49**, 359-364.
32. Melzig MF, Löser B, Bader G and Papsdorf G. Echtes Goldrutenkraut als entzündungshemmende Droge. Molekularpharmakologische Untersuchungen zur entzündungshemmenden Wirksamkeit von *Solidago-virgaurea*-Zubereitungen [European goldenrod as an anti-inflammatory drug. Molecular pharmacological investigation of the anti-inflammatory efficacy of *Solidago virgaurea* preparations]. *Z. Phytotherapie* 2000, **21**, 67-70 [GERMAN/English summary].
33. Borkowski B. Diuretische Wirkung einiger Flavondrogen [Diuretic effect of some flavone drugs]. *Planta Medica* 1960, **8**, 95-104 [GERMAN/English summary].
34. Schilcher H and Rau H. Nachweis der aquaretischen Wirkung von Birkenblätter- und Goldrutenkrautauszügen im Tierversuch [Evidence of the aquaretic effect of birch leaf and goldenrod infusions in animal experiments]. *Urologe B* 1988, **28**, 274-280 [GERMAN].
35. Chodera A, Dabrowska K, Sloderbach A, Skrzypczak L and Budzianowski J. Wplyw frakcji flawonoidowych gatunków rodzaju *Solidago* L. na diureze i stezenie elektrolitow [Influence of flavonoid fractions from species of the genus *Solidago* L. on diuresis and electrolyte concentrations]. *Acta Polon. Pharm.- Drug Res.* 1991, **48**, 35-37 [POLISH/English summary].
36. Budzianowski J. Urological Activity of Leiocarposide. *Drogenreport* 1999, **12**, 20-21.
37. Chodera A, Dabrowska K, Skrzypczak L and Budzianowski J. Further studies on diuretic activity of leiocarposide. *Acta Polon. Pharm.* 1986, **43**, 499-503 [POLISH/English summary].
38. Chodera A, Dabrowska K, Senzuk M, Wasik-Olejnik A, Skrzypczak L, Budzianowski J and Ellnain-Wojtaszek M. Studies on the diuretic action of a glucoside ester from the *Solidago* L. genus. *Acta Polon. Pharm.* 1985, **42**, 199-204 [POLISH/English summary].
39. Chodera A, Dabrowska K, Bobkiewicz-Kozlowska T, Tkaczyk J, Skrzypczak L and Budzianowski J. Effect of leiocarposide on experimental urolithiasis in rats. *Acta Polon. Pharm.* 1988, **45**, 181-186 [POLISH/English summary].
40. El-Ghazaly M, Khayyal MT, Okpanyi SN and Arens-Corell M. Study of the Anti-inflammatory Activity of *Populus tremula, Solidago virgaurea* and *Fraxinus excelsior. Arzneim.-Forsch./Drug Res.* 1992, **42**, 333-336.
41. Okpanyi SN, Schirpke-von Paczensky R and Dickson D. Anti-inflammatory, Analgesic and Antipyretic Effects of Various Plant Extracts and a Combination Thereof in Animal Models. *Arzneim.-Forsch./Drug Res.* 1989, **39**, 698-703 [GERMAN/English summary].
42. Metzner J, Hirschelmann R and Hiller K. Antiphlogistische und analgetische Wirkungen von Leiocarposid, einem phenolischen Bisglucosid aus *Solidago virgaurea* L. [Anti-inflammatory and analgesic effects of leiocarposide, a phenolic diglucoside from *Solidago virgaurea* L.]. *Pharmazie* 1984, **39**, 869-870 [GERMAN].
43. Fötsch G, Pfeifer S, Bartoszek M, Franke P and Hiller K. Metabolism of the phenolic glycosides leiocarposide and salicin. *Pharmazie* 1989, **44**, 555-558 [GERMAN/English summary].
44. Jacker H-J, Voigt G and Hiller K. Zum antiexsudativen Verhalten einiger Triterpensaponine [The antiexudative behaviour of some triterpene saponins]. *Pharmazie* 1982, **37**, 380-382 [GERMAN].
45. Gross SC, Goodarzi G, Watabe M, Bandyopadhyay S, Pai SK and Watabe K. Antineoplastic Activity of *Solidago virgaurea* on Prostatic Tumor Cells in an SCID Mouse Model. *Nutrition Cancer* 2002, **43**, 76-81.
46. Kraus J, Schneider M and Franz G. Antitumorpolysaccharide aus *Solidago* sp. *Dtsch. Apoth. Ztg.* 1986, **126**, 2045-2049 [GERMAN].
47. Plohmann B, Bader G, Hiller K and Franz G. Immunomodulatory and antitumoral effects of triterpenoid saponins. *Pharmazie* 1997, **52**, 953-957.
48. Brühwiler K, Frater-Schröder M, Kalbermatten R, Tobler M. Research project on *Solidago virgaurea* tincture. In: Abstracts of 4th and International Congress on Phytotherapy. Munich, 10-13 September 1992 (Abstract SL 20).
49. Laszig R. Goldrutenkraut bei chronischen/rezidivierenden Harnwegsinfekten [European goldenrod in chronic/recurrent urinary tract infections]. *Jatros Uro* 1999, **15**, 39-43 [GERMAN].
50. Laszig R, Smiszek R, Stammwitz U, Henneicke-von Zepelin H-H and Akçetin Z. Clinical Drug Monitorings Regarding Efficacy and Safety of a Monograph-Compliant Preparation of Golden Rod Extract. *Drogenreport* 1999, **12**, 38-40 [GERMAN].
51. Pfannkuch A and Stammwitz U. Wirksamkeit und Verträglichkeit eines monographiekonformen Goldrutenkraut-Extraktes bei Patienten mit Reizblase [Efficacy and tolerability of a monograph-conforming golden rod extract in patients suffering from irritable bladder]. *Z. Phytotherapie* 2002, **23**, 20-25 [GERMAN/English summary].
52. Schmitt M. Echte Goldrute normalisiert die Reizblase. Effektive und nebenwirkungsarme Behandlung abakterieller Cystitiden [European goldenrod normalises irritable bladder. Effective treatment of abacterial cystitis with minimal side effects]. *TW Urol Nephrol* 1996, **8**, 133-135 [GERMAN].
53. Solidage ou Verge d'Or. In: *Médicaments à base de plantes.* ISBN 2-911473-02-7. Saint-Denis Cedex, France: Agence du Médicament, 1998.
54. Solidago (Goldrute). German Commission E Monograph published in: Bundesanzeiger No. 193 of 15 October 1987; amended in Bundesanzeiger No. 50 of 13 March 1990.
55. Virgaurea. In: *British Herbal Pharmacopoeia 1983.* ISBN 0-903032-07-4. Bournemouth: British Herbal Medicine Association, 1983.
56. Chevallier A. Goldenrod - *Solidago virgaurea.* In: *Encyclopedia of Medicinal Plants, 2nd ed.* ISBN 0-7513-1209-6. London-New York: Dorling Kindersley, 2001:271.
57. Grieve M (edited by Leyel CF).Golden Rod. In: *A Modern Herbal* (first published 1931; revised 1973). ISBN 1-85501-249-9. London: Tiger Books International, 1994:361-362.
58. Stodola J and Volák J. Goldenrod. Translated into English in: Bunney S, editor. *The Illustrated Book of Herbs.* ISBN 0-7064-1489-6. London: Octopus Books, 1984:272.
59. Wichtl M and Neubeck M. Echtes Goldrutenkraut - Solidaginis virgaureae herba. In: Hartke K, Hartke H, Mutschler E, Rücker G and Wichtl M, editors. *Kommentar zum Deutschen Arzneibuch.* Stuttgart: Wissenschaftliche Verlagsgesellschaft, 2000 (13 Lfg.):G 26/2 [GERMAN].
60. Bauer HW and Wiedemann A. Diuretische, antiinflammatorische, spasmolytische und immunmodulatorische Therapie mit Goldrutenkraut. Eine aktuelle Übersicht [Diuretic, anti-inflammatory, spasmolytic and immunomodulatory therapy with European goldenrod herb. An up-to-date summary]. *Z. Phytotherapie* 2003, **24**, 218-221 [GERMAN/English summary].

REGULATORY GUIDELINES FROM OTHER EU COUNTRIES

FRANCE

Médicaments à base de plantes [53]: Solidage ou Verge d'Or, sommité fleurie.

Therapeutic indications accepted

Oral use
Traditionally used: to facilitate urinary and digestive elimination functions; to promote the renal elimination of water.

GERMANY

Commission E monograph [54]: Solidago (Goldrute).

Goldenrod, European

Uses
As irrigation therapy for inflammatory disorders of the lower urinary tract, urinary calculi and kidney gravel; for the prophylaxis of urinary calculi and kidney gravel.

Contraindications
None known.

Note: Avoid irrigation therapy in cases of oedema due to impaired cardiac or renal function.

Side effects
None known.

Interactions with other drugs
None known.

Dosage
Daily dose: 6-12 g of the herb or equivalent preparations.

Mode of administration
Comminuted drug for infusions and other galenic preparations for internal use.

Note: Ensure copious intake of fluids.

Actions
Diuretic, weakly spasmolytic, anti-inflammatory.

GRINDELIA

Compositae

Grindeliae herba

Synonyms: Gumweed, gumplant (common names used for most species of *Grindelia*).

Definition
Grindelia consists of the dried flowering tops of *Grindelia camporum* Greene, *G. squarrosa* (Pursh) Dunal, *G. robusta* Nutt. or *G. humilis* Hook. et Arn.

CONSTITUENTS

☐ ***Diterpenes*** Resin exuded from surface glands constitutes 10-16% of the dry weight of aerial parts of *G. camporum*, 10-13% of *G. squarrosa*, 5-6% of *G. robusta* and 6% of *G. humilis*. 50-80% of the crude resin consists of 'resin acids', principally grindelic acid, 7,8-epoxygrindelic acid and 17-acetoxygrindelic acid [1]. In a sample from *G. camporum*, for example, crude resin constituted 20%, 14% and 2% of the dry weight of flower heads, leaves and stems respectively; 47% of the flower head resin acids consisted of grindelic acid, 15% of 7,8-epoxygrindelic acid and 8% of 17-acetoxygrindelic acid [2].

Numerous other grindelane acids [3,4] and methyl esters [4] have been isolated from *G. camporum* and/or *G. squarrosa* resins. A few diterpenic acids of different skeletal structure, such as strictanonic acid, have also been isolated from *G. camporum* [5].

Grindelic acid was first isolated in 1961 from the resin of *G. robusta* [6]. Its absolute configuration (and hence that of all grindelane diterpenoids) was long disputed but has now been confirmed [7,8].

☐ ***Acetylenic compounds*** The C_{10} diacetylenic compounds matricarianol and matricarianol acetate have been isolated from aerial parts of *G. robusta* [9,10], *G. camporum* and *G. humilis* [11] together with other C_{10} acetylenic compounds. In all, 9 acetylenic compounds including aldehydes, alcohols and esters have been isolated from *G. camporum* and 19 from *G. humilis* [11].

☐ ***Flavonoids*** Methylated flavonols identified in resin (composed mainly of diterpenes) on the surface of aerial parts of *G. robusta* include kaempferol 3-methyl ether (isokaempferide) and 3,4′-dimethyl ether (ermanin), 6-hydroxykaempferol 3,6,7-trimethyl ether (penduletin), quercetin 3,3′-dimethyl ether, 3,7,3′-trimethyl ether (pachypodol) and 3,3′,4′-trimethyl ether, and quercetagetin 3,6,4′-trimethyl ether (centaureidin) and 3,6,7,3′-tetramethyl ether (chrysosplenetin) [12]. Quercetin, quercetin 3,3′-dimethyl ether, acacetin and kumatakenin have been isolated from *G. camporum* [4].

Some similar methylated flavonols and also the flavone luteolin have been identified in flower heads of *G. robusta* and *G. squarrosa* [13-15]. Chrysoeriol-7-glucuronide has been isolated from *G. squarrosa* [16].

☐ ***Triterpenoid saponins*** Grindelia sapogenin D, bayogenin and oleanolic acid have been identified as sapogenins after hydrolysis of a saponin fraction from *Grindelia robusta* [17].

☐ ***Phenolic acids*** *p*-Hydroxybenzoic, *p*-coumaric and vanillic acids have been identified in flower heads of *G. squarrosa* and *G. robusta* [13,18]; also ferulic, caffeic and chlorogenic acids in the leaves of *G. robusta* [18].

☐ ***Essential oil***, ca. 0.2% [19] containing mainly mono- and sesquiterpenes [19-21]. Steam-distilled oil from flowers and leaves of *G. robusta* contained α-pinene (ca. 13%), germacrene D (10-23%), β-pinene (ca. 3%), myrcene (2-7%) and β-caryophyllene (2-4%) [20] among some 140 constituents [19]. Oils from other species are qualitatively similar but quantitatively distinct with limonene (12-15%), α-pinene and germacrene D dominant in *G. camporum*, and α-pinene (10-35%) and limonene dominant in *G. squarrosa* [20].

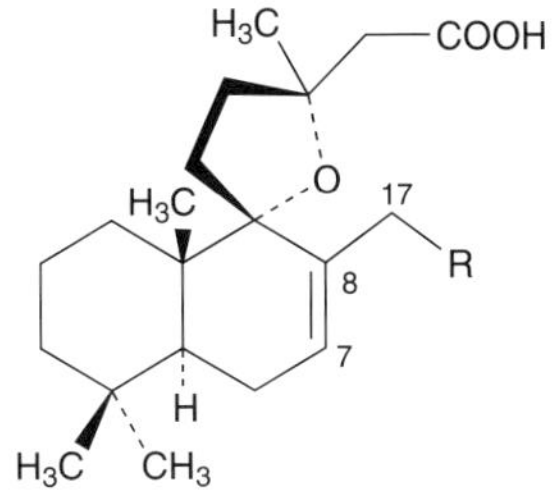

Grindelic acid R = H
17-Acetoxy-grindelic acid R = $OCOCH_3$

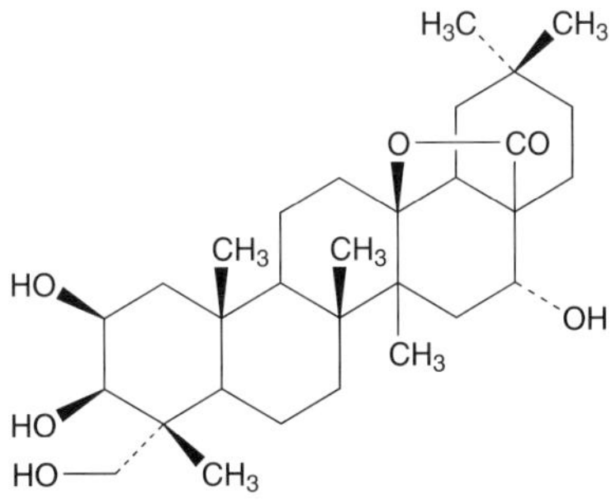

Grindelia sapogenin D

Published Assay Methods
Resin content [Ph. Fr.]. Resin content by extraction, total resin acids by titration [1] and individual acids (as methyl esters) by GC [1,3]. Essential oil constituents by GC/GC-MS [19].

PHARMACOLOGY

In vitro
Hydroethanolic extracts [13,17,22], resin fractions [13,17] and a polyphenolic fraction [13] from grindelia have shown inhibitory activity against various bacteria including *Staphylococcus aureus* and *Bacillus subtilis*. However, neither relevant flavonoids [22] nor a saponin fraction [17] exhibited antibacterial activity, which is at least partly attributable to the resin [17] and possibly to phenolic acids [18].

A 50% V/V methanolic extract of grindelia showed no antispasmodic activity on spontaneous or acetylcholine-induced contractions of isolated guinea pig ileum at concentrations up to 800 µg/ml [23]. However, in an earlier study, mild antispasmodic activity on contractions of guinea pig ileum was demonstrated with a fluid extract; ED_{50} values for acetylcholine-, histamine-, serotonin- and bradykinin-induced contractions were 150-200 µg/ml, 40 µg/ml, 10-50 µg/ml and 10-20 µg/ml respectively [13].

In vivo
A dry 80% ethanolic extract of grindelia (*G. robusta*) exhibited significant anti-inflammatory activity, dose-dependently inhibiting carrageenan-induced rat paw oedema by 41% ($p<0.01$) and 63% ($p<0.001$) after oral administration at 100 and 200 mg/kg body weight respectively, compared to 45% inhibition by indometacin at 5 mg/kg ($p<0.01$) [24]. In similar experiments, intraperitoneally administered grindelia fluid extract and a polyphenolic fraction also showed anti-inflammatory activity [13].

Respiratory tract fluid (RTF) was collected from the trachea of urethanized animals for 3 hours before and 4 hours after administration by stomach tube of fluid extract of grindelia in doses from 0.1 to 10 ml/kg body weight. In the 2nd hour after administration the output of RTF increased by 79% in cats but no effect was evident in rabbits or guinea pigs. Control animals showed increases or decreases in RTF output of less than 30% over the 4 hours. The results did not substantiate a useful expectorant effect of grindelia [25].

A fluid extract and polyphenolic fraction from grindelia, administered intraperitoneally to guinea pigs, showed no antispasmodic activity against histamine- or serotonin-induced bronchospasms and only slight antispasmodic activity at high dose levels (close to the toxic dose) in reducing the intensity of acetylcholine- or bradykinin-induced bronchospasms [13].

CLINICAL STUDIES

None published on mono-preparations of grindelia.

THERAPEUTICS

Actions
Anti-inflammatory [13,24], antispasmodic, expect-

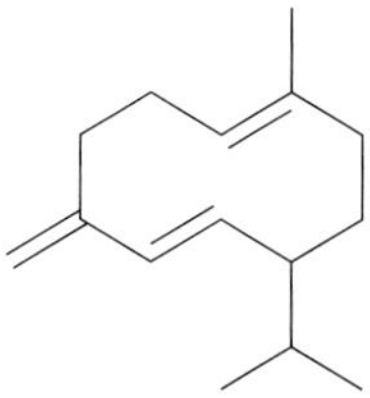

Germacrene D

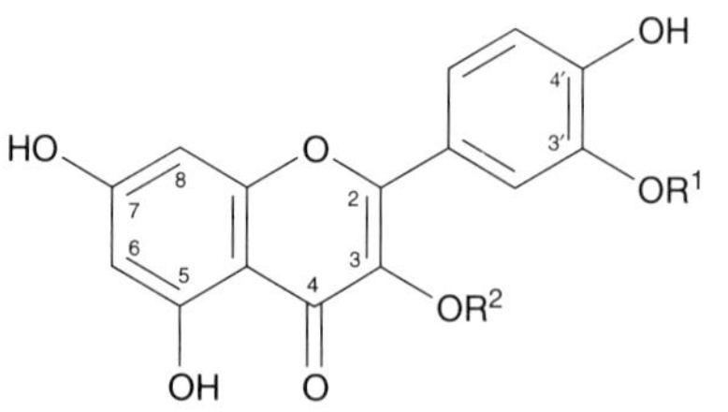

	R1	R2
Quercetin	H	H
Quercetin 3,3′-dimethyl ether	CH_3	CH_3

$$H_3C-CH=CH-C\equiv C-C\equiv C-CH=CH-CH_2OH$$

Matricarianol

orant, cardiac depressant [26], antibacterial [13,17,22].

Indications
None adequately substantiated by pharmacological or clinical studies.

Uses based on experience or tradition
Bronchitis, asthma [22,26], coughs [27], whooping cough [22,26]; catarrh of the upper respiratory tract [22,26,28].

Has also been used in the treatment of cystitis [26] and hay fever [22], and topically as a lotion for poison ivy dermatitis [26].

Contraindications
None known.

Side effects
In rare cases (or in large doses) may cause gastric [28] or renal [26] irritation.

Dosage
Three times daily: dried herb or as an infusion, 2-3 g; liquid extract (BPC 1949), 1:1 in 22.5% ethanol, 0.6-1.2 ml [26]; tincture 1:10 or 1:5 in ethanol 60-80% V/V, 1-3 ml [26,28].
As a lotion: liquid extract 1:10 in 10% ethanol [26].

SAFETY

No mortality occurred and no side effects were apparent in rats after a single oral dose at 2.5 g/kg body weight of a dry 80% ethanolic extract of grindelia (*G. robusta*) [24].

The intraperitoneal LD_{50} in mice of a commercial liquid extract of grindelia was determined as 250 mg/kg [13].

REGULATORY STATUS

Medicines

UK	Accepted for general sale, internal or external use [29].
France	Accepted for specified indication [27].
Germany	Commission E monograph published, with approved uses [28].

REFERENCES

Current Pharmacopoeial Monographs

Ph. Fr.	Grindélia
BHP	Grindelia

Literature References

1. Timmermann BN, McLaughlin SP and Hoffmann JJ. Quantitative Variation of Grindelane Diterpene Acids in 20 Species of North American *Grindelia*. *Biochem. Syst. Ecol.* 1987, **15**, 401-410.
2. Hoffmann JJ and McLaughlin SP. *Grindelia camporum*: Potential Cash Crop for the Arid Southwest. *Econ. Bot.* 1986, **40**, 162-169.
3. Timmermann BN, Luzbetak DJ, Hoffmann JJ, Jolad SD, Schram KH, Bates RB and Klenck RE. Grindelane diterpenoids from *Grindelia camporum* and *Chrysothamnus paniculatus*. *Phytochemistry* 1983, **22**, 523-525.
4. Timmermann BN, Hoffmann JJ, Jolad SD and Schram KH. Grindelane diterpenoids from *Grindelia squarrosa* and *G. camporum*. *Phytochemistry* 1985, **24**, 1031-1034.
5. Hoffmann JJ, Jolad SD, Timmermann BN, Bates RB and Camou FA. Two grindelane diterpenoids from *Grindelia camporum*. *Phytochemistry* 1988, **27**, 493-496.
6. Panizzi L, Mangoni L and Belardini M. The structure of grindelic acid, a new diterpene acid. *Tetrahedron Lett.* 1961, 376.
7. Paquette LA and Wang H-L. Total synthesis of (+)-grindelic acid by stereocontrolled oxonium ion activated pinacol ring expansion. Chemical proof of the absolute configuration of all grindelane diterpenes. *Tetrahedron Lett.* 1995, **36**, 6005-6008.
8. Adinolfi M, Greca MD, and Mangoni L. The absolute configuration of grindelic acid. *Phytochemistry* 1988, **27**, 1878-1881.
9. Schulte KE, Reisch J and Busch P. Matricarianol als Inhaltsstoff der Grindelia robusta. [Matricarianol as a constituent of Grindelia robusta]. *Arch. Pharm. (Weinheim)* 1964, **297**, 496-499 [GERMAN].
10. Bohlmann F, Kleine K-M and Bornowski H. Die Acetylenverbindungen der Gattung *Grindelia W.* [Acetylenic Compounds of the Genus *Grindelia* Willd.]. *Chem. Ber.* 1965, **98**, 369-371 [GERMAN].
11. Bohlmann F, Thefeld W and Zdero C. Polyacetylenic Compounds, 178. Constituents of *Grindelia* Species. *Chem. Ber.* 1970, **103**, 2245-2251 [GERMAN/English summary].
12. Timmermann B, Wollenweber E, Dörr M, Armbruster S, Valant-Vetschera KM and Fuentes ER. External Flavonoids in Two *Grindelia* Species. *Z. Naturforsch.* 1994, **49c**, 395-397.
13. Pinkas M, Didry N, Torck M, Bézanger L and Cazin J-C. Phenolic components from some species of Grindelia. *Ann. Pharm. Franç.* 1978, **36**, 97-104 [FRENCH/English summary].
14. Pinkas M, Torck M and Bézanger-Beauquesne L. Recherches sur la composition du *Grindelia squarrosa* Dunal et du *G. aphanactis* Rydb. (Composées). [Research on the composition of *Grindelia squarrosa* Dunal and *G. aphanactis* Rydb. (Compositae)]. *C.R. Acad. Sc. Paris* 1977, **284**, 1593-1596 [FRENCH/English summary].
15. Torck M, Pinkas M and Didry N. Recherches sur la composition du Grindelia squarrosa Dunal (Composées). [Research on the composition of Grindelia squarrosa Dunal (Compositae)]. *C.R. Acad. Sc. Paris* 1976, **282**, 1453-1455 [FRENCH].
16. Wagner H, Iyengar MA, Seligmann O and Hörhammer L. Chrysoeriol-7-Glucuronid in *Grindelia squarrosa*. *Phytochemistry* 1972, **11**, 2350 [GERMAN].
17. Kreutzer S, Schimmer O and Waibel R. Triterpenoid Sapogenins in the Genus *Grindelia*. *Planta Medica* 1990, **56**, 392-394 [GERMAN/English summary].
18. Didry N, Pinkas M and Torck M. Sur la composition chimique et l'activité antibactérienne des feuilles de diverses espèces de *Grindelia*. [The chemical composition and antibacterial activity of the leaves of some *Grindelia* species]. *Plantes Méd. Phytothér.* 1982, **16**, 7-15 [FRENCH].
19. Kaltenbach G, Schäfer M and Schimmer O. Volatile Constituents of the Essential Oil of *Grindelia robusta* Nutt. and *Grindelia squarrosa* Dun. *J. Essent. Oil Res.* 1993, **5**, 107-108.
20. Schäfer M, Schimmer O and Schultze W. Relative Amounts of Essential Oil Components in the Flowers, Leaves and Stems of Four *Grindelia* Species. *Planta Medica* 1993, **59** (Suppl.), A634.

21. Kaltenbach G and Schimmer O. Volatile Constituents of the Herbs of *Grindelia robusta* and *Grindelia squarrosa*. *Planta Medica* 1991, **57** (Suppl. 2), A82.
22. Schimmer O and Egersdörfer S. Grindelia-Arten - Die Grindelie. [Grindelia species - Grindelia]. *Z. Phytotherapie* 1988, **9**, 86-90 [GERMAN].
23. Izzo AA, Capasso R, Senatore F, Seccia S and Morrica P. Spasmolytic Activity of Medicinal Plants Used for the Treatment of Disorders Involving Smooth Muscles. *Phytotherapy Res.* 1996, **10**, S107-S108.
24. Mascolo N, Autore G, Capasso F, Menghini A and Fasulo MP. Biological Screening of Italian Medicinal Plants for Anti-Inflammatory Activity. *Phytotherapy Res.* 1987, **1**, 28-31.
25. Boyd EM and Palmer ME. The Effect of Quillaia, Senega, Squill, Grindelia, Sanguinaria, Chionanthus and Dioscorea upon the Output of Respiratory Tract Fluid. *Acta Pharmacol.* 1946, **2**, 235-246.
26. Grindelia. In: *British Herbal Pharmacopoeia 1983*. ISBN 0-903032-07-9. Bournemouth: British Herbal Medicine Association, 1983.
27. Grindélia. In: *Médicaments à base de plantes*. ISBN 2-911473-02-7. Saint-Denis Cedex, France: Agence du Médicament, 1998
28. Grindeliae herba (Grindeliakraut). German Commission E Monograph published in: Bundesanzeiger No. 11 of 17.01.91.
29. Grindelia. In: UK Statutory Instrument 1984 No. 769. The Medicines (Products other than Veterinary Drugs) (General Sale List) Order 1984. Schedule 1, Table A.

REGULATORY GUIDELINES FROM OTHER EU COUNTRIES

FRANCE

Médicaments à base de plantes [27]: Grindélia, sommité fleurie.

Therapeutic indications accepted

Oral use
Traditionally used in the symptomatic treatment of coughs.

GERMANY

Commission E monograph [28]: Grindeliae herba (Grindeliakraut).

Uses
Catarrhs of the upper respiratory tract.

Contraindications
None known.

Side effects
In rare cases, irritation of the gastric mucosa.

Interactions with other drugs
None known.

Dosage
Unless otherwise prescribed, daily dose: 4-6 g of the drug or 3-6 g of Grindelia fluid extract (in accordance with Erg. B6.); tincture (1:10 or 1:5, ethanol 60%-80% V/V), 1.5-3 ml; equivalent preparations.

Mode of administration
Comminuted drug for tea infusions and other galenical preparations for internal use.

Action
Antibacterial in vitro.

HAMAMELIS BARK

Hamamelidaceae

Hamamelidis cortex

Synonym: Witch Hazel Bark.

Definition
Hamamelis Bark consists of the dried bark from stems and branches of *Hamamelis virginiana* L.

Hamamelis virginiana is a shrub indigenous to the USA and Canada. The bark is usually collected in the Spring [1].

CONSTITUENTS

☐ ***Tannins***, up to about 12% [2] (DAC min. 4.0% by hide powder method), of both the hydrolysable and condensed types:

Gallotannins, principally hamamelitannin [3], a mixture of the α- and β-furanose forms of 2′,5-digalloylhamamelose in a ratio of about 2:1 [4]. Highly unstable α- and β-1-(4-hydroxybenzoyl) derivatives of hamamelitannin (which degrade to, and are probably precursors of, hamamelitannin), are also present [4].

Other galloylhamameloses identified in the bark include 2′- and 5-monogalloylhamameloses [5], 2′,4-digalloylhamamelose [6], 1,2′,5-trigalloylhamamelose [4], 2′,3,5-trigalloylhamamelose and its α- and β-1-(4-hydroxybenzoyl) derivatives [6].

From HPLC analysis of a hydroethanolic extract of hamamelis bark, hamamelitannin, proanthocyanidins and gallic acid were found to be in a ratio of 65:30:5 [3]. Another study found that about 20% of a 60%-ethanolic dry extract was hamamelitannin [7].

Condensed tannins (proanthocyanidins) [2], including procyanidin dimers such as catechin-[4α→8]-catechin, 3-*O*-galloyl-epicatechin-[4β→8]-catechin and epicatechin-[4β→8]-catechin-3-*O*-(4-hydroxybenzoate), and prodelphinidins such as epigallocatechin-[4β→8]-catechin, 3-*O*-galloyl epigallocatechin-[4β→8]-catechin and 3-*O*-galloyl epigallocatechin-[4β→8]-gallocatechin [6].

Oligomeric proanthocyanidins have been isolated consisting of catechin and gallocatechin units, some of which are 3-*O*-galloylated, with 4→8 linkages and a degree of polymerisation of 4-9 [6,8,9].

The monomers (+)-catechin, (+)-gallocatechin [2,6], (–)-epicatechin gallate and (–)-epigallocatechin gallate [2] are present, as well as free gallic acid [4].

☐ ***Polysaccharides*** consisting of highly-branched arabinans, an arabinogalactan, and various arabinorhamnogalacturonans and mannoglucans [10].

☐ ***Essential oil***, 0.1-0.5 % [11]. In a recent study of the steam distillate from fresh young twigs of *Hamamelis virginiana*, Engel et al. [12] obtained a yield of 0.09% of oil containing about 160 compounds, which are more fully described in the monograph on Hamamelis Water.

Published Assay Methods
Determination of tannins in herbal drugs [Ph. Eur. method 2.8.14]. Hamamelitannin by HPLC [8]. Volatile compounds in steam-distillate by GC-MS [12].

PHARMACOLOGY

In vitro

Anti-inflammatory activity
Hamamelitannin potently inhibited 5-lipoxygenase (from a cytosol fraction of RBL-1 cells) with an IC_{50} of 1.0 μM; three galloylated proanthocyanidins from hamamelis bark also showed strong activity with IC_{50} values of 6.6-18.7 μM. The galloylated

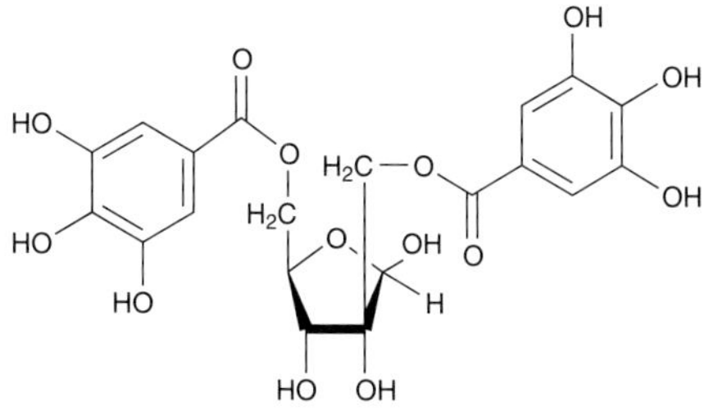

Hamamelitannin

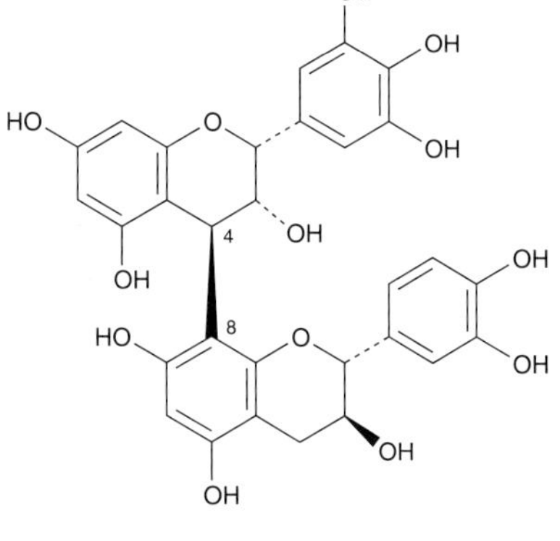

Epigallocatechin-[4β→8]-catechin

proanthocyanidins, especially an oligomer of 5-6 units with an IC_{50} of 9.4 μM, also potently inhibited acetyltransferase, while hamamelitannin was ineffective in this test [6].

Antiviral activity
Hamamelitannin and fractions consisting mainly of oligomeric and polymeric proanthocyanidins were obtained from a hamamelis bark 60%-ethanolic extract by ultrafiltration techniques. The fraction with MW ≥ 3 kDa (mainly tetramers and larger molecules) exhibited greater antiviral activity (ED_{50} of 6.3 μg/ml) against herpes simplex virus than the fraction of MW < 3 kDa (mainly monomers, dimers and trimers) or hamamelitannin [8].

Active-oxygen scavenging activity
Hamamelis bark extract [13,14] and hamamelitannin [13,15] have been found to have high active-oxygen scavenging activity; the galloyl groups of hamamelitannin appear to play an important role in this [15].

By electron spin resonance spin-trapping methods hamamelitannin was found to be a potent scavenger of superoxide anions, hydroxyl radicals and singlet oxygens [13,15,16]. Hamamelitannin showed higher activity than DL-α-tocopherol in scavenging lipid peroxides and was found to have antioxidative and strongly scavenging activity against organic radicals such as 1,1-diphenyl-2-picrylhydrazyl (DPPH) [15].

The high scavenging activity of hamamelitannin against superoxide anions was also demonstrated by its suppressive effect on the depolymerization of hyaluronic acid; it inhibited the rate of depolymerization by 73.8% compared to 24.7% for ascorbic acid and 84.4% for superoxide dismutase. Hamamelitannin also showed a dose-dependent protective effect against cytotoxicity induced by superoxide anions on cultured human dermal fibroblasts, increasing the survival rate of fibroblasts to 85.5% at 100 μM compared to 27% for controls [13], and similarly protected murine dermal fibroblasts against superoxide anions, hydroxyl radicals and singlet oxygens [15,17].

Pretreatment of murine dermal fibroblasts with hamamelitannin protected against cell damage induced by exposure to a high dose of UVB irradiation. This effect was related to active-oxygen scavenging (not UVB filtering) and it was concluded that hamamelitannin associates with fibroblasts via the hamamelose moiety [16].

Hamamelitannin (ED_{50} 29 ng/ml) and a low MW procyanidin fraction (MW < 3 kDa; ED_{50} 80 ng/ml) showed greater antioxidant activity than higher MW procyanidins (MW ≥ 3 kDa; ED_{50} 160 ng/ml) in a radical scavenging test based on chemiluminescence of lipids [8].

On the basis of its protective activity against cell damage through active-oxygen scavenging, hamamelis bark extract has been suggested as a potential anti-ageing or anti-wrinkle agent for the skin [14].

Other effects
The astringency of a tincture prepared from fresh hamamelis bark has been demonstrated using hide powder [18].

Polymeric proanthocyanidin fractions from hamamelis bark at 1-10 μg/ml strongly increased the proliferation of cultured human keratinocytes ($p<0.01$ to $p<0.05$) without significantly influencing differentiation [10].

In vivo
In the croton oil ear oedema test in mice, with test substances applied topically at 250 μg/ear, the anti-inflammatory effect of a 60%-ethanolic crude extract of hamamelis bark (43% inhibition of oedema; $p<0.05$) was found to be largely due to proanthocyanidins of molecular weight ≥ 3kDa (69% inhibition; $p<0.05$); a low MW fraction (MW < 3 kDa) produced no inhibition and hamamelitannin only 7% inhibition [8].

Pharmacological studies in humans
In a pilot study involving cumulative irritation of the skin of 7 healthy volunteers, pretreatment of the skin with a cream containing 1% of high MW proanthocyanidins from hamamelis bark reduced transepidermal water loss, erythema formation and the clinical score in sodium lauryl sulphate-induced dermatitis by more than the corresponding 'placebo' cream. The results suggested that polymeric proanthocyanidins are at least partly responsible for the effects of hamamelis bark in dermatology [10].

CLINICAL STUDIES

None published on mono-preparations from hamamelis bark (see Hamamelis Water for studies involving distillates).

THERAPEUTICS

Actions
Astringent [18-23], antihaemorrhagic [19], locally haemostyptic [20-22], anti-inflammatory [8,19-22], active-oxygen scavenger [13,14].

Indications
None adequately substantiated by pharmacological or clinical studies.

Uses based on experience or tradition
External: Small wounds, skin injuries and bruises, local inflammation of skin [1,20,21] and mucous membranes [20]; haemorrhoids [1,19-21] and varicose vein complaints [20,21].
Internal: Diarrhoea, mucous colitis, haemorrhoids [19,21].

Contraindications
None known.

Side effects
None known.

Interactions with other drugs
None known.

Dosage
External use Semi-solid and liquid preparations containing the equivalent of 5-10% of bark [20]; as a compress, lotion or mouthwash, diluted tincture of hamamelis BPC 1934 (1:10, 45% ethanol) [19] or a decoction of 5-10 g of bark to 250 ml of water [20].
Internal use Tincture BPC 1934, 2-4 ml [19] or an infusion of 2 g of dried bark [21], three times daily. In suppositories, an amount equivalent to 0.1-1 g of dried bark, up to three times daily [20,21].

SAFETY

External use of hamamelis bark preparations and local internal use as mouthwashes or suppositories present no safety concerns. Some texts no longer recommend oral use of hamamelis bark [22,23]; although no significant adverse effects are to be expected, caution should be exercised with respect to prolonged intake [21].

In the Ames mutagenicity test a tincture and a methanolic extract of hamamelis bark dose-dependently inhibited 2-nitrofluorene-induced mutagenicity in *Salmonella typhimurium* strain TA 98, by 60% and 54% respectively at 100 µl/plate. No antimutagenic effects were observed with hamamelitannin, (+)-catechin or a tannin-free tincture. The antimutagenic effect was found to be due to oligomeric proanthocyanidins and the effect increased with increasing degree of polymerisation [7].

REGULATORY STATUS

Medicines

UK	Accepted for general sale, internal or external use [24].
France	Not listed in *Médicaments à base de plantes* [25].
Germany	Commission E monograph published, with approved uses [20].

Food

Council of Europe	Permitted as flavouring, category N3 [26].

REFERENCES

Current Pharmacopoeial Monographs

BHP	Hamamelis Bark
DAC	Hamamelisrinde

Literature References

1. Pharmaceutical Society of Great Britain. Hamamelidis Cortex. In: *British Pharmaceutical Codex* 1934. London: Pharmaceutical Press, 1934.
2. Friedrich H and Krüger N. New Investigations on the Tannin of Hamamelis. I. The Tannin of the Bark of *H. virginiana*. *Planta Medica* 1974, **25**, 138-148 [GERMAN/English summary].
3. Vennat B, Pourrat H, Pouget MP, Gross D and Pourrat A. Tannins from *Hamamelis virginiana*: Identification of Proanthocyanidins and Hamamelitannin Quantification in Leaf, Bark, and Stem Extracts. *Planta Medica* 1988, **54**, 454-457.
4. Haberland C and Kolodziej H. Novel Galloylhamameloses from *Hamamelis virginiana*. *Planta Medica* 1994, **60**, 464-466.
5. Schilling G and Keller A. Monogalloylhamamelose from *Hamamelis virginiana*. *Z. Naturforsch.* 1986, **41c**, 253-257 [GERMAN/English summary].
6. Hartisch C and Kolodziej H. Galloylhamameloses and proanthocyanidins from *Hamamelis virginiana*. *Phytochemistry* 1996, **42**, 191-198.
7. Erdelmeier CAJ, Cinatl J, Rabenau H, Doerr HW, Biber A and Koch E. Antiviral and Antiphlogistic Activities of *Hamamelis virginiana* Bark. *Planta Medica* 1996, **62**, 241-245.
8. Hartisch C, Kolodziej H and von Bruchhausen F. Dual Inhibitory Activities of Tannins from *Hamamelis virginiana* and Related Polyphenols on 5-Lipoxygenase and Lyso-PAF: Acetyl-CoA Acetyltransferase. *Planta Medica* 1997, **63**, 106-110.
9. Dauer A, Metzner P and Schimmer O. Proanthocyanidins from the Bark of *Hamamelis virginiana* Exhibit Antimutagenic Properties against Nitroaromatic Compounds. *Planta Medica* 1998, **64**, 324-327.
10. Deters A, Dauer A, Schnetz E, Fartasch M and Hensel A. High molecular compounds (polysaccharides and proanthocyanidins) from *Hamamelis virginiana* bark: influence on human skin keratinocyte proliferation and differentiation, and influence on irritated skin. *Phytochemistry* 2001, **58**, 949-958.
11. Neugebauer H. Über die Wirkung der Destillate von *Hamamelis virginiana* und *Corylus avellana* [The action of distillates from *Hamamelis virginiana* and *Corylus avellana*]. *Pharmazie* 1948, **3**, 313-314 [GERMAN].
12. Engel R, Gutmann M, Hartisch C, Kolodziej H and Nahrstedt A. Study on the Composition of the Volatile Fraction of *Hamamelis virginiana*. *Planta Medica* 1998, **64**, 251-258.
13. Masaki H, Atsumi T and Sakurai H. Evaluation of super-oxide scavenging activities of Hamamelis extract and hamamelitannin. *Free Rad. Res. Comms.* 1993, **19**, 333-340.
14. Masaki H, Sakaki S, Atsumi T and Sakurai H. Active-Oxygen Scavenging Activity of Plant Extracts. *Biol. Pharm. Bull.* 1995, **18**, 162-166.
15. Masaki H, Atsumi T and Sakurai H. Hamamelitannin as a new potent active oxygen scavenger. *Phytochemistry* 1994, **37**, 337-343.
16. Masaki H, Atsumi T and Sakurai H. Protective activity of hamamelitannin on cell damage of murine skin fibroblasts induced by UVB irradiation. *J. Dermatol. Sci.* 1995, **10**, 25-34.
17. Masaki H, Atsumi T and Sakurai H. Protective Activity of Hamamelitannin on Cell Damage Induced by Superoxide

Anion Radicals in Murine Dermal Fibroblasts. *Biol. Pharm. Bull.* 1995, **18**, 59-63.
18. Gracza L. Adstringierende Wirkung von Phytopharmaka [Astringent effect of herbal drugs]. *Dtsch. Apoth. Ztg.* 1987, **127**, 2256-8.
19. Hamamelis Bark. In: *British Herbal Pharmacopoeia 1983*. ISBN 0-903032-07-4. Bournemouth: British Herbal Medicine Association, 1983.
20. Hamamelidis folium et cortex. German Commission E Monograph published in: Bundesanzeiger No. 154 of 21 August 1985; amended in Bundesanzeiger No. 50 of 13 March 1990.
21. Mills S and Bone K. Witchhazel. In: *Principles and Practice of Phytotherapy. Modern Herbal Medicine.* ISBN 0-443-06016-9. Edinburgh-London-New York: Churchill Livingstone, 2000:590-594.
22. Schulz V, Hänsel R and Tyler VE. Witch Hazel and Other Tannin-Containing Herbs. In: *Rational Phytotherapy - A Physicians' Guide to Herbal Medicine, 4th ed.* ISBN 3-540-67096-3. Berlin-Heidelberg-New York-London: Springer-Verlag, 2001:306-307.
23. Weiss RF. *Hamamelis virginiana* (Witch Hazel). In: *Herbal Medicine* (translated from the 6th German edition of *Lehrbuch der Phytotherapie*). ISBN 0-906584-19-1. Gothenburg: AB Arcanum, Beaconsfield, UK: Beaconsfield Publishers, 1988:344.
24. Hamamelis. In: UK Statutory Instrument 1994 No. 2410. The Medicines (Products Other Than Veterinary Drugs) (General Sale List) Amendment Order 1994. Schedule 1, Table A.
25. *Médicaments à base de plantes.* ISBN 2-911473-02-7. Saint-Denis Cedex, France: Agence du Médicament, 1998.
26. Hamamelis virginiana L., bark. In: *Flavouring Substances and Natural Sources of Flavourings, 3rd ed.* ISBN 2-7160-0081-6. Strasbourg: Council of Europe, 1981.

REGULATORY GUIDELINES FROM OTHER EU COUNTRIES

GERMANY

Commission E monograph [20]: Hamamelidis folium et cortex (Hamamelisblätter und -rinde).

Uses
Minor skin injuries, local inflammation of skin and mucous membranes.
Haemorrhoids, varicose vein complaints.

Contraindications
None known.

Side effects
None known.

Interactions with other drugs
None known.

Dosage

External use
Steam distillate (Hamamelis water): for compresses, undiluted or diluted 1:3 with water; in semi-solid preparations, 20-30%.
Extract preparations: in semi-solid and liquid preparations, the equivalent of 5-10% of drug.
Drug: for compresses and rinses, decoctions of 5-10 g of drug to 1 cupful (ca. 250 ml) of water.

Internal use (on mucous membranes)
Suppositories: use an amount equivalent to 0.1-1 g of the drug, 1-3 times daily
Other dosage forms: use an amount of preparation equivalent to 0.1-1 g of the drug, or hamamelis water undiluted or diluted with water, several times daily.

Mode of administration
Hamamelis leaf and bark: comminuted drug or infusions for external and internal use.
Fresh leaves and twigs of Hamamelis: steam distillate for external and internal use.

Actions
Astringent, anti-inflammatory, locally haemostyptic.

HAMAMELIS LEAF

Hamamelidaceae

Hamamelidis folium

Synonym: Witch Hazel Leaf.

Definition

Hamamelis Leaf consists of the dried leaves of *Hamamelis virginiana* L.

CONSTITUENTS

☐ ***Tannins***, 5-10% [1] (Ph. Eur. min. 3%) consisting of condensed tannins (proanthocyanidin oligomers and polymers composed of catechin and/or gallocatechin units, mainly with a degree of polymerization ≤ 6) together with hydrolysable gallotannins, including a small amount of hamamelitannin (see structure under Hamamelis Bark) [2-4].

(+)-Catechin [4,5], (+)-gallocatechin, (–)-epicatechin gallate and (–)-epigallocatechin gallate are also present [4].

☐ ***Flavonoids*** Kaempferol, quercetin [2,5] and their respective 3-galactosides (trifolin and hyperin) and 3-glucuronides [5]; also quercitrin and isoquercitrin [2].

☐ ***Phenolic acids*** Caffeic acid, gallic acid [2,3,5] and chlorogenic acid [5].

☐ ***Volatile fraction***, 0.04-0.14% on dry weight basis [6,7]. About 175 compounds have been detected (and 145 identified or partly characterized by GC-MS) in the steam-distillate, including aliphatic hydrocarbons (62.9%, of which heptacosane 16.1%, pentacosane 11.0% and tricosane 10.4%), diterpenes (10.4%, of which *trans*-phytol 9.8%), monoterpenes (7.4%, of which linalool 3.7%), sesquiterpenes (3.3%), fatty acids and their esters (3.6%), and aldehydes and ketones (4.6%) [6].

Surprisingly, neither the carbonyl compounds (α- and β-ionones, n-hexen-2-al and acetaldehyde) [7,8] nor safrole [9] previously reported by Messerschmidt were detected in the latest study [6].

Published Assay Methods

Tannin content by spectrophotometry (hide powder method) [Ph. Eur. method 2.8.14]. Procyanidin oligomers and hamamelitannin by HPLC; flavonoids by spectrophotometry; phenolic acids by TLC densitometry [2].

PHARMACOLOGY

In vivo

To estimate their venoconstrictive effect as a

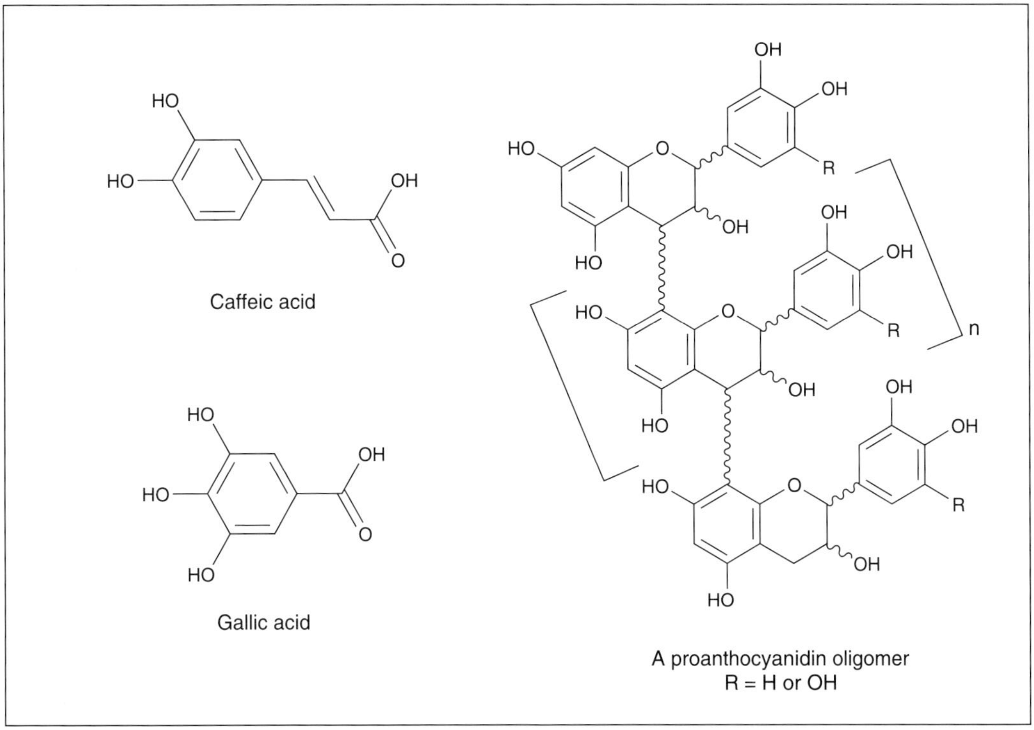

Caffeic acid

Gallic acid

A proanthocyanidin oligomer
R = H or OH

measure of venotonic activity, various hamamelis leaf extracts (as dry residues dissolved in isotonic solutions of equal concentration) were perfused at constant pressure through the hind quarters of rabbits and compared in terms of output on the venous side. All the extracts produced venoconstriction, the order of activity being fluid extract > tincture > hydroethanolic dry extract > aqueous dry extract [10].

A freeze-dried 70%-ethanolic extract of hamamelis leaf administered orally to rats at 200 mg/kg had no anti-inflammatory effect against carrageenan-induced paw oedema. Neither did it significantly inhibit paw swelling in injected limbs in Freund's adjuvant-induced arthritis when orally administered at 200 mg/kg/day for 19 days, although some inhibition was evident; in the non-injected (contralateral) limbs the extract significantly inhibited paw swelling ($p<0.05$) [11].

Pharmacological studies in humans

Topical application of a water-propylene glycol (1:1) extract from hamamelis leaf to the skin of 30 healthy volunteers led to a significant reduction in skin temperature over a period of about 1 hour compared to application of the solvent only, indicating a vasoconstrictive effect [12].

CLINICAL STUDIES

In an open pilot study, patients with neurodermitis atopica (a complex skin allergy, the causes of which are not fully understood, characterized by dry eczema with strong itching, inflammation and an inclination to microbial infection) were treated with hamamelis leaf extract in a cream applied twice daily for 2 weeks. From a total of 32 subacute or chronic cases, divided into 6 groups according to age and nature of symptoms, all showed some improvement, with rapid alleviation of itching; symptoms were eliminated in 6 patients and showed a considerable improvement in a further 21 cases [13].

THERAPEUTICS

Actions

Astringent [2,5,14-17], anti-inflammatory [5,11,14-16], locally haemostyptic [15,16], antihaemorrhagic [5,14], venoconstrictive [2,10,12,18].

Indications

None adequately substantiated by pharmacological or clinical studies.

Uses based on experience or tradition

External: Minor skin injuries, local inflammation of skin and mucous membranes [14-16], bruises [14,16]; varicose vein complaints [15,16,19] and haemorrhoids [14-16,19].

Hamamelis leaf extract appears to be beneficial in the topical treatment of dermitis atopica [13].

Internal: Diarrhoea [14,16], colitis [14].

Contraindications

None known.

Side effects

None known.

Interactions with other drugs

None known. Tannins can, however, inhibit the absorption of minerals [20].

Dosage

External use Hamamelis Ointment BPC 1973 (10% by weight of Hamamelis Liquid Extract BPC 1973 in an ointment base); semi-solid and liquid preparations containing the equivalent of 5-10% of leaf [15]; for compresses and rinses, decoctions of 5-10 g of leaf to 250 ml of water [15], or 20 ml of tincture diluted to 100 ml [16].

Local internal use For mouthwashes, a decoction of 2-3 g in 150 ml of water, several times daily [1]. As suppositories, Hamamelis Suppositories BPC 1973 (200 mg of Hamamelis Dry Extract BPC 1973 in a suitable base) or, more generally, suppositories containing the equivalent of 0.1-1 g of dried leaf [15].

Internal use Three times daily: dried leaf, 2 g or by infusion; Hamamelis Liquid Extract BPC 1973 (1:1, 45% ethanol), 2-4 ml three times daily [14,20].

SAFETY

Hamamelis leaf presents no safety concerns in topical use and has negligible oral toxicity. In rats the acute oral LD_{50} was too high to be established and no adverse effects were observed after oral doses of 100 mg/kg for 3 months [17,18]. However, in view of the tannin content, excessive ingestion should be avoided [20].

REGULATORY STATUS

Medicines

UK	Accepted for general sale, internal or external use [21].
France	Accepted for specified indications [19].
Germany	Commission E monograph published, with approved uses [15].

Food

Council of Europe	Permitted as flavouring, category N3 [22].

REFERENCES

Current Pharmacopoeial Monographs

Ph. Eur. Hamamelis Leaf

Literature References

1. Wichtl M and Egerer HP. Hamamelisblätter - Hamamelidis folium. In: Hartke K, Hartke H, Mutschler E, Rücker G and Wichtl M, editors. *Kommentar zum Europäischen Arzneibuch [Commentary on the European Pharmacopoeia]*. Stuttgart: Wissenschaftliche Verlagsgesellschaft, 1999 (11. Lfg.):H 6/1 [GERMAN].
2. Vennat B, Gross D, Pourrat A and Pourrat H. *Hamamelis virginiana*: Identification and Assay of Proanthocyanidins, Phenolic Acids and Flavonoids in Leaf Extracts. *Pharm. Acta Helv.* 1992, **67**, 11-14.
3. Vennat B, Pourrat H, Pouget MP, Gross D and Pourrat A. Tannins from *Hamamelis virginiana*: Identification of Proanthocyanidins and Hamamelitannin Quantification in Leaf, Bark and Stem Extracts. *Planta Medica* 1988, **54**, 454-457.
4. Friedrich H and Krüger N. New Investigations on the Tannin of Hamamelis. II. The Tannin of the Leaves of *H. virginiana*. *Planta Medica* 1974, **26**, 327-332 [GERMAN/English summary].
5. Sagareishvili TG, Yarosh EA and Kemertelidze EP. Phenolic compounds from leaves of *Hamamelis virginiana*. *Khim. Prir. Soedin.* 1999, (5), 674-675 [RUSSIAN], translated into English as: *Chem. Nat. Compd.* 1999, **35**, 585.
6. Engel R, Gutmann M, Hartisch C, Kolodziej H and Nahrstedt A. Study on the Composition of the Volatile Fraction of *Hamamelis virginiana*. *Planta Medica* 1998, **64**, 251-258.
7. Messerschmidt W. Zur Kenntnis des Wasserdampfdestillats der Blätter von *Hamamelis virginiana* L. 4. Mitteilung: Charakterisierung von Blattdroge und Destillat [Investigation of the steam distillate from leaves of *Hamamelis virginiana* L. Part 4. Characterization of the leaf drug and distillate]. *Dtsch. Apoth. Ztg.* 1971, **111**, 299-301 [GERMAN].
8. Messerschmidt W. Zur Kenntnis des Wasserdampfdestillats der Blätter von Hamamelis virg. L. 1. Mitt. [Investigation of the steam distillate from leaves of *Hamamelis virginiana* L. Part 1.]. *Arch. Pharm. (Weinheim)* 1967, **300**, 550-552 [GERMAN].
9. Messerschmidt W. Zur Kenntnis des Wasserdampfdestillats der Blätter von *Hamamelis virginiana* L. 3. Mitteilung: Über die Isolierung und Identifizierung von Safrol [Investigation of the steam distillate from leaves of *Hamamelis virginiana* L. Part 3. The isolation and identification of safrole]. *Arzneim.-Forsch.* 1968, **18**, 1618 [GERMAN/English summary].
10. Bernard P, Balansard P, Balansard G and Bovis A. Valeur pharmacodynamique toniveineuse des préparations galéniques à base de feuilles d'Hamamélis [Pharmacodynamic venotonic value of galenic preparations of hamamelis leaves]. *J. Pharm. Belg.* 1972, **27**, 505-512 [FRENCH/English summary].
11. Duwiejua M, Zeitlin IJ, Waterman PG and Gray AI. Anti-inflammatory Activity of *Polygonum bistorta, Guaiacum officinale* and *Hamamelis virginiana* in Rats. *J. Pharm. Pharmacol.* 1994, **46**, 286-290.
12. Diemunsch A-M and Mathis C. Effet vasoconstricteur de l'Hamamelis en application externe [Vasoconstrictive effect of hamamelis in external application]. *STP Pharma* 1987, **3**, 111-114 [FRENCH/English summary].
13. Wokalek H. Zur Bedeutung epidermaler Lipide und des Arachidonsäurestoffwechsels bei Neurodermitis atopica [The significance of epidermal lipids and arachidonic acid metabolism in neurodermitis atopica]. *Deutsche Dermatologe* 1993, **5**, 498-506 [GERMAN].
14. Hamamelis Leaf. In: *British Herbal Pharmacopoeia 1983*. ISBN 0-903032-07-4. Bournemouth: British Herbal Medicine Association, 1983.
15. Hamamelidis folium et cortex. German Commission E Monograph published in: Bundesanzeiger No. 154 of 21 August 1985; amended in Bundesanzeiger No. 50 of 13 March 1990.
16. Chevallier A. Witch Hazel. In: *Encyclopedia of Medicinal Plants, 2nd ed.* ISBN 0-7513-1209-6. London-New York: Dorling Kindersley, 2001:104.
17. Laux P and Oschmann R. Die Zaubernuß. *Hamamelis virginiana* L. *Z. Phytotherapie* 1993, **14**, 155-166 [GERMAN/English summary].
18. Bernard P. Les feuilles d'Hamamelis [Hamamelis leaves]. *Plantes Méd. Phytothér.* 1977, **11**, 184-188 [FRENCH].
19. Hamamélis, feuille. In: *Médicaments à base de plantes*. ISBN 2-911473-02-7. Saint-Denis Cedex, France: Agence du Médicament, 1998.
20. Barnes J, Anderson LA and Phillipson JD. Witch Hazel. In: *Herbal Medicines, 2nd ed.* ISBN 0-85369-474-5. London: Pharmaceutical Press, 2002:486-488.
21. Hamamelis. In: UK Statutory Instrument 1994 No. 2410. The Medicines (Products Other Than Veterinary Drugs) (General Sale List) Amendment Order 1994. Schedule 1, Table A.
22. Hamamelis virginiana L., leaves. In: *Flavouring Substances and Natural Sources of Flavourings, 3rd ed.* ISBN 2-7160-0081-6. Strasbourg: Council of Europe, 1981.

REGULATORY GUIDELINES FROM OTHER EU COUNTRIES

FRANCE

Médicaments à base de plantes [19]: Hamamélis, feuille.

Therapeutic indications accepted

Oral use
Traditionally used in subjective manifestations of venous insufficiency, such as heavy legs, and for haemorrhoidal symptoms.

Topical use
Traditionally used: in subjective manifestations of venous insufficiency, such as heavy legs, and for haemorrhoidal symptoms; in cases of ocular irritation or discomfort due to various causes (smoky atmosphere, sustained visual effort, bathing in the sea or swimming pool); locally in mouthwashes, for buccal hygiene.

GERMANY

Commission E monograph [15]: Hamamelidis folium et cortex (Hamamelisblätter und -rinde).
See the text under Hamamelis Bark

HAMAMELIS WATER

Hamamelidaceae

Hamamelidis aqua

Synonyms: Distilled Witch Hazel, Witch Hazel (USP).

Definition

Hamamelis water is a clear, colourless distillate prepared from recently cut and partially dried dormant twigs of *Hamamelis virginiana* L. by macerating in water, distilling, and adding the requisite quantity of ethanol to the distillate.

The USP monograph for Witch Hazel describes the method of preparation as:

- Macerate a weighed amount of the twigs for about 24 hours in about twice their weight of water, then distil until not less than 800 ml and not more than 850 ml of clear, colourless distillate is obtained from each 1000 g of the twigs taken. Add 150 ml of ethanol to each 850 ml of distillate and mix thoroughly.

The BPC 1973 monograph for Hamamelis Water [1] was broadly similar.

CONSTITUENTS

By the USP method of preparation, 1 kg of partially dried dormant twigs yields approximately 1 litre (980 g) of hamamelis water containing 14-15% of ethanol [USP]. The constituents are those of the volatile fraction, devoid of tannins [2].

Detailed analytical data on the constituents of hamamelis water prepared exactly by the USP or BPC 1973 method appear to be unavailable. However, in a recent study, milled *fresh* young twigs from *Hamamelis virginiana* were steam-distilled; they were harvested in May, not in the dormant period, since leaves were simultaneously but separately collected. Reporting the same data, Engel et al. stated 'bark of young twigs' [3], but the original dissertation by Hartisch [4] stated 'young twigs and twig tips were coarsely milled and then steam distilled'. The volatile fraction (0.09% of the crude drug on the dry weight basis) contained about 160 compounds: aliphatic hydrocarbons (45.4%, of which nonacosane 6.9%, heptacosane 5.4%), sesquiterpenes (20.2%, of which α-ylangene 11.1%, *trans*-nerolidol 2.73%), monoterpenes (8.3%, of which linalool 2.0%), phenylpropanoids (7.5%, of which *trans*-anethole 3.3%, eugenol 2.4%), aldehydes (6.1%, of which nonanal 2.7%) and small amounts of many other compounds [3,4].

Although not meeting USP criteria, it should be noted that in Germany a 'hamamelis distillate' distilled from *fresh leaves and twigs* has been used for more than a century and preparations containing it remain on the market; in fact, more of the published clinical studies relate to this material than to USP material. The hamamelis distillate is claimed to be standardized on carbonyl compounds (sometimes loosely called 'hamamelis ketones'), principally hex-2-en-1-al, acetaldehyde and α- and β-ionone; these compounds were identified in hamamelis leaf distillate by Messerschmidt [5], although more recently Engel et al. [3] could not confirm their presence apart from a trace of β-ionone (0.08% of the volatiles).

Published Assay Methods

GC-MS of volatiles from leaves and twigs [3].

PHARMACOLOGY

In vivo

Intravenous administration to rabbits of 2 or 4 ml

$H_3C-(CH_2)_{27}-CH_3$

Nonacosane

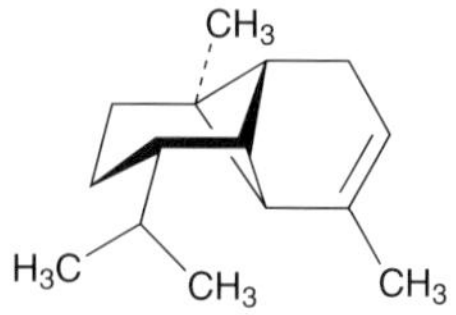

α-Ylangene

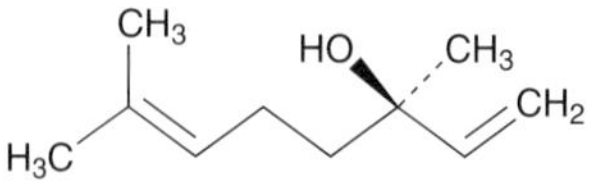

Linalool

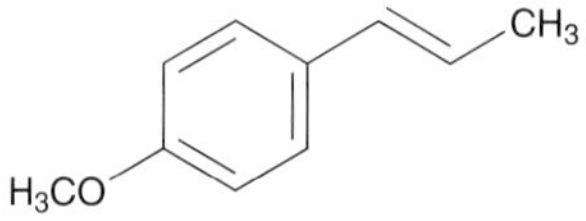

trans-Anethole

of a hamamelis leaf distillate reduced the bleeding time of small cuts (3-5 mm) made on rabbit ears by 33% and 37% respectively, and accelerated *ex vivo* blood coagulation from 4-7 minutes to 0.5 minutes [6].

Pharmacological studies in humans

As a test of anti-inflammatory activity in the alleviation of mild sunburn, areas of skin (test fields) on the backs of 30 healthy volunteers were exposed to UV-B light at four different dose levels ranging from 1 to 2 MED (minimal erythema doses); irradiated test fields were immediately treated with an oil-in-water aftersun lotion containing 10% of hamamelis water (USP grade) or the vehicle only, occluded from light and evaluated for suppression of erythema by chromametric assessment of skin reddening after 7, 24 and 48 hours. Irradiated but untreated (except for subsequent occlusion from light) test fields served as controls. From pooled chromametry measurements, in comparison with irradiated controls, erythema suppression in test fields treated with the hamamelis lotion ranged from 20% after 7 hours to 27% after 48 hours, while results for the vehicle-only lotion ranged from 10% after 7 hours to 12% after 48 hours. The hamamelis water preparation had significantly reduced erythema compared to the vehicle or untreated skin ($p = 0.00001$ in both cases), although the vehicle also caused a significant difference compared to untreated skin ($p = 0.00007$) [7]. In a subsequent study using this UV-irradiation technique and chromametric measurement on 40 healthy volunteers, the effect of the same hamamelis water lotion was greater than that of its vehicle but less than that of 0.25% hydrocortisone lotion; compared to irradiated controls 72 hours after irradiation at 1.4 MED, the 10% hamamelis water lotion, its vehicle and 0.25% hydrocortisone lotion had suppressed erythema by 38%, 24% and 67% respectively [8].

Creams containing a hamamelis distillate from fresh leaves and twigs at two concentrations, equivalent to 0.64 mg or 2.56 mg of hamamelis ketones per 100 g, in oil-in-water emulsions containing phosphatidylcholine (PC, which aids penetration into the skin), and a cream containing the lower concentration in an oil-in-water emulsion without PC, were evaluated for anti-inflammatory activity against erythema using visual scoring and chromametry. The effects were compared with those of creams containing hydrocortisone (1%) or chamomile (*Matricaria chamomilla*) extract (20 mg/g), four vehicle-only preparations (including the with and without PC vehicles mentioned above) and an untreated area of skin as a control in two randomized, double-blind studies, each involving 24 healthy volunteers. In the first study erythema was induced by UV irradiation; noteworthy reductions (i.e. $0.05 < p \leq 0.1$) in erythema 24 hours later were observed only from use of hydrocortisone 1% cream and low dose hamamelis-PC cream, hydrocortisone being more effective. In the second study erythema was induced by repeated stripping of the horny layer with adhesive tape; erythema 4-8 hours later was suppressed by hydrocortisone cream ($p<0.05$), while less pronounced but noteworthy reductions were observed with low and high dose hamamelis-PC creams, and also the chamomile extract cream. Thus hamamelis distillate in a PC-containing vehicle showed some anti-inflammatory activity, but a 4-fold increase in hamamelis distillate concentration did not increase activity [9].

In another experiment, an ointment containing a hamamelis distillate (25 g/100 g) from fresh leaves and twigs was applied to the skin of 22 healthy volunteers and 5 patients with atopic neurodermitis or psoriasis. Using fluvography (measurements of the thermal conductivity of the skin, which can be related to blood circulation in the skin), a decrease in blood circulation of the skin was demonstrated in most cases, suggesting a mild anti-inflammatory effect [10].

CLINICAL STUDIES

In a randomized, double-blind study, 72 patients suffering from moderately severe atopic eczema were treated on one side of the body with a cream containing a hamamelis distillate (5.35 g/100 g) from fresh leaves and twigs, and on the other side with its drug-free vehicle or 0.5% hydrocortisone cream. After 14 days the reduction in total scores for three basic criteria (itching, erythema and scaling) and even for minor criteria was significantly greater ($p<0.0001$) after application of hydrocortisone cream than after hamamelis distillate cream. The score for the hamamelis distillate cream did not differ from that of its vehicle; thus no anti-inflammatory efficacy was evident against severe atopic eczema [11].

In a randomized, double-blind study, 22 patients suffering from atopic dermatitis were simultaneously treated three times daily for 3 weeks on one forearm with an ointment containing a hamamelis distillate (25 g/100 g) from fresh leaves and twigs, and on the other forearm with bufexamac (50 mg/g) ointment. No statistical difference between the effects of the two ointments emerged from assessment of symptoms such as reddening, scaling, lichenification, itching and infiltration; both forearms showed clear improvements [12].

Another double-blind study compared the efficacy of two hamamelis preparations, one defined as an ointment containing a hamamelis distillate (25 g/ 100 g) from fresh leaves and twigs, applied to the hands of 116 patients with toxic-degenerative or endogenous eczema for 28-39 days. Improvements in symptoms (itching, burning sensations, infiltration, reddening, scaling) were observed in the majority of cases with both preparations [13].

Three topical agents, hamamelis water (BPC 1973), ice, and a foam containing 1% of hydrocortisone acetate and 1% of pramoxine hydrochloride, were compared for their efficacy in achieving analgesia for episiotomy pain in 300 postnatal mothers following forceps delivery. An oral analgesic was also taken at about the same dosage level in all three groups. Data from 266 women indicated that the three topical treatments were equally effective, with no significant differences in achieving analgesia on the first day, although subjective and professional assessment indicated that about one-third of all mothers derived little benefit from any agent. Ice tended to be the most helpful on days 3 and 5. From subsequent assessment of 126 mothers after 6 weeks no differences were found between the three groups in terms of healing, pain and intercourse patterns [14].

THERAPEUTICS

Actions
Mildly anti-inflammatory [7-10] and haemostatic [15,16]. Also stated to be astringent [16,17].

It is difficult to attribute the actions of hamamelis water to specific constituents since only a low content of volatiles, comprising a wide range of compounds, is present. The claimed astringent action [16,17] has been suggested as implausible in the absence of tannins [2]; however, intravenously administered leaf distillate had surprising effects on the blood of rabbits, shortening bleeding time and accelerating blood coagulation [6].

Indications
None adequately confirmed by clinical studies.

Uses based on experience or tradition
Topical use
Minor sores, inflammation or irritations of the skin such as cuts, grazes, insect bites [1,2,16-21], dermatitis [12], slight burns or scalds [20] and sunburn; bruises and sprains, muscle pains [2]; external haemorrhoids [2,16,18,21], varicose vein complaints [16,20,21]; as a mouthwash for inflamed mucosa [16] or bleeding gums [18]; as a nasal plug for nosebleeds [19-21]; as an eyewash [1] for conjunctivitis [21,22] and sore or tired eyes [21].

Contraindications
None known.

Side effects
None known.

Interactions with other drugs
None known.

Dosage
Topical use
Undiluted hamamelis water for application to cuts, grazes, insect stings, other skin complaints and haemorrhoids [17-19], as a mouthwash [18], and in a saturated cotton wool swab as a nasal plug for nosebleeds [19,21] or to place over eyelids [21]; for compresses, undiluted or diluted 1:3 with water; in semi-solid preparations, 20-30% [16].

As an eyewash, use diluted hamamelis water [1, 21,22], 10 drops to an eyebath half-filled with water [21].

SAFETY

Hamamelis water is generally considered harmless for external use and, although little used internally, for internal use at normal dose levels.

REGULATORY STATUS

Medicines

UK	Accepted for general sale, internal or external use [23].
France	Not listed in *Médicaments à base de plantes* [24].
Germany	Commission E monograph published, with approved uses [16].

Food
Not used in foods.

REFERENCES

Current Pharmacopoeial Monographs
USP Witch Hazel

Literature References

1. Pharmaceutical Society of Great Britain. Hamamelis Water. In: British Pharmaceutical Codex 1973. London: Pharmaceutical Press, 1973:825.
2. Hänsel R, Keller K, Rimpler H, Schneider G, editors. Hamamelis. In: *Hagers Handbuch der Pharmazeutischen Praxis, 5th ed. Volume 5: Drogen E-O.* Berlin: Springer-Verlag, 1993:367-384 [GERMAN].
3. Engel R, Gutmann M, Hartisch C, Kolodziej H and Nahrstedt A. Study on the Composition of the Volatile Fraction of *Hamamelis virginiana. Planta Medica* 1998, **64**, 251-258.
4. Hartisch C. Isolierung, Strukturaufklärung und antiinflammatorische Wirksamkeit von Polyphenolen aus *Hamamelis virginiana* L. sowie Analyse der wasserdampfflüchtigen Fraktion aus dem Cortexmaterial [Isolation, structure elucidation and anti-inflammatory efficacy of polyphenols from *Hamamelis virginiana* L. and analysis of the steam-volatile fraction from bark material]. Dissertation:

Fachbereich Pharmazie der Freien Universität Berlin, 1996.
5. Messerschmidt W. Zur Kenntnis des Wasserdampfdestillats der Blätter von Hamamelis virg. L. 1. Mitt. [Investigation of the steam distillate from leaves of *Hamamelis virginiana* L. Part 1]. *Arch. Pharm. (Weinheim)* 1967, **300**, 550-552 [GERMAN].
6. Neugebauer H. Über die Wirkung der Distillate von *Hamamelis virginiana* und *Corylus avellana* [The effects of distillates from *Hamamelis virginiana* and *Corylus avellana*]. *Pharmazie* 1948, **3**, 313-314 [GERMAN].
7. Hughes-Formella BJ, Bohnsack K, Rippke F, Benner G, Rudolph M, Tausch I and Gassmueller J. Anti-Inflammatory Effect of Hamamelis Lotion in a UVB Erythema Test. *Dermatology* 1998, **196**, 316-322.
8. Hughes-Formella BJ, Filbry A, Gassmueller J and Rippke F. Anti-Inflammatory Efficacy of Topical Preparations with 10% Hamamelis Distillate in a UV Erythema Test. *Skin Pharmacol. Appl. Skin Physiol.* 2002, **15**, 125-132.
9. Korting HC, Schäfer-Korting M, Hart H, Laux P and Schmid M. Anti-inflammatory activity of hamamelis distillate applied topically to the skin. Influence of vehicle and dose. *Eur. J. Clin. Pharmacol.* 1993, **44**, 315-318.
10. Sorkin B. Hametum Salbe, eine kortikoidfreie anti-inflammatorische Salbe [Hametum ointment, a corticoid-free anti-inflammatory ointment]. *Phys. Med. Rehab.* 1980, **21**, 53-57.
11. Korting HC, Schäfer-Korting M, Klövekorn W, Klövekorn G, Martin C and Laux P. Comparative efficacy of hamamelis distillate and hydrocortisone cream in atopic eczema. *Eur. J. Clin. Pharmacol.* 1995, **48**, 461-465.
12. Swoboda M and Meurer J. Therapie von Neurodermitis mit *Hamamelis-virginiana*-Extrakt in Salbenform. Eine Doppelblindstudie [Therapy of neurodermitis with an ointment containing *Hamamelis virginiana* extract. A double-blind study]. *Z. Phytotherapie* 1991, **12**, 114-117 [GERMAN].
13. Pfister R. Zur Problematik der Behandlung und Nachbehandlung chronischer Dermatosen. Eine klinische Studie über Hametum Salbe [Problems associated with treatment and follow-up treatment of chronic dermatoses. A clinical study with Hametum ointment]. *Fortschr. Med.* 1981, **99**, 1264-1268 [GERMAN/English summary].
14. Moore W and James DK. A random trial of three topical analgesic agents in the treatment of episiotomy pain following instrumental vaginal delivery. *J. Obstet. Gynaecol.* 1989, **10**, 35-39.
15. Reynolds JEF, editor. Hamamelis. In: *Martindale - The Extra Pharmacopoeia, 29th ed.* ISBN 0-85369-210-6. London: Pharmaceutical Press, 1989:778-779.
16. Hamamelidis folium et cortex. German Commission E Monograph published in: Bundesanzeiger No. 154 of 21 August 1985; amended in Bundesanzeiger No. 50 of 13 March 1990.
17. Chevallier A. Witch Hazel. In: *Encyclopedia of Medicinal Plants, 2nd ed.* ISBN 0-7513-1209-6. London-New York: Dorling Kindersley, 2001: 104.
18. McIntyre A. Witch Hazel. In: *The Complete Woman's Herbal.* ISBN 1-85675-135-X. London: Gaia Books, 1994: 78.
19. Ody P. Witch Hazel. In: *Medicinal Herbal - Herbal remedies for common ailments.* ISBN 0-7513-3005-1. London-New York: Dorling Kindersley, 2000:71.
20. Grieve M (edited by Leyel CF). Witch Hazel. In: *A Modern Herbal* (first published 1931; revised 1973). ISBN 1-85501-249-9. London: Tiger Books International, 1994:851.
21. Bartram T. Witch Hazel. In: *Encyclopaedia of Herbal Medicine.* ISBN 0-9515984-1-4. Christchurch, UK: Grace Publishers, 1995:57:455-456.
22. Laux P and Oschmann R. Die Zaubernuß [Witch Hazel]. *Hamamelis virginiana* L. *Z. Phytotherapie* 1993, **14**, 155-166 [GERMAN/English summary].
23. Hamamelis. In: UK Statutory Instrument 1994 No. 2410. The Medicines (Products Other Than Veterinary Drugs) (General Sale List) Amendment Order 1994. Schedule 1, Table A.
24. *Médicaments à base de plantes.* ISBN 2-911473-02-7. Saint-Denis Cedex, France: Agence du Médicament, 1998.

REGULATORY GUIDELINES FROM OTHER EU COUNTRIES

GERMANY

Commission E monograph [16]: Hamamelidis folium et cortex (Hamamelisblätter und -rinde).
Although not specifically included in the title of this monograph, hamamelis water (Hamameliswasser) is mentioned in the text - see under Hamamelis Bark.

HAWTHORN BERRY **Rosaceae**

Crataegi fructus

Synonyms: May blossom berry (*Crataegus monogyna*), Midland hawthorn berry (*C. laevigata*).

Definition

Hawthorn Berry consists of the dried, ripe false fruits of *Crataegus monogyna* Jacq. (Lindm.) or *C. laevigata* (Poiret) D.C. [*C. oxyacantha* L. emend. Jacq.; *C. oxyacanthoides* Thuill.] or their hybrids or a mixture of these false fruits.

CONSTITUENTS

□ ***Procyanidins***, 0.4-2.5% (average 1.35%) by spectrophotometry [1] (Ph. Eur. min. 1.0% by spectrophotometry, calculated as cyanidin chloride).

In *Crataegus monogyna* berries collected in the summer and autumn of 1985 and analysed by spectrophotometry, the content of oligomeric procyanidins was 4-10 times higher than the content of polymeric procyanidins and the total procyanidin content was found to be highest in immature berries (June-July). The data suggested that, for *ripe* berries, October may be the optimum harvesting time [2]:

	Procyanidin content (% dry weight)		
Date	**Oligomeric**	**Polymeric**	**Total**
21 June	3.43	0.34	3.98
16 July	3.18	0.47	3.81
3 September	1.30	0.30	1.72
2 October	1.74	0.38	2.22

In another study, *C. monogyna* berries harvested in mid-September (1992) were found to contain 1.25% of total procyanidins (by spectrophotometry), of which 0.25% was procyanidin B2 (by HPLC). The principal phenolic compound found in these berries was the monomer (–)-epicatechin (1.33% by HPLC) [3].

On the other hand, in a sample of *Crataegus laevigata* berries the content of oligomeric procyanidins (dimers to pentamers; no hexamer detected) was found to be only 0.15% by HPLC. The pattern of individual procyanidins was qualitatively similar to that of hawthorn leaf and flower (see separate monograph), but with dimers such as B-2 and trimers such as C-1 predominant [4].

□ ***Flavonoids*** (excluding epicatechin, a flavan-3-ol, mentioned above), 0.13-0.17% by HPLC, 0.04-0.15% by the DAB spectrophotometric method in *C. monogyna* (much lower amounts than found in Hawthorn leaf with flower), principally the flavonol *O*-glycoside hyperoside (0.11-0.17%) with a smaller amount of the flavone *C*-glycoside vitexin 2″-rhamnoside (0.01-0.03%) and a trace of rutin [2,3,5].

HPLC assays of flavonoids tend to give higher results than spectrophotometric methods, to some extent because *C*-glycosides are not hydrolyzed by acid and therefore are not extracted and determined by the latter methods [6].

□ ***Hydroxycinnamic acid derivatives*** Chlorogenic acid (0.14% in *C. monogyna*) [3].

□ ***Pentacyclic triterpenes***, 0.3-0.5%, including ursolic acid, crataegolic acid (=2α-hydroxyoleanolic acid) and oleanolic acid [7].

□ ***Other constituents*** include β-sitosterol, about 35% of sugars (glucose and fructose) and 3% of minerals [8].

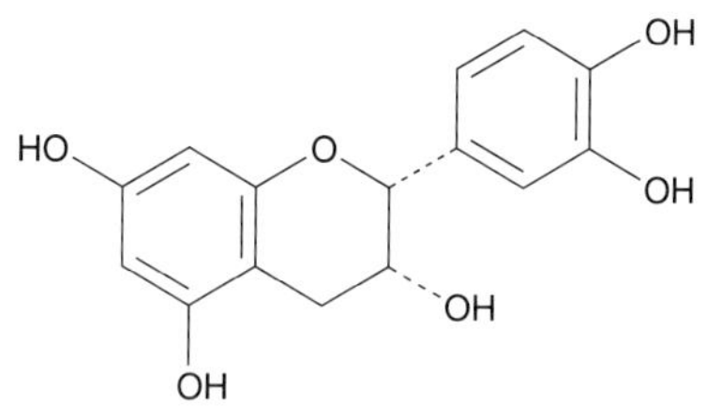

(–)-Epicatechin

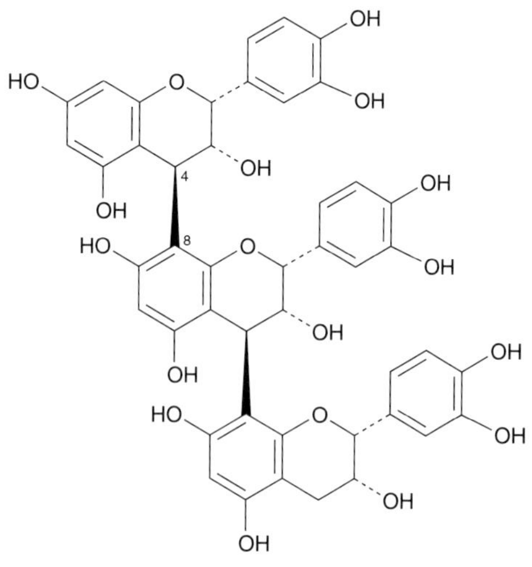

Procyanidin C-1

Published Assay Methods
Total procyanidins by spectrophotometry (after hydrolysis to cyanidin) [Ph. Eur.]. Procyanidins by HPLC [4]. Flavonoids by HPLC (after acid hydrolysis to quercetin and vitexin) [6,9].

PHARMACOLOGY

Very few pharmacological studies have been carried out on hawthorn berry apart from *in vitro* experiments demonstrating the antioxidant activity of extracts and phenolic constituents [3] and the human study summarized below. Since the qualitative profile of procyanidins and flavonoids in hawthorn berry is similar to that of the leaf and flower (albeit with lower amounts in the berry, especially in the case of flavonoids), pharmacodynamic effects similar to those of hawthorn leaf and flower have been assumed [10].

Pharmacological studies in humans
In a randomized, double-blind, placebo-controlled crossover study, 14 healthy male volunteers received daily, for periods of 28 days separated by a wash-out period of at least 4 weeks, 9.0 g of a liquid extract from *fresh* hawthorn berries (1:1.4, 60% ethanol, concentrated to 5:1 with 3% of procyanidins) and then placebo, or *vice versa*. A haemodynamic profile of each participant was recorded for up to 6 hours after the doses on day 1 and day 28. Compared to the placebo group, significant cardiovascular effects were evident in the verum group: increased mean arterial pressure in the supine position ($p<0.02$ on day 1, intensified to $p<0.001$ on day 28), increased total peripheral resistance ($p<0.05$ on days 1 and 28) and shortening of systolic time intervals (a cardiostimulatory effect, $p<0.03$ on days 1 and 28) [11]. The daily dose of 270 mg of procyanidins in this study was much higher than daily doses used in the clinical studies summarized below and at the top end of the dosage range used for hawthorn leaf and flower (see Table 1 in that monograph).

CLINICAL STUDIES

In a randomized, double-blind, placebo-controlled, multicentre study, 143 patients with NYHA class II heart failure (see Hawthorn Leaf and Flower monograph for definition) were treated daily for 8 weeks with 3 × 0.75 ml (= 3 × 30 drops) of either a standardized 49%-ethanolic extract from *fresh* hawthorn berry (drug to extract ratio 1:3.2, providing a daily dose of at least 6.4 mg of oligomeric procyanidins, 12.7 mg of total phenolic compounds; n = 69) or placebo (n = 74). Concomitant medications were not permitted during or within 4 weeks before commencement of the study period. The primary efficacy variable, exercise tolerance (the maximum wattage sustained for at least 1 minute during bicycle exercise testing), increased in both groups, but significantly by 8.3 watts more in the hawthorn group than in the placebo group ($p = 0.045$). No significant differences between groups were observed in the pressure-heart rate product (PHRP; systolic blood pressure in mm Hg × heart rate per minute ÷ 100) or in subjective cardiac symptoms at rest and at higher levels of exertion, although there was a downward trend in PHRP in favour of hawthorn berry. Patient/physician overall assessments were similar for the verum and placebo groups, 72% of patients considering the hawthorn berry preparation to have average to good efficacy (placebo group 62%) [12].

In a randomized, double-blind, placebo-controlled study [13], 88 patients with NYHA class II congestive heart failure were treated daily for 12 weeks (after a 2-week placebo run-in period) with 3 × 25 drops of either a standardized liquid extract from *fresh* hawthorn berry in 60% V/V ethanol (drug to extract ratio 1:1.3-1.5, not less than 300 mg of oligomeric procyanidins per 100 ml; n = 44) or placebo (n = 44). The majority of patients were also taking concomitant medications (ACE inhibitors and β-blockers; in some cases diuretics) before and during the study period and no changes in these were permitted. The following results were obtained:

- Total exercise time in bicycle ergonometry, the primary efficacy variable, increased in both groups, but by 38.9 seconds more in the hawthorn group (from 397.4 to 464.4) than in the placebo group (from 411.4 to 435.3).
- Using the Minnesota Questionnaire, the quality of life score fell by 31% (placebo group: 18%).
- The total score of the Dyspnoea Fatigue Index, assessed by the physicians, increased by 12% (placebo group: 8%).
- On a visual analogue scale patients assessed their decrease in dyspnoea as 11% (placebo group: 4%).

Although trends in favour of the hawthorn berry extract were evident for each parameter tested [13], the results did not attain statistical significance [14].

A recent systematic review of clinical studies using hawthorn berry in the treatment of heart complaints mentioned five studies, including the two summarized above. However, the three other studies involved the use of a combination product (hawthorn berry extract + camphor) [14].

Although one significant clinical result has been obtained with a preparation from *fresh* hawthorn berry [12], the evidence of efficacy of hawthorn berry mono-preparations in the treatment of NYHA class II heart failure is not yet convincing; further studies are needed. Standardized hawthorn leaf and flower preparations remain preferable for this indication in view of the weight of clinical evidence in their favour.

THERAPEUTICS

Actions
Mildly cardiotonic [11,12,15-17], strengthens cardiac and circulatory function [10-12], vasodilative [16,17], hypotensive [15,16], antioxidant [3,15,17] and mildly astringent [15].

Indications
None adequately substantiated by pharmacological or clinical studies.

Uses based on experience or tradition
Mild heart conditions such as angina pectoris, hypertension and myocardial weakness, and to minimise arterial degeneration caused by atherosclerosis [15-17].

Contraindications
None known.

Side effects
None known.

Interactions with other drugs
Concomitant use with other cardioactive and hypotensive drugs may require modification of dosages (or be inadvisable).

Dosage
Daily dose: Dried berry, 1.5-3.5 g as an infusion or decoction; liquid extract 1:2 in 25% ethanol, 3-7 ml [15,16]; tincture 1:5, 7.5-17.5 ml [15].

When used to treat heart conditions, hawthorn berry should be taken for a period of at least 2 months [15].

SAFETY

Bearing in mind the qualitative similarity in constituents, the general safety data summarized for hawthorn leaf and flower (see adjacent monograph) may be considered relevant to hawthorn berry.

Hawthorn berry should be used under the supervision of a qualified practitioner.

Mild adverse events, the vast majority assessed as unlikely to be related to the study medication, were reported by a total of 31 patients out of 113 taking oral hawthorn berry preparations for up to 3 months in two controlled clinical studies. Higher incidences of adverse events were reported in the placebo groups in both studies (a total of 38 patients out of 118) [12,13].

REGULATORY STATUS

Medicines

UK	No licences issued for products containing hawthorn berry.
France	Not listed in *Médicaments à base de plantes* [18].
Germany	Commission E monograph published; not approved for any indications [19].

Food

Council of Europe	Permitted as flavouring, category N2 [20].

REFERENCES

Current Pharmacopoeial Monographs
Ph. Eur. Hawthorn Berries

Literature References

1. Rohr G and Meier B. *Crataegus* - Pharmazeutische Qualität und Wirksamkeit [*Crataegus* - Pharmaceutical quality and efficacy]. *Dtsch. Apoth. Ztg.* 1997, **137**, 3740-3752 [GERMAN].
2. Kartnig T, Hiermann A and Azzam S. Investigations on the Procyanidin and Flavonoid Contents of *Crataegus monogyna* Drugs. *Sci. Pharm.* 1987, **55**, 95-100 [GERMAN/English summary].
3. Bahorun T, Trotin F, Pommery J, Vasseur J and Pinkas M. Antioxidant Activities of *Crataegus monogyna* Extracts. *Planta Medica* 1994, **60**, 323-328.
4. Svedström U, Vuorela H, Kostiainen R, Huovinen K, Laakso I and Hiltunen R. High-performance liquid chromatographic determination of oligomeric procyanidins from dimers up to the hexamer in hawthorn. *J. Chromatogr. A* 2002, **968**, 53-60.
5. Ammon HPT and Kaul R. *Crataegus.* Herz-Kreislauf-Wirkungen von Crataegusextrakten, Flavonoiden und Procyanidinen. Teil 1: Historisches und Wirkstoffe [*Crataegus.* Cardiac and circulatory effects of hawthorn extracts, flavonoids and procyanidins. Part 1. History and active principles]. *Dtsch. Apoth. Ztg.* 1994, **134**, 2433-2436. Teil 2: Wirkungen auf das Herz [Part 2: Effects on the heart]. *ibid* 1994, **134**, 2521-2535. Teil 3: Wirkungen auf den Kreislauf [Part 3: Effects on the circulation]. *ibid* 1994, **134**, 2631-2636.
6. Rehwald A, Meier B and Sticher O. Qualitative and quantitative reversed-phase high-performance liquid chromatography of flavonoids in Crataegus leaves and flowers. *J. Chromatogr. A* 1994, **677**, 25-33.
7. Steinegger E and Hänsel R. Weißdornpräparate [Hawthorn preparations]. In: *Pharmakognosie, 5th ed.* ISBN 3-540-55649-4. Berlin-Heidelberg-New York: Springer-Verlag, 1992:580-584 [GERMAN].
8. List PH and Hörhammer L, editors. Crataegus. In: *Hagers Handbuch der Pharmazeutischen Praxis, 4th ed.* Band IV. Berlin-Heidelberg-New York: Springer-Verlag, 1973: 324-334 [GERMAN].
9. Sticher O and Meier B. Hawthorn (*Crataegus*): Biological Activity and New Strategies for Quality Control. In: Lawson

LD and Bauer R, editors. *Phytomedicines of Europe - Chemistry and Biological Activity*. ACS Symposium Series 691. ISBN 0-8412-3559-7. Washington DC: American Chemical Society, 1998:241-262.
10. Wichtl M and Moser U. Weißdornfrüchte - Crataegi fructus. In: Hartke K, Hartke H, Mutschler E, Rücker G and Wichtl M, editors. *Kommentar zum Europäischen Arzneibuch*. Stuttgart: Wissenschaftliche Verlagsgesellschaft, 1999 (11 Lfg.):W 14/5 [GERMAN].
11. Belz GG and Loew D. Dose-response related efficacy in orthostatic hypotension of a fixed combination of D-camphor and an extract from fresh Crataegus berries and the contribution of the single components. *Phytomedicine* 2003, **10** (Suppl. IV), 61-67.
12. Degenring FH, Suter A, Weber M and Saller R. A randomised double blind placebo controlled clinical trial of a standardised extract of fresh Crataegus berries (Crataegisan®) in the treatment of patients with congestive heart failure NYHA II. *Phytomedicine* 2003, **10**, 363-369.
13. Rietbrock N, Hamel M, Hempel B, Mitrovic V, Schmidt T and Wolf GK. Efficacy of a Standardized Extract of Fresh Crataegus Berries on Exercise Tolerance and Quality of Life in Patients with Congestive Heart Failure (NYHA II). *Arzneim.-Forsch./Drug Res.* 2001, **51**, 793-798 [GERMAN/English summary].
14. Melzer J, Iten F and Saller R. Crataegus berries: heart complaints, congestive heart failure NYHA I and II - a systematic review. *Perfusion* 2003, **16**, 358-362.
15. Mills S and Bone K. Hawthorn - *Crataegus* spp. In: *Principles and Practice of Phytotherapy. Modern Herbal Medicine.* ISBN 0-443-06016-9. Edinburgh-London-New York: Churchill Livingstone, 2000:439-447.
16. Crataegus Fruit. In: *British Herbal Pharmacopoeia 1983*. ISBN 0-903032-07-4. Bournemouth: British Herbal Medicine Association, 1983.
17. Chevallier A. Hawthorn. In: *Encyclopedia of Medicinal Plants, 2nd ed.* ISBN 0-7513-1209-6. London-New York: Dorling Kindersley, 2001:90.
18. Aubépine [Hawthorn]. In: *Médicaments à base de plantes*. ISBN 2-911473-02-7. Saint-Denis Cedex, France: Agence du Médicament, 1998.
19. Crataegi fructus. German Commission E Monograph published in: Bundesanzeiger of 19 July 1994.
20. Crataegus oxyacantha; flowers, leaves, fruit. In: *Flavouring Substances and Natural Sources of Flavourings, 3rd ed.* ISBN 2-7160-0081-6. Strasbourg: Council of Europe, 1981.

REGULATORY GUIDELINES FROM OTHER EU COUNTRIES

GERMANY

Commission E monograph [19]: Crataegi fructus (Weißdornfrüchte).

Pharmacological properties, pharmacokinetics, toxicology

No scientific data are available on the pharmacology and toxicology of the drug. On the basis of the constituents of hawthorn berry, which differ only a little quantitatively (flavonoids) and qualitatively (oligomeric procyanidins) from those of hawthorn leaf and flower, pharmacodynamic effects similar to those of hawthorn leaf and flower can be assumed for hawthorn berry.

Clinical data

Areas of use

Hawthorn berry and preparations from it may be used for improvement of coronary circulation and for weak heart, heart and circulatory disorders, high blood pressure and arteriosclerosis. However, efficacy in the claimed areas of use has not been substantiated through clinical studies.

Risks

None known.

Assessment

Since efficacy in the claimed areas of use has not been substantiated, therapeutic use cannot be recommended.

The drug as well as aqueous, hydroalcoholic and wine infusions and fresh juice have traditionally been taken to strengthen and invigorate cardiac and circulatory function. This information is based solely on tradition and long-term experience.

HAWTHORN LEAF AND FLOWER Rosaceae

Crataegi folium cum flore

Synonyms: May Blossom (*Crataegus monogyna*), Midland Hawthorn (*C. laevigata*).

Definition

Hawthorn Leaf and Flower consists of the dried flower-bearing tips of *Crataegus monogyna* Jacq. (Lindm.), *C. laevigata* (Poiret) D.C. [*C. oxyacantha* L. emend. Jacq.; *C. oxyacanthoides* Thuill.] or their hybrids or, more rarely, other European *Crataegus* species including *C. pentagyna* Waldst. et Kit. ex Willd., *C. nigra* Waldst. et Kit. and *C. azarolus* L.

CONSTITUENTS

□ ***Procyanidins***: Total procyanidins, 1.7-4% by spectrophotometric methods [1,2]; oligomeric procyanidins (OPC; 2-6 epicatechin/catechin units), 1.6% in leaves, 1.2% in flowers by HPLC [3].

Oligomeric procyanidins consisting of 2-6 epicatechin and/or catechin units, mainly with C4→C8 links but including some C4→C6 links, have been isolated; they include the dimers B-2, B-4 and B-5, the trimers C-1, epicatechin-(4β→6)-epicatechin-(4β→8)-epicatechin and epicatechin-(4β→8)-epicatechin-(4β→6)-epicatechin, the tetramer D-1 and pentamer E-1 consisting of 4β→8 linked (–)-epicatechin units, and a hexamer (F) [4]. Procyanidin B-1 [5] and monomeric (–)-epicatechin [4,6,7] and (+)-catechin [7] are also present.

In *Crataegus laevigata* the predominant oligomers in descending order were found by HPLC to be D-1, C-1, E-1, B-2 and F [3].

□ ***Flavonoids*** (Ph. Eur. min. 1.5% by spectrophotometry, calculated as hyperoside), principally the flavone *C*-glycosides vitexin 2″-rhamnoside and its 4‴-acetyl derivative and the flavonol *O*-glycoside hyperoside, with smaller amounts of vitexin, isovitexin and rutin [1,5,8,9] and other flavones (apigenin, luteolin and their glycosides) [10] and flavonols (isoquercitrin and spiraeoside) [9]. The amounts of individual compounds vary according to the *Crataegus species*, hyperoside usually predominating in the flower (up to 2.0% by HPLC) and vitexin 2″-rhamnoside in the leaf (up to 1.6% by HPLC) [1].

HPLC assays of flavonoids give higher results than spectrophotometric methods since *C*-glycosides are not hydrolyzed by acid and therefore are not extracted and determined by the spectrophotometric methods [8].

□ ***Hydroxycinnamic acid derivatives*** including chlorogenic acid (0.6-1.0% in flowers, 0.7-0.9% in leaves) [9] and caffeic acid (0.16% in flowers, 0.07% in leaves) [7].

□ ***Pentacyclic triterpenes***, 0.5-1.4% in leaf, 0.7-1.2% in flower [11], principally ursolic acid and crataegolic acid (= 2α-hydroxyoleanolic acid) with a small amount of oleanolic acid [12,13].

□ ***Phytosterols*** β-Sitosterol [13] and, from stems and leaves (but not flowers) of *Crataegus monogyna*, cycloartenol (0.11% of dried material) with smaller amounts of 24-methylen-24-dihydrolanosterol and butyrospermol [14].

□ ***Polysaccharides*** Two neutral polysaccharides

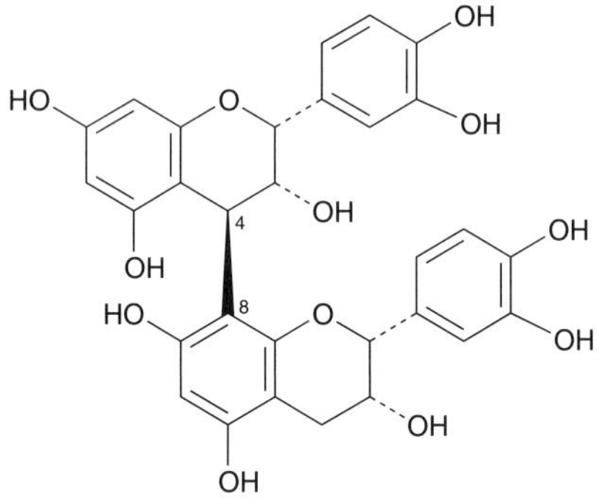

Procyanidin B-2
= (–)-Epicatechin-[4β→8]-(–)-epicatechin

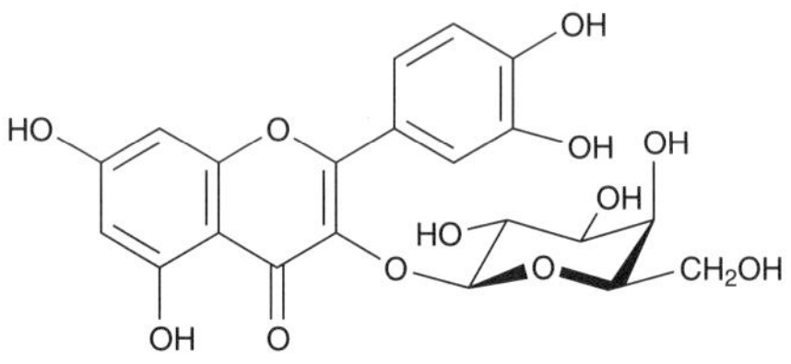

Hyperoside

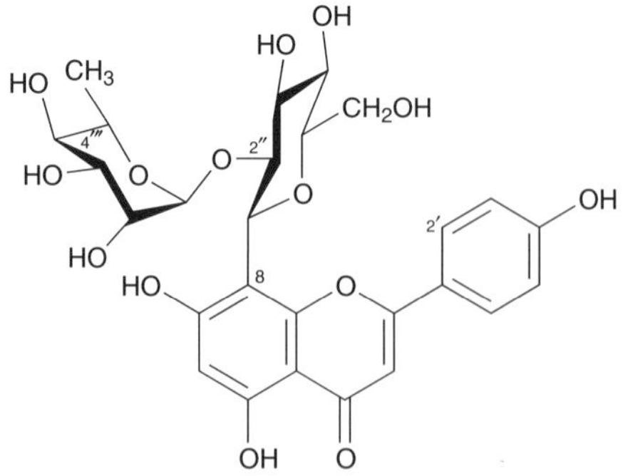

Vitexin 2″-rhamnoside

have been isolated and characterized, an arabinoxyloglucan with a β-(1→4)-glucose backbone and a highly-branched arabinogalactan with a β-(1→3)-galactose backbone and galactose-arabinose side chains [15].

□ ***Amines*** Phenethylamine, *o*-methoxyphenethylamine and tyramine in the flowers of *C. oxyacantha* [16]. Also small amounts of choline, acetylcholine and ethylamine [17].

□ ***Other constituents*** include purine derivatives such as adenine, adenosine and uric acid [11,17] and minerals, with a high potassium content [11].

Published Assay Methods

Oligomeric procyanidins by HPLC [2,3,18]. Oligomeric procyanidins and monomers by TLC-densitometry [6]. Procyanidins in products by spectrophotometry and HPLC [19].

Flavonoids by spectrophotometry [Ph. Eur.]. Flavonoids by HPLC (after acid hydrolysis of major flavonoids to vitexin and quercetin) [5,8]. Chlorogenic acid by HPLC [2,9].

PHARMACOLOGY

Hawthorn leaf and flower extracts, and flavonoid fractions, procyanidin fractions and single constituents from them, have been shown to increase myocardial contractility (a positive inotropic effect) and coronary blood flow *in vitro*; these effects have also been demonstrated *in vivo* by intravenous administration of hawthorn extracts to anaesthetized dogs. In various other *in vitro* and/or *in vivo* experiments, hawthorn leaf and flower extracts have been shown to reduce myocardial excitability (a negative bathmotropic effect) and protect against arrhythmias, to protect against ischaemia-reperfusion-induced damage to the heart, and to have vasorelaxant and hypotensive effects, reducing blood pressure and peripheral vascular resistance. Summaries of these pharmacological studies can be found in the ESCOP monograph on Crataegi folium cum flore [20], in an American Herbal Pharmacopoeia monograph [21] and in a review by Ammon and Kaul [22].

Although *in vitro* studies have suggested a number of possible mechanisms [20], the exact mode of action of hawthorn leaf and flower is not yet fully understood. It is clear, however, that oligomeric procyanidins and flavonoids play a major role in the cardiovascular activity.

CLINICAL STUDIES

The clinical severity of cardiac disease is internationally defined in accordance with a classification of functional capacity published since 1928 (and now in its ninth edition) by the New York Heart Association (NYHA) [23]. In brief, this defines four classes of functional capacity:

Patients with cardiac disease....

- but without resulting limitation of physical activity (Class I)
- resulting in slight limitation of physical activity (Class II)
- resulting in marked limitation of physical activity (Class III)
- resulting in inability to carry on any physical activity without discomfort (Class IV)

Controlled studies

Some 15 controlled clinical studies have been carried out since 1980 to evaluate the efficacy of hawthorn leaf and flower mono-preparations in the treatment of chronic heart failure. Parameters measured in assessing efficacy frequently include the Maximal Tolerated Workload (MTW; usually assessed by bicycle ergometry) and the Pressure-Heart Rate Product (PHRP; systolic blood pressure in mm Hg × heart rate per minute ÷ 100), as well as patients' records of Subjective Complaints (SC).

The more important placebo-controlled studies [24-35] are listed in Table 1. The majority involved patients of NYHA Class II and in all the studies the hawthorn leaf and flower preparations used contained one or the other of two extracts of hawthorn leaf and flower:

- a dry 45%-ethanolic extract standardized to 18.75% of oligomeric procyanidins (OPC)
- a dry hydroalcoholic extract standardized to 2.2% of flavonoids

Although standardized in different ways, these extracts (and others obtained by extraction with aqueous-alcoholic solvents, 40 to 70% ethanol or methanol) have similar spectra of constituents and are considered to have comparable quality profiles and pharmacological effects [36].

It should be noted that in the majority of studies concomitant medications, most commonly diuretics but sometimes even ACE inhibitors [32,33], were permitted. Also, it should be mentioned that in one study [29] the results were not statistically significant, but nevertheless the trends contributed to the meta-analysis.

The eight studies [25-29,32,34,35] marked with an asterisk in Table 1 provided data suitable for statistical pooling in a meta-analysis [37], from which conclusions could be drawn:

- Changes in maximal tolerated workload (MTW) measured in four studies [25,29,34,35] indicated a significant increase in MTW in patients receiving hawthorn extracts compared to those receiving placebo ($p<0.01$).
- Data from five studies [26-28,32,34] suggested a substantial beneficial effect in reducing the pressure-heart rate product (PHRP).

Patients receiving hawthorn extract showed improvement in symptoms such as dyspnoea and fatigue [24,29,30,35], and in two studies where the von Zerssen symptom score was used the data suggested a significant effect in favour of hawthorn [28,35].

One randomized, double-blind study in patients with NYHA class II cardiac insufficiency compared the effects of two different active treatments daily for 8 weeks: 3 × 300 mg of hawthorn leaf and flower extract (2.2% flavonoids; n = 68) or 3 × 12.5 mg of captopril (a synthetic drug used in the management of heart failure; n = 64). In both groups, significant increases in exercise tolerance ($p<0.001$) were observed as well as reductions in the pressure-heart rate product; the incidence and severity of symptoms also declined by about 50%. No significant difference was evident between the two treatments [38].

A randomized, double-blind, placebo-controlled pilot study in which mildly hypertensive patients were treated daily for 10 weeks with 500 mg of a dry hydroalcoholic extract from hawthorn leaf and flower did not reveal a statistically significant hypotensive effect. However, a trend in that direction was observed and, with hindsight, the dosage used was considered rather low [39].

Open studies

Two large surveillance studies have been carried on patients with cardiac insufficiency:

- 3664 NYHA class I-II patients were treated daily for 8 weeks with 3 × 300 mg of a hawthorn leaf and flower extract (2.2% flavonoids). Of the 1476 patients whose cardiac insufficiency was treated exclusively with the extract, the total symptom score (based on nine typical symptoms of heart failure) dropped from 6.9 to 1.7 for NYHA I patients and from 10.5 to 3.3 for NYHA II patients [40].
- 1011 NYHA class II patients were treated with 2 × 450 mg of a hawthorn leaf and flower extract (18.75% OPC) daily and monitored over a period of 24 weeks. Marked improvements were evident in clinical symptoms (better performance in the exercise tolerance test and reductions in fatigue, palpitations and exercise dyspnoea). Ankle oedema disappeared in 83% and nocturia in 50% of patients manifesting these symptoms. Mean blood pressure decreased

TABLE 1 Randomized, double-blind, placebo-controlled studies in the treatment of chronic heart failure

First author Year Reference number	Duration of treatment	Patients randomized (analyzed)	NYHA class	Preparation	Daily dosage	Parameters
Iwamoto 1981 [24]	6 weeks	102 (80)	II and III	Dry extract 18.75% OPC	180-270 mg (n = 35) or placebo (n = 45)	PHRP, SC
Hanak 1983 [25]*	3 weeks	60 (58)	I to II	Dry extract 18.75% OPC	180 mg (n = 29) or placebo (n = 29)	MTW
O'Connolly 1986 [26]*	6 weeks crossover	36 (34)	I to II	Dry extract 18.75% OPC	180 mg or placebo	PHRP
O'Connolly 1987 [27]*	6 weeks crossover	36 (31)	I to II	Dry extract 18.75% OPC	180 mg or placebo	PHRP
Leuchtgens 1993 [28]*	8 weeks	30 (30)	II	Dry extract 18.75% OPC	160 mg (n = 15) or placebo (n = 15)	PHRP, SC
Bödigheimer 1994 [29]*	4 weeks	85 (73)	II	Dry extract 2.2% flavonoids	300 mg (n = 36) or placebo (n = 37)	MTW
Schmidt 1994 [30]	8 weeks	78 (70)	II	Dry extract 2.2% flavonoids	600 mg (n =36) or placebo (n = 34)	MTW, PHRP
Förster 1994 [31]	8 weeks	72 (69)	II	Dry extract 2.2% flavonoids	900 mg (n = 36) or placebo (n = 36)	ET, SC
Weikl 1996 [32]*	8 weeks	136 (129)	II	Dry extract 18.75% OPC	160 mg (n = 63) or placebo (n = 66)	PHRP, SC
Eichstädt 2001 [33]	4 weeks	40 (40)	II	Dry extract 18.75% OPC	480 mg (n = 20) or placebo (n = 20)	LVEF, MTW
Zapfe 2001 [34]*	12 weeks	40 (40)	II	Dry extract 18.75% OPC	240 mg (n = 20) or placebo (n = 20)	MTW, PHRP
Tauchert 2002 [35]*	16 weeks	209 (209)	III	Dry extract 18.75% OPC	1800 mg (n = 69) 900 mg (n = 70) or placebo (n = 70)	MTW, SC

*Included in meta-analysis [37]

ET = Exercise Tolerance, LVEF = Left Ventricular Ejection Fraction, MTW = Maximal Tolerated Workload
PHRP = Pressure-Heart Rate Product, SC = Subjective Complaints

from 142.9/84.5 to 137.0/82.3 mm Hg and maximal exercise tolerance increased from 88.75 to 102.5 Watt [41].

THERAPEUTICS

Actions

Increases myocardial contractility (positively inotropic), increases coronary and myocardial blood flow, lessens myocardial excitability (negatively bathmotropic), antiarrhythmic, protects against myocardial damage, hypotensive, vasodilative, lowers peripheral vascular resistance; antioxidant and mildly astringent [5,20,21,42].

Indications

Mild cardiac insufficiency corresponding to NYHA classes I and II [24-35,37].

Other uses, based on experience or tradition

Mild heart conditions such as angina pectoris, cardiac arrhythmias and hypertension [42-44].

Contraindications

None known.

Side effects

None known.

Interactions with other drugs

Concomitant use with other cardioactive and hypotensive drugs may require modification of dosages (or be inadvisable).

Dosage

Daily dose: Hydroalcoholic extracts (4-7:1) standardized on oligomeric procyanidins or flavonoids, 160-900 mg [24-34]; dried leaf and flower, 1.5-3.5 g as infusion or decoction, or in tablets standardized with respect to oligomeric procyanidins and/or flavonoids; other comparable preparations [42].

When used to treat heart conditions, hawthorn should be taken for a period of at least 2 months [42].

SAFETY

Hawthorn leaf and flower has low toxicity and is well tolerated, adverse events usually being mild, infrequent and transient. The most common adverse event reported in the clinical studies listed in Table 1 was dizziness/vertigo and 5 studies reported no adverse events in verum patients [37]. During treatment of 3664 patients with 900 mg of extract daily for 8 weeks in a surveillance study, 48 patients (1.3%), of whom 19 discontinued treatment, reported adverse events including gastrointestinal upsets, palpitations, dizziness, headache, dyspnoea and hot flushes [40]. In a 24-week postmarketing surveillance study of 1011 patients only 14 adverse events were reported, of which only 2 were considered to have a possible (but unlikely) causal relationship with hawthorn therapy [41].

The wide range of daily dosages in Table 1 suggest that hawthorn leaf and flower extracts have a wide "therapeutic window" without risk of intoxication [37]. Patients with NYHA class III heart failure taking 1800 mg of an extract for 16 weeks reported fewer adverse events than those taking a lower daily dose of 900 mg or placebo [35]. However, hawthorn leaf and flower is not suitable for self-medication and should be used only under the supervision of a qualified practitioner.

In oral toxicity studies using a hawthorn leaf and flower extract (18.75% OPC), single doses of 3000 mg/kg caused neither mortality nor toxic signs in rats or mice, 300 mg/kg/day for 26 weeks caused no toxic effects in rats or dogs [45], and 1600 mg/kg produced no teratogenic effects in rats or rabbits [20]. A battery of standard mutagenic and clastogenic tests also gave negative results [45].

REGULATORY STATUS

Medicines

UK	No licences issued for products containing hawthorn leaf and flower.
France	Accepted for specified indications [46].
Germany	Commission E monograph published, with approved uses [47].

Food

Council of Europe	Permitted as flavouring, category N2 [48].

REFERENCES

Current Pharmacopoeial Monographs

Ph. Eur.	Hawthorn Leaf and Flower
USP	Hawthorn Leaf with Flower

Literature References

1. Kartnig T, Hiermann A and Azzam S. Investigations on the Procyanidin and Flavonoid Contents of *Crataegus monogyna* Drugs. *Sci. Pharm.* 1987, **55**, 95-100 [GERMAN/English summary].
2. Rohr GE, Meier B and Sticher O. Quantitative reversed-phase high-performance liquid chromatography of procyanidins in *Crataegus* leaves and flowers. *J. Chromatogr. A* 1999, **835**, 59-65.
3. Svedström U, Vuorela H, Kostiainen R, Huovinen K, Laakso I and Hiltunen R. High-performance liquid chromatographic determination of oligomeric procyanidins from dimers up to the hexamer in hawthorn. *J. Chromatogr. A* 2002, **968**, 53-60.

4. Svedström U, Vuorela H, Kostiainen R, Tuominen J, Kokkonen J, Rauha J-P et al. Isolation and identification of oligomeric procyanidins from *Crataegus* leaves and flowers. *Phytochemistry* 2002, **60**, 821-825.
5. Sticher O and Meier B. Hawthorn (*Crataegus*): Biological Activity and New Strategies for Quality Control. In: Lawson LD and Bauer R, editors. *Phytomedicines of Europe - Chemistry and Biological Activity*. ACS Symposium Series 691. ISBN 0-8412-3559-7. Washington DC: American Chemical Society, 1998:241-262.
6. Vanhaelen M and Vanhaelen-Fastre R. TLC-densitometric determination of 2,3-*cis*-procyanidin monomer and oligomers from hawthorn (*Crataegus laevigata* and *C. monogyna*). *J. Pharmaceut. Biomed. Analysis* 1989, **7**, 1871-1875.
7. Ficarra P, Ficarra R, Villari A, De Pasquale A, Monforte MT and Calabro ML. High-performance liquid chromatography and diffuse reflectance spectroscopy of flavonoids in Crataegus oxyacantha L. III - Analysis of 2-phenyl-chroman derivatives and caffeic acid. *Il Farmaco* 1990, **45**, 237-245.
8. Rehwald A, Meier B and Sticher O. Qualitative and quantitative reversed-phase high-performance liquid chromatography of flavonoids in Crataegus leaves and flowers. *J. Chromatogr. A* 1994, **677**, 25-33.
9. Lamaison JL and Carnat A. Teneur en principaux flavonoïdes des fleurs et des feuilles de *Crataegus monogyna* Jacq. et de *Crataegus laevigata* (Poiret) DC. (Rosaceae) [Content of the principal flavonoids in flowers and leaves of *Crataegus monogyna* Jacq. and of *Crataegus laevigata* (Poiret) DC. (Rosaceae)]. *Pharm. Acta Helv.* 1990, **65**, 315-320 [FRENCH/English summary].
10. Ficarra P, Ficarra R, De Pasquale A, Monforte MT and Calabro ML. High-performance liquid chromatography of flavonoids in Crataegus oxyacantha L. IV - Reversed-phase high-pressure liquid chromatography in flower, leaf and bud extractives of *Crataegus oxyacantha* L. *Il Farmaco* 1990, **45**, 247-255.
11. Steinegger E and Hänsel R. Weissdornpräparate [Hawthorn preparations]. In: *Pharmakognosie, 5th ed.* ISBN 3-540-55649-4. Berlin-Heidelberg-New York: Springer-Verlag, 1992:580-584 [GERMAN].
12. Tschesche R, Heesch A and Fugmann R. Über Triterpenoide, III. Mitteil.: Zur Kenntnis der Crataegolsäure [Triterpenoids, III. A study on crataegolic acid]. *Chem. Ber.* 1953, **86**, 626-629 [GERMAN].
13. Bersin T and Müller A. Über Inhaltsstoffe von *Crataegus oxyacantha* L. II. Mitteilung. β-Sitosterin und Oleanolsäure [Constituents of *Crataegus oxyacantha* L. II. β-Sitosterol and oleanolic acid]. *Helv. Chim. Acta* 1952, **35**, 1891-1895 [GERMAN].
14. García MD, Sáenz MT, Ahumada MC and Cert A. Isolation of three triterpenes and several aliphatic alcohols from *Crataegus monogyna* Jacq. *J. Chromatogr. A* 1997, **767**, 340-342.
15. Hensel A. Studies on neutral polysaccharides and their extractability from Crataegi folium cum flore. *Pharmazie* 1998, **53**, 572-577.
16. Wagner H and Grevel J. Cardioactive Drugs IV. Cardiotonic Amines from Crataegus oxyacantha. *Planta Medica* 1982, **45**, 98-101 [GERMAN/English summary].
17. Stuhlemmer U. Der Weißdorn - eine Pflanze nicht nur fürs Herz? [Hawthorn - a plant not only for the heart?]. *Z. Phytotherapie* 2003, **24**, 117-125 [GERMAN/English summary].
18. Rohr GE, Meier B and Sticher O. Evaluation of Different Detection Modes for the Analysis of Procyanidins in Leaves and Flowers of *Crataegus* spp. Part I. Diode Array and Electrochemical Detection. *Phytochem. Analysis* 2000, **11**, 106-112.
19. Wittig J, Leipolz I, Graefe EU, Jaki B, Treutter D and Veit M. Quantification of Procyanidins in Oral Herbal Medicinal Products Containing Extracts of *Crataegus* Species. *Arzneim.-Forsch./Drug Res.* 2002, **52**, 89-96.
20. European Scientific Cooperative on Phytotherapy. Crataegi folium cum flore - Hawthorn Leaf and Flower. In: *ESCOP Monographs - The Scientific Foundation for Herbal Medicinal Products, 2nd ed.* Stuttgart-New York: Thieme, Exeter, UK: ESCOP, 2003:98-106.
21. Upton R, editor. Hawthorn Leaf with Flower - *Crataegus* spp. Analytical, Quality Control and Therapeutic Monograph. In: *American Herbal Pharmacopoeia and Therapeutic Compendium.* Santa Cruz, CA: American Herbal Pharmacopoeia, 1999:1-29 (Available as a single monograph. Website: herbal-ahp.org).
22. Ammon HPT, Kaul R. *Crataegus.* Herz-Kreislauf-Wirkungen von Crataegusextrakten, Flavonoiden und Procyanidinen. Teil 1: Historisches und Wirkstoffe [*Crataegus.* Effects of hawthorn extracts, flavonoids and procyanidins on the heart and circulation. Part 1: History and constituents]. *Dtsch. Apoth. Ztg.* 1994, **134**, 2433-2436. Teil 2: Wirkungen auf das Herz [Part 2: Effects on the heart]. *ibid* 2521-2535. Teil 3: Wirkungen auf den Kreislauf [Effects on the circulation]. *ibid* 2631-2636 [GERMAN].
23. American Heart Association. AHA Medical/Scientific Statement. 1994 Revisions to Classification of Functional Capacity and Objective Assessment of Patients with Diseases of the Heart. *Circulation* 1994, **90**, 644-645.
24. Iwamoto M, Ishizaki T and Sato T. Klinische Wirkung von Crataegutt® bei Herzerkrankungen ischämischer und/oder hypertensiver Genese. Eine multizentrische Doppelblindstudie [Clinical effect of Crataegutt® in heart complaints of ischaemic and/or hypertensive origin]. *Planta Medica* 1981, **42**, 1-16 [GERMAN/English summary].
25. Hanak T and Brückel M-H. Behandlung von leichten stabilen Formen der Angina pectoris mit Crataegutt® novo. Eine placebokontrollierte Doppelblindstudie [Treatment of mild stable forms of angina pectoris with Crataegutt® novo. A placebo-controlled double-blind study]. *Therapiewoche* 1983, **33**, 4331-4333 [GERMAN].
26. O'Connolly M, Jansen W, Bernhöft G and Bartsch G. Treatment of Decreasing Cardiac Performance (NYHA Stages I to II) in Advanced Age with Crataegutt® novo. *Fortschr. Med.* 1986, **104**, 805-808 [GERMAN/English summary].
27. O'Connolly M, Bernhöft G and Bartsch G. Behandlung älterer, multimorbider Patienten mit stenokardischen Beschwerden. Eine placebokontrollierte Cross-over-Doppelblindstudie mit Crataegutt® novo [Treatment of older, multimorbid patients with stenocardiac conditions. A placebo-controlled, crossover, double-blind study with Crataegutt® novo]. *Therapiewoche* 1987, **37**, 3587-3600 [GERMAN/English summary].
28. Leuchtgens H. Crataegus Special Extract WS 1442 in Patients with Cardiac Insufficiency NYHA II. A Placebo-Controlled Double-Blind Study. *Fortschr. Med.* 1993, **111**, 352-354 [GERMAN/English summary].
29. Bödigheimer K and Chase D. Effectiveness of Hawthorn Extract at a Dosage of 3 × 100 mg per day. Multicentre Double-blind Study in 85 NYHA Class II Heart Failure Patients. *Münch. med. Wochenschr.* 1994, **136** (Suppl. 1), S7-S11 [GERMAN/English summary].
30. Schmidt U, Kuhn U, Ploch M and Hübner W-D. Efficacy of the Hawthorn (Crataegus) Preparation LI 132 in 78 patients with chronic congestive heart failure defined as NYHA functional class II. *Phytomedicine* 1994, **1**, 17-24.
Also published in German as:
Schmidt U, Kuhn U, Ploch M and Hübner W-D. Wirksamkeit des Extraktes LI 132 (600 mg/Tag) bei achtwöchiger Therapie. Plazebokontrollierte Doppelblindstudie mit Weißdorn an 78 herzinsuffizienten Patienten im Stadium II nach NYHA [Efficacy of Hawthorn Extract LI 132 (600 mg/day) during an Eight-Week Treatment. Placebo-controlled Double-blind Study in 78 NYHA Class II Heart Failure Patients]. *Münch. med. Wochenschr.* 1994, **136** (Suppl. 1), S13-S19 [GERMAN/English summary].
31. Förster A, Förster K, Bühring M and Wolfstädter HD. Crataegus for Moderately Reduced Left Ventricular Ejection Fraction. Ergospirometric Monitoring Study with 72 Patients in a Double-blind Comparison with Placebo. *Münch. med. Wochenschr.* 1994, **136** (Suppl. 1), S21-S26 [GERMAN/English summary].
32. Weikl A, Assmus K-D, Neukum-Schmidt A, Schmitz J, Zapfe G, Noh H-S and Siegrist J. Crataegus-Spezialextrakt WS 1442. Objectiver Wirksamkeitsnachweis bei Patienten

mit Herzinsuffizienz (NYHA II) [Crataegus special extract WS 1442. Objective confirmation of efficacy in patients with NYHA II cardiac insufficiency]. *Fortschr. Med.* 1996, **114**, 291-296 [GERMAN/English summary].
33. Eichstädt H, Störk T, Möckel M, Danne O, Funk P and Köhler S. Wirksamkeit und Verträglichkeit von Crataegus-Extrakt WS® 1442 bei herzinsuffizienten Patienten mit eingeschränkter linksventrikulärer Funktion. Eine plazebokontrollierte, randomisierte Doppelblindstudie mit radionuklidventrikulographischer Bestimmung der linksventrikulären Funktionsparameter in Ruhe und unter Belastung [Efficacy and tolerability of Crataegus extract WS® 1442 in heart failure patients with impaired left ventricular function. A placebo-controlled, randomized, double-blind study with determination of the left ventricular function parameter at rest and under load by radionuclide angiocardiography]. *Perfusion* 2001, **14**, 212-217 [GERMAN/English summary].
34. Zapfe G. Clinical Efficacy of Crataegus extract WS® 1442 in congestive heart failure NYHA class II. *Phytomedicine* 2001, **8**, 262-266.
35. Tauchert M. Efficacy and safety of crataegus extract WS 1442 in comparison with placebo in patients with chronic stable New York Heart Association class-III heart failure. *Am. Heart J.* 2002, **143**, 910-915.
36. Vierling W, Brand N, Gaedcke F, Sensch KH, Schneider E and Scholz M. Investigation of the pharmaceutical and pharmacological equivalence of different hawthorn extracts. *Phytomedicine* 2003, **10**, 8-16.
37. Pittler MH, Schmidt K and Ernst E. Hawthorn Extract for Treating Chronic Heart Failure: Meta-analysis of Randomized Trials. *Am. J. Med.* 2003, **114**, 665-674.
38. Tauchert M, Ploch M and Hübner W-D. Wirksamkeit des Weißdorn-Extraktes LI 132 im Vergleich mit Captopril. Multizentrische Doppelblindstudie bei 132 Patienten mit Herzinsuffizienz im Stadium II nach NYHA [Effectiveness of hawthorn extract LI 132 in comparison with captopril. Multicentric double-blind study in 132 patients with NYHA class II cardiac insufficiency]. *Münch. med. Wochenschr.* 1994, **136** (Suppl. 1), S27-S33 [GERMAN/English summary].
39. Walker AF, Marakis G, Morris AP and Robinson PA. Promising Hypotensive Effect of Hawthorn Extract: A Randomized Double-blind Pilot Study of Mild, Essential Hypertension. *Phytotherapy Res.* 2002, **16**, 48-54.
40. Schmidt U, Albrecht M, Podzuweit H, Ploch M and Maisenbacher J. Hochdosierte *Crataegus*-Therapie bei herzinsuffizienten Patienten NYHA-Stadium I und II [High-Dose *Crataegus* Therapy in Patients with NYHA Class I and II Cardiac Insufficiency]. *Z. Phytotherapie* 1998, **19**, 22-30 [GERMAN/English summary].
41. Tauchert M, Gildor A and Lipinski J. High-Dose Crataegus (Hawthorn) Extract WS 1442 for the Treatment of NYHA Class II Heart Failure Patients. *Herz* 1999, **24**, 465-474 [GERMAN/English summary].
42. Mills S and Bone K. Hawthorn - *Crataegus* spp. In: *Principles and Practice of Phytotherapy. Modern Herbal Medicine.* ISBN 0-443-06016-9. Edinburgh-London-New York: Churchill Livingstone, 2000:439-447.
43. Chevallier A. Hawthorn. In: *Encyclopedia of Medicinal Plants, 2nd ed.* ISBN 0-7513-1209-6. London-New York: Dorling Kindersley, 2001:90.
44. Wichtl M and Moser U. Weißdornblätter mit Blüten - Crataegi folium cum flore. In: Hartke K, Hartke H, Mutschler E, Rücker G and Wichtl M, editors. *Kommentar zum Deutschen Arzneibuch.* Stuttgart: Wissenschaftliche Verlagsgesellschaft, 2000 (13 Lfg.):W 13 [GERMAN].
45. Schlegelmilch R and Heywood R. Toxicity of *Crataegus* (Hawthorn) Extract (WS1442). *J. Am. Coll. Toxicol.* 1994, **13**, 103-111.
46. Aubépine. In: *Médicaments à base de plantes.* ISBN 2-911473-02-7. Saint-Denis Cedex, France: Agence du Médicament, 1998.
47. Crataegi folium cum flore. German Commission E Monograph published in: Bundesanzeiger No. 133 of 19 July 1994.
48. Crataegus oxyacantha; flowers, leaves, fruit. In: *Flavouring Substances and Natural Sources of Flavourings, 3rd ed.* ISBN 2-7160-0081-6. Strasbourg: Council of Europe, 1981.
49. Blumenthal M, senior editor. Hawthorn leaf with flower. In: *The Complete German Commission E Monographs - Therapeutic Guide to Herbal Medicines.* ISBN 0-9655555-0-X. Austin, Texas: American Botanical Council, 1998:142-144.

REGULATORY GUIDELINES FROM OTHER EU COUNTRIES

FRANCE

Médicaments à base de plantes [46]: Aubépine; fleur, sommité fleurie.

Therapeutic indications accepted

Oral use
Traditionally used: to reduce excitability in adults, particularly in cases of exaggerated perception of heart palpitations when any form of cardiac illness has been ruled out; in the symptomatic treatment of neurotonic states in adults and children, particularly in cases of minor sleep disorders.

GERMANY

Commission E monograph [47]: Crataegi folium cum flore (Weißdornblätter mit Blüten).

A lengthy section on Pharmacological Properties, Pharmacokinetics and Toxicology, of which an English translation is available [49], precedes the following text.

Uses
Declining cardiac performance corresponding to Functional Capacity Class II as defined by the New York Heart Association.

Contraindications
None known.

Side effects
None known.

Special precautions for use
If symptoms continue unchanged for over 6 weeks, or if fluid accumulates in the legs, a doctor should be consulted. If pains occur in the region of the heart, possibly radiating into the arms, upper abdomen or neck region, or in the event of shortness of breath, a medical diagnosis is absolutely essential.

Use during pregnancy and lactation
Nothing known.

Interactions with other drugs
None known.

Dosage
Unless otherwise prescribed, daily dose: 160-900 mg of native hydroalcoholic extract (ethanol 45% V/V or

methanol 70% V/V; drug to extract ratio 4-7:1, with defined flavonoid or procyanidin content) corresponding to 30-168.7 mg of oligomeric procyanidins, calculated as epicatechin, or 3.5-19.8 mg of flavonoids, calculated as hyperoside in accordance with DAB 10, divided into two or three sub-doses.

Hawthorn fluid extract DAB 10: the equivalent single and daily doses must be substantiated by clinical-pharmacological investigations or clinical studies.

Mode of administration: In liquid or solid oral dosage forms.
Duration of use: At least 6 weeks.

Overdose
Nothing known.

Special warnings
None.

Effects on ability to drive and operate machines
None known.

Note: The crude drug, as well as aqueous, hydroalcoholic or wine-based extracts and fresh plant juice, have traditionally been taken to strengthen and invigorate cardiac and circulatory functions. This information is based solely on tradition and long-term experience.

HEARTSEASE

Violaceae

Violae tricoloris herba

Synonym: Wild Pansy.

Definition
Heartsease consists of the dried flowering aerial parts of *Viola tricolor* L.

The European Pharmacopoeia monograph (2002) providing a specification for "dried flowering aerial parts of *Viola arvensis* Murray and/or *Viola tricolor* L." is entitled "Wild Pansy" - a rather unsatisfactory title since, in English usage, the common name "wild pansy" or "heartsease" is reserved for *Viola tricolor* L., while *Viola arvensis* Murray is distinguished as the "field pansy" [1]. To avoid confusion, the title Heartsease has been retained for this monograph, which covers only *Viola tricolor* L., the species more frequently used in the UK.

In some European countries the position has been seen differently. What are now designated as two separate species, *V. tricolor* L. and *V. arvensis* Murray, were previously treated as subspecies of *V. tricolor* [2]:

- *V. tricolor* L. ssp. *tricolor*. [= ssp. *vulgaris* (Koch) Oborný], of which a predominantly blue-flowered variety is the one usually cultivated. This is heartsease or wild pansy from the English point of view.
- *V. tricolor* L. ssp. *arvensis* (Murray) Gaudin, i.e. field pansy.

Both were accepted in former monographs of, for example, the Pharmacopée Française (Pensée sauvage - Viola tricolor) and the Deutscher Arzneimittel-Codex (Stiefmütterchenkraut - Violae tricoloris herba).

The garden pansy, *V.* × *wittrockiana* Gams, of which *V. tricolor* is one of several parent species [3], is not used medicinally.

CONSTITUENTS

□ ***Flavonoids***, up to 2.1% [4] (Ph. Eur. min. 1.5%, expressed as violanthin), principally rutin (quercetin 3-rutinoside, at one time called violaquercitrin; up to 0.8%) [4-6] together with quercetin, luteolin and luteolin 7-glucoside [7]. Also apigenin di-*C*-glycosides including violanthin (apigenin-6-*C*-β-D-glucoside-8-*C*-α-L-rhamnoside) [8,9], vicenin-2 and several others, the apigenin mono-*C*-glucosides vitexin and isovitexin (= saponaretin), and the luteolin mono-*C*-glucosides orientin and iso-orientin [9].

The highest concentration of rutin occurs in the flowers. In a variety of *Viola tricolor* not used

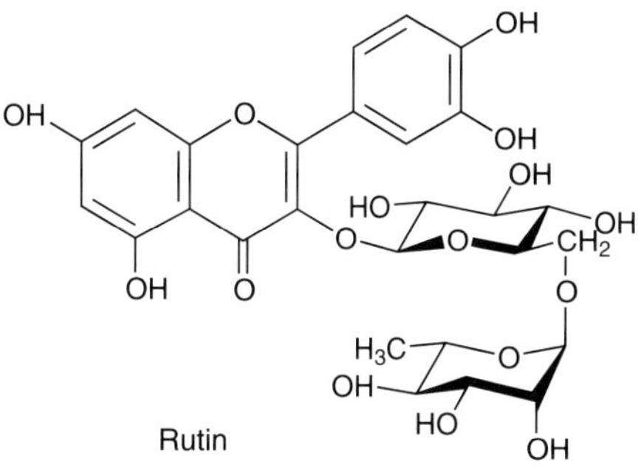

Rutin

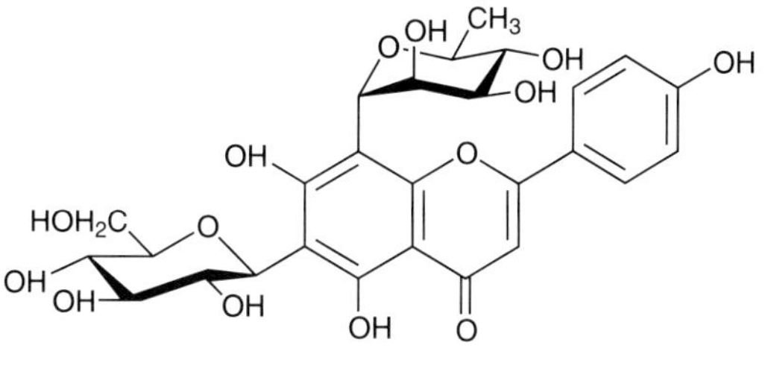

Violanthin

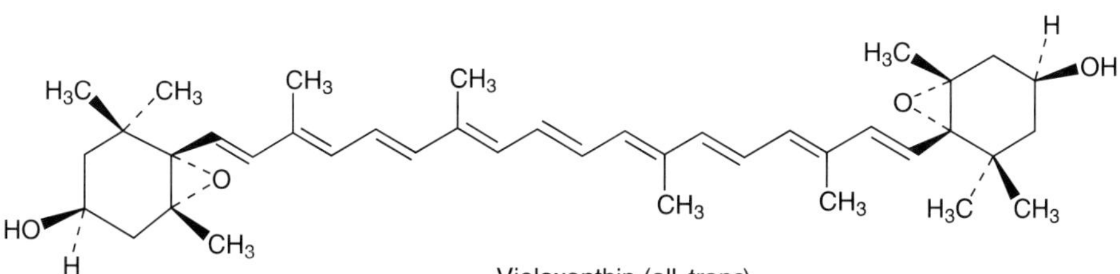

Violaxanthin (all-*trans*)

medicinally, var. Maxima (Giant Roggli), the flowers are reported to contain a remarkable 18-21% of rutin [10].

□ ***Polysaccharides***, ca. 10% of dry weight, maximal during flowering, containing principally glucose, galactose and arabinose residues (2 : 1.8 : 1.1) together with galacturonic acid, rhamnose and xylose [11,12].

□ ***Phenolic acids***, ca. 0.8%, including protocatechuic, *trans*-caffeic, gentisic, *p*-coumaric, *p*-hydroxybenzoic, *p*-hydroxyphenylacetic, vanillic and salicylic acids [7,13]; also methyl salicylate and violutin (methyl salicylate arabinosylglucoside) [14].

□ ***Carotenoids*** in the flowers: Yellow blossoms yielded 13 carotenoids totalling ca. 9.7 mg/g dry weight, principally 9-*cis*-violaxanthin (4.97 mg/g) and all-*trans*-violaxanthin (2.87 mg/g) [15] and including other *cis*- and four di-*cis*-violaxanthins [15,16], mainly as di-esters, esterified with fatty acids [17].

□ ***Anthocyanins*** Violanin, a violet, triglycosidic anthocyanin pigment containing delphinidin, D-glucose, L-rhamnose and *p*-coumaric acid, has been isolated from the flowers [18,19].

□ ***Cyclotides (macrocyclic peptides)*** Three cyclotides, named vitri A, varv A and varv E, have been isolated from aerial parts of *Viola tricolor* and their amino acid sequences determined. Each consists of about 30 amino acids with a head-to-tail cyclic backbone constrained by three disulphide bonds (cysteine to cysteine) at its core, forming a "cyclic cystine knot" arrangement [20].

Cyclotides have exceptional chemical and biological stability and display a range of biological activities [21].

□ ***Other constituents*** include β-sitosterol and the triterpenes α-amyrin and β-amyrin acetate [14].

No saponins were detected in *Viola tricolor* or *V. arvensis* in a 1993 investigation [22], casting considerable doubt on an earlier report of ca. 5% dry weight of triterpene saponins (with a haemolytic index of 4000) in *V. tricolor* [23]. A haemolytic peptide composed of 28 amino acids, violapeptide I, has been isolated from *V. arvensis* leaf (but not detected in *V. tricolor*) and its structure partly elucidated [22], although whether it is a cyclotide (see above) is not clear.

Published Assay Methods

Total flavonoids by spectrophotometry [Ph. Eur.].

PHARMACOLOGY

In vitro

A hydromethanolic extract from *Viola tricolor* flowering tops at concentrations of 100-800 µg/ml exhibited spasmogenic activity on isolated guinea pig ileum [24].

Contrary to an earlier report [19], no compounds with haemolytic activity were detected in *Viola tricolor* in a more recent study [22].

Three cyclotides, vitri A, varv A and varv E, isolated from aerial parts of *Viola tricolor* exhibited dose-dependent cytotoxic activity against two human cancer cell lines (lymphoma and myeloma) with IC_{50} values of 0.6-4 µM. These potencies are in the range of the clinically used anticancer drug doxorubicin [20].

In vivo

Anti-inflammatory activity of heartsease has been demonstrated in animals [14].

In an old experiment (original author not clear; no further data available), eczema was induced in rats by prolonged feeding with rye. Animals then fed a diet augmented with heartsease for 2 months markedly improved in comparison with control animals [2].

Heartsease showed no diuretic activity in another old (1937) experiment. When administered orally to rabbits at 2.5-7.5 g/kg body weight or to mice at 50-200 mg/kg it did not influence urine volume; at the dose of 200 mg/kg in mice, chloride excretion increased by 108% [25].

CLINICAL STUDIES

None published on mono-preparations of heartsease.

THERAPEUTICS

Published research on heartsease is very limited; reported actions and uses are largely based on the experience of practitioners in herbal medicine.

Actions

Anti-inflammatory [26,27].

Also claimed to be expectorant, diuretic [26-28], diaphoretic [22,28] and mildly laxative [2, 26,29].

Indications

None adequately substantiated by pharmacological or clinical studies.

Uses based on experience or tradition

Internally and/or externally for skin disorders, especially those of a seborrhoeal nature [26,30-32] including weeping and dry eczema [2,22,26, 28,29], acne, impetigo [2,22,29], skin rashes and eruptions [26,27], and milk-crust of infants [27, 29,31,32].

Has also been used in the treatment of acute bronchitis [26], whooping cough [2,26,29], coughs [30]; catarrhs of the respiratory tract [2,29], throat inflammation; feverish conditions [2]; urinary disorders including cystitis [26,29], polyuria and dysuria [26]; rheumatism [2,26]; varicose ulcers [27] and capillary fragility [26,29].

Contraindications
None known.

Side effects
None known.

Interactions with other drugs
None known.

Dosage
Adult internal dose, three times daily: dried herb, 2-4 g, usually as an infusion or tea; liquid extract 1:1 in 25% ethanol, 2-4 ml [26].
Children: proportion of adult dose according to age or body weight.
Externally, as a compress or poultice: 3-4 g of dried herb infused in 150 ml of hot water, several times daily.
A long period of treatment is recommended for a good response in chronic eczema [32].

SAFETY

No toxicological data is available but from practitioner experience and traditional use of heartsease, including internal use in babies [32], there are no apparent safety concerns at therapeutic dose levels.

REGULATORY STATUS

Medicines

UK	Accepted for general sale, internal or external use [33].
France	Accepted for specified indications [30].
Germany	Commission E monograph published, with approved uses [31].

Foods

USA	Permitted as flavouring, in alcoholic beverages only (21 CFR 172.510) [34].
Council of Europe	Permitted as flavouring, category 5 [35].

REFERENCES

Current Pharmacopoeial Monographs
Ph. Eur. Wild Pansy (flowering aerial parts)

Literature References

1. Blamey M and Grey-Wilson C. Violet Family - Violaceae. In: *The Illustrated Flora of Britain and Northern Europe.* ISBN 0-340-40170-2. London: Hodder & Stoughton, 1989: 250-253.
2. Hänsel R, Keller K, Rimpler H and Schneider G, editors. Viola. In: *Hagers Handbuch der Pharmazeutischen Praxis, 5th ed. Volume 6: Drogen P-Z.* ISBN 3-540-52639-0. Berlin-Heidelberg-New York-London: Springer-Verlag, 1994:1141-1153 [GERMAN].
3. Mabberley DJ. Viola. In: *The Plant-Book - A portable dictionary of the higher plants.* Cambridge-New York: Cambridge University Press, 1990.
4. Vincze-Vermes M, Marczal G and Pethes E. Occurrence of rutin in some Viola species. *Acta Agron. Acad. Sci. Hung.* 1974, **23**, 448-453.
5. Vincze M and Marczal G. Isolation of rutin from the herb of Viola tricolor. *Gyogyszereszet* 1972, **16** (2), 58-60 [HUNGARIAN]; through *Chem. Abstr.* 1972, **77**, 45573.
6. Bandyukova VA and Sergeeva NV. Rutin in some cultivated plants. *Khim. Prir. Soedin.* 1974, (4), 524 [RUSSIAN]; through *Chem. Abstr.* 1975, **82**, 54179.
7. Boruch T, Gora J, Bielawska M, Swiatek L and Luczak S. Extracts of plants and their cosmetic application. Part XI. Extracts from herb of Viola tricolor. *Pollena: Tluszcze, Srodki Piorace, Kosmet.* 1985, **29**, 38-40 [POLISH]; through *Chem. Abstr.* 1986, **104**, 31766.
8. Hörhammer L, Wagner H, Rosprim L, Mabry T and Rösler H. Über die Struktur neuer und bekannter Flavon-C-Glykoside I [The structure of newer and well-known flavone C-glycosides I]. *Tetrahedron Lett.* 1965, (22), 1707-1711 [GERMAN].
9. Wagner H, Rosprim L and Düll P. The Flavone-C-glycosides of *Viola tricolor* L. *Z. Naturforsch.* 1972, **27b**, 954-958 [GERMAN/English summary].
10. Krewson CF and Naghski J. Occurrence of rutin in plants. *Am. J. Pharm.* 1953, **125**, 190-200.
11. Franz G. Untersuchungen über die Schleimpolysaccharide von [Investigations on the mucilage polysaccharides of] *Tussilago farfara* L., *Symphytum officinalis* L., *Borago officinalis* L. und *Viola tricolor* L. *Planta Medica* 1969, **17**, 217-220 [GERMAN/English summary].
12. Zabaznaya EI. Polysaccharides of *Viola tricolor. Khim. Prir. Soedin.* 1985, (1), 116 [RUSSIAN], translated into English as: *Chem. Nat. Compd.* 1985, **21**, 113.
13. Komorowski T, Mosiniak T, Kryszczuk Z and Rosinski G. Phenolic acids in the Polish species Viola tricolor L. and Viola arvensis Murr. *Herba Pol.* 1983, **29**, 5-11 [POLISH]; through *Chem. Abstr.* 1984, **100**, 153820.
14. Papay V, Molnar B, Lepran I and Toth L. Study of chemical substances of Viola tricolor L. *Acta Pharm. Hung.* 1987, **57**, 153-158 [HUNGARIAN/English summary].
15. Molnar P and Szabolcs J. Occurrence of 15-*cis*-violaxanthin in *Viola tricolor. Phytochemistry* 1980, **19**, 623-627.
16. Molnar P, Szabolcs J and Radics L. Naturally occurring di-*cis*-violaxanthins from *Viola tricolor*: isolation and identification by 1H NMR spectroscopy of four di-*cis*-isomers. *Phytochemistry* 1986, **25**, 195-199.
17. Hansmann P and Kleinig H. Violaxanthin esters from *Viola tricolor* flowers. *Phytochemistry* 1982, **21**, 238-239.
18. Takeda K and Hayashi K. Anthocyanins. XL. Analytical evidence for the presence of the triglycosidic pattern in violanin. *Botan. Mag. (Tokyo)* 1963, **76**, 206-214; through *Chem. Abstr.* 1964, **60**, 9347.
19. Hayashi K and Takeda K. Anthocyanins. XXXVII. Violet flower color in the pansy, Viola tricolor. *Proc. Japan Acad.* 1962, **38**, 161-165; through *Chem. Abstr.* 1962, **57**, 14186.
20. Svangård E, Göransson U, Hocaoglu Z, Gullbo J, Larsson R, Claeson P and Bohlin L. Cytotoxic Cyclotides from *Viola tricolor. J. Nat. Prod.* 2004, **67**, 144-147.
21. Lindholm P, Göransson U, Johansson S, Claeson P, Gullbo J, Larsson R et al. Cyclotides: A Novel Type of Cytotoxic Agents. *Molecular Cancer Therapeutics* 2002, **1**, 365-369.

22. Schöpke T, Hasan Agha MI, Kraft R, Otto A and Hiller K. Compounds with hemolytic activity from *Viola tricolor* L. und *Viola arvensis* Murray. *Sci. Pharm.* 1993, **61**, 145-153 [GERMAN/English summary].
23. Tamas M, Grecu L and Rosca M. Investigations on triterpene saponins in Viola tricolor L. *Farmacia (Bucharest)* 1981, **29**, 99-103 [HUNGARIAN/English summary].
24. Izzo AA, Capasso R, Senatore F, Seccia S and Morrica P. Spasmolyic Activity of Medicinal Plants Used for the Treatment of Disorders Involving Smooth Muscles. *Phytotherapy Res.* 1996, **10** (Suppl. 1), S107-S108.
25. Vollmer H and Weidlich R. Untersuchungen über die diuretische Wirkung der Fructus juniperi, Radix levistici, Radix liquiritiae und Herba violae tricoloris an Kaninchen und Mausen [Investigations on the diuretic effect of Fructus juniperi, Radix levistici, Radix liquiritiae and Herba violae tricoloris on rabbits and mice]. *Naunyn Schmiederberg's Arch. Pharmakol. Exp. Pathol.* 1937, **186**, 574-583 [GERMAN].
26. Viola tricolor. In: *British Herbal Pharmacopoeia 1983*. ISBN 0-903032-07-4. Bournemouth: British Herbal Medicine Association, 1983.
27. Ody P. *Viola* spp. - Heartsease. In: *Medicinal Herbal, 2nd* ed. ISBN 0-7513-3005-1. London-New York: Dorling Kindersley, 2000:137.
28. Stodola J and Volák J. Wild Pansy. In: Bunney S, editor. *The Illustrated Book of Herbs*. ISBN 0-7064-1489-6. London: Octopus Books, 1984:302.
29. Rimkiene S, Ragazinskiene O and Savickiene N. The cumulation of wild pansy (*Viola tricolor* L.) accessions: the possibility of species preservation and usage in medicine. *Medicina (Kaunas, Lithuania)* 2003, **39**, 411-416.
30. Pensée sauvage. In: *Médicaments à base de plantes*. ISBN 2-911473-02-7. Saint-Denis Cedex, France: Agence du Médicament, 1998.
31. Violae tricoloris herba. German Commission E Monograph published in: Bundesanzeiger No. 50 of 13.03.86.
32. Weiss RF and Fintelmann V. Viola tricolor - Wild Pansy. In: *Herbal Medicine, 2nd ed.* ISBN 3-13-126332-6. Stuttgart: Georg Thieme Verlag, 2000:298-299.
33. Heartsease. In: UK Statutory Instrument 1994 No. 2410. The Medicines (Products Other Than Veterinary Drugs) (General Sale List) Amendment Order 1994. Schedule 1, Table A.
34. Pansy (*Viola tricolor* L.) (Section 172.510). In: USA Code of Federal Regulations, Title 21, Food and Drugs, Parts 170 to 199. Revised as of April 1, 2000.
35. Viola tricolor L., flowers, herb. In: *Natural Sources of Flavourings. Report No. 1*. ISBN 92-871-4324-2. Strasbourg: Council of Europe Publishing, 2000.

REGULATORY GUIDELINES FROM OTHER EU COUNTRIES

GERMANY

Commission E monograph [31]: Violae tricoloris herba (Stiefmütterchenkraut).

Uses
External use: Mild seborrhoeal skin disorders; milk-crust of infants.

Contraindications
None known.

Side effects
None known.

Interactions with other drugs
None known.

Dosage
Unless otherwise prescribed: three times daily, 1.5 g of dried herb to a cup of water as a tea infusion; equivalent preparations.

Mode of administration
Comminuted drug for infusions or decoctions and other galenic preparations for external use.

FRANCE

Médicaments à base de plantes [30]: Pensée sauvage, parties aériennes fleuries.

Therapeutic indications accepted
Oral use
Traditionally used in seborrhoeal skin conditions.
Traditionally used as adjuvant treatment of the pain associated with functional digestive disorders.
Traditionally used in the symptomatic treatment of coughs.

Topical use
Traditionally used in seborrhoeal skin conditions.
Traditionally used locally in mouthwashes, for buccal hygiene.

HORSE-CHESTNUT SEED Hippocastanaceae

Hippocastani semen

Definition
Horse-chestnut seed consists of the dried seeds of *Aesculus hippocastanum* L.

CONSTITUENTS

□ ***Triterpene glycosides***, i.e. saponins, 2-10% (DAB min. 3.0%, expressed as anhydrous aescin) of the oleanane type, occurring as a complex mixture collectively known as "aescin", which can be separated into fractions [1]:

β-Aescin (in some literature referred to simply as "aescin"). The sparingly water-soluble and crystallizable fraction, composed of triterpene glycosides of very similar structure. The aglycones are diesters of protoaescigenin and barringtogenol C, which differ only in that protoaescigenin has a hydroxyl group on C-24. An acetyl group on C-22 (in the case of aescins) or C-28 (in the case of isoaescins) is characteristic of β-aescin saponins and they are also esterified at C-21, most commonly with angelic acid or tiglic acid. All the saponins have a trisaccharide group at C-3, comprising glucuronic acid with substituent sugars at its 2-position (glucose, galactose or xylose) and 4-position (glucose) [1,2].

The structures of a number of individual saponins, designated as aescins Ia, Ib, IIa, IIb, IIIa [3], IIIb, IV, V and VI, and isoaescins Ia, Ib and V [4], have been fully elucidated. The two principal saponins in β-aescin, aescins Ia and Ib, both arising from protoaescigenin, have a 21-tigloyl and a 21-angeloyl group respectively, and 2-glucosyl and 4-glucosyl substituents on the glucuronic acid at C-3 [3].

Cryptoaescin A water-soluble fraction, obtained by counter-current distribution, containing only 28-acetyl compounds [1].

α-Aescin The readily water-soluble fraction obtained from the mother liquor after crystallization of β-aescin, containing 28-acetyl as well as 22-acetyl compounds; thus essentially a mixture of β-aescin and cryptoaescin [1].

□ ***Flavonoids***, ca. 0.3%, as di- and tri-*O*-glycosides of the flavonols quercetin and kaempferol. Nine such glycosides have been isolated, with glucose and xylose or rhamnose residues in the 3-position and, additionally in some cases, a glucose, 6-nicotinoylglucose or 6-indolinone hydroxyacetylglucose residue in the 3′-position of quercetin [5].

□ ***Condensed tannins (proanthocyanidins)*** in the pericarp (seed shell) including procyanidin dimers of the A-type (i.e. with doubly-linked structures), such as proanthocyanidins A2, A4, A6 and A7, and of the B-type (i.e. with singly-linked structures), such as proanthocyanidins B2, B5 and C1 [6,7]. Numerous procyanidin oligomers have also been isolated including singly-linked trimers such as epicatechin-(4β→6)-epicatechin-(4β→6)-epicatechin [6,8] and doubly-linked trimers such as epicatechin-(4β→8; 2β→7)-catechin-(4β→8)-epicatechin [8], aesculitannins A, B, C, D (trimers), E, F and G (tetramers), and cinnamtannins B_1 (a trimer) and B_2 (a tetramer). Monomeric (–)-epicatechin is also present [6].

□ ***Sterols*** Δ^7-Sterols (mainly Δ^7-stigmastadienol and α-spinasterol) and Δ^5-sterols (mainly sitosterol and stigmasterol), constituting 18% and 8% respectively of the unsaponifiable matter (0.014% of the dry weight of seed) have been identified

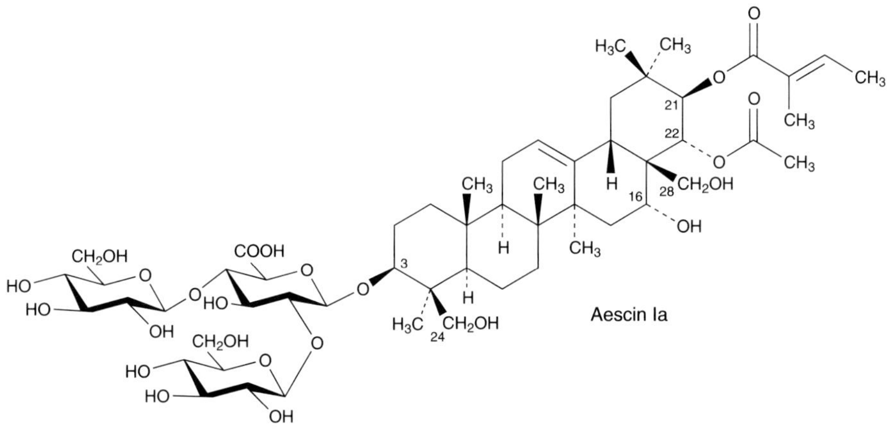

in fixed oil extracted from the seed [9]. Several 4α-methyl sterols (principally citrostadienol) are also present [10].

☐ *Other constituents* include volatile oil (0.8%) [11], fixed oil (ca. 6%), starch (ca. 40%) and protein (ca. 10%) [12].

Coumarins such as aesculin and fraxin, which are found in the bark and leaves of horse-chestnut, are absent from the seeds.

Published Assay Methods

Triterpene glycosides by spectrophotometry [DAB, Ph. Fr.], HPLC [1,13,14] and TLC densitometry [13].

PHARMACOLOGY

Note: In the following text the abbreviation "HCSE" stands for horse-chestnut seed extract(s).

In vitro

HCSE concentration-dependently contracted isolated canine saphenous vein; at 5×10^{-4} g/ml the maximum contraction of 43% was reached in 15 minutes and lasted 5 hours [15].

A 50%-methanolic extract from horse-chestnut seed exhibited antispasmodic activity in isolated guinea pig ileum, inhibiting spontaneous contractions of the circular smooth muscle (IC_{50} 632 μg/ml) and acetylcholine- and barium chloride-induced contractions of the longitudinal smooth muscle (IC_{50} values of 167 and 224 μg/ml respectively) [16].

In vivo

Anti-inflammatory and anti-oedematous effects

Orally administered HCSE dose-dependently inhibited carrageenan-induced rat paw oedema, by 5% at 150 mg/kg and 36% at 200 mg/kg ($p<0.05$) [15]. It was subsequently demonstrated that aescins Ia, Ib, IIa and IIb, isolated from horse-chestnut seed and orally administered at 200 mg/kg, inhibited carrageenan-induced rat paw oedema to varying extents over a period of 6 hours, aescin Ib being the most effective [17,18].

In earlier experiments, intravenously administered aescin significantly inhibited egg albumin-induced rat paw oedema, by 16% at 0.2 mg/kg and 53% at 2.5 mg/kg (both $p<0.001$) [19], while dextran-induced rat paw oedema was completely inhibited by aescin administered intraperitoneally at 4 mg/kg [20].

Venotonic effects

HCSE administered intravenously at 50 mg to anaesthetized dogs significantly increased femoral venous pressure ($p<0.001$) [15].

Skin capillary hyperpermeability induced in rats by histamine or serotonin was significantly reduced by HCSE administered orally at 200 mg/kg ($p<0.001$) [15], and dose-dependently by aescins Ia, Ib, IIa and IIb at 50-200 mg/kg ($p<0.001$ for aescins Ib, IIa and IIb; not significant for Ia) [17].

Pharmacological studies in humans

The inhibitory effect of orally administered HCSE on transcapillary filtration and hence oedema formation in venous disorders of the lower legs has been demonstrated in two randomized, placebo-controlled studies using plethysmographic devices. A single dose of 300 mg of HCSE taken by 12 healthy volunteers significantly lowered capillary filtration coefficients ($p<0.001$) over the course of 3 hours compared to placebo ($n = 14$) [21]. A subsequent double-blind crossover study involved 22 patients with chronic venous insufficiency. A single 600 mg dose of HCSE (standardized to 100 mg of aescin) significantly reduced the capillary filtration coefficient by 22% ($p = 0.006$) over the course of 3 hours compared to a slight increase with placebo [22].

Earlier placebo-controlled plethysmometric studies in healthy volunteers showed that orally administered single doses of HCSE increased venous tone and significantly decreased venous capacity in the lower leg [23,24].

The observation that the activity of three enzymes, the hydrolases β-*N*-acetylglucosaminidase, β-glucuronidase and arylsulphatase, was elevated by as much as 60-120% in the serum of varicose patients compared to that of healthy subjects provided an insight into how HCSE may exert effects on capillary permeability and capillary resistance. These enzymes catalyse the breakdown of proteoglycans, which form part of capillary walls, and thus may increase both the permeability and fragility of capillaries [25]. In a double-blind, placebo-controlled study, significant reductions of 25-30% in the activity of each of the three enzymes ($p<0.01$ to $p<0.05$) were observed after daily oral administration of 900 mg of HCSE (providing 150 mg of aescin) to varicose patients for 12 consecutive days [25,26].

Oral administration of a high daily dose of HCSE, 3 × 600 mg, for 12 days to patients with varicosis of the lower legs increased the flow velocity of venous blood between instep and groin (measured by means of injected ^{133}Xe) by about 30% ($p<0.001$), at the same time reducing blood viscosity by about 5% ($p<0.001$). The favourable effect on haemodynamics correlated with improvement in subjective symptoms in 73% of cases [27].

Pharmacokinetics

Several human studies have been performed with healthy volunteers to determine the pharmacokinetic profile of aescin, particularly the relative bioavailability of aescin from oral rapid-release and prolonged-release formulations of horse-chestnut seed extracts. The data are highly variable and reasons for this have been summarized by Loew et al. [28].

However, no major differences in bioavailability of aescin were evident between rapid-release tablets and prolonged-release capsules (both containing HCSE to providing 2 × 50 mg/day of aescin), each taken for 7 days by 18 healthy volunteers in an open, randomized, crossover study. Steady-state serum concentrations of β-aescin indicated that the two formulations were bioequivalent with respect to the extent of absorption and that parameters such as C_{max} (16.7-18.5 ng/ml after the first dose of the day) and t_{max} (2.1 hours) were comparable [29].

CLINICAL STUDIES

Horse-chestnut seed extracts (HCSE) are used for the treatment of chronic venous insufficiency (CVI), a common disorder of the legs with symptoms such as varicosis, oedema, dermatosclerosis, swelling, pain, sensation of tension, leg fatigue or heaviness, itching and cramp, all in the lower extremities. The standard conservative therapy for CVI is compression treatment (with compression stockings) but since this is inconvenient, often causes discomfort and is subject to poor compliance, oral treatments such as HCSE offer an attractive alternative [30]. Numerous randomized controlled studies have been carried out to evaluate the efficacy of HCSE in the treatment of CVI, with control groups receiving placebo, other oral preparations or compression therapy. The more important of these studies have been summarized in the ESCOP monograph [31].

From a recent systematic review [32] of 16 rigorous clinical studies it was concluded that HCSE (standardized to provide 100-150 mg of aescin daily) is an effective and safe short term treatment for CVI, with improvement in CVI-related signs and symptoms compared to placebo. A meta-analysis of pooled data from five studies [33-37] suggested a significant reduction in leg volume (measured by water displacement plethysmography) in favour of HCSE compared to placebo [32].

Results from 13 randomized controlled studies [33-41 and four others, two unpublished] were evaluated in another review. Wherever possible, data on outcomes for individual symptoms were pooled to enable meta-analyses, the results of which were significantly in favour of HCSE with respect to leg volume, ankle and calf circumference, and oedema; borderline ($p = 0.05$) with respect to pain and itching, and not significant with respect to leg fatigue/heaviness and calf cramp. The reviewers concluded that HCSE appeared to be an effective and safe treatment for CVI [42].

One study worthy of special mention involved comparison of the efficacy, in terms of oedema reduction, of HCSE and compression therapy in patients with chronic venous insufficiency. After a 2-week period of placebo run-in, 240 randomized patients, all of whom had substantial lower leg oedema due to CVI, were assigned to one of three treatments daily for 12 weeks: HCSE (2 × 50 mg of aescin; $n = 95$), therapy with elastic compression stockings ($n = 99$) or placebo ($n = 46$). The study was blinded in the HCSE and placebo groups. Patients allocated to compression treatment received a diuretic daily for the first 7 days and thereafter were provided with individually fitted compression stockings. Periodic measurements of lower leg volumes in the more severely affected limb by water displacement plethysmometry revealed significant oedema reductions in the HCSE ($p = 0.005$) and compression therapy ($p = 0.002$) groups after 12 weeks compared to the placebo group, and the two verum therapies were shown to be equivalent ($p<0.001$). The results indicated that both HCSE and compression stockings are effective therapies for the treatment of oedema resulting from chronic venous insufficiency, and that a 12-week course of HCSE may lead to a 25% reduction in mean leg oedema volume [37].

THERAPEUTICS

Actions

Increases venous tone [23,24] and inhibits transcapillary filtration (and hence oedema), particularly in the lower leg [21,22], anti-inflammatory [15,19, 20].

Indications

Conditions arising from chronic venous insufficiency in the lower legs, such as varicosis, oedema and swelling, pain, itching, feelings of heaviness and nocturnal cramp [32-43].

Where appropriate (and normally under medical supervision), horse-chestnut seed extract preparations may be used in conjunction with compression stockings or other non-invasive treatments [30,43].

Other uses, based on experience or tradition

Haemorrhoids [44,45]. Topically for haematoma, contusions and sports injuries involving oedema [45], and for disorders of cutaneous capillary fragility such as ecchymoses or petechiae [44].

Contraindications

None known.

Side effects

In isolated cases, mild gastrointestinal disorders, headache, dizziness or pruritus [32,42].

Interactions with other drugs

None known.

Dosage

Daily dose: Preparations providing 100-150 mg of triterpene glycosides (calculated as aescin), usually in the form of hydroethanolic extracts [32,42].

For topical use, a decoction from dried or fresh seed, or a hydroethanolic extract, in cream, gel or ointment [45].

SAFETY

Horse-chestnut seed extracts and aescin are generally well tolerated and have a good safety record. Adverse events reported in clinical studies have usually been mild and infrequent, the most common being gastrointestinal disorders such as constipation, diarrhoea, nausea and vomiting, as well as headache, dizziness and pruritus [32,42,46]. Analysis of pooled data from 8 randomized controlled studies showed no significant difference in adverse events between patients taking HCSE (n = 353) and those taking placebo (n = 307). No severe adverse events were reported in 3 observational studies involving a total of 10,725 patients taking HCSE and the mild adverse event rates ranged from 0.6% to 2.9% [42].

In other safety studies, HCSE showed no significant mutagenic [47] or teratogenic [48] potential. Further toxicological data have been summarized in the ESCOP monograph [31].

REGULATORY STATUS

Medicines

UK	Accepted for general sale, *external use* only [49].
France	Accepted for specified indications [44].
Germany	Commission E monograph published, with approved uses [43].

Food

Not used in foods.

REFERENCES

Current Pharmacopoeial Monographs

Ph. Fr.	Marron d'Inde
DAB	Roßkastaniensamen
USP	Horse Chestnut
BHP	Horse-chestnut Seed

Literature References

1. Wagner H, Reger H and Bauer R. Saponinhaltige Drogen und Fertigarzneimittel. HPLC-Analyse am Beispiel von Roßkastaniensamen [Saponin-containing herbal drugs and finished medicines. HPLC analysis taking horse-chestnut seed as an example]. *Dtsch. Apoth. Ztg.* 1985, **125**, 1513-1518 [GERMAN/English summary].
2. Wagner J, Schlemmer W and Hoffmann H. Über Inhaltsstoffe des Roßkastaniensamens. IX. Struktur und Eigenschaften der Triterpenglykoside [Constituents of horse-chestnut seed. IX. Structure and characteristics of the triterpene glycosides]. *Arzneim.-Forsch./Drug Res.* 1970, **20**, 205-209 [GERMAN/English summary].
3. Yoshikawa M, Murakami T, Matsuda H, Yamahara J, Murakami N and Kitagawa I. Bioactive Saponins and Glycosides. III. Horse Chestnut. (1): The Structures, Inhibitory Effects of Ethanol Absorption and Hypoglycemic Activity of Escins Ia, Ib, IIa, IIb and IIIa from the Seeds of *Aesculus hippocastanum* L. *Chem. Pharm. Bull.* 1996, **44**, 1454-1464.
4. Yoshikawa M, Murakami T, Yamahara J and Matsuda H. Bioactive Saponins and Glycosides. XII. Horse Chestnut. (2): Structures of Escins IIIb, IV, V and VI and Isoescins Ia, Ib and V, Acylated Polyhydroxyoleanene Triterpene Oligoglycosides from the Seeds of Horse Chestnut Tree (*Aesculus hippocastanum* L., Hippocastanaceae). *Chem. Pharm. Bull.* 1998, **46**, 1764-1769.
5. Hübner G, Wray V and Nahrstedt A. Flavonol oligosaccharides from the seeds of *Aesculus hippocastanum. Planta Medica* 1999, **65**, 636-642.
6. Morimoto S, Nonaka G-I and Nishioka I. Tannins and Related Compounds. LIX. Aesculitannins, Novel Proanthocyanidins with Doubly-Bonded Structures from *Aesculus hippocastanum* L. *Chem. Pharm. Bull.* 1987, **35**, 4717-4729.
7. Kaul R. Pflanzliche Procyanidine - Vorkommen, Klassifikation und pharmakologische Wirkungen [Plant procyanidins - Occurrence, classification and pharmacological effects]. *Pharm. unserer Zeit* 1996, **25**, 175-185 [GERMAN].
8. Santos-Buelga C, Kolodziej H and Treutter D. Procyanidin trimers possessing a doubly linked structure from *Aesculus hippocastanum. Phytochemistry* 1995, **38**, 499-504.
9. Stankovic SK, Bastic MB and Jovanovic JA. Composition of the sterol fraction in horse-chestnut. *Phytochemistry* 1984, **23**, 2677-2679.
10. Stankovic SK, Bastic MB and Jovanovic JA. 4α-Methylergosta-8,24(28)-dien-3β-ol, a minor sterol in the seed of horse-chestnut. *Phytochemistry* 1985, **24**, 2466-2469.
11. Buchbauer G, Jirovetz L, Wasicky M and Nikiforov A. Volatiles of Common Horsechestnut (*Aesculus hippocastanum* L.) (Hippocastanaceae) Peels and Seeds. *J. Essent. Oil Res.* 1994, **6**, 507-511.
12. Wichtl M and Egerer HP. Roßkastaniensamen - Hippocastani semen. In: Hartke K, Hartke H, Mutschler E, Rücker G and Wichtl M, editors. *Kommentar zum Deutschen Arzneibuch.* Stuttgart: Wissenschaftliche Verlagsgesellschaft, 2000 (13 Lfg.):R 21 [GERMAN].
13. Koçkar OM, Kara M, Kara S, Bozan B and Baser KHC. Quantitative determination of escin. A comparative study of HPLC and TLC-densitometry. *Fitoterapia* 1994, **65**, 439-443.
14. Yoshikawa M, Murakami T, Otuki K, Yamahara J and Matsuda H. Bioactive Saponins and Glycosides. XIII. Horse Chestnut. (3): Quantitative Analysis of Escins Ia, Ib, IIa and IIb by Means of High Performance Liquid Chromatography. *Yakugaku Zasshi* 1999, **119**, 81-87 [JAPANESE/English summary].
15. Guillaume M and Padioleau F. Veinotonic Effect, Vascular Protection, Antiinflammatory and Free Radical Scavenging Properties of Horse Chestnut Extract. *Arzneim.-Forsch./Drug Res.* 1994, **44**, 25-35.

16. Izzo AA, Capasso R, Senatore F, Seccia S and Morrica P. Spasmolytic Activity of Medicinal Plants Used for the Treatment of Disorders Involving Smooth Muscles. *Phytotherapy Res.* 1996, **10**, S107-S108.
17. Matsuda H, Li Y, Murakami T, Ninomiya K, Yamahara J and Yoshikawa M. Effects of Escins Ia, Ib, IIa and IIb from Horse Chestnut, the Seeds of *Aesculus hippocastanum* L., on Acute Inflammation in Animals. *Biol. Pharm. Bull.* 1997, **20**, 1092-1095.
18. Matsuda H, Li Y, Murakami T, Ninomiya K, Araki N, Yoshikawa M and Yamahara J. Antiinflammatory effects of escins Ia, Ib, IIa and IIb from horse chestnut, the seeds of *Aesculus hippocastanum* L. *Bioorg. Med. Chem. Lett.* 1997, **7**, 1611-1616.
19. Girerd RJ, Di Pasquale G, Steinetz BG, Beach VL and Pearl W. The anti-edema properties of aescin. *Arch. Int. Pharmacodyn.* 1961, **133**, 127-137.
20. Damas P, Volon G, Damas J and Lecomte J. Sur l'action antioedème de l'escine [The anti-oedematous action of aescin]. *Bull. Soc. Roy. Sci. Liège* 1976, **45**, 436-442 [FRENCH/English summary].
21. Pauschinger P, Wörz E and Zwerger E. Die Messung des Filtrationskoeffizienten am menschlichen Unterschenkel und seine pharmakologische Beeinflussung [Measurement of filtration coefficients in the human lower leg and their pharmacological influence]. *Med. Welt* 1981, **32**, 1953-1955 [GERMAN].
22. Bisler H, Pfeifer R, Klüken N and Pauschinger P. Effect of horse-chestnut seed extract on transcapillary filtration in chronic venous insufficiency. *Dtsch. med. Wschr.* 1986, **111**, 1321-1329 [GERMAN/English summary].
23. Nehring U. Zum Nachweis der Wirksamkeit von Roßkastanienextrakt auf den Venentonus nach oraler Applikation [Evidence of the effectiveness of horse-chestnut seed extract on venous tone after oral administration]. *Med. Welt* 1966, **17**, 1662-1665 [GERMAN].
24. Ehringer H. Zum venentonisierenden Prinzip des Roßkastanienextraktes. Wirkung von reinem Roßkastanienextrakt und von Aescin auf Venenkapazität, Venentonus und Durchblutung der Extremitäten [The venotonic principle of horse-chestnut seed extracts. Effect of pure horse-chestnut seed extract and of aescin on venous capacity, venous tone and circulation in the extremities]. *Med. Welt* 1968, **19**, 1781-1785 [GERMAN].
25. Kreysel HW, Nissen HP and Enghofer E. Erhöhte Serumaktivitäten lysosomaler Enzyme bei Varikosis. Beeinflussung durch einen Roßkastaniensamenextrakt [Elevated serum activity of lysosomal enzymes in varicosis. Influence of a horse-chestnut seed extract]. *Therapiewoche* 1983, **33**, 1098-1104 [GERMAN/English summary].
26. Kreysel HW, Nissen HP and Enghofer E. A possible role of lysosomal enzymes in the pathogenesis of varicosis and the reduction in their serum activity by Venostasin®. *VASA* 1983, **4**, 377-382.
27. Klemm J. Strömungsgeschwindigkeit von Blut in varikösen Venen der unteren Extremitäten. Einfluss eines Venentherapeutikums (Venostasin®) [Flow velocity of blood in varicose veins of the lower extremities. Influence of a venous remedy (Venostasin®)]. *Münch. med. Wschr.* 1982, **124**, 579-582 [GERMAN/English summary].
28. Loew D, Schrödter A, Schwankl W and März RW. Measurement of the Bioavailablity of Aescin-Containing Extracts. *Methods Findings Exp. Clin. Pharmacol.* 2000, **22**, 537-542.
29. Kunz K, Lorkowski G, Petersen G, Samcova E, Schaffler K and Wauschkuhn CH. Bioavailability of Escin after Administration of Two Oral Formulations Containing Aesculus Extract. *Arzneim.-Forsch./Drug Res.* 1998, **48**, 822-825.
30. Blaschek W. Rosskastaniensamen-Extrakte (RKSE) bei chronisch venöser Insuffizienz (CVI) [Horse-chestnut seed extracts (HCSE) for chronic venous insufficiency (CVI)]. *Z. Phytotherapie* 2004, **25**, 21-30 [GERMAN/English summary].
31. European Scientific Cooperative on Phytotherapy. Hippocastani semen - Horse-chestnut Seed. In: *ESCOP Monographs - The Scientific Foundation for Herbal Medicinal Products, 2nd ed.* Stuttgart-New York: Thieme; Exeter, UK: ESCOP, 2003:248-256.
32. Pittler MH and Ernst E. Horse chestnut seed extract for chronic venous insufficiency. *Cochrane Database Syst. Rev.* 2004, (2), CD003230.
33. Rudofsky G, Neiß A, Otto K and Seibel K. Ödemprotektive Wirkung und klinische Wirksamkeit von Roßkastaniensamenextrakt im Doppelblindversuch [Oedema-protective action and clinical efficacy of horse-chestnut seed extract in a double-blind study]. *Phlebol. Proktol.* 1986, **15**, 47-54 [GERMAN/English summary].
34. Steiner M and Hillemanns HG. Untersuchung zur ödemprotektiven Wirkung eines Venentherapeutikums [Investigation of the oedema-protective action of a venous remedy]. *Münch. med. Wschr.* 1986, **128**, 551-552 [GERMAN/English summary].
35. Steiner M and Hillemanns HG. Venostasin retard in the management of venous problems during pregnancy. *Phlebology* 1990, **5**, 41-44.
36. Diehm C, Vollbrecht D, Amendt K, Comberg HU. Medical edema protection - clinical benefit in patients with chronic deep vein incompetence. A placebo controlled double blind study. *VASA* 1992, **21**, 188-192.
37. Diehm C, Trampisch HJ, Lange S and Schmidt C. Comparison of leg compression stocking and oral horse-chestnut seed extract therapy in patients with chronic venous insufficiency. *Lancet* 1996, **347**, 292-294.
38. Neiss A and Böhm C. Zum Wirksamkeitsnachweis von Roßkastaniensamenextrakt beim varikösen Symptomenkomplex [Evidence for the effectiveness of horse-chestnut seed extract in the varicose symptom complex]. *Münch. med. Wschr.* 1976, **118**, 213-216 [GERMAN].
39. Friederich HC, Vogelsberg H and Neiss A. Ein Beitrag zur Bewertung von intern wirksamen Venenpharmaka [A contribution to the evaluation of internally active venous remedies]. *Z. Hautkr.* 1978, **53**, 369-374 [GERMAN].
40. Pilz E. Ödeme bei Venenerkrankungen [Oedemas in venous disorders]. *Med. Welt.* 1990, **41**, 1143-1144 [GERMAN/English summary].
41. Rehn D, Unkauf M, Klein P, Jost V and Lücker PW. Comparative Clinical Efficacy and Tolerability of Oxerutins and Horse Chestnut Extract in Patients with Chronic Venous Insufficiency. *Arzneim.-Forsch./Drug Res.* 1996, **46**, 483-487.
42. Siebert U, Brach M, Sroczynski G and Überla K. Efficacy, routine effectiveness and safety of horsechestnut seed extract in the treatment of chronic venous insufficiency. A meta-analysis of randomized controlled trials and large observational studies. *Internat. Angiol.* 2002, **21**, 305-315.
43. Hippocastani semen (Roßkastaniensamen). German Commission E Monograph published in Bundesanzeiger No. 71 of 15 April 1994.
44. Marronnier d'Inde. In: *Médicaments à base de plantes.* ISBN 2-911473-02-7. Saint-Denis Cedex, France: Agence du Médicament, 1998.
45. Mills S and Bone K. Horsechestnut seed (*Aesculus hippocastanum* L.) In: *Principles and Practice of Phytotherapy. Modern Herbal Medicine.* ISBN 0-443-06016-9. Edinburgh-London-New York: Churchill Livingstone, 2000:448-455.
46. Sirtori CR. Aescin: pharmacology, pharmacokinetics and therapeutic profile. *Pharmacol. Res.* 2001, **44**, 183-193.
47. Schimmer O, Krüger A, Paulini H and Haefele F. An evaluation of 55 commercial plant extracts in the Ames mutagenicity test. *Pharmazie* 1994, **49**, 448-451.
48. Liehn HD, Franco PA, Hampel H and Hofrichter G. A toxicological study of extractum Hippocastani semen (EHS). *Panminerva Med* 1972, **14**, 84-91.
49. Horse-chestnut (Aesculus). In: UK Statutory Instrument 1994 No. 2410. The Medicines (Products Other Than Veterinary Drugs) (General Sale List) Amendment Order 1994. Schedule 1, Table B (External use only).

REGULATORY GUIDELINES FROM OTHER EU COUNTRIES

FRANCE

Médicaments à base de plantes [44]: Marronnier d'Inde, graine = marron.

Therapeutic indications accepted

Oral and/or topical use
Traditionally used: in the symptomatic treatment of functional disorders of cutaneous capillary fragility, such as ecchymoses or petechiae; in subjective manifestations of venous insufficiency, such as 'heavy legs'; and in haemorrhoidal symptomatology.

GERMANY

Commission E monograph [43]: Hippocastani semen (Roßkastaniensamen).

Composition of the drug
A dry extract made from horse-chestnut seed, *Aesculus hippocastanum* L. [Fam. Hippocastanaceae], adjusted to a triterpene glycoside content of 16-20% (calculated as anhydrous aescin).

Pharmacological properties, pharmacokinetics, toxicology
A brief summary of pharmacological findings and toxicological data in the monograph is omitted here.

Uses
Treatment of complaints associated with pathological conditions of leg veins (chronic venous insufficiency), such as pain and feeling of heaviness in the legs, nocturnal cramp in the calf, itching and swelling of the legs.
Note: Other non-invasive measures prescribed by a physician, such as bandaging of the legs, wearing of compression stockings or cold water treatments, should be observed in all cases.

Contraindications
None known.

Side effects
In isolated cases, itching, nausea, vomiting or other gastrointestinal complaints.

Special precautions for use
None.

Use during pregnancy and lactation
No restriction known.

Interactions with other drugs
None known.

Dosage
Daily dose: 100 mg of aescin corresponding to 2 × 250-312.5 mg of extract in a delayed release dosage form.

Overdosage
Nothing known.

Special warnings
None

Effects on ability to drive and operate machines
None.

HYDRANGEA

Hydrangeaceae

Hydrangeae arborescentis rhizoma

Synonyms: Wild Hydrangea, Seven Barks.

Definition
Hydrangea consists of the dried rhizomes and roots of *Hydrangea arborescens* L.

Found throughout the eastern USA growing on rocky banks along rivers and streams, *Hydrangea arborescens* is a shrub 5-10 feet high with large clusters of white flowers [1].

The more familiar cultivated hydrangeas are usually varieties of *H. macrophylla* Seringe (syn. *H. hortensia*), a species indigenous to the Far East; the leaves and twigs of one variety are official in the Pharmacopoeia of Japan.

Although considerable phytochemical and pharmacological investigation has been carried out on *H. macrophylla* leaf, very little scientific research has been published on the rhizome/root of *Hydrangea arborescens*.

CONSTITUENTS

No recent data are available and few constituents are known except in the most general terms. Starch, sugars, saponins, resin, fixed oil and volatile oil have been reported present, as well as a "characteristic glucoside, hydrangin" (isolated in 1887), but no tannin [1].

The nature of the "hydrangin" in hydrangea is not clear [2]. Some texts state that it is a cyanogenic glycoside present at about 1.0% [3]. However, "hydrangin" is also a synonym for the coumarin umbelliferone [4], which has been found in *Hydrangea arborescens* leaf [5] but is not a glycoside.

PHARMACOLOGY

No pharmacological or clinical data are available.

THERAPEUTICS

Actions
Diuretic [6,7] and antilithic [6].

Indications
None adequately substantiated by pharmacological or clinical studies.

Uses based on experience or tradition
Treatment of urinary calculi [1,6-8]; reported to relieve pain caused by the presence and passage of urinary calculi [8] - it is thought to encourage their expulsion and to help dissolve those that remain [9].

Other genito-urinary complaints such as cystitis, urethritis and prostatitis [6,9].

Contraindications
Avoid during pregnancy [10].

Side effects
None known.

Interactions with other drugs
None known.

Dosage
Three times daily: dried rhizome and root, 2-4 g or by decoction; liquid extract 1:1 in 25% alcohol, 2-4 ml; tincture 1:5 in 45% alcohol, 2-10 ml [6].

SAFETY

Hydrangea has been classified by the United States FDA as a herb of undefined safety [10]. Since the presence of a cyanogenic glycoside is suspected, a degree of caution is necessary; hydrangea is not recommended for prolonged use and dosage recommendations should not be exceeded [3].

An overdose is said to cause vertigo and a feeling of tightness of the chest [1].

REGULATORY STATUS

Medicines

UK	Accepted for general sale, internal or external use [11].
France	Not listed in *Médicaments à base de plantes* [12].
Germany	No Commission E monograph published.

Food
Not used in foods.

REFERENCES

Current Pharmacopoeial Monographs

BHP	Hydrangea

Literature References

1. Wood HC and LaWall CH, editors. Hydrangea N.F. In: *United States Dispensatory, Centennial (22nd) Edition.* Philadelphia-London: JB Lippincott Company, 1937:532-533.
2. Leung AY. Hydrangea. In: *Encyclopedia of Common Natural Ingredients Used in Food, Drugs and Cosmetics.* ISBN 0-471-04954-9. New York-Chichester: John Wiley, 1980:201-202.
3. McGuffin M, Hobbs C, Upton R and Goldberg A, editors. *Hydrangea arborescens* L. In: American Herbal Products Association's *Botanical Safety Handbook.* Boca Raton-Boston-London: CRC Press, 1997:62.
4. Budavari S, editor. Hydrangea. In: *The Merck Index - An Encyclopedia of Chemicals, Drugs and Biologicals, 12th ed.* Whitehouse Station, NJ: Merck & Co., 1996.
5. Billek G and Kindl H. Über die phenolischen Inhaltsstoffe der Familie Saxifragaceae [Phenolic constituents of the Saxifragaceae family]. *Monatsh. Chem* 1962, **93**, 85-98 [GERMAN].
6. Hydrangea. In: *British Herbal Pharmacopoeia 1983.* ISBN 0-903032-07-9. Bournemouth: British Herbal Medicine Association, 1983.
7. Grieve M (edited by Leyel CF). Hydrangea. In: *A Modern Herbal* (first published 1931; revised 1973). ISBN 1-85501-249-9. London: Tiger Books International, 1994:424-425.
8. Ellingwood F. Hydrangea - *Hydrangea arborescens.* In: *A Systematic Treatise on Materia Medica and Therapeutics.* Chicago: Chicago Medical Press, 1900:538-539.
9. Chevallier A. Wild Hydrangea - *Hydrangea arborescens.* In: *Encyclopedia of Medicinal Plants, 2nd ed.* ISBN 0-7513-1209-6. London-New York: Dorling Kindersley, 2001:220.
10. Barnes J, Anderson LA and Phillipson JD. Hydrangea. In: *Herbal Medicines - A guide for healthcare professionals, 2nd ed.* ISBN 0-85369-474-5. London-Chicago: Pharmaceutical Press, 2002:302.
11. Hydrangea. In: UK Statutory Instrument 1994 No. 2410. The Medicines (Products Other Than Veterinary Drugs) (General Sale List) Amendment Order 1994. Schedule 1, Table A.
12. *Médicaments à base de plantes.* ISBN 2-911473-02-7. Saint-Denis Cedex, France: Agence du Médicament, 1998.

HYSSOP

Labiatae

Hyssopi herba

Definition
Hyssop consists of the dried leaves and flowering tops of *Hyssopus officinalis* L.

CONSTITUENTS

☐ ***Essential oil***, usually 0.5-1% from dried herb [1], although yields ranging from 0.1% from fresh leaves [2] to 4.5% from dried herb [3] have been reported. The composition is extremely varied depending on the source and variety or chemotype.

Essential oil distilled from *Hyssopus officinalis* from Italy (Piedmont) contained isopinocamphone (43.3%), limonene (12.2%), β-pinene (11.1%) and pinocamphone (4.4%) [4]. Isopinocamphone was also predominant in commercial oil from Hungary: isopinocamphone (32.6%), β-pinene (22.9%), pinocamphone (12.2%) [5]. Pinocamphone, rather than isopinocamphone, has been reported as predominant in oils from Canada and India [6], and pinocamphone, isopinocamphone or pinocarvone in different phenotypes grown in Finland [7].

Some hyssop essential oils vary even more in composition. The principal components of oil from *Hyssopus officinalis* grown in Spain were 1,8-cineole (52.9%) and β-pinene (16.8%), with only small amounts of isopinocamphone (less than 3%) and pinocamphone (0.15%) [8]. Oil from Montenegro contained methyleugenol (38.3%), limonene (37.4%) and β-pinene (9.6%) [1].

Oil distilled from *Hyssopus officinalis* L. var. *decumbens* (Jordan et Fourr.) Briq. grown in France, which has morphological differences from *H. officinalis* L., contained linalool (51.7%), 1,8-cineole (12.3%) and limonene (5.1%) [4].

Thus no compound is consistently predominant among the more than 50 components, mainly terpenes, identified [1] in hyssop essential oils. None of the results summarized above fully meet the ISO 9841 standard (1991) for hyssop oil, which specifies 34.5-50% of isopinocamphone, 13.5-23% of β-pinene and 5.5-17.5% of pinocamphone [4].

☐ ***Flavonoids***, principally the flavone glycoside diosmin (3.2% in mature dried leaves, 4% in sepals) [9]. Vicenin-2 is also present [10] but, in contrast to earlier reports, hesperidin was not found in a recent investigation [9].

☐ ***Phenylpropanoids*** including rosmarinic acid (0.5%) [11-13], caffeic acid [13] and isoferulyl-D-glucose ester (0.08% in leaves) [9]. The total content of hydroxycinnamic acid derivatives has been determined as 2.2% of dry weight [11,12].

☐ ***Triterpenes*** Ursolic acid (0.5%) and oleanolic acid (0.3%) [14].

☐ ***Other constituents*** include rosmanol-9-ethyl ether [15], inositol, polysaccharides [16], the diterpene marrubiin and tannins (5-8%) [17].

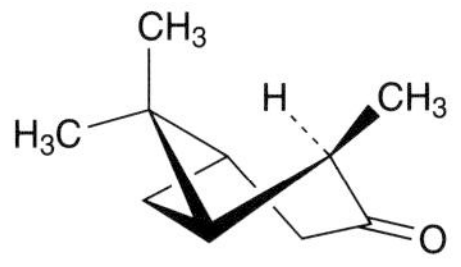

Isopinocamphone

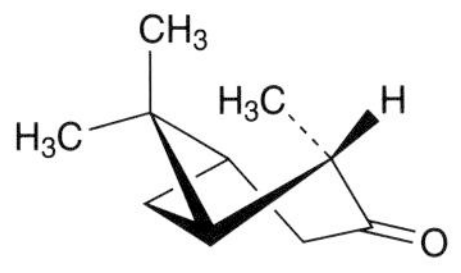

Pinocamphone

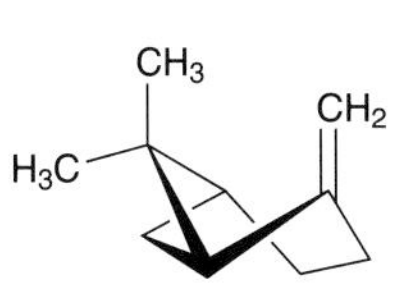

β-Pinene

Published Assay Methods
Essential oil components by GC and GC-MS [1,2,4,7]. Diosmin by HPLC [9].

PHARMACOLOGY

In vitro

Spasmolytic activity
In tests on medicinal plants traditionally used in respiratory disorders, a 67%-methanolic dry extract of hyssop at 0.56 mg/ml produced relaxation of up to 20% (relative to the maximum relaxation produced by terbutaline at 2.2 μmol/litre) against carbachol-induced contractions of isolated guinea pig trachea [18].

Essential oil from French-grown *Hyssopus officinalis* var. *decumbens*, of which the three major components were linalool (49%), 1,8-cineole (14.9%) and limonene (5.0%), concentration-

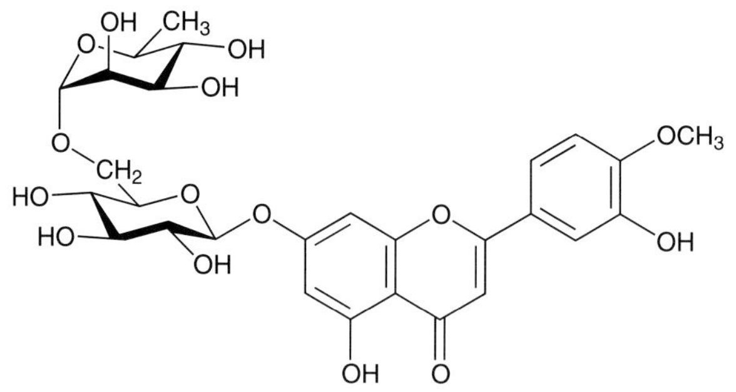

Diosmin

dependently inhibited acetylcholine- and barium chloride-induced contractions of isolated guinea pig ileum with IC_{50} values of 37 µg/ml and 60 µg/ml respectively. When tested as pure compounds, linalool also inhibited the contractions with IC_{50} values of 10 µg/ml and 51 µg/ml respectively, while 1,8-cineole and limonene had a weak spasmogenic action [19].

Antioxidant activity
Essential oil and various extract fractions from hyssop did not show useful antioxidant activity in comparison with sage and thyme [3]. In antioxidant activity tests using the reagent DPPH, the EC_{50} for hyssop was 60 µg/ml compared to 39 µg/ml for sage and 35 µg/ml for thyme [11]. However, rosmanol-9-ethyl ether isolated from hyssop (and sage) had antioxidant activity greater than that of butylated hydroxytoluene, an antioxidant used in the food industry [15].

Antimicrobial activity
In antimicrobial screening tests, essential oil from Italian *Hyssopus officinalis* showed generally negligible antibacterial activity, except against *Staphylococcus aureus*. French-grown *Hyssopus officinalis* var. *decumbens* showed broader activity, particularly against *Enterococcus faecalis* and *Escherichia coli*, and this appeared to be due to its linalool content [4]. Oils of both types were active against *Candida* yeasts [4], as was a chloroform extract from Spanish hyssop [20].

Methanolic and aqueous extracts from hyssop showed strong antiviral activity against HIV-1, and an unidentified polysaccharide (MAR-10) isolated from hyssop leaf exhibited strong anti-HIV-1 activity in several assay systems, with no toxic or inhibitory effects on lymphocyte proportions or functions [16]. An aqueous extract from hyssop also exhibited activity against *Herpes simplex* virus, attributed to unidentified tannins; however, it was less potent than extracts of *Melissa officinalis* [21].

In vivo
Sedative properties of linalool, the predominant component of essential oil from *Hyssopus officinalis* L. var. *decumbens*, have been demonstrated (see the Coriander monograph) [22].

CLINICAL STUDIES

None published on mono-preparations of hyssop.

THERAPEUTICS

Actions
Expectorant, carminative [5,23-25], spasmolytic [18,19], pectoral [25].

Also said to be diaphoretic [23-25] and sedative [23].

Indications
None adequately substantiated by pharmacological or clinical studies.

Uses based on experience or tradition
Bronchitis [23,24,26,27], common colds [23,24], chronic nasal catarrh [23,25,27], coughs, asthma; as a gargle for sore throat or hoarseness [27].
Topical use: Congested nose due to colds [26].

Contraindications
Pregnancy.

Side effects
None known at therapeutic dose levels.

Interactions with other drugs
None known.

Dosage
Adults, three times daily: dried herb, usually in infusion, 2-4 g; liquid extract 1:1 in 25% ethanol, 2-4 ml [23]; tincture 1:5 in 45% alcohol, 5-10 ml.

Excessive doses and prolonged use should be avoided (see Safety section).

SAFETY

Between 1978 and 1981 researchers at the Poison Control Centre in Marseille highlighted 4 cases of intoxication characterized by clonic or tonicoclonic convulsions after oral ingestion of relatively large amounts of hyssop essential oil for therapeutic purposes; for example, half a teaspoonful administered to an asthmatic 6-year-old girl, 30 drops taken by an 18 year-old girl for a common cold [28,29]. Similar effects were produced in dogs and guinea pigs [28]. Studies in rats using electrocorticography showed that the convulsant action of hyssop oil was of central nervous system origin and that pinocamphone induced the same electrocortical seizures associated with myoclonic activities [29]. When administered intraperitoneally, hyssop oil produced convulsant effect in rats at 0.13 g/kg body weight and was lethal at doses above 1.25 g/kg; cumulative effects of lower doses were also demonstrated. The lethal intraperitoneal dose of pinocamphone in rats was found to be 0.05 ml/kg. Although not specifically tested, isopinocamphone was thought to have similar properties [29,30].

An *in vitro* study by the same researchers demonstrated that hyssop essential oil, and a mixture of pinocamphone and isopinocamphone, concentration-dependently inhibited the respiration (consumption of oxygen) of slices of rat cerebral cortex, an indication that the epileptogenic properties could be due to metabolic inhibition [31].

Considerable caution should therefore be exercised with hyssop essential oil and it should be used only under professional supervision. Therapeutic doses of dried herb and preparations from it appear to present no toxicological hazard. Selection of herb with a low content of isopinocamphone and pinocamphone, and also of methyleugenol due to its carcinogenic potential [32], would be prudent.

REGULATORY STATUS

Medicines

UK	Accepted for general sale, internal or external use [33].
France	Accepted for specified indications [26].
Germany	Commission E monograph published: not approved for any indications [34].

Food

USA	Generally recognized as safe (herb, 21 CFR 182.10; essential oil and extracts, 182.20) [35].
Council of Europe	Permitted as flavouring, category N2 [36].

REFERENCES

Current Pharmacopoeial Monographs

Ph. Fr.	Hysope
BHP	Hyssop

Literature References

1. Gorunovic MS, Bogavac PM, Chalchat JC and Chabard JL. Essential Oil of *Hyssopus officinalis* L., Lamiaceae, of Montenegro Origin. *J. Essent. Oil. Res.* 1995, **7**, 39-43.
2. Schulz G and Stahl-Biskup E. Essential Oils and Glycosidic Bound Volatiles from Leaves, Stems, Flowers and Roots of *Hyssopus officinalis* L. (Lamiaceae). *Flavour Fragrance J.* 1991, **6**, 69-73.
3. Dapkevicius A, Venskutonis R, van Beek TA and Linssen JPH. Antioxidant Activity of Extracts Obtained by Different Isolation Procedures from some Aromatic Herbs Grown in Lithuania. *J. Sci. Food Agric.* 1998, **77**, 140-146.
4. Mazzanti G, Battinelli L and Salvatore G. Antimicrobial properties of the linalol-rich essential oil of *Hyssopus officinalis* L. var. *decumbens* (Lamiaceae). *Flavour Fragrance J.* 1998, **13**, 289-294.
5. Joulain D. Contribution à l'étude de la composition chimique de l'huile essentielle d'hysope [Contribution to the study of the chemical composition of essential oil of hyssop] (*Hyssopus officinalis* Linnaeus). *Rivista Ital. Essenze Profumi P.O.S.* 1976, **58**, 479-485 [FRENCH].
6. Lawrence BM. Chemical components of Labiatae oils and their exploitation. In: Harley RM and Reynolds T, editors. *Advances in Labiate Science*. Kew: Royal Botanic Gardens, 1992:399-436.
7. Kerrola K, Galambosi B and Kallio H. Volatile Components and Odor Intensity of Four Phenotypes of Hyssop (*Hyssopus officinalis*). *J. Agric. Food Chem.* 1994, **42**, 776-781.
8. García Vallejo MC, Guijarro Herraiz J, Pérez-Alonso MJ and Velasco-Negueruela A. Volatile Oil of *Hyssopus officinalis* L. from Spain. *J. Essent. Oil. Res.* 1995, **7**, 567-568.
9. Marin FR, Ortuño A, Benavente-García O and Del Río JA. Distribution of Flavone Glycoside Diosmin in *Hyssopus officinalis* Plants: Changes During Growth. *Planta Medica* 1998, **64**, 181-182.
10. Husain SZ and Markham KR. The glycoflavone vicenin-2 and its distribution in related genera within the Labiatae. *Phytochemistry* 1981, **20**, 1171-1173.
11. Lamaison JL, Petitjean-Freytet C, Duband F and Carnat AP. Rosmarinic acid content and antioxidant activity in French Lamiaceae. *Fitoterapia* 1991, **62**, 166-171.
12. Lamaison JL, Petitjean-Freytet C and Carnat AP. Rosmarinic acid, total hydroxycinnamic derivative contents and antioxidant activity of medicinal Apiaceae, Boraginaceae and Lamiaceae. *Ann. Pharm. Fr.* 1990, **48**, 103-108 [FRENCH/English summary].
13. Varga E, Hadjú Z, Veres K, Máthé I, Németh É, Pluhár Z and Bernáth J. Investigation of production biological and chemical variation of *Hyssopus officinalis* L. *Acta Pharm. Hung.* 1998, **68**, 183-188 [HUNGARIAN/English summary].

14. Brieskorn CH, Eberhardt KH and Briner M. Biogenetische Zusammenhänge zwischen Oxytriterpensäuren und ätherischem Öl bei einigen pharmazeutisch wichtigen Labiaten [Biogenetic relationships between oxytriterpene acids and essential oil in some pharmaceutically important Labiatae]. *Arch. Pharm. (Weinheim)* 1953, **286**, 501-506 [GERMAN].
15. Djarmati Z, Jankov RM, Schwirtlich E, Djulinac B and Djordjevic A. High Antioxidant Activity of Extracts Obtained from Sage by Supercritical CO_2 Extraction. *JAOCS* 1991, **68**, 731-734.
16. Gollapudi S, Sharma HA, Aggarwal S, Byers LD, Ensley HE and Gupta S. Isolation of a previously unidentified polysaccharide (MAR-10) from *Hyssopus officinalis* that exhibits strong activity against human immunodeficiency virus type 1. *Biochem. Biophys. Res. Commun.* 1995, **210**, 145-151.
17. Leung AY and Foster S. Hyssop. In: *Encyclopedia of Common Natural Ingredients Used in Food, Drugs and Cosmetics.* ISBN 0-471-50826-8. New York-Chichester: John Wiley, 1996: 312-314.
18. Bergendorff O, Franzén C, Jeppsson A-B, Sterner O and Waldeck B. Screening of some European medicinal plants for spasmolytic activity on isolated guinea-pig trachea. *Internat. J. Pharmacognosy* 1995, **33**, 356-358.
19. Mazzanti G, Lu M and Salvatore G. Spasmolytic Action of the Essential Oil from *Hyssopus officinalis* L. var. *decumbens* and its Major Components. *Phytotherapy Res.* 1998, **12** (Suppl. 1), S92-S94.
20. Recio MC, Ríos JL and Villar A. Antimicrobial Activity of Selected Plants Employed in the Spanish Mediterranean Area. Part II. *Phytotherapy Res.* 1989, **3**, 77-80.
21. Herrmann EC and Kucera LS. Antiviral Substances in Plants of the Mint Family (Labiatae). III. Peppermint (*Mentha piperita*) and other Mint Plants. *Proc. Soc. Exptl. Biol. Med.* 1967, **124**, 874-878.
22. Elisabetsky E, Coelho de Souza GP, Dos Santos MAC, Siquieira IR and Amador TA. Sedative properties of linalool. *Fitoterapia* 1995, **66**, 407-414.
23. Hyssopus. In: *British Herbal Pharmacopoeia 1983.* ISBN 0-903032-07-4. Bournemouth: British Herbal Medicine Association, 1983.
24. Ody P. Hyssop. In: *The Complete Guide Medicinal Herbal.* ISBN 0-7513-3005-1. London-New York: Dorling Kindersley, 2000:76.
25. Grieve M (edited by Leyel CF). Hyssop. In: *A Modern Herbal* (first published 1931; revised 1973). ISBN 1-85501-249-9. London: Tiger Books International, 1994:426.
26. Hysope. In: *Médicaments à base de plantes.* ISBN 2-911473-02-7. Saint-Denis Cedex, France: Agence du Médicament, 1998.
27. Winter C. Hyssopus. In: Blaschek W, Hänsel R, Keller K, Reichling J, Rimpler H and Schneider G, editors. *Hagers Handbuch der Pharmazeutischen Praxis, 5th ed. Supplement Volume 2: Drogen A-K.* ISBN 3-540-61618-7. Berlin-Heidelberg-New York-London: Springer, 1998:867-873 [GERMAN].
28. Arditti J, Jean Ph, Faizende J, Bernard J, Moisan D and Jouglard J. Trois observations d'intoxication par des essences végétales convulsivantes [Three observations of intoxication by convulsant essential oils]. *Ann. Méd. Nancy* 1978, **17**, 371-374 [French/English summary].
29. Millet Y, Jouglard J, Steinmetz MD, Tognetti P, Joanny P and Arditti J. Toxicity of Some Essential Plant Oils. Clinical and Experimental Study. *Clin. Toxicol.* 1981, **18**, 1485-1498.
30. Millet Y, Tognetti P, Lavaire-Pierlovisi M, Steinmetz M-D, Arditti J and Jouglard J. Experimental study of the toxic convulsant properties of commercial preparations of essences of sage and hyssop. *Rev. E.E.G. Neurophysiol.* 1979, **9**, 12-18 [French/English summary].
31. Steinmetz MD, Joanny P and Millet Y. Action d'huiles essentielles de sauge, thuya, hysope et de certains constituants, sur la respiration de coupes de cortex cérébral in vitro [Action of essential oils of sage, thuja, hyssop and certain constituents on the respiration of slices of cerebral cortex in vitro]. *Plantes Méd. Phytothér.* 1985, **19**, 35-47 [FRENCH/English summary].
32. De Vincenzi M, Silano M, Stacchini P and Scazzocchio B. Constituents of aromatic plants: I. Methyleugenol. *Fitoterapia* 2000, **71**, 216-221.
33. Hyssop. In: UK Statutory Instrument 1984 No. 769. The Medicines (Products Other Than Veterinary Drugs) (General Sale List) Order 1984. Schedule 1, Table A.
34. Hyssopus officinalis (Ysop). German Commission E Monograph published in: Bundesanzeiger No. 162 of 29 August 1992.
35. Hyssop. In sections 182.10 and 182.20 of USA Code of Federal Regulations, Title 21, Food and Drugs, Parts 170 to 199. Revised as of April 1, 2000.
36. Hyssopus officinalis L., herb. In: *Flavouring Substances and Natural Sources of Flavourings, 3rd ed.* ISBN 2-7160-0081-6. Strasbourg: Council of Europe, 1981.

REGULATORY GUIDELINES FROM OTHER EU COUNTRIES

FRANCE

Médicaments à base de plantes [26]: Hysope, feuille, sommité fleurie.

Therapeutic indications accepted

Oral use
Traditionally used in the course of acute benign bronchial affections.

Topical use
Traditionally used in cases of congested nose, from colds.

GERMANY

Commission E monograph [34]: *Hyssopus officinalis* (Ysop): Hyssopi herba (Ysopkraut), Hyssopi aetheroleum (Ysopöl).

Pharmacological properties, pharmacokinetics, toxicology

Hyssop herb: None known.
Hyssop oil causes clonic spasms and tonicoclonic convulsions in rats after intraperitoneal administration at a dosage of 0.13 g/kg body weight.

Clinical data

1. Uses
Preparations from hyssop herb are used for stimulation of the circulation in a natural way, for intestinal catarrhs, for treatment of illnesses of the respiratory tract, colds, chest and lung ailments, for the prevention of frostbite, digestive disorders, intestinal ailments, menstrual complaints, heart problems and eye pains.

Efficacy in the claimed areas of use is not substantiated.

2. Risks
Hyssop herb: None known.
Hyssop oil: Three cases of poisoning have been recorded, in adults after taking 10 and 30 drops of hyssop oil and in a 6-year-old child after 2-3 drops over several days, leading to clonic or tonicoclonic spasms in each case.

Assessment

Since efficacy in the claimed areas of use is not substantiated, therapeutic use cannot be justified.

There are no objections to the use of up to 5% of hyssop herb as a flavour enhancer in tea mixtures.

ICELAND MOSS

Parmeliaceae

Lichen islandicus

Definition
Iceland Moss consists of the dried thalli of *Cetraria islandica* (L.) Acharius *sensu latiore*.

Botanically *Cetraria islandica* is not a moss; it is a lichen, a symbiotic partnership between an alga and a fungus.

CONSTITUENTS

The constituents summarized below relate to *Cetraria islandica* (L.) Ach. from northern Europe. They may not be entirely typical of related varieties which might be implied to fall within the European Pharmacopoeia definition of Iceland moss by the designation *sensu latiore* (s.l.). For example, *Cetraria islandica* var. *polaris* Rassad from Kamchatka and other regions around the Sea of Okhotsk (and possibly Alaska) contains a similar amount of fumarprotocetraric acid, but no protolichesterinic acid [1].

□ ***Lichen acids*** Fumarprotocetraric acid, a β-orcinol depsidone (2.6-11.5%) [1-3], together with protocetraric acid (0.2-0.3%) [3] and, in some samples, a small amount of cetraric acid [1]; and (+)-protolichesterinic acid (0.1-0.5%), an aliphatic α-methylene-γ-lactone [2,4].

□ ***Polysaccharides***, 25-50% [5,6], principally lichenan (lichenin), a cellulose-like, linear β-glucan composed of (1→3) and (1→4)-linked β-D-glucose residues in a ratio of 3:7 [7-10] with a MW of ca. 20-35 kD [11], and isolichenan (isolichenin), a starch-like, linear α-glucan composed of (1→3) and (1→4)-linked α-D-glucose residues in a ratio of about 3:2 [5,10,12] and a MW of ca. 6-8 kD [11].

Other polysacccharides include an α-glucan (denoted as Ci-3) resembling isolichenan and consisting of (1→3) and (1→4)-linked α-D-glucose residues in a ratio of 2:1, but with a much higher degree of polymerization and a MW of ca. 2000 kD [11]; an acidic, branched polysaccharide containing D-glucose and D-glucuronic acid units [13]; and one or more branched galactomannans [14-16].

Yields of 17.4% lichenan, 1.7% isolichenan and 7.6% galactomannan have been achieved from dried crude drug [5].

□ ***Minerals*** In mg/kg dry weight of material from southern Finland: iron 530, magnesium 270, calcium 48, lead 30, arsenic 0.8, cadmium 0.3, mercury 0.07 and other trace elements [17].

□ ***Other constituents*** Small amounts of numerous other compounds have been identified: hydrocarbons (mainly 1,8-heptadecadiene), fatty acids (linoleic, oleic and linolenic acids) [18];

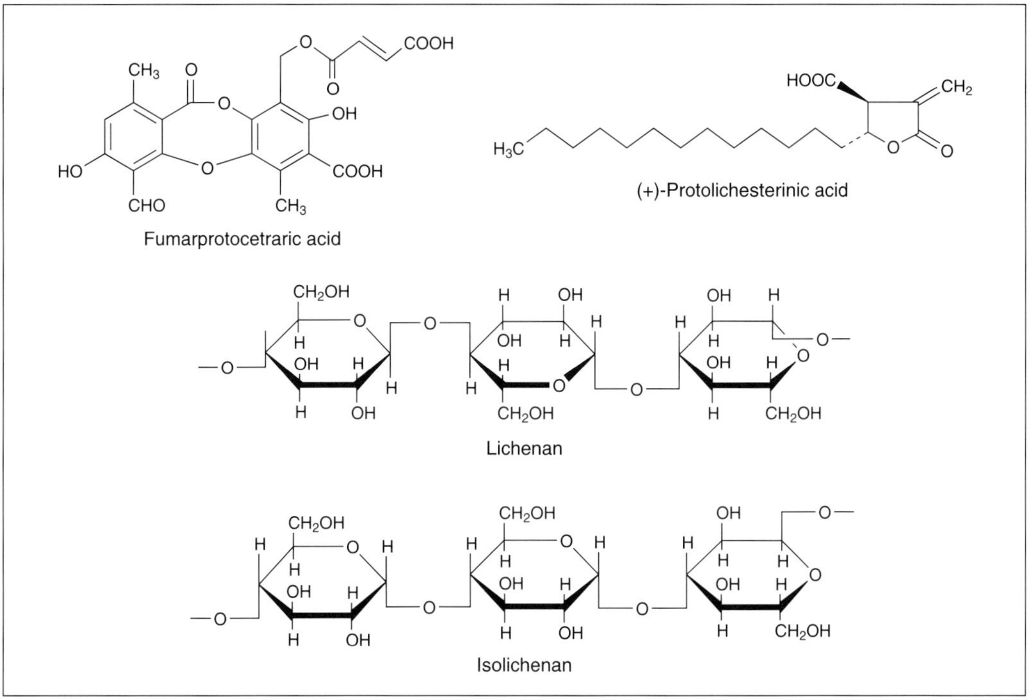

sterols such as ergosterol [18] and ergosterol peroxide [1]; triterpenes (lupeol and α-amyrin), the sesquiterpene lactone bakkenolide A and monoterpenes (carvone, camphor and borneol) [18].

The presence of usnic acid was reported in the 1950s [17], but none has been detected in more recent work [1,19].

Published Assay Methods
Fumarprotocetraric acid and protolichesterinic acid by HPLC [2].

PHARMACOLOGY

In vitro

Polysaccharides
Immunomodulating activity, demonstrated by enhancement of *in vitro* phagocytosis using human granulocytes, was exhibited by two polysaccharides isolated from Iceland moss, an alkali-soluble galactomannan denoted as KI-M-7 (68% relative stimulation at 100 μg/ml, compared to 100% for the positive control) [14,20] and a water-soluble neutral α-D-glucan denoted as Ci-3 (46% relative stimulation at 100 μg/ml) [11,20]. A traditionally-prepared Iceland Moss hot water extract and a polysaccharide fraction from it also showed phagocytic activity [21].

Various polysaccharide fractions [21] and particularly the α-D-glucan Ci-3 [11] produced anti-complementary effects, an indication of potential anti-inflammatory activity [20]; Ci-3 at 100 μg/ml reduced complementary-induced haemolysis by about 80% [11].

In a study of the bioadhesive effects of purified (> 95%) polysaccharides from medicinal plants on porcine buccal membranes, polysaccharides from Iceland moss showed only slight adhesion to epithelial tissue whereas moderate adhesion was observed with polysaccharides from *Althea officinalis* and *Plantago lanceolata* and strong adhesion with polysaccharides from *Fucus vesiculosus* and *Calendula officinalis* [22].

Lichenan exhibited strong antiviral activity in leaves of tobacco plants, reducing the number of necrotic lesions due to local infection with tobacco mosaic virus by ca. 80% at 250 μg/ml and suppressing systemic infection with potato virus Y to the same degree at 1000 μg/ml [23].

Protolichesterinic acid
(+)-Protolichesterinic acid inhibited the enzyme 5-lipoxygenase in porcine leucocytes with an IC_{50} of 20 μM; 5-lipoxygenase is a catalyst in the biosynthesis of leukotrienes, which are potent bronchoconstrictors and are involved in inflammatory processes [4]. Subsequently it was shown that (+)-protolichesterinic acid inhibited leukotriene B_4 biosynthesis in stimulated bovine polymorphonuclear leukocytes ($p<0.05$) with an IC_{50} of 9 μM [24].

Antiproliferative and cytotoxic effects exhibited by protolichesterinic acid may be related to its 5-lipoxygenase inhibitory activity. At an ED_{50} between 1.1 and 24.6 μg/ml protolichesterinic acid caused a significant reduction in DNA synthesis in three malignant human cell lines (T-47D and ZR-75-1 from breast carcinomas and K-562 from erythro-leukaemia); significant cell death occurred in all three cell lines at concentrations above 20 μg/ml. The proliferative response of mitogen-stimulated peripheral blood lymphocytes was also inhibited with a mean ED_{50} of 8.4 μg/ml. In contrast, DNA synthesis in, and proliferation and survival of, normal skin fibroblasts were not affected at doses of up to 20 μg/ml [25].

Protolichesterinic acid has also been shown to be a potent inhibitor of human immunodeficiency virus-1 reverse transcriptase at an IC_{50} of 24 μM [26].

Inhibitory activity of protolichesterinic acid (sodium salt and free form) against 35 strains of *Helicobacter pylori* has been demonstrated, with MICs of 16-64 μg/ml. The MIC_{90} (90% of the strains inhibited) was 32 μg/ml, considerably higher than that of ampicillin (0.125 μg/ml) and erythromycin (0.25 μg/ml) but only twice as high as that of metronidazole (16 μg/ml). *H. pylori* is considered to contribute to the aetiology of gastric and duodenal ulcer and gastritis [27].

In the late 1940s protolichesterinic acid was reported to be active against *Mycobacterium tuberculosis* [28]. However, in a recent study of antimycobacterial activity against *Mycobacterium aurium*, a non-pathogenic organism with a similar sensitivity profile to *M. tuberculosis*, the MIC of protolichesterinic acid was 250 μg/ml (compared to 0.25 for streptomycin), which did not merit further investigation [29].

In vivo
A traditionally-prepared hot water extract [21] and an alkali-soluble galactomannan isolated from Iceland moss [14] exhibited significant immunostimulating activity in the *in vivo* carbon clearance assay in mice, markedly increasing the rate of reticuloendothelial phagocytosis. The rate of carbon elimination was stimulated by a mean ration of 1.9 compared to controls.

In the evaluation of substances with potential for improvement of cognitive impairment, such as senile amnesia, Japanese researchers noted that extracts of thallophytic plants, including lichens, were highly regarded in Chinese traditional medicine for improvement of senile cognition as long ago as the Tang dynasty (618-977 AD). Their recent research in rodents has shown that isolichenan, isolated from Iceland moss and orally administered, could be useful in this respect. Isolichenan had no effect on the cognitive performance of healthy rats or mice. However, oral isolichenan at 100 mg/kg significantly repaired the effect of β-amyloid peptide-induced memory impairment ($p<0.05$) in rats subjected to the Morris water maze test, which depends heavily on intact hippocampal function. Similarly, when the learning ability of mice was impaired by pretreatment with 30% ethanol, oral isolichenan significantly improved memory acquisition in passive-avoidance tests ($p<0.01$ at 100 mg in step-through tests, 400 mg/kg in step-down tests) [30,31].

CLINICAL STUDIES

In a comparative, double-blind, randomized study, three parallel groups of patients with inflammation and dryness of the oral cavity due to breathing only through the mouth after nasal surgery were treated daily for 5 days, commencing on the day after surgery, with 10 pastilles each containing: 0.048 g (group 1, n = 23) or 0.3 g (group 2, n = 18) or 0.5 g (group 3, n = 22) of Iceland moss; there was no placebo group on ethical grounds. From assessments on a 0-3 scale of coating, dryness and inflammation of the mucosa, conspicuousness of lymph nodes, tongue coating and symptoms such as hoarseness and sore throat, all three groups showed a similar and substantial degree of improvement over the 5-day treatment; the lowest dose, 10 × 0.048 g or ca. 0.5 g daily, therefore appeared to be adequate. All three preparations were well tolerated [32].

In an open study 100 patients with pharyngitis, laryngitis or acute or chronic bronchial catarrh were treated with pastilles containing 160 mg of an aqueous extract of Iceland moss. 1-2 pastilles were sucked slowly at 2-3 hour intervals for periods of 4 days to 3 weeks depending on the condition. The results were assessed as positive in 86 cases and no side effects were reported [33].

THERAPEUTICS

Actions
Demulcent [34-36] and antitussive [35]; immunomodulatory [20,21], bitter tonic [6,35,37].

In aqueous preparations the polysaccharides in Iceland moss have mucilaginous effects and are thought to form thin polysaccharide layers which shield irritated mucus membranes in the upper respiratory tract, leading to rehydration, desensitisation of peripheroreceptors and decrease of local inflammation, and therefore a reduction of dry coughing [22].

Indications
None adequately substantiated by pharmacological or clinical studies.

Uses based on experience or tradition
Irritation or inflammation of the oral and pharyngeal mucosa and associated dry coughs [32,33,38]; hoarseness and sore throat [11,32], bronchitis [34, 39], bronchial asthma [4,11], respiratory catarrh [33-36,39]; digestive complaints [34-36], gastritis [4] and loss of appetite [6,38].

Has also been used in the treatment of gastric and duodenal ulcer [27,29], irritable bowel syndrome [35], cachexia [34] and tumours [11].

In earlier days, used as a galactagogue [40].

Contraindications
None known.

Side effects
None known.

Interactions with other drugs
None known.

Dosage
Adult dose Three or four times daily: 1-2 g of dried lichen as a decoction or infusion [6,34,37,38]; tincture (1:5 in 40% alcohol), 1-1.5 ml [34]; equivalent preparations.

Daily dosages of 12 g or more in infusions have also been recommended [35,39].

In the form of pastilles to be sucked slowly, aqueous extract equivalent to 0.5-3 g of dried lichen per day [32].

The best preparation to use depends on whether demulcent polysaccharide mucilage or bitter lichen acids, or both, are appropriate for the indication. In a cough remedy, the bitter lichen acids may be detrimental to taste and can be minimised by briefly boiling the lichen and discarding the first infusion before preparing a tea or cough syrup. As a tonic bitter, where lichen acids are important, a cold or hot maceration (without boiling), or alternatively an ethanolic preparation, minimises the mucilage content. If both mucilage and bitter acids are desirable, the lichen should be boiled and then strained [37].

SAFETY

At therapeutic dose levels Iceland moss is well tolerated without side effects [32,33] and no reports of toxicity or drug interactions have arisen from its use [20]. In olden times it was used as an emergency food, and even in bread and jellies, in Arctic areas after traditional pretreatment with alkaline wood ash and boiling to remove the lichen acids [17].

As 50% of the diet, untreated lichen proved toxic to mice, which died within 4-5 days; pre-boiling increased survival by only 2 days whereas ash-soaked and boiled material increased survival times to 20-22 days. Ash-soaked and 10-minute boiled material as 25% of the diet was well tolerated for 6 weeks by mice and for 3-months by rats. Blood, urine and histological tests on the rats gave generally normal results apart from some kidney damage, attributed to the lead content of the lichen [17].

Protolichesterinic acid showed no appreciable cytotoxic activity in *in vitro* tests with a variety of cultured mammalian cells [26].

Lichens have the ability to accumulated radionuclides. Contamination of some Iceland moss habitats by radioactive fallout from the Chernobyl disaster in 1986 had a substantial impact on the availability of acceptable material. Samples collected in southern Finland in 1983 had cesium-137 levels in the range 51 to 199 Bq/kg (lichen dry weight); in 1990 the range was 479 to 39,300 Bq/kg and only one of nine samples collected had less than the European Union maximum for foodstuffs (600 Bq/kg) [41]; the half-life of cesium-137 is 30.2 years [42].

REGULATORY STATUS

Medicines

UK	Accepted for general sale, internal or external use [43].
France	Not listed in *Médicaments à base de plantes* [44].
Germany	Commission E monograph published, with approved uses [38].

Foods

USA	Permitted as flavouring in alcoholic beverages only (21 CFR 172.510) [45].
Council of Europe	Permitted as flavouring, category N2 [46].

REFERENCES

Current Pharmacopoeial Monographs

Ph. Eur. Iceland Moss

Literature References

1. Stepanenko LS, Skirina IF, Dmitrenok PS and Khotimchenko SV. Characteristics of the Far-Eastern lichen *Cetraria islandica*. *Khim. Prir. Soedin.* 1996, (1), 82-88 [RUSSIAN], translated into English as: *Chem. Nat. Compd.* 1996, **32**, 66-70.
2. Gudjónsdóttir GA and Ingólfsdóttir K. Quantitative determination of protolichesterinic and fumarprotocetraric acids in *Cetraria islandica* by high-performance liquid chromatography. *J. Chromatogr. A* 1997, **757**, 303-306.
3. Huovinen K, Härmälä P, Hiltunen R and v. Schantz M. Variation of Fumarprotocetraric and Protocetraric Acids in *Cetraria islandica* and *C. ericetorum*. *Planta Medica* 1986, **52**, 508.
4. Ingolfsdottir K, Breu W, Huneck S, Gudjonsdottir GA, Müller-Jakic B and Wagner H. *In vitro* inhibition of 5-lipoxygenase by protolichesterinic acid from *Cetraria islandica*. *Phytomedicine* 1994, **1**, 187-191.
5. Krämer P, Wincierz U, Grübler G, Tschakert J, Voelter W and Mayer H. Rational Approach to Fractionation, Isolation and Characterization of Polysaccharides from the Lichen Cetraria islandica. *Arzneim.-Forsch./Drug Res.* 1995, **45**, 726-731.
6. Wichtl M and Henke D. Isländisches Moos. In: Hartke K, Hartke H, Mutschler E, Rücker G and Wichtl M, editors. *Kommentar zum Europäischen Arzneibuch* [*Commentary on the European Pharmacopoeia*]. Stuttgart: Wissenschaftliche Verlagsgesellschaft, 2001 (14. Lfg.):I 31/05 [GERMAN].
7. Cunningham WL and Manners DJ. Studies on Carbohydrate-Metabolizing Enzymes. 11. The hydrolysis of lichens by enzyme preparations from malted barley and *Rhizopus arrhizus*. *Biochem. J.* 1964, **90**, 596-602.
8. Perlin AS and Suzuki S. The structure of lichenin: selective enzymolysis studies. *Can. J. Chem.* 1962, **40**, 50-56.
9. Peat S, Whelan WJ and Roberts JG. The Structure of Lichenin. J. Chem. Soc. 1957, 3916-3924.
10. Chanda NB, Hirst EL and Manners DJ. A Comparison of isoLichenin and Lichenin from Iceland Moss (Cetraria islandica). *J. Chem. Soc.* 1957, 1951-1958.
11. Olafsdottir ES, Ingólfsdottir K, Barsett H, Smestad Paulsen B, Jurcic K and Wagner H. Immunologically active (1$\rightarrow$3)-(1$\rightarrow$4)-α-D-glucan from *Cetraria islandica*. *Phytomedicine* 1999, **6**, 33-39.
12. Peat S, Whelan WJ, Turvey JR and Morgan K. The Structure of Isolichenin. *J. Chem. Soc.* 1961, 623-629.
13. Hranisavljevic-Jakovljevic M, Miljkovic-Stojanovic J, Dimitrijevic R and Micovic VM. An alkali-soluble polysaccharide from the oak lichen, *Cetraria islandica* (L.) Ach. *Carbohydr. Res.* 1980, **80**, 291-295.
14. Ingolfsdottir K, Jurcic K, Fischer B and Wagner H. Immunologically Active Polysaccharide from *Cetraria islandica*. *Planta Medica* 1994, **60**, 527-531.
15. Gorin PAJ and Iacomini M. Polysaccharides of the Lichens *Cetraria islandica* and *Ramalina usnea*. *Carbohydr. Res.* 1984, **128**, 119-132.
16. Teixeira AZA, Iacomini M and Gorin PAJ. An unusual glucomannan from *Tornabenia intricata*. *Phytochemistry* 1992, **31**, 3467-3470.
17. Airaksinen MM, Peura P and Antere S. Toxicity of Iceland Lichen and Reindeer Lichen. *Arch. Toxicol.* 1986, **9** (Suppl.), 406-409.
18. Solberg Y. Chemical constituents of the lichen species *Cetraria islandica*. *J. Hattori Bot. Lab.* 1986, **60**, 391-406.
19. Sticher O. Über die antibakterielle Wirksamkeit von Lichen islandicus mit besonderer Berücksichtigung der Inhaltsstoffe. 1. Mitteilung [The antibacterial effectiveness of Lichen islandicus with particular regard to the constituents. Part 1]. *Pharm. Acta Helv.* 1965, **40**, 385-394 [GERMAN].
20. Ingólfsdóttir K. Bioactive compounds from Iceland moss. In: Paulsen BS, editor. *Bioactive Carbohydrate Polymers.* Dordrecht: Kluwer Academic, 2000:25-36.
21. Ingólfsdóttir K, Jurcic K and Wagner H. Immunomodulating polysaccharides from aqueous extracts of *Cetraria islandica* (Iceland moss). *Phytomedicine* 1998, **5**, 333-339.
22. Schmidgall J, Schnetz E and Hensel A. Evidence for Bioadhesive Effects of Polysaccharides and Polysaccharide-Containing Herbs in an *ex vivo* Bioadhesion Assay on

Buccal Membranes. *Planta Medica* 2000, **66**, 48-53.
23. Stübler D and Buchenauer H. Antiviral Activity of the Glucan Lichenan (Poly-β{1→3, 1→4}D-anhydroglucose). 1. Biological Activity in Tobacco Plants. *J. Phytopathol.* 1996, **144**, 37-43.
24. Kumar KC S and Müller K. Lichen Metabolites. 1. Inhibitory Action against Leukotriene B_4 Biosynthesis by a Non-Redox Mechanism. *J. Nat. Prod.* 1999, **62**, 817-820.
25. Ögmundsdóttir HM, Zoëga GM, Gissurarson SR and Ingólfsdóttir K. Anti-proliferative Effects of Lichen-derived Inhibitors of 5-Lipoxygenase on Malignant Cell-lines and Mitogen-stimulated Lymphocytes. *J. Pharm. Pharmacol.* 1998, **50**, 107-115.
26. Pengsuparp T, Cai L, Constant H, Fong HHS, Lin L-Z, Kinghorn AD et al. Mechanistic evaluation of new plant-derived compounds that inhibit HIV-1 reverse transcriptase. *J. Nat. Prod.* 1995, **58**, 1024-31.
27. Ingolfsdottir K, Hjalmarsdottir MA, Sigurdsson A, Gudjonsdottir GA, Brynjolfsdottir A and Steingrimsson O. In Vitro Susceptibility of *Helicobacter pylori* to Protolichesterinic Acid from the Lichen *Cetraria islandica*. *Antimicrob. Agents Chemother.* 1997, **41**, 215-217.
28. Vartia KO. Antibiotics in lichens. In: Ahmadjian V, Hale ME, editors. *The Lichens.* New York: Academic Press, 1973:547-561.
29. Ingólfsdóttir K, Chung GAC, Skúlason VG, Gissurarson SR and Vilhelmsdóttir M. Antimycobacterial activity of lichen metabolites in vitro. *Eur. J. Pharm. Sci.* 1998, **6**, 141-144.
30. Smriga M, Chen J, Zhang J-T, Narui T, Shibata S, Hirano E and Saito H. Isolichenan, an α-glucan isolated from lichen *Cetrariella islandica,* repairs impaired learning behaviors and facilitates hippocampal synaptic plasticity. *Proc. Japan Acad. Ser. B.* 1999, **75**, 219-223.
31. Smriga M and Saito H. Effect of Selected Thallophytic Glucans on Learning Behaviour and Short-term Potentiation. *Phytotherapy Res.* 2000, **14**, 153-155.
32. Kempe C, Grüning H, Stasche N and Hörmann K. Isländisch-Moos-Pastillen zur Prophylaxe bzw. Heilung von oralen Schleimhautirritationen und ausgetrockneter Rachenschleimhaut [Iceland moss pastilles for the prophylaxis and healing of oral mucosal irritation and for dryness of the pharyngeal mucosa]. *Laryngo-Rhino-Otol.* 1997, **76**, 186-188 [GERMAN/English summary].
33. Vorberg G. Flechtenwirkstoffe lindern Reizzustände der Atemwege. Neben den entzündungshemmenden Eigenschaften wirkt sich der Schleimhautschutz besonders günstig aus [Active substances in lichens alleviate irritation of the respiratory tract. In addition to anti-inflammatory properties they have a particularly favourable effect in protecting the mucosa]. *Ärztl. Praxis* 1981, **33**, 3068 {GERMAN].
34. Cetraria. In: *British Herbal Pharmacopoeia 1983.* ISBN 0-903032-07-4. Bournemouth: British Herbal Medicine Association, 1983.
35. Chevallier A. Iceland Moss. In: *Encyclopedia of Medicinal Plants, 2nd ed.* ISBN 0-7513-1209-6. London-New York: Dorling Kindersley, 2001:186.
36. Weiss RF and Fintelmann V. In: *Herbal Medicine, 2nd ed.* (translated from the 9th German edition of *Lehrbuch der Phytotherapie*). ISBN 3-13-126332-6. Stuttgart-New York: Thieme, 2000:61-62.
37. Weiss RF. *Cetraria islandica*. In: *Herbal Medicine* (translated from the 6th German edition of *Lehrbuch der Phytotherapie*). ISBN 0-906584-19-1. Gothenburg: AB Arcanum, Beaconsfield, UK: Beaconsfield Publishers, 1988:48-50.
38. Lichen islandicus (Isländisches Moos): German Commission E Monograph published in Bundesanzeiger No. 43 of 02.03.89.
39. Isländisches Moos. In: Braun R, editor. *Standardzulassungen für Fertigarzneimittel - Text und Kommentar* [Standard licences for finished medicines - Text and commentary]. Stuttgart: Deutscher Apotheker Verlag, Frankfurt: Govi-Verlag, 1989.
40. Brückner C. In Mitteleuropa genutzte Heilpflanzen mit milchsekretionsfördernder Wirkung (Galactagoga) [Plants used in central European folk medicine to stimulate milk secretion (galactagogues)]. *Gleditschia* 1989, **2**, 189-201 [GERMAN/English summary].
41. Huovinen K and Jaakkola T. *Lichen islandicus* and the Chernobyl Fallout in Finland. *Planta Medica* 1991, **57**, A24.
42. Nedic O, Stankovic A, Stankovic S and Kraincanic M. Chemical Localization of ^{137}Cs in the Lichen *Cetraria islandica. Arch. Environ. Contam. Toxicol.* 1995, **29**, 380-383.
43. Iceland Moss. In: UK Statutory Instrument 1994 No. 2410. The Medicines (Products Other Than Veterinary Drugs) (General Sale List) Amendment Order 1994. Schedule 1, Table A.
44. *Médicaments à base de plantes.* ISBN 2-911473-02-7. Saint-Denis Cedex, France: Agence du Médicament, 1998.
45. Iceland Moss. In: Section 172.510 of USA Code of Federal Regulations, Title 21, Food and Drugs, Parts 170 to 199. Revised as of April 1, 2000.
46. Cetraria islandica (L.) Ach., thallus. In: *Flavouring Substances and Natural Sources of Flavourings, 3rd ed.* ISBN 2-7160-0081-6. Strasbourg: Council of Europe, 1981.

REGULATORY GUIDELINES FROM OTHER EU COUNTRIES

GERMANY

Commission E monograph [38]: Lichen islandicus (Isländisches Moos).

Uses
(a) Irritation of the oral and pharyngeal mucosa and associated dry coughs
(b) Loss of appetite.

Contraindications
None known

Side effects
None known.

Interactions with other drugs
None known.

Dosage
Unless otherwise prescribed, daily dose: 4-6 g of the drug; equivalent preparations.

Mode of administration
Use (a): Comminuted drug in tea infusions and other galenical preparations for internal use.
Use (b): Comminuted drug, preferably in cold macerates and other bitter-tasting preparations for internal use.

Action
Relieves irritation, weakly antimicrobial.

IRISH MOSS

Chondri thallus

Synonyms: Chondrus, Carrageen.

Definition

Irish Moss consists of the dried, partially bleached, red alga *Chondrus crispus* (L.) Stackh., alone or mixed with *Mastocarpus stellatus* (Stackh. in With.) Guiry comb. nov. [*Gigartina mamillosa* (Gooden. et Woodw.) J. Agardh.].

The botanical name of the latter species was revised to *Mastocarpus stellatus* (Stackh. in With.) Guiry comb. nov. in 1984. A synonym, *G. stellata* (Stackh.) Batters, is not considered to be definitive; it may refer to several entities [1].

Since *Chondrus crispus* and *Mastocarpus stellatus* occur in the same habitat in the intertidal zone of rocky shores and most collectors do not distinguish between them, the proportion of *Mastocarpus stellatus* in commercial material depends on their relative abundance; it ranged from 5% to 20% in retail samples [2].

Chondrus crispus is diplobiontic, i.e. its life history has two isomorphic phases, described as sporophytes and gametophytes [3].

CONSTITUENTS

☐ *Carrageenan*, 30-60% of dry weight [4,5], a generic term applied to a family of hydrophilic polysaccharides which can be extracted from Irish moss and closely related species of red seaweeds. Carrageenans are linear sulphated galactans of MW up to 600,000 with a backbone of alternating 3-linked β-D-galactose and 4-linked α-D-galactose or 4-linked 3,6-anhydro-D-galactose, the position and degree of sulphation depending on the type [4,6]; they occur as sodium, potassium or calcium salts [7]. *Chondrus crispus* (and similarly *Mastocarpus stellatus*) produces different types of carrageenan in the two phases of its life history.

Gametophytes contain mainly kappa (κ)-carrageenan with a smaller proportion of iota (ι)-carrageenan [3,8] and ca. 10% of lamda (λ)-carrageenan [9]. Recent work confirmed the presence of a κ/ι hybrid carrageenan with a mixed chain of both κ- and ι-repeating units rather than pure κ- and ι-chains. Gelling carrageenans (κ and ι, or κ/ι) have chains with a random coil structure, which changes to an ordered helical conformation on gelation [6].

Sporophytes contain predominantly λ-carrageenan [3] or a variant, ξ-carrageenan [8].

☐ ***Lipids***, including monoglycosyldiacylglycerols, diglycosyldiacylglycerols and more polar lipids in which the predominant sugar component is galactose [10,11] and the fatty acids are predominantly polyunsaturated, the main ones being eicosapentaenoic (20:5ω3), arachidonic (20:4ω6), oleic (C18:1ω9) and palmitic (16:0) acids [10-13]. *Trans*-3-hexadecenoic and *trans*-3-tetradecenoic acids have been identified as minor fatty acids [13].

The total fatty acids content appears to be about 1.5-2.1% of dry weight [11], although a much lower amount of 0.06-0.07% of dry weight has also been reported [12].

☐ ***Sterols***, 0.011-0.019% of dry weight [12,14]. Cholesterol represents over 94% of the total sterols; small amounts of campesterol, stigmasterol, sitosterol and others are present [12].

☐ ***Other constituents*** Protein, iodine and bromine, iron and various other minerals [15] including 2-12 ppm of arsenic [7].

The amino acid hordenine (*N,N*-dimethyltyramine) does not occur in *Chondrus crispus* but has been found in *Mastocarpus stellatus* at 1500-5500 µg/g

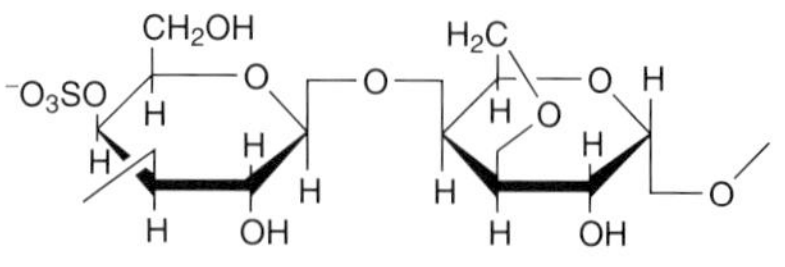

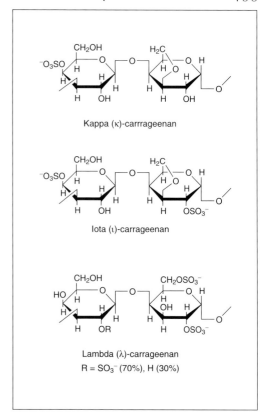

Kappa (κ)-carrrageenan

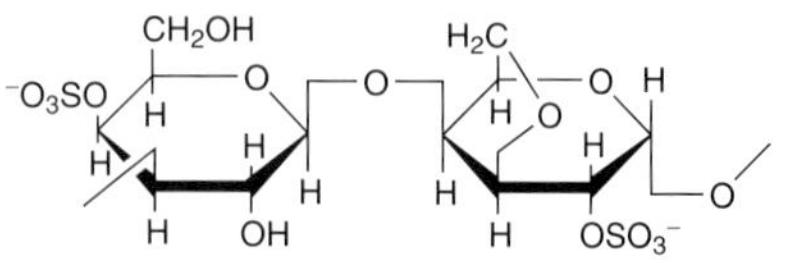

Iota (ι)-carrageenan

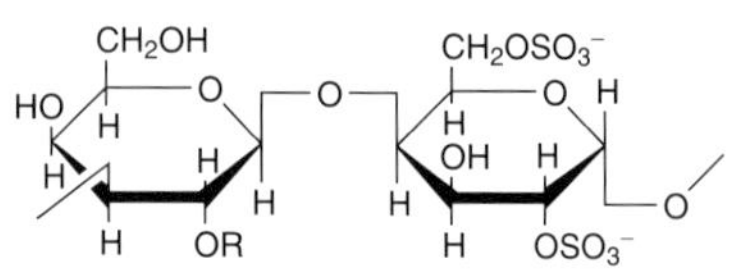

Lambda (λ)-carrageenan

R = SO_3^- (70%), H (30%)

dry weight; the level declines by 40-90% after open-air bleaching [2].

Published Assay Method
Separation of κ-, ι- and λ-carrageenans by capillary electrophoresis [16].

PHARMACOLOGY

The therapeutically relevant effects of Irish moss are mainly due to its content of carrageenan. Refined (but not degraded) carrageenan is widely used in foods and pharmaceutical preparations as a suspending, gelling and stabilizing agent. For a review of the physiological effects of carrageenan see Stancioff [4].

In vitro
Lamda (λ)-carrageenan has anticoagulant activity and bears structural similarities to heparin, a well-known anticoagulant. However, λ-carrageenan strongly inhibited the clotting activity of thrombin (a serine protease) directly, in the absence of protease inhibitors, prolonging the fibrinogen clotting time by a factor of 8 at a concentration as low as 5.5×10^{-9} mol/litre. In contrast, heparin showed comparable effects on clotting time only in the presence of protease inhibitors, principally antithrombin [17]. It has been demonstrated that, whereas the effect of heparin is mainly mediated by antithrombin, λ-carrageenan directly inhibits the amidolytic activity of thrombin and ionic interactions appear to be involved [18]. Since carrageenans are not absorbed from the gastrointestinal tract, the anticoagulant properties are not relevant to oral use of Irish moss.

A crude aqueous fraction from Irish moss exhibited inhibitory activity against 12 species of bacteria (eg. *Streptococcus* and *Staphylococcus*) and fungi out of 44 in a 1.25 mg/ml solution; a refined fraction had 64 times stronger activity against *Streptococcus mutans* than the crude fraction [19].

In vivo
Carrageenan injected subcutaneously into animals induces collagen proliferation with resultant formation of a granuloma; when injected into a rodent's paw, a reproducible inflammatory oedematous condition results. These effects have been used in pharmacological screening tests but are not relevant to the oral use of Irish moss [4].

At high oral dose levels, several physiological effects of carrageenan, which can be attributed to the hydrophilic and polyanionic properties of the macromolecule, have been demonstrated in animals:

- Interference with the activity of the proteolytic enzyme pepsin, which is involved in gastric digestion of protein in food. The interaction appears to be complexation with the protein in food rather than with the enzyme. No peptic inhibition was observed in rats at carrageenan to protein ratios lower than 0.1; even at the high ratio of 0.3 peptic activity was reduced by only 10-20%.
- Reduction in the volume and acidity of histamine-stimulated gastric secretion, which may be related to complexation with mucin on the stomach wall.
- Hypocholesterolaemic activity. In rats fed on a diet including 1% cholesterol and 10% carrageenan, liver cholesterol remained at the normal level and the total lipid level was greatly reduced.
- Increased water content of the bowel and softening of the stool. This effect is common to all hydrophilic polysaccharides resistant to digestion, a number of which are used as bulk-forming laxatives [4].

Pharmacokinetics
Breakdown of carrageenan in the gut is insignificant and there is no evidence that it is absorbed by test animals with the possible exceptions of guinea pigs and rabbits; 100% recovery was obtained from the faeces of dogs [4].

CLINICAL STUDIES

None published on mono-preparations of Irish moss.

THERAPEUTICS

Actions
Antitussive, demulcent, emollient [20,21], weakly antibacterial [19]. Bulk-forming laxative in high doses [4].

Indications
None adequately substantiated by pharmacological or clinical studies.

Uses based on experience or tradition
Internal: Coughs and bronchitis [7,20-23]. Dyspepsia, gastritis; urinary infections such as cystitis [20,21]; in constipation, as a bulk-forming laxative [24].
External: As a lotion for chapped hands or dermatitis [20,21].

Contraindications
None known.

Side effects
None known.

Interactions with other drugs
None known.

Dosage
Single dose: dried thallus, 1-3 g as a decoction (1 in 40) [22].

Daily dosages of 15-30 g per day have been recommended [20].

SAFETY

Carrageenan is not broken down or absorbed in the body and, at the levels used in food, it has no adverse physiological effects in humans [4]. The establishment of an acceptable daily intake (ADI) for refined, non-degraded carrageenan was not deemed necessary by the FAO/WHO Expert Committee on Food Additives in 1984 [25].

Depolymerized carrageenan (MW < 20,000), once used in France for the treatment of peptic ulcers, has shown no toxicity in man but caused mucosal erosions in the caecum of guinea pigs and, at high doses, also effected cell changes in the colon of rats and monkeys. Degraded carrageenan was demonstrated as being partly absorbed by the epithelial cells, deposited in the Kupffer cells of the liver and found in the urine. A broad margin of safety for food grade carrageenan in the diet is assured by low functional use levels and a minimum molecular weight of 100,000 [4].

Although hordenine (present in *Mastocarpus stellatus*, but not *Chondrus crispus*) is known to inhibit uptake of the neurotransmitter noradrenaline into sympathetic nerves, the amount present in commercial Irish moss was found to be 10-490 µg/g dry weight, considerably less than in foods such as cheeses and yeast extracts [2]. The pharmacological effects of orally ingested hordenine have not been determined, but it is unlikely to have any adverse effects at this level.

REGULATORY STATUS

Medicines

UK	Accepted for general sale, internal or external use [26].
France	Accepted for specified indications [24].
Germany	No Commission E monograph published.

Food

USA	Carrageenan approved as a food additive (21 CFR 172.620); Chondrus extract (carrageenan), as a stabilizer, generally recognized as safe (21 CFR 182.7255) [27].
Council of Europe	Permitted as flavouring, category N2 [28].

REFERENCES

Current Pharmacopoeial Monographs

ÖAB	Carrageen - Irländische Alge
BHP 1996	Irish Moss

Literature References

1. Guiry MD, West JA, Kim D-H and Masuda M. Reinstatement of the genus *Mastocarpus* Kützing (Rhodophyta). *Taxon* 1984, **33**, 53-63.
2. Barwell CJ, Canham CA and Guiry MD. Hordenine Content of the Marine Alga *Mastocarpus stellatus* and the Algal Food Product Carrageen. *Phytotherapy Res.* 1989, **3**, 67-69.
3. McCandless EL, West JA and Guiry MD. Carrageenan Patterns in the Gigartinaceae. *Biochem. Syst. Ecol.* 1983, **11**, 175-182.
4. Stancioff DJ and Renn DW. Physiological Effects of Carrageenans. In: Jeanes A and Hodge J, editors. *Physiological Effects of Food Carbohydrates.* ACS Symposium Series 15. ISBN 0-8412-0246-X. Washington DC: American Chemical Society, 1975:282-295.
5. Chopin T, Bodeau-Bellion C, Floch JY, Guittet E and Lallemand JY. Seasonal study of carrageenan structures from female gametophytes of *Chondrus crispus* Stackhouse (Rhodophyta). *Hydrobiologia* 1987, **151-152**, 535-539; through *Chem. Abstr.* 1987, **108**, 3411.
6. van de Velde F, Peppelman HA, Rollema HS and Tromp RH. On the structure of κ/ι-hybrid carrageenans. *Carbohydr. Res.* 2001, **331**, 271-283.
7. Pharmaceutical Society of Great Britain. Chondrus. In: *British Pharmaceutical Codex 1959.* London: Pharmaceutical Press, 1959.
8. Matsuhiro B and Urzua CC. Heterogeneity of carrageenans from *Chondrus crispus. Phytochemistry* 1992, **31**, 531-534.
9. De Lestang Bremond G, Quillet M and Bremond M. λ-Carrageenan in the gametophytes of *Chondrus crispus. Phytochemistry* 1987, **26**, 1705-1707.
10. Jamieson GR and Reid EH. The component fatty acids of some marine algal lipids. *Phytochemistry* 1972, **11**, 1423-1432.
11. Pettitt TR, Jones AL and Harwood JL. Lipids of the marine red algae *Chondrus crispus* and *Polysiphonia lanosa. Phytochemistry* 1989, **28**, 399-405.
12. Tasende MG. Fatty acid and sterol composition of gametophytes and sporophytes of Chondrus crispus (Gigartinaceae, Rhodophyta). *Scientia Marina* 2000, **64**, 421.
13. Lamberto M and Ackman RG. Confirmation by Gas Chromatography/Mass Spectrometry of Two Unusual *trans*-3-Monoethylenic Fatty Acids from the Nova Scotian Seaweeds *Palmaria palmata* and *Chondrus crispus. Lipids* 1994, **29**, 441-444.
14. Saito A and Idler DR. Sterols in Irish moss (*Chondrus crispus*). *Can. J. Biochem.* 1966, **44**, 1195-1199.
15. Launert E. *Chondrus crispus.* In: *The Hamlyn Guide to Edible and Medicinal Plants of Northern Europe.* ISBN 0-600-35281-1. London-New York: Hamlyn, 1981:228-229.
16. Mangin CM, Goodall DM and Roberts MA. Separation of ι-, κ- and λ-carrageenans by capillary electrophoresis. *Electrophoresis* 2001, **22**, 1460-1467.
17. Lange U and Nowak G. Studies on lamda-carrageenan - thrombin interactions. I. Effect of lamda-carrageenan on the clotting activity of thrombin. *Pharm. Pharmacol. Lett.* 1994, **3**, 176-178.
18. Lange U and Nowak G. Studies on lamda-carrageenan - thrombin interactions. II. Effect of lamda-carrageenan

on the amidolytic activity of thrombin. *Pharm. Pharmacol. Lett.* 1994, **3**, 179-182.
19. Natsuno T, Mikami M and Saito K. A potent inhibitor of bacterial growth from the seaweed Chondrus crispus. *Shigaku* 1986, **74**, 412-421 [JAPANESE]; through *Chem. Abstr.* 1987, **106**, 30026.
20. Chondrus. In: *British Herbal Pharmacopoeia 1983*. ISBN 0-903032-07-4. Bournemouth: British Herbal Medicine Association, 1983.
21. Chevallier A. Carragheen, Irish moss. In: *The Encyclopedia of Medicinal Plants*. ISBN 0-7513-0314-3. London-New York-Stuttgart: Dorling Kindersley, 1996:187.
22. Todd RG, editor. Chondrus. In: *Martindale - Extra Pharmacopoeia, 25th edition*. London: Pharmaceutical Press, 1967:78-79.
23. Wagner H. Carrageen - Irländisches Moos. In: *Pharmazeutische Biologie. 2. Drogen und ihre Inhaltsstoffe*. ISBN 3-437-20408-4. Stuttgart-New York: Gustav Fischer, 1988:288-289 [GERMAN].
24. Carragaheen. In: *Médicaments à base de plantes*. ISBN 2-911473-02-7. Saint-Denis Cedex, France: Agence du Médicament, 1998.
25. Reynolds JEF, editor. Carrageenan. In: *Martindale - The Extra Pharmacopoeia, 29th edition*. ISBN 0-85369-210-6. London: Pharmaceutical Press, 1989:1433-1434.
26. Chondrus. In: UK Statutory Instrument 1984 No. 769. The Medicines (Products Other Than Veterinary Drugs) (General Sale List) Order 1984. Schedule 1, Table A.
27. Carrageenan (section 172.620), Chondrus extract (section 182.7255). In: USA Code of Federal Regulations, Title 21, Food and Drugs, Parts 170 to 199. Revised as of April 1, 2000.
28. Chondrus crispus (L.) Stackh., thallus. In: *Flavouring Substances and Natural Sources of Flavourings, 3rd ed.* ISBN 2-7160-0081-6. Strasbourg: Council of Europe, 1981.

REGULATORY GUIDELINES FROM OTHER EU COUNTRIES

FRANCE

Médicaments à base de plantes [24]: Carragaheen, thalle.

Therapeutic indications accepted

Oral use
As a bulk-forming laxative, for the symptomatic treatment of constipation.

JAVA TEA

Labiatae

Orthosiphonis folium

Synonym: Known as Kumis Kucing in South-East Asia.

Definition

Java Tea consists of the dried leaves and tops of stems of *Orthosiphon stamineus* Benth. [*O. aristatus* Miq.; *O. spicatus* Bak.], usually harvested shortly before flowering.

CONSTITUENTS

□ ***Flavonoids*** Highly methoxylated flavones, 0.2-0.43%, principally sinensetin (5,6,7,3′4′-pentamethoxyflavone, 0.1-0.2%) [1-12] and tetramethylscutellarein (5,6,7,4′-tetramethoxyflavone, ca. 0.1%) [1-10] together with eupatorin (5,3′-dihydroxy-6,7,4′-trimethoxyflavone), 3′-hydroxy-5,6,7,4′- tetramethoxyflavone [2-7], 5-hydroxy-6,7,3′4′-tetramethoxyflavone [1,3-5,9,10] and smaller amounts of other tetra- and tri-, and some di-, methoxylated flavones [3,4,10].

Flavones are present exclusively as aglycones, whereas the flavonols kaempferol and quercetin are present as 3-*O*-glucosides [12].

□ ***Highly oxygenated diterpenes*** Orthosiphols A [8,9,13-16], B [8,9,14-16], C [14], D and E [8], F to I [10,17] and J [10]; neoorthosiphols A and B [9,16], orthosiphonones A and B [9,15], staminols A [10,17] and B [10], norstaminol A, and staminolactones A and B [10,18].

□ ***Benzochromenes:*** methylripariochromene A, in apparently highly variable amount; isolated as 4% of the dried flowering herb by Guérin et al. [19] and as 0.63% of dried leaf by Shibuya et al. [9,15], but not found by Sumaryono et al. [12]. Small amounts of orthochromene A and acetovanillochromene have also been isolated [9,15].

□ ***Caffeic acid derivatives***, principally rosmarinic acid, ca. 0.1% [8,10,12,20,21], followed by 2,3-dicaffeoyl tartrate [12]. Caffeoyl tartrate, lithospermic acid derivatives (see below) and free caffeic acid are also present [10,12].

Quantitatively, the caffeic acid derivatives (67% of the total phenolic compounds in Java tea) predominate over the flavones (33%) [12]. The total of hydroxycinnamic acid derivatives has been determined as 0.9% [21].

□ ***Lithospermic acid derivatives*** in small amounts. In contrast to the one dihydrocaffeic acid substituent of lithospermic acid itself (not detected in Java tea), compounds with two dihydrocaffeic substituents or two dihydro-*p*-hydroxycinnamic acid substituents, or one of each type, have been identified [12].

□ ***Essential oil***, ca. 0.02%, containing mainly sesquiterpenes such as β-caryophyllene and its oxide,

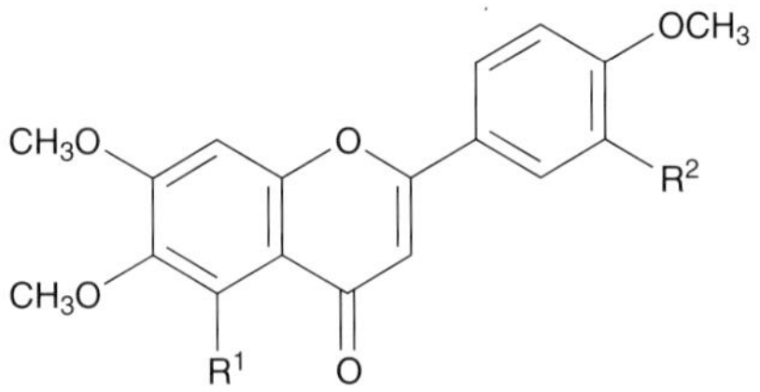

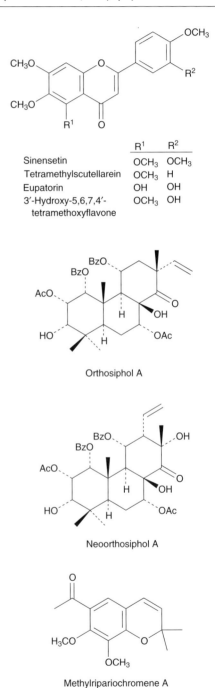

	R^1	R^2
Sinensetin	OCH_3	OCH_3
Tetramethylscutellarein	OCH_3	H
Eupatorin	OH	OH
3′-Hydroxy-5,6,7,4′-tetramethoxyflavone	OCH_3	OH

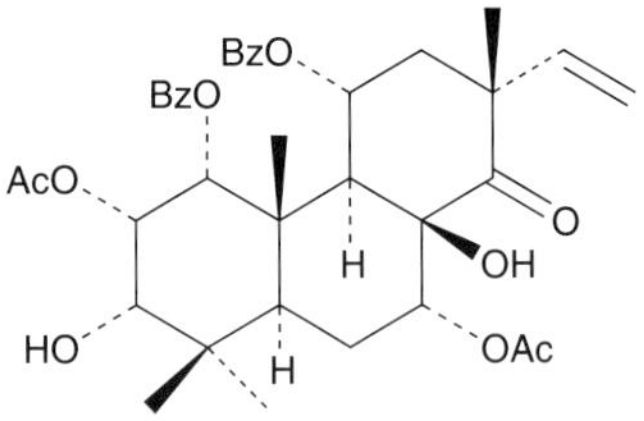

Orthosiphol A

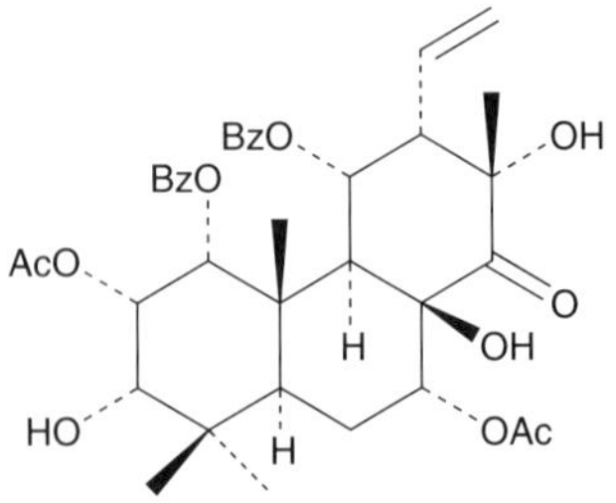

Neoorthosiphol A

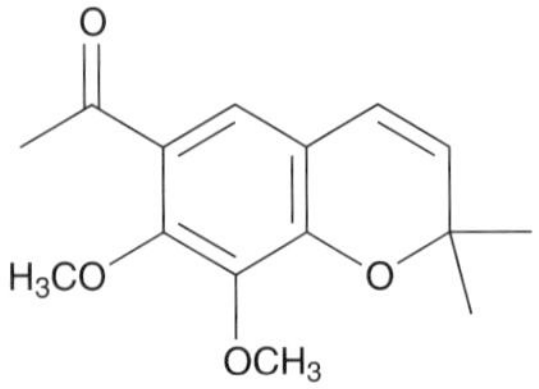

Methylripariochromene A

δ-cadinene, β-selinene and α-guaiene, with lesser amounts of monoterpenes [22].

☐ ***Potassium*** A high potassium content of about 3% is widely quoted [23]. The only recent data available, from analysis of a tea preparation, indicated extraction of 2.2% of potassium from dried leaf and flower [24].

☐ ***Other constituents*** include β-sitosterol, vomifoliol, aurantiamide acetate, triterpene acids (betulinic, oleanolic and ursolic) [10], the coumarin esculetin [12] and meso-inositol [23]. The presence of saponins has been reported [25,26], to the extent of 4.5% of the crude drug [25], but this needs confirmation.

Published Assay Methods

Methoxylated flavones by HPLC [6]. Sinensetin by TLC/spectrophotometry [11]. Rosmarinic acid by HPLC [20].

PHARMACOLOGY

In vitro

An ethyl acetate extract from Java tea, and sinensetin and tetramethylscutellarein extracted from it, inhibited the oxidation of linoleic acid catalyzed by 15-lipoxygenase (from soya beans) with IC_{50} values of 0.018% w/v, 114 μM and 110 μM respectively, compared to 98 μM for quercetin (a well-known lipoxygenase inhibitor) as a positive control; similar results were obtained with arachidonic acid as substrate [5]. Flavones from Java tea also exhibited radical scavenging activity and protected 15-lipoxygenase from air-induced oxidative inactivation [27].

Methylripariochromene A isolated from Java tea concentration-dependently suppressed contractions induced by high K^+, phenylephrine or prostaglandin $F_{2\alpha}$ in endothelium-denuded rat thoracic aorta. Acetovanillochromene and orthochromene A showed similarly potent dilating activity on high K^+-induced contractions [9,28,29]. Methylripariochromene A also caused a marked suppression of contractile force, without significant reduction in beating rate, in isolated guinea pig atria [28].

In vivo

Diuretic effects of Java tea extracts

Extracts of Java tea administered intragastrically to rats as single doses in water, a dry aqueous (5:1) extract at 18.0 mg/kg and 180 mg/kg, and a dry hydroethanolic (7:1) extract at 13.5 mg/kg and 135 mg/kg, significantly increased urine volumes over a 6-hour period ($p \le 0.05$) compared to those of control animals given the same volume of water. Both dose levels of the aqueous extract (but not the hydroethanolic extract) significantly increased sodium elimination ($p = 0.009$); and the higher dose levels of aqueous and hydroethanolic extracts significantly increased chloride elimination ($p = 0.009$ and $p = 0.02$ respectively). No significant changes were observed in elimination of potassium or urea [30].

In another study, neither a dry aqueous extract of Java tea at 125, 750 and 1000 mg/kg nor furosemide at 100 mg/kg, administered to rats by stomach tube, increased urine volumes significantly compared to control animals given water, although average urine volumes were 33.4 mg after Java tea extract at 750 mg/kg compared to 24.6 mg after furosemide at 100 mg/kg and 26.8 mg for controls. The extract and furosemide increased excretion of sodium/potassium/chloride by factors of 2.0/2.0/2.8 and 5.8/1.3/4.2 respectively. The authors concluded that Java tea extract does not act as an aquaretic and that the rat is a rather poor model for furosemide [31].

A hydroalcoholic extract, administered intraperitoneally to rats in hypotonic saline at a dose equivalent to 50 mg/kg of Java tea, significantly increased urine volume ($p<0.001$ at 8 hours, $p<0.01$ at 24 hours), comparable to the effect of hydrochlorothiazide at 10 mg/kg, and urinary potassium excretion at 8 hours ($p<0.05$) compared to control animals; 100% of the hypotonic saline overload was eliminated within 4.75 hours (hydrochlorothiazide at 10 mg/kg: 5.33 hours). The diuretic effect was not attributable to the potassium content of Java tea [32].

Urine volume and excretion of electrolytes (sodium, potassium and chloride) increased in dogs after intravenous infusion of a hydroethanolic (50% V/V) extract of Java tea at 18.8 mg/kg/min, although with considerably less effect than furosemide (prime dose of 0.3 mg/kg i.v. and maintaining dose of 7 μg/kg/min i.v.) [33].

Diuretic effects of constituents

Methylripariochromene A increased urinary volume, about 3-fold over 3 hours ($p<0.01$), after oral administration to fasted rats at 100 mg/kg; the effect was comparable to that of hydrochlorothiazide at 25 mg/kg [28,29].

Sinensetin and 3′-hydroxy-5,6,7,4′-tetramethoxyflavone administered intravenously to rats at 1 mg/kg increased urine volume compared to control animals, with a lesser diuretic effect than hydrochlorothiazide at 1 mg/kg and a greater time lag, possibly due to action via metabolites [7].

Other effects

The hypoglycaemic effect of a dried aqueous extract from Java tea, administered orally at 1.0 g/kg, was demonstrated in both normal and streptozotocin

(STZ)-induced diabetic rats, and also in normal rats in an oral glucose tolerance test (glucose load of 1.5 g/kg); blood glucose levels decreased significantly ($p<0.05$) compared to control animals. In STZ-induced diabetic rats the effect was comparable to that of 10 mg/kg of glibenclamide [26].

A hydroethanolic (50% V/V) extract of Java tea significantly decreased ($p<0.05$) locomotor activity in mice within 30 minutes after intraperitoneal administration at 1.0 g/kg [33].

Methylripariochromene A caused dose-dependent decreases in systolic blood pressure over a 24-hour period ($p<0.01$) and heart rate over a 6-hour period ($p<0.01$) after subcutaneous administration to conscious, stroke-prone, spontaneously hypertensive rats at 100 mg/kg [28,29]. Thus, including effects noted above, methylripariochromene A produces diuretic and vasodilating effects and reduces cardiac output - activities related to antihypertensive activity [28].

Orthosiphols A and B, applied topically at 200 µg per ear, potently inhibited (by 42% and 50% respectively) inflammation of the mouse ear induced by 2 µg of 12-*O*-tetradecanoylphorbol-13-acetate [14].

Pharmacological studies in humans

Diuretic effects
Early pharmacological studies (1927-28) in three individuals, involving self-administration of aqueous infusions of Java tea, demonstrated increases in urine volume [34-36].

However, in a double-blind, placebo-controlled, crossover study, no influence was observed on 12- or 24-hour urine volume or excretion of sodium or potassium after administration of 600 ml (3 × 200 ml at 4-hour intervals) of an aqueous decoction equivalent to 10 g of Java tea to 40 healthy young volunteers [37].

In another study, a decoction of Java tea (described as *Orthosiphon grandiflorus* Bolding, a synonym for *O. stamineus*) was administered to 6 healthy male volunteers as 250 ml four times in one day at 6-hour intervals. Equal amounts of water were ingested by the same volunteers on a separate control day. Java tea produced no significant changes in urine volume, or in excretion of sodium, potassium or chloride, compared to the control day. From urine analysis, the decoction significantly increased excretion of oxalate ($p<0.05$) and increases were also noted in excretion of calcium ($p<0.1$), citrate and uric acid, while titratable acidity decreased ($p<0.05$) and the pH increased during the first 6-hour period. It was concluded that Java tea may be beneficial in prevention of uric acid stone formation, primarily due to decreased acidity of the urine [24].

Choleretic effect
In early experiments (1935) on healthy volunteers, it was shown by means of duodenal probes and x-rays that intravenous administration of a Java tea preparation increased the production of bile and its liberation from the gall bladder [38].

CLINICAL STUDIES

No controlled clinical studies have been published on mono-preparations of Java tea.

In 14 case studies (reported in 1936) on patients with azotaemic uraemia associated with various other ailments, daily treatment for 10-15 days with 5 × 100 ml of a 12% infusion of Java tea increased urine volumes substantially (in some cases more than two-fold within 4-5 days), together with increased elimination of urea and chloride [39].

In an open study on 67 patients with uratic diathesis, of whom 34 received Java tea and 33 *Equisetum arvense* decoctions for 3 months, Java tea produced a 9% lower diuretic effect than *Equisetum arvense* and did not affect the plasma level or excretion of uric acid [40].

THERAPEUTICS

Actions
Diuretic [30,32,33,39], uricosuric [24].

Antihyperglycaemic [26] and sedative [33] effects of Java tea extracts, as well as antihypertensive [28] and topical anti-inflammatory [14] effects of constituents, have been demonstrated in animals. Methylripariochromene A and other chromenes exhibit spasmolytic effects *in vitro* [28].

Although Java Tea is used primarily as a diuretic in Europe [41,42], published evidence of a diuretic effect in humans is inadequate, relying largely on open case studies reported over 65 years ago [34-36,39]. No increases in urine volume or excretion of electrolytes were observed in the two studies with healthy volunteers in the 1990s [24,37], one of which had a double-blind, placebo-controlled, crossover design [37]; aqueous extracts were used in both studies.

On balance, Java tea and some of its constituents (particularly methylripariochromene A) appear to have weak diuretic activity. Conclusions from animal studies are ambiguous with aqueous extracts [30,31] but consistent with hydroalcoholic extracts, albeit via several routes of administration [30,32,33]. Since the constituents for which a diuretic effect has been demonstrated tend to be lipophilic, hydroalcoholic extracts might be more effective in humans, but this remains to be investigated.

Indications
None adequately substantiated by pharmacological or clinical studies.

Uses based on experience or tradition
To increase urine volume in bacterial and inflammatory disorders of the urinary tract and to eliminate renal gravel [42].

In South-East Asia, for the treatment of hypertension and diabetes [16] and as a diuretic, uricosuric and renal stone elimination agent [24].

Contraindications
None known.

Side effects
None known.

Dosage
Adult daily dose: Dried herb, 6-12 g, in infusion or as equivalent extracts [23,42].

SAFETY

The intraperitoneal LD_{50} in mice of a 50% hydroethanolic extract of Java tea was determined as 19.6 g/kg [33].

In a somatic segregation assay using *Aspergillus nidulans*, no genotoxic effects were observed from an ethanolic extract of Java tea at 1.4 mg/ml [43].

REGULATORY STATUS

Medicines

UK	No licences issued for products containing Java tea.
France	Accepted for specified indications [41].
Germany	Commission E monograph published, with approved uses [42].

REFERENCES

Current Pharmacopoeial Monographs
Ph. Eur. Java Tea

Literature References

1. Bombardelli E, Bonati A, Gabetta B and Mustich G. Flavonoid constituents of Orthosiphon stamineus Benth. *Fitoterapia* 1972, **43**, 35-40.
2. Schneider G and Tan HS. Die lipophilen Flavone von Folia Orthosiphonis [The lipophilic flavones of Folia Orthosiphonis]. *Dtsch. Apoth. Ztg.* 1973, **113**, 201-202 [GERMAN].
3. Wollenweber E and Mann K. Further Flavonoids from *Orthosiphon spicatus*. *Planta Med.* 1985, **51**, 459-460 [GERMAN].
4. Malterud KE, Hanche-Olsen IM and Smith-Kielland I. Flavonoids from *Orthosiphon spicatus*. *Planta Med.* 1989, **55**, 569-570.
5. Lyckander IM and Malterud KE. Lipophilic flavonoids from *Orthosiphon spicatus* as inhibitors of 15-lipoxygenase. *Acta Pharm. Nord.* 1992, **4**, 159-166.
6. Pietta PG, Mauri PL, Gardana C and Bruno A. High-performance liquid chromatography with diode-array detection of methoxylated flavones in Orthosiphon leaves. *J. Chromatogr.* 1991, **547**, 439-442.
7. Schut GA and Zwaving JH. Pharmacological investigation of some lipophilic flavonoids from *Orthosiphon aristatus*. *Fitoterapia* 1993, **64**, 99-102.
8. Takeda Y, Matsumoto T, Terao H, Shingu T, Futatsuishi Y, Nohara T and Kajimoto T. Orthosiphol D and E, minor diterpenes from *Orthosiphon stamineus*. *Phytochemistry* 1993, **33**, 411-415.
9. Ohashi K, Bohgaki T, Matsubara T and Shibuya H. Indonesian Medicinal Plants. XXIII. Chemical Structures of Two New Migrated Pimarane-type Diterpenes, Neo-orthosiphols A and B, and Suppressive Effects on Rat Thoracic Aorta of Chemical Constituents Isolated from the Leaves of *Orthosiphon aristatus* (Lamiaceae). *Chem. Pharm. Bull.* 2000, **48**, 433-435.
10. Tezuka Y, Stampoulis P, Banskota AH, Awale S, Tran KQ, Saiki I and Kadota S. Constituents of the Vietnamese Medicinal Plant *Orthosiphon stamineus*. *Chem. Pharm. Bull.* 2000, **48**, 1711-1719.
11. Nagell A. Qualitätssicherung von Arzneidrogen. Teil 1: Schachtelhalmkraut, Holunderblüten, Steinkleekraut und Orthosiphonblätter. [Quality assurance of plant drugs. Part 1: Horsetail, Elder Flower, Melilot and Java Tea]. *Dtsch. Apoth. Ztg.* 1987, **127**, 7-10 [GERMAN].
12. Sumaryono W, Proksch P, Wray V, Witte L and Hartmann T. Qualitative and Quantitative Analysis of the Phenolic Constituents from *Orthosiphon aristatus*. *Planta Med.* 1991, **57**, 176-180.
13. Masuda T, Masuda K and Nakatani N. Orthosiphol A, a Highly Oxygenated Diterpene from the Leaves of *Orthosiphon stamineus*. *Tetrahedron Lett.* 1992, **33**, 945-946.
14. Masuda T, Masuda K, Shiragami S, Jitoe A and Nakatani N. Orthosiphol A and B, Novel Diterpenoid Inhibitors of TPA (12-*O*-tetradecanoylphorbol-13-acetate)-Induced Inflammation, from *Orthosiphon stamineus*. *Tetrahedron* 1992, **48**, 6787-6792.
15. Shibuya H, Bohgaki T, Matsubara T, Watarai M, Ohashi K and Kitagawa I. Indonesian Medicinal Plants. XXII. Chemical Structures of the Two New Isopimarane-Type Diterpenes, Orthosiphonones A and B, and a New Benzochromene, Orthochromene A, from the Leaves of *Orthosiphon aristatus* (Lamiaceae). *Chem. Pharm. Bull.* 1999, **47**, 695-698.
16. Shibuya H, Bohgaki T and Ohashi K. Two Novel Migrated Pimarane-type Diterpenes, Neoorthosiphols A and B, from the Leaves of *Orthosiphon aristatus* (Lamiaceae). *Chem. Pharm. Bull.* 1999, **47**, 911-912.
17. Stampoulis P, Tezuka Y, Banskota AH, Tran KQ, Saiki I and Kadota S. Staminol A, a Novel Diterpene from *Orthosiphon stamineus*. *Tetrahedron Lett.* 1999, **40**, 4239-4242.
18. Stampoulis P, Tezuka Y, Banskota AH, Tran KQ, Saiki I and Kadota S. Staminolactones A and B and Norstaminol A: Three Highly Oxygenated Staminane-Type Diterpenes from *Orthosiphon stamineus*. *Org. Lett.* 1999, **1**, 1367-1370.
19. Guérin J-C, Reveillère HP, Ducrey P and Toupet L. *Orthosiphon stamineus* as a potent source of methylripariochromene A. *J. Nat. Prod.* 1989, **52**, 171-173.
20. Gracza L and Ruff P. Occurrence and Analysis of Phenylpropane Derivatives in Medicinal Plants, V. Rosmarinic Acid in Drugs of Pharmacopeias and its Determination by HPLC. *Arch. Pharm. (Weinheim)* 1984, **317**, 339-345 [GERMAN/English summary].

21. Lamaison JL, Petitjean-Freytet C and Carnat A. Rosmarinic acid, total hydroxycinnamic derivatives and antioxidant activity of medicinal Apiaceae, Boraginaceae and Labiatae. *Ann. Pharm. Fr.* 1990, **48**, 103-108 [FRENCH/English summary].
22. Schut GA and Zwaving JH. Content and Composition of the Essential Oil of *Orthosiphon aristatus*. *Planta Med.* 1986, **52**, 240-241.
23. Wichtl M and Schäfer-Korting M. Orthosiphonblätter. In: DAB 10-Kommentar. Wissenschaftliche Erläuterungen zum Deutschen Arzneibuch, 10. Ausgabe 1991. Stuttgart: Wissenschaftliches Verlagsgesellschaft, 1994 (4. Lfg) [GERMAN].
24. Nirdnoy M and Muangman V. Effects of Folia orthosiphonis on Urinary Stone Promoters and Inhibitors. *J. Med. Assoc. Thai.* 1991, **74**, 318-321.
25. Efimova FV and Inaishvili AD. Java tea (Orthosiphon stamineus) saponins. *Aktual. Vop. Farm.* 1968 (pub. 1970), 17-18 [RUSSIAN]; through *Chem. Abstr.* 1972, **76**, 56594.
26. Mariam A, Asmawi MZ and Sadikun A. Hypoglycaemic activity of the aqueous extract of *Orthosiphon stamineus*. *Fitoterapia* 1996, **67**, 465-468.
27. Lyckander IM and Malterud KE. Lipophilic flavonoids from *Orthosiphon spicatus* prevent oxidative inactivation of 15-lipoxygenase. *Prostagland. Leukotr. Essent. Fatty Acids* 1996, **54**, 239-246.
28. Matsubara T, Bohgaki T, Watarai M, Suzuki H, Ohashi K and Shibuya H. Antihypertensive Actions of Methylripariochromene A from *Orthosiphon aristatus*, an Indonesian Traditional Medicinal Plant. *Biol. Pharm. Bull.* 1999, **22**, 1083-1088.
29. Ohashi K, Bohgaki T and Shibuya H. Antihypertensive Substance in the Leaves of Kumis Kucing (*Orthosiphon aristatus*) in Java Island. *Yakugaku Zasshi* 2000, **120**, 474-482 [JAPANESE/English summary].
30. Casadebaig-Lafon J, Jacob M, Cassanas G, Marion C and Puech A. Elaboration d'extraits végétaux adsorbés, réalisation d'extraits secs d'*Orthosiphon stamineus* Benth. [Elaboration of adsorbed vegetable extracts and application to dry extracts of *Orthosiphon stamineus* Benth.]. *Pharm. Acta Helv.* 1989, **64**, 220-224 [FRENCH/English summary].
31. Englert J and Harnischfeger G. Diuretic Action of Aqueous *Orthosiphon* Extract in Rats. *Planta Medica* 1992, **58**, 237-238.
32. Beaux D, Fleurentin J and Mortier F. Effect of Extracts of *Orthosiphon stamineus* Benth., *Hieracium pilosella* L., *Sambucus nigra* L. and *Arctostaphylos uva-ursi* (L.) Spreng. in Rats. *Phytotherapy Res.* 1998, **12**, 498-501.
33. Chow S-Y, Liao J-F, Yang H-Y and Chen C-F. Pharmacological Effects of Orthosiphonis Herba. *J. Formosan Med. Assoc.* 1979, **78**, 953-660 [CHINESE/English summary].
34. Schumann R. Über die diuretische Wirkung von Koemis-Koetjing [The diuretic effect of Koemis-Koetjing] (Dissertation). Philipps-Universität, Marburg, 1927:1-39 [GERMAN].
35. Gürber A. Der indische Nierentee, Koemis-Koetjing [Indian kidney tea, Koemis-Koetjing]. *Dtsch. Med. Wochenschr.* 1927, (31), 1299-1301 [GERMAN].
36. Westing J. Weitere Untersuchungen über die Wirkung der Herba Orthosiphonis auf den menschlichen Harn [Further investigations on the effect of Herba Orthosiphonis on human urine] (Dissertation). Philipps-Universität, Marburg, 1928:1-23 [GERMAN].
37. Doan DD, Nguyen NH, Doan HK, Nguyen TL, Phan TS, van Dau N et al. Studies on the individual and combined diuretic effects of four Vietnamese traditional herbal remedies (*Zea mays, Imperata cylindrica, Plantago major* and *Orthosiphon stamineus*). *J. Ethnopharmacol.* 1992, **36**, 225-231.
38. Rutenbeck H. Klinische Untersuchungen über ein neues Präparat aus Koemis-Koetjing, dem indischen Nierentee [Clinical investigations on a new preparation from Koemis-Koetjing, Indian kidney tea]. *Dtsch. Med. Wochenschr.* 1935, (10), 377-378 [GERMAN].
39. Mercier F and Mercier L-J. L'*Orthosiphon stamineus*, Médicament hépato-rénal. Stimulant de la dépuration urinaire. *Le Bulletin Médical* 1936, (1 August), 523-31 [FRENCH].
40. Tiktinsky OL, Bablumyan YA. The therapeutic effect of Java tea and Equisetum arvense in patients with uratic diathesis. *Urol. Nefrol.* 1983, (1), 47-50 [RUSSIAN/English summary].
41. Orthosiphon. In: *Médicaments à base de plantes.* ISBN 2-911473-02-7. Saint-Denis Cedex, France: Agence du Médicament, 1998.
42. Orthosiphonis folium (Orthosiphonblätter). German Commission E Monograph published in: Bundesanzeiger No. 50 of 13.03.86 with a revision in Bundesanzeiger No. 50 of 13.03.90.
43. Ramos Ruiz A, De la Torre RA, Alonso N, Villaescusa A, Betancourt J and Vizoso A. Screening of medicinal plants for induction of somatic segregation activity in *Aspergillus nidulans*. *J. Ethnopharmacol.* 1996, **52**, 123-127.

REGULATORY GUIDELINES FROM OTHER EU COUNTRIES

FRANCE

Médicaments à base de plantes [41]: Orthosiphon, tige feuillée.

Therapeutic indications accepted

Oral use
Traditionally used to facilitate urinary and digestive elimination functions.
Traditionally used as an adjuvant to slimming regimes.
Traditionally used to promote the renal elimination of water.

GERMANY

Commission E monograph [42]: Orthosiphonis folium (Orthosiphonblätter).

Uses
Irrigation therapy in bacterial and inflammatory complaints of the lower urinary tract and renal gravel.

Contraindications
None known.
Caution: No irrigation therapy in cases of oedema due to impaired heart and kidney function.

Side effects
None known.

Interactions with other drugs
None known.

Dosage
Unless otherwise prescribed, daily dosage: 6-12 g of the drug or equivalent preparations.

Mode of administration
Comminuted drug for infusions and other galenic preparations for oral use.

Actions
Diuretic, weak antispasmodic.

JUNIPER

Cupressaceae

Juniperi pseudo-fructus

Definition
Juniper consists of the dried, ripe cone berries of *Juniperus communis* L.

CONSTITUENTS

□ ***Essential oil***, up to 3% V/m (Ph. Eur. min. 1.0% V/m), of very variable composition but consisting mainly of monoterpene hydrocarbons, principally α-pinene (24-80%) together with β-pinene (up to 27%), myrcene (up to 22%), sabinene (up to 29%), limonene (up to 11%) and others. Monoterpene alcohols including terpinen-4-ol (up to 17%) and α-terpineol, and sequiterpenes such as β-caryophyllene and germacrene D, are also present [1-6]. About 105 constituents occur in the oil [1].

Analysis of essential oil from 15 batches of juniper berry from various sources gave results in the ranges: α-pinene (24.1-55.4%), β-pinene (2.1-6.0%), myrcene (7.3-22.0%), sabinene (1.4-28.8%), limonene (2.3-10.9%), terpinen-4-ol (0.7-17.0%), α-terpineol (up to 1.7%), terpinolene (0.7-1.9%), γ-terpinene (0.5-5.8%), α-terpinene (0.5-2.6%), α-thujene (0.6-1.9%) and β-caryophyllene (1.3-2.3%) [4].

Commercial juniper berry oil is rarely a true distillate from the berries and may be a by-product from gin or brandy manufacture, derived from fermented berries [5].

□ ***Diterpenoids*** Myrcecommunic (= isocommunic), *cis*- and *trans*-communic, sandaracopimaric, isopimaric, torulosic, imbricatolic and imbricatalic acids [7]; also some of the corresponding aldehydes (myrcecommunal, *cis*-communal, sandaracopimaral, isopimaral, torulosal) and alcohols (*cis*-communol, sandaracopimarol, isopimarol, torulosol), and various other diterpenoids [8].

□ ***Condensed tannins*** (proanthocyanidins) A small amount (5 mg/kg) of proanthocyanidins has been isolated [9]. In a different study, (+)-catechin, (−)-epicatechin, (+)-gallocatechin, (−)-epigallocatechin, (+)-afzelechin and (−)-epiafzelechin were identified [10].

□ ***Flavonoids*** Flavonols and flavones including isoquercitrin, rutin [11], quercitrin, apigenin and luteolin [12]; the 7-glucosides of hypolaetin, scutellarein, apigenin, 7-hydroxy-4',5,6-trimethoxyflavone [11] and luteolin [12]; the 6-xylosides of 6-hydroxyluteolin and scutellarein; quercetin 3-arabinosylglucoside [11], and kaempferol 3-glucoside and 3-rhamnoside [12].

The biflavones robustaflavone, podocarpusflavone A and hinokiflavone have also been isolated [12].

□ ***Other constituents*** include fatty alcohols (10-nonacosanol and 5,10-nonacosadiol), β-sitosterol [8], sugars (fructose, glucose and glucuronic acid) and ascorbic acid [13].

Published Assay Methods
Essential oil content [Ph. Eur. 2]. Essential oil components by GC [1-4] and GC-MS [1-3].

PHARMACOLOGY

In vitro
Juniper oil exhibited only weak antimicrobial activity against a range of organisms. Minimum inhibitory concentrations were 2.0% (V/V) against *Staphylococcus aureus* and *Candida albicans*, and 4.0% against *Escherichia coli*, compared to 0.03% with thyme oil against all three organisms[14].

In vivo

Diuretic effects
In older (1937) studies, oral administration to rabbits of an infusion equivalent to 750 mg of juniper increased urine volume by 20% compared to animals given water only; in mice a dose equivalent to 50 mg of juniper increased urine volume by 38%

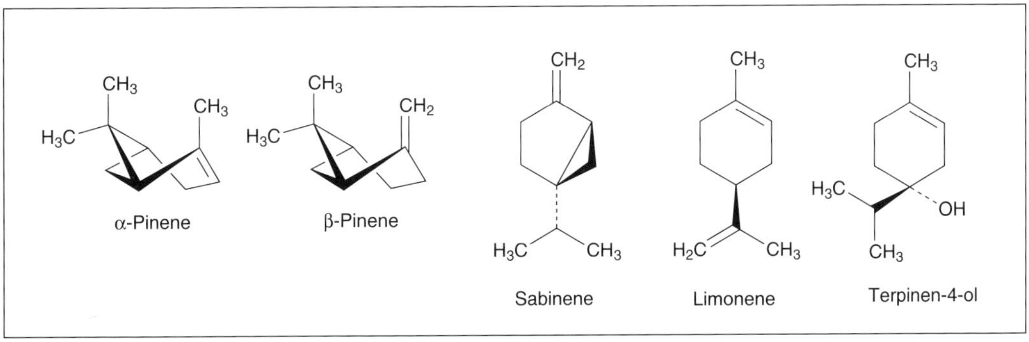

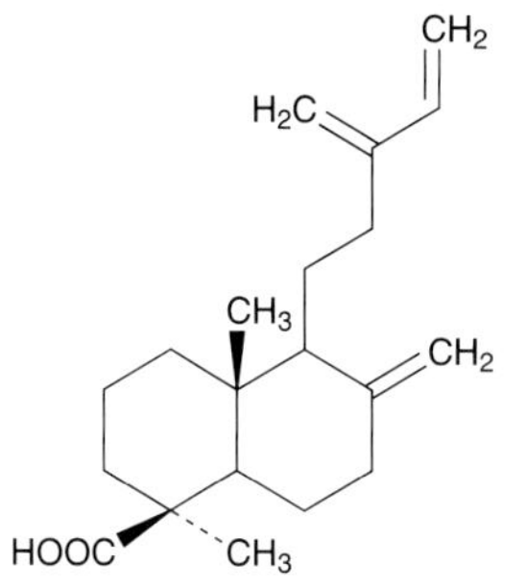

Myrcecommunic acid

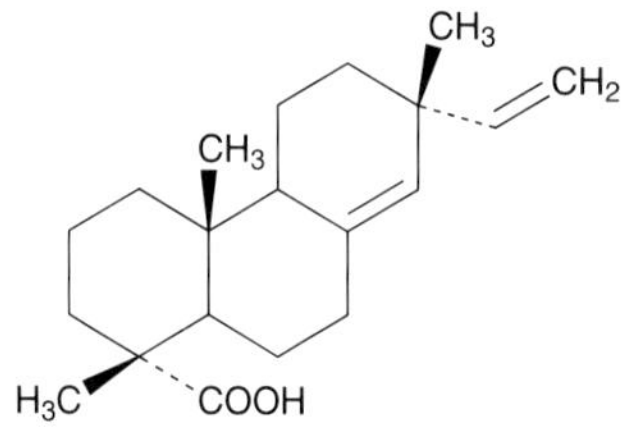

Sandaracopimaric acid

[15]; in rats a dose equivalent to 125 mg of juniper increased urine volume by 36% [16]. However, in all three cases twice or half the above doses produced much less or no effect.

No increase in urine volume or excretion of sodium, potassium or chloride was observed in rats over a 6-hour period after oral administration of a lyophilised aqueous extract of juniper at 1000 mg/kg body weight, compared to the effect of the same volume of water [17].

Oral administration of a 10% aqueous infusion of juniper or a 0.1% aqueous solution of juniper oil (with solubiliser) to groups of rats at 5 ml/100 g body weight caused, in comparison with the effect of water only, reductions of 6% in diuresis over a 24-hour period; this was equivalent to the effect of 0.004 IU/100 g of antidiuretic hormone (ADH, vasopressin; administered intraperitoneally). An aqueous 0.01% solution of terpinen-4-ol at 5 ml/100 g caused a reduction of 30% in diuresis ($p<0.01$), equivalent to 0.4 IU/100 g of ADH. However, with continued daily administration at the same dose levels, the two juniper preparations and terpinen-4-ol stimulated diuresis on days 2 and 3, although only the 10% aqueous infusion of juniper exerted significant diuretic activity (+ 43% on day 2; + 44% on day 3; $p<0.05$). Thus the diuretic effect appeared to be due partly to the essential oil and partly to hydrophilic constituents [18].

Oral administration of juniper oil to rats at 100 or 333 mg/kg/day for 28 days produced no significant diuresis [19].

Juniper oil administered subcutaneously to rats at 1.0 mg/kg significantly increased urine volume after 4 hours and 24 hours compared to physiological saline. Terpinen-4-ol was identified as the principal diuretic component of the oil; at 0.1 mg/kg s.c. it increased urine volume with more than twice the effect of the oil [20] and also increased excretion of sodium, potassium and chloride [21].

A 1% infusion, or volatile oil (10 mg/kg body weight), from unripened juniper berries, administered intragastrically to rats, produced a more effective diuretic response than the same preparations from matured fruits. It was also observed that the aqueous residue from unripened berries after distillation of the volatile oil had a marked diuretic effect [22].

In summary, the evidence of diuretic activity is rather contradictory with respect to juniper aqueous extracts and juniper oil.

Anti-inflammatory effect
An orally administered dry 80% ethanolic extract of juniper inhibited carrageenan-induced rat paw oedema by 60% ($p<0.001$) at 100 mg/kg and 79% at 200 mg/kg, compared to 45% inhibition by indometacin at 5 mg/kg ($p<0.01$) [23].

Antifertility effects
Extracts of juniper berry or seeds, administered orally to female rats at 300-500 mg/kg body weight, showed dose-dependent anti-implantation activity [24,25] and also abortifacient activity [24]. The antifertility effects have been attributed to anti-progestational activity [26].

Other effects
An orally administered decoction of juniper showed significant hypoglycaemic activity in normoglycaemic rats after single doses equivalent to 250-500 mg of juniper per kg and in streptozotocin-induced diabetic rats after 24-day treatment with the equivalent of 125 mg of juniper per kg; the effects were attributed to an increase in peripheral absorption of glucose, independent of plasma insulin levels [27]. On the other hand, a study in streptozotocin-induced diabetic mice failed to show any antihyperglycaemic effect [28].

A lyophilised aqueous extract of juniper, administered intravenously to anaesthetised normotensive rats at 25 mg/kg body weight, produced a transient rise in arterial pressure followed by a decrease of 27%. The same extract at 1200 mg/kg had an analgesic effect of 178% in a hot plate test in mice [17].

CLINICAL STUDIES

None published on mono-preparations of juniper.

THERAPEUTICS

Actions
Carminative and stomachic [29-31]; anti-inflammatory [23], weakly antimicrobial [14]. Also stated to be emmenagogic [30] and rubefacient [31].

In vivo studies of diuretic activity after oral administration of infusions, extracts or essential oil have yielded conflicting results [15-19].

Indications
None adequately substantiated by pharmacological or clinical studies.

Uses based on experience or tradition
Internal Dyspeptic complaints [29,30,32,33] and as an appetite stimulant [34]; cystitis [29,30] and other benign urinary tract disorders [34]; rheumatism [29-31], arthritis and gout [30].
External Rheumatic and arthritic pain [29-31], particularly as juniper oil preparations.

Contraindications
Pregnancy [24,30-32], renal inflammation [29-32].

Side effects
Prolonged use or overdosing may cause kidney damage [31,32].

Interactions with other drugs
None known.

Dosage
Dried berries, 6-12 g daily, divided into 3 or 4 doses [29,32,33], as an infusion or liquid extract (1:1 in 25% ethanol) [29].

SAFETY

No mortality occurred and no side effects were apparent in rats after a single oral dose of a dry 80% ethanolic extract of juniper berry at 2.5 g/kg body weight [23]. The intraperitoneal LD_{50} of a lyophilised aqueous extract in mice was determined as 3.0 g/kg [17].

The acute oral LD_{50} of juniper oil has been determined as 6.28 g/kg in rats [35]; the acute dermal LD_{50} exceeded 5 g/kg in rabbits [36].

Extracts of juniper have shown anti-implantation and abortifacient activity in rats [24] but there is no evidence, and it seems unlikely, that juniper oil is responsible for the reproductive toxicity [37]. No evidence of teratogenicity was observed in rats [24].

Nephrotoxicity
Juniper and juniper oil have long been associated with adverse effects such as kidney irritation or damage on the basis of very old reports, dating from as far back as 1844 up to 1937. The conclusion from a comprehensive review of the old primary literature was that such reports were unreliable; they related only to juniper oil at high dose levels and adverse effects were probably due to contamination with turpentine oil. For medicinal purposes it is, of course, important to use juniper oil of pharmaceutical quality, with a relatively low content of pinenes and a high terpinen-4-ol content, manufactured exclusively from mature berries (juniper oil for certain purposes may be distilled from a mixture of ripe and unripe berries, needles and wood) [38,39].

In a toxicological study, two batches of juniper oil of good pharmaceutical quality (α- and β-pinenes to terpinen-4-ol ratios of 3:1 and 5:1) were administered orally to male rats daily for 28 days, the first batch at 100, 333 or 1000 mg/kg body weight and the second batch at 100, 333 or 900 mg/kg; another group of rats received terpinen-4-ol at 400 mg/kg/day. Biochemical, pathological and histological investigations revealed that neither the juniper oils nor terpinen-4-ol had induced changes in function or morphology of the kidneys and they were assessed as non-toxic at therapeutic dose levels [19].

REGULATORY STATUS

Medicines

UK	Accepted for general sale, internal or external use [40].
France	Accepted for specified indications [34].
Germany	Commission E monograph published, with approved uses [32].

Food

USA	Generally recognized as safe (21 CFR 182.20) [41].
Council of Europe	Permitted as flavouring, category N2 [42].

REFERENCES

Current Pharmacopoeial Monographs
Ph. Eur. Juniper

Literature References

1. Chatzopoulou PS and Katsiotis ST. Study of the Essential Oil from *Juniperus communis* "Berries" (Cones) Growing Wild in Greece. *Planta Medica* 1993, **59**, 554-556.
2. Chatzopoulou PS and Katsiotis ST. Procedures influencing the yield and the quality of the essential oil from *Juniperus communis* L. berries. *Pharm. Acta Helv.* 1995, **70**, 247-253.
3. Koukos PK and Papadopoulou KI. Essential Oil of *Juniperus communis* L. grown in Northern Greece: Variation of Fruit Oil Yield and Composition. *J. Essent. Oil. Res.* 1997, **9**, 35-39.
4. Schilcher H, Emmrich D, Koehler C. Gaschromatographischer Vergleich von ätherischen Wacholderölen und deren toxikologische Bewertung [Gas chromatographic comparison of juniper essential oils and their toxicological evaluation]. *Pharm. Ztg. Wiss.* 1993, **138**, 85-91 [GERMAN/English summary].
5. Formácek V and Kubeczka K-H. Juniper berry oil. In: *Essential oils analysis by capillary gas chromatography and carbon-13 NMR spectroscopy.* ISBN 0-471-26218-8. Chichester-New York: John Wiley, 1982: 125-129.
6. Ochocka JR, Asztemborska M, Zook DR, Sybilska D, Perez G and Ossicini L. Enantiomers of monoterpenic hydrocarbons in essential oils from *Juniperus communis. Phytochemistry* 1997, **44**, 869-873.
7. De Pascual Teresa J, San Feliciano A and Barrero AF. Composition of Juniperus communis (common juniper) fruit. *An. Quim.* 1973, **69**, 1065-1067 [SPANISH]; through *Chem. Abstr.* 1974, **81**, 74847.
8. De Pascual Teresa J, Barrero AF, San Feliciano A and Sanchez Bellido I. Componentes de las arcestidas de Juniperus communis L. IV. Fracción neutra [Components of the berries of Juniperus communis L. IV. Neutral fraction]. An. Quim. 1977, **73**, 568-573 [SPANISH/English summary].
9. Schulz JM and Herrmann K. Occurrence of Catechins and Proanthocyanidins in Spices. V. Phenolics of Spices. *Z. Lebensm. Unters. Forsch.* 1980, **171**, 278-280 [GERMAN/English summary].
10. Friedrich H and Engelshowe R. Tannin Producing Monomeric Substances in Juniperus communis L. *Planta Medica* 1978, **33**, 251-257 [GERMAN/English summary].
11. Lamer-Zarawska E. Phytochemical studies on flavonoids and other compounds of juniper fruits (Juniperus communis L.). *Pol. J. Chem.* 1980, **54**, 213-219; through *Chem. Abstr.* 1980, **93**, 128746.
12. Hiermann A, Kompek A, Reiner J, Auer H and Schubert-Zsilavecz M. Investigation of flavonoid pattern in fruits of *Juniperus communis* L. *Sci. Pharm.* 1996, **64**, 437-444 [GERMAN/English summary].
13. Panaiotov IM. Sugar content of juniper berries. *Bulgar. Akad. Nauk. Izvest. Khim. Inst.* 1958, **6**, 113-119; through *Chem. Abstr.* 1960, **54**, 18693.
14. Hammer KA, Carson CF and Riley TV. Antimicrobial activity of essential oils and other plant extracts. *J. Applied Microbiol.* 1999, **86**, 985-990.
15. Vollmer H and Weidlich R. Untersuchungen über die diuretische Wirkung der Fructus juniperi, Radix levistici, Radix liquiritiae und Herba violae tricoloris an Kaninchen und Mäusen [Investigations of the diuretic effect of Fructus juniperi, Radix levistici, Radix liquiritiae and Herba violae tricoloris in rabbits and mice]. *Naunyn-Schmiedebergs Arch. Exp. Path. Pharmakol.* 1937, **186**, 574-583 [GERMAN]
16. Vollmer H and Hübner K. Untersuchungen über die diuretische Wirkung der Fructus juniperi, Radix levistici, Radix ononidis, Folia betulae, Radix liquiritiae und Herba equiseti an Ratten [Investigations of the diuretic effect of Fructus juniperi, Radix levistici, Radix ononidis, Folia betulae, Radix liquiritiae and Herba equiseti in rats]. *Naunyn-Schmiedebergs Arch. Exp. Path. Pharmakol.* 1937, **186**, 592-605 [GERMAN].
17. Lasheras B, Turillas P and Cenarruzabeitia E. Étude pharmacologique préliminaire de *Prunus spinosa* L. Amelanchier ovalis Medikus, *Juniperus communis* L. et *Urtica dioica* L. *Plantes Méd. Phytothér.* 1986, **20**, 219-226 [FRENCH/English summary].
18. Stanic G, Samarzija I and Blazevic N. Time-dependent Diuretic Response in Rats Treated with Juniper Berry Preparations. *Phytotherapy Res.* 1998, **12**, 494-497.
19. Schilcher H and Leuschner F. Studies of Potential Nephrotoxic Effects of Juniper Essential Oil. *Arzneim.-Forsch./Drug Res.* 1997, **47**, 855-858 [GERMAN/English summary].
20. Janku I, Háva M, Motl O. Ein diuretisch wirksamer Stoff aus Wacholder (*Juniperus communis* L.) [An effective diuretic substance from juniper (*Juniperus communis* L.)]. *Experientia* 1957, **13**, 255-256 [GERMAN/English summary].
21. Janku I, Háva M, Kraus R, Motl O. Das diuretische Prinzip des Wacholders [The diuretic principle of juniper]. *Naunyn-Schmiedebergs Arch. Exp. Path. Pharmakol.* 1960, **238**, 112-113 [GERMAN].
22. Rácz-Kotilla E, Csedö C and Rácz G. The diuretic action of unripened fruits of Juniper (*Juniperus communis* L.). *Farmacia (Bucharest)* 1971, **19**, 165-169 [ROMANIAN/English summary].
23. Mascolo N, Autore G, Capasso F, Menghini A and Fasulo MP. Biological Screening of Italian Medicinal Plants for Anti-inflammatory Activity. *Phytotherapy Res.* 1987, **1**, 28-31.
24. Agrawal OP, Santosh B and Mathur R. Antifertility Effects of Fruits of Juniperus communis. *Planta Medica* 1980, (Suppl), 98-101.
25. Prakash AO. Potentialities of Some Indigenous Plants for Antifertility Activity. *Int. J. Crude Drug Res.* 1986, **24**, 19-24.
26. Prakash AO, Sisodia B and Mathur R. Biological profile of butanolic extract of dried fruits of *Juniperus communis. Fitoterapia* 1994, **65**, 248-252.
27. Sánchez de Medina F, Gámez MJ, Jiménez I, Jiménez J, Osuna JI and Zarzuelo A. Hypoglycemic activity of Juniper "Berries". *Planta Medica* 1994, **60**, 197-200.
28. Gray AM and Flatt PR. Nature's own pharmacy: the diabetes perspective. *Proc. Nutr. Soc.* 1997, **56**, 507-517.
29. Juniperus. In: *British Herbal Pharmacopoeia 1983.* ISBN 0-903032-07-4. Bournemouth: British Herbal Medicine Association, 1983.
30. Chevallier A. Juniper. In: *The Encyclopedia of Medicinal Plants.* ISBN 0-7513-0314-3. London-New York-Stuttgart: Dorling Kindersley, 1996:223.
31. Stodola J and Volák J. Juniper. Translated into English in: Bunney S, editor. *The Illustrated Book of Herbs.* ISBN 0-7064-1489-6. London: Octopus Books, 1984:174.
32. Juniperi fructus (Wacholderbeeren). German Commission E Monograph published in: Bundesanzeiger No. 228 of 5.12.84.
33. Wacholderbeeren [Juniper berries]. In: Braun R, editor. *Standardzulassungen für Fertigarzneimittel - Text und Kommentar.* Stuttgart: Deutscher Apotheker Verlag, Frankfurt: Govi-Verlag, 1986.
34. Genévrier [Juniper]. In: *Médicaments à base de plantes.* ISBN 2-911473-02-7. Saint-Denis Cedex, France: Agence du Médicament, 1998.
35. von Skramlik E. Über die Giftigkeit und Verträglichkeit von ätherischen Ölen [The toxicity and tolerability of essential oils]. *Pharmazie* 1959, **14**, 435-445 [GERMAN].
36. Opdyke DLJ. Monographs on fragrance raw materials: Juniper berry oil. *Food Cosmet. Toxicol.* 1976, **14**, 333.
37. Tisserand R and Balacs J. Juniper. In: *Essential Oil Safety.* London: Churchill Livingstone, 1995:142.
38. Schilcher H and Heil BM. Nephrotoxicity of juniper berry preparations: A critical review of the literature from 1844 to 1993. *Z Phytotherapie* 1994, **15**, 205-213 [GERMAN/English summary].
39. Schilcher H. Wacholderbeeröl bei Erkrankungen der ableitenden Harnwege? [Juniper oil in ailments of the lower urinary tract?]. *Med. Monatsschr. Pharm.* 1995, **18**, 198-199 [GERMAN].
40. Juniper. In: UK Statutory Instrument 1984 No. 769. The Medicines (Products Other Than Veterinary Drugs) (General Sale List) Order 1984. Schedule 1, Table A.
41. Juniper (berries). In: Section 182.20 of USA Code of Federal Regulations, Title 21, Food and Drugs, Parts 170 to 199. Revised as of April 1, 2000.

42. Juniperus communis L., fruits. In: *Flavouring Substances and Natural Sources of Flavourings, 3rd ed.* ISBN 2-7160 0081-6. Strasbourg: Council of Europe, 1981.

REGULATORY GUIDELINES FROM OTHER EU COUNTRIES

FRANCE

Médicaments à base de plantes [34]: Genévrier, pseudo-fruit (= cône femelle).

Therapeutic indications accepted

Oral use
Traditionally used: to stimulate the appetite; to promote the renal elimination of water; as an adjuvant in diuretic treatments of benign urinary complaints.

GERMANY

Commission E monograph [32]: Juniperi fructus (Wacholderbeeren).

Uses
Dyspeptic complaints.

Contraindications
Pregnancy, inflammatory kidney ailments.

Side effects
Prolonged use or overdosing may cause kidney damage.

Interactions with other drugs
None known.

Dosage
Unless otherwise prescribed, daily dose: from 2 g up to a maximum of 10 g of dried juniper berries, equivalent to 20-100 mg of the essential oil.

Mode of administration
Whole, crushed or powdered drug for infusions and decoctions, alcoholic extracts and wine infusions. Essential oil.
Liquid and solid dosage forms exclusively for oral use.
Note: Combination with other plant drugs in 'bladder and kidney teas' and similar preparations may be appropriate.

Actions
Increased urine excretion and a direct effect on contraction of smooth muscle have been demonstrated

KAVA-KAVA

Piperaceae

Piperis methystici rhizoma

Definition

Kava-Kava consists of the rhizome, usually free from roots and sometimes scraped, of *Piper methysticum* G. Forst., cut into pieces and dried.

In the UK and various other countries the sale of kava-kava products is currently prohibited due to reports of potential hepatotoxicity and consequent action by regulatory authorities [1,2]. The benefit-risk profile of kava-kava remains a matter of controversy [3-5], but no satisfactory explanation for the adverse data has yet emerged and it seems that further research will be needed to resolve this perplexing toxicological problem [6].

CONSTITUENTS

☐ ***Kavalactones (kavapyrones)***, 4-18% (average 11%) [7]. The six major ones, representing about 96% of total kavalactones, are (+)-kavain, (+)-dihydrokavain, (+)-methysticin, (+)-dihydromethysticin, yangonin and demethoxyyangonin [7-10]. Proportions of individual compounds vary, depending more on chemotype than environmental factors. Based on HPLC analysis of 121 cultivars (6 chemotypes) from 51 islands in Polynesia, Micronesia and Melanesia, (+)-dihydrokavain, (+)-kavain or (+)-methysticin is usually predominant [7]. So far 18 kavalactones have been been isolated [8].
☐ ***Chalcones*** Flavokavins A, B [8,11] and C [8] have been isolated as minor constituents; they are yellow pigments.
☐ ***Alkaloids*** Very small amounts of cepharadione A, a fluorescent orange-coloured compound [12], the pyrrolidine alkaloids *N*-cinnamoylpyrrolidine and *N*-(3-methoxycinnamoyl)-pyrrolidine [13,14].

The rather unstable piperidine alkaloid pipermethystine has been reported as a minor component of kava-kava root [15], but was not detected in commercial root powders from Fiji, Tonga or Hawaii. It is, however, present in amounts of 0.1-0.4% in basal stem peelings from various cultivars of *Piper methysticum*, and stem peelings have apparently been included in some raw material destined for the pharmaceutical industry [16].
☐ ***Other constituents*** include bornyl cinnamate, stigmasterol [14], free aromatic and aliphatic acids [17] and glutathione [18].

Published Assay Methods

HPLC of kavalactones [7-9]. Capillary electrophoresis of kavalactones [10]. Separation and quantification of kavalactone enantiomers (from synthetic racemates) [19,20].

PHARMACOLOGY

Kava-kava has been shown to have anxiolytic, sedative, muscle relaxant, anticonvulsant, neuroprotective, analgesic and local anaesthetic effects, attributed mainly to the activity of the lipid-soluble kavalactone constituents [21,22]. Its pharmacological properties are postulated to include enhanced ligand binding to $GABA_A$ receptors (through a non-benzodiazepine mechanism), blockade of voltage-gated sodium ion channels, diminished excitatory neurotransmitter

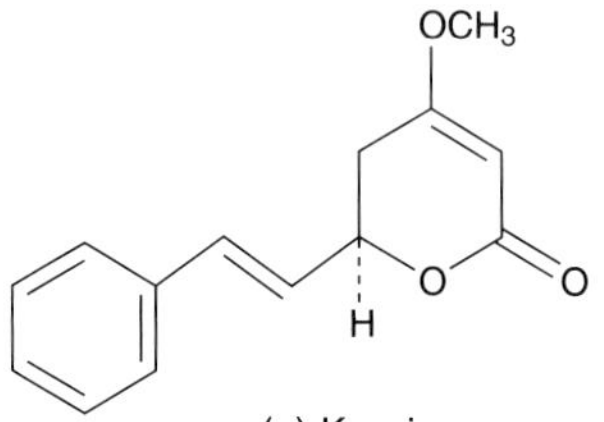

(+)-Kavain

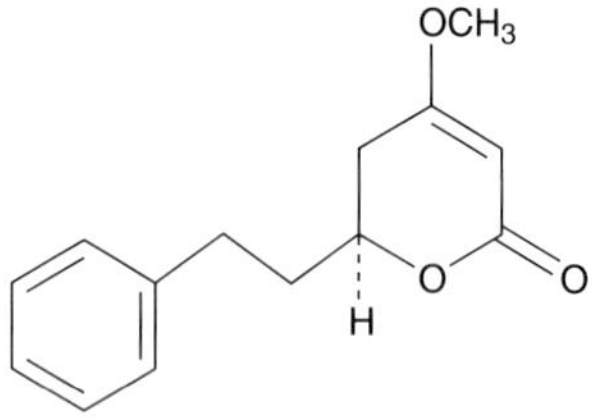

(+)-Dihydrokavain

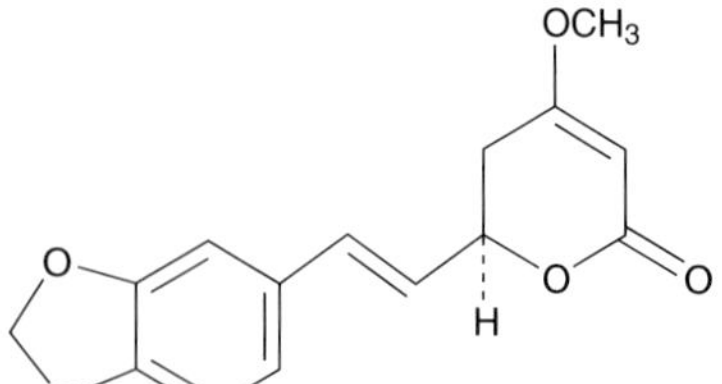

(+)-Methysticin

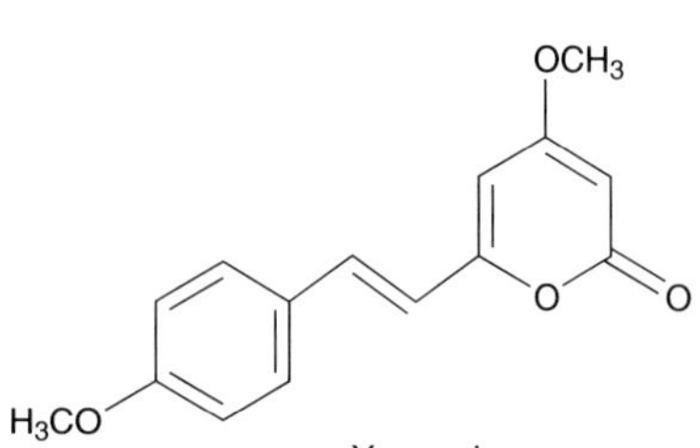

Yangonin

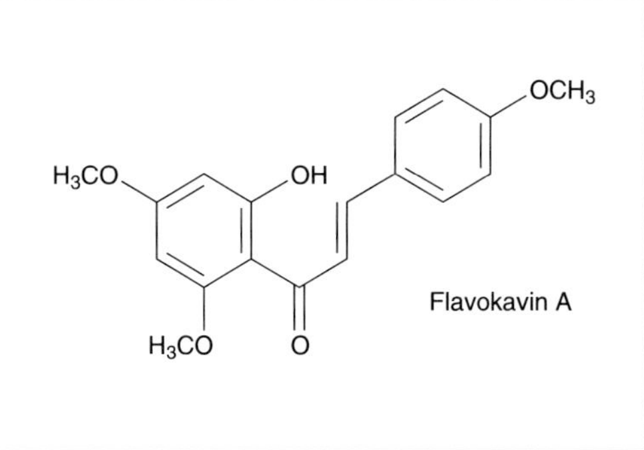

Flavokavin A

release due to calcium ion channel blockade, reduced neuronal reuptake of noradrenaline (norepinephrine), reversible inhibition of monoamine oxidase B and suppression of the synthesis of thromboxane A2 (which antagonises $GABA_A$ receptor function) [21,23].

A summary of the extensive *in vitro* and *in vivo* studies carried out with kava-kava extracts and isolated kavalactones can be found in the ESCOP monograph [2].

Pharmacological studies in humans

Healthy volunteers have participated in a number of controlled studies to evaluate the effects of kava-kava extracts:

- Neither a dry acetone-water extract (70% kavalactones; 3 × 200 mg/day for 5 days) [24] nor aqueous preparations [25] from kava-kava were found to have any significant effect on the cognitive performance of young volunteers in psychometric tests. In contrast, the benzodiazepine drug oxazepam (15 mg the day before and 75 mg on the test day) greatly reduced performance [24].
- Electro-encephalograms and electro-oculograms recorded during the sleep of volunteers aged 20-31 years after they had taken 3 × 50 mg or 3 × 100 mg of an acetone-water extract of kava-kava suggested, in comparison with those recorded in a placebo group, improvement in sleep quality: a tendency towards more rapid onset of sleep, shorter periods of light sleep and more prolonged periods of deep sleep [26].
- A dry acetone-water extract (3 × 100 mg or 3 × 200 mg daily for 7 days) from kava-kava produced changes typical of anxiolytics in the encephalograms of volunteers aged 24-47 years. The extract had no sedative-hypnotic effects even after 600 mg/day and the results suggested an increase in vigilance, while psychometric tests indicated increased activation and an improvement in emotional stability [27]. A later study in which male volunteers aged 18-33 years were given a single dose of an ethanolic kava-kava extract containing 120 mg of kavalactones also demonstrated increased vigilance, with better performance in sustained concentration and reaction time tests [28].
- Assessment of 20 volunteers using the State-Trait Inventory showed that a single 300 mg oral dose of a kava-kava extract (30% kavalactones) led to increased cheerfulness ($p<0.001$ compared to placebo) and could act as an "exhilarant", particularly in those with a cheerful temperament, but did not influence seriousness or bad mood. Improvements in cognitive performance were also observed in tests of visual attention and short-term memory retrieval [29].

Pharmacokinetics

In mice, kavalactones have been shown to readily cross the blood-brain barrier with attainment of maximal concentrations of kavain and dihydrokavain in mouse brain about 5 minutes after intraperitoneal injection. Penetration of kavalactones into the mouse brain appeared to be synergistically increased when they were administered together rather than individually. Furthermore, marked increases in pharmacological potency of some kavalactones have been observed when given orally in combination with others, suggesting a synergistic action in their absorption from the intestine [23,30].

Following ingestion by healthy male volunteers of a kava-kava beverage (about 10 × 100 ml aliquots over a period of 1 hour) prepared by the traditional method of aqueous extraction, all 7 major and several minor kavalactones were identified in human urine. Metabolic transformations included reduction of the double bond and/or demethylation of the methoxyl group of the α-pyrone ring system. In contrast to findings in rats, no dihydroxylated metabolites of kavalactones or products from opening of the α-pyrone ring were identified in human urine [31].

After ingestion of 200 mg of kavain by humans, approx. 80% is absorbed, of which up to 98% is metabolized on first pass through the liver, mainly to more hydrophilic *p*-hydroxykavain (as its sulphate conjugate). Maximum plasma levels of *p*-hydroxykavain sulphate conjugate (50 ng/ml) and kavain (18 ng/ml) are attained within 1.7-1.8 hours. The elimination half-life of p-hydroxykavain sulphate is about 29 hours, while elimination of kavain is biphasic with half-lives of 50 minutes for the first phase and 9 hours for the second [32].

CLINICAL STUDIES

Controlled studies

Table 1 lists in chronological order 15 controlled studies carried out with mono-preparations of kava-kava. Seven studies [33-39] are summarized below; summaries of the other studies [40-47] can be found in the ESCOP monograph [2].

Six randomized, placebo-controlled, double-blind studies [33-38] have been subjected to meta-analysis (see below). In each of these studies the same acetone-water (75% w/w of acetone) dry extract of kava-kava, containing 70% of kava-lactones, was used and reductions in Hamilton Anxiety Scale (HAMA) scores were the main criterion for assessment of efficacy:

- In an 8-week study, women aged 45-60 years in the peri- or post-menopausal phase with anxiety, restlessness and sleep disorders and also psychosomatic symptoms correlating with gynaecological dysfunction were treated daily with 3 × 100 mg of extract (n = 20) or placebo (n = 20). After 1 week the average HAMA score in the verum group had decreased by over 50% (from 31.1 to 14.7), significantly more (p<0.001) than in the placebo group (30.1 to 27.5), and the difference widened by the end of weeks 4 and 8 (p<0.0005). Results from the Depressive Status Inventory (DSI) scale, Clinical Global Impressions (CGI) scale and Kuppermann Index (severity of climacteric symptoms) were also favourable to kava-kava treatment [33].
- In a 4-week study patients with non-psychotic anxiety syndromes were treated daily with 3 × 100 mg of extract (n = 29) or placebo (n = 29). After 1 week the HAMA total score had decreased significantly in the kava-kava group compared to the placebo group and this difference widened during the course of the study (p = 0.0035 after 4 weeks). Results for HAMA sub-scores for somatic and mental anxiety, and from CGI and the Adjectives Check List, were also in favour of the kava-kava extract [34].
- In a 25-week study, 101 outpatients suffering from non-psychotic anxiety diagnosed in accordance with DSM-III-R criteria were treated daily with 3 × 100 mg of extract (n = 52) or placebo (n = 49). Patients taking the kava-kava extract had significantly better HAMA total scores by week 8 (p = 0.02) than those on placebo and the difference increased during subsequent weeks (p<0.001 at weeks 16, 20 and 24). Verum patients also showed significantly greater improvements in HAMA sub-scores for somatic and mental anxiety (p = 0.02 by week 8), in CGI rating (p = 0.001 after 12 weeks; p = 0.015 after 24 weeks) and in a Self-report Symptom Inventory (p<0.05 from week 12) [35].
- Patients with non-psychotic nervous anxiety, tension and restlessness diagnosed in accordance with DSM-III-R, initial HAMA total scores not exceeding 14 (to exclude severe disorders) and a history of uninterrupted treatment with benzodiazepines (mean duration 21 months) were included in a 5-week study. Existing benzodiazepine medication was tapered off to zero at a steady rate over the first 2 weeks, while over the first week the patients received either kava-kava extract, gradually increasing from 50 mg/day to 3 × 100 mg/day (n = 20), or placebo (n = 20). In the final 3 weeks of the study, therefore, the patients were receiving only 3 × 100 mg/day of kava-kava extract or placebo. Compared to the placebo group, significant decreases in scores were evident in the kava-kava group on the HAMA scale (p = 0.01) and the Bf-S subjective well-being scale (p = 0.002), and these results were supported by the secondary efficacy measures of CGI and the Erlangen Anxiety and Aggression Scale (EAAS). Over the 5-week period, the median HAMA score in the kava-kava group decreased by 7.5, whereas in the placebo group it increased by 1 point [36].
- Patients with sleep disturbances associated with anxiety disorders of non-psychotic origin (diagnosed in accordance with DSM-III-R) were assigned to treatment with 200 mg/day of kava-kava extract (n = 34) or placebo (n = 27) for 4 weeks. Compared to the placebo group, patients in the kava-kava group showed significantly greater improvements with respect to subscores for "quality of sleep" (p = 0.007) and "recuperative effect after sleep" (p = 0.018) in a sleep questionnaire, and in the HAMA psychic anxiety subscore (p = 0.002), but not in HAMA total score (p = 0.10). Trends on the Bf-S subjective well-being scale and the CGI scale were in favour of the kava-kava extract [37].
- Patients with non-psychotic anxiety (diagnosed in accordance with DSM-III-R) were assigned to treatment with kava-kava extract (3 × 50 mg/day; n = 25) or placebo (n = 25) for 4 weeks. Problems were encountered with intention-to-treat evaluation and placebo effects were considerable, but from per-protocol analysis HAMA total scores improved significantly in the kava group (p = 0.03) compared to the placebo group, as did scores in HAMA subscales for "somatic anxiety" (p = 0.03) and "psychic anxiety" (p = 0.04). Trends favourable to kava-kava extract treatment in secondary variables such as the CGI, EAAS and and the Brief Personality Structure Scale (KEPS) did not reach statistical significance. This was not a particularly well-conducted study [38].

In a further randomized, double-blind study (not suitable for the meta-analyses described below), patients with neurotic anxiety diagnosed in accordance with DSM-III-R and with mean total scores of over 25 on the Hamilton Anxiety Scale

TABLE 1 CONTROLLED CLINICAL STUDIES WITH KAVA-KAVA EXTRACTS in chronological order

First author Year Reference number	Number of patients Verum/RT	Diagnosis	Type of preparation	Daily dosage		Duration (days)	Reference therapy (RT)	Main efficacy outcomes for the kava-kava group in comparison with the reference therapy group(s)
				Extract	Kava-lactones			
Bhate 1989 [40]	28/28	Anxiety before surgery	Ethanolic extract (20% kavalactones)	1 × 300 mg	60 mg	2	Placebo	Significantly less anxiety ($p<0.05$); better sleep quality ($p<0.05$), psychostatus ($p<0.01$) and postoperative assessment ($p<0.01$).
Warnecke 1990 [41]	20/20	Menopausal anxiety	Ethanolic extract (20% kavalactones)	2 × 150 mg	60 mg	84	Placebo	Reduced severity of climacteric symptoms and anxiety disorders ($p<0.001$).
Warnecke 1991 [33]	20/20	Menopausal anxiety	Acetone-water extract (70% kavalactones)	3 × 100 mg	210 mg	56	Placebo	Significantly greater reduction in HAMA total score ($p<0.0005$).
Kinzler 1991 [34]	29/29	Anxiety disorders	Acetone-water extract (70% kavalactones)	3 × 100 mg	210 mg	28	Placebo	Significantly greater reduction in HAMA total score ($p = 0.0035$).
Woelk 1993 [42]	57/59/56	Anxiety disorders	Acetone-water extract (70% kavalactones)	3 × 100 mg	210 mg	42	Oxazepam 15 mg/day or Bromazepam 9 mg/day	No significant differences between groups in HAMA total score reduction.
Volz 1997 [35]	52/48	Non-psychotic anxiety	Acetone-water extract (70% kavalactones)	3 × 100 mg	210 mg	168	Placebo	Significantly greater reduction in HAMA total score ($p<0.001$).
Mittman 2000 [43]	26/27	Anxiety before surgery	Spissum extract	Not stated	100 mg	2	Benzodiazepines	Comparable efficacy in the two groups.
De Leo 2000 [44]	24/16	Menopausal anxiety	Extract (55% kavain)	1 × 100 mg + HRT	Not stated	183	Placebo + HRT	Significantly greater reduction in HAMA total score ($p = 0.05$).
Malsch 2001 [36]	20/20	Non-psychotic anxiety	Acetone-water extract (70% kavalactones)	3 × 100 mg	210 mg	28	Placebo	Significantly greater reductions in HAMA total score ($p = 0.01$) and Bf-S ($p = 0.002$).
Connor 2002 [47]	17/18	Generalized anxiety disorder	Not stated	Not stated	280 mg	28	Placebo	No significant differences between groups in HAMA total score reduction or other criteria (high placebo effect).
Boerner 2003 [45]	43/42/42	Generalized anxiety disorder	Ethanolic extract (30% kavalactones)	1 × 400 mg	120 mg	56	Buspirone 10 mg/day or Opipramol 100 mg/day	No significant differences between groups in HAMA total score reduction.
Cagnacci 2003 [46]	20/20/40	Menopausal anxiety	Extract (55% kavain)	1 × 100 mg or 1 × 200 mg + 1 g Calcium	Not stated	91	Calcium only	Significantly greater reduction in State Trait Anxiety Inventory score: 100 mg ($p<0.025$); 200 mg ($p<0.0003$).
Gastpar 2003 [39]	71/70	Non-psychotic anxiety	Acetone-water extract (70% kavalactones)	3 × 50 mg	105 mg	28	Placebo	No significant difference in ASI scores, but analysis of variance indicated superiority of kava-kava ($p = 0.01$)
Lehrl 2004 [37]	34/23	Sleep disturbances associated with non-psychotic anxiety	Acetone-water extract (70% kavalactones)	1 × 200 mg	140 mg	28	Placebo	Significantly greater improvements in sleep questionnaire subscores ($p = 0.007$ and $p = 0.018$) and HAMA psychic anxiety ($p = 0.002$), but not in HAMA total score.
Geier 2004 [38]	25/25	Non-psychotic anxiety	Acetone-water extract (70% kavalactones)	3 × 50 mg	105 mg	28	Placebo	Significantly greater reduction in HAMA total score ($p = 0.03$).

(HAMA) were assigned to treatment with 3 × 50 mg/day of the same acetone-water extract of kava-kava, corresponding to 105 mg/day of kavalactones (n = 71), or placebo (n = 70), for 4 weeks. The primary outcome measure, average total score in the Anxiety Status Inventory, decreased substantially in both groups and the difference between groups was not significant (p>0.05); however, a different statistical analysis indicated superiority of the kava-kava extract over placebo (p<0.01). Results from the Bf-S self-rated well-being scale and the CGI scale were in favour of the extract, while the EAAS and KEPS showed only minor differences between groups. The authors noted that, despite several results favouring the kava-kava extract, differences versus placebo were not as large as in previous studies which employed the same extract at 300 mg/day (210 mg/day of kavalactones) [39].

Meta-analyses
Data from six randomized, double-blind, placebo-controlled clinical studies [33-38] were found to be suitable for pooling to enable combined evaluation as a meta-analysis. Taking somewhat different approaches, two meta-analyses have been performed on this data [48,49]. The same acetone-water dry extract of kava-kava was used in all six studies, which included a total of 345 patients (180 taking the extract, 165 placebo) and assessed a common outcome measure, the total score on the Hamilton Anxiety Scale (HAMA).

The results of the first meta-analysis suggested a significantly greater reduction in HAMA total score in patients receiving kava-kava extract compared with those receiving placebo (p = 0.01). Subsequent sensitivity analyses indicated a relatively large treatment effect (p = 0.0002) from the two largest studies assessing patients with non-psychotic anxiety and a HAMA total score of 19 or above who received 210 mg/day of kavalactones [34,35] but, on the other hand, a *non*-significant effect (p = 0.6) from two studies [37,38] which included patients with non-psychotic anxiety and a HAMA total score of 16 or 19 or above who received relatively small doses equivalent to 105 to 140 mg/day of kava-lactones. From their meta-analysis and a review of other randomized, placebo-controlled studies the authors concluded that kava-kava appears to be an effective symptomatic treatment option for anxiety [48].

Individual patient data was made available for use in the second meta-analysis, which thus supplemented the earlier one. Using a binary outcome method, i.e. taking an improvement in HAMA score of at least 50% compared to baseline as a success, significant overall efficacy of the six studies was indicated (p<0.0001), but an alternative method indicated only borderline overall efficacy. The authors concluded that the kava-kava extract was an effective treatment for patients with non-psychotic anxiety disorders. They also noted that the extract appeared to be more effective in females and in younger patients [49].

From both meta-analyses it became clear that lower daily doses of extract, 200 mg [37] or 150 mg [38], used in more recent studies had been less effective than the 300 mg used in earlier studies [33-36]. A return to the daily dose of 300 mg (i.e. 210 mg of kavalactones) was therefore recommended by one group of authors [49].

Open studies
Four open (mainly post-marketing surveillance) studies carried out in the 1990s involved a total of over 6500 patients with various states of anxiety and reported favourable results with kava-kava preparations [50-53]. Summaries of these studies can be found in the ESCOP monograph [2].

THERAPEUTICS

Actions
Anxiolytic, tranquillizer, mild sedative, centrally-induced muscle relaxant, anticonvulsant, neuro-protective, mild analgesic and local anaesthetic [2,21,54,55].
Also stated to be antiseptic and diuretic [56-58].

Indications
Anxiety, nervous tension or restlessness of non-psychotic origin [2,33-46,54,55], including meno-pausal anxiety [33,41,44,46].

Other uses, based on experience or tradition
Inflammations and infections of the genito-urinary tract in both men and women [54,56-58].

Contraindications
Existing liver diseases, alcohol abuse [2].

Side effects
Usually none at recommended dosage levels. The question of potential hepatotoxicity is covered in the Safety section.

Excessive or chronic use of kava-kava may lead to reversible symptoms such as yellowing of the skin and nails, a typical scaly rash due to pellagroid dermatopathy and/or disturbed vision [2,54,55].

Interactions with other drugs
None confirmed [2].

Dosage
Adult daily dose: Standardized preparations corresponding to 60-210 mg of kavalactones [33-46]; dried rhizome, 1.5-3 g, or in decoction; liquid extract (1:2), 3-6 ml [54].

Treatment should usually be for 1 month; at most 2 months [3].

Note: The maximum daily dose stated above, corresponding to 210 mg of kavalactones, is based on efficacy considerations. This was the daily dose in some of the more convincing placebo-controlled clinical studies (see Table 1) [33-36], in line with the manufacturer's recommendation in the 1990s for the kava-kava extract used. However, in the wake of reports associating kava-kava extracts with rare cases of hepatotoxicity, European recommended daily doses are now generally within the limits of 60-120 mg of kavalactones [2,59], as recommended in 1990 (before the above clinical studies) by the German Commission E [55]. Meta-analyses indicate that daily doses used in the most recent clinical studies, corresponding to 105-140 mg of kavalactones, were somewhat less effective than 210 mg in the treatment of anxiety [48,49]. On this basis some authors (including two members of Commission E), have recommended a return to the daily dose corresponding to 210 mg of kavalactones [49]. This is, of course, academic in countries where kava has been withdrawn from the market.

SAFETY

Clinical safety data

Kava-kava extracts are well tolerated by most users and, in general, adverse events are rare, mild and reversible. Over 500 patients have been treated with kava-kava extracts in controlled clinical studies and more than 6500 in open studies; adverse events, mainly gastrointestinal complaints or allergic reactions, were reported in about 2.3% of patients. In placebo-controlled studies, the level of adverse events in patients treated with kava-kava was similar to that in placebo groups [2,60].

Controlled studies in healthy volunteers demonstrated that kava-kava extracts at normal dosage levels have no negative influence on the ability to drive or use machines [61,62] and no additive or potentiating effect in combination with alcohol [63].

Preclinical safety data

The oral LD_{50} in mice and rats of an acetone-water extract from kava-kava (11-20:1, 70% kavalactones) was found to be greater than 1500 mg/kg body weight [3,64,65]. Oral LD_{50} values in mice for individual kavalactones range from over 800 mg/kg for methysticin to 1130 mg/kg for kavain and over 1500 mg/kg for yangonin [66]. Chronic toxicity testing of the acetone-water extract for up to 6 months in rats and beagle dogs, and of an ethanolic kava-kava extract in rats, gave acceptable results. Neither the Ames test nor the micronucleus test in mice revealed any mutagenic potential of the acetone-water extract [2,3,64,65].

In cytotoxicity tests, acetone-water and ethanolic extracts gave no signs of hepatotoxicity in rat hepatocytes and human HepG2 cells. Six kavalactones showed dose-dependent cytotoxicity, more pronounced in rat hepatocytes than human HepG2 cells; kavain was the most toxic with an EC_{50} value of 45 µg/ml in rat hepatocytes. However, this was considered to give a wide safety margin for human use [2,3,64].

Potential hepatotoxicity

From the late 1990s rare case reports began to appear worldwide linking the medicinal use of kava-kava preparations at normal dosage levels to severe liver damage, in extreme cases resulting in death or liver transplants [1,2]. Although many of the reports were badly documented and have been disputed, the number suggesting probable or possible association between kava-kava and liver damage was sufficient to cause widespread concern. During the period 2001-2003 regulatory authorities in the UK, France, Germany and various other countries took action to halt the sale of kava-kava preparations. Such decisions have been criticized on the basis that they did not sufficiently take into account the large body of positive evidence of efficacy and tolerability of kava-kava [3-5]. However, there appears to be no immediate prospect of products returning to the market in these countries, although regulatory stances are reviewed from time to time.

Considerable effort is being devoted to research in this controversial area and various hypotheses have been postulated as to a possible mechanism of kava-kava hepatotoxicity, so far without a satisfactory answer [6]. It remains unclear how the safety profile of kava-kava compares with those of other agents (such as benzodiazepines) used in the management of anxiety. For a safety review of kava-kava, including the regulatory position in various countries, see Ulbricht et al. [1].

REGULATORY STATUS

Medicines

UK*	Accepted for general sale, internal or external use. Maximum single dose: 625 mg [67].
France*	Not listed in *Médicaments à base de plantes* [68].
Germany*	Commission E monograph published, with approved uses [55].

* The sale of kava-kava products is currently prohibited in these countries; see the Safety section above.

REFERENCES

Current Pharmacopoeial Monographs

DAC	Kava-Kava-Wurzelstock
BHP	Kava-Kava

Literature References

1. Ulbricht C, Basch E, Boon H, Ernst E, Hammerness P, Sollars D et al. Safety review of kava (*Piper methysticum*) by the Natural Standard Research Collaboration. *Expert Opin. Drug Saf.* 2005, **4**, 779-794.
2. European Scientific Cooperative on Phytotherapy. Piperis methystici rhizoma - Kava-Kava. In: *ESCOP Monographs - The Scientific Foundation for Herbal Medicinal Products, 2nd ed.* Stuttgart-New York: Thieme; Exeter, UK: ESCOP, 2003:365-382.
3. Loew D and Gaus W. Kava-Kava. Tragödie einer Fehlbeurteilung [Tragedy of a flawed assessment]. *Z. Phytotherapie* 2002, **23**, 267-281 [GERMAN/English summary].
4. Society for Medicinal Plant Research. Relevant Hepatotoxic Effects of Kava Still Need to be Proven. A Statement of the Society for Medicinal Plant Research. *Planta Medica* 2003, **69**, 971-972.
5. Mills SY and Steinhoff B. Kava-kava: a lesson for the phytomedicine community. *Phytomedicine* 2003, **10**, 261-262.
6. Anke J and Ramzan I. Kava Hepatotoxicity: Are we any Closer to the Truth? *Planta Medica* 2004, **70**, 193-196.
7. Lebot V and Levesque J. Genetic control of kavalactone chemotypes in *Piper methysticum* cultivars. *Phytochemistry* 1996, **43**, 397-403.
8. He X-G, Lin L-Z and Lian L-Z. Electrospray High Performance Liquid Chromatography-Mass Spectrometry in Phytochemical Analysis of Kava (*Piper methysticum*) Extract. *Planta Medica* 1997, **63**, 70-74.
9. Shao Y, He K, Zheng B and Zheng Q. Reversed-phase high-performance liquid chromatographic method for quantitative analysis of the six major kavalactones in *Piper methysticum. J. Chromatogr. A* 1998, **825**, 1-8.
10. Lechtenberg M, Quandt B, Kohlenberg F-J and Nahrstedt A. Qualitative and quantitative micellar electrokinetic chromatography of kavalactones from dry extracts of *Piper methysticum* Forst. and commercial drugs. *J. Chromatogr. A* 1999, **848**, 457-464.
11. Hänsel R, Ranft G and Bähr P. Zwei Chalkonpigmente aus *Piper methysticum* Forst. [Two chalcone pigments from *Piper methysticum* Forst.]. *Z. Naturforsch.* 1963, **18b**, 370-373 [GERMAN].
12. Jaggy H and Achenbach H. Cepharadione A from *Piper methysticum. Planta Medica* 1992, **58**, 111.
13. Achenbach H and Karl W. The Isolation of Two New Pyrrolidides from *Piper methysticum* Forst. *Chem. Ber.* 1970, **103**, 2535-2540 [GERMAN/English summary].
14. Cheng D, Lidgard RO, Duffield PH, Duffield AM and Brophy JJ. Identification by Methane Chemical Ionization Gas Chromatography/Mass Spectrometry of the Products Obtained by Steam Distillation and Aqueous Acid Extraction of Commercial *Piper methysticum. Biomed. Environ. Mass Spectrom.* 1988, **17**, 371-376.
15. Smith RM. Pipermethystine, a novel pyridone alkaloid from *Piper methysticum. Tetrahedron* 1979, **35**, 437-439.
16. Dragull K, Yoshida WY and Tang C-S. Piperidine alkaloids from *Piper methysticum. Phytochemistry* 2003, **63**, 193-198.
17. Achenbach H and Karl W. Investigation of the Acids from *Piper methysticum* Forst. *Chem. Ber.* 1971, **104**, 1468-1477 [GERMAN/English summary].
18. Whitton PA, Lau A, Salisbury A, Whitehouse J and Evans CS. Kava lactones and the kava-kava controversy. *Phytochemistry* 2003, **64**, 673-679.
19. Boonen G, Beck M-A and Häberlein H. Contribution to the quantitative and enantioselective determination of kavapyrones by high-performance liquid chromatography on ChiraSpher NT material. *J. Chromatogr. B* 1997, **702**, 240-244.
20. Häberlein H, Boonen G and Beck M-A. *Piper methysticum*: Enantiomeric Separation of Kavapyrones by High Performance Liquid Chromatography. *Planta Medica* 1997, **63**, 63-65.
21. Singh YN and Singh NN. Therapeutic potential of kava in the treatment of anxiety disorders. *CNS Drugs* 2002, **16**, 731-743.
22. Cairney S, Maruff P and Clough AR. The neurobehavioural effects of kava. *Aust. NZ J. Psychiatry* 2002, **36**, 657-662.
23. Spinella M. The Importance of Pharmacological Synergy in Psychoactive Herbal Medicines. *Altern. Med. Rev.* 2002, **7**, 130-137.
24. Heinze HJ, Münte TF, Steitz J and Matzke M. Pharmacopsychological Effects of Oxazeparn and Kava Extract in a Visual Search Paradigm assessed with Event-Related Potentials. *Pharmacopsychiatry* 1994, **27**, 224-230.
25. Russell PN, Bakker D and Singh NN. The effects of kava on alerting and speed of access of information from long-term memory. *Bull. Psychonomic Soc.* 1987, **25**, 236-237.
26. Emser W and Bartylla K. Verbesserung der Schlafqualität. Zur Wirkung von Kava-Extrakt WS 1490 auf das Schlafmuster bei Gesunden [Improvement of sleep quality. Effect of kava extract WS 1490 on the sleep pattern of healthy subjects]. *TW Neurologie Psychiatrie* 1991, **5**, 636-642 [GERMAN/English summary].
27. Johnson D, Frauendorf A, Stecker K and Stein U. Neurophysiologisches Wirkprofil und Verträglichkeit von Kava-Extrakt WS 1490. Eine Pilotstudie mit randomisierter Auswertung [Neurophysiological effect profile and tolerability of kava extract WS 1490. A randomized pilot study]. *TW Neurologie Psychiatrie* 1991, **5**, 349-354 [GERMAN/English summary].
28. Gessner B and Cnota P. Untersuchung der Vigilanz nach Applikation von Kava-Kava-Extrakt, Diazepam oder Placebo [A study of vigilance after administration of kava-kava extract, diazepam or placebo]. *Z. Phytotherapie* 1994, **15**, 30-37 [GERMAN/English summary].
29. Thompson R, Ruch W and Hasenöhrl RU. Enhanced cognitive performance and cheerful mood by standardized extracts of *Piper methysticum* (Kava-kava). *Hum. Psychopharmacol. Clin. Exp.* 2004, **19**, 243-250.
30. Keledjian J, Duffield PH, Jamieson DD, Lidgard RO and Duffield AM. Uptake into Mouse Brain of Four Compounds Present in the Psychoactive Beverage Kava. *J. Pharm. Sci.* 1988, **77**, 1003-1006.
31. Duffield AM, Jamieson DD, Lidgard RO, Duffield PH and Bourne DJ. Identification of some human urinary metabolites of the intoxicating beverage Kava. *J. Chromatogr.* 1989, **475**, 273-281.
32. Hänsel R and Woelk H, editors. Bioverfügbarkeit, Pharmakokinetik [Bioavailability, Pharmacokinetics]. In: *Spektrum Kava Kava, 2nd ed.* Basel: Aesopus Verlag, 1994:35-38 [GERMAN].
33. Warnecke G. Psychosomatische Dysfunktionen im weiblichen Klimakterium. Klinische Wirksamkeit und Verträglichkeit von Kava-Extrakt WS 1490 [Psychosomatic dysfunction in the female climacteric. Clinical efficacy and tolerability of kava extract WS 1490]. *Fortschr. Med.* 1991, **109**, 119-122 [GERMAN/English summary].
34. Kinzler E, Krömer J and Lehmann E. Clinical Efficacy of a Kava Extract in Patients with Anxiety Syndrome. Double-blind placebo controlled study over 4 weeks. *Arzneim.-Forsch./Drug Res.* 1991, **41**, 584-588 [GERMAN/English summary]. Subsequently published in English as:
   Lehmann E, Kinzler E, Friedemann J. Efficacy of a special Kava extract (*Piper methysticum*) in patients with states of anxiety, tension and excitedness of non-mental origin. A double-blind placebo-controlled study of four weeks treatment. *Phytomedicine* 1996, **3**, 113-119.
35. Volz H-P, Kieser M. Kava kava Extract WS 1490 versus Placebo in Anxiety Disorders. A Randomized Placebo controlled 25-week Outpatient Trial. *Pharmacopsychiatry* 1997, **30**, 1-5.
36. Malsch U and Kieser M. Efficacy of kava-kava in the treatment of non-psychotic anxiety, following pretreatment with benzodiazepines. *Psychopharmacology* 2001, **157**, 277-283.
37. Lehrl S. Clinical efficacy of kava extract WS® 1490 in sleep disturbances associated with anxiety disorders. Results of a multicenter, randomized, placebo-controlled, double-blind clinical trial. *J. Affect. Disord.* 2004, **78**, 101-110.
38. Geier FP and Konstantinowicz T. Kava Treatment in Patients

with Anxiety. *Phytotherapy Res.* 2004, **18**, 297-300.
39. Gastpar M and Klimm HD. Treatment of anxiety, tension and restlessness states with Kava special extract WS® 1490 in general practice: A randomized placebo-controlled double-blind multicenter trial. *Phytomedicine* 2003, **10**, 631-639.
40. Bhate H, Gerster G and Gracza E. Orale Prämedikation mit Zubereitungen aus Piper methysticum bei operativen Eingriffen in Epiduralanästhesie [Oral premedication with preparations from Piper methysticum in surgical operations under epidural anaesthesia]. *Erfahrungsheilkunde* 1989, **6**, 339-345 [GERMAN/English summary].
41. Warnecke G, Pfaender H, Gerster G and Gracza E. Wirksamkeit von Kawa-Kawa-Extrakt beim Klimakterischen Syndrom. Eine Doppelblindstudie mit einem neuen Monopräparat [Efficacy of kava-kava extract in the climacteric syndrome. A double-blind study with a new mono-preparation]. *Z. Phytotherapie* 1990, **11**, 81-86 [GERMAN/English summary].
42. Woelk H, Kapoula O, Lehrl S, Schröter K and Weinholz P. Behandlung von Angst-Patienten. Doppelblindstudie: Kava-Spezialextrakt WS 1490 versus Benzodiazepine [Treatment of anxiety patients. Double-blind study: Kava special extract WS 1490 versus benzodiazepines]. *Z. Allg. Med.* 1993, **69**, 271-277 [GERMAN].
43. Mittman U, Schmidt M and Vrastyakova J. Akut-anxiolytische Wirksamkeit von Kava-Spissum-Spezialextrakt und Benzodiazepinen als Prämedikation bei chirurgischen Eingriffen - Ergebnisse einer randomisierten, referenzkontrollierten Studie [Acute anxiolytic efficacy of a kava special spissum extract and benzodiazepines as pre-medication in surgical operations. Results of a randomized, reference-controlled study]. *J. Pharmakol. Ther.* 2000, **9**, 99-108 [GERMAN/English summary].
44. De Leo V, La Marca A, Lanzetta D, Palazzi S, Torricelli M, Facchini C and Morgante G. Valutazione dell'associazione di estratto di Kava-Kava e terapia ormonale sostitutiva nel trattamento d'ansia in postmenopausa [Evaluation of the association of kava-kava extract and hormone replacement therapy in the treatment of anxiety in postmenopause]. *Minerva Ginecol.* 2000, **52**, 263-267 [ITALIAN/English summary].
45. Boerner RJ, Sommer H, Berger W, Kuhn U, Schmidt U and Mannel M. Kava-kava extract LI 150 is as effective as Opipramol and Buspirone in Generalised Anxiety Disorder - An 8-week randomized, double-blind multi-centre clinical trial in 129 out-patients. *Phytomedicine* 2003, **10** (Suppl. 4), 38-49.
46. Cagnacci A, Arangino S, Renzi A, Zanni AL, Malmusi S and Volpe A. Kava-Kava administration reduces anxiety in perimenopausal women. *Maturitas* 2003, **44**, 103-109.
47. Connor KM and Davidson JRT. A placebo-controlled study of kava-kava in generalized anxiety disorder. *Int. Clin. Psychopharmacol.* 2002, **17**, 185-188.
48. Pittler MH and Ernst E. Kava extract for treating anxiety. *Cochrane Database Syst. Rev.* 2003, (1), CD003383.
49. Witte S, Loew D and Gaus W. Meta-Analysis of the Efficacy of the Acetonic Kava-Kava Extract WS®1490 in Patients with Non-Psychotic Anxiety Disorders. *Phytotherapy Res.* 2005, **19**, 183-188.
50. Siegers C-P, Honold E, Krall B, Meng G and Habs M. Ergebnisse der Anwendungsbeobachtung L 1090 mit Laitan® Kapseln. Verträglichkeit in 96% der Fälle sehr gut oder gut [Results of observational study L 1090 with Laitan® capsules. Tolerability very good or good in 96% of cases]. *Ärztl. Forsch.* 1992, **39**, 7-11 [GERMAN].
51. Spree MH and Croy H-H. Antares® - ein standardisiertes Kava-Kava-Präparat mit dem Spezialextrakt KW 1491. Therapeutische Ergebnisse und Verträglichkeit [Antares® - a standardized kava-kava-preparation with special extract KW 1491. Therapeutic results and tolerability]. *Der Kassenarzt* 1992, (17), 44-51 [GERMAN].
52. Scherer J. Kava-Kava Extract in Anxiety Disorders: An Outpatient Observational Study. *Adv. Ther.* 1998, **15**, 261-269.
53. Neto JT. Eficácia e tolerabilidade do extrato de kava-kava WS 1490 em estados de ansiedade. Estudo multicêntrico brasileiro [Efficacy and tolerability of kava-kava extract WS 1490 in anxiety disorders. Multicentric Brazilian study]. *Rev. Bras. Med.* 1999, **56**, 280-284 [PORTUGUESE/English summary].
54. Mills S and Bone K. Kava (*Piper methysticum* Forst. f.). In: *Principles and Practice of Phytotherapy. Modern Herbal Medicine.* ISBN 0-443-06016-9. Edinburgh-London-New York: Churchill Livingstone, 2000:456-464.
55. Piperis methystici rhizoma (Kava-Kava-Wurzelstock). German Commission E Monograph published in: Bundesanzeiger No. 101 of 01.06.90.
56. Singh YN. Kava: an overview. *J. Ethnopharmacol.* 1992, **37**, 13-45.
57. Pharmaceutical Society of Great Britain. Kava. In: *British Pharmaceutical Codex 1934.* London: Pharmaceutical Press, 1934:573-574.
58. Piper methysticum. In: *British Herbal Pharmacopoeia 1983.* ISBN 0-903032-07-4. Bournemouth: British Herbal Medicine Association, 1983.
59. Rote Liste Service GmbH, editor. Pflanzliche Psychopharmaka: Anxiolytica [Herbal Medicines: Anxiolytics]. In: *Rote Liste 2002. Arzneimittelverzeichnis für Deutschland* [*Red List 2002. Index of Medicines for Germany*]. Aulendorf: Editio Cantor Verlag, 2002: Section 71.A.2.
60. Stevinson C, Huntley A and Ernst E. A Systematic Review of the Safety of Kava Extract in the Treatment of Anxiety. *Drug Safety* 2002, **25**, 251-261.
61. Herberg K-W. Safety-related performance after intake of kava extract, bromazepam and their combination. *Z. Allg. Med.* 1996, **72**, 973-977 [GERMAN/English summary].
62. Herberg K-W. Fahrtüchtigkeit nach Einnahme von Kava-Spezial-Extrakt WS 1490. Doppelblinde, placebokontrollierte Probandenstudie [Ability to drive after intake of kava special extract WS 1490. Double-blind, placebo-controlled study in healthy subjects]. *Z. Allg. Med.* 1991, **67**, 842-846 [GERMAN].
63. Herberg K-W. The Influence of Kava Special Extract WS 1490 on Safety-relevant Performance Alone and in Combination with Ethyl Alcohol. *Blutalkohol* 1993, **30**, 96-105 [GERMAN/English summary].
64. Teschke R, Gaus W and Loew D. Kava extracts: Safety and risks including rare hepatotoxicity. *Phytomedicine* 2003, **10**, 440-446.
65. Hölzl J, Juretzek W, Schneider G and Stahl-Biskup E. *Piper.* In: Hänsel R, Keller K, Rimpler H and Schneider G, editors. *Hagers Handbuch der Pharmazeutischen Praxis. 5th ed. Volume 6: Drogen P-Z.* Berlin-Heidelberg-New York-London: Springer Verlag 1992:191-221.
66. Kretzschmar R and Meyer HJ. Comparative studies on the anticonvulsant activity of the pyrone compounds of *Piper methysticum* Forst. *Arch. Int. Pharmacodyn.* 1969, **177**, 261-277 [GERMAN/English summary].
67. Kava. In: UK Statutory Instrument 1994 No. 2410. The Medicines (Products Other Than Veterinary Drugs) (General Sale List) Amendment Order 1994. Schedule 1, Table A.
68. *Médicaments à base de plantes.* ISBN 2-911473-02-7. Saint-Denis Cedex, France: Agence du Médicament, 1998.

REGULATORY GUIDELINES FROM OTHER EU COUNTRIES

GERMANY

Commission E monograph [55]: Piperis methystici rhizoma (Kava-Kava-Wurzelstock).

Uses
Conditions involving nervous anxiety, stress and restlessness.

Contraindications
Pregnancy and lactation, endogenous depression.

Side effects
None known.
Note: Prolonged intake may lead to temporary yellow colouring of the skin, hair and nails, in which case this medication should be discontinued. In rare cases allergic skin reactions may occur. Accommodation disorders, enlargement of the pupils and disturbance of the oculomotor balance have also been reported.

Interactions with other drugs
Potentiation of the effect of centrally acting substances, such as alcohol, barbiturates and psychotropic drugs, is possible.

Dosage
Unless otherwise prescribed, daily dose: drug or preparations equivalent to 60-120 mg of kavapyrones.

Mode of administration
Comminuted drug and other galenic preparations for internal use.

Duration of administration
No more than 3 months without medical advice.
Note: Even with appropriate use, this medicine may influence visual performance and ability to react when driving or operating machines.

Actions
Anxiolytic. Narcosis-potentiating (sedative), anticonvulsive, spasmolytic and central muscle-relaxing effects have been demonstrated in animals.

LADY'S MANTLE

Rosaceae

Alchemillae herba

Definition
Lady's Mantle consists of the dried flowering aerial parts of *Alchemilla vulgaris* L. *sensu latiore.*

Alchemilla is an extremely large and complex genus. Demarcation of individual species, even from the more common representatives, is difficult, and this has led to uncertainties of classification and differing accounts in the literature. Up to 1990 *Alchemilla vulgaris* L., with up to 30 subspecies, was generally considered to be the collective species or "aggregate", rich in varying forms, commonly called lady's mantle. In the following decade, based on a revised classification, the alternative name *Alchemilla xanthochlora* Rothm. was widely adopted in the literature [1]. The first version (2000) of the European Pharmacopoeia monograph for Alchemilla (Alchemillae herba) defined "the dried flowering aerial parts of *Alchemilla xanthochlora* Rothm. (*Alchemilla vulgaris* L. *sensu latiore*)". However, in the current version (2003) "*A. xanthochlora*" has been omitted and the botanical name is given simply as *Alchemilla vulgaris* L. *sensu latiore.*

CONSTITUENTS

□ ***Ellagitannins***, principally the dimer agrimoniin (3.5-3.8% by HPLC) together with pedunculagin (1.2%) and another dimer, laevigatin F (0.9%) [2].
The tannin content is often reported as 5-8% by the gravimetric hide powder method [1,3] but has been found as high as 12-13% in the herb [4,5], 15% in the leaves and 12% in the flowers [6]; the European Pharmacopoeia requires not less than 6.0%. The highest tannin content occurs during the flowering period [7].
□ ***Flavonoids*** Flavonol glycosides, 2.2-2.5% in leaves, 1.0-1.9% in flowers [8], principally quercetin 3-glucuronide (1.2%) [9] together with quercetin 3-glucoside (isoquercitrin), 3-rutinoside (rutin) [10] and 3-arabinoside [10,11], and kaempferol 3-(6''-*p*-coumaroyl)-glucoside [10].
About 1% of leucocyanidin (a flavan-3,4-diol) occurs in the flowers [8].
□ ***Other constituents*** include phytosterols and aliphatic hydrocarbons [4].

Published Assay Methods
Determination of tannins in herbal drugs [Ph. Eur. method 2.8.14].

PHARMACOLOGY

In vitro tests for anti-inflammatory activity showed that *Alchemilla vulgaris* aqueous extract strongly inhibited platelet activating factor-induced exocytosis of elastase in human neutrophils, but not prostaglandin synthesis in bovine seminal vesicles [12]. In the hen's egg chorioallantoic membrane (HET-CAM) assay a dry hydroethanolic extract from *Alchemilla vulgaris* at a concentration of 500 µg/pellet inhibited membrane irritation by 91-100%, an anti-inflammatory effect comparable to that of hydrocortisone, phenylbutazone or diclofenac sodium at 50 µg/pellet [13].

Effects of lady's mantle (*A. xanthochlora*) extracts attributed to the tannin content include inhibition of lipid peroxidation, superoxide anion scavenging activity [14] and antibacterial activity against *Staphylococcus aureus* and *Bacillus subtilis* [4]. No antispasmodic effects of lady's mantle were observed in tests on isolated guinea-pig ileum [15]. Leucocyanidin (leucocianidol) is reputed to have beneficial effects on capillary circulation [16].

CLINICAL STUDIES

In an open study involving 341 girls aged between 11 and 17 years, followed up for 6 years, a Romanian clinic investigated the efficacy of a fluid extract of *Alchemilla vulgaris* (5.8% tannins, 2.2% flavonoid glycosides) in juvenile menometrorrhagia. Oral administration of 50-60 drops of the fluid extract 3-5 times daily gave favourable results, stopping genital haemorrhage within 3-5 days. The extract also had an antihaemorrhagic effect when used prophylactically for 10-15 days before menstruation. No side effects were observed and the preparation was considered harmless [5].

THERAPEUTICS

Actions
Astringent [17], antihaemorrhagic [5,17], anti-inflammatory [12,13].

Indications
None adequately substantiated by pharmacological or clinical studies.

Uses based on experience or tradition
Internal use: Mild diarrhoea [17-19], menorrhagia and metrorrhagia [5,17].
Internal or external use: Venous insufficiency, such as 'heavy legs' and haemorrhoids [18].
External use: Wound healing and inflammatory skin

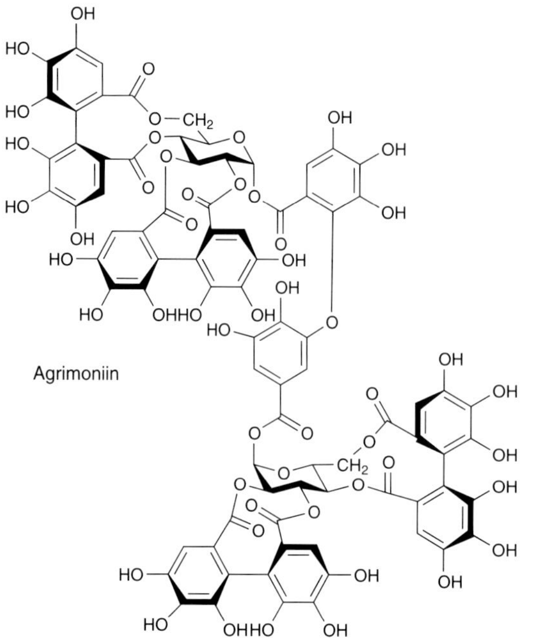

Agrimoniin

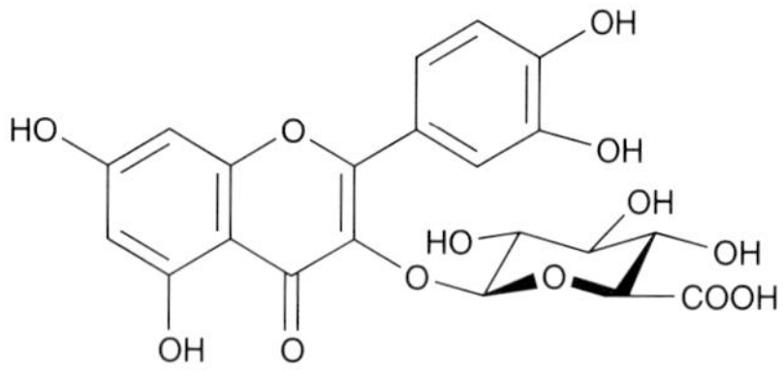

Quercetin 3-glucuronide

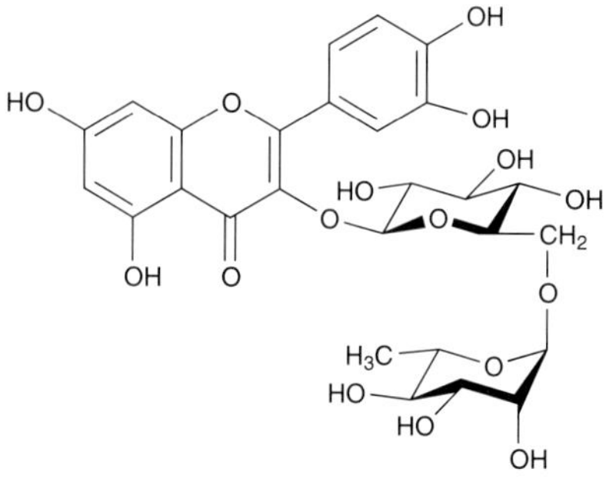

Rutin (quercetin 3-rutinoside)

ailments [12,14,20]; as a douche in leucorrhoea [17,21]; as a douche or ointment in pruritus vulvae [17,20]; as a mouthwash or gargle for mouth ulcers, sore throat or laryngitis [20].

Contraindications
Avoid during pregnancy [20].

Side effects
None known.

Interactions with other drugs
None known.

Dosage
Internal use: Three times daily, 2-4 g of dried herb or as an infusion or equivalent preparation [17,19]; liquid extract (1:1) in 25% ethanol, 2-3 ml.
External use: As a douche, 6 g/100 ml of water.

SAFETY

No side effects or significant changes in clinical biochemistry parameters were observed after administration of high daily doses of a lady's mantle fluid extract to over 300 teenage girls at intervals over periods of up to 6 years [5].

In the Ames mutagenicity test with *Salmonella typhimurium* strains TA98 and TA100, commercial 'Alchemillae tinctura' (1:5 in ethanol 70%; species not defined) showed no mutagenicity without activation and weak mutagenicity after activation with S9 mix [22]. On the other hand, Alchemillae tinctura inhibited 2-nitrofluorene-induced mutagenicity in *Salmonella typhimurium* strains TA98 and TA100, the antimutagenic activity being attributed to the tannin content [23].

REGULATORY STATUS

Medicines

UK	Accepted for general sale, internal or external use [24].
France	Accepted for specified indications [18].
Germany	Commission E monograph published, with approved uses [19].

Foods

Council of Europe	Permitted as flavouring, category N2 [25].

REFERENCES

Current Pharmacopoeial Monographs
Ph. Eur. Alchemilla

Literature References

1. Scholz E and Rimpler H. Phytochemie der Gerbstoffdrogen der deutschsprachigen Arzneibücher [Phytochemistry of tannin drugs of German language pharmacopoeias]. *Österreich. Apoth.-Ztg.* 1994, **48**, 138-141 [GERMAN].
2. Geiger C, Scholz E and Rimpler H. Ellagitannins from

Alchemilla xanthochlora and *Potentilla erecta*. *Planta Medica* 1994, **60**, 384-385.
3. Scholz E. Pflanzliche Gerbstoffe. Pharmakologie und Toxikologie [Plant tannins. Pharmacology and toxicology]. *Dtsch. Apoth. Ztg.* 1994, **34**, 3167-3179 [GERMAN].
4. Schimmer O and Felser C. *Alchemilla xanthochlora* Rothm. - der Frauenmantel [*Alchemilla xanthochlora* Rothm. - Lady's Mantle]. *Z. Phytotherapie* 1992, **13**, 207-214 [GERMAN/English summary].
5. Petcu P, Andronescu E, Gheorgheci V, Cucu-Cabadaief L and Zsigmond Z. The management of juvenile meno-metrorrhagia with *Alchemilla vulgaris* L. fluid extract. *Clujul Medical* 1979, **52**, 266-270 [ROMANIAN/English summary].
6. Lamaison JL, Carnat A and Petitjean-Freytet C. Teneur en tanins et activité inhibitrice de l'élastase chez les Rosaceae [Tannin content and elastase inhibiting activity in Rosaceae]. *Ann. Pharm. Fr.* 1990, **48**, 335-340 [FRENCH/English summary].
7. Tuka L and Popescu H. Determination of tannins in the plants of *Alchemilla mollis* (Buser) Rothm. and *Alchemilla vulgaris* L. *Clujul Med.* 1979, **52**, 78-83 [ROMANIAN]; through *Chem. Abstr.* 1979, **91**, 198835.
8. Tuka L and Tamas M. Determination of flavonoids in *Alchemilla mollis* (Buser) Rothm. and *Alchemilla vulgaris* L. (Lady's Mantle). *Farmacia (Bucharest)* 1977, **25**, 247-252 [ROMANIAN/English summary].
9. Lamaison JL, Carnat A, Petitjean-Freyet C and Carnat AP. La quercétine-3-glucuronide, principal flavonoïde de l'Alchémille, *Alchemilla xanthochlora* Rothm. (Rosaceae). *Ann. Pharm. Fr.* 1991, **49**, 186-189 [FRENCH/English summary].
10. D'Agostino M, Dini I, Ramundo E and Senatore F. Flavonoid Glycosides of *Alchemilla vulgaris* L. *Phytotherapy Res.* 1998, **12**, S162-S163.
11. Fraisse D, Heitz A, Carnat A, Carnat A-P and Lamaison J-L. Quercetin 3-arabinopyranoside, a major flavonoid compound from *Alchemilla xanthochlora*. *Fitoterapia* 2000, **71**, 463-464.
12. Tunón H, Olavsdotter C and Bohlin L. Evaluation of anti-inflammatory activity of some Swedish medicinal plants. Inhibition of prostaglandin biosynthesis and PAF-induced exocytosis. *J. Ethnopharmacol.* 1995, **48**, 61-76.
13. Paper DH, Müller K and Franz G. Frauenmantel, Schachtelhalm und Stechpalme. Die entzündungshemmende Wirkung der Urtinkturen [Lady's Mantle, Horsetail and Holly. The inflammation-inhibiting effect of mother tinctures]. In: Chrubasik S and Wink M, editors. *Rheumatherapie mit Phytopharmaka.* ISBN 3-7773-1304-1. Stuttgart: Hippokrates Verlag, 1997:145-148 [GERMAN].
14. Filípek J. The effect of Alchemilla xanthochlora water extract on lipid peroxidation and superoxide anion scavenging activity. *Pharmazie* 1992, **47**, 717-718.
15. Izzo AA, Capasso R, Senatore F, Seccia S and Morrica P. Spasmolytic Activity of Medicinal Plants Used for the Treatment of Disorders Involving Smooth Muscles. *Phytotherapy Res.* 1996, **10**, S107-S108.
16. Reynolds JEF, editor. Leucocianidol. In: Martindale - The Extra Pharmacopoeia, 29th ed. London: Pharmaceutical Press, 1989:1584.
17. Alchemilla. In: *British Herbal Pharmacopoeia 1983.* ISBN 0-903032-07-4. Bournemouth: British Herbal Medicine Association, 1983.
18. Alchémille vulgaire. In: *Médicaments à base de plantes.* ISBN 2-911473-02-7. Saint-Denis Cedex, France: Agence du Médicament, 1998.
19. Alchemillae herba (Frauenmantelkraut). German Commission E Monograph published in: Bundesanzeiger No. 173 of 18.09.86.
20. Ody P. *Alchemilla xanthochlora* - Lady's Mantle. In: *Medicinal Herbal, 2nd ed.* ISBN 0-7513-3005-1. London: Dorling Kindersley, 2000:32.
21. Weiss RF and Fintelmann V. Alchemilla vulgaris (Alchemilla xanthochlora), Lady's mantle. In: *Herbal Medicine, 2nd ed.* ISBN 3-13-126332-6. Stuttgart-New York: Thieme Verlag, 2000:338-339.
22. Schimmer O, Krüger A, Paulini H and Haefele F. An evaluation of 55 commercial plant extracts in the Ames mutagenicity test. *Pharmazie* 1994, **49**, 448-451.
23. Schimmer O and Lindenbaum M. Tannins with Antimutagenic Properties in the Herb of *Alchemilla* Species and *Potentilla anserina*. *Planta Medica* 1995, **61**, 141-145.
24. Lady's Mantle. In: UK Statutory Instrument 1994 No. 2410. The Medicines (Products Other Than Veterinary Drugs) (General Sale List) Amendment Order 1994. Schedule 1, Table A.
25. Alchemilla vulgaris L., herb. In: *Flavouring Substances and Natural Sources of Flavourings, 3rd ed.* ISBN 2-7160-0081-6. Strasbourg: Council of Europe, 1981.

REGULATORY GUIDELINES FROM OTHER EU COUNTRIES

FRANCE

Médicaments à base de plantes [18]: Alchémille vulgaire, parties aériennes.

Therapeutic indications accepted

Oral use
Traditionally used in subjective manifestations of venous insufficiency, such as heavy legs, and for haemorrhoidal symptoms.
Traditionally used in the symptomatic treatment of mild diarrhoea.

Topical use
Traditionally used used in subjective manifestations of venous insufficiency, such as heavy legs.
Traditionally used for haemorrhoidal symptoms.
Traditionally used topically in mouthwashes, for buccal hygiene.

GERMANY

Commission E monograph [19]: Alchemillae herba (Frauenmantelkraut).

Uses
Mild, non-specific diarrhoea.

Contraindications
None known.

Side effects
None known.

Interactions with other drugs
None known.

Dosage
Unless otherwise prescribed, average daily dose: 5-10 g of the drug; equivalent preparations.

Mode of administration
Comminuted drug for infusions, decoctions or other galenic preparations for oral use.

Duration of administration
If the diarrhoea persists for more than 3-4 days, consult a doctor.

Action
Astringent.

LILY OF THE VALLEY

Convallariaceae

Convallariae herba

Definition
Lily of the Valley consists of the dried flowering aerial parts of *Convallaria majalis* L.

CONSTITUENTS

☐ *Cardenolides (cardiac glycosides)*, 0.1-0.5% (with more in the flowers than in the leaves) [1,2]. About 40 glycosides have been identified in *Convallaria majalis*, at least 23 in the aerial parts [2], the pattern varying considerably depending on the source of the plant material [3] and the vegetative period [4].

Cardenolides have a tetracyclic steroidal ring system with an α,β-unsaturated γ-lactone ring at C-17. In lily of the valley the aglycones are strophanthidin and related compounds including strophanthidol, periplogenin, bipindogenin, sarmentogenin, 19-hydroxysarmentogenin, sarmentologenin, sarmentosigenin and cannogenol [5,6]. The cardiac glycoside complex usually consists of about two thirds mono- and one third diglycosides [2].

From HPLC analysis of 13 samples of lily of the valley (flowering herb) the main cardiac glycosides were found to be convallatoxin (strophanthidin 3-rhamnoside; 11-45%), convallatoxol (strophanthidol 3-rhamnoside; 10-23%), convalloside (strophanthidin 3-glucorhamnoside; none to 35%), lokundjoside (bipindogenin 3-rhamnoside; 3-27%) and deglucocheirotoxin (strophanthidin 3-gulomethyloside; none to 15%) [2].

Western European plants contain relatively large amounts of convallatoxin and convallatoxol, while those from eastern Austria and Slovenia contain more lokundjoside and eastern European plants also more convalloside [3].

☐ ***Flavonoids*** Glycosides of isorhamnetin, kaempferol and quercetin, including the 3-galactosides, 3-galactorhamnosides and 3-galactodirhamnosides [7]. In other work the aglycones isorhamnetin, kaempferol, quercetin, luteolin, apigenin and chrysoeriol were identified after acid hydrolysis [8].

☐ ***Essential oil***, of which the principal components were found to be hydroxycitronellal (49.5%) and citronellol (10.8%) [9].

☐ ***Other constituents*** include azetidine-2-carboxylic acid [10], chelidonic acid [11,12], caffeic acid methyl ester [8] and a trace of progesterone (up to 57 μg/100 g of fresh leaf) [13].

Published Assay Methods
Individual and total cardenolides by HPLC [2]. Convallatoxin by TLC-densitometry [14].

PHARMACOLOGY

Although the pharmacological effects of cardiac glycosides, notably those from *Digitalis* species, are well known, specific pharmacological data on lily of the valley are very limited; they can be found only in older studies and almost exclusively for convallatoxin [12].

The main pharmacodynamic property of cardiac glycosides is their ability to increase the force of myocardial contraction. Beneficial effects in patients with heart failure (increased cardiac output; decreased heart size, venous pressure and blood volume; diuresis and relief of oedema)

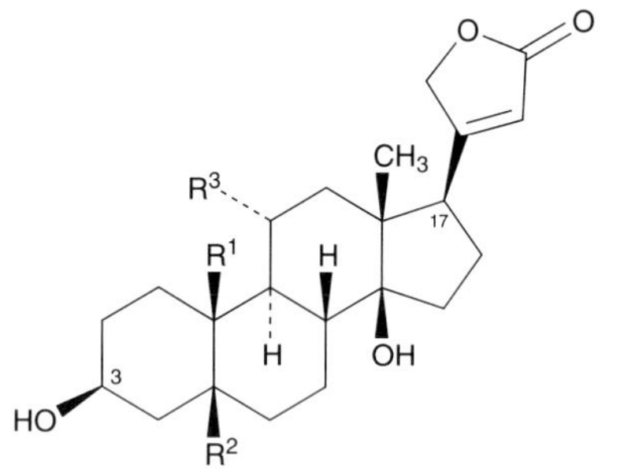

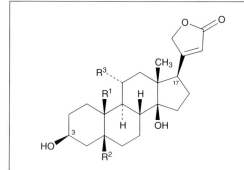

Cardenolide aglycones

	R^1	R^2	R^3
Strophanthidin	CHO	OH	H
Strophanthidol	CH_2OH	OH	H
Cannogenol	CH_2OH	H	H
Periplogenin	CH_3	OH	H
Bipindogenin	CH_3	OH	OH
Sarmentogenin	CH_3	H	OH
Sarmentosigenin	CHO	OH	OH
Sarmentologenin	CH_2OH	OH	OH

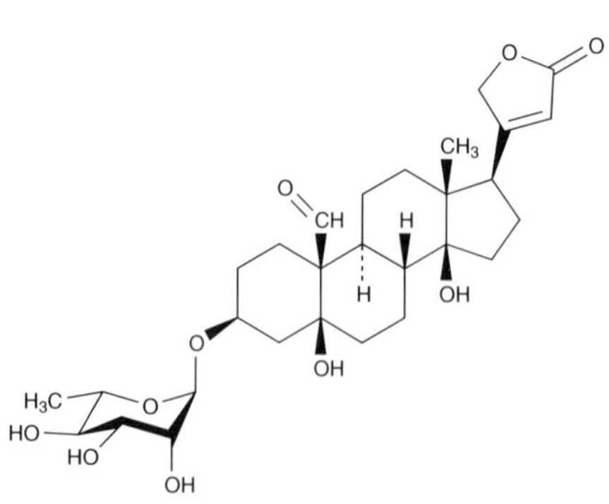

Convallatoxin
(Strophanthidin 3-rhamnoside)

result mainly from the increased contractile force, a positive inotropic action. The second important action is to slow the ventricular rate in atrial fibrillation or flutter. The mechanisms responsible for these beneficial effects are complex. Cardiac glycosides exert direct effects on the heart that modify both its mechanical and electrical activity. They also act directly on the smooth muscle of the vascular system. In addition, they exert a number of effects on neural tissue and thus indirectly influence the mechanical and electrical activity of the heart and modify vascular resistance and capacitance [15].

In vivo

Dose-dependent venoconstriction in the hind legs was observed in anaesthetized cats after intravenous administration of a lily of the valley extract [16].

Essential oil of lily of the valley, applied to the skin of volunteers as an ethanolic solution, was 94.6% effective in repelling mosquitoes (mainly *Aedes communis* and *A. cinereus*) in field tests carried out in Sweden; the effect was of the same order of magnitude as that of commercial mosquito repellents [9].

Pharmacokinetics

Whereas digitoxin and digoxin (cardiac glycosides from *Digitalis* species) are 70-100% absorbed from the gastrointestinal tract [17], only about 10% of convallatoxin is absorbed after oral administration. In the liver it is mainly reduced to convallatoxol. Six hours after intraperitoneal administration of convallatoxin to guinea pigs the highest concentrations were found in the kidneys, skeletal muscle, liver and heart muscle; 13% was eliminated in the urine and 10% in the faeces. The full dose was excreted within 2 days [18].

CLINICAL STUDIES

None published on mono-preparations of lily of the valley.

THERAPEUTICS

Because of the low therapeutic latitude between efficacy and toxicity of cardiac glycosides, lily of the valley preparations have to a large extent been replaced by pure cardiac glycosides from *Digitalis* in the treatment of chronic heart failure.

However, lily of the valley is still used in a number of drug preparations in Europe and by herbal practitioners to strengthen heart function in mild forms of cardiac insufficiency. It is better tolerated than foxglove as it does not accumulate within the body to the same degree. Relatively low doses are required to support heart rate and rhythm and to cause diuresis [19].

Actions

Cardiac tonic and diuretic [20]; has actions on the heart similar to those of cardiac glycosides from *Digitalis*, such as digitoxin and digoxin [17].

It should be noted that, while the cardiac glycosides in lily of the valley behave pharmacodynamically like those of *Digitalis*, they are different in pharmacokinetic behaviour, being absorbed to a much lesser extent and eliminated more rapidly.

Indications

Mild cardiac insufficiency, heart decline due to physiological changes in old age, chronic pulmonary heart disease [21]. Arrhythmia, oedema of cardiac origin, cardiac asthma [22].

Contraindications

Potassium deficiency [21].

Side effects

Nausea, vomiting, cardiac arrhythmias [21].

Interactions with other drugs

Increased effect and therefore also increased side effects when taken simultaneously with quinidine, calcium, saluretics, laxatives or long-term glucocorticoid therapy [21].

Dosage

Three times daily: standardized lily of the valley powder, 60-200 mg [21,22], or equivalent preparations. The standardized powder of the DAB has activity corresponding to 0.2% of convallatoxin [23].

Caution: Lily of the valley is not suitable for self-medication.

SAFETY

Lily of the valley should be used only under medical supervision [19,24,25] and only in the form of preparations with known cardenolide content and activity [26].

The intravenous lethal dose in guinea pigs of the glycoside complex of lily of the valley was determined as 0.19 mg/kg body weight, while that of pure convallatoxin was 0.31 mg/kg (indicating that some of the glycosides are more toxic than convallatoxin) [27].

Intraperitoneal LD_{50} values for convallatoxin, convallatoxol and G-strophanthin (ouabain) were compared in cats, mice, rats and guinea pigs. Convallatoxol showed the strongest toxicity in cats

(LD_{50}: 0.14 mg/kg body weight), but in mice (30 mg/kg) and rats (56 mg/kg) it was distinctly less toxic than convallatoxin (10 mg/kg) or G-strophanthin (20 mg/kg). In guinea pigs there was little difference in toxicity between the three glycosides (LD_{50}: 0.2-0.3 mg/kg) [12].

Lily of the valley has been designated by the USA Food and Drug Administration as a herb that should not be used in foods, beverages or drugs [28].

REGULATORY STATUS

Medicines

UK	Pharmacy only, with exemption for herbal practitioners up to 150 mg per dose, 450 mg daily [29].
France	Not listed in *Médicaments à base de plantes* [30].
Germany	Commission E monograph published, with approved uses [21].

Food

Not used in foods.

REFERENCES

Current Pharmacopoeial Monographs

DAB	Maiglöckchenkraut
ÖAB	Herba Convallariae - Maiglöckchenkraut
BHP	Lily of the Valley Leaf

Literature References

1. Jurenitsch J, Kopp B, Bamberg-Kubelka E and Kubelka W. Bestimmung des Einzel- und Gesamtcardenolidgehaltes in *Convallaria majalis* L. mittels Hochleistungsflüssigchromatographie [Determination of the content of individual and total cardenolides in *Convallaria majalis* L. by high performance liquid chromatography]. *J. Chromatogr.* 1982, **240**, 235-242 [GERMAN].
2. Krenn L, Schlifelner L, Stimpfl T and Kopp B. A new HPLC method for the quantification of cardenolides in *Convallaria majalis* L. *Pharmazie* 1996, **51**, 906-909.
3. Bleier W, Kaiser S, Kubelka W and Wichtl M. Beziehungen zwischen Standort und Glykosid-Zusammensetzung bei *Convallaria majalis* L. 6. Mitteilung über Convallaria-Glykoside [Relationship between habitat and glycoside composition in *Convallaria majalis* L. Part 6 on Convallaria glycosides]. *Pharm. Acta Helv.* 1967, **42**, 423-447 [GERMAN].
4. Kopp B, Kubelka W and Jentzsch K. Jahreszeitliche Änderungen von Cardenolidgehalt und -verteilung in den ober- und unterirdischen Organen von *Convallaria majalis* L. [Seasonal changes in cardenolide content and distribution in the aerial and underground organs of *Convallaria majalis* L.]. *Sci. Pharm.* 1981, **49**, 265-281 [GERMAN].
5. Kopp B and Kubelka W. Neue Cardenolide aus Convallaria majalis. 14. Mitteilung über Convallaria-Glykoside: Bipindogenin-, Sarmentologenin- und Sarmentosigenin-Glykoside [New cardenolides from Convallaria majalis. Part 14 on Convallaria glycosides: bipindogenin, sarmentologenin und sarmentosigenin glycosides]. *Planta Medica* 1982, **45**, 87-94 [GERMAN/English summary].
6. Kopp B and Kubelka W. Neue Cardenolide aus Convallaria majalis. 15. Mitteilung über Convallaria-Glykoside: Strophanthidin-, Cannogenol-, 19-Hydroxy-sarmentogenin- und Sarmentogenin-Glykoside [New cardenolides from Convallaria majalis. Part 14 on Convallaria glycosides: strophanthidin, cannogenol, 19-hydroxysarmentogenin und sarmentogenin glycosides]. *Planta Medica* 1982, **45**, 195-202 [GERMAN/English summary].
7. Malinowski J and Strzelecka H. Flavonoid compounds of *Convallaria majalis* herb. *Acta Polon. Pharm.* 1976, **33**, 767-776 [POLISH/English summary].
8. Kartnig T, Hiermann A and Vrecer C. Flavonoids of Convallaria majalis. *Planta Medica* 1978, **33**, 412-413 [GERMAN/English summary].
9. Thorsell W, Mikiver A, Malander I and Túnon H. Efficacy of plant extracts and oils as mosquito repellents. *Phytomedicine* 1998, **5**, 311-323.
10. Fowden L. Azetidine-2-carboxylic acid: a new constituent of plants. *Nature* 1955, **176**, 347-348.
11. Wichtl M and Moser U. Maiglöckchenkraut - Convallariae herba. In: Hartke K, Hartke H, Mutschler E, Rücker G and Wichtl M, editors. *Kommentar zum Deutschen Arzneibuch.* Stuttgart: Wissenschaftliche Verlagsgesellschaft, 2000 (13. Lfg.):M 20 [GERMAN].
12. Hänsel R, Keller K, Rimpler H and Schneider G, editors. Convallaria. In: *Hagers Handbuch der Pharmazeutischen Praxis, 5th ed. Volume 4: Drogen A-D.* ISBN 3-540-52631-5. Berlin-Heidelberg-New York-London: Springer-Verlag, 1992:975-987 [GERMAN].
13. Kopp B and Löffelhardt W. Determination of Progesterone in Vegetative Organs and Cell Organelles of *Convallaria majalis* L. by Radioimmunoassay. *Z. Naturforsch* 1980, **35c**, 41-44.
14. Matysik G, Kowalski J and Staszewska M. Quantitative Determination of Convallatoxin from Herba Convallariae. *Chromatographia* 1996, **43**, 559-562.
15. Hoffmann BF and Bigger JT. Digitalis and Allied Cardiac Glycosides. In: Goodman Gilman A, Rall TW, Nies AS and Taylor P, editors. *Goodman and Gilman's The Pharmacological Basis of Therapeutics, 8th ed.* ISBN 0-08-040296-8. New York-Oxford: Pergamon, 1990: 814-839.
16. Lehmann HD. Effect of Plant Glycosides on Resistance Vessels and Capacitance Vessels. *Arzneim.-Forsch./Drug Res.* 1984, **34**, 423-429 [GERMAN/English summary].
17. Parfitt K, editor. Convallaria. In: *Martindale - The complete drug reference, 32nd edition.* ISBN 0-85369-429-X. London: Pharmaceutical Press, 1999:1567.
18. Loew DA and Loew AD. Pharmakokinetik von herzglykosidhaltigen Pflanzenextrakten. *Z. Phytotherapie* 1994, **15**, 197-202 [GERMAN/English summary].
19. Chevallier A. Lily of the Valley - *Convallaria majalis.* In: *Encyclopedia of Medicinal Plants, 2nd ed.* ISBN 0-7513-1209-6. London-New York: Dorling Kindersley, 2001:194.
20. Grieve M (edited by Leyel CF). Lily-of-the-Valley. In: *A Modern Herbal* (first published 1931; revised 1973). ISBN 1-85501-249-9. London: Tiger Books International, 1994:480-482.
21. Convallariae herba. German Commission E Monograph published in: Bundesanzeiger No. 76 of 23 April 1987; amended in Bundesanzeiger No. 22 of 1 February 1990.
22. Convallaria. In: *British Herbal Pharmacopoeia 1983.* ISBN 0-903032-07-4. Bournemouth: British Herbal Medicine Association, 1983.
23. Eingestelltes Maiglöckchenpulver - Convallariae pulvis normatus [Standardized lily of the valley powder - Convallariae pulvis normatus]. In: *Deutsches Arzneibuch* [German Pharmacopoeia].
24. Ody P. Lily-of-the-Valley. In: *The Complete Guide - Medicinal Herbal.* ISBN 0-7513-3005-1. London-New York: Dorling Kindersley, 2000:229.
25. Stodola J and Volák J. Lily-of-the-Valley. Translated into English in: Bunney S, editor. *The Illustrated Book of Herbs.* ISBN 0-7064-1489-6. London: Octopus Books, 1984:117.
26. Loew D. Phytotherapie bei der Herzinsuffizienz. *Z. Phyto-*

therapie 1997, **18**, 92-96 [GERMAN/English summary].
27. Fuchs L, Wichtl M and Peithner G. Vergleichende chemische und biologische Untersuchung verschiedener Drogenmuster von *Convallaria majalis*. 3. Mitteilung über Convallaria-Glykoside. *Arzneim.-Forsch.* 1963, **13**, 220-222 [GERMAN/English summary].
28. Anon. Herbs Hazardous to Your Health. *American Pharmacy* 1984, **NS24**, 120-121.
29. UK Statutory Instrument 1977 No. 2130: The Medicines (Retail Sale or Supply of Herbal Remedies) Order 1977.
30. *Médicaments à base de plantes*. ISBN 2-911473-02-7. Saint-Denis Cedex, France: Agence du Médicament, 1998.

REGULATORY GUIDELINES FROM OTHER EU COUNTRIES

GERMANY

Commission E monograph [21]: Convallariae herba (Maiglöckchenkraut).

Uses
Mild cardiac insufficiency, heart decline due to physiological changes in old age, chronic cor pulmonale (pulmonary heart disease).

Contraindications
Therapy with digitalis glycosides; potassium deficiency.

Side effects
Nausea, vomiting, cardiac arrhythmias.

Interactions with other drugs
Increased effect and therefore also increased side effects when taken simultaneously with quinidine, calcium, saluretics, laxatives or long-term glucocorticoid therapy.

Dosage
Unless otherwise prescribed, average daily dose: 0.6 g of standardized lily of the valley powder or equivalent preparations.

Mode of administration
Comminuted herb and other galenic preparations for oral use.

Action
Positively inotropic on the myocardium, "economises" the exertion of the heart, lowers elevated left ventricular end-diastolic pressure and pathologically elevated venous pressure; venotonic, diuretic, natriuretic, kaliuretic.

LOVAGE ROOT

Umbelliferae

Levistici radix

Definition

Lovage Root consists of the dried rhizomes and roots of *Levisticum officinale* Koch.

CONSTITUENTS

□ ***Essential oil***, 0.6-1.0% [1] (Ph.Eur. min. 0.4% V/m in whole drug, 0.3% V/m in cut drug), consisting predominantly of phthalides: Z-ligustilide (= *cis*-3-n-butylidene-4,5-dihydrophthalide, 67.5%; with 1.3% of the *trans* isomer), 3-n-butylidenephthalide (1.5% *cis*, 0.7% *trans*), *cis*-3-n-validene-4,5-dihydrophthalide (= *cis*-ternine, 1.4%) and small amounts of other phthalides [1,2]. Ligustilide dimers have also been isolated [3].

Among over 100 compounds identified in the oil are also pentylcyclohexadiene (7.5%), β-phellandrene (3.8%), β-pinene (2.9%), α-pinene (2.1%) and other mono- and sequiterpenes [1].

Results from other analyses [3-10] show broadly similar results, but with considerable quantitative variation depending on the source of the material and the maturity of the roots [5]. In one investigation, much higher contents of essential oil and ligustilide were reported in the root: 4.1-4.8% and 1.9-2.5% respectively during the vegetative growth and senescent stages, and 3.8% and 1.2% respectively at the fruit formation stage [11].

□ ***Coumarins***, ca. 3.2% [12], including umbelliferone [12-14], coumarin [12,14] and others. Also the furanocoumarin bergapten [13] and possibly apterin [15].

□ ***Phenylpropanoids*** Chlorogenic, caffeic [16] and ferulic [17] acids, and a small amount of coniferyl ferulate [4].

□ ***Polyacetylenes*** Falcarindiol (0.14-0.2%) [3,4].

□ ***Other constituents*** include linoleic acid [4], succinic acid, amino acids and sucrose [17].

Many similarities have been noted between the root constituents of lovage and *Angelica sinensis* (Oliv.) Diels, known as danggui or dong quai; in fact, lovage root is known in China as "European danggui" [4,18]. HPLC patterns for the two drugs were found to be almost identical (in the system used), differing only in the higher falcarindiol content of lovage root [4].

Published Assay Methods

Volatile constituents by GC and GC-MS [1,2,5]. Z-ligustilide by HPLC [7]. HPLC and LC-MS of crude drug extracts [4]. Furanocoumarins by HPLC [19].

PHARMACOLOGY

In vitro

Inhibition of cyclooxygenase and 5-lipoxygenase by a lovage root extract, and hence an influence on arachidonic acid metabolism, has been demonstrated. Neither ligustilide nor ferulic acid produced these effects whereas linoleic acid, which is present in a remarkably high amount, contributed to the inhibitory activity of the extract [20].

Spasmolytic activity of phthalides

Following tests which showed that light petroleum and ethanolic extracts from *Angelica sinensis* significantly inhibited acetylcholine-induced spasms in isolated duodenal muscle, ligustilide

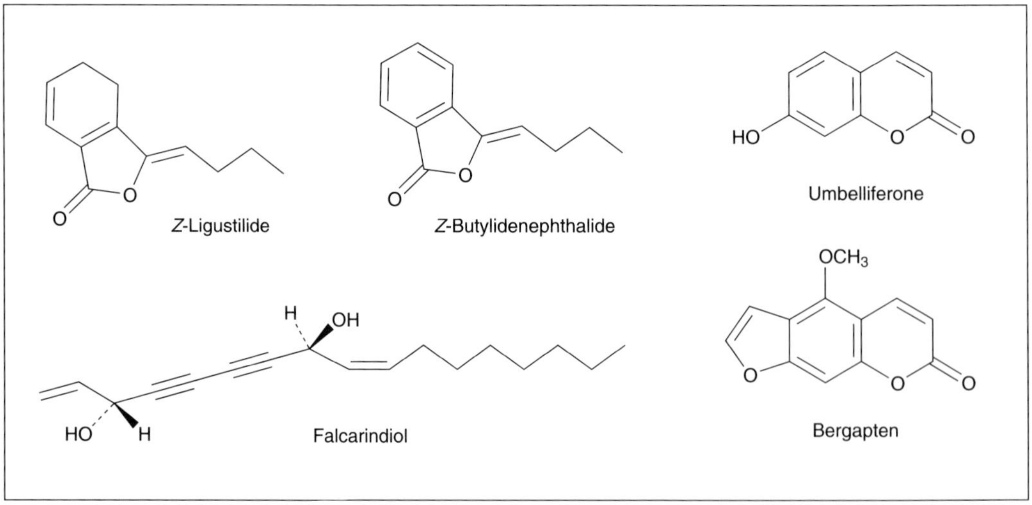

was identified as the spasmolytic principle [21]. Ligustilide, and to a lesser extent 3-butylidenephthalide, also inhibited acetylcholine-induced spasm of isolated female rat jejunum [22].

Ligustilide and butylidenephthalide inhibited contraction of isolated uterus from the non-pregnant rat induced by prostaglandin $F_{2\alpha}$, oxytocin and acetylcholine, butylidenephthalide being the more active [23,24]. In subsequent tests, butylidenephthalide inhibited the contractile responses of isolated guinea pig ileum, vas deferens and taenia coli to various agonists, exhibiting non-specific antispasmodic activity significantly weaker ($p<0.001$) than that of papaverine [23].

In other tests, ligustilide at 0.0325-0.13 ml/ml exhibited a concentration-dependent antispasmodic effect on acetylcholine-, histamine- and barium chloride-induced contractions in tracheal strips isolated from the guinea pig ($p<0.001$ at 0.13 ml/ml), and a relaxant effect on tracheal strips under normal tension ($p<0.01$ at 0.13 ml/ml); addition of propanolol did not alter these effects [25].

In vivo

Diuretic activity
An aqueous infusion of lovage root, administered to rats at 250-1000 mg crude drug per animal, did not produce diuresis; the urine volume was unchanged [26]. Other early experiments (1935-37) in mice and rabbits showed modest increases in urine volume. Overall, despite the traditional use of lovage root as a diuretic, animal studies cannot be considered to have convincingly demonstrated a diuretic effect relevant to humans [18,27]; the same applies to a number of other traditional diuretics and rats have not proved a reliable model for diuresis experiments.

Oestrogenic activity
An aqueous dry extract of lovage root, subcutaneously injected into rats, exhibited oestrogenic activity per g equivalent to 8 IU of oestradiol [28]; this may account for the traditional use of lovage as an emmenagogue.

Spasmolytic effects of constituents
Ligustilide administered intraperitonally to guinea pigs at 0.14 ml/kg body weight significantly impeded the asthmatic reaction induced by acetylcholine and histamine, with a potency approximately equal to that of aminophylline at 50 mg/kg ($p<0.001$). In a lung overflow experiment, ligustilide administered intravenously to anaesthetised guinea pigs at 0.08 ml/kg caused a complete or partial block of the reaction to histamine at 2-10 μg/kg [25].

Ferulic acid dose-dependently inhibited spontaneous uterine contractions of rats in oestrus with an intravenous ID_{50} of 47.9 mg/kg body weight compared to 4.5 mg/kg for papaverine; when administered orally at 300 mg/kg the maximum inhibition was about 30%, equivalent to papaverine at 30 mg/kg [29]. The same research group also demonstrated that ferulic acid has anti-inflammatory activity [30].

Sedative effects of phthalides
No data appears to be available with respect to the sedative activity of ligustilide or 3-n-butylidenephthalide. However, it has been demonstrated that two similar phthalides, sedanenolide and 3-n-butylphthalide (both with a butyl rather than butylidene substituent group), have mild central depressant activity; they prolonged pentobarbital-induced sleeping time after intraperitoneal administration to mice and also exhibited weak sedative activities when administered alone [31].

Pharmacological studies in humans
An early study (1941) in healthy volunteers showed that lovage root tea produced a small increase in urine volume and a clear increase in excretion of chloride and total nitrogen [32].

CLINICAL STUDIES

None published on mono-preparations of lovage root.

THERAPEUTICS

Actions
Spasmolytic [4,25,33,34], carminative [35,36], mildly diuretic [27,32,34-37], weakly estrogenic [28] and probably sedative [31].

Also stated to be expectorant [27,35,36]; emmenagogic, antimicrobial [35,37]; stomachic, cholagogic and antirheumatic [36].

Indications
None adequately substantiated by pharmacological or clinical studies.

Uses based on experience or tradition
Inflammatory complaints of the lower urinary tract [33-37] and renal gravel [33,34] or lithuria [35]. Menstrual disorders [18,27] including dysmenorrhoea, delayed menses [35], heavy menstrual bleeding and period pain [37]. Digestive disorders including flatulent colic, heartburn and loss of appetite [35-37].

Has also been use in the treatment of catarrh of the respiratory tract, oedematous swellings [18] and rheumatism [36], and topically for aphthous ulcers (as a mouthwash) and tonsillitis (as a gargle) [35].

Contraindications
Pregnancy [36,37].
Inflammatory disorders of the kidney [33,36]; oedema due to impaired cardiac or renal function [33].

Side effects
None known.

Interactions with other drugs
None known.

Dosage
Up to 3 times daily: dried root, 1-3 g [33-35] or as an infusion [34] or decoction [35]; liquid extract 1:1 in 45% ethanol [35], 1-3 ml.

SAFETY

The acute oral LD_{50} of lovage root in mice has been reported as 3.4 g/kg body weight [27].

Although certain furanocoumarins are potentially phototoxic, an extract of lovage showed no phototoxic or photomutagenic activity in a *Chlamydomonas reinhardii* test system [38].

REGULATORY STATUS

Medicines

UK	No licences issued for products containing lovage.
France	Not listed in *Médicaments à base de plantes* [39].
Germany	Commission E monograph published, with approved uses [33].

Food

USA	Permitted as flavouring (21 CFR 172.510) [40]
Council of Europe	Permitted as flavouring, category N2 [41].

REFERENCES

Current Pharmacopoeial Monographs
Ph. Eur. Lovage Root

Literature References

1. Toulemonde B and Noleau I. Volatile constituents of lovage (*Levisticum officinale* Koch). In: Lawrence BM, Mookherjee BD and Willis BJ, editors. *Flavors and Fragrances: A World Perspective*. Amsterdam: Elsevier, 1988:641-657.
2. Toulemonde B, Paul F and Noleau I. Phthalides from lovage (*Levisticum officinale* Koch). In: Martens M, Dalen GA and Russwurm H, Jr. *Flavour Science and Technology*. ISBN 0-471-91743-5. New York: John Wiley, 1987:89-94.
3. Cichy M, Wray V and Höfle G. New Constituents of *Levisticum officinale* Koch (Lovage). *Liebigs Ann. Chem.* 1984, 397-400 [GERMAN/English summary].
4. Zschocke S, Liu J-H, Stuppner H and Bauer R. Comparative Study of Roots of *Angelica sinensis* and Related Umbelliferous Drugs by Thin Layer Chromatography, High-Performance Liquid Chromatography and Liquid Chromatography-Mass Spectrometry. *Phytochem. Analysis* 1998, **9**, 283-290.
5. Cu J-Q, Pu F, Shi Y, Perineau F, Delmas M and Gaset A. The Chemical Composition of Lovage Headspace and Essential Oils Produced by Solvent Extraction with Various Solvents. *J. Ess. Oil Res.* 1990, **2**, 53-59.
6. Stahl-Biskup E and Wichtmann E-M. Composition of the Essential Oils from Roots of some Apiaceae in Relation to the Development of their Oil Duct Systems. *Flavour Fragrance J.* 1991, **6**, 249-255.
7. Segebrecht S and Schilcher H. Ligustilide: Guiding Component for Preparations of *Levisticum officinale* Roots. *Planta Medica* 1989, **55**, 572-573.
8. Gijbels MJM, Scheffer JJC and Baerheim Svendsen A. Phthalides in the Essential Oil from Roots of Levisticum officinale. *Planta Medica* 1982, **44**, 207-211.
9. Gijbels MJM, Scheffer JJC and Baerheim Svendsen A. Z-Butylidenephthalide in the Essential Oil from Roots of Levisticum officinale. *Planta Medica* 1980, (Suppl.), 41-47.
10. Fehr D. On the Essential Oil of Levisticum officinale. I. Investigations on the Oil from Fruit, Leaves, Stems and Roots. *Planta Medica* 1980, (Suppl.), 34-40 [GERMAN/English summary].
11. Liu T, Lu R, Li W and Liu J. Growth dynamics and changes of active constituent accumulation in Levisticum officinale Koch root. *Zhongyao Tongbao* 1982, **7** (4), 2-3 [CHINESE] through *Chem. Abstr.* 1983, **98**, 14420.
12. Dauksha AD. Phytochemical study of Levisticum officinale. *Aktual. Vop. Farm.* 1968 (pub. 1970), 23-24; through *Chem. Abstr.* 1972, **76**, 70136.
13. Hörhammer L, Wagner H and Kraemer-Heydweiller D. Neue Methoden im Pharmakognostischen Unterricht. 12. Mitteilung: Identifizierung von Umbelliferenwurzeln und Nachweis der wichtigsten Verfälschungen mit Hilfe der Dünnschichtchromatographie [New methods in the teaching of pharmacognosy. Part 12. Identification of roots of the Umbelliferae and detection of the most important adulterants by means of thin-layer chromatography]. *Dtsch. Apoth. Ztg.* 1966, **106**, 267-272 [GERMAN].
14. Albulescu D, Palade M and Dafincescu M. Contribution to the study of coumarin derivatives from *Levisticum officinale* Koch. *Farmacia (Bucharest)* 1975, **23**, 159-165 [ROMANIAN/English summary].
15. Fischer FC and Baerheim Svendsen A. Apterin. A common furanocoumarin glycoside in the Umbelliferae. *Phytochemistry* 1976, **15**, 1079-1080.
16. Baerheim Svendsen A. Über das Vorkommen der Chlorogen- und Kaffeesäure in der Pflanzenfamilie der Umbelliferen. 2. Mitteilung über Papierchromatographie in der phytochemischen Analyse [The occurrence of chlorogenic and caffeic acids in the Umbelliferae family. Part 2. Paper chromatography in the phytochemical analysis]. *Pharm. Acta Helv.* 1951, **26**, 253-258 [GERMAN].
17. Lu R, Lin M, Liu T and Fang Q. Studies on the chemical constituents of Ou Dang Gui (Levisticum officinale). *Zhongcaoyao* 1981, **12**, 485-486 [CHINESE]; through *Chem. Abstr.* 1982, **97**, 3545.
18. Hänsel R, Keller K, Rimpler H and Schneider G, editors. Levisticum. In: *Hagers Handbuch der Pharmazeutischen Praxis, 5th ed. Volume 5: Drogen E-O.* ISBN 3-540-52638-2. Berlin-Heidelberg-New York-London: Springer-Verlag, 1993:664-670 [GERMAN].
19. Zogg GC, Nyiredy S and Sticher O. Apiaceenwurzeln. Qualitative und quantitative Furanocumarinbestimmung in Apiaceenwurzeln [Qualitative and quantitative determination of furanocoumarins in roots of the Apiaceae]. *Dtsch. Apoth. Ztg.* 1989, **129**, 717-722 [GERMAN].
20. Zschocke S, Stuppner H and Bauer R. Analytical and pharmacological investigations of *Angelica sinensis* ("Danggui") and comparison with other Umbelliferous

drugs. In: Abstracts of 2nd International Congress on Phytomedicine. Munich, 11-14 September 1996. Published as: *Phytomedicine* 1996, **3** (Suppl. 1), 279 (Abstract P-98).
21. Trivedi B, Volicer L and Motl O. A Spasmolytic Substance from the Drug "Tang-kuej" (*Angelica sinensis* Diels). *Ceskoslov. Farm.* 1966, **15**, 206-209 [CZECH/English summary].
22. Mitsuhashi H, Nagai U, Muramatsu T and Tashiro H. Studies on the Constituents of Umbelliferae Plants. II. Isolation of the Active Principles of Ligusticum Root. *Chem. Pharm. Bull.* 1960, **8**, 243-245.
23. Ko W-C. A newly isolated antispasmodic - butylidene-phthalide. *Japan. J. Pharmacol.* 1980, **30**, 85-91.
24. Ko W-C, Lin S-C, Yeh C-Y and Wang Y-T. Alkylphthalides isolated from *Ligusticum wallichii* Franch. and their in vitro inhibitory effect on rat uterine contraction induced by prostaglandin $F_{2\alpha}$. *T'ai-wan I Hsueh Hui Tsa Chih (J. Formosan Med. Assoc.)* 1977, **76**, 669-677; through *Chem. Abstr.* 1978, **88**, 130721.
25. Tao J-Y, Ruan Y-P, Mei Q-B, Liu S, Tian Q-L, Chen Y-Z et al. Studies on the antiasthmatic action of ligustilide of dang-gui, Angelica sinensis (Oliv.) Diels. *Acta Pharmacol. Sin.* 1984, **19**, 561-565 [CHINESE/English summary].
26. Vollmer H and Hübner K. Untersuchungen über die diuretische Wirkung der Fructus juniperi, Radix levistici, Radix ononidis, Folia betulae, Radix liquiritiae und Herba equiseti an Ratten [Investigations on the diuretic effect of Fructus juniperi, Radix levistici, Radix ononidis, Folia betulae, Radix liquiritiae and Herba equiseti in rats]. *Naunyn-Schmiederbergs Arch. exp. Path. Pharmakol.* 1937, **186**, 592-605 [GERMAN].
27. Vollman C. Levisticum officinale - Der Liebstöckel [Levisticum officinale - Lovage]. *Z. Phytotherapie* 1988, **9**, 128-132 [GERMAN].
28. San Martin R. Sobre el valor estrogeno en algunas especies vegetales. Actividad del *Levisticum officinale* [The estrogenic potency of some plant species. Activity of *Levisticum officinale*]. *Farmacognosia (Madrid)* 1958, **18**, 179-186 [SPANISH/English summary].
29. Ozaki Y and Ma J-P. Inhibitory Effects of Tetramethyl-pyrazine and Ferulic Acid on Spontaneous Movement of Rat Uterus *in Situ*. *Chem. Pharm. Bull.* 1990, **38**, 1620-1623.
30. Ozaki Y. Anti-inflammatory Effect of Tetramethylpyrazine and Ferulic Acid. *Chem. Pharm. Bull.* 1992, **40**, 954-956.
31. Bjeldanes LF and Kim I-S. Sedative activity of celery oil constituents. *J. Food Sci.* 1978, **43**, 143-144.
32. Braun R. *Dtsch. Heilpflanze* 1941, 7, 21; cited by Vollman [27].
33. Levistici radix. German Commission E monograph published in: Bundesanzeiger No. 101 of 1 June 1990 [GERMAN].
34. Weiss RF and Fintelmann V. Levisticum officinale, Lovage. In: *Herbal Medicine, 2nd ed.* (translated from the 9th German edition of *Lehrbuch der Phytotherapie*). ISBN 3-13-126332-6. Stuttgart-New York: Thieme, 2000:229.
35. Levisticum. In: *British Herbal Pharmacopoeia 1983.* ISBN 0-903032-07-4. Bournemouth: British Herbal Medicine Association, 1983.
36. Stodola J and Volák J. Lovage. Translated into English in: Bunney S, editor. *The Illustrated Book of Herbs.* ISBN 0-7064-1489-6. London: Octopus Books, 1984:180.
37. Chevallier A. Lovage. In: *The Encyclopedia of Medicinal Plants.* ISBN 0-7513-0314-3. London-New York-Stuttgart: Dorling Kindersley, 1996:226.
38. Schimmer O. Determination of the Phototoxic and Photomutagenic Potency of Plant Extracts and Commercial Products Containing Furocoumarins Using *Chlamydomonas* as a Test System. *Planta Medica* 1983, **47**, 79-82 [GERMAN/English summary].
39. *Médicaments à base de plantes.* ISBN 2-911473-02-7. Saint-Denis Cedex, France: Agence du Médicament, 1998.
40. Lovage. In: Section 172.510 of USA Code of Federal Regulations, Title 21, Food and Drugs, Parts 170 to 199. Revised as of April 1, 2000.
41. Levisticum officinale Koch, roots. In: Flavouring Substances and *Natural Sources of Flavourings, 3rd ed.* ISBN 2-7160-0081-6. Strasbourg: Council of Europe, 1981.

REGULATORY GUIDELINES FROM OTHER EU COUNTRIES

GERMANY

Commission E monograph [33]: Levistici radix (Liebstöckelwurzel).

Uses
Irrigation in inflammatory ailments of the lower urinary tract. Irrigation therapy for the prevention of kidney gravel.

Contraindications
Lovage preparations should not be used in acute inflammatory disorders of the kidney parenchyma or impaired kidney function.

No irrigation therapy in oedema due to impaired cardiac or renal function.

Side effects
None known.

Interactions with other drugs
None known.

Dosage
Unless otherwise prescribed, daily dose: 4-8 g of the drug, or equivalent preparations.

Mode of administration
Comminuted drug and other galenic preparations for internal use.
Note: A plentiful intake of liquid is necessary during irrigation therapy.
Note: With prolonged use of lovage, exposure to ultraviolet light and intensive sun should be avoided.

Action
The essential oil containing ligustilide is spasmolytic.

MARSHMALLOW LEAF **Malvaceae**

Althaeae folium

Definition
Marshmallow Leaf consists of the dried leaves of *Althaea officinalis* L. harvested shortly before the flowering period.

CONSTITUENTS

□ ***Polysaccharides***, in which glucuronic acid, galacturonic acid, rhamnose, glucose, galactose, xylose and arabinose residues have been identified [1-3]. The principal water-soluble polysaccharide (denoted as Althaea-mucilage OL) has a MW of ca. 180,000 and consists mainly of the repeating structure (1→4)-[β-D-glucuronic acid-(1→3)]-α-D-galacturonic acid-(1→2)-α-L-rhamnose, with about 1% acetyl groups and 3% protein [3,4]. A water-soluble and virtually linear D-glucan with α-(1→6) links has also been isolated [5].

The mucilage content in dried leaf has been determined as ca. 9.8%, compared to ca. 11.2% in dried marshmallow root [1].

□ ***Flavonoids***, Hypolaetin 8-gentiobioside (0.25-0.4%) [6-9] and tiliroside [= kaempferol 3-(6″-*p*-coumaroyl)-glucoside] (0.13-0.25%) [6-8] with smaller amounts of astragalin (= kaempferol 3-glucoside) [6,7,10], isoquercitrin [6,10], quercetin 4′-glucoside [7], hypolaetin 8-glucoside [9], hypolaetin 4′-methyl ether 8-glucoside and hypolaetin 4′-methyl ether 8-glucoside-3′-sulphate [7,10].

The flowers (excluded from the leaf definition) have a higher flavonoid content including dihydrokaempferol 4′-glucoside (0.8-0.9%), astragalin and tiliroside [6-8,11,12].

□ ***Phenolic acids***, including caffeic, *p*-coumaric, ferulic, *p*-hydroxybenzoic, *p*-hydroxyphenylacetic, protocatechuic, salicylic, sinapic, syringic and vanillic acids [13].

□ ***Coumarins*** Scopoletin has been identified [13].

□ ***Other constituents*** include β-sitosterol, stigmasterol, α- and β-amyrin, various fatty acids [14], and free sucrose and glucose [2].

Published Assay Methods
Mucilage content [Ph. Fr. X]. Flavonoid glycosides by HPLC [6,7,11]. Total flavonoid aglycones by spectrophotometry [8]. Phenolic acids and coumarins by HPLC [13].

PHARMACOLOGY

In vitro
Althaea-mucilage OL exhibited weak anti-complement activity at concentrations of 100-1000 µg/ml [15]. Tiliroside, on the other hand, exhibited potent anti-complement activity on the classical pathway of the complement system with an IC_{50} of 5.4×10^{-5} M [16]. Inhibition of complement activity can be an indicator of anti-inflammatory activity.

In vivo

Anti-inflammatory activity
Tiliroside inhibited croton oil-induced dermatitis of mouse ear with an ID_{50} of 0.036 µM and activity of 0.8 in relation to 1.0 for indometacin [17].

Whether hypolaetin 8-gentiobioside (the principal flavonoid in marshmallow leaf) is anti-inflammatory has not been determined. However, hypolaetin 8-glucoside, which is present in marshmallow leaf to a small extent [9] and might also be formed in the body as a metabolite of hypolaetin 8-gentiobioside, has been shown to possesses anti-inflammatory activity [18-20]. When administered

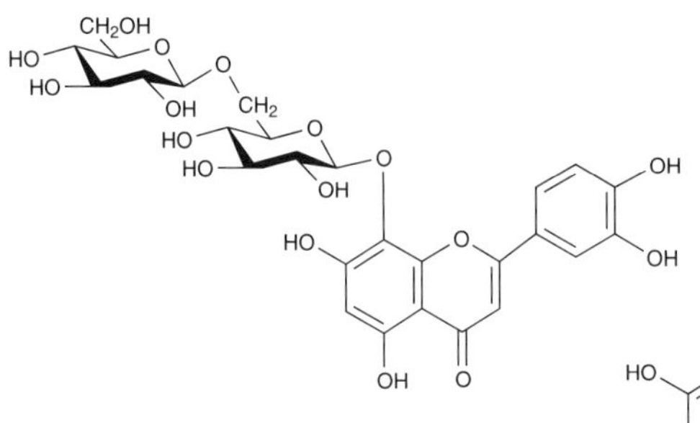

Hypolaetin 8-gentiobioside

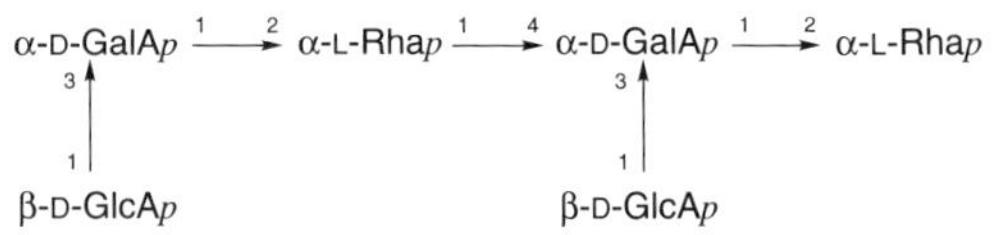

Repeating component of the principal polysaccharide

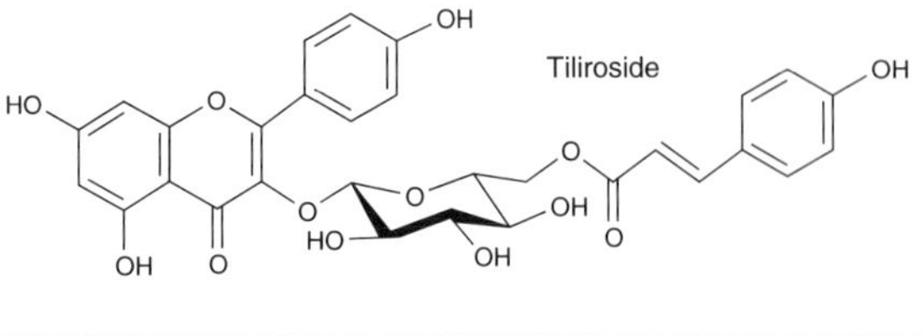

Tiliroside

intraperitoneally to rats, hypolaetin 8-glucoside dose-dependently inhibited carrageenan-induced paw oedema, by 74% after 3 hours at a dose of 90 mg/kg body weight ($p<0.01$) compared to 49% inhibition by phenylbutazone at the same dose. The anti-inflammatory effect of hypolaetin 8-glucoside declined more rapidly than that of phenylbutazone, but did not cause gastric erosions whereas phenylbutazone was damaging [20]. In other studies hypolaetin 8-glucoside showed gastric anti-ulcer activity in rats [21] and was more potent than troxerutin in inhibiting histamine-induced capillary permeability in rats [19].

Hypoglycaemic activity
When administered intraperitoneally to mice, Althaea-mucilage OL isolated from marshmallow leaf exhibited significant hypoglycaemic activity, reducing plasma glucose levels after 7 hours to 79% ($p<0.05$) and 54% ($p<0.01$) of the control level at 10 and 100 mg/kg respectively [22].

CLINICAL STUDIES

None published on mono-preparations of marshmallow leaf.

THERAPEUTICS

Actions
Demulcent, emollient [23], weakly anti-inflammatory [7,11,15,17], vulnerary [24].

Indications
None adequately substantiated by pharmacological or clinical studies.

Uses based on experience or tradition
Internal: Irritation and inflammation of the oral and pharyngeal mucosa, dry irritating coughs [24-26], respiratory catarrh and bronchitis [23]; digestive tract disorders [26,27] including enteritis and peptic ulcer [24]; urinary tract disorders including cystitis and urethritis [23,24].
External: Mouth and throat inflammations (as a gargle) [26,27]; skin disorders including abrasions, fissures, insect stings [27], boils, abscesses and ulcers [23,26].

Contraindications
None known.

Side effects
None known.

Interactions with other drugs
None known.

Dosage
Up to three times daily: dried leaf, 2-5 g as an infusion or equivalent preparation; liquid extract (1:1 in 25% ethanol), 2-5 ml [23].
Topically: 5% powdered leaf in an ointment base [23].

SAFETY

No specific toxicity data are available but from the known constituents and the use of marshmallow in foods there are no reasons for concern regarding safety [24].

REGULATORY STATUS

Medicines

UK	No licences issued for products containing marshmallow leaf, but marshmallow root is accepted for general sale, internal or external use [28].
France	Accepted for specified indications [27].
Germany	Commission E monograph published, with approved uses [25].

Foods

USA	Marshmallow leaf not listed, but root and flowers permitted as flavouring (21 CFR 172.510) [29].
Council of Europe	Permitted as flavouring, category N2 [30].

REFERENCES

Current Pharmacopoeial Monographs
Ph. Eur. Marshmallow Leaf

Literature References

1. Franz G. Die Schleimpolysaccharide von *Althaea officinalis* und *Malva sylvestris* [The mucilage polysaccharides of *Althaea officinalis* and *Malva sylvestris*]. *Planta Medica* 1966, **14**, 90-110 [GERMAN/English summary].
2. Karawya MS, Balbaa SI and Afifi MSA. Investigation of the carbohydrate contents of certain mucilaginous plants. *Planta Medica* 1971, **20**, 14-23.
3. Tomoda M, Shimizu N, Suzuki H and Takasu T. Plant Mucilages. XXVIII. Isolation and Characterization of a Mucilage, "Althea-mucilage OL", from the Leaves of *Althaea officinalis*. *Chem. Pharm. Bull.* 1981, **29**, 2277-2282.
4. Shimizu N and Tomoda M. Carbon-13 Nuclear Magnetic Resonance Spectra of Alditol-Form Oligosaccharides having the Fundamental Structural Units of the Malvaceae Plant Mucilages and a Related Polysaccharide. *Chem. Pharm. Bull.* 1985, **33**, 5539-5542.
5. Kardosová A, Rosik J, Toman R and Capek P. Glucan isolated from leaves of *Althaea officinalis* L. *Collect. Czech. Chem. Commun.* 1983, **48**, 2082-2087.
6. Gudej J and Dzido TH. Quantitative determination of flavonoid glycosides in leaves and flowers from some species of Althaea genus using HPLC technique. *Acta Polon. Pharm. - Drug Res.* 1991, **48**, 59-62.
7. Gudej J and Bieganowska ML. Chromatographic Investigations of Flavonoid Compounds in the Leaves and Flowers of Some Species of the Genus *Althaea*. *Chromatographia*

1990, **30**, 333-336.
8. Gudej J. Determination of flavonoids in leaves, flowers and roots of Althaea officinalis L. *Farm. Pol.* 1990, **46**, 153-155 [POLISH/English summary].
9. Gudej J. Flavonoid compounds of leaves of *Althaea officinalis* L. (Malvaceae). II. 8-Hydroxyluteolin (hypolaetin) heterosides. *Acta Polon. Pharm.* 1987, **44**, 369-373 [POLISH/English summary].
10. Gudej J. Flavonoid compounds of leaves of *Althaea officinalis* L. (Malvaceae). I. Glucosido-esters and monoglucosides. *Acta Polon. Pharm.* 1985, **42**, 192-198 [POLISH/English summary].
11. Dzido TH, Soczewinski E and Gudej J. Computer-aided optimization of high-performance liquid chromatographic analysis of flavonoids from some species of the genus *Althaea*. *J. Chromatogr.* 1991, **550**, 71-76.
12. Gudej J. Polyphenolic compounds of flowers of *Althaea officinalis* L. (Malvaceae). *Acta Polon. Pharm.* 1988, **45**, 340-345 [POLISH/English summary].
13. Gudej J and Bieganowska ML. Chromatographic investigations of phenolic acids and coumarins in the leaves and flowers of some species of the genus Althaea. *J. Liq. Chromatogr.* 1990, **13**, 4081-4092.
14. Karawya MS, Balbaa SI and Afifi MS. Lipids of Egyptian Althaea, Malva and Plantago Species. *Egypt. J. Pharm. Sci.* 1979, **20**, 291-298.
15. Yamada H, Nagai T, Cyong J-C, Otsuka Y, Tomoda M, Shimizu N and Shimada K. Relationship between chemical structure and anti-complementary activity of plant polysaccharides. *Carbohydrate Res.* 1985, **144**, 101-111.
16. Jung KY, Oh SR, Park S-H, Lee IS, Ahn KS, Lee JJ and Lee H-K. Anti-complement Activity of Tiliroside from the Flower Buds of *Magnolia fargesii*. *Biol. Pharm. Bull.* 1998, **21**, 1077-1078.
17. Della Loggia R, Del Negro P, Bianchi P, Romussi G and Tubaro A. Topical Anti-inflammatory Activity of some Flavonoids from *Quercus ilex* Leaves. *Planta Medica* 1989, **55**, 109-110.
18. Alcaraz MJ, Moroney M and Hoult JRS. Effects of Hypolaetin-8-O-glucoside and its Aglycone in *in vivo* and *in vitro* Tests for Anti-inflammatory Agents. *Planta Medica* 1989, **55**, 107-108.
19. Villar A, Gascó MA and Alcaraz MJ. Some aspects of the inhibitory activity of hypolaetin-8-glucoside in acute inflammation. *J. Pharm. Pharmacol.* 1987, **39**, 502-507.
20. Villar A, Gasco MA and Alcaraz MJ. Anti-inflammatory and anti-ulcer properties of hypolaetin-8-glucoside, a novel plant flavonoid. *J. Pharm. Pharmacol.* 1984, **36**, 820-823.
21. Alcaraz MJ and Tordera M. Studies on the Gastric Anti-ulcer Activity of Hypolaetin-8-glucoside. *Phytotherapy Res.* 1988, **2**, 85-88.
22. Tomoda M, Shimizu N, Oshima Y, Takahashi M, Murakami M and Hikino H. Hypoglycemic Activity of Twenty Plant Mucilages and Three Modified Products. *Planta Medica* 1987, **53**, 8-12.
23. Althaea Leaf. In: *British Herbal Pharmacopoeia 1983*. ISBN 0-903032-07-4. Bournemouth: British Herbal Medicine Association, 1983.
24. Newall CA, Anderson LA and Phillipson JD. Marshmallow. In: *Herbal Medicines - A Guide for Health-care Professionals*. ISBN 0-85369-289-0. London: Pharmaceutical Press, 1996:188.
25. Althaeae folium (Eibischblätter). German Commission E Monograph published in: *Bundesanzeiger* No. 43 of 02.03.89.
26. Hänsel R, Keller K, Rimpler H and Schneider G, editors. Althaea. In: *Hagers Handbuch der Pharmazeutischen Praxis. 5th ed. Volume 4: Drogen A-D*. ISBN 3-540-52631-5. Berlin-Heidelberg-New York-London: Springer-Verlag, 1992:233-239 [GERMAN].
27. Guimauve. In: *Médicaments à base de plantes*. ISBN 2-911473-02-7. Saint-Denis Cedex, France: Agence du Médicament, 1998.
28. Marshmallow Root. In: UK Statutory Instrument 1994 No. 2410. The Medicines (Products Other Than Veterinary Drugs) (General Sale List) Amendment Order 1994. Schedule 1, Table A.
29. Althea root and flowers (Section 172.510). In: USA Code of Federal Regulations, Title 21, Food and Drugs, Parts 170 to 199. Revised as of April 1, 2000.
30. Althaea officinalis L., leaves. In: Flavouring Substances and Natural Sources of Flavourings, 3rd ed. ISBN 2-7160-0081-6. Strasbourg: Council of Europe, 1981.

REGULATORY GUIDELINES FROM OTHER EU COUNTRIES

FRANCE

Médicaments à base de plantes [27]: Guimauve, feuille.

Therapeutic indications accepted

Oral use
Traditionally used as adjuvant treatment of the painful component of functional digestive disorders.
Traditionally used in the symptomatic treatment of coughs.
Laxative with a bulk-forming effect.

Topical use
Traditionally used as a soothing and antipruriginous local treatment of dermatological ailments, as a trophic protector in the treatment of chaps, abrasions or fissures and against insect stings.
Traditionally used locally (mouthwash/gargle, pastille) as an antalgesic in ailments of the buccal cavity and/or the pharynx.

GERMANY

Commission E monograph [25]: Althaeae folium (Eibischblätter).

Uses
Irritation of the oral and pharyngeal mucosa and associated irritable dry cough.

Contraindications
None known.

Side effects
None known.

Interactions with other drugs
None known.
Absorption of other drugs taken simultaneously may be delayed.

Dosage
Unless otherwise prescribed, daily dose: 5 g of dried leaf or equivalent preparations.

Mode of administration
Comminuted drug for aqueous infusions and other galenic preparations for internal use.

Action
Relieves irritation.

MATÉ

Aquifoliaceae

Mate folium

Synonyms: Yerba Maté, Paraguay Tea.

Definition

Maté consists of the leaves of *Ilex paraguariensis* A. St.-Hil., cured by brief but strong heating then more gently dried.

Ilex paraguariensis is an evergreen tree found in the subtropical-to-Mediterranean climate of the southern provinces of Brazil and adjacent areas of Argentina and Paraguay. About 70% of the leaf crop in Brazil is derived from coppiced wild trees, but cultivation in plantations is increasing. Although processing techniques may vary according to the scale of operations, in general the leaves are subjected on the day of harvesting to brief but strong heating (e.g. by passing them through a heated, rotating metal cylinder at 150°C for 80 seconds) to inactivate enzymes, especially polyphenoloxidases; otherwise the leaves would go black due to fermentation and degradation. Subsequently the leaves are dried at about 60°C, then comminuted to the required size, to produce what may be called "green maté". For some markets, the leaves are subjected to an additional roasting process (e.g. in a heated metal drum with an air temperature of about 100°C) to produce "roasted maté". Monographs for both green maté (Grüne Mateblätter) and roasted maté (Geröstete Mateblätter) appear in the Deutscher Arzneimittel-Codex. For the local beverage known as "chimarrão" in Brazil, a powdered form of green maté containing a proportion of powdered twigs (to produce a milder taste) is used [1,2].

CONSTITUENTS

☐ *Methylxanthines* (also referred to as purines or purine alkaloids), notably caffeine (0.8-1.9%; Ph. Fr. min. 1.0%, DAC min. 0.6%) and theobromine (0.1-0.9%) [3-6]. A trace of theophylline (about 0.005%) is also present [7].

☐ ***Hydroxycinnamic acid derivatives*** Chlorogenic, neochlorogenic and cryptochlorogenic acids (i.e. 5-, 3- and 4-caffeoylquinic acids respectively*), 3,4-, 3,5- and 4,5-dicaffeoylquinic acids and a small amount of free caffeic acid (0.02%) [3,9,10]. The predominant compounds are chlorogenic, neochlorogenic and 3,5-dicaffeoylquinic acids. In green maté the total amount of caffeoyl derivatives is about 9.5% [3,9]; however, the total was found to be considerably lower (about 2.9%) in what may have been roasted maté [3].

☐ ***Flavonoids*** Small amounts of flavonols: quercetin (0.003%), kaempferol (0.001%), rutin (=quercetin 3-rutinoside, 0.06%) [9], isoquercitrin (=quercetin 3-glucoside) [2,11] and kaempferol 3-rutinoside [11].

☐ *Triterpenoid saponins* Five bidesmosidic saponins, matesaponins 1 [12], 2, 3, 4 [13] and 5 [14], with ursolic acid as the aglycone, a glycosyl group (up to three sugars) at C-3 and a glycosyl ester group (up to three sugars) at C-28. Matesaponin 1 is ursolic acid 3-*O*-[glucosyl-(1→3)-arabinosyl]-(28→1)-glucosyl ester.

Two further saponins have been identified as isomers of matesaponins 1 and 2 with oleanolic acid as the aglycone [15].

☐ ***Other constituents*** A relatively high mineral content (average in dried leaf, as mg/100 g: potassium 1200, calcium 760, magnesium 586 and manganese 194; in hot water infusions the average manganese level was 117 mg/100 g) [16] and modest amounts of B vitamins and ascorbic acid [2].

A nitrile compound (0.02%) detected in the leaves [17] was subsequently identified as menisdaurin [18].

No condensed or hydrolysable tannins appear to be present [3,19].

*Numbered in accordance with IUPAC recommendations [8].

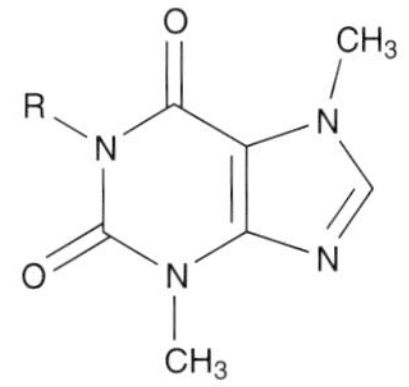

Caffeine	R = CH_3
Theobromine	R = H

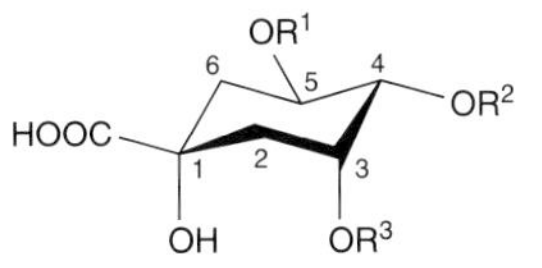

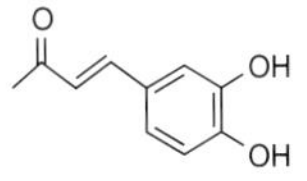

caffeoyl group

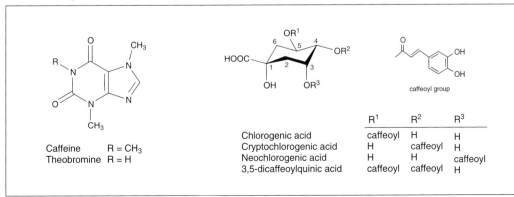

	R^1	R^2	R^3
Chlorogenic acid	caffeoyl	H	H
Cryptochlorogenic acid	H	caffeoyl	H
Neochlorogenic acid	H	H	caffeoyl
3,5-dicaffeoylquinic acid	caffeoyl	caffeoyl	H

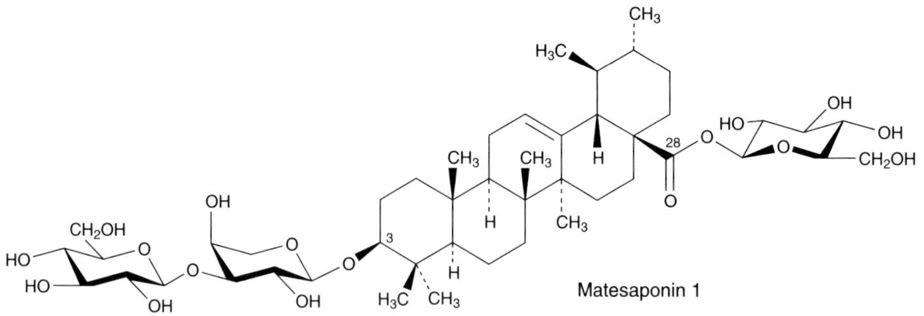

Published Assay Methods
Methylxanthines (caffeine and theobromine) by HPLC [3,4,6] and HP capillary electrophoresis [5]. Hydroxycinnamic acid derivatives by HPLC [3,9,10]. Flavonoids by HPLC [9]. Minerals by capillary ion electrophoresis [16].

PHARMACOLOGY

In vitro

Antioxidant activity
A freeze-dried aqueous extract from maté concentration-dependently inhibited lipid peroxidation in rat liver microsomes (IC_{50}: 18-28 μg/ml) and hydrogen peroxide-induced peroxidation of red blood cell membranes (IC_{50}: 100 μg/ml), and proved to be an effective scavenger of superoxide anions (IC_{50}: 15 μg/ml) [20]. The antioxidant activity has been attributed largely to phenolic compounds, notably the caffeoylquinic acids present. A similar maté extract showed radical scavenging activity comparable to, and chain-breaking antioxidant activity greater than, that of chlorogenic acid alone [10].

An aqueous extract concentration-dependently inhibited copper-induced oxidation of low density lipoprotein (LDL, isolated from human blood) at concentrations between 7.5 and 37.7 μg/ml. On a weight-for-weight basis, the extract was as effective an antioxidant as ascorbic acid or butylated hydroxytoluene [21].

In vivo

Stimulation of the central nervous system
In animals, the stimulant actions of caffeine are manifested as enhanced spontaneous locomotor activity, enhanced electrical activity in brain regions and effects on coordination paradigms requiring vigilance. In humans, caffeine increases vigilance, decreases psychomotor reaction time and increases sleep latency and waking time. Caffeine may also influence intellectual performance if this is compromised by boredom or tiredness. Precise mechanisms underlying the stimulant actions of caffeine remain poorly defined, but dose-dependent stimulation of locomotor activity in a number of species has been attributed to the blockade by caffeine of tonically active central inhibitory adenosine receptors [22].

Chlorogenic acid was found to have a dose-dependent central stimulating effect, about one sixth of that caused by caffeine, after oral administration to rats at 3.75-15 mg/kg [23].

Choleretic effects
A lyophilized aqueous extract from maté, administered intravenously to rats significantly and dose-dependently increased bile flow, by 18% within 60 minutes at 250 mg/kg ($p<0.01$); this increase was sustained for at least 120 minutes, resulting in a 61% cumulative increase in excreted bile over the 120-minute period compared to saline as control. Intraduodenal administration of the extract at 250 mg/kg also caused a significant increase in bile flow ($p<0.01$). No increases in bile acid excretion were observed and the maté extract had no effect on intestinal propulsion [24].

Anti-inflammatory effects
A dry methanolic extract of maté, applied topically at 2 mg/ear, inhibited 12-*O*-tetradecanoylphorbol-13-acetate (TPA)-induced ear oedema in mice by 69% ($p<0.01$) six hours after TPA treatment [25].

Pharmacological studies in humans

Antioxidant effect
Copper-induced autoxidation of low-density lipoprotein (LDL) in plasma from blood taken from healthy fasting human volunteers one hour after drinking (over a period of one hour) 500 ml of a maté tea was significantly inhibited in comparison with the oxidability of LDL in plasma from blood drawn immediately before the intake of maté tea ($p<0.001$). Since no differences were observed in

the oxidability of isolated LDL from the plasma samples, it was concluded that antioxidants in maté tea are absorbed and reach sufficiently high levels in plasma to inhibit copper-induced LDL autoxidation by increasing aqueous phase antioxidant capacity [26].

In a double-blind study of thermogenic effects, a single large dose (1.5 g) of freeze-dried aqueous extract of maté was administered to 6 healthy young volunteers while 6 others received placebo. Maté caused a significant reduction in heart rate ($p = 0.043$), but only a borderline decrease in respiratory quotient ($p = 0.054$), which indicates enhancement of the proportion of fat oxidized, a favourable effect for decreasing body fat. No significant changes were observed in energy expenditure or blood pressure. The potential of maté for the treatment of human obesity therefore appeared to be poor [27].

Caffeine is efficiently absorbed from the gastro-intestinal tract and peak plasma concentrations occur 15 to 120 minutes after ingestion. An oral dose of 1 mg/kg in humans (considered equivalent to a cup of coffee) produces plasma concentrations of 1-2 μg/ml. The half-life of caffeine in adults is 2.5-4.5 hours; it is extensively metabolized in the liver and excreted in the urine as 1-methyluric acid, 1-methylxanthine, 7-methylxanthine and other compounds [22,28].

To some extent a complex is formed between caffeine and caffeoylquinic acids in maté; this influences the pharmacokinetics of caffeine and hence may modify some of its pharmacodynamic effects [2].

CLINICAL STUDIES

None published on mono-preparations of maté.

THERAPEUTICS

Actions

Stimulant to the central nervous system [29,30], choleretic [24], antioxidant [26], diuretic [20,29, 30], mildly analgesic [29,30] and topical anti-inflammatory [20,25].

The stimulant and diuretic properties of maté are largely due to the high content of caffeine. Choleretic and antioxidant activity may be attributed to phenolic constituents, notably the caffeoyl derivatives.

Indications

None adequately substantiated by pharmacological or clinical studies of maté.

Uses based on experience or tradition

Mental and physical fatigue [30-32]; headache [29,30], particularly when associated with fatigue [29].

Has also been used in the treatment of mild depression and rheumatic pains [29,30], as an adjuvant in slimming regimes [32] and in the treatment of migraine, and as a fortifying beverage in much the same way as tea [30].

Contraindications

None known. However, it is prudent to limit caffeine intake during pregnancy [28].

Side effects

None known.

Interactions with other drugs

The metabolic clearance of caffeine from the body may be enhanced or retarded by concomitant use of certain other drugs [28].

Dosage

Three times daily: 1-2 g of dried leaf or an equivalent preparation [29,31] such as an infusion or liquid extract 1:1 in 25% alcohol [29]

Excessive or long-term use of maté should be avoided [33].

SAFETY

In parts of South America where the "gaucho" culture is widespread, including Argentina, Uruguay, Paraguay and southern Brazil, the drinking of maté as a hot beverage (*mate-chimarrão*) has been associated with high incidences of oesophageal cancer. A number of studies have reported a link between maté drinking and cancer or precancerous lesions of the upper digestive tract. Traditionally the maté leaf is infused with hot water in a gourd (the hard shell of a local fruit) and the infusion is sucked through a silver tube with a flattened perforated disc on the lower end to act as a filter. Since large amounts may be drunk at rather high temperatures, thermal injury is thought to be a factor in carcinogenesis. Whatever the case, a review by the International Agency for Research on Cancer concluded that "hot maté drinking is probably carcinogenic to humans" [34,35].

In the Ames test, a lyophilized aqueous extract of maté showed no mutagenic potential with *Salmonella typhimurium* strains TA97 and TA 98 but gave a mutagenic response with strains TA 100 and TA 102. Lysogenic induction studies in strains of *Escherichia coli* confirmed that the extract had genotoxic properties and other results indicated that active oxygen species appeared to play an essential role in this genotoxicity. The extract also increased the frequency of chromosomal aberrations in human peripheral lymphocytes. On the other hand, no clastogenicity was detected *in vivo* after oral administration of the extract to rats; there was no significant increase in chromosomal aberrations in bone marrow cells from the rats compared to a control group. It was concluded that the overall results supported epidemiological data suggesting that maté can potentiate carcinogenesis in the human oropharynx and oesophagus [35].

REGULATORY STATUS

Medicines

UK	Accepted for general sale, internal or external use [36].
France	Accepted for specified indications [32].
Germany	Commission E monograph published, with approved uses [31].

Food

USA	Generally recognized as safe (21 CFR 182.20) [37].
Council of Europe	Permitted as flavouring, category N2 [38].

REFERENCES

Current Pharmacopoeial Monographs

Ph. Fr.	Maté vert
DAC	Grüne Mateblätter (green maté)
	Geröstete Mateblätter (roasted maté)
BHP	Maté

Literature References

1. Ohem N. Auf den Spuren des Mate. 5000 Kilometer durch den Süden Brasiliens [On the maté trail. 5000 kilometres through southern Brazil]. *Dtsch. Apoth. Ztg.* 1990, **130**, 1769-1773 [GERMAN].
2. Ohem N, Hölzl J. Der Mate - eine Genuß- und Heilpflanze aus dem mittleren Südamerika [Maté - a beverage and medicinal plant from central South America]. *Pharm Ztg.* 1990, **135**, 2737-2746 [GERMAN].
3. Clifford MN and Ramirez-Martinez JR. Chlorogenic Acids and Purine Alkaloids Contents of Maté (*Ilex paraguariensis*) Leaf and Beverage. *Food Chem.* 1990, **35**, 13-21.
4. Filip R, Lopez P, Coussio J and Ferraro G. Mate Substitutes or Adulterants: Study of Xanthine Content. *Phytotherapy Res.* 1998, **12**, 129-131.
5. Pomilio AB, Trajtemberg S and Vitale AA. High-Performance Capillary Electrophoresis Analysis of *mate* infusions prepared from stems and leaves of *Ilex paraguariensis* using Automated Micellar Electrokinetic Capillary Chromatography. *Phytochem. Analysis* 2002, **13**, 235-241.
6. Saldaña MDA, Zetzl C, Mohamed RS and Brunner G. Extraction of Methylxanthines from Guaraná Seeds, Maté Leaves and Cocoa Beans Using Supercritical Carbon Dioxide and Ethanol. *J. Agric. Food Chem.* 2002, **50**, 4820-4826.
7. Saldaña MDA, Mohamed RS, Baer MG and Mazzafera P. Extraction of Purine Alkaloids from Maté (*Ilex paraguariensis*) Using Supercritical CO_2. *J. Agric. Food Chem.* 1999, **47**, 3804-3808.
8. IUPAC Commission on the Nomenclature of Organic Chemistry (CNOC) and IUPAC-IUB Commission on Biochemical Nomenclature (CBN). Nomenclature of Cyclitols: Recommendations, 1973. *Biochem. J.* 1976, **153**, 23-31.
9. Filip R, López P, Giberti G, Coussio J and Ferraro G. Phenolic compounds in seven South American *Ilex* species. *Fitoterapia* 2001, **72**, 774-778.
10. Carini M, Maffei Facino R, Aldini G, Calloni M and Colombo L. Characterization of Phenolic Antioxidants from Maté (*Ilex paraguariensis*) by Liquid Chromatography/Mass Spectrometry and Liquid Chromatography/Tandem Mass Spectrometry. *Rapid Commun. Mass Spectrom.* 1998, **12**, 1813-1819.
11. Ohem N and Hölzl J. Some New Investigations on *Ilex paraguariensis*: Flavonoids and Triterpenes. *Planta Medica* 1988, **54**, 576 (Abstract P1-12).
12. Gosmann G, Schenkel EP and Seligmann O. A new saponin from mate, *Ilex paraguariensis*. *J. Nat. Prod.* 1989, **52**, 1367-1370.
13. Gosmann G, Guillaume D, Taketa ATC and Schenkel EP. Triterpenoid saponins from *Ilex paraguariensis*. *J. Nat. Prod.* 1995, **58**, 438-441.
14. Kraemer KH, Taketa ATC, Schenkel EP, Gosmann G and Guillaume D. Matesaponin 5, a highly polar saponin from *Ilex paraguariensis*. *Phytochemistry* 1996, **42**, 1119-1122.
15. Martinet A, Ndjoko K, Terreaux C, Marston A, Hostettmann K and Schutz Y. NMR and LC-MS Characterisation of Two Minor Saponins from *Ilex paraguariensis*. *Phytochem. Analysis* 2001, **12**, 48-52.
16. Carducci CN, Dabas PC and Muse JO. Determination of Inorganic Cations by Capillary Ion Electrophoresis in *Ilex paraguariensis* (St. H.), a Plant Used to Prepare Tea in South America. *J. AOAC Internat.* 2000, **83**, 1167-1173.
17. Willems M. Quantitative Determination and Distribution of a Cyanogenic Glucoside in *Ilex aquifolium*. *Planta Medica* 1989, **55**, 195.
18. Nahrstedt A and Wray V. Structural revision of a putative cyanogenic glucoside from *Ilex aquifolium*. *Phytochemistry* 1990, **29**, 3934-3936.
19. Mazzafera P. Maté drinking: caffeine and phenolic acid intake. *Food Chemistry* 1997, **60**, 67-71.
20. Schinella GR, Troiani G, Dávila V, de Buschiazzo PM and Tournier HA. Antioxidant Effects of an Aqueous Extract of *Ilex paraguariensis*. *Biochem. Biophys. Res. Commun.* 2000, **269**, 357-360.
21. Gugliucci A and Stahl AJC. Low density lipoprotein oxidation is inhibited by extracts of *Ilex paraguariensis*. *Biochem. Molec. Biol. Internat.* 1995, **35**, 47-56.
22. Sawynok J. Pharmacological Rationale for the Clinical Use of Caffeine. *Drugs* 1995, **49**, 37-50.
23. Czok G and Lang K. Zur erregenden Wirkung von Chlorogensäure [The stimulant action of chlorogenic acid]. *Arzneim.-Forsch.* 1961, **11**, 448-450 [GERMAN/English summary].
24. Gorzalczany S, Filip R, del Rosario Alonso M, Miño J, Ferraro GE and Acevedo C. Choleretic effect and intestinal propulsion of 'mate' (*Ilex paraguariensis*) and its substitutes or adulterants. *J. Ethnopharmacol.* 2001, **75**, 291-294.
25. Yasukawa K, Yamaguchi A, Arita J, Sakurai S, Ikeda A and Takido M. Inhibitory Effect of Edible Plant Extracts on 12-*O*-Tetradecanoylphorbol-13-acetate-induced Ear Oedema in Mice. *Phytotherapy Res.* 1993, **7**, 185-189.
26. Gugliucci A. Antioxidant Effects of Ilex paraguariensis: Induction of Decreased Oxidability of Human LDL *in Vivo*. *Biochem. Biophys. Res. Commun.* 1996, **224**, 338-344.
27. Martinet A, Hostettmann K and Schutz Y. Thermogenic effects of commercially available plant preparations aimed at treating human obesity. *Phytomedicine* 1999, **6**, 231-238.
28. Parfitt K, editor. Caffeine. In: *Martindale - The complete drug reference, 32nd edition.* ISBN 0-85369-429-X. London:

Pharmaceutical Press, 1999:749-751.
29. Ilex. In: *British Herbal Pharmacopoeia 1983*. ISBN 0-903032-07-4. Bournemouth: British Herbal Medicine Association, 1983.
30. Chevallier A. Maté - *Ilex paraguariensis*. In: *Encyclopedia of Medicinal Plants, 2nd ed.* ISBN 0-7513-1209-6. London-New York: Dorling Kindersley, 2001:222.
31. Mate folium. German Commission E Monograph published in: Bundesanzeiger No. 85 of 5 May 1988.
32. Maté. In: *Médicaments à base de plantes*. ISBN 2-911473-02-7. Saint-Denis Cedex, France: Agence du Médicament, 1998.
33. McGuffin M, Hobbs C, Upton R and Goldberg A, editors. *Ilex paraguayensis* St. Hil. In: American Herbal Products Association's *Botanical Safety Handbook*. Boca Raton-Boston-London: CRC Press, 1997:63.
34. Victora CG, Muñoz N, Horta BL and Ramos EO. Patterns of Maté Drinking in a Brazilian City. *Cancer Res.* 1990, **50**, 7112-7115.
35. Fonseca CAS, Otto SS, Paumgartten FJR and Leitão AC. Nontoxic, Mutagenic and Clastogenic Activities of *Mate-Chimarrão* (*Ilex paraguariensis*). *J. Environ. Pathol. Toxicol. Oncol.* 2000, **19**, 333-346.
36. Mate. In: UK Statutory Instrument 1984 No. 769. The Medicines (Products Other Than Veterinary Drugs) (General Sale List) Order 1984. Schedule 1, Table A.
37. Maté. In: Section 182.20 of USA Code of Federal Regulations, Title 21, Food and Drugs, Parts 170 to 199. Revised as of April 1, 2000.
38. Ilex paraguariensis St.-Hilaire, leaves. In: *Flavouring Substances and Natural Sources of Flavourings, 3rd ed.* ISBN 2-7160-0081-6. Strasbourg: Council of Europe, 1981.

REGULATORY GUIDELINES FROM OTHER EU COUNTRIES

FRANCE

Médicaments à base de plantes [32]: Maté, feuille.

Therapeutic indications accepted

Oral use
Traditionally used: in functional asthenia; as an adjuvant in slimming regimes; to promote the renal elimination of water.

Local use
Traditionally used as an adjuvant in slimming regimes.

GERMANY

Commission E monograph [31]: Mate folium (Mateblätter).

Uses
Mental and physical fatigue.

Contraindications
None known.

Side effects
None known.

Interactions with other drugs
None known.

Dosage
Unless otherwise prescribed, average daily dose: 3 g of the drug or equivalent preparations.

Mode of administration
Comminuted drug for infusions; powdered drug for other galenic preparations for internal use.

Actions
Analeptic, diuretic, positively inotropic, positively chronotropic, glycogenolytic, lipolytic.

MELILOT

Leguminosae-Papilionoideae

Meliloti herba

Synonyms: Ribbed Melilot, Yellow Melilot, Yellow Sweet Clover, King's Clover, *Melilotus arvensis* Wallr.

Definition

Melilot consists of the dried aerial parts of *Melilotus officinalis* (L.) Lam.

A further species, *Melilotus altissima* Thuill., was included in the former DAC monograph.

CONSTITUENTS

□ ***Coumarins*** Coumarin, 0.3-0.8% [1,2] (Ph. Eur. min. 0.3%), and also 3,4-dihydrocoumarin (melilotin), scopoletin and umbelliferone [3].

Fresh melilot contains only a low level of free coumarin, but *cis*- and *trans*-*o*-hydroxycinnamic acid glucosides are stored in the vacuoles. When the tissues are ruptured, an endogenous β-glucosidase specific to *cis*-*o*-hydroxycinnamic acid glucoside hydrolyses the latter to the unstable free acid (coumarinic acid), which spontaneously lactonises to coumarin. The β-glucosidase remains efficient in dried material and during water extraction at room temperature *cis*-*o*-hydroxycinnamic acid glucoside is fully converted to coumarin. *Trans*-*o*-hydroxycinnamic acid glucoside (melilotoside) remains unchanged under these conditions [1], but can also be converted to coumarin under other conditions [3,4].

□ ***Cinnamic acid derivatives*** including, as mentioned above, *trans*-2-hydroxycinnamic acid glucoside (up to 0.4%) [1]. Also melilotic acid (= dihydro-*o*-coumaric acid, 0.2%) and caffeic acid (0.1%) with smaller amounts of ferulic, *o*- and *p*-coumaric, salicylic and other acids [5].

□ ***Triterpene saponins*** Oleanene saponins including soyasaponin I, astragaloside VIII, wistariasaponin D, melilotus-saponin O_2 [6], azukisaponin II [7] and azukisaponin V carboxylate [7,8]. They are based on one or another of three sapogenols identified earlier, soyasapogenols B and E [9] and melilotigenin [10], and all have a 3-glucuronyl group, to which one or two further sugar residues are attached by 1→2 links; for example, soyasaponin I is 3-rhamnosyl-(1→2)-galactosyl-(1→2)-glucuronyl soyasapogenol B [6].

□ ***Volatile compounds*** Over 80 compounds have been identified by GC-MS in a volatile fraction from melilotus, mainly monoterpenes and aliphatics [11].

□ ***Flavonoids*** Robinin (kaempferol 3-rhamno-[1→6]-galactoside 7-rhamnoside) [7,12] and the corresponding quercetin glycoside, clovin [7]. A kaempferol 3-galacto-gluco-arabino-rhamnoside has also been reported [12].

□ ***Other constituents*** Dicoumarol and the antifungal isoflavonoid medicarpin, which can arise in melilot due to fungal infection and spoilage, should be absent from properly dried material [13,14]; a method for detection of dicoumarol appears in the DAC monograph.

Published Assay Methods

Coumarin content by HPLC [1,15,DAC] and TLC densitometry [2].

PHARMACOLOGY

In vitro

Neither an aqueous nor a 67%-methanolic extract from melilot exhibited any spasmolytic activity on carbachol-induced contractions of isolated guinea pig trachea at concentrations of up to 0.6 mg/ml [17].

The pulse rate, vascular amplitude and tone of isolated segments from guinea pig lymph vessels were considerably increased by coumarin at a dilution of 10^{-7} [16].

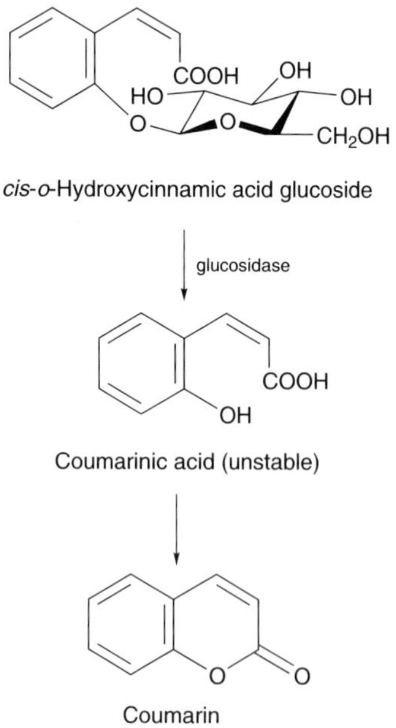

cis-o-Hydroxycinnamic acid glucoside

Coumarinic acid (unstable)

Coumarin

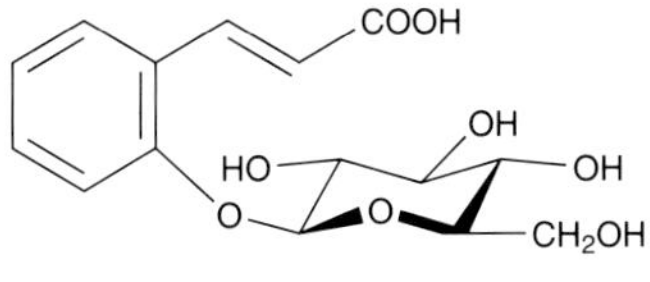

Melilotoside

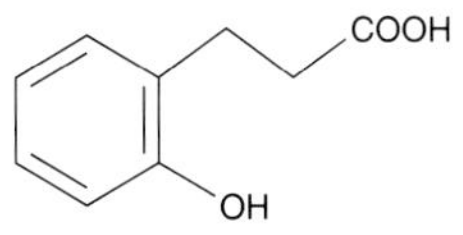

Melilotic acid

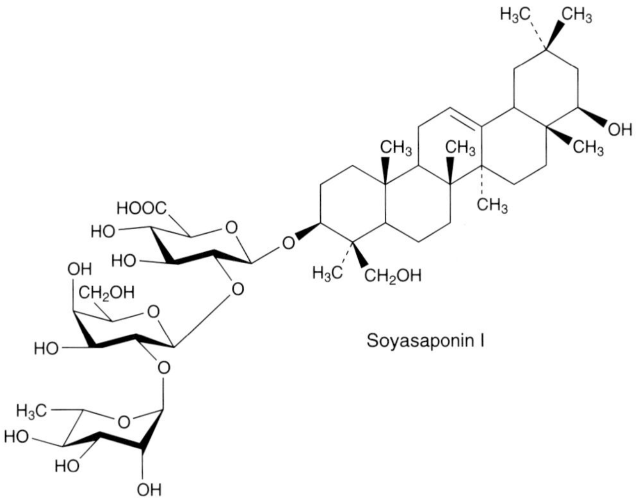

Soyasaponin I

In vivo

Anti-inflammatory activity
A standardized hydroalcoholic melilot liquid extract (1:1, 0.25% coumarin, 0.38% flavone), administered intraperitoneally to rabbits at 10 ml/kg, had an anti-inflammatory effect on turpentine oil-induced acute inflammation in rabbits. From tests on blood samples compared to controls, the extract moderately reduced the level of serum citrulline ($p<0.01$, indicating reduced nitric oxide synthesis), decreased phagocytic activity and reduced the proportion of neutrophils ($p<0.001$, indicating a reduction in bone marrow acute phase reponse). Coumarin at 25 mg/kg gave similar results [18].

Intraperitoneal pre-treatment of rats with coumarin (isolated from melilot) at 50 mg/kg reduced carrageenan-induced paw oedema by 42% after 4 hours and 33% after 6 hours compared to animals treated with normal saline solution; the effect was comparable to that of 1.5 mg/kg of flufenamic acid [19].

Intraperitoneal injection of a melilot extract into rats at 2.5 mg/kg before or immediately after thermal injury to the leg significantly reduced the rate of swelling ($p<0.01$) and inhibited the occurrence of necrosis and induration of the injury compared to controls in which 3rd degree burns were observed [20].

An ethanol-soluble fraction containing saponins and flavonoid glycosides (in which azukisaponin V was the main constituent), isolated from a melilot extract and injected subcutaneously into carboxymethylcellulose pouches on the dorsum of rats, potently inhibited leucocyte migration into the pouches by 48% at 2.2 mg/rat and 56% at 4.4 mg/rat ($p<0.01$) compared to 39.6% inhibition by aspirin at 15 mg/rat ($p<0.01$). In the same test pure azukisaponin V dose-dependently inhibited leucocyte migration by 30% at 2 mg/rat ($p<0.01$) and 49% at 6 mg/rat compared to 69% by aspirin at 20 mg/rat ($p<0.001$) [8]. Subsequently, similar tests confirmed the inhibitory activity of azukisaponin V, while azukisaponin II and a flavonoid fraction were found to be ineffective [7].

Anti-oedematous effect of coumarin
Dogs with experimentally-induced thrombophlebitis were treated with coumarin, administered intramuscularly at 4 mg/kg/day. The maximum oedematous swelling of the extremities in coumarin-treated animals (116% of initial value) was significantly less ($p<0.0025$) than in untreated animals (157%) and healing was achieved in a shorter time, 7 days compared to 17 days in untreated animals ($p<0.0005$) [21].

Effects of polysaccharide fraction
Daily oral administration of a purified polysaccharide fraction from an aqueous extract of melilot to rats once daily for 30 days at 50 or 500 µg/kg body weight increased their physical work capacity (determined in swimming tests) by 38.5% ($p<0.001$ at 50 µg/kg) by day 10. Their body weight increased gradually thoughout the 30-day period and at the end was 19.8% higher than that of untreated controls. The external appearance and appetite of the animals improved, and they became calmer. After the same treatment in mice, their immunocompetent organs (spleen and thymus) and blood were examined in detail; both doses led to significant decreases in spleen weight, significant increases in thymus weight

and significant increases in erythrocyte, leucocyte and particularly lymphocyte counts in peripheral blood. In mice injected intraperitoneally with rat erythrocytes, those treated with the polysaccharide fraction at 50 µg/kg had 57.7 antibody-producing cells per 10^6 spleen cells on day 4 compared to 19.2 in untreated controls. In rats with lead acetate-induced anaemia, control animals exhibited about 3-fold falls in haemoglobin and erythrocytes whereas those treated with the polysaccharide fraction had almost normal haemoglobin and erythrocyte levels, while their leucocyte counts were above normal. It was concluded that the polysaccharide fraction from melilot showed well-defined immunostimulating, antianaemic and general adaptogenic effects [22].

Pharmacokinetics
Coumarin administered orally to 6 human volunteers as a single dose of 0.857 mg/kg was rapidly absorbed but less than 4% reached systemic circulation. The rest of the dose appeared quantitatively in systemic circulation as 7-hydroxycoumarin and its glucuronide, suggesting an extensive first-pass effect. The biological half-lives of coumarin and 7-hydroxycoumarin glucuronide were 1.02 and 1.15 hours respectively, and about 90% of the dose was eliminated in the urine as 7-hydroxycoumarin glucuronide [23]. 7-Hydroxycoumarin (umbelliferone) is thought to be the pharmacologically active moiety, since the glucuronide, as a polar substance, should have no pharmacological activity [24].

CLINICAL STUDIES

The published clinical studies available on mono-preparations of melilot are uncontrolled and not entirely convincing. To some extent the indications for melilot appear to be based on extrapolation from clinical studies using coumarin and/or combinations of melilot with coumarin or rutin [25].

Lymphoedema
In an open study, a melilot extract (20 mg, containing 4 mg of coumarin) was administered daily for 12 weeks to 25 women with lymphoedema of the upper limbs following lymphadenectomy for breast cancer. From average circumference measurements a marked reduction in affected limb volume was evident after 6 weeks and the results were highly significant after 12 weeks ($p<0.0005$ for armpit, upper arm, forearm and hand) without noteworthy changes in body weight [26].

In another open study, 17 patients with the same condition were treated daily for 6 months with a dry extract of melilotus providing 8 mg of coumarin (combined with 30 mg of rutin). Of the 14 patients evaluated (3 did not report for follow-up) the condition improved in 11, with an average reduction of 4.7% in circumference of the upper arm, although individual reductions varied widely from 1% to 20%; no improvement was observed in the other 3 treated patients. The symptomatology of 2 further patients, not treated but considered as controls, worsened during the study period [27].

As pure compounds, benzopyrones such as coumarin (5,6-benzo-α-pyrone) have been used in the treatment of lymphoedema at much higher doses, coumarin at 100-400 mg/day for up to 6 months [28]. Casley-Smith reviewed the pathophysiology of lymphoedema and the action of benzopyrones in slowly reducing it. Oedema occurs when the lymphatic load of filtered fluid and protein from plasma exceeds the lymphatic transport capacity. Tissue protein is as important as fluid since a surplus of macromolecules holds excess fluid in the tissues, and tissue protein is removed by proteolysis as well as by lymphatic drainage. High protein oedemas have > 1 g/dl of plasma protein in the tissues; if the oedema lasts several weeks, this promotes chronic inflammation and its associated aftermaths. Benzopyrones have multiple actions but one consistent effect - they reduce high-protein oedema. While they increase pumping of collecting lymphatics, their main action in alleviating oedema is via macrophage stimulation. Normally, macrophages lyse some of the plasma protein filtered into tissues but benzopyrones increase macrophage lytic activity and induce many more of these macrophages to arrive at the site of tissue swelling. In chronic lymphoedema, moreover, the macrophages are dormant or less active and the benzopyrones seem to restore normal activity. In high-protein oedema, the benzopyrones promote proteolysis and the fragments are resorbed directly back into the bloodstream; with removal of the excess protein oedema subsides. In chronic lymphoedema, removal of the protein eliminates the stimulus for excess fibrosis which gradually disappears as tissue collagenases facilitate remodelling. The effectiveness of coumarin in a variety of high protein oedemas and a few lymphoedemas has been repeatedly demonstrated in numerous clinical trials; it has also been found effective in filaritic lymphoedema and elephantiasis [28].

Chronic venous insufficiency
Treatment of 20 patients suffering from chronic venous insufficiency with a dry extract of melilot at 200 mg/day for 15 days significantly reduced malleolar (ankle) oedema ($p<0.0005$), nocturnal cramps ($p<0.05$) and feelings of heaviness in the legs [29].

Mastalgia
In an open study, 50 women with cyclic or non-

cyclic mastalgia were treated with an undefined melilot extract once daily for two periods of 2 months with a 1-month interval. Of 31 patients who complied with the study protocol, 74% reported positive results and 26% found no benefit from the treatment [30].

THERAPEUTICS

Actions

Anti-oedematous [25,31], anti-inflammatory [7, 18-20].

Coumarin improves lymph kinetics [31,32], particularly in high-protein oedemas [28], and improves venous return [25,31,32].

The polysaccharide fraction is reported to have immunostimulating, antianaemic and general adaptogenic effects [22].

Indications

Internal use: Complaints arising from chronic venous insufficiency in the legs, such as varicose veins and associated pains, swelling, nocturnal cramp, itching and feeling of heaviness [29,31-34].

Other uses, based on experience or tradition

Internal use: Lymphoedema arising from various causes including lymphadenectomy [26,27]; symptoms of cutaneous capillary fragility, such as ecchymoses or petechiae [34]; haemorrhoids [9,33,34]; phlebitis [9,31-33]; indigestion and flatulence; minor sleep disorders [33,34]; rheumatic pains [9,33]; and burns [20,25].

External use: Bruises, sprains and superficial bleeding [31].

Contraindications

None known.

Side effects

In rare cases headaches [31].

Interactions with other drugs

Although not an anticoagulant, coumarin retards the onset of blood coagulation [25]; melilot should not be used in conjunction with anticoagulants [33] and caution is advised with aspirin [25].

Dosage

Adult daily dose: Preparations containing the equivalent of up to 10 g of dried herb, in divided doses. For preparations of known coumarin content, the equivalent of up to 30 mg of coumarin [31], or up to 1 mg/kg body weight [25].

SAFETY

Toxicity data on melilot and its extracts appear to be unavailable, but extensive data are available for coumarin and have been reviewed by Cohen [35] and more recently by Lake [36].

The acute oral LD_{50} of coumarin has been reported to range from 290 to 680 mg/kg in various rat strains and from 196 to 780 mg/kg in the mouse. However, coumarin exhibits marked species differences in both metabolism and toxicity [36].

Hepatotoxicity has been observed in the mouse, rat and dog but these species have metabolic pathways for coumarin different from those of baboons and humans, where 7-hydroxylation is predominant and acts as a detoxification pathway. No hepatotoxic effects were observed in baboons after administration of coumarin in the diet at 22.5 mg/kg/day for 16-24 months [36].

In clinical studies using coumarin at high dose levels, 2 cases of hepatotoxicity were reported from studies involving 1106 lymphoedema patients taking 400 mg of coumarin daily for a mean duration of 14.6 months. Other studies involving 2173 patients with cancer or chronic infections, the majority of whom received coumarin at 100 mg/day for 1 month followed by 50 mg/day for 2 years, reported a similar incidence level: 8 patients (0.37%) developed elevated liver enzymes (serum transaminases) after total doses of between 1 g and 15 g of coumarin. In all of these patients serum transaminase levels returned to normal after cessation of coumarin treatment [36].

At lower dose levels, no adverse effects were reported during a clinical study in which 25 women received 20 mg (containing 4 mg of coumarin) of a melilot extract daily for 12 weeks [26]. In another study, in which 17 women received melilot extract containing 8 mg of coumarin daily for 6 months, there were 2 reports each of dyspepsia and increased diuresis in the first month, and 1 report each of a laxative effect and a rash on the forearm after 3 months [27].

Most of the available data suggest that coumarin is not a genotoxic agent [36].

Intravenous administration to pregnant rabbits of coumarin at 10 and 100 times the therapeutic dose during the sensitive phase of foetal development (6th to 18th day of gestation) produced no signs of teratogenicity compared to controls; earlier findings in mice and rats were similar [37].

In contrast to various coumarin derivatives, notably dicoumarol, coumarin itself is not an anticoagulant, since its anticoagulant effectiveness is only 1/1000 to 1/5000th of that of dicoumarol [23].

REGULATORY STATUS

Medicines

UK	No licences issued for products containing melilot.
France	Accepted for specified indications [34].
Germany	Commission E monograph published, with approved uses [31].

Food

Council of Europe	Permitted as flavouring, category N2, with coumarin content in foods limited to less than 1 mg/kg, in beverages 2 mg/kg and in alcoholic beverages 10 mg/kg [38].

REFERENCES

Current Pharmacopoeial Monographs

Ph. Eur. Melilot

Literature References

1. Bourgaud F, Poutaraud A and Guckert A. Extraction of Coumarins from Plant Material (Leguminosae). *Phytochem. Analysis* 1994, **5**, 127-132.
2. Nagell A. Qualitätssicherung von Arzneidrogen. Teil I. Schachtelhalmkraut, Holunderblüten, Steinkleekraut und Orthosiphonblätter [Quality Assurance of Plant Drugs. Part 1. Equisetum, Elder Flower, Melilot and Java Tea]. *Dtsch. Apoth. Ztg.* 1987, **127**, 7-10 [GERMAN].
3. Steinegger E and Hänsel R. Steinkleekraut. In: *Pharmakognosie, 5th ed.* ISBN 3-540-55649-4. Berlin-Heidelberg-New York: Springer-Verlag, 1992:381 [GERMAN].
4. Schwarz-Schulz B and Wissinger-Gräfenhahn U. Melilotus. In: Blaschek W, Hänsel R, Keller K, Reichling J, Rimpler H and Schneider G, editors. *Hagers Handbuch der Pharmazeutischen Praxis, 5th ed. Supplement Volume 3: Drogen L-Z.* ISBN 3-540-61619-5. Berlin-Heidelberg-New York-London: Springer, 1998:195-211 [GERMAN].
5. Dombrowicz E, Swiatek L, Guryn R and Zadernowski R. Phenolic acids in herb *Melilotus officinalis. Pharmazie* 1991, **46**, 156-157.
6. Hirakawa T, Okawa M, Kinjo J and Nohara T. A New Oleanene Glucuronide Obtained from the Aerial Parts of *Melilotus officinalis. Chem. Pharm. Bull.* 2000, **48**, 286-287.
7. Kang SS, Lee YS and Lee EB. Saponins and Flavonoid Glycosides from Yellow Sweetclover. *Arch. Pharm. Res.* 1988, **11**, 197-202.
8. Kang SS, Lee YS and Lee EB. Isolation of Azukisaponin V Possessing Leucocyte Migration Inhibitory Activity from *Melilotus officinalis. Kor. J. Pharmacogn.* 1987, **18**, 89-93.
9. Kang SS, Lim C-H and Lee SY. Soyasapogenols B and E from *Melilotus officinalis. Arch. Pharm. Res.* 1987, **10**, 9-13.
10. Kang SS and Woo WS. Melilotigenin, a new sapogenin from *Melilotus officinalis. J. Nat. Prod.* 1988, **51**, 335-338.
11. Wörner M and Schreier P. Volatile constituents of sweet clover (*Melilotus officinalis* L. Lam.). *Z. Lebensm. Unters. Forsch.* 1990, **190**, 425-428.
12. Sutiashvili MG and Alaniya MD. Flavonoids of *Melilotus officinalis. Khim. Prir. Soedin.* 1999, (5), 673-674 [RUSSIAN], translated into English as: *Chem. Nat. Compd.* 1999, **35**, 584.
13. Ingham JL. Phytoalexin production by high- and low-coumarin cultivars of *Melilotus alba* and *Melilotus officinalis. Can. J. Bot.* 1978, **56**, 2230-3.
14. Ingham JL. Medicarpin as a Phytoalexin of the Genus *Melilotus. Z. Naturforsch.* 1977, **32c**, 449-452.
15. Vande Casteele K, Geiger H and Van Sumere CF. Separation of phenolics (benzoic acids, cinnamic acids, phenylacetic acids, quinic acid esters, benzaldehydes and acetophenones, miscellaneous phenolics) and coumarins by reversed-phase high-performance liquid chromatography. *J. Chromatogr.* 1983, **258**, 111-124.
16. Mislin H. Die Wirkung von Cumarin aus *Melilotus officinalis* auf die Funktion des Lymphangions [The effect of coumarin from *Melilotus officinalis* on the function of lymph vessels]. *Arzneim.-Forsch./Drug Res.* 1971, **21**, 852-853 [GERMAN/English summary].
17. Bergendorff O, Franzén C, Jeppsson A-B, Sterner O and Waldeck B. Screening of Some European Medicinal Plants for Spasmolytic Activity on Isolated Guinea-Pig Trachea. *Internat. J. Pharmacog.* 1995, **33**, 356-358.
18. Plesca-Manea L, Pârvu AE, Pârvu M, Taamas M, Buia R and Puia M. Effects of *Melilotus officinalis* on Acute Inflammation. *Phytotherapy Res.* 2002, **16**, 316-319.
19. Földi-Börcsök E, Bedall FK and Rahlfs VW. Die antiphlogistische und ödemhemmende Wirkung von Cumarin aus *Melilotus officinalis* [The anti-inflammatory and oedema-inhibiting action of coumarin from *Melilotus officinalis*]. *Arzneim.-Forsch./Drug Res.* 1971, **21**, 2025-2030 [GERMAN/English summary].
20. Nishikawa M, Yamashita A, Ando K and Mitsuhiro S. The suppressive effect of melilotus extract on thermal edema of rats. *Folia Pharmacol. Japon.* 1983, **81**, 193-209 [JAPANESE/English summary].
21. Földi M, Zoltán ÖT and Piukovich I. Die Wirkung von Rutin und Cumarin auf den Verlauf einer experimentellen Thrombophlebitis [The effect of rutin and coumarin on the course of experimental thrombophlebitis]. *Arzneim.-Forsch./Drug Res.* 1970, **20** (Suppl. 11a), 1629-1630.
22. Podkolzin AA, Dontsov VI, Sychev IA, Kobeleva GY and Kharchenko ON. Immunomodulating, Antianemic and Adaptogenic Effects of Polysaccharides from Plaster Clover (*Melilotus officinalis*). *Byull. Eksp. Biol. Med.* 1996, **121**, 661-663 [RUSSIAN], translated into English as: *Bull. Exptl. Biol. Med.* 1996:597-599; also through *Chem. Abstr.* 1996, **125**, 265395.
23. Ritschel WA, Brady ME, Tan HSI, Hoffmann KA, Yiu IM and Grummich KW. Pharmacokinetics of Coumarin and its 7-Hydroxy-Metabolites upon Intravenous and Peroral Administration of Coumarin in Man. *Eur. J. Clin. Pharmacol.* 1977, **12**, 457-461.
24. Ritschel WA, Brady ME and Tan HSI. First-pass effect of coumarin in man. *Internat. J. Clin. Pharmacol. Biopharm.* 1979, **17**, 99-103.
25. Mills S and Bone K. Melilotus. In: *Principles and Practice of Phytotherapy. Modern Herbal Medicine.* ISBN 0-443-06016-9. Edinburgh-London-New York: Churchill Livingstone, 2000:483-489.
26. Muraca MG and Baroncelli TA. Post-mastectomy lymphedema of the upper limbs. Treatment with extract of Melilotus officinalis. *Gazz. Med. Ital. - Arch. Sci. Med.* 1999, **158**, 133-136 [ITALIAN/English summary].
27. Pastura G, Mesiti M, Saitta M, Romeo D, Settineri N, Maisano R et al. Linfedema dell'arto superiore in pazienti operati per carcinoma della mammella: esperienza clinica con estratto cumarinico di Melilotus officinalis [Lymphoedema of the upper limbs in patients after operations for breast cancer: clinical experience with a coumarinic extract from Melilotus officinalis]. *Clin. Ter.* 1999, **150**, 403-408 [ITALIAN/English summary].
28. Casley-Smith JR and Casley-Smith JR. The pathophysiology of lymphedema and the action of benzopyrones in reducing it. *Lymphology* 1988, **21**, 190-194.
29. Stefanini L, Gigli P, Galassi A, Pierallini F, Tillieci A and Scalabrino A. Pharmacological treatment and/or balneotherapy of chronic venous insufficiency. *Gazz. Med. Ital. - Arch. Sci. Med* 1996, **155**, 179-185 [ITALIAN/English summary].

30. Mazzocchi B, Andrei A, Bonifazi VF and Algeri R. Trattamento con estratto di Melilotus officinalis della mastodinia ciclica e non ciclica delle donne afferenti presso un ambulatorio senologico [Treatment with extract of Melilotus officinalis of cyclic and non-cyclic mastalgia in women referred to a breast clinic]. *Gazz. Med. Ital. - Arch. Sci. Med.* 1997, **156**, 221-224 [ITALIAN/English summary].
31. Meliloti herba. German Commission E Monograph published in: Bundesanzeiger No. 50 of 13 March 1986; amended in Bundesanzeiger No. 50 of 13 March 1990.
32. Weiss RF and Fintelmann V. Melilotus officinalis, Melilot. In: *Herbal Medicine, 2nd ed.* (translated from the 9th German edition of *Lehrbuch der Phytotherapie*). ISBN 3-13-126332-6. Stuttgart-New York: Thieme, 2000:180-181.
33. Chevallier A. Melilot. In: *Encyclopedia of Medicinal Plants, 2nd ed.* ISBN 0-7513-1209-6. London-New York: Dorling Kindersley, 2001:233.
34. Mélilot. In: *Médicaments à base de plantes.* ISBN 2-911473-02-7. Saint-Denis Cedex, France: Agence du Médicament, 1998.
35. Cohen AJ. Critical review of the toxicology of coumarin with special reference to interspecies differences in metabolism and hepatotoxic response and their significance to man. *Food Cosmet. Toxicol.* 1979, **17**, 277-289.
36. Lake BG. Coumarin Metabolism, Toxicity and Carcinogenicity: Relevance for Human Risk Assessment. *Food Chem. Toxicol.* 1999, **37**, 423-453.
37. Grote W and Weinmann I. Überprüfung der Wirkstoffe Cumarin und Rutin im teratologischen Versuch an Kaninchen [Investigation of the active substances coumarin and rutin in teratological studies in rabbits]. *Arzneim.-Forsch./Drug Res.* 1973, **23**, 1319-1320 [GERMAN/English summary].
38. Melilotus officinalis (L.) Lam., flower tips. In: *Flavouring Substances and Natural Sources of Flavourings, 3rd ed.* ISBN 2-7160-0081-6. Strasbourg: Council of Europe, 1981.

REGULATORY GUIDELINES FROM OTHER EU COUNTRIES

FRANCE

Médicaments à base de plantes [34]: Mélilot, sommité fleurie.

Therapeutic indications accepted

Oral and/or topical use
Traditionally used: in the symptomatic treatment of functional disorders of cutaneous capillary fragility, such as ecchymoses or petechiae; in subjective manifestations of venous insufficiency, such as 'heavy legs'; and in haemorrhoidal symptomatology.

Oral use
Traditionally used: in the symptomatic treatment of digestive disorders such as: epigastric distension, sluggish digestion, eructation, flatulence; as adjuvant treatment of the painful component of functional digestive disorders; and in the symptomatic treatment of neurotonic states in adults and children, particularly in cases of minor sleep disorders.

Topical use
Traditionally used in cases of ocular irritation or discomfort due to various causes (smoky atmosphere, sustained visual effort, bathing in the sea or swimming pool).

GERMANY

Commission E monograph [31]: Meliloti herba (Steinkleekraut).

Uses

Internal use: Complaints arising from chronic venous insufficiency, such as pains and feelings of heaviness in the legs, nocturnal cramp in the legs, itching and swelling.
Supportive treatment of thrombophlebitis, post-thrombotic syndrome, haemorrhoids and lymphatic congestion.
External use: Bruises, sprains and superficial bleeding.

Contraindications

None known.

Side effects

In rare cases headaches.

Interactions with other drugs

None known.

Dosage

Unless otherwise prescribed, average daily oral dose: dried herb or preparations equivalent to 3-30 mg of coumarin.
For parenteral use, the equivalent of 1.0-7.5 mg of coumarin.
The effective dosage of fixed combination preparations containing melilot for external use must be substantiated for each preparation.

Mode of administration

Comminuted drug for infusions and other galenic preparations for oral use. Liquid dosage forms for parenteral use. Ointments, liniments, poultices and herbal cushions for external use; ointments and suppositories for rectal use.

Actions

Anti-oedematous in inflammatory and congestive oedema through increase in venous return and improvement in lymph kinetics. Experimental studies in animals have shown acceleration of wound healing.

MELISSA LEAF

Labiatae

Melissae folium

Synonym: Balm leaf, lemon balm leaf.

Definition

Melissa Leaf consists of the dried leaves of *Melissa officinalis* L.

There are two subspecies of *Melissa officinalis* L., the lemon-scented subsp. *officinalis* being the official drug; essential oil of the foetid subsp. *altissima* lacks monoterpene aldehydes of the citral type [1,2].

CONSTITUENTS

☐ ***Hydroxycinnamic acid derivatives***, 6-11% [2, 3] (Ph. Eur. min. 4.0%, expressed as rosmarinic acid), principally rosmarinic acid (a dimer of caffeic acid, 2-5%) [2-4] and caffeic acid (over 2%) [5,6]. Melitric acids A and B, both of which are trimers of caffeic acid [7], and the methyl esters of rosmarinic acid and caffeic acid [6] have been isolated. Chlorogenic acid [1,8] and small amounts of *p*-coumaric (0.09%), ferulic (0.01%) and other acids [5] are also present.

☐ ***Benzoic acid derivatives*** A 1,3-benzodioxole derivative and protocatechuic acid [6].

☐ ***Tannins*** True tannins, in the sense of proanthocyanidins or gallo- and ellagitannins, are not present in melissa leaf, nor in the Labiatae generally. However, a substantial proportion of the polyphenols (mainly hydroxycinnamic acid derivatives) are adsorbed by hide powder and will therefore give a positive result by this method for the determination of tannins [4,8]. Thus 4-14% of tannins have been reported for melissa leaf [4,9] and these substances are sometimes referred to as 'Labiatae tannins'[1,10].

☐ ***Flavonoids***, ca. 0.5% [2], principally luteolin 3′-glucuronide (0.3%) [11,12] with smaller amounts of luteolin [12], luteolin 7-glucoside (cynaroside) [12-14], 7-glucuronide and 7-glucoside-3′-glucuronide [12], apigenin 7-glucoside (cosmosiin) [12,13], isoquercitrin and rhamnocitrin [13].

☐ ***Triterpenes*** Ursolic acid (0.6%) and oleanolic acid (0.2%) [15].

☐ ***Essential oil***, usually 0.1-0.4% [2,16-18], the highest levels normally occurring in September/October and under Mediterranean climatic conditions; an exceptionally high content of 0.97% was reported for Brazilian leaf [19]. The main components are monoterpene aldehydes, the citral isomers geranial (citral A, *trans*) and neral (citral B, *cis*) in a ratio of about 4:3 representing 45-90% of the oil and citronellal 1-40%. Other components include β-caryophyllene and its oxide, linalool, geranyl acetate, geraniol, nerol and 6-methyl-5-hepten-2-one [2,16-22].

☐ ***Other constituents*** include the glucosides of geraniol, nerol, eugenol, benzyl alcohol and various other volatile aglycones [23-25].

Published Assay Methods

Total hydroxycinnamic derivatives by spectrophotometry [Ph. Eur.]. Rosmarinic acid by HPLC [2]. Essential oil components by GC-MS [16,17,21].

PHARMACOLOGY

In vitro

Aqueous extracts from melissa leaf exhibited antiviral activity against *Herpes simplex*, vaccinia, influenza [26], Newcastle disease [27] and HIV-1 [28] viruses. This activity, which is virustatic rather than cytotoxic, is attributed mainly to the

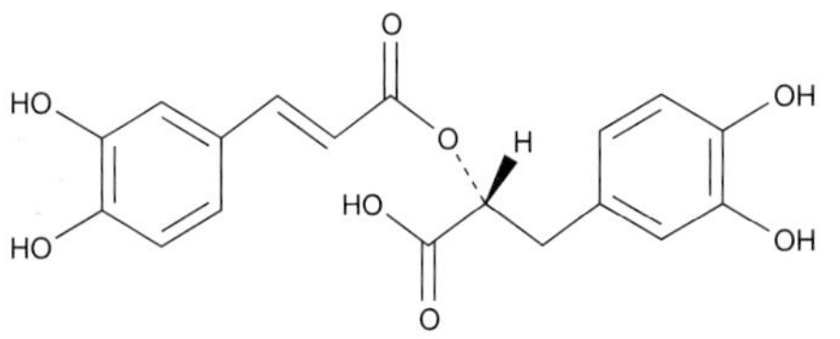

Rosmarinic acid

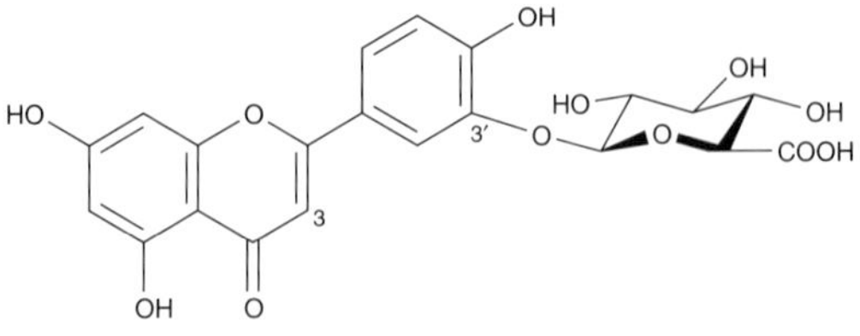

Luteolin 3′-glucuronide

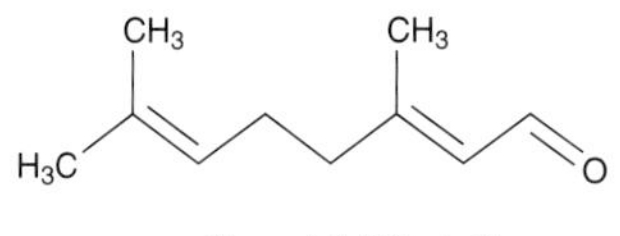

Geranial (Citral A)

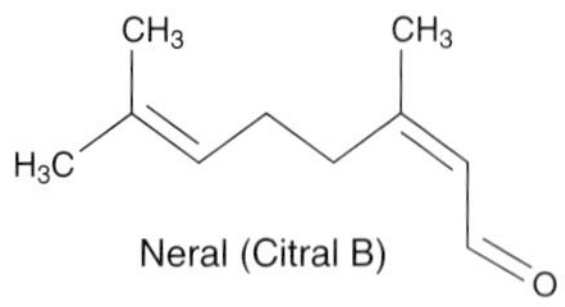

Neral (Citral B)

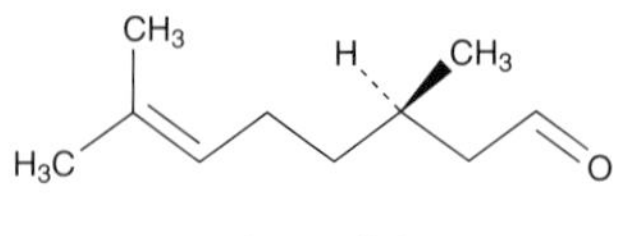

Citronellal

presence of caffeic acid derivatives ("Labiatae tannins") [10].

In screening tests on European medicinal plants reputed to enhance mental function, an 80%-ethanolic extract of melissa leaf exhibited CNS cholinergic receptor binding activity. It displaced $[^3H]$-(*N*)-nicotine from nicotinic receptors and $[^3H]$-(*N*)-scopolamine from muscarinic receptors in homogenates of human cerebral cortical cell membranes with IC_{50} values below 1 mg dried leaf/ml for some samples. The nature of the receptor-specific constituents remains unclear [29]. Using identical methodology the respective IC_{50} values obtained for a 30%-methanolic extract (used in a human cognitive performance study) were 11 mg/ml and 4 mg/ml [30].

A 30%-alcoholic dry extract from fresh (pre-frozen) melissa leaf showed antispasmodic activity against spontaneous contractions of isolated rat duodenum, but not against carbachol-induced contractions [31]. An earlier study found that no significant spasmolytic activity against acetylcholine- or histamine-induced contractions of guinea pig ileum was exhibited by a hydroethanolic extract from melissa leaf at concentrations of 2.5-10 ml/litre [32]. Melissa leaf essential oil has considerable spasmolytic activity, as demonstrated in a number of studies [33-35].

Antioxidant and radical scavenging activity has been demonstrated for hydroalcoholic extracts of melissa leaf and this correlates fairly well with the content of hydroxycinnamic acid derivatives [6,36,37]. Rosmarinic acid contributes over 50% of the antioxidant activity and a 1,3-benzodioxole derivative (present at a much lower concentration in the leaf) showed even higher radical scavenging activity [6].

Melissa essential oil has been shown to have antimicrobial and antioxidant activity [16] and to be cytotoxic to a range of human cancer cell lines [19].

In vivo

Sedative effects

A dry 30%-ethanolic extract from melissa leaf, administered intraperitoneally to mice, dose-dependently reduced behavioural activity in familiar and non-familiar environments with a maximum effect at the equivalent of 25 mg of crude drug/kg. At lower doses (equivalent to 3-6 mg of crude drug/kg) the extract induced sleep in mice treated with an infra-hypnotic dose of pentobarbital and also prolonged pentobarbital-induced sleep. High doses of the extract (equivalent to 400 mg/kg of crude drug) produced peripheral analgesic effects in the acetic acid-induced writhing test [31,38]. Comparable dose levels (relative to the crude drug) of melissa leaf essential oil had no significant sedative effects in mice after intraperitoneal administration [38]. However, an earlier study found that the essential oil produced sedative effects when orally administered at 3.16 mg/kg and higher [39].

Anti-ulcerogenic effects

An ethanolic liquid extract from melissa leaf, orally administered at 2.5-10 ml/kg, dose-dependently inhibited indometacin-induced gastric ulceration in rats. This effect was associated with reduced acid output, increased mucin secretion, and an increase in prostaglandin E_2 release and a decrease in leukotriene levels in the gastric mucosa [40].

Pharmacological studies in humans

Three randomized, double-blind, placebo-controlled, crossover studies have been carried out on healthy volunteers by the same research group to investigate the effects of melissa leaf on cognition, mood and stress.

In the first study, 20 volunteers (average age 19 years) received, on four separate days at 7-day intervals, single doses of 300, 600 or 900 mg of a dry 30%-methanolic melissa leaf extract (with 10% of inert excipients) or a placebo. Assessment of cognitive performance on each treatment day, before and 1, 2.5, 4 and 6 hours after treatment, using the Cognitive Drug Research (CDR) computerized test battery and two serial subtraction tasks indicated a sustained improvement in accuracy of attention after a 600 mg dose. On the other hand, striking impairments in quality of memory were observed 2.5 and 4 hours after the two higher doses. Reduction of working memory was more pronounced at 1 and 2.5 hours after the higher doses. Self-rated assessment of mood using Bond-Lader visual analogue scales showed that calmness was elevated at 1 and 2.5 hours after the 300 mg dose, while alertness was reduced at all time points following the 900 mg dose. Subsequent *in vitro* tests showed negligible nicotinic and muscarinic binding activity of the extract in question [30].

In the second study, 8 samples of dried melissa leaf were first tested *in vitro* for nicotinic and muscarinic receptor-binding properties in human post mortem occipital cortex tissue and the sample with the most favourable profile, was used in behavioural experiments. At 7-day intervals, doses of 600, 1000 or 1600 mg of encapsulated dried melissa leaf or a matching placebo were taken by 20 volunteers (average age 19 years), and cognitive performance and mood were assessed before and 1, 3 and 6 hours after treatment using the CDR test battery and Bond-Lader scales as described above. The most notable cognitive and mood effects were improved memory performance and increased 'calmness' at all time points after the highest (1600 mg) dose, suggesting that at or above this dose level, melissa leaf can improve cognitive performance and mood [41].

In the third study 18 volunteers (average age 29 years) took, again at 7-day intervals, single doses of 300 or 600 mg of the same melissa leaf extract as described for the first study, or a placebo. Before and 1 hour after treatment the participants completed a 20-minute version of the Defined Intensity Stressor Simulation (DISS) battery, which is known to increase negative ratings of mood and engender physiological responses concomitant with increased stress. The 600 mg dose ameliorated the negative mood effects of the DISS with increased self-ratings of calmness and decreased self-ratings of alertness (using Bond-Lader mood scales), without detrimental effects on the performance of DISS tasks [42].

Taken together, the three studies suggested a robust effect of melissa leaf on mood [42].

CLINICAL STUDIES

Herpes simplex
In a randomized, double-blind, placebo-controlled study, 116 patients with *Herpes simplex* skin lesions, most frequently *Herpes labialis* (i.e. *Herpes simplex* affecting the lips or perioral skin, commonly called cold sores), the clinical symptoms of which appeared not more than 72 hours before treatment, treated the affected skin areas 2-4 times daily for 5-10 days with either a cream containing 1% of a lyophilised aqueous extract from melissa leaf (70:1; n = 58) or a placebo cream (n = 58). Clinical symptoms (reddening, swelling, blisters etc.) were assessed after 2 days and at the end of treatment (after 5 days on average). After 2 days reddening ($p<0.01$) and swelling ($p<0.05$) were significantly less in the verum group than in the placebo group. In the cases of *Herpes labialis*, the size of lesions was significantly less in the verum group after 5 days ($p = 0.012$). Global assessments by physicians and patients indicated significant acceleration of the healing process in the verum group ($p<0.05$) [43,44]. An earlier open study, in which 115 patients with cutaneous *Herpes simplex* lesions were treated with the same cream, also showed that the healing times were reduced and furthermore suggested that recurrence-free intervals were extended in comparison with topical virustatic preparations containing idoxuridine and tromantidine hydrochloride [44,45].

In a further randomized, double-blind, placebo-controlled study, patients with a history of recurrent *Herpes labialis* (cold sores), experiencing at least four episodes per year, were treated topically with either the same melissa extract cream (n = 34) or a placebo cream (n = 32), applied to the affected area 4 times daily for 5 days. For the primary target parameter, a symptom score derived from the severity ratings for complaints, size of affected area and number of blisters on day 2 of therapy, there was a significant difference in favour of the verum group ($p<0.05$). This difference on the second day of treatment is particularly important because the complaints in patients suffering from *Herpes labialis* are usually most intensive at that time [46].

Dementia
A randomized, double-blind, placebo-controlled study investigated the effects of melissa leaf in patients with mild to moderate Alzheimer's disease, aged 65-80 years and with initial scores of 12 or higher on the cognitive subscale of the Alzheimer's Disease Assessment Scale (ADAS-cog) and 2 or lower on the Clinical Dementia Rating (CDR) scale. The patients received 60 drops/day of either a liquid extract of melissa leaf (1:1, 45% ethanol, containing not less than 500 µg of citral per ml; n = 21) or a placebo liquid (n = 21) for 4 months and had regular contact with a caregiver. Melissa leaf treatment produced significantly better outcomes on cognitive function than placebo with respect to both the ADAS-cog ($p<0.01$) and the CDR scale ($p<0.0001$), and agitation appeared to be less common in the melissa group [47].

Aromatherapy treatment with melissa essential oil has been investigated in the management of agitation in severe dementia. This double-blind, placebo-controlled study involved 72 patients of mean age 78.5 years with clinically significant agitation in the context of severe dementia. Patients were treated topically twice daily for 4 weeks with a lotion containing 10% of melissa essential oil, providing a daily total of 200 mg of the oil (n = 36), or a placebo lotion containing sunflower oil (n = 36). Lotion was gently applied twice a day to the patient's face and both arms. In the melissa oil group the Cohen-Mansfield Agitation Inventory (CMAI) score decreased by 35% ($p<0.0001$; placebo group, 11%;) and 21 patients attained a 30% improvement in CMAI score (placebo group, 5 patients; $p<0.0001$). Quality of Life indices measured by Dementia Care Mapping also improved significantly more in the melissa oil group; the percentage of time spent socially withdrawn decreased ($p = 0.005$) and time engaged in constructive activities increased ($p = 0.001$) [48].

THERAPEUTICS

Actions
Sedative and peripheral analgesic [31,38], promotes calmness and positive mood [30,41,42];

virustatic [10,26-28], antioxidant [6,36,37], mildly antispasmodic [31].

Also stated to be carminative [49-52] and diaphoretic [50-52].

Indications

External use: Treatment of *Herpes simplex* skin lesions, especially on the lips and/or perioral skin (*Herpes labialis* or cold sores) [43-46].

Other uses, based on experience or tradition

Internal use: Sleep disorders of nervous origin [49, 53], restlessness and irritability [51]; as a tonic for mild depression, anxiety [50-52] and neurasthenia [50]; digestive ailments [49-53] such as dyspepsia, eructation and flatulence [50,53].

Contraindications

None known.

Side effects

None known.

Interactions with other drugs

None known.

Dosage

*Internal use*Three times daily: dried leaf, 2-4 g as an infusion [49,50]; liquid extract 1:1 in 45% alcohol, 2-4 ml [50]; or equivalent preparations.

External use For *Herpes simplex/labialis* episodes, 2-4 times daily for 5-10 days, apply a cream containing 1% of a dry aqueous extract of melissa leaf (70:1) in a suitable base [43-46].

SAFETY

In the human studies summarized above melissa leaf (internal or external use) and melissa oil (external use) preparations were well tolerated and no significant adverse effects were reported.

Tinctures of melissa leaf gave negative results in two mutagenicity tests, the Ames test [54] and a somatic segregation assay using *Aspergillus nidulans* [55]. Tests in guinea pigs revealed only a low risk of sensitization from melissa leaf extract [56].

REGULATORY STATUS

Medicines

UK	Accepted for general sale, internal or external use [57].
France	Accepted for specified indications [53].
Germany	Commission E monograph published, with approved uses [49].

Food

USA	Generally recognized as safe (21 CFR 182.10 and 182.20) [58].
Council of Europe	Permitted as flavouring, category N2 [59].

REFERENCES

Current Pharmacopoeial Monographs

Ph. Eur. Melissa Leaf

Literature References

1. Hänsel R, Keller K, Rimpler H and Schneider G, editors. Melissa. In: *Hagers Handbuch der Pharmazeutischen Praxis, 5th ed. Volume 5: Drogen E-O.* ISBN 3-540-52638-2. Berlin Heidelberg-New York-London: Springer-Verlag, 1993:810-821 [GERMAN].
2. Carnat AP, Carnat A, Fraisse D and Lamaison JL. The aromatic and polyphenolic composition of lemon balm (*Melissa officinalis* L. subsp. *officinalis*) tea. *Pharm. Acta Helv.* 1998, **72**, 301-305.
3. Lamaison JL, Petitjean-Freytet C and Carnat A. Lamiacées médicinales á propriétés antioxydantes, sources potentielles d'acide rosmarinique [Medicinal Labiatae with antioxidant properties, potential sources of rosmarinic acid]. *Pharm. Acta Helv.* 1991, **66**, 185-188 [FRENCH/English summary].
4. Gracza L and Ruff P. Rosmarinsäure in Arzneibuchdrogen und ihre HPLC-Bestimmung [Rosmarinic acid in pharmacopoeial plant drugs and their determination by HPLC]. *Arch. Pharm. (Weinheim)* 1984, **317**, 339-345 [GERMAN/English summary].
5. Schulz JM and Herrmann K. Occurrence of Hydroxybenzoic Acids and Hydroxycinnamic Acids in Spices. IV. Phenolics of Spices. *Z. Lebensm. Unters. Forsch.* 1980, **171**, 193-199 [GERMAN/English summary].
6. Tagashira M and Ohtake Y. A New Antioxidative 1,3-Benzodioxole from *Melissa officinalis. Planta Medica* 1998, **64**, 555-558.
7. Agata I, Kusakabe H, Hatano T, Nishibe S and Okuda T. Melitric Acids A and B, New Trimeric Caffeic Acid Derivatives from *Melissa officinalis. Chem. Pharm. Bull.* 1993, **41**, 1608-1611.
8. Litvinenko VI, Popova TP, Simonjan AV, Zoz IG and Sokolov VS. "Tannins" and Derivatives of Hydroxycinnamic Acid in Labiatae. *Planta Medica* 1975, **27**, 372-380 [GERMAN/English summary].
9. Karuza-Stojakovic L, Smit Z and Petricic J. The Question of Estimation of Tannins in Drugs. *Planta Medica* 1988, **54**, 574-575.
10. Koch-Heitzmann I and Schultze W. 2000 Jahre *Melissa officinalis.* Von der Bienenpflanze zum Virustatikum [2000 years of *Melissa officinalis.* From bee plant to virustatic]. *Z. Phytotherapie* 1988, **9**, 77-85 [GERMAN].
11. Heitz A, Carnat A, Fraisse D, Carnat A-P and Lamaison J-L. Luteolin 3'-glucuronide, the major flavonoid from *Melissa officinalis* subsp. *officinalis. Fitoterapia* 2000, **71**, 201-202.
12. Patora J, Klimek B. Flavonoids from lemon balm (*Melissa officinalis* L., Lamiaceae). *Acta Pol. Pharm.* 2002, **59**, 139-143.
13. Mulkens A and Kapetanidis I. Flavonoïdes des feuilles de *Melissa officinalis* L (Lamiaceae) [Flavonoids of the leaves of *Melissa officinalis* L. (Labiatae)]. *Pharm. Acta Helv.* 1987, **62**, 19-22 [FRENCH/English summary].
14. Thieme H and Kitze C. Über das Vorkommen von Flavonoiden in *Melissa officinalis* L. [The occurrence of flavonoids in *Melissa officinalis* L.]. *Pharmazie* 1973, **28**, 69-70 [GERMAN].
15. Brieskorn CH and Krause W. Weitere Triterpene aus *Melissa*

officinalis. Arch. Pharm. (Weinheim) 1974, **307**, 603-612 [GERMAN].

16. Mimica-Dukic N, Bozin B, Sokovic M and Simin N. Antimicrobial and Antioxidant Activities of *Melissa officinalis* L. (Lamiaceae) Essential Oil. *J. Agric. Food Chem.* 2004, **52**, 2485-2489.
17. Mulkens A and Kapetanidis I. Etude de l'huile essentielle de *Melissa officinalis* L. (Lamiaceae) [Study of the essential oil of *Melissa officinalis* L. (Labiatae)]. *Pharm. Acta Helv.* 1988, **63**, 266-270 [FRENCH/English summary].
18. Tittel G, Wagner H and Bos R. Chemical Composition of the Essential Oil from Melissa. *Planta Medica* 1982, **46**, 91-98.
19. de Sousa AC, Alviano DS, Blank AF, Alves PB, Alviano CS and Gattass CR. *Melissa officinalis* L. essential oil: antitumoral and antioxidant properties. *J. Pharm. Pharmacol.* 2004, **56**, 677-681.
20. Adzet T, Ponz R, Wolf E and Schulte E. Content and Composition of *M. officinalis* Oil in Relation to Leaf Position and Harvest Time. *Planta Medica* 1992, **58**, 562-564.
21. Mrlianová M, Tekel'ová D, Felklová M, Reinöhl V and Tóth J. The Influence of the Harvest Cut Height on the Quality of the Herbal Drugs Melissae folium and Melissae herba. *Planta Medica* 2002, **68**, 178-180.
22. Enjalbert F, Bessière JM, Pellecuer J, Privat G and Doucet G. Analyse des Essences de Mélisse [Analysis of Essential Oils from Melissa]. *Fitoterapia* 1983, **54**, 59-65 [FRENCH/English summary].
23. Mulkens A, Stephanou F and Kapetanidis I. Hétérosides à génines volatiles dans les feuilles de *Melissa officinalis* L (Lamiaceae) [Glycosides of volatile aglycones in the leaves of *Melissa officinalis* L. (Labiatae)]. *Pharm. Acta Helv.* 1985, **60**, 276-278 [FRENCH/English summary].
24. Mulkens A, Kapetanidis I. Eugenylglucoside, a new natural phenylpropanoid heteroside from *Melissa officinalis. J. Nat. Prod.* 1988, **51**, 496-498.
25. Baerheim Svendsen A and Merkx IJM. A Simple Method for Screening of Fresh Plant Material for Glycosidic Bound Volatile Compounds. *Planta Medica* 1989, **55**, 38-40.
26. May G and Willuhn G. Antiviral Activity of Aqueous Extracts from Medicinal Plants in Tissue Cultures. *Arzneim.-Forsch./Drug Res.* 1978, **28**, 1-7 [GERMAN/English summary].
27. Kucera LS and Herrmann EC. Antiviral Substances in Plants of the Mint Family (Labiatae). I. Tannin of *Melissa officinalis. Proc. Soc. Exp. Biol. Med.* 1967, **124**, 865-869.
28. Yamasaki K, Nakano M, Kawahata T, Mori H, Otake T, Ueba N et al. Anti-HIV-1 Activity of Herbs in Labiatae. *Biol. Pharm. Bull.* 1998, **21**, 829-833.
29. Wake G, Court J, Pickering A, Lewis R, Wilkins R and Perry E. CNS acetylcholine receptor activity in European medicinal plants traditionally used to improve failing memory. *J. Ethnopharmacol.* 2000, **69**, 105-114.
30. Kennedy DO, Scholey AB, Tildesley NTJ, Perry EK and Wesnes KA. Modulation of mood and cognitive performance following acute administration of *Melissa officinalis* (lemon balm). *Pharmacol. Biochem. Behavior* 2002, **72**, 953-964.
31. Soulimani R, Younos C, Fleurentin J, Mortier F, Misslin R and Derrieux G. Recherche de l'activité biologique de *Melissa officinalis* L. sur le système nerveux central de la souris *in vivo* et le duodenum de rat *in vitro* [Research into the biological activity of *Melissa officinalis* L. on the central nervous system of the mouse *in vivo* and the rat duodenum *in vitro*]. *Plantes Méd. Phytothér.* 1993, **26**, 77-85 [FRENCH/English summary].
32. Forster HB, Niklas H and Lutz S. Antispasmodic Effects of Some Medicinal Plants. *Planta Medica* 1980, **40**, 309-319.
33. Reiter M and Brandt W. Relaxant Effects on Tracheal and Ileal Smooth Muscles of the Guinea Pig. *Arzneim.-Forsch./Drug Res.* 1985, **35**, 408-414.
34. Brandt W. Spasmolytische Wirkung ätherische Öle [Spasmolytic effects of essential oils]. *Z. Phytotherapie* 1988, **9**, 33-39 [GERMAN].
35. Sadraei H, Ghannadi A and Malekshahi K. Relaxant effect of essential oil of *Melissa officinalis* and citral on rat ileum contractions. *Fitoterapia* 2003, **74**, 445-452.
36. Lamaison JL, Petitjean-Freytet C, Duband F and Carnat AP. Rosmarinic acid content and antioxidant activity in French Lamiaceae. *Fitoterapia* 1991, **62**, 166-171.
37. Hohmann J, Zupkó I, Rédei D, Csányi M, Falkay G, Máthé I and Janicsák G. Protective Effects of the Aerial Parts of *Salvia officinalis, Melissa officinalis* and *Lavandula angustifolia* and their Constituents against Enzyme-Dependent and Enzyme-Independent Lipid Peroxidation. *Planta Medica* 1999, **65**, 576-578.
38. Soulimani R, Fleurentin J, Mortier F, Misslin R, Derrieu G and Pelt J-M. Neurotropic Action of the Hydroalcoholic Extract of *Melissa officinalis* in the Mouse. *Planta Medica* 1991, **57**, 105-109.
39. Wagner H and Sprinkmeyer L. Über die pharmakologische Wirkung von Melissengeist [The pharmacological effect of Melissengeist]. *Dtsch. Apoth. Ztg.* 1973, **113**, 1159-1166 [GERMAN].
40. Khayyal MT, El-Ghazaly MA, Kenawy SA, Seif-El-Nasr M, Mahran LG, Kafafi YAH and Okpanyi SN. Antiulcerogenic Effect of Some Gastrointestinally Acting Plant Extracts and their Combination. *Arzneim.-Forsch./Drug Res.* 2001, **51**, 545-553.
41. Kennedy DO, Wake G, Savelev S, Tildesley NTJ, Perry EK, Wesnes KA and Scholey AB. Modulation of Mood and Cognitive Performance Following Acute Administration of Single Doses of *Melissa officinalis* (Lemon Balm) with Human CNS Nicotinic and Muscarinic Receptor-Binding Properties. *Neuropsychopharmacology* 2003, **28**, 1871-1881.
42. Kennedy DO, Little W and Scholey AB. Attenuation of Laboratory-Induced Stress in Humans After Acute Administration of *Melissa officinalis* (Lemon Balm). *Psychosomatic Med.* 2004, **66**, 607-613.
43. Vogt H-J, Tausch I, Wölbling RH and Kaiser PM. Eine placebo-kontrollierte Doppelblind-Studie. Melissenextrakt bei *Herpes simplex*. Wirksamkeit und Verträglichkeit von Lomaherpan® Creme. Größte Effektivität bei frühzeitiger Behandlung [A placebo-controlled double-blind study. Melissa extract for *Herpes simplex*. Efficacy and tolerability of Lomaherpan® Crème. Greatest effectiveness from earlier treatment]. *Der Allgemeinarzt* 1991, **13**, 832-841 [GERMAN].
44. Wölbling RH and Leonhardt K. Local therapy of herpes simplex with dried extract from *Melissa officinalis. Phytomedicine* 1994, **1**, 25-31.
45. Wölbling RH, Milbradt R. Klinik und Therapie des Herpes simplex. Vorstellung eines neuen phytotherapeutischen Wirkstoffes [Clinical aspects and therapy of *Herpes simplex*. Introduction of a new phytotherapeutic active substance]. *Therapiewoche* 1984, **34**, 1193-1200 [GERMAN/English summary].
46. Koytchev R, Alken RG and Dundarov S. Balm mint extract (Lo-701) for topical treatment of recurring Herpes labialis. *Phytomedicine* 1999, **6**, 225-230.
47. Akhondzadeh S, Noroozian M, Mohammadi M, Ohadinia S, Jamshidi AH and Khani M. *Melissa officinalis* extract in the treatment of patients with mild to moderate Alzheimer's disease: a double blind, randomised, placebo controlled trial. *J. Neurol. Neurosurg. Psychiatry* 2003, **74**, 863-866.
48. Ballard CG, O'Brien JT, Reichelt K and Perry EK. Aromatherapy as a Safe and Effective Treatment for the Management of Agitation in Severe Dementia: The Results of a Double-Blind, Placebo-Controlled Trial with Melissa. *J. Clin. Psychiatry* 2002, **63**, 553-558.
49. Melissae folium. German Commission E Monograph published in: Bundesanzeiger No. 228 of 5 December 1984; amended in Bundesanzeiger No. 50 of 13 March 1990.
50. Melissa. In: *British Herbal Pharmacopoeia 1983*. ISBN 0-903032-07-4. Bournemouth: British Herbal Medicine Association, 1983.
51. Chevallier A. Lemon Balm, Balm - *Melissa officinalis*. In: *Encyclopedia of Medicinal Plants, 2nd ed.* ISBN 0-7513-1209-6. London-New York: Dorling Kindersley, 2001:115.

52. Stodola J and Volák J. Balm, Lemon Balm. Translated into English in: Bunney S, editor. *The Illustrated Book of Herbs*. ISBN 0-7064-1489-6. London: Octopus Books, 1984:191.
53. Mélisse. In: *Médicaments à base de plantes*. ISBN 2-911473-02-7. Saint-Denis Cedex, France: Agence du Médicament, 1998.
54. Schimmer O, Krüger A, Paulini H and Haefele F. An evaluation of 55 commercial plant extracts in the Ames mutagenicity test. *Pharmazie* 1994, **49**, 448-450.
55. Ramos Ruiz A, De la Torre RA, Alonso N, Villaescusa A, Betancourt J and Vizoso A. Screening of medicinal plants for induction of somatic segregation activity in *Aspergillus nidulans*. *J. Ethnopharmacol.* 1996, **52**, 123-127.
56. Hausen BM and Schulze R. Comparative Study of the Sensitizing Capacity of Some Commonly Used Antiviral Drugs. *Dermatosen* 1986, **34**, 163-170 [GERMAN/English summary].
57. Balm. In: UK Statutory Instrument 1984 No. 769. The Medicines (Products Other Than Veterinary Drugs) (General Sale List) Order 1984. Schedule 1, Table A.
58. Balm (lemon balm). In: Sections 182.10 and 182.20 of USA Code of Federal Regulations, Title 21, Food and Drugs, Parts 170 to 199. Revised as of April 1, 2000.
59. Melissa officinalis L., herb. In: *Flavouring Substances and Natural Sources of Flavourings, 3rd ed.* ISBN 2-7160-0081-6. Strasbourg: Council of Europe, 1981.

REGULATORY GUIDELINES FROM OTHER EU COUNTRIES

FRANCE

Médicaments à base de plantes [53]: Mélisse, feuille, sommité fleurie.

Therapeutic indications accepted

Oral use
Traditionally used: in the symptomatic treatment of digestive disorders such as epigastric distension, sluggish digestion, eructation, flatulence; as adjuvant treatment of the painful component of functional digestive disorders; and in the symptomatic treatment of neurotonic states in adults and children, particularly in cases of minor sleep disorders.

GERMANY

Commission E monograph [49]: Melissae folium (Melissenblätter).

Uses
Sleep disorders of nervous origin. Functional gastrointestinal complaints.

Contraindications
None known.

Side effects
None known.

Interactions with other drugs
None known.

Dosage
Unless otherwise prescribed, 1.5-4.5 g of dried leaf per cup as an infusion, several times daily according to need.

Mode of administration
Cut or powdered drug, liquid or dry extract for infusions and other galenic preparations. Comminuted drug and its preparations for internal use.

Note: Combinations with other sedative and/or carminative herbal drugs may be beneficial.

Actions
Sedative, carminative.

MILK THISTLE FRUIT

Compositae

Silybi mariani fructus

Synonyms: St. Mary's Thistle Fruit, Cardui mariae fructus.

Definition

Milk Thistle Fruit consists of the mature fruits, devoid of the pappi, of *Silybum marianum* L. Gaertner.

Native to the Mediterranean region, milk thistle is naturalized in hot dry areas from central Europe to central Asia, the Americas and southern Australia. It may be found casually throughout a large part of Europe and is cultivated in Germany, Austria and eastern European countries [1,2].

CONSTITUENTS

□ ***Flavanonol derivatives**** A mixture known as silymarin (1.5-3%, Ph. Eur. min. 1.5% by HPLC, expressed as silibinin), consisting mainly of silibinin (diastereoisomeric silibinin A and silibinin B), isosilibinin (diastereoisomeric isosilibinin A and isosilibinin B), silicristin and silidianin, together with related compounds [3,4].

HPLC assay of two samples of milk thistle fruit gave the following average results: silibinin diastereoisomers 1.90%, isosilibinin diastereoisomers 0.485%, silicristin 1.055% and silidianin 0.435%; total 3.875% [5].

* The term "flavonolignans" is often used for these compounds, but it is somewhat misleading since they are not true lignans (dimeric β,β-linked phenylpropanoids) [6].
Recommended international non-proprietary names (rINN) are used here. Alternatives names or spellings such as silybin or silibin (= silibinin), silychristin and silydianin also appear in the literature.

□ ***Flavonoids*** Taxifolin, quercetin [7], dihydrokaempferol [8], kaempferol, apigenin, chrysoeriol, eriodictyol and naringenin [2].
□ ***Fatty oil***, 23-27%, consisting mainly of linoleic (35-55%) and oleic (24-30%) acids together with palmitic (8-12%), linolenic (3-7%), behenic (3-9%) and other fatty acids [9,10].
□ ***Sterols***, ca. 0.18%, principally β-sitosterol [10].
□ ***Other constituents*** include dehydrodiconiferyl alcohol [11] and 5,7-dihydroxychromone [12].

Published Assay Methods

Silymarin by HPLC [Ph. Eur.]. Silymarin components by HPLC and capillary electrophoresis [5,13]. Silymarin by spectrophotometry (DAB method up to 1999) [14].

PHARMACOLOGY

Standardized extracts (Silymarin)

Highly concentrated and refined dry extracts have been used in most of the pharmacological and clinical studies on milk thistle fruit. A current DAB monograph [15] provides a definition for such extracts with analysis by HPLC:

Mariendistelfrüchtetrockenextrakt
(Milk Thistle Fruit Dry Extract)
Dry extract from milk thistle fruit containing not less than 40.0% and not more than 80% of silymarin, calculated as silibinin ($C_{25}H_{22}O_{10}$; M_r 482.4) in relation to anhydrous extract. Of the total content of silymarin 40-65% is silibinin A + silibinin B, 10-20% is isosilibinin A + isosilibinin B and 20-45% is silicristin + silidianin.

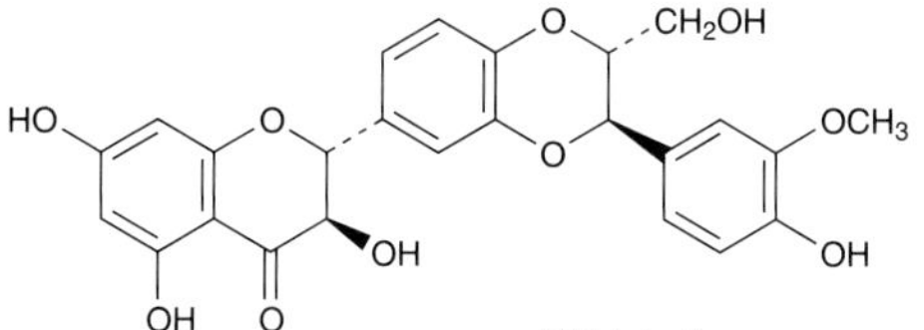

Silibinin A

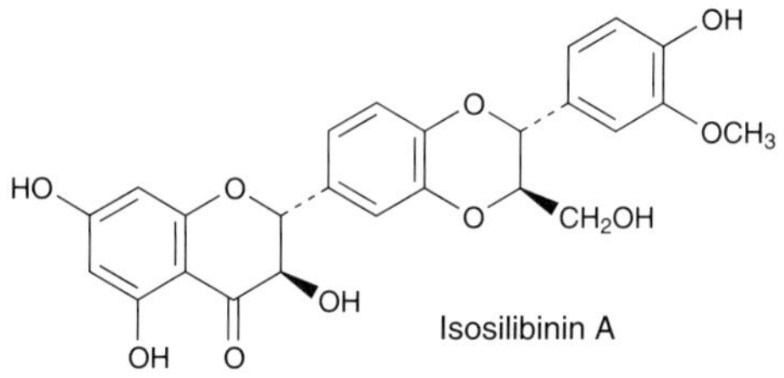

Isosilibinin A

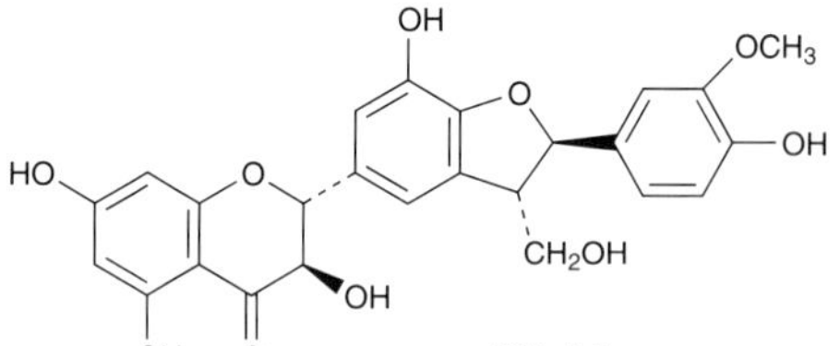

Silicristin

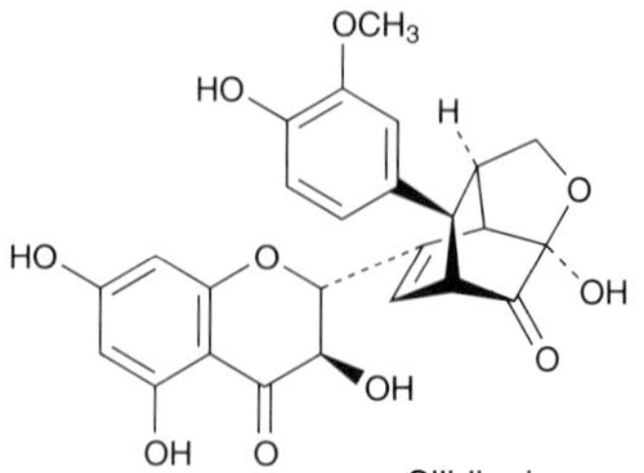

Silidianin

However, in the majority of studies reported up to the year 2000 the silymarin content of the extract used was determined by an earlier spectrophotometric method of the DAB [14], which gave higher values than the HPLC method: the extract (about 40:1, extracted with ethyl acetate) contained 75-81% of silymarin calculated as silibinin [16]. For dosage calculation purposes, it can be taken that the silymarin assay result of a dry extract by the HPLC method of the current DAB is about 77% of the figure obtained by the superseded DAB spectrophotometric method.

It is important to note that, rather confusingly, the term "silymarin" is used in the literature to mean two different things depending on the context:

- In the phytochemical and pharmacopoeial sense, the mixture of flavanonol derivatives described under Constituents
- In most of the pharmacological and clinical literature, standardized dry extracts from milk thistle fruit containing (when determined by spectrophotometry) 60-80% of silymarin, calculated as silibinin. In the following text such extracts are denoted by Silymarin with a capital S.

Pharmacological activities

Extensive research has been conducted on the pharmacological activities of Silymarin and its major component silibinin, but the mechanisms by which their hepatoprotective actions are exerted are still poorly understood. However, the published data indicate that they act in four different ways:

- as antioxidants, free radical scavengers and regulators of the intracellular content of glutathione
- as cell membrane stabilizers and permeability regulators, preventing hepatotoxic agents from entering hepatocytes
- as promoters of ribosomal RNA synthesis, stimulating liver regeneration
- as "antifibrotics", inhibiting the transformation of stellate hepatocytes into myofibroblasts, the process responsible for deposition of collagen fibres leading to cirrhosis.

The key mechanism affording hepatoprotection appears to be free radical scavenging [17].

Anti-inflammatory, anti-lipid peroxidative, immunomodulating and anticarcinogenic properties of Silymarin have also been documented.

The wide range of published *in vitro* and *in vivo* studies are not described here, but reviews of the pharmacology of milk thistle fruit extracts (Silymarin) and silibinin are available in the literature [1,17-19].

Virtually all human studies with Silymarin have been carried out on patients. As it would be somewhat arbitrary to separate those evaluating only changes in liver function parameters from the minority reporting clinical outcomes, all human studies are summarized under Clinical studies.

Pharmacokinetics

Human studies involving the oral administration of Silymarin have usually reported on the pharmacokinetic parameters of silibinin. Since it is almost insoluble in water, silibinin is poorly absorbed and its bioavailability is rather low; 3-8% of an oral dose is excreted into the urine, while 20-40% is recovered from the bile as glucuronide and sulphate conjugates. The bioavailability of silibinin from different commercial Silymarin preparations of the same declared content can vary considerably and may depend on factors such as the presence of accompanying substances with a solubilising character [18].

After oral administration of single doses of a Silymarin preparation containing 102, 153, 203 or 254 mg of silibinin to 6 healthy volunteers in a four-way crossover study, mean plasma levels of silibinin (both diastereoisomers) correlated well with the dose, although variations between one individual and another were remarkably high Depending on the dose, mean peak plasma levels of unconjugated silibinin were 117-317 ng/ml, while those of total silibinin (unconjugated and conjugated) were much higher at 524-1383 ng/ml, attained after about 1.7 hours. The elimination half-life of total silibinin was estimated as about 6 hours [20].

CLINICAL STUDIES

Standardized dry extracts of the type defined at the beginning of the Pharmacology section and denoted by Silymarin have been used in the majority of clinical studies of milk thistle fruit in the treatment of liver disorders.

Some studies have involved the use of silibinin as an isolated chemical constituent, but such studies are not classed as herbal medicine and are therefore mentioned only briefly here. Silibinin itself is practically insoluble in water, but in the form of a silibinin-phosphatidylcholine complex [1] or silibinin-β-cyclodextrin its bioavailability for oral use is claimed to be enhanced; three minor clinical studies using these substances are included in the meta-analysis described below. Silibinin given intravenously as its water-soluble disodium dihemisuccinate is a frequently used therapy (in conjunction with standard treatments) for acute poisoning by the deathcap mushroom, *Amanita phalloides* [19,21]. Pooling of data from 452 case studies of *A. phalloides* poisoning revealed a highly significant difference in mortality in favour of silibinin (9.8% mortality vs. 18.3% with standard treatments; $p<0.01$) [18], confirming the effectiveness of the principal component of silymarin in response to specific hepatotoxins.

Liver disease

Milk thistle has been used in the treatment of liver diseases for centuries [18]. Over the past 30 years the efficacy of oral Silymarin has been evaluated in patients with liver disease of various aetiologies, principally chronic alcoholic liver disease (the majority having cirrhosis of the liver) but also hepatitis or a combination of alcoholic liver disease and hepatitis, and other causes such as exposure to industrial solvents. Only a few studies focussed on clinical outcomes, of which by far the most important in patients with liver cirrhosis is survival; the majority of studies evaluated changes in indices of liver function.

Beneficial responses to Silymarin in the treatment of liver disease and liver damage have been demonstrated in many clinical studies, but the question of efficacy remains controversial. As pointed out in recent systematic reviews of controlled studies in this field, there are considerable difficulties in drawing overall conclusions from the available data due to various confounding factors including [18,22,23]:

Poor methodological quality of many studies
Relatively small numbers of patients
Variability in aetiologies
Varying severity of the liver diseases studied
Concomitant therapies
Inconsistencies in the use of (or abstinence from) alcohol, and the detection and reporting of it.

The intrinsic ability of liver injury to improve on removal of hepatotoxins, e.g. discontinuation of alcohol use, or resolution of acute hepatitis has usually not been taken sufficiently into account [22]. In the alcoholic patient, abstinence - if achieved - is probably the major 'intervention' in the pathogenic process of cirrhosis and it is likely to dilute any benefit from other therapeutic interventions [18].

Systematic reviews and meta-analyses

A recent systematic review (with meta-analyses) of milk thistle fruit in the oral treatment of liver diseases [23] included thirteen randomized, mainly placebo-controlled, clinical studies involving a total of 915 patients. Silymarin was used in 10 of the studies [24-33], a silibinin-phosphatidylcholine complex in 2 studies [34,35] and silibinin-β-cyclodextrin in 1 study [36]. From assessment of methodological criteria, three studies [25,26,33] were considered to have somewhat higher quality than the others.

The studies could be divided into four groups according to aetiology:

- Chronic alcoholic liver disease: 657 patients, of whom the majority had cirrhosis [24-31,36].
- Hepatitis B: 28 patients with acute hepatitis B [32].
- Hepatitis C: 10 patients with chronic hepatitis C [34].
- More than one aetiology: 200 patients with alcoholic liver disease, some with and some without hepatitis C virus antibody positivity [33]; 20 patients with hepatitis B and hepatitis C [35].

Assessment of the data led to the following conclusions (among others) [23]:

- Milk thistle fruit significantly reduced all-cause mortality in patients with alcoholic liver disease ($p = 0.04$) [24-31,36]. In verum groups 16/325 patients died (4.9%) compared to 28/332 patients (8.4%) in control groups.
- Furthermore, a significant effect of milk thistle fruit on liver-related mortality in patients with alcoholic liver disease ($p = 0.02$) was demonstrated by combining results from the four studies which reported this factor. Three of these studies included patients with alcoholic liver disease only [24-26], while one included patients with alcoholic liver disease or alcoholic liver disease + hepatitis C virus antibody positivity [33]. In verum groups 16/422 patients died (3.8%) compared to 31/422 patients (7.3%) in control groups. Unfortunately, subgroup analysis showed no significant effect in the three studies categorized as of higher quality [25,26,33]; the effect was essentially based on one study in which less than 100 patients had alcohol-induced liver disease [24].
- With regard to liver biochemical parameters, milk thistle fruit significantly improved (reduced) serum levels of bilirubin and gamma-glutamyl transferase (GGT) (both $p<0.05$), and also had a significant beneficial (reducing) effect on serum levels of aspartine aminotransferase (AST) and alanine aminotransferase (ALT) when analyzed by a "fixed effect" meta-analytical model.
- Combining the results of all 13 studies failed to demonstrate a significant effect of milk thistle fruit on all-cause mortality. In verum groups 34/456 patients died (7.9%) compared to 45/459 patients (9.8%) in control groups.

Earlier systematic reviews concluded that:

"the available evidence supports the therapeutic use of silymarin in alcohol-induced liver diseases, including liver cirrhosis....obviously as a supportive element in the broader context of the management of the alcoholic patient" [18].

"oral silymarin dosages of 420 mg/day have shown some therapeutic potential, with good tolerability, in the treatment of alcoholic cirrhosis" and have also been shown "to improve indices of liver function (AST, ALT, GGT and bilirubin) in patients with liver disease of various aetiologies, including those exposed to toxic levels of toluene and xylene; however, it was largely ineffective in patients with viral hepatitis" [19].

Other reviews since the year 2000 have drawn more neutral conclusions on the basis of insufficient evidence:

"Data are too limited to exclude a substantial benefit or harm of milk thistle on mortality, and also to support recommending it for the treatment of liver disease" [37].

"Milk thistle's efficacy is not established. Published evidence is clouded by poor design and reporting. Laboratory tests are the most common outcome measure studied and possible benefit has been shown most frequently, but inconsistently, for aminotransferases. Survival and other clinical outcomes have been studied less, with mixed results" [38].

Mortality rate of patients with cirrhosis of the liver
Liver cirrhosis ranks among the top 12 causes of death worldwide and 6th in Europe. According to Saller, the only established therapy for patients with alcoholic liver disease is to stop alcohol consumption. For alcoholic cirrhosis, therapy is generally supportive and aims at improving nutrition, encouraging abstinence and treating complications [18].

The two largest randomized, double-blind, placebo-controlled studies which have investigated the effects of Silymarin on the survival of patients with cirrhosis of the liver [24,33], summarized below, yielded contrasting results and illustrate some of the difficulties encountered in studies of this kind.

In a 1989 study [24], 170 patients (of whom 91 had alcohol-induced cirrhosis, 79 non-alcoholic cirrhosis) were randomized to daily treatment with either 3 × 140 mg of Silymarin (n = 87) or placebo (n = 83). Treatment was nominally for 2 years, but was extended for patients recruited earliest until the last patients completed, hence the mean observation period was 41 months. Although no significant beneficial effect on patient mortality was achieved by the end of the study period (i.e. $p > 0.05$), a trend in favour of Silymarin was evident: mortality rates were 23% (20 out of 87) in the Silymarin group and 33% (27 out of 83) in the placebo group ($p = 0.07$). Three significant results emerged from sub-analyses:

- Among patients with alcohol-induced cirrhosis, irrespective of degree of severity, significantly fewer died in the Silymarin group (10/46, 22%; $p = 0.01$) than in the placebo group (19/45, 42%).
- Independent of the aetiology, in patients originally having a Child-Turcotte A (the least severe) classification of cirrhosis, the survival rate was significantly improved by treatment with Silymarin ($p<0.03$).
- The cumulative 4-year patient survival rate in the Silymarin group (58%) was significantly higher than in the placebo group (38%; $p<0.036$).

In a later study, 200 alcoholics with alcohol-induced liver cirrhosis were assigned to treatment with either Silymarin at 3 × 150 mg/day (n = 103) or placebo (n = 97) for at least 2 years. For a variety of reasons, including the deaths of 14.6% of patients receiving Silymarin (8.7% from liver disease) and 14.4% on placebo (13.4% from liver disease), only 125 patients (58 receiving Silymarin, 67 on placebo) completed the study period. In the Silymarin group 39 patients continued to drink alcohol compared to 28 in the placebo group. Rather late in the study, when the stored sera from only 75 patients (30 verum, 45 placebo) were still available, it was found that hepatitis C antibodies were present in the sera of 43% (13/30) of these patients in the Silymarin group and 36% (16/45) in the placebo group, suggesting the co-existence of hepatitis C infection and cirrhosis in a fairly high proportion of patients; none of the patients on Silymarin but 4 on placebo died. The 5-year (intention-to-treat) survival rate was 71% in Silymarin-treated patients compared to 76% in the placebo group (difference not significant). Although some trends in favour of Silymarin were evident, the authors concluded that Silymarin had no effect on survival or the clinical course of liver cirrhosis in alcoholics - at the same time accepting that the sample size may have been too small to exclude the possibility that Silymarin has conclusive beneficial effects on mortality in such patients [33].

Effects on liver function
The ability of silymarin to normalize routinely tested parameters of liver function, such as serum levels of aspartine aminotransferase (AST, also called glutamic-oxalacetic transaminase or GOT), alanine aminotransferase (ALT, also called glutamic-pyruvic transaminase or GPT), gamma-glutamyl transferase (GGT), bilirubin, alkaline phosphatase and albumin, which become abnormal during liver-related diseases, has been investigated in a number of randomized, double-blind, placebo-controlled studies [25,30,39-41].

Patients with chronic alcoholic liver disease were randomized to receive 3 × 140 mg of Silymarin (n = 17) or placebo (n = 19) daily for 6 months. Compared to placebo, Silymarin treatment led to significant decreases in mean serum levels of bilirubin ($p<0.05$), AST ($p<0.05$), GGT ($p<0.05$) and procollagen-III-peptide (an indicator of fibrogenesis, $p<0.02$) and a non-significant decrease in ALT. Only the GGT level decreased significantly ($p<0.05$) in the placebo group [30]. However, since alcohol consumption decreased significantly in both groups ($p<0.001$) this in itself would have resulted in improvement of liver function parameters.

Patients aged 23-61 years with varying stages of alcohol-induced liver disease (10 with fatty degeneration of the liver, 10 with chronic alcoholic hepatitis, 9 with cirrhosis of the liver) were treated daily for 2 months with 3 × 140 mg of Silymarin (n = 15) or placebo (n = 14). Compared to baseline values, significant decreases in mean serum levels of AST (–38%; $p<0.05$), ALT (–42%; $p<0.01$) and bilirubin (–46%; $p<0.05$), and a significant increase in prothrombin time (+ 22%; $p<0.05$), were observed in the Silymarin group, but not in the placebo group. Subjective complaints also decreased significantly in the Silymarin group: epigastric complaints ($p<0.01$), fatigue ($p<0.05$), anorexia ($p<0.01$) and nausea ($p<0.01$) [39].

Similarly, treatment of patients (mainly young soldiers serving in a UN peace-keeping force) with relatively mild acute and subacute liver disease, indicated by elevated serum transaminase levels and mostly induced by alcohol abuse, with 3 × 140 mg of Silymarin (n = 47) for 4 weeks significantly reduced serum levels of AST and ALT (both $p<0.01$) compared to those receiving placebo (n = 50). Histological examinations (after blind liver biopsy) of about one third of the patients revealed significantly greater improvement in the Silymarin group ($p = 0.022$). Alcohol intake was not permitted during the study, although how many patients complied was not reported [40].

Patients with toxic liver damage, mainly alcohol-induced and confirmed by biopsies and serological tests, were treated daily for 4 weeks with 420 mg of Silymarin (n = 31) or placebo (n = 35). Abnormally elevated levels of serum ALT returned to the normal range by day 13 in the Silymarin group compared to day 24 in the placebo group ($p<0.05$) [41].

In contrast, no significant changes in routine liver function parameters (AST, ALT, GGT etc.) were observed in a more recent randomized, double-blind, placebo-controlled study after treatment of 60 alcoholics with cirrhosis of the liver daily for 6 months with 3 × 150 mg of Silymarin or placebo - despite the fact that all 49 patients who completed the study (24 Silymarin, 25 placebo) reported abstinence from alcohol during the study period. This study also investigated the antiperoxidative effects of Silymarin on "oxidative stress" in the patients. A significant increase was found in total erythrocyte glutathione levels ($p<0.001$), as well as significant reductions in levels of platelet malondialdehyde ($p<0.015$) and serum amino-terminal propeptide of procollagen type III ($p<0.033$), indicating modest favourable changes in the level of oxidative stress [25].

Beneficial effects of Silymarin on toxic liver damage resulting from occupational exposure to solvents have been clearly demonstrated. Workers in a Hungarian chemical plant with abnormal liver function parameters due to long-term exposure to toluene and/or xylene vapour were treated with 3 × 140 mg of Silymarin daily for 1 month (n = 30) and compared with an untreated control group (n = 19). Mean serum levels of AST, ALT and GGT decreased by 24%, 32% and 43% respectively compared to baseline, while no improvement was observed in the control group [42]. In an earlier study, daily treatment of 35 workers in Italy suffering from long-term exposure to mainly halogenated solvents with 420 mg of Silymarin for 15-20 days reduced mean serum levels of AST, ALT and GGT by about 51%, 55% and 57% respectively [43].

When administered concomitantly with tacrine (a cholinesterase inhibitor) Silymarin did not significantly reduce or prevent the hepatotoxic effects of tacrine in a controlled study involving 222 patients suffering from Alzheimer's disease. No significant differences in serum AST and ALT levels were observed between the silymarin and placebo groups [44].

Hepatitis C
Silymarin had no effect on chronic hepatitis C virus (HCV) infections in two recent studies. Daily treatment of chronic HCV in 88 residents of an Egyptian village with 373 mg of Silymarin for 12 months did not improve symptoms, ALT levels or hepatic fibrosis compared to a placebo group [45]. No improvement in liver function parameters (AST, ALT and GGT) was evident from retrospective analysis of data relating to 40 patients with chronic HCV treated for 125 days on average with 420-1260 mg of Silymarin per day [46].

THERAPEUTICS

Actions
Hepatoprotective, antioxidant and free radical scavenger, regulator of cell membrane permeability, stimulates liver tissue regeneration, antifibrotic and anti-inflammatory [17,19].

Indications
Inflammatory conditions and cirrhosis of the liver [47,48], particularly as supportive treatment in patients with alcoholic liver disease with cirrhosis [18,19,23,24] and/or abnormal liver function [19, 23,30,39-41]; liver damage following exposure to chemical toxins [19,42,43].

Other uses, based on experience or tradition
Liver and gall bladder problems [48] including jaundice and gall bladder colic [49]; dyspeptic complaints [47] such as flatulence and bloating;

loss of appetite [50].

Contraindications
None known.

Side effects
None known for dried fruits. A mild laxative effect of Silymarin preparations has occasionally been reported [47].

Interactions with other drugs
No clinically relevant interactions have been reported [18].

Dosage

Adult daily dose, divided into 2-3 single doses: Milk thistle extract corresponding to 165-330 mg of silymarin* [19,37,47] as determined by HPLC using the DAB method [15]; 4-9 g of dried fruits or 4-9 ml of liquid extract 1:1 [48].

Taking a lecithin supplement simultaneously with milk thistle preparations has been recommended (on the basis that phosphatidylcholine in the lecithin enhances the absorption and bioavailability of silymarin) [48].

* This approximates to 210-420 mg of silymarin when determined by the now superseded pre-2000 spectrophotometric method of the DAB [14].

SAFETY

Treatment with milk thistle appears to be safe and well tolerated. The frequency of adverse effects is low and, in clinical trials, indistinguishable from that of placebo [37,38]. A systematic review of 13 controlled studies involving a total of 915 patients found that no serious adverse events occurred in either the control groups (0/459 patients, most of whom received placebo) or groups treated with preparations derived from milk thistle fruit (0/456 patients, who received Silymarin in 10 studies and silibinin complexes in 3 studies); non-serious adverse events occurred in 20/459 (4.4%) patients in control groups compared to 16/456 (3.5%) in milk thistle fruit groups [23].

No adverse events were reported after daily oral administration of up to 700 mg of Silymarin (corresponding to 254 mg of silibinin) to 6 healthy volunteers for four consecutive days in a pharmacokinetic study [20]. Silymarin has been given to hepatitis C patients at dose levels as high as 1260 mg/day for 16 weeks without adverse effects [46].

No deaths occurred within 48 hours after a single oral administration of aqueous, ethanolic or petroleum ether extracts from milk thistle fruit to mice at dose levels between 0.5 and 2 g/kg body weight [51].

In tests of the oral toxicity of Silymarin in rodents no adverse effects were observed:

- after administration of a single dose to mice at up to 20 g/kg or to dogs at 1g/kg bodyweight.
- after daily administration to rats of 1 g/kg for 15 days or 100 mg/kg for 16 weeks or 22 weeks.

Furthermore, after oral administration of Silymarin to rats at 1 g/kg/day on days 8-12 of pregnancy and to rabbits at 100 mg/kg/day on day 8-17 of pregnancy, no embryotoxic effects were evident in the rats on day 21 or in the rabbits on day 28 [52].

REGULATORY STATUS

Medicines

UK	Accepted for general sale, internal or external use [53].
France	Accepted for specified indication [54].
Germany	Commission E monograph published, with approved uses [47].

Food
Not used in foods.

REFERENCES

Current Pharmacopoeial Monographs

Ph. Eur.	Milk-Thistle Fruit
USP	Milk Thistle

Literature References

1. Morazzoni P and Bombardelli E. *Silybum marianum (Carduus marianus)*. *Fitoterapia* 1995, **66**, 3-42.
2. Liersch R, Grimminger W, Leng-Peschlow E and Mengs U. Silybum. In: Blaschek W, Hänsel R, Keller K, Reichling J, Rimpler H and Scheider G, editors. *Hagers Handbuch der Pharmazeutischen Praxis, 5th ed. Folgeband 3: Drogen L-Z*. Berlin-Heidelberg-New York: Springer-Verlag, 1998:548-568 [GERMAN].
3. Kim N-C, Graf TN, Sparacino CM, Wani MC and Wall ME. Complete isolation and characterization of silybins and isosilybins from milk thistle (*Silybum marianum*). *Org. Biomol. Chem.* 2003, **1**, 1684-1689.
4. Lee DY-W and Liu Y. Molecular Structure and Stereochemistry of Silybin A, Silibyn B, Isosilibyn A and Isosilybin B, Isolated from *Silybum marianum* (Milk Thistle). *J. Nat. Prod.* 2003, **66**, 1171-1174 with correction: *ibid.* 1632.
5. Kvasnicka F, Bíba B, Sevcík R, Voldrich M and Krátká J. Analysis of the active components of silymarin. *J. Chromatogr. A.* 2003, **990**, 239-245.
6. Wichtl M and Kober S. Mariendistelfrüchte - Cardui mariae fructus. In: Hartke K, Hartke H, Mutschler E, Rücker G and Wichtl M, editors. *Kommentar zum Deutschen Arzneibuch* [*Commentary on the German Pharmacopoeia*]. Stuttgart: Wissenschaftliche Verlagsgesellschaft, 2000 (13 Lfg.): M 27 [GERMAN].
7. Wagner H, Seligmann O, Hörhammer L and Seitz M. Zur Struktur von Silychristin, einem zweiten Silymarin-isomeren

aus *Silybum marianum* [The structure of silychristin, a second silymarin isomer from *Silybum marianum*]. *Tetrahedron Lett.* 1971, (22), 1895-1899 [GERMAN].
8. Kaloga M. Isolation of Dihydrokaempferol from *Silybum marianum* L. Gaertn. *Z. Naturforsch.* 1981, **36b**, 524-525 [GERMAN/English summary].
9. Szentmihályi K, Then M, Illés V, Perneczky S, Sándor Z, Lakatos B and Vinkler P. Phytochemical Examination of Oils Obtained from the Fruit of Milk Thistle (*Silybum marianum* L. Gaertner) by Supercritical Fluid Extraction. *Z. Naturforsch.* 1998, **53c**, 779-784.
10. Funes JA, Gros EG, Bertoni MH and Cattaneo P. *Silybum marianum* L. Gaertn. (Cardo marino, cardo asnal) (Compositae). Chemical composition of seminal oil and seed meal. *An. Asoc. Quim. Argent.* 1979, **67**, 29-39 [SPANISH]; through *Chem. Abstr.* **93**, 41569.
11. Weinges K, Müller R, Kloss P and Jaggy H. Phenolic Natural Products, XIII. Isolation and Determination of the Constitution of an Optically Active Dehydrodiconiferyl Alcohol from the Seeds of the Milk Thistle *Silybum marianum* (Gaertn.). *Liebigs Ann. Chem.* 1970, **736**, 170-172 [GERMAN/English summary].
12. Szilagyi I, Tetenyi P, Antus S, Seligmann O, Chari VM, Seitz M and Wagner H. Isolation and structure of silymonin and silandrin, two new flavanolignans from *Silybum marianum* (L.) Gaertn., flore albo. *Stud. Org. Chem. (Amsterdam)* 1981, **11**, 345-351; through *Chem. Abstr.* **97**, 212666.
13. Quaglia MG, Bossù E, Donati E, Mazzanti G and Brandt A. Determination of silymarin in the extract from dried *Silybum marianum* fruits by high performance liquid chromatography and capillary electrophoresis. *J. Pharmaceut. Biomed. Analysis* 1999, **19**, 435-442.
14. Wichtl M and Schäfer-Korting M. Mariendistelfrüchte - Cardui mariae fructus. In: Hartke K and Mutschler E, editors. *DAB 9-Kommentar, Volume 3, Monographs M-Z.* Stuttgart: Wissenschaftliche Verlagsgesellschaft, 1988:2226-2230 [GERMAN].
15. Mariendistelfrüchtetrockenextrakt - Cardui mariae fructus extractum siccum. In: *Deutsches Arzneibuch* [German Pharmacopoeia] 2003.
16. Rote Liste® Service GmbH, editor. Pflanzliche Lebertherapeutika [Herbal medicines for the liver]: Legalon® 140 Kapseln (Madaus AG, Cologne). In: *Rote Liste 1998* [*Red List 1998*]. Aulendorf: Editio Cantor, 1998: Section 57. A.1.
17. Fraschini F, Demartini G and Eposti D. Pharmacology of Silymarin. *Clin. Drug Invest.* 2002, **22**, 51-65.
18. Saller R, Meier R and Brignoli R. The Use of Silymarin in the Treatment of Liver Diseases. *Drugs* 2001, **61**, 2035-2063.
19. Wellington K and Blair J. Silymarin: A Review of its Clinical Properties in the Management of Hepatic Disorders. *BioDrugs* 2001, **15**, 465-489.
20. Weyhenmeyer R, Mascher H and Birkmayer J. Study on dose-linearity of the pharmacokinetics of silibinin diastereomers using a new stereospecific assay. *Int. J. Clin. Pharmacol. Therapy Toxicol.* 1992, **30**, 134-138.
21. Parfitt K, editor. Silymarin, Silibinin, Silicristin, Silidianin. In: *Martindale - The complete drug reference, 32nd ed.* ISBN 0-85369-429-X. London: Pharmaceutical Press, 1999:993-994.
22. Flora K, Hahn M, Rosen H and Benner K. Milk thistle (*Silybum marianum*) for the therapy of liver disease. *Am. J. Gastroenterol.* 1998, **93**, 139-143.
23. Rambaldi A, Jacobs BP, Iaquinto G and Gluud C. Milk Thistle for Alcoholic and/or Hepatitis B or C Liver Diseases - a Systematic Cochrane Hepato-Biliary Group Review with Meta-Analyses of Randomized Clinical Trials. *Am. J. Gastroenterol.* 2005, **100**, 2583-2591.
24. Ferenci P, Dragosics B, Dittrich H, Frank H, Benda L, Lochs H et al. Randomized controlled trial of silymarin treatment in patients with cirrhosis of the liver. *J. Hepatol.* 1989, **9**, 105-113.
25. Lucena MI, Andrade RJ, de la Cruz JP, Rodriguez-Mendizabal M, Blanco E and Sanchez de la Cuesta F. Effects of silymarin MZ-80 on oxidative stress in patients with alcoholic cirrhosis. Results of a randomized, double-blind, placebo-controlled clinical study. *Int. J. Clin. Pharmacol. Ther.* 2002, **40**, 2-8.
26. Trinchet JC, Coste T, Levy VG, Vivet F, Duchatelle V, Legendre C et al. A randomized double blind trial of silymarin in 116 patients with alcoholic hepatitis. *Gastroenterol. Clin. Biol.* 1989, **13**, 120-124 [FRENCH/English summary].
27. Bunout D, Hirsch S, Petermann M, de la Maza MP, Silva G, Kelly M et al. Effects of silymarin on alcoholic liver disease. A controlled trial. *Rev. Méd. Chil.* 1992, **120**, 1370-1375 [SPANISH/English summary].
28. Velussi M, Cernigoi AM, De Monte A, Dapas F, Caffau C and Zilli M. Long-term (12 months) treatment with an anti-oxidant drug (silymarin) is effective on hyperinsulinemia, exogenous insulin need and malondialdehyde levels in cirrhotic diabetic patients. *J. Hepatol.* 1997, **26**, 871-879.
29. Láng I, Nékám K, Deák G, Müzes G, Gonzalez-Cabello R, Gergely P et al. Immunomodulatory and hepatoprotective effects of in vivo treatment with free radical scavengers. *Ital. J. Gastroenterol.* 1990, **22**, 283-287.
30. Fehér J, Deák G, Müzes G, Láng I, Niederland V, Nékám K and és Kárteszi M. Hepatoprotective activity of silymarin (Legalon®) therapy in patients with chronic alcoholic liver disease. *Orvosi Hetilap* 1989, **130**, 2723-2727 [HUNGARIAN/English summary].
31. Salvagnini M, Martines D, Piccoli A et al. *J. Hepatol.* 1985, (Suppl. 1), S124. Cited in Ref. 23.
32. Magliulo E, Gagliardi B and Fiori GP. Results of a double-blind study on the effect of silymarin in the treatment of acute viral hepatitis, carried out at two medical centres. *Med. Klin.* 1978, **73**, 1060-1065 [GERMAN/English summary].
33. Parés A, Planas R, Torres M, Caballería J, Viver JM, Acero D et al. Effects of silymarin in alcoholic patients with cirrhosis of the liver: results of a controlled double-blind, randomized and multicenter trial. *J. Hepatol.* 1998, **28**, 615-621.
34. Buzzelli G, Moscarella S, Barbagli S et al. *J. Hepatol.* 1994, **21** (Suppl. 1), S100. Cited in Ref. 23.
35. Buzzelli G, Moscarella S, Giusti A, Duchini A, Marena C and Lampertico M. A pilot study on the liver protective effect of silybin-phosphatidylcholine complex (IdB1016) in chronic active hepatitis. *Int. J. Clin. Pharmacol. Ther. Toxicol.* 1993, **31**, 456-460.
36. Lirussi F, Beccarello A, Zanette G, De Monte A, Donadon V, Velussi M and Crepaldi E. Silybin-β-cyclodextrin in the treatment of patients with diabetes mellitus and alcoholic liver disease. Efficacy study of a new preparation of an anti-oxidant agent. *Diab. Nutr. Metab.* 2002, **15**, 222-231.
37. Jacobs BP, Dennehy C, Ramirez G, Sapp J and Lawrence VA. Milk Thistle for the Treatment of Liver Disease: A Systematic Review and Meta-analysis. *Am. J. Med.* 2002, **113**, 506-515.
38. Mulrow C, Lawrence V, Jacobs B, Dennehy C, Sapp J, Ramirez G et al. *Milk thistle: effects on liver disease and cirrhosis and clinical adverse effects. Evidence Report/ Technology Assessment No. 21.* AHRQ Publication No. 01-E025. Rockville MD: Agency for Healthcare Research and Quality, October 2000 (158 pp).
39. Di Mario F, Farini R, Okolicsanyi L and Naccarato RL. Die Wirkung von Legalon auf die Leberfunktionsproben bei Patienten mit alkoholbedingter Lebererkrankung: Doppelblindstudie [The effect of Legalon on liver function tests in patients with alcohol-induced liver disease: Double-blind study]. In: De Ritis F, Csomos G and Braatz R, editors. *Der toxisch-metabolische Leberschaden* (Proceedings of Legalon Symposium, Hamburg, 13 June 1980). Lübeck: Hansisches Verlagskontor, 1981:54-58 [GERMAN].
40. Salmi HA and Sarna S. Effect of Silymarin on Chemical, Functional and Morphological Alterations of the Liver. A Double-Blind Controlled Study. *Scand. J. Gastroenterol.* 1982, **17**, 517-521.
41. Fintelmann V and Albert A. Nachweis der therapeutischen Wirksamkeit von Legalon® bei toxischen Lebererkrankungen im Doppelblindversuch [Evidence of the therapeutic efficacy of Legalon® in toxic liver diseases in a double-blind study]. *Therapiewoche* 1980, **30**, 5589-5594 [GERMAN].
42. Szilárd S, Szentgyörgyi D and Demeter I. Protective effect of Legalon® in workers exposed to organic solvents. *Acta Med. Hung.* 1988, **45**, 249-256.

43. Boari C, Montanari FM, Galletti GP, Rizzoli D, Baldi E, Caudarella R and Gennari P. Therapeutische Wirkungen von Silymarin bei berufsbedingten toxischen Hepatopathien [Therapeutic effects of silymarin on toxic hepatopathies caused by occupational hazards]. In: De Ritis F, Csomos G and Braatz R, editors. *Der toxisch-metabolische Leberschaden* (Proceedings of Legalon Symposium, Hamburg, 13 June 1980). Lübeck: Hansisches Verlagskontor, 1981;46-53 [GERMAN].
44. Allain H, Schück S, Lebreton S, Streng-Hesse A, Braun W, Gandon JM and Brissot P. Aminotransferase Levels and Silymarin in de novo Tacrine-Treated Patients with Alzheimer's Disease. *Dement. Geriatr. Cogn. Disord.* 1999, **10**, 181-185.
45. Tanamly MD, Tadros F, Labeeb S, Makld H, Shehata M, Mikhail N et al. Randomised double-blinded trial evaluating silymarin for chronic hepatitis C in an Egyptian village: study description and 12 month results. *Digest. Liver Dis.* 2004, **36**, 752-759.
46. Huber R, Futter I and Lüdtke R. Oral silymarin for chronic hepatitis C - A retrospective analysis comparing three dose regimens. *Eur. J. Med. Res.* 2005, **10**, 68-70.
47. Cardui mariae fructus. German Commission E Monograph published in: Bundesanzeiger No. 50 of 13 March 1986.
48. Mills S and Bone K. St. Mary's thistle - *Silybum marianum* (L.) Gaertn. In: *Principles and Practice of Phytotherapy. Modern Herbal Medicine.* ISBN 0-443-06016-9. Edinburgh-London-New York: Churchill Livingstone, 2000:553-562.
49. Barnes J, Anderson LA and Phillipson JD. Milk Thistle. In: *Herbal Medicines - A guide for healthcare professionals, 2nd ed.* ISBN 0-85369-474-5. London-Chicago: Pharmaceutical Press, 2002:341-348.
50. Schulz V, Hänsel R and Tyler VE. Medicinal Teas and Their Actions: Milk thistle fruit. In: *Rational Phytotherapy - A Physicians' Guide to Herbal Medicine, 4th ed.* ISBN 3-540-67096-3. Berlin-Heidelberg-New York-London: Springer-Verlag, 2001:27-30.
51. Pandey GP and Shrivastava DN. Phytochemical and acute toxicity studies of *Silybum marianum* and *Wedelia calendulacea*. *Indian Vet. J.* 1990, **67**, 773-776.
52. Hahn G, Lehmann HD, Kürten M, Uebel H, Vogel G, Baumann J et al. Pharmacology and Toxicology of Silymarin, the Antihepatotoxic Agent of *Silybum marianum* (L.) Gaertn. *Arzneim.-Forsch./Drug Res.* 1968, **18**, 698-704 [GERMAN/English summary].
53. St. Mary's Thistle. In: UK Statutory Instrument 1984 No. 769. The Medicines (Products other than Veterinary Drugs) (General Sale List) Order 1984. Schedule 1, Table A.
54. Chardon-Marie. In: *Médicaments à base de plantes.* ISBN 2-911473-02-7. Saint-Denis Cedex, France: Agence du Médicament, 1998.

REGULATORY GUIDELINES FROM OTHER EU COUNTRIES

FRANCE

Médicaments à base de plantes [54]: Chardon-Marie, fruit.

Therapeutic indications accepted

Oral use
Traditionally used in the symptomatic treatment of functional digestive disorders attributed to a hepatic origin.

GERMANY

Commission E monograph [47]: Cardui mariae fructus (Mariendistelfrüchte).

Uses
Dried fruits: Dyspeptic complaints.
Preparations: Toxic damage to the liver; supportive treatment in chronic inflammatory liver diseases and cirrhosis of the liver.

Contraindications
None known.

Side effects
Dried fruits: None known.
Preparations: A mild laxative effect has occasionally been reported.

Interactions with other drugs
None known.

Dosage
Unless otherwise prescribed, average daily dose:
Dried fruits: 12-15 g.
Preparations: The equivalent of 200-400 mg of silymarin, calculated as silibinin.

Mode of administration
Comminuted drug for infusions and other galenic preparations for oral use.

Actions
Silymarin acts as an antagonist in numerous models of liver damage: the poisons phalloidin and α-amanitin from green *Amanita* mushrooms, lanthanides, carbon tetrachloride, galactosamine, thioacetamide and the hepatotoxic virus FV_3 of cold-blooded animals.

The therapeutic efficacy of silymarin rests on two targets or mechanisms of action. Silymarin alters the structure of the external cell membrane of hepatocytes in such a way that liver poisons cannot penetrate. It also stimulates the activity of nucleolar polymerase A, resulting in increased synthesis of ribosomal protein; thus the regenerative ability of the liver is activated and the formation of new hepatocytes stimulated.

MUGWORT

Compositae

Artemisiae herba

Definition
Mugwort consists of the dried leaves and flowering tops of *Artemisia vulgaris* L.

Two varieties can be distinguished: *A. vulgaris* var. *vulgaris*, found in Europe and central and northern Asia (naturalized in north America), and *A. vulgaris* var. *indica* (Willd.) Maxim., found in southern and eastern Asia [1].

CONSTITUENTS

☐ ***Phenolic acids*** 3,5-Dicaffeoylquinic acid (2.0%), 1,5-dicaffeoylquinic acid (cynarin, 0.3%) [2], caffeic acid (0.47%) and small amounts of 11 other phenolic acids [3].

☐ ***Coumarins***, ca. 1.9% [4] including esculin, esculetin, umbelliferone, scopoletin, coumarin [4] and 6-methoxy-7,8-methylenedioxycoumarin (dracunculin) [5].

☐ ***Flavonoids*** Quercetin 3-glucoside (isoquercitrin) and 3-rutinoside (rutin) in the leaves [6]. 5,3′-dihydroxy-3,7,4′-trimethoxyflavone (ayanin) in the (presumed) aerial parts [7].

20 flavonoids have been isolated from dried whole plants, the most abundant being eriodictyol and luteolin (each > 40 mg/kg) with smaller amounts of apigenin, quercetin, isorhamnetin, homoeriodictyol, diosmetin, eupafolin, chrysoeriol, jaceosidin and tricin, together with the glycosides kaempferol 3-glucoside (astragalin), 3-rhamnoside, 3-rutinoside and 7-glucoside, quercetin 3-glucoside (isoquercitrin), 3-galactoside (hyperin) and 3-rutinoside (rutin), luteolin 7-glucoside and apigenin-8-C-glucoside (vitexin) [8].

☐ ***Essential oil***, up to 0.3% [9], consisting mainly of monoterpenes but varying widely in composition according to phytogeographical origin; 1,8-cineole, camphor and/or thujones are characteristic, and usually the most abundant, components [10].

In plants grown in Italy 1,8-cineole (up to 26.8%) or camphor (up to 20%) were predominant, with up to 9% of borneol and 5.7% of β-thujone but only a trace of α-thujone [11].

From French Mugwort, cineole (up to 8.7%) or α-terpineol (up to 9%) were the principal monoterpenes with 0-4.2% of thujone [9]; in a different investigation, cineole and camphor predominated, with smaller amounts of borneol and β-thujone [12].

Oil from Moroccan Mugwort contained 30% of camphor, 35% of thujones and various other monoterpenes [13].

Leaf oil from Mugwort grown in southern India contained α-thujone (56.3%), β-thujone (7.5%), *p*-cymene (3.3%), camphor (3.0%), β-pinene (2.2%), α-terpineol (2.2%), geraniol (1.5%), caryophyllene (1.5%), γ-cadinene (1.2%) and linalool (1.1%) [14].

Exceptionally, in oil from fresh aerial parts of plants grown in England, linalool (65%) was predominant; other components included 1,8-cineole (7%), neryl acetate (5%), isothujone (4%), neothujol (4%) and α-pinene (4%) [15].

In volatile oil from the flowers only, sabinene (15.9%), myrcene (13.7%) and cineole (9.7%) were the main components [16].

☐ ***Sequiterpenes*** The sequiterpene lactones psilostachyin, psilostachyin C [17] and vulgarin [18]. Also two eudesmane acids and a eudesmane alcohol [19].

☐ ***Triterpenes*** The pentacyclic triterpene alcohol fernenol [20,21], α-amyrin and its acetate [21] and quinovic acid [7].

☐ ***Polyacetylenes*** Heptadeca-1,7,9-triene-11,13,15-triyne and traces of *cis*-dehydromatricaria ester and tetradeca-6-ene-8,10,12-triyne-3-one in the flowers, but no polyacetylenes detected in other aerial parts [22].

☐ ***Other constituents*** include quebrachitol (2-methyl inositol) [23,24] and a small amount of inositol [24], β-sitosterol and stigmasterol [21],

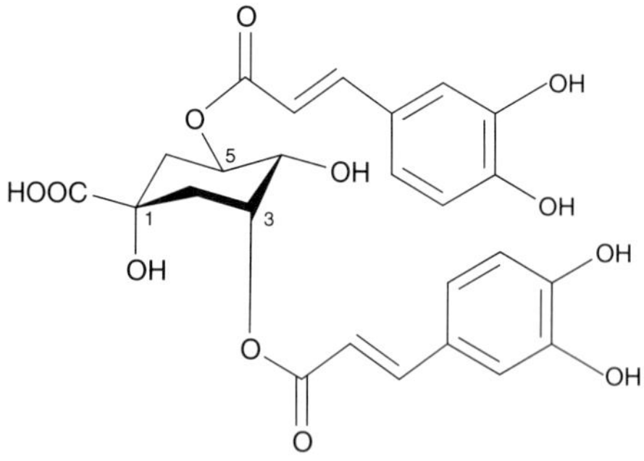

3,5-Dicaffeoylquinic acid

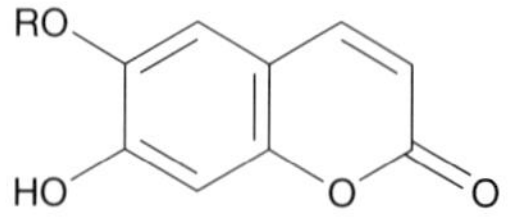

Esculin R = glucosyl
Esculetin R = H

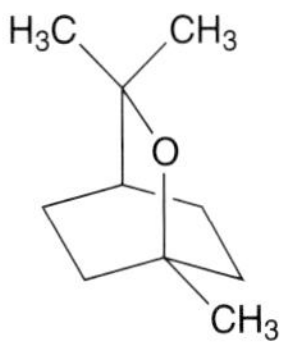

1,8-Cineole

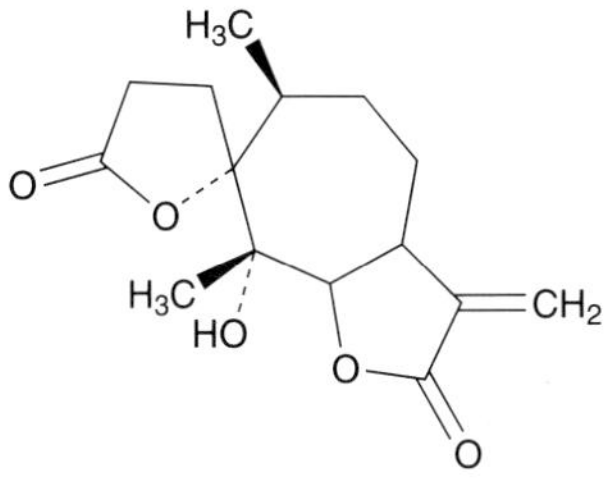

Psilostachyin

and the cyanogenic glucoside prunasin (mandelonitrile glucoside, ca. 0.008%) [25].

Published Assay Methods

Phenolic acids by GC [3]. Total essential oil by distillation [Ph. Fr.]. Essential oil components by GC and GC-MS [14,16]. Thujone by GC [26].

PHARMACOLOGY

In vitro

An aqueous decoction from *Artemisia vulgaris* var. *indica* leaf inhibited *Streptococcus mutans* serotype c (a bacterium associated with dental caries) with a minimum inhibitory concentration of 7.8 mg of crude drug per ml of medium [27]. At a dilution of 1:1000, essential oil from mugwort leaf inhibited the growth of *Staphylococcus aureus, Pseudomonas aeruginosa, Klebsiella pneumoniae* and *Aspergillus niger* [28].

In vivo

A crude 80%-ethanolic extract of mugwort (whole plant) showed weak estrogenic activity and an ethyl acetate fraction exhibited 5% estrogenic activity relative to 17β-estradiol. On further investigation, eriodictyol (one of the major flavonoids present) and apigenin were shown to be dose-dependent weak estrogens [8].

CLINICAL STUDIES

None published on mono-preparations of mugwort.

THERAPEUTICS

Actions

Emmenagogic, choleretic, orexigenic, stomachic, anthelmintic [29].

The emmenagogic properties of mugwort may be due to the phytoestrogenic flavonoids present [8]. Choleretic properties of caffeoylquinic acids have been demonstrated [30].

Indications

None adequately substantiated by pharmacological or clinical studies.

Uses based on experience or tradition

Functional amenorrhoea [29], dysmenorrhoea [8, 29,31]. Loss of appetite [29,31], nervous dyspepsia [29] and other digestive ailments [3]; threadworm and roundworm infestation [29].

Contraindications

Pregnancy and lactation.

Side effects

None known.

Dosage

Three times daily: dried herb, 0.5-2 g as an infusion; liquid extract 1:1 in 25% alcohol, 0.5-2 ml [29]; equivalent dry extracts.

SAFETY

Mugwort is edible and is used as a flavouring and culinary herb [8]. Although recorded in ancient Indian literature (and reiterated in reviews) as abortifacient [32], an ethanolic extract of the whole plant showed no stimulant action on isolated guinea pig uterus [33].

Thujone has neurotoxic potential, α-thujone being more toxic than β-thujone. However, it is rapidly metabolized [34] and unlikely to have toxicological significance in therapeutic doses of mugwort from European sources, provided that material with a relatively low content of thujones is used. The Council of Europe limit for thujones (α and β) in foodstuffs was set at 0.5 mg/kg [35] in 1981, but a more recent evaluation (still in progress) defines the tolerable daily intake of thujone as 0.01 mg per kg body weight per day [36], hence 0.7 mg for a 70 kg person. Appropriate extraction procedures can reduce the thujone level in extracts [26].

REGULATORY STATUS

Medicines

UK No licences issued for products

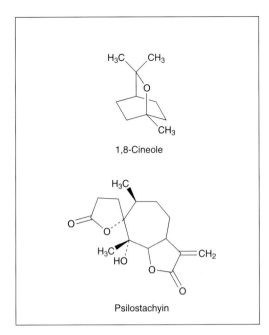

	containing mugwort.
France	Accepted for specified indications [31].
Germany	Commission E monograph published: not approved for any indications [37].

Foods

Council of Europe	Permitted as flavouring, category 4 (with limits on camphor, eucalyptol, polyacetylene compounds and thujone) [38].

REFERENCES

Current Pharmacopoeial Monographs

Ph. Fr.	Armoise
BHP	Mugwort

Literature References

1. Hänsel R, Keller K, Rimpler H and Schneider G, editors. Artemisia. In: *Hagers Handbuch der pharmazeutischen Praxis,* 5th ed. Volume 4: Drogen A-D. ISBN 3-540-52631-5. Berlin-Heidelberg-New York-London: Springer-Verlag, 1992: 357-377 [GERMAN].
2. Carnat A, Heitz A, Fraisse D, Carnat A-P and Lamaison J-L. Major dicaffeoylquinic acids from *Artemisia vulgaris. Fitoterapia* 2000, **71**, 587-589.
3. Swiatek L, Grabias B and Kalemba D. Phenolic acids in certain medicinal plants of the genus *Artemisia. Pharm. Pharmacol. Lett.* 1998, **8**, 158-160.
4. Ikhsanova MA, Berezovskaya TR and Serykh EA. Coumarins of *Artemisia vulgaris. Khim. Prir. Soedin.* 1986, (1), 110 [RUSSIAN]; through *Chem. Abstr.* 1986, **104**, 203928.
5. Murray RDH and Stefanovic M. 6-Methoxy-7,8-methylenedioxycoumarin from *Artemisia dracunculoides* and *Artemisia vulgaris. J. Nat. Prod.* 1986, **49**, 550-551.
6. Hoffman B and Herrmann K. Flavonol Glycosides of Mugwort (Artemisia vulgaris L.), Tarragon (Artemisia dracunculus L.) and Absinth (Artemisia absinthium L.). *Z. Lebensm. Unters. Forsch.* 1982, **174**, 211-215 [GERMAN/English summary].
7. Stefanovic M, Dermanovic M and Verencevic M. Chemical investigation of the plant species Artemisia vulgaris L. (Compositae). *Glas. Hem. Drus. Beograd.* 1982, **47** (3), 7-12; though *Chem. Abstr.* 1982, **96**, 177968.
8. Lee S-J, Chung H-Y, Maier CG-A, Wood AR, Dixon RA and Mabry TJ. Estrogenic Flavonoids from *Artemisia vulgaris* L. *J. Agric. Food Chem.* 1998, **46**, 3325-3329.
9. Carnat AP, Gueugnot J, Lamaison JL, Guillot J and Pourrat H. Mugwort: *Artemisia vulgaris* L. and *Artemisia verlotiorum* Lamotte. *Ann. Pharm. Fr.* 1985, **43**, 397-405 [FRENCH/English summary].
10. Stangl R and Greger H. Monoterpenes and Systematics of the genus *Artemisia* (Asteraceae - Anthemidae). *Plant Syst. Evol.* 1980, **136**, 125-136 [GERMAN/English summary].
11. Nano GM, Bicchi C, Frattini C and Gallino M. On the composition of some oils from *Artemisia vulgaris. Planta Medica* 1976, **30**, 211-215.
12. Hurabielle M, Malsot M and Paris M. Contribution à l'étude chimique de deux huiles d'Artemisia: Artemisia herba-alba Asso et Artemisia vulgaris Linnaeus; intérêt chimiotaxonomique. [Contribution to the chemical study of two oils from Artemisia: Artemisia herba-alba Asso and Artemisia vulgaris Linnaeus; chemotaxonomic interest]. *Riv. Ital. EPPOS* 1981, **53**, 296-299 [FRENCH].
13. Näf-Müller R, Pickenhagen W and Willhalm B. New Irregular Monoterpenes in *Artemisia vulgaris. Helv. Chim. Acta* 1981, **64**, 1424-1430.
14. Misra LN and Singh SP. α-Thujone, the major component of the essential oil from *Artemisia vulgaris* growing wild in Nilgiri hills. *J. Nat. Prod.* 1986, **49**, 941.
15. Banthorpe DV, Baxendale D, Gatford C and Williams SR. Monoterpenes of some *Artemisia* and *Tanacetum* species grown in England. *Planta Medica* 1971, **20**, 147-152.
16. Michaelis K, Vostrowsky O, Paulini H, Zintl R and Knobloch K. Das ätherische Öl aus Blüten von *Artemisia vulgaris* L. [The Essential Oil from Flowers of *Artemisia vulgaris* L.]. *Z. Naturforsch.* 1982, **37c**, 152-158 [GERMAN/English summary].
17. Stefanovic M, Jokic A and Behbud A. Psilostachyin and psilostachyin C from Yugoslav *Artemisia vulgaris* and *Ambrosia artemisiifolia. Glas. Hem. Drus. Beograd* 1972, **37**, 463-468; through *Chem. Abstr.* 1974, **80**, 80080.
18. Marco JA and Barbera O. Natural Products from the Genus Artemisia L. In: Atta-ur-Rahman, editor. *Studies in Natural Product Chemistry, Volume 7.* ISBN 0-444-88829-2. Amsterdam-Oxford-New York-Tokyo: Elsevier, 1990:201-264.
19. Marco JA, Sanz JF and del Hierro P. Two eudesmane acids from *Artemisia vulgaris. Phytochemistry* 1991, **30**, 2403-2404.
20. Kundu SK, Chatterjee A and Rao AS. Isolation of fernenol from *Artemisia vulgaris* L. *Aust. J. Chem.* 1968, **21**, 1931-1933.
21. Kundu SK, Chatterjee A and Rao AS. Chemical Investigation of *Artemisia vulgaris* L. *J. Indian Chem. Soc.* 1969, **46**, 584-594.
22. Drake D and Lam J. Polyacetylenes of *Artemisia vulgaris. Phytochemistry* 1974, **13**, 455-457.
23. Plouvier V. The presence of quebrachitol in some Artemisia species. *Ann. Pharm. Fr.* 1949, **7**, 192-195 [FRENCH]; through *Chem. Abstr.* 1950, **44**, 192.
24. Scholda R, Billek G and Hoffmann-Ostenhof O. Untersuchungen über die Biosynthese der Cyclite, 3. Mitt.: Bildung von Methyläthern des L-Inosits aus meso-Inosit in Blättchen von *Artemisia vulgaris* und *Artemisia dracunculus.* [Studies on the biosynthesis of cyclitols. 3. Formation of methyl ethers of L-inositol from meso-inositol in leaflets of *Artemisia vulgaris* and *Artemisia dracunculus*]. *Monatsh. Chem.* 1964, **95**, 541 [GERMAN].
25. Mizushina Y, Takahashi N, Ogawa A, Tsurugaya K, Koshino H, Takemura M et al. The Cyanogenic Glucoside Prunasin (D-Mandelonitrile-β-D-Glucoside) is a Novel Inhibitor of DNA Polymerase β. *J. Biochem.* 1999, **126**, 430-436.
26. Tegtmeier M and Harnischfeger G. Methods for the Reduction of Thujone Content in Pharmaceutical Preparations of *Artemisia, Salvia* and *Thuja. Eur. J. Pharm. Biopharm.* 1994, **40**, 337-340.
27. Chen C-P, Lin C-C and Namba T. Screening of Taiwanese crude drugs for antibacterial activity against *Streptococcus mutans. J. Ethnopharmacol.* 1989, **27**, 285-295.
28. Kaul VK, Nigam SS and Dhar KL. Antimicrobial Activities of the Essential Oils of *Artemisia absinthium* Linn., *Artemisia vestita* Wall and *Artemisia vulgaris* Linn. *Indian J. Pharmacy* 1976, **38**, 21-22.
29. Artemisia vulgaris. In: *British Herbal Pharmacopoeia 1983.* ISBN 0-903032-07-9. Bournemouth: British Herbal Medicine Association, 1983.
30. Lietti A. Choleretic and Cholesterol Lowering Properties of two Artichoke Extracts. *Fitoterapia* 1977, **48**, 153-158.
31. Armoise, feuille, sommité fleurie. In: *Médicaments à base de plantes.* ISBN 2-911473-02-7. Saint-Denis Cedex, France: Agence du Médicament, 1998.
32. Saha JC, Savini EC and Kasinathan S. Ecbolic properties of Indian medicinal plants. Part 1. *Indian J. Med. Res.* 1961, **49**, 130-151.
33. Jamwal KS and Anand KK. Preliminary screening of some reputed abortifacient indigenous plants. *Indian J. Pharmacy* 1962, **24**, 218-220.
34. Höld KM, Sirisoma NS, Ikeda T, Narahashi T and Casida JE. α-Thujone (the active component of absinthe): γ-Aminobutyric acid type A receptor modulation and metabolic detoxification. *Proc. Natl. Acad. Sci. USA* 2000, **97**, 3826-3831.

35. Provisional limits for active principles: thujones (α and β). In: *Flavouring Substances and Natural Sources of Flavourings, 3rd ed.* ISBN 2-7160-0081-6. Strasbourg: Council of Europe, 1981:29-30.
36. List of "active principles" currently under evaluation by the committee: thujone. In: *Natural Sources of Flavourings. Report No. 1.* ISBN 92-871-4324-2. Strasbourg: Council of Europe Publishing, 2000:19-20.
37. Artemisia vulgaris (Beifuß). German Commission E Monograph published in: Bundesanzeiger No. 122 of 06.07.88.
38. Artemisia vulgaris L. In: *Natural Sources of Flavourings. Report No. 1.* ISBN 92-871-4324-2. Strasbourg: Council of Europe Publishing, 2000:81-83.

REGULATORY GUIDELINES FROM OTHER EU COUNTRIES

FRANCE

Médicaments à base de plantes [31]: Armoise, feuille, sommité fleurie.

Therapeutic indications accepted
Oral use
Traditionally used for painful periods.
Traditionally used to stimulate the appetite.

GERMANY

Commission E monograph [37]: Artemisiae vulgaris herba (Beifußkraut).

Uses
Mugwort herb is used in illnesses and complaints of the gastrointestinal tract, such as colic, diarrhoea, constipation, cramps, weakness of digestion, to stimulate the secretion of gastric juice and bile, as a laxative in obesity and as a "hepatic"; also as an anthelmintic, for hysteria, epilepsy, persistent vomiting, convulsion in children, menstrual disorders and irregular periods, to promote circulation and as a sedative.

The efficacy of mugwort preparations in the claimed areas of use is not proven.

Risks
An abortient action has been reported. Allergic reactions may arise after previous sensitization.

Assessment
Since efficacy in the claimed areas of use is not substantiated, therapeutic use cannot be approved.

MULLEIN

Scrophulariaceae

Verbasci flos/folium

Synonyms: Great Mullein, Aaron's Rod (*V. thapsus*); Large-flowered Mullein (*V. densiflorum*); Orange Mullein (*Verbascum phlomoides*).

Definitions

Mullein Flower consists of the dried flowers, reduced to corolla and androecium, of *Verbascum thapsus* L., *V. densiflorum* Bertol. [*V. thapsiforme* Schrad.] and/or *V. phlomoides* L.

Mullein Leaf consists of the dried leaves of *Verbascum thapsus* L., *V. densiflorum* Bertol. and/or *V. phlomoides* L.

Verbascum thapsus is found throughout Europe and abundantly naturalized in the USA [1]. The leaf of *V. thapsus* is the most frequently used form of mullein in the UK; at one time a monograph on *V. thapsus* leaf appeared in the U.S.N.F. (and subsequently in the BHP 1983). In continental Europe on the other hand, the tradition has been to use the flowers of *V. densiflorum* and *V. phlomoides*; these species are less common in the UK and not found in the USA, although the flowers were at one time official in the U.S.N.F.

A monograph for mullein flower now appears in the European Pharmacopoeia, whereas the British Herbal Pharmacopoeia defines only mullein leaf. Both flower and leaf are covered in this text.

CONSTITUENTS

MULLEIN FLOWER

□ ***Iridoid glycosides***, 0.56% in *V. phlomoides*, 0.13% in *V. densiflorum* [2,3], including aucubin, catalpol, 6-xylosylaucubin and 6-xylosylcatalpol in *V. densiflorum* [4,5] and *V. phlomoides* [5,6]. *V. densiflorum* flower contains 10-fold less aucubin but 2-fold more catalpol than *V. phlomoides* flower [7].

Also, 6-(4″-p-coumaroyl)-xylosylaucubin (named phlomoidoside) and another iridoid ester glycoside, specioside, in *V. phlomoides* flower [8].

□ ***Flavonoids***, 0.57% in *V. phlomoides*, 0.22% in *V. densiflorum* [9], although up to 4% of flavonoids has been claimed [10].

In the flower of *V. thapsus* ssp. *thapsus*, 6-hydroxyluteolin 7-glucoside, 3′-methylquercetin and 7,4′-dihydroxyflavone 4′-rhamnoside [11].

In *V. densiflorum* flower, apigenin and luteolin and their 7-glucosides, quercetin 7-glucoside and 3,7-diglucoside, tamarixetin 7-rutinoside and diosmin (diosmetin 7-rutinoside), the glycosides of luteolin and quercetin being predominant [12].

In *V. phlomoides* flower, tamarixetin 7-rutinoside (predominant) [12-14], tamarixetin 7-glucoside [12,14], apigenin and luteolin [12,13] and their 7-glucosides [13], diosmin [12,14], chrysoeriol, eriodictyol, kaempferol, quercetin and rutin [13]. The reported presence of hesperidin [15] was not confirmed in a later investigation [12].

□ ***Phenylethanoid glycosides*** Verbascoside (acteoside), ca. 0.6% in *V. densiflorum* flower [16], but only traces in *V. phlomoides* flower; traces of forsythoside B (verbascoside 6′-apioside) in both species [8,16,17].

□ ***Triterpene saponins*** Verbascosaponin [8,18-20], a monodesmosidic oleanane saponin with an ether bridge between C13 and C-28 and a group of four neutral sugar residues at the 3-position, was first isolated in 1980 from *V. phlomoides*

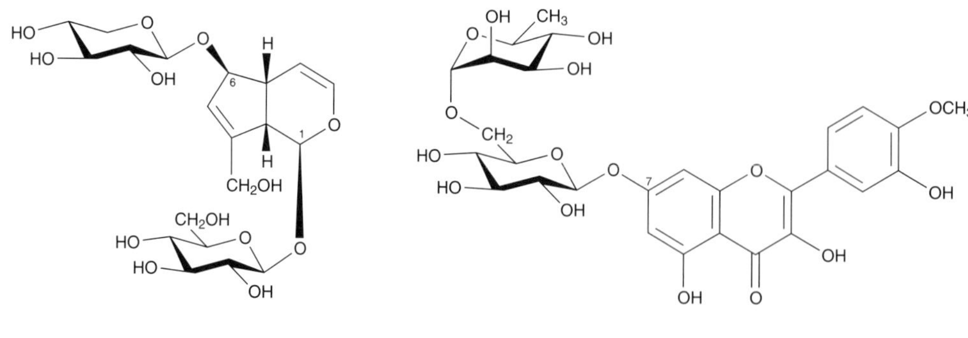

6-Xylosylaucubin

Tamarixetin 7-rutinoside

flower [18,21]; the structure was revised in 1992 [19,20]. The closely-related verbascosaponin A [8,19], verbascosaponin B [20] and desrhamnosyl verbascosaponin [8] have also been isolated from *V. phlomoides* flower.

From *V. thapsus* flower four saponins of fairly similar structure have been isolated and named thapsuins A and B and hydroxythapsuins A and B [22].

No saponins have been confirmed in *V. densiflorum* flower [9].

□ ***Polysaccharides***, 2-3%. Water-soluble acidic polysaccharides, principally a highly-branched arabinogalactan with a β-1,6-linked galactan backbone (MW 70,000), and neutral polysaccharides (an arabinogalactan and a xyloglucan) have been isolated from commercial mullein flower (*V. phlomoides* and/or *V. densiflorum*) [23].

□ ***Phenolic acids*** Vanillic, *p*-hydroxybenzoic, *p*-coumaric, ferulic, protocatechuic and *p*-hydroxycinnamic acids have been identified in the flowers of *V. densiflorum* and *V. phlomoides* [24]. Also *p*-coumaric acid glucoside in *V. phlomoides* flower [6].

□ ***Other constituents*** Phytosterols (β-sitosterol and ergosterol peroxide) and oleanolic acid in *V. thapsus* flower [25]; phytosterol glycosides [6,26] and digiprolactone (a bicyclic monoterpene) [6] in *V. phlomoides* flower; fixed oil in flowers of *V. phlomoides* (2.4%) and *V. densiflorum* (1.6%), in which the main fatty acids are palmitic and linolenic acids [24]; amino acids and free sugars in *V. densiflorum* flower [27,28]; carotenoids and xanthophylls [29].

MULLEIN LEAF

The available phytochemical data is very limited.

□ ***Iridoid glycosides*** Aucubin (0.2-0.5%) and catalpol in *V. thapsus* shoots [30,31] and the leaves of *V. densiflorum* and *V. phlomoides* [5].

Other researchers detected no iridoids by TLC in aerial parts (before flowering) of *V. thapsus* ssp. *thapsus* [32], although no less than 23 iridoids have been isolated from fresh *whole plant* of *V. thapsus* [33].

□ ***Flavonoids*** 6-Hydroxyluteolin 7-glucoside, 3′-methylquercetin and 7,4′-dihydroxyflavone 4′-rhamnoside in leaves of *V. thapsus* ssp. *thapsus* [11].

□ ***Saponins*** From the aerial parts of *V. densiflorum* six saponins (all structurally related to verbascosaponin) have been isolated: desrhamnosyl verbascosaponin, songarosaponins C and D, buddlejasaponins I and IV, and ilwensia saponin [34].

□ ***Polysaccharides*** of undetermined structure but composed of galactose, rhamnose, arabinose and xylose residues occur in *V. densiflorum* leaf, the highest mucilage content coinciding with the flowering period [35].

□ ***Other constituents*** Triterpenes (mainly β-amyrin) and phytosterols (mainly β-sitosterol) in *V. thapsus* leaf [36].

Published Assay Methods

Verbascoside by TLC/UV spectrophotometry [16].

PHARMACOLOGY

In vitro

Antimicrobial activity

A lyophilized infusion from *V. densiflorum* flower exhibited antiviral activity against several influenza A strains, an influenza B strain and fowl plague virus [27], and virucidal activity against *Herpes simplex* virus type 1 [27,28]. An earlier study also demonstrated antiviral activity of *V. thapsus* flower against influenza A and B viruses [37]. Furthermore, the lyophilized infusion from *V. densiflorum* flower

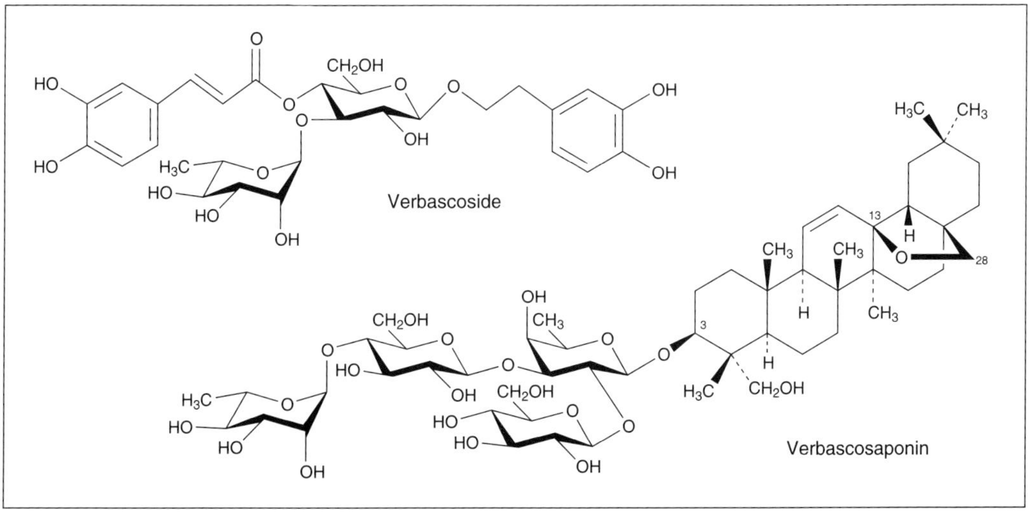

showed synergistic antiviral activity in combination with amantadine derivatives (drugs used in the prophylaxis and treatment of influenza A virus infections) against an avian influenza virus strain in chick embryo fibroblast cultures [38].

At 200 μg/ml the ethyl acetate fraction from a methanolic extract of *V. densiflorum* flower inhibited HIV-1 reverse transcriptase by a modest 39%, while the aqueous fraction was inactive [39].

A dry methanolic extract from *V. thapsus* leaf exhibited antimicrobial activity against Gram-positive *Staphyloccus aureus*, but not against Gram-negative bacteria (*Escherichia coli* and *Pseudomonas aeruginosa*) or the fungus *Candida albicans* [40]. A more recent screen gave similar antibacterial results [41].

Other activities
In screening for substances with anti-tumour activity, aqueous extracts from *V. densiflorum* flower had a strong inhibitory effect on the elongation step of protein biosynthesis in isolated rat liver microsomes. The saponin fraction was shown to be mainly responsible; it strongly inhibited the incorporation of [^{14}C]leucine into proteins and the target site for inhibition was the ribosome fraction from rat liver cells [42].

Aqueous and 67%-methanolic dry extracts from *V. thapsus* flower showed no spasmolytic activity on isolated guinea pig trachea [43].

No effects were evident on mucociliary transport velocity in isolated ciliated epithelium from the frog oesophagus 90 seconds after application of 200 μl of an infusion from *V. densiflorum* flower (4.6 g per 100 ml of water) [44].

In vivo
No anti-inflammatory activity towards carrageen-induced rat paw oedema was exhibited by a dry 80%-ethanolic extract from *V. thapsus* flower after oral administration at 100 mg/kg body weight [45].

Pharmacological activities of constituents
Although relatively few pharmacological studies on mullein preparations have been reported, the pharmacological activities of certain constituents, notably the iridoid aucubin and the phenylethanoid glycoside verbascoside (acteoside), have been extensively studied and may explain some of the effects of mullein.

Aucubin

Anti-inflammatory activity
Aucubin administered orally at 100 mg/kg inhibited carrageenan-induced rat paw oedema by 33% after 3 hours ($p<0.01$), compared to 44% inhibition by indometacin at 7 mg/kg, and aucubin administered topically at 1 mg/ear inhibited 12-*O*-tetradecanoylphorbol acetate (TPA)-induced mouse ear oedema by 80% after 4 hours ($p<0.01$), compared to 87% inhibition by indometacin at 0.5 mg/ear. Catalpol showed no significant anti-inflammatory activity in either test [46].

Hepatoprotective activity
Aucubin administered intravenously at 100 mg/kg significantly protected beagle dogs from lethal poisoning caused by ingestion of *Amanita virosa* mushrooms [47]. It has also been reported that aucubin protected mice from hepatic damage induced by carbon tetrachloride intoxication [48].

Verbascoside
A wide spectrum of *in vitro* and *in vivo* biological activities of verbascoside, including anti-inflammatory (inhibition of 5-lipoxygenase), antioxidant (free radical scavenging), anticancer (inhibition of protein kinase C), cardiovascular and antinephritic effects have been reviewed by Deepak et al. [49].

Anti-inflammatory activity
Verbascoside inhibited formation of the 5-lipoxygenase products 5-HETE and leukotriene B_4 in human polymorphonuclear leukocytes. Leukotrienes are involved in immunoregulation and in inflammatory processes and diseases such as asthma [50]. Verbascoside was found to have nitric oxide radical scavenging activity, which possibly contributes to its anti-inflammatory effect [51].

Verbascoside administered orally at 150 mg/kg inhibited carrageenan-induced rat paw oedema by 94% after 3 hours ($p<0.02$), compared to 40% inhibition by indometacin at 10 mg/kg ($p<0.01$) [52]. In the arachidonic acid-induced mouse ear oedema test verbascoside inhibited oedema by 14% at 3 mg/ear ($p<0.05$) [53].

Analgesic activity
Orally-administered verbascoside inhibited acetic acid-induced writhing and tail pressure pain in mice at 300 mg/kg and 100 mg/kg respectively ($p<0.001$ in both cases) [54].

Cardiovascular activity
In isolated, perfused rat hearts (Langendorff model) verbascoside increased heart rate by 37%, the force of contraction by 9% and coronary perfusion rate by 68% [55]. On the other hand, verbascoside administered intravenously to normotensive, anaesthetized rats had a hypotensive effect; the median effective dose of 10 mg/kg reduced mean arterial blood pressure by 39% for 2-3 minutes, while heart rate also decreased [56].

Other activities
Verbascoside inhibited proliferation of a human gastric carcinoma cell line by 53% ($p<0.01$) at 20 µmol/litre. When the verbascoside-treated cells were inoculated subcutaneously into nude mice the rate of tumour development decreased by 75% compared to that of animals receiving untreated cells. These effects were thought to be related to antioxidant properties of verbascoside [57].

CLINICAL STUDIES

None published on mono-preparations of mullein flower or leaf.

THERAPEUTICS

From the available data, no appreciable differences in actions or uses can be discerned between mullein flower and mullein leaf.

Actions
Expectorant and demulcent [58-60]; the expectorant action of the saponins is complemented by the irritation-soothing effect of the mucilage polysaccharides [10]. Also mildly diuretic [6,59,60] and antiviral [27,28,37]. In external use, vulnerary and emollient [59,60].

Anti-inflammatory effects of aucubin [46] and verbascoside [49,52,53] have been demonstrated.

Indications
None adequately substantiated by pharmacological or clinical studies.

Uses based on experience or tradition
Internal: Bronchitis and tracheitis [59,61], coughs and colds, catarrh of the upper respiratory tract [59-62].
External: As a wound healer [61] and in the treatment of haemorrhoids [60,61,63] and minor dermatological ailments [62]. Also for inflamed mucosa [3,59,62,63], sore throat [3,64], ear infections and earache [61,63].

Contraindications
None known.

Side effects
None known.

Interactions with other drugs
None known.

Dosage
Leaf Three times daily: dried leaf, 4-8 g or by infusion; liquid extract 1:1 in 25% alcohol, 4-8 ml [59].

Flower Daily dose: 3-4 g of dried flower or equivalent preparations [58].

An olive oil macerate of leaf or flower has been recommended for topical application to inflamed mucosa [59,63], ear infections/earache and haemorrhoids [61]. Mouthwashes, gargles or lozenges are recommended for inflammation of the mouth or throat [62,64].

SAFETY

Although toxicological data are very limited, general experience and the absence of adverse reports suggest that mullein flower and leaf have acceptable levels of safety when used appropriately at normal dosage levels [65].

In the brine shrimp lethality assay, methanolic and ethanolic extracts and an aqueous infusion from *V. thapsus* leaf (all corresponding to 0.5 g dried leaf per ml) showed toxicity only at high concentrations with LC_{50} values of approx. 1000-5000 mg/ml [41].

REGULATORY STATUS

Medicines

UK	No licences issued for products containing mullein leaf or flower.
France	Mullein flower accepted for specified indications [62].
Germany	Commission E monograph for mullein flower published, with approved uses [58].

Food

USA	Mullein flower permitted as flavouring in alcoholic beverages only (21 CFR 172.510) [66].
Council of Europe	Permitted as flavouring: flower and flowering top, category N2; leaf, category N3 [67].

REFERENCES

Current Pharmacopoeial Monographs

Ph. Eur.	Mullein Flower
BHP	Mullein Leaf

Literature References

1. Wood HC and LaWall CH, editors. Verbascum. In: United States Dispensatory, Centennial (22nd) Edition. Philadelphia-London, JB Lippincott Company, 1937: 1634.
2. Swiatek L and Adamczyk U. Content of glycosides of aucubin type in the drug *Flos Verbasci*. *Farm. Pol.* 1983, **39**, 275-277 [POLISH/English summary].

3. Grzybek J and Szewczyk A. *Verbascum*-Arten - Königskerze oder Wollblume. *Z. Phytotherapie* 1996, **17**, 389-398 [GERMAN/English summary].
4. Swiatek L, Salama O and Sticher O. 6-O-β-D-Xylopyranosyl-catalpol, a New Iridoid Glycoside from Verbascum thapsiforme. *Planta Medica* 1982, **45**, 153.
5. Swiatek L, Luczak S and Grabias B. Occurrence of iridoids in various organs of Verbascum phlomoides L. and Verbascum thapsiforme Schrad. *Farm. Pol.* 1984, **40**, 415-418 [POLISH/English summary].
6. Osváth K, Pápay V and Tóth L. Active constituents of the flowers of *Verbascum phlomoides* L. and their therapeutical application [HUNGARIAN/English summary]. *Herba Hungarica* 1982, **21**, 141-147.
7. Swiatek L and Adamczyk U. Content of catalpol in the drug Flos Verbasci. *Farm. Pol.* 1985, **41**, 19-21 [POLISH]; through *Chem. Abstr.* 1985, **103**, 110005.
8. Klimek B. Hydroxycinnamoyl ester glycosides and saponins from flowers of *Verbascum phlomoides*. *Phytochemistry* 1996, **43**, 1281-1284.
9. Klimek B. Comparative analysis of carbohydrates, flavonoids and saponins in six *Verbascum* species. *Farm. Pol.* 1991, **47**, 571-576 [POLISH/English summary].
10. Willuhn G. Verbasci flos - Wollblumen. In: Wichtl M, editor. *Teedrogen und Phytopharmaka - Ein Handbuch für die Praxis auf wissenschaftlicher Grundlage, 3rd ed.* ISBN 3-8047-1453-6. Stuttgart: Wissenschaftliche Verlagsgesellschaft, 1997:608-610.
11. Souleles C and Geronikaki A. Flavonoids from *Verbascum thapsus*. *Sci. Pharm.* 1989, **57**, 59-61.
12. Klimek B and Królikowska M. Flavonoid compounds of the flowers of *Verbascum thapsiforme* Schrad. and *V. phlomoides* L. (Scrophulariaceae). *Acta Pol. Pharm.* 1984, **41**, 259-264 [POLISH/English summary].
13. Pápay V, Toth L, Osváth K and Bujtás Gy. Über die Flavonoide von *Verbascum phlomoides* L. [The flavonoids of *Verbascum phlomoides* L.]. *Pharmazie* 1980, **35**, 334-335 [GERMAN].
14. Tschesche R, Delhvi S and Sepúlveda S. Tamarixetin glycosides from the flowers of *Verbascum phlomoides*. *Phytochemistry* 1979, **18**, 1248-1249.
15. Hein S. Untersuchungen über die Flavonoide und Saponine in Verbascum-Arten, insbesondere in den Blüten von Verbascum phlomoides [Investigations on the flavonoids and saponins of Verbascum species, especially of Verbascum phlomoides]. *Planta Medica* 1959, **7**, 185-205 [GERMAN/English summary].
16. Klimek B. Verbascoside in the flowers of some *Verbascum* species. *Acta Polon. Pharm.* 1991, **48**, 51-54.
17. Klimek B. 6′-O-Apiosyl-verbascoside in the flowers of mullein (*Verbascum* species). *Acta Polon. Pharm.* 1996, **53**, 137-140; through *Chem. Abstr.* **126**, 57484.
18. Tschesche R, Sepúlveda S and Braun TM. Über das Saponin der Blüten von *Verbascum phlomoides* L. [The saponin of the flowers of *Verbascum phlomoides* L.]. *Chem. Ber.* 1980, **113**, 1754-1760 [GERMAN/English summary].
19. Schröder H and Haslinger E. The Structure of Verbascosaponin. *Liebigs Ann. Chem.* 1993, 413-418.
20. Schröder H and Haslinger E. Multidimensional NMR Techniques for the Elucidation of Oligosaccharide Structures: Verbascosaponin and a Further Saponin from Wool Flower. *Liebigs Ann. Chem.* 1993, 959-965.
21. Sepulveda S and Tschesche R. A new saponin isolated from *Verbascum phlomoides* L. *Contrib. Cient. Tecnol. (Univ. Tec. Estado, Santiago, Chile)* 1980, **10**, 5-14 [SPANISH]; through *Chem. Abstr.* **94**, 99778.
22. de Pascual Teresa J, Diaz F and Grande M. Componentes del Verbascum thapsus L. III. - Contribución al estudio de las saponinas [Constituents of Verbascum thapsus L. III. - Contribution to the study of the saponins]. *An. Quim.* 1980, **76**, 107-110 [SPANISH/English summary].
23. Kraus J and Franz G. Schleimpolysaccharide aus Wollblumen [Mucilage polysaccharides from mullein]. *Dtsch. Apoth. Ztg.* 1987, **127**, 665-669 [GERMAN].
24. Swiatek L, Kurowska A and Rotkiewicz D. Analysis of fatty and phenolic acids in Flos Verbasci. *Herba Polonica* 1984, **30**, 173-181 [POLISH/English summary].
25. Zhang C, Wang J, Zhu F and Wu D. Studies on the chemical constituents of flannel mullein (*Verbascum thapsus*). *Zhongcaoyao* 1996, **27**, 261-262 [CHINESE]; through *Chem. Abstr.* **125**:190625.
26. Sepulveda S, Delhvi S and Tschesche R. Partial determination of the structure by spectroscopy methods of a new phytosterol isolated from *Verbascum phlomoides* L. flowers. *Contrib. Cient. Tecnol. (Univ. Tec. Estado, Santiago, Chile)* 1980, **10**, 15-21 [SPANISH]; through *Chem. Abstr.* **94**, 99779.
27. Zgórniak-Nowosielska I, Grzybek J, Manolova N, Serkedjieva J and Zawilinska B. Antiviral activity of Flos verbasci infusion against influenza and *Herpes simplex* viruses. *Archiv. Immunol. Ther. Exp.* 1991, **39**, 103-108.
28. Slagowska A, Zgórniak-Nowosielska I and Grzybek J. Inhibition of *Herpes simplex* virus replication by Flos verbasci infusion. *Pol. J. Pharmacol. Pharm.* 1987, **39**, 55-61.
29. Steinegger E and Hänsel R. Hinweise auf Karotinoidführung in Drogen. In: *Pharmakognosie, 5th ed.* ISBN 3-540-55649-4. Berlin-Heidelberg-New York: Springer-Verlag, 1992:244-245 [GERMAN].
30. Gröger D and Simchen P. Zur Kenntnis iridoider Pflanzenstoffe [Contribution to the knowledge of iridoid plant constituents]. *Pharmazie* 1967, **22**, 315-321 [GERMAN].
31. Hüni JES, Hiltebrand H, Schmid H, Gröger D, Johne S and Mothes K. Zur Biosynthese des Verbenalins und Aucubins [Biosynthesis of verbenalin and aucubin]. *Experientia* 1966, **22**, 656 [GERMAN].
32. Seifert K, Schmidt J, Lien NT and Johne S. Iridoids from *Verbascum* Species. *Planta Medica* 1985, 409-411 [GERMAN/English summary].
33. Warashina T, Miyase T and Ueno A. Iridoid Glycosides from *Verbascum thapsus* L. *Chem. Pharm. Bull.* 1991, **39**, 3261-3264.
34. Miyase T, Horikoshi C, Yabe S, Miyasaka S, Melek FR and Kusano G. Saikosaponin Homologues from *Verbascum* spp. The Structures of Mulleinsaponins I-VII. *Chem. Pharm. Bull.* 1997, **45**, 2029-2033.
35. Naglschmid F, Kull U and Jeremias K. Physiological investigations on leaf mucilages. I. Research on the mucilages of *Verbascum densiflorum*. *Biochem. Physiol. Pflanz.* 1982, **177**, 671-685 [GERMAN]; through *Chem. Abstr.* **97**, 107238.
36. Hooper SN and Chandler RF. Herbal remedies of the maritime Indians: phytosterols and triterpenes of 67 plants. *J. Ethnopharmacol.* 1984, **10**, 181-194.
37. Skwarek T. Effects of some plant preparations on influenza virus propagation. I. Effects of plant preparations on propagation of the influenza virus in cultures of chicken embryo fibroblasts and in chicken embryos. *Acta Polon. Pharm.* 1979, **36**, 605-612 [POLISH/English summary].
38. Serkedjieva J. Combined Antiinfluenza Virus Activity of Flos verbasci Infusion and Amantidine Derivatives. *Phytotherapy Res.* 2000, **14**, 571-574.
39. Grzybek J, Wongpanich V, Mata-Greenwood E, Angerhofer CK, Pezzuto JM and Cordell GA. Biological evaluation of selected plants from Poland. *Internat. J. Pharmacognosy* 1997, **35**, 1-5.
40. Meurer-Grimes B, McBeth DL, Hallihan B and Delph S. Antimicrobial activity in medicinal plants of the Scrophulariaceae and Acanthaceae. *Internat. J. Pharmacognosy* 1996, **34**, 243-248.
41. Turker AU and Camper ND. Biological activity of common mullein, a medicinal plant. *J. Ethnopharmacol.* 2002, **82**, 117-125.
42. Paszkiewicz-Gadek A, Grochowska K and Galasinski W. Effect of the Aqueous Extract and Saponin Fraction from the Flowers of *Verbascum thapsiforme* on Protein Biosynthesis in a Rat Liver Ribosomal System. *Phytotherapy Res.* 1990, **4**, 177-181.
43. Bergendorff O, Franzén C, Jeppsson A-B, Sterner O and Waldeck B. Screening of some European medicinal plants for spasmolytic activity on isolated guinea-pig trachea. *Internat. J. Pharmacognosy* 1995, **33**, 356-358.
44. Müller-Limmroth W and Fröhlich H-H. Wirkungsnachweis

einiger phytotherapeutischer Expektorantien auf den mukoziliaren Transport [Evidence of the effects of some phytotherapeutic expectorants on mucociliary transport]. *Fortschr. Med.* 1980, **98**, 95-101 [GERMAN].
45. Mascolo N, Autore G, Capasso F, Menghini A and Fasulo MP. Biological Screening of Italian Medicinal Plants for Anti-Inflammatory Activity. *Phytotherapy Res.* 1987, **1**, 28-31.
46. Recio MC, Giner RM, Máñez S and Ríos JL. Structural Considerations on the Iridoids as Anti-Inflammatory Agents. *Planta Medica* 1994, **60**, 232-234.
47. Chang I-M and Yamaura Y. Aucubin: a New Antidote for Poisonous *Amanita* Mushrooms. *Phytotherapy Res.* 1993, **7**, 53-56.
48. Chang I-M. Antiviral Activity of Aucubin against Hepatitis B Virus Replication. *Phytotherapy Res.* 1997, **11**, 189-192.
49. Deepak M, Umashankar DC and Handa SS. Verbascoside - a promising phenylpropanoid. *Indian Drugs* 1999, **36**, 336-345.
50. Kimura Y, Okuda H, Nishibe S and Arichi S. Effects of Caffeoylglycosides on Arachidonate Metabolism in Leukocytes. *Planta Medica* 1987, **53**, 148-153.
51. Xiong Q, Tezuka Y, Kaneko T, Li H, Tran LQ, Hase K et al. Inhibition of nitric oxide by phenylethanoids in activated macrophages. *Eur. J. Pharmacol.* 2000, **400**, 137-144.
52. Schapoval EES, Winter de Vargas MR, Chaves CG, Bridi R, Zuanazzi JA and Henriques AT. Antiinflammatory and antinociceptive activities of extracts and isolated compounds from *Stachytarpheta cayennensis*. *J. Ethnopharmacol.* 1998, **60**, 53-59.
53. Murai M, Tamayama Y and Nishibe S. Phenylethanoids in the Herb of *Plantago lanceolata* and Inhibitory Effect on Arachidonic Acid-Induced Mouse Ear Edema. *Planta Medica* 1995, **61**, 479-480.
54. Nakamura T, Okuyama E, Tsukada A, Yamazaki M, Satake M, Nishibe S et al. Acteoside as the Analgesic Principle of Cedron (*Lippia triphylla*), a Peruvian Medicinal Plant. *Chem. Pharm. Bull.* 1997, **45**, 499-504.
55. Pennacchio M, Syah YM, Alexander E and Ghisalberti EL. Mechanism of Action of Verbascoside on the Isolated Rat Heart: Increases in Level of Prostacyclin. *Phytotherapy Res.* 1999, **13**, 254-255.
56. Ahmad M, Rizwani GH, Aftab K, Ahmad VU, Gilani AH and Ahmad SP. Acteoside: a New Antihypertensive Drug. *Phytotherapy Res.* 1995, **9**, 525-527.
57. Li J, Zheng Y, Zhou H, Su B and Zheng R. Differentiation of Human Gastric Adenocarcinoma Cell Line MGc80-3 Induced by Verbascoside. *Planta Medica* 1997, **63**, 499-502.
58. Verbasci flos (Wollblumen). German Commission E monograph published in: Bundesanzeiger No. 22 of 1 February 1990.
59. Verbascum. In: *British Herbal Pharmacopoeia 1983.* ISBN 0-903032-07-4. Bournemouth: British Herbal Medicine Association, 1983.
60. Ody P. Mullein - *Verbascum thapsus*. In: *The Complete Guide - Medicinal Herbal.* ISBN 0-7513-3005-1. London-New York: Dorling Kindersley, 2000:134.
61. Chevallier A. Mullein - *Verbascum thapsus*. In: *Encyclopedia of Medicinal Plants, 2nd ed.* ISBN 0-7513-1209-6. London-New York: Dorling Kindersley, 2001:281.
62. Bouillon blanc, fleur mondée. In: *Médicaments à base de plantes.* ISBN 2-911473-02-7. Saint-Denis Cedex, France: Agence du Médicament, 1998.
63. Grieve M (edited by Leyel CF). Great Mullein - *Verbascum thapsus*. In: *A Modern Herbal* (first published 1931; revised 1973). ISBN 1-85501-249-9. London: Tiger Books International, 1994:562-566.
64. Schulz V, Hänsel R and Tyler VE. Herbal Cough Remedies. In: *Rational Phytotherapy - A Physicians' Guide to Herbal Medicine, 4th ed.* ISBN 3-540-67096-3. Berlin-Heidelberg-New York-London: Springer-Verlag, 2001:180-184.
65. McGuffin M, Hobbs C, Upton R and Goldberg A, editors. *Verbascum thapsus* L., *Verbascum densiflorum* Bertoloni, *Verbascum phlomoides* L. In: American Herbal Products Association's *Botanical Safety Handbook.* ISBN 0-8493-1675-8. Boca Raton-Boston-London: CRC Press, 1997:121.
66. Mullein flowers (*Verbascum phlomoides* L. or *V. thapsiforme* Schrad.). In: Section 172.510 of USA Code of Federal Regulations, Title 21, Food and Drugs, Parts 170 to 199. Revised as of April 1, 2000.
67. *Verbascum thapsiforme* Schrad., *Verbascum thapsus* L., *Verbascum phlomoides* L., flowers, flower tips, leaves. In: *Flavouring Substances and Natural Sources of Flavourings, 3rd ed.* ISBN 2-7160-0081-6. Strasbourg: Council of Europe, 1981.

REGULATORY GUIDELINES FROM OTHER EU COUNTRIES

FRANCE

Médicaments à base de plantes [62]: Bouillon blanc, fleur mondée.

Therapeutic indications accepted

Oral use
Traditionally used: as adjuvant treatment of the painful component of functional digestive disorders; in the symptomatic treatment of coughs.

Topical use
Traditionally used: as a soothing and antipruriginous local treatment of dermatological ailments, as a trophic protector in the treatment of chaps, abrasions or fissures and against insect stings; locally (mouthwash/gargle, pastille) as an antalgesic in ailments of the buccal cavity and/or the pharynx; locally in mouthwashes, for buccal hygiene.

GERMANY

Commission E monograph [58]: Verbasci flos (Wollblumen).

Uses
Catarrh of the upper respiratory tract.

Contraindications
None known.

Side effects
None known.

Interactions with other drugs
None known.

Dosage
Unless otherwise prescribed, daily dose: 3-4 g of the drug or equivalent preparations.

Mode of administration
Comminuted drug for infusions and other galenic preparations for oral use.

Actions
Soothes irritation, expectorant.

NETTLE ROOT

Urticaceae

Urticae radix

Synonym: Stinging nettle root.

Definition
Nettle Root consists of the dried rhizomes and roots of *Urtica dioica* L.

CONSTITUENTS

□ ***Lectins*** *Urtica dioica* agglutinin (UDA), 0.1%, first isolated in 1984 [1]. This small plant lectin, the smallest known with a MW of 8.5 kDa, is a monomeric protein consisting of 89 amino acid residues including two 43-amino acid, glycine- and cysteine-rich domains [2]. It has been shown to be a complex mixture of at least 6 isolectins with similar but not identical properties [3].
□ ***Polysaccharides***, ca. 0.85%. Five polysaccharides have been isolated, of which two are glucans with [1→4]-linked glucose units but differing in MW (15 and 50 kDa), degree of branching and acidity; two are rhamnogalacturonans of MW 18 and 210 kDa; and the fifth is an acidic arabinogalactan of MW 70 kDa consisting of a [1→3]-linked galactan chain with arabinose side chains [4,5].
□ ***Lignans*** including (+)-neo-olivil and acetylated derivatives [6-8], (–)-secoisolariciresinol [7,9,10], (–)-isolariciresinol, dehydrodiconiferyl alcohol, pinoresinol and traces of 3,4-divanillyltetrahydro furan [7]; also lignan glucosides [8,11].
□ ***Homovanillyl alcohol*** and its 4′-glucoside [8].
□ ***Sterols*** β-Sitosterol (ca. 0.05%) and its glucoside [12-14], and several other sterols and sterol glucosides [15].
□ ***Ceramides*** Two groups of ceramides, consisting of a sphingoid base (2-amino-1,3,4-trihydroxy-8-octadecene) with an amido link from the amino group to an unbranched C_{20}-C_{25} fatty acid or corresponding 2-hydroxy fatty acid, have been isolated [16].
□ ***Hydroxy fatty acids*** (10*E*,12*Z*)-9-hydroxy-10,12-octadecadienoic acid [17]; (9*Z*,11*E*)-13-hydroxy-9,11-octadecadienoic acid [10] and the isomeric 9,10,13-trihydroxy-11-octadecenoic and 9,12,13-trihydroxy-10-octadecenoic acids [9].
□ ***Terpenes*** Three monoterpene diols and their monoglucosides [18], and the triterpenes oleanolic acid and ursolic acid [10].
□ ***Fatty alcohols*** 14-Octacosanol [10].
□ ***Coumarins*** Scopoletin, ca. 0.0002% [12-14].

Published Assay Methods
Lectin content by ELISA and/or HPLC [19]; β-sitosterol and scopoletin by HPLC [14].

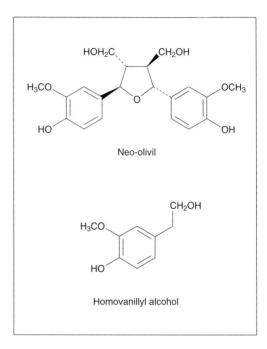

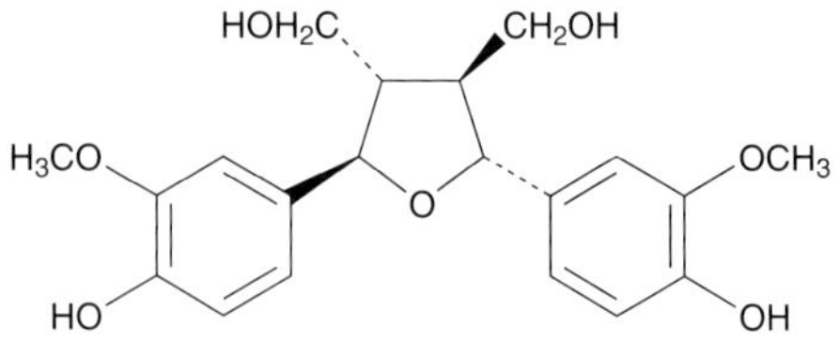

Neo-olivil

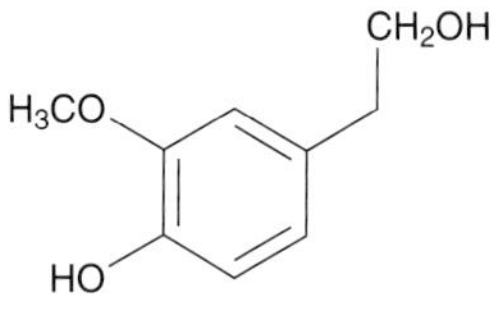

Homovanillyl alcohol

PHARMACOLOGY

Nettle root was first used in urinary tract disorders in the 1950s. Today it is used mainly in the symptomatic treatment of early stages of benign prostatic hyperplasia (BPH), a common condition in ageing men caused by non-malignant growth of both the stromal and epithelial elements of the prostate gland. Progressive enlargement of the prostate can lead to impediment of urination with various 'lower urinary tract symptoms' (LUTS), both irritative (urgency, frequency, nocturia) and obstructive (hesitancy, weak flow, incomplete emptying of the bladder). More than 50% of men over 50 years of age have histological signs of BPH and up to 40% of men over 70 will complain of symptoms [20].

Despite its clinical importance the aetiology of BPH is not fully understood. It is triggered by various hormones and mediators. Among the hypotheses advanced to explain the development of BPH are: an increased concentration of sex hormone binding globulin (SHBG); increased activity of enzymes such as 5α-reductase (testosterone → dihydrotestosterone) and/or aromatase (testosterone → oestrogen); and increased concentrations of prostaglandins and leukotrienes (inflammation mediators) [21].

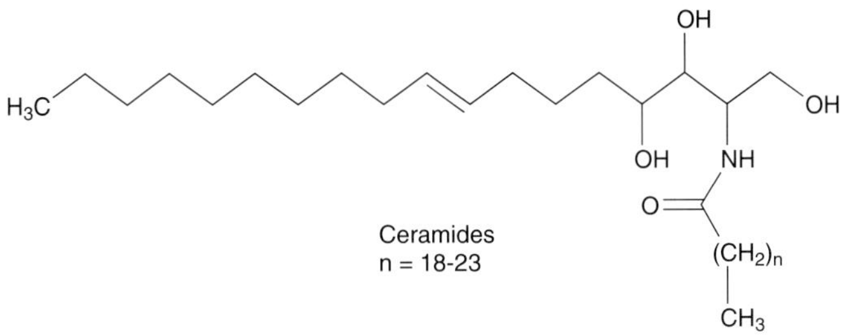

Ceramides
n = 18-23

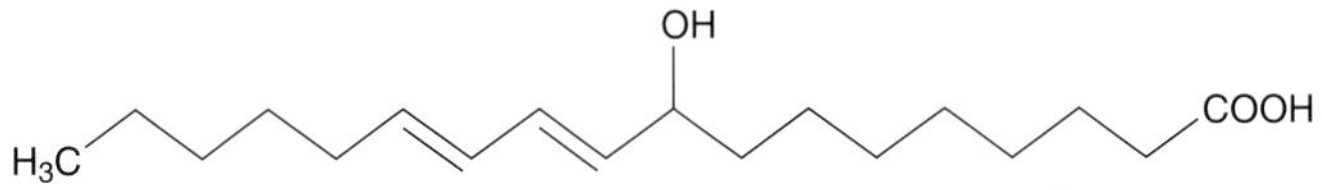

9-Hydroxy-10,12-octadecadienoic acid

In vitro
As the aetiology of BPH is multifactorial, it has not been possible so far to develop therapeutically relevant *in vitro* or *in vivo* models allowing the bioguided fractionation of a plant extract in the search for active principles useful in treating BPH [4,22].

Extracts from nettle root have been shown

- to inhibit the capacity of sexual hormone binding globulin (SHBG) in human blood plasma to bind to 5α-dihydrotestosterone [23].
- to inhibit Na^+,K^+-ATPase activity of human BPH tissue cells, which may suppress prostate cell metabolism and growth [24].
- to inhibit the proliferation of human prostatic epithelial LNCaP (lymph node carcinoma of the prostate) cells with growth reduction of 30% at a concentration of 10^{-6} mg/ml; no antiproliferative effect was observed on human prostatic stromal cells [25].
- to inhibit cell proliferation in cultures of prostatic cells taken from BPH patients [26].
- to have *no* 5α-reductase activity when incubated with a preparation of human prostatic tissue (containing 5α-reductase) and testosterone [27].

Although numerous activities of fractions and isolated constituents from nettle root have also been demonstrated, and hypotheses put forward as to their relevance to BPH [20,28], it remains unclear which constituents of nettle root have beneficial effects in the treatment of BPH.

In vivo
A crude polysaccharide fraction from nettle root, administered orally at 40 mg/kg, showed considerable anti-inflammatory activity in the carrageenan-induced rat paw oedema test [29].

A dry 20%-methanolic nettle root extract did not inhibit testosterone- or dihydrotestosterone-stimulated growth of the prostate gland in castrated rats, suggesting that the extract had no anti-androgenic activity [27].

Pharmacological studies in humans
When prostatic tissue obtained (as a result of prostatectomy) from BPH patients previously treated with nettle root extract was examined by fluorescence microscopy, granular fluorescence was observed. This fluorescence was not observed in prostatic tissue from control patients not treated with nettle root extract, but could be reproduced *in vitro*, with comparable structure but lower intensity, by incubation of such tissue with nettle root extract. The results were interpreted as evidence that nettle root constituents or their metabolites were present in prostatic tissue from BPH patients treated with a nettle root extract [30].

Microscopical examination of prostatic tissue from BPH patients, obtained by biopsy before and after 6 months of therapy with nettle root extract, confirmed ultrastructural changes in the smooth muscle cells and epithelial cells [31].

Prostatic cells from 33 BPH patients treated with nettle root extract for about 6 months were investigated by fluorescence microscopy. Compared to normal prostatic cells, a decrease in homogenous granules was detected in hyperplastic cells from the BPH patients, indicating that biological activity in these cells had decreased [32].

Pharmacokinetics
After oral administration of 20 mg of purified *Urtica dioica* agglutinin (UDA) to volunteers and patients, 30-50% of the UDA was excreted in the faeces and less than 1% in the urine.

CLINICAL STUDIES

Five controlled studies (Table 1) and 11 open studies (Table 2) have been carried out with mono-preparations of nettle root in patients with the early stages of benign prostatic hyperplasia.

Controlled studies
A dry 20% methanolic extract was used in four of the controlled studies and a liquid preparation in one study, as listed in Table 1, with the following results:

- In the Vontobel study, significant improvements were observed in two objective parameters in the verum group: average micturition volume increased by 43.7% ($p = 0.027$) compared to a decrease of 9% in the placebo group, and the average serum level of sexual hormone binding globulin (SHBG) fell by 2.43 nmol/litre ($p = 0.0005$) compared to an increase in the placebo group. Although subjective improvements in dysuric symptoms were noted in both patient groups, differerences in urinary flow rates and residual urine volume did not reach statistical significance [33].

- In the Dathe study, the verum group's average urinary flow rate increased by 14% (placebo group: 2%); the residual urine volume decreased by 40% (placebo group: 8%) and, in patients with an initial residual volume of less than 100 ml, by 52% (placebo group: 14%). No significant differences were noted in subjective symptoms [34].

- Twice the dosage of the earlier studies was used in the Fischer study. Significant decreases in micturition frequency and SHBG levels and an improvement in subjective well-being scores (all $p<0.05$) were observed in the verum group after 6 months [35].

- In the Schneider study, the extract dose level (459 mg/day) was midway between the previous ones (300-600 mg/day) and taken over a longer period of 12 months. The International Prostate Symptom Score (IPSS) decreased significantly more in the verum group (from 18.7 to 13.0; $p = 0.023$) than in the placebo group (from 18.5 to 13.8). Objective improvements in maximum urinary flow rate and residual urine volume, and subjective improvements in the quality of life index, were substantial in both groups, but differences between groups were not statistically significant [36].

- In the Engelmann study, patients were treated daily for 3 months with either 2 × 3 ml of an aqueous liquid preparation, equivalent to 4.68 g of a fluid extract (1:1, 16% ethanol) ($n = 20$), or placebo ($n = 21$). The IPSS decreased significantly more in the verum group (from 18.2 to 8.7; $p = 0.002$) than in the placebo group (from 17.7 to 12.9). In the verum group residual urinary volume decreased by 19.2 ml (placebo group: 10.7 ml) and maximal urinary flow increased by 7.1 ml/second (placebo group: 4.4 ml/second), but the differences were not statistically significant [37].

Although all the above studies found that nettle root produced significant improvement in certain parameters, the pattern was by no means consistent. For example, substantial improvements in urinary flow rate and residual urine volume (obstructive symptoms) were reported in the Dathe study, but no statistically significant improvements were evident in these parameters in the more recent Schneider and Engelmann studies, where significant decreases in IPSS scores were primarily due to improvements in more subjective criteria (irritative symptoms).

Opinions on the efficacy of nettle root in the symptomatic treatment of BPH therefore remain divided. While some consider it to be a "viable alternative in the medical treatment of benign prostatic hyperplasia and associated urinary tract symptoms" [20], others share the view that so far its efficacy is inadequately proven [49-51].

TABLE 1 Controlled Clinical Studies with Nettle Root

First author Year Reference number	Duration of treatment	Number of patients	Type of preparation	Daily dosage	Comparison treatment
Vontobel 1985 [33]	9 weeks	50	Dry extract (20% methanol)	2 × 150 mg*	Placebo
Dathe 1987 [34]	4-6 weeks	79	Dry extract (20% methanol)	2 × 150 mg*	Placebo
Fischer 1992 [35]	6 months	40	Dry extract (20% methanol)	2 × 300 mg*	Placebo
Schneider 2004 [36]	12 months	246	Dry extract (20% methanol)	459 mg	Placebo
Engelmann 1996 [37]	3 months	41	Liquid preparation	2 × 3 ml	Placebo

*Dosages stated here relate to native extracts. Dosages reported in the published papers were double these amounts, but referred to dry 20%-methanolic native extract with an equal amount of diluent.

TABLE 2 Open Clinical Studies with Nettle Root

First author Year Reference number	Duration of treatment	Number of patients	Type of preparation	Daily dosage
Tosch 1983 [38]	3-4 months	5492	Dry 20%-methanolic extract	2 × 150-300 mg*
Stahl 1984 [39]	10 weeks	4051	Dry 20%-methanolic extract	2 × 300 mg*
Friesen 1988 [40]	20 weeks	4480	Dry 20%-methanolic extract	2 × 150-300 mg*
Kaldewey 1995 [41]	6 months	1319	Dry 70%-ethanolic extract	2 × 189-378 mg*
Djulepa 1982 [42]	3-24 months	89	Dry 20%-methanolic extract	2 × 150 mg*
Vandierendounck 1986 [43]	10 weeks	111	Dry 20%-methanolic extract	2 × 300 mg*
Maar 1987 [44]	6 months	39	Dry 20%-methanolic extract	2 × 150-300 mg*
Bauer 1988 [45]	12 weeks	253	Dry 20%-methanolic extract	2 × 300 mg*
Feiber 1988 [46]	4-24 weeks	26	Dry 20%-methanolic extract	2 × 300 mg*
Goetz 1989 [47]	2 months	10	Liquid extract (1:1, 40% ethanol)	30-150 drops
Belaiche 1991 [48]	6 months	67	Liquid extract (1:5, 40% ethanol)	3 × 5 ml

*Dosages stated here relate to native extracts.

Open studies
As listed in Table 2, four very large multicentric open studies [38-41] involving a total of over 15,300 patients with benign prostatic hyperplasia have been carried out, as well as a number of smaller open studies. These are not summarized in detail here, but each study reported improvements in certain efficacy parameters after treatment with nettle root preparations. However, since placebo effects in BPH treatment are often considerable, as demonstrated in the controlled studies above, conclusions from open studies with regard to efficacy are not very convincing.

THERAPEUTICS

Indications
Symptomatic treatment of micturition disorders in the early stages of benign prostatic hyperplasia [33-37,52,53].

Contraindications
None known.

Side effects
Mild gastrointestinal upsets in sensitive individuals.

Interactions with other drugs
None known.

Dosage
Daily dose: 300-600 mg of dry 20%-methanolic extract of nettle root [33-36], or equivalent preparations [37].

SAFETY

No serious adverse effects were reported from the clinical studies listed in Tables 1 and 2, in which over 16,000 patients were treated with nettle root extracts for periods of up to 12 months at daily doses ranging from 300 mg to 756 mg of hydroalcoholic dry native extract of nettle root. The majority of complaints were mild gastrointestinal upsets. In an open study involving 1319 patients, the incidence of adverse events probably or possibly related to treatment with nettle root extract was 1.0% [41] and in the most recent controlled study the level of adverse events was higher in the placebo group than in the verum group [36].

REGULATORY STATUS

Medicines
UK	Accepted for general sale, internal or external use [54].
France	Accepted for specified indications [53].
Germany	Commission E monograph published, with approved uses [52].

Foods
Not used in foodstuffs.

REFERENCES

Current Pharmacopoeial Monographs
DAB	Brennesselwurzel
USP	Stinging Nettle

Literature References

1. Peumans WJ, De Ley M and Broekaert WF. An unusual lectin from stinging nettle (*Urtica dioica*) rhizomes. *FEBS Letters* 1984, **177**, 99-103.
2. Beintema JJ and Peumans WJ. The primary structure of stinging nettle (*Urtica dioica*) agglutinin. A two-domain member of the hevein family. *FEBS Letters* 1992, **299**, 131-134.

3. Van Damme EJM, Broekaert WF and Peumans WJ. The *Urtica dioica* Agglutinin is a Complex Mixture of Isolectins. *Plant Physiol.* 1988, **86**, 598-601.
4. Wagner H, Willer F, Samtleben R and Boos G. Search for the antiprostatic principle of stinging nettle (*Urtica dioica*) roots. *Phytomedicine* 1994, **1**, 213-224.
5. Wagner H, Willer F and Samtleben R. Lektine und Polysaccharide - die Wirkprinzipien der *Urtica-dioica*-Wurzel? [Lectins and polysaccharides - the active principles of *Urtica dioica* root?]. In: Boos G, editor. *Benigne Prostatahyperplasie.* Frankfurt: PMI, 1994:115-22 [GERMAN].
6. Schöttner M, Reiner J and Tayman FSK. (+)-Neo-olivil from roots of *Urtica dioica. Phytochemistry* 1997, **46**, 1107-1109.
7. Schöttner M, Ganßer D and Spiteller G. Lignans from the Roots of *Urtica dioica* and their Metabolites Bind to Human Sex Hormone Binding Globulin (SHBG). *Planta Medica* 1997, **63**, 529-32
8. Chaurasia N and Wichtl M. Phenylpropane und Lignane aus der Wurzel von Urtica dioica L. [Phenylpropanes and lignans from the root of Urtica dioica L.]. *Dtsch. Apoth. Ztg.* 1986, **126**, 1559-1563 [GERMAN].
9. Ganßer D and Spiteller G. Plant Constituents Interfering with Human Sex Hormone-Binding Globulin. Evaluation of a Test Method and its Application to *Urtica dioica* Root Extracts. *Z. Naturforsch.* 1995, **50c**, 98-104.
10. Ganßer D and Spiteller G. Aromatase Inhibitors from *Urtica dioica* Roots. *Planta Medica* 1995, **61**, 138-140.
11. Kraus R and Spiteller G. Lignan Glucosides from Roots of *Urtica dioica. Liebigs Ann. Chem.* 1990, 1205-1213 [GERMAN/English summary].
12. Chaurasia N and Wichtl M. Scopoletin, 3-β-Sitosterin und Sitosterin-3-β-D-glucosid aus Brennesselwurzel (Urticae radix). *Dtsch. Apoth. Ztg.* 1986, **126**, 81-83 [GERMAN].
13. Schilcher H and Effenberger S. Scopoletin und β-Sitosterol - zwei geeignete Leitsubstanzen für Urticae radix [Scopoletin and β-Sitosterol - two suitable marker substances for Urticae radix]. *Dtsch. Apoth. Ztg.* 1986, **126**, 79-81 [GERMAN].
14. Lichius JJ and Muth C. The Inhibiting Effects of *Urtica dioica* Root Extracts on Experimentally Induced Prostatic Hyperplasia in the Mouse. *Planta Medica* 1997, **63**, 307-310.
15. Chaurasia N and Wichtl M. Sterols and steryl glycosides from *Urtica dioica. J. Nat. Prod.* 1987, **50**, 881-885.
16. Kraus R and Spiteller G. Ceramides from *Urtica dioica* Roots. *Liebigs Ann. Chem.* 1991, 125-128.
17. Kraus R, Spiteller G and Bartsch W. (10*E*,12*Z*)-9-Hydroxy-10,12-octadecadiensäure, ein Aromatase-Hemmstoff aus dem Wurzelextrakt von *Urtica dioica* [(10*E*,12*Z*)-9-hydroxy-10,12-octadecadienoic acid, an aromatase inhibitor from the root extract of *Urtica dioica*]. *Liebigs Ann Chem* 1991, 335-339 [GERMAN/English summary].
18. Kraus R and Spiteller G. Terpene diols and terpene diol glucosides from roots of *Urtica dioica. Phytochemistry* 1991, **30**, 1203-1206.
19. Willer F, Wagner H and Schecklies E. Urtica-Wurzelextrakte. Standardisierung mit Hilfe der ELISA-Technik und der HPLC [Urtica root extract. Standardization using the ELISA technique and HPLC]. *Dtsch. Apoth. Ztg.* 1991, **131**, 1217-1221 [GERMAN].
20. Koch E. Extracts from Fruits of Saw Palmetto (*Sabal serrulata*) and Roots of Stinging Nettle (*Urtica dioica*): Viable Alternatives in the Medical Treatment of Benign Prostatic Hyperplasia and Associated Lower Urinary Tract Symptoms. *Planta Medica* 2001, **67**, 489-500.
21. Schilcher H. Herbal Drugs in the Treatment of Benign Prostatic Hyperplasia. In: Lawson LD and Bauer R, editors. *Phytomedicines of Europe: Chemistry and Biological Activity.* ACS Symposium Series 691. ISBN 0-8412-3559-7. Washington DC: American Chemical Society, 1998:62-73.
22. Wagner H, Geiger WN, Boos G and Samtleben R. Studies on the binding of Urtica dioica agglutinin (UDA) and other lectins in an in vitro epidermal growth factor receptor test. *Phytomedicine* 1994, **1**, 287-290.
23. Schmidt K. The action of Radix Urticae extracts on the sexual hormone binding globulin of the blood plasma in benign prostatic hyperplasia. *Fortschr. Med.* 1983, 713-716 [GERMAN/English summary].
24. Hirano T, Homma M and Oka K. Effects of Stinging Nettle Root Extracts and Their Steroidal Components on the Na^+, K^+-ATPase of the Benign Prostatic Hyperplasia. *Planta Medica* 1994, **60**, 30-3.
25. Konrad L, Müller H-H, Lenz C, Laubinger H, Aumüller G and Lichius JJ. Antiproliferative Effect on Human Prostate Cancer Cells by a Stinging Nettle Root (*Urtica dioica*) Extract. *Planta Medica* 2000, **66**, 44-47.
26. Rausch U, Aumüller G, Eicheler W, Gutschank W, Beyer G and Ulshöfer B. Der Einfluß von Phytopharmaka auf BPH-Gewebe und Explantatkulturen in vitro [The influence of phytomedicines on BPH tissues and explantat cultures in vitro]. In: Rutishauser G, editor. *Klinische und experimentelle Urologie 22: Benigne Prostatahyperplasie III.* ISBN 3-88603-404-6. München-Bern-Wien-New York: Zuckschwerdt, 1992:116-124 [GERMAN].
27. Rhodes L, Primka RL, Berman C, Vergult G, Gabriel M, Pierre-Malice M and Gibelin B. Comparison of Finasteride (Proscar®), a 5α Reductase Inhibitor, and Various Commercial Plant Extracts in In Vitro and In Vivo 5α Reductase Inhibition. *The Prostate* 1993, **22**, 43-51.
28. European Scientific Cooperative on Phytotherapy. Urticae radix - Nettle Root. In: *ESCOP Monographs - The Scientific Foundation for Herbal Medicinal Products, 2nd ed.* Stuttgart-New York: Thieme, Exeter, UK: ESCOP, 2003:528-535.
29. Wagner H, Willer F and Kreher B. Biologically Active Compounds from the Aqueous Extract of *Urtica dioica. Planta Medica* 1989, **55**, 452-454 [GERMAN/English summary].
30. Dunzendorfer U. Der Nachweis von Reaktionseffekten des Extractum Radicis Urticae (ERU) im menschlichen Prostatagewebe durch Fluoreszenzmikroskopie [The identification of reaction effects of Extractum Radicis Urticae (ERU) in human prostatic tissue by fluorescence microscopy]. *Z. Phytotherapie* 1984, **5**, 800-804 [GERMAN].
31. Oberholzer M, Schamböck A, Rugendorff EW, Mihatsch M, Rist M, Buser M and Heitz PU. Elektronenmikroskopische Ergebnisse bei medikamentös behandelter benigner Prostatahyperplasie (BPH) [Electron microscopy results in the medicinal treatment of benign prostatic hyperplasia (BPH)]. In: Bauer HW, editor. *Klinische und experimentelle Urologie 14: Benigne Prostatahyperplasie.* ISBN 3-88603-196-9. München-Bern-Wien-San Francisco: Zuckschwerdt, 1987:13-17 [GERMAN].
32. Ziegler H. Fluoreszenzmikroskopische Untersuchungen von Prostatazellen unter Einwirkung von Extract Radicis Urticae (ERU) [Investigation by fluorescence microscopy of prostate cells treated with nettle root extract]. *Fortschr. Med.* 1983, **101**, 2112-2114 [GERMAN/English summary].
33. Vontobel HP, Herzog R, Rutishauser G and Kres H. Results of a double-blind study on the efficacy of ERU [Extractum Radix Urticae] capsules in the conservative treatment of benign prostatic hyperplasia. *Urologe A* 1985, **24**, 49-51 [GERMAN/English summary].
34. Dathe G and Schmid H. Phytotherapie der benignen Prostatahyperplasie (BPH). Doppelblindstudie mit Extraktum Radicis Urticae (ERU) [Phytotherapy of benign prostatic hyperplasia. Double-blind study with Extractum Radicis Urticae (ERU)]. *Urologe B* 1987, *27*, 223-226 [GERMAN].
35. Fischer M and Wilbert D. Wirkprüfung eines Phytopharmakons zur Behandlung der benignen Prostatahyperplasie (BPH) [Trial of a phytomedicine for the treatment of benign prostatic hyperplasia (BPH)]. In: Rutishauser G, editor. *Klinische und experimentelle Urologie 22: Benigne Prostatahyperplasie III.* ISBN 3-88603-404-6. München-Bern-Wien-New York: Zuckschwerdt, 1992:79-84 [GERMAN].
36. Schneider T and Rübben H. Extract of stinging nettle roots (Bazoton®-uno) in long-term treatment of benign prostatic syndrome (BPS). Results of a randomized, double-blind, placebo-controlled multicenter study after 12 months. *Urologe [A]* 2004, **43**, 302-306 [GERMAN/English summary].
37. Engelmann U, Boos G and Kres H. Therapie der benignen

Prostatahyperplasie mit Bazoton Liquidum. Ergebnisse einer doppelblinden, placebokontrollierten, klinischen Studie [Therapy of benign prostatic hyperplasia with Bazoton Liquid. Results of a double-blind, placebo-controlled, clinical study]. *Urologe B* 1996, **36**, 287-291 [GERMAN].
38. Tosch U and Müssiggang H. Medikamentöse Behandlung der benignen Prostatahyperplasie [Medicinal treatment of benign prostatic hyperplasia]. *Euromed* 1983, (6), 334-336 [GERMAN].
39. Stahl H-P. Die Therapie prostatischer Nykturie mit standardisierten Extraktum Radix Urticae (ERU) [Treatment of prostatic nocturia with standardized Extractum Radix Urticae (ERU)]. *Z. Allgemeinmed.* 1984, **60**, 128-132 [GERMAN].
40. Friesen A. Statistische Analyse einer Multizenter-Langzeitstudie mit ERU [Statistical analysis of a multicentric long-term study with ERU (Extractum Radix Urticae)]. In: Bauer HW, editor. *Klinische und experimentelle Urologie 19: Benigne Prostatahyperplasie II.* ISBN 3-88603-302-3. München-Bern-Wien-New York: Zuckschwerdt, 1988: 121-130 [GERMAN].
41. Kaldewey W. Behandlung der benignen Prostatahyperplasie und der Prostatitis mit einem standardisierten Urticae-radix-Extrakt. Eine multizentrische Studie in 279 urologischen Praxen [Treatment of benign prostatic hyperplasia and prostatitis with a standardized Urticae radix extract. A multicentric study in 279 urological practices]. *Urologe B* 1995, **35**, 430-433 [GERMAN].
42. Djulepa J. Zweijährige Erfahrung in der Therapie des Prostata-Syndroms. Die Ergebnisse einer konservativen Behandlung mit Bazoton® [Two-year experience in the therapy of prostate syndrome. Results of a conservative treatment with Bazoton®]. *Ärztl. Praxis* 1982, **34**, 2199-2202 [GERMAN].
43. Vandierendounck EJ and Burkhardt P. Extractum radicis Urticae bei Fibromyoadenom der Prostata mit nächtlicher Pollakisurie. Studie zur Prüfung der Wirkung von ZY 15095 (Simic®) [Extractum radicis Urticae for fibromyoma of the prostate with nocturnal pollakiuria. Study to evaluate the effect of ZY 15095 (Simic®)]. *Therapiewoche Schweiz.* 1986, **2**, 892-895 [GERMAN].
44. Maar K. Rückbildung der Symptomatik von Prostataadenomen. Ergebnisse einer sechsmonatigen konservativen behandlung mit ERU-Kapseln [Retrogression of the symptomatology of prostate adenoma. Results of a six-month conservative treatment with ERU Capsules]. *Fortschr. Med.* 1987, **105**, 18-20 [GERMAN/English summary].
45. Bauer HW, Sudhoff F and Dressler S. Endokrine Parameter während der Behandlung der benignen Prostatahyperplasie mit ERU [Endocrine parameters during treatment of benign prostatic hyperplasia with ERU]. In: Bauer HW, editor. *Klinische und experimentelle Urologie 19: Benigne Prostatahyperplasie II.* München-Bern-Wien-New York: Zuckschwerdt, 1988:44-9 [GERMAN].
46. Feiber H. Sonographische Verlaufsbeobachtungen zum Einfluß der medikamentösen Therapie der benignen Prostatahyperplasie (BPH) [Sonographic monitoring of the influence of medicinal therapy on benign prostatic hyperplasia (BPH)]. In: Bauer HW, editor. *Klinische und experimentelle Urologie 19: Benigne Prostatahyperplasie II.* München-Bern-Wien-New York: Zuckschwerdt, 1988:75-82 [GERMAN].
47. Goetz P. Die Behandlung der benignen Prostatahyperplasie mit Brennesselwurzeln [Treatment of benign prostatic hyperplasia with nettle root]. *Z. Phytotherapie* 1989, **10**, 175-178 [GERMAN/English summary].
48. Belaiche P and Lievoux O. Clinical Studies on the Palliative Treatment of Prostatic Adenoma with Extract of *Urtica* Root. *Phytotherapy Res.* 1991, **5**, 267-269.
49. Wichtl M and Grimm U. Brennesselwurzel - Urticae radix. In: Hartke K, Hartke H, Mutschler E, Rücker G and Wichtl M, editors. *Kommentar zum Deutschen Arzneibuch.* Stuttgart: Wissenschaftliche Verlagsgesellschaft, 2000 (13 Lfg.):B 54 [GERMAN].
50. Lowe FC and Fagelman E. Phytotherapy in the treatment of benign prostatic hyperplasia: An update. *Urology* 1999, **53**, 671-678.
51. Wilt TJ, Ishani A, Rutks I and MacDonald R. Phytotherapy for benign prostatic hyperplasia. In: Loew D, Blume H and Dingermann T, editors. *Phytopharmaka V. Forschung und klinische Anwendung.* ISBN 3-7985-1203-5. Darmstadt: Steinkopff, 1999:165-177.
52. Urticae radix (Brennesselwurzel). German Commission E Monograph published in: Bundesanzeiger No. 173 of 18.09.86; amended in Bundesanzeiger No. 43 of 2.03.89, No. 50 of 13.03.90 and No. 11 of 17.01.91.
53. Ortie dioïque. In: *Médicaments à base de plantes.* ISBN 2-911473-02-7. Saint-Denis Cedex, France: Agence du Médicament, 1998.
54. Nettle (Urtica dioica). In: UK Statutory Instrument 1990 No. 1129. The Medicines (Products Other Than Veterinary Drugs) (General Sale List) Amendment Order 1990. Schedule 1, Table A.

REGULATORY GUIDELINES FROM OTHER EU COUNTRIES

FRANCE

Médicaments à base de plantes [53]: Ortie dioïque, organes souterrains.

Therapeutic indications accepted

Oral use
Traditionally used to promote the renal elimination of water.
Traditionally used as an adjuvant in micturition disorders of prostatic origin.

GERMANY

Commission E monograph [52]: Urticae radix (Brennesselwurzel).

Uses
Micturition disorders in prostatic adenoma stages I and II.

Contraindications
None known.

Side effects
Occasionally, mild gastro-intestinal upsets.

Interactions with other drugs
None known.

Dosage
Unless otherwise prescribed, daily dose: 4-6 g of the drug or equivalent preparations.

Mode of administration
Comminuted drug for infusions and other galenic preparations for internal use.

Actions
Increase in urinary volume.
Increase in maximum urinary flow.
Reduction in residual urine.
Note: This medication improves only the symptoms of an enlarged prostate, without reducing the enlargement. Therefore please consult your doctor at regular intervals.

OAK BARK

Fagaceae

Quercus cortex

Synonyms: Common, English or Pedunculate Oak Bark (*Quercus robur*); Sessile or Durmast Oak Bark (*Quercus petraea*).

Definition

Oak Bark consists of dried bark from the fresh young branches of *Quercus robur* L. [*Q. pedunculata* Ehrh.], *Quercus petraea* (Matt.) Liebl. [*Q. sessiliflora* Salisb.] or *Quercus pubescens* Willd.

CONSTITUENTS

☐ ***Hydrolysable tannins*** The ellagitannins 2,3-(S)-hexahydroxydiphenoylglucose, pedunculagin, castalagin and its epimer vescalagin, the flavano-ellagitannins acutissimin A, acutissimin B, eugenigrandin A, guajavin B and stenophyllanin C, and the procyanidinoellagitannin mongolicanin have been isolated from *Quercus petraea* bark [1].

Castalagin and vescalagin were found in the inner bark but not the outer bark of *Quercus robur*; other hexahydroxydiphenoyl esters were found in both inner and outer bark [2].

The structures of castalagin, vescalagin, acutissimins A and B and mongolicanin were revised in 1990 [3].

☐ ***Condensed tannins (proanthocyanidins)*** *Quercus robur* bark [4] and *Quercus petraea* bark [5] contain a mixture of oligomeric and polymeric proanthocyanidins, mainly with [4→8] linkages, together with related monomers.

More than 20 compounds have been isolated from *Quercus robur* bark including monomeric (+)-catechin, (+)-catechin 3-gallate, (+)-gallocatechin, (–)-epicatechin, (–)-epicatechin 3-gallate, (–)-epigallocatechin and (–)-epigallocatechin 3-gallate; six dimers, for example (+)-catechin-[4α→8]-(+)-catechin (procyanidin B-3); and six oligomers consisting of 3-8 units, designated as proanthocyanidins D14-D19 [4]. Catechin-[6′→8]-catechin, gallocatechin-[6′→8]-catechin [6] and the trimer catechin-[6′→8]-catechin-[4→8]-catechin [7] have also been isolated from *Quercus robur* bark but were not found in *Q. petraea* bark [5].

Compounds isolated from *Quercus petraea* bark include monomeric (+)-catechin and (+)-gallocatechin, and the dimers catechin-[4α→8]-catechin and gallocatechin-[4α→8]-catechin. The proanthocyanidins had an average degree of polymerization of 6.1 and a procyanidin to prodelphinidin ratio of 6:4 [5].

The total tannin content of oak bark is usually in the range 8-15% [4,8] (Ph. Eur. min. 3.0%).

Published Assay Methods

Determination of tannins in herbal drugs [Ph. Eur. method 2.8.14].

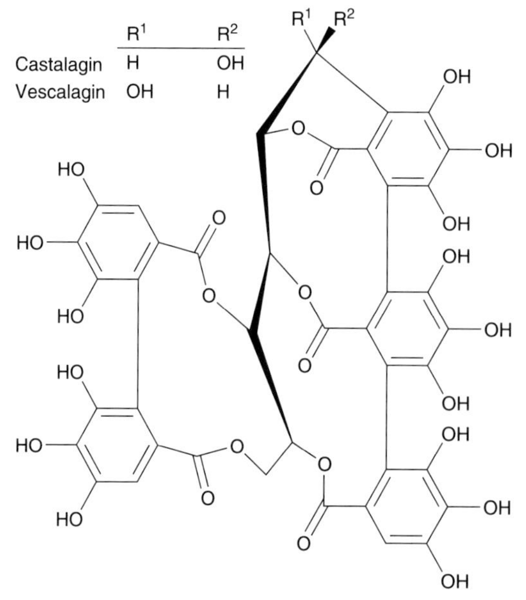

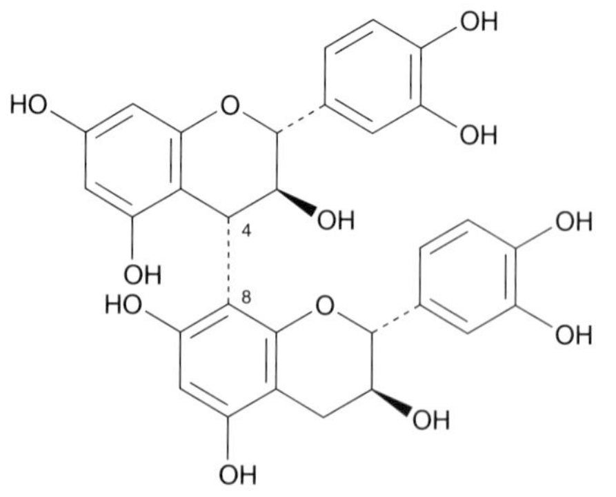

(+)-Catechin-[4α→8]-(+)-catechin
(Procyanidin B-3)

PHARMACOLOGY

In vitro

Although ellagitannins represent 77% of the total tannins in *Quercus petraea* bark, their relative astringencies are rather low (from 0.20 for pedunculagin to 0.46 for eugenigrandin A, compared to 1.0 for a standard tannin) and they contribute only 45% of the astringency of the bark. The astringency of the crude drug is mainly attributed to oligomeric proanthocyanidins, the proanthocyanidin fraction having a relative astringency of 1.14 [1].

In antibacterial screening of 48 plants traditionally used in the treatment of infected skin lesions, an aqueous extract from *Quercus robur* bark showed outstanding antibacterial activity against *Staphylococcus aureus* and *Escherichia coli* with a minimum inhibitory concentration of 0.08 mg dry extract per ml [9]. An aqueous extract from *Quercus robur* bark also exhibited antiviral activity against herpes, influenza and vaccine viruses [10].

A 50% ethanolic extract from *Quercus robur* bark exhibited strong scavenging activity against superoxide anion and singlet oxygen with IC_{50} values of 1.0 and 16.1 µg (dry extract)/ml respectively (both less than those of ascorbic acid), and at 50 µg/ml a strong protective effect ($p<0.01$) on fibroblasts exposed to active oxygen species, 69.9% expressed as the survival ratio. The results suggest that the bark contains chain-breaking antioxidants which are able to inhibit peroxidation chain reactions [11].

Tannins of natural or synthetic origin are used in topical anti-inflammatory therapy of skin ailments; *in vitro* effects related to anti-inflammatory activity have been demonstrated with a few tannins [12], but not specifically with oak bark tannins.

CLINICAL STUDIES

None published on mono-preparations of oak bark.

THERAPEUTICS

Actions

Astringent, haemostatic, antibacterial, anti-inflammatory [1,9,13,14].

Indications

None adequately substantiated by pharmacological or clinical studies.

Uses based on experience or tradition

Internal: Acute diarrhoea [13,15].

External: Haemorrhoids [13,16]; leucorrhoea [13]; inflammation of the oral/pharyngeal mucosa (including tonsillitis) or anal/genital area [13,15]; inflammatory skin complaints [15], acute or weeping eczema [14,16], boils and abscesses, varicose leg ulcers, dermatitis, chilblains and sweaty feet [16].

Contraindications

Internal use: None known.

External use: Full baths are not recommended for extensive eczema or skin damage; partial baths should be applied [15].

Side effects

None known.

Interactions with other drugs

Internal use: Absorption of alkaloids or other alkaline drugs may be inhibited [15].

Dosage

Internal daily dose: Dried bark or by decoction, 3-6 g; liquid extract 1:1 in 25% alcohol, 3-6 ml. For acute diarrhoea, take in frequent small doses [13] for no longer than 3-4 days.

External use: 20 g of bark per litre of water [15] in decoction, as an enema for haemorrhoids [13]; as a mouthwash or gargle for oral/pharyngeal use [13,15]; as a compress for application to the anal/genital area [15], skin complaints and varicose leg ulcers; as a fomentation for boils or abscesses [16]; as a douche for leucorrhoea [13] or as a styptic. 100 g of bark per litre of water in decoction as a partial bath for chilblains or sweaty feet [16].

REGULATORY STATUS

Medicines

UK	Accepted for general sale, internal or external use [17].
France	Not listed in *Médicaments à base de plantes* [18].
Germany	Commission E monograph published, with approved uses [15].

Foods

Council of Europe	*Quercus robur* bark permitted as flavouring, category N2 [19].

REFERENCES

Current Pharmacopoeial Monographs

Ph. Eur. Oak Bark

Literature References

1. König M, Scholz E, Hartmann R, Lehmann W and Rimpler H. Ellagitannins and complex tannins from *Quercus petraea* Bark. *J. Nat. Prod.* 1994, **57**, 1411-1415.

2. Scalbert A, Monties B and Favre J-M. Polyphenols of *Quercus robur*. Adult tree and *in vitro* grown calli and shoots. *Phytochemistry* 1988, **27**, 3483-3488.
3. Nonaka G-i, Sakai T, Tanaka T, Mihashi K and Nishioka I. Tannins and Related Compounds. XCVII. Structure Revision of C-Glycosidic Ellagitannins, Castalagin, Vescalagin, Casuarinin and Stachyurin, and Related Hydrolyzable Tannins. *Chem. Pharm. Bull.* 1990, **38**, 2151-2156.
4. Kuliev ZA, Vdovin AD, Abdullaev ND, Makhmatkulov AB and Malikov VM. Study of the catechins and proanthocyanidins of Quercus robur. *Khim. Prir. Soedin.* 1997, (6), 819-833 [RUSSIAN], translated into English as: *Chem. Nat. Compd.* 1997, **33**, 642-652.
5. Pallenbach E, Scholz E, König M and Rimpler H. Proanthocyanidins from *Quercus petraea* Bark. *Planta Medica* 1993, **59**, 264-268.
6. Ahn B-Z and Gstirner F. Catechin-dimers Contained in Oak Bark. *Arch. Pharm. (Weinheim)* 1971, **304**, 666-673 [GERMAN/English summary].
7. Ahn B-Z. A Catechin-trimer from Oak Bark. *Arch. Pharm. (Weinheim)* 1974, **307**, 186-197 [GERMAN/English summary].
8. Scholz E and Rimpler H. Phytochemie der Gerbstoffdrogen der deutschsprachigen Arzneibücher. [Phytochemistry of tannin-containing drugs of German language pharmacopoeias]. *Österreich. Apoth. Ztg.* 1994, **48**, 138-141 [GERMAN].
9. Brantner A and Grein E. Antibacterial activity of plant extracts used externally in traditional medicine. *J. Ethnopharmacol.* 1994, **44**, 35-40.
10. May G and Willuhn G. Antiviral Activity of Aqueous Extracts from Medicinal Plants in Tissue Cultures. *Arzneim.-Forsch./ Drug Res.* 1978, **28**, 1-7 [GERMAN/English summary].
11. Masaki H, Sakaki S, Atsumi T and Sakurai H. Active-Oxygen Scavenging Activity of Plant Extracts. *Biol. Pharm. Bull.* 1995, **18**, 162-166.
12. Mrowietz U, Ternowitz T and Wiedow O. Selective Inactivation of Human Neutrophil Elastase by Synthetic Tannin. *J. Invest. Dermatol.* 1991, **97**, 529-533.
13. Quercus. In: *British Herbal Pharmacopoeia 1983*. ISBN 0-903032-07-9. Bournemouth: British Herbal Medicine Association, 1983.
14. Grimme H and Augustin M. Phytotherapy in Chronic Dermatoses and Wounds: What is the Evidence? *Forsch. Komplementärmed.* 1999, **6** (Suppl. 2), 5-8 [GERMAN/ English summary].
15. Quercus cortex (Eichenrinde): German Commission E Monograph published in: Bundesanzeiger No. 22 of 1 February 1990.
16. Weiss RF and Fintelmann V. Dermatologic Disease. In: *Herbal Medicine*, 2nd ed. (translated from the 9th German Edition of *Lehrbuch der Phytotherapie*). ISBN 3-13-126332-6. Stuttgart: Thieme, 2000:293-313.
17. Oak Bark. In: UK Statutory Instrument 1994 No. 2410. The Medicines (Products Other Than Veterinary Drugs) (General Sale List) Amendment Order 1994. Schedule 1, Table A.
18. *Médicaments à base de plantes*. ISBN 2-911473-02-7. Saint-Denis Cedex, France: Agence du Médicament, 1998.
19. Quercus pedunculata Ehrh. (Quercus robur L.). In: *Flavouring Substances and Natural Sources of Flavourings, 3rd ed.* ISBN 2-7160-0081-6. Strasbourg: Council of Europe, 1981.

REGULATORY GUIDELINES FROM OTHER EU COUNTRIES

GERMANY

Commission E monograph [15]: Quercus cortex (Eichenrinde).

Uses
External use: Inflammatory skin complaints.
Internal use: Non-specific acute diarrhoea. Local treatment of mild inflammation in the oral/pharyngeal or genital/anal areas.

Contraindications
Internal use: None known.
External use: Widespread skin damage. Baths: irrespective of the particular active substances, full baths should not be taken in cases of: widespread weeping eczema or skin injuries; feverish and infectious illnesses; cardiac insufficiency classes III and IV (NY Heart Association); hypertonia class 4 (WHO).

Side effects
None known.

Interactions with other drugs
External use: None known.
Internal use: Absorption of alkaloids and other alkaline drugs may be reduced or prevented.

Dosage
Unless otherwise prescribed, internal daily dose: 3 g of the drug; equivalent preparations.
For rinses, compresses or gargles, 20 g of the drug per litre of water; equivalent preparations.
For full or partial baths, 5 g of the drug per litre of water; equivalent preparations.

Mode of administration
Comminuted drug for decoctions and other galenic preparations for internal or external use.

Duration of administration
If diarrhoea persists for more than 3-4 days, consult a doctor. In other indications: not more than 2-3 weeks.

Actions
Astringent, virostatic.

PARSLEY ROOT Umbelliferae

Petroselini radix

Synonyms: *Petroselinum crispum* has numerous botanical synonyms including *P. sativum* Hoffm., *P. hortense* Hoffm., *Carum petroselinum* Benth. et Hook.f. and *Apium petroselinum* L.

Definition

Parsley Root consists of the dried roots of *Petroselinum crispum* (Mill.) Nyman ex A.W. Hill.

Two subspecies of *Petroselinum crispum* can be distinguished [1]:

- ssp. *crispum*, cultivated for the leaf as smooth-leaved and curly-leaved varieties.
- ssp. *tuberosum*, cultivated for the thicker root (similar in shape and colour to a parsnip).

Some texts define parsley root for use in herbal medicine as ssp. *tuberosum*; it is not entirely clear whether the root of ssp. *crispum* is also used to some extent.

CONSTITUENTS

☐ ***Flavonoids***, ca. 1.6% of dry weight, the principal one being apiin (apigenin 7-apiosylglucoside) [1].

☐ ***Essential oil***, reported as 0.1-0.3% of dry weight in ssp. *tuberosum*, 0.2-0.5% in ssp. *crispum* (curly-leaved variety) and 0.45-0.75% in ssp. *crispum* (smooth-leaved variety) [1].

The constituents of ether-extracted oils from roots of ssp. *tuberosum* and ssp. *crispum* were found to be qualitatively similar but showed quantitative differences among some 44 components. Polyacetylenes were predominant in ssp. *tuberosum* roots, whereas phenylpropanoids (mainly apiole and myristicin) were predominant in ssp. *crispum*. The proportions of phytochemical groups, as percentages of the ether-extracted oil, were [2]:

	ssp. *tuberosum*	ssp. *crispum*
Polyacetylenes	45.9	16.8
Phenylpropanoids	14.7	37.5
Phthalides	13.2	7.2
Terpenes	12.8	30.7
Furanocoumarins	3.5	3.0
	90.1%	95.2%

The following constituents include those identified in the ether-extracted oil.

☐ ***Polyacetylenes*** The C_{17} acetylenic alcohol falcarinol with a smaller amount of falcarindiol [2,3].

☐ ***Phenylpropanoids***, principally the methylenedioxy-benzene derivatives apiole and myristicin [2,4]. The ratio of apiole to myristicin was reported as about 1:1 in ssp. *tuberosum* and 3:1 in ssp. *crispum* [2].

☐ ***Phthalides*** Sedanenolide, *E*-ligustilide, 3-n-butylphthalide and others [2]. Senkyunolide has also been reported in ssp. *tuberosum* [5].

☐ ***Terpenes***, principally the monoterpenes β-pinene and β-phellandrene, and the sesquiterpene β-sesquiphellandrene [2].

☐ ***Furanocoumarins*** Xanthotoxin, bergapten, isopimpinellin and others [2]. Oxypeucedanin (88 µg/g of fresh weight) was found to be the major furanocoumarin in roots of ssp. *crispum* (described only as a 'curled leaf variety') [6]. Isoimperatorin has also been isolated from ssp. *crispum* (described only as *Petroselinum sativum* L.) [7].

Published Assay Methods

Ether-extracted oil components by GC and GC-MS [2]. Apiole and myristicin in distilled oil by GC [4].

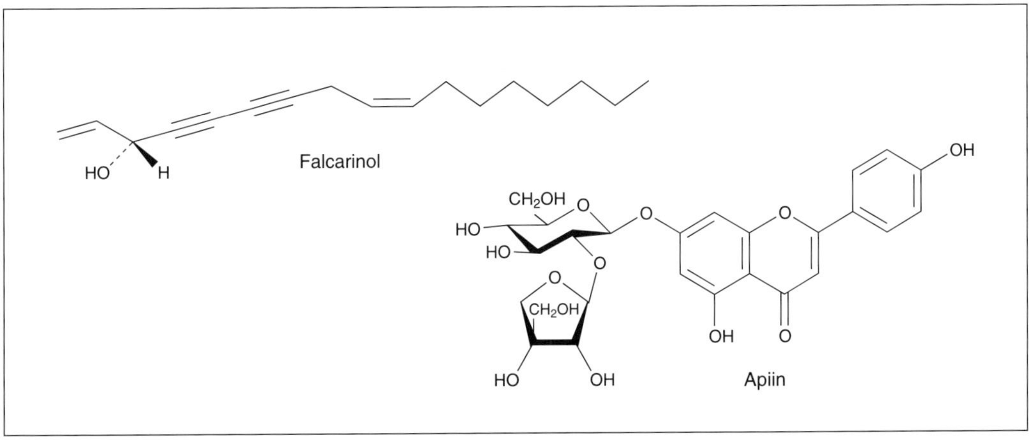

PHARMACOLOGY

Few pharmacological studies have been carried out on parsley root.

In vitro

Apiin strongly inhibited pyrazine cation free radical formation in model chemical systems by 71-88%; this was interpreted as antimutagenic potential [8].

In vivo

Orally administered myristicin induced increased activity of the detoxifying enzyme glutathione *S*-transferase in several mouse target tissues, showing high activity in the liver and small intestinal mucosa; this was taken as an indication that myristicin has anticarcinogenic potential [9]. However, it should be noted that myristicin and apiole are methoxysafroles, and safrole itself is known to be carcinogenic and hepatotoxic.

CLINICAL STUDIES

None published on mono-preparations of parsley root.

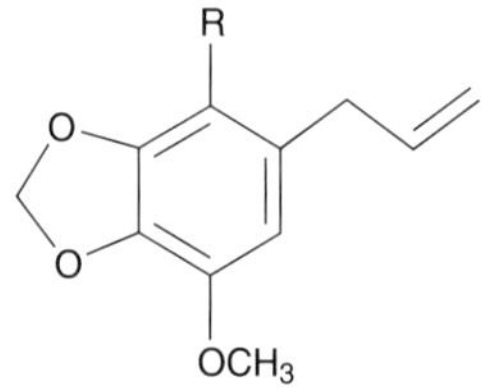

Apiole R = OCH_3
Myristicin R = H

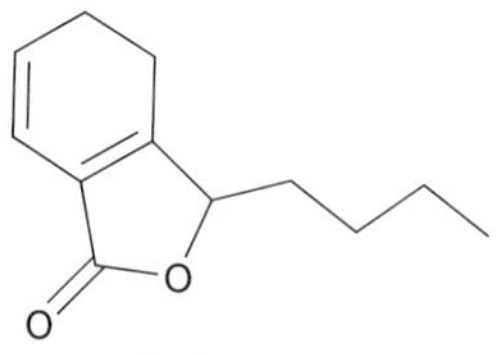

Sedanenolide

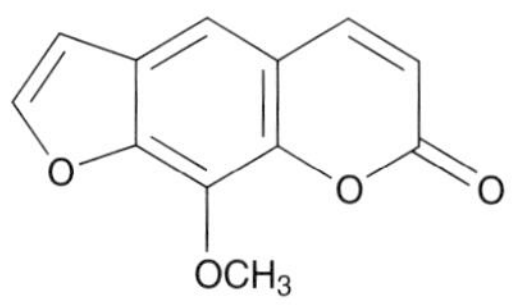

Xanthotoxin

THERAPEUTICS

Actions

Diuretic [10-12], carminative [10,11], spasmolytic [10] and emmenagogic [10,12].

The volatile oil is a strong uterine stimulant [13]; apiole extracted from parsley (fruits) was at one time used as an emmenagogue and diuretic [14]. It has been suggested that the diuretic effect of parsley root is mainly due to apiole and myristicin [4,15].

Indications

None adequately substantiated by pharmacological or clinical studies.

Uses based on experience or tradition

Digestive complaints such as flatulence [10,11, 13], dyspepsia [10] and intestinal colic; urinary tract complaints including cystitis [10,13], dysuria [10] and renal gravel [11,16]; dysmenorrhoea and functional amenorrhoea [10,13,17]; myalgia (internal or topical use) [10] and rheumatic conditions [13].

Contraindications

Pregnancy; inflammatory kidney disorders [16].

Side effects

In rare cases, contact allergic reactions of skin are possible [3].

Interactions with other drugs

None known.

Dosage

Three times daily: dried root, 2-3 g or by infusion or decoction [10,12,16]; liquid extract 1:1 in 25% alcohol, 2-3 ml [10,12].

The use of isolated essential oil is not recommended due to its potential toxicity.

SAFETY

In the Ames test, parsley herb (which has many constituents in common with parsley root, including apiole and myristicin) exhibited no mutagenic potential using *Salmonella typhimurium* strains TA98 or TA102 [18].

Contact dermatitis and skin irritation from parsley root are possible, especially due to the sensitization and allergenic potential of falcarinol and falcarindiol [3].

Intravenous LD_{50} values of apiole and myristicin in mice were determined as 200 and 500 mg/kg respectively [15].

Apiole has been used as an abortifacient and has caused deaths, the lowest known doses causing these effects being 0.9 g taken for 8 consecutive days, and 2.1 g for 3 days, respectively. Oral use of the essential oil is therefore considered inadvisable [19]. Although these data are scarcely relevant to therapeutic doses of parsley root or its preparations, it is prudent to avoid medicinal use during pregnancy.

REGULATORY STATUS

Medicines

UK	Accepted for general sale, internal or external use [20].
France	Accepted for specified indications [17].
Germany	Commission E monograph published, with approved uses [16].

Food

USA	Generally recognized as safe (21 CFR 182.10 and 182.20) [21].
Council of Europe	Permitted as flavouring, category N2 [22].

REFERENCES

Current Pharmacopoeial Monographs

BHP Parsley Root

Literature References

1. Warncke D. *Petroselinum crispum* - Die Gartenpetersilie [The garden parsley]. *Z. Phytotherapie* 1994, **15**, 50-58 [GERMAN/English summary].
2. Spraul MH, Nitz S and Drawert F. About the chemical composition of parsley root and seed extractives. *Chem. Mikrobiol. Technol. Lebensm.* 1991, **13**, 179-182.
3. Nitz S, Spraul MH and Drawert F. C_{17} Polyacetylenic Alcohols as the Major Constituents in Roots of *Petroselinum crispum* Mill. ssp. *tuberosum*. *J. Agric. Food Chem.* 1990, **38**, 1445-1447.
4. Marczal G, Balogh M and Verzár-Petri G. Phenol-ether components of diuretic effect in Parsley, I. *Acta Agron. Acad. Sci. Hung.* 1977, **26**, 7-13.
5. Gijbels MJM, Fischer FC, Scheffer JJC and Baerheim Svendsen A. Phthalides in Roots of *Apium graveolens, A. graveolens* var. *rapaceum, Bifora testiculata* and *Petroselinum crispum* var. *tuberosum*. *Fitoterapia* 1985, **56**, 17-23.
6. Chaudhary SK, Ceska O, Têtu C, Warrington PJ, Ashwood-Smith MJ and Poulton GA. Oxypeucedanin, a Major Furocoumarin in Parsley, *Petroselinum crispum*. *Planta Medica* 1986, **52**, 462-464.
7. Bohlmann F. Notiz über die Inhaltsstoffe von Petersilie- und Sellerie-Wurzeln [Note on the constituents of parsley and celery roots]. *Chem. Ber.* 1967, **100**, 3454-3456 [GERMAN].
8. Milic BL and Milic NB. Protective Effects of Spice Plants on Mutagenesis. *Phytotherapy Res.* 1998, **12**, S3-S6.
9. Zheng G-Q, Kenney PM and Lam LKT. Myristicin: A Potential Cancer Chemopreventive Agent from Parsley Leaf Oil. *J. Agric. Food Chem.* 1992, **40**, 107-110.
10. Petroselinum. In: *British Herbal Pharmacopoeia 1983*. ISBN 0-903032-07-4. Bournemouth: British Herbal Medicine Association, 1983.
11. Grieve M (edited by Leyel CF). Parsley. In: *A Modern Herbal* (first published 1931; revised 1973). ISBN 1-85501-249-9. London: Tiger Books International, 1994:611-614.
12. Todd RG, editor. Parsley. In: *Extra Pharmacopoeia: Martindale, 25th edition*. London: Pharmaceutical Press, 1967:1540.
13. Chevallier A. Parsley. In: *The Encyclopedia of Medicinal Plants*. ISBN 0-7513-0314-3. London-New York-Stuttgart: Dorling Kindersley, 1996:244.
14. Pharmaceutical Society of Great Britain. Apiol. In: *British Pharmaceutical Codex 1934*. London: Pharmaceutical Press, 1934:145.
15. Buchanan RL. Toxicity of spices containing methylenedioxybenzene derivatives: a review. *J. Food Safety* 1978, **1**, 275-293.
16. Petroselini herba/radix. German Commission E Monograph published in: Bundesanzeiger No. 43 of 2 March 1989.
17. Persil [Parsley]. In: *Médicaments à base de plantes*. ISBN 2-911473-02-7. Saint-Denis Cedex, France: Agence du Médicament, 1998.
18. Mahmoud I, Alkofahi A and Abdelaziz A. Mutagenic and Toxic Activities of Several Spices and Some Jordanian Medicinal Plants. *Int. J. Pharmacognosy* 1992, **30**, 81-85.
19. Tisserand R and Balacs T. Apiol (parsley apiol). In: *Essential Oil Safety - A Guide for Health Care Professionals*. Edinburgh: Churchill-Livingstone, 1995:183.
20. Parsley. In: UK Statutory Instrument 1994 No. 2410. The Medicines (Products Other Than Veterinary Drugs) (General Sale List) Amendment Order 1994. Schedule 1, Table A.
21. Parsley, *Petroselinum crispum* (Mill.) Mansf. In: Sections 182.10 and 182.20 of USA Code of Federal Regulations, Title 21, Food and Drugs, Parts 170 to 199. Revised as of April 1, 2000.
22. Petroselinum sativum Hoffm., roots. In: *Flavouring Substances and Natural Sources of Flavourings, 3rd ed.* ISBN 2-7160-0081-6. Strasbourg: Council of Europe, 1981.

REGULATORY GUIDELINES FROM OTHER EU COUNTRIES

FRANCE

Médicaments à base de plantes [17]: Persil; fruit, racine.

Therapeutic indications accepted

Oral use
Traditionally used for painful periods.
Traditionally used to promote the renal elimination of water.

GERMANY

Commission E monograph [16]: Petroselini herba/radix (Petersilienkraut/wurzel).

Uses

Irrigation in complaints of the lower urinary tract and in the prevention and treatment of renal gravel.

Contraindications

Pregnancy; inflammatory kidney disorders.

Caution: Irrigation therapy not to be used in cases of oedema due to impaired cardiac or renal function.

Side effects
In rare cases, allergic reactions of skin or mucosa are possible. Particularly in light-skinned persons, phototoxic reactions are possible.

Interactions with other drugs
None known.

Dosage
Unless otherwise prescribed, daily dose: 6 g of the drug; equivalent preparations.

Mode of administration
Comminuted drug for infusions and other galenic preparations with a comparably low content of essential oil, for oral use.

Caution: Isolated essential oil should not be used due to its toxicity.
Copious amounts of fluid should be taken during irrigation therapy.

PILEWORT HERB/ROOT

Ranunculaceae

Ranunculi ficariae herba/radix

Synonym: Lesser Celandine.

Definition

Pilewort Herb consists of the dried flowering aerial parts, and Pilewort Root of the dried tuberous roots, of *Ranunculus ficaria* L. [*Ficaria ranunculoides* Moench, *Ficaria verna* Huds.].

Traditions differ with respect to the part of the plant used in phytotherapy. The herb (and sometimes the whole plant) has been used in the UK, while the tuberous root is generally used in France.

CONSTITUENTS

HERB

☐ ***Triterpene saponins*** (0.7% of dry material), with hederagenin and oleanolic acid as sapogenins and glucose, rhamnose and arabinose as glycosidic sugars [1].

☐ ***Lactones*** Protoanemonin, a vesicant oil, obtained by steam distillation from fresh plant material was found to be distributed in a very organ-specific way, the highest amounts being present in stems (0.26% of fresh weight; 67% of total protoanemonin in the plant) and flowers (0.19% of fresh weight; 25% of the total protoanemonin) with very little in the leaves (0.012%) [2]. Since 1 g of protoanemonin is equivalent to 2.688 g of the glucoside ranunculin (see next paragraph), these figures indicate 0.7% of ranunculin in fresh stems, 0.5% in fresh flowers and 0.03% in fresh leaves.

Although not demonstrated specifically for pilewort it has been shown that, in intact plants of species of the Ranunculaceae family, protoanemonin is glucosidically bound in the form of ranunculin, which is hydrolysed by an endogenous enzyme to protoanemonin during maceration of fresh plant tissue; it can also be obtained by steam distillation of the fresh plant. Ranunculin (a stable, water-soluble solid) can be extracted from freeze-dried plant material with methanol and assayed or isolated [3,4]. Protoanemonin gradually and spontaneously dimerizes to anemonin, a water-insoluble substance with no vesicant properties [5], hence neither ranunculin nor protoanemonin are likely to be present in stored, air-dried material.

☐ ***Flavonoids*** Flavonol-*O*-glycosides including the 3-glucosides (i.e. astragalin and isoquercitrin), 3-rutinosides (i.e. nicotiflorin and rutin) and 3-rutinoside-7-glucosides of kaempferol and quercetin, as well as free kaempferol. Also flavone-*C*-glycosides including apigenin 8-*C*-glucoside (vitexin), apigenin 8-*C*-(2″-*O*-glucosyl)-glucoside (flavosativaside) and luteolin 8-*C*-glucoside (orientin) [6-9].

From HPLC analysis after acid hydrolysis, which hydrolyses *O*-glycosides (but not *C*-glycosides) to the corresponding aglycones, the flavonoid content during the flowering period was 3.9-4.7% in leaves (predominantly as flavone-*C*-glycosides) and 5.7-6.7% in flowers (predominantly as flavonol aglycones) [9].

☐ ***Phenolic acids*** Caffeic, *p*-coumaric, ferulic, sinapic, *p*-hydroxybenzoic, protocatechuic, vanillic and *p*-hydroxyphenylacetic acids [6].

ROOT

☐ ***Triterpene saponins*** based mainly on the aglycone hederagenin and to a minor extent on oleanolic acid [1,10]. Although the glycosidic structures have not been fully clarified, the principal saponin is a hederagenin 3-glucoside with one or more other glucose residues [10]; another (minor) one is thought to be hederagenin 3-arabinoside 28-rhamno-diglucoside [11,12]

The saponin content has been reported as 2-2.5% in fresh roots at the stage of maximum tuberisation [13]; other authors have reported 1.8% in dried overwintering tubers and 0.5% in dried young tubers [1].

☐ ***Lactones*** Compared to the relatively high amounts in stems and flowers (see Herb above), only

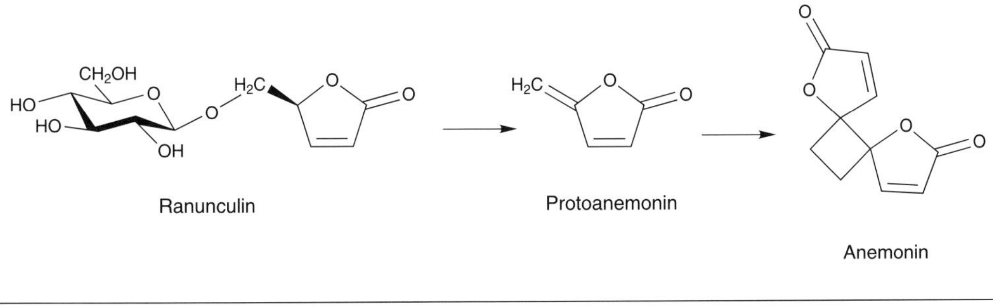

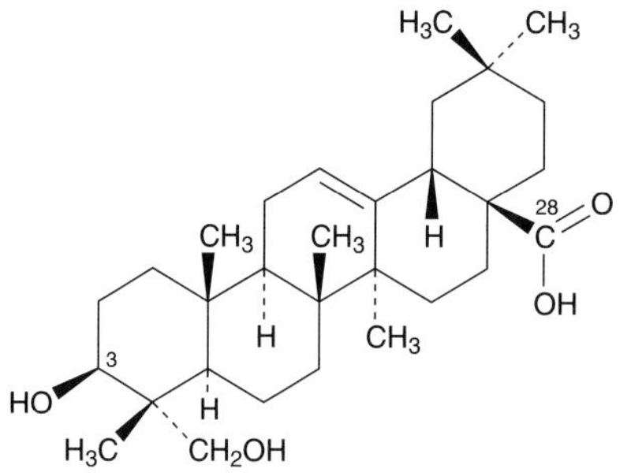

Hederagenin

a small amount of protoanemonin was obtained by steam distillation from fresh pilewort roots (0.047% of fresh weight; 4% of total protoanemonin in the whole plant) [2]; this is equivalent to about 0.13% of ranunculin in fresh roots.

□ ***Other constituents*** Gentiobiose (1%) [14], β-sitosterol and its glucoside [13] and a small amount of tannins (0.1%) [15].

Published Assay Methods

Hederagenin and oleanolic acid by HPLC [16]. Ranunculin in freeze-dried material by HPLC [3]. Protoanemonin in fresh plant by HPLC [5].

PHARMACOLOGY

Remarkably for a herbal drug which is official in the French Pharmacopoeia and has been found useful in the experience of many [13,17-19], although dismissed as ineffective by others [20], almost no modern pharmacological or clinical data on pilewort can be found in the scientific literature.

Pilewort has been used for centuries as a remedy for haemorrhoids (piles). It was so described by Gerard (1597) and Culpeper (1652) in days when the doctrine of signatures was still prevalent and, as the common name of the plant suggests, it seems likely that the use of pilewort in the treatment of haemorrhoids was to some extent based on a similarity in appearance between the elongated tubers and certain haemorrhoidal symptoms [18,20].

In 1904 Sir James Sawyer, a senior physician at a Birmingham hospital, published his formulae for pilewort ointment and suppositories from "whole fresh plant" (presumably including the tuberous roots), used for several years "with much therapeutic success" in patients suffering from haemorrhoids [21]. These formulae, almost unchanged except for "fresh herb" instead of "whole fresh plant", were subsequently included in the BPC from 1911 to 1934 [22].

While the flowering aerial parts have generally been preferred in the UK [17-19], French tradition [13,23] and the Pharmacopée Française have favoured use of the tuberous roots. Pilewort finds little recognition in Germany.

At one time internal use of pilewort as infusions was advocated [13,17,18]. Only external use in ointments or suppositories is now recommended [19,23,24]. Two reports by French authors [Palliez et al. (1968) and Delacroix (1969), cited in 9] described topical treatment of haemorrhoids with pilewort root preparations.

THERAPEUTICS

Actions

Stated to be astringent and locally demulcent [17].

Indications

None adequately substantiated by pharmacological or clinical studies.

Uses based on experience or tradition

Topical use only: Haemorrhoids [13,17-19,22-24], including internal or prolapsed piles, with or without haemorrhage [17].

Contraindications

None known.

Side effects

None known.

Interactions with other drugs

None known.

Dosage

Ointment or suppositories prepared from up to 30% of fresh [21,22] or 3% of dried [17] pilewort in a suitable base.

Note: If fresh pilewort is used, prolonged heating should be applied during ointment preparation, as described in the BPC 1934 [22] to ensure the absence of protoanemonin.

SAFETY

Although protoanemonin is a disagreeable vesicant (blistering agent) [5], it is unstable and gradually (or more rapidly during heat processing) dimerizes to anemonin, which has no vesicant properties. Protoanemonin is unlikely to be present in dried plant material or preparations, but care should be taken in the handling of fresh pilewort, especially the herb.

The intraperitoneal LD_{50} of anemonin in mice was determined as 150 mg/kg body weight [25].

REGULATORY STATUS

Medicines

UK	Accepted for general sale, internal or external use [26].
France	Accepted for specified indications [23].
Germany	No Commission E monograph published.

Food

Not used in foods.

REFERENCES

Current Pharmacopoeial Monographs

Ph. Fr.	Ficaire (tuberous root)
BHP	Pilewort (herb)

Literature References

1. Figurkin BA and Figurkina LN. Triterpene glycosides of *Ficaria verna* Huds. *Rastit. Resur.* 1976, **12**, 557-559 [RUSSIAN], through *Chem. Abstr.* 1977, **86**, 27654.
2. Bonora A, Botta B, Menziani-Andreoli E and Bruni A. Organ-specific Distribution and Accumulation of Protoanemonin in *Ranunculus ficaria* L. *Biochem. Physiol. Pflanzen.* 1988, **183**, 443-447.
3. Bai Y, Benn MH, Majak W and McDiarmid R. Extraction and HPLC Determination of Ranunculin in Species of the Buttercup Family. *J. Agric. Food Chem.* 1996, **44**, 2235-2238.
4. Hill R and van Heyningen R. Ranunculin: The Precursor of the Vesicant Substance of the Buttercup. *Biochem. J.* 1951, **49**, 332-335.
5. Bonora A, Dall'Olio G and Bruni A. Separation and Quantitation of Protoanemonin in Ranunculaceae by Normal- and Reversed-Phase HPLC. *Planta Medica* 1985, **51**, 364-367.
6. Gudej J and Tomczyk M. Polyphenolic compounds from flowers of *Ficara verna* Huds. *Acta Polon. Pharm.* 1999, **56**, 475-476; through *Chem. Abstr.* **133**, 205403.
7. Tomczyk M, Gudej J and Sochacki M. Flavonoids from *Ficaria verna* Huds. *Z. Naturforsch.* 2002, **57c**, 440-444.
8. Tomczyk M and Gudej J. Quercetin and kaempferol glycosides from *Ficaria verna* flowers and their structure studied by 2D NMR spectroscopy. *Polish J. Chem.* 2002, **76**, 1601-1605.
9. Tomczyk M and Gudej J. Quantitative Analysis of Flavonoids in the Flowers and Leaves of *Ficaria verna* Huds. *Z. Naturforsch.* 2003, **58c**, 762-764.
10. Pourrat H, Regerat F, Lamaison J-L and Pourrat A. Utilisation d'une souche d'*Aspergillus niger* pour la purification de la saponine principale des tubercules de Ficaire, *Ficaria ranunculoides* Moench [Purification of the main saponin from tubers of pilewort, *Ficaria ranunculoides* Moench, using a strain of *Aspergillus niger*]. *Ann. Pharm. Fr.* 1979, **37**, 441-444 [FRENCH/English summary].
11. Pourrat H, Texier O and Regerat F. Utilisation d'une souche d'*Aspergillus niger* pour la purification d'un rhamnoglucoside d'hédéragénine des tubercules de Ficaire, *Ficaria ranunculoides* Moench. *Ann. Pharm. Fr.* 1982, **40**, 373-376 [FRENCH/English summary].
12. Texier O, Ahond A, Regerat F and Pourrat H. A triterpenoid saponin from *Ficaria ranunculoides* tubers. *Phytochemistry* 1984, **23**, 2903-2905.
13. Pourrat A and Pourrat H. La Ficaire - *Ficaria ranunculoides* Moench. *Plantes Méd. Phytothér.* 1969, **3**, 288-295 [FRENCH].
14. Barthomeuf C, Regerat F and Pourrat H. Isolation and identification of gentiobiose in Ranunculaceae. *Lett. Bot.* 1987, (4-5), 359-363 [FRENCH]; through *Chem. Abstr.* **109**, 51773.
15. Kolesnik OV. Preliminary phytochemical study of certain Ranunculus species. *Sb. Nauchn. Tr. Dnepropetr. Gos. Med. Inst.*1961, **19**, 191-192 [RUSSIAN], through *Chem. Abstr.* 1963, **59**, 7856.
16. Brisse-Le Menn F, Duclos MP, Larpent C, Mahe C and Patin H. Dosage par chromatographie en phase liquide de l'hédéragénine et de l'acide oléanolique contenus dans les tubercules de ficaire [HPLC analysis of hederagenin and oleanolic acid in pilewort tubers]. *Analusis* 1990, **18**, 250-254 [FRENCH/English summary].
17. Ranunculus. In: *British Herbal Pharmacopoeia 1983.* ISBN 0-903032-07-4. Bournemouth: British Herbal Medicine Association, 1983.
18. Grieve M (edited by Leyel CF). Lesser Celandine. In: *A Modern Herbal* (first published 1931; revised 1973). ISBN 1-85501-249-9. London: Tiger Books International, 1994:179-182.
19. Chevallier A. Lesser Celandine - *Ranunculus ficaria.* In: *Encyclopedia of Medicinal Plants, 2nd ed.* ISBN 0-7513-1209-6. London-New York: Dorling Kindersley, 2001:260.
20. Weiss RF. *Ranunculus ficaria* (Lesser Celandine). In: *Herbal Medicine* (translated from the 6th German edition of *Lehrbuch der Phytotherapie*). ISBN 0-906584-19-1. Gothenburg: AB Arcanum, Beaconsfield, UK: Beaconsfield Publishers, 1988:116.
21. Sawyer J. Pilewort ointment and suppository. *Br. Med. J.* 1904, (1), 14.
22. Pharmaceutical Society of Great Britain. Ficaria - Pilewort, Unguentum Ficariae - Pilewort Ointment. In: *British Pharmaceutical Codex 1934.* London: Pharmaceutical Press, 1934: 465-466 and 1506.
23. Ficaire, racine tubérisée. In: *Médicaments à base de plantes.* ISBN 2-911473-02-7. Saint-Denis Cedex, France: Agence du Médicament, 1998.
24. Stodola J and Volák J. Lesser Celandine - Pilewort. Translated into English in: Bunney S, editor. *The Illustrated Book of Herbs.* ISBN 0-7064-1489-6. London: Octopus Books, 1984:240.
25. Budavari S, editor. Anemonin. In: *The Merck Index: An encyclopedia of chemicals, drugs and biologicals, 12th edition.* ISBN 0-911910-12-3. Whitehouse Station, NJ: Merck & Co., 1996:108 (monograph 681).
26. Pilewort. In: UK Statutory Instrument 1994 No. 2410. The Medicines (Products Other Than Veterinary Drugs) (General Sale List) Amendment Order 1994. Schedule 1, Table A.

REGULATORY GUIDELINES FROM OTHER EU COUNTRIES

FRANCE

Médicaments à base de plantes [23]: Ficaire, racine tubérisée.

Therapeutic indications accepted

Topical use

Traditionally used: in subjective manifestations of venous insufficiency, such as heavy legs; for haemorrhoidal symptoms.

POKE ROOT

Phytolaccae radix

Synonym: Pokeweed Root.

Definition

Poke Root consists of the dried roots of *Phytolacca americana* L. (*P. decandra* L.) collected in autumn.

Phytolacca americana is a large perennial herb, reaching heights of up to 12 feet, with large leaves (about 1 foot long), white flowers and purple berries. It is indigenous to North America.

CONSTITUENTS

☐ ***Triterpene saponins*** At least 10 compounds [1] including phytolaccosides A [2], B [3,4], D [2], D2 [5], E [2], F [5] and G [4].

The aglycones are jaligonic acid, its 30-methyl ester (known as phytolaccagenin) and esculentic acid 30-methyl ester. Most of the saponins are monodesmosidic with 1-3 glycosidic sugars at C-3 (xylose with or without glucose and, in phytolaccoside F, with both glucose and rhamnose). The principal saponin is phytolaccoside E [1,6], based on phytolaccagenin with a glucosyl-(1→4)-xylosyl group at C-3 [2].

Another research group applied the term "phytolaccasaponins" to such compounds and isolated phytolaccasaponin E (= phytolaccoside E), phytolaccasaponin G (= phytolaccoside B) and a bidesmosidic compound named phytolaccasaponin B [7].

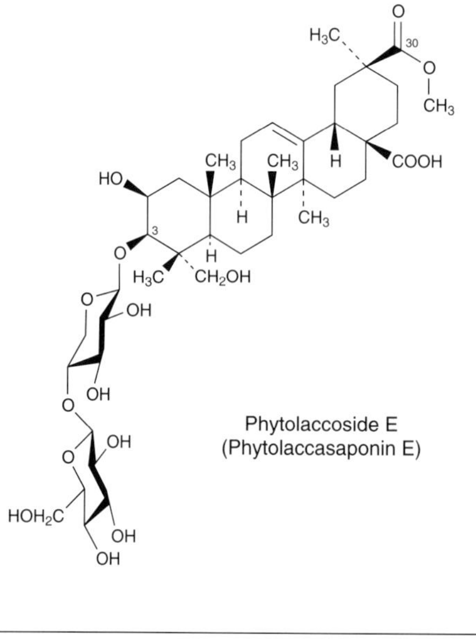

Phytolaccoside E
(Phytolaccasaponin E)

Free jaligonic acid and phytolaccagenin have also been isolated from poke root [6,8].

☐ ***Lectins*** A lectin isolated by Reisfeld et al. in the 1960s [9] was subsequently found to consist of 5 mitogenic proteins, designated as Pa-1 to Pa-5 [10,11]. However, their structures were not fully characterized.

In later work mitogenic lectins termed "pokeweed lectins" (PLs) were isolated from poke root and designated as PL-A, PL-B (the largest), PL-C [12] and PL-D (the smallest, with two isolectins, PL-D1 and PL-D2) [13]. They are chitin-binding, homologous proteins of different molecular sizes:

PL-A A glycoprotein closely related to, but smaller than, PL-B; MW of about 22 kDA [12].

PL-B A glycoprotein consisting of 295 amino acid residues in seven repetitive chitin-binding domains (complete sequence determined) and two oligosaccharides N-linked to asparagine96 and asparagine139; MW 34,493 [14]. The oligosaccharide has a complex arrangement of three mannose, one xylose, one fucose and two N-acetylglucosamine residues [15].

PL-C A polypeptide chain of 126 amino acid residues forming three repetitive chitin-binding domains (complete sequence determined); MW 13,747 [16]. The crystal structure has been determined [17].

PL-D1 A chain of 84 amino acid residues in two repetitive chitin-binding domains; MW 9,317 [13]. The crystal structure has been determined [18].

PL-D2 An isolectin of PL-D1, identical in sequence but lacking two C-terminal residues [18].

☐ ***Antiviral protein*** A ribosome-inactivating protein with a single chain and a molecular weight of about 30,000, designated as PAP-R (pokeweed antiviral protein from root). It is similar in structure (same aminoterminal sequence) to and probably an isoform of PAP, pokeweed antiviral protein from the *leaf* of *Phytolacca americana*, on which considerable research has been carried out in recent years based on its ability to inhibit the transmission of viruses [19].

☐ ***Sterols*** including α-spinasterol, Δ^7-stigmastenol, their glucosides and 6′-palmityl glucosides [8].

☐ ***Other constituents***: Starch, gum, sucrose, oxalates [20].

PHARMACOLOGY

In vitro

Pokeweed lectins

Pokeweed lectin (a combination of lectins from

the root) possesses three distinct biological activities: haemagglutination, leukagglutination and mitogenicity (i.e. the capacity to transform resting peripheral blood lymphocytes into "blast-like" cells *in vitro*) [9].

Among the pokeweed lectins designated Pa-1 to Pa-5 in early work, Pa-1 was found to be mitogenic for both murine B-cells and T-cells; the others were T-cell mitogens only [11,21]. In haemagglutination assays, Pa-1 and Pa-2 were shown to have essentially the same carbohydrate-binding specificity and they bind primarily to sugar chains of band-3 glycoprotein on human erythrocytes [22]

The five pokeweed lectins, PL-A, PL-B, PL-C, PL-D1 and PL-D2, are chitin-binding proteins (specific for N-acetylglucosamine-containing saccharides) and have mitogenic activity, i.e. they stimulate peripheral lymphocytes to undergo mitosis by binding to their cell surfaces. PL-B (a glycoprotein) has the largest molecular mass of approximately 34 kDa and the most potent haemagglutinating and mitogenic activities, which have been ascribed to its seven-domain structure [14]. PL-C has almost no haemagglutinating activity [12].

Pokeweed antiviral protein
The antiviral activity of PAP (pokeweed antiviral protein from *leaf*) has been demonstrated against a number of animal viruses including polio [23], herpes simplex, influenza and human immunodeficiency viruses (HIV) [24]. PAP-R (pokeweed antiviral protein from root) is less studied so far, but appears likely to have similar activity in view of its structural similarity to PAP.

In vivo

Anti-inflammatory activity
The saponin fraction from poke root, administered intraperitoneally to rats at 5-30 mg/kg showed potent anti-inflammatory activity, significantly and dose-dependently inhibiting carrageenan-induced paw oedema with an ED_{50} of 15.1 mg/kg; at 30 mg/kg it caused 63.2% inhibition ($p<0.01$) compared to 47.7% inhibition by cortisone actetate at the same dose level [1,25]. When administered orally, a 6-fold higher dose of the saponin fraction was necessary to produce a similar degree of inhibition. Intraperitoneal administration of phytolaccagenin (the major aglycone of poke root saponins) at 30 mg/kg produced 46.2% inhibition of paw oedema, an effect comparable to that of cortisone acetate at the same dose level and more potent than that of two other triterpenoids known to be effective in acute inflammation, oleanolic acid and glycyrrhetinic acid (both 35% inhibition at 30 mg/kg) [1].

In the granuloma pouch model in rats, intramuscular administration of the saponin fraction from poke root at 60 mg/kg daily for 7 days led to only weak inhibition of granuloma and exudate formation, while hydrocortisone acetate at 10 mg/kg produced significant inhibition. It was concluded that the saponin fraction is likely to be more effective as an anti-oedema agent than as an inhibitor of pathological connective tissue behaviour [1].

Pharmacological studies in humans
In a study designed to evaluate thermogenic effects of plant preparations, administration of a single dose of 3 ml of a tincture of poke (assumed to be root) to four healthy volunteers caused no apparent changes in heart rate, blood pressure, energy expenditure or respiratory quotient [26].

CLINICAL STUDIES

None published on mono-preparations of poke root.

THERAPEUTICS

Actions
Anti-inflammatory [1,25,27,28].
Also stated to be expectorant and potentially immunostimulant, and a depurative for skin complaints acting primarily via the lymphatic system [28].

Indications
None adequately substantiated by pharmacological or clinical studies.

Uses based on experience or tradition
Internal: Inflammatory conditions or infections of the upper respiratory tract [28-30] such as tonsillitis, laryngitis [28,29] and chronic respiratory catarrh [29,30]; lymphatic adenitis and mumps [28,29]. Has also been used to treat chronic rheumatism [29-32].
External: In ointments for skin irritations, infections and infestations [28] such as scabies, tinea, sycosis or acne [29-31]; as a poultice for mastitis and mammary abscess [28-30].

Contraindications
Pregnancy and lactation [27,28,30].
Lymphocytic leukaemia and gastrointestinal irritation [28].

Side effects
Emetic and purgative in large doses [29-32].

Interactions with other drugs
None known.

Dosage
Adult daily dose: dried root, 0.2-1 g [28,29,32]

or as a decoction; tincture 1:5 in 45% ethanol, 0.15-0.7 ml [28].

Cautions: Poke root should be used only under professional supervision [30,33]. Recommended doses should not be exceeded; toxic in overdose [28,30]. The fresh root should not be used [27,28]. The powdered root is sternutatory [32].

SAFETY

Poke root is not suitable for self-medication and should only be taken under professional supervision [30,33]. It may be safely prescribed at the recommended dosage [28] but requires careful control, since it is decidedly toxic if taken orally in excessive amounts.

In a classic case report, even the infusion from half a teaspoonful of poke root in a cup of boiling water caused severe gastrointestinal upset with vomiting, abdominal pain and diarrhoea followed by hypertension and tachycardia, involving emergency treatment in hospital [34]. Reviews of the toxicology of poke root can be found in the literature [28,35,36].

The oral LD_{50} of the saponin fraction from poke root was found to be >1.5 g/kg body weight in mice. Intraperitoneal LD_{50} values for the saponin fraction were 181 mg/kg in mice and 208 mg/kg in rats, and for the aglycone phytolaccagenin > 2.0 g/kg in mice [1]. The intraperitoneal LD_{50} of pokeweed antiviral protein from root (PAP-R) was determined as 1.2 mg/kg [19].

Due to their molecular size, pokeweed mitogenic lectins and antiviral proteins are unlikely to be significantly absorbed into the bloodstream after oral doses, except if the gastrointestinal tract is damaged [28].

Pokeweed antiviral protein (PAP, in this case derived from leaf rather than root), which has been shown to have broad spectrum antiviral activity, was well tolerated by HIV-1-infected adult patients after intravenous administration of a single dose of 5 µg/kg of a PAP immunoconjugate; no significant adverse reactions were observed and effective plasma levels were achieved [37].

REGULATORY STATUS

Medicines

UK	Accepted for general sale, internal or external use. Maximum internal dose: 120 mg [38].
France	Not listed in *Médicaments à base de plantes* [39].
Germany	No Commission E monograph published.

Food

Not used in foods.

REFERENCES

Current Pharmacopoeial Monographs

PPRC	Radix Phytolaccae (Shanglu)
BHP	Poke Root

Literature References

1. Woo WS and Shin KH. Anti-inflammatory action of Phytolacca saponin. *J. Pharm. Soc. Korea* 1976, **20**, 149-155.
2. Woo WS, Kang SS, Wagner H, Seligman O and Chari VM. Triterpenoid Saponins from the Roots of *Phytolacca americana. Planta Medica* 1978, **34**, 87-92.
3. Woo WS and Kang SS. Phytolaccoside B: Triterpene glucoside from *Phytolacca americana. Phytochemistry* 1976, **15**, 1315-1317.
4. Woo WS and Kang SS. The Structure of Phytolaccoside G. *J. Pharm. Soc. Korea (Yakhak Hoe Chi)* 1977, **21**, 159-162; also through *Chem. Abstr.* 1978, **88**, 191324.
5. Kang SS and Woo WS. Two New Saponins from *Phytolacca americana. Planta Medica* 1987, **53**, 338-340.
6. Woo WS, Chi H-J and Kang SS. Constituents of *Phytolacca* Species (II). Comparative Examination on Constituents of the Roots of *Phytolacca americana, P. esculenta* and *P. insularis. Korean J. Pharmacog.* 1976, **7**, 51-54.
7. Suga Y, Maruyama Y, Kawanishi S and Shoji J. Studies on the Constituents of Phytolaccaceous Plants. I. On the Structures of Phytolaccasaponins B, E and G from the Roots of *Phytolacca americana* L. *Chem. Pharm. Bull.* 1978, **26**, 520-525.
8. Woo WS. Steroids and pentacyclic triterpenoids from *Phytolacca americana. Phytochemistry* 1974, **13**, 2887-2889.
9. Reisfeld RA, Börjeson J, Chessin LN and Small PA. Isolation and characterization of a mitogen from pokeweed (*Phytolacca americana*). *Proc. Natl. Acad. Sci. USA* 1967, **58**, 2020-2027.
10. Waxdal MJ. Isolation, Characterization and Biological Activities of Five Mitogens from Pokeweed. *Biochemistry* 1974, **13**, 3671-3677.
11. Yokoyama K, Yano O, Terao T and Osawa T. Purification and biological activities of pokeweed (*Phytolacca americana*) mitogens. *Biochim. Biophys. Acta* 1976, **427**, 443-452.
12. Kino M, Yamaguchi K-i, Umekawa H and Funatsu G. Purification and Characterization of Three Mitogenic Lectins from the Roots of Pokeweed (*Phytolacca americana*). *Biosci. Biotech. Biochem.* 1995, **59**, 683-688.
13. Yamaguchi K, Mori A and Funatsu G. Amino Acid Sequence and Some Properties of Lectin-D from the Roots of Pokeweed (*Phytolacca americana*). *Biosci. Biotech. Biochem.* 1996, **60**, 1380-1382.
14. Yamaguchi K, Yurino N, Kino M, Ishiguro M and Funatsu G. The Amino Acid Sequence of Mitogenic Lectin-B from the Roots of Pokeweed (*Phytolacca americana*). *Biosci. Biotech. Biochem.* 1997, **61**, 690-698.
15. Kimura Y, Yamaguchi K-i and Funatsu G. Structural Analysis of N-linked Oligosaccharide of Mitogenic Lectin-B from the Roots of Pokeweed (*Phytolacca americana*). *Biosci. Biotech. Biochem.* 1996, **60**, 537-540.
16. Yamaguchi K-i, Mori A and Funatsu G. The Complete Amino Acid Sequence of Lectin-C from the Roots of Pokeweed (*Phytolacca americana*). *Biosci. Biotech. Biochem.* 1995, **59**, 1384-1385.
17. Hayashida M, Fujii T, Hamasu M, Ishiguro M and Hata Y. Similarity between Protein-Protein and Protein-Carbohydrate Interactions, Revealed by Two Crystal Structures

of Lectins from the Roots of Pokeweed. *J. Mol. Biol.* 2003, **334**, 551-565.
18. Fujii T, Hayashida M, Hamasu M, Ishiguro M and Hata Y. Structures of two lectins from the roots of pokeweed (*Phytolacca americana*). *Acta Cryst.* 2004, **D60**, 665-673.
19. Bolognesi A, Barbieri L, Abbondanza A, Falasca AI, Carnicelli D, Battelli MG and Stirpe F. Purification and properties of new ribosome-inactivating proteins with RNA *N*-glycosidase activity. *Biochim. Biophys. Acta* 1990, **1087**, 293-302.
20. Ahmed ZF, Zufall CJ and Jenkins GL. A Contribution to the Chemistry and Toxicology of the Root of *Phytolacca americana* L. *J. Am. Pharm. Assoc.* 1949, **38**, 443-448.
21. Waxdal MJ and Basham TY. B and T-cell stimulatory activities of multiple mitogens from pokeweed. *Nature* 1974, **251**, 163-164.
22. Yokoyama K, Terao T and Osawa T. Carbohydrate-binding specificity of pokeweed mitogens. *Biochim. Biophys. Acta* 1978, **538**, 384-396.
23. Ussery MA, Irvin JD and Hardesty B. Inhibition of poliovirus replication by a plant antiviral peptide. *Ann. N. Y. Acad. Sci.* 1977, **284**, 431-443.
24. Tumer NE, Hudak K, Di R, Coetzer C, Wang P and Zoubenko O. Pokeweed Antiviral Protein and Its Applications. *Curr. Topics Microbiol. Immunol.* 1999, **240**, 139-158.
25. Woo WS, Shin KH and Kang SS. Constituents of *Phytolacca* Species (I). Anti-inflammatory Saponins. *Korean J. Pharmacog.* 1976, **7**, 47-50.
26. Martinet A, Hostettmann K and Schutz Y. Thermogenic effects of commercially available plant preparations aimed at treating human obesity. *Phytomedicine* 1999, **6**, 231-238.
27. McIntyre A. Poke root. In: *The Complete Woman's Herbal.* ISBN 1-85675-135-X. London: Gaia Books, 1999:179.
28. Mills S and Bone K. Poke root (*Phytolacca decandra* L.). In: *Principles and Practice of Phytotherapy. Modern Herbal Medicine.* ISBN 0-443-06016-9. Edinburgh-London-New York: Churchill Livingstone, 2000:515-518.
29. Phytolacca. In: *British Herbal Pharmacopoeia 1983.* ISBN 0-903032-07-4. Bournemouth: British Herbal Medicine Association, 1983.
30. Chevallier A. Poke Root - *Phytolacca decandra.* In: *Encyclopedia of Medicinal Plants, 2nd ed.* ISBN 0-7513-1209-6. London-New York: Dorling Kindersley, 2001:247.
31. Grieve M (edited by Leyel CF). Poke Root. In: *A Modern Herbal* (first published 1931; revised 1973). ISBN 1-85501-249-9. London: Tiger Books International, 1994:648-649.
32. Pharmaceutical Society of Great Britain. Phytolacca. In: The British Pharmaceutical Codex 1934. London: Pharmaceutical Press, 1934: 802-803.
33. McGuffin M, Hobbs C, Upton R and Goldberg A, editors. *Phytolacca americana* L. In: American Herbal Products Association's *Botanical Safety Handbook.* Boca Raton-Boston-London: CRC Press, 1997:85.
34. Lewis WH and Smith PR. Poke Root Herbal Tea Poisoning. *JAMA* 1979, 242, 2759-2760.
35. De Smet PAGM. *Phytolacca americana.* In: De Smet PAGM, Keller K, Hänsel R and Chandler RF, editors. *Adverse Effects of Herbal Drugs, Volume 2.* Berlin-Heidelberg: Springer-Verlag, 1993:253-261.
36. Knight-Trent AH and Cupp MJ. Pokeweed. In: Cupp MJ, editor. *Toxicology and Clinical Pharmacology of Herbal Products.* Totowa, New Jersey: Humana Press, 2000:237-243.
37. Uckun FM, Bellomy K, O'Neill K, Messinger Y, Johnson T and Chen C-L. Toxicity, Biological Activity and Pharmacokinetics of TXU (Anti-CD7)-Pokeweed Antiviral Protein in Chimpanzees and Adult Patients Infected with Human Immunodeficiency Virus. *J. Pharmacol. Exptl. Ther.* 1999, **291**, 1301-1307.
38. Poke Root (Phytolacca). In: UK Statutory Instrument 1994 No. 2410. The Medicines (Products Other Than Veterinary Drugs) (General Sale List) Amendment Order 1994. Schedule 1, Table A.
39. *Médicaments à base de plantes.* ISBN 2-911473-02-7. Saint-Denis Cedex, France: Agence du Médicament, 1998.

PUMPKIN SEED

Cucurbitaceae

Cucurbitae peponis semen

Definition

Pumpkin Seed consists of the dried, ripe seeds of appropriate cultivars of *Cucurbita pepo* L.

Cucurbita pepo L. has many cultivars, which variously yield vegetable marrows, courgettes (zucchini), and even hard-shelled ornamental gourds, as well as pumpkins and squash - and the term 'pumpkin' is applied to a number of *Cucurbita* species [1]. The species of *Cucurbita*, including *C. pepo*, *C. maxima* and *C. moschata*, which, as pumpkins, are cultivated for the oil from their seeds - and within the 'oil pumpkin' types of *C. pepo* the varieties which have been developed for particular characteristics and systematically classified by the Russian pumpkin cultivator Grebenshchikov (Greb.) - have been described by Schilcher [2].

Modern therapeutic use of pumpkin seed, primarily in urological disorders such as benign prostatic hyperplasia, requires reproducibility of dosage from consistent medicinal products. In this respect, a reliable source of seeds from a botanically well-defined pumpkin cultivar is obviously important. The human pharmacological and clinical studies so far published relate mainly to a cultivar with seeds which have a soft testa (seed coat) and a high sterol content: *Cucurbita pepo* L. convar. *citrullinina* Greb. var. *styriaca* Greb., which is cultivated in southern Europe (Austria, Hungary and Slovenia) [3,4]. The soft-coated seeds are dark green, in contrast to the generally white seeds of hard-coated varieties [2].

The monograph on Cucurbita in BPC 1934 [5] specified the seeds of *Cucurbita maxima* Duchesne, described as 'melon pumpkin seed', for use as a taenicide (a vermicide to kill tapeworms), References to such use of pumpkin seed may still be found in current texts.

CONSTITUENTS

Older data reported in the literature on the composition of pumpkin seeds are rather inconsistent, because in many cases details of the variety and cultivar, or even the full botanical name, are not given [6]. Constituent data on seeds from *Cucurbita pepo* L. convar. *citrullinina* var. *styriaca* has been summarised by Schilcher [2].

☐ ***Fatty oil***, 45-52% [2,7,8]. When obtained from pumpkin seeds by pressing, the oil has a dark red to green colour (due to its content of carotenoids and chlorophylls), a red fluorescence and a nutty taste [3,4,9].

The *glyceride fraction* contains:
Fatty acids, of which over 80% are unsaturated, mainly linoleic (C18:2, 42-64%) and oleic (C18:1, 20-38%) acids, and 19% saturated, mainly palmitic (C16:0, ca. 13%) and stearic (C18:0, ca. 6%) acids [2,4,7,9,10].

The *unsaponifiable fraction* contains:
Sterols, up to 0.5% of the oil (55-60% of the unsaponifiable fraction) [2,11], predominantly Δ^7-sterols, which are considered to be the key active constituents of pumpkin seed in the treatment of benign prostatic hyperplasia (Δ^7, or delta-7, signifies

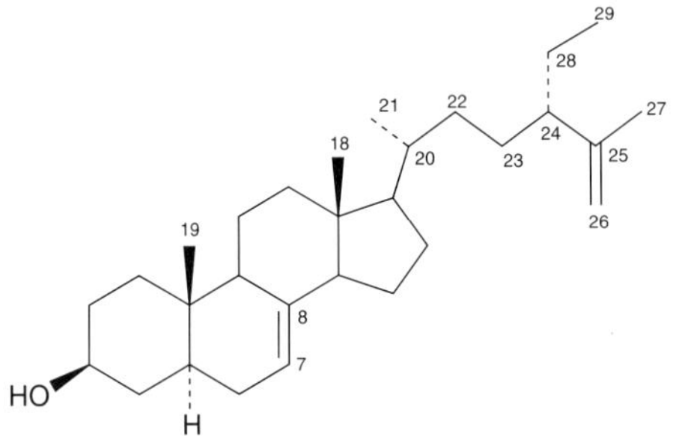

$\Delta^{7,25}$-Stigmastadienol

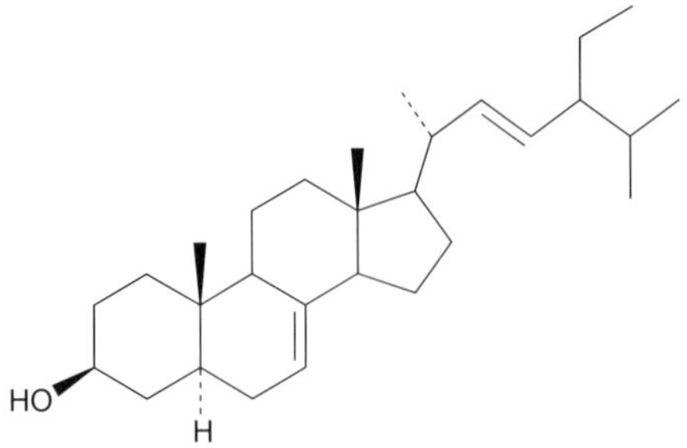

$\Delta^{7,22}$-Stigmastadienol (α-spinasterol)

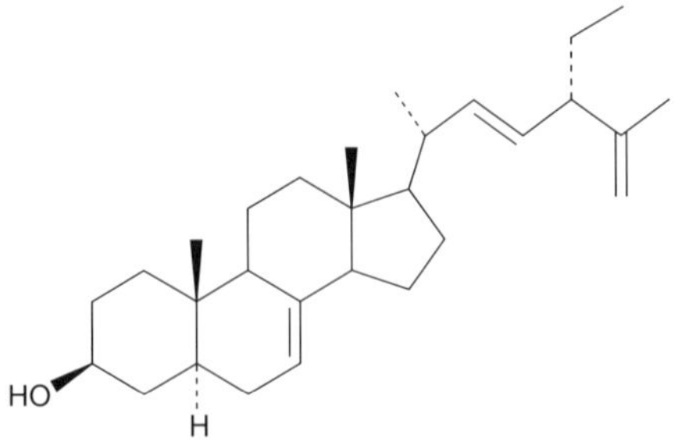

$\Delta^{7,22,25}$-Stigmastatrienol

a double bond between C-7 and C-8). Much smaller amounts of Δ^5- and Δ^8-sterols are also present.

Four Δ^7-sterols account for 75-88% of the total sterols [10-12] and 40-50% of the unsaponifiable part of the oil [3]: $\Delta^{7,25}$-stigmastadienol, $\Delta^{7,22}$-stigmastadienol (α-spinasterol), $\Delta^{7,22,25}$-stigmastatrienol and $\Delta^{7,24(28)}$-stigmastadienol (Δ^7-avenasterol) [3,10-12]. Glucosides of the first three have also been identified in the seeds [13].

In the literature, different authors use varying chemical terminology for the names of sterols; for example, $\Delta^{7,25}$-stigmastadienol [10] is also described as $\Delta^{7,25(27)}$-stigmastadien-3β-ol [6], 5α-stigmasta-7,25-dien-3β-ol [3] and 24β-ethyl-5α-cholesta-7,25(27)-dien-3β-ol [12].

The predominance of Δ^7-sterols in pumpkin seed oil is in contrast to the sterol fractions of most seed oils, in which Δ^5-sterols (30-60%) are usually predominant [3].

Squalene, 39-46% of the unsaponifiable part of the oil [3]; this can be used as a marker to differentiate pumpkin seed oil from other vegetable oils [2].

Tocopherols, ca. 360-540 mg per kg of oil, comprising β- and γ- (but not α-) tocopherols [2,7,9].

Carotenoids, 15 ppm [9], mainly lutein (50%) and β-carotene (10-12%) with smaller amounts of cryptoxanthins and various other carotenoids [9,14].

Chlorophylls, 13 ppm, mainly chlorophyll b and phaeophytin a [9].

□ ***Sesquiterpenoids***, including oxycerotic acid, (+)-abscisic acid, (+)-2-trans-abscisic acid, (+)-dehydrovomifoliol and (+)-vomifoliol [15].

□ ***Other constituents*** include protein (30-34%) and carbohydrates (6-10%) [2]; minerals, particularly phosphorus, potassium, magnesium, calcium, iron, zinc and trace elements [8], notably a relatively high selenium content (up to 0.4 µg/g) [2]; cucurbitine (3-amino-3-carboxypyrrolidine, 0.2-0.6%) [16]; small amounts of gibberellins, a kaurenolide [17], cucurbic acid and other acids and esters [18].

Peponin, a single-chain, ribosome-inactivating protein with a MW of about 30 kDA, was isolated from pumpkin seed by bioactivity-guided fractionation [19].

Published Assay Methods

Sterols as trimethylsilyl ethers by GC [10 and Ph. Eur. method 2.4.23]; fatty acids as methyl esters by GC [10 and Ph. Eur. method 2.4.22]

PHARMACOLOGY

Pumpkin seed preparations are used mainly in the symptomatic treatment of early stages of benign prostatic hyperplasia (BPH), a common condition in ageing men caused by non-malignant growth of both the stromal and epithelial elements of the prostate gland. Progressive enlargement of the prostate can lead to impediment of urination with various symptoms, both irritative (urgency, frequency, nocturia) and obstructive (hesitancy, weak flow, incomplete emptying of the bladder). More than 50% of men over 50 years of age have histological signs of BPH and up to 40% of men over 70 will complain of symptoms.

In vitro

Although the pathogenesis of BPH is not yet fully understood, dihydrotestosterone (DHT), which is formed from testosterone in the prostate, is thought to have a key role in its development; DHT is enriched in the nuclei of prostatic cells and activates proliferation. Delta-7-sterols present in pumpkin seed have structural and conformational similarities to DHT and it has been demonstrated that they can displace DHT from its binding sites. Cultured human fibroblasts were incubated for 24 hours with a mixture of delta-7 sterols from pumpkin seed, then DHT was added and after a further 24-hour incubation the excess of free DHT was determined by radioassay. The results showed that pumpkin seed sterols concentration-dependently reduced DHT binding to the cells (38% binding of 120 ng of DHT in the presence of 240 ng of delta-7-sterols) compared to controls (68% binding of DHT in the absence of delta-7-sterols) [20].

Peponin, a single-chain protein isolated from pumpkin seed, has been shown to be a potent inhibitor of human immunodeficiency virus Type 1 reverse transcriptase (HIV-1 RT) with an IC_{50} of 12.7 µg/ml [19].

The activity of pumpkin seeds as a taenifuge (to expel tapeworms) is attributed to the presence of cucurbitine, which has been shown to inhibit the growth of *Schistosoma japonicum* [16].

In vivo

Oil extracted from pumpkin seeds grown in Yunnan, China, and administered intravenously to rabbits at 0.5 ml per day for 7 days, was found to reduce bladder pressure and urethral pressure ($p<0.01$) [21].

Pumpkin seed oil administered intramuscularly to rats with Freund's adjuvant-induced arthritis at 100 mg/kg daily for 29 days markedly reduced the chronic phase of inflammation as indicated by a significant reduction in hind paw oedema ($p<0.05$) and, by its antioxidant activity, modulated the effects of superoxide and peroxide radicals during arthritic inflammation [22].

Pharmacological studies in humans

On the 3rd and 4th days before prostatectomy operations due to benign prostatic hyperplasia (BPH), 6 volunteer patients took 90 mg of a mixture of five delta-7 sterols isolated from pumpkin seed (*Cucurbita pepo* L. convar. *citrullinina* var. *styriaca*), while a similar control group of patients took no sterols. Serum parameters tested before, and 1, 2 and 3 days after, taking the sterol mixture, showed a significant daily decline in acid phosphatase ($p<0.05$) and prostate-specific antigen ($p<0.05$) levels, while unbound testosterone levels increased ($p<0.05$ on day 3); sexual hormone binding globulin and total testosterone levels remained unchanged.

Although these results could not be fully explained, it was clear that the pumpkin seed sterol mixture had an influence on prostate-specific hormone metabolism. Delta-7-sterols, which have a structural conformation similar to that of dihydrotestosterone (DHT), are not ubiquitous in higher plants (in contrast to delta-5-sterols, such as sitosterol, stigmasterol and campesterol). Elevated DHT levels are a typical indication of BPH - and DHT, rather than testosterone, is thought to be responsible for proliferative activity in the prostate. Analyses following the prostatectomies revealed a significantly lower level of DHT ($p = 0.05$) in prostate tissues from the pumpkin seed sterol group (0.94 ng/g) compared to those from the control group (1.28 ng/g). Whether this reduction in DHT, in the direction of normal levels, was due to inhibition of 5-alpha-reductase or to reduction of intraprostate binding capacity could not be ascertained from the experiment. Attempts to assay delta-7-sterols in tissue from removed prostates proved technically difficult but qualitative identification was achieved in five cases [23].

CLINICAL STUDIES

Controlled studies

Patients with benign prostatic hyperplasia at stages I and II as defined by Alken [24], participating in a randomized, double-blind, multicentric study, received two placebo capsules daily for a 1-month run-in period, then daily for 12 months either 2 × 500 mg of a viscous extract (15-25:1, extraction solvent: ethanol 92% m/m) from pumpkin seed (*Cucurbita pepo* L. convar. *citrullinina* Greb. var. *styriaca* Greb.) (n = 233) or placebo (n = 243). The main target parameter was improvement in the International Prostate Symptom Score (IPSS) [25], which was 17.6 in the verum group and 17.7 in the placebo group before the treatment phase. A minimum improvement in IPSS of 5 points (defined as a therapy response) at the end of the 12-month treatment was achieved in 65% of patients treated with pumpkin seed extract, compared to 54% in the placebo group, a statistically significant difference ($p = 0.021$ for the intention-to-treat population). Continuous improvement in IPSS over the 12-month treatment period was evident in the pumpkin seed group, while the placebo group showed no appreciable further changes after the 6th month. In patients in the pumpkin seed group greater improvement was noted in six out of seven individual symptoms included in the overall IPSS, although only 'sensation of incomplete bladder emptying' ($p = 0.035$) and 'difficulty in starting urination' ($p = 0.019$) reached statistical significance compared to the placebo group. Patients taking the pumpkin seed extract also had a significant reduction in daytime micturition frequency compared to those on placebo, but no significant differences were detected in night-time micturition frequency, residual urine volume, uroflowmetry, quality of life scores, PSA values or prostate volume. Overall, the results of this study (the first controlled study with a pumpkin seed preparation) were positive but hardly spectacular in view of the substantial 'placebo effect'; further controlled studies to confirm efficacy are clearly needed. Based on the results, the authors suggested that the mechanism of action of pumpkin seed extract is mainly an influence on relevant smooth musculature of the bladder and prostate [26].

Open studies

In evaluating results from open studies it is important to bear in mind that a substantial 'placebo effect', amounting to 5 points in the IPSS, is possible - as evident from the controlled study above [26].

2245 Patients, of whom 85% were aged 50-80 years, with benign prostatic hyperplasia at stage I or early stage II (as defined by Alken) took 500 or 1000 mg daily of a pumpkin seed extract (the same extract as in the above controlled study) for 3 months in an open surveillance study; 60% of the patients had not previously received any treatment for BPH. Significant improvements in International Prostate Symptom Scores (IPSS) were noted by the physicians: an overall decrease of 41% (7.7 points, from 18.64 to 10.94) with greater decreases in stage I (46%) than in stage II (38%) patients. Quality of Life Index questionnaires completed by patients showed an overall improvement of 46% (decrease of 1.55 points, 3.36 to 1.81), again with greater improvement in those at an early stage of BPH. Average frequencies of passing water dropped from 6.7 to 5.2 in the daytime and 2.7 to 1.3 during the night [27].

In an earlier open study, 101 persons with micturition problems (62 men, of whom 43 had prostate hypertrophy and 19 had irritable bladder; 39 women with irritable bladder) were treated daily for 8 weeks with 3 tablespoonsful (about 19 g) of ground pumpkin seed (*Cucurbita pepo* L. convar. *citrullinina* Greb. var. *styriaca* Greb.). From data recorded by the patients, the average micturition index (daily amount of urine in ml divided by the number of micturitions per day) improved from 141 to 175 over the 8-week period, an increase of

24%. Subjectively assessed micturition problems in men with prostate hypertrophy decreased in 50-70% of patients [28].

Beneficial effects on urinary flow and residual urine were reported (with insufficient detail) in two other open studies:

- A 1962 paper presenting 16 case reports on BPH patients who consumed about 3 tablespoonsful (subsequently 1-2 as a maintenance dose) of pumpkin seed granulate daily for several months [29].
- A more recent study in which about 25 BPH patients were treated orally with pumpkin seed oil for 12 weeks [30].

THERAPEUTICS

Actions
Reduction of dihydrotestosterone levels in prostate tissues [23]; strengthening of bladder function with improvement of sphincter and detrusor coordination [20]; anti-inflammatory [22].

Indications
Symptomatic treatment of micturition disorders in the early stages of benign prostatic hyperplasia [26,31].

Other uses, based on experience or tradition
Irritable bladder [28,31]; functional disorders of the bladder and problems in passing water [32].

Contraindications
None known.

Side effects
None known.

Interactions with other drugs
None known.

Dosage
Daily dose: 10-30 g of pumpkin seed, as ground seed or an equivalent amount of ethanolic extract or pumpkin seed oil [26,31,32].

Pumpkin seed preparations should be taken for at least several weeks or months to achieve optimum effects [32].

SAFETY

Pumpkin seeds are generally considered safe; entire seeds and pumpkin seed oil are widely consumed as food [2,10,11]. In a controlled clinical study [26] pumpkin seed extract was well tolerated with only a few minor adverse effects attributable to the preparation.

REGULATORY STATUS

Medicines

UK	No licences issued for products containing pumpkin seed.
France	Not listed in *Médicaments à base de plantes* [33].
Germany	Commission E monograph published, with approved uses [31].

REFERENCES

Current Pharmacopoeial Monographs

DAB	Kürbissamen
BHP	Pumpkin Seed

Literature References

1. Mabberley DJ. Cucurbita. In: *The Plant-Book: A portable dictionary of the higher plants.* Cambridge-New York: Cambridge University Press, 1990:158.
2. Schilcher H. *Cucurbita*-Species - Kürbis-Arten. *Z. Phytotherapie* 1986, **7**, 19-23 [GERMAN].
3. Sauter M, Schilcher H and Segebrecht S. "Kürbiskernöl" und seine Verfälschungen. Identitäts- und Reinheitsprüfung von Kürbissamenöl mit Hilfe der Dünnschichtchromatographie ["Pumpkin seed oil" and its adulteration. Testing for identity and purity of pumpkin seed oil with the aid of thin-layer chromatography]. *Pharm. Ztg.* 1985, **130**, 73-75 [GERMAN].
4. Murkovic M, Hillebrand A, Winkler J, Leitner E and Pfannhauser W. Variability of fatty acid content in pumpkin seeds (*Cucurbita pepo* L.). *Z. Lebensm. Unters. Forsch.* 1996, **203**, 216-219.
5. Pharmaceutical Society of Great Britain. Cucurbita. In: *British Pharmaceutical Codex 1934.* London: Pharmaceutical Press, 1934:374-375.
6. Bombardelli E and Morazzoni P. *Cucurbita pepo* L. *Fitoterapia* 1997, **68**, 291-302.
7. Schuster W, Zipse W and Marquard R. Influence of Genotype and Place of Cultivation on Various Components of Oil Pumpkin Seeds (*Cucurbita pepo* L.). *Fette Seifen Anstrichmittel* 1983, **85**, 56-64 [GERMAN/English summary].
8. Mansour EH, Dworschák E, Lugasi A, Barna E and Gergely A. Nutritive Value of Pumpkin (*Cucurbita pepo* Kakai 35) Seed Products. *J. Sci. Food Agric.* 1993, **61**, 73-78.
9. Vogel P. Studies on Pumpkin Seed Oil. *Fette Seifen Anstrichmittel* 1978, **80**, 315-317 [GERMAN/English summary].
10. Tsaknis J, Lalas S and Lazos ES. Characterization of crude and purified pumpkin seed oil. *Grasas y Aceites* 1997, **48**, 267-272.
11. Bastic M, Bastic Lj, Jovanovic JA and Spiteller G. Sterols in Pumpkin Seed Oil. *J. Am. Oil Chem. Soc.* 1977, **54**, 525-527.
12. Akihisa T, Thakur S, Rosenstein FU and Matsumoto T. Sterols of Cucurbitaceae: The Configurations at C-24 of 24-Alkyl-Δ^5-, Δ^7 and Δ^8-Sterols. *Lipids* 1986, **21**, 39-47.
13. Rauwald H-W, Sauter M and Schilcher H. A 24β-ethyl-Δ^7-steryl glucopyranoside from *Cucurbita pepo* seeds. *Phytochemistry* 1985, **24**, 2746-2748.
14. Matus Z, Molnár P and Szabó LG. Main carotenoids in pressed seed (Cucurbitae semen) of oil-pumpkin (*Cucurbita pepo* convar. *pepo* var. *styriaca*). *Acta Pharm. Hung.* 1993, **63**, 247-256 [HUNGARIAN/English summary].
15. Fukui H, Koshimizu K, Usuda S and Yamazaki Y. Isolation of Plant Growth Regulators from Seeds of *Cucurbita pepo* L. *Agric. Biol. Chem.* 1977, **41**, 175-180.
16. Mihranian VH and Abou-Chaar CI. Extraction, Detection and Estimation of Cucurbitin in Cucurbita Seeds. *Lloydia* 1968, **31**, 23-29.

17. Fukui H, Nemori R, Koshimizu K and Yamazaki Y. Structures of Gibberellins A_{39}, A_{48}, A_{49} and a New Kaurenolide in *Cucurbita pepo* L. *Agric. Biol. Chem.* 1977, **41**, 181-187.
18. Fukui H, Koshimizu K, Yamazaki Y and Usuda S. Structures of Plant Growth Inhibitors in Seeds of *Cucurbita pepo* L. *Agric. Biol. Chem.* 1977, **41**, 189-194.
19. Gerhäuser C, Samtleben R, Tan GT, Pezzuto JM, Lottspeich F and Wagner H. Peponin, a new ribosome-inactivating protein isolated from the seeds of *Cucurbita pepo* L., inhibits human immunodeficiency virus Type 1 reverse transcriptase. *Pharm. Pharmacol. Lett.* 1993, **3**, 71-75.
20. Schilcher H and Schneider H-J. Beurteilung von Kürbissamen in fixer Kombination mit weiteren pflanzlichen Wirkstoffen zur Behandlung des Symptomenkomplexes bei BPH [Evaluation of pumpkin seeds in fixed combination with other active substances from plants for treatment of the BPH symptom complex]. *Urologe [B]* 1990, **30**, 62-66 [GERMAN].
21. Zhang X, Ouyang J, Zhang Y, Tayalla B, Zhou X and Zhou S. Effect of the Extracts of Pumpkin Seeds on the Urodynamics of Rabbits: An Experimental Study. *J. Tongji Med. Univ.* 1994, **14**, 235-238.
22. Fahim AT, Abd-El Fattah AA, Agha AM and Gad MZ. Effect of pumpkin-seed oil on the level of free radical scavengers induced during adjuvant arthritis in rats. *Pharmacol. Res.* 1995, **31**, 73-79.
23. Schilcher H, Dunzendorfer U and Ascali F. Delta 7-sterole, das prostatotrope Wirkprinzip in Kürbissamen? [Delta-7 sterols, the prostatotropic active principle in pumpkin seeds?]. *Urologe [B]* 1987, **27**, 316-319 [GERMAN].
24. Alken CE. Konservative Behandlung des Prostata-Adenoms und Stadien-Einteilung [Conservative treatment of prostatic adenoma and classification of stages]. *Urologe [B]* 1973, **13**, 95-98 [GERMAN].
25. Cockett AT, Aso Y, Denis L, Murphy G, Khoury S, Abrams P et al. 1994 Recommendations of the International Consensus Committee concerning: The International Prostate Symptom Score (I-PSS) and Quality of Life Assessment. In: Cockett ATK, Khoury S, Aso Y, Chatelain C, Denis L, Griffiths K and Murphy G, editors. *The 2nd International Consultation on Benign Prostatic Hyperplasia (BPH). Paris - June 27-30, 1993: Proceedings 2.* Jersey, Channel Islands: Scientific Communication International, 1993:553-555.
26. Bach D. Placebokontrollierte Langzeittherapiestudie mit Kürbissamenextrakt bei BPH-bedingten Miktionsbeschwerden [Placebo-controlled long term therapy study with pumpkin seed extract in micturition disorders caused by BPH]. *Urologe [B]* 2000, **40**, 437-443 [GERMAN]. Erratum (Tables 4 and 5): *ibid.* 2001, **41**, 42.
27. Schiebel-Schlosser G and Friederich M. Kürbissamen in der Phytotherapie der BPH. Eine Anwendungsbeobachtung [Pumpkin seed in the phytotherapy of BPH. A drug monitoring study]. *Z. Phytotherapie* 1998, **19**, 71-76 [GERMAN/English summary].
Also published as:
Friederich M, Theurer C and Schiebel-Schlosser G. Prosta Fink Forte capsules in the treatment of benign prostatic hyperplasia. Multicentric surveillance study in 2245 patients. *Forsch. Komplementärmed. Klass. Naturheilkd.* 2000, **7**, 200-204 [GERMAN].
28. Nitsch-Fitz R, Egger H, Wutzl H and Maruna H. Einsatz des Kürbiskern-Diätetikums "Kürbis Granufink" bei Patienten mit Prostatahypertrophie in Wiener Allgemeinpraxen [Use of the pumpkin seed dietetic preparation "Kürbis Granufink" in patients with prostatic hypertrophy in Vienna general practices]. *Erfahrungsheilkunde* 1979, **12**, 1009-1013 [GERMAN].
29. Auel W. Zur Heilwirkung des Kürbiskerns beim prostatischen Symptomenkomplex [The therapeutic effect of pumpkin seed on the prostate symptom complex]. *Der Landarzt* 1962, **38**, 372-373 [GERMAN].
30. Sabo E, Berenji J, Stoikov J and Bogdanovic J. Pharmacodynamic effect of pumpkin seed oil (Oleum cucurbitae pepo) in patients with prostate adenoma. *Fundam. Clin. Pharmacol.* 1999, **13** (Suppl. 1), 360s (Abstract PW103).
31. Cucurbitae peponis semen. German Commission E Monograph published in: Bundesanzeiger No. 223 of 30 November 1985, amended in Bundesanzeiger No. 11 of 17 January 1991.
32. Braun R, editor. Kürbissamen [Pumpkin seed]. In: *Standardzulassungen für Fertigarzneimittel - Text und Kommentar [Standard authorisations for finished medicines - Text and commentary]*. Stuttgart: Deutscher Apotheker Verlag, Frankfurt: Govi-Verlag, 1986 [GERMAN].
33. *Médicaments à base de plantes.* ISBN 2-911473-02-7. Saint-Denis Cedex, France: Agence du Médicament, 1998.

REGULATORY GUIDELINES FROM OTHER EU COUNTRIES

GERMANY

Commission E monograph [31]: Cucurbitae peponis semen (Kürbissamen)

Uses
Irritable bladder; micturition problems in prostate adenoma stages I to II.

Contraindications
None known.

Side effects
None known.

Interactions with other drugs
None known.

Dosage
Unless otherwise prescribed, average daily dose: 10 g of seeds or equivalent preparations.

Mode of administration
Whole or coarsely cut seeds and other galenic preparations for internal use.

Action
The clinical efficacy found empirically lacks adequate pharmacological studies due to the unavailability of suitable models.

Note: This medicine improves only the symptoms of an enlarged prostate, without eliminating the enlargement. Therefore, please consult your doctor at regular intervals.

QUEEN'S DELIGHT **Euphorbiaceae**

Stillingiae radix

Synonyms: Queen's Root, Yaw Root.

Definition
Queen's Delight consists of the roots of *Stillingia sylvatica* L., freed from rootlets and usually sliced, then carefully dried.

Stillingia sylvatica is a low sub-shrub, 20-120 cm tall, with a woody rhizome, native to sandy, pine-barren regions of the southeastern United States from Virginia to Florida and west to Texas and New Mexico [1,2]. The botanical name *Stillingia sylvatica* Garden ex L. has also been used and two subspecies can be distinguished, ssp. *sylvatica* and ssp. *tenuis*, although the latter is found only in extreme south-eastern Florida [1].

At one time queen's delight was official in the U.S. National Formulary [3] and a monograph on it appeared in the BPC 1934 [4]. The dried root should not be stored for more than 2 years due to gradual chemical changes on ageing [2,4].

CONSTITUENTS

□ ***Diterpene esters***, of which nine have been isolated and called stillingia factors S1 to S9 [5-7].

Seven of these, stillingia factors S1-S6 [5] and S9 [6], have daphnane structures based on 5β,12β-dihydroxyresiniferonol-6α,7α-oxide. Taking S1 and S9 as examples (see diagram), S2-S5 vary with respect to

- n: either 2 or 4
- R: either CH_3-$(CH_2)_{11}$-CH=CH-CO– or CH_3-$(CH_2)_{12}$-CO–

S6 (also known as gnidilatidin or yuanhuacin) has a structure identical to S9 except that the long chain at C-12 is replaced by a benzoyloxy group [7].

S7 (also known as prostratin) and S8 have tigliane structures and are 12-deoxyphorbol esters; S8 differs from S7 (see diagram) in having a 5β-hydroxy group and also R = CH_3-$(CH_2)_{14}$-CO– [5,7].

All these compounds are present in very small amounts. The yields obtained *from a methanolic extract (not the dried root itself)* were: S1, 0.014%; S2 + S3, 0.012%; S4 + S5, 0.005%; S6, 0.009%; S7, 0.003%; S8, 0.0009% [5,7] and S9, 0.024% [6,7]; a total of about 0.07%. Since methanolic extract yields of only 1.4-3.7% were obtained from dried root [6], the total amount of diterpene esters in dried root appears to be around 0.001-0.003%.

□ ***Other constituents*** are not well characterized, but include essential oil (3-4%), an acrid fixed oil, an acrid resin (sylvacrol, 5-8%), tannin (10-12%) and starch. The presence of an alkaloid named stillingine was reported in 1885, but its structure has not been identified [2,7].

PHARMACOLOGY

In vivo

Skin irritant effects
Various diterpene esters, especially from Euphorbiaceae, are irritating to the skin and tumour-promoting. The sap from *Stillingia sylvatica* roots is well known to be irritant, causing swelling and inflammation of the skin and mucous membranes [5]. A diterpene ester used in pharmacology as a standard irritant and tumour-promoter, 12-*O*-tetradecanoylphorbol-13-acetate (TPA, a component of croton oil from seeds of *Croton tiglium* L.,

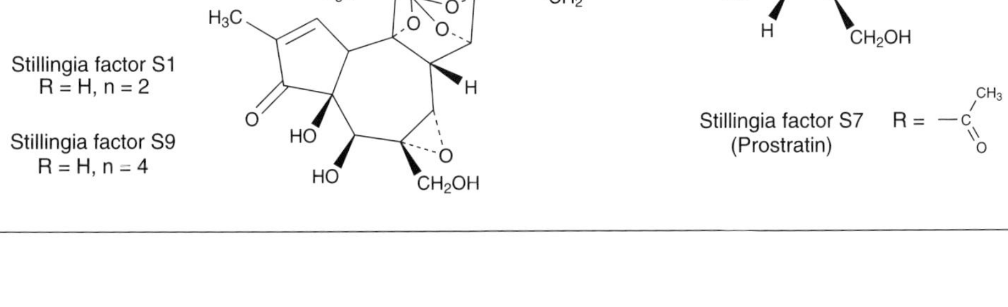

Stillingia factor S1
R = H, n = 2

Stillingia factor S9
R = H, n = 4

Stillingia factor S7
(Prostratin)

Euphorbiaceae), has a tigliane structure very similar (except at C-12) to that of S7 and S8.

The skin irritant effects of stillingia factors S1-S9 have been quantified as ID_{50} values, the minimum irritant doses (ID) which, 24 hours after application to the mouse ear in a standard test, cause distinct reddening (i.e. erythema) to the ears of 50% of mice compared to untreated controls. S7 was only weakly irritant, but S1-S6, S8 and S9 were moderately strongly to strongly irritant (ID_{50}: 0.036 to 0.11 µg) compared to TPA (ID_{50}: 0.010 µg) as the positive control. S9, the stillingia factor present in the highest amount in the root, had an ID_{50} of 0.036 µg, not much higher than that of TPA (0.010 µg). In the same test, an ethyl acetate extract from the root was moderately irritant (ID_{50}: 2.7 µg, corresponding to ca. 0.42 mg of root) [6,7].

Tumour promotion
Some diterpene esters are tumour-promoting when applied over long periods to the "initiated" dorsal skin of mice and this effect can be measured in a standardized, two-stage, initiation-promotion model of carcinogenesis. After a single initiation with 7,12-dimethylbenz[*a*]anthracene (DMBA), test substances were applied twice weekly to the backs of mice and the resultant skin tumour rates, tumour yields and latency times observed. Application of an ethyl acetate extract at 2.5 mg (corresponding to 0.39 g of root) for 24 weeks produced a tumour rate of 73% and a tumour yield of 3 per animal with a latency time of 14.2 weeks. When stillingia factors S8 and S9 were applied at 12 µg and 13.6 µg respectively (each corresponding to about 20 nmol) for 24 weeks, S8 caused moderately strong tumour promotion (tumour rate, 50%; tumour yield, 1; latency time 17.5 weeks) while S9 was strongly tumour-promoting (tumour rate, 50%; tumour yield, 2.8; latency time 22.4 weeks). As a positive control, TPA applied at 3.1 µg (5 nmol) was very strongly tumour-promoting (tumour rate, 88%; tumour yield, 7.5; latency time 13.3 weeks) [6,7].

CLINICAL STUDIES

None published on mono-preparations of queen's delight.

THERAPEUTICS

Actions
Due to its mildly irritant properties [BPC 1934] queen's delight acts reflexively as a sialagogue and expectorant [1,4,8,9].

Also stated to be diaphoretic, astringent and spasmolytic, and to be a dermatological agent [9].

Indications
None substantiated by pharmacological or clinical studies.

Uses based on experience or tradition
Internal: Bronchitis and laryngitis; exudative skin eruptions [8-10] with lymphatic involvement; haemorrhoids [9].
External: As a lotion for haemorrhoids, eczema and psoriasis [10].

In earlier times queen's delight was also used in the treatment of syphilis [1,3,8] and scrofula [8,10].

Contraindications
Pregnancy and lactation [11].

Side effects
None known at recommended dosage levels. In large doses, queen's delight is emetic and purgative [3,4,8,10], and causes a burning sensation in the alimentary canal [8].

Interactions with other drugs
None known.

Dosage
Three times daily: dried root, 1-2 g or by decoction [4,9]; liquid extract 1:1 in 25% alcohol, 0.5-2 ml [3,8,9]; tincture 1:5 in 45% alcohol, 2-8 ml [8].

Recommended dose levels should not be exceeded. See the Safety section below.

SAFETY

Except in licensed medicines, which are limited to a maximum single dose of 320 mg [12], queen's delight should be used only under professional supervision [10].

No case reports appear to have been published of adverse effects of queen's delight. However, the sap of the root is reported to be inflammatory and produces swellings on the skin, and oral overdoses of root preparations to cause dizziness, burning in the mouth, throat and gastrointestinal tract, diarrhoea, nausea, vomiting, coughs, depression, difficulty in urination, irritable itching and skin eruptions [7].

Although their concentrations in the root are very low, the diterpene esters in queen's delight are highly toxic. The intraperitoneal LD_{50} of stillingia factor S6 (gnidilatidin) in mice was determined as 1.7 mg/kg body weight [7] and intraperitoneal administration of 56 µg of S7 (prostratin) to an 18 g mouse (i.e. about 3 mg/kg) caused death within 2 hours [13].

Tumour promoters of the irritant diterpene ester type have been described as "co-carcinogens" and as "*per se* essentially non-carcinogenic amplifiers" of carcinogenesis [14]. *In vivo* tumour-promoting activities of an ethyl acetate extract and diterpene esters (notably S9) from queen's delight have been demonstrated [6,7]. In Germany, where it is used only in homoeopathic preparations, queen's delight has been restricted to dilutions of at least D3 since 1989; further limitation to D4 has been recommended on the basis of scientific study in animals [6].

In the light of research data on the skin irritant and tumour-promoting activities of its diterpene esters [6,7] and the lack of scientific evidence to support its reputed herbal uses [11], the risk-benefit ratio for queen's delight seems particularly unfavourable. Internal use at phytotherapeutic dose levels is difficult to justify and external use also seems undesirable. It would perhaps be prudent to avoid the use of queen's delight altogether.

REGULATORY STATUS

Medicines

UK	Accepted for general sale, internal or external use; maximum single dose, 320 mg [12].
France	Not listed in *Médicaments à base de plantes* [15].
Germany	No Commission E monograph published.

Food

Not used in food.

REFERENCES

Current Pharmacopoeial Monographs

BHP Queen's Delight

Literature References

1. Rogers DJ. A revision of Stillingia in the New World. *Ann. Missouri Bot. Gard.* 1951, **38**, 207-259.
2. Youngken HW and Vander Wyk RW. Studies of National Formulary drugs. *J. Am. Pharm. Assoc.* 1939, **28**, 17-33.
3. Wood HC and LaWall CH, editors. Stillingia N.F. In: *United States Dispensatory, Centennial (22nd) Edition.* Philadelphia-London: JB Lippincott Company, 1937:1028-1029.
4. Pharmaceutical Society of Great Britain. Stillingia. In: *The British Pharmaceutical Codex 1934.* London: Pharmaceutical Press, 1934:1008.
5. Adolf W and Hecker E. New irritant diterpene esters from roots of *Stillingia sylvatica* L. Euphorbiaceae. *Tetrahedron Lett.* 1980, **21**, 2887-2890.
6. Zahn P. Über iatrogene - inbesondere kanzerogene - Risiken homöopathischer Urtinkturen aus Wolfsmilchgewächsen (Euphorbiaceae). Umsetzung einer allgemeinen Strategie zur Abschätzung irritierender und tumorpromovierender Risikopotentiale in spezielle Prüfpläne und deren Ergebnisse bei einigen homöopathischen Urtinkturen [Iatrogenic - especially carcinogenic - risks associated with homoeopathic mother tinctures from certain plants of the Euphorbiaceae. Conversion of a general strategy for estimation of irritant and tumour-promoting risk potential into specialized testing plans, and their results with a few homoeopathic mother tinctures [Dissertation]. Heidelberg: Ruprecht-Karls-Universtät, 1998 [GERMAN].
7. Zahn P and Hecker E. Stillingia. In: Blaschek W, Hänsel R, Keller K, Reichling J, Rimpler H and Schneider G, editors. *Hagers Handbuch der Pharmazeutischen Praxis, 5th ed. Supplement Volume 3: Drogen L-Z.* ISBN 3-540-61619-5. Berlin-Heidelberg-New York-London: Springer, 1998:579-583 [GERMAN].
8. Grieve M (edited by Leyel CF). Queen's Delight - *Stillingia sylvatica.* In: *A Modern Herbal* (first published 1931; revised 1973). ISBN 1-85501-249-9. London: Tiger Books International, 1994:664.
9. Stillingia. In: *British Herbal Pharmacopoeia 1983.* ISBN 0-903032-07-4. Bournemouth: British Herbal Medicine Association, 1983.
10. Chevallier A. Queen's Delight - *Stillingia sylvatica.* In: *Encyclopedia of Medicinal Plants, 2nd ed.* ISBN 0-7513-1209-6. London-New York: Dorling Kindersley, 2001:272.
11. Barnes J, Anderson LA and Phillipson JD. Queen's Delight. In: *Herbal Medicines - A guide for healthcare professionals, 2nd ed.* ISBN 0-85369-474-5. London-Chicago: Pharmaceutical Press, 2002:395-396.
12. Queen's Delight. In: UK Statutory Instrument 1994 No. 2410. The Medicines (Products Other Than Veterinary Drugs) (General Sale List) Amendment Order 1994. Schedule 1, Table A.
13. Cashmore AR, Seelye RN, Cain BF, Mack H, Schmidt R and Hecker E. The structure of prostratin: a toxic tetracyclic diterpene ester from *Pimelea prostrata. Tetrahedron Lett.* 1976, (20), 1737-1738.
14. Hecker E. Tumour promoters of the irritant diterpene ester type as risk factors of cancer in man. *Bot. J. Linnean Soc.* 1987, **94**, 197-219.
15. *Médicaments à base de plantes.* ISBN 2-911473-02-7. Saint-Denis Cedex, France: Agence du Médicament, 1998.

RASPBERRY LEAF

Rosaceae

Rubi idaei folium

Definition

Raspberry Leaf consists of the dried leaflets of *Rubus idaeus* L., harvested in spring or early summer.

CONSTITUENTS

□ ***Hydrolysable tannins***, principally ellagitannins [1] and especially sanguiin H-6 [2,3], thought to arise from oxidative coupling of α- and β-1-O-galloyl-2,3:4,6-bis-(*S*)-hexahydroxydiphenoyl-D-glucoses, which have been isolated from raspberry leaf together with 2,3:4,6-bis-(S)-hexahydroxy-diphenoyl-D-glucose [3]. The gallotannins 1,2,6-trigalloylglucose and pentagalloyl-D-glucose [4], and free gallic and ellagic acids [5], have also been isolated.

The total tannin content by the hide powder method in raspberry leaf from 12 cultivated varieties was found to be in the range 2.6-6.7% (average 4.7%) [6], while a much higher figure of 11.2% was reported in another study [7].

By HPLC, the content of ellagic acid was 2.1-4.1% (average 3.2%) [6].

□ ***Flavonoids*** Kaempferol and quercetin and their 3-glucosides (i.e. astragalin and isoquercitrin), 3-galactosides [8-10], 3-glucuronides and 3-xylosyl-glucuronides [10]. Also kaempferol 3-arabinoside and 3-(6″-*p*-coumaroyl)-glucoside (i.e. tiliroside) [8], and rutin (quercetin 3-rutinoside) [11].

From HPLC analysis after acid hydrolysis of glycosides, the total amounts of flavonol aglycones in raspberry leaf from 12 cultivated varieties were in the range 0.29-0.57% (0.17-0.31% for kaempferol and 0.10-0.32% for quercetin) [6], corresponding to around 0.5-1.0% of flavonol glycosides in the leaf. The total flavonoid content by spectrophotometry has been reported as 0.5-0.8% expressed as hyperoside (kaempferol 3-galactoside) [6] and as 2.8-5.6% expressed as rutin [9]; the latter range seems too high and needs confirmation.

□ ***Phenolic acids*** Caffeic, *p*-coumaric, ferulic, protocatechuic, gentisic, *p*-hydroxybenzoic, vanillic and other acids [12].

□ ***Other constituents*** include methyl gallate [8], ascorbic acid [13], minerals including calcium, magnesium, zinc and trace elements [14], and small amounts of volatiles such as 2-hexenal and 3-hexenol [15].

Published Assay Methods

Determination of tannins in herbal drugs [Ph. Eur. method 2.8.14]. Total flavonoids by spectrophotometry [6,9]. Flavonoid aglycones (after acid hydrolysis of glycosides) and ellagic acid by HPLC [6].

PHARMACOLOGY

In vitro

In an early study (1954) aqueous extracts of rasp-

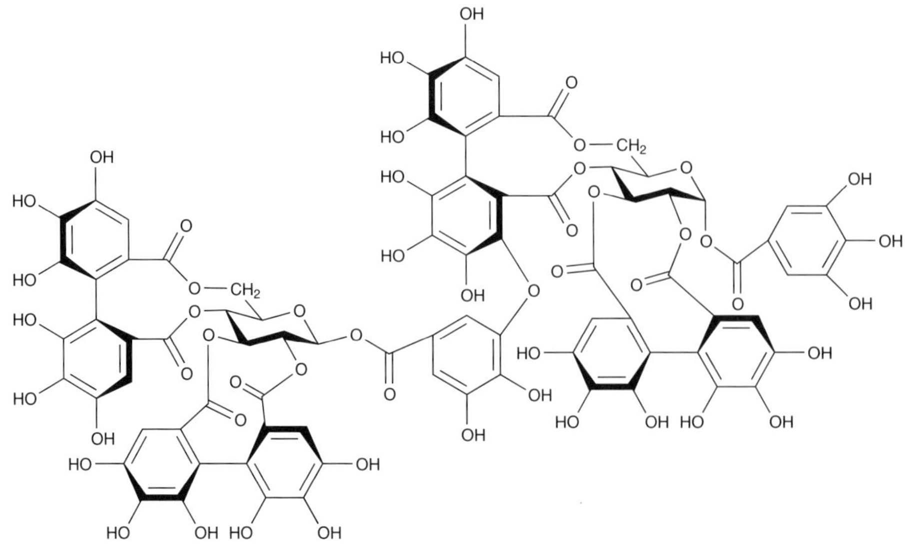

Sanguiin H-6

berry leaf were shown to contain unidentified active principles which stimulated smooth muscle, some fractions producing much greater stimulation of isolated guinea pig uterine muscle than of other smooth muscle, but also anticholinesterase activity and spasmolytic activity in other experiments. The mutually antagonistic actions made it difficult to predict what the overall clinical effect might be [16].

Chromatographically separated fractions from a chloroform extract of raspberry leaf produced relaxant effects on isolated guinea pig ileum but no active constituents were identified [17]. Further work by the same group indicated that unidentified compounds of a relatively polar nature exert dose-dependent relaxant activity on isolated guinea pig ileum [18].

A saline infusion of raspberry leaf had little or no effect on strips from human and rat non-pregnant uteri but inhibited contractions of strips from human (at 10-16 weeks of pregnancy) and rat pregnant uteri; inhibition lasted several minutes then intrinsic contractions resumed. The researchers noted that in uteri in which a pharmacological effect was observed (pregnant human and rat uteri) the intrinsic rhythm over a 20-minute period, while the extract remained in contact with the tissue, appeared to become more regular in most cases and contractions were less frequent [19].

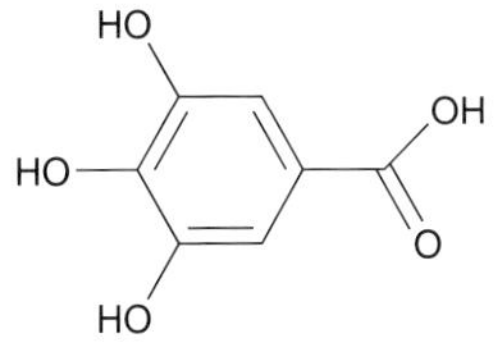

Gallic Acid

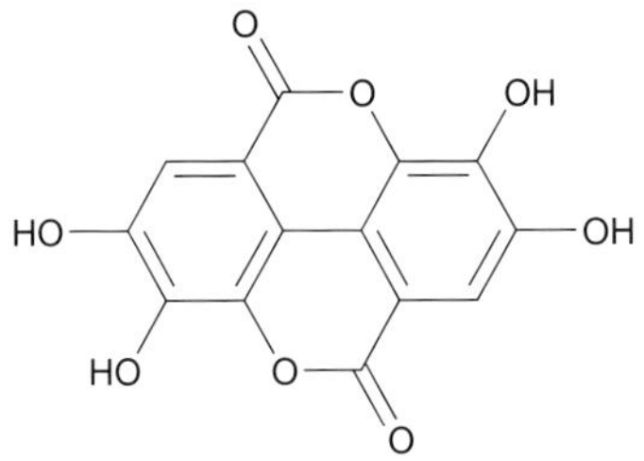

Ellagic acid

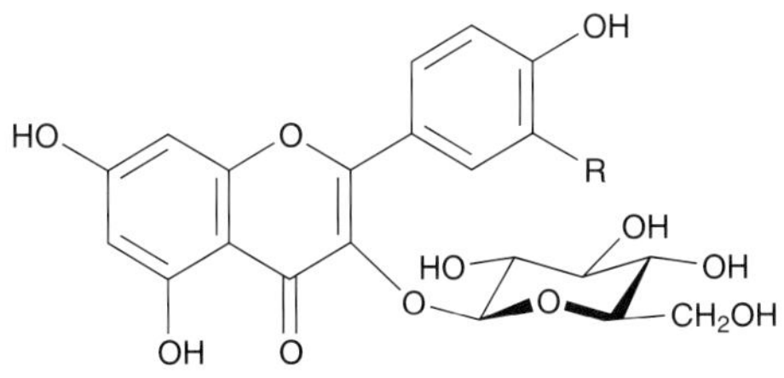

Astragalin R = H
Isoquercitrin R = OH

Raspberry leaf showed an appreciable amount of antigonadotrophic activity *in vitro*, determined by inactivation of pregnant mares' serum gonadotrophin, which subsequently had a reduced effect on ovarian weight increase in female rats compared to controls. The activity was seasonally variable and declined on storage of dried leaf for 15 months [20].

In screening tests on medicinal plants, raspberry leaf exhibited oestrogenic activity, enhancing proliferation of the oestrogen-sensitive MCF-7 breast cancer cell line. Compared to controls, proliferation of 163% and 178% was observed with a dry methanolic extract from raspberry leaf at concentrations of 1 and 10 µg/ml respectively, compared to proliferation of 130% and 157% with a soybean isoflavone glycoside fraction at the same concentrations. So far this intriguing observation does not appear to have been followed up [21].

In vivo
From a complicated series of experiments reported in 1941, Burn and Withell found that in cats an intravenously administered infusion of raspberry leaf had a rather variable relaxant effect on the uterus and intestine when in tone, but produced contraction in rabbit uterus. Relaxation was also produced in isolated uterus of dog, cat and rabbit when in tone, but contractions when not in tone; only contractions occurred in guinea pig uterus. The name 'fragarine' was proposed for the unknown active principle, although no specific active substance has ever been identified [22].

Pharmacological studies in humans
Clinical observations on three women 5-8 days *after* childbirth using an intra-uterine bag method showed that a single oral dose of raspberry leaf extract (1.3-2.6 g) diminished the force and frequency of uterine contractions and eliminated secondary contractions within 30 minutes of administration [23].

In summary, the results of early pharmacological studies were somewhat paradoxical, apparently demonstrating that raspberry leaf can produce both uterine contractions and relaxant effects. Bamford et al. offered an interpretation in 1970: 'A major problem in obstetrics is in coordination of uterine action and it may be that raspberry leaf extract is able to modify the course of labour favourably by producing more coordinated uterine contractions' [19].

CLINICAL STUDIES

The consumption of raspberry leaf (usually as a tea or in tablet form) during pregnancy has been popular for generations. In the early 1940s, nursing staff at a Worcestershire maternity hospital reported favourably on the effect of raspberry leaf tea in 'making things easier' [23]. No current statistics are available for the UK but the use of raspberry leaf remains popular with some expectant mothers. From a partial survey in 1999 of members of the American College of Nurse-Midwives, 90 respondents used herbal preparations to stimulate labour (compared to 82 who did not); 63% had used raspberry leaf among other herbal preparations, either by direct prescribing or suggestion to expectant mothers [24]. Raspberry leaf is also recommended by some obstetricians and midwives in Australia in the belief that it may shorten labour and ease childbirth [25]. However, no clinical data were available until recently.

In a retrospective study (no influence from the investigators on the consumption of raspberry leaf) carried out by midwives on women who gave birth in 1998 at a hospital in Sydney, Australia, 57 women who had taken raspberry leaf preparations (the raspberry leaf group, RL) were compared with 51 women who had not (the control group, C) by means of medical records and a questionnaire completed by participants. The two groups were reasonably comparable in age, weight, parity, ethnicity and level of obstetric care. Individual self-dosage in the raspberry leaf group had varied widely, from 1 to 6 cups of raspberry leaf tea daily or from 1 to 8 tablets, commencing as early as week 8 of gestation: 13% commenced between weeks 8-28, 59% between weeks 30-34 and 28% between weeks 35-39, with duration of consumption over continuous periods of 1-32 weeks.

Although most of the differences in labour and birth outcomes did not reach statistical significance (which required $p \leq 0.05$), the quantitative data revealed trends in favour of raspberry leaf. Average gestation periods (GP) were similar in both groups (GP_{RL} 283.9 days, GP_C 281.5 days), but the standard deviation (SD_{RL} 8.20, SD_C 12.10) was markedly lower in the raspberry leaf group than in the control group ($p = 0.067$). There was less likelihood of artificial rupture of membranes in the raspberry leaf group (22/57, 38.6%) than in the control group (27/51, 52.9%) ($p = 0.13$). Excluding mothers who gave birth by caesarean section, the mean time (T) in the first stage of labour was substantially lower (T_{RL} 301.6 minutes, T_C 387.8 minutes; $p = 0.165$) and the spread of time (SD) significantly lower (SD_{RL} 212.5, SD_C 349.8; $p = 0.007$) in the raspberry leaf group than in the control group. The percentage of normal deliveries was slightly larger in the raspberry leaf group (44/57, 77.2%) than in the control group (34/51, 66.7%).

Thus, while extraneous variables were not controlled and interpretation of the data should be treated with caution, the results suggested that ingestion of raspberry leaf may decrease the likelihood of pre- or post-term delivery, may shorten the labour process and may reduce the need for medical intervention. In the questionnaires, a majority of the treatment group indicated that raspberry leaf was perceived to shorten labour (68%) and would be taken in future pregnancies (84%) [25].

Subsequently, a randomized, double-blind clinical study was carried out at a Sydney hospital in 1999-2000 on low-risk nulliparous women, who received 2 tablets daily, each containing 0.4 g of raspberry leaf extract (3:1), equivalent to 2.4 g of dried leaf daily (n = 96), or placebo (n = 96), from week 33 of gestation until commencement of labour.

The anticipated effect of a shorter first stage of labour was not observed. However, there were promising findings in the raspberry leaf group:

- A shortening of the second stage of labour by 12% (mean difference of 9.6 minutes; $p = 0.28$, not statistically significant).
- More women than would be expected by chance had normal vaginal births (62.4% vs. 50.6% in the placebo group) with accordingly a lower rate of forceps or vacuum-assisted deliveries (19.3% vs. 30.4% in the placebo group; $p = 0.19$); this was considered by the researchers to be clinically (although not statistically) significant and may have been associated with the reduction in length of the second stage of labour. The level of emergency caesarean sections was similar in the two groups. More mothers in the raspberry leaf group experienced spontaneous rupture of membranes and therefore had less need for artificial rupture of membranes to initiate or accelerate labour.

The results prompted consideration as to whether the dosage, acknowledged as conservative in the first study of its kind, had been too conservative - and whether a higher dose than 2.4 g of raspberry leaf per day, or commencement at an earlier gestational stage, might contribute to a more clinically significant outcome. Overall, taking into account a wide range of clinical data, it was concluded that raspberry leaf not only seems to be safe but may be of benefit for women and their babies during the labour and birth process, with an increase in maternal satisfaction [26].

THERAPEUTICS

Actions

Astringent, parturifacient [27-29].

Indications
None adequately substantiated by pharmacological or clinical studies.

However, the encouraging trends observed in two clinical studies of the effects of raspberry leaf in childbirth [25,26] suggest that further controlled studies would be useful.

Uses based on experience or tradition
To facilitate parturition [25-29].
Painful and profuse menstruation [16,23,28,29]; diarrhoea; stomatitis and tonsillitis (as a mouthwash) [27,29,30]; externally as a wash for superficial wounds and ulcers [29,30].

Contraindications
Early stages of pregnancy.
Raspberry leaf preparations should only be taken during the final 8-10 weeks of pregnancy [29].

Side effects
None known.
Constipation reported by a few women (4 out of 96) taking raspberry leaf, compared to none in the placebo group, in a controlled clinical study was not clearly attributable to the preparation since it is a common pregnancy complaint [26].

Interactions with other drugs
None known.

Dosage
2-3 times daily: dried leaf 3-4 g, or as a 5% infusion or equivalent extract.
Higher doses of up to twice this amount (maximum: 24 g dried leaf per day) have also been recommended [27,28].

SAFETY

Historically, no adverse events appear to have been reported in the literature with respect to consumption of raspberry leaf by expectant mothers. No complications were reported by American nurse-midwives from the use of raspberry leaf tea 'freely in late pregnancy as an uterine tonic' [24].

In the clinical studies undertaken in Australian hospital maternity units, 57 expectant mothers in the retrospective study [25] and 96 in the controlled study [26] consumed raspberry leaf. Its safety was assessed, in comparison with the control/placebo groups, from variables in the recorded clinical and physiological data, such as maternal blood loss at birth, maternal diastolic blood pressure, presence of meconium-stained fluid, newborn Apgar score at 5 minutes, newborn birth weight, newborn admission to neonatal intensive or special care facilities and the occurrence of participant-reported side effects.

Basically, no significant differences in these variables, and no concerns regarding the safety of raspberry leaf for mother or baby, emerged from either study. In the retrospective study, participants reported one case of diarrhoea and one of increased frequency of Braxton Hicks contractions (normal contractions of pregnancy); if attributable to raspberry leaf, they might have been avoided by lower dosage [25]. In the controlled study, the only complaints exclusive to the raspberry leaf group were four cases of constipation, which could be attributed to the astringency of raspberry leaf or to its being a common pregnancy complaint [26].

REGULATORY STATUS

Medicines

UK	Accepted for general sale, internal or external use (although no product licences relating to use during pregnancy have been granted) [31].
France	Not listed in *Médicaments à base de plantes* [32].
Germany	Commission E monograph published: not approved for any indications [33].

Food

Council of Europe	Permitted as flavouring, category N2 [34].

REFERENCES

Current Pharmacopoeial Monographs

BHP	Raspberry Leaf
DAC	Himbeerblätter

Literature References

1. Haslam E. Natural Polyphenols (Vegetable Tannins) as Drugs: Possible Modes of Action. *J. Nat. Prod.* 1996, **59**, 205-215.
2. Haslam E, Lilley TH, Cai Y, Martin R and Magnolato D. Traditional Herbal Medicines - The Role of Polyphenols. *Planta Medica* 1989, **55**, 1-8.
3. Gupta RK, Al-Shafi SMK, Layden K and Haslam E. The Metabolism of Gallic Acid and Hexahydroxydiphenic Acid in Plants. Part 2. Esters of (*S*)-Hexahydroxydiphenic Acid with D-Glucopyranose ($^4C_1$). *J. Chem. Soc. Perkin Trans. I.* 1982, 2525-2534.
4. Haddock EA, Gupta RK, Al-Shafi SMK and Haslam E. The Metabolism of Gallic Acid and Hexahydroxydiphenic Acid in Plants. Part 1. Introduction. Naturally Occurring Galloyl Esters. *J. Chem. Soc. Perkin Trans. I.* 1982, 2515-2524.
5. Marczal G. A Rubi idaei folium cseranyagtartalmának kvalitativ vizsgálata [Qualitative investigations on the tannin content of Rubi idaei folium]. *Herba Hungarica* 1963, **2**, 343-360 [HUNGARIAN/German summary].
6. Gudej J and Tomczyk M. Determination of Flavonoids, Tannins and Ellagic Acid in Leaves from *Rubus* L. Species. *Arch. Pharmacal. Res.* 2004, **27**, 1114-1119.
7. Lamaison JL, Carnat A and Petitjean-Freytet C. Tannin content and elastase inhibiting activity in the Rosaceae

family. *Ann. Pharm. Fr.* 1990, **48**, 335-340 [FRENCH/English summary].
8. Gudej J. Kaempferol and quercetin glycosides from *Rubus idaeus* L. leaves. *Acta Polon. Pharm.* 2003, **60**, 313-316.
9. Nikitina VS, Shendel GV, Gerchikov AY and Efimenko NB. Flavonoids from raspberry and blackberry leaves and their antioxidant activities. *Khim.-Farm. Zh.* 2000, **34** (11), 25-27 [RUSSIAN], translated into English as *Pharmaceut. Chem. J.* 2000, **34** (11), 596-598.
10. Henning W. Flavonol Glycosides of Strawberries (*Fragaria × ananassa* Duch.), Raspberries (*Rubus idaeus* L.) und Blackberries (*Rubus fruticosus* L.). 14. Phenolics of Fruits. *Z. Lebensm. Unters. Forsch.* 1981, **173**, 180-187 [GERMAN/English summary].
11. Khabibullaeva LA and Khazanovich RL. Phytochemical study of raspberry leaves. *Mater. Yubileinoi Resp. Nauchn. Konf. Farm., Posvyashch. 50-Letiyu Obraz. SSSR. September 1972.* (Pub. 1972): 98-99 [RUSSIAN]; through *Chem. Abstr.* 1975, **83**, 4960.
12. Krzaczek T. Phenolic acids in some tannin drugs from the Rosaceae family. *Farm. Pol.* 1984, **40**, 475-477 [POLISH]; through *Chem. Abstr.* 1985, **102**, 146198.
13. Fejer SO, Johnston FB, Spangelo LPS and Hammill MM. Ascorbic acid in red raspberry fruit and leaves. *Can. J. Plant Sci.* 1970, **50**, 457-461; through *Chem. Abstr.* 1970, **73**, 106273.
14. Hughes M, Chaplin MH and Dixon AR. Elemental Composition of Red Raspberry leaves as a Function of Time of Season and Position of Cane. *Hortscience* 1979, **14**, 46-47.
15. Czygan F-C. Die Himbeere - *Rubus idaeus*. Portrait einer Arzneipflanze [Raspberry - *Rubus idaeus*. Portrait of a medicinal plant]. *Z. Phytotherapie* 1995, **16**, 366-374 [GERMAN/English summary].
16. Beckett AH, Belthle FW and Fell KR. The active constituents of raspberry leaves. A preliminary investigation. *J. Pharm. Pharmacol.* 1954, **6**, 785-796.
17. Patel AV, Obiyan J, Patel N, and Dacke CG. Raspberry leaf extract relaxes intestinal smooth muscle in vitro. *J. Pharm. Pharmacol.* 1995, **47**, 1129.
18. Rojas-Vera J, Patel AV and Dacke CG. Relaxant activity of raspberry (*Rubus idaeus*) leaf extract in guinea-pig ileum in vitro. *Phytotherapy Res.* 2002, **16**, 665-668.
19. Bamford DS, Percival RC and Tothill AU. Raspberry leaf tea: a new aspect of an old problem. *Brit. J. Pharmacol.* 1970, **40**, 161P-162P.
20. Graham RCB and Noble RL. Comparison of *in vitro* activity of various species of *Lithospermum* and other plants to inactivate gonadotrophin. *Endocrinology* 1955, **56**, 239-47.
21. Yoshikawa M, Uemura T, Shimoda H, Kishi A, Kawahara Y and Matsuda H. Medicinal Foodstuffs. XVIII. Phytoestrogens from the Aerial Part of *Petroselinum crispum* Mill. (Parsley) and Structures of 6''-Acetylapiin and a New Monoterpene Glycoside, Petroside. *Chem. Pharm. Bull.* 2000, **48**, 1039-1044.
22. Burn JH and Withell ER. A principle in raspberry leaves which relaxes uterine muscle. *Lancet* 1941, (2), 1-3.
23. Whitehouse B. Fragarine: an inhibitor of uterine action. *Brit. Med. J.* 1941, (13 Sept.), 370-371.
24. McFarlin BL, Gibson MH, O'Rear J and Harman P. A National Survey of Herbal Preparation Use by Nurse-Midwives for Labor Stimulation. Review of the Literature and Recommendations for Practice. *J. Nurse-Midwifery* 1999, **44**, 205-216.
25. Parsons M, Simpson M and Ponton T. Raspberry leaf and its effect on labour: safety and efficacy. *Australian College of Midwives Incorporated Journal* 1999, **12** (3), 20-25.
26. Simpson M, Parsons M, Greenwood J and Wade K. Raspberry leaf in pregnancy: its safety and efficacy in labor. *J. Midwifery Women's Health* 2001, **546**, 51-59.
27. Rubus. In: *British Herbal Pharmacopoeia 1983*. ISBN 0-903032-07-4. Bournemouth: British Herbal Medicine Association, 1983.
28. Pharmaceutical Society of Great Britain. Rubi idaei folium - Raspberry leaf. In: *British Pharmaceutical Codex 1949*. London: Pharmaceutical Press, 1949:772-773.
29. Chevallier A. Raspberry. In: *The Encyclopedia of Medicinal Plants*. ISBN 0-7513-0314-3. London-New York-Stuttgart: Dorling Kindersley, 1996:262.
30. Grieve M (edited by Leyel CF). Raspberry. In: *A Modern Herbal* (First published 1931; revised 1973). ISBN 1-85501-249-9. London: Tiger Books International, 1994:671-672.
31. Raspberry. In: UK Statutory Instrument 1994 No. 2410. The Medicines (Products Other Than Veterinary Drugs) (General Sale List) Amendment Order 1994. Schedule 1, Table A.
32. *Médicaments à base de plantes*. ISBN 2-911473-02-7. Saint-Denis Cedex, France: Agence du Médicament, 1998.
33. Rubi idaei folium. German Commission E Monograph published in: Bundesanzeiger No. 193 of 15.10.87.
34. Rubus idaeus L., leaves. In: *Flavouring Substances and Natural Sources of Flavourings, 3rd ed.* ISBN 2-7160-0081-6. Strasbourg: Council of Europe, 1981.

REGULATORY GUIDELINES FROM OTHER EU COUNTRIES

GERMANY

Commission E monograph [33]: Rubi idaei folium (Himbeerblätter).

Uses

Raspberry leaf is used for disorders and ailments of the gastrointestinal tract, the respiratory tract, the cardiovascular system and the mouth and throat; also for skin rashes and inflammation, influenza, fever, menstrual disorders, diabetes and vitamin deficiency, as a diaphoretic, diuretic and choleretic, and to 'purify the blood and skin'.

The claimed uses are not proven.

Risks

None known

Assessment

Since efficacy in the claimed areas of use is not substantiated, therapeutic use cannot be supported.

ROSEMARY LEAF

Labiatae

Rosmarini folium

Definition
Rosemary Leaf consists of the dried leaves of *Rosmarinus officinalis* L.

The dried flowering tops of *Rosmarinus officinalis* have also been used medicinally and were official in the Pharmacopée Française up to 2002.

CONSTITUENTS

□ ***Essential oil***, 0.4-2.4% [1-3] (Ph. Eur. min. 1.2% V/m), of very variable composition. The principal components are usually 1,8-cineole (up to 89%), α-pinene (up to 29%) and camphor (up to 23%); other components include bornyl acetate, borneol, camphene, *p*-cymene, β-pinene and α-terpineol [2-8].

In oil distilled from Dalmatian leaf the main components were 1,8-cineole (30.5%), α-pinene (20.4%) and camphor (11.7%) [5], and from 8 samples, probably of flowering tops, of Spanish origin, 1,8-cineole (18-23%), α-pinene (13-23%) and camphor (19-23%) [2]. From two different chemotypes cultivated in Tuscany, one yielded oil containing 1,8-cineole (8.5%), α-pinene (28.6%) and camphor (9.3%) while the other gave oil containing 1,8-cineole (43.3%), α-pinene (18.6%) and camphor (4.6%) [9].

□ ***Hydroxycinnamic acid derivatives***, ca. 3.5% (Ph. Eur. min. 3.0% expressed as rosmarinic acid), principally rosmarinic acid (a dimer of caffeic acid, 2.0-2.5% by HPLC) [10,11]. Caffeic acid (0.7%) and small amounts of sinapic, p-coumaric, ferulic and other hydroxycinnamic (and benzoic) derivatives are also present [12].

□ ***Phenolic diterpenes*** Carnosic acid, a tricyclic diterpene, which is converted by oxidation into carnosol. In turn, carnosol can degrade further to produce other phenolic diterpenes with γ-lactone structures, such as rosmanol, epirosmanol and 7-methylepirosmanol [13,14]. Thus the nature and amount of individual phenolic diterpenes in a sample is related to its status (dry or fresh leaf, storage conditions, method of extraction etc.) [15].

Reliable quantitative determination of carnosic acid can be problematical due to its instability, particularly in polar solvents [16]. When extracted with supercritical carbon dioxide (which avoids oxidation) and determined by HPLC, the content of carnosic acid in samples of rosemary leaf cultivated in Spain was usually in the range of 0.2-0.4%, the highest figure being 0.735% [17]. Another study, using several extraction methods and HPLC assay found 0.19-0.28% of carnosic acid and 0.015-0.03% of carnosol in dried leaf [15]. In a study of the variation in carnosic acid content of rosemary leaf over a 12-month period, a level of 0.4% in February rose briefly to over 1.0% in young leaves in March and remained over 0.6% during summer and autumn (dry weight basis, extracted with dimethyl sulfoxide, determined by HPLC) [13].

Rosmariquinone, a related (but not phenolic) diterpene, is also present in rosemary leaf [18].

□ ***Triterpenes*** Ursolic acid (up to 4%) and oleanolic acid (ca. 1.0%) [19-21], and the 3-acetyl derivatives of these [20]. Also rofficerone (3-oxo-20β-hydroxyurs-12-ene), α- and β-amyrin, α- and β-amyrenone [20], betulin [22] and betulinic acid [21,23].

□ ***Flavonoids*** Flavones and flavone glycosides including genkwanin (apigenin 7-methyl ether)

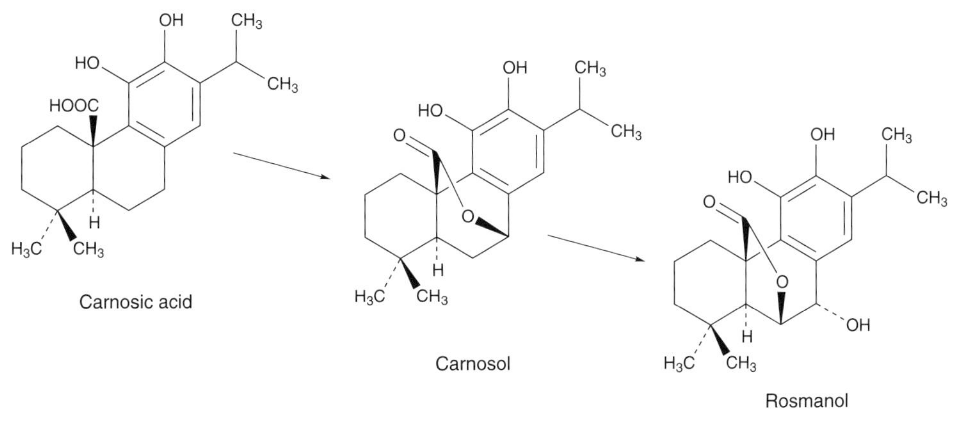

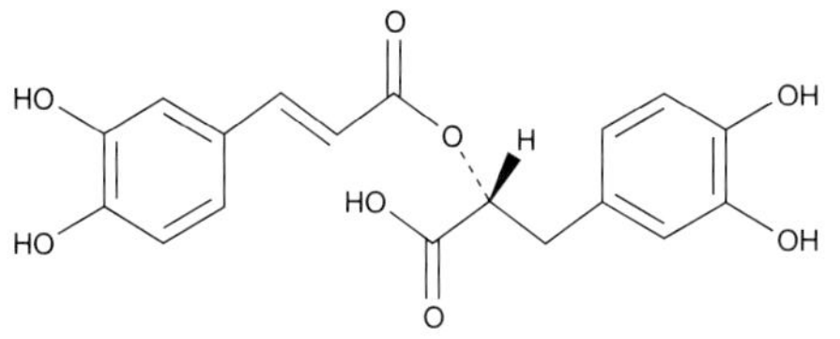

Rosmarinic acid

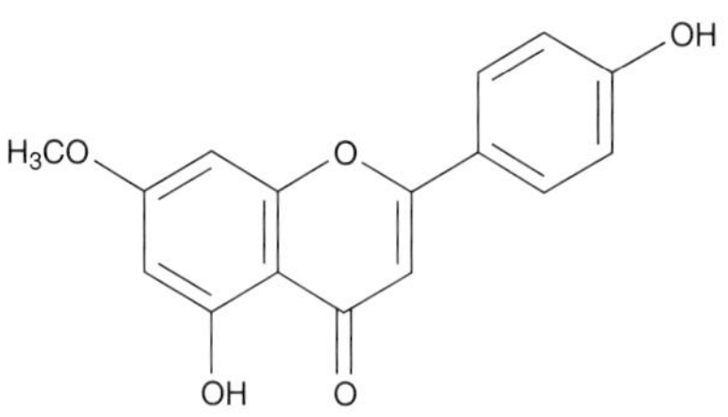

Genkwanin

[13,23,24] and its 4′-glucoside (phegopolin) [25], 6-methoxygenkwanin (cirsimaritin) [22] and its 4′-glucoside (cirsimarin) [25], 4′-methoxygenkwanin [26], apigenin 7-glucoside (apigetrin), isoscutellarein 7-glucoside [13], hispidulin 7-glucoside (homoplantaginin), diosmin [25], luteolin 3′-glucuronide and its 3″- and 4″-acetyl derivatives [25,27], 6-methoxyluteolin 7-glucoside (nepitrin) [24,25] and others.

Also the flavanone hesperidin (hesperetin 7-rutinoside) [25,27].

Published Assay Methods
Total hydroxycinnamic acid derivatives by spectrophotometry [Ph. Eur.]. Phenolic diterpenes by HPLC [13,15,17].

PHARMACOLOGY

In vitro

Antioxidant activity
Antioxidant activity is one of the most important properties of rosemary leaf extracts; it is comparable to that of the synthetic antioxidants butylated hydroxyanisole (BHA) and butylated hydroxytoluene (BHT). Rosemary leaf extracts are therefore used as food additives to stabilise fat-containing foodstuffs against oxidation. About 90% of the antioxidant activity can be attributed to carnosol and carnosic acid [28].

Carnosic acid, carnosol, rosmanol and epirosmanol potently inhibited superoxide anion production in the xanthine/xanthine oxidase system and completely inhibited lipid peroxidation in rat liver mitochondria and microsomes at concentrations of 3-30 μM, demonstrating their ability to protect tissues and cells against oxidative stresses [29].

Other effects
Antimicrobial and antispasmodic activities of rosemary leaf essential oil have been demonstrated; a summary of the data may be found in the ESCOP monograph [30].

In vivo

Anti-inflammatory effects
A dry 80%-ethanolic extract from rosemary leaf showed moderate anti-inflammatory activity, inhibiting carrageenan-induced paw oedema in rats by 27% ($p<0.05$) after oral administration at 100 mg/kg body weight, while indometacin at 5 mg/kg produced 45% inhibition ($p<0.01$) [31].

Topical application of 3.6 mg of a dry methanolic extract from rosemary leaf to the backs of mice twice a day for 4 days inhibited skin inflammation and hyperplasia induced by 12-*O*-tetradecanoylphorbol-13-acetate (TPA) [Ho 1994/2]. A similar extract, applied topically to the ears of mice at 0.02-0.24 mg/ear, inhibited arachidonic acid-induced oedema by 16-54% [28].

Rosmarinic acid pre-administered intramuscularly to rats at 0.3-3 mg/kg inhibited cobra venom factor-induced paw oedema ($p<0.05$) [32].

Diuretic effects
Oral administration to rats of an aqueous extract corresponding to rosemary leaf at 0.8 g/kg for 7 days had a somewhat delayed diuretic effect. The increase in urine volume was significant on days 5-7 compared to controls ($p<0.01$ for the peak effect on day 5). Surprisingly, twice this dosage (1.6 g/kg daily) had a much lesser effect, which did not reach statistical significance. Urinary excretion of sodium, potassium and chloride also increased, the most significant effects being on day 6 in the 0.8 g/kg group ($p<0.001$ in each case) [33].

Anti-ulcerogenic effects
The anti-ulcerogenic activity of a 70%-ethanolic extract from rosemary aerial parts was demonstrated in rats in several experiments. After oral administration at 1000 mg/kg the extract reduced the index of indometacin-induced ulcerative lesions (by 44%, $p<0.05$ compared to saline), as did cimetidine at 100 mg/kg ($p<0.001$) as positive control. It also reduced the index of ethanol-induced lesions (by 74.6%, $p<0.01$), as did carbenoxolone at 200 mg/kg as positive control ($p<0.01$). In the reserpine-induced ulcer model, the extract reduced the index by 51.8% ($p<0.01$), as did atropine at 10

mg/kg as positive control ($p<0.01$) [34].

Tumour inhibition
A dry methanolic extract from rosemary leaf, applied topically to the dorsal skin of mice, inhibited the initiation and promotion of tumours by various carcinogens. Further experiments demonstrated that carnosol and ursolic acid are the constituents mainly responsible for these effects [14,28].

Oral administration of a rosemary extract to rats as 1% of their diet for 21 weeks reduced the frequency of 7,12-dimethylbenz[*a*]anthracene (DMBA)-induced mammary carcinoma to 40% compared to 76% in the control group [35].

CNS stimulation
Inhalation of rosemary oil vapour (headspace analysis: 39.0% 1,8-cineole, 19.2% α-pinene, 13.9% β-pinene, 9.3% limonene, 8.4% camphor) by mice, or oral administration of rosemary oil at 20-40 µl per mouse, produced dose-related increases in blood levels of 1,8-cineole. Both methods of administration led to a 4-fold stimulation of locomotor activity ($p<0.001$) about an hour after inhalation or ingestion. This suggested a direct pharmacological action on the central nervous system, but no conclusion could be drawn as to which component(s) of the oil had the stimulatory effect, 1,8-cineole serving only as a marker substance [36].

Other effects
Choleretic, cholagogic and hepatoprotective effects of rosemary leaf extracts, and antispasmodic activity of the essential oil have also been demonstrated [30].

Pharmacological studies in humans
In a study assessing the olfactory impact of essential oil aromas on cognitive performance and mood, healthy volunteers were exposed to the vapours of rosemary oil ($n = 48$) or water ($n = 48$, as control) under ambient conditions in testing cubicles while completing a battery of computerized cognitive tests and a visual analogue mood questionnaire. To prevent expectancy effects, the participants were deceived as to the genuine aim of the study until completion of testing. Compared to the control, rosemary oil enhanced performance slightly with respect to overall quality of memory and significantly with respect to secondary memory factors ($p<0.05$), but impaired the speed of memory ($p<0.05$) and had no effect on working memory. With regard to mood after completion of the cognitive assessment battery, the rosemary oil group was more alert ($p<0.05$) and more content ($p<0.01$) than the control group [37].

Pharmacokinetics
Rosmarinic acid orally administered to rats at 200 mg/kg was excreted in the urine (32% within 48 hours) as six metabolites, mainly *m*-hydroxyphenylpropionic acid and *trans-m*-coumaric acid 3-sulphate. Four of the metabolites were also detected in the plasma, but none in the bile [38].

1,8-Cineole could be detected in the blood of mice after inhalation of rosemary essential oil vapour [36].

CLINICAL STUDIES

None published on mono-preparations of rosemary leaf.

THERAPEUTICS

Actions
Antioxidant [28,29], spasmolytic [39-42], carminative [40-42], anti-inflammatory [14,28,31], diuretic [33,40], antimicrobial [40], anti-ulcerogenic [34], tumour-inhibiting [14,28], choleretic, cholagogic [30,43] and hepatoprotective [30]. In external use, rubefacient [39,40,46] and mildly analgesic [40].

Rosemary has a general stimulant and tonic effect on the circulation, nervous system and digestion [41,42,44,45].

Indications
None adequately substantiated by pharmacological or clinical studies.

Uses based on experience or tradition
Internal: Digestive complaints including dyspepsia, flatulence and bloating [39,40,43]; as a tonic to raise the spirits in mild depressive states and to aid recovery from debility or chronic illness [40,42,44]; as a circulatory stimulant in cases of circulatory weakness, including hypotension [45].

Has been used to ease headaches [40,44] caused by feeble circulation [47]. Stated to increase the flow of blood to the head, thereby stimulating the brain and enhancing mental performance [41,44]; to some extent this is supported by one study in healthy volunteers [37].

External: Rheumatic ailments [39,46], myalgia, sciatica [40] and neuralgia [40,46].

Has been used in hair lotions to improve blood flow to the scalp [44], to encourage hair growth and as a remedy for dandruff [47].

Contraindications
None known.

Side effects
None known.

Interactions with other drugs
None known.

Dosage

Internal daily dose: Dried leaf, 4-6 g [39], or as an infusion or liquid extract (1:1 in 45% alcohol) [40].

External use: As an infusion for compresses or hair rinses [42]. As a tincture (1:5, 70% ethanol) [35]. As a bath additive, a decoction from 50 g of dried leaf to a full bath [39]. Essential oil (4-6%) diluted with almond oil [42] or in semi-solid preparations [39] for application to joints, muscles etc.

SAFETY

Besides being a familiar culinary herb, rosemary leaf is widely accepted for therapeutic use, internally or externally. During pregnancy, however, it should not be taken in amounts greatly exceeding those encountered in foods on the basis that, although evidence is elusive, it is traditionally reputed to be abortifacient, emmenagogic and an uterine stimulant [48,49].

A single dose of a 15%-alcoholic extract from rosemary flowering tops, administered intraperitoneally to rats and mice at 2 g/kg caused neither deaths nor behavioural changes over a period of 15 days and no abnormalities were revealed during autopsy [50].

A rosemary extract exhibited strongly antimutagenic effects in *Salmonella typhimurium* strain TA102 against mutagenicity induced by *tert*-butyl hydroperoxide. The effect was attributed to the antioxidant properties of the extract [51].

REGULATORY STATUS

Medicines

UK	Accepted for general sale, internal or external use [52].
France	Accepted for specified indications [43].
Germany	Commission E monograph published, with approved uses [39].

Food

USA	Generally recognized as safe (21 CFR 182.10 and 182.20) [53].
Council of Europe	Permitted as flavouring, category N2 [54].

REFERENCES

Current Pharmacopoeial Monographs

Ph. Eur. Rosemary Leaf

Literature References

1. Angioni A, Barra A, Ceretti E, Barile D, Coïsson JD, Arlorio M et al. Chemical Composition, Plant Genetic Differences, Antimicrobial and Antifungal Activity Investigation of the Essential Oil of *Rosmarinus officinalis* L. *J. Agric. Food Chem.* 2004, **52**, 3530-3535.
2. Svoboda KP and Deans SG. A Study of the Variability of Rosemary and Sage and their Volatile Oils on the British Market: their Antioxidative Properties. *Flavour Fragrance J.* 1992, **7**, 81-87.
3. Panizzi L, Flamini G, Cioni PL and Morelli I. Composition and antimicrobial properties of essential oils of four Mediterranean Lamiaceae. *J. Ethnopharmacol.* 1993, **39**, 167-170.
4. Daferera DJ, Ziogas BN and Polissiou MG. GC-MS Analysis of Essential Oils from Some Greek Aromatic Plants and Their Fungitoxicity on *Penicillium digitatum*. *J. Agric. Food Chem.* 2000, **48**, 2576-2581.
5. Mastelic J and Kustrak D. Essential oil and glycosidically bound volatiles in aromatic plants. II. Rosemary (*Rosmarinus officinalis* L., Lamiaceae). *Acta Pharm. (Zagreb)* 1997, **47**, 139-142.
6. Pérez-Alonso MJ, Velasco-Negueruela A, Duru ME, Harmandar M and Esteban JL. Composition of the Essential Oils of *Ocimum basilicum* var. *glabratum* and *Rosmarinus officinalis* from Turkey. *J. Essent. Oil Res.* 1995, **7**, 73-75.
7. Boatto G, Pintore G, Palomba M, de Simone F, Ramundo E and Iodice C. Composition and antibacterial activity of *Inula helenium* and *Rosmarinus officinalis* essential oils. *Fitoterapia* 1994, **65**, 279-280.
8. Lawrence BM. Chemical components of Labiatae oils and their exploitation. In: Harley RM and Reynolds T, editors. *Advances in Labiate Science*. Kew: Royal Botanic Gardens, 1992:399-436.
9. Flamini G, Cioni PL, Morelli I, Macchia M and Ceccarini L. Main Agronomic-Productive Characteristics of Two Ecotypes of *Rosmarinus officinalis* L. and Chemical Composition of Their Essential Oils. *J. Agric. Food Chem.* 2002, **50**, 3512-3517.
10. Lamaison JL, Petitjean-Freytet C, Duband F and Carnat AP. Rosmarinic acid content and antioxidant activity in French Lamiaceae. *Fitoterapia* 1991, **62**, 166-171.
11. Gracza L and Ruff P. Rosmarinsäure in Arzneibuchdrogen und ihre HPLC-Bestimmung [Rosmarinic acid in pharmacopoeial plant drugs and its determination by HPLC]. *Arch. Pharm. (Weinheim)* 1984, **317**, 339-345 [GERMAN/English summary].
12. Schulz JM and Herrmann K. Occurrence of Hydroxybenzoic Acids and Hydroxycinnamic Acids in Spices. IV. Phenolics of Spices. *Z. Lebensm. Unters. Forsch.* 1980, **171**, 193-199 [GERMAN/English summary].
13. del Baño MJ, Lorente J, Castillo J, Benavente-García O, del Río JA, Ortuño A et al. Phenolic Diterpenes, Flavones, and Rosmarinic Acid Distribution during the Development of Leaves, Flowers, Stems and Roots of *Rosmarinus officinalis*. Antioxidant Activity. *J. Agric. Food Chem.* 2003, **51**, 4247-4253.
14. Ho C-T, Ferraro T, Chen Q, Rosen RT and Huang M-T. Phytochemicals in Teas and Rosemary and Their Cancer-Preventive Properties. In: Ho C-T, Osawa T, Huang M-T, Rosen RT, editors. *Food Phytochemicals for Cancer Prevention II: Teas, Spices and Herbs*. ACS Symposium Series 547. Washington DC: American Chemical Society, 1994:2-19.
15. Bicchi C, Binello A and Rubiolo P. Determination of Phenolic Diterpene Antioxidants in Rosemary (*Rosmarinus officinalis* L.) with Different Methods of Extraction and Analysis. *Phytochem. Analysis* 2000, **11**, 236-242.
16. Thorsen MA and Hildebrandt KS. Quantitative determination of phenolic diterpenes in rosemary extracts. Aspects of accurate quantification. *J. Chromatogr. A* 2003, **995**, 119-125.
17. Hidalgo PJ, Ubera JL, Tena MT and Valcárcel M. Determination of the Carnosic Acid Content in Wild and Cultivated *Rosmarinus officinalis*. *J. Agric. Food. Chem.* 1998, **46**, 2624-2627.
18. Houlihan CM, Ho C-T and Chang SS. The Structure of Rosmariquinone - A New Antioxidant Isolated from

Rosmarinus officinalis L. *JAOCS* 1985, **62**, 96-98.
19. Brieskorn CH, Eberhardt KH and Briner M. Biogenetische Zusammenhänge zwischen Oxytriterpensäuren und ätherischem Öl bei einigen pharmazeutisch wichtigen Labiaten [Biogenetic relationships between oxytriterpene acids and essential oils in some pharmaceutically important Labiatae]. *Arch. Pharm. (Weinheim)* 1953, **286**, 501-506 [GERMAN].
20. Ganeva Y, Tsankova E, Simova S, Apostolova B and Zaharieva E. Rofficerone: A New Triterpenoid from *Rosmarinus officinalis. Planta Medica* 1993, **59**, 276-277.
21. Abe F, Yamauchi T, Nagao T, Kinjo J, Okabe H, Higo H and Akahane H. Ursolic Acid as a Trypanocidal Constituent in Rosemary. *Biol. Pharm. Bull.* 2002, **25**, 1485-1487.
22. Arisawa M, Hayashi T, Ohmura K, Nagayama K, Shimizu M and Morita N. Chemical and pharmaceutical studies on medicinal plants in Paraguay: Studies on "Romero", Part 2. *J. Nat. Prod.* 1987, **50**, 1164-1166.
23. Hayashi T, Arisawa M, Bandome T, Namose Y, Shimizu M, Suzuki S et al. Studies on Medicinal Plants in Paraguay: Studies on "Romero", Part I. *Planta Medica* 1987, **53**, 394.
24. Brieskorn CH and Michel H. Flavone aus dem Blatt von *Rosmarinus officinalis* [Flavones from the leaf of *Rosmarinus officinalis*]. *Tetrahedron Lett.* 1968, (30), 3447-3448 [GERMAN].
25. Aeschbach R, Philipossian G and Richli U. Flavonoid glycosides from rosemary: separation, isolation and identification. *Bull. Liaison - Groupe Polyphenols* 1986, **13**, 56-58 [FRENCH]; through *Chem. Abstr.* 108:34769.
26. Brieskorn CH and Dömling HJ. Zum Vorkommen von 5-Hydroxy-7,4'-dimethoxyflavon im Blatt von Rosmarinus officinalis [Occurrence of 5-hydroxy-7,4'-dimethoxyflavone in the leaf of *Rosmarinus officinalis*]. *Arch. Pharm. (Weinheim)* 1967, **300**, 1042-1044 [GERMAN].
27. Okamura N, Haraguchi H, Hashimoto K and Yagi A. Flavonoids in *Rosmarinus officinalis* leaves. *Phytochemistry* 1994, **37**, 1463-1466.
28. Huang M-T, Ho C-T, Wang ZY, Ferraro T, Lou Y-R, Stauber K et al. Inhibition of Skin Tumorigenesis by Rosemary and Its Constituents Carnosol and Ursolic Acid. *Cancer Res.* 1994, **54**, 701-708.
29. Haraguchi H, Saito T, Okamura N and Yagi A. Inhibition of Lipid Peroxidation and Superoxide Generation by Diterpenoids from *Rosmarinus officinalis. Planta Medica* 1995, **61**, 333-336.
30. European Scientific Cooperative on Phytotherapy. Rosmarini folium - Rosemary Leaf. In: *ESCOP Monographs - The Scientific Foundation for Herbal Medicinal Products, 2nd ed.* Stuttgart-New York: Thieme; Exeter, UK: ESCOP, 2003:429-436.
31. Mascolo N, Autore G, Capasso F, Menghini A and Fasulo MP. Biological Screening of Italian Medicinal Plants for Anti-inflammatory Activity. *Phytotherapy Res.* 1987, **1**, 28-31.
32. Englberger W, Hadding U, Etschenberg E, Graf E, Leyck S, Winkelmann J and Parnham MJ. Rosmarinic acid: a new inhibitor of complement C3-convertase with anti-inflammatory activity. *Int. J. Immunopharmacol.* 1988, **10**, 729-737.
33. Haloui M, Louedec L, Michel J-B and Lyoussi B. Experimental diuretic effects of *Rosmarinus officinalis* and *Centaurium erythraea. J. Ethnopharmacol.* 2000, **71**, 465-472.
34. Corrêa Dias P, Foglio MA, Possenti A and de Carvalho JE. Antiulcerogenic activity of crude hydroalcoholic extract of *Rosmarinus officinalis* L. *J. Ethnopharmacol.* 2000, **69**, 57-62.
35. Hänsel R, Keller K, Rimpler H and Schneider G, editors. Rosmarinus. In: *Hagers Handbuch der Pharmazeutischen Praxis, 5th ed. Volume 6: Drogen P-Z.* ISBN 3-540-52639-0. Berlin-Heidelberg-New York-London: Springer-Verlag, 1994:490-503 [GERMAN].
36. Kovar KA, Gropper B, Friess D and Ammon HPT. Blood Levels of 1,8-Cineole and Locomotor Activity of Mice After Inhalation and Oral Administration of Rosemary Oil. *Planta Medica* 1987, **53**, 315-318.
37. Moss M, Cook J, Wesnes K ands Duckett P. Aromas of rosemary and lavender essential oils differentially affect cognition and mood in healthy adults. *Intern. J. Neurosci.* 2003, **113**, 15-38.
38. Nakazawa T and Ohsawa K. Metabolism of Rosmarinic Acid in Rats. *J. Nat. Prod.* 1998, **61**, 993-996.
39. Rosmarini folium. German Commission E Monograph published in: Bundesanzeiger No. 223 of 30 November 1985; amended in Bundesanzeiger No. 221 of 28 November 1986 and Bundesanzeiger No. 50 of 13 March 1990.
40. Rosmarinus. In: *British Herbal Pharmacopoeia 1983.* ISBN 0-903032-07-4. Bournemouth: British Herbal Medicine Association, 1983.
41. McIntyre A. Rosemary - *Rosmarinus officinalis.* In: *The Complete Woman's Herbal.* ISBN 1-85675-135-X. London: Gaia Books, 1994:56.
42. Ody P. *Rosmarinus officinalis* - Rosemary. In: *The Complete Guide - Medicinal Herbal.* ISBN 0-7513-3005-1. London-New York: Dorling Kindersley, 2000:112.
43. Romarin. In: *Médicaments à base de plantes.* ISBN 2-911473-02-7. Saint-Denis Cedex, France: Agence du Médicament, 1998.
44. Chevallier A. Rosemary - *Rosmarinus officinalis.* In: *Encyclopedia of Medicinal Plants, 2nd ed.* ISBN 0-7513-1209-6. London-New York: Dorling Kindersley, 2001:128.
45. Weiss RF. *Rosmarinus officinalis* (Rosemary). In: *Herbal Medicine* (translated from the 6th German edition of *Lehrbuch der Phytotherapie*). ISBN 0-906584-19-1. Gothenburg: AB Arcanum, Beaconsfield, UK: Beaconsfield Publishers, 1988:185-186.
46. Stodola J and Volák J. Rosemary. Translated into English in: Bunney S, editor. *The Illustrated Book of Herbs.* ISBN 0-7064-1489-6. London: Octopus Books, 1984:250.
47. Grieve M (edited by Leyel CF). Rosemary. In: *A Modern Herbal* (first published 1931; revised 1973). ISBN 1-85501-249-9. London: Tiger Books International, 1994:681-683.
48. McGuffin M, Hobbs C, Upton R and Goldberg A, editors. *Rosmarinus officinalis* L. In: American Herbal Products Association's *Botanical Safety Handbook.* Boca Raton-Boston-London: CRC Press, 1997:99.
49. Barnes J, Anderson LA and Phillipson JD. Rosemary. In: *Herbal Medicines - A guide for healthcare professionals, 2nd ed.* ISBN 0-85369-474-5. London-Chicago: Pharmaceutical Press, 2002:403-407.
50. Mongold JJ, Camillieri S, Susplugas P, Taillade C, Masse JP and Serrano JJ. Activité cholagogue/cholérétique d'un extrait lyophilisé de *Rosmarinus officinalis* L. *Plantes Méd. Phytothér.* 1991, **25**, 6-11 [FRENCH/English summary].
51. Minnunni M, Wolleb U, Mueller O, Pfeifer A and Aeschbacher HU. Natural antioxidants as inhibitors of oxygen species induced mutagenicity. *Mutation Res.* 1992, **269**, 193-200.
52. Rosemary. In: UK Statutory Instrument 1994 No. 2410. The Medicines (Products Other Than Veterinary Drugs) (General Sale List) Amendment Order 1994. Schedule 1, Table A.
53. Rosemary. In: Sections 182.10 and 182.20 of USA Code of Federal Regulations, Title 21, Food and Drugs, Parts 170 to 199. Revised as of April 1, 2000.
54. Rosmarinus officinalis L., leaves. In: *Flavouring Substances and Natural Sources of Flavourings, 3rd ed.* ISBN 2-7160-0081-6. Strasbourg: Council of Europe, 1981.

REGULATORY GUIDELINES FROM OTHER EU COUNTRIES

FRANCE

Médicaments à base de plantes [43]: Romarin; feuille, sommité fleurie.

Therapeutic indications accepted

Oral use
Traditionally used: in the symptomatic treatment of

digestive disorders such as epigastric distension, sluggish digestion, eructation and flatulence; to facilitate urinary and digestive elimination functions; as a choleretic or cholagogue.

Topical use
Traditionally used: in the event of blocked nose in colds; locally in mouthwashes, for buccal hygiene.

GERMANY

Commission E monograph [39]: Rosmarini folium (Rosmarinblätter).

Uses
Internal: Dyspeptic complaints.
External: Supportive therapy for rheumatic ailments; circulatory problems.

Contraindications
None known.

Side effects
None known.

Interactions with other drugs
None known.

Dosage
Internal Daily dose: 4-6 g of the drug, 10-20 drops of essential oil or equivalent preparations.
External 50 g of the drug to a full bath; 6-10% of essential oil in semi-solid and liquid preparations; equivalent preparations.

Mode of administration
Comminuted drug for infusions; powdered drug, dry extract and other galenic preparations for internal and external use.

Actions
Experimentally: spasmolytic on the bile duct and small intestine, positively inotropic, increases coronary flow. In humans: rubefacient, promotes circulation (external use).

SAGE LEAF

Labiatae

Salviae officinalis folium

Synonyms: Common or Dalmatian sage leaf.

Definition
Sage Leaf consists of the dried leaves of *Salvia officinalis* L.

Monographs on (common or Dalmatian) sage leaf from *Salvia officinalis* L. and three-lobed sage leaf from *Salvia fructicosa* Mill. [*S. triloba* L. fil.] appear in the European Pharmacopoeia. Certain other well-known *Salvia* species, such as *S. lavandulaefolia* (or *lavandulifolia*) Vahl (Spanish sage) and *S. sclarea* L. (clary sage) are used primarily for their essential oils.

CONSTITUENTS

□ ***Essential oil***, up to 3% [1] (Ph. Eur. min. 1.5% V/m for whole dried leaf, 1.0% V/m for cut dried leaf), of very variable composition depending on the source, time of harvesting and other factors. The principal components are monoterpenoids such as α-thujone (10-60%), β-thujone (4-36%), camphor (5-20%) and 1,8-cineole (2-15%), together with sesquiterpenes such as α-humulene, β-caryophyllene and viridiflorol [1-3].
□ ***Hydroxycinnamic acid derivatives***, about 3.5%, principally the caffeic acid dimer rosmarinic acid (up to 3.3%) [4]. Caffeic acid trimers (melitric acid A, methyl melitrate A, sagecoumarin and salvianolic acid K) [5,6] and a tetramer (sagerinic acid) [6] have also been isolated.

Collectively, these and similar compounds are sometimes described as "tannins" or "Labiatae tannins" since they may be adsorbed by hide powder to some extent in methods for the determination of tannins in herbal drugs (e.g. Ph. Eur. method 2.8.14). However, they are not genuine tannins in the sense of condensed tannins (proanthocyanidins) or hydrolysable tannins (gallo- and ellagitannins).

Other hydroxycinnamic compounds present include 6-feruloyl-glucose [7] and a polyalcohol derivative of it [8], three hydroxycinnamic esters of disaccharides, e.g. 1-caffeoyl-(6′-apiosyl)-glucoside [9] and free caffeic acid [8].
□ ***Phenolic diterpenes*** Carnosic acid, a tricyclic diterpene, occurs in the fresh leaf [10] and to some extent in the dried leaf [11] and certain types of extract [12]. However, carnosic acid is fairly unstable and readily auto-oxidises to form lactones (see the diagram in the Rosemary Leaf monograph), especially the bitter-tasting lactone carnosol (0.35%) [10]. In turn, carnosol can degrade further to produce other phenolic diterpenes with lactone structures, such as rosmanol, epirosmanol, 7-methoxyrosmanol and galdosol, which have been identified in sage leaf [11,13] and/or sage oleoresin [12].

Safficinolide and sageone [14], methyl carnosate, the lactone sagequinone methide A [11], and other related diterpenes [11] have also been isolated. Some of these compounds may be artefacts formed during extraction and isolation.
□ ***Triterpenes*** Pentacyclic triterpene acids, mainly ursolic acid (up to 3.5%) and oleanolic acid (up to 0.4%), and the triterpene alcohols α- and β-amyrin (0.18% and 0.10% respectively) [15].
□ ***Flavonoids***, ca. 1.1% [16], principally flavones and their glycosides including: luteolin, its 7-glucoside, 7-glucuronide, 3′-glucuronide and 7-methyl ether; 6-hydroxyluteolin, its 7-glucoside and 7-

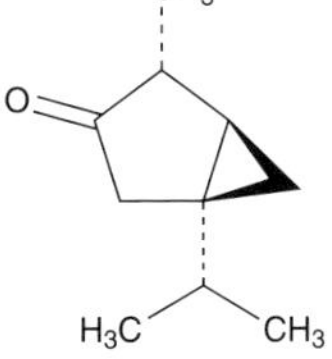

α-Thujone

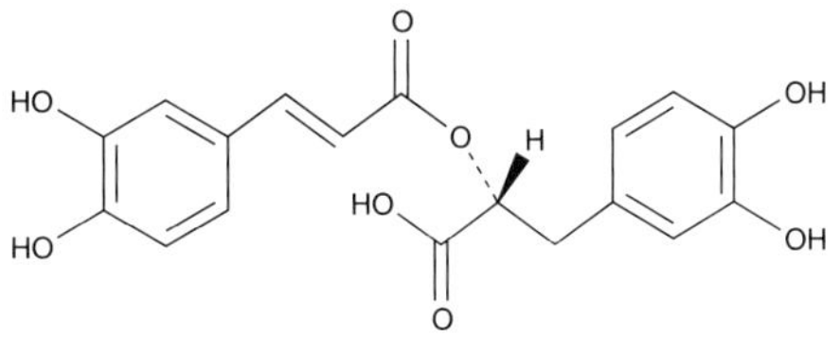

Rosmarinic acid

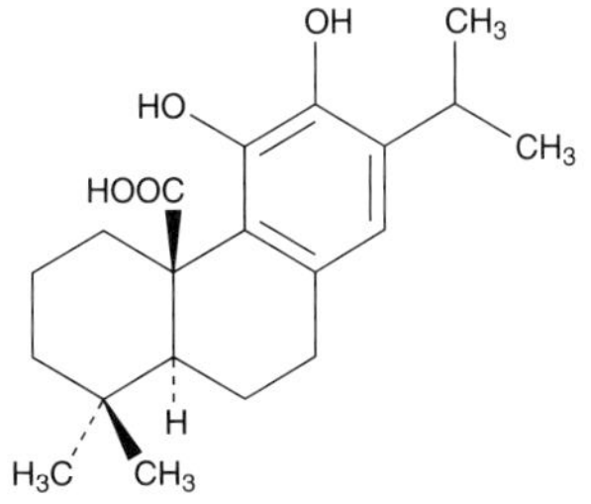

Carnosic acid

glucuronide; 6-methoxyluteolin and its 7-methyl ether; apigenin, its 7-glucoside and 7-methyl ether (= genkwanin); 6-methoxyapigenin (= hispidulin) and its 7-methyl ether (cirsimaritin); vicenin-2 (= apigenin 6,8-di-*C*-glucoside) [13,17-19] and 5-methoxysalvigenin [20].

☐ ***Phenolic glycosides***, a diverse range including, in addition to the glycosides mentioned under Hydroxycinnamic acid derivatives and Flavonoids, picein (4-hydroxyacetophenone glucoside), 4-hydroxyacetophenone 4-(6′-apiosyl)-glucoside, *cis*- and *trans*-*p*-coumaric acid 4-(2′-apiosyl)-glucoside, isolariciresinol 3-glucoside, 1-hydroxypinoresinol 1-glucoside and others [7,8,19].

☐ ***Polysaccharides*** Crude fractions rich in water-soluble arabinogalactans and also high-MW pectin and glucuronoxylan-related polysaccharides have been isolated from aerial parts of sage [21,22].

☐ ***Other constituents*** include small amounts of benzoic acid derivatives (*p*-hydroxybenzoic, gentisic, syringic and other acids) [8,23] and phytosterols (β-sitosterol and stigmasterol, 0.001%) [15,18].

Published Assay Methods

Rosmarinic acid by HPLC [24]. Phenolic diterpenes and rosmarinic acid by HPLC [25].

PHARMACOLOGY

In vitro

Antioxidant activity

Sage leaf extracts exhibit strong antioxidant activity, largely attributable to various phenolic constituents including phenolic diterpenes such as carnosol [8] and hydroxycinnamic acid derivatives, notably rosmarinic acid [4].

In a carotene bleaching test, the antioxidative activity of a dry acetone extract (15:1) from sage leaf was found to be 101-116% of that of the synthetic antioxidant butylated hydroxytoluene (BHT) [26].

Lipid peroxidation in both enzyme-dependent and enzyme-independent test systems were inhibited more effectively by a dry 50%-methanolic extract from aerial parts of sage leaf than by α-tocopheryl acid succinate (as a positive control). The antioxidant activity was attributed mainly to phenolic compounds, rosmarinic acid being the main contributor due to its high concentration in the extract [27,28].

Affinity to human benzodiazepine receptors

A methanolic extract from sage leaf showed affinity to human brain benzodiazepine receptors (from post-mortem frontal cortex) by competitive displacement of ^{3}H-flumazenil, a specific benzodiazepine antagonist. Activity-guided analysis revealed five benzodiazepine receptor-active constituents, of which three are flavones and two diterpenes. Compared to diazepam (IC_{50}: 0.05 µM) the diterpene galdosol (IC_{50}: 0.8 µM) and the flavone hispidulin (IC_{50}: 1.3 µM) were the most active; 7-methoxyrosmanol (IC_{50}: 7.2 µM) also exhibited strong affinity, while apigenin (IC_{50}: 30 µM) and cirsimaritin (IC_{50}: 350 µM) were considerably less active [13].

Other activities

Sage oil has strong antimicrobial properties, attributed principally to the presence of thujones. Inhibitory activity of the oil against Gram-positive and Gram-negative bacteria and against a range of fungi has been demonstrated [29,30]. Antiviral activity (against vesicular stomatitis virus) was exhibited by a methanolic extract from sage aerial parts and two phenolic diterpene constituents (safficinolide and sageone) [14].

Sage oil had only a relatively weak spasmolytic effect on isolated guinea pig tracheal and ileal smooth muscle in comparison with oils from other Labiatae such as melissa leaf or thyme [31].

An 80%-ethanolic extract from sage leaf exhibited dose-dependent cholinesterase-inhibiting activity. It was a more selective inhibitor of butyrylcholinesterase (IC_{50}: 0.054 mg/ml) than of acetylcholinesterase (IC_{50}: 0.365 mg/ml) [32].

It has recently been shown that water-soluble polysaccharides isolated from aerial parts of sage possess immunomodulatory activity [21,22].

In vivo

Topically applied chloroform extracts from sage leaf (obtained from four different plant populations) dose-dependently inhibited croton oil-induced ear oedema in mice with an ID_{50} corresponding to dried leaf at 2-4 mg/cm^2. Almost 50% of the extract proved to be ursolic acid which, as an isolated compound, exhibited strong anti-inflammatory activity in the same test with an ID_{50} of 0.14 µMoles/cm^2, almost twice as potent as indometacin with an ID_{50} of 0.26 µMoles/cm^2 [33].

Pharmacological studies in humans

In a double-blind, placebo-controlled, crossover study, 30 healthy young volunteers (17 males, 13 females; mean age 24 years) were given, on three separate days at 7-day intervals in accordance with a randomized scheme, different single-dose treatments in identical opaque capsules: 300 mg or 600 mg of dried sage leaf, or placebo. On each test day, pre-dose and at 1 hour and 4 hours post-dose, each participant underwent mood assessment, requiring completion of Bond-Lader mood scales and the State Trait Anxiety Inventory (STAI) before and after a 20-minute performance on the Defined Intensity Stress Simulator (DISS) computerized multitasking battery. The last comprised a set of four cognitive and psychomotor tasks presented concurrently on a split (quartered) screen layout, to which responses had to be made with an external mouse, giving attention simultaneously to all four tasks while monitoring the cumulative score (reflecting accuracy and speed of response) in the centre of the screen. The DISS engenders increases in self-ratings of negative mood, arousal and stress-related physiological responses.

Both doses of sage leaf led to post-dose improved ratings of mood before performing on the DISS, with the lower dose reducing anxiety and the higher dose increasing 'alertness', 'calmness' and 'contentedness' on the Bond-Lader scales. However, the lower dose reduced alertness on the DISS and, as a result of performing on the DISS, the previously reduced anxiety effect of this dose was abolished. After the higher dose, task performance on the DISS battery improved at both post-dose sessions, but after the lower dose task performance decreased. The results indicated that single doses of sage leaf can improve cognitive performance and mood in healthy young participants, although the lower dose (300 mg) appeared to fall somewhat below the level required for beneficial effects. It is possible that inhibition of cholinesterases by sage leaf (demonstrated only *in vitro*) could be involved in the mechanism causing these effects [32].

CLINICAL STUDIES

In a randomized, double-blind, placebo-controlled study, patients aged 65-80 years of age with a diagnosis of mild to moderate dementia and probable Alzheimer's disease were treated for 16 weeks with 60 drops/day of either a sage leaf liquid extract (1:1, 45% ethanol; n = 15) or a placebo liquid (n = 15). Compared with the placebo group, patients in the sage leaf group experienced significant benefits in cognitive function by the end of treatment, as indicated by improved scores in the Clinical Dementia Rating (CDR; $p<0.003$) and the Alzheimer's Disease Assessment Scale (ADAS-Cog; $p = 0.03$). Within the limitations of a fairly small number of patients and short period of follow-up, the results suggested efficacy of the sage leaf extract in the management of mild to moderate Alzheimer's disease [34].

Several open studies, carried out mainly in the 1930s on patients or healthy volunteers but including a larger 1989 study (unpublished) on 80 patients with idiopathic hyperhidrosis (the secretion of an abnormally large amount of sweat), supported the longstanding belief that sage leaf aqueous extracts have anti-hyperhidrotic activity [35].

THERAPEUTICS

Actions

Antioxidant [4,26-28], anti-inflammatory [33], antimicrobial [29,30], carminative [36,37], weakly spasmolytic [31,37], astringent [36-39], antihidrotic (inhibits perspiration) [37-40]. Considered to be a stimulant and tonic to the digestion and nervous system [36,39].

Recent human studies have demonstrated beneficial effects of sage leaf on cognitive performance and mood in healthy young volunteers [32] and cognitive function in elderly patients with mild to moderate Alzheimer's disease [34].

Indications

None adequately substantiated by pharmacological or clinical studies.

Uses based on experience or tradition

Internal: Digestive disorders such as dyspepsia, flatulence, poor digestion and bloating [37-40]; to reduce excessive perspiration [37-40,42], e.g. in the menopause [39,42]. Also taken as a gentle, stimulating tonic [39].

Topical (as a gargle or mouthwash): Inflammations of the mouth or throat mucosa, such as pharyngitis, tonsillitis, stomatitis, gingivitis and glossitis [36-40].

Contraindications

Sage leaf should not be taken during pregnancy or lactation (except in amounts present as a flavouring in foods) [35,42]. Epileptics are also advised to avoid it due to the convulsant potential of thujones [40].

Side effects

None reported.

Interactions with other drugs

None known.

Dosage

Internal daily dose: 3-6 of dried leaf, usually as an infusion [37,38]; liquid extract 1:1 in 45% ethanol, 2-6 ml [34,37].

For topical use in mouthwashes and gargles: 2.5 g of dried leaf to 100 ml of water as an infusion [38].

SAFETY

The amount of sage leaf consumed as a culinary herb in food presents no hazard, but a degree of caution is necessary with larger amounts due to the presence of thujones and camphor in the essential oil. Recommended dosages should not be exceeded or taken over prolonged periods, and sage leaf preparations should be avoided during pregnancy and lactation [43]. The pure essential oil should never be used [44].

In a randomized clinical study, 15 elderly patients treated with 60 drops/day of a sage leaf liquid extract (1:1, 45% ethanol) for 16 weeks experienced slightly more mild gastrointestinal complaints than those receiving placebo, but the differences were not statistically significant [34].

The oral LD_{50} of the essential oil in rats was found to be 2.6 g/kg [45]. α-Thujone, which is more toxic than β-thujone [46] and is present as a higher proportion of the essential oil [2], is a convulsant. Its intraperitoneal LD_{50} in mice is about 45 mg/kg, while 60 mg/kg causes a tonic convulsion leading to death within 1 minute. The mechanism of α-thujone neurotoxicity has been shown to be modulation of the γ-aminobutyric acid (GABA) type A receptor. However, α-thujone is rapidly detoxified in mice by conversion to less toxic metabolites [46].

In tests for mutagenicity neither ethanolic extracts [47,48] nor the essential oil [49] from sage leaf showed any mutagenic potential.

REGULATORY STATUS

Medicines

UK	Accepted for general sale, internal or external use [50].
France	Accepted for specified indications [41].
Germany	Commission E monograph published, with approved uses [38].

Food

USA	Generally recognized as safe (21 CFR 182.10 and 182.20) [51].
Council of Europe	Permitted as flavouring, category N2 with provisional limits on the content of thujones (α and β) in the finished product (0.5 mg/kg, with some exceptions) [52].

REFERENCES

Current Pharmacopoeial Monographs

Ph. Eur. Sage Leaf (Salvia officinalis)

Literature References

1. Pitarevic I, Kuftinec J, Blazevic N and Kustrak D. Seasonal variation of essential oil yield and composition of Dalmatian sage, *Salvia officinalis*. *J. Nat. Prod.* 1984, **47**, 409-412.
2. Lawrence BM. Progress in Essential Oils. *Perfumer & Flavorist* 1998, **23** (March/April), 47-57.
3. Lawrence BM. Chemical components of Labiatae oils and their exploitation. In: Harley RM and Reynolds T, editors. *Advances in Labiate Science*. Kew: Royal Botanic Gardens, 1992:399-436.
4. Lamaison JL, Petitjean-Freytet C, Duband F and Carnat AP. Rosmarinic acid content and antioxidant activity in French Lamiaceae. *Fitoterapia* 1991, **62**, 166-171.
5. Lu Y, Foo LY and Wong H. Sagecoumarin, a novel caffeic acid trimer from *Salvia officinalis*. *Phytochemistry* 1999, **52**, 1149-1152.
6. Lu Y and Foo LY. Rosmarinic acid derivatives from *Salvia officinalis*. *Phytochemistry* 1999, **51**, 91-94.
7. Wang M, Li J, Rangarajan M, Shao Y, LaVoie EJ, Huang T-C and Ho C-T. Antioxidative Phenolic Compounds from Sage (*Salvia officinalis*). *J. Agric. Food Chem.* 1998, **46**, 4869-4873.
8. Wang M, Kikuzaki H, Zhu N, Sang S, Nakatani N and Ho C-T. Isolation and structure elucidation of two new glycosides from sage (*Salvia officinalis* L.). *J. Agric. Food Chem.* 2000, **48**, 235-238.
9. Wang M, Shao Y, Li J, Zhu N, Rangarajan M, LaVoie EJ and Ho C-T. Antioxidative phenolic glycosides from sage (*Salvia officinalis*). *J. Nat. Prod.* 1999, **62**, 454-456.
10. Brieskorn CH. Salbei - seine Inhaltsstoffe und sein therapeutischer Wert [Sage - its constituents and therapeutic value]. *Z. Phytotherapie* 1991, **12**, 61-69 [GERMAN/English summary].
11. Tada M, Hara T, Hara C and Chiba K. A quinone methide from *Salvia officinalis*. *Phytochemistry* 1997, **45**, 1475-1477.
12. Cuvelier M-E, Berset C and Richard H. Antioxidant Constituents in Sage (*Salvia officinalis*). *J. Agric. Food. Chem.* 1994, **42**, 665-669.
13. Kavvadias D, Monschein V, Sand P, Riederer P and Schreier P. Constituents of Sage (*Salvia officinalis*) with *in vitro* Affinity to Human Brain Benzodiazepine Receptor. *Planta Medica* 2003, **69**, 113-117.
14. Tada M, Okuno K, Chiba K, Ohnishi E and Yoshii T. Antiviral diterpenes from *Salvia officinalis*. *Phytochemistry* 1994, **35**, 539-541.
15. Brieskorn CH and Kapadia Z. Bestandteile von Salvia officinalis. XXIV. Triterpenalkohole, Triterpensäuren und Pristan im Blatt von *Salvia officinalis* L. [Constituents of Salvia officinalis. XXIV. Triterpene alcohols, triterpene acids and pristan in leaves of *Salvia officinalis* L.]. *Planta Medica* 1980, **38**, 86-90 [GERMAN/English summary].
16. Tamas M, Fagarasan E and Ionescu C. Phytochemical study of Salviae folium. *Farmacia (Bucharest)* 1986, **34**, 181-186 [ROMANIAN]; through *Chem. Abstr.* 106:81597.
17. Brieskorn CH, Biechele W. The Flavones from *Salvia officinalis* L. *Arch. Pharm.* 1971, **304**, 557-561 [GERMAN/English summary].
18. Masterova I, Uhrin D, Kettmann V and Suchy V. Phytochemical study of *Salvia officinalis* L. *Chem. Papers* 1989, **43**, 797-803; through *Chem. Abstr.* 112:73917.
19. Lu Y and Foo LY. Flavonoid and phenolic glycosides from *Salvia officinalis*. *Phytochemistry* 2000, **55**, 263-267.
20. Brieskorn CH and Kapadia Z. Constituents of *Salvia officinalis* XXIII: 5-methoxysalvigenin in leaves of *Salvia officinalis*. *Planta Medica* 1979, **35**, 376-378.
21. Capek P, Hríbalová V, Svandová E, Ebringerová A, Sasinková V and Masarová J. Characterization of immunomodulatory polysaccharides from *Salvia officinalis* L. *Int. J. Biol. Macromol.* 2003, **33**, 113-119.
22. Capek P and Hríbalová V. Water-soluble polysaccharides from *Salvia officinalis* L. possessing immunomodulatory activity. *Phytochemistry* 2004, **65**, 1983-1992.
23. Schulz JM and Herrmann K. Occurrence of Hydroxybenzoic Acids and Hydroxycinnamic Acids in Spices. IV. Phenolics of Spices. *Z. Lebensm. Unters. Forsch.* 1980, **171**, 193-199 [GERMAN/English summary].
24. Carnat AP, Carnat A, Fraisse D and Lamaison JL. The aromatic and polyphenolic composition of lemon balm (*Melissa officinalis* L. subsp. *officinalis*) tea. *Pharm. Acta Helv.* 1998, **72**, 301-305.
25. del Baño MJ, Lorente J, Castillo J, Benavente-García O, del Río JA, Ortuño A et al. Phenolic Diterpenes, Flavones, and Rosmarinic Acid Distribution during the Development of Leaves, Flowers, Stems and Roots of *Rosmarinus officinalis*. Antioxidant Activity. *J. Agric. Food Chem.* 2003, **51**, 4247-

4253.

26. Dapkevicius A, Venskutonis R, van Beek TA and Linssen JPH. Antioxidant Activity of Extracts Obtained by Different Isolation Procedures from some Aromatic Herbs Grown in Lithuania. *J. Sci. Food Agric.* 1998, **77**, 140-146.
27. Hohmann J, Zupkó I, Rédei D, Csányi M, Falkay G, Máthé I and Janicsák G. Protective effects of the aerial parts of *Salvia officinalis, Melissa officinalis* and *Lavandula angustifolia* and their constituents against enzyme-dependent and enzyme-independent lipid peroxidation. *Planta Medica* 1999, **65**, 576-578.
28. Zupkó I, Hohmann J, Rédei D, Falkay G, Janicsák G and Máthé I. Antioxidant Activity of Leaves of *Salvia* Species in Enzyme-Dependent and Enzyme-Independent Systems of Lipid Peroxidation and their Phenolic Constituents. *Planta Medica* 2001, **67**, 366-368.
29. Jalsenjak V, Peljnjak S and Kustrak D. Microcapsules of sage oil: essential oils content and antimicrobial activity. *Pharmazie* 1987, **42**, 419-420.
30. Hammer KA, Carson CF and Riley TV. Antimicrobial activity of essential oils and other plant extracts. *J. Applied Microbiol.* 1999, **86**, 985-990.
31. Reiter M and Brandt W. Relaxant Effects on Tracheal and Ileal Smooth Muscles of the Guinea Pig. *Arzneim.-Forsch./Drug Res.* 1985, **35**, 408-414.
32. Kennedy DO, Pace S, Haskell C, Okello EJ, Milne A and Scholey AB. Effects of Cholinesterase Inhibiting Sage (*Salvia officinalis*) on Mood, Anxiety and Performance on a Psychological Stressor Battery. *Neuropsychopharmacology* 2006, **31**, 845-852.
33. Baricevic D, Sosa S, Della Loggia R, Tubaro A, Simonovska B, Krasna A and Zupancic A. Topical anti-inflammatory activity of *Salvia officinalis* L. leaves: the relevance of ursolic acid. *J. Ethnopharmacol.* 2001, **75**, 125-132.
34. Akhondzadeh S, Noroozian M, Mohammadi M, Ohadinia S, Jamshidi AH and Khani M. *Salvia officinalis* extract in the treatment of patients with mild to moderate Alzheimer's disease: a double blind, randomized and placebo-controlled trial. *J. Clin. Pharmacy Ther.* 2003, **28**, 53-59.
35. European Scientific Cooperative on Phytotherapy. Salviae officinalis folium. In: *ESCOP Monographs - The Scientific Foundation for Herbal Medicinal Products, 2nd ed.* Stuttgart-New York: Thieme; Exeter, UK: ESCOP, 2003:452-455.
36. Grieve M (edited by Leyel CF). Sage, Common. In: *A Modern Herbal* (first published 1931; revised 1973). ISBN 1-85501-249-9. London: Tiger Books International, 1994:700-705.
37. Salvia. In: *British Herbal Pharmacopoeia 1983.* ISBN 0-903032-07-4. Bournemouth: British Herbal Medicine Association, 1983.
38. Salviae folium. German Commission E Monograph published in: Bundesanzeiger No. 90 of 15 May 1985; amended in Bundesanzeiger No. 50 of 13 March 1990.
39. Chevallier A. Sage - *Salvia officinalis.* In: *Encyclopedia of Medicinal Plants, 2nd ed.* ISBN 0-7513-1209-6. London-New York: Dorling Kindersley, 2001:131.
40. Stahl-Biskup E, Wichtl M and Neubeck M. Salbeiblätter - Salviae officinalis folium. In: Hartke K, Hartke H, Mutschler E, Rücker G and Wichtl M, editors. *Kommentar zum Europäischen Arzneibuch [Commentary on the European Pharmacopoeia].* Stuttgart: Wissenschaftliche Verlagsgesellschaft, 1999 (12 Lfg.):S 6 [GERMAN].
41. Sauge officinale. In: *Médicaments à base de plantes.* ISBN 2-911473-02-7. Saint-Denis Cedex, France: Agence du Médicament, 1998.
42. Weiss RF. Influenza and Colds - Other Drugs. In: *Herbal Medicine* (translated from the 6th German edition of *Lehrbuch der Phytotherapie*). ISBN 0-906584-19-1. Gothenburg: AB Arcanum, Beaconsfield, UK: Beaconsfield Publishers, 1988:228-229.
43. Barnes J, Anderson LA and Phillipson JD. Sage. In: *Herbal Medicines - A guide for healthcare professionals, 2nd ed.* ISBN 0-85369-474-5. London-Chicago: Pharmaceutical Press, 2002:408-411.
44. Tisserand R and Balacs T. Sage (Dalmatian). In: *Essential Oil Safety - A Guide for Health Care Professionals.* ISBN 0-443-05260-3. Edinburgh: Churchill-Livingstone, 1995:167.
45. von Skramlik E. Über die Giftigkeit und Verträglichkeit von ätherischen Ölen [The toxicity and tolerability of essential oils]. *Pharmazie* 1959, **14**, 435-445 [GERMAN].
46. Höld KM, Sirisoma NS, Ikeda T, Narahashi T and Casida JE. α-Thujone (the active component of absinthe): γ-Aminobutyric acid type A receptor modulation and metabolic detoxification. *Proc. Natl. Acad. Sci. USA* 2000, **97**, 3826-3831.
47. Mahmoud I, Alkofahi A and Abdelaziz A. Mutagenic and Toxic Activities of Several Spices and Some Jordanian Medicinal Plants. *Int. J. Pharmacognosy* 1992, **30**, 81-85.
48. Schimmer O, Krüger A, Paulini H and Haefele F. An evaluation of 55 commercial plant extracts in the Ames mutagenicity test. *Pharmazie* 1994, **49**, 448-451.
49. Zani F, Massimo G, Benvenuti S, Bianchi A, Albasini A, Melegari M et al. Studies on the genotoxic properties of essential oils with *Bacillus subtilis* rec-assay and *Salmonella*/microsome reversion assay. *Planta Medica* 1991, **57**, 237-241.
50. Sage. In: UK Statutory Instrument 1990 No. 1129. The Medicines (Products Other Than Veterinary Drugs) (General Sale List) Amendment Order 1990. Schedule 1, Table A.
51. Sage. In: Sections 182.10 and 182.20 of USA Code of Federal Regulations, Title 21, Food and Drugs, Parts 170 to 199. Revised as of April 1, 2000.
52. Salvia officinalis L., herb, leaf. In: *Flavouring Substances and Natural Sources of Flavourings, 3rd ed.* ISBN 2-7160-0081-6. Strasbourg: Council of Europe, 1981.

REGULATORY GUIDELINES FROM OTHER EU COUNTRIES

FRANCE

Médicaments à base de plantes [41]: Sauge officinale, feuille.

Therapeutic indications accepted

Oral use
Traditionally used in the symptomatic treatment of digestive disorders such as epigastric distension, sluggish digestion, eructation and flatulence.

Topical use
Traditionally used locally in mouthwashes, for buccal hygiene.

GERMANY

Commission E monograph [38]: Salviae folium (Salbeiblätter).

Uses
Internal Dyspeptic complaints; excessive perspiration.
External Inflammation of the mouth and throat mucosa.

Contraindications
The pure essential oil and alcoholic extracts should not be taken during pregnancy.

Side effects
Prolonged ingestion of alcoholic extracts or pure essential oil can cause epileptiform convulsions.

Interactions with other drugs
None known.

Sage Leaf

Dosage
Unless otherwise prescribed:
Internal Daily dose: 4-6 g of the drug; 0.1-0.3 g of essential oil; 2.5-7.5 g of tincture (in accordance with Erg. DAB 6); 1.5-3 g of fluid extract (in accordance with Erg. DAB 6).
Gargles and rinses 2.5 g of the drug or 2-3 drops of essential oil to 100 ml of water as an infusion, or 5 g of alcoholic extract to a glass of water.

Mode of administration
Cut drug for infusions; alcoholic extracts and distillates for gargles, rinses and other topical applications, as well as for internal use; also as pressed juice from the fresh plant.

Actions
Antibacterial, fungistatic, virustatic, astringent, promotes secretion and inhibits perspiration.

SAW PALMETTO FRUIT

Palmae

Serenoae repentis fructus

Synonyms: Sabal, Sabalis serrulatae fructus.

Definition

Saw Palmetto Fruit consists of the partially dried ripe fruits of *Serenoa repens* (Bartram) Small [*Serenoa serrulata* Hook.f., *Sabal serrulata* (Michaux) Nichols].

Serenoa repens is a low shrubby palm which flourishes along the Atlantic coast of the USA from South Carolina to Florida. Colonies of the plant can cover huge areas among pine woods and sand dunes The fan-shaped leaves have long petioles with sharp and rigid serrations, hence the common name saw palmetto. The fruits (also known as berries, and botanically as drupes) are 2-3 cm long, ovoid, green or yellow before ripening and almost black when ripe, and contain a single hard seed. Commercial supplies of the fruits are harvested from the wild [1-3].

CONSTITUENTS

The dried fruits consist of approximately 36% outer rind (epicarp), 16% flesh (mesocarp or sarcocarp), 10% seed shell (endocarp) and 38% seed [1,3].

Lipido-sterolic extracts are used in the majority of saw palmetto fruit preparations and consequently most analyses tend to focus on the constituents present in such extracts. Considering the extensive use of saw palmetto fruit preparations, the published analytical data are rather limited.

LIPIDO-STEROLIC FRACTION

One of three different extraction solvents is generally used in the commercial production of lipido-sterolic extracts from saw palmetto fruit: hexane, ethanol 90% or hypercritical carbon dioxide (CO_2). Approximate yields of extracts based on laboratory-scale extractions have been reported as 11-12% with hexane, 20% with ethanol [4] and 11-14% with CO_2 [5]. Total fatty acid contents of 93-94% have been reported for CO_2 extracts [5,6]. Constituent profiles of the extracts appear to be qualitatively similar and, as far as is known, quantitative differences arising from different extraction solvents or extraction conditions (as well as natural variation between batches) are not of such magnitude as to influence therapeutic efficacy.

The following classes of compounds are found in the lipido-sterolic fraction:

☐ ***Free fatty acids*** The major portion of the lipido-sterolic fraction, representing about 90% of a hexane extract [7] and 85% or more of a CO_2 extract [5], comprising C_6 to C_{18} fatty acids and particularly rich in oleic and lauric acids. The major components (as percentages of the lipophilic fraction) are oleic (C18:1, *cis*-9 mono-unsaturated; 23-36%), lauric (C12:0, saturated; 22-30%), myristic (C14:0, saturated; 8-17%) and palmitic (C16:0, saturated; 6-14%) acids. Smaller amounts of caproic (C6:0), caprylic (C8:0), capric (C10:0), stearic (C18:0), linoleic (C18:2, up to 5%) and linolenic (C18:3) acids are also present [1,5,6,8,9].

Free fatty acids occur mainly in the fruit flesh. It has been suggested that, in the flesh but not the seeds, a particularly active lipase splits fatty acids from triglycerides during ripening and drying of the fruits [1,4]; an alternative view is that no enzyme is present for biosynthesis of triglycerides [8].

☐ ***Triglycerides*** (triacylglycerols, i.e. fatty acids combined with glycerol) in the seeds, composed of fatty acids in similar ratios to the free ones, with oleic acid mainly in the 2-position and lauric acid in 1- and 3-positions [8].

☐ ***Fatty acid esters*** Propyl and ethyl esters of C_6-C_{18} fatty acids (mainly even-numbered ones) with traces of corresponding methyl and butyl esters, the predominant compound being propyl laurate.

Hexane extracts from four batches of dried fruits contained 5.7-7.1% of fatty acid esters, of which propyl laurate represented 27-42%, propyl caprylate 13-17% and ethyl laurate 5-16% (the esters were steam-distilled from the extracts then determined by GC). In contrast, ethanol 90% extracts from the

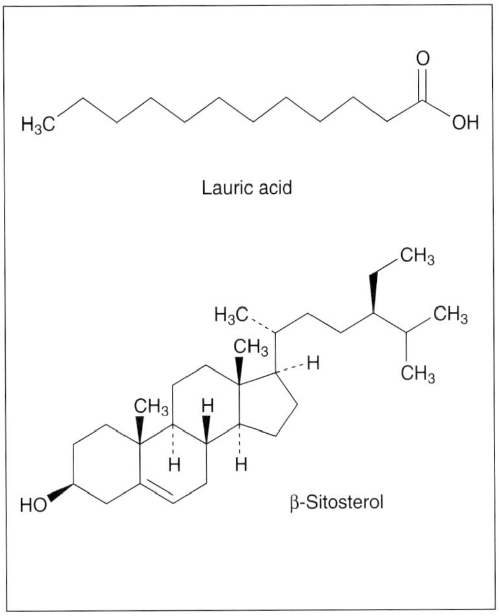

same batches of fruits contained only 0.5-2.8% of fatty acid esters, predominantly ethyl esters, of which ethyl laurate represented 55-62%, with only traces of methyl, propyl and butyl esters [10]. No comparable data is available for CO_2 extracts.

Statements that ethyl esters are the predominant fatty acid esters in the dried fruits [2,3,11-13] seem questionable, as does the notion that ethyl esters arise from enzymic esterification of free fatty acids during shipment or storage [3] (since the fruits were at one time shipped in barrels to which a small quantity of ethanol was added as a preservative) [11]. Ethyl esters may be the predominant esters in lipido-sterolic extracts obtained by extraction of the dried fruits with ethanol [12,13] because quantitatively more abundant propyl esters are not extracted efficiently by ethanol.

Two glyceryl esters, the monoacylglycerides 1-monolaurin and 1-monomyristin, have been isolated from an ethanolic extract [14].

□ ***Phytosterols***, 0.2-0.3%, principally β-sitosterol (0.22%), campesterol (0.07%) and stigmasterol (0.03%) [5] together with β-sitosterol 3-glucoside and 3-diglucoside, and various esters of β-sitosterol including the palmitate, myristate, laurate, 6-*O*-myristyl glucoside, 6-*O*-lauryl glucoside and 6-*O*-capryl glucoside [15].

Cycloartenol and 24-methylene-cycloartenol have also been reported [16,17].

□ ***Fatty alcohols*** Octacosanol (0.15-0.2%), hexacosanol (0.02%), triacontanol (0.03%) and tetracosanol (0.004%) [5,16,17].

OTHER CONSTITUENTS

□ ***Flavonoids*** The flavonoid glycosides isoquercitrin, rutin, kaempferol 3-glucoside and rhoifolin (apigenin 7-rhamnoglucoside) [15].

□ ***Polysaccharides*** An acidic polysaccharide isolated from an aqueous extract had a MW of about 100,000 and was composed mainly of galactose (38%), arabinose (19%) and unidentified uronic acids (14%) [18].

□ ***Miscellaneous*** Sugars, mannitol [1,4], carotenoids [16], and small amounts of ceramides, sphingolipids [1] and free anthranilic acid [19]. Also, the sesquiterpene farnesol, the diterpene geranylgeraniol and the triterpene lupeol [17].

Published Assay Methods

Total fatty acids by GC [Ph. Eur.]. Individual fatty acids as methyl esters by GC [USP]. Fatty acids, fatty alcohols and phytosterols by GC [5]. Fatty acids and fatty acid esters by GC [12] and supercritical fluid chromatography [13].

PHARMACOLOGY

Therapeutic effects of saw palmetto fruit on the genito-urinary tract have been known since the 19th century. Correspondence in the late 1890s between the Arnold Arboretum of Harvard University and the Royal Botanic Gardens, Kew, expressed particular interest in its effects on dysfunction of the prostate gland, and saw palmetto fruit was made official in the USP in 1900 [20]. Liquid Extract of Sabal BPC 1934 (1:1, ethanol 90%) [21] would have had a constituent profile comparable to that of lipido-sterolic extracts used today in the symptomatic treatment of benign prostatic hyperplasia (BPH).

In vitro and in vivo

Based on extensive research a number of contributing mechanisms have been proposed to explain the mode of action of saw palmetto fruit extracts in alleviating symptoms of BPH, but so far little consensus has been achieved:

- Antiandrogenic activity.
  Dihydrotestosterone (DHT), the major androgenic hormone in the prostate, is derived from testosterone in a conversion catalyzed by the enzyme 5α-reductase. Excessive accumulation of DHT is thought to contribute to the development of BPH. Some *in vitro* studies have demonstrated that saw palmetto fruit extracts can inhibit 5α-reductase [22,23] and this has been attributed to the free fatty acids present [6]. However, another study found minimal 5α-reductase inhibition in direct comparison with finasteride (a known 5α-reductase inhibitor) [24]. Inhibition of the binding of DHT to androgen receptors in prostate cells has also been demonstrated, again with conflicting results.
- Spasmolytic activity and inhibition of α_1-adrenoreceptor binding in relation to the tone of smooth muscle in the bladder neck and prostate (which is mediated by α-adrenoreceptors).
- Anti-inflammatory [15] and anti-oedematous activity.
- Anti-oestrogenic activity.

Pharmacological studies in this area are too numerous and complicated to describe in detail here, but the more important papers have been summarized in an ESCOP monograph [25] and other reviews [26,27].

Pharmacological studies in humans

BPH patients randomly assigned to treatment with 320 mg of a saw palmetto fruit hexane extract daily for 3 months (n = 10) or to an untreated control group (n = 15) subsequently underwent prostatectomy. In prostatic tissue from the group treated with the extract significant reductions were observed in concentrations of dihydrotestosterone (DHT; p<0.001) and epidermal growth factor (p<0.01), whereas testosterone levels increased (p<0.001) [28].

In contrast, in healthy male volunteers randomly treated daily for 1 week with 5 mg of finasteride (n = 10), 2 × 160 mg of a saw palmetto fruit hexane extract (n = 11) or placebo (n = 11), median serum levels of DHT were significantly reduced only in the finasteride group, by 65% after the first dose and 60% after 8 days (both $p<0.001$ vs hexane extract and placebo) [29].

Pharmacokinetics
In a study carried out to investigate the fate of three constituents of saw palmetto fruit after oral ingestion, male rats were given 10 mg of a hexane extract supplemented with ^{14}C-radioactively-labelled oleic acid, lauric acid or β-sitosterol. From whole body radiograms and assays of radioactivity, nothing remarkable was observed with regard to the distribution of lauric acid or β-sitosterol in various organs and tissues, but with ^{14}C-labelled oleic acid a greater uptake was evident in the prostate than in other genital organs (seminal vesicles and bladder) or in the liver or brain [9].

CLINICAL STUDIES

Benign prostatic hyperplasia (BPH), non-malignant enlargement of the prostate gland which can lead to irritative and/or obstructive lower urinary tract symptoms (LUTS), is very common in ageing men throughout the world. The management of LUTS associated with clinically symptomatic BPH remains controversial. Treatment options range from watchful waiting, for those wishing to delay any active therapy, to minimally invasive treatments such as transurethral needle ablation of the prostate or transurethral microwave therapy and, if necessary, to surgical interventions. Most patients present with difficulties of urination, for which various pharmaceutical treatments are available including 5α-reductase inhibitors, α-blockers and plant extracts such as saw palmetto lipido-sterolic extract [30].

Since the early 1980s numerous clinical studies in the treatment of LUTS and BPH have been performed with saw palmetto fruit extracts, particularly hexane extracts and in some of the more recent studies with hypercritical CO_2 extracts, but few with ethanol extracts. Many of the earlier studies would not satisfy modern guidelines for Good Clinical Practice (GCP) and standard questionnaires to derive subjective symptom scores, such as the International Prostate Symptom Score (IPSS), were not introduced until the 1990s. Nevertheless, most of the published studies have evaluated the effects of extracts on objective parameters such as peak urinary flow rate, residual urine volume and frequency of diurnal and nocturnal urination.

The IPSS, derived from and virtually identical to the American Urological Association Symptom Index (AUASI), is based on the patient's answers on a scale of 0-5 to seven simple questions about potential problems in passing urine: urgency, daytime and night-time urinary frequency, hesitancy, intermittency, sensation of incomplete voiding and force of urine stream [31].

Clinical studies with hexane extracts from saw palmetto fruit
The majority of clinical studies carried out since 1983 in patients with LUTS suggestive of BPH have involved the use of one product (Permixon®) containing a hexane extract from saw palmetto fruit, at the daily dosage of 2 × 160 mg of extract. Summaries of many of the individual studies can be found in the ESCOP monograph [25]. A meta-analysis of a sort was carried out on 17 of these studies, of which 9 were placebo-controlled [32-39 + one unpublished], 4 were comparisons with synthetic drugs [7,40,41 + one unpublished], 1 compared two different dose levels of the extract [unpublished] and 3 were large open studies [42,43 + one unpublished]. Data from the four unpublished studies were obtained from the manufacturer's technical reports. Results derived from the pooled data suggested that:

- The extract was associated with a mean reduction in IPSS of 4.78 (based on 6 studies, of which 4 unpublished).
- The mean placebo effect on peak urinary flow rate was an increase of 1.20 ml/sec and the estimated effect of the extract was a further increase of 1.02 ml/sec ($p = 0.04$).
- Placebo was associated with a reduction of 0.63 in the mean number of nocturnal voids; a further reduction of 0.38 was attributable to the extract ($p<0.001$). However, in the largest placebo-controlled study (unpublished; involving a total of 396 patients) no difference was found between verum and placebo groups for this parameter.

The authors concluded that, compared to placebo, the extract produced significant improvements in peak flow rate and nocturia and a 5-point reduction in the IPSS [30]. Taking into account that only 9/17 studies included placebo groups (hence 3315 patients took the extract while 500 took placebo), that in 6/9 placebo-controlled studies the size of groups was less than 50 patients whereas the three open studies included 592, 500 and 154 patients, that 7/9 of the placebo-controlled studies were carried out over 20 years ago (1983-1986), before modern GCP guidelines were introduced, and that data lacking in some studies had to be "imputed" from other studies, the shortcomings of this exercise are apparent. While confirming mild to moderate beneficial effects of the extract, it tended to emphasize the considerable placebo effect in LUTS treatment and the paucity of well-executed and adequately powered placebo-controlled studies for hexane extracts. Another review of clinical studies with the same extract covered much of the same ground and was faced with similar limitations [44].

Comparisons with synthetic drugs
The effects of daily treatment with 2 ×160 mg of saw palmetto fruit hexane extract (n = 553) were compared with those of 5 mg of finasteride (a 5α-reductase inhibitor; n = 545) in men with moderate BPH in a 26-week, randomized, double-blind study carried out at 87 urology centres in nine European countries; 467 patients taking the extract and 484 taking finasteride completed the study. Compared to baseline values, both the hexane extract and finasteride reduced the IPSS (by 37% and 39% respectively; both $p<0.001$) and quality of life scores (by 38% and 41% respectively), with no significant difference between groups. Significant increases ($p<0.001$) were observed in peak urinary flow rate (25% and 30% respectively; $p = 0.035$ in favour of finasteride) with no statistical difference between groups in the percentage of responders showing an improvement of 3 ml/sec. Finasteride reduced residual urine volume more than the extract ($p = 0.017$), and markedly reduced prostate volume by 18% ($p<0.001$; hexane extract, 6%) and serum PSA levels by 41% ($p<0.001$; hexane extract, no change). On the other hand, the hexane extract fared better in a sexual function questionnaire ($p<0.001$). It was concluded that both treatments relieved the symptoms of BPH in about two-thirds of patients but, unlike finasteride, saw palmetto fruit has little effect on so-called androgen-dependent parameters [7].

In a large double-blind study conducted at 98 centres in eleven European countries, 704 men of mean age 65.6 years with symptomatic BPH (IPSS ≥10) participated initially in a 4-week placebo run-in period during which the mean IPSS decreased by 1.5, from 16.8 to 15.3. The patients were then randomized to receive daily for 12 months either 320 mg of a hexane extract from saw palmetto fruit (n = 350) or 0.4 mg of tamsulosin (an α-blocker; n = 354). Endpoint analysis performed on the per-protocol population of 542 patients (hexane extract, n = 269; tamsulosin, n = 273) revealed a further decrease of 4.4 in the IPSS in each group with no differences between groups in improvement of irritative and obstructive symptoms. Similar increases in peak urinary flow rate were observed in the two groups, 1.9 ml/second in the saw palmetto fruit group and 1.8 ml/second in the tamsulosin group. Fluctuations in PSA values and prostate volumes were slight. The only significant difference noted was a more frequent occurrence of ejaculation disorders in the tamsulosin group than in the saw palmetto fruit group (15 vs. 2). It was concluded that the saw palmetto fruit extract and tamsulosin are equivalent in the treatment of LUTS in men with BPH during 12 months of therapy [45].

From the same study, a subset analysis of 124 patients showed the hexane extract to be marginally superior to tamsulosin in reducing LUTS in patients (65 taking the extract; 59 taking tamsulosin) with severe BPH, i.e. IPSS ≥ 19 at the time of randomization. After 12 months the IPSS had decreased by 7.8 with the hexane extract and 5.8 with tamsulosin ($p = 0.051$), while irritative symptoms improved significantly more with the extract (−2.9, $p = 0.049$) than with tamsulosin (−1.9) [46].

Earlier and smaller studies comparing the effects of the saw palmetto fruit hexane extract with those of other α-blockers in men with LUTS associated with BPH, a 3-week comparison with alfuzosin involving 63 patients [41] and a 12-week comparison with prazosin involving 45 patients [40], found both treatments effective but the α-blockers rather more effective.

Clinical studies with CO_2 extracts from saw palmetto fruit
In a randomized double-blind study, patients aged 45-72 years suffering from moderate symptoms of BPH were assigned to treatment with 2 × 160 mg of a hypercritical CO_2 extract (n = 20) or placebo (n = 20) daily for 90 days. Compared to the placebo group, the number of daytime and nocturnal urinations substantially decreased in the verum group and residual urine volume, determined by ultrasound, decreased significantly from 110 ml to 45 ml ($p<0.01$; increase in the placebo group from 102 to 110 ml). Accordingly, subjective scores in the verum group for dysuria, incomplete voiding and feelings of pain or pressure significantly decreased ($p<0.01$ after 60 days) [47].

A randomized, double-blind, placebo-controlled study carried out in Belgium in patients with symptoms of BPH (including mean peak urinary flow rates of 10-11 ml/second) evaluated the effects of daily treatment for 3 months with either 2 × 160 mg of a CO_2 extract (n = 106) or placebo (n = 99). By the end of treatment, compared to the placebo group, significant improvements were observed in the extract group with respect to total symptom score ($p<0.01$) and quality of life score ($p<0.001$), urinary volume, pollakiuria and nocturia (all three $p<0.05$), and dysuria and urgency (both $p<0.01$). Differences between groups did not reach statistical significance for maximal and mean urinary flow rates or for residual urine volume, although trends in favour of the extract were noted with respect to these parameters [48].

In another randomized, double-blind, placebo-controlled study, carried out in Australia, men of average age 63 years with symptoms of BPH (maximum urinary flow rate of 5-15 ml/sec for a voided volume of at least 150 ml) were randomly assigned to treatment with 2 × 160 mg of a CO_2 extract (n = 50) or placebo (n = 50) daily for 12 weeks. During the study period all participants had some improvement in their symptoms of BPH but there were no significant beneficial effects of the extract over placebo. IPSS scores declined significantly in both groups (p<0.001) but with no difference between groups (p = 0.131). Peak urinary flow rates improved in both groups (p<0.001), from 11.1 to 12.6 ml/sec in the verum group and from 11.2 to 15.6 ml/sec in the placebo group. To the study authors it appeared that simply having some attention and talking about their condition was therapeutic for these men. In the 74 men who were sexually active, scores in the Rosen International Index of Erectile Function (IIEF) did not change significantly in either group [49].

The largest double-blind, placebo-controlled study published to date evaluating the effects of a saw palmetto fruit CO_2 extract in BPH was recently carried out in the USA to a high standard of clinical practice. It involved 225 men of average age 63 years with moderate-to-severe symptoms of BPH (average AUASI score of 15.4; peak urinary flow rate of less than 15 ml per second), who were randomly assigned to daily treatment with 2 × 160 mg of the extract (n = 112) or identical placebo (n = 113) for 1 year. No significant differences were observed between saw palmetto and placebo groups with respect to change in AUASI score, maximal urinary flow rate, residual urine volume, quality of life or prostate size. During a one-month, single-blind, placebo run-in period there was a small but significant decrease (improvement) in AUASI score in both groups (mean change among all participants, –1.49), leading to "baseline" scores of 15.7 in the saw palmetto group and 15.0 in the placebo group; during the one-year study period there were further small decreases from baseline of –0.68 and –0.72 respectively, but no significant difference between groups in the mean change over time [50]. In this study the greatest changes in both of the primary outcome measures (AUASI scores and peak urinary flow rates) occurred during the one-month placebo run-in period, indicating considerable placebo effects. Furthermore, it should be emphasized that the patients in this study had moderate-to-severe symptoms of BPH, whereas the majority of clinical studies have involved men with mild to moderate symptoms.

Other controlled studies

In a double-blind, placebo-controlled study, men of average age 65 years with LUTS were randomly assigned after a 1-month placebo run-in period to treatment with either 2 × 160 mg of an undefined saw palmetto fruit extract (n = 41; mean initial IPSS of 16.7) or placebo (n = 44; mean initial IPSS of 15.8) daily for 6 months. The IPSS improved (decreased) significantly more in the extract group, by 4.4 compared to 2.2 in the placebo group (p = 0.038). Peak urinary flow rate improved slightly in both groups but with no difference in magnitude between groups. No significant differences between groups were observed in quality of life scores or the results of a sexual function questionnaire [51].

Clinical reviews

From a systematic review of 21 randomized studies (18 of which were double-blinded), involving a total of 3139 men with obstructive and/or irritative LUTS attributable to BPH, the evidence suggested that saw palmetto fruit extracts provide mild to moderate improvement in urinary tract symptoms (assessed by symptom scale scores) and urinary flow rates when compared to placebo, and similar improvements when compared to finasteride but with fewer adverse events [52]. A earlier review by the same authors drew the same conclusions, while noting that the evidence was limited by the short duration of studies and the variability of study design [53]. Clinical reviews relating to a specific hexane extract have been discussed above [30,44].

Conclusions

Results from at least 45 clinical studies (of which 16 were placebo-controlled) in the treatment of lower urinary tract symptoms associated with BPH with mono-preparations containing saw palmetto fruit lipido-sterolic extracts can be found to varying extents in the literature from 1983 to the present. From the vast majority of studies the results suggest beneficial effects of the extracts compared to placebo or baseline values, or effects equivalent to those of drugs such as finasteride, tamsulosin, prazosin and alfuzosin. Inevitably, considering the time-span, a considerable proportion of these studies would not satisfy modern guidelines for Good Clinical Practice. It is also clear that placebo effects can be high, on occasion 30-40% improvement in peak urinary flow rate for example [39,49]; this diminishes the value of clinical reviews which do not take placebo effects sufficiently into account, while the value of clinical studies which include a placebo run-in period is enhanced. Overall, the weight of evidence indicates that saw palmetto fruit extracts can induce improvements in mild to moderate lower urinary tract symptoms. However, unfavourable results from recent placebo-controlled clinical studies [49,50] leave the question of efficacy controversial. The need for further randomized, controlled studies of high quality is self-evident.

THERAPEUTICS

Actions

Anti-inflammatory, anti-oedematous, spasmolytic, possibly antiandrogenic [25-27,54,55].

Indications
Micturition disorders (such as weak flow, incomplete voiding, frequent daytime and night-time urination) associated with mild to moderate benign prostatic hyperplasia [25,30,32-39,44,47,48,54-56].

Other uses, based on experience or tradition
Inflammation of the genito-urinary tract, especially cystitis [55].

Contraindications
None known.

Side effects
Occasionally, minor gastrointestinal complaints [25].

Interactions with other drugs
None reported.

Dosage
Daily dose: 320 mg of saw palmetto fruit lipido-sterolic extract [25,30,32-39,44,47,48,54-56]; liquid extract BPC 1934 (1:1, ethanol 90%), 2-4 ml [57]; dried fruits, 2-4 g [55,57].

Although a twice-daily dose of 160 mg of a lipido-sterolic extract is usually recommended, the authors of an open clinical study involving 176 patients with BPH concluded that a single daily dose of 320 mg appeared to be equally effective and enhanced patient compliance [58].

SAFETY

Saw palmetto lipido-sterolic extracts are well tolerated and present no safety concerns at normal dosage levels. The incidence of reported adverse effects in clinical studies is usually similar in saw palmetto fruit and placebo groups [47-50]. In long-term open clinical studies a hexane extract has been taken by BPH patients at 320 mg/day for periods of 2-5 years without apparent adverse effects [44]. The overall rates of patient withdrawal from 21 randomized clinical studies involving 3139 men assigned to treatment with placebo, saw palmetto fruit extracts or finasteride were 7%, 9% and 11% respectively [52].

No significant differences between saw palmetto fruit and placebo groups have been found from questionnaires on sexual and erectile function [49,51], assessment of clinical biochemistry parameters (serum PSA, creatinine and testosterone levels, and standard blood tests) or measurement of prostate volume (by sonography) [47,50].

From toxicological tests, the oral LD_{50} in rats of a hexane extract from saw palmetto fruit was found to be very high at 54 ml/kg (= 49 g/kg) and no toxic effects were apparent after a dose of 10 ml/kg. No deaths occurred in mice after an oral dose of the extract at 50 ml/kg [20,59]. Subacute and chronic tests also confirmed the virtually non-toxic nature of a hexane extract and mutagenicity tests (including the Ames test) gave negative results [20].

REGULATORY STATUS

Medicines

UK	Accepted for general sale, internal or external use [60].
France	Not listed in *Médicaments à base de plantes* [61]; approved as a prescription medicine [62].
Germany	Commission E monograph published, with approved uses [56].

Food
Not used in foods.

REFERENCES

Current Pharmacopoeial Monographs

Ph. Eur.	Saw Palmetto Fruit
USP	Saw Palmetto

Literature References

1. Bombardelli E and Morazzoni P. *Serenoa repens* (Bartram) J.K. Small. *Fitoterapia* 1997, **68**, 99-113.
2. Hiermann A, Hübner W and Schulz V. Serenoa. In: Hänsel R, Keller K, Rimpler H and Schneider G, editors. *Hagers Handbuch der Pharmazeutischen Praxis, 5th ed. Volume 6: Drogen P-Z.* ISBN 3-540-52639-0. Berlin-Heidelberg-New York-London: Springer-Verlag, 1994:680-687 [GERMAN].
3. Harnischfeger G and Stolze H. *Serenoa repens* - Die Sägezahnpalme. *Z. Phytotherapie* 1989, **10**, 71-76 [GERMAN/English summary].
4. Neuzil E and Cousse H. Le Palmier-Scie, *Serenoa repens.* Aspects botaniques et chimiques [Saw Palmetto, *Serenoa repens.* Botanical and chemical aspects]. *Bull. Soc. Pharm. Bordeaux* 1993, **132**, 121-141 [FRENCH/English summary].
5. Cristoni A, Morazzoni P and Bombardelli E. Chemical and pharmacological study on hypercritical CO_2 extracts of *Serenoa repens* fruits. *Fitoterapia* 1997, **4**, 355-358.
6. Niederprüm H-J, Schweikert H-U and Zänker KS. Testosterone 5α-reductase inhibition by free fatty acids from *Sabal serrulata* fruits. *Phytomedicine* 1994, **1**, 127-133.
7. Carraro J-C, Raynaud J-P, Koch G, Chisholm GD, Di Silverio F, Teillac P et al. Comparison of Phytotherapy (Permixon®) with Finasteride in the Treatment of Benign Prostate Hyperplasia: A Randomized International Study of 1,098 Patients. *Prostate* 1996, **29**, 231-240.
8. Wajda-Dubos J-P, Farines M, Soulier J and Cousse H. Étude comparative de la fraction lipidique des pulpes et graines de *Serenoa repens* (*Palmaceae*) [Comparative study of the lipid fraction from pulp and seeds of *Serenoa repens* (*Palmaceae*)]. *OCL (Montrouge)* 1996, **3**, 136-139 [FRENCH/English summary].
9. Chevalier G, Benard P, Cousse H and Bengone T. Distribution study of radioactivity in rats after oral administration of the lipido-sterolic extract of Serenoa repens (Permixon®) supplemented with [1-^{14}C]-lauric acid, [1-^{14}C]-oleic acid or [4-^{14}C]-β-sitosterol. *Eur. J. Drug Metab. Pharmacokinet.*

1997, **22**, 73-83.
10. Unpublished.
11. Wood HC and LaWall CH, editors. Sabal N.F. In: *United States Dispensatory, Centennial (22nd) Edition*. Philadelphia-London: JB Lippincott Company, 1937:939-940.
12. De Swaef SI and Vlietinck AJ. Simultaneous quantitation of lauric acid and ethyl laureate in *Sabal serrulata* by capillary gas chromatography and derivatisation with trimethyl-sulphonium hydroxide. *J. Chromatogr. A* 1996, **719**, 479-482.
13. De Swaef SI, Kleiböhmer W and Vlietinck AJ. Supercritical Fluid Chromatography of Free Fatty Acids and Ethyl Esters in Ethanolic Extracts of *Sabal serrulata*. *Phytochem. Analysis* 1996, **7**, 223-227.
14. Shimada H, Tyler VE and McLaughlin JL. Biologically Active Acylglycerides from the Berries of Saw Palmetto (*Serenoa repens*). *J. Nat. Prod.* 1997, **60**, 417-418.
15. Hiermann A. Über Inhaltsstoffe von Sabalfrüchten und deren Prüfung auf entzündungshemmende Wirkung [Constituents of Sabal fruits and investigation of their anti-inflammatory activity]. *Arch. Pharm. (Weinheim)* 1989, **322**, 111-114 [GERMAN/English summary].
16. Hatinguais P, Belle R, Basso Y, Ribet JP, Bauer M and Pousset JL. Composition de l'extrait hexanique de fruits de *Serenoa repens* Bartram. *Trav. Soc. Pharm. Montpellier* 1981, **41**, 253-262 [FRENCH/English summary].
17. Jommi G, Verotta L, Gariboldi P and Gabetta B. Constituents of the Lipophilic Extract of the Fruits of *Serenoa repens* (Bart.) Small. *Gazz. Chim. Ital.* 1988, **118**, 823-826.
18. Wagner H and Flachsbarth H. A New Antiphlogistic Principle from *Sabal serrulata* I. *Planta Medica* 1981, **41**, 244-251 [GERMAN/English summary].
19. Hänsel R, Schöpflin G and Rimpler H. Notiz über das Vorkommen von Anthranilsäure in Sabalfrüchten (*Serenoa repens*) [The occurrence of anthranilic acid in sabal fruits (*Serenoa repens*)]. *Planta Medica* 1966, **14**, 261-265 [GERMAN].
20. Neuzil E and Cousse H. Le Palmier-Scie, *Serenoa repens*. Aspects pharmacologiques. Utilisation thérapeutique actuelle [Saw Palmetto, *Serenoa repens*. Pharmacological aspects and current therapeutic uses]. *Bull. Soc. Pharm. Bordeaux* 1993, **132**, 142-163 [FRENCH/English summary].
21. Pharmaceutical Society of Great Britain. Extractum Sabal Liquidum - Liquid Extract of Sabal. In: *British Pharmaceutical Codex 1934*. London: Pharmaceutical Press, 1934:1249.
22. Weisser H, Tunn S, Behnke B and Krieg M. Effects of the Sabal serrulata Extract IDS 89 and Its Subfractions on 5 - Reductase Activity in Human Benign Prostatic Hyperplasia. *Prostate* 1996, **28**, 300-306.
23. Hagenlocher M, Romalo G and Schweikert H-U. Specific Inhibition of 5α-Reductase by a New Extract of *Sabal serrulata*. *Akt. Urol.* 1993, **24**, 147-150 [GERMAN/English summary].
24. Rhodes L, Primka RL, Berman C, Vergult G, Gabriel M, Pierre-Malice M and Gibelin B. Comparison of Finasteride (Proscar®), a 5α Reductase Inhibitor, and Various Commercial Plant Extracts in In Vitro and In Vivo 5α Reductase Inhibition. *Prostate* 1993, **22**, 43-51.
25. European Scientific Cooperative on Phytotherapy. Serenoae repentis fructus (Sabal fructus) - Saw Palmetto Fruit. In: *ESCOP Monographs - The Scientific Foundation for Herbal Medicinal Products, 2nd ed.* Stuttgart-New York: Thieme; Exeter, UK: ESCOP, 2003:477-486.
26. Koch E. Extracts from Fruits of Saw Palmetto (*Sabal serrulata*) and Roots of Stinging Nettle (*Urtica dioica*): Viable Alternatives in the Medical Treatment of Benign Prostatic Hyperplasia and Associated Lower Urinary Tract Symptoms. *Planta Medica* 2001, **67**, 489-500.
27. Plosker GL and Brogden RN. *Serenoa repens* (Permixon®). A Review of its Pharmacology and Therapeutic Efficacy in Benign Prostatic Hyperplasia. *Drugs and Aging* 1996, **9**, 379-395.
28. Di Silverio F, Monti S, Sciarra A, Varasano PA, Martini C, Lanzara S et al. Effects of Long-Term Treatment with *Serenoa repens* (Permixon®) on the Concentrations and Regional Distribution of Androgens and Epidermal Growth Factor in Benign Prostatic Hyperplasia. *Prostate* 1998, **37**, 77-83.
29. Strauch G, Perles P, Vergult G, Gabriel M, Gibelin B, Cummings S et al. Comparison of Finasteride (Proscar®) and *Serenoa repens* (Permixon®) in the Inhibition of 5-Alpha Reductase in Healthy Male Volunteers. *Eur. Urol.* 1994, **26**, 247-252.
30. Boyle P, Robertson C, Lowe F and Roehrborn C. Updated meta-analysis of clinical trials of *Serenoa repens* extract in the treatment of symptomatic benign prostatic hyperplasia. *BJU International* 2004, **93**, 751-756.
31. Cockett AT, Aso Y, Denis L, Murphy G, Khoury S, Abrams P et al. 1994 Recommendations of the International Consensus Committee concerning: The International Prostate Symptom Score (I-PSS) and Quality of Life Assessment. In: Cockett ATK, Khoury S, Aso Y, Chatelain C, Denis L, Griffiths K, Murphy G, editors. *The 2nd International Consultation on Benign Prostatic Hyperplasia (BPH). Paris, June 27-30, 1993: Proceedings 2*. Jersey, Channel Islands: Scientific Communication International, 1993:553-64.
32. Mandressi A, Tarallo U, Maggioni A, Tombolini P, Rocco F and Quadraccia S. Terapia medica dell'adenoma prostatico: confronto della efficacia dell'estratto di Serenoa repens (Permixon®) versus l'estratto di Pigeum africanum e placebo [Medical therapy of prostatic adenoma: comparison of the efficacy of *Serenoa repens* extract (Permixon®) versus *Pygeum africanum* and placebo]. *Urologia* 1983, **50**, 752-757 [ITALIAN].
33. Emili E, Lo Cigno M and Petrone U. Risultati clinici su un nuovo farmaco nella terapia dell'ipertrofia della prostata (Permixon) [Clinical results on a new medicine for the treatment of prostate hypertrophy (Permixon)]. *Urologia* 1983, **50**, 1042-1049 [ITALIAN].
34. Boccafoschi C and Annoscia S. Confronto fra estratto di Serenoa repens e placebo mediante prova clinica controllata in pazienti con adenomatosi prostatica [Comparison between *Serenoa repens* extract and placebo in a controlled clinical study in patients with prostatic adenoma]. *Urologia* 1983, **50**, 1257-1268 [ITALIAN].
35. Champault G, Patel JC and Bonnard AM. A double-blind trial of an extract of the plant *Serenoa repens* in benign prostatic hyperplasia. *Br. J. Clin. Pharmacol.* 1984, **18**, 461-462.
36. Cukier J, Ducassou J, Le Guillou M, Leriche A, Lobel B, Toubol J et al. Permixon versus placebo. Résultats d'une étude multicentrique. *Compt. Rend. Thér. Pharmacol. Clin.* 1985, **4**, 15-21 [FRENCH/English summary].
37. Tasca A, Barulli M, Cavazzana A, Zattoni F, Artibani W and Pagano F. Trattamento della sintomatologia ostruttiva da adenoma prostatico con estratto di Serenoa repens. Studio clinico in doppio cieca vs. placebo [Treatment of obstructive symptomatology due to prostate adenoma with *Serenoa repens* extract. Double-blind clinical study vs. placebo]. *Minerva Urol. Nefrol.* 1985, **37**, 87-91 [ITALIAN/English summary].
38. Reece Smith H, Memon A, Smart CJ and Dewbury K. The Value of Permixon in Benign Prostatic Hypertrophy. *Brit. J. Urol.* 1986, **58**, 36-40.
39. Descotes JL, Rambeaud JJ, Deschaseaux P and Faure G. Placebo-Controlled Evaluation of the Efficacy and Tolerability of Permixon® in Benign Prostatic Hyperplasia after Exclusion of Placebo Responders. *Clin. Drug Invest.* 1995, **9**, 291-297.
40. Adriazola Semino M, Lozano Ortega JL, Garcia Cobo E, Tejeda Bañez E and Romero Rodriguez F. Tratamiento sintomático de la hipertrofia benigna de próstata. Estudio comparativo entre Prazosin y *Serenoa repens* [Symptomatic treatment of benign prostatic hypertrophy. Comparative study between prazosin and *Serenoa repens*]. *Arch. Esp. Urol.* 1992, **45**, 211-213 [SPANISH/English summary].
41. Grasso M, Montesano A, Buonaguidi A, Castelli M, Lania C, Rigatti P et al. Comparative effects of alfuzosin versus *Serenoa repens* in the treatment of symptomatic benign prostatic hyperplasia. *Arch. Esp. Urol.* 1995, **48**, 97-103.
42. Foroutan F. Wirksamkeit und Verträglichkeit von Permixon®

bei einem größeren Patientenkollektiv (592 Patienten) unter Praxisbedingungen [Efficacy and tolerability of Permixon® in a large group of patients (592 patients) under practice conditions]. *J. Urologie Urogynäkol.* 1997, **2**, 17 [GERMAN].

43. Authie D and Cauquil J. Appréciation de l'efficacité de Permixon® en pratique quotidienne. Étude multicentrique [Evaluation of the efficacy of Permixon in everyday practice. Multicentric study]. *Compt. Rend. Thér.* 1987, **56**, 4-13 [FRENCH/English summary].
44. Gerber GS and Fitzpatrick JM. The role of a lipido-sterolic extract of *Serenoa repens* in the management of lower urinary tract symptoms associated with benign prostatic hyperplasia. *BJU International* 2004, **94**, 338-344.
45. Debruyne F, Koch G, Boyle P, Da Silva FC, Gillenwater JG, Hamdy FC et al. Comparison of a Phytotherapeutic Agent (Permixon) with an α-blocker (Tamsulosin) in the Treatment of Benign Prostatic Hyperplasia: A 1-year Randomized International Study. *Eur. Urol.* 2002, **41**, 497-507.
46. Debruyne F, Boyle P, Da Silva FC, Gillenwater JG, Hamdy FC, Perrin P et al. Evaluation of the Clinical Benefit of Permixon and Tamsulosin in Severe BPH Patients - PERMAL Study Subset Analysis. *Eur. Urol.* 2004, **45**, 773-780.
47. Mattei FM, Capone M and Acconcia A. Medikamentöse Therapie der benignen Prostatahyperplasie mit einem Extrakt der Sägepalme [Medicinal treatment of benign prostatic hyperplasia with an extract from saw palmetto]. *TW Urol. Nephrol.* 1990, **2**, 346-350 [GERMAN/English summary].
48. Braeckman J, Denis L, de Leval J, Keuppens F, Cornet A, De Bruyne R et al. A double-blind, placebo-controlled study of the plant extract *Serenoa repens* in the treatment of benign hyperplasia of the prostate. *Eur. J. Clin. Res.* 1997, **9**, 247-259.
49. Willetts KE, Clements MS, Champion S, Ehsman S and Eden JA. *Serenoa repens* extract for benign prostate hyperplasia: a randomized controlled trial. *BJU International* 2003, **92**, 267-270.
50. Bent S, Kane C, Shinohara K, Neuhaus J, Hudes ES, Goldberg H and Avins AL. Saw Palmetto for Benign Prostatic Hyperplasia. *New Engl. J. Med.* 2006, **354**, 557-566.
51. Gerber GS, Kuznetsov D, Johnson BC and Burstein JD. Randomized, double-blind, placebo-controlled trial of saw palmetto in men with lower urinary tract symptoms. *Urology* 2001, **58**, 960-965.
52. Wilt TJ, Ishani A and MacDonald R. Serenoa repens for benign prostatic hyperplasia. *Cochrane Database Syst. Rev.* 2002, (3), CD001423.
53. Wilt TJ, Ishani A, Stark G, MacDonald R, Lau J and Mulrow C. Saw Palmetto Extracts for Treatment of Benign Prostatic Hyperplasia. *JAMA* 1998, **280**, 1604-1609.
54. World Health Organization. Fructus Serenoae Repentis. In: *WHO monographs on selected medicinal plants, Volume 2.* ISBN 92-4-154537-2. Geneva: World Health Organization, 2002:285-299.
55. Mills S and Bone K. Saw palmetto - *Serenoa repens* (Bartram) Small. In: *Principles and Practice of Phytotherapy. Modern Herbal Medicine.* ISBN 0-443-06016-9. Edinburgh-London-New York: Churchill Livingstone, 2000:523-533.
56. Sabal fructus. German Commission E Monograph published in: Bundesanzeiger No. 43 of 2 March 1989; amended in Bundesanzeiger No. 22 of 1 February 1990 and Bundesanzeiger 11 of 17 January 1991.
57. Serenoa. In: *British Herbal Pharmacopoeia 1983.* ISBN 0-903032-07-4. Bournemouth: British Herbal Medicine Association, 1983.
58. Fabricius PG and Vahlensieck W. Therapie bei benignen Prostatahyperplasie. Sabalfrucht-Extrakt: Einmalgabe reicht! [Therapy of benign prostatic hyperplasia. Sabal fruit extract: a single dose suffices!]. *Therapiewoche* 1993, **43**, 1616-1620 [GERMAN/English summary].
59. Tarayre JP, Delhon A, Lauressergues H and Stenger A. Anti-edematous action of a hexane extract from *Serenoa repens* Bartr. drupes. *Ann. Pharm. Fr.* 1983, **41**, 559-570 [FRENCH/English summary].
60. Saw Palmetto. In: UK Statutory Instrument 1994 No. 2410. The Medicines (Products Other Than Veterinary Drugs) (General Sale List) Amendment Order 1994. Schedule 1, Table A.
61. *Médicaments à base de plantes.* ISBN 2-911473-02-7. Saint-Denis Cedex, France: Agence du Médicament, 1998.
62. Serenoa repens. In: *Vidal® 2000. Le Dictionnaire, 76th ed.* Paris: Editions du Vidal, 2000.

REGULATORY GUIDELINES FROM OTHER EU COUNTRIES

GERMANY

Commission E monograph [56]: Sabal fructus (Sägepalmenfrüchte).

Uses
Micturition problems in benign prostatic hyperplasia stages I to II.

Contraindications
None known.

Side effects
In rare cases, stomach upsets.

Interactions with other drugs
None known.

Dosage
Daily dose: 1-2 g of the drug or 320 mg of components extractable with lipophilic solvents (e.g. hexane or ethanol 90% V/V); other equivalent preparations.

Mode of administration
Comminuted drug and other galenic preparations for oral use.

Actions
Antiandrogenic (hexane extract); antiexudative (ethanol extract).

Note: This medication only alleviates the symptoms associated with an enlarged prostate, without reducing the enlargement. Therefore please consult your physician at regular intervals.

SHEPHERD'S PURSE Cruciferae

Bursae pastoris herba

Definition
Shepherd's Purse consists of the dried aerial parts of *Capsella bursa-pastoris* (L.) Medik., harvested towards the end of the flowering period when seed pods are present.

CONSTITUENTS

☐ ***Flavonoids*** Kaempferide (kaempferol 4′-methyl ether), quercetin 3-methyl ether, gossypetin hexamethyl ether, diosmin, robinetin, garbanzol (= 3,7,4′-trihydroxyflavone) [1], hesperidin [2] and small amounts of luteolin 7-rutinoside [3] and rutin (quercetin 3-rutinoside) [2,3].
☐ ***Organic acids*** Fumaric [4], malic, oxalic, tartaric, pyruvic, sulphanilic and glutamic acids [5].
Ascorbic acid (136 mg/100 g in leaves) is also present [6].
☐ ***Amino acids***, 2.3% [7], of which 22 have been identified including proline (the major one) [7,8], tyramine [7], α- and γ-aminobutyric acid, α-aminoadipic acid and ornithine [8].
☐ ***Mustard oil glucosides*** Sinigrin (allylglucosinolate) [9,10], 9-methylsulfinylnonylglucosinolate and 10-methylsulfinyldecylglucosinolate [10].
☐ ***Essential oil***, ca. 0.02%, containing over 70 components, the characteristic major one being camphor (20%). Other components include *cis*-3-hexen-1-ol (15%), aliphatic hydrocarbons (ca. 27%), and α-phellandrene (8%) and various other terpenoids [11].
☐ ***Other constituents*** β-Sitosterol [10], choline (ca. 0.2%) and histamine [12], sugars and minerals, especially potassium [5]. Alkaloids have been reported [12], but their presence remains in doubt [13]. Acetylcholine has also been reported [14] but not detected by others [15].

PHARMACOLOGY

In vitro
Aqueous and 50%-methanolic extracts of shepherd's purse dose-dependently shortened the recalcification time of human citrated plasma by 50-60%, indicating a significant accelerating effect on blood coagulation [16].

The tonus of isolated rabbit and guinea pig uterine horn was enhanced by an aqueous infusion (1-2 mg crude drug per ml) from shepherd's purse [17]. An unidentified, water-soluble substance (at least partly polypeptide) from shepherd's purse exerted contractile activity on isolated rat uterus in an oxytocin-like manner [18].

Fractions from an ethanolic extract of shepherd's purse exhibited negative inotropic and chronotropic activity on isolated heart muscle [15] and induced contractions in various isolated smooth muscles (small intestine of guinea pigs, aortic strip of rabbits, tracheal muscle of guinea pigs, uterine muscle of rats) [15,19].

A hydroethanolic extract of shepherd's purse exhibited only weak antibacterial activity against a range of organisms [20].

Fumaric acid isolated from shepherd's purse markedly reduced the growth and viability of

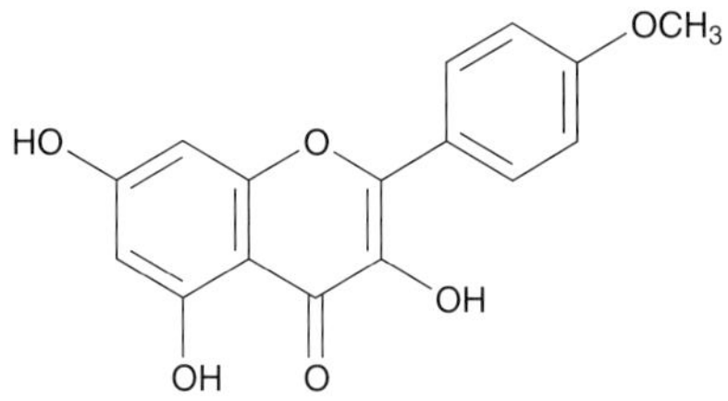

Kaempferide (kaempferol-4′-methyl ether)

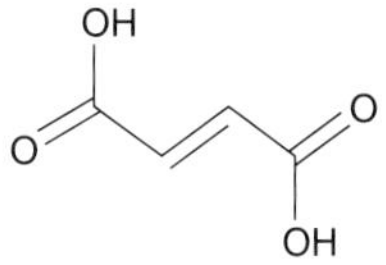

Fumaric acid

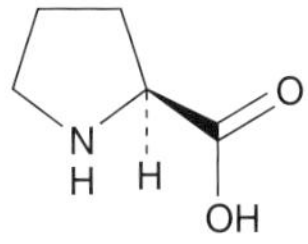

Proline

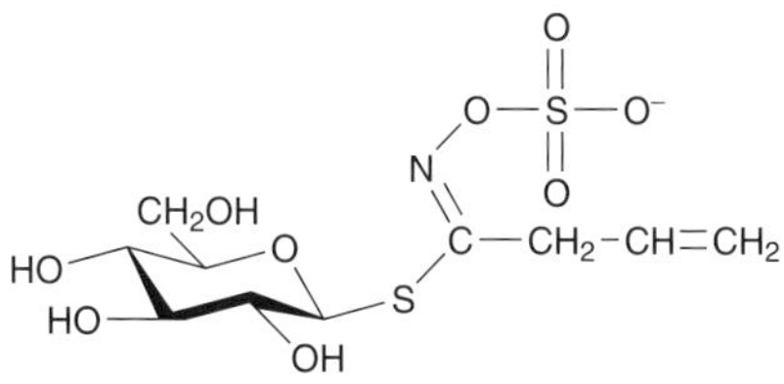

Sinigrin

cultured Ehrlich, MH134 and L1210 mouse tumour cells at 0.3-1.2 mg/ml but had no adverse effect on mouse and chick embryo cells (normal cells) [21].

In vivo

Effects on blood circulation
A transient decrease in blood pressure, not antagonized by atropine, was observed after intravenous administration of extracts of shepherd's purse to various animals (dogs, cats, rabbits and rats) [14,15,19].

Fractions from an ethanolic extract of shepherd's purse had a coronary vasodilative effect and increased peripheral blood flow in dogs [19].

Diuretic activity
An ethanol-soluble fraction from shepherd's purse exhibited diuretic activity, increasing urine volume and glomerular filtration rate when administered orally to mice at 2 mg/g [22].

Anti-inflammatory activity
Intraperitoneal administration of a water-soluble fraction from shepherd's purse inhibited dextran-induced rat paw oedema by 50% at 300 mg/kg (dose dependent) and carrageenan-induced rat paw oedema by 30% at 20 mg/kg (no further increase at higher doses) [22].

Effect on the uterus
An unidentified, water-soluble substance (at least partly polypeptide) from shepherd's purse increased spontaneous activity of rat uterus *in vivo* [18].

Other effects
Fractions from an ethanolic extract of shepherd's purse prolonged hexobarbitone-induced sleeping time in mice [19].

The water-soluble fraction showed anti-ulcer properties in rats and inhibited histamine-induced capillary permeability in guinea pigs [22]. Flavonoids from shepherd's purse reduced the permeability of blood vessels in white mice [2].

An ethanolic extract from shepherd's purse, administered intraperitoneally to mice at 140 mg/kg/day for 25 days, retarded the growth of Ehrlich solid tumour by 50-80%; the activity was attributed to fumaric acid, which caused significant and dose-dependent inhibition at 10 mg/kg/day ($p<0.01$) [4].

CLINICAL STUDIES

None published on mono-preparations of shepherd's purse.

THERAPEUTICS

Actions
Antihaemorrhagic [13,23-25], haemostatic [13,16, 24,26] and astringent [24-27]; uterine stimulant [13, 17,18,27], diuretic [22,24,26], anti-inflammatory, inhibits capillary permeability [22], increases peripheral blood flow [19,27], mildly hypotensive [15, 19], antitumour [4].

Also stated to be urinary antiseptic [23,27].

Indications
None adequately substantiated by pharmacological or clinical studies.

Uses based on experience or tradition
Internal: Menorrhagia [23,25,27,28], metrorrhagia [13,28]; haematuria [23-25], haemorrhoids [24,29]; diarrhoea; acute catarrhal cystitis [23-25,27].
Topical: Superficial, bleeding skin injuries [28], nosebleeds [24,25,28].

Contraindications
Pregnancy [25,27].

Side effects
None known.

Interactions with other drugs
None known.

Dosage
Internal: Three times daily: dried herb, 2-4 g, usually as an infusion [23,28,30]; liquid extract (1:1 in 25% ethanol), 2-4 ml [23]; equivalent preparations.

Up to 15 g of dried herb (as infusion) may be taken daily, divided into 3-4 doses [25,28].
Topical: Dried herb, 3-5 g as an infusion with 150 ml of water [28], applied as a poultice or compress; in nose bleeds as a cotton wool swab inserted in the nostril [27].

Excessive use of shepherd's purse should be avoided [26].

SAFETY

The LD_{50} of water-soluble and ethanol-insoluble fractions from shepherd's purse were determined as 31.5 g/kg (subcutaneous) and 1.5 g/kg (intraperitoneal) respectively in mice [19].

Sinigrin (which also occurs in black mustard seed and horseradish) has shown mutagenic potential in some *in vitro* test systems but presents no identifiable carcinogenic risk in man [31].

REGULATORY STATUS

Medicines
UK Accepted for general sale, internal

	or external use [32].
France	Accepted for specified indications [29].
Germany	Commission E monograph published, with approved uses [28].

Food

Not used in foods.

REFERENCES

Current Pharmacopoeial Monographs

Ph. Fr.	Bourse à pasteur
DAC	Hirtentäschelkraut

Literature References

1. Wohlfart R, Gademann R and Kirchner C-P. Physiologisch-chemische Betrachtungen über Änderungen am Flavonoidmuster von Capsella bursa-pastoris [Physiological-chemical observations on the flavonoid pattern of Capsella bursa-pastoris]. *Dtsch. Apoth. Ztg.* 1972, **112**, 1158-1160 [GERMAN].
2. Jurisson S. Flavonoid substances of Capsella bursa-pastoris. *Farmatsiya (Moscow)* 1973, **22** (5), 34-35 [RUSSIAN]; through *Chem. Abstr.* 1974, **80**, 24822.
3. Olechnowicz-Stepien W and Krug H. Flavonoid compounds of *Capsella bursa-pastoris* Moench. Part I. *Dissertationes Pharmaceuticae* 1965, **17**, 389-394 [POLISH/English summary].
4. Kuroda K, Akao M, Kanisawa M and Miyaki K. Inhibitory Effect of *Capsella bursa-pastoris* Extract on Growth of Ehrlich Solid Tumor in Mice. *Cancer Res.* 1976, **36**, 1900-1903.
5. Nagai K. Studies on Capsella bursa-pastoris. I. Carboxylic acids, amino acids, carbohydrates, alcohols and inorganic components in C. bursa-pastoris. *Yakugaku Kenkyu* 1960, **32**, 617-626; through *Chem. Abstr.* 1961, **55**, 12551.
6. Jones E and Hughes RE. Foliar ascorbic acid in some Angiosperms. *Phytochemistry* 1983, **22**, 2493-2499.
7. Kolos-Pethes E and Marczal G. Pharmacognosy of herba bursae pastoris. *Gyogyszereszet* 1966, **10**, 465-467 [HUNGARIAN]; through *Chem. Abstr.* 1967, **66**, 88678.
8. Maillard C, Barlatier A, Debrauwer L, Calaf R, Balansard G and Boudon G. Identification des acides aminés des parties aériennes de Bourse-à-pasteur, *Capsella bursa-pastoris* Moench. Intérêt dans le contrôle analytique [Identification of amino acids in the aerial parts of shepherd's purse, *Capsella bursa-pastoris* Moench. Analytical aspects]. *Ann. Pharm. Fr.* 1988, **46**, 211-216 [FRENCH/English summary].
9. Park RJ. The occurrence of mustard oil glucosides in *Lepidium hyssopifolium* Desv., L. *bonariense* (L.) and *Capsella bursa pastoris* (L.) Medic. *Aust. J. Chem.* 1967, **20**, 2799-2801.
10. Nazmi Sabri N, Sarg T and Seif-el-Din AA. Phytochemical Investigation of *Capsella bursa-pastoris* (L.) Medik. Growing in Egypt. *Egypt. J. Pharm. Sci.* 1975, **16**, 521-522; also through *Chem. Abstr.* 1978, **89**, 160097.
11. Miyazawa M, Uetake A and Kameoka H. The Constituents of the Essential Oils from *Capsella bursa-pastoris* Medik. *Yakugaku Zasshi* 1979, **99**, 1041-1043 [JAPANESE/English summary].
12. Jurisson S. Determination of active substances of Capsella bursa-pastoris (shepherd's purse). *Tartu Riikliku Ulikooli Toim.* 1971, No. 270, 71-79 [ESTONIAN]; through *Chem. Abstr.* 1972, **76**, 23018.
13. San Martin Casamada R. Capsella bursa-pastoris L. (Crucifères). *Plantes Méd. Phytothér.* 1977, **11**, 181-183 [FRENCH].
14. Nagai K. Capsella bursa-pastoris. II. The blood pressure depressing components and their pharmacological action and the steam-distilled components in C. bursa-pastoris. *Yakugaku Kenkyu* 1961, **33**, 48-54; through *Chem. Abstr.* 1961, **55**, 14823.
15. Kuroda K and Kaku T. Pharmacological and chemical studies on the alcohol extract of Capsella bursa-pastoris. *Life Sciences* 1969, **8**, 151-155.
16. Vermathen M and Glasl H. Effect of the Herb Extract of *Capsella bursa-pastoris* on Blood Coagulation. *Planta Medica* 1993, **59** (Suppl.), A670.
17. Shipochliev T. Extracts from a group of medicinal plants enhancing the uterine tonus. *Vet. Sci. (Sofia)* 1981, **18** (4), 94-98 [RUSSIAN/English summary].
18. Kuroda K and Takagi K. Physiologically Active Substance in *Capsella bursa-pastoris. Nature* 1968, **220**, 707-708.
19. Kuroda K and Takagi K. Studies on Capsella bursa-pastoris. I. General pharmacology of the ethanol extract of the herb. *Arch. Int. Pharmacodyn.* 1969, **178**, 382-391.
20. Moskalenko SA. Preliminary screening of Far-Eastern ethnomedicinal plants for antibacterial activity. *J. Ethnopharmacol.* 1986, **15**, 231-259.
21. Kuroda K and Akao M. Antitumor and anti-intoxication activities of fumaric acid in cultured cells. *Gann* 1981, **72**, 777-782.
22. Kuroda K and Takagi K. Studies on Capsella bursa-pastoris. II. Diuretic, anti-inflammatory and anti-ulcer action of ethanol extracts of the herb. *Arch. Int. Pharmacodyn.* 1969, **178**, 392-399.
23. Capsella. In: *British Herbal Pharmacopoeia 1983.* ISBN 0-903032-07-4. Bournemouth: British Herbal Medicine Association, 1983.
24. Grieve M (edited by Leyel CF). Shepherd's Purse. In: *A Modern Herbal* (First published 1931; revised 1973). ISBN 1-85501-249-9. London: Tiger Books International, 1994:738-739.
25. Chevallier A. Shepherd's Purse. In: *The Encyclopedia of Medicinal Plants.* ISBN 0-7513-0314-3. London-New York-Stuttgart: Dorling Kindersley, 1996:181.
26. Stodola J and Volák J. Shepherd's Purse. Translated into English in: Bunney S, editor. *The Illustrated Book of Herbs.* ISBN 0-7064-1489-6. London: Octopus Books, 1984:47.
27. Ody P. Shepherd's Purse. In: *The Complete Guide Medicinal Herbal.* ISBN 0-7513-3005-1. London-New York: Dorling Kindersley, 2000:49.
28. Bursae pastoris herba. German Commission E Monograph published in: Bundesanzeiger No. 173 of 18 September 1986; amended in Bundesanzeiger No. 50 of 13 March 1990.
29. Bourse à pasteur. In: *Médicaments à base de plantes.* ISBN 2-911473-02-7. Saint-Denis Cedex, France: Agence du Médicament, 1998.
30. Braun R, editor. Hirtentäschelkraut (No. 1539.99.99). In: Standardzulassungen für Fertigarzneimittel - Text und Kommentar. Stuttgart: Deutscher Apotheker Verlag, Frankfurt: Govi-Verlag, 1986.
31. Steinegger E and Hänsel R. Unbedenklichkeit pflanzlicher Arzneimittel [Safety of plant medicines]. In: Pharmakognosie, 5th ed. ISBN 3-540-55649-4. Berlin-Heidelberg-New York: Springer-Verlag, 1992:23-24.
32. Shepherd's Purse. In: UK Statutory Instrument 1994 No. 2410. The Medicines (Products Other Than Veterinary Drugs) (General Sale List) Amendment Order 1994. Schedule 1, Table A.

REGULATORY GUIDELINES FROM OTHER EU COUNTRIES

FRANCE

Médicaments à base de plantes [29]: Bourse à pasteur, parties aériennes fleuries.

Therapeutic indications accepted

Oral and/or topical use

Traditionally used in subjective manifestations of venous

insufficiency, such as 'heavy legs'.
Traditionally used in haemorrhoidal symptomatology.

GERMANY

Commission E monograph [28]: Bursae pastoris herba (Hirtentäschelkraut).

Uses
Internal: Symptomatic treatment of mild menorrhagia and metrorrhagia; topical use in nose bleeding.
External: Superficial, bleeding injuries to the skin.

Contraindications
None known.

Side effects
None known.

Interactions with other drugs
None known.

Dosage
Unless otherwise prescribed, average daily dose: 10-15 g of dried herb or equivalent preparations; fluid extract (in accordance with DAB Erg. B6), 5-8 g. Topical use: 3-5 g of dried herb to 150 ml of infusion.

Mode of administration
Comminuted drug for infusions and other galenic preparations for internal use, and for topical use.

Actions
Only from parenteral administration: muscarine-like effects with dose-dependent lowering and elevation of blood pressure; positively inotropic and chronotropic action on the heart and increase in uterine contraction.

SKULLCAP

Labiatae

Scutellariae herba

Synonyms: Virginian, American, blue or mad-dog skullcap (*Scutellaria lateriflora*); marsh, common or greater skullcap (*Scutellaria galericulata*).

The spelling 'scullcap' has also been used, particularly in older literature, but 'skullcap' is generally accepted in current texts.

Definition

Skullcap consists of the dried flowering aerial parts of *Scutellaria lateriflora* L. or *S. galericulata* L.

There are numerous species of *Scutellaria*. The BPC 1934 monograph on Scutellaria [1] included both *Scutellaria lateriflora* and *S. galericulata*, the former generally being more favoured in herbal textbooks; neither is well researched, although considerable interest has been shown in *S. lateriflora* during the past few years.

S. lateriflora is a perennial herb indigenous to North America, growing in wet places from eastern Canada to Florida and westward to British Columbia, Oregon and New Mexico [2]. *S. galericulata* is found throughout Europe, in parts of temperate Asia, and also in North America [3].

Reference by Yaghmai [4] to *S. lateriflora* "growing wild in northern Iran, near the Caspian Sea" seems questionable. According to Hosokawa [5], discrimination between dried aerial parts of *S. lateriflora* and *S. galericulata* on the basis of their morphology is difficult.

The root of *Scutellaria baicalensis* Georgi (Baikal skullcap) is one of the most important herbal drugs in traditional Chinese medicine [6] and more extensively researched than the aerial parts of *S. lateriflora* or *galericulata*. Although pharmacological studies of *S. baicalensis* root itself would not be pertinent to this monograph, some pharmacological data are included on constituents (e.g. flavones) isolated from *S. baicalensis* but common to all three species.

CONSTITUENTS

Scutellaria lateriflora

□ ***Flavonoids***, principally flavone 7-glucuronides, such as baicalin, with a smaller amount of free flavones. After room temperature extraction with 70% ethanol, the following 7-glucuronides were identified [7] and determined by HPLC (as % of dry weight of *extract*; the herb to extract ratio was not stated) [2]: baicalin (12.0%), 2,3-dihydrobaicalin (6.3%), lateriflorin (2.6%), ikonnikoside I (2.5%), scutellarin (1.3%) and oroxylin A 7-glucuronide (0.8%). Extraction with hot water (85°C) gave a fairly similar extract, somewhat higher in baicalin (13.1%) but lower in dihydrobaicalin (3.7%) and ikonnikoside I (1.4%).

A more lipophilic solvent was necessary for extraction of free flavones. After supercritical fluid extraction with carbon dioxide + 10% ethanol, HPLC analysis gave the following results (again as % of dry weight of *extract*): oroxylin A (1.9%), baicalein (1.0%) and wogonin (0.5%) [2]. The presence of lateriflorein (5,6,7-trihydroxy-2′-methoxyflavone, the aglycone of lateriflorin) has also been reported [7,8].

The flavonoids of *S. lateriflora* herb had not been investigated for 40 years, since Plouvier isolated scutellarin in 1963 [9], until the recent phytochemical studies [2,7,8].

□ ***Diterpenes*** with neo-clerodane structures:

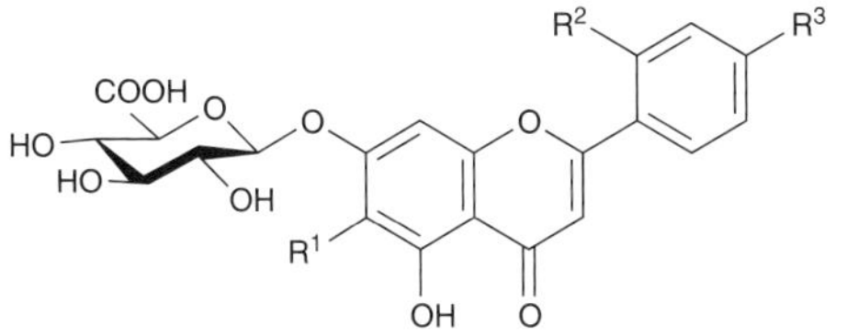

	R^1	R^2	R^3
Baicalin	OH	H	H
Lateriflorin	OH	OCH_3	H
Oroxylin A 7-glucuronide	OCH_3	H	H
Chrysin 7-glucuronide	H	H	H
Ikonnikoside I	OH	OH	H
Scutellarin	OH	H	OH

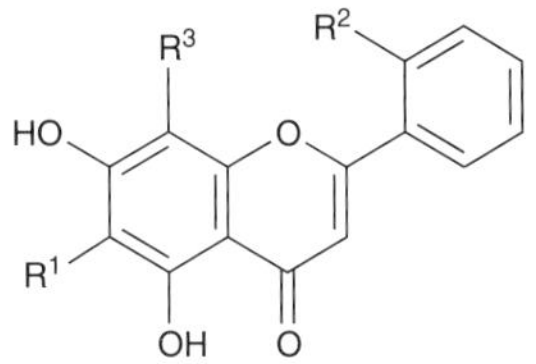

	R^1	R^2	R^3
Baicalein	OH	H	H
Lateriflorein	OH	OCH_3	H
Oroxylin A	OCH_3	H	H
Chrysin	H	H	H
Wogonin	H	H	OCH_3

ajugapitin, scutecyprol A and scutelaterins A, B and C [10].
☐ ***Amino acids***, principally gamma (or γ)-aminobutyric acid (GABA, ca. 0.55% of dried herb), followed by glutamine (ca. 0.34% of dried herb) and smaller amounts of tryptophan, phenylalanine, proline and various other amino acids. GABA was efficiently extracted with 70% ethanol, but for glutamine the highest yield was obtained by extraction with hot water at 100°C and under pressure (10 Mpa) [2]. In another study, 3.1% of glutamine was found in a dry aqueous extract [11].
☐ ***Essential oil***, 0.06%, composed mainly of sesquiterpenes (78%) including δ-cadinene (27%), calamenene (15%), β-elemene (9%), α-cubebene (4%) and α-humulene (4%); at least 73 compounds are present [4].
☐ ***Leaf Wax***, 1.2% of dry weight. 35% of the epicuticular wax consists of alkyl esters (C_{16}-C_{28} *n*-alkanols and C_{14}-C_{26} *n*-acids) [12]; 20% consists of

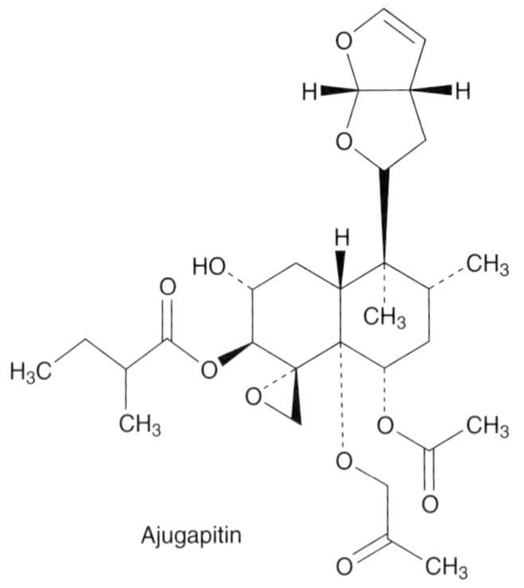

Ajugapitin

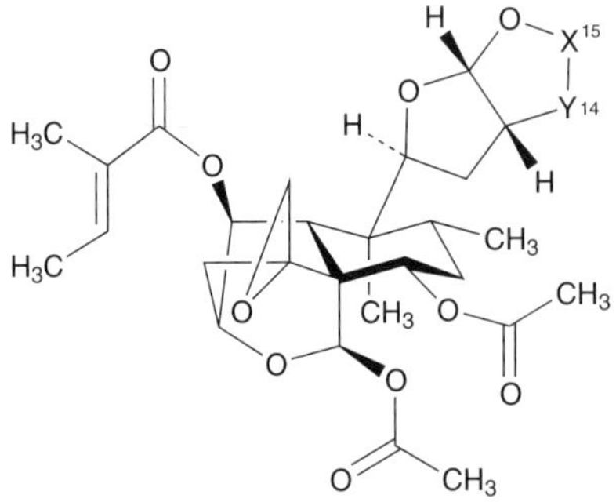

	X—Y
14,15-Dihydrojodrellin T	$H_2C—CH_2$
Jodrellin T	$HC{=}CH$

C_{23}-C_{37} hydrocarbons, the major components being *n*-tritriacontane (C_{33}, 38%), *n*-pentatriacontane (C_{35}, 24%) and *n*-hentatriacontane (C_{31}, 14%) [13,14].
☐ ***Other constituents*** include the iridoid glucoside catalpol [15] and undefined tannins [16].

Only a trace of melatonin (0.09 μg/g) was found in *Scutellaria lateriflora*, compared to a relatively high amount in *S. baicalensis* leaf (7.11 μg/g) [17].

Scutellaria galericulata

☐ ***Flavonoids*** Chrysin 7-glucuronide was isolated in 1955 as 2.6% of dry leaf weight [18] and the presence of scutellarin was reported in 1961 [19]. Subsequently, 21 flavonoids were identified in *Scutellaria galericulata* leaf from various regions of the USSR: the 7-glucuronides and aglycones of the flavones chrysin, scutellarein, baicalein, oroxylin-A, wogonin, apigenin, luteolin and 6-hydroxyluteolin, and of the flavanones dihydronorwogonin and dihydrobaicalein [20-22], and also baicalein 7-rhamnoside (galeroside) [20-23].
☐ ***Diterpenes*** with neo-clerodane structures: 14,15-dihydrojodrellin T, jodrellin T [24,25], jodrellin B, galericulin [24] and scutegalins A, B [26], C and D [25].
☐ ***Phenolic acids*** Caffeic acid and *p*-hydroxycinnamic acid [20]. The total content of hydroxycinnamic derivatives was found to be 0.7% [27, 28].
☐ ***Essential oil*** containing caryophyllene (29%), trans-β-farnesene (17%), menthone (10%), 1-octene-3-ol (8%), β-cubebene (3.3%), α-humulene, germacrene D and limonene [3].
☐ ***Other constituents*** include the iridoid glucoside catalpol [15] and 2.9-3.5% of tannins [19].

Published Assay Methods
Flavonoid glycosides and aglycones by HPLC [2,11,29]. Amino acids by HPLC [11] and HPLC-MS [2]. Essential oil by GC and GC-MS [4]. Isolation of flavonoid marker compounds [7,18].

PHARMACOLOGY

Flavonoids and amino acids are thought to be the main constituents contributing to the anxiolytic activity of skullcap [2,11].

In vitro

Receptor binding activities
Hot water and 70%-ethanolic dry extracts from skullcap (*S. lateriflora*) showed affinity for the 5-HT_7 serotonin receptor, inhibiting the binding of [³H]-LSD to the receptor by 87% and 57% respectively at 100 μg/ml. This activity was found to be at least partly due to flavonoid constituents, the highest inhibition of [³H]-LSD binding being shown by the flavone glucuronides scutellarin and

ikonnikoside I with IC_{50} values of 63.4 and 135 μM respectively [7].

Four flavones isolated from *Scutellaria baicalensis* root exhibited binding affinity for the benzodiazepine site of the $GABA_A$ receptor in rat forebrain synaptosomes, the order of affinity being wogonin (strong) > baicalein (strong) > scutellarein (moderate) > baicalin (weak) [6]. Three of these compounds are present in aerial parts of *Scutellaria lateriflora* (albeit in the quantitative order of baicalin > baicalein > wogonin) and all four have been identified in aerial parts of *Scutellaria galericulata* (amounts not known).

Antimicrobial activity
Dichloromethane and methanol extracts from *Scutellaria lateriflora* aerial parts exhibited antibacterial activity against *Escherichia coli* and antifungal activity against *Cladosporium cucumerinum*. The methanol extract was also active against the yeast *Candida albicans* [30].

In vivo

Anxiolytic activity
Behavioural tests were conducted to determine whether a single 100 mg oral dose of a dry aqueous extract from skullcap (*S. lateriflora*) imparted anxiolytic responses in rats. Compared to untreated control animals, treated rats spent more time in the centre in an "open field" exploration test (p<0.01), and entered the open arms more frequently and spent more time in the open in the elevated plus maze test (p<0.05), but did not behave differently in a social interaction test. Positive results in two out of the three tests were interpreted as indicating significant effects of skullcap in reducing anxiety levels in rats [11].

Anxiolytic-like effects of intraperitoneally administered baicalein (10 mg/kg) and baicalin (20 mg/kg) were demonstrated in the Vogel lick-shock conflict test in mice; a significantly increased number of shocks were tolerated over a period of 9 minutes. Chlordiazepoxide (a benzodiazepine receptor agonist) had a similar effect, while the effects were antagonized by co-administration of flumazenil (a benzodiazepine receptor antagonist). It was suggested that the anxiolytic-like effects may be mediated through activation of the benzodiazepine binding site of the $GABA_A$ receptor [31].

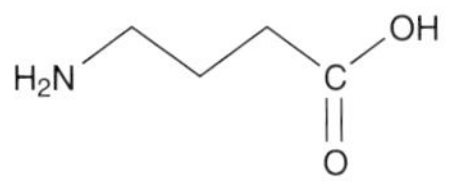

γ-Aminobutyric acid (GABA)

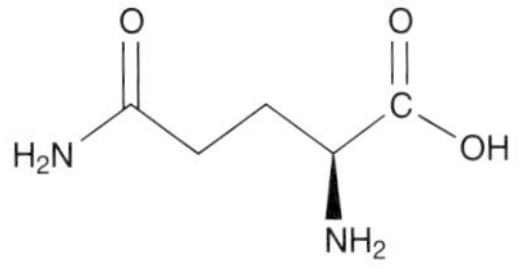

Glutamine

Wogonin given orally to mice at 7.5-30 mg/kg elicited an anxiolytic response similar to that of diazepam in the elevated plus maze test and the effect was blocked by co-administration of flumazenil. Taken together with results from holeboard and horizontal wire tests on wogonin-treated mice, the data suggested that wogonin exerts its anxiolytic effect through positive allosteric modulation of the $GABA_A$ receptor complex via interaction at the benzodiazepine site. Its anxiolytic effect was not accompanied by sedative or myorelaxant side effects typical of benzodiazepines [32].

Chrysin (present in *Scutellaria galericulata*) administered intraperitoneally to rats dose-dependently reduced spontaneous locomotor activity at 25-100 mg/kg (p<0.01 at 50 mg/kg) and had an anxiolytic effect at the low dose of 1 mg/kg in the light-dark experimental model of anxiety (p<0.05). The anxiolytic effect appeared to be related to benzodiazepine receptor activation [33].

Other effects
Aqueous and alcoholic extracts of *Scutellaria galericulata* (20%) administered intravenously to cats and rabbits at 1.0 or 1.5 ml/kg had no pronounced effect on blood pressure, even in experimental hypertension. The extracts did not depress the central nervous system in frogs nor exert an antispasmodic effect in strychnine poisoning [34].

Scutellarin has been reported to have marked effects in increasing cerebral blood flow, decreasing the resistance of cerebral vessels, and also inhibiting ADP-induced platelet aggregation [35].

Wogonin administered orally to rats at 10 mg/kg on days 1-7 *post coitum* exhibited 100% anti-implantational activity, compared to the formation of 30 foetuses in 5 control animals. The same dose administered intramuscularly proved mildly oestrogenic, significantly increasing uterine weight (p<0.001 compared to controls), but with less effect than conjugated oestrogen at 0.1 μg/kg [36].

Pharmacological studies in humans
Nineteen healthy volunteers (15 women and 4 men, aged 20-70 years) participating in a double-blind,

placebo-controlled crossover study of skullcap (*S. lateriflora*) were supplied with coded packets containing four different preparations in capsule form, to be taken orally at times and in settings of the participants' choice (without observation from the investigators), but on separate days at least 2 days apart and all within a 2-week period: 350 mg of freeze-dried skullcap herb, 100 mg and 200 mg of freeze-dried skullcap extract, and placebo capsules. After taking each preparation, the participants were required to subjectively assess and record, at baseline and 30, 60, 90, and 120 minutes after ingestion, using an "acute psychoactivity self-rating scale", their experiences with regard to three variables: energy (from sedating to stimulating), cognition (from diminished to increased) and anxiety (from relaxed to tense).

Of the three variables, the effect on anxiety was the most pronounced, all three preparations producing noteworthy results compared to both placebo and baseline, with the 200 mg dose of skullcap extract having the greatest effect. Lesser impacts were observed with respect to energy and cognition. It was concluded that the data clearly indicated an anxiolytic effect from *S. lateriflora* without any major impairment of intellect or vitality [37].

Pharmacokinetics

Baicalin (baicalein 7-glucuronide) given orally to rats is poorly absorbed as such from the rat gut, but it is hydrolysed by intestinal bacteria to its aglycone baicalein, which is readily absorbed and then efficiently conjugated back to baicalin in the plasma [38].

With regard to the amino acids GABA (γ-aminobutyric acid) and glutamine in skullcap (*S. lateriflora*), glutamine can pass the blood brain barrier whereas GABA cannot do so; glutamine can then be taken up by nerve terminals and subsequently metabolized to GABA [39]. To the extent that these amino acids may act on brain receptors, the content of glutamine in skullcap preparations appears, therefore, to be the more important from the activity viewpoint [2].

CLINICAL STUDIES

None published on mono-preparations of skullcap.

In clinical studies in China involving patients with cerebral thrombosis, cerebral embolism or paralysis caused by stroke, scutellarin administered to 469 cases, intramuscularly at 2 × 5 mg or intravenously at 10-15 mg daily for 10 days and generally continued for three more courses, was effective in 88% of cases. After oral administration at 3 × 40 mg daily in 165 other cases, scutellarin was effective in 93 and produced rudimentary restoration in a further 65 [35].

THERAPEUTICS

Actions

Anxiolytic [11,37], nervine tonic, antispasmodic [40-44], anticonvulsive [41,45], sedative [40,41,45] and mildly astringent [42,43].

Indications

None adequately substantiated by pharmacological or clinical studies.

Uses based on experience or tradition

Nervous disorders due to anxiety, tension or stress [1,40-45] including hysteria, panic attacks, neurasthenia, restlessness, sleep disorders, headaches, migraine, neuralgia, nervous exhaustion and depression [40-43]; to assist withdrawal from benzodiazepines [41]; premenstrual tension [41,44] and period pain [40].

Has also been used in the treatment of epilepsy (particularly grand mal) [43-45], chorea [45] and hiccough [1,42].

Contraindications

None known.

Side effects

None known.

Interactions with other drugs

None known.

Skullcap preparations (*S. lateriflora*) were found to inhibit the human cytochrome P450 3A4 enzyme in a standard *in vitro* test. As this hepatic enzyme is involved in the metabolization of various drugs, the possibility of herb-drug interactions may exist [11].

Dosage

Three times daily: dried herb, 1-2 g [1,45] or as an infusion of 2 g in 50 ml [40]; liquid extract 1:1 in 25% ethanol, 2-4 ml [42,45]; tincture 1:5 in 45% ethanol, 2 ml [40,45].

SAFETY

No formal toxicological data have been published on *Scutellaria lateriflora* or *galericulata*, but from evaluation of available information the American Herbal Products Association has classified *S. lateriflora* as a herb that can be safely consumed when used appropriately [46].

At one time some commercial supplies of skullcap were reported to have been adulterated or substituted with a *Teucrium* species [45,47]. This apparently related to adulteration of *Scutellaria lateriflora* with *Teucrium canadense* [48], both plants being indigenous to the same regions of North America [49] - not with European *Teucrium chamaedrys* which, during the early 1990s in France, caused acute hepatotoxicity in humans [50] and was subsequently confirmed as hepatotoxic in mice [51]. A few inconclusive case reports in the UK [52], attributing hepatotoxic effects to herbal combination products in which skullcap was one of the stated herbal ingredients, caused some concern over a decade ago but there is no evidence that skullcap is hepatotoxic and it remains on the UK General Sale List [53]. As with any herbal raw material, it is essential to confirm the identity of each batch of skullcap. Suitable methods have been published to identify *Scutellaria lateriflora* and to distinguish it specifically from *Teucrium canadense* (and *T. chamaedrys*) by microscopy, TLC and HPLC-MS [8].

REGULATORY STATUS

Medicines

UK	Accepted for general sale, internal or external use [53].
France	Not listed in *Médicaments à base de plantes* [54].
Germany	No Commission E monograph issued.

Food

Not used in foods.

REFERENCES

Current Pharmacopoeial Monographs

BHP	Skullcap

Literature References

1. Pharmaceutical Society of Great Britain. Scutellaria. In: *British Pharmaceutical Codex 1934*. London: Pharmaceutical Press, 1934:941-942.
2. Bergeron C, Gafner S, Clausen E and Carrier DJ. Comparison of the Chemical Composition of Extracts from *Scutellaria lateriflora* Using Accelerated Solvent Extraction and Supercritical Fluid Extraction versus Standard Hot Water or 70% Ethanol Extraction. *J. Agric. Food Chem.* 2005, **53**, 3076-3080.
3. Lawrence BM, Hogg JW, Terhune SJ, Morton JK and Gill LS. Terpenoid composition of some Canadian Labiatae. *Phytochemistry* 1972, **11**, 2636-2638.
4. Yaghmai MS. Volatile Constituents of *Scutellaria lateriflora* L. *Flavour Fragrance J.* 1988, **3**, 27-31.
5. Hosokawa K, Minami M, Kawahara K, Nakamura I and Shibata T. Discrimination among Three Species of Medicinal *Scutellaria* Plants using RAPD Markers. *Planta Medica* 2000, **66**, 270-272.
6. Hui KM, Wang XH and Xue H. Interaction of Flavones from the Roots of *Scutellaria baicalensis* with the Benzodiazepine Site. *Planta Medica* 2000, **66**, 91-93.
7. Gafner S, Bergeron C, Batcha LL, Reich J, Arnason JT, Burdette JE et al. Inhibition of [^{3}H]-LSD Binding to 5-HT$_7$ Receptors by Flavonoids from *Scutellaria lateriflora*. *J. Nat. Prod.* 2003, **66**, 535-537.
8. Gafner S, Bergeron C, Batcha LL, Angerhofer CK, Sudberg S, Sudberg EM et al. Analysis of *Scutellaria lateriflora* and its adulterants *Teucrium canadense* and *Teucrium chamaedrys* by LC-UV/MS, TLC and digital photomicroscopy. *J. AOAC Int.* 2003, **86**, 453-460.
9. Plouvier V. Sur la recherche des hétérosides flavoniques dans quelques groupes botaniques [Investigation of flavonoid glycosides in some botanical groups]. *Comptes Rendus Acad. Sci. Paris* 1963, **257**, 4061-4063 [FRENCH].
10. Bruno M, Cruciata M, Bondi ML, Piozzi F, de la Torre MC, Rodríguez B and Servettaz O. Neo-clerodane diterpenoids from *Scutellaria lateriflora*. *Phytochemistry* 1998, **48**, 687-691.
11. Awad R, Arnason JT, Trudeau V, Bergeron C, Budzinski JW, Foster BC and Merali Z. Phytochemical and biological analysis of Skullcap (*Scutellaria lateriflora* L.): A medicinal plant with anxiolytic properties. *Phytomedicine* 2003, **10**, 640-649.
12. Yaghmai S. Epicuticular wax esters of the leaves of *Scutellaria lateriflora* L. *Iran. J. Chem. Chem. Eng.* 1988, **10-11** Part A, 21-27 (English), 14-18 (Persian); through *Chem. Abstr.* 1989, **111**, 130680.
13. Yaghmai MS and Benson GG. The wax hydrocarbons of *Scutellaria lateriflora* L. *J. Nat. Prod.* 1979, **42**, 228-230.
14. Yaghmai S and Khayat MH. Epicuticular wax alkanes of *Scutellaria lateriflora* L. leaves. *Iran. J. Chem. Chem. Eng.* 1987, **9** (Part A), 26-30 (English), 3-8 (Persian); through *Chem. Abstr.* 1988, **108**, 183638.
15. Kooiman P. The occurrence of iridoid glycosides in the Labiatae. *Acta Bot. Neerl.* 1972, **21**, 417-427.
16. Budavari S, editor. Scutellaria. In: *The Merck Index - An encyclopedia of chemicals, drugs and biologicals, 12th ed.* Whitehouse Station, NJ: Merck, 1996:1446 (monograph 8557).
17. Murch SJ, Simmons CB and Saxena PK. Melatonin in feverfew and other medicinal plants. *Lancet* 1997, **350**, 1598-1599.
18. Marsh CA. Glucuronide Metabolism in Plants. 2. The isolation of flavone glucosiduronic acids from plants. *Biochem. J.* 1955, **59**, 58-62.
19. Denisova EK. The physical and anatomical properties of *Scutellaria galericulata*. *Uch. Zap. Pyatigorskii Gos. Farmatsevt. Inst.* 1961, **5**, 79-82 [RUSSIAN]; through *Chem. Abstr.* 1963, **59**, 11183.
20. Popova TP, Pakalns D, Chernykh NA, Zoz IG and Litvinenko VI. Intraspecific variability of phenolic compounds in *Scutellaria galericulata*. *Rastit. Resur.* 1976, **12** (2), 232-236 [RUSSIAN]; through *Chem. Abstr.* 1976, **85**, 59587.
21. Popova TP, Litvinenko VI, Gella EV and Ammosov AS. Chemical composition and medicinal properties of *Scutellaria galericulata*. *Farm. Zh. (Kiev)* 1972, **27** (5), 58-61 [UKRAINIAN]; through *Chem. Abstr.* 1973, **78**, 40407.
22. Barberan FAT. The Flavonoid Compounds of the Labiatae. *Fitoterapia* 1986, **57**, 67-95.
23. Gella EV, Beshko NP, Popova TP and Litvinenko VI. Galeroside, a new flavonoid glycoside from *Scutellaria galericulata*. *Khim. Prir. Soedin.* 1972, (2), 242 [RUSSIAN]; translated into English as *Chem. Nat. Compd.* 1972, **8**, 239; also through *Chem. Abstr.* 1972, **77**, 58845.
24. Cole MD, Anderson JC, Blaney WM, Fellows LE, Ley SV, Sheppard RN and Simmonds MSJ. Neo-clerodane insect antifeedants from *Scutellaria galericulata*. *Phytochemistry* 1990, **29**, 1793-1796.
25. Rodríguez B, de la Torre MC, Rodríguez B and Gómez-Serranillos P. *Neo*-clerodane diterpenoids from *Scutellaria galericulata*. *Phytochemistry* 1996, **41**, 247-253.
26. Rodríguez B, de la Torre MC, Rodríguez B, Bruno M, Piozzi F, Savona G et al. *Neo*-clerodane insect antifeedants from *Scutellaria galericulata*. *Phytochemistry* 1993, **33**, 309-315.
27. Lamaison JL, Petitjean-Freytet C, Duband F and Carnat AP. Rosmarinic acid content and antioxidant activity in French Lamiaceae. *Fitoterapia* 1991, **62**, 166-171.

28. Lamaison JL, Petitjean-Freytet C and Carnat AP. Rosmarinic acid, total hydroxycinnamic derivative contents and antioxidant activity of medicinal Apiaceae, Boraginaceae and Lamiaceae. *Ann. Pharm. Fr.* 1990, **48**, 103-108 [FRENCH/English summary].
29. Nishikawa K, Furukawa H, Fujioka T, Fujii H, Mihashi K, Shimomura K and Ishimaru K. Phenolics in Tissue Cultures of *Scutellaria. Natural Medicines* 1999, **53**, 209-213.
30. Bergeron C, Marston A, Gauthier R and Hostettmann K. Screening of Plants Used by North American Indians for Antifungal, Bactericidal, Larvicidal and Molluscicidal Activities. *Internat. J. Pharmacognosy* 1996, **34**, 233-242.
31. Liao JF, Hung WY and Chen CF. Anxiolytic-like effects of baicalein and baicalin in the Vogel conflict test in mice. *Eur. J. Pharmacol.* 2003, **464**, 141-146.
32. Hui KM, Huen MS, Wang HY, Zheng H, Sigel E, Baur R et al. Anxiolytic effect of wogonin, a benzodiazepine receptor ligand isolated from *Scutellaria baicalensis* Georgi. *Biochem. Pharmacol.* 2002, **64**, 1415-1424.
33. Zanoli P, Avallone R and Baraldi M. Behavioral characterisation of the flavonoids apigenin and chrysin. *Fitoterapia* 2000, **71** (Suppl. 1), S117-S123.
34. Kurnakov BA. Pharmacology of skullcap. *Farmakol. Toksikol.* 1957, **20** (6), 79-80 [RUSSIAN]; through *Chem. Abstr.* 1958, **52**, 14026.
35. Xiao P and Chen K. Recent Advances in Clinical Studies of Chinese Medicinal Herbs. 1. Drugs Affecting the Cardiovascular System. *Phytotherapy Res.* 1987, **1**, 53-57.
36. Singh P, Jain S, Bhala M, Goyal RB, Jayaprakash D and Lohiya NK. Wogonin, 5,7-Dihydroxy-8-methoxyflavone, as Oestrogenic and Anti-implantational Agent in the Rat. *Phytotherapy Res.* 1990, **4**, 86-89.
37. Wolfson P and Hoffmann DL. An investigation into the efficacy of *Scutellaria lateriflora* in healthy volunteers. *Altern. Ther. Health Med.* 2003, **9**, 74-78.
38. Akao T, Kawabata K, Yanagisawa E, Ishihara K, Mizuhara Y, Wakui Y et al. Baicalin, the predominant flavone glucuronide of Scutellariae radix, is absorbed from the rat gastrointestinal tract as the aglycone and restored to its original form. *J. Pharm. Pharmacol.* 2000, **52**, 1563-1568.
39. Cavadas C, Araújo I, Cotrim MD, Amaral T, Cunha AP, Macedo T and Fontes Ribeiro C. In vitro Study on the Interaction of Valeriana officinalis L. Extracts and their Amino Acids on $GABA_A$ Receptor in Rat Brain. *Arzneim.-Forsch./Drug Res.* 1995, **45**, 753-755.
40. Chevallier A. Skullcap. In: *The Encyclopedia of Medicinal Plants.* ISBN 0-7513-0314-3. London-New York-Stuttgart: Dorling Kindersley, 1996:134.
41. Bartram T. Skullcap. In: *Encyclopaedia of Herbal Medicine.* ISBN 0-9515984-1-4. Christchurch, UK: Grace Publishers, 1995:394.
42. Grieve M (edited by Leyel CF). Scullcaps. In: *A Modern Herbal* (first published 1931; revised 1973). ISBN 1-85501-249-9. London: Tiger Books International, 1994:724-725.
43. McIntyre A. Skullcap. In: *The Complete Woman's Herbal.* ISBN 1-85675-135-X. London: Gaia Books, 1994:38.
44. Ody P. Skullcap. *The Complete Guide Medicinal Herbal.* ISBN 0-7513-3005-1. London-New York: Dorling Kindersley, 2000:118.
45. Scutellaria. In: *British Herbal Pharmacopoeia 1983.* ISBN 0-903032-07-4. Bournemouth: British Herbal Medicine Association, 1983.
46. McGuffin M, Hobbs C, Upton R and Goldberg A, editors. *Scutellaria lateriflora* L. In: American Herbal Products Association's *Botanical Safety Handbook.* ISBN 0-8493-1675-8. Boca Raton-Boston-London: CRC Press, 1997:105.
47. Phillipson JD and Anderson LA. Herbal remedies used in sedative and antirheumatic preparations: Part 1. *Pharm. J.* 1984, **233**, 80-82 (Part 2, *ibid.* 111-115).
48. Barnes J, Anderson LA and Phillipson JD. Scullcap. In: *Herbal Medicines - A guide for healthcare professionals, 2nd ed.* ISBN 0-85369-474-5. London-Chicago: Pharmaceutical Press, 2002:425-427.
49. Denison E. Mint Family - Lamiaceae (Labiatae): *Teucrium canadense*; *Scutellaria* species. In: *Missouri Wildflowers. A Field Guide to Wildflowers of Missouri and Adjacent Areas.* Missouri Department of Conservation, 1973:227.
50. Stickel F, Egerer G and Seitz HK. Hepatotoxicity of botanicals. *Public Health Nutr.* 2000, **3**, 113-124.
51. Kouzi SA, McMurtry RJ and Nelson SD. Hepatotoxicity of Germander (*Teucrium chamaedrys* L.) and One of Its Constituent Neoclerodane Diterpenes Teucrin A in the *Mouse. Chem. Res. Toxicol.* 1994, **7**, 850-856.
52. MacGregor FB, Abernethy VE, Dahabra S, Cobden I and Hayes PC. Hepatotoxicity of herbal remedies. *Brit. Med. J.* 1989, **299**, 1156-1157.
53. Scullcap. In: UK Statutory Instrument 1984 No. 769. The Medicines (Products Other Than Veterinary Drugs) (General Sale List) Order 1984. Schedule 1, Table A.
54. *Médicaments à base de plantes.* ISBN 2-911473-02-7. Saint-Denis Cedex, France: Agence du Médicament, 1998.

ST. JOHN'S WORT

Hypericaceae (Guttiferae)

Hyperici herba

Synonym: Perforate St. John's Wort.

Definition

St. John's Wort consists of the dried flowering tops of *Hypericum perforatum* L.

Common throughout Europe except the far north, *Hypericum perforatum* is an erect perennial with yellow flowers. Translucent glands in the leaves, looking like tiny perforations when held up to the light, have given the plant its specific epithet. The common name relates to St. John the Baptist and *Hypericum* is reputed to be derived from the Greek *hyper* (over) and *eikon* (image). In medieval Europe garlands of St. John's Wort were hung over pictures of the saint during midsummer festivals (the 24th of June is St. John's Day).

CONSTITUENTS

□ ***Phloroglucinol derivatives***, principally hyperforin and its homologue adhyperforin. The content of hyperforin is typically quoted as 2-4% [1-4] and of adhyperforin as 0.2-1.9% [3], but the amounts can be very variable [5]. In 21 samples of flowering aerial parts grown in Slovenia (separated into green "herb" and flowers, then dried), hyperforin content in the herb ranged from 0.5% to 11% (average 6.0%) and in the flowers from 2.6% to 18.6% (average 13.6%) [6]. In another study the average content of hyperforin was 6.6% in just-opened flowers and 7.5% in overblown flowers [7].

Hyperforin and adhyperforin are very susceptible to oxidation and particularly unstable in non-polar solvents or when exposed to light. However, hyperforin can be stabilized with suitable antioxidants [2] and St. John's wort extracts with a standardized content of hyperforin are available [8].

□ ***Naphthodianthrones***, 0.06-0.4% (Ph. Eur. min. 0.08% of total hypericins, expressed as hypericin), principally hypericin (0.03-0.09%) and pseudohypericin (0.03-0.34%), which occur mainly in the flowers [9,10].

Their biosynthetic precursors protohypericin and protopseudohypericin (which are converted to hypericin and pseudohypericin respectively on exposure to light), and a small amount of cyclopseudohypericin, are also present and included in the analytical term 'total hypericins' [11].

□ ***Flavonoids***, up to 4%, mainly glycosides of the flavonol quercetin: hyperoside (0.7-1.2%), rutin (0.3-0.8%), isoquercitrin (0.3-0.7%), quercitrin (ca. 0.2%), quercetin 3-glucuronide (miquelianin, 0.1-0.3%) [10] and others [12].

The biflavones I3, II8-biapigenin [13] and I3',II8-biapigenin (amentoflavone) [14] are present in amounts of 0.1-0.5% and 0.01-0.05% respectively. They occur exclusively in the flowers and flower buds [15].

□ ***Tannins***, 6-15% (depending on the method of determination), consisting mainly of procyanidins (condensed tannins) [4,9,15]. Procyanidins A2, B1, B2, B3, B5, B7 and C1 have been isolated, together with the flavanol monomers catechin and epicatechin. The average size of the polymers was estimated as 4-5 flavanol units [16].

□ ***Xanthones*** in trace amounts, notably 1,3,6,7-tetrahydroxyxanthone [15] and its 2-*C*-glucoside (mangiferin) [12,17].

□ ***Essential oil***, 0.1-0.25% [15]. Steam-distillation

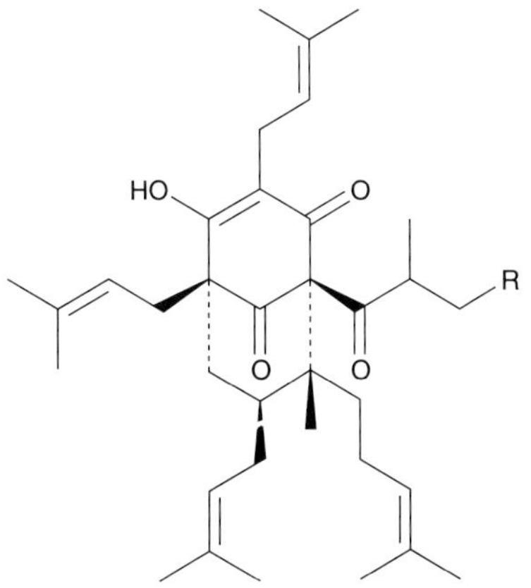

Hyperforin R = H
Adhyperforin R = CH_3

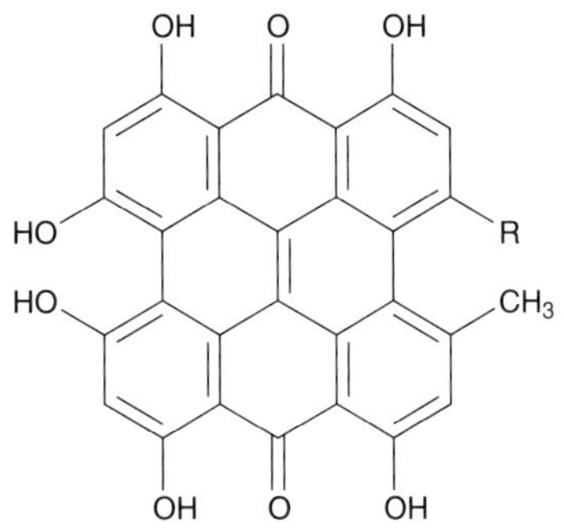

Hypericin R = CH_3
Pseudohypericin R = CH_2OH

of dried flowering tops yielded an oil in which the principal components identified were 2-methyloctane (16%) and α-pinene (10.6%) [18]. In steam-distilled leaf oil of Indian origin 58 components were identified, α-pinene (67%) being dominant; the other components included caryophyllene, geranyl acetate and nonane (each about 5%) [19].

☐ ***Other constituents*** include small amounts of chlorogenic acid [20] and other caffeoylquinic and *p*-coumaroylquinic acids [12], and also free amino acids (about 0.3%) [21].

For a review of the constituents of St. John's wort see Nahrstedt and Butterweck [15].

Published Assay Methods

Total hypericins by spectrophotometry [Ph. Eur. and USP]. Naphthodianthrones and flavonoids by spectrophotometry and HPLC [10]. Simultaneous determination of hyperforin, adhyperforin, hypericin and pseudohypericin by HPLC [22]. Rapid HPLC analysis of naphthodianthrones and phloroglucinols in extracts [23].

PHARMACOLOGY

As befits one of the most clinically tested of herbs, a wide range of pharmacological studies has been carried out with extracts from St. John's wort, primarily in relation to their antidepressant effects. Although the mode of action is not yet fully understood, it has been demonstrated that the extracts have pharmacological properties comparable to those of synthetic antidepressants. Furthermore, naphthodianthrones, hyperforin and flavonoid constituents have been shown to possess relevant activity. Since an extensive summary of these and other studies may be found in the ESCOP monograph [24], they are not covered in detail here.

Pharmacokinetics

Several pharmacokinetic studies have been carried out following oral administration of St. John's wort extracts to healthy volunteers [25-27]. After a single dose of 612 mg of a 50%-ethanolic dry extract the following maximum plasma concentrations and elimination half-lives were determined: hypericin, 3.1 ng/ml and 23.8 hours; pseudohypericin, 8.5 ng/ml and 25.4 hours; hyperforin, 83.5 ng/ml and 19.6 hours; quercetin (two peaks), 47.7 and 43.8 ng/ml, and 4.2 hours. Plasma levels under steady state conditions after a daily dose of 612 mg of the extract for 14 days were fairly similar [27].

CLINICAL STUDIES

The efficacy of standardized hydroalcoholic extracts of St. John's wort has been assessed in over 40 controlled, double-blind studies and at least 20 observational studies. Summaries of the more important individual studies published up to 2003 may be found in the ESCOP monograph [24].

Randomized controlled studies have shown that, in mild to moderate depression, St. John's wort extracts are more effective than placebo and comparable in effectiveness to synthetic antidepressants. These conclusions have been confirmed by meta-analyses of the pooled data from a substantial number of studies, as summarized below, thus providing a higher level of evidence than that of any individual study.

Data from 30 controlled clinical studies in which extracts of St. John's wort were compared with placebo (19 studies) or synthetic antidepressants including fluoxetine, amitriptyline, sertraline, maprotiline and imipramine (15 studies) were pooled to enable two meta-analyses. Four of the studies involved all three arms and were included in both analyses. In most of the studies the patients suffered from mild to moderate depression, but a few studies related to severe depression. The results demonstrated [28]:

- for St. John's wort (n = 1086) versus placebo (n = 1043), a highly significant superiority of St. John's wort preparations (mean response 53.3% vs. 32.7%; $p<0.00001$).
- for St. John's wort (n = 1117) versus synthetic antidepressants (n = 1114), similar effectiveness (mean response 53.2% vs. 51.3%; $p = 0.5$) and, in the sub-group of patients with mild to moderate depression, superiority of St. John's wort preparations (mean response 59.5% vs. 52.9%; $p = 0.01$).

An earlier meta-analysis of the data from 22 randomized controlled studies (in both mild to moderate depression and major depression) showed that St. John's wort preparations were significantly more effective than placebo and of similar efficacy to synthetic antidepressants. Sub-analysis of data from 6 placebo-controlled and 4 synthetic antidepressant comparator studies satisfying stricter methodological criteria led to the same conclusions. No evidence was found of publication bias [29].

The data from 37 randomized double-blind studies (26 placebo-controlled and 14 comparisons with synthetic antidepressants, involving a total of 4925 patients) were analysed in a systematic review using the responder rate ratio (RR = responder rate in the treatment group/responder rate in the control group) as the main criterion of efficacy. Although results from placebo-controlled studies were found to be markedly heterogeneous, the overall evidence again confirmed that in adults with mild to moderate depression St. John's wort extracts improved symptoms more than placebo and to an extent comparable to that of synthetic antidepressants. In patients suffering from major depression St. John's wort extracts produced only minimal benefits compared to placebo [30].

To eliminate questionable methodology, another meta-analysis concentrated on well-designed studies with strictly defined depression criteria. Pooled data from 6 randomized, double-blind studies (2 placebo-controlled, 4 comparisons with tricyclic antidepressants or TCAs: maprotiline, amitriptyline or imipramine), involving a total of 651 patients with mainly mild to moderately severe depressive disorders, confirmed that St. John's wort preparations were more effective than placebo (1.5 times more likely to result in an antidepressant response) and similar in effectiveness to low-dose TCAs [31].

Although non-randomized "observational" studies carry less weight and sometimes have relatively poor methodological quality, collectively they can contribute to the evidence base, not least to safety data. From a systematic review of 16 such studies, involving a total of 38,804 patients taking one of 12 different mono-preparations (some based on the same extracts) for 4-6 weeks, it was concluded that St. John's Wort extracts are well tolerated and seemed to be effective in routine treatment of mild to moderate depressive disorders [32].

Hitherto, conclusions relating to the efficacy of St. John's wort extracts in major depression have been based primarily on two studies from which no superiority over placebo was evident [33,34]. However, in a more recent study not yet incorporated into meta-analyses, a St. John's wort extract (3-7:1, standardized to 3-6% of hyperforin and 0.12-0.28% of hypericin) proved to be at least as effective as paroxetine (a synthetic antidepressant of the SSRI type) in the treatment of moderate to severe major depression [8].

A therapeutic use of St. John's wort which has stood the test of time, having been recommended by the English physician John Gerard in *The Herball* or *Generall Historie of Plantes* in 1597 and some 400 years later by the German Commission E [35], is as a vulnerary in the form of an oil macerate (originally in olive oil) [36,37]. The wound healing action has been attributed to hyperforin [36] but no clinical data appear to be available.

THERAPEUTICS

Actions
Antidepressant, antiviral, antiseptic [24,27,38], anti-inflammatory [38,39] and vulnerary [35-37].

Indications
Treatment of mild to moderate depressive disorders [24,28-31].

Other uses, based on experience or tradition
Internal: Depressive moods, anxiety (including menopausal anxiety) and nervous restlessness [35,37].

External: Treatment of burns, wounds, bruises, swellings [35-37,40] and shingles [37].

Contraindications
Avoid concomitant use with drugs which are known or suspected to interact with St John's wort (see Interactions below).

Side effects
Occasionally, mild gastro-intestinal disturbances, nausea, restlessness, fatigue, headache or allergic reactions [24].

Interactions with other drugs
Considerable caution is necessary in the concomitant use of St. John's wort with other drugs, since numerous reports have indicated the possibility of interactions. It is important in this respect to read the in-pack leaflet supplied with the product.

St. John's wort has been shown to lower plasma concentrations and/or the pharmacological effect of tricyclic antidepressants such as amitriptyline, anticoagulants such as phenprocoumon and warfarin, oral contraceptives (ethinyloestradiol/desogestrel) and also alprazolam, cyclosporin, digoxin, fexofenadine, indinavir, methadone, simvastatin, theophylline and others [41]. It induces activity of cytochrome P450 enzymes (particularly CYP3A4) in the liver and may therefore result in accelerated metabolization and elimination of various drugs. Hyperforin has been shown to contribute to this effect [42]. As a further mechanism of interaction, St. John's wort appears to increase expression and enhance the function of a drug transporter, P-glycoprotein [43].

St. John's wort should not be taken concurrently with other antidepressants; in combination with those of the serotonin reuptake inhibitor type (e.g. sertraline, paroxetine, nefazodone) it can cause serotonergic syndrome [41].

Dosage
Adult daily dose: 450-1050 mg (typically 900 mg) of dry extracts (4-7:1, 50-60% ethanol) [24]; 900 mg of hydroalcoholic extract standardized (by HPLC) to 3-6% of hyperforin and 0.12-0.28% of hypericin [8,44]; 3-4.5 ml of tincture (1:5, ethanol 50% V/V) [24]; equivalent preparations.
For tea infusions, 2-5 g of dried herb [24,37].

External: Infused oil from St. John's wort flowers [36,37].

SAFETY

As a mono-therapy St. John's Wort has a particularly encouraging safety profile. However, as mentioned above, caution is necessary in considering its concurrent use with prescribed drugs since there is a high potential for interactions [41]. The first reports of interactions (with phenprocoumon, digoxin and theophylline) appeared in 1999 and numerous other have followed.

Results from controlled clinical studies with almost 5,000 patients [30] and observational studies involving a further 34,800 patients [32] show that St. John's Wort extracts are well tolerated and have a good safety record. When side effects occur, they are usually mild and transient [45]; from one systematic review, those most frequently occurring were found to be dry mouth (3.7%), headaches (1.8%), nausea and vomiting (1.6%), abdominal pain (1.3%), dizziness (1.0%), fatigue/sedation (1.2%), vertigo and dizziness (1.0%), and restlessness (1.0%) [29].

St. John's Wort extracts cause fewer adverse effects than tricyclic antidepressants (TCAs) and marginally fewer than selective serotonin reuptake inhibitors (SSRIs) [28,30]. Pooled data from 7 comparative studies revealed that 49% of patients taking TCAs complained of at least one type of adverse effect, compared to 28% of those taking St. John's wort extracts ($p<0.00001$); this led to drop out rates of 8.3% with TCAs compared to 2.3% with St. John's wort ($p<0.0001$). St. John's wort extracts also tended to be more tolerable than SSRIs, but the differences were not significant [28].

No evidence of mutagenicity was evident from *in vitro* or *in vivo* studies of a St. John's wort extract [46]. An orally administered St. John's wort extract did not affect normal reproduction and development of offspring through to the second generation in mice [47], and no signs of maternal toxicity were observed after oral administration of an extract to pregnant rats during the period of organogenesis (days 9-15 of pregnancy) [48].

Although hypericin can potentially cause photosensitization, plasma hypericin levels during antidepressant therapy are far too low to induce phototoxic skin reactions [45].

REGULATORY STATUS

Medicines

UK	Accepted for general sale, *external use only* [49].
France	Accepted for specified indications [50].
Germany	Commission E monograph published, with approved uses [35].

Food

Council of Europe	Permitted as flavouring, category 5, with limit of 0.4 mg/kg for hypericin in beverages (no limit in food); limit for xanthones under evaluation [51].

REFERENCES

Current Pharmacopoeial Monographs

Ph. Eur.	St. John's Wort
USP	St. John's Wort

Literature References

1. Orth HCJ, Rentel C and Schmidt PC. Isolation, Purity Analysis and Stability of Hyperforin as a Standard Material from *Hypericum perforatum* L. *J. Pharm. Pharmacol.* 1999, 51, 193-200.
2. Orth HCJ and Schmidt PC. Stability and Stabilization of Hyperforin. *Drugs made in Germany* 1999, **42**, 110-113.
3. Upton R. editor. St. John's Wort - *Hypericum perforatum.* Quality Control, Analytical and Therapeutic Monograph. In: American Herbal Pharmacopoeia and Therapeutic Compendium. Santa Cruz, CA: American Herbal Pharmacopoeia, 1997:1-32 (Available as a single monograph. Website: herbal-ahp.org).
4. Hänsel R, Keller K, Rimpler H and Schneider G, editors. Hypericum. In: *Hagers Handbuch der Pharmazeutischen Praxis, 5th ed. Volume 5: Drogen E-O.* ISBN 3-540-52638-2. Berlin-Heidelberg-New York-London: Springer-Verlag, 1993:474-495 [GERMAN].
5. Bergonzi MC, Bilia AR, Gallori S, Guerrini D and Vincieri FF. Variability in the Content of the Constituents of Hypericum perforatum L. and Some Commercial Extracts. *Drug Dev. Ind. Pharm.* 2001, **27**, 491-497.
6. Umek A, Kreft S, Kartnig T and Heydel B. Quantitative Phytochemical Analyses of Six *Hypericum* Species Growing in Slovenia. Planta Medica 1999, **65**, 388-390.
7. Tekel'ová D, Repcák M, Zemková E and Tóth J. Quantitative Changes of Dianthrones, Hyperforin and Flavonoids Content in the Flower Ontogenesis of *Hypericum perforatum. Planta Medica* 2000, **66**, 778-780.
8. Szegedi A, Kohnen R, Dienel A and Kieser M. Acute treatment of moderate to severe depression with hypericum extract WS 5570 (St. John's wort): randomized controlled double blind non-inferiority trial versus paroxetine. *BMJ* 2005, **330**, 503-507.
9. Brantner A, Kartnig T and Quehenberger F. Comparative phytochemical investigations of *Hypericum perforatum* L. and *Hypericum maculatum* Crantz. *Sci. Pharm.* 1994, **62**, 261-276 [GERMAN/English summary].
10. Girzu-Amblard M, Carnat A, Fraisse D, Carnat A-P and Lamaison J-L. Flavonoid and dianthranoid levels of St. John's wort flowering tops. *Ann. Pharm. Fr.* 2000, **58**, 341-345 [FRENCH/English summary].
11. Krämer W and Wiartalla R. Determination of Naphthodianthrones in St. John's Wort (*Hypericum perforatum*). *Pharm. Ztg. Wiss.* 1992, **137**, 202-207 [GERMAN/English summary].
12. Jürgenliemk G and Nahrstedt A. Phenolic Compounds from *Hypericum perforatum. Planta Medica* 2002, **68**, 88-91.
13. Berghöfer R, Hölzl J. Biflavonoids in *Hypericum perforatum.* Part 1. Isolation of I3, II8-Biapigenin. *Planta Medica* 1987, **53**, 216-217.
14. Berghöfer R, Hölzl J. Isolation of I3',II8-Biapigenin (Amentoflavone) from *Hypericum perforatum. Planta*

Medica 1989, **55**, 91.
15. Nahrstedt A and Butterweck V. Biologically Active and Other Chemical Constituents of the Herb of *Hypericum perforatum* L. *Pharmacopsychiatry* 1997, **30** (Suppl.) 129-134.
16. Ploss O, Petereit F and Nahrstedt A. Procyanidins from the herb of *Hypericum perforatum. Pharmazie* 2001, **56**, 509-511.
17. Seabra RM, Vasconcelos MH, Cruz Costa MA and Correia Alves A. Phenolic compounds from *Hypericum perforatum* and *H. undulatum. Fitoterapia* 1992, **63**, 474.
18. Chialva F, Gabri G, Liddle PAP and Ulian F. Indagine sulla composizione dell'olio essenziale di Hypericum perforatum L. e di Teucrium chamaedrys L. [Investigation of the composition of essential oils from *Hypericum perforatum* L. and *Teucrium chamaedrys* L.]. *Riv. Ital. E.P.P.O.S.* 1981, **63**, 286-288 [ITALIAN].
19. Weyerstahl P, Splittgerber U, Marschall H and Kaul VK. Constituents of the Leaf Essential Oil of *Hypericum perforatum* L. from India. *Flavour Fragrance J.* 1995, **10**, 365-370.
20. Ollivier B, Balansard G, Maillard C and Vidal E. Separation and Identification of Phenolic Acids by HPLC and UV Spectral Analysis. Application to Parietaria (*Parietaria officinalis* L.) and Saint John's Wort (*Hypericum perforatum* L.). *J. Pharm. Belg.* 1985, **40**, 173-177 [FRENCH/English summary].
21. Lapke C, Nündel M, Wendel G, Schilcher H and Riedel E. Concentrations of Free Amino Acids in Herbal Drugs. *Planta Medica* 1993, **59** (Suppl.), A627.
22. Gray DE, Rottinghaus GE, Garrett HEG and Pallardy SG. Simultaneous Determination of the Predominant Hyperforins and Hypericins in St. John's Wort (*Hypericum perforatum* L.) by Liquid Chromatography. *J. AOAC. Int.* 2000, **83**, 944-949.
23. Tolonen A, Hohtola A and Jalonen J. Fast High-Performance Liquid Chromatographic Analysis of Naphthodianthrones and Phloroglucinols from *Hypericum perforatum* Extracts. *Phytochem. Analysis* 2003, **14**, 306-309.
24. European Scientific Cooperative on Phytotherapy. Hyperici herba - St. John's Wort. In: *ESCOP Monographs - The Scientific Foundation for Herbal Medicinal Products, 2nd ed.* Stuttgart-New York: Thieme; Exeter, UK: ESCOP, 2003:257-281.
25. Kerb R, Brockmöller J, Staffeldt B, Ploch M and Roots I. Single-Dose and Steady-State Pharmacokinetics of Hypericin and Pseudohypericin. *Antimicrob. Agents Chemother.* 1996, **40**, 2087-2093.
26. Brockmöller J, Reum T, Bauer S, Kerb R, Hübner W-D and Roots I. Hypericin and Pseudohypericin: Pharmacokinetics and Effects on Photosensitivity in Humans. *Pharmacopsychiatry* 1997, **30** (Suppl. 2), 94-101.
27. Schulz H-U, Schürer M, Bässler D and Weiser D. Investigation of the Bioavailability of Hypericin, Pseudohypericin, Hyperforin and the Flavonoids Quercetin and Isorhamnetin Following Single and Multiple Oral Dosing of a Hypericum Containing Tablet. *Arzneim.-Forsch./Drug Res.* 2005, **55**, 15-22.
28. Röder C, Schaefer M and Leucht S. Meta-Analysis of Effectiveness and Tolerability of Treatment of Mild to Moderate Depression with St. John's Wort. *Fortschr. Neurol. Psychiat.* 2004, **72**, 330-343 [GERMAN/English summary].
29. Whiskey E, Werneke U and Taylor D. A systematic review and meta-analysis of *Hypericum perforatum* in depression: a comprehensive clinical review. *Int. Clin. Psychopharmacol.* 2001, **16**, 239-252.
30. Linde K, Mulrow C, Berner M and Egger E. St. John's Wort for depression. *Cochrane Database Syst. Rev.* 2005, Issue 3, CD000448.
31. Kim HL, Streltzer J and Goebert D. St. John's Wort for Depression. A Meta-Analysis of Well-Defined Clinical Trials. *J. Nerv. Ment. Dis.* 1999, **187**, 532-538.
32. Linde K and Knüppel L. Large-scale observational studies of hypericum extracts in patients with depressive disorders - a systematic review. *Phytomedicine* 2005, **12**, 148-157.
33. Shelton RC, Keller MB, Gelenberg A, Dunner DL, Hirschfeld R, Thase ME et al. Effectiveness of St. John's Wort in Major Depression. A Randomized Controlled Trial. *JAMA* 2001, **285**, 1978-1986.
34. Hypericum Depression Trial Study Group. Effect of *Hypericum perforatum* (St John's Wort) in Major Depressive Disorder. A Randomized Controlled Trial. *JAMA* 2002, **287**, 1807-1814.
35. Hyperici herba. German Commission E Monograph published in: Bundesanzeiger No. 228 of 5 December 1984, amended in Bundesanzeiger of 13 March 1990.
36. Maisenbacher P and Kovar K-A. Analysis and Stability of Hyperici Oleum. *Planta Medica* 1992, **58**, 351-354.
37. Mills S and Bone K. St. John's wort (*Hypericum perforatum* L.). In: *Principles and Practice of Phytotherapy. Modern Herbal Medicine.* ISBN 0-443-06016-9. Edinburgh-London-New York: Churchill Livingstone, 2000:542-552.
38. Barnes J, Anderson LA and Phillipson JD. St. John's Wort (*Hypericum perforatum* L.): a review of its chemistry, pharmacology and clinical properties. *J. Pharm. Pharmacol.* 2001, **53**, 583-600.
39. Mattace Raso G, Pacilio M, Di Carlo G, Esposito E, Pinto L and Meli R. In-vivo and in-vitro anti-inflammatory effect of *Echinacea purpurea* and *Hypericum perforatum. J. Pharm. Pharmacol.* 2002, **54**, 1379-1383.
40. Hölzl J. Inhaltsstoffe und Wirkmechanismen des Johanniskrautes [Constituents and mode of action of St. John's wort]. *Z Phythotherapie* 1993, **14**, 255-264 [GERMAN/English summary].
41. Izzo AA. Drug interactions with St. John's Wort (*Hypericum perforatum*): a review of the clinical evidence. *Int. J. Clin. Pharmacol. Ther.* 2004, **42**, 139-148.
42. Moore LB, Goodwin B, Jones SA, Wisely GB, Serabjit-Singh CJ, Willson TM et al. St. John's wort induces hepatic drug metabolism through activation of the pregnane X receptor. *Proc. Natl. Acad. Sci. USA* 2000, **97**, 7500-7502.
43. Hennessy M, Kelleher D, Spira JP, Barry M, Kavanagh P, Back D et al. St. John's Wort increases expression of P-glycoprotein: Implications for drug interactions. *Br. J. Clin. Pharmacol.* 2002, **53**, 75-82.
44. Lecrubier Y, Clerc G, Didi R and Kieser M. Efficacy of St. John's Wort Extract WS 5570 in Major Depression: A Double-Blind, Placebo-Controlled Trial. *Am. J. Psychiatry* 2002, **159**, 1361-1366.
45. Greeson JM, Sanford B and Monti DA. St. John's wort (*Hypericum perforatum*): a review of the current pharmacological, toxicological and clinical literature. *Psychopharmacology* 2001, **153**, 402-414.
46. Leuschner J. Preclinical Toxicological Profile of Hypericum Extract LI 160. In: Abstracts of 2nd International Congress on Phytomedicine. Munich, 11-14 September 1996. Published as: *Phytomedicine* 1996, **3** (Suppl. 1), 104 (Abstract SL-80).
47. Rayburn WF, Gonzalez CL, Christensen D and Stewart JD. Effect of prenatally administered hypericum (St. John's wort) on growth and physical maturation of mouse offspring. *Am. J. Obstet. Gynecol.* 2001, **184**, 191-195.
48. Borges LV, do Carmo Cancino JC, Peters VM, Las Casas L and de Oliveira Guerra M. Development of Pregnancy in Rats Treated with *Hypericum perforatum. Phytotherapy Res.* 2005, **19**, 885-887.
49. Hypericum (St. John's Wort). In: UK Statutory Instrument 1994 No. 2410. The Medicines (Products Other Than Veterinary Drugs) (General Sale List) Amendment Order 1994. Schedule 1, Table B (External use only).
50. Millepertuis, sommité fleurie. In: *Médicaments à base de plantes.* ISBN 2-911473-02-7. Saint-Denis Cedex, France: Agence du Médicament, 1998.
51. Hypericum perforatum L. In: *Natural Sources of Flavourings. Report No. 1.* ISBN 92-871-4324-2. Strasbourg: Council of Europe Publishing, 2000:203-204.

REGULATORY GUIDELINES FROM OTHER EU COUNTRIES

FRANCE

Médicaments à base de plantes [50]: Millepertuis, sommité fleurie.

Therapeutic indications accepted

Topical use
Traditionally used: as a soothing and antipruriginous local treatment of dermatological ailments, as a trophic protector in the treatment of chaps, abrasions or fissures and against insect stings; in cases of sunburn, superficial and limited burns, and erythema of the buttocks; locally (mouthwash/gargle, pastille) as an antalgesic in ailments of the buccal cavity and/or the pharynx.

GERMANY

Commission E monograph [35]: Hyperici herba (Johanniskraut).

Uses

Internal: Psychovegetative disorders, depressive moods, anxiety and/or nervous restlessness. Oily St. John's wort preparations for dyspeptic complaints.
External: Oily St. John's wort preparations for the treatment and after-treatment of acute and contused injuries, myalgia and first-degree burns.

Contraindications

None known.

Side effects

Photosensitization is possible, especially in light-skinned persons.

Interactions with other drugs

None known.

Dosage

Unless otherwise prescribed, average daily dose for internal use: 2-4 g of herb or 0.2-1 mg of total hypericin in other dosage forms.

Mode of administration

Cut or powdered herb, liquid and solid preparations for oral use. Liquid and semi-solid preparations for external use. Preparations made with fatty oils for external and internal use.

Actions

A mild antidepressive effect of the herb and its preparations has been reported in numerous accounts of medical experience. From experimental findings hypericin is considered to be a monoamine oxidase inhibitor. Oily preparations of St. John's wort have anti-inflammatory activity.

THYME **Labiatae**

Thymi herba

Synonyms: Garden or Common Thyme (*Thymus vulgaris*), Spanish Thyme (*T. zygis*).

Definition

Thyme consists of the leaves and flowers, separated from the previously dried stems, of *Thymus vulgaris* L. or *Thymus zygis* L. or a mixture of both species.

Thymus vulgaris L., a subshrub with usually pink-violet flowers, is native to the Mediterranean area but widely cultivated elsewhere. *Thymus zygis* L., with a similar appearance but differentiated by white flowers, is found almost exclusively on the Iberian peninsula.

CONSTITUENTS

□ ***Essential oil*** Chemotypes with different essential oil compositions have been reported for both *Thymus vulgaris* and *T. zygis* [1,2]. Since only thyme with essential oil rich in phenolic terpenes (thymol and carvacrol) meets pharmacopoeial requirements (Ph. Eur. min. 1.2% V/m of essential oil, of which not less than 40% consists of thymol and carvacrol), it is necessary to be selective. Thyme (*T. vulgaris*) grown in countries as varied as Greece [3], Italy [4,5], Cuba [6] and Mongolia [7] has satisfied pharmacopoeial criteria for essential oil composition with the following components: thymol (31.4-63.6%), carvacrol (2.2-12.4%), *p*-cymene (10.0-23.5%), γ-terpinene (4.3-17.6%), smaller amounts of other monoterpenes such as myrcene, linalool, borneol and 1,8-cineole, and sesquiterpenes such as β-caryophyllene. In a vegetative cycle study, the highest yield of essential oil and highest phenolic terpene content were obtained from young (2-year-old) plants in July [4].

Oil distilled from *Thymus zygis* grown in Spain had similar components, with a very high level of phenolic terpenes: thymol (74.0%), carvacrol (4.8%), *p*-cymene (17.0%) and γ-terpinene (11.1%) [8].

In contrast, oil from a chemotype of *Thymus vulgaris* from Spain contained barely a trace of thymol or carvacrol, the principal volatile components being 1,8-cineole and linalool [9], and a chemotype of *T. zygis* ssp. *gracilis*, also from Spain, yielded essential oil containing over 90% of linalool [2].

□ ***Monoterpene glycosides*** Glucosides and galactosides of thymol and carvacrol [10] as well as glycosides of other volatile compounds [11].

□ ***Biphenyls*** 3,4,3′,4′-Tetrahydroxy-5,5′-diisopropyl-2,2′-dimethylbiphenyl (see diagram) [12-14] and four similar compounds [12,15]; the first may be regarded as a dimer of *p*-cymene-2,3-diol, which has also been isolated from thyme leaf [14].

□ ***Flavonoids*** of various types: flavones such as luteolin, apigenin [16] and their 7-glucosides and 7-rutinosides, apigenin 6,8-di-*C*-glucoside (vicenin-2) [17,18], luteolin 7-glucuronide [14], 6-hydroxyluteolin [19] and genkwanin [16,20]; the highly oxygenated flavones cirsilineol, 8-methoxycirsilineol [16,20,21] and thymonin [21]; flavanones such as eriodictyol [13,14,16], naringenin, sakuranetin [16] and hesperidin [17]; and dihydroflavonols such as taxifolin and dihydrokaempferol [14,16].

□ ***Phenylpropanoids*** Rosmarinic acid (up to 2.6%) [14,16,22,23] and a phenylpropanoid trimer [14] as well as caffeic acid (ca. 0.3%) [16,24] and small amounts of ferulic, *p*-coumaric and sinapic acids [24].

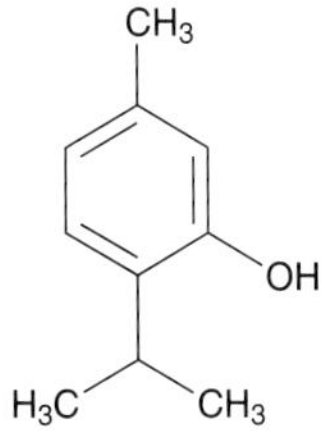

Thymol

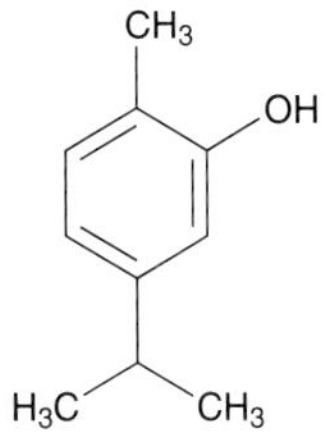

Carvacrol

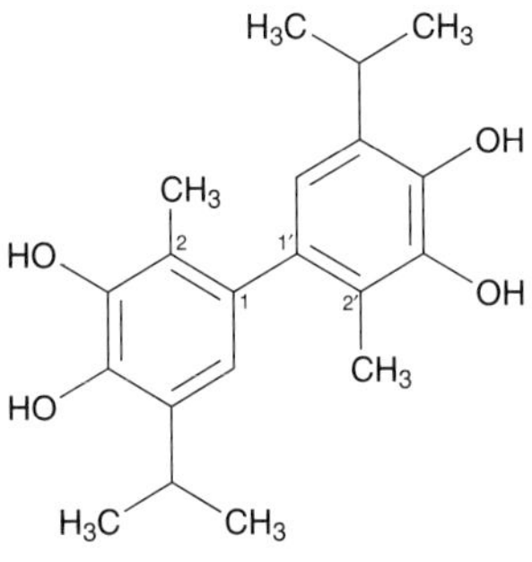

A biphenyl compound

The content of hydroxycinnamic derivatives in thyme was determined as 3.8% [22,23].

☐ ***Hydroxybenzoic compounds*** Small amounts of *p*-hydroxybenzoic, vanillic, protocatechuic and syringic acids [24] and their glucosides and glucose esters [25].

☐ ***Acetophenone glycosides*** 4-Hydroxyacetophenone glucoside (picein), its 3-methoxy derivative (androsin) and two related glycosides [26].

☐ ***Triterpenes*** Ursolic acid (1.7%) and oleanolic acid (0.6%) [27].

☐ ***Polysaccharides*** Two polysaccharides have been isolated but not fully characterized; one has arabinogalactan characteristics in part [28], the other is an acidic polysaccharide consisting mainly of galacturonic acid and glucuronic acid residues [29].

☐ ***Other constituents*** include small amounts of saturated aliphatic hydrocarbons and phytosterols [9].

No genuine tannins occur in thyme or other Labiatae; substances present which are precipitable with hide powder are thought to be polyphenolic compounds derived from caffeic, rosmarinic and other hydroxycinnamic acids [30].

Published Assay Methods

Thymol and carvacrol by GC [Ph. Eur.]. Essential oil components by GC-MS [4]. Thymol by spectrophotometry [31]. Flavonoids and rosmarinic acid by HPLC [16].

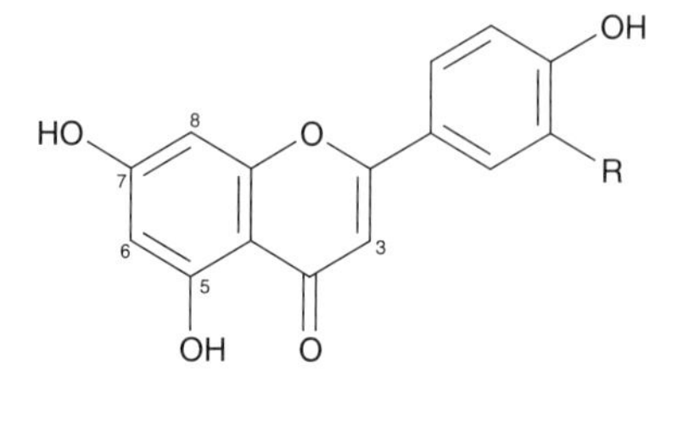

Apigenin R = H
Luteolin R = OH

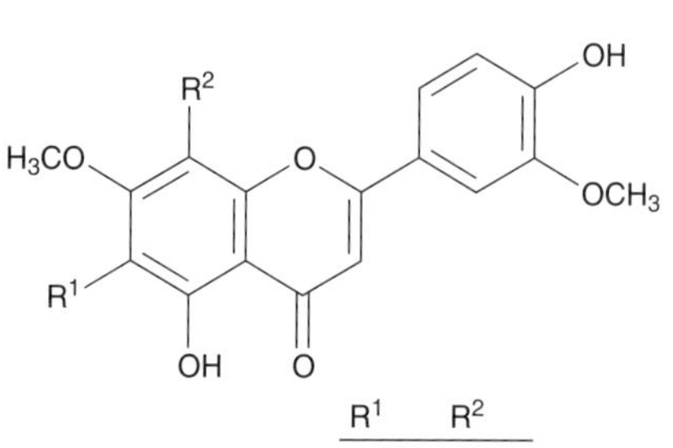

	R^1	R^2
Thymonin	OH	OCH_3
Cirsilineol	OCH_3	H

PHARMACOLOGY

In vitro

Antimicrobial activity

Thyme has long been valued for its antimicrobial properties; the ancient Egyptians used it as an embalming ingredient. Thyme extracts and thyme essential oil are strongly antibacterial and antifungal.

An aqueous extract of thyme dose-dependently inhibited the growth of the bacterium *Helicobacter pylori* (a human pathogen involved in chronic gastritis and peptic ulceration); the inhibition was 100% at 3.5 mg/ml [32]. An acetone extract inhibited the growth of drug-sensitive and drug-resistant strains of *Mycobacterium tuberculosis* with a minimum inhibitory concentration of 0.5 mg/ml in both cases [33]. The growth of a range of fungi including *Candida albicans* and *Aspergillus niger* was strongly inhibited by a hydroalcoholic extract from thyme [34].

In an assessment of the antibacterial activity of a range of essential oils (black pepper, clove, geranium, nutmeg, oregano and thyme) against 25 different genera of bacteria (9 Gram-positive, 16 Gram-negative), thyme oil showed the widest spectrum of activity, which correlated well with the high activity of its phenolic components, thymol and carvacrol [35]. In an earlier study against an almost identical range of bacteria, thyme oil exhibited one of the highest inhibitory activities among 50 essential oils tested [36].

Using the broth microdilution method, the minimum inhibitory concentration of thyme essential oil was 0.03% V/V against *Staphylococcus aureus, Escherichia coli* and the yeast *Candida albicans* (for the last two, the lowest MIC among 20 oils tested) [37]. The essential oil also exerts strong antifungal activity against dermatophytes [38].

Spasmolytic activity

Dose-dependent spasmolytic effects on isolated guinea pig trachea and/or ileum have been demonstrated with hydroethanolic thyme fluid extracts [39,40] and also with thyme essential oil [41] and the isolated flavones cirsilineol, 8-methoxycirsilineol and thymonin [42].

Antioxidant activity

Antioxidative properties of a dry acetone extract (29:1) from thyme were demonstrated in a carotene bleaching test; the extract had 81% of the activity of the synthetic antioxidant butylated hydroxytoluene (BHT) [43]. In other studies, ethanolic and supercritical carbon dioxide extracts of thyme had about 60% of the antioxidant activity of BHT [44], and a methanolic extract (from *Thymus zygis*) showed potent activity as a scavenger of superoxide and peroxyl radicals [45]. At a concentration of 500 ppm a dry 80%-methanolic extract of thyme inhibited the autoxidation of methyl linoleate by 97% [46].

Thyme essential oil at 250-1000 ppm significantly and dose-dependently inhibited the autoxidation of evening primrose oil over a 7-day period ($p<0.001$); it was as effective as α-tocopherol and more effective than ascorbyl palmitate [47]. Potent antioxidative effects of the oil have also been demonstrated in other test systems [48,49].

Among the constituents of thyme which contribute to antioxidative activity are thymol, carvacrol [48] and certain biphenyls and flavonoids [13,20,50].

Other effects
A negative effect on mucociliary transport velocity in isolated ciliated epithelium from the frog oesophagus was evident 90 seconds after application of 200 µl of an infusion from thyme (4.6 g per 100 ml of water); mucociliary activity was inhibited by 35%, in contrast to an increase in activity after applying a corresponding infusion of aniseed or fennel fruit [51]. In contrast, stimulation of ciliary movement by thyme has been observed *in vivo* (see *Expectorant effects* below).

A 50%-ethanolic extract of thyme exhibited weak binding both to oestrogen receptors (equivalent to 2 µg of oestradiol per 2 g of thyme) and to progesterone receptors (equivalent to 4 µg of progesterone per 2 g of thyme) in intact human breast cancer cells [52]. These preliminary results need further investigation but may offer some credence to a traditional belief that thyme can influence the menstrual cycle.

Thymol and carvacrol at a concentration of 37 µM inhibited cyclooxygenase activity and hence the biosynthesis of prostaglandins (mediators of inflammation) in sheep seminal vesicles by 87.5% and 94% respectively [53].

Two polysaccharides isolated from thyme exhibited significant and dose-dependent anticomplementary activity via both classical and alternative pathways ($p<0.01$ to $p<0.05$) [28,29].

In vivo

Expectorant effects
Subcutaneously administered thyme liquid extract was found to stimulate ciliary movement and cause hypersecretion in the upper respiratory tract of cats [54].

Anti-inflammatory activity
A dry ethanolic extract from thyme, administered orally to rats at 162 mg/kg, significantly inhibited carrageenan-induced paw oedema by 42% after 2 hours ($p<0.05$); the effect was comparable to that of phenylbutazone at 123 mg/kg [55].

Using a model in which complement activation plays a role, intramuscularly-administered rosmarinic acid inhibited rat paw oedema induced by cobra venom factor by 40% at 0.32 mg/kg ($p<0.05$); it was less effective after intravenous administration due to being rapidly metabolized. On the other hand, rosmarinic acid had little effect on rat paw oedema induced by *t*-butyl hydroperoxide, which is not a known activator of the complement system [56].

Antioxidant effects
Beneficial antioxidant effects of long-term supplementation of the diet of rats with thyme essential oil or thymol have been demonstrated in several studies:

- Thyme essential oil (3.9 mg/day for 17 months) maintained significantly higher levels of polyunsaturated fatty acids (PUFAs), particularly arachidonic acid ($p<0.001$) and docosahexaenoic acid (DHA; $p<0.05$), within the retinal phospholipids of the ageing rats, mainly at the expense of monounsaturated oleic acid. Since a decrease in DHA concentration is thought to be among the causes of visual impairment, the antioxidant capacity of thyme oil might have potential in the prevention of age-related macular degeneration [57].
- Thyme essential oil or thymol (42.5 mg/kg/day for 21 months) maintained levels of the same two PUFAs in phospholipid fractions from liver, brain, kidney and heart tissues significantly higher than those in age-matched controls ($p<0.001$ to $p<0.05$) [58,59]. Furthermore, higher superoxide dismutase activity in liver and heart, higher glutathione peroxidase activity in liver, kidney and brain, and higher total antioxidant status in all these organs were observed in treated animals than in age-matched controls [59,60].

Other effects
Intraperitoneal pretreatment of rats with *T. zygis* essential oil at 125 mg/kg body weight provided considerable protection against carbon tetrachloride-induced hepatotoxicity [8].

Pharmacokinetics
In treating acute and chronic respiratory ailments such as bronchitis, the effectiveness of preparations containing thyme essential oil depends on bioavailability at the bronchial mucosa. After oral administration of tablets or capsules containing a thyme dry extract (6-10:1, 70% ethanol) to healthy volunteers the first traces of thymol were detected in exhaled air (using sensors fitted to a gas mask) after

30 and 60 minutes respectively; after 140 minutes thymol was no longer detectable [61,62].

When 12 healthy male volunteers ingested a single tablet containing 160 mg of a thyme dry extract (6-10:1, 70% ethanol; corresponding to 1.08 mg of thymol) no free thymol could be detected in plasma or urine. However, the metabolite thymol sulphate was detectable in plasma, and thymol sulphate and thymol glucuronide were found in the urine. The elimination half-life of thymol was 10.2 hours and about 16% of the dose was excreted as metabolites in 24-hour urine [63]

CLINICAL STUDIES

Patients with productive coughs resulting from uncomplicated respiratory infections were treated daily for 5 days with 3 × 10 ml of either a thyme syrup (n = 31) or a bromhexine preparation (n = 29) in a randomized, double-blind study. No significant difference was evident between the two preparations in self-reported alleviation of cough complaints on days 2 and 5 of treatment. The results could indicate that the remedies had comparable efficacy - or, as the authors pointed out, that neither had any positive influence on natural recovery [64].

THERAPEUTICS

Actions

Expectorant [54,64-67], spasmolytic [39,40,65, 66], antitussive, carminative [66,67], strongly antimicrobial [32-38], anti-inflammatory [55], antioxidant [57-60].

Indications

None adequately substantiated by pharmacological or clinical studies.

Uses based on experience or tradition

Internal: Symptoms of bronchitis and whooping cough [65,66,68]; productive cough [64,69] associated with catarrhs of the upper respiratory tract [65,68]; asthma [66,70].
Gastrointestinal ailments including dyspepsia, gastritis and flatulence [66,69].
External: As an antiseptic mouthwash or gargle for inflammations of the mouth and throat [66,68,69]. Applied to the skin, as a treatment for minor wounds and sores [69], insect bites and stings, athlete's foot and other fungal infections, and scabies and lice [70].

Contraindications

None known. However, during pregnancy it is prudent to limit internal use of thyme to an amount not greatly exceeding that used in foods [71].

Side effects

None known.

Interactions with other drugs

None known.

Dosage

Three times daily: dried herb, 1-2 g as an infusion [65,66] or equivalent liquid or dry extract.
Externally, a 5% infusion is suitable as a compress [65] or mouthwash; well-diluted thyme oil may be applied to skin infections.

SAFETY

In a surveillance study involving patients with acute bronchitis treated with preparations containing thyme extracts for up to 10 days, no adverse reactions were reported by 21 patients who took thyme fluid extract in a mono-preparation. The rate of adverse events (mainly gastrointestinal) was less than 1% in a further 3139 adults and 1490 children who took a combination preparation containing a dry extract of thyme [72].

Single oral doses of a dry ethanolic thyme extract at 0.5-3.0 g/kg body weight (corresponding to 4.3-26.0 g/kg of crude drug) caused decreased locomotor activity and a slight slowing down of respiration in mice. The same extract administered orally to mice for 3 months at 100 mg/kg/day (corresponding to crude drug at 870 mg/kg/day) caused increases in weights of liver ($p<0.05$) and testes ($p<0.01$); 3 out of 10 male and 1 out of 10 female animals died [73].

The oral LD_{50} of *Thymus vulgaris* essential oil in rats [74] and the intraperitoneal LD_{50} of *Thymus zygis* oil in mice [8] were determined as 2.84 g/kg and 600 mg/kg body weight respectively. No toxic effects were observed in rats after the addition of 1.0% of thymol to their diet for 19 weeks [75]. Thyme oil (*T. vulgaris*) showed no mutagenic potential in the Ames mutagenicity test or the *Bacillus subtilis* rec-assay [76].

REGULATORY STATUS

Medicines

UK	Accepted for general sale, internal or external use [77].
France	Accepted for specified indications [69].
Germany	Commission E monograph published, with approved uses [65].

Food

USA	Generally recognized as safe (21 CFR 182.10 and 182.20) [78].

Council of Europe	Permitted as flavouring, category N2 [79].

REFERENCES

Current Pharmacopoeial Monographs

Ph. Eur. Thyme

Literature References

1. Stahl-Biskup E. The Chemical Composition of *Thymus* Oils: A Review of the Literature 1960-1989. *J. Ess. Oil Res.* 1991, **3**, 61-82.
2. Lawrence BM. Progress in Essential Oils. *Perfumer Flavorist* 1998, **23** (Jan-Feb), 39-50.
3. Daferera DJ, Ziogas BN and Polissiou MG. GC-MS Analysis of Essential Oils from Some Greek Aromatic Plants and Their Fungitoxicity on *Penicillium digitatum*. *J. Agric. Food Chem.* 2000, **48**, 2576-2581.
4. Hudaib M, Speroni E, Di Pietra AM and Cavrini V. GC/MS evaluation of thyme (*Thymus vulgaris* L.) oil composition and variations during the vegetative cycle. *J. Pharmaceut. Biomed. Analysis* 2002, **29**, 691-700.
5. Panizzi L, Flamini G, Cioni PL and Morelli I. Composition and antimicrobial properties of essential oils of four Mediterranean Lamiaceae. *J. Ethnopharmacol.* 1993, **39**, 167-170.
6. Pino JA, Estarrón M and Fuentes V. Essential Oil of Thyme (*Thymus vulgaris* L.) Grown in Cuba. *J. Essent. Oil. Res.* 1997, **9**, 609-610.
7. Shatar S and Altantsetseg S. Essential Oil Composition of Some Plants Cultivated in Mongolian Climate. *J. Essent. Oil Res.* 2000, **12**, 745-750.
8. Jiménez J, Navarro MC, Montilla MP, Martin A and Martinez A. *Thymus zygis* Oil: Its Effects on CCl_4-Induced Hepatotoxicity and Free Radical Scavenger Activity. *J. Essent. Oil Res.* 1993, **5**, 153-158.
9. Guillén MD and Manzanos MJ. Composition of the extract in dichloromethane of the aerial parts of a Spanish wild growing plant *Thymus vulgaris* L. *Flavour Fragr. J.* 1998, **13**, 259-262.
10. Skopp K and Hörster H. Sugar Bound Regular monoterpenes, Part 1. Thymol and Carvacrol Glycosides in *Thymus vulgaris*. *Planta Medica* 1976, **29**, 208-215 [GERMAN/English summary].
11. van den Dries JMA and Baerheim Svendsen A. A Simple method for Detection of Glycosidic Bound Monoterpenes and Other Volatile Compounds Occurring in Fresh Plant Material. *Flavour Fragrance J.* 1989, **4**, 59-61.
12. Miura K, Inagaki T and Nakatani N. Structure and Activity of New Deodorant Biphenyl Compounds from Thyme (*Thymus vulgaris* L.). *Chem. Pharm. Bull.* 1989, **37**, 1816-1819.
13. Haraguchi H, Saito T, Ishikawa H, Date H, Kataoka S, Tamura Y and Mizutani K. Antiperoxidative Components in *Thymus vulgaris*. *Planta Medica* 1996, **62**, 217-221.
14. Dapkevicius A, van Beek TA, Lelyveld GP, van Veldhuizen A, de Groot A, Linssen JPH and Venskutonis R. Isolation and Structure Elucidation of Radical Scavengers from *Thymus vulgaris* Leaves. *J. Nat. Prod.* 2002, **65**, 892-896.
15. Nakatani N, Miura K and Inagaki T. Structure of New Deodorant Biphenyl Compounds from Thyme (*Thymus vulgaris* L.) and Their Activity Against Methyl Mercaptan. *Agric. Biol. Chem.* 1989, **53**, 1375-1381.
16. Adzet T, Vila R and Cañigueral S. Chromatographic analysis of polyphenols of some Iberian *Thymus*. *J. Ethnopharmacol.* 1988, **24**, 147-154.
17. Wang M, Li J, Ho GS, Peng X and Ho C-T. Isolation and identification of antioxidative flavonoid glycosides from thyme (*Thymus vulgaris* L.). *J. Food Lipids* 1998, **5**, 313-321.
18. Schulz H and Albroscheit G. High-performance liquid chromatographic characterization of some medicinal plant extracts used in cosmetic formulas. *J. Chromatogr.* 1988, **442**, 353-361.
19. Adzet T and Martinez Vergés F. Luteolin and 6-Hydroxyluteolin: Taxonomically Important Flavones in the Genus Thymus. *Planta Medica* 1980, (Suppl.), 52-55.
20. Miura K and Nakatani N. Antioxidative activity of flavonoids from Thyme (*Thymus vulgaris* L.). *Agric. Biol. Chem.* 1989, **53**, 3043-3045: through *Chem. Abstr.* 1990, **112**, 115744.
21. Van Den Broucke CO, Dommisse RA, Esmans EL and Lemli JA. Three methylated flavones from *Thymus vulgaris*. *Phytochemistry* 1982, **21**, 2581-2583.
22. Lamaison JL, Petitjean-Freytet C and Carnat A. Rosmarinic acid, total hydroxycinnamic acid contents and antioxidant activity of medicinal Apiaceae, Boraginaceae and Lamiaceae. *Ann. Pharm. Fr.* 1990, **48**, 103-108 [FRENCH/English summary].
23. Lamaison JL, Petitjean-Freytet C, Duband F and Carnat AP. Rosmarinic acid content and antioxidant activity in French Lamiaceae. *Fitoterapia* 1991, **62**, 166-171.
24. Schulz JM and Herrmann K. Analysis of hydroxybenzoic and hydroxycinnamic acids in plant material. Determination by gas-liquid chromatography. *J. Chromatogr.* 1980, **195**, 95-104.
25. Klick S and Herrmann K. Determination of hydroxybenzoic acid compounds in spices and some other plant foods. *Z. Lebensm. Unters. Forsch.* 1988, **187**, 444-450 [GERMAN/English summary].
26. Wang M, Kikuzaki H, Lin C-C, Kahyaoglu A, Huang M-T, Nakatani N, Ho C-T. Acetophenone Glycosides from Thyme (*Thymus vulgaris* L.). *J. Agric. Food Chem.* 1999, **47**, 1911-1914.
27. Brieskorn CH, Eberhardt KH and Briner M. Biogenetische Zusammenhänge zwischen Oxytriterpensäuren und ätherischem Öl bei einigen pharmazeutisch wichtigen Labiaten [Biogenetic relationships between oxytriterpenic acids and essential oil in some pharmaceutically important Labiatae]. *Arch. Pharm. (Weinheim)* 1953, **286**, 501-506 [GERMAN].
28. Chun H, Jun WJ, Shin DH, Hong BS, Cho HY and Yang HC. Purification and Characterization of Anti-complementary Polysaccharide from Leaves of *Thymus vulgaris*. *Chem. Pharm. Bull.* 2001, **49**, 762-764.
29. Chun H, Shin DH, Hong BS, Cho HY and Yang HC. Purification and Biological Activity of Acidic Polysaccharide from Leaves of *Thymus vulgaris* L. *Biol. Pharm. Bull.* 2001, **24**, 941-946.
30. Litvinenko VI, Popova TP, Simonjan AV, Zoz IG and Sokolov VS. "Tannins" and Derivatives of Hydroxycinnamic Acid in Labiatae. *Planta Medica* 1975, **27**, 372-380 [GERMAN/English summary].
31. Backheet EY. Micro Determination of Eugenol, Thymol and Vanillin in Volatile Oils and Plants. *Phytochem. Analysis* 1998, **9**, 134-140.
32. Tabak M, Armon R, Potasman I and Neeman I. *In vitro* inhibition of *Helicobacter pylori* by extracts of thyme. *J. Appl. Bacteriol.* 1996, **80**, 667-672.
33. Lall N and Meyer JJM. In vitro inhibition of drug-resistant and drug-sensitive strains of *Mycobacterium tuberculosis* by ethnobotanically selected South African plants. *J. Ethnopharmacol.* 1999, **66**, 347-354.
34. Guérin J-C and Réveillère H-P. Antifungal activity of plant extracts used in therapy. II. Study of 49 plant extracts against 9 fungi species. *Ann. Pharm. Fr.* 1985, **43**, 77-81 [FRENCH/English summary].
35. Dorman HJD and Deans SG. Antimicrobial agents from plants: antibacterial activity of plant volatile oils. *J. Applied Microbiol.* 2000, **88**, 308-316.
36. Deans SG and Ritchie G. Antibacterial properties of plant essential oils. *Internat. J. Food Microbiol.* 1987, **5**, 165-180.
37. Hammer KA, Carson CF and Riley TV. Antimicrobial activity of essential oils and other plant extracts. *J. Applied Microbiol.* 1999, **86**, 985-990.
38. Janssen AM, Scheffer JJC, Parhan-Van Atten AW and Baerheim Svendsen A. Screening of some essential oils

for their activities on dermatophytes. *Pharm. Weekblad Sci. Ed.* 1988, **10**, 277-280.

39. Van Den Broucke C, Lemli J and Lamy J. Action spasmolytique des flavones de différentes espèces de *Thymus* [Spasmolytic action of flavones in various species of *Thymus*]. *Plantes Méd. Phytothér.* 1982, **16**, 310-317 [FRENCH/English summary].
40. Meister A, Bernhardt G, Christoffel V and Buschauer A. Antispasmodic Activity of *Thymus vulgaris* Extract on the Isolated Guinea-Pig Trachea: Discrimination Between Drug and Ethanol Effects. *Plant Medica* 1999, **65**, 512-516.
41. Reiter M and Brandt W. Relaxant Effects on Tracheal and Ileal Smooth Muscles of the Guinea Pig. *Arzneim.-Forsch./Drug Res.* 1985, **35**, 408-414.
42. Van Den Broucke CO and Lemli JA. Spasmolytic activity of the flavonoids from Thymus vulgaris. *Pharm. Weekbl. Sci. Ed.* 1983, **5**, 9-14.
43. Dapkevicius A, Venskutonis R, van Beek TA and Linssen JPH. Antioxidant Activity of Extracts Obtained by Different Isolation Procedures from some Aromatic Herbs Grown in Lithuania. *J. Sci. Food Agric.* 1998, **77**, 140-146.
44. Simandi B, Hajdu V, Peredi K, Czukor B, Nobik-Kovacs A and Kery A. Antioxidant activity of pilot-plant alcoholic and supercritical carbon dioxide extracts of thyme. *Eur. J. Lipid Sci. Technol.* 2001, **103**, 355-358.
45. Soares JR, Dinis TCP, Cunha AP and Almeida LM. Antioxidant activities of some extracts of *Thymus zygis*. *Free Rad. Res.* 1997, **26**, 469-478.
46. Kähkönen MP, Hopia AI, Vuorela HJ, Rauha J-P, Pihlaja K, Kujala TS and Heinonen M. Antioxidant Activity of Plant Extracts Containing Phenolic Compounds. *J. Agric. Food Chem.* 1999, **47**, 3954-3962.
47. Youdim KA, Dorman HJD and Deans SG. The Antioxidant Effectiveness of Thyme Oil, α-Tocopherol and Ascorbyl Palmitate on Evening Primrose Oil Oxidation. *J. Essent. Oil Res.* 1999, **11**, 643-648.
48. Dorman HJD, Surai P and Deans SG. *In Vitro* Antioxidant Activity of a Number of Plant Essential Oils and Phytoconstituents. *J. Essent. Oil. Res.* 2000, **12**, 241-248.
49. Teissedre PL and Waterhouse AL. Inhibition of Oxidation of Human Low-Density Lipoproteins by Phenolic Substances in Different Essential Oils Varieties. *J. Agric. Food Chem.* 2000, **48**, 3801-3805.
50. Nakatani N. Natural Antioxidants from Spices. In: Huang M-T, Ho C-T and Lee CY, editors. *Phenolic Compounds in Food and Their Effects on Health II. Antioxidants and Cancer Prevention.* ACS Symposium Series 507. ISBN 0-8412-2476-5. Washington DC: American Chemical Society, 1992:72-86.
51. Müller-Limmroth W and Fröhlich H-H. Wirkungsnachweis einiger phytotherapeutischer Expektorantien auf den mukoziliaren Transport [Evidence of the effects of some phytotherapeutic expectorants on mucociliary transport]. *Fortschr. Med* 1980, **98**, 95-101 [GERMAN].
52. Zava DT, Dollbaum CM and Blen M. Estrogen and Progestin Bioactivity of Foods, Herbs and Spices. *Proc. Soc. Exp. Biol. Med.* 1998, **217**, 369-378.
53. Wagner H, Wierer M and Bauer R. *In vitro* Inhibition of Prostaglandin Biosynthesis by Essential Oils and Phenolic Compounds. *Planta Medica* 1986, **52**, 184-187 [GERMAN/English summary].
54. Van Dongen K and Leusink H. The action of opium-alkaloids and expectorants on the ciliary movements in the air passages. *Arch. Int. Pharmacodyn.* 1953, **93**, 261-276.
55. Haen E. Pharmacological activities of *Thymus vulgaris* and *Hedera helix*. In: Abstracts of 2nd International Congress on Phytotherapy, Munich, 11-14 September 1996. Published as: *Phytomedicine* 1996, **3** (Suppl. 1), 144 (Abstract SL-115).
56. Englberger W, Hadding U, Etschenberg E, Graf E, Leyck S, Winkelmann J and Parnham MJ. Rosmarinic acid: a new inhibitor of complement C3-convertase with anti-inflammatory activity. *Int. J. Immunopharm.* 1988, **10**, 729-737.
57. Recsan Z, Pagliuca G, Piretti MV, Penzes LG, Youdim KA, Noble RC and Deans SG. Effect of Essential Oils on the Lipids of the Retina in the Ageing Rat: A Possible Therapeutic Use. *J. Essent. Oil. Res.* 1997, **9**, 53-56.
58. Youdim KA and Deans SG. Beneficial effects of thyme oil on age-related changes in the phospholipid C_{20} and C_{22} polyunsaturated fatty acid composition of various rat tissues. *Biochem. Biophys. Acta* 1999, **1438**, 140-146.
59. Youdim KA and Deans SG. Effect of thyme oil and thymol dietary supplementation on the antioxidant status and fatty acid composition of the ageing rat brain. *Br. J. Nutr.* 2000, **83**, 87-93.
60. Youdim KA and Deans SG. Dietary supplementation of thyme (*Thymus vulgaris* L.) essential oil during the lifetime of the rat: its effects on the antioxidant status in liver, kidney and heart tissues. *Mech. Ageing Dev.* 1999, **109**, 163-175.
61. Bischoff R, Ismail C, März R, Bischoff G. Exhalationsmonitoring mit Online-Analyse Geräten - ppb und sub-ppb Analytik mit neuartigen Sensoren [Exhalation monitoring with on-line analytical instrumentation - ppb and sub-ppb analysis with a new types of sensor]. *Biomedizin Technik* 1998, **43**, 266-267 [GERMAN].
62. Schindler G, Bischoff R, Kohlert C, März R, Ismail C, Veit M et al. Comparison between the concentrations in exhaled air and plasma of an essential oil compound (thymol) after oral administration. In: Abstracts of 3rd International Congress on Phytomedicine. Munich, 11-13 October 2000. Published as: *Phytomedicine* 2000, **7** (Suppl 2), 30 (Abstract SL-58).
63. Kohlert C, Schindler G, März RW, Abel G, Brinkhaus B, Derendorf H et al. Systemic Availability and Pharmacokinetics of Thymol in Humans. *J. Clin. Pharmacol.* 2002, **42**, 731-737.
64. Knols G, Stal PC and van Ree JW. Produktieve hoest: tijm of broomhexine? Een dubbelblind gerandomiseerd onderzoek [Productive cough: thyme or bromhexine? A double-blind, randomized study]. *Huisarts Wet.* 1994, **37**, 392-394 [DUTCH/English summary].
65. Thymi herba. German Commission E Monograph published in: Bundesanzeiger No. 228 of 5 December 1984; amended in Bundesanzeiger No. 50 of 13 March 1990 and Bundesanzeiger No. 226 of 2 December 1992.
66. Parfitt K, editor. Thyme. In: *Martindale - The complete drug reference, 32nd edition.* ISBN 0-85369-429-X. London: Pharmaceutical Press, 1999:1636-1637.
67. Thymus vulgaris. In: *British Herbal Pharmacopoeia 1983.* ISBN 0-903032-07-4. Bournemouth: British Herbal Medicine Association, 1983.
68. Wichtl M and Henke D. Thymian - Thymi herba. In: Hartke K, Hartke H, Mutschler E, Rücker G and Wichtl M, editors. *Kommentar zum Europäischen Arzneibuch.* Stuttgart: Wissenschaftliche Verlagsgesellschaft, 1999 (12 Lfg.):T 44 [GERMAN].
69. Thym. In: *Médicaments à base de plantes.* ISBN 2-911473-02-7. Saint-Denis Cedex, France: Agence du Médicament, 1998.
70. Chevallier A. Thyme - *Thymus vulgaris.* In: *Encyclopedia of Medicinal Plants, 2nd ed.* ISBN 0-7513-1209-6. London-New York: Dorling Kindersley, 2001:143.
71. Barnes J, Anderson LA and Phillipson JD. Thyme. In: *Herbal Medicines - A guide for healthcare professionals, 2nd ed.* ISBN 0-85369-474-5. London-Chicago: Pharmaceutical Press, 2002:462-464.
72. Ernst E, März R and Sieder C. A controlled multi-centre study of herbal versus synthetic secretolytic drugs for acute bronchitis. *Phytomedicine* 1997, **4**, 287-293.
73. Qureshi S, Shah AH, Al-Yahya MA and Ageel AM. Toxicity of *Achillea fragrantissima* and *Thymus vulgaris* in mice. *Fitoterapia* 1991, **62**, 319-323.
74. von Skramlik E. Über die Giftigkeit und Verträglichkeit von ätherischen Ölen [The toxicity and tolerability of essential oils]. *Pharmazie* 1959, **14**, 435-445.
75. Hagan EC, Hansen WH, Fitzhugh OG, Jenner PM, Jones WI, Taylor JM et al. Food Flavourings and Compounds of Related Structure. II. Subacute and Chronic Toxicity. *Food Cosmet. Toxicol.* 1967, **5**, 141-157.
76. Zani F, Massimo G, Benvenuti S, Bianchi A, Albasini A,

Melegari M et al. Studies on the Genotoxic Properties of Essential Oils with *Bacillus subtilis rec*-Assay and *Salmonella*/Microsome Reversion Assay. *Planta Medica* 1991, **57**, 237-241.
77. Thyme. In: UK Statutory Instrument 1984 No. 769. The Medicines (Products Other Than Veterinary Drugs) (General Sale List) Order 1984. Schedule 1, Table A.
78. Thyme. In: Sections 182.10 and 182.20 of USA Code of Federal Regulations, Title 21, Food and Drugs, Parts 170 to 199. Revised as of April 1, 2000.
79. *Thymus vulgaris* L., aerial parts, leaves; *Thymus zygis* L., aerial parts. In: *Flavouring Substances and Natural Sources of Flavourings, 3rd ed.* ISBN 2-7160-0081-6. Strasbourg: Council of Europe, 1981.

REGULATORY GUIDELINES FROM OTHER EU COUNTRIES

FRANCE

Médicaments à base de plantes [69]: Thym, feuille, sommité fleurie.

Therapeutic indications accepted

Oral use
Traditionally used: in the symptomatic treatment of digestive disorders such as epigastric distension, sluggish digestion, eructation and flatulence; in the symptomatic treatment of coughs.

Topical use
Traditionally used: for the treatment of small wounds and sores after copious washing (with soap and water) and for the elimination of spots; in cases of congested nose, from colds; locally (mouthwash/gargle, pastille) as an antalgesic in ailments of the buccal cavity and/or the pharynx; locally in mouthwashes, for buccal hygiene.

GERMANY

Commission E monograph [65]: Thymi herba (Thymiankraut).

Uses
Symptoms of bronchitis and whooping cough; catarrhs of the upper respiratory tract.

Contraindications
None known.

Side effects
None known.

Interactions with other drugs
None known.

Dosage
Unless otherwise prescribed: 1-2 g of the herb per cup as an infusion, several times daily according to need; 1-2 g of liquid extract, one to three times daily; for compresses, a 5% infusion.

Mode of administration
Cut or powdered herb, liquid extract or dry extract for infusions and other galenic preparations. Liquid and solid dosage forms for internal and external use.

Note: Combinations with other expectorant drugs may be appropriate.

Actions
Bronchospasmolytic, expectorant, antibacterial.

VERVAIN

Verbenaceae

Verbenae herba

Synonym: Verbena (not to be confused with Lemon Verbena, an entirely different species).

Definition

Vervain consists of the dried, flowering aerial parts of *Verbena officinalis* L.

Verbena officinalis is an upright perennial, 30-75 cm in height, with slender spikes of pale pink flowers. It is cultivated in Eastern Europe for medicinal use [1].

CONSTITUENTS

□ ***Iridoid glucosides*** Verbenalin (= cornin, ca. 0.34%), hastatoside (ca. 0.30%) [2-7], 3,4-dihydroverbenalin [8], dihydrocornin [4] and aucubin [5,9].

□ ***Hydroxycinnamic acid derivatives*** Verbascoside (= acteoside, ca. 0.23%) [2-6,10], isoverbascoside, martynoside [4] and eukovoside [6].

□ ***Flavonoids*** Flavone glycosides, especially luteolin 7-diglucuronide [4,11], apigenin 7-diglucuronide [4] and apigenin 7-glucuronide; also luteolin 7-glucoside, apigenin 7-galactoside, pedalitin 6-glucoside [12], acacetin 7-diglucuronide [4], and the 7-glycosides (sugar groups not identified) of 6-hydroxyluteolin and scutellarein (= 6-hydroxyapigenin) [5,13].

The flavone aglycones apigenin and 4′-hydroxywogonin have been isolated [14], and a number of highly oxygenated 6-*O*-substituted flavone aglycones are present including sorbifolin (5,6,4′-trihydroxy-7-methoxyflavone), pedalitin (5,6,3′4′-tetrahydroxy-7-methoxyflavone), nepetin (5,7,3′4′-tetrahydroxy-6-methoxyflavone) [15] and artemetin (5-hydroxy-3,6,7,3′4′-pentamethoxyflavone) [9].

□ ***Triterpenes*** Ursolic acid (ca. 0.26%) [2,3,9,16], oleanolic acid, 3-epiursolic acid, 3-epioleanolic acid [3], 3α,24-dihydroxy-urs-12-en-28-oic acid, 3α,24-dihydroxy-olean-12-en-28-oic acid [3,16] and lupeol [9].

□ ***Sterols*** β-sitosterol and its glucoside [2,3,9], and daucosterol [8].

Published Assay Methods

Verbenalin, hastatoside and verbascoside simultaneously by HPLC [2]. Iridoids, hydroxycinnamic acid derivatives and flavone glycosides simulta-

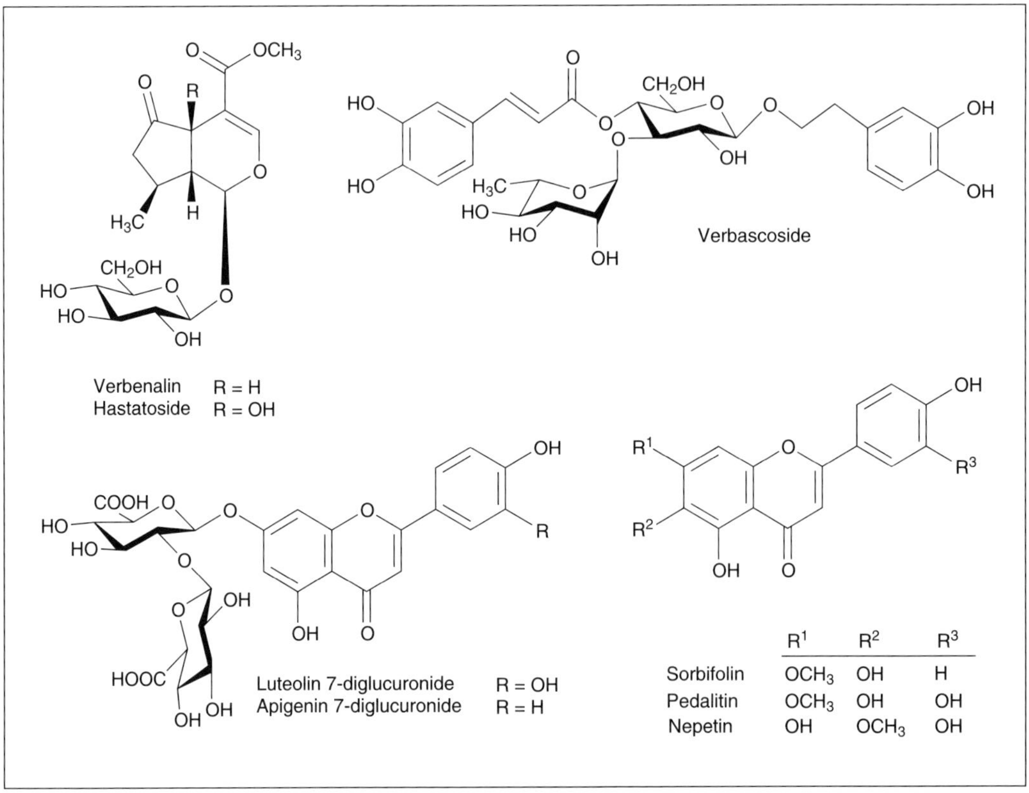

neously by HPLC [4,5]. Verbenalin by HPLC [17]. Verbascoside by HPLC [10]. Ursolic acid by HPLC [18] or HPTLC/densitometry [2].

PHARMACOLOGY

In vitro

Oestrogenic activity
In screening tests on medicinal plants vervain leaf exhibited oestrogenic activity, enhancing proliferation of the oestrogen-sensitive MCF-7 breast cancer cell line. Compared to controls, a dry methanolic extract from vervain leaf significantly increased proliferation levels by 47% and 52% at concentrations of 1 and 10 μg/ml respectively (both $p<0.01$), similar enhancement of proliferation to that produced by a soybean isoflavone glycoside fraction at the same concentrations (30% and 57% respectively) [19].

Uterine activity
Preparations of isolated rat uterus were contracted synergistically by vervain and prostaglandin PGE_2, and additively by vervain and prostaglandin $PGF_{2\alpha}$, according to the brief abstract of a study published in Chinese [20].

Phagocytic activity
A dilute hydroethanolic extract from vervain increased phagocytic activity in non-stimulated and zymosan-treated freshly isolated neutrophils from peripheral human blood [21,22].

Antiviral activity
A dry extract from vervain inhibited the spread of viruses affecting the respiratory system: respiratory syncytial virus (IC_{50}: 15-50 μg/ml), influenza A/Chile 1/83 virus (IC_{50}: 50-100 μg/ml) and parainfluenza type 1 [21,23]. A dry ethanolic extract from *Verbena officinalis* whole plant exhibited antiviral activity against murine cytomegalovirus (double-strand DNA) and Sindbis virus (single-strand RNA) at minimum effective concentrations of 65 μg/ml and 30 μg/ml respectively [24].

In vivo

Anti-inflammatory effects
A 50% methanolic extract from leaves of *Verbena officinalis* (drug to extract ratio 3:1), applied topically as 6 doses of 4.15 mg at 30-minute intervals (total 25 mg/ear), significantly reduced 12-*O*-tetradecanoylphorbate acetate (TPA)-induced oedema of the ear of mice by 63.8% ($p<0.01$) compared to controls, similar to the anti-inflammatory effect of indometacin at 0.5 mg/ear (68.5%). Pure verbenalin (3 mg/ear) had rather less effect than the extract, suggesting that several constituents contribute to the anti-inflammatory effect of vervain [25].

Oral administration of the 50% methanolic extract at a very high dose of 800 mg/kg inhibited carrageenan-induced rat paw oedema by 26.5% after 4 hours ($p = 0.02$), but lower doses were ineffective. It was concluded that topical use of vervain at the site of inflammation is more effective than oral use [25].

Petroleum ether, chloroform and methanol dry extracts from vervain (obtained by successive extraction from the same material), orally administered to rats at 500 mg/kg, inhibited carrageenan-induced paw oedema by 46.1%, 56.9% and 54.4% respectively ($p<0.001$) after 3 hours compared to a control group; ibuprofen at 50 mg/kg produced 70.6% inhibition. The anti-inflammatory activity thus appeared to be due to both polar and non-polar constituents [3].

Secretion-enhancing effects
An extract from vervain in 19% ethanol, equivalent to 39 mg of vervain herb per kg body weight (about 50 times the human dose of vervain in a combination product), administered intragastrically to rabbits, significantly increased bronchial secretion to 2.18 ml in 3 hours ($p<0.01$) compared to 1.55 ml and 1.05 ml in control groups given 19% ethanol or 0.9% sodium chloride respectively [26].

Antitussive effects
An aqueous extract from vervain extended by 16-44% the time to coughing provoked in mice 20 minutes after intraperitoneal administration and 60-90 minutes after oral administration. Verbenalin at 0.2 g/kg extended the time by 21-30% [27].

Phagocytic activity
No phagocytic activity was observed after intraperitoneal administration of a 95%-ethanolic extract from vervain or its unsaponifiable fraction to mice at 50 mg/kg body weight 24 hours before inoculation with *Escherichia coli* [28].

Galactagogic effect of verbenalin
Intravenous administration of 'verbenin' isolated from vervain (and later confirmed identical to verbenalin [26,29]) to 5 lactating rabbits at 50 mg/kg increased milk secretion by 55-114% in the first hour and produced an average increase of 71% in the amount of milk secreted over a 24-hour period. Gastric or subcutaneous administration gave similar overall, but rather delayed, effects. Administration of 10 mg/kg intravenously increased the average daily amount of milk by 24%. The quality of the milk, assessed by turbidity measurement and weight of residue after evaporation, was not appreciably changed [30].

For a review of the pharmacological activity of verbascoside see Deepak et al. [31].

CLINICAL STUDIES

None published on mono-preparations of vervain.

THERAPEUTICS

Actions
Anti-inflammatory [3,25], mildly sedative [32,33], oestrogenic [19], galactagogic [30], increases bronchial secretion [26], antitussive [27], antiviral [21,23,24].

Indications
None adequately substantiated by pharmacological or clinical studies.

Uses based on experience or tradition
Internal use: Nervous tension, irritability, mild anxiety or stress, nervous exhaustion [32,33]; symptomatic relief of minor conditions associated with menstruation, such as amenorrhoea [33] and headaches or migraines [32], or with the menopause [34]. Stimulation of the flow of breastmilk in nursing mothers [29,33,35].

Has also been used in the treatment of mild depression and debility of convalescence after fevers, particularly influenza; early stages of fevers; jaundice [36]; and coughs [37] and catarrhs [37] of the upper respiratory tract.
External use: Skin inflammation due to abrasions, fissures, superficial burns or insect bites [37].

Contraindications
Pregnancy [33,34,39,40].

Side effects
None known.

Dosage
Three times daily: Dried herb or as an infusion, 2-4 g; liquid extract 1:1 in 25% ethanol, 2-4 ml; tincture 1:5 in 40% ethanol, 5-10 ml [36].

SAFETY

Although the available toxicological data are very limited, vervain appears to have an acceptable safety profile for medicinal use at normal dosage levels, with the proviso that it should not be taken during pregnancy [39,40].

Compared to control animals, no significant differences in respiration rate, pulse frequency, red blood cell count, Quick % (a biochemical test of liver function) or serum levels of calcium, sodium and potassium were evident in rabbits after oral administration of an extract of vervain 10 times over a period of 80 hours at approximately 50 times the human dosage [26].

Verbenalin caused neither mortality nor apparent toxic effects in mice over a period of 72 hours after oral or intraperitoneal administration as a single dose of up to 3.0 g/kg [41].

REGULATORY STATUS

Medicines

UK	Accepted for general sale, internal or external use [42].
France	Accepted for specified indications [37].
Germany	Commission E monograph published: not approved for any indications [38].

Foods

USA	Permitted as flavouring in alcoholic beverages only [43].
Council of Europe	Permitted as flavouring, category N2 [44].

REFERENCES

Current Pharmacopoeial Monographs
BHP Vervain

Literature References

1. Hänsel R, Keller K, Rimpler H and Schneider G, editors. Verbena. In: *Hagers Handbuch der Pharmazeutischen Praxis, 5th ed. Volume 6: Drogen P-Z.* ISBN 3-540-52639-0. Berlin-Heidelberg-New York-London: Springer-Verlag, 1994:1106-1116 [GERMAN].
2. Deepak M and Handa SS. Quantitative Determination of the Major Constituents of *Verbena officinalis* using High Performance Thin Layer Chromatography and High Pressure Liquid Chromatography. *Phytochem. Analysis* 2000, **11**, 351-355.
3. Deepak M and Handa SS. Anti-inflammatory Activity and Chemical Composition of Extracts of *Verbena officinalis*. *Phytotherapy Res.* 2000, **14**, 463-465.
4. Mende R and Wichtl M. Eisenkraut - *Verbena officinalis* L. Beiträge zur Analytik, zu Inhaltsstoffen und zu biologischen Wirkungen [Vervain - *Verbena officinalis* L. Contribution to Analytical Methods, Constituents and Biological Effects]. *Dtsch. Apoth. Ztg.* 1998, **138**, 2905-2910 [GERMAN].
5. Calvo MI, San Julian A and Fernández M. Identification of the Major Compounds in Extracts of *Verbena officinalis* (Verbenaceae) by HPLC with Post-Column Derivatization. *Chromatographia* 1997, **46**, 241-244.
6. Lahloub MF, Salama OM and Mansour ES. Phenylpropanoid and iridoid glycosides from *Verbena officinalis* herb growing in Egypt. *Bull. Fac. Pharm. Cairo Univ.* 1990, **28**, 75-77.
7. Rimpler H and Schäfer B. Hastatoside, a New Iridoid from *Verbena hastata* L. and *Verbena officinalis* L. *Z. Naturforsch.* 1979, **34c**, 311-318 [GERMAN/English summary].
8. Zhang T, Ruan JL and Lu ZM. Studies on chemical constituents of aerial parts of *Verbena officinalis*. *Zhongguo Zhong Yao Za Zhi* 2000, **25**, 676-678 [CHINESE]; through PubMed abstract.
9. Makboul AM. Chemical Constituents of *Verbena officinalis*.

Fitoterapia 1986, **57**, 50-51.
10. Hänsel R and Kallmann S. Verbascoside, a Main Constituent of Verbena officinalis. *Arch. Pharm. (Weinheim)* 1986, **319**, 227-230 [GERMAN/English summary].
11. Carnat A, Carnat A-P, Chavignon O, Heitz A, Wylde R and Lamaison J-L. Luteolin 7-Diglucuronide, the Major Flavonoid Compound from *Aloysia triphylla* and *Verbena officinalis*. *Planta Medica* 1995, **61**, 490.
12. Reynaud J, Couble A and Raynaud J. *O*-Glycosylflavonoïdes de *Verbena officinalis* L. (Verbénacées). *Pharm. Acta Helv.* 1992, **67**, 216-217 [FRENCH/English summary].
13. Tomás-Barberán FA, Grayer-Barkmeijer RJ, Gil MI and Harborne JB. Distribution of 6-hydroxy-, 6-methoxy- and 8-hydroxyflavone glycosides in the Labiatae, the Scrophulariaceae and related families. *Phytochemistry* 1988, **27**, 2631-2645.
14. Tian J, Zhao YM and Luan XH. Studies on the chemical constituents in herb of *Verbena officinalis*. *Zhongguo Zhong Yao Za Zhi* 2005, **30**, 268-269 [CHINESE]; through PubMed abstract.
15. Reynaud J, Couble A and Raynaud J. Les Flavonoides de *Verbena officinalis* L. (Verbénacées). *J. Plant Physiol.* 1989, **135**, 380-381 [FRENCH/English summary].
16. Deepak M and Handa SS. 3α,24-Dihydroxy-urs-12-en-28-oic acid from *Verbena officinalis*. *Phytochemistry* 1998, **49**, 269-271.
17. Semenova OP, Timerbaev AR and Bonn GK. Application of high-performance liquid chromatography to the determination of bitter principles of pharmaceutical relevance. *J. Chromatogr. A* 1994, **667**, 327-333.
18. Liu CH and Liu Y. Determination of ursolic acid in herb of *Verbena officinalis* by HPLC. *Zhongguo Zhong Yao Za Zhi* 2002, **27**, 916-918 [CHINESE]; through PubMed abstract.
19. Yoshikawa M, Uemura T, Shimoda H, Kishi A, Kawahara Y and Matsuda H. Medicinal Foodstuffs. XVIII. Phytoestrogens from the Aerial Part of *Petroselinum crispum* Mill. (Parsley) and Structures of 6″-Acetylapiin and a New Monoterpene Glycoside, Petroside. *Chem. Pharm. Bull.* 2000, **48**, 1039-1044.
20. Research Group on Reproductive Physiology. Effect of Verbena herb (*Verbena officinalis*) on the uterus. II. Interaction between Verbena Herb and prostaglandins. *Tung Wu Hsueh Pao* 1974, **20**, 340-345 [CHINESE]; through *Chem. Abstr.* 1975, **82**, 149650.
21. Mende-Weber R, Schmolz M, Christoffel V and Wichtl M. Verbena officinalis L. - New compounds and new biological activities from a former well known plant. In: Abstracts of 2nd International Congress on Phytomedicine, Munich, 11-14 September 1996. Published as: *Phytomedicine* 1996, **3** (Suppl. 1), 147 (Abstract SL-118).
22. Schmolz M. Immunological features of extracts from Radix Gentianae, Flore Primulae, Flores Sambuci, Herba Verbenae and Herba Rumicis as well as from a combination thereof (Sinupret®). In: Abstracts of 4th and International Congress on Phytotherapy, Munich, 10-13 September 1992 (Abstract SL 36).
23. Glatthaar B and Christoffel V. Antiviral activity in vitro of Sinupret® drops and its components. In: Abstracts of 5th Annual Symposium on Complementary Health Care. Exeter, 10-12 December 1998. Published as: *FACT - Focus on Alternative and Complementarry Therapies* 1998, **3**, 183-184.
24. Yip L, Pei S, Hudson JB and Towers GHN. Screening of medicinal plants from Yunnan Province in southwest China for antiviral activity. *J. Ethnopharmacol.* 1991, **34**, 1-6.
25. Calvo MI, Vilalta N, San Julián A and Fernández M. Anti-inflammatory activity of leaf extract of *Verbena officinalis* L. *Phytomedicine* 1998, **5**, 465-467.
26. Chibanguza G, März R and Sterner W. Zur Wirksamkeit und Toxizität eines pflanzlichen Secretolytikums und seiner Einzeldrogen. [Effectiveness and toxicity of a secretolytic plant drug combination and its components]. *Arzneim.-Forsch./Drug Res.* 1984, **34**, 32-36 [GERMAN/English summary].
27. Kui C and Tang R. Studies on the antitussive constituents of *Verbena officinalis*. *Zhongyao Tongbao (Bull. Chin. Materia Med.)* 1985, **10**, 467 [CHINESE], summarized in [1].
28. Delaveau P, Lallouette P and Tessier AM. Drogues Végétales Stimulant l'Activité Phagocytaire du Système Réticulo-endothélial [Plant Drugs Stimulating the Phagocytic Activity of the Reticulo-endothelial System]. *Planta Medica* 1980, **40**, 49-54 [FRENCH/English summary].
29. Brückner C. In Mitteleuropa genutzte Heilpflanzen mit milchsekretionsfördernder Wirkung (Galactagoga) [Medicinal plants used in central Europe with a milk secretion promoting effect (galactagogues)]. *Gleditschia* 1989, **17**, 189-201 [GERMAN/English summary].
30. Kuwajima K. Chemische und pharmakologische Untersuchungen über das Verbenin, ein galaktogog wirkendes Glycosid von Verbena officinalis L. [Chemical and pharmacological studies on verbenin, a galactagogic glycoside from Verbena officinalis L.]. *Tohoku J. Exptl. Med.* 1939, **36**, 28-43 [GERMAN].
31. Deepak M, Umashankar DC and Handa SS. Verbascoside - a promising phenylpropanoid. *Indian Drugs* 1999, **36**, 336-345.
32. Chevallier A. Vervain - Verbena officinalis. In: *Encyclopedia of Medicinal Plants, 2nd ed.* ISBN 0-7513-1209-6. London-New York: Dorling Kindersley, 2001:149.
33. McIntyre A. Vervain - *Verbena officinalis*. In: *The Complete Woman's Herbal*. ISBN 1-85675-135-X. London: Gaia Books, 1994:61.
34. Steinegger E and Hänsel R. Eisenkraut. In: *Pharmakognosie, 5th ed.* ISBN 3-540-55649-4. Berlin-Heidelberg-New York-London: Springer-Verlag, 1992:704-705 [GERMAN].
35. Brückner C. Anwendung und Wert in Europa gebräuchlicher lactationsfördernder Heilpflanzen (Galactagoga) [Use and value of lactation-promoting medicinal plants (galactagogues) commonly used in Europe]. *Pädiatr. Grenzgeb.* 1989, **28**, 403-410 [GERMAN/English summary].
36. Verbena. In: *British Herbal Pharmacopoeia 1983*. ISBN 0-903032-07-9. Bournemouth: British Herbal Medicine Association, 1983.
37. Verveine officinale. In: *Médicaments à base de plantes*. ISBN 2-911473-02-7. Saint-Denis Cedex, France: Agence du Médicament, 1998.
38. Verbenae herba (Eisenkraut). German Commission E monograph published in: Bundesanzeiger No. 22 of 01.02.90.
39. Barnes J, Anderson LA and Phillipson JD. Vervain. In: *Herbal Medicines - A guide for healthcare professionals. 2nd ed.* ISBN 0-85369-474-5. London-Chicago: Pharmaceutical Press, 2002:477-478.
40. McGuffin M, Hobbs C, Upton R and Goldberg A, editors. *Verbena officinalis* L. In: American Herbal Products Association's *Botanical Safety Handbook*. Boca Raton-Boston-London: CRC Press, 1997:121.
41. Singh B, Saxena A, Chandan BK, Anand KK, Suri OP, Suri KA and Satti NK. Hepatoprotective activity of verbenalin on experimental liver damage in rodents. *Fitoterapia* 1998, **69**, 135-140.
42. Verbena. In: UK Statutory Instrument 1984 No. 769. The Medicines (Products other than Veterinary Drugs) (General Sale List) Order 1984. Schedule 1, Table A.
43. Vervain, European. In: Section 172.510 of USA Code of Federal Regulations, Title 21, Food and Drugs, Parts 170 to 199. Revised as of April 1, 2000.
44. Verbena officinalis L., herb. In: *Flavouring Substances and Natural Sources of Flavourings, 3rd ed.* ISBN 2-7160-0081-6. Strasbourg: Council of Europe, 1981.

REGULATORY GUIDELINES FROM OTHER EU COUNTRIES

FRANCE

Médicaments à base de plantes [37]: Vervaine officinale, parties aériennes.

Vervain

Therapeutic indications accepted

Oral use
Traditionally used in the symptomatic treatment of coughs.

Topical use
Traditionally used: as a soothing and antipruriginous local treatment of dermatological ailments, as a trophic protector in the treatment of chaps, abrasions or fissures and against insect stings; in cases of sunburn, superficial and limited burns, and erythema of the buttocks.

GERMANY

Commission E monograph [38]: Verbenae herba (Eisenkraut).

Uses
Vervain preparations are used in illnesses and complaints of the oral and pharygeal mucosa such as angina or sore throat, and illnesses of the respiratory tract such as coughs, asthma and whooping cough; also for pain, cramp, exhaustion, nervous disorders, digestive disorders, liver and gall bladder illnesses, jaundice, illnesses and complaints of the kidneys and lower urinary tract, in menopausal complaints, irregular menstruation and to promote lactation during breast-feeding; also for rheumatic conditions, gout, metabolic disorders, anaemia, dropsy, and externally for poorly healing wounds, abscesses and burns.

Efficacy in the claimed areas of use is not substantiated.

Risks
None known.

Evaluation
Since efficacy in the claimed areas of use is not substantiated, therapeutic use cannot be approved.

On the basis of its secretion-enhancing effect, a positive contribution to the efficacy of fixed combinations for catarrhs of the upper respiratory tract is conceivable. However, this contribution must be established for specific preparations.

Action
Stimulates secretion.

VIOLET LEAF/FLOWER

Violaceae

Violae odoratae folium/flos

Synonym: Sweet Violet Leaf/Flower.

Definitions

Violet Leaf consists of the dried leaves of *Viola odorata* L., harvested in late spring.

Violet Flower consists of the dried flowers of *Viola odorata* L.

Two varieties of violet, Parma and Victoria, are cultivated, mainly for the perfumery industry. Violet flower extracts appear to be no longer produced commercially due to the prohibitive cost, but leaf extraction is still carried out [1].

The Pharmacopée Francaise definition of violet flower includes *Viola lutea* Hudson (mountain pansy or "violette d'Auvergne") and *V. calcarata* L. ("violette des Alpes") as well as *V. odorata* L. ("violette odorante").

CONSTITUENTS

LEAF

☐ ***Volatiles***, 0.002% [2]. In leaves of *Viola odorata* var. Parma, the volatile fraction consisted essentially of aliphatic hydrocarbons and related oxygenated compounds. Extraction with hexane yielded pentadec-3-enal (16%), nona-2,6-dienal (13%), hexadec-1-ene (13%), octadec-1-ene (11%), nona-2,6-dienol (5%) and other compounds [1]. In the absolute (extracted with a more powerful solvent, 1,1,2-trichloro-1,2,2-trifluoroethane), the main components were octadeca-9,12-dienoic acid (40-58%), hexadecanoic acid (8-17%), nona-2,6-dienal (5-18%), nona-2,6-dienol (2%), *cis*-hex-3-enol (4%), 2,6,11-trimethyldodecane (0.3-10%), dodecanol (0.4-9%) and other compounds. No ionones were detected [1].

Summarizing data from earlier studies on violet leaf oil (1934-1945), Bedoukian [3] listed the presence of 2-*trans*-6-*cis*-nonadienal (10 times more than in the flower oil) [4] and 2-*trans*-6-cis-nonadienol, these two being largely responsible for the odour of violet leaves, and also n-hexanol, an n-hexenol, 4-methyl-*cis*-2-hexenol and 4-isopropyl-2-pentenol, *n*-2-octenol, a tertiary octenol, benzyl alcohol and traces of eugenol.

☐ ***Flavonoids***, less than 0.5%; two unidentified flavonoids have been detected in the herb [5].

☐ ***Saponins*** Unidentified saponins were detected in violet leaf in a 1937 haemolysis study [6]. No modern phytochemical data are available.

☐ ***Salicylates*** Methyl salicylate as a glycoside [7]; in older literature the glycoside is stated to be monotropitin (gaultherin), the 2-primeveroside of methyl salicylate [5].

☐ ***Triterpenes*** The pentacyclic triterpenes friedelin (0.016%) [8,9] and 3β-friedanol [9].

☐ ***Macrocyclic peptides (cyclotides)*** Two cyclotides named vodo M and vodo N, both consisting of 29 amino acids with a head-to-tail cyclic backbone constrained by three disulphide bonds (cysteine to cysteine) at its core, have recently been isolated from aerial parts of *Viola odorata* [10]. Twelve other cyclotides, cycloviolacins O1-O12, were isolated from violet in 1999; each consists of about 30 amino acids in the same "cyclic cystine knot" arrangement [11,12].

Cyclotides have exceptional chemical and biological stability and display a range of biological

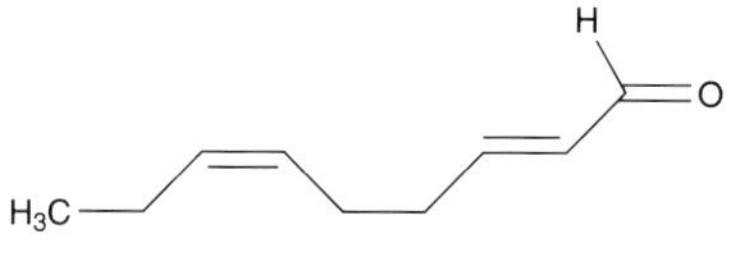

2-*trans*-6-*cis*-Nonadienal

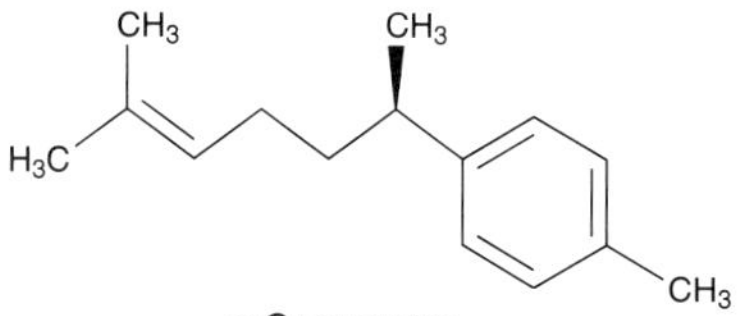

α-Curcumene

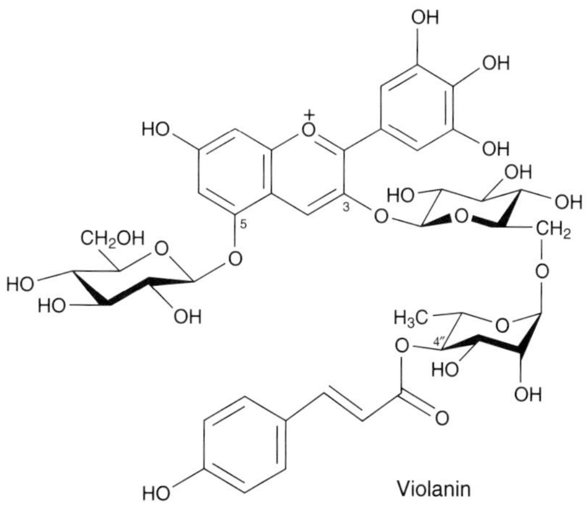

Violanin

activities [10,12].
☐ ***Phenolic acids***, including ferulic and sinapic acids [13].
☐ ***Other constituents*** β-sitosterol (0.033%) [8].

Although the presence of alkaloids is mentioned in the literature [14,15], none appear to have been confirmed in violet leaf or flower. From violet *root* the isolation of an alkaloid of undetermined structure was reported in 1961, with the suggested name of "odoratine" [16]

FLOWER

☐ ***Volatiles***, 0.003% [17]. The volatile fraction obtained by vacuum distillation under nitrogen from a violet flower extract contained diethylphthalate (26.2%), (+)-α-curcumene (17.7%), (–)-zingiberene (17.4%), dihydro-β-ionone (10.8%), (+)-α-ionone (8.2%), (+)-dihydro-α-ionone (1.9%), 2,6-nonadienal (1.9%), α-ionol (1.1%) and smaller amounts of undecan-2-one, vanillin, α-ionone and isoborneol [18].

Summarizing data from earlier studies on violet flower oil (1934-1942), Bedoukian also listed the presence of 2-*trans*-6-*cis*-nonadienal and 2-*trans*-6-*cis*-nonadienol (these two being largely responsible for the odour of violet flower), and also n-hexanol, a heptenol, an octadienol, benzyl alcohol and eugenol [3].
☐ ***Flavonoids*** Rutin (quercetin 3-rutinoside, 0.4%) and two other flavonol (probably kaempferol) glycosides. The total flavonoid content by colorimetry was 1.1% [19].
☐ ***Saponins*** The presence of unidentified saponins in violet flower was confirmed in a 1937 haemolysis study; the content was lower than that of the leaf [6]. Earlier authors had found only questionable evidence of saponins [20]. No modern phytochemical data are available.
☐ ***Salicylates*** Methyl salicylate as a glycoside [7].
☐ ***Anthocyanins***, 4.0%, including violanin {delphinidin 3-(4″-*p*-coumaroyl)-rutinoside-5-glucoside} [19].
☐ ***Polysaccharides*** of undetermined composition. The mucilage content of the dried flowers was found to be 18.0% [19].
☐ ***Other constituents*** include minerals (8.5%) [19], reducing sugars and vitamin C (0.025%) [21].

Published Assay Methods
Leaf volatiles by GC and GC-MS [1].

PHARMACOLOGY

In vitro

Antimicrobial activity
A dry 50%-ethanolic macerate from violet leaf exhibited no antimicrobial activity against *Escherichia coli*, *Pseudomonas aeruginosa*, *Staphylococcus aureus* or *Candida albicans* [22]. An earlier study indicated modest activity of a dry aqueous extract from violet flower against *E. coli*, *S. aureus*, *Bacillus proteus* and two *Streptomyces* species [21].

Cytotoxic activity of cyclotides
The pharmacological activity of cyclotides (macrocyclic peptides) is a current area of research. A cyclotide isolated from violet aerial parts, cycloviolacin O2, exhibited strong, dose-dependent cytotoxic activity (IC_{50}: 0.1-0.3 μM) against a panel of 10 human tumour cell lines (originating, for example, from small cell lung cancer and renal adenoma), leading to total cell death at concentrations as low as 0.5 μM. The cytotoxic activity was also evident in primary cultures of tumour cells from patients; the IC_{50} against chronic lymphocytic leukaemia cells was 0.1 μM compared to 0.87 μM against healthy human lymphocytes. The cytotoxic mode of action appears to be different to that of antitumour drugs in clinical use [12].

Such cytotoxic activity might be relevant to the former use of violet leaf in the UK in the treatment of cancer [23-25].

In vivo

Anti-inflammatory effects
A decoction from violet herb produced significant anti-inflammatory effects in rats ($p<0.05$), inhibiting hyaluronidase-, egg white- and dextran-induced oedema of the hind limb after oral or subcutaneous administration at 1 ml/100 g body weight and cotton pellet-induced granuloma after oral administration at 0.5 ml/100 g [14].

Antipyretic effects
Hexane, chloroform and water-soluble fractions from violet leaf, orally administered to rabbits at 150 mg/kg body weight, significantly reduced yeast-induced pyrexia ($p<0.05$); the effects were comparable to that of aspirin at 150 mg/kg [26].

Diuretic effects
When administered intragastrically to rats, an aqueous infusion, a dry methanolic extract (77.4 mg/animal) and ash (34.3 mg/animal) from violet leaf, each corresponding to 300 mg of dried leaf per animal, significantly increased the volume of urine excreted over a period of 5 hours ($p<0.005$), in each case with greater effect than theophylline at 5 mg/kg; modest kaliuretic and natriuretic effects were also observed. The diuretic effects were attributed to flavonoid glycosides and potassium [27].

Testing for antineoplastic activity
A freeze-dried 50%-ethanolic extract from violet leaf exhibited no antineoplastic (anti-tumour) activity against L-1210 lymphoid leukaemia, Lewis lung

carcinoma and sarcoma 180 in mouse test-systems, nor against human epidermoid carcinoma using the *in vitro* KB cell culture test-system [28].

Other effects
Intravenous administration to rats of an aqueous infusion or a methanolic extract of violet leaf at dose levels corresponding to 300 mg of dried leaf had no effect on arterial pressure or respiration [27].

CLINICAL STUDIES

None published on mono-preparations of violet leaf or flower.

THERAPEUTICS

Note: *The information in this section is largely based on data and texts relating to violet leaf or herb. Very little specific information is available for violet flower.*

Actions
Anti-inflammatory [14], antipyretic [26], diuretic [14,21,27]. Also stated to be expectorant [5,14, 15,24], diaphoretic and demulcent [15,21].

Violet leaf has a long-standing reputation as an antitumour agent [23,24]. Pharmacological testing of a 50%-ethanolic extract failed to confirm any such activity [28]. However, recent research demonstrating the cytotoxic activity of cyclotides [12], of which a number are present in *Viola odorata* [10-12], opens up an intriguing field for investigation.

Indications
None adequately substantiated by pharmacological or clinical studies.

Uses based on experience or tradition
Internal: As an infusion or syrup for coughs [15, 17,21,29,30], colds [15,21] and naso-pharyngeal catarrh [15,17,21,24,30], whooping cough, asthma, hoarseness [17] and inflammatory ailments of the respiratory tract such as bronchitis [14,17, 24,30], laryngitis [14], pharyngitis and tonsillitis [21]. Has also been used in sleep disorders and nervous restlessness [17,21].
External: As an aqueous or semi-solid preparation for the treatment of skin complaints such as dermatitis, inflammation, chaps, bruises, sores and insect stings [17,22,29].

In earlier days, violet leaf was used in the UK (internally and externally) in the treatment of cancer, particularly of the breast and alimentary canal [23,25]. It may still feature in alternative cancer therapies [15,24,30], especially after surgery as protection against metastasis [24,30].

Contraindications
None known.

Side Effects
None known.

Dosage
Three times daily: dried herb, 2-4 g as an infusion [17,24]; liquid extract 1:1 in 25% alcohol, 2-4 ml; liquid extract (from fresh leaf) 2:1 in 45% alcohol, 2-4 ml [24].

SAFETY

Violet leaf has been assessed as safe to be consumed when used appropriately [31].

Hexane, chloroform and water-soluble fractions from violet leaf were well tolerated by rabbits after single oral doses of up to 1.6 g/kg body weight [26].

In topical testing, violet leaf absolute caused no phototoxic effects in animals and, at 2% in petrolatum, was found to be non-irritant and non-sensitizing in humans [32,33].

REGULATORY STATUS

Medicines

UK	No licences issued for products containing violet leaf or flower.
France	Violet flower accepted for specified indications [29].
Germany	No Commission E monograph issued for violet leaf or flower as an individual plant drug. In a "substance characteristics" monograph, violet herb was not approved as a component of combination products due to insufficient evidence of efficacy [34].

Food

USA	Essential oil and natural extractives of violet leaf or flower generally recognized as safe (21 CFR 182.20) [35].
Council of Europe	Permitted as flavouring: leaves, category 5; flowers, category 1 [36].

REFERENCES

Current Pharmacopoeial Monographs

BHP	Violet Leaf
Ph. Fr.	Violette (flower)

Literature References

1. Cu JQ, Perineau F and Gaset A. Volatile components of Violet leaves. *Phytochemistry* 1992, **31**, 571-573.
2. Ruzicka L and Schinz H. Veilchenriechstoffe IV. Über das Veilchenblätteröl. Zur Konstitution des Veilchenblätter-aldehyds, Nonadien-(2,6)-al-(1) [Violet odour substances IV. Violet leaf oil. The structure of the violet leaf aldehyde, nonadien-(2,6)-al-(1)]. *Helv. Chim. Acta* 1934, **17**, 1592-1601 [GERMAN].
3. Bedoukian PZ. Violet odor in perfumery. *Perfumer & Flavorist* 1978, **3** (Feb/March), 29-32.
4. Ruzicka L and Schinz H. Veilchenriechstoffe, 13. Mitt. Über das ätherische Öl der Veilchenblüten [Violet odour substances, Part 13. The volatile oil of violet flowers]. *Helv. Chim. Acta* 1942, **25**, 760-774 [GERMAN].
5. Vincze-Vermes M, Marczal G and Pethes E. Occurrence of rutin in some *Viola* species. *Acta Agron. Acad. Sci. Hung.* 1974, **23**, 448-453.
6. Roberg M. Über das Vorkommen und die Verteilung von Saponinen in Kräuterdrogen. II [The occurrence and distribution of saponins in herbal drugs. Part II]. *Arch. Pharm.* 1937, **275**, 145-166 [GERMAN].
7. Kroeber L. *Viola odorata* L., das Wohlriechende Veilchen in alter und neuer Betrachtungsweise [*Viola odorata* L., the fragrant violet considered from old and new perspectives]. *Pharmazie* 1946, **1**, 85-90 [GERMAN]; also through *Chem. Abstr.* 1947, **41**, 6022.
8. Ladwa PH and Dutta NL. Chemical investigation of *Viola odorata*. *Indian J. Appl. Chem.* 1969, **32**, 399-400; through *Chem. Abstr.* 1971, **75**, 1331.
9. Biglino G. Constituents of violet wax. *Corsi Semin. Chim.* 1968, **11**, 72-73 [ITALIAN]; through *Chem. Abstr.* 1970, **72**, 14065.
10. Svangård E, Göransson U, Smith D, Verma C, Backlund A, Bohlin L and Claeson P. Primary and 3-D modelled structures of two cyclotides from *Viola odorata*. *Phytochemistry* 2003, **64**, 135-142.
11. Craik DJ, Daly NL, Bond T and Waine C. Plant Cyclotides: A Unique Family of Cyclic and Knotted Proteins that Defines the Cyclic Cystine Knot Structural Motif. *J. Mol. Biol.* 1999, **294**, 1327-1336.
12. Lindholm P, Göransson U, Johansson S, Claeson P, Gullbo J, Larsson R et al. Cyclotides: A Novel Type of Cytotoxic Agents. *Molecular Cancer Therapeutics* 2002, **1**, 365-369.
13. Komorowski T, Mosiniak T, Kryszczuk Z and Rosinski G. Phenolic acids in domestic species *Viola tricolor* L. and *Viola arvensis* Murr. *Herba Pol.* 1983, **29**, 5-11 [POLISH/English summary].
14. Kroutil M and Kroutilová J. Comparison of anti-inflammatory action of extracts from violet (*Viola odorata* L.) and from ipecacuanha (*Uragoga ipecacuanha* Baill.). *Acta Univ. Palackianae Olomucensis, Fac. Med.* 1968, **48**, 55-63 [in English]; also through *Chem. Abstr.* 1969, **71**, 59307.
15. Chevallier A. *Viola odorata* - Sweet Violet. In: *Encyclopedia of Medicinal Plants, 2nd ed.* ISBN 0-7513-1209-6. London-New York: Dorling Kindersley, 2001:282.
16. Frenclowa I. Research and chemical investigations of active compounds from *Viola odorata* L. I. Isolation of alkaloid from roots and shags. *Acta Polon. Pharm.* 1961, **18**, 187-195 [POLISH/English summary].
17. Hänsel R, Keller K, Rimpler H and Schneider G, editors. Viola. In: *Hagers Handbuch der Pharmazeutischen Praxis, 5th ed. Volume 6: Drogen P-Z.* ISBN 3-540-52639-0. Berlin-Heidelberg-New York-London: Springer-Verlag, 1994.
18. Uhde G and Ohloff G. Parmon, eine Phantomverbindung im Veilchenblütenöl [Parmon, a phantom compound in violet flower oil]. *Helv. Chim. Acta* 1972, **55**, 2621-2625 [GERMAN/English summary].
19. Lamaison JL, Petitjean-Freytet C and Carnat A. La fleur de Violette: Étude comparée de *Viola lutea* Huds., *V. calcarata* L. et *V. odorata* L. [Violet flower: comparative study of *Viola lutea* Huds., *V. calcarata* L. and *V. odorata* L.]. *Plantes Méd. Phytothér.* 1991, **25**, 79-88 [FRENCH/English summary].
20. Kofler L and Steidl G. Über das Vorkommen und die Verteilung von Saponinen in pflanzlichen Drogen. I. Blüten [The occurrence and distribution of saponins in plant drugs. I. Flowers]. *Arch. Pharm.* 1932, **270**, 398-402 [GERMAN].
21. Zaidi SSA, Ashraf M and Bhatty MK. Biochemical studies on *Viola odorata*. *Pakistan J. Sci. Ind. Res.* 1984, **27**, 295-296.
22. Cáceres A, Girón LM, Alvarado SR and Torres MF. Screening of antimicrobial activity of plants popularly used in Guatemala for the treatment of dermatomucosal diseases. *J. Ethnopharmacol.* 1987, **20**, 223-237.
23. *Viola* - Violet. In: *British Pharmaceutical Codex 1907.* London: Pharmaceutical Society of Great Britain, 1907.
24. Viola odorata. In: *British Herbal Pharmacopoeia 1983.* ISBN 0-903032-07-4. Bournemouth: British Herbal Medicine Association, 1983.
25. Grieve M (edited by Leyel CF). Violet, Sweet. In: *A Modern Herbal* (first published 1931; revised 1973). ISBN 1-85501-249-9. London: Tiger Books International, 1994:834-839.
26. Khattak SG, Gilani SN and Ikram M. Antipyretic studies on some indigenous Pakistani medicinal plants. *J. Ethnopharmacol.* 1985, **14**, 45-51.
27. Rebuelta M, Vivas JM, San Roman L and G-Serranillos Fdez M. Étude de l'effet diurétique de différentes préparations des feuilles de *Viola odorata* L. [Study of the diuretic effect of various preparations of the leaves of *Viola odorata* L.]. *Plantes Méd. Phytothér.* 1983, **17**, 215-221 [FRENCH].
28. Charlson AJ. Antineoplastic constituents of some southern African plants. *J. Ethnopharmacol.* 1980, **2**, 323-335.
29. Violette, fleur. In: *Médicaments à base de plantes.* ISBN 2-911473-02-7. Saint-Denis Cedex, France: Agence du Médicament, 1998.
30. Ody P. Sweet violet and heartsease - *Viola* spp. In: *The Complete Guide - Medicinal Herbal.* ISBN 0-7513-3005-1. London-New York: Dorling Kindersley, 2000:137.
31. McGuffin M, Hobbs C, Upton R and Goldberg A, editors. *Viola odorata* L. In: American Herbal Products Association's *Botanical Safety Handbook.* Boca Raton-Boston-London: CRC Press, 1997:77.
32. Opdyke DLJ. Monographs on fragrance raw materials: Violet leaf absolute. *Food Cosmet. Toxicol.* 1976, **14**, 893.
33. Tisserand R and Balacs T. Safety Index: Part 1. In: *Essential Oil Safety - A Guide for Health Care Professionals.* Edinburgh: Churchill-Livingstone, 1995:201-211.
34. Stoffcharakteristik: Violae odoratae rhizoma/herba (Märzveilchen). German Commission E Monograph published in: Bundesanzeiger of 17 June 1994.
35. Violet flowers, violet leaf. In: Section 182.20 of USA Code of Federal Regulations, Title 21, Food and Drugs, Parts 170 to 199. Revised as of April 1, 2000.
36. Viola odorata L., flowers, leaves. In: *Natural Sources of Flavourings. Report No. 1.* ISBN 92-871-4324-2. Strasbourg: Council of Europe Publishing, 2000.

REGULATORY GUIDELINES FROM OTHER EU COUNTRIES

FRANCE

Médicaments à base de plantes [29]: Violette, fleur.

Therapeutic indications accepted

Oral use
Traditionally used in the symptomatic treatment of coughs.

Topical use
Traditionally used as a soothing and antipruriginous local treatment of dermatological ailments, as a trophic protector in the treatment of chaps, abrasions or fissures and against insect stings.

WHITE DEADNETTLE Labiatae

Lamii albi herba

Synonym: Archangel.

Definition

White Deadnettle consists of the dried flowering aerial parts of *Lamium album* L.

Although only the flowering herb is commonly used in the UK, the flower (corolla) is also used medicinally in continental Europe and is official in the Pharmacopée Française. The available phytochemical data suggest higher concentrations of some key constituents, such as flavonoids and saponins, in the flowers [1].

CONSTITUENTS

□ ***Iridoids***, principally lamalbid (ca. 0.25% from fresh whole plants) [2-4] with smaller amounts of caryoptoside (6-deoxy-lamalbid), alboside A and alboside B, the last being an equilibrium mixture of three compounds [2].

□ ***Phenylpropanoids*** Chlorogenic acid (ca. 1% in the flowers) [5,6], lamalboside (= 2^R-galactosylacteoside = 2^R-galactosylverbascoside, ca. 0.8% in the flowers), and small amounts of *trans*- and *cis*-acteoside (= verbascoside) [5]. Hydroxycinnamic acids present include *p*-coumaric, caffeic, ferulic and isoferulic acids [1].

□ ***Hydroxybenzoic acids*** *p*-Hydroxybenzoic in the herb, and also gentisic, protocatechuic and syringic acids in the flowers [1].

□ ***Flavonoids***, ca. 0.4% in the flowering herb [1] including isoquercitrin (quercetin 3-glucoside) and kaempferol 3-glucoside [5,7,8].

In the flowers, quercimeritrin (= quercetin 7-glucoside, ca. 1%) is the predominant flavonoid, together with kaempferol 3-diglucoside and 4′-glucoside [9,10]. Small amounts of *cis*- and *trans*-tiliroside [= kaempferol 3-(6″-*p*-coumaroyl)-glucoside] and rutin are also present [5].

□ ***Triterpenoid saponins*** of unidentified structure (3.5% in leaves, 14.5% in flowers). Four aglycones were evident from TLC, one corresponding to gypsogenin [6].

□ ***Tannins***, of both the condensed and hydrolysable types, 6-7% in leaves, 3-5% in flowers [6,7].

□ ***Other constituents*** include the alkaloid stachydrine (2.0%) [11], the hemiterpene glucoside hemialboside (0.01% of fresh weight) [12], a novel C_{13} glucoside, 9ξ-O-β-D-glucosyloxy-5-megastigmen-4-one [13], ascorbic acid (9 mg/g) [14], polysaccharides and a small amount of essential oil [7].

PHARMACOLOGY

In vivo

Moderate anti-inflammatory and diuretic effects of a hydroethanolic dry extract of white deadnettle flowers and a mixture of triterpene saponins isolated from the herb have been demonstrated in rats [15]:

- The extract orally administered at 280 mg/kg body weight inhibited kaolin-induced rat paw oedema by 33%, compared to 38% inhibition by the saponins intramuscularly administered at 200 mg/kg and 59% inhibition by oral phenylbutazone at 50 mg/kg.

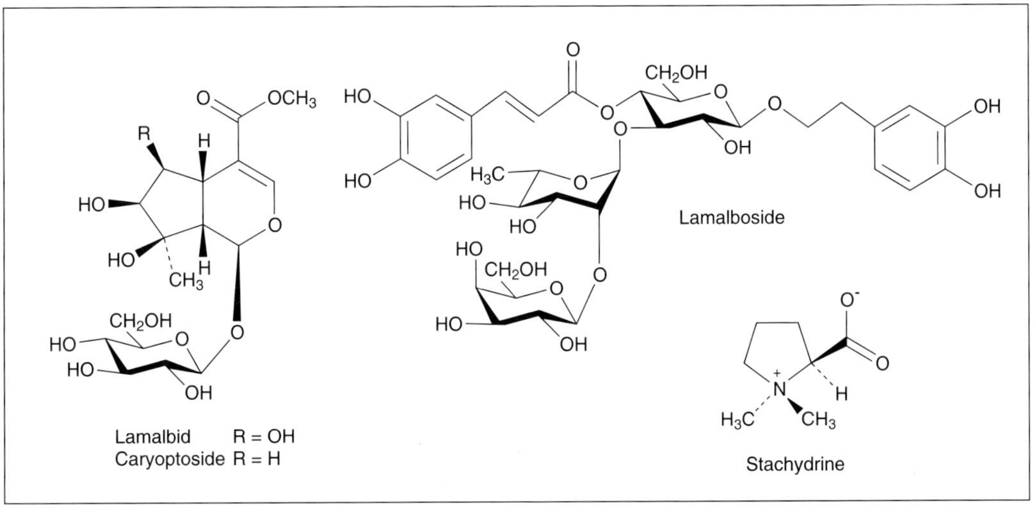

- Urine volumes over a 10-hour period after oral administration of the extract at 300 mg/kg body weight, the saponins at 30 mg/kg and hydrochlorothiazide at 2.5 mg/kg were 15, 10 and 34 ml/kg respectively, compared to 2 ml from control animals.

The saponin mixture intravenously administered into the carotid artery at 100-500 µg per animal also produced dose-dependent short term hypotensive effects in rats [15].

CLINICAL STUDIES

None published on mono-preparations of white deadnettle.

THERAPEUTICS

No distinction is made below between the flowering herb and the flowers only. It would be impracticable to do so on a rational basis in view of varying traditional usage and the very limited pharmacological data.

Actions

Astringent [16-19], haemostatic [17,18], anti-inflammatory [15,18,19], diuretic [15,18-20], expectorant [18,19].

Indications

None adequately substantiated by pharmacological or clinical studies.

Uses based on experience or tradition

Internal: Leucorrhoea [7,18,21-23]; menstrual disorders such as menorrhagia [16,18], dysmenorrhoea [7] and painful periods [16]. Catarrhs of the upper respiratory tract [18,19,21,23]. Gastrointestinal complaints [15,24] such as irritation of the gastric mucosa, flatulence [24] or irritable bowel [18].
Topical: Leucorrhoea (as a douche) [18,21,22], inflammation of the oropharyngeal mucosa [21, 23]; superficial skin inflammations [23], minor wounds, bruises and burns [17,18]; itching scalp and dandruff [20]; haemorrhoids [16,18] and varicose veins [16].

Contraindications

None known.

Side effects

None known.

Interactions with other drugs

None known.

Dosage

Internal use Up to three times daily: dried herb (or flowers), 1-3 g, usually as an infusion; equivalent preparations [18,21,23,24].
External use Infusions: as a gargle, 2-3 g per 100 ml of water; as a compress or vaginal douche, 5-10 g per 100 ml [18,21].

SAFETY

The herb is generally considered harmless; it has been used to make aromatic tea as a beverage [22] and the tender young leaves can be eaten like spinach [18,19].

REGULATORY STATUS

Medicines

UK	No licences issued for products containing white deadnettle.
France	Flowers or flowering herb accepted for specified indications [20].
Germany	Separate Commission E monographs published on the flowers, with approved uses [23], and on the flowering herb, with no approved uses [25]. The Standardzulassung gives approved uses of the flowering herb [24].

REFERENCES

Current Pharmacopoeial Monographs

Flowering Herb

DAC	Taubnesselkraut
BHP	White Deadnettle

Flower (corolla) only

Ph. Fr.	Lamier Blanc

Literature References

1. Góra J, Swiatek L, Kurowska A, Kalemba D and Boruch T. Chemical comparative studies of the herb and flowers of *Lamium album* L. *Acta Polon. Pharm.* 1983, **40**, 389-393 [POLISH/English summary].
2. Damtoft S. Iridoid glucosides from *Lamium album*. *Phytochemistry* 1992, **31**, 175-178.
3. Eigtved P, Jensen SR and Nielsen BJ. A Novel Iridoid Glucoside Isolated from *Lamium album* L. *Acta Chem. Scand.* 1974, **B 28**, 85-91.
4. Brieskorn CH and Ahlborn R. Lamalbid, ein neues Iridoid aus Flores Lamii albi. *Tetrahedron Lett.* 1973, **41**, 4037-4038 [GERMAN].
5. Budzianowski J and Skrzypczak L. Phenylpropanoid esters from *Lamium album* flowers. *Phytochemistry* 1995, **38**, 997-1001.
6. Hodisan V, Rosca M, Grecu L and Muica E. Contributions to the study of the chemical composition of *Lamium album* L. (I.). *Contributii Botanice, Universitatea Babes-Bolyai din Cluj-Napoca, Gradina Botanica* 1977, 215-221 [ROMANIAN/English summary]; also through *Chem. Abstr.* 1978, **89**, 39380.

7. Kwasniewski V. Zur Kenntnis der Inhaltsstoffe der Blüten der Taubnessel. *Planta Medica* 1959, **7**, 35-40 [GERMAN/English summary].
8. Tamas M, Hodisan V and Muica E. Study on flavones from Lamium album L. (Labiatae family). *Clujul Med.* 1978, **51**, 266-270 [ROMANIAN]; through *Chem. Abstr.* 1979, **90**, 83647.
9. Duchnowska A and Borkowski B. Polyphenolic compounds in flowers of the genus *Lamium*. *Dissertationes Pharmaceuticae (Warsaw)* 1964, **16**, 101-104 [POLISH/English summary].
10. Duchnowska A and Borkowski B. Flavonoids in the flowers of *Lamium album*. *Dissertationes Pharmaceuticae (Warsaw)* 1964, **16**, 91-99 [POLISH/English summary].
11. Pulatova TP. Alkaloid content of some plants of the family Labiatae. *Khim. Prir. Soedin.* 1969, **5**(1), 62-63 [RUSSIAN], translated into English as: *Chem. Nat. Compd.* 1969, **5**, 55.
12. Damtoft S and Jensen SR. Hemialboside, a hemiterpene glucoside from *Lamium album*. *Phytochemistry* 1995, **39**, 923-924.
13. Sarker SD, Dinan L, Sik V and Rees HH. 9ξ-O-β-D-glucopyranosyloxy-5-megastigmen-4-one from *Lamium album*. *Phytochemistry* 1997, **45**, 1431-1433.
14. Istratescu Guti L. Ascorbic acid content of Melophyta plants. Note V. Ascorbic acid content of some plants of the Tubiflorae order. *Farmacia (Bucharest)* 1985, **33**, 113-115 [ROMANIAN]; through *Chem. Abstr.* 1985, **103**, 211163.
15. Kory M, Hodisan V, Toader S and Gugu P. Pharmacodynamic investigations on the species of Lamium album L. *Clujul Med.* 1982, **55**, 156-160 [ROMANIAN/English summary]; also through *Chem. Abstr.* 1983, **98**, 46480.
16. Chevallier A. White Deadnettle. In: *The Encyclopedia of Medicinal Plants.* ISBN 0-7513-0314-3. London-New York-Stuttgart: Dorling Kindersley, 1996:224.
17. Grieve M, edited by Leyel CF. White Deadnettle. In: *A Modern Herbal* (first published in 1931). ISBN 1-85501-249-9. London: Tiger Books International, 1994: 579-580.
18. Bartram T. White Deadnettle. In: Encyclopaedia of Herbal Medicine. ISBN 0-9515984-1-4. Christchurch, UK: Grace Publishers, 1995:57.
19. Stodola J and Volák J. White Deadnettle. Translated into English in: Bunney S, editor. *The Illustrated Book of Herbs.* ISBN 0-7064-1489-6. London: Octopus Books, 1984:177.
20. Lamier blanc ou Ortie blanche. In: *Médicaments à base de plantes.* ISBN 2-911473-02-7. Saint-Denis Cedex, France: Agence du Médicament, 1998.
21. Weiss RF and Fintelmann V. Lamium album. In: *Herbal Medicine, 2nd ed.* (translated from the 9th German edition of *Lehrbuch der Phytotherapie*). ISBN 3-13-126332-6. Stuttgart-New York; Thieme, 2000: 338 and 416.
22. Weiss RF. Lamium album (Deadnettle). In: *Herbal Medicine* (translated from the 6th German edition of *Lehrbuch der Phytotherapie*). ISBN 0-906584-19-1. Gothenburg: AB Arcanum, Beaconsfield, UK: Beaconsfield Publishers, 1988:313-314.
23. Lamii albi flos. German Commission E Monograph published in: Bundesanzeiger No. 76 of 23 April 1987.
24. Braun R, editor. Weißes Taubnesselkraut (Standardzulassung No. 1359.99.99). In: Standardzulassungen für Fertigarzneimittel - Text und Kommentar. Stuttgart: Deutscher Apotheker Verlag, Frankfurt: Govi-Verlag, 1986.
25. Lamii albi herba. German Commission E Monograph published in: Bundesanzeiger No. 128 of 14 July 1993.

REGULATORY GUIDELINES FROM OTHER EU COUNTRIES

FRANCE (flowering herb or flowers only)

Médicaments à base de plantes [20]: Lamier blanc ou Ortie blanche, corolle mondée, sommité fleurie.

Therapeutic indications accepted

Oral use
Traditionally used to facilitate urinary and digestive elimination functions; to promote the renal elimination of water.

Topical use
Traditionally used in itching and desquamation of the scalp with dandruff.

GERMANY (flowering herb)

Commission E monograph [25]: Lamii albi herba (Weißes Taubnesselkraut).

Pharmacological properties, pharmacokinetics, toxicology
Nothing known.

Uses
Preparations from white deadnettle herb are used in support of the treatment of gastrointestinal ailments such as irritation of the gastric mucosa, bloatedness or flatulence, and for strengthening the intestine.

Combination preparations of white deadnettle herb are used for nervousness, restlessness and irritation, for sleep disorders, for invigoration, relaxation and stimulation, during the menopause, for female ailments of all kinds, menstrual disorders, "blood purifying", metabolic stimulation in support of gallbladder and liver function, proneness to biliary gravel, to stimulate the appetite, for neutralization of gastric hyperacidity, to promote digestion, in flatulence, for stimulation of pancreatic function, regulation of the blood lipid level, irrigation of the urinary tract in inflammatory and spasmodic bladder ailments, functioning of the prostate gland, stimulation of the heart and blood circulation, in dizziness, flickering of the eyes, tinnitus, for increased blood supply to the heart, increased heart capacity, improvement of lymph flow and stimulation of lymph formation, strengthening of the respiratory tract, dissolving mucus, and improvement in vitality and general weakness, especially after illness or surgery.

Risks
None known.

Assessment
Since efficacy in the claimed areas of use is not substantiated, therapeutic use cannot be recommended.

Standardzulassung *published 1986 (valid up to 1996) for a standard medicinal tea: Weißes Taubnesselkraut [24].*

The labelling text included:

Uses
In support of the treatment of gastrointestinal ailments such as irritation of the gastric mucosa, bloatedness and flatulence.

Dosage instruction and mode of administration
Pour boiling water (ca. 150 ml) over 3-4 teaspoonsful (3-4 g) of white deadnettle herb and after 10-15 minutes filter through a tea strainer. Unless otherwise prescribed, drink 1 cup of freshly prepared warm infusion several times daily between meals.

White Deadnettle

GERMANY (flowers only)

Commission E monograph [23]: Lamii albi flos (Weiße Taubnesselblüten).

Uses

Internal: Catarrh of the upper respiratory tract; local treatment of mild inflammation of the mouth and throat mucosa, and for non-specific fluor albus (leucorrhoea).
External: Mild, superficial inflammations of the skin.

Contraindications

None known.

Side effects

None known.

Interactions with other drugs

None known.

Dosage

Unless otherwise prescribed, average internal daily dose: 3 g of dried flowers. External use: 5 g of dried flowers for a hip-bath. Equivalent preparations.

Mode of administration

Dried flowers for infusions and other galenic preparations for internal use, and for rinses, baths and wet compresses.

WILD THYME

Labiatae

Serpylli herba

Synonyms: Creeping Thyme [1], Breckland Thyme (*Thymus serpyllum* L.), Large Thyme (*T. pulegioides* L.) [2].

Definition
Wild Thyme consists of the dried flowering aerial parts of *Thymus serpyllum* L.s.l. or *Thymus pulegioides* L.

Although somewhat weaker in action, wild thyme has a spectrum of activity and medicinal uses resembling those of thyme [3,4]. Its therapeutic value is to a large extent dependent on the amount and composition of its essential oil. However, in comparison with thyme (for which the European Pharmacopoeia accepts only two species, *Thymus vulgaris* and *T. zygis*), selection of the most appropriate species and chemotype for medicinal wild thyme is more complicated.

Thymus serpyllum L.s.l. is a "collective species" (hence s.l. = sensu latiore, in the wide sense), rich in forms, chemotypes and karyotypes, which occurs in quite diverse habitats and ecological conditions in temperate Eurasia. Although the different forms show considerable variability in appearance and morphological characteristics (and also a high tendency to hybridization), they can be broadly described as low-lying perennial herbs with reddish to violet, and sometimes white, flowers in composite spikes or whorls. Among the many individual species which have been considered to belong to this collective species, the more important ones from a medicinal viewpoint appear to be *Thymus serpyllum* L. sensu stricto and *Thymus pulegioides* L.

Some taxonomists no longer include *Thymus pulegioides* L. within the collective *Thymus serpyllum* L.s.l. [3,5]. However, the available data suggest that "carvacrol chemotypes" of *T. pulegioides* offer the most reliable source of phenol-rich, low-citral wild thyme for medicinal use bearing in mind that, as in the case of thyme, monoterpenic phenols (i.e. carvacrol and thymol) are important to the pharmacological activity. As far back as 1965 it was recommended that medicinal wild thyme should come only from low-citral forms of *Thymus pulegioides* [6] and a 1993 review defined *T. pulegioides* L. as the only botanical source [5]. In these circumstances continued widespread use of the synonym "Serpylli herba" for wild thyme has become rather inappropriate.

The European Pharmacopoeia monograph for Wild Thyme (2003) defines *Thymus serpyllum* L.s.l. as the botanical source with no mention of *T. pulegioides* L. A minimum content of essential oil (3.0 ml/kg) is specified, but only a qualitative TLC test is included for the presence of carvacrol and thymol; this seems inadequate in view of the importance of these monoterpenic phenols to the activity. Former monographs of the DAB and Ph. Helv. stipulated a minimum content of phenols (0.1% in the DAB 1999).

CONSTITUENTS

□ ***Essential oil***, 0.1-0.6% [3; Ph. Eur. min. 0.3% V/m] of very variable composition.

Based on their essential oils, at least eight chemotypes of *Thymus pulegioides* have been reported [7,8], for example carvacrol, citral-geraniol [7] and α-terpenyl acetate [8] chemotypes. It is therefore necessary to be selective and for medicinal use a carvacrol chemotype is normally the most appropriate. Over a period of three years in three locations near Vilnius, Lithuania, carvacrol chemotypes gave the following essential oil composition: carvacrol 16.0-25.5%, β-bisabolene 11.1-20.2%, β-caryophyllene 11.1-19.1%, γ-terpinene 5.8-16.2%, *p*-cymene 5.5-10.4%, thymol 3.3-9.8% and carvacrol methyl ether 5.6-8.6% [7]. In an earlier study, 8 samples of flowering *Thymus pulegioides* L. from Poland, Germany and the Czech Republic

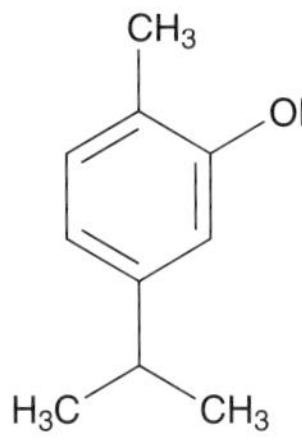

Carvacrol

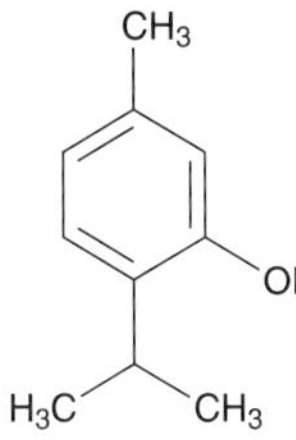

Thymol

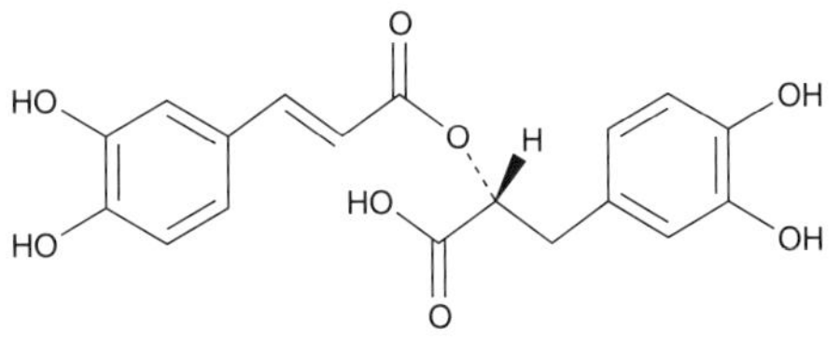

Rosmarinic acid

yielded an average of 0.33% of essential oil containing linalool + linalyl acetate (22.3-45.0%), carvacrol (4.9-32.5%), geraniol (2.5-9.6%), geranyl acetate (1.6-4.1%) and thymol (1.0-4.0%) [6].

In contrast, carvacrol and thymol occur at lower levels in (or are absent from) essential oils of European *T. serpyllum*, at least in samples from Baltic countries:

- Samples of *T. serpyllum* s.l. growing wild in Lithuania (three forms with violet, reddish or white flowers) yielded 0.4-0.6% of essential oil with high contents of 1,8-cineole (16.3-19.0%), myrcene (9.7-10.7%) and β-caryophyllene (9.5-11.3%), but completely devoid of carvacrol and thymol [1].
- Out of 20 samples of *T. serpyllum* L. harvested from wild plants growing in 20 different locations in Estonia, only one sample gave a yield of essential oil (4 ml/kg) meeting the Ph. Eur. requirement of not less than 3 ml/kg; the other 19 yielded 0.6-2.5 ml/kg; all the oils contained low levels of carvacrol (0.1-3.5%) and all but one contained thymol (0.2-2.9%). The predominant components varied, usually including nerolidol (up to 70%), caryophyllene oxide (up to 45%), myrcene (up to 20%), β-caryophyllene (up to 13%) and germacrene D (up to 12%), and occasionally geranyl acetate (up to 46%), linalyl acetate (up to 31%) or linalool (up to 23%) [9].

On the other hand, essential oil obtained (with a high yield of 0.9% m/m) from *T. serpyllum* L. growing wild in Iran contained 18.7% of thymol and 0.4% of carvacrol together with γ-terpinene (22.7%), *p*-cymene (20.7%) and germacrene D (5.1%) [10].

□ ***Hydroxycinnamic derivatives***, 3.3% including 2.3% of rosmarinic acid [11] and 0.6% of caffeic acid [12].

□ ***Flavonoids*** Flavone glycosides including apigenin 7-glucoside, luteolin 7-glucoside and 7-diglucoside (and a luteolin arabinogalactoside), diosmetin 7-glucuronide and a scutellarein glucoglucuronide [13].

In contrast to thyme (*Thymus vulgaris*), no methoxylated flavones appear to be present in *T. serpyllum* or *T. pulegioides* [14].

□ ***Triterpenes*** Oleanolic acid (ca. 0.5%) and ursolic acid (ca. 0.9%) [15].

Published Assay Methods

GC and GC-MS of the essential oil components [7,9].

PHARMACOLOGY

In vitro

Antimicrobial activity

A dry 80%-ethanolic extract from wild thyme (*Thymus serpyllum* L. from Italy) exhibited antibacterial activity against *Staphylococcus aureus, Bacillus subtilis, Salmonella typhi* and *Proteus mirabilis*, but not *Klebsiella pneumoniae* or *Pseudomonas aeruginosa* [16]. Essential oil from wild thyme (*T. serpyllum* L.; 18.7% thymol) exhibited strong antibacterial activity against *Escherichia coli, S. aureus, B. subtilis* and *K. pneumoniae*, but not against *P. aeruginosa* [10].

An aqueous extract from wild thyme (*T. serpyllum*) inhibited the growth of *Herpes simplex* virus and Newcastle disease virus in disc-plaque suppression tests [17].

Spasmolytic activity

A fluid extract (1:2; 25% ethanol) from wild thyme (*T. serpyllum* L. from Belgium) dose-dependently inhibited acetylcholine-induced contractions of isolated guinea pig ileum at 0.133-0.266 ml/20 ml (by about 60% at the higher concentration), but a fluid extract from *T. pulegioides* L. (from Italy) was ineffective. Neither extract had a relaxant effect on carbachol-induced contractions of isolated guinea pig trachea [14].

Pharmacokinetics

Data on the pharmacokinetics of thymol are summarized in the Thyme monograph.

CLINICAL STUDIES

None published on mono-preparations of wild thyme.

THERAPEUTICS

Actions

Spasmolytic [3,4,14,18,19], carminative [3,19], expectorant [20], antimicrobial [10,17-19], vulnerary [19].

Indications

None adequately substantiated by pharmacological or clinical studies.

Uses based on experience or tradition

Internal: Catarrhs of the upper respiratory tract [3, 4,18], bronchitis [19-21], bronchial catarrh [19], coughs and colds [21,22], whooping cough [4, 19-21], laryngitis [4,19,21].

Digestive disorders [20,22] such as flatulent dyspepsia [4,19] and colic [21].

External: Treatment of small wounds, sores, ulcers [19,21,22] and mastitis [19,21].

Contraindications

None known. However, as with thyme, it is prudent to limit internal use of wild thyme during pregnancy to an amount not greatly exceeding that used in foods.

Side effects
None known.

Interactions with other drugs
None known.

Dosage
Three times daily: dried herb, 1-3 g or by infusion; liquid extract, 1:1 in 45% alcohol, 1-3 ml [18,19].

SAFETY

Neither formal safety data nor human studies have been published on wild thyme but the available literature suggests that wild thyme is well tolerated at normal therapeutic dose levels.

REGULATORY STATUS

Medicines

UK	No licences issued for products containing wild thyme.
France	Accepted for specified indications [22].
Germany	Commission E monograph published, with approved uses [18].

Food

USA	Generally recognized as safe (21 CFR 182.10 and 182.20) [23].
Council of Europe	Permitted as flavouring, category N2 [24].

REFERENCES

Current Pharmacopoeial Monographs
Ph. Eur. Wild Thyme

Literature References

1. Loziene K, Vaiciuniene J and Venskutonis PR. Chemical Composition of the Essential Oil of Creeping Thyme (*Thymus serpyllum* s.l.) Growing Wild in Lithuania. *Planta Medica* 1998, **64**, 772-773.
2. Blamey M and Grey-Wilson C. Thymes - *Thymus*. In: *The Illustrated Flora of Britain and Northern Europe*. ISBN 0-340-40170-2. London: Hodder & Stoughton, 1989:342.
3. Stahl-Biskup E, Wichtl M and Neubeck M. Quendelkraut - Serpylli herba. In: Hartke K, Hartke H, Mutschler E, Rücker G and Wichtl M, editors. *Kommentar zum Deutschen Arzneibuch*. Stuttgart: Wissenschaftliche Verlagsgesellschaft, 2000 (13. Lfg.):Q 2 [GERMAN].
4. Grieve M (edited by Leyel CF). Thyme, wild. In: *A Modern Herbal* (first published 1931; revised 1973). ISBN 1-85501-249-9. London: Tiger Books International, 1994:813-815.
5. Czygan F-C and Hänsel R. Thymian und Quendel - Arznei und Gewürzpflanzen [Thyme and wild thyme - medicinal and condiment plants]. *Z. Phytotherapie* 1993, **14**, 104-110 [GERMAN/English summary].
6. Messerschmidt W. Gas- und dünnschichtchromatographische Untersuchungen der ätherischen Öle einiger Thymusarten. II. Der Einfluß verschiedener Herkünfte auf die Zusammensetzung des ätherischen Öls von Herba Thymi und Herba Serpylli und Vorschläge für ihre chromatographische Beurteilung [Gas and thin-layer chromatographic investigations of essential oils of some *Thymus* species. II. The influence of varied origins on the essential oils of Herba Thymi and Herba Serpylli and proposals for their chromatographic evaluation]. *Planta Medica* 1965, **13**, 56-72 [GERMAN/English summary].
7. Mockute D and Bernotiene G. The Main Citral-Geraniol and Carvacrol Chemotypes of the Essential Oil of *Thymus pulegioides* L. Growing Wild in Vilnius District (Lithuania). *J. Agric. Food Chem.* 1999, **47**, 3787-3790.
8. Mockute D and Bernotiene G. The α-terpenyl acetate chemotype of essential oil of *Thymus pulegioides* L. *Biochem. Syst. Ecol.* 2001, **29**, 69-76.
9. Raal A, Paaver U, Arak E and Orav A. Content and composition of the essential oil of *Thymus serpyllum* L. growing wild in Estonia. *Medicina (Kaunas)* 2004, **40**, 795-800.
10. Rasooli I and Mirmostafa SA. Antibacterial properties of *Thymus pubescens* and *Thymus serpyllum* essential oils. *Fitoterapia* 2002, **73**, 244-250.
11. Lamaison JL, Petitjean-Freytet C and Carnat A. Rosmarinic acid, total hydroxycinnamic acid contents and antioxidant activity of medicinal Apiaceae, Boraginaceae and Lamiaceae. *Ann. Pharm. Fr.* 1990, **48**, 103-108 [FRENCH/English summary].
12. Steinegger E and Hänsel R. Quendelkraut. In: *Pharmakognosie, 5th ed.* ISBN 3-540-55649-4. Berlin-Heidelberg-New York: Springer-Verlag, 1992:333-334.
13. Olechnowicz-Stepien W and Lamer-Zarawska E. Investigation of flavonoid fractions of some crude drugs from the family Labiatae (Herba Serpylli L., Herba Thymi L., Herba Majoranae L., Herba Origani L.). *Herba Polonica* 1975, **21**, 347-356.
14. Van Den Broucke C, Lemli J and Lamy J. Action spasmolytique des flavones de différentes espèces de *Thymus* [Spasmolytic action of the flavones of various species of *Thymus*]. *Plantes Méd. Phytothér.* 1982, **16**, 310-317 [FRENCH/English summary].
15. Brieskorn CH, Eberhardt KH and Briner M. Biogenetische Zusammenhänge zwischen Oxytriterpensäuren und ätherischem Öl bei einigen pharmazeutisch wichtigen Labiaten [Biogenetic relationships between oxytriterpenic acids and essential oil in some pharmaceutically important Labiatae]. *Arch. Pharm. (Weinheim)* 1953, **286**, 501-506 [GERMAN].
16. Izzo AA, Di Carlo G, Biscardi D, De Fusco R, Mascolo N, Borrelli F et al. Biological Screening of Italian Medicinal Plants for Antibacterial Activity. *Phytotherapy Res.* 1995, **9**, 281-286.
17. Herrmann EC and Kucera LS. Antiviral Substances in Plants of the Mint Family (Labiatae). III. Peppermint (*Mentha piperita*) and other Mint Plants. *Proc. Soc. Exptl. Biol. Med.* 1967, **124**, 874-878.
18. Serpylli herba. German Commission E Monograph published in: Bundesanzeiger No. 193 of 15 October 1987; amended in Bundesanzeiger No. 50 of 13 March 1990.
19. Thymus serpyllum. In: *British Herbal Pharmacopoeia 1983*. ISBN 0-903032-07-4. Bournemouth: British Herbal Medicine Association, 1983.
20. Stodola J and Volák J. Breckland Thyme, Wild Thyme. Translated into English in: Bunney S, editor. *The Illustrated Book of Herbs*. ISBN 0-7064-1489-6. London: Octopus Books, 1984:280.
21. Chevallier A. Wild Thyme - *Thymus serpyllum*. In: *Encyclopedia of Medicinal Plants, 2nd ed.* ISBN 0-7513-1209-6. London-New York: Dorling Kindersley, 2001:276.
22. Serpolet. In: *Médicaments à base de plantes*. ISBN 2-911473-02-7. Saint-Denis Cedex, France: Agence du Médicament, 1998.
23. Thyme, wild or creeping. In: Sections 182.10 and 182.20

of USA Code of Federal Regulations, Title 21, Food and Drugs, Parts 170 to 199. Revised as of April 1, 2000.
24. *Thymus serpyllum* L., aerial parts. In: *Flavouring Substances and Natural Sources of Flavourings, 3rd ed.* ISBN 2-7160-0081-6. Strasbourg: Council of Europe, 1981.

REGULATORY GUIDELINES FROM OTHER EU COUNTRIES

FRANCE

Médicaments à base de plantes [22]: Serpolet, feuille, sommité fleurie.

Therapeutic indications accepted

Oral use
Traditionally used: in the symptomatic treatment of digestive disorders such as epigastric distension, sluggish digestion, eructation and flatulence; in the symptomatic treatment of coughs.

Topical use
Traditionally used: for the treatment of small wounds and sores after copious washing (with soap and water) and for the elimination of spots; in cases of congested nose, from colds; locally (mouthwash/gargle, pastille) as an antalgesic in ailments of the buccal cavity and/or the pharynx; locally in mouthwashes, for buccal hygiene.

GERMANY

Commission E monograph [18]: Serpylli herba (Quendelkraut).

Uses
Catarrhs of the upper respiratory tract.

Contraindications
None known.

Side effects
None known.

Interactions with other drugs
None known.

Dosage
Daily dose: 4-6 g of the herb or equivalent preparations.

Mode of administration
Comminuted herb for infusions and other preparations for internal use.

Actions
Antimicrobial, spasmolytic.

WILD YAM

Dioscoreae villosae rhizoma

Synonyms: Colic root, rheumatism root.

Definition
Wild Yam consists of the dried rhizome and roots of *Dioscorea villosa* L.

Dioscorea is a large genus of approximately 850 species, the majority of which grow in humid tropical and subtropical areas of the world and include a number of yams cultivated for their edible tubers. *Dioscorea villosa* L., one of only three *Dioscorea* species native to North America, grows in the eastern USA from Massachusetts to northern Florida; it is neither cultivated nor edible [1]. At one time a monograph on wild yam (as Dioscorea N.F.) appeared in the U.S. National Formulary [2].

During and after World War II, the rapidly increasing demand for steroidal drugs led to a worldwide search for plant sources of starting materials which could be converted into therapeutically useful steroid compounds, such as oral contraceptives and corticosteroids (e.g. cortisone). The steroidal sapogenin diosgenin, obtained from *Dioscorea* species (although not commercially from *D. villosa*), became the compound most widely used for this purpose.

CONSTITUENTS

☐ ***Steroidal saponins***, principally dioscin, a 3-glycoside of diosgenin (22α-spirost-5-en-3β-ol) in which the first sugar is glucose, to which two units of rhamnose are attached. Gracillin (a similar trioside of diosgenin except with the 4'-rhamnose unit replaced by glucose) [3,4] is also probably present, together with smaller amounts of glycosides based on pennogenin (22α-spirost-5-en-3β,17α-diol) and other sapogenins [5]. Diosgenin is not found in the free state in the rhizome [6].

Knowing that diosgenin could be obtained from *Dioscorea* species and could be chemically converted to progesterone and other steroidal hormones, Marker and colleagues in Pennsylvania, looking for American sources of diosgenin, isolated it (after acid hydrolysis) from rhizomes of *Dioscorea villosa* in 1940 [7]. However, since the yield of diosgenin from *D. villosa* is relatively low, interest soon turned to more promising *Dioscorea* species and habitats south of the border.

Tubers of *Dioscorea composita* and *D. floribunda* from Mexico/Central America, which have been used by the pharmaceutical industry as rich sources of diosgenin, may contain up to 13% and 10% of sapogenins respectively [8]. By comparison, *D. villosa* rhizome has been reported to yield, on the dry basis, 1.3% of steroidal sapogenins (a sample from Illinois) [9], 0.7-1.1% of diosgenin [5] and, using an improved technique, 2.3% of diosgenin [6].

☐ ***Other constituents*** include starch [2] and tannins [3].

An alkaloid called dioscorine [2,10] and a storage protein called dioscorin [11] have been reported in the tubers of some species of *Dioscorea*, but evidence of their presence in *D. villosa* is lacking.

Published Assay Methods
Diosgenin by GC [12] and TLC-densitometry [13].

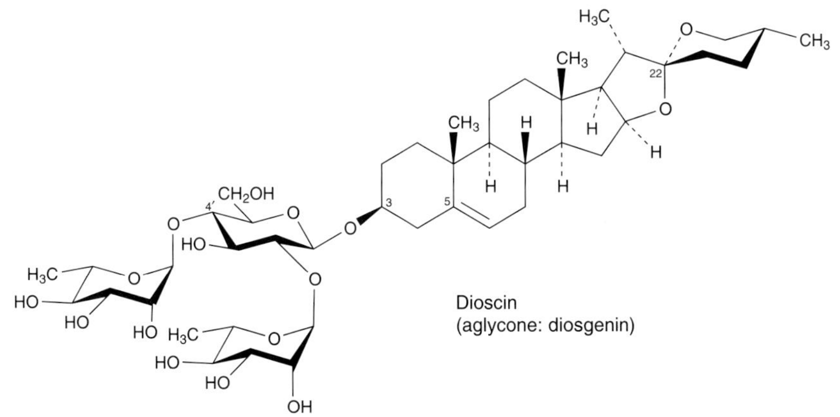

Dioscin
(aglycone: diosgenin)

PHARMACOLOGY

Pharmacological studies using wild yam (as crude drug or extracts) are very limited. On the other hand, the pharmacology of diosgenin has been extensively studied. Wild yam contains steroidal saponins (glycosides), principally dioscin, rather than sapogenins (aglycones) such as diosgenin. It appears probable that dioscin is hydrolysed to diosgenin by human gut flora, but no direct evidence is available to confirm this.

In vitro

In a tissue culture screening procedure for steroid hormone activity, wild yam root showed no oestrogenic or progestational activity; it exhibited weak anti-oestrogenic activity [14]. Similarly, a 50%-ethanolic extract from wild yam showed no appreciable oestrogenic or progestogenic activity in competitive assays of binding to oestrogen and progesterone receptors in intact human breast cancer cells [15].

Saliva from women taking diosgenin-containing preparations (including wild yam) was found not to possess any progesterone bioactivity; in fact, the saliva contained only very low base levels of progesterone. These data support the view that diosgenin (or its glycoside dioscin, as present in wild yam) is not converted to progesterone in the human body [15].

A hydroethanolic fluid extract from wild yam had only a slight lowering effect on the amplitude of contractions of isolated uterus from virgin and pregnant guinea pigs, while an aqueous infusion was inactive [16].

Dioscin markedly and dose-dependently inhibited the proliferation of Hela cells, a human cervical cancer cell line, with an IC_{50} of 4.4 µM [17], and was also shown to induce mitotic arrest and apoptosis (cell death) in several human leukaemia cell lines [18].

Assuming that diosgenin is released *in vivo* by enzymic hydrolysis of dioscin, results from recent research appear to support the traditional use of wild yam in the treatment of rheumatoid arthritis. This inflammatory joint disease, in which perpetuation of chronic synovitis leads to bone and cartilage degradation, is characterized by the proliferation of synoviocytes, which generate prostanoids, important mediators found at elevated levels in inflamed tissues. Using fresh synovial biopsy material obtained from 6 rheumatoid arthritis patients undergoing hip surgery, fibroblast-like synoviocytes (FLS) were cultured and cell proliferation was evaluated in the presence or absence of diosgenin. Diosgenin at 40 µM induced significant inhibition of human rheumatoid arthritis FLS cell growth ($p<0.05$) with induction of apoptosis [19].

In vivo

Effects of diosgenin

Subcutaneous administration of diosgenin to ovariectomized mice at 20 and 40 mg/kg/day for 15 days stimulated the growth of mammary epithelium, suggesting oestrogenic activity [20].

Administration of diosgenin (500 mg/capsule) to ovariectomized rats for 33 days by means of sustained release capsules implanted in the peritoneal cavity inhibited the progression of osteoporotic bone loss evident in ovariectomized but untreated control animals; to varying degrees, oestrogen and dehydroepiandrosterone had similar effects [21].

Intragastrically administered diosgenin inhibited the growth rate of tumours after inoculation of several types of tumour cells into mice [22].

Diosgenin influences the absorption and excretion of cholesterol in rodents:

- When administered to mice as 1% of their diet for 15 days, diosgenin reduced cholesterol absorption to about one-third of that observed in control mice, reduced liver cholesterol levels, increased faecal excretion of cholesterol and reduced faecal excretion of bile acids [23].
- Given orally to rats as 1% of their diet for 5 days, diosgenin stimulated biliary output of cholesterol more than 3-fold ($p<0.05$); the increase was shown to be bile-salt-dependent [24].
- Diosgenin increased bile flow (especially the bile acid-independent fraction) and biliary output of cholesterol and total glutathione in rats. The choleretic activity was attributed to increases in liver canalicular membrane fluidity and transporter activity [25].
- Intragastrically-administered diosgenin showed antihypercholesterolaemic activity in rodents fed on a high-cholesterol diet; at 80-160 mg/kg it had a significant preventive effect against hypercholesterolaemia in mice and at 100-200 mg/kg reduced serum total cholesterol in rats [26].

Pharmacokinetics

Diosgenin was found to be poorly absorbed in rats, dogs and monkeys after a single oral dose of [4-^{14}C]-diosgenin. All of the absorbed radioactivity was eliminated via the bile and virtually all of the radioactivity was excreted in the faeces. No serum diosgenin was detected after a single large dose to dogs, but up to 15 µg/ml of unchanged diosgenin was found in serum after doses of 100 mg/kg/day for 4 weeks [27].

In 5 human subjects receiving 3 × 1 g of diosgenin daily for 4 weeks (approx. 40 mg/kg/day), serum levels (checked weekly) were low and irregular (< 1 μg/ml) and there was no evidence of accumulation in the serum [27].

CLINICAL STUDIES

In a double-blind, placebo-controlled crossover study, healthy women (average age 53 years) suffering from troublesome symptoms of the menopause were assigned to treatment in random order with an active cream and a matching placebo cream, each for a period of 3 months. The active cream contained wild yam extract (100 mg/g), *Salvia officinalis* oil (100 mg/g), *Pelargonium graveolens* oil (100 mg/g), α-tocopheryl acetate (10 mg/g) and linseed oil. One teaspoonful of either cream was applied twice daily to the skin of arms, legs or abdomen. From 50 women initially randomized, only 23 completed the study. No significant effects were observed on body weight or blood pressure, or on biochemical or hormonal parameters. Some symptom scores showed improvement from baseline but no statistical differences were evident between the active cream and placebo. Thus topical use of a wild yam extract appeared to have little effect on menopausal symptoms [28].

THERAPEUTICS

Actions
Spasmolytic, anti-inflammatory [29-31], cholagogic [29], antirheumatic, mildly diaphoretic [29,30], diuretic [30-32].

Indications
None substantiated by pharmacological or clinical studies.

Uses based on experience or tradition
Biliary and intestinal colic [29-31,33]; cholecystitis, diverticulitis; dysmenorrhoea [29,30], ovarian and uterine pain [29-31]; acute phase of rheumatoid arthritis [29]; rheumatic and arthritic ailments generally [29-32]; cramps and muscle tension [29, 30], nausea of pregnancy [31,33].

Contraindications
None known.

Side effects
In large doses has a nauseating effect [2].

Interactions with other drugs
None known.

Dosage
Three times daily: dried root, 2-4 g or by infusion or decoction [2,29]; liquid extract 1:1 in 45% alcohol, 2-4 ml [29,33]; tincture 1:5 in 45% alcohol, 2-10 ml [29].

SAFETY

In acute oral toxicity tests a wild yam extract produced for cosmetic purposes showed no toxicity in rats at 0.5 g/kg, but 2 g/kg caused hypoactivity, dyspnoea and the death of 1 in 10 animals. Genotoxicity tests in bacterial and mammalian systems gave negative results. The extract showed no oestrogenic activity in the juvenile rat uterotrophic assay [34].

REGULATORY STATUS

Medicines

UK	No licences issued for products containing wild yam.
France	Not listed in *Médicaments à base de plantes* [35].
Germany	No Commission E monograph issued.

REFERENCES

Current Pharmacopoeial Monographs
BHP Wild Yam

Literature References

1. Al-Shehbaz IA and Schubert BG. The Dioscoreaceae in the southeastern United States. *J. Arnold Arboretum* 1989, **70**, 57-95.
2. Wood HC and LaWall CH, editors. Dioscorea N.F. In: *United States Dispensatory, Centennial (22nd) Edition.* Philadelphia-London, JB Lippincott Company, 1937:401-402.
3. Steinegger E and Hänsel R. Steroidsaponine. In: *Pharmakognosie, 5th ed.* ISBN 3-540-55649-4. Berlin-Heidelberg-New York: Springer-Verlag, 1992:214-219 [GERMAN].
4. Zou C-C, Hou S-J, Shi Y, Lei P-S, and Liang X-T. The synthesis of gracillin and dioscin; two typical representatives of spirostanol glycosides. *Carbohydr. Res.* 2003, **338**, 721-727.
5. Blunden G and Hardman R. Thin-layer chromatography of *Dioscorea* sapogenins. *J. Chromatogr.* 1964, **15**, 273-276.
6. Sauvaire Y and Baccou JC. L'obtention de la Diosgénine, (25R)-Spirost-5-ène-3β-ol; Problèmes de l'hydrolyse acide des saponines [Obtaining diosgenin, (25R)-spirost-5-ene-3β-ol; problems of acid hydrolysis of saponins]. *Lloydia* 1978, **41**, 247-256 [FRENCH/English summary].
7. Marker RE, Turner DL and Ulshafer PR. Sterols. CIV. Diosgenin from Certain American Plants. *J. Am. Chem. Soc.* 1940, **62**, 2542-2543.
8. Martin FW. The Species of Dioscorea Containing Sapogenin. *Econ. Bot.* 1969, **23**, 373-379.
9. Wall ME, Garvin JW, Willaman JJ, Jones Q and Schubert BG. Steroidal Sapogenins LX. Survey of Plants for Steroidal Sapogenins and Other Constituents. *J. Pharm. Sci.* 1961, **50**, 1001-1034.
10. Budavari S, editor. Dioscorine. In: *The Merck Index: An encyclopedia of chemicals, drugs and biologicals, 12th*

edition. ISBN 0-911910-12-3. Whitehouse Station, NJ: Merck & Co., 1996:557 (monograph 3347).

11. Shewry PR. Tuber Storage Proteins. *Ann. Bot.* 2003, **91**, 755-769.
12. Rozanski A. A Simplified Method of Extraction of Diosgenin from *Dioscorea* Tubers and its Determination by Gas-Liquid Chromatography. *Analyst* 1972, **97**, 968-972.
13. Blunden G, Hardman R and Morrison JC. Quantitative Estimation of Diosgenin in *Dioscorea* Tubers by Densitometric Thin-Layer Chromatography. *J. Pharm. Sci.* 1967, **56**, 948-950.
14. Rosenberg Zand RS, Jenkins DJA and Diamandis EP. Effects of natural products and nutraceuticals on steroid hormone-regulated gene expression. *Clin. Chim. Acta* 2001, **312**, 213-219.
15. Zava DT, Dollbaum CM and Blen M. Estrogen and Progestin Bioactivity of Foods, Herbs and Spices. *Proc. Soc. Exp. Biol. Med.* 1998, **217**, 369-378.
16. Pilcher JD, Burman GE and Delzell WR. The action of the so-called female remedies on the excized uterus of the guinea pig. *Arch. Intern. Med.* 1916, **18**, 557-583; through *Chem. Abstr.* 1917, **11**, 495-496.
17. Cai J, Liu M, Wang Z and Ju Y. Apoptosis Induced by Dioscin in Hela Cells. *Biol. Pharm. Bull.* 2002, **25**, 193-196.
18. Liu M-J, Wang Z, Ju Y, Zhou J, Wang Y and Wong RN-S. The Mitotic-Arresting and Apoptosis-Inducing Effects of Diosgenyl Saponins on Human Leukemia Cell Lines. *Biol. Pharm. Bull.* 2004, **27**, 1059-1065.
19. Liagre B, Vergne-Salle P, Corbiere C, Charissoux JL and Beneytout JL. Diosgenin, a plant steroid, induces apoptosis in human rheumatoid arthritis synoviocytes with cyclooxygenase-2 overexpression. *Arthritis Res. Ther.* 2004, **6**, R373-R383.
20. Aradhana, Rao AR and Kale RK. Diosgenin - a growth stimulator of mammary gland of ovariectomized mouse. *Indian J. Exp. Biol.* 1992, **30**, 367-370; throught *Chem. Abstr.* **116**, 248828.
21. Higdon K, Scott A, Tucci M, Benghuzzi H, Tsao A, Puckett A et al. The use of estrogen, DHEA and diosgenin in a sustained delivery setting as a novel treatment approach for osteoporosis in the ovariectomized adult rat model. *Biomed. Sci. Instrument.* 2001, **37**, 281-286.
22. Wang LJ, Wang Y, Chen SW, Ma JS, Fu Q and Wang BX. The antitumor activity of diosgenin *in vivo* and *in vitro*. *Zhongguo Zhong Yao Za Zhi* 2002, **27**, 777-779 [CHINESE]; through PubMed abstract.
23. Uchida K, Takase H, Nomura Y, Takeda K, Takeuchi N and Ishikawa Y. Changes in biliary and fecal bile acids in mice after treatments with diosgenin and β-sitosterol. *J. Lipid Res.* 1984, **25**, 236-245.
24. Thewles A, Parslow RA and Coleman R. Effect of diosgenin on biliary cholesterol transport in the rat. *Biochem. J.* 1993, **291**, 793-798.
25. Yamaguchi A, Tazuma S, Ochi H and Chayama K. Choleretic action of diosgenin is based upon the increases in canalicular membrane fluidity and transporter activity mediating bile acid independent bile flow. *Hepatol. Res.* 2003, **25**, 287-295.
26. Ma HY, Zhao ZT, Wang LJ, Wang Y, Zhou QL and Wang BX. Comparative study on anti-hypercholesterolemia activity of diosgenin and total saponin of *Dioscorea panthaica*. *Zhongguo Zhong Yao Za Zhi* 2002, **27**, 528-531 [CHINESE]; through PubMed abstract.
27. Cayen MN, Ferdinandi ES, Greselin E and Dvornik D. Studies on the disposition of diosgenin in rats, dogs, monkeys and man. *Atherosclerosis* 1979, **33**, 71-87.
28. Komesaroff PA, Black CVS, Cable V and Sudhir K. Effects of wild yam extract on menopausal symptoms, lipids and sex hormones in healthy menopausal women. *Climacteric* 2001, **4**, 144-150.
29. Dioscorea. In: *British Herbal Pharmacopoeia 1983.* ISBN 0-903032-07-4. Bournemouth: British Herbal Medicine Association, 1983.
30. Chevallier A. Wild Yam. In: *Encyclopedia of Medicinal Plants, 2nd ed.* ISBN 0-7513-1209-6. London-New York: Dorling Kindersley, 2001:93.
31. McIntyre A. Wild Yam - *Dioscorea villosa*. In: *The Complete Woman's Herbal.* ISBN 1-85675-135-X. London: Gaia Books, 1994:29.
32. Grieve M (edited by Leyel CF). Wild Yam - *Dioscorea villosa*. In: *A Modern Herbal* (first published 1931; revised 1973). ISBN 1-85501-249-9. London: Tiger Books International, 1994:863.
33. List PH and Hörhammer L, editors. Dioscorea. In: *Hagers Handbuch der Pharmazeutischen Praxis, 4th ed.* Band IV. Berlin-Heidelberg-New York: Springer-Verlag, 1973:673-677 [GERMAN].
34. Anon. Final Report of the Amended Safety Assessment of *Dioscorea villosa* (Wild Yam) Root Extract. *Int. J. Toxicol.* 2004, **23** (Suppl. 2), 49-54.
35. *Médicaments à base de plantes.* ISBN 2-911473-02-7. Saint-Denis Cedex, France: Agence du Médicament, 1998.

WORMWOOD

Compositae

Absinthii herba

Definition
Wormwood consists of the dried basal leaves or slightly leafy flowering tops, or of a mixture of these parts, of *Artemisia absinthium* L.

CONSTITUENTS

☐ ***Sesquiterpene lactones***, up to 0.7% [1] with the highest content during the flowering period [2], principally the guaianolides absinthin (average 0.24%) and artabsin (average 0.10%) [3], absinthin being a dimer of artabsin [4]. Isoabsinthin [5], artabsinolides A-D [1], absintholide [6] and various other sesquiterpene lactones have also been isolated.

Sesquiterpene lactones give the bitter taste to wormwood. The Ph. Eur requires a bitterness value of not less than 10,000 compared to that of quinine hydrochloride, which is set at 200,000. Absinthin has a bitterness value of 12,700,000 and artabsin 490,000 [3], hence absinthin contributes most of the bitterness. Since tests on wormwood samples from varied sources indicated an average bitterness of 30,500 with a lower limit of 25,000 the Ph. Eur. limit seems rather low [2].

☐ ***Essential oil***, 0.1-1.0% [7-10] (Ph. Eur. min. 0.2% V/m), of very variable composition with a number of chemotypes, but consisting mainly of oxygenated monoterpenes together with monoterpene hydrocarbons and sesquiterpenoids. The principal component may be *cis*-epoxyocimene (up to 76%) [7,8,10] or β-thujone (up to 60%) [9-12], or in exceptional cases *cis*-chrysanthenyl acetate (up to 60%), *trans*-sabinyl acetate (up to 84%) [10] or even α-thujone (up to 67%) [13]. However, the α-thujone content is usually below 3% [7-12].

Chemotypes completely devoid of α- and β-thujones, with essential oil containing mainly *cis*-epoxyocimene (Spain) [8] or *cis*-epoxyocimene + *cis*-chrysanthenyl acetate (France and Spain) [7,8] have been reported.

☐ ***Phenolic acids***, about 0.9%, of which 0.77% is caffeic acid (mostly in ester form) and the remainder mainly *p*-hydroxyphenylacetic, ferulic, vanillic and sinapic acids in free and bound forms [14].

☐ ***Flavonols*** Artemetin (0.4%) [1] and small amounts of the 3-glucosides and 3-rhamnoglucosides (= 3-rutinosides) of quercetin, isorhamnetin, patuletin and spinacetin [15].

☐ ***Other constituents*** Tannins of unidentified type, 6-7% in leaves and flowers [16]; a phytosterol, 24ζ-ethylcholesta-7,22-dien-3β-ol [17] and two homoditerpene peroxides [18].

Published Assay Methods
Absinthin by HPLC [19]. Essential oil components by GC [7,9] and GC-MS [7,8].

PHARMACOLOGY

Not many modern pharmacological studies have been carried out on wormwood. Its pharmacological properties and therapeutic uses largely depend on two distinct groups of constituents.

- Sesquiterpene lactones provide the aromatic bitter characteristics and are of key importance in uses relating to digestion.
- The components of the essential oil are particularly important to antimicrobial, anthelmintic and certain other properties of wormwood, including any influence on mental function, and thujones (mainly β-thujone) probably play a vital role in such activities.

Wormwood chemotypes completely devoid of thujones are increasingly reported. Such chemotypes may be advantageous in the "digestive" uses of wormwood, but less appropriate for the other uses. It is disappointing to find that the thujone content of wormwood used in pharmacological studies, even recent work, has not always been determined.

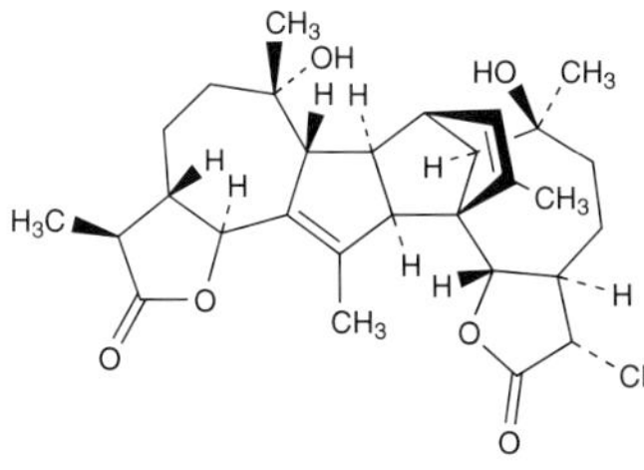

Absinthin

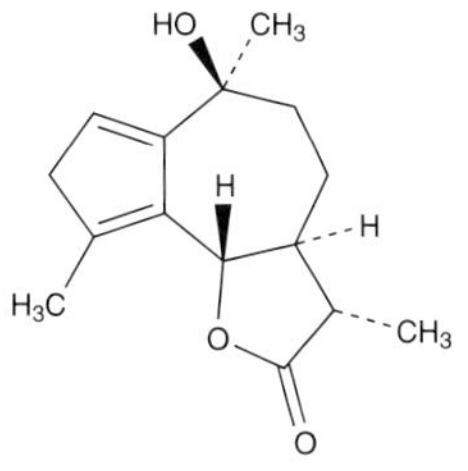

Artabsin

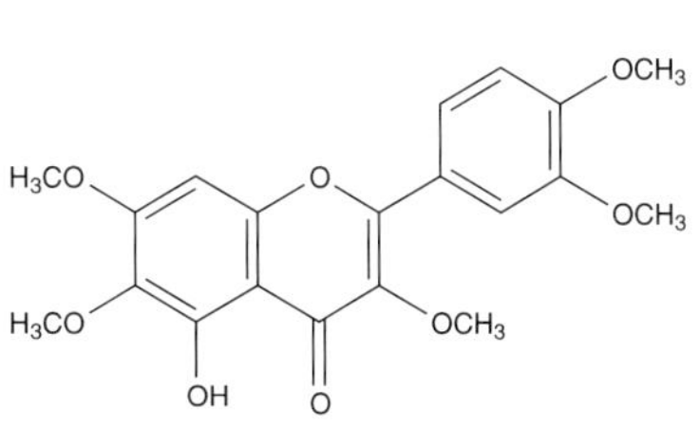

Artemetin

In vitro

Thujone-free essential oil (principal components: *cis*-epoxyocimene + *cis*-chrysanthenyl acetate) at 0.05-0.2 mg/ml showed no antibacterial activity against Gram-positive *Staphylococcus aureus* or Gram-negative *Escherichia coli* and *Enterococcus hirae*, but exhibited antifungal activity against *Candida albicans* and *Saccharomyces cerevisiae* with IC_{50} values of 0.1 and 0.2 mg/ml (and complete inhibition of growth at double these concentrations) [7].

In an investigation of medicinal plants reputed to enhance or restore mental functions (including memory), the human CNS cholinergic receptor binding activity of ethanolic extracts from two samples of wormwood was evaluated in homogenates of human cerebral cortical cell membranes.

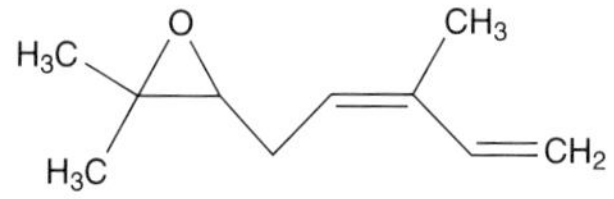

cis-Epoxyocimene

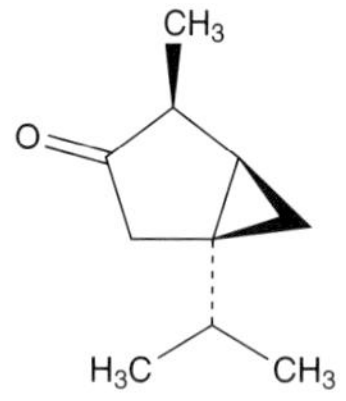

β-Thujone

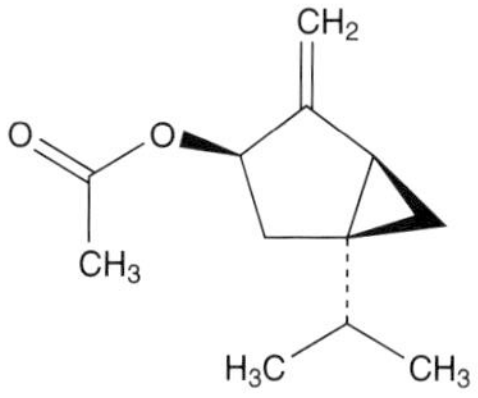

trans-Sabinyl acetate

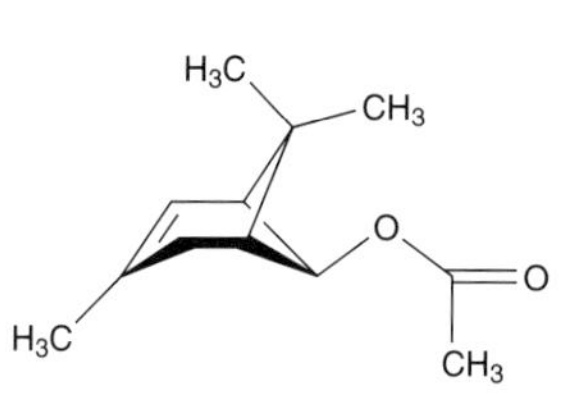

cis-Chrysanthenyl acetate

The extracts dose-dependently displaced [^{3}H]-(*N*)-nicotine and [^{3}H]-(*N*)-scopolamine from nicotinic and muscarinic receptors respectively with IC_{50} values of 0.9-4.1 mg/ml. Although choline was present in the extracts, the concentrations were far too low to account for the displacement activity and the nature of the receptor-specific cholinergic compounds was not clear [20].

In vivo

In experiments using dogs, bile secretion increased 3-fold after intravenous administration of a decoction corresponding to 5 g of wormwood. Isolated absinthin had no effect on gastric secretions when administered by tube directly into the stomach of dogs. However, absinthin given orally stimulated the secretion of gastric juice and increased total acid and free hydrochloric acid in the stomach, demonstrating that gastric secretion is reflexively stimulated from the mouth by bitter principles [21].

Hepatoprotective effects of oral pre-treatment with a dry 80%-methanolic extract from wormwood against acetaminophen (paracetamol)- and carbon tetrachloride-induced hepatotoxicity have been demonstrated in rodents ($p<0.01$ to $p<0.05$); oral post-treatment with the extract was effective in the case of acetaminophen only ($p<0.01$). The extract also prolonged pentobarbital-induced sleeping time ($p<0.05$) and increased strychnine lethality after oral administration to mice, effects which suggested inhibitory activity on microsomal drug-metabolizing enzymes in the liver [22].

Yeast-induced pyrexia in rabbits was significantly reduced by orally administered hexane-, chloroform- and water-soluble fractions from wormwood ($p<0.05$) [23], and also by a sterol isolated from an ethanolic extract of wormwood [17].

Pharmacological studies in humans

In 15 patients with hepatopathy (various liver disorders), administration of 20 mg of a dry ethanolic extract from wormwood produced substantial increases in biliary and pancreatic secretions ($p<0.01$), as evident from increased levels of bilirubin, cholesterol, lipase and amylase in duodenal fluid [24].

Pharmacokinetics

Absinthin administered orally to rats was rapidly absorbed and attained its maximum blood level within 60 minutes; the elimination half-life was about 4 hours [25].

CLINICAL STUDIES

None published on mono-preparations of wormwood.

THERAPEUTICS

Actions
Aromatic bitter [25-28], appetite stimulant [29,30], tonic [30,31], choleretic [27,30,32], anthelmintic [27,30-32], antipyretic [23], antifungal [7] and hepatoprotective [22].

Wormwood is one of the bitterest herbs known [33]. It reflexively stimulates the secretion of gastric, biliary and pancreatic secretions [21,24,25,28], thus improving digestive functions.

Indications
None adequately substantiated by pharmacological or clinical studies.

Uses based on experience or tradition
Dyspeptic complaints [28,32] including flatulence and mild gastrointestinal spasms [2]; stimulation of weak and underactive digestions [28,31]; biliary dyskinesia [26,27]; loss of appetite [26,29,32].

Also used as a tonic with a general strengthening effect in debility and convalescence [27,28,30], especially in influenza and colds [27], and as an anthelmintic for elimination of worm infestations [28,32].

Contraindications
Pregnancy [28,30]; gastric and duodenal ulcers [2].

Side effects
None at recommended dose levels. Depending on the thujone content, excessive doses can lead to vomiting, severe diarrhoea, dazed feelings and spasms [2].

Interactions with other drugs
None known.

Dosage
Three times daily: dried herb, 1-2 g as an infusion; liquid extract 1:1 in 25% alcohol, 1-2 ml [32]; tincture 1:10 in 70% alcohol [34], 5-10 ml.

The duration of treatment should not exceed 3-4 weeks [27].

SAFETY

Safety considerations in the oral use of wormwood revolve mainly around the neurotoxic potential of thujones, at one time notorious due to their presence in the liqueur absinthe, of which wormwood was a key ingredient. High consumption of absinthe, a popular and fashionable drink in France in the late 19th century, could have dire consequences, from a dazed condition to intellectual enfeeblement and hallucinations; ultimately absinthe was banned [33]. Such excesses have no bearing on the therapeutic use of wormwood. At normal dosage levels wormwood preparations contain so little thujone that there is considered to be no risk of toxic effects [27]; the low-level presence of thujone may be regarded as beneficial, and for certain indications essential. However, as noted under Constituents, the amount of thujone isomers in the essential oil is highly variable, from none to more than 60%. It is therefore useful to monitor the level of thujones and, for most purposes, to select a wormwood chemotype with relatively low levels. Methods are available to minimise the thujone content in wormwood preparations [35].

A single oral dose of a dry 80%-methanolic wormwood extract at up to 4.0 g/kg caused neither deaths nor apparent behavioural changes in mice [22]. In a 13-week repeated dose toxicity study, rats were given a commercial wormwood extract in their drinking water at levels of 0, 0.125, 0.5 or 2%. All the animals survived and no differences of toxicological significance were evident between treated and control groups with respect to water and food consumption, body weight gain, organ weights, histopathological examinations and haematological and serum biochemical parameters. The "no observed adverse effect level" for the extract was concluded to be at least 2%, equivalent to 1.27 g/kg/day in male rats and 2.06 g/kg/day in females. Unfortunately, the method of preparation of the extract and its thujone content were not reported [36].

Neither a tincture nor a fluid extract from wormwood showed any mutagenic potential in the Ames test [37].

Wormwood essential oil should never be used medicinally [26]. The oral LD_{50} of the oil in rats was determined as 0.96 g/kg body weight [38], but since the thujone content was not reported this information is of limited value. β-Thujone, which usually exceeds α-thujone as a proportion of the essential oil, is less toxic than the α-diastereoisomer [39].

Antifertility screening of medicinal plants revealed that a 50%-ethanolic extract from wormwood, given orally to female rats at 200 mg/kg daily on days 1-7 after mating, reduced pregnancy implantations by 66%. When given only on days 11-13, the number of foetuses per rat on day 20 was substantially diminished [40]. On this basis wormwood should be avoided during pregnancy.

REGULATORY STATUS

Medicines
UK No licences issued for products con-

	taining wormwood.
France	Accepted for specified indications [29].
Germany	Commission E monograph published, with approved uses [26].

Food

USA	Permitted as flavouring provided the finished food is thujone-free (21 CFR 172.510) [41].
Council of Europe	Permitted as flavouring, category 5 (with limits on camphor and thujone under evaluation) [42].

REFERENCES

Current Pharmacopoeial Monographs

Ph. Eur. Wormwood

Literature References

1. Beauhaire J and Fourrey J-L. Structure of artabsinolides. Photooxygenation studies on artabsin. *J. Chem. Soc. Perkin I* 1982:861-864.
2. Wichtl M and Neubeck M. Wermutkraut - Absinthii herba. In: Hartke K, Hartke H, Mutschler E, Rücker G and Wichtl M, editors. *Kommentar zum Europäischen Arzneibuch.* Stuttgart: Wissenschaftliche Verlagsgesellschaft, 1999 (12 Lfg.):W 16 [GERMAN].
3. Schneider G and Mielke B. Analysis of the bitter principles absinthin, artabsin and matricin from *Artemisia absinthium* L. Part II. Isolation and determination. *Dtsch. Apoth. Ztg.* 1979, **119**, 977-982 [GERMAN/English summary].
4. Beauhaire J, Fourrey JL, Vuilhorgne M and Lallemand JY. Dimeric sesquiterpene lactones: structure of absinthin. *Tetrahedron Lett.* 1980, **21**, 3191-3194.
5. Beauhaire J, Fourrey JL, Lallemand JY and Vuilhorgne M. Dimeric sesquiterpene lactone. Structure of isoabsinthin. Acid isomerization of absinthin derivatives. *Tetrahedron Lett.* 1981, **22**, 2269-2272.
6. Beauhaire J, Fourrey J-L and Guittet E. Structure of absintholide, a new guaianolide dimer of *Artemisia absinthium* L. *Tetrahedron Lett.* 1984, **25**, 2751-2754.
7. Juteau F, Jerkovic I, Masotti V, Milos M, Mastelic J, Bessière J-M and Viano J. Composition and Antimicrobial Activity of the Essential Oil of *Artemisia absinthium* from Croatia and France. *Planta Medica* 2003, **69**, 158-161.
8. Ariño A, Arberas I, Renobales G, Arriaga S and Domínguez JB. Essential Oil of *Artemisia absinthium* L. from the Spanish Pyrenees. *J. Essent. Oil Res.* 1999, **11**, 182-184.
9. Nin S, Arfaioli P and Bosetto M. Quantitative Determination of Some Essential Oil Components of Selected *Artemisia absinthium* Plants. *J. Essent. Oil Res.* 1995, **7**, 271-277.
10. Chialva F, Liddle PAP and Doglia G. Chemotaxonomy of Wormwood (*Artemisia absinthium* L.). I. Composition of the Essential Oil of Several Chemotypes. *Z. Lebensm. Unters. Forsch.* 1983, **176**, 363-366.
11. Vostrowsky O, Brosche T, Ihm H, Zintl R and Knobloch K. On the Essential Oil Components from *Artemisia absinthium* L. *Z. Naturforsch.* 1981, **36c**, 369-377 [GERMAN/English summary].
12. Sacco T and Chialva F. Chemical Characteristics of the Oil from *Artemisia absinthium* Collected in Patagonia (Argentina). *Planta Medica* 1988, **54**, 93.
13. Lawrence BM. Progress in Essential Oils. *Perfumer & Flavorist* 1998, **23** (Jan/Feb), 39-50.
14. Swiatek L, Grabias B and Kalemba D. Phenolic acids in certain medicinal plants of the genus *Artemisia. Pharm. Pharmacol. Lett.* 1998, **8**, 158-160.
15. Hoffman B and Herrmann K. Flavonol Glycosides of Mugwort (*Artemisia vulgaris* L.), Tarragon (*Artemisia dracunculus* L.) and Absinth (*Artemisia absinthium* L.). *Z. Lebensm. Unters. Forsch.* 1982, **174**, 211-215 [GERMAN/English summary].
16. Shlyapyatis YY. Biology and biochemistry of the common wormwood: 8. Accumulation dynamics of tannic substances, ascorbic acid and carotene. *Liet. TSR Mokslu Akad. Darb. Ser. C Biol. Mokslai* 1975, **1**, 43-48 [RUSSIAN]; through *Biol. Abstr.* 1976, **61**, 28166.
17. Ikram M, Shafi N, Mir I, Do MN, Nguyen P and Le Quesne PW. 24ζ-Ethylcholesta-7,22-dien-3β-ol: A Possibly Antipyretic Constituent of *Artemisia absinthium. Planta Medica* 1987, **53**, 389.
18. Rücker G, Manns D and Wilbert S. Homoditerpene peroxides from *Artemisia absinthium. Phytochemistry* 1992, **31**, 340-342.
19. Perez-Souto N, Lynch RJ, Measures G and Hann JT. Use of high-performance liquid chromatographic peak deconvolution and peak labelling to identify antiparasitic components in plant extracts. *J. Chromatogr.* 1992, **593**, 209-215.
20. Wake G, Court J, Pickering A, Lewis R, Wilkins R and Perry E. CNS acetylcholine receptor activity in European medicinal plants traditionally used to improve failing memory. *J. Ethnopharmacol.* 2000, **69**, 105-114.
21. Kreitmair H. *Artemisia absinthium* L. - der echte Wermut [*Artemisia absinthium* L. - the real wormwood]. *Pharmazie* 1951, **6**, 27-28 [GERMAN].
22. Gilani AH and Janbaz KH. Preventive and Curative Effects of *Artemisia absinthium* on Acetaminophen and CCl_4-induced Hepatotoxicity. *Gen. Pharmacol.* 1995, **26**, 309-315.
23. Khattak SG, Gilani SN and Ikram M. Antipyretic studies on some indigenous Pakistani medicinal plants. *J. Ethnopharmacol.* 1985, **14**, 45-51.
24. Baumann JC. Über die Wirkung von Chelidonium, Curcuma, Absinth und Carduus marianus auf die Galle- und Pankreassekretion bei Hepatopathien [The effect of Chelidonium, Curcuma, Wormwood and Carduus marianus on biliary and pancreatic secretions in hepatopathy patients]. *Med. Mschr.* 1975, **29**, 173-180 [GERMAN].
25. Hose S. Der Wermut - *Artemisia absinthium* L. Arzneipflanze für Kranke und "Kultige". *Z. Phytotherapie* 2002, **23**, 187-194 [GERMAN/English summary].
26. Absinthii herba. German Commission E Monograph published in: Bundesanzeiger No. 228 of 5 December 1984.
27. Weiss RF. (Wormwood). In: *Herbal Medicine* (translated from the 6th German edition of *Lehrbuch der Phytotherapie*). ISBN 0-906584-19-1. Gothenburg: AB Arcanum, Beaconsfield (UK): Beaconsfield Publishers, 1988: 79-82.
28. Chevallier A. Wormwood - *Artemsia absinthium.* In: *Encyclopedia of Medicinal Plants, 2nd ed.* ISBN 0-7513-1209-6. London-New York: Dorling Kindersley, 2001:66.
29. Absinthe. In: *Médicaments à base de plantes.* ISBN 2-911473-02-7. Saint-Denis Cedex, France: Agence du Médicament, 1998.
30. McIntyre A. Wormwood - *Artemisia absinthium.* In: *The Complete Woman's Herbal.* ISBN 1-85675-135-X. London: Gaia Books, 1994:128.
31. Grieve M (edited by Leyel CF). Wormwood, common - *Artemisia absinthium.* In: *A Modern Herbal* (first published 1931; revised 1973). ISBN 1-85501-249-9. London: Tiger Books International, 1994:858-860.
32. Artemisia absinthium. In: *British Herbal Pharmacopoeia 1983.* ISBN 0-903032-07-4. Bournemouth: British Herbal Medicine Association, 1983.
33. Arnold WN. Absinthe. *Scientific American* 1989, June, 86-91.
34. Pharmaceutical Society of Great Britain. Tinctura Absinthii. *British Pharmaceutical Codex 1934.* London: Pharmaceutical Press, 1934:1465.
35. Tegtmeier M and Harnischfeger G. Methods for the Reduction of Thujone Content in Pharmaceutical

Preparations of *Artemisia, Salvia* and *Thuja. Eur. J. Pharm. Biopharm.* 1994, **40**, 337-340.
36. Muto T, Watanabe T, Okamura M, Moto M, Kashida Y and Mitsumori K. Thirteen-week repeated dose toxicity study of wormwood (*Artemisia absinthium*) extract in rats. *J. Toxicol. Sci.* 2003, **28**, 471-478.
37. Schimmer O, Krüger A, Paulini H and Haefele F. An evaluation of 55 commercial plant extracts in the Ames mutagenicity test. *Pharmazie* 1994, **49**, 448-451.
38. Opdyke DLJ. Monographs on fragrance raw materials: Artemisia oil (wormwood). *Food Cosmet. Toxicol.* 1975, **13**, 721-722.
39. Höld KM, Sirisoma NS, Ikeda T, Narahashi T and Casida JE. α-Thujone (the active component of absinthe): γ-Aminobutyric acid type A receptor modulation and metabolic detoxification. *Proc. Natl. Acad. Sci. USA* 2000, **97**, 3826-3831.
40. Rao VSN, Menezes AMS and Gadelha MGT. Antifertility screening of some indigenous plants of Brasil. *Fitoterapia* 1988, **59**, 17-20.
41. Artemisia (wormwood). In: Section 172.510 of USA Code of Federal Regulations, Title 21, Food and Drugs, Parts 170 to 199. Revised as of April 1, 2000.
42. Artemisia absinthium L. In: *Natural Sources of Flavourings. Report No. 1.* ISBN 92-871-4324-2. Strasbourg: Council of Europe Publishing, 2000:61-64.

REGULATORY GUIDELINES FROM OTHER EU COUNTRIES

FRANCE

Médicaments à base de plantes [29]: Absinthe, feuille, sommité fleurie.

Therapeutic indications accepted

Oral use
Traditionally used to stimulate the appetite.

GERMANY

Commission E monograph [26]: Absinthii herba (Wermutkraut).

Uses
Loss of appetite, dyspeptic complaints, biliary dyskinesia.

Contraindications
None known.

Side effects
None known.

Interactions with other drugs
None known.

Dosage
Unless otherwise prescribed, average daily dose: 2-3 g of the herb as an aqueous infusion.

Mode of administration
Cut herb for infusions and decoctions; powdered herb, and also extracts or tinctures, as liquid or solid dosage forms for oral use.

Note: Combinations with other bitters or aromatics may be helpful.
As the active part of the oil, thujone is a convulsive poison in toxic doses. Therefore the isolated essential oil should never be used.

Actions
As an aromatic bitter, the effect is due to the bitter principles and essential oil. No useful recent pharmacological data are available.

INDEX

Monograph titles are listed in capitals and Latin botanical names in italics.
Chemical constituents of plants are listed only where the structure is illustrated.

BHMA BOOKS IN PRINT

British Herbal Pharmacopoeia 1983
Quality specifications and therapeutics for 232 plant drugs.
Although the specifications have been superseded, this pioneering work provides unique summaries of therapeutics in the view of herbal practitioners of the time.

British Herbal Pharmacopoeia 1996
Quality specifications for 169 plant drugs, including many not found in official pharmacopoeias.

British Herbal Compendium, Volume 1
A handbook of scientific information on widely used plant drugs
Companion to the British Herbal Pharmacopoeia
First published in 1992; 84 monographs

British Herbal Compendium, Volume 2
A handbook of scientific information on widely used plant drugs.
Companion to the British Herbal Pharmacopoeia
First published in 2006; 80 monographs

A Guide to Traditional Herbal Medicines, 2003 edition
A sourcebook of accepted traditional uses of medicinal plants within Europe

Further information may be obtained from the website of the British Herbal Medicine Association:
www.bhma.info